RANDOM HOUSE
WEBSTER'S

D1550706

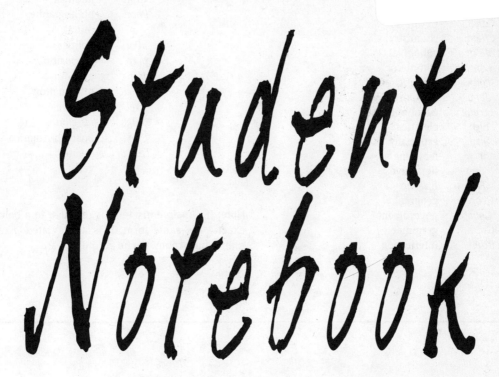

Student

Notebook

SPANISH
DICTIONARY

Spanish–English ◆ *English–Spanish*
español–inglés ◆ *inglés–español*

RANDOM HOUSE
NEW YORK

ENGLISH ABBREVIATIONS/ABREVIATURAS INGLESAS

a.	adjective		*interrog.*	interrogative
abbr.	abbreviation		*Leg.*	legal
adv.	adverb		*m.*	masculine
Aero.	aeronautics		*Mech.*	mechanics
Agr.	agriculture		*Mex.*	Mexico
Anat.	anatomy		*Mil.*	military
art.	article		*Mus.*	music
Auto.	automotive		*n.*	noun
Biol.	biology		*Naut.*	nautical
Bot.	botany		*Phot.*	photography
Carib.	Caribbean		*pl.*	plural
Chem.	chemistry		*Pol.*	politics
Colloq.	colloquial		*prep.*	preposition
Com.	commerce		*pron.*	pronoun
conj.	conjunction		*Punct.*	punctuation
dem.	demonstrative		*rel.*	relative
Econ.	economics		*Relig.*	religion
Elec.	electrical		*S.A.*	Spanish America
esp.	especially		*Theat.*	theater
f.	feminine		*v.*	verb
Fig.	figurative			
Fin.	finance			
Geog.	geography			
Govt.	government			
Gram.	grammar			
interj.	interjection			

Note: If a main entry term is repeated in a boldface subentry in exactly the same form, it is abbreviated. Example: **comedor** *n.m.* dining room. **coche c.,** dining car.

SPANISH STRESS

In a number of words, spoken stress is marked by an accent (´): *nación, país, médico, día.*

Words which are not so marked are, generally speaking, stressed on the next-to-the-last syllable if they end in a vowel, *n,* or *s;* and on the last syllable if they end in a consonant other than *n* or *s.*

Note: An accent is placed over some words to distinguish them from others having the same spelling and pronunciation but differing in meaning.

SPANISH ALPHABETIZATION

In Spanish, *ch* and *ll* are no longer considered to be separate letters of the alphabet. They are now alphabetized as they would be in English. However, words with *ñ* are alphabetized after *n.*

PRONUNCIATION KEY FOR SPANISH

IPA Symbols	Key Words	Approximate Equivalents
a	alba, banco, cera	father, depart
e	esto, del, parte, mesa	bet; like rain when e ends syllable and is not followed by r, rr, or t
i	ir, fino, adiós, muy	like beet, but shorter
o	oler, flor, grano	like vote, but shorter
u	un, luna, cuento, vergüenza, guarda	fool, group
b	bajo, ambiguo, vaca	by, abet
β	hablar, escribir, lavar	like vehicle, but with lips almost touching
d	dar, desde, andamio, dueña	deal, adept
ð	pedir, edredón, verdad	that, gather
f	fecha, afectar, golf	fan, after
g	gato, grave, gusto, largo, guerra	garden, ugly
h	gemelo, giro, junta, bajo	horse
k	cacao, claro, cura, cuenta, que, quinto	kind, actor
l	lado, lente, habla, papel	lot, altar
ʎ	(in Spain) llama, calle, olla	like million, but with tongue behind teeth
m	mal, amor	more, commit
n	nada, nuevo, mano, bien	not, enter
ɲ	ñapa, año	canyon, companion
ŋ	angosto, aunque	ring, anchor
p	peso, guapo	pill, applaud
r	real, faro, deber	like rice, but with single flap of tongue on roof of mouth
rr	perro, sierra	like rice, but with trill, or vibration of tongue, against upper teeth
s	sala, espejo, mas; (in Latin America) cena, hacer, vez	say, clasp
θ	(in Spain) cena, hacer, cierto, cine, zarzuela, lazo, vez	thin, myth
t	tocar, estado, cenit	table, attract
y	ya, ayer; (in Latin America) llama, calle	you, voyage
tʃ	chica, mucho	chill, batch

Diphthongs

ai, ay	baile, hay	high, rye
au	audacia, laudable	out, round
ei, ey	veinte, seis, rey	ray
ie	miel, tambien	fiesta
oi, oy	estoico, hoy	coin, loyal
ua	cuanto	quantity
ue	buena, suerte	sway, quaint

Guía de Pronunciación del Inglés

Símbolos del AFI	Ejemplos
/æ/	*ingl.* hat; como la **a** de *esp.* p**a**ro, pero más cerrada
/ei/	*ingl.* stay; *esp.* r**ei**na
/ɛə/ [followed by /r/]	*ingl.* hair; *esp.* v**e**r
/ɑ/	*ingl.* father; similar a las **a**s de *esp.* c**a**sa, pero más larga
/ɛ/	*ingl.* bet; *esp.* **e**ntre
/i/	*ingl.* bee; como la **i** de *esp.* v**i**da, pero más larga
/ɪə/ [followed by /r/]	*ingl.* hear; como la **i** de *esp.* ven**i**r, pero menos cerrada
/ɪ/	*ingl.* sit; como la **i** de *esp.* Ch**i**le, pero menos cerrada
/ai/	*ingl.* try; *esp.* h**ay**
/ɒ/	*ingl.* hot; *esp.* p**o**ner
/o/	*ingl.* boat; similar a la **o** de *esp.* sac**o**, pero más cerrada
/ɔ/	*ingl.* saw; similar a la **o** de *esp.* c**o**rte, pero más cerrada
/ɔi/	*ingl.* toy; *esp.* h**oy**
/ʊ/	*ingl.* book; como la **u** de *esp.* ins**u**lto, pero menos cerrada
/u/	*ingl.* too; como la **u** de *esp.* l**u**na, pero más larga
/au/	*ingl.* cow; *esp.* p**au**sa
/ʌ/	*ingl.* up; entre la **o** de *esp.* b**o**rde y la **a** de *esp.* b**a**rro
/ɜ/ [followed by /r/]	*ingl.* burn; *fr.* fl**eu**r
/ə/	*ingl.* alone; *fr.* d**e**main
/·/	*ingl.* fire (fi·r); *fr.* bastill**e**
/b/	*ingl.* boy; como la **b** de *esp.* **b**oca, pero más aspirada
/tʃ/	*ingl.* child; *esp.* mu**ch**o
/d/	*ingl.* dad; *esp.* **d**ar
/f/	*ingl.* for; *esp.* **f**echa
/g/	*ingl.* give; *esp.* **g**ato
/h/	*ingl.* happy; como la **j** de *esp.* **j**abón, pero más aspirada y menos aspera
/dʒ/	*ingl.* just; *it.* **g**iorno
/k/	*ingl.* kick; similar a la **k** de *esp.* **k**ilogramo, pero más aspirada
/l/	*ingl.* love; *esp.* **l**ibro
/m/	*ingl.* mother; *esp.* li**m**bo
/n/	*ingl.* now; *esp.* **n**oche
/ŋ/	*ingl.* sing; *esp.* bla**n**co
/p/	*ingl.* pot; como las **p**s de *esp.* **p**a**p**a, pero más aspirada
/r/	*ingl.* read; como la **r** de *esp.* pa**r**a, pero con la lengua elevada hacia el paladar, sin tocarlo
/s/	*ingl.* see; *esp.* ha**s**ta
/ʃ/	*ingl.* shop; *fr.* **ch**er**ch**er
/t/	*ingl.* ten; similar a la **t** de *esp.* **t**omar, pero más aspirada
/θ/	*ingl.* thing; *esp.* (en España) **c**erdo, **z**apato
/ð/	*ingl.* father; *esp.* co**d**o
/v/	*ingl.* victory; como la **b** de *esp.* ha**b**a, pero es labiodental en vez de bilabial
/w/	*ingl.* witch; como la **u** de *esp.* p**u**esto, pero con labios más cerrados
/y/	*ingl.* yes; *esp.* **y**acer
/z/	*ingl.* zipper; *fr.* **z**éro
/ʒ/	*ingl.* pleasure; *fr.* **j**eune

Las consonantes /l̩/, /m̩/, y /n̩/ son similar a las **l**, **m**, y **n** del español, pero alargada y resonante

Spanish–English

español–inglés

A

a /a/ *prep.* to; at.
abacería /aβaθe'ria; aβase'ria/ *n. f.* grocery store.
abacero /aβa'θero; aβa'sero/ *n. m.* grocer.
ábaco /'aβako/ *n. m.* abacus.
abad /a'βaδ/ *n. m.* abbot.
abadía /aβa'δia/ *n. f.* abbey.
abajar /aβa'har/ *v.* lower; go down.
abajo /a'βaho/ *adv.* down; downstairs.
abandonar /aβando'nar/ *v.* abandon.
abandono /aβan'dono/ *n. m.* abandonment.
abanico /aβa'niko/ *n. m.* fan. —**abanicar,** *v.*
abaratar /aβara'tar/ *v.* cheapen.
abarcar /aβar'kar/ *v.* comprise; clasp.
abastecer /aβaste'θer; aβaste'ser/ *v.* supply, provide.
abatido /aβa'tiδo/ *a.* dejected, despondent.
abatir /aβa'tir/ *v.* knock down; dismantle; depress, dishearten.
abdicación /aβδika'θion; aβδika'sion/ *n. f.* abdication.
abdicar /aβδi'kar/ *v.* abdicate.
abdomen /aβ'δomen/ *n. m.* abdomen.
abdominal /aβδomi'nal/ *a.* **1.** abdominal. —*n.* **2.** *m.* sit-up.
abecé /aβe'θe; aβe'se/ *n. m.* ABCs, rudiments.
abecedario /aβeθe'δario; aβese'δario/ *n. m.* alphabet; reading book.
abeja /a'βeha/ *n. f.* bee.
abejarrón /aβeha'rron/ *n. m.* bumblebee.
aberración /aβerra'θion; aβerra'sion/ *n. f.* aberration.
abertura /aβer'tura/ *n. f.* opening, aperture, slit.
abeto /a'βeto/ *n. m.* fir.
abierto /a'βierto/ *a.* open; overt.
abismal /aβis'mal/ *a.* abysmal.
abismo /a'βismo/ *n. m.* abyss, chasm.
ablandar /aβlan'dar/ *v.* soften.
abnegación /aβnega'θion; aβnega'sion/ *n. f.* abnegation.
abochornar /aβot͡for'nar/ *v.* overheat; embarrass.
abogado /aβo'gaδo/ **-da** *n.* lawyer, attorney.
abolengo /aβo'lengo/ *n. m.* ancestry.
abolición /aβoli'θion; aβoli'sion/ *n. f.* abolition.
abolladura /aβoʎa'δura; aβoya'δura/ *n. f.* dent. —**abollar,** *v.*
abominable /aβomi'naβle/ *a.* abominable.
abominar /aβomi'nar/ *v.* abhor.
abonado /aβo'naδo/ **-da** *n. m. & f.* subscriber.
abonar /aβo'nar/ *v.* pay; fertilize.
abonarse /aβo'narse/ *v.* subscribe.
abono /a'βono/ *n. m.* fertilizer; subscription; season ticket.
aborigen /aβor'ihen/ *a. & n.* aboriginal.
aborrecer /aβorre'θer; aβorre'ser/ *v.* hate, loathe, abhor.
abortar /aβor'tar/ *v.* abort, miscarry.
aborto /a'βorto/ *n. m.* abortion.
abovedar /aβoβe'δar/ *v.* vault.
abrasar /aβra'sar/ *v.* burn.
abrazar /aβra'θar; aβra'sar/ *v.* embrace, clasp.
abrazo /a'βraθo; a'βraso/ *n. m.* embrace.
abrelatas /aβre'latas/ *n. m.* can opener.
abreviar /aβre'βiar/ *v.* abbreviate, abridge, shorten.
abreviatura /aβreβia'tura/ *n. f.* abbreviation.
abrigar /aβri'gar/ *v.* harbor, shelter.
abrigarse /aβri'garse/ *v.* bundle up.
abrigo /a'βrigo/ *n. m.* overcoat; shelter; (*pl.*) wraps.
abril /a'βril/ *n. m.* April.

abrir /a'βrir/ *v.* open; *Med.* lance.
abrochar /aβro't͡far/ *v.* clasp.
abrogación /aβroga'θion; aβroga'sion/ *n. f.* abrogation, repeal.
abrogar /aβro'gar/ *v.* abrogate.
abrojo /a'βroho/ *n. m.* thorn.
abrumar /aβru'mar/ *v.* overwhelm, crush, swamp.
absceso /aβs'θeso; aβ'sseso/ *n. m.* abscess.
absolución /aβsolu'θion; aβsolu'sion/ *n. f.* absolution; acquittal.
absoluto /aβso'luto/ *a.* absolute; downright.
absolver /aβsol'βer/ *v.* absolve, pardon.
absorbente /aβsor'βente/ *a.* absorbent.
absorber /aβsor'βer/ *v.* absorb.
absorción /aβsor'θion; aβsor'sion/ *n. f.* absorption.
abstemio /aβs'temio/ *a.* abstemious.
abstenerse /aβste'nerse/ *v.* abstain; refrain.
abstinencia /aβsti'nenθia; aβsti'nensia/ *n. f.* abstinence.
abstracción /aβstrak'θion; aβstrak'sion/ *n. f.* abstraction.
abstracto /aβ'strakto/ *a.* abstract.
abstraer /aβstra'er/ *v.* abstract.
absurdo /aβ'surδo/ *a.* **1.** absurd. —*n.* **2.** *m.* absurdity.
abuchear /aβut͡fe'ar/ *v.* boo.
abuela /a'βuela/ *n. f.* grandmother.
abuelo /a'βuelo/ *n. m.* grandfather; (*pl.*) grandparents.
abultado /aβul'taδo/ *a.* bulky.
abultamiento /aβulta'miento/ *n. m.* bulge. —**abultar,** *v.*
abundancia /aβun'danθia; aβun'dansia/ *n. f.* abundance, plenty.
abundante /aβun'dante/ *a.* abundant, plentiful.
abundar /aβun'dar/ *v.* abound.
aburrido /aβu'rriδo/ *a.* boring, tedious.
aburrimiento /aβurri'miento/ *n. m.* boredom.
aburrir /aβu'rrir/ *v.* bore.
abusar /aβu'sar/ *v.* abuse, misuse.
abusivo /aβu'siβo/ *a.* abusive.
abuso /a'βuso/ *n. m.* abuse.
abyecto /aβ'yekto/ *a.* abject, low.
a.C., *abbr.* (**antes de Cristo**) BC.
acá /a'ka/ *adv.* here.
acabar /aka'βar/ *v.* finish. **a. de...,** to have just....
acacia /a'kaθia; a'kasia/ *n. f.* acacia.
academia /aka'δemia/ *n. f.* academy.
académico /aka'δemiko/ *a.* academic.
acaecer /akae'θer; akae'ser/ *v.* happen.
acanalar /akana'lar/ *v.* groove.
acaparar /akapa'rar/ *v.* hoard; monopolize.
acariciar /akari'θiar; akari'siar/ *v.* caress, stroke.
acarrear /akarre'ar/ *v.* cart, transport; occasion, entail.
acaso /a'kaso/ *n. m.* chance. **por si a.,** just in case.
acceder /akθe'δer; akse'δer/ *v.* accede.
accesible /akθe'siβle; akse'siβle/ *a.* accessible.
acceso /ak'θeso; ak'seso/ *n. m.* access, approach.
accesorio /akθe'sorio; akse'sorio/ *a.* accessory.
accidentado /akθiδen'taδo; aksiδen'taδo/ *a.* hilly.
accidental /akθiδen'tal; aksiδen'tal/ *a.* accidental.
accidente /akθi'δente; aksi'δente/ *n. m.* accident, wreck.
acción /ak'θion; ak'sion/ *n. f.* action, act; *Com.* share of stock.
accionista /akθio'nista; aksio'nista/ *n. m. & f.* shareholder.
acechar /aθe't͡far; ase't͡far/ *v.* ambush, spy on.
acedia /a'θeδia; a'seδia/ *n. f.* heartburn.

aceite /a'θeite; a'seite/ *n. m.* oil.
aceite de hígado de bacalao /a'θeite de i'gaδo de baka'lao; a'seite/ cod-liver oil.
aceitoso /aθei'toso; asei'toso/ *a.* oily.
aceituna /aθei'tuna; asei'tuna/ *n. f.* olive.
aceleración /aθelera'θion; aselera'sion/ *n. f.* acceleration.
acelerar /aθele'rar; asele'rar/ *v.* accelerate, speed up.
acento /a'θento; a'sento/ *n. m.* accent.
acentuar /aθen'tuar; asen'tuar/ *v.* accent, accentuate, stress.
acepillar /aθepi'ʎar; asepi'yar/ *v.* brush; plane (wood).
aceptable /aθep'taβle; asep'taβle/ *a.* acceptable.
aceptación /aθepta'θion; asepta'sion/ *n. f.* acceptance.
aceptar /aθep'tar; asep'tar/ *v.* accept.
acequia /a'θekia; a'sekia/ *n. f.* ditch.
acera /a'θera; a'sera/ *n. f.* sidewalk.
acerca de /a'θerka de; a'serka de/ *prep.* about, concerning.
acercar /aθer'kar; aser'kar/ *v.* bring near.
acercarse /aθer'karse; aser'karse/ *v.* approach, come near, go near.
acero /a'θero; a'sero/ *n. m.* steel.
acero inoxidable /a'θero inoksi'δaβle; a'sero inoksi'δaβle/ stainless steel.
acertar /aθer'tar; aser'tar/ *v.* guess right. **a. en,** hit (a mark).
acertijo /aθer'tiho; aser'tiho/ *n. m.* puzzle, riddle.
achicar /at͡fi'kar/ *v.* diminish, dwarf; humble.
acidez /aθi'δeθ; asi'δes/ *n. f.* acidity.
ácido /'aθiδo; 'asiδo/ *a.* **1.** sour. —*n.* **2.** *m.* acid.
aclamación /aklama'θion; aklama'sion/ *n. f.* acclamation.
aclamar /akla'mar/ *v.* acclaim.
aclarar /akla'rar/ *v.* brighten; clarify, clear up.
acoger /ako'her/ *v.* welcome, receive.
acogida /ako'hiδa/ *n. f.* welcome, reception.
acometer /akome'ter/ *v.* attack.
acomodador /akomoδa'δor/ *n. m.* usher.
acomodar /akomo'δar/ *v.* accommodate, fix up.
acompañamiento /akompaɲa'miento/ *n. m.* accompaniment; following.
acompañar /akompa'ɲar/ *v.* accompany.
acondicionar /akondiθio'nar; akondisio'nar/ *v.* condition.
aconsejable /akonse'haβle/ *a.* advisable.
aconsejar /akonse'har/ *v.* advise.
acontecer /akonte'θer; akonte'ser/ *v.* happen.
acontecimiento /akonteθi'miento; akontesi'miento/ *n. m.* event, happening.
acorazado /akora'θaδo; akora'saδo/ *a.* **1.** *m.* battleship. —*a.* **2.** armor-plated, ironclad.
acordarse /akor'δarse/ *v.* remember, recollect.
acordeón /akorδe'on/ *n. m.* accordion.
acordonar /akorδo'nar/ *v.* cordon off.
acortar /akor'tar/ *v.* shorten.
acosar /ako'sar/ *v.* beset, harry.
acostar /ako'star/ *v.* lay down; put to bed.
acostarse /akos'tarse/ *v.* lie down; go to bed.
acostumbrado /akostum'braδo/ *a.* accustomed; customary.
acostumbrar /akostum'brar/ *v.* accustom.
acrecentar /akreθen'tar; akresen'tar/ *v.* increase.
acreditar /akreδi'tar/ *v.* accredit.
acreedor /akree'δor/ **-ra** *n.* creditor.

acróbata /a'kroβata/ *n. m. & f.* acrobat.
acrobático /akro'βatiko/ *a.* acrobatic.
actitud /akti'tuδ/ *n. f.* attitude.
actividad /aktiβi'δaδ/ *n. f.* activity.
activista /akti'βista/ *a. & n.* activist.
activo /ak'tiβo/ *a.* active.
acto /'akto/ *n. m.* act.
actor /ak'tor/ *n. m.* actor.
actriz /ak'triθ; ak'tris/ *n. f.* actress.
actual /ak'tual/ *a.* present; present day.
actualidades /aktuali'δaδes/ *n. f.pl.* current events.
actualmente /aktual'mente/ *adv.* at present; nowadays.
actuar /ak'tuar/ *v.* act.
acuarela /akua'rela/ *n. f.* watercolor.
acuario /a'kuario/ *n. m.* aquarium.
acuático /a'kuatiko/ *a.* aquatic.
acuchillar /akut͡fi'ʎar; akut͡fi'yar/ *v.* slash, knife.
acudir /aku'δir/ *v.* rally; hasten; be present.
acuerdo /a'kuerδo/ *n. m.* accord, agreement; settlement. **de a.,** in agreement, agreed.
acumulación /akumula'θion; akumula'sion/ *n. f.* accumulation.
acumular /akumu'lar/ *v.* accumulate.
acuñar /aku'ɲar/ *v.* coin, mint.
acupuntura /akupun'tura/ *n. f.* acupuncture.
acusación /akusa'θion; akusa'sion/ *n. f.* accusation, charge.
acusado /aku'saδo/ **-da** *a. & n.* accused; defendant.
acusador /akusa'δor/ **-ra** *n.* accuser.
acusar /aku'sar/ *v.* accuse; acknowledge.
acústica /a'kustika/ *n. f.* acoustics.
adaptación /aδapta'θion; aδapta'sion/ *n. f.* adaptation.
adaptador /aδapta'δor/ *n. m.* adapter.
adaptar /aδap'tar/ *v.* adapt.
adecuado /aδe'kuaδo/ *a.* adequate.
adelantado /aδelan'taδo/ *a.* advanced; fast (clock).
adelantamiento /aδelanta'miento/ *n. m.* advancement, promotion.
adelantar /aδelan'tar/ *v.* advance.
adelante /aδe'lante/ *adv.* ahead, forward, onward, on.
adelanto /aδe'lanto/ *n. m.* advancement, progress, improvement.
adelgazar /aδelga'θar; aδelga'sar/ *v.* make thin.
ademán /aδe'man/ *n. m.* attitude; gesture.
además /aδe'mas/ *adv.* in addition, besides, also.
adentro /a'δentro/ *adv.* in, inside.
adepto /a'δepto/ *a.* adept.
aderezar /aδere'θar; aδere'sar/ *v.* prepare; trim.
adherirse /aδe'rirse/ *v.* adhere, stick.
adhesivo /aδe'siβo/ *a.* adhesive.
adicción /aδik'θion; aδik'sion/ *n. f.* addiction.
adición /aδi'θion; aδi'sion/ *n. f.* addition.
adicional /aδiθio'nal; aδisio'nal/ *a.* additional, extra.
adicto /a'δikto/ **-ta** *a. & n.* addicted; addict.
adinerado /aδine'raδo/ **-a** *a.* wealthy.
adiós /a'δios/ *n. m. & interj.* good-bye, farewell.
adivinar /aδiβi'nar/ *v.* guess.
adjetivo /aδhe'tiβo/ *n. m.* adjective.
adjunto /aδ'hunto/ *a.* enclosed.
administración /aδministra'θion; aδministra'sion/ *n. f.* administration.
administrador /aδministra'δor/ **-ra** *n.* administrator.
administrar /aδminis'trar/ *v.* administer; manage.
administrativo /aδministra'tiβo/ *a.* administrative.
admirable /aδmi'raβle/ *a.* admirable.
admiración. /aδmira'θion; aδmira'prim;sion/ *n. f.* admiration; wonder.

admirar /aðmiˈrar/ v. admire.

admisión /aðmiˈsion/ n. f. admission.

admitir /aðmiˈtir/ v. admit, acknowledge.

ADN, abbr. (ácido deoxirribonucleico) DNA (deoxyribonucleic acid).

adobar /adoˈβar/ v. marinate.

adolescencia /aðolesˈθenθia; aðolesˈsensia/ n. f. adolescence, youth.

adolescente /aðolesˈθente; aðolesˈsente/ a. & n. adolescent.

adónde /aˈðonde/ adv. where.

adondequiera /a,ðondeˈkiera/ conj. wherever.

adopción /aðopˈθion; aðopˈsion/ n. f. adoption.

adoptar /aðopˈtar/ v. adopt.

adoración /aðoraˈθion; aðoraˈsion/ n. f. worship, love, adoration. —**adorar**, v.

adormecer /aðormeˈθer; aðormeˈser/ v. drowse.

adornar /aðorˈnar/ v. adorn; decorate.

adorno /aˈðorno/ n. m. adornment, trimming.

adquirir /aðkiˈrir/ v. acquire, obtain.

adquisición /aðkisiˈθion; aðkisiˈsion/ n. f. acquisition, attainment.

aduana /aˈðuana/ n. f. custom house, customs.

adujada /aðuˈhaða/ n. f. Naut. coil of rope.

adulación /aðulaˈθion; aðulaˈsion/ n. f. flattery.

adular /aðuˈlar/ v. flatter.

adulterar /aðulteˈrar/ v. adulterate.

adulterio /aðulˈterio/ n. m. adultery.

adulto /aˈðulto/ **-ta** a. & n. adult.

adusto /aˈðusto/ a. gloomy; austere.

adverbio /aðˈβerβio/ n. m. adverb.

adversario /aðβerˈsario/ n. m. adversary.

adversidad /aðβersiˈðað/ n. f. adversity.

adverso /aðˈβerso/ a. adverse.

advertencia /aðβerˈtenθia; aðβerˈtensia/ n. f. warning.

advertir /aðβerˈtir/ v. warn; notice.

adyacente /aðyaˈθente; aðyaˈsente/ a. adjacent.

aéreo /ˈaereo/ a. aerial; air.

aerodeslizador /aeroðesliˈθaðor; aeroðeslisaˈðor/ n. m. hovercraft.

aeromoza /aeroˈmoθa; aeroˈmosa/ n. f. stewardess, flight attendant.

aeroplano /aeroˈplano/ n. m. light plane.

aeropuerto /aeroˈpuerto/ n. m. airport.

aerosol /aeroˈsol/ n. m. aerosol, spray.

afable /aˈfaβle/ a. affable, pleasant.

afanarse /afaˈnarse/ v. toil.

afear /afeˈar/ v. deface, mar, deform.

afectación /afektaˈθion; afektaˈsion/ n. f. affectation.

afectar /afekˈtar/ v. affect.

afecto /aˈfekto/ n. m. affection, attachment.

afeitada /afeiˈtaða/ n. f. shave. —**afeitarse**, v.

afeminado /afemiˈnaðo/ a. effeminate.

afición /afiˈθion; afiˈsion/ n. f. fondness, liking; hobby.

aficionado /afiθioˈnaðo; afisioˈnaðo/ a. fond.

aficionado -da n. fan, devotee; amateur.

aficionarse a /afiθioˈnarse a; afisioˈnarse a/ v. become fond of.

afilado /afiˈlaðo/ a. sharp.

afilar /afiˈlar/ v. sharpen.

afiliación /afiliaˈθion; afiliaˈsion/ n. f. affiliation.

afiliado /afiˈliaðo/ **-da** n. affiliate. —**afiliar**, v.

afinar /afiˈnar/ v. polish; tune up.

afinidad /afiniˈðað/ n. f. relationship, affinity.

afirmación /afirmaˈθion; afirmaˈsion/ n. f. affirmation, statement.

afirmar /afirˈmar/ v. affirm, assert.

afirmativa /afirmaˈtiβa/ n. f. affirmative. —**afirmativo**, a.

aflicción /aflikˈθion; aflikˈsion/ n. f. affliction; sorrow, grief.

afligido /afliˈhiðo/ a. sorrowful, grieved.

afligir /afliˈhir/ v. grieve, distress.

aflojar /afloˈhar/ v. loosen.

afluencia /aˈfluenθia; aˈfluensia/ n. f. influx.

afortunado /afortuˈnaðo/ a. fortunate, successful, lucky.

afrenta /aˈfrenta/ n. f. insult, outrage, affront. —**afrentar**, v.

afrentoso /afrenˈtoso/ a. shameful.

africano /afriˈkano/ **-na** a. & n. African.

afuera /aˈfuera/ adv. out, outside.

afueras /aˈfueras/ n. f.pl. suburbs.

agacharse /agaˈtʃarse/ v. squat, crouch; cower.

agarrar /agaˈrrar/ v. seize, grasp, clutch.

agarro /aˈgarro/ n. m. clutch, grasp.

agencia /aˈhenθia; aˈhensia/ n. f. agency.

agencia de colocaciones /aˈhenθia de kolokaˈθiones; aˈhensia de kolokaˈsiones/ employment agency.

agencia de viajes /aˈhenθia de ˈbiahes; aˈhensia de ˈbiahes/ travel agency.

agente /aˈhente/ n. m. & f. agent, representative.

agente de aduana /aˈhente de aˈðuana/ mf. customs officer.

agente inmobiliario /aˈhente imoβiˈliario/ **-ria** n. real-estate agent.

ágil /ˈahil/ a. agile, spry.

agitación /ahitaˈθion; ahitaˈsion/ n. f. agitation, ferment.

agitado /ahiˈtaðo/ a. agitated; excited.

agitador /ahitaˈðor/ n. m. agitator.

agitar /ahiˈtar/ v. shake, agitate, excite.

agobiar /agoˈβiar/ v. oppress, burden.

agosto /aˈgosto/ n. m. August.

agotamiento /a,gotaˈmiento/ n. m. exhaustion.

agotar /agoˈtar/ v. exhaust, use up, sap.

agradable /agraˈðaβle/ a. agreeable, pleasant.

agradar /agraˈðar/ v. please.

agradecer /agraðeˈθer; agraðeˈser/ v. thank; appreciate, be grateful for.

agradecido /agraðeˈθiðo; agraðeˈsiðo/ a. grateful, thankful.

agradecimiento /agraðeθiˈmiento; agraðesiˈmiento/ n. m. gratitude, thanks.

agravar /agraˈβar/ v. aggravate, make worse.

agravio /aˈgraβio/ n. m. wrong. —**agraviar**, v.

agregado /agreˈgaðo/ a. & n. aggregate; Pol. attaché.

agregar /agreˈgar/ v. add; gather.

agresión /agreˈsion/ n. f. aggression; Leg. battery.

agresivo /agreˈsiβo/ a. aggressive.

agresor /agreˈsor/ **-ra** n. aggressor.

agrícola /aˈgrikola/ a. agricultural.

agricultor /agrikulˈtor/ n. m. farmer.

agricultura /agrikulˈtura/ n. f. agriculture, farming.

agrio /ˈagrio/ a. sour.

agrupar /agruˈpar/ v. group.

agua /ˈagua/ n. f. water. —**aguar**, v.

aguacate /aguaˈkate/ n. m. avocado, alligator pear.

aguafuerte /,aguaˈfuerte/ n. f. etching.

agua mineral /ˈagua mineˈral/ mineral water.

aguantar /aguanˈtar/ v. endure, stand, put up with.

aguardar /aguarˈðar/ v. await; expect.

aguardiente /aguarˈðiente/ n. m. brandy.

aguas abajo /ˈaguas aˈβaho/ adv. downriver, downstream.

aguas arriba /ˈaguas aˈrriβa/ adv. upriver, upstream.

agudo /aˈguðo/ a. sharp, keen, shrill; acute.

agüero /aˈguero/ n. m. omen.

águila /ˈagila/ n. f. eagle.

aguja /aˈguha/ n. f. needle.

agujero /aguˈhero/ n. m. hole.

aguzar /aguˈθar; aguˈsar/ v. sharpen.

ahí /aˈi/ adv. there.

ahogar /aoˈgar/ v. drown; choke; suffocate.

ahondar /aonˈdar/ v. deepen.

ahora /aˈora/ adv. now.

ahorcar /aorˈkar/ v. hang (execute).

ahorrar /aoˈrrar/ v. save, save up; spare.

ahorros /aˈorros/ n. m.pl. savings.

ahumar /auˈmar/ v. smoke.

airado /aiˈraðo/ a. angry, indignant.

aire /ˈaire/ n. m. air. —**airear**, v.

aire acondicionado /ˈaire akondiˈθionaðo; ˈaire akondisioˈnaðo/ air conditioning.

aislamiento /aislaˈmiento/ n. m. isolation.

aislar /aisˈlar/ v. isolate.

ajedrez /aheˈðreθ; aheˈðres/ n. m. chess.

ajeno /aˈheno/ a. alien; someone else's.

ajetreo /aheˈtreo/ n. m. hustle and bustle.

ají /aˈhi/ n. m. chili.

ajo /ˈaho/ n. m. garlic.

ajustado /ahusˈtaðo/ a. adjusted; trim; exact.

ajustar /ahusˈtar/ v. adjust.

ajuste /aˈhuste/ n. m. adjustment, settlement.

al /al/ contr. of a + el.

ala /ˈala/ n. f. wing; brim (of hat).

alabanza /alaˈβanθa; alaˈβansa/ n. f. praise. —**alabar**, v.

alabear /alaβeˈar/ v. warp.

ala delta /ˈala ˈdelta/ hang glider.

alambique /alamˈbike/ n. m. still.

alambre /aˈlambre/ n. m. wire. **a. de púas**, barbed wire.

alarde /aˈlarðe/ n. m. boasting, ostentation.

alargar /alarˈgar/ v. lengthen; stretch out.

alarma /aˈlarma/ n. f. alarm. —**alarmar**, v.

alba /ˈalβa/ n. f. daybreak, dawn.

albanega /alβaˈnega/ n. f. hair net.

albañil /alβaˈɲil/ n. m. bricklayer; mason.

albaricoque /alβariˈkoke/ n. m. apricot.

alberca /alˈβerka/ n. f. swimming pool.

albergue /alˈβerge/ n. m. shelter. —**albergar**, v.

alborotar /alβoroˈtar/ v. disturb, make noise, brawl, riot.

alboroto /alβoˈroto/ n. m. brawl, disturbance, din, tumult.

álbum /ˈalβum/ n. m. album.

álbum de recortes /ˈalβum de reˈkortes/ scrapbook.

alcachofa /alkaˈtʃofa/ n. f. artichoke.

alcalde /alˈkalde/ n. m. mayor.

alcance /alˈkanθe; alˈkanse/ n. m. reach; range, scope.

alcanfor /alkanˈfor/ n. m. camphor.

alcanzar /alkanˈθar; alkanˈsar/ v. reach, overtake, catch.

alcayata /alkaˈyata/ n. f. spike.

alce /ˈalθe; ˈalse/ n. m. elk.

alcoba /alˈkoβa/ n. f. bedroom; alcove.

alcoba de huéspedes /alˈkoβa de ˈuespeðes/ guest room.

alcoba de respeto /alˈkoβa de rresˈpeto/ guest room.

alcohol /alˈkool/ n. m. alcohol.

alcohólico /alkoˈoliko/ **-ca** a. & n. alcoholic.

aldaba /alˈdaβa/ n. f. latch.

aldea /alˈdea/ n. f. village.

alegación /alegaˈθion; alegaˈsion/ n. f. allegation.

alegar /aleˈgar/ v. allege.

alegrar /aleˈgrar/ v. make happy, brighten.

alegrarse /aleˈgrarse/ v. be glad.

alegre /aˈlegre/ a. glad, cheerful, merry.

alegría /aleˈgria/ n. f. gaiety, cheer.

alejarse /aleˈharse/ v. move away, off.

alemán /aleˈman/ **-ana** a. & n. German.

Alemania /aleˈmania/ n. f. Germany.

alentar /alenˈtar/ v. cheer up, encourage.

alergia /alerˈhia/ n. f. allergy.

alerta /aˈlerta/ adv. on the alert.

aleve /aˈleβe/ **alevoso** a. treacherous.

alfabeto /alfaˈβeto/ n. m. alphabet.

alfalfa /alˈfalfa/ n. f. alfalfa.

alfarería /alfareˈria/ n. f. pottery.

alférez /alˈfereθ; alˈferes/ n. m. (naval) ensign.

alfil /alˈfil/ n. m. (chess) bishop.

alfiler /alfiˈler/ n. m. pin.

alfombra /alˈfombra/ n. f. carpet, rug.

alforja /alˈforha/ n. f. knapsack; saddlebag.

alga /ˈalga/ n. f. seaweed.

alga marina /ˈalga maˈrina/ seaweed.

algarabía /algaraˈβia/ n. f. jargon; din.

álgebra /ˈalheβra/ n. f. algebra.

algo /ˈalgo/ pron. & adv. something, somewhat; anything.

algodón /algoˈðon/ n. m. cotton.

algodón hidrófilo /algoˈðon iˈðrofilo/ absorbent cotton.

alguien /ˈalgien/ pron. somebody, someone; anybody, anyone.

algún /alˈgun/ **-no -na** a. & pron. some; any.

alhaja /alˈaha/ n. f. jewel.

aliado /aˈliaðo/ **-da** a. & n. allied; ally. —**aliar**, v.

alianza /aˈlianθa; aˈliansa/ n. f. alliance.

alicates /aliˈkates/ n. m.pl. pliers.

aliento /aˈliento/ n. m. breath. **dar a.**, encourage.

aligerar /aliheˈrar/ v. lighten.

alimentar /alimenˈtar/ v. feed, nourish.

alimento /aliˈmento/ n. m. nourishment, food.

alinear /alineˈar/ v. line up; Pol. align.

aliñar /aliˈɲar/ v. dress (a salad).

aliño /aˈliɲo/ n. m. salad dressing.

alisar /aliˈsar/ v. smooth.

alistamiento /alistaˈmiento/ n. m. enlistment.

alistar /alisˈtar/ v. make ready, prime.

alistarse /alisˈtarse/ v. get ready; Mil. enlist.

aliviar /aliˈβiar/ v. alleviate, relieve, ease.

alivio /aˈliβio/ n. m. relief.

allá /aˈʎa; aˈya/ adv. there. **más a.**, beyond, farther on.

allanar /aʎaˈnar; ayaˈnar/ v. flatten, smooth, plane.

allí /aˈʎi; aˈyi/ adv. there. **por a.**, that way.

alma /ˈalma/ n. f. soul.

almacén /almaˈθen; almaˈsen/ n. m. department store; storehouse, warehouse.

almacenaje /almaθeˈnahe; almaseˈnahe/ n. m. storage.

almacenar /almaθeˈnar; almaseˈnar/ v. store.

almanaque /almaˈnake/ n. m. almanac.

almeja /alˈmeha/ n. f. clam.

almendra /alˈmendra/ n. f. almond.

almíbar /alˈmiβar/ n. m. syrup.

almidón /almiˈðon/ n. m. starch. —**almidonar**, v.

almirante /almiˈrante/ n. m. admiral.

almohada /almoˈaða/ n. f. pillow.

almuerzo /al'muerθo; al'muerso/ *n. m.* lunch. —**almorzar,** *v.*

alojamiento /aloha'miento/ *n. m.* lodging, accommodations.

alojar /alo'har/ *v.* lodge, house.

alojarse /alo'harse/ *v.* stay, room.

alquiler /alki'ler/ *n. m.* rent. —**alquilar,** *v.*

alrededor /alreðe'ðor/ *adv.* around.

alrededores /alreðe'ðores/ *n. m.pl.* environs.

altanero /alta'nero/ *a.* haughty.

altar /al'tar/ *n. m.* altar.

altavoz /ˌalta'βoθ; ˌalta'βos/ *n. m.* loudspeaker.

alteración /altera'θion; altera'sion/ *n. f.* alteration.

alterar /alte'rar/ *v.* alter.

alternativa /alterna'tiβa/ *n. f.* alternative. —**alternativo,** *a.*

alterno /al'terno/ *a.* alternate. —**alternar,** *v.*

alteza /al'teθa; al'tesa/ *n. f.* highness.

altivo /al'tiβo/ *a.* proud, haughty; lofty.

alto /'alto/ *a.* **1.** high, tall; loud. —*n.* **2.** *m.* height, story (house).

altura /al'tura/ *n. f.* height, altitude.

alud /a'luð/ *n. m.* avalanche.

aludir /alu'ðir/ *v.* allude.

alumbrado /alum'braðo/ *n. m.* lighting.

alumbrar /alum'brar/ *v.* light.

aluminio /alu'minio/ *n. m.* aluminum.

alumno /a'lumno/ **-na** *n.* student, pupil.

alusión /alu'sion/ *n. f.* allusion.

alza /'alθa; 'alsa/ *n. f.* rise; boost.

alzar /al'θar; al'sar/ *v.* raise, lift.

ama /'ama/ *n. f.* housewife, mistress (of house). **a. de llaves,** housekeeper.

amable /a'maβle/ *a.* kind; pleasant, sweet.

amalgamar /amalga'mar/ *v.* amalgamate.

amamantar /amaman'tar/ *v.* suckle, nurse.

amanecer /amane'θer; amane'ser/ *n.* **1.** *m.* dawn, daybreak. —*v.* **2.** dawn; awaken.

amante /a'mante/ *n. m. & f.* lover.

amapola /ama'pola/ *n. f.* poppy.

amar /a'mar/ *v.* love.

amargo /a'margo/ *a.* bitter.

amargón /amar'gon/ *n. m.* dandelion.

amargura /amar'gura/ *n. f.* bitterness.

amarillo /ama'riʎo; ama'riyo/ *a.* yellow.

amarradero /amarra'ðero/ *n. m.* mooring.

amarrar /ama'rrar/ *v.* hitch, moor, tie up.

amartillar /amarti'ʎar; amarti'yar/ *v.* hammer; cock (a gun).

amasar /ama'sar/ *v.* knead, mold.

ámbar /'ambar/ *n. m.* amber.

ambarino /amba'rino/ *a.* amber.

ambición /ambi'θion; ambi'sion/ *n. f.* ambition.

ambicionar /ambiθio'nar; ambisio'nar/ *v.* aspire to.

ambicioso /ambi'θioso; ambi'sioso/ *a.* ambitious.

ambientalista /ambienta'lista/ *n. m. & f.* environmentalist.

ambiente /am'biente/ *n. m.* environment, atmosphere.

ambigüedad /ambigue'ðað/ *n. f.* ambiguity.

ambiguo /am'biguo/ *a.* ambiguous.

ambos /'ambos/ *a. & pron.* both.

ambulancia /ambu'lanθia; ambu'lansia/ *n. f.* ambulance.

amenaza /ame'naθa; ame'nasa/ *n. f.* threat, menace.

amenazar /amena'θar; amena'sar/ *v.* threaten, menace.

ameno /a'meno/ *a.* pleasant.

americana /ameri'kana/ *n. f.* suit coat.

americano /ameri'kano/ **-na** *a. & n.* American.

ametralladora /ametraʎa'ðora; ametraya'ðora/ *n. f.* machine gun.

amigable /ami'gaβle/ *a.* amicable, friendly.

amígdala /a'migðala/ *n. f.* tonsil.

amigo /a'migo/ **-ga** *n.* friend.

aminorar /amino'rar/ *v.* lessen, reduce.

amistad /amis'tað/ *n. f.* friendship.

amistoso /amis'toso/ *a.* friendly.

amniocéntesis /amnioθen'tesis; amniosen'tesis/ *n. m.* amniocentesis.

amo /'amo/ *n. m.* master.

amonestaciones /amonesta'θiones; amonesta'siones/ *n. f.pl.* banns.

amonestar /amones'tar/ *v.* admonish.

amoníaco /amo'niako/ *n. m.* ammonia.

amontonar /amonto'nar/ *v.* amass, pile up.

amor /a'mor/ *n. m.* love. **a. propio,** self-esteem.

amorío /amo'rio/ *n. m.* romance, love affair.

amoroso /amo'roso/ *a.* amorous; loving.

amortecer /amorte'θer; amorte'ser/ *v.* deaden.

amparar /ampa'rar/ *v.* aid, befriend; protect, shield.

amparo /am'paro/ *n. m.* protection.

ampliar /amp'liar/ *v.* enlarge; elaborate.

amplificar /amplifi'kar/ *v.* amplify.

amplio /'amplio/ *a.* ample, roomy.

ampolla /am'poʎa; am'poya/ *n. f.* bubble; bulb; blister.

amputar /ampu'tar/ *v.* amputate.

amueblar /amue'βlar/ *v.* furnish.

analfabeto /analfa'βeto/ **-ta** *a. & n.* illiterate.

analgésico /anal'hesiko/ *n. m.* pain killer.

análisis /a'nalisis/ *n. m.* analysis.

analizar /anali'θar; anali'sar/ *v.* analyze.

analogía /analo'hia/ *n. f.* analogy.

análogo /a'nalogo/ *a.* similar, analogous.

anarquía /anar'kia/ *n. f.* anarchy.

anatomía /anato'mia/ *n. f.* anatomy.

ancho /'antʃo/ *a.* wide, broad.

anchoa /an'tʃoa/ *n. f.* anchovy.

anchura /an'tʃura/ *n. f.* width, breadth.

anciano /an'θiano; an'siano/ **-na** *a. & n.* old, aged (person).

ancla /'ankla/ *n. f.* anchor. —**anclar,** *v.*

anclaje /an'klahe/ *n. m.* anchorage.

andamio /an'damio/ *n. m.* scaffold.

andar /an'dar/ *v.* walk; move, go.

andén /an'den/ *n. m.* (railroad) platform.

andrajoso /andra'hoso/ *a.* ragged, uneven.

anécdota /a'nekðota/ *n. f.* anecdote.

anegar /ane'gar/ *v.* flood, drown.

anestesia /anes'tesia/ *n. f.* anesthetic.

anexar /anek'sar/ *v.* annex.

anexión /anek'sion/ *n. f.* annexation.

anfitrión /anfitri'on/ **-na** *n.* host.

ángel /'anhel/ *n. m.* angel.

angosto /aŋ'gosto/ *a.* narrow.

anguila /aŋ'gila/ *n. f.* eel.

angular /aŋgu'lar/ *a.* angular.

ángulo /'aŋgulo/ *n. m.* angle.

angustia /aŋ'gustia/ *n. f.* anguish, agony.

angustiar /aŋgus'tiar/ *v.* distress.

anhelar /ane'lar/ *v.* long for.

anidar /ani'ðar/ *v.* nest, nestle.

anillo /a'niʎo; a'niyo/ *n. m.* ring; circle.

animación /anima'θion; anima'sion/ *n. f.* animation; bustle.

animado /ani'maðo/ *a.* animated, lively; animate.

animal /ani'mal/ *a. & n.* animal.

ánimo /'animo/ *n. m.* state of mind, spirits; courage.

aniquilar /aniki'lar/ *v.* annihilate, destroy.

aniversario /aniβer'sario/ *n. m.* anniversary.

anoche /a'notʃe/ *adv.* last night.

anochecer /anotʃe'θer; anotʃe'ser/ *n.* **1.** *m.* twilight, nightfall. —*v.* **2.** get dark.

anónimo /a'nonimo/ *a.* anonymous.

anorexia /ano'reksia/ *n. f.* anorexia.

anormal /anor'mal/ *a.* abnormal.

anotación /anota'θion; anota'sion/ *f.* annotation.

anotar /ano'tar/ *v.* annotate.

ansia /'ansia/ **ansiedad** *n. f.* anxiety.

ansioso /an'sioso/ *a.* anxious.

antagonismo /antago'nismo/ *n. m.* antagonism.

antagonista /antago'nista/ *n. m. & f.* antagonist, opponent.

anteayer /antea'yer/ *adv.* day before yesterday.

antebrazo /ante'βraθo; ante'βraso/ *n. m.* forearm.

antecedente /anteθe'ðente; antese'ðente/ *a. & m.* antecedent.

anteceder /anteθe'ðer; antese'ðer/ *v.* precede.

antecesor /anteθe'sor; antese'sor/ *n. m.* ancestor.

antemano /ante'mano/ *de a.,* in advance.

antena /an'tena/ *n. f.* antenna.

antena parabólica /an'tena para'βolika/ satellite dish.

anteojos /ante'ohos/ *n. m.pl.* eyeglasses.

antepasado /antepa'saðo/ *n. m.* ancestor.

antepenúltimo /antepe'nultimo/ *a.* antepenultimate.

anterior /ante'rior/ *a.* previous, former.

antes /'antes/ *adv.* before; formerly.

antibala /anti'bala/ *a.* bulletproof.

anticipación /antiθipa'θion; antisipa'sion/ *n. f.* anticipation.

anticipar /antiθi'par; antisi'par/ *v.* anticipate; advance.

anticonceptivo /antikonθep'tiβo; antikonsep'tiβo/ *a. & n.* contraceptive.

anticongelante /antikoŋge'lante/ *m.* antifreeze.

anticuado /anti'kuaðo/ *a.* antiquated, obsolete.

antídoto /an'tiðoto/ *n. m.* antidote.

antigüedad /antigue'ðað/ *n. f.* antiquity; antique.

antiguo /an'tiguo/ *a.* former; old; antique.

antihistamínico /antiista'miniko/ *m.* antihistamine.

antílope /an'tilope/ *n. m.* antelope.

antinuclear /antinukle'ar/ *a.* antinuclear.

antipatía /antipa'tia/ *n. f.* antipathy.

antipático /anti'patiko/ *a.* disagreeable, nasty.

antiséptico /anti'septiko/ *a. & m.* antiseptic.

antojarse /anto'harse/ *v.* **se me antoja...** etc., I desire..., take a fancy to..., etc.

antojo /an'toho/ *n. m.* whim, fancy.

antorcha /an'tortʃa/ *n. f.* torch.

antracita /antra'θita; antra'sita/ *n. f.* anthracite.

anual /a'nual/ *a.* annual, yearly.

anudar /anu'ðar/ *v.* knot; tie.

anular /anu'lar/ *v.* annul, void.

anunciar /anun'θiar; anun'siar/ *v.* announce; proclaim, advertise.

anuncio /a'nunθio; a'nunsio/ *n. m.* announcement; advertisement.

añadir /aɲa'ðir/ *v.* add.

añil /a'ɲil/ *n. m.* bluing; indigo.

año /'aɲo/ *n. m.* year.

apacible /apa'θiβle; apa'siβle/ *a.* peaceful, peaceable.

apaciguamiento /aˌpaθigua'miento;

aˌpasigua'miento/ *n. m.* appeasement.

apaciguar /apaθi'guar; apasi'guar/ *v.* appease; placate.

apagado /apa'gaðo/ *a.* dull.

apagar /apa'gar/ *v.* extinguish, quench, put out.

apagón /apa'gn/ *n. m.* blackout.

aparador /apara'ðor/ *n. m.* buffet, cupboard.

aparato /apa'rato/ *n. m.* apparatus; machine; appliance, set.

aparcamiento /aparka'miento/ *n. m.* parking lot; parking space.

aparecer /apare'θer; apare'ser/ *v.* appear, show up.

aparejo /apa'reho/ *n. m.* rig. —**aparejar,** *v.*

aparentar /aparen'tar/ *v.* pretend; profess.

aparente /apa'rente/ *a.* apparent.

apariencia /apa'rienθia; apa'riensia/ **aparición** *n. f.* appearance.

apartado /apar'taðo/ *a.* **1.** aloof; separate. —*n.* **2.** *m.* post-office box.

apartamento /aparta'mento/ *n. m.* apartment. **a. en propiedad,** condominium.

apartar /apar'tar/ *v.* separate; remove.

aparte /a'parte/ *adv.* apart; aside.

apartheid /apar'teið/ *n. m.* apartheid.

apasionado /apasio'naðo/ *a.* passionate.

apatía /apa'tia/ *n. f.* apathy.

apearse /ape'arse/ *v.* get off, alight.

apedrear /apeðre'ar/ *v.* stone.

apelación /apela'θion; apela'sion/ *n. f.* appeal. —**apelar,** *v.*

apellido /ape'ʎiðo; ape'yiðo/ *n. m.* family name.

apellido materno /ape'ʎiðo ma'terno; ape'yiðo ma'terno/ mother's family name.

apellido paterno /ape'ʎiðo pa'terno; ape'yiðo pa'terno/ father's family name.

apenas /a'penas/ *adv.* scarcely, hardly.

apéndice /a'pendiθe; a'pendise/ *n. m.* appendix.

apercibir /aperθi'βir; apersi'βir/ *v.* prepare, warn.

aperitivo /aperi'tiβo/ *n. m.* appetizer.

aperos /a'peros/ *n. m.pl.* implements.

apestar /apes'tar/ *v.* infect; stink.

apetecer /apete'θer; apete'ser/ *v.* desire, have appetite for.

apetito /ape'tito/ *n. m.* appetite.

ápice /'apiθe; 'apise/ *n. m.* apex.

apilar /api'lar/ *v.* stack.

apio /'apio/ *n. m.* celery.

aplacar /apla'kar/ *v.* appease; placate.

aplastar /aplas'tar/ *v.* crush, flatten.

aplaudir /aplau'ðir/ *v.* applaud, cheer.

aplauso /a'plauso/ *n. m.* applause.

aplazar /apla'θar; apla'sar/ *v.* postpone, put off.

aplicable /apli'kaβle/ *a.* applicable.

aplicado /apli'kaðo/ *a.* industrious, diligent.

aplicar /apli'kar/ *v.* apply.

aplomo /a'plomo/ *n. m.* aplomb, poise.

apoderado /apoðe'raðo/ **-da** *n.* attorney.

apoderarse de /apoðe'rarse de/ *v.* get hold of, seize.

apodo /a'poðo/ *n. m.* nickname. —**apodar,** *v.*

apologético /apolo'hetiko/ *a.* apologetic.

apoplejía /apople'hia/ *n. f.* apoplexy.

aposento /apo'sento/ *n. m.* room, flat.

apostar /apos'tar/ *v.* bet, wager.

apóstol /a'postol/ *n. m.* apostle.

apoyar /apo'yar/ *v.* support, prop; lean.

apoyo /a'poyo/ *n. m.* support; prop; aid; approval.

apreciable /apre'θiaβle; apre'siaβle/ *a.* appreciable.

apreciar /apreˈθiar; apreˈsiar/ v. appreciate, prize.

aprecio /aˈpreθio; aˈpresio/ n. m. appreciation, regard.

apremio /aˈpremio/ n. m. pressure, compulsion.

aprender /aprenˈder/ v. learn.

aprendiz /aprenˈdiθ; aprenˈdis/ n. m. apprentice.

aprendizaje /aprendiˈθahe; aprendiˈsahe/ n. m. apprenticeship.

aprensión /aprenˈsion/ n. f. apprehension.

aprensivo /aprenˈsiβo/ a. apprehensive.

apresurado /apresuˈraðo/ a. hasty, fast.

apresurar /apresuˈrar/ v. hurry, speed up.

apretado /apreˈtaðo/ a. tight.

apretar /apreˈtar/ v. squeeze, press; tighten.

apretón /apreˈton/ n. m. squeeze.

aprieto /aˈprieto/ n. m. plight, predicament.

aprobación /aproβaˈθion; aproβaˈsion/ n. f. approbation, approval.

aprobar /aproˈβar/ v. approve.

apropiación /apropiaˈθion; apropiaˈsion/ n. f. appropriation.

apropiado /aproˈpiaðo/ a. appropriate. —**apropiar,** v.

aprovechar /aproβeˈtʃar/ v. profit by.

aprovecharse /aproβeˈtʃarse/ v. take advantage.

aproximado /aproksiˈmaðo/ a. approximate.

aproximarse a /aproksiˈmarse a/ v. approach.

aptitud /aptiˈtuð/ n. f. aptitude.

apto /ˈapto/ a. apt.

apuesta /aˈpuesta/ n. f. bet, wager, stake.

apuntar /apunˈtar/ v. point, aim; prompt; write down.

apunte /aˈpunte/ n. m. annotation, note; promptings, cue.

apuñalar /apuɲaˈlar/ v. stab.

apurar /apuˈrar/ v. hurry; worry.

apuro /aˈpuro/ n. m. predicament, scrape, trouble.

aquel /aˈkel/ **aquella** dem. a. that.

aquél /aˈkel/ **aquélla** dem. pron. that (one); the former.

aquello /aˈkeʎo; aˈkeyo/ dem. pron. that.

aquí /aˈki/ adv. here. **por a.,** this way.

aquietar /akieˈtar/ v. allay; lull, pacify.

ara /ˈara/ n. f. altar.

árabe /ˈaraβe/ a. & n. Arab, Arabic.

arado /aˈraðo/ n. m. plow. —**arar,** v.

arándano /aˈrandano/ n. m. cranberry.

araña /aˈraɲa/ n. f. spider. **a. de luces,** chandelier.

arbitración /arβitraˈθion; arβitraˈsion/ n. f. arbitration.

arbitrador /arβitraˈðor/ **-ra** n. arbitrator.

arbitraje /arβiˈtrahe/ n. m. arbitration.

arbitrar /arβiˈtrar/ v. arbitrate.

arbitrario /arβiˈtrario/ a. arbitrary.

árbitro /ˈarβitro/ n. m. arbiter, umpire, referee.

árbol /ˈarβol/ n. m. tree; mast.

árbol genealógico /ˈarβol heneaˈlohiko/ family tree.

arbusto /arˈβusto/ n. m. bush, shrub.

arca /ˈarka/ n. f. chest; ark.

arcada /arˈkaða/ n. f. arcade.

arcaico /arˈkaiko/ a. archaic.

arce /ˈarθe; ˈarse/ n. m. maple.

archipiélago /artʃiˈpielago/ n. m. archipelago.

archivador /artʃiβaˈðor/ n. m. file cabinet.

archivo /arˈtʃiβo/ n. m. archive; file. —**archivar,** v.

arcilla /arˈθiʎa; arˈsiya/ n. f. clay.

arco /ˈarko/ n. m. arc; arch; (archer's) bow. **a. iris,** rainbow.

arder /arˈðer/ v. burn.

ardid /arˈðið/ n. m. stratagem, cunning.

ardiente /arˈðiente/ a. ardent, burning, fiery.

ardilla /arˈðiʎa; arˈðiya/ n. f. squirrel.

ardor /arˈðor/ n. m. ardor, fervor.

ardor de estómago /arˈðor de esˈtomago/ heartburn.

arduo /ˈarðuo/ a. arduous.

área /ˈarea/ n. f. area.

arena /aˈrena/ n. f. sand; arena.

arenoso /areˈnoso/ a. sandy.

arenque /aˈrenke/ n. m. herring.

arete /aˈrete/ n. earring.

argentino /arhenˈtino/ **-na** a. & n. Argentine.

argüir /arˈguir/ v. dispute, argue.

árido /ˈariðo/ a. arid.

aristocracia /aristoˈkraθia; aristoˈkrasia/ n. f. aristocracy.

aristócrata /arisˈtokrata/ n. f. aristocrat.

aristocrático /aristoˈkratiko/ a. aristocratic.

aritmética /aritˈmetika/ n. f. arithmetic.

arma /ˈarma/ n. f. weapon, arm.

armadura /armaˈðura/ n. f. armor; reinforcement; framework.

armamento /armaˈmento/ n. m. armament.

armar /arˈmar/ v. arm.

armario /arˈmario/ n. m. cabinet, bureau, wardrobe.

armazón /armaˈθon; armaˈson/ n. m. framework, frame.

armería /armeˈria/ n. f. armory.

armisticio /armisˈtiθio; armisˈtisio/ n. m. armistice.

armonía /armoˈnia/ n. f. harmony.

armonioso /armoˈnioso/ a. harmonious.

armonizar /armoniˈθar; armoniˈsar/ v. harmonize.

arnés /arˈnes/ n. m. harness.

aroma /aˈroma/ n. f. aroma, fragrance.

aromático /aroˈmatiko/ a. aromatic.

arpa /ˈarpa/ n. f. harp.

arquear /arkeˈar/ v. arch.

arquitecto /arkiˈtekto/ n. m. architect.

arquitectura /arkitekˈtura/ n. f. architecture.

arquitectural /arkitektuˈral/ a. architectural.

arrabal /arraˈβal/ n. m. suburb.

arraigar /arraiˈgar/ v. take root, settle.

arrancar /arranˈkar/ v. pull out, tear out; start up.

arranque /aˈrranke/ n. m. dash, sudden start; fit of anger.

arrastrar /arrasˈtrar/ v. drag.

arrebatar /arreβaˈtar/ v. snatch, grab.

arrebato /arreˈβato/ n. m. sudden attack, fit of anger.

arrecife /arreˈθife; arreˈsife/ n. m. reef.

arreglar /arreˈglar/ v. arrange; repair, fix; adjust, settle.

arreglárselas /arreˈglarselas/ v. manage, shift for oneself.

arreglo /aˈrreglo/ n. m. arrangement, settlement.

arremangarse /arremaɲˈgarse/ v. roll up one's sleeves; roll up one's pants.

arremeter /arremeˈter/ v. attack.

arrendar /arrenˈdar/ v. rent.

arrepentimiento /arrepentiˈmiento/ n. m. repentance.

arrepentirse /arrepenˈtirse/ v. repent.

arrestar /arresˈtar/ v. arrest.

arriba /aˈrriβa/ adv. up; upstairs.

arriendo /aˈrriendo/ n. m. lease.

arriero /aˈrriero/ n. m. muleteer.

arriesgar /arriesˈgar/ v. risk.

arrimarse /arriˈmarse/ v. lean.

arrodillarse /arroðiˈʎarse; arroðiˈyarse/ v. kneel.

arrogancia /arroˈganθia; arroˈgansia/ n. f. arrogance.

arrogante /arroˈgante/ a. arrogant.

arrojar /arroˈhar/ v. throw, hurl; shed.

arrollar /arroˈʎar; arroˈyar/ v. roll, coil.

arroyo /aˈrroyo/ n. m. brook; gully; gutter.

arroz /aˈrroθ; aˈrros/ n. m. rice.

arruga /aˈrruga/ n. f. ridge; wrinkle.

arrugar /arruˈgar/ v. wrinkle, crumple.

arruinar /arruiˈnar/ v. ruin, destroy, wreck.

arsenal /arseˈnal/ n. m. arsenal; armory.

arsénico /arˈseniko/ n. m. arsenic.

arte /ˈarte/ n. m. (f. in pl.) art, craft; wiliness.

arteria /arˈteria/ n. f. artery.

artesa /arˈtesa/ n. f. trough.

artesano /arteˈsano/ **-na** n. artisan, craftsman.

ártico /ˈartiko/ a. arctic.

articulación /artikulaˈθion; artikulaˈsion/ n. f. articulation; joint.

articular /artikuˈlar/ v. articulate.

artículo /arˈtikulo/ n. m. article.

artífice /arˈtifiθe; arˈtifise/ n. m. & f. artisan.

artificial /artifiˈθial; artifiˈsial/ a. artificial.

artificio /artiˈfiθio; artiˈfisio/ n. m. artifice, device.

artificioso /artifiˈθioso; artifiˈsioso/ a. affected.

artillería /artiˈʎeria; artiyeˈria/ n. f. artillery.

artista /arˈtista/ n. m. & f. artist.

artístico /arˈtistiko/ a. artistic.

artritis /arˈtritis/ n. f. arthritis.

arzobispo /arθoˈβispo; arsoˈβispo/ n. m. archbishop.

as /as/ n. m. ace.

asado /aˈsaðo/ a. & n. roast.

asaltador /asaltaˈðor/ **-ra** n. assailant.

asaltante /asalˈtante/ n. m. & f. mugger.

asaltar /asalˈtar/ v. assail, attack.

asalto /aˈsalto/ n. m. assault. —**asaltar,** v.

asamblea /asamˈβlea/ n. f. assembly.

asar /aˈsar/ v. roast; broil, cook (meat).

asaz /aˈsaθ; aˈsas/ adv. enough; quite.

ascender /asθenˈder; assenˈder/ v. ascend, go up; amount.

ascenso /asˈθenso; asˈsenso/ n. m. ascent.

ascensor /asθenˈsor; assenˈsor/ n. m. elevator.

ascensorista /asθensoˈrista; assensoˈrista/ n. m. & f. (elevator) operator.

asco /ˈasko/ n. m. nausea; disgusting thing. **qué a.,** how disgusting.

aseado /aseˈaðo/ a. tidy. —**asear,** v.

asediar /aseˈðiar/ v. besiege.

asedio /aˈseðio/ n. m. siege.

asegurar /aseguˈrar/ v. assure; secure.

asegurarse /aseguˈrarse/ v. make sure.

asemejarse a /asemeˈharse a/ v. resemble.

asentar /asenˈtar/ v. settle; seat.

asentimiento /asentiˈmiento/ n. m. assent. —**asentir,** v.

aseo /aˈseo/ n. m. neatness, tidiness.

aseos /aˈseos/ n. m.pl. restroom.

asequible /aseˈkiβle/ a. attainable; affordable.

aserción /aserˈθion; aserˈsion/ n. f. assertion.

aserrar /aseˈrrar/ v. saw.

asesinar /asesiˈnar/ v. assassinate; murder, slay.

asesinato /asesiˈnato/ n. m. assassination, murder.

asesino /aseˈsino/ **-na** n. murderer, assassin.

aseveración /aseβeraˈθion; aseβeraˈsion/ n. f. assertion.

aseverar /aseβeˈrar/ v. assert.

asfalto /asˈfalto/ n. m. asphalt.

así /aˈsi/ adv. so, thus, this way, that way. **a. como,** as well as. **a. que,** as soon as.

asiático /aˈsiatiko/ **-ca** a. & n. Asiatic.

asiduo /aˈsiðuo/ a. assiduous.

asiento /aˈsiento/ n. m. seat; chair; site.

asiento delantero /aˈsiento delanˈtero/ front seat.

asiento trasero /aˈsiento traˈsero/ back seat.

asignar /asigˈnar/ v. assign; allot.

asilo /aˈsilo/ n. m. asylum, sanctuary.

asimilar /asimiˈlar/ v. assimilate.

asir /aˈsir/ v. grasp.

asistencia /asisˈtenθia; asisˈtensia/ n. f. attendance, presence.

asistir /asisˈtir/ v. be present, attend.

asno /ˈasno/ n. m. donkey.

asociación /asoθiaˈθion; asosiaˈsion/ n. f. association.

asociado /asoˈθiaðo; asoˈsiaðo/ n. m. associate, partner.

asociar /asoˈθiar; asoˈsiar/ v. associate.

asolar /asoˈlar/ v. desolate; burn, parch.

asoleado /asoleˈaðo/ a. sunny.

asomar /asoˈmar/ v. appear, loom up, show up.

asombrar /asomˈβrar/ v. astonish, amaze.

asombro /aˈsombro/ n. m. amazement, astonishment.

aspa /ˈaspa/ n. f. reel. —**aspar,** v.

aspecto /asˈpekto/ n. m. aspect.

aspereza /aspeˈreθa; aspeˈresa/ n. f. harshness.

áspero /ˈaspero/ a. rough, harsh.

aspiración /aspiraˈθion; aspiraˈsion/ n. f. aspiration.

aspirador /aspiraˈðor/ n. m. vacuum cleaner.

aspirar /aspiˈrar/ v. aspire.

aspirina /aspiˈrina/ n. f. aspirin.

asqueroso /askeˈroso/ a. dirty, nasty, filthy.

asta /ˈasta/ n. f. shaft.

asterisco /asteˈrisko/ n. m. asterisk.

astilla /asˈtiʎa; asˈtiya/ n. f. splinter, chip. —**astillar,** v.

astillero /astiˈʎero; astiˈyero/ n. m. dry dock.

astro /ˈastro/ n. m. star.

astronauta /astroˈnauta/ n. m. & f. astronaut.

astronave /astroˈnaβe/ n. f. spaceship.

astronomía /astronoˈmia/ n. f. astronomy.

astucia /asˈtuθia; asˈtusia/ n. f. cunning.

astuto /asˈtuto/ a. astute, sly, shrewd.

asumir /asuˈmir/ v. assume.

asunto /aˈsunto/ n. m. matter, affair, business; subject.

asustar /asusˈtar/ v. frighten, scare, startle.

atacar /ataˈkar/ v. attack, charge.

atajo /aˈtaho/ n. m. shortcut.

ataque /aˈtake/ n. m. attack, charge; spell, stroke.

ataque cardíaco /aˈtake karˈðiako/ heart attack.

atar /aˈtar/ v. tie, bind, fasten.

atareado /atareˈaðo/ a. busy.

atascar /atasˈkar/ v. stall, stop, obstruct.

atasco /aˈtasko/ n. m. traffic jam.

ataúd /ataˈuð/ n. m. casket, coffin.

atavío /ataˈβio/ n. m. dress; gear, equipment.

atemorizar /atemoriˈθar; atemoriˈsar/ v. frighten.

atención /atenˈθion; atenˈsion/ n. f. attention.

atender /atenˈder/ v. heed; attend to, wait on.

atenerse a /ateˈnerse a/ v. count on, depend on.

atentado /atenˈtaðo/ n. m. crime, offense.

atento /a'tento/ *a.* attentive, courteous.

ateo /a'teo/ *n. m.* atheist.

aterrizaje /aterri'θahe; aterri'sahe/ *n. m.* landing (of aircraft).

aterrizaje forzoso /aterri'θahe for'θoso; aterri'sahe for'soso/ emergency landing, forced landing.

aterrizar /aterri'θar; aterri'sar/ *v.* land.

atesorar /ateso'rar/ *v.* hoard.

atestar /ates'tar/ *v.* witness.

atestiguar /atesti'guar/ *v.* attest, testify.

atinar /ati'nar/ *v.* hit upon.

atisbar /atis'βar/ *v.* scrutinize, pry.

Atlántico /at'lantiko/ *n. m.* Atlantic.

atlántico *a.* Atlantic.

atlas /'atlas/ *n. m.* atlas.

atleta /at'leta/ *n. m. & f.* athlete.

atlético /at'letiko/ *a.* athletic.

atletismo /atle'tismo/ *n. m.* athletics.

atmósfera /at'mosfera/ *n. f.* atmosphere.

atmosférico /atmos'feriko/ *a.* atmospheric.

atolladero /atoʎa'ðero; atoya'ðero/ *n. m.* dead end, impasse.

atómico /a'tomiko/ *a.* atomic.

átomo /'atomo/ *n. m.* atom.

atormentar /atormen'tar/ *v.* torment, plague.

atornillar /atorni'ʎar; atorni'yar/ *v.* screw.

atracción /atrak'θion; atrak'sion/ *n. f.* attraction.

atractivo /atrak'tiβo/ *a.* **1.** attractive. —*n.* **2.** *m.* attraction.

atraer /atra'er/ *v.* attract; lure.

atrapar /atra'par/ *v.* trap, catch.

atrás /a'tras/ *adv.* back; behind.

atrasado /atra'saðo/ *a.* belated; backward; slow (clock).

atrasar /atra'sar/ *v.* delay, retard; be slow.

atraso /a'traso/ *n. m.* delay; backwardness; (*pl.*) arrears.

atravesar /atraβe'sar/ *v.* cross.

atreverse /atre'βerse/ *v.* dare.

atrevido /atre'βiðo/ *a.* daring, bold.

atrevimiento /atreβi'miento/ *n. m.* boldness.

atribuir /atri'βuir/ *v.* attribute, ascribe.

atributo /atri'βuto/ *n. m.* attribute.

atrincherar /atrintʃe'rar/ *v.* entrench.

atrocidad /atroθi'ðað; atrosi'ðað/ *n. f.* atrocity, outrage.

atronar /atro'nar/ *v.* deafen.

atropellar /atrope'ʎar; atrope'yar/ *v.* trample; fell.

atroz /a'troθ; a'ntros/ *a.* atrocious.

atún /a'tun/ *n. m.* tuna.

aturdir /atur'ðir/ *v.* daze, stun, bewilder.

audacia /au'ðaθia; au'ðasia/ *n. f.* audacity.

audaz /au'ðaθ; au'ðas/ *a.* audacious, bold.

audible /au'ðiβle/ *a.* audible.

audífono /au'ðifono/ *n. m.* hearing aid.

audiovisual /auðioβi'sual/ *a.* audiovisual.

auditorio /auði'torio/ *n. m.* audience.

aula /'aula/ *n. f.* classroom, hall.

aullar /au'ʎar; au'yar/ *v.* howl, bay.

aullido /au'ʎiðo; au'yiðo/ *n. m.* howl.

aumentar /aumen'tar/ *v.* augment; increase, swell.

aun /a'un/ **aún** *adv.* still; even. **a. cuando,** even though, even if.

aunque /'aunke/ *conj.* although, though.

áureo /'aureo/ *a.* golden.

aureola /aure'ola/ *n. f.* halo.

auriculares /auriku'lares/ *n. m.pl.* headphones.

aurora /au'rora/ *n. f.* dawn.

ausencia /au'senθia; au'sensia/ *n. f.* absence.

ausentarse /ausen'tarse/ *v.* stay away.

ausente /au'sente/ *a.* absent.

auspicio /aus'piθio; aus'pisio/ *n. m.* auspice.

austeridad /austeri'ðað/ *n. f.* austerity.

austero /aus'tero/ *a.* austere.

austriaco /aus'triako/ **-ca** *a. & n.* Austrian.

auténtico /au'tentiko/ *a.* authentic.

auto /'auto/ **automóvil** *n. m.* auto, automobile.

autobús /auto'βus/ *n. m.* bus.

autocine /auto'θine; auto'sine/ **autocinema** *n. m.* drive-in (movie theater).

automático /auto'matiko/ *a.* automatic.

autonomía /autono'mia/ *n. f.* autonomy.

autopista /auto'pista/ *n. f.* expressway.

autor /au'tor/ *n. m.* author.

autoridad /autori'ðað/ *n. f.* authority.

autoritario /autori'tario/ *a.* authoritarian; authoritative.

autorizar /autori'θar; autori'sar/ *v.* authorize.

autostop /auto'stop/ *n. m.* hitchhiking. **hacer a.,** to hitchhike.

auxiliar /auksi'liar/ *a.* **1.** auxiliary. —*v.* **2.** assist, aid.

auxilio /auk'silio/ *n. m.* aid, assistance.

avaluar /aβa'luar/ *v.* evaluate, appraise.

avance /a'βanθe; a'βanse/ *n. m.* advance. —**avanzar,** *v.*

avaricia /aβa'riθia; aβa'risia/ *n. f.* avarice.

avariento /aβa'riento/ *a.* miserly, greedy.

avaro /a'βaro/ **-ra** *a. & m.* miser; miserly.

ave /'aβe/ *n. f.* bird.

avellana /aβe'ʎana; aβe'yana/ *n. f.* hazelnut.

Ave María /aβema'ria/ *n. m.* Hail Mary.

avena /a'βena/ *n. f.* oat.

avenida /aβe'niða/ *n. f.* avenue; flood.

avenirse /aβe'nirse/ *v.* compromise; agree.

aventajar /aβenta'har/ *v.* surpass, get ahead of.

aventar /aβen'tar/ *v.* fan; scatter.

aventura /aβen'tura/ *n. f.* adventure.

aventurar /aβentu'rar/ *v.* venture, risk, gamble.

aventurero /aβentu'rero/ **-ra** *a. & n.* adventurous; adventurer.

avergonzado /aβergon'θaðo; aβergon'saðo/ *a.* ashamed, abashed.

avergonzar /aβergon'θar; aβergon'sar/ *v.* shame, abash.

avería /aβe'ria/ *n. f.* damage. —**averiar,** *v.*

averiguar /aβeri'guar/ *v.* ascertain, find out.

aversión /aβer'sion/ *n. f.* aversion.

avestruz /aβes'truθ; aβes'trus/ *n. m.* ostrich.

aviación /aβia'θion; aβia'sion/ *n. f.* aviation.

aviador /aβia'ðor/ **-ra** *n.* aviator.

ávido /'aβiðo/ *a.* avid; eager.

avión /a'βion/ *n. m.* airplane.

avisar /aβi'sar/ *v.* notify, let know; warn, advise.

aviso /a'βiso/ *n. m.* notice, announcement; advertisement; warning.

avispa /a'βispa/ *n. f.* wasp.

avivar /aβi'βar/ *v.* enliven, revive.

axila /ak'sila/ *n. f.* armpit.

aya /'aya/ *n. f.* governess.

ayatolá /aya'tola/ *n. m.* ayatollah.

ayer /a'yer/ *adv.* yesterday.

ayuda /a'yuða/ *n. f.* help, aid. —**ayudar,** *v.*

ayudante /ayu'ðante/ *a.* assistant, helper; adjutant.

ayuno /a'yuno/ *n. m.* fast. —**ayunar,** *v.*

ayuntamiento /ayunta'miento/ *n. m.* city hall.

azada /a'θaða; a'saða/ *n. f.,* **azadón,** *m.* hoe.

azafata /aθa'fata; asa'fata/ *n. f.* stewardess, flight attendant.

azar /a'θar; a'sar/ *n. m.* hazard, chance. **al a.,** at random.

azotar /aθo'tar; aso'tar/ *v.* whip, flog; belabor.

azote /a'θote; a'sote/ *n. m.* scourge, lash.

azúcar /a'θukar; a'sukar/ *n. m.* sugar.

azucarero /aθuka'rero; asuka'rero/ *n. m.* sugar bowl.

azúcar moreno /a'θukar mo'reno; a'sukar mo'reno/ brown sugar.

azul /a'θul; a'sul/ *a.* blue.

azulado /aθu'laðo; asu'laðo/ *a.* blue, bluish.

azulejo /aθu'leho; asu'leho/ *n. m.* tile; bluebird.

azul marino /a'θul ma'rino; a'sul ma'rino/ navy blue.

B

baba /'baβa/ *n. f.* drivel. —**babear,** *v.*

babador /baβa'ðor, ba'βero/ *n. m.* bib.

babucha /ba'βutʃa/ *n. f.* slipper.

bacalao /baka'lao/ *n. m.* codfish.

bachiller /batʃi'ʎer; batʃi'yer/ **-ra** *n.* bachelor (degree).

bacía /ba'θia; ba'sia/ *n. f.* washbasin.

bacterias /bak'terias/ *n. f.pl.* bacteria.

bacteriología /bakteriolo'hia/ *n. f.* bacteriology.

bahía /ba'ia/ *n. f.* bay.

bailador /baila'ðor/ **-ra** *n.* dancer.

bailar /bai'lar/ *v.* dance.

bailarín /baila'rin/ **-ina** *n.* dancer.

baile /'baile/ *n. m.* dance.

baja /'baha/ *n. f.* fall (in price); *Mil.* casualty.

bajar /ba'har/ *v.* lower; descend.

bajeza /ba'heθa; ba'hesa/ *n. f.* baseness.

bajo /'baho/ *prep.* **1.** under, below. —*a.* **2.** low; short; base.

bala /'bala/ *n. f.* bullet; ball; bale.

balada /ba'laða/ *n. f.* ballad.

balancear /balanθe'ar; balanse'ar/ *v.* balance; roll, swing, sway.

balanza /ba'lanθa; ba'lansa/ *n. f.* balance; scales.

balbuceo /balβu'θeo; balβu'seo/ *n. m.* stammer; babble. —**balbucear,** *v.*

Balcanes /bal'kanes/ *n. m.pl.* Balkans.

balcón /bal'kon/ *n. m.* balcony.

balde /'balde/ *n. m.* bucket, pail. **de b.,** gratis. **en b.,** in vain.

balística /ba'listika/ *n. f.* ballistics.

ballena /ba'ʎena; ba'yena/ *n. f.* whale.

balneario /balne'ario/ *n. m.* bathing resort; spa.

balompié /balom'pie/ *n. m.* football.

balón /ba'lon/ *n. m.* football; *Auto.* balloon tire.

baloncesto /balon'θesto; balon'sesto/ *n. m.* basketball.

balota /ba'lota/ *n. f.* ballot, vote. —**balotar,** *v.*

balsa /'balsa/ *n. f.* raft.

bálsamo /'balsamo/ *n. m.* balm.

baluarte /ba'luarte/ *n. m.* bulwark.

bambolearse /bambole'arse/ *v.* sway.

bambú /bam'βu/ *n.* bamboo.

banal /ba'nal/ *a.* banal, trite.

banana /ba'nana/ *n. f.* banana.

banano /ba'nano/ *n. m.* banana tree.

bancarrota /banka'rrota/ *n. f.* bankruptcy.

banco /'banko/ *n. m.* bank; bench; school of fish.

banco cooperativo /'banko koopera'tiβo/ credit union.

banda /'banda/ *n. f.* band.

bandada /ban'daða/ *n. f.* covey; flock.

banda sonora /'banda so'nora/ *n. f.* soundtrack.

bandeja /ban'deha/ *n. f.* tray.

bandera /ban'dera/ *n. f.* flag; banner; ensign.

bandido /ban'diðo/ **-da** *n.* bandit.

bando /'bando/ *n. m.* faction.

bandolero /bando'lero/ **-ra** *n.* bandit, robber.

banquero /ban'kero/ **-ra** *n.* banker.

banqueta /ban'keta/ *n. f.* stool; (Mex.) sidewalk.

banquete /ban'kete/ *n. m.* feast, banquet.

banquillo /ban'kiʎo; ban'kiyo/ *n. m.* stool.

bañar /ba'ɲar/ *v.* bathe.

bañera /ba'ɲera/ *n. f.* bathtub.

baño /'baɲo/ *n. m.* bath; bathroom.

bar /bar/ *n. m.* bar, pub.

baraja /ba'raha/ *n. f.* pack of cards; game of cards.

baranda /ba'randa/ *n. f.* railing, banister.

barato /ba'rato/ *a.* cheap.

barba /'barβa/ *n. f.* beard; chin.

barbacoa /barβa'koa/ *n. f.* barbecue; stretcher.

barbaridad /barβari'ðað/ *n. f.* barbarity; *Colloq.* excess (in anything).

bárbaro /'barβaro/ *a.* barbarous; crude.

barbería /barβe'ria/ *n. f.* barbershop.

barbero /bar'βero/ *n. m.* barber.

barca /'barka/ *n. f.* (small) boat.

barcaza /bar'kaθa; bar'kasa/ *n. f.* barge.

barco /'barko/ *n. m.* ship, boat.

barniz /bar'niθ; bar'nis/ *n. m.* varnish. —**barnizar,** *v.*

barómetro /ba'rometro/ *n. m.* barometer.

barón /ba'ron/ *n. m.* baron.

barquilla /bar'kiʎa; bar'kiya/ *n. f.* *Naut.* log.

barra /'barra/ *n. f.* bar.

barraca /ba'rraka/ *n. f.* hut, shed.

barrear /barre'ar/ *v.* bar, barricade.

barreno /ba'rreno/ *n. m.* blast, blasting. —**barrenar,** *v.*

barrer /ba'rrer/ *v.* sweep.

barrera /ba'rrera/ *n. f.* barrier.

barricada /barri'kaða/ *n. f.* barricade.

barriga /ba'rriga/ *n. f.* belly.

barril /ba'rril/ *n. m.* barrel; cask.

barrio /'barrio/ *n. m.* district, ward, quarter.

barro /'barro/ *n. m.* clay, mud.

base /'base/ *n. f.* base; basis. —**basar,** *v.*

base de datos /'base de 'datos/ database.

bastante /bas'tante/ *a.* **1.** enough, plenty of. —*adv.* **2.** enough; rather, quite.

bastar /bas'tar/ *v.* suffice, be enough.

bastardo /bas'tarðo/ **-a** *a. & n.* bastard.

bastear /baste'ar/ *v.* baste.

bastidor /basti'ðor/ *n. m.* wing (in theater).

bastón /bas'ton/ *n. m.* (walking) cane.

bastos /'bastos/ *n. m.pl.* clubs (cards).

basura /ba'sura/ *n. f.* refuse, dirt; garbage; junk.

basurero /basu'rero/ **-ra** *n.* scavenger.

batalla /ba'taʎa; ba'taya/ *n. f.* battle. —**batallar,** *v.*

batallón /bata'ʎon; bata'yon/ *n. m.* batallion.

batata /ba'tata/ *n. f.* sweet potato.

bate /'bate/ *n. m.* bat. —**batear,** *v.*

batería /bate'ria/ *n. f.* battery.

batido /ba'tiðo/ *n. m.* (cooking) batter; milkshake.

batidora /bati'ðora/ *n. f.* mixer (for food).

batir /ba'tir/ v. beat; demolish; conquer.

baúl /ba'ul/ n. m. trunk.

bautismo /bau'tismo/ n. m. baptism.

bautista /bau'tista/ n. m. & f. Baptist.

bautizar /bauti'θar; bauti'sar/ v. christen, baptize.

bautizo /bau'tiθo; bau'tiso/ n. m. baptism.

baya /'baia/ n. f. berry.

bayoneta /bayo'neta/ n. f. bayonet.

beato /be'ato/ a. blessed.

bebé /be'βe/ n. m. baby.

beber /be'βer/ v. drink.

bebible /be'βiβle/ a. drinkable.

bebida /be'βiða/ n. f. drink, beverage.

beca /'beka/ n. f. grant, scholarship.

becado /be'kaðo/ -da n. scholar.

becerro /be'θerro; be'serro/ n. m. calf; calfskin.

beldad /bel'dað/ n. f. beauty.

belga /'belga/ a. & n. Belgian.

Bélgica /'belhika/ n. f. Belgium.

belicoso /beli'koso/ a. warlike.

beligerante /belihe'rante/ a. & n. belligerent.

bellaco /be'ʎako; be'yako/ a. **1.** sly, roguish. —n. **2.** m. rogue.

bellas artes /'beʎas 'artes; 'beyas 'artes/ n. f.pl. fine arts.

belleza /be'ʎeθa; be'yesa/ n. f. beauty.

bello /'beʎo; 'beyo/ a. beautiful.

bellota /be'ʎota; be'yota/ n. f. acorn.

bendecir /bende'θir; bende'sir/ v. bless.

bendición /bendi'θion; bendi'sion/ n. f. blessing, benediction.

bendito /ben'dito/ a. blessed.

beneficio /bene'fiθio; bene'fisio/ m. benefit. —**beneficiar,** v.

beneficioso /benefi'θioso; benefi'sioso/ a. beneficial.

benevolencia /beneβo'lenθia; beneβo'lensia/ n. f. benevolence.

benévolo /be'neβolo/ a. benevolent.

benigno /be'nigno/ a. benign.

beodo /be'oðo/ -da a. & n. drunk.

berenjena /beren'hena/ n. f. eggplant.

beso /'beso/ n. m. kiss. —**besar,** v.

bestia /'bestia/ n. f. beast, brute.

betabel /beta'βel/ n. m. beet.

Biblia /'biβlia/ n. f. Bible.

bíblico /'biβliko/ a. Biblical.

biblioteca /biβlio'teka/ n. f. library.

bicarbonato /bikarβo'nato/ n. m. bicarbonate.

bicicleta /biθi'kleta; bisi'kleta/ n. f. bicycle.

bien /bien/ adv. **1.** well. —n. **2.** good; (pl.) possessions.

bienes inmuebles /'bienes i'mueβles/ n. m.pl. real estate.

bienestar /bienes'tar/ n. m. well-being, welfare.

bienhechor /biene'tʃor/ -ra n. benefactor.

bienvenida /biembe'niða/ n. f. welcome.

bienvenido /biembe'niðo/ a. welcome.

biftec /bif'tek/ n. m. steak.

bifurcación /bifurka'θion; bifurka'sion/ n. f. fork. —**bifurcar,** v.

bigamia /bi'gamia/ n. f. bigamy.

bígamo /'bigamo/ -a n. bigamist.

bigotes /bi'gotes/ n. m.pl. mustache.

bikini /bi'kini/ n. m. bikini.

bilingüe /bi'lingue/ a. bilingual.

bilingüismo /bilin'guismo/ n. m. bilingualism.

bilis /'bilis/ n. f. bile.

billar /bi'ʎar; bi'yar/ n. m. billiards.

billete /bi'ʎete; bi'yete/ n. m. ticket; bank note, bill.

billete de banco /bi'ʎete de 'banko; bi'yete de 'banko/ bank note.

billón /bi'ʎon; bi'yon/ n. m. billion.

bingo /'bingo/ n. m. bingo.

biodegradable /bioðegra'ðaβle/ a. biodegradable.

biografía /biogra'fia/ n. f. biography.

biología /biolo'hia/ n. f. biology.

biombo /'biombo/ n. m. folding screen.

bisabuela /bisa'βuela/ n. f. great-grandmother.

bisabuelo /bisa'βuelo/ n. m. great-grandfather.

bisel /bi'sel/ n. m. bevel. —**biselar,** v.

bisonte /bi'sonte/ n. m. bison.

bisté /bis'te/ **bistec** n. m. steak.

bisutería /bisute'ria/ n. f. costume jewelry.

bizarro /bi'θarro; bi'sarro/ a. brave; generous; smart.

bizco /'biθko/ -ca n. **1.** cross-eyed person. —a. **2.** cross-eyed, squinting.

bizcocho /biθ'kotʃo; bis'kotʃo/ n. m. biscuit, cake.

blanco /'blanko/ a. **1.** white; blank. —n. **2.** m. white; target.

blandir /blan'dir/ v. brandish, flourish.

blando /'blando/ a. soft.

blanquear /blanke'ar/ v. whiten; bleach.

blasfemar /blasfe'mar/ v. blaspheme, curse.

blasfemia /blas'femia/ n. f. blasphemy.

blindado /blin'daðo/ a. armored.

blindaje /blin'dahe/ n. m. armor.

bloque /'bloke/ n. m. block. —**bloquear,** v.

bloqueo /blo'keo/ n. m. blockade. —**bloquear,** v.

blusa /'blusa/ n. f. blouse.

bobada /bo'βaða/ n. f. stupid, silly thing.

bobo /'boβo/ -ba a. & n. fool; foolish.

boca /'boka/ n. f. mouth.

bocado /bo'kaðo/ n. m. bit; bite, mouthful.

bocanada /boka'naða/ n. f. puff (of smoke); mouthful (of liquor).

bocazas /bo'kaθas/ n. m. & f. Colloq. bigmouth.

bochorno /bo'tʃorno/ n. m. sultry weather; embarrassment.

bocina /bo'θina; bo'sina/ n. f. horn.

boda /'boða/ n. f. wedding.

bodega /bo'ðega/ n. f. wine cellar; Naut. hold; (Carib.) grocery store.

bofetada /bofe'taða/ n. f. **bofetón,** m. slap.

boga /'boga/ n. f. vogue; fad.

bogar /bo'gar/ v. row (a boat).

bohemio /bo'emio/ -a a. & n. Bohemian.

boicoteo /boiko'teo/ n. m. boycott. —**boicotear,** v.

boina /'boina/ n. f. beret.

bola /'bola/ n. f. ball.

bola de nieve /'bola de 'nieβe/ snowball.

bolas de billar /'bolas de bi'ʎar; 'bolas de bi'yar/ billiard balls.

bolera /bo'lera/ n. f. bowling alley.

boletín /bole'tin/ n. m. bulletin.

boletín informativo /bole'tin informa'tiβo/ news bulletin.

boleto /bo'leto/ n. m. ticket. **b. de embarque,** boarding pass.

boliche /bo'litʃe/ n. m. bowling alley.

bolígrafo /bo'ligrafo/ n. m. ballpoint pen.

boliviano /boli'βiano/ -a a. & n. Bolivian.

bollo /'boʎo; 'boyo/ n. m. bun, loaf.

bolos /'bolos/ n. m.pl. bowling.

bolsa /'bolsa/ n. f. purse; stock exchange.

bolsa de agua caliente /'bolsa de 'agua ka'liente/ hot-water bottle.

bolsillo /bol'siʎo; bol'siyo/ n. m. pocket.

bomba /'bomba/ n. f. pump; bomb; gas station.

bombardear /bombarðe'ar/ v. bomb, bombard, shell.

bombear /bombe'ar/ v. pump.

bombero /bom'βero/ n. m. fireman.

bombilla /bom'βiʎa; bom'βiya/ n. f. (light) bulb.

bonanza /bo'nanθa; bo'nansa/ n. f. prosperity; fair weather.

bondad /bon'dað/ n. f. kindness; goodness.

bondadoso /bonda'ðoso/ a. kind, kindly.

bongó /boŋ'go/ n. m. bongo drum.

bonito /bo'nito/ a. pretty.

bono /'bono/ n. m. bonus; Fin. bond.

boqueada /boke'aða/ n. f. gasp; gape. —**boquear,** v.

boquilla /bo'kiʎa; bo'kiya/ n. f. cigarette holder.

bordado /bor'ðaðo/ n. m., **bordadura,** f. embroidery.

bordar /bor'ðar/ v. embroider.

borde /'borðe/ n. m. border, rim, edge, brink, ledge.

borde de la carretera /'borðe de la karre'tera/ roadside.

borla /'borla/ n. f. tassel.

borracho /bo'rratʃo/ -a a. & n. drunk.

borrachón /borra'tʃon/ -na a. drunkard.

borrador /borra'ðor/ n. m. eraser.

borradura /borra'ðura/ n. f. erasure.

borrar /bo'rrar/ v. erase, rub out.

borrasca /bo'rraska/ n. f. squall, storm.

borrico /bo'rriko/ n. m. donkey.

bosque /'boske/ n. m. forest, wood.

bosquejo /bos'keho/ n. m. sketch, draft. —**bosquejar,** v.

bostezo /bos'teθo; bos'teso/ n. m. yawn. —**bostezar,** v.

bota /'bota/ n. f. boot.

botalón /bota'lon/ n. m. Naut. boom.

botánica /bo'tanika/ n. f. botany.

botar /bo'tar/ v. throw out, throw away.

bote /'bote/ n. m. boat; can, box.

bote salvavidas /'bote salβa'βiðas/ lifeboat.

botica /bo'tika/ n. f. pharmacy, drugstore.

boticario /boti'kario/ n. m. pharmacist, druggist.

botín /bo'tin/ n. m. booty, plunder, spoils.

botiquín /boti'kin/ n. m. medicine chest.

boto /'boto/ a. dull, stupid.

botón /bo'ton/ n. m. button.

botones /bo'tones/ n. m. bellboy (in a hotel).

bóveda /'boβeða/ n. f. vault.

boxeador /boksea'ðor/ n. m. boxer.

boxeo /bok'seo/ n. m. boxing. —**boxear,** v.

boya /'boya/ n. f. buoy.

boyante /bo'yante/ a. buoyant.

bozal /bo'θal; bo'sal/ n. m. muzzle.

bragas /'bragas/ n. f.pl. panties.

bramido /bra'miðo/ n. m. roar, bellow. —**bramar,** v.

brasa /'brasa/ n. f. embers, grill. —**brasear,** v.

brasileño /brasi'leɲo/ -ña a. & n. Brazilian.

bravata /bra'βata/ n. f. bravado.

bravear /braβe'ar/ v. bully.

braza /'braθa; 'brasa/ n. f. fathom.

brazada /bra'θaða; bra'saða/ n. f. (swimming) stroke.

brazalete /braθa'lete; brasa'lete/ n. m. bracelet.

brazo /'braθo; 'braso/ n. m. arm.

brea /'brea/ n. f. tar, pitch.

brecha /'bretʃa/ n. f. gap, breach.

brécol /'brekol/ n. m. broccoli.

bregar /bre'gar/ v. scramble.

breña /'breɲa/ n. f. rough country with brambly shrubs.

Bretaña /bre'taɲa/ n. f. Britain.

breve /'breβe/ a. brief, short. **en b.,** shortly, soon.

brevedad /breβe'ðað/ n. f. brevity.

bribón /bri'βon/ -na n. rogue, rascal.

brida /'briða/ n. f. bridle.

brigada /bri'gaða/ n. f. brigade.

brillante /bri'ʎante; bri'yante/ a. **1.** brilliant, shiny. —n. **2.** m. diamond.

brillo /'briʎo; 'briyo/ n. m. shine, glitter. —**brillar,** v.

brinco /'brinko/ n. m. jump; bounce, skip. —**brincar,** v.

brindis /'brindis/ n. m. toast. —**brindar,** v.

brío /'brio/ n. m. vigor.

brioso /'brioso/ a. vigorous, spirited.

brisa /'brisa/ n. f. breeze.

brisa marina /'brisa ma'rina/ sea breeze.

británico /bri'taniko/ a. British.

brocado /bro'kaðo/ -da a. & n. brocade.

brocha /'brotʃa/ n. f. brush.

broche /'brotʃe/ n. m. brooch, clasp, pin.

broma /'broma/ n. f. joke. —**bromear,** v.

bronca /'bronka/ n. f. Colloq. quarrel, row, fight.

bronce /'bronθe; 'bronse/ n. m. bronze; brass.

bronceador /bronθea'ðor; bronsea'ðor/ n. m. suntan lotion, suntan oil.

bronquitis /bron'kitis/ n. f. bronchitis.

brotar /bro'tar/ v. gush; sprout; bud.

brote /'brote/ n. m. bud, shoot.

bruja /'bruha/ n. f. witch.

brújula /'bruhula/ n. f. compass.

bruma /'bruma/ n. f. mist.

brumoso /bru'moso/ a. misty.

brusco /'brusko/ a. brusque; abrupt, curt.

brutal /bru'tal/ a. savage, brutal.

brutalidad /brutali'ðað/ n. f. brutality.

bruto /'bruto/ -ta a. **1.** brutish; ignorant. —n. **2.** blockhead.

bucear /buθe'ar; buse'ar/ v. dive.

bueno /'bueno/ a. good, fair; well (in health).

buey /buei/ n. m. ox, steer.

búfalo /'bufalo/ n. m. buffalo.

bufanda /bu'fanda/ n. f. scarf.

bufón /bu'fon/ -ona a. & n. fool, buffoon, clown.

búho /'buo/ n. m. owl.

buhonero /buo'nero/ n. m. peddler, vendor.

bujía /bu'hia/ n. f. spark plug.

bulevar /bule'βar/ n. m. boulevard.

bulimia /bu'limia/ n. f. bulimia.

bullicio /bu'ʎiθio; bu'yisio/ n. m. bustle, noise.

bullicioso /buʎi'θioso; buyi'sioso/ a. boisterous, noisy.

bulto /'bulto/ n. m. bundle; lump.

buñuelo /bu'ɲuelo/ n. m. bun.

buque /'buke/ n. m. ship.

buque de guerra /'buke de 'gerra/ warship.

buque de pasajeros /'buke de pasa'heros/ passenger ship.

burdo /'burðo/ a. coarse.

burgués /bur'ges/ -esa a. & n. bourgeois.

burla /'burla/ n. f. mockery; fun.

burlador /burla'ðor/ -ra n. trickster, jokester.

burlar /bur'lar/ v. mock, deride.

burlarse de /bur'larse de/ v. scoff at; make fun of.

burro /'burro/ n. m. donkey.

busca /'buska/ n. f. search, pursuit, quest.

buscar /bus'kar/ v. seek, look for; look up.

busto /'busto/ n. m. bust.

butaca /bu'taka/ n. f. armchair; Theat. orchestra seat.

buzo /'buθo; 'buso/ n. m. diver.

buzón /bu'θon; bu'son/ n. m. mailbox.

C

cabal /ka'βal/ a. exact; thorough.

cabalgar /kaβal'gar/ v. ride horseback.

caballeresco /kaβaʎe'resko; kaβaye-'resko/ *a.* gentlemanly, chivalrous.

caballería /kaβaʎe'ria; kaβaye'ria/ *n. f.* cavalry; chivalry.

caballeriza /kaβaʎe'riθa; kaβaye'risa/ *n. f.* stable.

caballero /kaβa'ʎero; kaβa'yero/ *n. m.* gentleman; knight.

caballete /kaβa'ʎete; kaβa'yete/ *n. m.* sawhorse; easel; ridge (of roof).

caballo /ka'βaʎo; ka'βayo/ *n. m.* horse.

cabaña /ka'βaɲa/ *n. f.* cabin; booth.

cabaré /kaβa're/ *n. m.* nightclub.

cabaretero /kaβare'tero/ **-a** *n. m. & f.* nightclub owner.

cabecear /kaβeθe'ar; kaβese'ar/ *v.* pitch (as a ship).

cabecera /kaβe'θera; kaβe'sera/ *n. f.* head (of bed, table).

cabello /ka'βeʎo; ka'βeyo/ *n. m.* hair.

caber /ka'βer/ *v.* fit into, be contained in. **no cabe duda,** there is no doubt.

cabeza /ka'βeθa; ka'βesa/ *n. f.* head; warhead.

cabildo /ka'βildo/ *n. m.* city hall.

cabildo abierto /ka'βildo a'βierto/ town meeting.

cabizbajo /kaβiθ'βaho; kaβis'βaho/ *a.* downcast.

cablegrama /kaβle'grama/ *n. m.* cablegram.

cabo /'kaβo/ *n. m.* end; *Geog.* cape; *Mil.* corporal. **llevar a c.,** carry out, accomplish.

cabra /'kaβra/ *n. f.* goat.

cacahuete /kaka'uete/ *n. m.* peanut.

cacao /ka'kao/ *n. m.* cocoa; chocolate.

cacerola /kaθe'rola; kase'rola/ *n. f.* pan, casserole.

cachondeo /katʃon'deo/ *n. m.* fun, hilarity.

cachondo /ka'tʃondo/ *a.* funny; *Colloq.* horny.

cachorro /ka'tʃorro/ *n. m.* cub; puppy.

cada /'kaða/ *a.* each, every.

cadáver /ka'ðaβer/ *n. m.* corpse.

cadena /ka'ðena/ *n. f.* chain.

cadera /ka'ðera/ *n. f.* hip.

cadete /ka'ðete/ *n. m.* cadet.

caer /ka'er/ *v.* fall.

café /ka'fe/ *n. m.* coffee; café.

café exprés /ka'fe eks'pres/ espresso.

café soluble /ka'fe so'luβle/ instant coffee.

cafetal /kafe'tal/ *n. m.* coffee plantation.

cafetera /kafe'tera/ *n. f.* coffee pot.

caída /ka'iða/ *n. f.* fall, drop; collapse.

caimán /kai'man/ *n. m.* alligator.

caja /'kaha/ *n. f.* box, case; checkout counter.

caja de ahorros /'kaha de a'orros/ savings bank.

caja de cerillos /'kaha de θe'riʎos; 'kaha de se'riyos/ matchbox.

caja de fósforos /'kaha de 'fosforos/ matchbox.

caja torácica /'kaha to'raθika; 'kaha to'rasika/ rib cage.

cajero /ka'hero/ **-ra** cashier.

cajón /ka'hon/ *n. m.* drawer.

cal /kal/ *n. f.* lime.

calabaza /kala'βaθa; kala'βasa/ *n. f.* calabash, pumpkin.

calabozo /kala'βoθo; kala'βoso/ *n. m.* jail, cell.

calambre /ka'lambre/ *n. m.* cramp.

calamidad /kalami'ðað/ *n. f.* calamity, disaster.

calcetín /kalθe'tin; kalse'tin/ *n. m.* sock.

calcio /'kalθio; 'kalsio/ *n. m.* calcium.

calcular /kalku'lar/ *v.* calculate, figure.

cálculo /'kalkulo/ *n. m.* calculation, estimate.

caldera /kal'dera/ *n. f.* kettle, caldron; boiler.

caldo /'kaldo/ *n. m.* broth.

calefacción /kalefak'θion; kalefak-'sion/ *n. f.* heat, heating.

calendario /kalen'dario/ *n. m.* calendar.

calentar /kalen'tar/ *v.* heat, warm.

calidad /kali'ðað/ *n. f.* quality, grade.

caliente /ka'liente/ *a.* hot, warm.

calificar /kalifi'kar/ *v.* qualify.

callado /ka'ʎaðo; ka'yaðo/ *a.* silent, quiet.

callarse /ka'ʎarse; ka'yarse/ *v.* quiet down; keep still; stop talking.

calle /'kaʎe; 'kaye/ *n. f.* street.

callejón /kaʎe'hon; kaye'hon/ *n. m.* alley.

calle sin salida /'kaʎe sin sa'liða; 'kaye sin sa'liða/ dead end.

callo /'kaʎo; 'kayo/ *n. m.* callus, corn.

calma /'kalma/ *n. f.* calm, quiet.

calmado /kal'maðo/ *a.* calm.

calmante /kal'mante/ *a.* soothing, calming.

calmar /kal'mar/ *v.* calm, quiet, lull, soothe.

calor /ka'lor/ *n.* heat, warmth. **tener c.,** to be hot, warm; feel hot, warm. **hacer c.,** to be hot, warm (weather).

calorífero /kalo'rifero/ *a.* **1.** heat-producing. —*n.* **2.** *m.* radiator.

calumnia /ka'lumnia/ *n. f.* slander. —**calumniar,** *v.*

caluroso /kalu'roso/ *a.* warm, hot.

calvario /kal'βario/ *n. m.* Calvary.

calvo /'kalβo/ *a.* bald.

calzado /kal'θaðo; kal'saðo/ *n. m.* footwear.

calzar /kal'θar; kal'sar/ *v.* wear (as shoes).

calzoncillos /kalθon'θiʎos; kalson'si-yos/ *n. m.pl.* shorts.

calzones /kal'θones; kal'sones/ *n. m.pl.* trousers.

cama /'kama/ *n. f.* bed.

cámara /'kamara/ *n. f.* chamber; camera.

camarada /kama'raða/ *n. m. & f.* comrade.

camarera /kama'rera/ *n. f.* chambermaid; waitress.

camarero /kama'rero/ *n. m.* steward; waiter.

camarón /kama'ron/ *n. m.* shrimp.

camarote /kama'rote/ *n. m.* stateroom, berth.

cambiar /kam'βiar/ *v.* exchange, change, trade; cash.

cambio /'kambio/ *n. m.* change, exchange. **en c.,** on the other hand.

cambista /kam'βista/ *n. m. & f.* money changer; banker, broker.

cambur /kam'βur/ *n. m.* banana.

camello /ka'meʎo; ka'meyo/ *n. m.* camel.

camilla /ka'miʎa; ka'miya/ *n. f.* stretcher.

caminar /kami'nar/ *v.* walk.

caminata /kami'nata/ *n. f.* tramp, hike.

camino /ka'mino/ *n. m.* road; way.

camión /ka'mion/ *n. m.* truck.

camisa /ka'misa/ *n. f.* shirt.

camisería /kamise'ria/ *n. f.* haberdashery.

camiseta /kami'seta/ *n. f.* undershirt; T-shirt.

campamento /kampa'mento/ *n. m.* camp.

campana /kam'pana/ *n. f.* bell.

campanario /kampa'nario/ *n. m.* bell tower, steeple.

campaneo /kampa'neo/ *n. m.* chime.

campaña /kam'paɲa/ *n. f.* campaign.

campeón /kampe'on/ **-na** *n.* champion.

campeonato /kampeo'nato/ *n. m.* championship.

campesino /kampe'sino/ **-na** *n.* peasant.

campestre /kam'pestre/ *a.* country, rural.

campo /'kampo/ *n. m.* field; (the) country.

campo de concentración /'kampo de konθentra'θion; 'kampo de konsentra'sion/ concentration camp.

campo de golf /'kampo de 'golf/ golf course.

Canadá /kana'ða/ *n. m.* Canada.

canadiense /kana'ðiense/ *a. & n.* Canadian.

canal /ka'nal/ *n. m.* canal; channel.

Canal de la Mancha /ka'nal de la 'mantʃa/ *n. m.* English Channel.

canalla /ka'naʎa; ka'naya/ *n. f.* rabble.

canario /ka'nario/ *n. m.* canary.

canasta /ka'nasta/ *n. f.* basket.

cáncer /'kanθer; 'kanser/ *n. m.* cancer.

cancha de tenis /'kantʃa de 'tenis/ *n. f.* tennis court.

canciller /kanθi'ʎer; kansi'yer/ *n. m.* chancellor.

canción /kan'θion; kan'sion/ *n. f.* song.

candado /kan'daðo/ *n. m.* padlock.

candela /kan'dela/ *n. f.* fire; light; candle.

candelero /kande'lero/ *n. m.* candlestick.

candidato /kandi'ðato/ **-ta** *n.* candidate; applicant.

candidatura /kandiða'tura/ *n. f.* candidacy.

canela /ka'nela/ *n. f.* cinnamon.

cangrejo /kaŋ'greho/ *n. m.* crab.

caníbal /ka'niβal/ *n. m.* cannibal.

caniche /ka'nitʃe/ *n. m.* poodle.

canje /'kanhe/ *n. m.* exchange, trade. —**canjear,** *v.*

cano /'kano/ *a.* gray.

canoa /ka'noa/ *n. f.* canoe.

cansado /kan'saðo/ *a.* tired, weary.

cansancio /kan'sanθio; kan'sansio/ *n. m.* fatigue.

cansar /kan'sar/ *v.* tire, fatigue, wear out.

cantante /kan'tante/ *n. m. & f.* singer.

cantar /kan'tar/ *n.* **1.** *m.* song. —*v.* **2.** sing.

cántaro /'kantaro/ *n. m.* pitcher.

cantera /kan'tera/ *n. f.* (stone) quarry.

cantidad /kanti'ðað/ *n. f.* quantity, amount.

cantina /kan'tina/ *n. f.* bar, tavern; restaurant.

canto /'kanto/ *n. m.* chant, song, singing; edge.

caña /'kaɲa/ *n. f.* cane, reed; sugar cane; small glass of beer.

cañón /ka'ɲon/ *n. m.* canyon; cannon; gun barrel.

caoba /ka'oβa/ *n. f.* mahogany.

caos /'kaos/ *n. m.* chaos.

caótico /ka'otiko/ *a.* chaotic.

capa /'kapa/ *n. f.* cape, cloak; coat (of paint).

capacidad /kapaθi'ðað; kapasi'ðað/ *n. f.* capacity; capability.

capacitar /kapaθi'tar; kapasi'tar/ *v.* enable.

capataz /kapa'taθ; kapa'tas/ *n. m.* foreman.

capaz /ka'paθ; ka'pas/ *a.* capable, able.

capellán /kape'ʎan; kape'yan/ *n. m.* chaplain.

caperuza /kape'ruθa; kape'rusa/ *n. f.* hood.

capilla /ka'piʎa; ka'piya/ *n. f.* chapel.

capital /kapi'tal/ *n.* **1.** *m.* capital. **2.** *f.* capital (city).

capitalista /kapita'lista/ *a. & n.* capitalist.

capitán /kapi'tan/ *n. m.* captain.

capitular /kapitu'lar/ *v.* yield.

capítulo /ka'pitulo/ *n. m.* chapter.

capota /ka'pota/ *n. f.* hood.

capricho /ka'pritʃo/ *n. m.* caprice; fancy, whim.

caprichoso /kapri'tʃoso/ *a.* capricious.

cápsula /'kapsula/ *n. f.* capsule.

capturar /kaptu'rar/ *v.* capture.

capucha /ka'putʃa/ *n. f.* hood.

capullo /ka'puʎo; ka'puyo/ *n. m.* cocoon.

cara /'kara/ *n. f.* face.

caracol /kara'kol/ *n. m.* snail.

carácter /ka'rakter/ *n. m.* character.

característica /karakte'ristika/ *n. f.* characteristic.

característico /karakte'ristiko/ *a.* characteristic.

caramba /ka'ramba/ mild exclamation.

caramelo /kara'melo/ *n. m.* caramel; candy.

carátula /ka'ratula/ *n. f.* dial.

caravana /kara'βana/ *n. f.* caravan.

carbón /kar'βon/ *n. m.* carbon; coal.

carbonizar /karβoni'θar; karβoni'sar/ *v.* char.

carburador /karβura'ðor/ *n. m.* carburetor.

carcajada /karka'haða/ *n. f.* burst of laughter.

cárcel /'karθel; 'karsel/ *n. f.* prison, jail.

carcelero /karθe'lero; karse'lero/ *n. m.* jailer.

carcinogénico /karθino'heniko; karsino'heniko/ *a.* carcinogenic.

cardenal /karðe'nal/ *n. m.* cardinal.

cardiólogo /kar'ðiologo/ **-a** *m & f.* cardiologist.

carecer /kare'θer; kare'ser/ *v.* lack.

carestía /kares'tia/ *n. f.* scarcity; famine.

carga /'karga/ *n. f.* cargo; load, burden; freight.

cargar /kar'gar/ *v.* carry; load; charge.

cargo /'kargo/ *n. m.* load; charge, office.

caricatura /karika'tura/ *n. f.* caricature; cartoon.

caricaturista /karikatu'rista/ *n. m. & f.* caricaturist; cartoonist.

caricia /ka'riθia; ka'risia/ *n. f.* caress.

caridad /kari'ðað/ *n. f.* charity.

cariño /ka'riɲo/ *n. m.* affection, fondness.

cariñoso /kari'ɲoso/ *a.* affectionate, fond.

carisma /ka'risma/ *n. m.* charisma.

caritativo /karita'tiβo/ *a.* charitable.

carmesí /karme'si/ *a. & m.* crimson.

carnaval /karna'βal/ *n. m.* carnival.

carne /'karne/ *n. f.* meat, flesh; pulp.

carne acecinada /'karne aθeθi'naða; 'karne asesi'naða/ *n. f.* corned beef.

carnero /kar'nero/ *n. m.* ram; mutton.

carnicería /karniθe'ria; karnise'ria/ *n. f.* meat market; massacre.

carnicero /karni'θero; karni'sero/ **-ra** *n.* butcher.

carnívoro /kar'niβoro/ *a.* carnivorous.

caro /'karo/ *a.* dear, costly, expensive.

carpa /'karpa/ *n. f.* tent.

carpeta /kar'peta/ *n. f.* folder; briefcase.

carpintero /karpin'tero/ *n. m.* carpenter.

carrera /ka'rrera/ *n. f.* race; career.

carrera de caballos /ka'rrera de ka'βaʎos; ka'rrera de ka'βayos/ horse race.

carreta /ka'rreta/ *n. f.* wagon, cart.

carrete /ka'rrete/ *n. m.* reel, spool.

carretera /karre'tera/ *n. f.* road, highway.

carril /ka'rril/ *n. m.* rail.

carrillo /ka'rriʎo; ka'rriyo/ *n. m.* cart (for baggage or shopping).

carro /'karro/ *n. m.* car, automobile; cart.

carroza /ka'rroθa; ka'rrosa/ *n. f.* chariot.

carruaje /ka'rruahe/ *n. m.* carriage.

carta /'karta/ *n. f.* letter; (*pl.*) cards.

cartel /kar'tel/ *n. m.* placard, poster; cartel.

cartelera /karte'lera/ *n. f.* billboard.

cartera /kar'tera/ *n. f.* pocketbook, handbag, wallet; portfolio.

cartero /kar'tero/ **(-ra)** *n.* mail carrier.

cartón /kar'ton/ *n. m.* cardboard.

cartón piedra /kar'ton 'pieðra/ *n. m.* papier-mâché.

cartucho /kar'tutʃo/ *n. m.* cartridge; cassette.

casa /'kasa/ *n. f.* house, dwelling; home.

casaca /ka'saka/ *n. f.* dress coat.

casa de pisos /'kasa de 'pisos/ apartment house.

casado /ka'saðo/ *a.* married.

casamiento /kasa'miento/ *n. m.* marriage.

casar /ka'sar/ *v.* marry, marry off.

casarse /ka'sarse/ *v.* get married. **c. con**, marry.

cascabel /kaska'βel/ *n. m.* jingle bell.

cascada /kas'kaða/ *n. f.* waterfall, cascade.

cascajo /kas'kaho/ *n. m.* gravel.

cascanueces /kaska'nueθes; kaska-'nueses/ *n. m.* nutcracker.

cascar /kas'kar/ *v.* crack, break, burst.

cáscara /'kaskara/ *n. f.* shell, rind, husk.

casco /'kasko/ *n. m.* helmet; hull.

casera /ka'sera/ *n. f.* landlady; housekeeper.

caserío /kase'rio/ *n. m.* settlement.

casero /ka'sero/ *a.* **1.** homemade. —*n.* **2.** *m.* landlord, superintendent.

caseta /ka'seta/ *n. f.* cottage, hut.

casi /'kasi/ *adv.* almost, nearly.

casilla /ka'siʎa; ka'siya/ *n. f.* booth; ticket office; pigeonhole.

casimir /kasi'mir/ *n. m.* cashmere.

casino /ka'sino/ *n. m.* club; clubhouse.

caso /'kaso/ *n. m.* case. **hacer c. a,** pay attention to.

casorio /ka'sorio/ *n. m.* informal wedding.

caspa /'kaspa/ *n. f.* dandruff.

casta /'kasta/ *n. f.* caste.

castaña /kas'taɲa/ *n. f.* chestnut.

castaño /kas'taɲo/ *a.* **1.** brown. —*n.* **2.** *m.* chestnut tree.

castañuela /kasta'ɲuela/ *n. f.* castanet.

castellano /kaste'ʎano; kaste'yano/ **-na** *a. & n.* Castilian.

castidad /kasti'ðað/ *n. f.* chastity.

castigar /kasti'gar/ *v.* punish, castigate.

castigo /kas'tigo/ *n. m.* punishment.

castillo /kas'tiʎo; kas'tiyo/ *n. m.* castle.

castizo /kas'tiθo; kas'tiso/ *a.* pure, genuine; noble.

casto /'kasto/ *a.* chaste.

castor /kas'tor/ *n. m.* beaver.

casual /ka'sual/ *adj.* accidental, coincidental.

casualidad /kasuali'ðað/ *n. f.* coincidence. **por c.,** by chance.

casuca /ka'suka/ *n. f.* hut, shanty, hovel.

cataclismo /kata'klismo/ *n. m.* cataclysm.

catacumba /kata'kumba/ *n. f.* catacomb.

catadura /kata'ðura/ *n. f.* act of tasting; appearance.

catalán /kata'lan/ **-na** *a. & n.* Catalonian.

catálogo /ka'talogo/ *n. m.* catalogue. —**catalogar,** *v.*

cataputta /kata'putta/ *n. f.* catapult.

catar /ka'tar/ *v.* taste; examine, try; bear in mind.

catarata /kata'rata/ *n. f.* cataract, waterfall.

catarro /ka'tarro/ *n. m.* head cold, catarrh.

catástrofe /ka'tastrofe/ *n. f.* catastrophe.

catecismo /kate'θismo; kate'sismo/ *n. m.* catechism.

cátedra /'kateðra/ *n. f.* professorship.

catedral /kate'ðral/ *n. f.* cathedral.

catedrático /kate'ðratiko/ **-ca** *n.* professor.

categoría /katego'ria/ *n. f.* category.

categórico /kate'goriko/ *a.* categorical.

catequismo /kate'kismo/ *n. m.* catechism.

catequizar /kateki'θar; kateki'sar/ *v.* catechize.

cátodo /'katoðo/ *n. m.* cathode.

catolicismo /katoli'θismo; katoli-'sismo/ *n. m.* Catholicism.

católico /ka'toliko/ **-ca** *a. & n.* Catholic.

catorce /ka'torθe; ka'torse/ *a. & pron.* fourteen.

catre /'katre/ *n. m.* cot.

cauce /'kauθe; 'kause/ *n. m.* riverbed; ditch.

cauchal /kau'tʃal/ *n. m.* rubber plantation.

caucho /'kautʃo/ *n. m.* rubber.

caución /kau'θion; kau'sion/ *n. f.* precaution; security, guarantee.

caudal /kau'ðal/ *n. m.* means, fortune; (*pl.*) holdings.

caudaloso /kauða'loso/ *a.* prosperous, rich.

caudillaje /kauði'ʎahe; kauði'yahe/ *n. m.* leadership; tyranny.

caudillo /kau'ðiʎo; kau'ðiyo/ *n. m.* leader, chief.

causa /'kausa/ *n. f.* cause. —**causar,** *v.*

cautela /kau'tela/ *n. f.* caution.

cauteloso /kaute'loso/ *n. m.* cautious.

cautivar /kauti'βar/ *v.* captivate.

cautiverio /kauti'βerio/ *n. m.* captivity.

cautividad /kautiβi'ðað/ *n. f.* captivity.

cautivo /kau'tiβo/ **-va** *a. & n.* captive.

cauto /'kauto/ *a.* cautious.

cavar /ka'βar/ *v.* dig.

caverna /ka'βerna/ *n. f.* cavern, cave.

cavernoso /kaβer'noso/ *a.* cavernous.

cavidad /kaβi'ðað/ *n. f.* cavity, hollow.

cavilar /kaβi'lar/ *v.* criticize, cavil.

cayado /ka'yaðo/ *n. m.* shepherd's staff.

cayo /'kayo/ *n. m.* small rocky islet, key.

caza /'kaθa; 'kasa/ *n. f.* hunting, pursuit, game.

cazador /kaθa'ðor; kasa'ðor/ *n. m.* hunter.

cazar /ka'θar; ka'sar/ *v.* hunt.

cazatorpedero /kaθatorpe'ðero; kasatorpe'ðero/ *n. m.* torpedo-boat, destroyer.

cazo /'kaθo; 'kaso/ *n. m.* ladle, dipper; pot.

cazuela /ka'θuela; ka'suela/ *n. f.* crock.

cebada /θe'βaða; se'βaða/ *n. f.* barley.

cebiche /θe'bitʃe/ *n. m.* dish of marinated raw fish.

cebo /'θeβo; 'seβo/ *n. m.* bait. —**cebar,** *v.*

cebolla /θe'βoʎa; se'βoya/ *n. f.* onion.

cebolleta /θeβo'ʎeta; seβo'yeta/ *n. f.* spring onion.

ceceo /θe'θeo; se'seo/ *n. m.* lisp. —**cecear,** *v.*

cecina /θe'θina; se'sina/ *n. f.* dried beef.

cedazo /θe'ðaθo; se'ðaso/ *n. m.* sieve, sifter.

ceder /θe'ðer; se'ðer/ *v.* cede; transfer; yield.

cedro /'θeðro; 'seðro/ *n. m.* cedar.

cédula /'θeðula; 'seðula/ *n. f.* decree. **c. personal,** identification card.

céfiro /'θefiro; 'sefiro/ *n. m.* zephyr.

cegar /θe'gar; se'gar/ *v.* blind.

ceguedad /θege'ðað, θe'gera, sege-'ðað, se'gera/ **ceguera** *n. f.* blindness.

ceja /'θeha; 'seha/ *n. f.* eyebrow.

cejar /θe'har; se'har/ *v.* go backwards; yield, retreat.

celada /θe'laða; se'laða/ *n. f.* trap; ambush.

celaje /θe'lahe; se'lahe/ *n. m.* appearance of the sky.

celar /θe'lar; se'lar/ *v.* watch carefully, guard.

celda /'θelda; 'selda/ *n. f.* cell.

celebración /θeleβra'θion; seleβra-'sion/ *n. f.* celebration.

celebrante /θele'βrante; sele'βrante/ *n. m.* officiating priest.

celebrar /θele'βrar; sele'βrar/ *v.* celebrate, observe.

célebre /'θeleβre; 'seleβre/ *a.* celebrated, noted, famous.

celebridad /θeleβri'ðað; seleβri'ðað/ *n. f.* fame; celebrity; pageant.

celeridad /θeleri'ðað; seleri'ðað/ *n. f.* speed, rapidity.

celeste /θe'leste; se'leste/ *a.* celestial.

celestial /θeles'tial; seles'tial/ *a.* heavenly.

celibato /θeli'βato; seli'βato/ *n. m.* celibacy.

célibe /'θeliβe; 'seliβe/ *a.* **1.** unmarried. —*n.* **2.** *m. & f.* unmarried person.

celista /θe'lista; se'lista/ *n. m. & f.* cellist.

cellisca /θe'ʎiska; se'yiska/ *n. f.* sleet. —**cellisquear,** *v.*

celo /'θelo; 'selo/ *n. m.* zeal; (*pl.*) jealousy.

celofán /θelo'fan; selo'fan/ *n. m.* cellophane.

celosía /θelo'sia; selo'sia/ *n. f.* Venetian blind.

celoso /θe'loso; se'loso/ *a.* jealous, zealous.

céltico /'θeltiko; 'seltiko/ *a.* Celtic.

célula /'θelula; 'selula/ *n. f. Biol.* cell.

celuloide /θelu'loiðe; selu'loiðe/ *n. m.* celluloid.

cementar /θemen'tar; semen'tar/ *v.* cement.

cementerio /θemen'terio; semen-'terio/ *n. m.* cemetery.

cemento /θe'mento; se'mento/ *n. m.* cement.

cena /'θena; 'sena/ *n. f.* supper.

cenagal /θena'gal; sena'gal/ *n. m.* swamp, marsh.

cenagoso /θena'goso; sena'goso/ *a.* swampy, marshy, muddy.

cenar /θe'nar; se'nar/ *v.* dine, eat.

cencerro /θen'θerro; sen'serro/ *n. m.* cowbell.

cendal /θen'dal; sen'dal/ *n. m.* thin, light cloth; gauze.

cenicero /θeni'θero; seni'sero/ *n. m.* ashtray.

ceniciento /θeni'θiento; seni'siento/ *a.* ashen.

cenit /'θenit; 'senit/ *n. m.* zenith.

ceniza /θe'niθa; se'nisa/ *n. f.* ash, ashes.

censo /'θenso; 'senso/ *n. m.* census.

censor /θen'sor; sen'sor/ *n. m.* censor.

censura /θen'sura; sen'sura/ *n. f.* reproof, censure; censorship.

censurable /θensu'raβle; sensu'raβle/ *a.* objectionable.

censurar /θensu'rar; sensu'rar/ *v.* censure, criticize.

centavo /θen'taβo; sen'taβo/ *n. m.* cent.

centella /θen'teʎa; sen'teya/ *n. f.* thunderbolt, lightning.

centellear /θente'ʎe'ar; senteye'ar/ *v.* twinkle, sparkle.

centelleo /θente'ʎeo; sente'yeo/ *n. m.* sparkle.

centenar /θente'nar; sente'nar/ *n. m.* (a) hundred.

centenario /θente'nario; sente'nario/ *n. m.* centennial, centenary.

centeno /θen'teno; sen'teno/ *n. m.* rye.

centígrado /θen'tigraðo; sen'tigraðo/ *a.* centigrade.

centímetro /θenti'metro; senti'metro/ *n. m.* centimeter.

céntimo /'θentimo; 'sentimo/ *n. m.* cent.

centinela /θenti'nela; senti'nela/ *n. m.* sentry, guard.

central /θen'tral; sen'tral/ *a.* central.

centralita /θentra'lita; sentra'lita/ *n. f.* switchboard.

centralizar /θentrali'θar; sentrali'sar/ *v.* centralize.

centrar /θen'trar; sen'trar/ *v.* center.

céntrico /'θentriko; 'sentriko/ *a.* central.

centro /'θentro; 'sentro/ *n. m.* center.

centroamericano /θentroameri'kano; sentroameri'kano/ **-na** *a. & n.* Central American.

centro de mesa /'θentro de 'mesa; 'sentro de 'mesa/ centerpiece.

ceñidor /θeɲi'ðor; seɲi'ðor/ *n. m.* belt, sash; girdle.

ceñir /θe'ɲir; se'ɲir/ *v.* gird.

ceño /'θeɲo; 'seɲo/ *n. m.* frown.

ceñudo /θe'ɲuðo; se'ɲuðo/ *a.* frowning, grim.

cepa /'θepa; 'sepa/ *n. f.* stump.

cepillo /θe'piʎo; se'piyo/ *n. m.* brush; plane. —**cepillar,** *v.*

cera /'θera; 'sera/ *n. f.* wax.

cerámica /θe'ramika; se'ramika/ *n. m.* ceramics.

cerámico /θe'ramiko; se'ramiko/ *a.* ceramic.

cerca /'θerka; 'serka/ *adv.* **1.** near. —*n.* **2.** *f.* fence, hedge.

cercado /θer'kaðo; ser'kaðo/ *n. m.* enclosure; garden.

cercamiento /θerka'miento; serka-'miento/ *n. m.* enclosure.

cercanía /θerka'nia; serka'nia/ *n. f.* proximity.

cercano /θer'kano; ser'kano/ *a.* near, nearby.

cercar /θer'kar; ser'kar/ *v.* surround.

cercenar /θerθe'nar; serse'nar/ *v.* clip; lessen, reduce.

cerciorar /θerθio'rar; sersio'rar/ *v.* make sure; affirm.

cerco /'θerko; 'serko/ *n. m.* hoop; siege.

cerda /'θerða; 'serða/ *n. f.* bristle.

cerdo /'θerðo; 'serðo/ **-da** *n.* hog.

cerdoso /θer'ðoso; ser'ðoso/ *a.* bristly.

cereal /θere'al; sere'al/ *a. & m.* cereal.

cerebro /θe'reβro; se'reβro/ *n. m.* brain.

ceremonia /θere'monia; sere'monia/ *n. f.* ceremony.

ceremonial /θeremo'nial; seremo-'nial/ *a. & m.* ceremonial, ritual.

ceremonioso /θeremo'nioso; seremo'nioso/ *a.* ceremonious.

cereza /θe'reθa; se'resa/ *n. f.* cherry.

cerilla /θe'riʎa; se'riya/ *n. f.*, **cerillo**, *m.* match.

cerner /θer'ner; ser'ner/ *v.* sift.

cero /'θero; 'sero/ *n. m.* zero.

cerrado /θe'rraðo; se'rraðo/ *a.* closed; cloudy; obscure; taciturn.

cerradura /θerra'ðura; serra'ðura/ *n. f.* lock.

cerrajero /θerra'hero; serra'hero/ *n. m.* locksmith.

cerrar /θe'rrar; se'rrar/ *v.* close, shut.

cerro /'θerro; 'serro/ *n. m.* hill.

cerrojo /θe'rroho; se'rroho/ *n. m.* latch, bolt.

certamen /θer'tamen; ser'tamen/ *n. m.* contest; competition.

certero /θer'tero; ser'tero/ *a.* accurate, exact; certain, sure.

certeza /θer'teθa; ser'tesa/ *n. f.* certainty.

certidumbre /θerti'ðumbre; serti-'ðumβre/ *n. f.* certainty.

certificado /θertifi'kaðo; sertifi'kaðo/ *n. m.* certificate.

certificado de compra /θertifi'kaðo de 'kompra; sertifi'kaðo de 'kompra/ proof of purchase.

certificar /θertifi'kar; sertifi'kar/ *v.* certify; register (a letter).

cerúleo /θe'ruleo; se'ruleo/ *a.* cerulean, sky-blue.

cervecería /θerβeθe'ria; serβese'ria/ *n. f.* brewery; beer saloon.

cervecero /θerβe'θero; serβe'sero/ *n. m.* brewer.

cerveza /θer'βeθa; ser'βesa/ *n. f.* beer.

cesante /θe'sante; se'sante/ *a.* unemployed.

cesar /θe'sar; se'sar/ *v.* cease.

césped /'θespeð; 'sespeð/ *n. m.* sod, lawn.

cesta /'θesta; 'sesta/ *n. f.*, **cesto,** *m.* basket.

cetrino /θe'trino; se'trino/ *a.* yellow, lemon-colored.

cetro /'θetro; 'setro/ *n. m.* scepter.

chabacano /tʃaβa'kano/ *a.* vulgar.

chacal /tʃa'kal/ *n. m.* jackal.

chacó /'tʃako/ *n. m.* shako.

chacona /tʃa'kona/ *n. f.* chaconne.

chacota /tʃa'kota/ *n. f.* fun, mirth.

chacotear /tʃakote'ar/ *v.* joke.

chacra /'tʃakra/ *n. f.* small farm.

chafallar /tʃafa'ʎar; tʃafa'yar/ *v.* mend badly.

chagra /'tʃagra/ *n. m.* rustic; rural person.

chal /tʃal/ *n. m.* shawl.

chalán /tʃa'lan/ *n. m.* horse trader.

chaleco /tʃa'leko/ *n. m.* vest.

chaleco salvavidas /tʃa'leko salβa'βiðas/ life jacket.

chalet /tʃa'le; tʃa'let/ *n. m.* chalet.

challí /tʃa'ʎi; tʃa'yi/ *n. m.* challis.

chamada /tʃa'maða/ *n. f.* brushwood.

chamarillero /tʃamari'ʎero; tʃamari'yero/ *n. m.* gambler.

chamarra /tʃa'marra/ *n. f.* coarse linen jacket.

chambelán /tʃambe'lan/ *n. m.* chamberlain.

champaña /tʃam'paɲa/ *n. m.* champagne.

champú /tʃam'pu/ *n. m.* shampoo.

chamuscar /tʃamus'kar/ *v.* scorch.

chancaco /tʃan'kako/ *a.* brown.

chance /'tʃanθe/ *n. m. & f.* opportunity, break.

chancear /tʃanθe'ar; tʃanse'ar/ *v.* jest, joke.

chanciller /tʃanθi'ʎer; tʃansi'yer/ *n. m.* chancellor.

chancillería /tʃanθiʎe'ria; tʃansiye'ria/ *n. f.* chancery.

chancla /'tʃankla/ *n. f.* old shoe.

chancleta /tʃan'kleta/ *n. f.* slipper.

chanclos /'tʃanklos/ *n. m.pl.* galoshes.

chancro /'tʃankro/ *n. m.* chancre.

changador /tʃaŋga'ðor/ *n. m.* porter; handyman.

chantaje /tʃan'tahe/ *n. m.* blackmail.

chantajista /tʃanta'hista/ *n. m. & f.* blackmailer.

chantejear /tʃantehe'ar/ *v.* blackmail.

chanto /'tʃanto/ *n. m.* flagstone.

chantre /'tʃantre/ *n. m.* precentor.

chanza /'tʃanθa; 'tʃansa/ *n. f.* joke, jest. **—chancear,** *v.*

chanzoneta /tʃanθo'neta; tʃanso'neta/ *n. f.* chansonette.

chapa /'tʃapa/ *n. f.* (metal) sheet, plate; lock.

chapado en oro /tʃa'paðo en 'oro/ *a.* gold-plated.

chapado en plata /tʃa'paðo en 'plata/ *a.* silver-plated.

chaparrada /tʃapa'rraða/ *n. f.* downpour.

chaparral /tʃapa'rral/ *n. m.* chaparral.

chaparreras /tʃapa'rreras/ *n. f.pl.* chaps.

chaparrón /tʃapa'rron/ *n. m.* downpour.

chapear /tʃape'ar/ *v.* veneer.

chapeo /tʃa'peo/ *n. m.* hat.

chapero /tʃa'pero/ *n. m. Colloq.* male homosexual prostitute.

chapitel /tʃapi'tel/ *n. m.* spire, steeple; (architecture) capital.

chapodar /tʃapo'ðar/ *v.* lop.

chapón /tʃa'pon/ *n. m.* inkblot.

chapotear /tʃapote'ar/ *v.* paddle or splash in the water.

chapoteo /tʃapo'teo/ *n. m.* splash.

chapucear /tʃapuθe'ar; tʃapuse'ar/ *v.* fumble, bungle.

chapucero /tʃapu'θero; tʃapu'sero/ *a.* sloppy, bungling.

chapurrear /tʃapurre'ar/ *v.* speak (a language) brokenly.

chapuz /tʃa'puθ; tʃa'pus/ *n. m.* dive; ducking.

chapuzar /tʃapu'θar; tʃapu'sar/ *v.* dive; duck.

chaqueta /tʃa'keta/ *n. f.* jacket, coat.

chaqueta deportiva /tʃa'keta depor'tiβa/ sport jacket.

charada /tʃa'raða/ *n. f.* charade.

charamusca /tʃara'muska/ *n. f.* twisted candy stick.

charanga /tʃa'raŋga/ *n. f.* military band.

charanguero /tʃaraŋ'guero/ *n. m.* peddler.

charca /'tʃarka/ *n. f.* pool, pond.

charco /'tʃarko/ *n. m.* pool, puddle.

charla /'tʃarla/ *n. f.* chat; chatter, prattle. **—charlar,** *v.*

charladuría /tʃarlaðu'ria/ *n. f.* chatter.

charlatán /tʃarla'tan/ **-ana** *n.* charlatan.

charlatanismo /tʃarlata'nismo/ *n. m.* charlatanism.

charol /tʃa'rol/ *n. m.* varnish.

charolar /tʃaro'lar/ *v.* varnish; polish.

charquear /tʃarke'ar/ *v.* jerk (beef).

charquí /tʃar'ki/ *n. m.* jerked beef.

charrán /tʃa'rran/ *a.* roguish.

chascarillo /tʃaska'riʎo; tʃaska'riyo/ *n. m.* risqué story.

chasco /'tʃasko/ *n. m.* disappointment, blow; practical joke.

chasis /'tʃasis/ *n. m.* chassis.

chasquear /tʃaske'ar/ *v.* fool, trick; disappoint; crack (a whip).

chasquido /tʃas'kiðo/ *n. m.* crack (sound).

chata /'tʃata/ *n. f.* bedpan.

chatear /tʃate'ar/ *v.* chat (on the Internet).

chato /'tʃato/ *a.* flat-nosed, pugnosed.

chauvinismo /tʃauβi'nismo/ *n. m.* chauvinism.

chauvinista /tʃauβi'nista/ *n. & a.* chauvinist.

chelín /tʃe'lin/ *n. m.* shilling.

cheque /'tʃeke/ *n. m.* (bank) check.

chica /'tʃika/ *n. f.* girl.

chicana /tʃi'kana/ *n. f.* chicanery.

chicha /'tʃitʃa/ *n. f.* an alcoholic drink.

chícharo /'tʃitʃaro/ *n. f.* pea.

chicharra /tʃi'tʃarra/ *n. f.* cicada; talkative person.

chicharrón /tʃitʃa'rron/ *n. m.* crisp fried scrap of meat.

chichear /tʃitʃe'ar/ *v.* hiss in disapproval.

chichón /tʃi'tʃon/ *n. m.* bump, bruise, lump.

chicle /'tʃikle/ *n. m.* chewing gum.

chico /'tʃiko/ *a.* **1.** little. **—***n.* **2.** *m.* boy.

chicote /tʃi'kote/ *n. m.* cigar; cigar butt.

chicotear /tʃikote'ar/ *v.* whip, flog.

chifladura /tʃifla'ðura/ *n. f.* mania; whim; jest.

chiflar /tʃi'flar/ *v.* whistle; become insane.

chiflido /tʃi'fliðo/ *n. m.* shrill whistle.

chile /'tʃile/ *n. m.* chili.

chileno /tʃi'leno/ **-na** *a. & n.* Chilean.

chillido /tʃi'ʎiðo; tʃi'yiðo/ *n. m.* shriek, scream, screech. **—chillar,** *v.*

chillón /tʃi'ʎon; tʃi'yon/ *a.* shrill.

chimenea /tʃime'nea/ *n. f.* chimney, smokestack; fireplace.

china /'tʃina/ *n. f.* pebble; maid; Chinese woman.

chinarro /tʃi'narro/ *n. m.* large pebble, stone.

chinche /'tʃintʃe/ *n. f.* bedbug; thumbtack.

chincheta /tʃin'tʃeta/ *n. f.* thumbtack.

chinchilla /tʃin'tʃiʎa; tʃin'tʃiya/ *n. f.* chinchilla.

chinchorro /tʃin'tʃorro/ *n. m.* fishing net.

chinela /tʃi'nela/ *n. f.* slipper.

chinero /tʃi'nero/ *n. m.* china closet.

chino /'tʃino/ **-na** *a. & n.* Chinese.

chipirón /tʃipi'ron/ *n. m.* baby squid.

chiquero /tʃi'kero/ *n. m.* pen for pigs, goats, etc.

chiquito /tʃi'kito/ **-ta** *a.* **1.** small, tiny. **—***n.* **2.** *m. & f.* small child.

chiribitil /tʃiriβi'til/ *n. m.* small room, den.

chirimía /tʃiri'mia/ *n. f.* flageolet.

chiripa /tʃi'ripa/ *n. f.* stroke of good luck.

chirla /'tʃirla/ *n. f.* mussel.

chirle /'tʃirle/ *a.* insipid.

chirona /tʃi'rona/ *n. f.* prison, jail.

chirrido /tʃi'rriðo/ *n. m.* squeak, chirp. **—chirriar,** *v.*

chis /tʃis/ *interj.* hush!

chisgarabís /tʃisgara'βis/ *n.* meddler; unimportant person.

chisguete /tʃis'gete/ *n. m.* squirt, splash.

chisme /'tʃisme/ *n. m.* gossip. **—chismear,** *v.*

chismero /tʃis'mero/ **-ra** *n.* gossiper.

chismoso /tʃis'moso/ *adj.* gossiping.

chispa /'tʃispa/ *n. f.* spark.

chispeante /tʃispe'ante/ *a.* sparkling.

chispear /tʃispe'ar/ *v.* sparkle.

chisporrotear /tʃisporrote'ar/ *v.* emit sparks.

chistar /tʃis'tar/ *v.* speak.

chiste /'tʃiste/ *n. m.* joke, gag; witty saying.

chistera /tʃis'tera/ *n. f.* fish basket; top hat.

chistoso /tʃis'toso/ *a.* funny, comic, amusing.

chito /'tʃito/ *interj.* hush!

chiva /'tʃiβa/ *n. f.* female goat.

chivato /tʃi'βato/ *n. m.* kid, young goat.

chivo /'tʃiβo/ *n. m.* male goat.

chocante /tʃo'kante/ *a.* striking; shocking; unpleasant.

chocar /tʃo'kar/ *v.* collide, clash, crash; shock.

chocarrear /tʃokarre'ar/ *v.* joke, jest.

chochear /tʃotʃe'ar/ *v.* be in one's dotage.

chochera /tʃo'tʃera/ *n. f.* dotage, senility.

choclo /'tʃoklo/ *n. m.* clog; overshoe; ear of corn.

chocolate /tʃoko'late/ *n. m.* chocolate.

chocolate con leche /tʃoko'late kon 'letʃe/ milk chocolate.

chocolatería /tʃokolate'ria/ *n. f.* chocolate shop.

chofer /'tʃofer/ **chófer** *n. m.* chauffeur, driver.

chofeta /tʃo'feta/ *n. f.* chafing dish.

cholo /'tʃolo/ *n. m.* half-breed.

chopo /'tʃopo/ *n. m.* black poplar.

choque /'tʃoke/ *n. m.* collision, clash, crash; shock.

chorizo /tʃo'riθo; tʃo'riso/ *n. m.* sausage.

chorrear /tʃorre'ar/ *v.* spout; drip.

chorro /'tʃorro/ *n. m.* spout; spurt, jet. **llover a chorros,** to pour (rain).

choto /'tʃoto/ *n. m.* calf, kid.

choza /'tʃoθa; 'tʃosa/ *n. f.* hut, cabin.

chozno /'tʃoθno; 'tʃosno/ **-na** *n.* great-great-great-grandchild.

chubasco /tʃu'βasko/ *n. m.* shower, squall.

chubascoso /tʃuβas'koso/ *a.* squally.

chuchería /tʃutʃe'ria/ *n. f.* trinket, knickknack.

chucho /'tʃutʃo/ *n. m. Colloq.* mutt.

chulería /tʃule'ria/ *n. f.* pleasant manner.

chuleta /tʃu'leta/ *n. f.* chop, cutlet.

chulo /'tʃulo/ *n. m.* rascal, rogue; joker.

chupa /'tʃupa/ *n. f.* jacket.

chupada /tʃu'paða/ *n. f.* suck, sip.

chupado /tʃu'paðo/ *a.* very thin.

chupaflor /tʃupa'flor/ *n. m.* hummingbird.

chupar /tʃu'par/ *v.* suck.

churrasco /tʃu'rrasko/ *n. m.* roasted meat.

churros /'tʃuros/ *n. m.pl.* long, slender fritters.

chuscada /tʃus'kaða/ *n. f.* joke, jest.

chusco /'tʃusko/ *a.* funny, humorous.

chusma /'tʃusma/ *n. f.* mob, rabble.

chuzo /'tʃuθo; 'tʃuso/ *n. m.* pike.

CI, *abbr.* **(coeficiente intelectual)** IQ (intelligence quotient).

ciberespacio /θiβeres'paθio/ *n. m.* cyberspace.

cibernauta /θiβer'nauta/ *n. m. & f.* cybernaut.

cicatero /θika'tero; sika'tero/ *a.* stingy.

cicatriz /θika'triθ; sika'tris/ *n. f.* scar.

cicatrizar /θikatri'θar; sikatri'sar/ *v.* heal.

ciclamato /θi'klamato; si'klamato/ *n. m.* cyclamate.

ciclista /θi'klista; si'klista/ *m & f.* cyclist.

ciclo /'θiklo; 'siklo/ *n. m.* cycle.

ciclón /θi'klon; si'klon/ *n. m.* cyclone.

ciego /'θiego; 'siego/ **-ga** *a.* **1.** blind. **—***n.* **2.** blind person.

cielo /'θielo; 'sielo/ *n. m.* heaven; sky, heavens; ceiling.

ciempiés /θiem'pies; siem'pies/ *n. m.* centipede.

cien /θien; sien/ **ciento** *a. & pron.* hundred. **por c.,** per cent.

ciénaga /'θienaga; 'sienaga/ *n. f.* swamp, marsh.

ciencia /'θienθia; 'siensia/ *n. f.* science.

cieno /'θieno; 'sieno/ *n. m.* mud.

científico /θien'tifiko; sien'tifiko/ **-ca** *a.* **1.** scientific. **—***n.* **2.** scientist.

cierre /'θierre; 'sierre/ *n. m.* fastener, snap, clasp.

cierto /'θierto; 'sierto/ *a.* certain, sure, true.

ciervo /'θierβo; 'sierβo/ *n. m.* deer.

cierzo /'θierθo; 'sierso/ *n. m.* northerly wind.

cifra /'θifra; 'sifra/ *n. f.* cipher, number. **—cifrar,** *v.*

cigarra /θi'garra; si'garra/ *n. f.* locust.

cigarrera /θiga'rrera; siga'rrera/ **cigarrillera** *f.* cigarette case.

cigarrillo /θiga'rriʎo; siga'rriyo/ *n. m.* cigarette.

cigarro /θi'garro; si'garro/ *n. m.* cigar; cigarette.

cigüeña /θi'gueɲa; si'gueɲa/ *n. f.* stork.

cilíndrico /θi'lindriko; si'lindriko/ *a.* cylindrical.

cilindro /θi'lindro; si'lindro/ *n. m.* cylinder.

cima /'θima; 'sima/ *n. f.* summit, peak.

cimarrón /θima'rron; sima'rron/ *a.* **1.** wild, untamed. **—***n.* **2.** *m.* runaway slave.

címbalo /'θimbalo; 'simbalo/ *n. m.* cymbal.

cimbrar /θim'βrar, θimbre'ar; sim'βrar, simbre'ar/ *v.* shake, brandish.

cimientos /θi'mientos; si'mientos/ *n. m.pl.* foundation.

cinc /θink; sink/ *n. m.* zinc.

cincel /θin'θel; sin'sel/ *n. m.* chisel. **—cincelar,** *v.*

cincha /'θintʃa; 'sintʃa/ *n. f.* (harness) cinch. **—cinchar,** *v.*

cinco /'θinko; 'sinko/ *a. & pron.* five.

cincuenta /θin'kuenta; sin'kuenta/ *a. & pron.* fifty.

cine /'θine; 'sine/ *n. m.* movies; movie theater.

cíngulo /'θiŋgulo; 'siŋgulo/ *n. m.* cingulum.

cínico /'θiniko; 'siniko/ **-ca** *a. & n.* cynical; cynic.

cinismo /θi'nismo; si'nismo/ *n. m.* cynicism.

cinta /'θinta; 'sinta/ *n. f.* ribbon, tape; (movie) film.

cintilar /θinti'lar; sinti'lar/ *v.* glitter, sparkle.

cinto /'θinto; 'sinto/ *n. m.* belt; girdle.

cintura /θin'tura; sin'tura/ *n. f.* waist.

cinturón /θintu'ron; sintu'ron/ *n. m.* belt.

cinturón de seguridad /θintu'ron de seguri'ðað; sintu'ron de seguri'ðað/ safety belt.

ciprés /θi'pres; si'pres/ *n. m.* cypress.

circo /'θirko; 'sirko/ *n. m.* circus.

circuito /θir'kuito; sir'kuito/ *n. m.* circuit.

circulación /θirkula'θion; sirkula'sion/ *n. f.* circulation.

circular /θirku'lar; sirku'lar/ *a. & m.* **1.** circular. —*v.* **2.** circulate.

círculo /'θirkulo; 'sirkulo/ *n. m.* circle, club.

circundante /θirkun'dante; sirkun'dante/ *a.* surrounding.

circundar /θirkun'dar; sirkun'dar/ *v.* encircle, surround.

circunferencia /θirkunfe'renθia; sirkunfe'rensia/ *n. f.* circumference.

circunlocución /θirkunloku'θion; sirkunloku'sion/ *n.* circumlocution.

circunscribir /θirkunskri'βir; sirkunskri'βir/ *v.* circumscribe.

circunspección /θirkunspek'θion; sirkunspek'sion/ *n.* decorum, propriety.

circunspecto /θirkuns'pekto; sirkuns'pekto/ *a.* circumspect.

circunstancia /θirkuns'tanθia; sirkuns'tansia/ *n. f.* circumstance.

circunstante /θirkuns'tante; sirkuns'tante/ *n. m.* bystander.

circunvecino /θirkumbe'θino; sirkumbe'sino/ *a.* neighboring, adjacent.

cirio /'θirio; 'sirio/ *n. m.* candle.

cirrosis /θi'rrosis; si'rrosis/ *n. f.* cirrhosis.

ciruela /θi'ruela; si'ruela/ *n. f.* plum, prune.

cirugía /θiru'hia; siru'hia/ *n. f.* surgery.

cirujano /θiru'hano; siru'hano/ *n. m.* surgeon.

cisne /'θisne; 'sisne/ *n. m.* swan.

cisterna /θis'terna; sis'terna/ *n. f.* cistern.

cita /'θita; 'sita/ *n. f.* citation; appointment, date.

citación /θita'θion; sita'sion/ *n. f.* citation; (legal) summons.

citar /θi'tar; si'tar/ *v.* cite, quote; summon; make an appointment with.

cítrico /'θitriko; 'sitriko/ *a.* citric.

ciudad /θiu'ðað; siu'ðað/ *n. f.* city.

ciudadanía /θiuðaða'nia; siuðaða'nia/ *n. f.* citizenship.

ciudadano /θiuða'ðano; siuða'ðano/ **-na** *n.* citizen.

ciudadela /θiuða'ðela; siuða'ðela/ *n. f.* fortress, citadel.

cívico /'θiβiko; 'siβiko/ *a.* civic.

civil /θi'βil; si'βil/ *a. & n.* civil; civilian.

civilidad /θiβili'ðað; siβili'ðað/ *n. f.* politeness, civility.

civilización /θiβiliθa'θion; siβilisa'sion/ *n. f.* civilization.

civilizador /θiβiliθa'ðor; siβilisa'ðor/ *a.* civilizing.

civilizar /θiβili'θar; siβili'sar/ *v.* civilize.

cizallas /θi'θaʎas; si'sayas/ *n. f.pl.* shears. —**cizallar,** *v.*

cizaña /θi'θaɲa; si'saɲa/ *n. f.* weed; vice.

clamar /kla'mar/ *v.* clamor.

clamor /kla'mor/ *n. m.* clamor.

clamoreo /klamo'reo/ *n. m.* persistent clamor.

clamoroso /klamo'roso/ *a.* clamorous.

clandestino /klandes'tino/ *a.* secret, clandestine.

clara /'klara/ *n. f.* white (of egg).

claraboya /klara'βoya/ *n. m.* skylight; bull's-eye.

clara de huevo /'klara de 'ueβo/ egg white.

clarear /klare'ar/ *v.* clarify; become light, dawn.

clarete /kla'rete/ *n. m.* claret.

claridad /klari'ðað/ *n. f.* clarity.

clarificar /klarifi'kar/ *v.* clarify.

clarín /kla'rin/ *n. m.* bugle, trumpet.

clarinete /klari'nete/ *n. m.* clarinet.

clarividencia /klariβi'ðenθia; klariβi'ðensia/ *n. f.* clairvoyance.

clarividente /klariβi'ðente/ *a.* clairvoyant.

claro /'klaro/ *a.* clear; bright; light (in color); of course.

clase /'klase/ *n. f.* class; classroom; kind, sort.

clase nocturna /'klase nok'turna/ evening class.

clásico /'klasiko/ *a.* classic, classical.

clasificar /klasifi'kar/ *v.* classify, rank.

claustro /'klaustro/ *n. m.* cloister.

claustrofobia /klaustro'foβia/ *n. f.* claustrophobia.

cláusula /'klausula/ *n. f.* clause.

clausura /klau'sura/ *n. f.* cloister; inner sanctum; closing.

clavado /kla'βaðo/ *a.* **1.** nailed. —*n.* **2.** *m. & f.* dive.

clavar /kla'βar/ *v.* nail, peg, pin.

clave /'klaβe/ *n. f.* code; *Mus.* key.

clavel /kla'βel/ *n. m.* carnation.

clavetear /klaβete'ar/ *v.* nail.

clavícula /kla'βikula/ *n. f.* collarbone.

clavija /kla'βiha/ *n. f.* pin, peg.

clavo /'klaβo/ *n. m.* nail, spike; clove.

clemencia /kle'menθia; kle'mensia/ *n. f.* clemency.

clemente /kle'mente/ *a.* merciful.

clementina /klemen'tina/ *n. f.* tangerine.

clerecía /klere'θia; klere'sia/ *n. f.* clergy.

clerical /kleri'kal/ *a.* clerical.

clérigo /'klerigo/ *n. m.* clergyman.

clero /'klero/ *n. m.* clergy.

cliente /'kliente/ *n. m. & f.* customer, client.

clientela /klien'tela/ *n. f.* clientele, practice.

clima /'klima/ *n. m.* climate.

clímax /'klimaks/ *n. m.* climax.

clínca de reposo /'klinka de rre'poso/ convalescent home.

clínica /'klinika/ *n. f.* clinic.

clínico /'kliniko/ *a.* clinical.

clíper /'kliper/ *n. m.* clipper ship.

cloaca /klo'aka/ *n. f.* sewer.

cloquear /kloke'ar/ *v.* cluck, cackle.

cloqueo /klo'keo/ *n. m.* cluck.

cloro /'kloro/ *n. m.* chlorine.

club /kluβ/ *n. m.* club, association.

club juvenil /kluβ huβe'nil/ youth club.

clueca /'klueka/ *n. f.* brooding hen.

coacción /koak'θion; koak'sion/ *n.* compulsion.

coagular /koagu'lar/ *v.* coagulate, clot.

coágulo /ko'agulo/ *n. m.* clot.

coalición /koali'θion; koali'sion/ *n. f.* coalition.

coartada /koar'taða/ *n. f.* alibi.

coartar /koar'tar/ *v.* limit.

cobarde /ko'βarðe/ *a. & n.* cowardly; coward.

cobardía /koβar'ðia/ *n. f.* cowardice.

cobayo /ko'βayo/ *n. m.* guinea pig.

cobertizo /koβer'tiθo; koβer'tiso/ *n. m.* shed.

cobertor /koβer'tor/ *n. m.*, **cobija,** *f.* blanket.

cobertura /koβer'tura/ *n. f.* cover, wrapping.

cobijar /koβi'har/ *v.* cover; protect.

cobrador /koβra'ðor/ *n. m.* collector.

cobranza /ko'βranθa; ko'βransa/ *n. f.* collection or recovery of money.

cobrar /ko'βrar/ *v.* collect; charge; cash.

cobre /'koβre/ *n. m.* copper.

cobrizo /ko'βriθo; ko'βriso/ *a.* coppery.

cobro /'koβro/ *n. m.* collection or recovery of money.

coca /'koka/ *n. f.* coca leaves.

cocaína /koka'ina/ *n. f.* cocaine.

cocal /ko'kal/ *n. m.* coconut plantation.

cocear /koθe'ar; kose'ar/ *v.* kick; resist.

cocer /ko'θer; ko'ser/ *v.* cook, boil, bake.

coche /'kotʃe/ *n. m.* coach; car, automobile.

cochecito de niño /kotʃe'θito de 'niɲo; kotʃe'sito de 'niɲo/ baby carriage.

coche de choque /'kotʃe de 'tʃoke/ dodgem.

cochera /ko'tʃera/ *n. f.* garage.

cochero /ko'tʃero/ *n. m.* coachman; cab driver.

cochinada /kotʃi'naða/ *n. f.* filth; herd of swine.

cochino /ko'tʃino/ *n. m.* pig, swine.

cocido /ko'θiðo; ko'siðo/ *n. m.* stew.

cociente /ko'θiente; ko'siente/ *n. m.* quotient.

cocimiento /koθi'miento; kosi'miento/ *n. m.* cooking.

cocina /ko'θina; ko'sina/ *n. f.* kitchen.

cocinar /koθi'nar; kosi'nar/ *v.* cook.

cocinero /koθi'nero; kosi'nero/ **-ra** *n.* cook.

coco /'koko/ *n. m.* coconut; coconut tree.

cocodrilo /koko'ðrilo/ *n. m.* crocodile.

cóctel /kok'tel/ *n. m.* cocktail.

codazo /ko'ðaθo; ko'ðaso/ *n. m.* nudge with the elbow.

codicia /ko'ðiθia; ko'ðisia/ *n. f.* avarice, greed; lust.

codiciar /koðiθi'ar; koðisi'ar/ *v.* covet.

codicioso /koðiθi'oso; koðisi'oso/ *a.* covetous; greedy.

código /'koðigo/ *n. m.* (law) code.

codo /'koðo/ *n. m.* elbow.

codorniz /koðor'niθ; koðor'nis/ *n. f.* quail.

coeficiente /koefi'θiente; koefi'siente/ *n. m.* quotient.

coeficiente intelectual /koefi'θiente intelek'tual; koefi'siente intelek'tual/ intelligence quotient.

coetáneo /koe'taneo/ *a.* contemporary.

coexistir /koeksis'tir/ *v.* coexist.

cofrade /ko'fraðe/ *n. m.* fellow member of a club, etc.

cofre /'kofre/ *n. m.* coffer; chest; trunk.

coger /ko'her/ *v.* catch; pick; take.

cogote /ko'gote/ *n. m.* nape.

cohecho /ko'etʃo/ *n. m.* bribe. —**cohechar,** *v.*

coheredero /koere'ðero/ **-ra** *n.* coheir.

coherente /koe'rente/ *a.* coherent.

cohesión /koe'sion/ *n. f.* cohesion.

cohete /ko'ete/ *n. m.* firecracker; rocket.

cohibición /koiβi'θion; koiβi'sion/ *n.* restraint; repression.

cohibir /koi'βir/ *v.* restrain; repress.

coincidencia /koinθi'ðenθia; koinsi'ðensia/ *n. f.* coincidence.

coincidir /koinθi'ðir; koinsi'ðir/ *v.* coincide.

cojear /kohe'ar/ *v.* limp.

cojera /ko'hera/ *n. m.* limp.

cojín /ko'hin/ *n. m.* cushion.

cojinete /kohi'nete/ *n. m.* small cushion, pad.

cojo /'koho/ **-a** *a.* **1.** lame. —*n.* **2.** lame person.

col /kol/ *n. f.* cabbage.

cola /'kola/ *n. f.* tail; glue; line, queue. **hacer c.,** stand in line.

colaboración /kolaβora'θion; kolaβora'sion/ *n. f.* collaboration.

colaborar /kolaβo'rar/ *v.* collaborate.

cola de caballo /'kola de ka'βaʎo; 'kola de ka'βayo/ ponytail.

coladera /kola'ðera/ *n. f.* strainer.

colador /kola'ðor/ *n. m.* colander, strainer.

colapso /ko'lapso/ *n. m.* collapse, prostration.

colar /ko'lar/ *v.* strain; drain.

colateral /kolate'ral/ *a.* collateral.

colcha /'koltʃa/ *n. f.* bedspread, quilt.

colchón /kol'tʃon/ *n. m.* mattress.

colear /kole'ar/ *v.* wag the tail.

colección /kolek'θion; kolek'sion/ *n. f.* collection, set.

coleccionar /kolekθio'nar; koleksio'nar/ *v.* collect.

colecta /ko'lekta/ *n. f.* collection; collect (a prayer).

colectivo /kolek'tiβo/ *a.* collective.

colector /kolek'tor/ *n. m.* collector.

colega /ko'lega/ *n. m. & f.* colleague.

colegial /kole'hial/ *n. m.* college student.

colegiatura /kolehia'tura/ *n. f.* scholarship; tuition.

colegio /ko'lehio/ *n. m.* (private) school, college.

colegir /kole'hir/ *v.* infer, deduce.

cólera /'kolera/ *n.* **1.** *f.* rage, wrath. **2.** *m.* cholera.

colérico /ko'leriko/ *adj.* angry, irritated.

colesterol /koleste'rol/ *n. m.* cholesterol.

coleta /ko'leta/ *n. f.* pigtail; postscript.

coleto /ko'leto/ *n. m.* leather jacket.

colgado /kol'gaðo/ **-da** *n.* **1.** crazy person. —*a.* **2.** hanging, pending.

colgador /kolga'ðor/ *n. m.* rack, hanger.

colgaduras /kolga'ðuras/ *n. f.pl.* drapery.

colgante /kol'gante/ *a.* hanging.

colgar /kol'gar/ *v.* hang up, suspend.

colibrí /koli'βri/ *n. m.* hummingbird.

coliflor /koli'flor/ *n. f.* cauliflower.

coligarse /koli'garse/ *v.* band together, unite.

colilla /ko'liʎa; ko'liya/ *n. f.* butt of a cigar or cigarette.

colina /ko'lina/ *n. f.* hill, hillock.

colinabo /koli'naβo/ *n. m.* turnip.

colindante /kolin'dante/ *a.* neighboring, adjacent.

colindar /kolin'dar/ *v.* neighbor, abut.

coliseo /koli'seo/ *n. m.* theater; coliseum.

colisión /koli'sion/ *n. f.* collision.

collado /ko'ʎaðo; ko'yaðo/ *n. m.* hillock.

collar /ko'ʎar; ko'yar/ *n. m.* necklace; collar.

colmar /kol'mar/ *v.* heap up, fill liberally.

colmena /kol'mena/ *n. f.* hive.

colmillo /kol'miʎo; kol'miyo/ *n. m.* eyetooth; tusk; fang.

colmo /'kolmo/ *n. m.* height, peak, extreme.

colocación /koloka'θion; koloka'sion/ *n. f.* place, position; employment, job; arrangement.

colocar /kolo'kar/ *v.* place, locate, put, set.

colombiano /kolom'biano/ **-na** *a. & n.* Colombian.

colon /'kolon/ *n. m.* colon (of intestines).

colonia /ko'lonia/ *n. f.* colony; eau de Cologne.

Colonia *n. f.* Cologne.

colonial /kolo'nial/ *a.* colonial.

colonización /koloniθa'θion; kolonisa'sion/ *n. f.* colonization.

colonizador /koloniθa'ðor; koloni-sa'ðor/ **-ra** n. colonizer.

colonizar /koloni'θar; koloni'sar/ v. colonize.

colono /ko'lono/ n. m. colonist; tenant farmer.

coloquio /ko'lokio/ n. m. conversation, talk.

color /ko'lor/ n. m. color. **—colorar,** v.

coloración /kolora'θion; kolora'sion/ n. f. coloring.

colorado /kolo'raðo/ a. red, ruddy.

colorar /kolo'rar/ v. color, paint; dye.

colorete /kolo'rete/ n. m. rouge.

colorformo /kolor'formo/ n. m. chloroform.

colorido /kolo'riðo/ n. m. color, coloring. **—colorir,** v.

colosal /kolo'sal/ a. colossal.

columbrar /kolum'brar/ v. discern.

columna /ko'lumna/ n. f. column, pillar, shaft.

columpiar /kolum'piar/ v. swing.

columpio /ko'lumpio/ n. m. swing.

coma /'koma/ n. f. coma; comma.

comadre /ko'maðre/ n. f. midwife; gossip; close friend.

comadreja /koma'ðreha/ n. f. weasel.

comadrona /koma'ðrona/ n. f. midwife.

comandancia /koman'danθia; koman'dansia/ n. m. command; command post.

comandante /koman'dante/ n. m. commandant; commander; major.

comandar /koman'dar/ v. command.

comandita /koman'dita/ n. f. silent partnership.

comanditario /komandi'tario/ **-ra** n. silent partner.

comando /ko'mando/ n. m. command.

comarca /ko'marka/ n. f. region; border, boundary.

comba /'komba/ n. f. bulge.

combar /kom'bar/ v. bend; bulge.

combate /kom'bate/ n. m. combat. **—combatir,** v.

combatiente /komba'tiente/ a. & m. combatant.

combinación /kombina'θion; kombina'sion/ n. f. combination; slip (garment).

combinar /kombi'nar/ v. combine.

combustible /kombus'tiβle/ a. **1.** combustible. —n. **2.** m. fuel.

combustión /kombus'tion/ n. f. combustion.

comedero /kome'ðero/ n. m. trough.

comedia /ko'meðia/ n. f. comedy; play.

comediante /kome'ðiante/ n. m. actor; comedian.

comedido /kome'ðiðo/ a. polite, courteous; obliging.

comedirse /kome'ðirse/ v. to be polite or obliging.

comedor /kome'ðor/ n. m. dining room. **coche c.,** dining car.

comendador /komenda'ðor/ n. m. commander.

comensal /komen'sal/ n. m. table companion.

comentador /komenta'ðor/ **-ra** n. commentator.

comentario /komen'tario/ n. m. commentary.

comento /ko'mento/ n. m. comment. **—comentar,** v.

comenzar /komen'θar; komen'sar/ v. begin, start, commence.

comer /ko'mer/ v. eat, dine.

comercial /komer'θial; komer'sial/ a. commercial.

comercializar /komerθiali'θar; komersiali'sar/ v. market.

comerciante /komer'θiante; komer'siante/ **-ta** n. merchant, trader, businessperson.

comerciar /komer'θiar; komer'siar/ v. trade, deal, do business.

comercio /ko'merθio; ko'mersio/ n. m. commerce, trade, business; store.

comestible /komes'tiβle/ a. **1.** edible. —n. **2.** m. (pl.) groceries, provisions.

cometa /ko'meta/ n. **1.** m. comet. **2.** f. kite.

cometer /kome'ter/ v. commit.

cometido /kome'tiðo/ n. m. commission; duty; task.

comezón /kome'θon; kome'son/ n. f. itch.

comicios /ko'miθios; ko'misios/ n. m.pl. primary elections.

cómico /'komiko/ **-ca** a. & n. comic, comical; comedian.

comida /ko'miða/ n. f. food; dinner; meal.

comidilla /komi'ðiʎa; komi'ðiya/ n. f. light meal; gossip.

comienzo /ko'mienθo; ko'mienso/ n. m. beginning.

comilitona /komili'tona/ n. f. spread, feast.

comillas /ko'miʎas; ko'miyas/ n. f.pl. quotation marks.

comilón /komi'lon/ **-na** n. glutton; heavy eater.

comisario /komi'sario/ n. m. commissary.

comisión /komi'sion/ n. f. commission. **—comisionar,** v.

comisionado /komisio'naðo/ **-da** n. agent, commissioner.

comisionar /komisio'nar/ v. commission.

comiso /ko'miso/ n. m. (law) confiscation of illegal goods.

comistrajo /komis'traho/ n. m. mess, hodgepodge.

comité /komi'te/ n. m. committee.

comitiva /komi'tiβa/ n. f. retinue.

como /'komo/ conj. & adv. like, as.

cómo adv. how.

cómoda /'komoða/ n. f. bureau, chest (of drawers).

cómodamente /komoða'mente/ adv. conveniently.

comodidad /komoði'ðað/ n. f. convenience, comfort; commodity.

comodín /komo'ðin/ n. m. joker (playing card).

cómodo /'komoðo/ a. comfortable; convenient.

comodoro /komo'ðoro/ n. m. commodore.

compacto /kom'pakto/ a. compact.

compadecer /kompaðe'θer; kompaðe'ser/ v. be sorry for, pity.

compadraje /kompa'ðrahe/ n. m. clique.

compadre /kom'paðre/ n. m. close friend.

compaginar /kompahi'nar/ v. put in order; arrange.

compañerismo /kompaɲe'rismo/ n. m. companionship.

compañero /kompa'ɲero/ **-ra** n. companion, partner.

compañía /kompa'ɲia/ n. f. company.

comparable /kompa'raβle/ a. comparable.

comparación /kompara'θion; kompara'sion/ n. f. comparison.

comparar /kompa'rar/ v. compare.

comparativamente /komparatiβa'mente/ adv. comparatively.

comparativo /kompara'tiβo/ a. comparative.

comparecer /kompare'θer; kompare'ser/ v. appear.

comparendo /kompa'rendo/ n. m. summons.

comparsa /kom'parsa/ n. f. carnival masquerade; retinue.

compartimiento /komparti'miento/ n. m. compartment.

compartir /kompar'tir/ v. share.

compás /kom'pas/ n. m. compass; beat, rhythm.

compasar /kompa'sar/ v. measure exactly.

compasión /kompa'sion/ n. f. compassion.

compasivo /kompa'siβo/ a. compassionate.

compatibilidad /kompatiβili'ðað/ n. f. compatibility.

compatible /kompa'tiβle/ a. compatible.

compatriota /kompa'triota/ n. m. & f. compatriot.

compeler /kompe'ler/ v. compel.

compendiar /kompen'diar/ v. summarize; abridge.

compendiariamente /kompendiaria'mente/ adv. briefly.

compendio /kom'pendio/ n. m. summary; abridgment.

compendiosamente /kompendiosa'mente/ adv. briefly.

compensación /kompensa'θion; kompensa'sion/ n. f. compensation.

compensar /kompen'sar/ v. compensate.

competencia /kompe'tenθia; kompe'tensia/ n. f. competence; competition.

competente /kompe'tente/ a. competent.

competentemente /kompetente'mente/ adv. competently.

competición /kompeti'θion; kompeti'sion/ n. f. competition.

competidor /kompeti'ðor/ **-ra** a. & n. competitive; competitor.

competir /kompe'tir/ v. compete.

compilación /kompila'θion; kompila'sion/ n. f. compilation.

compilar /kompi'lar/ v. compile.

compinche /kom'pintʃe/ n. m. pal.

complacencia /kompla'θenθia; kompla'sensia/ n. f. complacency.

complacer /kompla'θer; kompla'ser/ v. please, oblige, humor.

complaciente /kompla'θiente; kompla'siente/ a. pleasing, obliging.

complejidad /komplehi'ðað/ n. f. complexity.

complejo /kom'pleho/ **-ja** a. & n. complex.

complemento /komple'mento/ n. m. complement; Gram. object.

completamente /kompleta'mente/ adv. completely.

completamiento /kompleta'miento/ n. m. completion, finish.

completar /komple'tar/ v. complete.

completo /kom'pleto/ a. complete, full, perfect.

complexión /komplek'sion/ n. f. nature, temperament.

complicación /komplika'θion; komplika'sion/ n. f. complication.

complicado /kompli'kaðo/ a. complicated.

complicar /kompli'kar/ v. complicate.

cómplice /'kompliθe; 'komplise/ n. m. & f. accomplice, accessory.

complicidad /kompliθi'ðað; komplisi'ðað/ n. f. complicity.

complot /kom'plot/ n. m. conspiracy.

componedor /kompone'ðor/ **-ra** n. typesetter.

componenda /kompo'nenda/ n. f. compromise; settlement.

componente /kompo'nente/ a. & m. component.

componer /kompo'ner/ v. compose; fix, repair.

componible /kompo'niβle/ a. reparable.

comportable /kompor'taβle/ a. endurable.

comportamiento /komportamiento/ n. m. behavior.

comportarse /kompor'tarse/ v. behave.

comporte /kom'porte/ n. m. behavior.

composición /komposi'θion; komposi'sion/ n. f. composition.

compositivo /komposi'tiβo/ a. synthetic; composite.

compositor /komposi'tor/ **-ra** n. composer.

compost /kom'post/ n. m. compost.

compostura /kompos'tura/ n. f. composure; repair; neatness.

compota /kom'pota/ n. f. (fruit) sauce.

compra /'kompra/ n. f. purchase. **ir de compras,** to go shopping.

comprador /kompra'ðor/ **-ra** n. buyer, purchaser.

comprar /kom'prar/ v. buy, purchase.

comprender /kompren'der/ v. comprehend, understand; include, comprise.

comprensibilidad /komprensiβili'ðað/ n. f. comprehensibility.

comprensible /kompren'siβle/ a. understandable.

comprensión /kompren'sion/ n. f. comprehension, understanding.

comprensivo /kompren'siβo/ n. m. comprehensive.

compresa /kom'presa/ n. f. medical compress.

compresión /kompre'sion/ n. f. compression.

comprimir /kompri'mir/ v. compress; restrain, control.

comprobación /komproβa'θion; komproβa'sion/ n. f. proof.

comprobante /kompro'βante/ a. **1.** proving. —n. **2.** m. proof.

comprobar /kompro'βar/ v. prove; verify, check.

comprometer /komprome'ter/ v. compromise.

comprometerse /komprome'terse/ v. become engaged.

compromiso /kompro'miso/ n. m. compromise; engagement.

compuerta /kom'puerta/ n. f. floodgate.

compuesto /kom'puesto/ n. m. composition; compound.

compulsión /kompul'sion/ n. f. compulsion.

compulsivo /kompul'siβo/ a. compulsive.

compunción /kompun'θion; kompun'sion/ n. f. compunction.

compungirse /kompuɲ'girse/ v. regret, feel remorse.

computación /komputa'θion; komputa'sion/ n. f. computation.

computador /komputa'ðor/ n. m. computer.

computadora de sobremesa /komputa'ðora de soβre'mesa/ n. f. desktop computer.

computadora doméstica /komputa'ðora do'mestika/ n. f. home computer.

computar /kompu'tar/ v. compute.

cómputo /'komputo/ n. m. computation.

comulgar /komul'gar/ v. take communion.

comulgatorio /komulga'torio/ n. m. communion altar.

común /ko'mun/ a. common, usual.

comunal /komu'nal/ a. communal.

comunero /komu'nero/ n. m. commoner.

comunicable /komuni'kaβle/ a. communicable.

comunicación /komunika'θion; komunika'sion/ n. f. communication.

comunicante /komuni'kante/ n. m. & f. communicant.

comunicar /komuni'kar/ v. communicate; convey.

comunicativo /komunika'tiβo/ a. communicative.

comunidad /komuni'ðað/ n. f. community.

comunión /komu'nion/ n. f. communion.

comunismo /komu'nismo/ n. m. communism.

comunista /komu'nista/ a. & n. communistic; communist.

comúnmente /komu'mente/ adv. commonly; usually; often.

con /kon/ prep. with.

concavidad /konkaβi'ðað/ n. f. concavity.

cóncavo /'konkaβo/ a. **1.** concave. —n. **2.** m. concavity.

concebible /konθe'βiβle; konse'βiβle/ *a.* conceivable.

concebir /konθe'βir; konse'βir/ *v.* conceive.

conceder /konθe'ðer; konse'ðer/ *v.* concede.

concejal /konθe'hal; konse'hal/ *n. m.* councilman.

concejo /kon'θeho; kon'seho/ *n. m.* city council.

concento /kon'θento; kon'sento/ *n. m.* harmony (of singing voices).

concentración /konθentra'θion; konsentra'sion/ *n. f.* concentration.

concentrar /konθen'trar; konsen'trar/ *v.* concentrate.

concepción /konθep'θion; konsep'sion/ *n. f.* conception.

conceptible /konθep'tiβle; konsep'tiβle/ *a.* conceivable.

concepto /kon'θepto; kon'septo/ *n. m.* concept; opinion.

concerniente /konθer'niente; konser'niente/ *a.* concerning.

concernir /konθer'nir; konser'nir/ *v.* concern.

concertar /konθer'tar; konser'tar/ *v.* arrange.

concertina /konθer'tina; konser'tina/ *n. f.* concertina.

concesión /konθe'sion; konse'sion/ *n. f.* concession.

concha /'kontʃa/ *n. f. S.A.* shell.

conciencia /konθi'enθia; kon'siensia/ *n. f.* conscience; consciousness; conscientiousness.

concienzudo /konθien'θuðo; konsien'suðo/ *a.* conscientious.

concierto /kon'θierto; kon'sierto/ *n. m.* concert.

conciliación /konθilia'θion; konsilia'sion/ *n. f.* conciliation.

conciliador /konθilia'ðor; konsilia'ðor/ **-ra** *n.* conciliator.

conciliar /konθi'liar; konsi'liar/ *v.* conciliate.

concilio /kon'θilio; kon'silio/ *n. m.* council.

concisión /konθi'sion; konsi'sion/ *n. f.* conciseness.

conciso /kon'θiso; kon'siso/ *a.* concise.

concitar /konθi'tar; konsi'tar/ *v.* instigate, stir up.

conciudadano /konθiuða'ðano; konsiuða'ðano/ **-na** *n.* fellow citizen.

concluir /kon'kluir/ *v.* conclude.

conclusión /konklu'sion/ *n. f.* conclusion.

conclusivo /konklu'siβo/ *a.* conclusive.

concluso /kon'kluso/ *a.* concluded; closed.

concluyentemente /konkluyente'mente/ *adv.* conclusively.

concomitante /konkomi'tante/ *a.* concomitant, attendant.

concordador /konkorða'ðor/ **-ra** *n.* moderator; conciliator.

concordancia /konkor'ðanθia; konkor'ðansia/ *n. f.* agreement, concord.

concordar /konkor'ðar/ *v.* agree; put or be in accord.

concordia /kon'korðia/ *n. f.* concord, agreement.

concretamente /konkreta'mente/ *adv.* concretely.

concretar /konkre'tar/ *v.* summarize; make concrete.

concretarse /konkre'tarse/ *v.* limit oneself to.

concreto /kon'kreto/ *a. & m.* concrete.

concubina /konku'βina/ *n. f.* concubine, mistress.

concupiscente /konkupis'θente; konkupis'sente/ *a.* lustful.

concurrencia /konku'rrenθia; konku'rrensia/ *n. f.* assembly; attendance; competition.

concurrente /konku'rrente/ *a.* concurrent.

concurrido /konku'rriðo/ *a.* heavily attended or patronized.

concurrir /konku'rrir/ *v.* concur; attend.

concurso /kon'kurso/ *n. m.* contest, competition; meeting.

conde /'konde/ *n. m.* (title) count.

condecente /konde'θente; konde'sente/ *a.* appropriate, proper.

condecoración /kondekora'θion; kondekora'sion/ *n. f.* decoration; medal; badge.

condecorar /kondeko'rar/ *v.* decorate with a medal.

condena /kon'dena/ *n. f.* prison sentence.

condenación /kondena'θion; kondena'sion/ *n. f.* condemnation.

condenar /konde'nar/ *v.* condemn; damn; sentence.

condensación /kondensa'θion; kondensa'sion/ *n. f.* condensation.

condensar /konden'sar/ *v.* condense.

condesa /kon'desa/ *n. f.* countess.

condescendencia /kondesθen'denθia; kondessen'densia/ *n. f.* condescension.

condescender /kondesθen'der; kondessen'der/ *v.* condescend, deign.

condescendiente /kondesθen'diente; kondessen'diente/ *a.* condescending.

condición /kondi'θion; kondi'sion/ *n. f.* condition.

condicional /kondiθio'nal; kondisio'nal/ *a.* conditional.

condicionalmente /kondiθional'mente; kondisional'mente/ *adv.* conditionally.

condimentar /kondimen'tar/ *v.* season, flavor.

condimento /kondi'mento/ *n. m.* condiment, seasoning, dressing.

condiscípulo /kondis'θipulo; kondis'sipulo/ **-la** *n.* schoolmate.

condolencia /kondo'lenθia; kondo'lensia/ *n. f.* condolence, sympathy.

condolerse de /kondo'lerse de/ *v.* sympathize with.

condominio /kondo'minio/ *n. m.* condominium.

condómino /kon'domino/ *n. m.* co-owner.

condonar /kondo'nar/ *v.* condone.

cóndor /'kondor/ *n. m.* condor (bird).

conducción /konduk'θion; konduk'sion/ *n. f.* conveyance.

conducente /kondu'θente; kondu'sente/ *a.* conducive.

conducir /kondu'θir; kondu'sir/ *v.* conduct, escort, lead; drive.

conducta /kon'dukta/ *n. f.* conduct, behavior.

conducto /kon'dukto/ *n. m.* pipe, conduit; sewer.

conductor /konduk'tor/ **-ra** *n.* driver; conductor.

conectar /konek'tar/ *v.* connect.

conejera /kone'hera/ *n. f.* rabbit warren; place of ill repute.

conejillo de Indias /kone'hiʎo de 'indias; kone'hiyo de 'indias/ guinea pig.

conejo /ko'neho/ **-ja** *n.* rabbit.

conexión /konek'sion/ *n. f.* connection; coupling.

conexivo /konek'siβo/ *a.* connective.

conexo /ko'nekso/ *a.* connected, united.

confalón /konfa'lon/ *n. m.* ensign, standard.

confección /konfek'θion; konfek'sion/ *n. f.* workmanship; ready-made article; concoction.

confeccionar /konfekθio'nar; konfeksio'nar/ *v.* concoct.

confederación /konfeðera'θion; konfeðera'sion/ *n. f.* confederation.

confederado /konfeðe'raðo/ **-da** *a. & n.* confederate.

confederar /konfeðe'rar/ *v.* confederate, unite, ally.

conferencia /konfe'renθia; konfe'rensia/ *n. f.* lecture; conference. **c. interurbana**, long-distance call.

conferenciante /konferen'θiante;

konferen'siante/ *n. m. & f.* lecturer, speaker.

conferenciar /konferen'θiar; konferen'siar/ *v.* confer.

conferencista /konferen'θista; konferen'sista/ *n. m. & f.* lecturer, speaker.

conferir /konfe'rir/ *v.* confer.

confesar /konfe'sar/ *v.* confess.

confesión /konfe'sion/ *n. f.* confession.

confesionario /konfesio'nario, konfeso'nario/ *n. m.* confessional.

confesor /konfe'sor/ **-ra** *n.* confessor.

confeti /kon'feti/ *n. m.pl.* confetti.

confiable /kon'fiaβle/ *a.* dependable.

confiado /kon'fiaðo/ *a.* confident; trusting.

confianza /kon'fianθa; kon'fiansa/ *n. f.* confidence, trust, faith.

confiar /kon'fiar/ *v.* entrust; trust, rely.

confidencia /konfi'ðenθia; konfi'ðensia/ *n. f.* confidence, secret.

confidencial /konfiðen'θial; konfiðen'sial/ *a.* confidential.

confidente /konfi'ðente/ *n. m. & f.* confidant.

confidentemente /konfiðente'mente/ *adv.* confidently.

confín /kon'fin/ *n. m.* confine.

confinamiento /konfina'miento/ *n. m.* confinement.

confinar /konfi'nar/ *v.* confine, imprison; border on.

confirmación /konfirma'θion; konfirma'sion/ *n. f.* confirmation.

confirmar /konfir'mar/ *v.* confirm.

confiscación /konfiska'θion; konfiska'sion/ *n. f.* confiscation.

confiscar /konfis'kar/ *v.* confiscate.

confitar /konfi'tar/ *v.* sweeten; make into candy or jam.

confite /kon'fite/ *n. m.* candy.

confitería /konfite'ria/ *n. f.* confectionery; candy store.

confitura /konfi'tura/ *n. f.* confection.

conflagración /konflagra'θion; konflagra'sion/ *n. f.* conflagration.

conflicto /kon'flikto/ *n. m.* conflict.

confluencia /kon'fluenθia; kon'fluensia/ *n. f.* confluence, junction.

confluir /kon'fluir/ *v.* flow into each other.

conformación /konforma'θion; konforma'sion/ *n. f.* conformation.

conformar /konfor'mar/ *v.* conform.

conforme /kon'forme/ *a.* **1.** acceptable, right, as agreed; in accordance, in agreement. —*conj.* **2.** according, as.

conformidad /konformi'ðað/ *n. f.* conformity; agreement.

conformismo /konfor'mismo/ *n. m.* conformism.

conformista /konfor'mista/ *n. m. & f.* conformist.

confortar /konfor'tar/ *v.* comfort.

confraternidad /konfraterni'ðað/ *n. f.* brotherhood, fraternity.

confricar /konfri'kar/ *v.* rub vigorously.

confrontación /konfronta'θion; konfronta'sion/ *n. f.* confrontation.

confrontar /konfron'tar/ *v.* confront.

confucianismo /konfuθia'nismo; konfusia'nismo/ *n. m.* Confucianism.

confundir /konfun'dir/ *v.* confuse; puzzle, mix up.

confusamente /konfusa'mente/ *adv.* confusedly.

confusión /konfu'sion/ *n. f.* confusion, mix-up; clutter.

confuso /kon'fuso/ *a.* confused; confusing.

confutación /konfuta'θion; konfuta'sion/ *n. f.* disproof.

confutar /konfu'tar/ *v.* refute, disprove.

congelable /konɡe'laβle/ *a.* congealable.

congelación /konɡela'θion; kon-

hela'sion/ *n. f.* congealment; deep freeze.

congelado /konɡe'laðo/ *a.* frozen, congealed.

congelar /konɡe'lar/ *v.* congeal, freeze.

congenial /konɡe'nial/ *a.* congenial; analogous.

congeniar /konɡe'niar/ *v.* be congenial.

congestión /konɡes'tion/ *n. f.* congestion.

conglomeración /konɡlomera'θion; konɡlomera'sion/ *n. f.* conglomeration.

congoja /kon'ɡoha/ *n. f.* grief, anguish.

congraciamiento /konɡraθia'miento; konɡrasia'miento/ *n. m.* flattery; ingratiation.

congraciar /konɡra'θiar; konɡra'siar/ *v.* flatter; ingratiate oneself.

congratulación /konɡratula'θion; konɡratula'sion/ *n. f.* congratulation.

congratular /konɡratu'lar/ *v.* congratulate.

congregación /konɡreɡa'θion; konɡreɡa'sion/ *n. f.* congregation.

congregar /konɡre'ɡar/ *v.* congregate.

congresista /konɡre'sista/ *n. m. & f.* congressional representative.

congreso /kon'ɡreso/ *n. m.* congress; conference.

conjetura /konhe'tura/ *n. f.* conjecture. —**conjeturar,** *v.*

conjetural /konhetu'ral/ *a.* conjectural.

conjugación /konhuɡa'θion; konhuɡa'sion/ *n. f.* conjugation.

conjugar /konhu'ɡar/ *v.* conjugate.

conjunción /konhun'θion; konhun'sion/ *n. f.* union; conjunction.

conjuntamente /konhunta'mente/ *adv.* together, jointly.

conjunto. /kon'hunto/ *a.* **1.** joint, unified. —*n.* **2.** *m.* whole.

conjuración /konhura'θion; konhura'sion/ *n. f.* conspiracy, plot.

conjurado /konhu'raðo/ **-da** *n.* conspirator, plotter.

conjurar /konhu'rar/ *v.* conjure.

conjuro /kon'huro/ *n. m.* exorcism; spell; plea.

conllevador /konʎeβa'ðor; konyeβa'ðor/ *n. m.* helper, aide.

conmemoración /komemora'θion; komemora'sion/ *n. f.* commemoration; remembrance.

conmemorar /komemo'rar/ *v.* commemorate.

conmemorativo /komemora'tiβo/ *a.* commemorative, memorial.

conmensal /komen'sal/ *n. m.* messmate.

conmigo /ko'miɡo/ *adv.* with me.

conmilitón /komili'ton/ *n. m.* fellow soldier.

conminación /komina'θion; komina'sion/ *n. f.* threat, warning.

conminar /komi'nar/ *v.* threaten.

conminatorio /komina'torio/ *a.* threatening, warning.

conmiseración /komisera'θion; komisera'sion/ *n. f.* sympathy.

conmoción /komo'θion; komo'sion/ *n. f.* commotion, stir.

conmovedor /komoβe'ðor/ *a.* moving, touching.

conmover /komo'βer/ *v.* move, affect, touch.

conmutación /komuta'θion; komuta'sion/ *n. f.* commutation.

conmutador /komuta'ðor/ *n. m.* electric switch.

conmutar /komu'tar/ *v.* exchange.

connatural /konnatu'ral/ *a.* innate, inherent.

connotación /konnota'θion; konnota'sion/ *n. f.* connotation.

connotar /konno'tar/ *v.* connote.

connubial /konnu'βial/ *a.* connubial.

connubio /ko'nnuβio/ *n. m.* matrimony.

cono /'kono/ *n. m.* cone.
conocedor /konoθe'ðor; konose'ðor/ **-ra** *n.* expert, connoisseur.
conocer /kono'θer; kono'ser/ *v.* know, be acquainted with; meet, make the acquaintance of.
conocible /kono'θiβle; kono'siβle/ *a.* knowable.
conocido /kono'θiðo; kono'siðo/ **-da** *a.* **1.** familiar, well-known. —*n.* **2.** acquaintance, person known.
conocimiento /konoθi'miento; konosi'miento/ *n. m.* knowledge, acquaintance; consciousness.
conque /'konke/ *conj.* so then; and so.
conquista /kon'kista/ *n. f.* conquest.
conquistador /konkista'ðor/ **-ra** *n.* conqueror.
conquistar /konkis'tar/ *v.* conquer.
consabido /konsa'βiðo/ *a.* aforesaid.
consagración /konsagra'θion; konsagra'sion/ *n. f.* consecration.
consagrado /konsa'graðo/ *a.* consecrated.
consagrar /konsa'grar/ *v.* consecrate, dedicate, devote.
consanguinidad /konsaŋguini'ðað/ *n. f.* consanguinity.
consciente /kons'θiente; kons'siente/ *a.* conscious, aware.
conscientemente /konsθiente-'mente; konssiente'mente/ *adv.* consciously.
conscripción /konskrip'θion; konskrip'sion/ *n. f.* conscription for military service.
consecución /konseku'θion; konseku'sion/ *n. f.* attainment.
consecuencia /konse'kuenθia; konse'kuensia/ *n. f.* consequence.
consecuente /konse'kuente/ *a.* consequent; consistent.
consecuentemente /konsekuente-'mente/ *adv.* consequently.
consecutivamente /konsekutiβa-'mente/ *adv.* consecutively.
consecutivo /konseku'tiβo/ *a.* consecutive.
conseguir /konse'gir/ *v.* obtain, get, secure; succeed in, manage to.
conseja /kon'seha/ *n. f.* fable.
consejero /konse'hero/ **-ra** *n.* adviser, counselor.
consejo /kon'seho/ *n. m.* council; counsel; (piece of) advice. **c. de redacción,** editorial board.
consenso /kon'senso/ *n. m.* consensus.
consentido /konsen'tiðo/ *a.* spoiled, bratty.
consentimiento /konsenti'miento/ *n. m.* consent.
consentir /konsen'tir/ *v.* allow, permit.
conserje /kon'serhe/ *n. m.* superintendent, keeper.
conserva /kon'serβa/ *n. f.* conserve, preserve.
conservación /konserβa'θion; konserβa'sion/ *n. f.* conservation.
conservador /konserβa'ðor/ **-ra** *a.* & *n.* conservative.
conservar /konser'βar/ *v.* conserve.
conservativo /konserβa'tiβo/ *a.* conservative, preservative.
conservatorio /konserβa'torio/ *n. m.* conservatory.
considerable /konsiðe'raβle/ *a.* considerable, substantial.
considerablemente /konsiðeraβle'mente/ *adv.* considerably.
consideración /konsiðera'θion; konsiðera'sion/ *n. f.* consideration.
consideradamente /konsiðeraða'mente/ *adv.* considerably.
considerado /konsiðe'raðo/ *a.* considerate; considered.
considerando /konsiðe'rando/ *conj.* whereas.
considerar /konsiðe'rar/ *v.* consider.
consigna /kon'signa/ *n. f.* watchword.

consignación /konsigna'θion; konsigna'sion/ *n. f.* consignment.
consignar /konsig'nar/ *v.* consign.
consignatorio /konsigna'torio/ **-ria** *n.* consignee; trustee.
consigo /kon'sigo/ *adv.* with herself, with himself, with oneself, with themselves, with yourself, with yourselves.
consiguiente /konsi'giente/ *a.* **1.** consequent. —*n.* **2.** *m.* consequence.
consiguientemente /konsigiente-'mente/ *adv.* consequently.
consistencia /konsis'tenθia; konsis'tensia/ *n. f.* consistency.
consistente /konsis'tente/ *a.* consistent.
consistir /konsis'tir/ *v.* consist.
consistorio /konsis'torio/ *n. m.* consistory.
consocio /kon'soθio; kon'sosio/ *n. m.* associate; partner; comrade.
consola /kon'sola/ *n. f.* console.
consolación /konsola'θion; konsola'sion/ *n. f.* consolation.
consolar /konso'lar/ *v.* console.
consolativo /konsola'tiβo/ *a.* consolatory.
consolidación /konsoliða'θion; konsoliða'sion/ *n. f.* consolidation.
consolidado /konsoli'ðaðo/ *a.* consolidated.
consolidar /konsoli'ðar/ *v.* consolidate.
consonancia /konso'nanθianb; konso'nansia/ *n. f.* agreement, accord, harmony.
consonante /konso'nante/ *a.* & *f.* consonant.
consonar /konso'nar/ *v.* rhyme.
consorte /kon'sorte/ *n. m.* & *f.* consort, mate.
conspicuo /kons'pikuo/ *a.* conspicuous.
conspiración /konspira'θion; konspira'sion/ *n. f.* conspiracy, plot.
conspirador /konspira'ðor/ **-ra** *n.* conspirator.
conspirar /konspi'rar/ *v.* conspire, plot.
constancia /kons'tanθia; kons'tansia/ *n. f.* perseverance; record.
constante /kons'tante/ *a.* constant.
constantemente /konstante'mente/ *adv.* constantly.
constar /kons'tar/ *v.* consist; be clear, be on record.
constelación /konstela'θion; konstela'sion/ *n. f.* constellation.
consternación /konsterna'θion; konsterna'sion/ *n. f.* consternation.
consternar /konster'nar/ *v.* dismay.
constipación /konstipa'θion; konstipa'sion/ *n. f.* head cold.
constipado /konsti'paðo/ *a.* **1.** having a head cold. —*n.* **2.** *m.* head cold.
constitución /konstitu'θion; konstitu'sion/ *n. f.* constitution.
constitucional /konstituθio'nal; konstitusio'nal/ *a.* constitutional.
constitucionalidad /konstituθional i'ðað; konstitusionali'ðað/ *n. f.* constitutionality.
constituir /konsti'tuir/ *v.* constitute.
constitutivo /konstitu'tiβo/ *n. m.* constituent.
constituyente /konstitu'yente, konstitu'tiβo/ *a.* constituent.
constreñidamente /konstreɲiða-'mente/ *adv.* compulsively; with constraint.
constreñimiento /konstreɲi'miento/ *n. m.* compulsion; constraint.
constreñir /konstre'ɲir/ *v.* constrain.
constricción /konstrik'θion; konstrik'sion/ *n. f.* constriction.
construcción /konstruk'θion; konstruk'sion/ *n. f.* construction.
constructivo /konstruk'tiβo/ *a.* constructive.
constructor /konstruk'tor/ **-ra** *n.* builder.
construir /kons'truir/ *v.* construct, build.

consuelo /kon'suelo/ *n. m.* consolation.
cónsul /'konsul/ *n. m.* consul.
consulado /konsu'laðo/ *n. m.* consulate.
consular /konsu'lar/ *a.* consular.
consulta /kon'sulta/ *n. f.* consultation.
consultación /konsulta'θion; konsulta'sion/ *n. f.* consultation.
consultante /konsul'tante/ *n. m.* & *f.* consultant.
consultar /konsul'tar/ *v.* consult.
consultivo /konsul'tiβo/ *a.* consultative.
consultor /konsul'tor/ **-ra** *n.* adviser.
consumación /konsuma'θion; konsuma'sion/ *n. f.* consummation; end.
consumado /konsu'maðo/ *a.* consummate, downright.
consumar /konsu'mar/ *v.* consummate.
consumidor /konsumi'ðor/ **-ra** *n.* consumer.
consumir /konsu'mir/ *v.* consume.
consumo /kon'sumo/ *n. m.* consumption.
consunción /konsun'θion; konsun'sion/ *n. m.* consumption, tuberculosis.
contabilidad /kontaβili'ðað/ *n. f.* accounting, bookkeeping.
contabilista /kontaβi'lista/ **contable** *n. m.* & *f.* accountant.
contacto /kon'takto/ *n. m.* contact.
contado /kon'taðo/ *n. m.* **al c.,** (for) cash.
contador /konta'ðor/ **-ra** *n.* accountant, bookkeeper; meter.
contagiar /konta'hiar/ *v.* infect.
contagio /kon'tahio/ *n. m.* contagion.
contagioso /konta'hioso/ *a.* contagious.
contaminación /kontamina'θion; kontamina'sion/ *n. f.* contamination, pollution. **c. del aire, c. atmosférica,** air pollution.
contaminar /kontami'nar/ *v.* contaminate, pollute.
contar /kon'tar/ *v.* count; relate, recount, tell. **c. con,** count on.
contemperar /kontempe'rar/ *v.* moderate.
contemplación /kontempla'θion; kontempla'sion/ *n. f.* contemplation.
contemplador /kontempla'ðor/ **-ra** *n.* thinker.
contemplar /kontem'plar/ *v.* contemplate.
contemplativamente /kontemplatiβa'mente/ *adv.* thoughtfully.
contemplativo /kontempla'tiβo/ *a.* contemplative.
contemporáneo /kontempo'raneo/ **-nea** *a.* & *n.* contemporary.
contención /konten'θion; konten'sion/ *n. f.* contention.
contencioso /konten'θioso; konten'sioso/ *a.* quarrelsome; argumentative.
contender /konten'der/ *v.* cope, contend; conflict.
contendiente /konten'diente/ *n. m.* & *f.* contender.
contenedor /kontene'ðor/ *n. m.* container.
contener /konte'ner/ *v.* contain; curb, control.
contenido /konte'niðo/ *n. m.* contents.
contenta /kon'tenta/ *n. f.* endorsement.
contentamiento /kontenta'miento/ *n. m.* contentment.
contentar /konten'tar/ *v.* content, satisfy.
contentible /konten'tiβle/ *a.* contemptible.
contento /kon'tento/ *a.* **1.** contented, happy. —*n.* **2.** *m.* contentment, satisfaction, pleasure.
contérmino /kon'termino/ *a.* adjacent, abutting.

contestable /kontes'taβle/ *a.* disputable.
contestación /kontesta'θion; kontesta'sion/ *n. f.* answer. —**contestar,** *v.*
contestador automático /kontesta'ðor auto'matiko/ *n. m.* answering machine.
contextura /konteks'tura/ *n. f.* texture.
contienda /kon'tienda/ *n. f.* combat; match; strife.
contigo /kon'tigo/ *adv.* with you.
contiguamente /kontigua'mente/ *adv.* contiguously.
contiguo /kon'tiguo/ *a.* adjoining, next.
continencia /konti'nenθia; konti'nensia/ *n. f.* continence, moderation.
continental /konti'nental/ *a.* continental.
continente /konti'nente/ *n. m.* continent; mainland.
continentemente /kontinente-'mente/ *adv.* in moderation.
contingencia /kontin'henθia; kontin'hensia/ *n. f.* contingency.
contingente /kontin'hente/ *a.* contingent; incidental.
continuación /kontinua'θion; kontinua'sion/ *n. f.* continuation. **a c.,** thereupon, hereupon.
continuamente /kontinua'mente/ *adv.* continuously.
continuar /konti'nuar/ *v.* continue, keep on.
continuidad /kontinui'ðað/ *n. f.* continuity.
continuo /kon'tinuo/ *a.* continual; continuous.
contorcerse /kontor'θerse; kontor'serse/ *v.* writhe, twist.
contorción /kontor'θion; kontor'sion/ *n. f.* contortion.
contorno /kon'torno/ *n. m.* contour; profile, outline; neighborhood.
contra /'kontra/ *prep.* against.
contraalmirante /kontraalmi'rante/ *n. m.* rear admiral.
contraataque /kontraa'take/ *n. m.* counterattack.
contrabajo /kontra'βaho/ *n. m.* double bass.
contrabalancear /kontraβalanθe'ar; kontraβalanse'ar/ *v.* counterbalance.
contrabandear /kontraβande'ar/ *v.* smuggle.
contrabandista /kontraβan'dista/ *n. m.* & *f.* smuggler.
contrabando /kontra'βando/ *n. m.* contraband, smuggling.
contracción /kontrak'θion; kontrak'sion/ *n. f.* contraction.
contracepción /kontraθep'θion; kontrasep'sion/ *n. f.* contraception, birth control.
contractual /kontrak'tual/ *a.* contractual.
contradecir /kontraðe'θir; kontraðe'sir/ *v.* contradict.
contradicción /kontraðik'θion; kontraðik'sion/ *n. f.* contradiction.
contradictorio /kontraðik'torio/ *adj.* contradictory.
contraer /kontra'er/ *v.* contract; shrink.
contrahacedor /kontraaθe'ðor; kontraase'ðor/ **-ra** *n.* imitator.
contrahacer /kontraa'θer; kontraa-'ser/ *v.* forge.
contralor /kontra'lor/ *n. m.* comptroller.
contramandar /kontraman'dar/ *v.* countermand.
contraorden /kontra'orðen/ *n. f.* countermand.
contraparte /kontra'parte/ *n. f.* counterpart.
contrapesar /kontrape'sar/ *v.* counterbalance; offset.
contrapeso /kontra'peso/ *n. m.* counterweight.
contraproducente /kontrap-

roðu'θente; kontraproðu'sente/ *a.* counterproductive.

contrapunto /kontra'punto/ *n. m.* counterpoint.

contrariamente /kontraria'mente/ *adv.* contrarily.

contrariar /kontra'riar/ *v.* contradict; vex; antagonize; counteract.

contrariedad /kontrarie'ðað/ *n. f.* contrariness; opposition; contradiction; disappointment; trouble.

contrario /kon'trario/ *a. & m.* contrary, opposite.

contrarrestar /kontrarres'tar/ *v.* resist; counteract.

contrasol /kontra'sol/ *n. m.* sunshade.

contraste /kon'traste/ *n. m.* contrast. —**contrastar,** *v.*

contratar /kontra'tar/ *v.* engage, contract.

contratiempo /kontra'tiempo/ *n. m.* accident; misfortune.

contratista /kontra'tista/ *n. m. & f.* contractor.

contrato /kon'trato/ *n. m.* contract.

contribución /kontriβu'θion; kontriβu'sion/ *n. f.* contribution; tax.

contribuir /kontri'βuir/ *v.* contribute.

contribuyente /kontriβu'yente/ *n. m. & f.* contributor; taxpayer.

contrición /kontri'θion; kontri'sion/ *n. f.* contrition.

contristar /kontris'tar/ *v.* afflict.

contrito /kon'trito/ *a.* contrite, remorseful.

control /kon'trol/ *n. m.* control. —**controlar,** *v.*

controlador aéreo /kontrola'ðor a'ereo/ *n. m.* air traffic controller.

controversia /kontro'βersia/ *n. f.* controversy.

controversista /kontroβer'sista/ *n. m. & f.* controversialist.

controvertir /kontroβer'tir/ *v.* dispute.

contumacia /kontu'maθia; kontu'masia/ *n. f.* stubbornness.

contumaz /kontu'maθ; kontu'mas/ *adj.* stubborn.

contumelia /kontu'melia/ *n. f.* contumely; abuse.

conturbar /kontur'βar/ *v.* trouble, disturb.

contusión /kontu'sion/ *n. f.* contusion; bruise.

convalecencia /kombale'θenθia; kombale'sensia/ *n. f.* convalescence.

convalecer /kombale'θer; kombale'ser/ *v.* convalesce.

convaleciente /kombale'θiente; kombale'siente/ *a.* convalescent.

convecino /kombe'θino; kombe'sino/ **-na** *a.* **1.** near, close. —*n.* **2.** neighbor.

convencedor /kombenθe'ðor; kombense'ðor/ *adj.* convincing.

convencer /komben'θer; komben'ser/ *v.* convince.

convencimiento /kombenθi'miento; kombensi'miento/ *n. m.* conviction, firm belief.

convención /komben'θion; komben'sion/ *n. f.* convention.

convencional /kombenθio'nal; kombensio'nal/ *a.* conventional.

conveniencia /kombe'nienθia; kombe'niensia/ *n. f.* suitability; advantage, interest.

conveniente /kombe'niente/ *a.* suitable; advantageous, opportune.

convenio /kom'benio/ *n. m.* pact, treaty; agreement.

convenir /kombe'nir/ *v.* assent, agree, concur; be suitable, fitting, convenient.

convento /kom'bento/ *n. m.* convent.

convergencia /komber'henθia; komber'hensia/ *n. f.* convergence.

convergir /komber'hir/ *v.* converge.

conversación /kombersa'θion; kombersa'sion/ *n. f.* conversation.

conversar /komber'sar/ *v.* converse.

conversión /komber'sion/ *n. f.* conversion.

convertible /komber'tiβle/ *a.* convertible.

convertir /komber'tir/ *v.* convert.

convexidad /kombeksi'ðað/ *n. f.* convexity.

convexo /kom'bekso/ *a.* convex.

convicción /kombik'θion; kombik'sion/ *n. f.* conviction.

convicto /kom'bikto/ *a.* found guilty.

convidado /kombi'ðaðo/ **-da** *n.* guest.

convidar /kombi'ðar/ *v.* invite.

convincente /kombin'θente; kombin'sente/ *a.* convincing.

convite /kom'bite/ *n. m.* invitation, treat.

convocación /komboka'θion; komboka'sion/ *n. f.* convocation.

convocar /kombo'kar/ *v.* convoke, assemble.

convoy /kom'boi/ *n. m.* convoy, escort.

convoyar /kombo'yar/ *v.* convey; escort.

convulsión /kombul'sion/ *n. f.* convulsion.

convulsivo /kombul'siβo/ *a.* convulsive.

conyugal /konyu'gal/ *a.* conjugal.

cónyuge /'konyuhe/ *n. m. & f.* spouse, mate.

coñac /ko'nak/ *n. m.* cognac, brandy.

cooperación /koopera'θion; koopera'sion/ *n. f.* cooperation.

cooperador /koopera'ðor/ *a.* cooperative.

cooperar /koope'rar/ *v.* cooperate.

cooperativa /koopera'tiβa/ *n. f.* (food, etc.) cooperative, co-op.

cooperativo /koopera'tiβo/ *a.* cooperative.

coordinación /koorðina'θion; koorðina'sion/ *n. f.* coordination.

coordinar /koorði'nar/ *v.* coordinate.

copa /'kopa/ *n. f.* goblet.

copartícipe /kopar'tiθipe; kopar'tisipe/ *m & f.* partner.

copete /ko'pete/ *n. m.* tuft; toupee.

copia /'kopia/ *n. f.* copy. —**copiar,** *v.*

copiadora /kopia'ðora/ *n. f.* copier.

copioso /ko'pioso/ *a.* copious.

copista /ko'pista/ *n. m. & f.* copyist.

copla /'kopla/ *n. f.* popular song.

coplero /kop'lero/ *n. m.* poetaster.

cópula /'kopula/ *n. f.* connection.

coqueta /ko'keta/ *n. f.* flirt. —**coquetear,** *v.*

coraje /ko'rahe/ *n. m.* courage, bravery; anger.

coral /ko'ral/ *a.* **1.** choral. —*n.* **2.** *m.* coral.

coralino /kora'lino/ *a.* coral.

Corán /ko'ran/ *n. m.* Koran.

corazón /kora'θon; kora'son/ *n. m.* heart.

corazonada /koraθo'naða; koraso'naða/ *n. f.* foreboding.

corbata /kor'βata/ *n. f.* necktie.

corbeta /kor'βeta/ *n. f.* corvette.

corcho /'kortʃo/ *n. m.* cork.

corcova /kor'koβa/ *n. f.* hump, hunchback.

corcovado /korko'βaðo/ **-da** *a. & n.* hunchback.

cordaje /kor'ðahe/ *n. m.* rigging.

cordel /kor'ðel/ *n. m.* string, cord.

cordero /kor'ðero/ *n. m.* lamb.

cordial /kor'ðial/ *a.* cordial; hearty.

cordialidad /korðiali'ðað/ *n. f.* cordiality.

cordillera /korði'ʎera; korði'yera/ *n. f.* mountain range.

cordón /kor'ðon/ *n. m.* cord; (shoe) lace.

cordura /kor'ðura/ *n. f.* sanity.

Corea /ko'rea/ *n. f.* Korea.

coreano /kore'ano/ **-a** *a. & n.* Korean.

coreografía /koreogra'fia/ *n. f.* choreography.

corista /ko'rista/ *n. f.* chorus girl.

corneja /kor'neha/ *n. f.* crow.

córneo /'korneo/ *a.* horny.

corneta /kor'neta/ *n. f.* bugle, horn, cornet.

corniforme /korni'forme/ *a.* horn-shaped.

cornisa /kor'nisa/ *n. f.* cornice.

cornucopia /kornu'kopia/ *n. f.* cornucopia.

coro /'koro/ *n. m.* chorus; choir.

corola /ko'rola/ *n. f.* corolla.

corolario /koro'lario/ *n. m.* corollary.

corona /ko'rona/ *n. f.* crown; halo; wreath.

coronación /korona'θion; korona'sion/ *n. f.* coronation.

coronamiento /korona'miento/ *n. m.* completion of a task.

coronar /koro'nar/ *v.* crown.

coronel /koro'nel/ *n. m.* colonel.

coronilla /koro'niʎa; koro'niya/ *n. f.* crown, top of the head.

corporación /korpora'θion; korpora'sion/ *n. f.* corporation.

corporal /korpo'ral/ *adj.* corporeal, bodily.

corpóreo /kor'poreo/ *a.* corporeal.

corpulencia /korpu'lenθia; korpu'lensia/ *n. f.* corpulence.

corpulento /korpu'lento/ *a.* corpulent, stout.

corpuscular /korpusku'lar/ *a.* corpuscular.

corpúsculo /kor'puskulo/ *n. m.* corpuscle.

corral /ko'rral/ *n. m.* corral, pen, yard.

correa /ko'rrea/ *n. f.* belt, strap.

correa transportadora /korrea transporta'ðora/ conveyor belt.

corrección /korrek'θion; korrek'sion/ *n. f.* correction.

correcto /ko'rrekto/ *a.* correct, proper, right.

corrector /korrek'tor/ **-ra** *n.* corrector, proofreader.

corredera /korre'ðera/ *n. f.* race course.

corredizo /korre'ðiθo; korre'ðiso/ *a.* easily untied.

corredor /korre'ðor/ *n. m.* corridor; runner.

corregible /korre'hiβle/ *a.* corrigible.

corregidor /korrehi'ðor/ *n. m.* corrector; magistrate, mayor.

corregir /korre'hir/ *v.* correct.

correlación /korrela'θion; korrela'sion/ *n. f.* correlation.

correlacionar /korrelaθio'nar; korrelasio'nar/ *v.* correlate.

correlativo /korrela'tiβo/ *a.* correlative.

correo /ko'rreo/ *n. m.* mail.

correoso /korre'oso/ *a.* leathery.

correr /ko'rrer/ *v.* run.

correría /korre'ria/ *n. f.* raid; escapade.

correspondencia /korrespon'denθia; korrespon'densia/ *n. f.* correspondence.

corresponder /korrespon'der/ *v.* correspond.

correspondiente /korrespon'diente/ *a. & m.* corresponding; correspondent.

corresponsal /korrespon'sal/ *n. m.* correspondent.

corretaje /korre'tahe/ *n. m.* brokerage.

correvedile /korreβe'ðile/ *n. m.* tale bearer; gossip.

corrida /ko'rriða/ *n. f.* race. **c. (de toros),** bullfight.

corrido /ko'rriðo/ *a.* abashed; expert.

corriente /ko'rriente/ *a.* **1.** current, standard. —*n.* **2.** *f.* current, stream. **3.** *m.* **al c.,** informed, up to date. **contra la c.,** against the current; upriver, upstream.

corroboración /korroβora'θion; korroβora'sion/ *n. f.* corroboration.

corroborar /korroβo'rar/ *v.* corroborate.

corroer /korro'er/ *v.* corrode.

corromper /korrom'per/ *v.* corrupt.

corrompido /korrom'piðo/ *a.* corrupt.

corrupción /korrup'θion; korrup'sion/ *n. f.* corruption.

corruptela /korrup'tela/ *n. f.* corruption; vice.

corruptibilidad /korruptiβili'ðað/ *n. f.* corruptibility.

corruptor /korrup'tor/ **-ra** *n.* corrupter.

corsario /kor'sario/ *n. m.* corsair.

corsé /kor'se/ *n. m.* corset.

corso /'korso/ *n. m.* piracy.

cortacésped /korta'θespeð; korta'sespeð/ *n. m.* lawnmower.

cortadillo /korta'ðiʎo; korta'ðiyo/ *n. m.* small glass.

cortado /kor'taðo/ *a.* cut.

cortadura /korta'ðura/ *n. f.* cut.

cortante /kor'tante/ *a.* cutting, sharp, keen.

cortapisa /korta'pisa/ *n. f.* obstacle.

cortaplumas /korta'plumas/ *n. m.* penknife.

cortar /kor'tar/ *v.* cut, cut off, cut out.

corte /'korte/ *n. f.* court, *m.* cut.

cortedad /korte'ðað/ *n. f.* smallness; shyness.

cortejar /korte'har/ *v.* pay court to, woo.

cortejo /kor'teho/ *n. m.* court; courtship; sweetheart.

cortés /kor'tes/ *a.* civil, courteous, polite.

cortesana /korte'sana/ *n. f.* courtesan.

cortesano. 1. /korte'sano/ *a.* **1.** courtly, courteous. —*n.* **2.** *m.* courtier.

cortesía /korte'sia/ *n. f.* courtesy.

corteza /kor'teθa; kor'tesa/ *n. f.* bark; rind; crust.

cortijo /kor'tiho/ *n. m.* farmhouse.

cortina /kor'tina/ *n. f.* curtain.

corto /'korto/ *a.* short.

corva /'korβa/ *n. f.* back of the knee.

cosa /'kosa/ *n. f.* thing. **c. de,** a matter of, roughly.

cosecha /ko'setʃa/ *n. f.* crop, harvest. —**cosechar,** *v.*

coser /ko'ser/ *v.* sew, stitch.

cosmético /kos'metiko/ *a. & m.* cosmetic.

cósmico /'kosmiko/ *a.* cosmic.

cosmonauta /kosmo'nauta/ *n. m. & f.* cosmonaut.

cosmopolita /kosmopo'lita/ *a. & n.* cosmopolitan.

cosmos /'kosmos/ *n. m.* cosmos.

coso /'koso/ *n. m.* arena for bull fights.

cosquilla /kos'kiʎa; kos'kiya/ *n. f.* tickle. —**cosquillar,** *v.*

cosquilloso /koski'ʎoso; koski'yoso/ *a.* ticklish.

costa /'kosta/ *n. f.* coast; cost, expense.

costado /kos'taðo/ *n. m.* side.

costal /kos'tal/ *n. m.* sack, bag.

costanero /kosta'nero/ *a.* coastal.

costar /kos'tar/ *v.* cost.

costarricense /kostarri'θense; kostarri'sense/ *a. & n.* Costa Rican.

coste /'koste/ *n. m.* cost, price.

costear /koste'ar/ *v.* defray, sponsor; sail along the coast of.

costilla /kos'tiʎa; kos'tiya/ *n. f.* rib; chop.

costo /'kosto/ *n. m.* cost, price.

costoso /kos'toso/ *a.* costly.

costra /'kostra/ *n. f.* crust.

costumbre /kos'tumbre/ *n. f.* custom, practice, habit.

costura /kos'tura/ *n. f.* sewing; seam.

costurera /kostu'rera/ *n. f.* seamstress, dressmaker.

costurero /kostu'rero/ *n. m.* sewing basket.

cota de malla /'kota de 'maʎa; 'kota de 'maya/ coat of mail.

cotejar /kote'har/ *v.* compare.

cotidiano /koti'ðiano/ *a.* daily; every-day.

cotillón /koti'ʎon; koti'yon/ *n. m.* cotillion.

cotización /kotiθa'θion; kotisa'sion/ *n. f.* quotation.

cotizar /koti'θar; koti'sar/ *v.* quote (a price).

coto /'koto/ *n. m.* enclosure; boundary.

cotón /ko'ton/ *n. m.* printed cotton cloth.

cotufa /ko'tufa/ *n. f.* Jerusalem artichoke.

coturno /ko'turno/ *n. m.* buskin.

covacha /ko'βatʃa/ *n. f.* small cave.

coxal /kok'sal/ *a.* of the hip.

coy /koi/ *n. m.* hammock.

coyote /ko'yote/ *n. m.* coyote.

coyuntura /koyun'tura/ *n. f.* joint; juncture.

coz /koθ; kos/ *n. f.* kick.

crac /krak/ *n. m.* failure.

cráneo /'kraneo/ *n. m.* skull.

craniano /kra'niano/ *a.* cranial.

crapuloso /krapu'loso/ *a.* drunken.

crasiento /kra'siento/ *a.* greasy, oily.

craso /'kraso/ *a.* fat; gross.

cráter /'krater/ *n. m.* crater.

craza /'kraθa; 'krasa/ *n. f.* crucible.

creación /krea'θion; krea'sion/ *n. f.* creation.

creador /krea'ðor/ **-ra** *a. & n.* creative; creator.

crear /kre'ar/ *v.* create.

creativo /krea'tiβo/ *a.* creative.

crébol /'kreβol/ *n. m.* holly tree.

crecer /kre'θer; kre'ser/ *v.* grow, grow up; increase.

creces /'kreθes; 'kreses/ *n. f.pl.* increase, addition.

crecidamente /kreθiða'mente; kresiða'mente/ *adv.* abundantly.

crecido /kre'θiðo; kre'siðo/ *a.* increased, enlarged; swollen.

creciente /kre'θiente; kre'siente/ *a.* **1.** growing. —*n.* **2.** *m.* crescent.

crecimiento /kreθi'miento; kresi'miento/ *n. m.* growth.

credenciales /kreðen'θiales; kreðen'siales/ *f.pl.* credentials.

credibilidad /kreðiβili'ðað/ *n. f.* credibility.

crédito /'kreðito/ *n. m.* credit.

credo /'kreðo/ *n. m.* creed, belief.

crédulamente /kreðula'mente/ *adv.* credulously, gullibly.

credulidad /kreðuli'ðað/ *n. f.* credulity.

crédulo /'kreðulo/ *a.* credulous.

creedero /kree'ðero/ *a.* credible.

creedor /kree'ðor/ *a.* credulous, believing.

creencia /kre'enθia; kre'ensia/ *n. f.* belief.

creer /kre'er/ *v.* believe; think.

creíble /kre'iβle/ *a.* credible, believable.

crema /'krema/ *n. f.* cream.

cremación /krema'θion; krema'sion/ *n. f.* cremation.

crema dentífrica /'krema den'tifrika/ toothpaste.

cremallera /krema'ʎera; krema'yera/ *n. f.* zipper.

crémor tártaro /'kremor 'tartaro/ *n. m.* cream of tartar.

cremoso /kre'moso/ *a.* creamy.

creosota /kreo'sota/ *n. f.* creosote.

crepitar /krepi'tar/ *v.* crackle.

crepuscular /krepusku'lar/ *a.* of or like the dawn or dusk; crepuscular.

crépusculo /kre'puskulo/ *n. m.* dusk, twilight.

crescendo /kres'θendo; kres'sendo/ *n. m.* crescendo.

crespo /'krespo/ *a.* curly.

crespón /kres'pon/ *n. m.* crepe.

cresta /'kresta/ *n. f.* crest; heraldic crest.

crestado /kres'taðo/ *a.* crested.

creta /'kreta/ *n. f.* chalk.

cretáceo /kre'taθeo; kre'taseo/ *a.* chalky.

cretinismo /kreti'nismo/ *n. m.* cretinism.

cretino /kre'tino/ **-na** *n. & a.* cretin.

cretona /kre'tona/ *n. f.* cretonne.

creyente /kre'yente/ *a.* **1.** believing. —*n.* **2.** believer.

creyón /kre'yon/ *n. m.* crayon.

cría /'kria/ *n. f.* (stock) breeding; young (of an animal), litter.

criada /kri'aða/ *n. f.* maid.

criadero /kria'ðero/ *n. m. Agr.* nursery.

criado /kri'aðo/ **-da** *n.* servant.

criador /kria'ðor/ *a.* fruitful, prolific.

crianza /kri'anθa; kri'ansa/ *n. f.* breeding; upbringing.

criar /kri'ar/ *v.* raise, rear; breed.

criatura /kria'tura/ *n. f.* creature; infant.

criba /'kriβa/ *n. f.* sieve.

cribado /kri'βaðo/ *a.* sifted.

cribar /kri'βar/ *v.* sift.

crimen /'krimen/ *n. m.* crime.

criminal /krimi'nal/ *a. & n.* criminal.

criminalidad /kriminali'ðað/ *n. f.* criminality.

criminalmente /kriminal'mente/ *adv.* criminally.

criminología /kriminolo'hia/ *n. f.* criminology.

criminoso /krimi'noso/ *a.* criminal.

crines /'krines/ *n. f.pl.* mane of a horse.

crinolina /krino'lina/ *n. f.* crinoline.

criocirugía /krioθiru'hia; kriosiru'hia/ *n. f.* cryosurgery.

criollo /'krioʎo; 'krioyo/ **-lla** *a. & n.* native; Creole.

cripta /'kripta/ *n. f.* crypt.

criptografía /kriptogra'fia/ *n. f.* cryptography.

crisantemo /krisan'temo/ *n. m.* chrysanthemum.

crisis /'krisis/ *n. f.* crisis.

crisis nerviosa /'krisis ner'βiosa/ nervous breakdown.

crisma /'krisma/ *n. m.* chrism.

crisol /kri'sol/ *n. m.* crucible.

crispamiento /krispa'miento/ *n. m.* twitch, contraction.

crispar /kris'par/ *v.* contract (the muscles); twitch.

cristal /kri'stal/ *n. m.* glass; crystal; lens.

cristalería /kristale'ria/ *n. f.* glassware.

cristalino /krista'lino/ *a.* crystalline.

cristalización /kristaliθa'θion; kristalisa'sion/ *n. f.* crystallization.

cristalizar /kristali'θar; kristali'sar/ *v.* crystallize.

cristianar /kristia'nar/ *v.* baptize.

cristiandad /kristian'dað/ *n. f.* Christendom.

cristianismo /kristia'nismo/ *n. m.* Christianity.

cristiano /kris'tiano/ **-na** *a. & n.* Christian.

Cristo /'kristo/ *n. m.* Christ.

criterio /kri'terio/ *n. m.* criterion; judgment.

crítica /'kritika/ *n. f.* criticism; critique.

criticable /kriti'kaβle/ *a.* blameworthy.

criticador /kritika'ðor/ *a.* critical.

criticar /kriti'kar/ *v.* criticize.

crítico /'kritiko/ **-ca** *a. & n.* critical; critic.

croar /kro'ar/ *v.* croak.

crocante /kro'kante/ *n. m.* almond brittle.

crocitar /kroθi'tar; krosi'tar/ *v.* crow.

cromático /kro'matiko/ *a.* chromatic.

cromo /'kromo/ *n. m.* chromium.

cromosoma /kromo'soma/ *n. m.* chromosome.

cromotipia /kromo'tipia/ *n. f.* color printing.

crónica /'kronika/ *n. f.* chronicle.

crónico /'kroniko/ *a.* chronic.

cronicón /kroni'kon/ *n. m.* concise chronicle.

cronista /kro'nista/ *n. m. & f.* chronicler.

cronología /kronolo'hia/ *n. f.* chronology.

cronológicamente /kronolohika'mente/ *adv.* chronologically.

cronológico /krono'lohiko/ *a.* chronologic.

cronometrar /kronome'trar/ *v.* time.

cronómetro /kro'nometro/ *n. m.* stopwatch; chronometer.

croqueta /kro'keta/ *n. f.* croquette.

croquis /'krokis/ *n. m.* sketch; rough outline.

crótalo /'krotalo/ *n. m.* rattlesnake; castanet.

cruce /'kruθe; 'kruse/ *n. m.* crossing, crossroads, junction.

crucero /kru'θero; kru'sero/ *n. m.* cruiser.

crucífero /kru'θifero; kru'sifero/ *a.* cross-shaped.

crucificado /kruθifi'kaðo; krusifi'kaðo/ *a.* crucified.

crucificar /kruθifi'kar; krusifi'kar/ *v.* crucify.

crucifijo /kruθi'fiho; krusi'fiho/ *n. m.* crucifix.

crucifixión /kruθifik'sion; krusifik'sion/ *n. f.* crucifixion.

crucigrama /kruθi'grama; krusi'grama/ *n. m.* crossword puzzle.

crudamente /kruða'mente/ *adv.* crudely.

crudeza /kru'ðeθa; kru'ðesa/ *n. f.* crudeness.

crudo /'kruðo/ *a.* crude, raw.

cruel /kruel/ *a.* cruel.

crueldad /kruel'dað/ *n. f.* cruelty.

cruelmente /kruel'mente/ *adv.* cruelly.

cruentamente /kruenta'mente/ *adv.* bloodily.

cruento /'kruento/ *a.* bloody.

crujía /kru'hia/ *n. f.* corridor.

crujido /kru'hiðo/ *n. m.* creak.

crujir /kru'hir/ *v.* crackle; creak; rustle.

cruórico /kru'oriko/ *a.* bloody.

crup /krup/ *n. m.* croup.

crupié /kru'pie/ *n. m. & f.* croupier.

crustáceo /krus'taθeo; krus'taseo/ *n. & a.* crustacean.

cruz /kruθ; krus/ *n. f.* cross.

cruzada /kru'θaða; kru'saða/ *n. f.* crusade.

cruzado /kru'θaðo; kru'saðo/ **-da** *n.* crusader.

cruzamiento /kruθa'miento; krusa'miento/ *n. m.* crossing.

cruzar /kru'θar; kru'sar/ *v.* cross.

cruzarse con /kru'θarse kon; kru'sarse kon/ *v.* to (meet and) pass.

cuaderno /kua'ðerno/ *n. m.* notebook.

cuadra /'kuaðra/ *n. f.* block; (hospital) ward.

cuadradamente /kuaðraða'mente/ *adv.* exactly, precisely; completely, in full.

cuadradillo /kuaðra'ðiʎo; kuaðra'ðiyo/ *n. m.* lump of sugar.

cuadrado /kua'ðraðo/ **-da** *a. & n.* square.

cuadrafónico /kuaðra'foniko/ *a.* quadraphonic.

Cuadragésima /kuaðra'hesima/ *n. f.* Lent.

cuadragesimal /kuaðrahesi'mal/ *a.* Lenten.

cuadrángulo /kua'ðraŋgulo/ *n. m.* quadrangle.

cuadrante /kua'ðrante/ *n. m.* quadrant; dial.

cuadrar /kua'ðrar/ *v.* square; suit.

cuadricular /kuaðriku'lar/ *a.* in squares.

cuadrilátero /kuaðri'latero/ *a.* quadrilateral.

cuadrilla /kua'ðriʎa; kua'ðriya/ *n. f.* band, troop, gang.

cuadro /'kuaðro/ *n. m.* picture; painting; frame. **a cuadros,** checked, plaid.

cuadro de servicio /'kuaðro de ser'βiθio; 'kuaðro de ser'βisio/ timetable.

cuadrupedal /kuaðrupe'ðal/ *a.* quadruped.

cuádruplo /'kuaðruplo/ *a.* fourfold.

cuajada /kua'haða/ *n. f.* curd.

cuajamiento /kuaha'miento/ *n. m.* coagulation.

cuajar /kua'har/ *v.* coagulate; overdecorate.

cuajo /'kuaho/ *n. m.* rennet; coagulation.

cual /kual/ *rel. pron.* which.

cuál *a. & pron.* what, which.

cualidad /kuali'ðað/ *n. f.* quality.

cualitativo /kualita'tiβo/ *a.* qualitative.

cualquiera /kual'kiera/ *a. & pron.* whatever, any; anyone.

cuando /'kuando/ *conj.* when.

cuando *adv.* when. **de cuando en cuando,** from time to time.

cuantía /kuan'tia/ *n. f.* quantity; amount.

cuantiar /kuan'tiar/ *v.* estimate.

cuantiosamente /kuantiosa'mente/ *adv.* abundantly.

cuantioso /kuan'tioso/ *a.* abundant.

cuantitativo /kuantita'tiβo/ *a.* quantitative.

cuanto /'kuanto/ *a., adv. & pron.* as much as, as many as; all that which. **en c.,** as soon as. **en c. a,** as for. **c. antes,** as soon as possible. **c. más... tanto más,** the more... the more. **unos cuantos,** a few.

cuánto *a. & adv.* how much, how many.

cuaquerismo /kuake'rismo/ *n. m.* Quakerism.

cuáquero /'kuakero/ **-ra** *n. & a.* Quaker.

cuarenta /kua'renta/ *a. & pron.* forty.

cuarentena /kuaren'tena/ *n. f.* quarantine.

cuaresma /kua'resma/ *n. f.* Lent.

cuaresmal /kuares'mal/ *a.* Lenten.

cuarta /'kuarta/ *n. f.* quarter; quadrant; quart.

cuartear /kuarte'ar/ *v.* divide into quarters.

cuartel /kuar'tel/ *n. m. Mil.* quarters; barracks; *Naut.* hatch. **c. general,** headquarters. **sin c.,** giving no quarter.

cuartelada /kuarte'laða/ *n. f.* military uprising.

cuarterón /kuarte'ron/ *n. & a.* quadroon.

cuarteto /kuar'teto/ *n. m.* quartet.

cuartillo /kuar'tiʎo; kuar'tiyo/ *n. m.* pint.

cuarto /'kuarto/ *a.* **1.** fourth. —*n.* **2.** *m.* quarter; room.

cuarto de baño /'kuarto de 'baɲo/ bathroom.

cuarto de dormir /'kuarto de dor'mir/ bedroom.

cuarto para invitados /'kuarto para imbi'taðos/ guest room.

cuarzo /'kuarθo; 'kuarso/ *n. m.* quartz.

cuasi /'kuasi/ *adv.* almost, nearly.

cuate /'kuate/ *a. & n.* twin.

cuatrero /kua'trero/ *n. m.* cattle rustler.

cuatrillón /kuatri'ʎon; kuatri'yon/ *n. m.* quadrillion.

cuatro /'kuatro/ *a. & pron.* four.

cuatrocientos /kuatro'θientos; kuatro'sientos/ *a. & pron.* four hundred.

cuba /'kuβa/ *n. f.* cask, tub, vat.

cubano /ku'βano/ **-na** *a. & n.* Cuban.

cubero /ku'βero/ *n. m.* cooper.

cubeta /ku'βeta/ *n. f.* small barrel, keg.

cúbico /'kuβiko/ *a.* cubic.

cubículo /ku'βikulo/ *n. m.* cubicle.

cubierta /ku'βierta/ n. f. cover; envelope; wrapping; tread (of a tire); deck.
cubiertamente /kuβierta'mente/ adv. secretly, stealthily.
cubierto /ku'βierto/ n. m. place (at table).
cubil /ku'βil/ n. m. lair.
cubismo /ku'βismo/ n. m. cubism.
cubito de hielo /ku'βito de 'ielo/ n. m. ice cube.
cubo /'kuβo/ n. m. cube; bucket.
cubo de la basura /'kuβo de la ba'sura/ trash can.
cubrecama /kuβre'kama/ n. f. bedspread.
cubrir /ku'βrir/ v. cover.
cubrirse /ku'βrirse/ v. put on one's hat.
cucaracha /kuka'ratʃa/ n. f. cockroach.
cuchara /ku'tʃara/ n. f. spoon, tablespoon.
cucharada /kutʃa'raða/ n. f. spoonful.
cucharita /kutʃa'rita/ **cucharilla** n. f. teaspoon.
cucharón /kutʃa'ron/ n. m. dipper, ladle.
cuchicheo /kutʃi'tʃeo/ n. m. whisper. —**cuchichear**, v.
cuchilla /ku'tʃiʎa; ku'tʃiya/ n. f. cleaver.
cuchillada /kutʃi'ʎaða; kutʃi'yaða/ n. f. slash.
cuchillería /kutʃiʎe'ria; kutʃiye'ria/ n. f. cutlery.
cuchillo /ku'tʃiʎo; ku'tʃiyo/ n. m. knife.
cucho /'kutʃo/ n. m. fertilizer.
cuchufleta /kutʃu'fleta/ n. f. jest.
cuclillo /ku'kliʎo; ku'kliyo/ n. m. cuckoo.
cuco /'kuko/ a. sly.
cuculla /ku'kuʎa; ku'kuya/ n. f. hood, cowl.
cuelga /'kuelga/ n. f. cluster, bunch.
cuelgacapas /kuelga'kapas/ n. m. coat rack.
cuello /'kueʎo; 'kueyo/ n. m. neck; collar.
cuenca /'kuenka/ n. f. socket; (river) basin; wooden bowl.
cuenco /'kuenko/ n. m. earthen bowl.
cuenta /'kuenta/ n. f. account; bill. **darse c.**, to realize. **tener en c. a**, to keep in mind.
cuenta bancaria /'kuenta ban'karia/ bank account.
cuenta de ahorros /'kuenta de a'orros/ savings account.
cuentagotas /kuenta'gotas/ n. m. dropper (for medicine).
cuentista /kuen'tista/ n. m. & f. storyteller; informer.
cuento /'kuento/ n. m. story, tale.
cuerda /'kuerða/ n. f. cord; chord; rope; string; spring (of clock). **dar c. a**, to wind (clock).
cuerdamente /kuerða'mente/ adv. sanely; prudently.
cuerdo /'kuerðo/ a. sane; prudent.
cuerno /'kuerno/ n. m. horn.
cuero /'kuero/ n. m. leather; hide.
cuerpo /'kuerpo/ n. m. body; corps.
cuervo /'kuerβo/ n. m. crow, raven.
cuesco /'kuesko/ n. m. pit, stone (of fruit).
cuesta /'kuesta/ n. f. hill, slope. **llevar a cuestas**, to carry on one's back.
cuestación /kuesta'θion; kuesta'sion/ n. f. solicitation for charity.
cuestión /kues'tion/ n. f. question; affair; argument.
cuestionable /kuestio'naβle/ a. questionable.
cuestionar /kuestio'nar/ v. question; discuss; argue.
cuestionario /kuestio'nario/ n. m. questionnaire.
cuete /'kuete/ n. m. firecracker.
cueva /'kueβa/ n. f. cave; cellar.
cuguar /ku'guar/ n. m. cougar.
cugujada /kugu'haða/ n. f. lark.

cuidado /kui'ðaðo/ n. m. care, caution, worry. **tener c.**, to be careful.
cuidadosamente /kuiðaðosa'mente/ adv. carefully.
cuidadoso /kuiða'ðoso/ a. careful, painstaking.
cuidante /kui'ðante/ n. caretaker, custodian.
cuidar /kui'ðar/ v. take care of.
cuita /'kuita/ n. f. trouble, care; grief.
cuitado /kui'taðo/ a. unfortunate; shy, timid.
cuitamiento /kuita'miento/ n. m. timidity.
culata /ku'lata/ n. f. haunch, buttock; butt of a gun.
culatada /kula'taða/ n. f. recoil.
culatazo /kula'taθo; kula'taso/ n. m. blow with the butt of a gun; recoil.
culebra /ku'leβra/ n. f. snake.
culero /ku'lero/ a. lazy, indolent.
culinario /kuli'nario/ a. culinary.
culminación /kulmina'θion; kulmina'sion/ n. f. culmination.
culminar /kulmi'nar/ v. culminate.
culpa /'kulpa/ n. f. fault, guilt, blame. **tener la c.**, to be at fault. **echar la culpa a**, to blame.
culpabilidad /kulpaβili'ðað/ n. f. guilt, fault, blame.
culpable /kul'paβle/ a. at fault, guilty, to blame, culpable.
culpar /kul'par/ v. blame, accuse.
cultamente /kulta'mente/ adv. politely, elegantly.
cultivable /kulti'βaβle/ a. arable.
cultivación /kultiβa'θion; kultiβa'sion/ n. f. cultivation.
cultivador /kultiβa'ðor/ -ra n. cultivator.
cultivar /kulti'βar/ v. cultivate.
cultivo /kul'tiβo/ n. m. cultivation; (growing) crop.
culto /'kulto/ a. 1. cultured, cultivated. —n. 2. m. cult; worship.
cultura /kul'tura/ n. f. culture; refinement.
cultural /kultu'ral/ a. cultural.
culturar /kultu'rar/ v. cultivate.
culturismo /kultu'rismo/ n. m. body building.
culturista /kultu'rista/ n. m. & f. body builder.
cumbre /'kumbre/ n. m. summit, peak.
cumpleaños /kumple'aɲos/ n. m.pl. birthday.
cumplidamente /kumpliða'mente/ adv. courteously, correctly.
cumplido /kum'pliðo/ a. polite, polished.
cumplimentar /kumplimen'tar/ v. compliment.
cumplimiento /kumpli'miento/ n. m. fulfillment; compliment.
cumplir /kum'plir/ v. comply; carry out, fulfill; reach (years of age).
cumulativo /kumula'tiβo/ a. cumulative.
cúmulo /'kumulo/ n. m. heap, pile.
cuna /'kuna/ n. f. cradle.
cundir /kun'dir/ v. spread; expand; propagate.
cuneiforme /kunei'forme/ a. cuneiform, wedge-shaped.
cuneo /ku'neo/ n. m. rocking.
cuña /'kuɲa/ n. f. wedge.
cuñada /ku'ɲaða/ n. f. sister-in-law.
cuñado /ku'ɲaðo/ n. m. brother-in-law.
cuñete /ku'ɲete/ n. m. keg.
cuota /'kuota/ n. f. quota; dues.
cuotidiano /kuoti'ðiano/ a. daily.
cupé /ku'pe/ n. m. coupé.
Cupido /ku'piðo/ n. m. Cupid.
cupo /'kupo/ n. m. share; assigned quota.
cupón /ku'pon/ n. m. coupon.
cúpula /'kupula/ n. f. dome.
cura /'kura/ n. m. priest; f. treatment, (medical) care. **c. de urgencia**, first aid.
curable /ku'raβle/ a. curable.

curación /kura'θion; kura'sion/ n. f. healing; cure; (surgical) dressing.
curado /ku'raðo/ a. cured, healed.
curador /kura'ðor/ -ra n. healer.
curandero /kuran'dero/ -ra n. healer, medicine man.
curar /ku'rar/ v. cure, heal, treat.
curativo /kura'tiβo/ a. curative, healing.
curia /'kuria/ n. f. ecclesiastical court.
curiosear /kuriose'ar/ v. snoop, pry, meddle.
curiosidad /kuriosi'ðað/ n. f. curiosity.
curioso /ku'rioso/ a. curious.
curro /'kurro/ a. showy, loud, flashy.
cursante /kur'sante/ n. student.
cursar /kur'sar/ v. frequent; attend.
cursi /'kursi/ a. vulgar, shoddy, in bad taste.
curso /'kurso/ n. m. course.
curso por correspondencia /'kurso por korrespon'denθia; 'kurso por korrespon'densia/ n. m. correspondence course.
cursor /kur'sor/ n. m. cursor.
curtidor /kurti'ðor/ n. m. tanner.
curtir /kur'tir/ v. tan.
curva /'kurβa/ n. f. curve; bend.
curvatura /kurβa'tura, kurβi'ðað/ n. f. curvature.
cúspide /'kuspiðe/ n. f. top, peak.
custodia /kus'toðia/ n. f. custody.
custodiar /kusto'ðiar/ v. guard, watch.
custodio /kus'toðio/ n. m. custodian.
cutáneo /ku'taneo/ a. cutaneous.
cutícula /ku'tikula/ n. f. cuticle.
cutis /'kutis/ n. m. or f. skin, complexion.
cutre /'kutre/ a. shoddy.
cuyo /'kuyo/ a. whose.

D

dable /'daβle/ a. possible.
dactilógrafo /dakti'lografo/ -fa n. typist.
dádiva /'daðiβa/ n. f. gift.
dadivosamente /daðiβosa'mente/ adv. generously.
dadivoso /daði'βoso/ a. generous, bountiful.
dado /'daðo/ n. m. die.
dador /da'ðor/ -ra n. giver.
dados /'daðos/ n. m.pl. dice.
daga /'daga/ n. f. dagger.
dalia /'dalia/ n. f. dahlia.
dallador /daʎa'ðor; daya'ðor/ n. m. lawn mower.
dallar /da'ʎar; da'yar/ v. mow.
daltonismo /dalto'nismo/ n. m. color blindness.
dama /'dama/ n. f. lady.
damasco /da'masko/ n. m. apricot; damask.
damisela /dami'sela/ n. f. young lady, girl.
danés /da'nes/ -esa a. & n. Danish, Dane.
danza /'danθa; 'dansa/ n. f. (the) dance. —**danzar**, v.
danzante /dan'θante; dan'sante/ -ta n. dancer.
dañable /da'ɲaβle/ a. condemnable.
dañar /da'ɲar/ v. hurt, harm; damage.
dañino /da'ɲino/ a. harmful.
daño /'daɲo/ n. m. damage; harm.
dañoso /da'ɲoso/ a. harmful.
dar /dar/ v. give; strike (clock). **d. a**, face, open on. **d. con**, find, locate. **¡Dalo por hecho!** Consider it done!
dardo /'darðo/ n. m. dart.
dársena /'darsena/ n. f. dock.
datar /da'tar/ v. date.
dátil /'datil/ n. m. date (fruit).
dativo /da'tiβo/ n. m. & a. dative.
datos /'datos/ n. m.pl. data.
de /de/ prep. of; from; than.
debajo /de'βaho/ adv. underneath. **d. de**, under.

debate /de'βate/ n. m. debate.
debatir /deβa'tir/ v. debate, argue.
debe /'deβe/ n. m. debit.
debelación /deβela'θion; deβela'sion/ n. f. conquest.
debelar /deβe'lar/ v. conquer.
deber /de'βer/ v. 1. owe; must; be to, be supposed to. —n. 2. m. obligation.
deberes /de'βeres/ n. m.pl. homework.
debido /de'βiðo/ a. due.
débil /'deβil/ a. weak, faint.
debilidad /deβili'ðað/ n. f. weakness.
debilitación /deβilita'θion; deβilita'sion/ n. f. weakness.
debilitar /deβili'tar/ v. weaken.
débito /'deβito/ n. m. debit.
debutar /deβu'tar/ v. make a debut.
década /'dekaða/ n. f. decade.
decadencia /deka'ðenθia; dekaðen'sia/ n. f. decadence, decline, decay.
decadente /deka'ðente/ a. decadent, declining, decaying.
decaer /deka'er/ v. decay, decline.
decalitro /deka'litro/ n. m. decaliter.
decálogo /de'kalogo/ n. m. decalogue.
decámetro /de'kametro/ n. m. decameter.
decano /de'kano/ n. m. dean.
decantado /dekan'taðo/ a. much discussed; overexalted.
decapitación /dekapita'θion; dekapitasion/ n. f. beheading.
decapitar /dekapi'tar/ v. behead.
decencia /de'θenθia; de'sensia/ n. f. decency.
decenio /de'θenio; de'senio/ n. m. decade.
decente /de'θente; de'sente/ a. decent.
decentemente /deθente'mente; desente'mente/ adv. decently.
decepción /deθep'θion; desep'sion/ n. f. disappointment, letdown; delusion.
decepcionar /deθepθio'nar; desepsio'nar/ v. disappoint, disillusion.
dechado /de'tʃaðo/ n. m. model; sample; pattern; example.
decibelio /deθi'βelio; desi'βelio/ n. m. decibel.
decididamente /deθiðiða'mente; desiðiða'mente/ adv. decidedly.
decidir /deθi'ðir; desi'ðir/ v. decide.
decigramo /deθi'gramo; desi'gramo/ n. m. decigram.
decilitro /deθi'litro; desi'litro/ n. m. deciliter.
décima /'deθima; 'desima/ n. f. ten-line stanza.
decimal /deθi'mal; desi'mal/ a. decimal.
décimo /'deθimo; 'desimo/ a. tenth.
decir /de'θir; de'sir/ v. tell, say. **es d.**, that is (to say).
decisión /deθi'sion; desi'sion/ n. f. decision.
decisivamente /deθisiβa'mente; desisiβa'mente/ adv. decisively.
decisivo /deθi'siβo; desi'siβo/ a. decisive.
declamación /deklama'θion; deklama'sion/ n. f. declamation; speech.
declamar /dekla'mar/ v. declaim.
declaración /deklara'θion; deklara'sion/ n. f. declaration; statement; plea.
declaración de la renta /deklara'θion de la 'rrenta; deklara'sion de la 'rrenta/ tax return.
declarar /dekla'rar/ v. declare, state.
declarativo /dekla'ratiβo, deklara'torio/ a. declarative.
declinación /deklina'θion; deklina'sion/ n. f. descent; decay; decline; declension.
declinar /dekli'nar/ v. decline.
declive /de'kliβe,/ n. m. declivity, slope.
decocción /dekok'θion; dekok'sion/ n. f. decoction.

decomiso /deko'miso/ *n. m.* seizure, confiscation.

decoración /dekora'θion; dekora'sion/ *n. f.* decoration, trimming.

decorado /deko'raðo/ *n. m. Theat.* scenery, set.

decorar /deko'rar/ *v.* decorate, trim.

decorativo /dekora'tiβo/ *a.* decorative, ornamental.

decoro /de'koro/ *n. m.* decorum; decency.

decoroso /deko'roso/ *a.* decorous.

decrecer /dekre'θer; dekre'ser/ *v.* decrease.

decrépito /de'krepito/ *a.* decrepit.

decreto /de'kreto/ *n. m.* decree. —**decretar,** *v.*

dedal /de'ðal/ *n. m.* thimble.

dédalo /'deðalo/ *n. m.* labyrinth.

dedicación /deðika'θion; deðika'sion/ *n. f.* dedication.

dedicar /deði'kar/ *v.* devote; dedicate.

dedicatoria /deðika'toria/ *n. f.* dedication, inscription.

dedo /'deðo/ *n. m.* finger, toe.

dedo anular /'deðo anu'lar/ ring finger.

dedo corazón /'deðo kora'θon; 'deðo kora'son/ middle finger.

dedo índice /'deðo 'indiθe; 'deðo 'indise/ index finger.

dedo meñique /'deðo me'ɲike/ little finger, pinky.

dedo pulgar /'deðo pul'gar/ thumb.

deducción /deðuk'θion; deðuk'sion/ *n. f.* deduction.

deducir /deðu'θir; deðu'sir/ *v.* deduce; subtract.

defectivo /defek'tiβo/ *a.* defective.

defecto /de'fekto/ *n. m.* defect, flaw.

defectuoso /defek'tuoso/ *a.* defective, faulty.

defender /defen'der/ *v.* defend.

defensa /de'fensa/ *n. f.* defense.

defensivo /defen'siβo/ *a.* defensive.

defensor /defen'sor/ -**ra** *n.* defender.

deferencia /defe'renθia; defe'rensia/ *n. f.* deference.

deferir /defe'rir/ *v.* defer.

deficiente /defi'θiente; defi'siente/ *a.* deficient.

déficit /'defiθit; 'defisit/ *n. m.* deficit.

definición /defini'θion; defini'sion/ *n. f.* definition.

definido /defi'niðo/ *a.* definite.

definir /defi'nir/ *v.* define; establish.

definitivamente /definitiβa'mente/ *adv.* definitely.

definitivo /defini'tiβo/ *a.* definitive.

deformación /deforma'θion; deforma'sion/ *n. f.* deformation.

deformar /defor'mar/ *v.* deform.

deforme /de'forme/ *a.* deformed; ugly.

deformidad /deformi'ðað/ *n. f.* deformity.

defraudar /defrau'ðar/ *v.* defraud.

defunción /defun'θion; defun'sion/ *n. f.* death.

degeneración /dehenera'θion; dehenera'sion/ *n. f.* degeneration.

degenerado /dehene'raðo/ *a.* degenerate. —**degenerar,** *v.*

deglutir /deglu'tir/ *v.* swallow.

degollar /dego'ʎar; dego'yar/ *v.* behead.

degradación /degraða'θion; degraða'sion/ *n. f.* degradation.

degradar /degra'ðar/ *v.* degrade, debase.

deidad /dei'ðað/ *n. f.* deity.

deificación /deifika'θion; deifika-'sion/ *n. f.* deification.

deificar /deifi'kar/ *v.* deify.

deífico /de'ifiko/ *a.* divine, deific.

deísmo /de'ismo/ *n. m.* deism.

dejadez /deha'ðeθ; deha'ðes/ *n. f.* neglect, untidiness; laziness.

dejado /de'haðo/ *a.* untidy; lazy.

dejar /de'har/ *v.* let, allow; leave. **d. de,** stop, leave off. **no d. de,** not fail to.

dejo /'deho/ *n. m.* abandonment; negligence; aftertaste; accent.

del /del/ *contr. of* **de** + **el.**

delantal /delan'tal/ *n. m.* apron; pinafore. **delantal de niña,** pinafore.

delante /de'lante/ *adv.* ahead, forward; in front.

delantero /delan'tero/ *a.* forward, front, first.

delator /dela'tor/ *n. m.* informer; accuser.

delegación /delega'θion; delega'sion/ *n. f.* delegation.

delegado /dele'gaðo/ -**da** *n.* delegate. —**delegar,** *v.*

deleite /de'leite/ *n. m.* delight. —**deleitar,** *v.*

deleitoso /delei'toso/ *a.* delightful.

deletrear /dcletre'ar/ *v.* spell; decipher.

delfín /del'fin/ *n. m.* dolphin; dauphin.

delgadez /delga'ðeθ; delgaðes/ *n. f.* thinness, slenderness.

delgado /del'gaðo/ *a.* thin, slender, slim, slight.

deliberación /deliβera'θion; deliβera-'sion/ *n. f.* deliberation.

deliberadamente /deliβeraða'mente/ *adv.* deliberately.

deliberar /deliβe'rar/ *v.* deliberate.

deliberativo /deliβera'tiβo/ *a.* deliberative.

delicadamente /delikaða'mente/ *adv.* delicately.

delicadeza /delika'ðeθa; delika'ðesa/ *n. f.* delicacy.

delicado /deli'kaðo/ *a.* delicate, dainty.

delicia /deli'θia; deli'sia/ *n. f.* delight; deliciousness.

delicioso /deli'θioso; deli'sioso/ *a.* delicious.

delincuencia /delin'kuenθia; delin'kuensia/ *n. f.* delinquency.

delincuencia de menores /delin'kuenθia de me'nores; delin'kuensia de me'nores/ **delincuencia juvenil** juvenile delinquency.

delincuente /delin'kuente/ *a. & n.* delinquent; culprit, offender.

delineación /delinea'θion; delinea'sion/ *n. f.* delineation, sketch.

delinear /deline'ar/ *v.* delineate, sketch.

delirante /deli'rante/ *a.* delirious.

delirar /deli'rar/ *v.* rave, be delirious.

delirio /de'lirio/ *n. m.* delirium; rapture, bliss.

delito /de'lito/ *n. m.* crime, offense.

delta /'delta/ *n. m.* delta (of river); hang glider.

demacrado /dema'kraðo/ *a.* emaciated.

demagogia /dema'gohia/ *n. f.* demagogy.

demagogo /dema'gogo/ *n. m.* demagogue.

demanda /de'manda/ *n. f.* demand, claim.

demandador /demanda'ðor/ -**ra** *n.* plaintiff.

demandar /deman'dar/ *v.* sue; demand.

demarcación /demarka'θion; demarka'sion/ *n. f.* demarcation.

demarcar /demar'kar/ *v.* demarcate, limit.

demás /de'mas/ *a. & n.* other; (the) rest (of). **por d.,** too much.

demasía /dema'sia/ *n. f.* excess; audacity; iniquity.

demasiado /dema'siaðo/ *a. & adv.* too; too much; too many.

demencia /de'menθia; de'mensia/ *n. f.* dementia; insanity.

demente /de'mente/ *a.* demented.

democracia /demo'kraθia; demo'krasia/ *n. f.* democracy.

demócrata /de'mokrata/ *n. m. & f.* democrat.

democrático /demo'kratiko/ *a.* democratic.

demoler /demo'ler/ *v.* demolish, tear down.

demolición /demoli'θion; demoli-'sion/ *n. f.* demolition.

demonio /de'monio/ *n. m.* demon, devil.

demontre /de'montre/ *n. m.* devil.

demora /de'mora/ *n. f.* delay, —**demorar,** *v.*

demostración /demostra'θion; demostra'sion/ *n. f.* demonstration.

demostrador /demostra'ðor/ -**ra** *n.* demonstrator.

demostrar /demos'trar/ *v.* demonstrate, show.

demostrativo /demostra'tiβo/ *a.* demonstrative.

demudar /demu'ðar/ *v.* change; disguise, conceal.

denegación /denega'θion; denega'sion/ *n. f.* denial; refusal.

denegar /dene'gar/ *v.* deny; refuse.

dengue /'dengue/ *n. m.* prudishness; dengue.

denigración /denigra'θion; denigra'sion/ *n. f.* defamation, disgrace.

denigrar /deni'grar/ *v.* defame, disgrace.

denodado /deno'ðaðo/ *a.* brave, dauntless.

denominación /denomina'θion; denomina'sion/ *n. f.* denomination.

denominar /denomi'nar/ *v.* name, call.

denotación /denota'θion; denota'sion/ *n. f.* denotation.

denotar /deno'tar/ *v.* denote, betoken, express.

densidad /densi'ðað/ *n. f.* density.

denso /'denso/ *a.* dense.

dentado /den'taðo/ *a.* toothed; serrated; cogged.

dentadura /denta'ðura/ *n. f.* set of teeth.

dentadura postiza /denta'ðura pos'tiθa; denta'ðura pos'tisa/ false teeth, dentures.

dental /den'tal/ *a.* dental.

dentífrico /den'tifriko/ *n. m.* dentifrice, toothpaste.

dentista /den'tista/ *n. m. & f.* dentist.

dentistería /dentiste'ria/ *n. f.* dentistry.

dentro /'dentro/ *adv.* within, inside. **d. de poco,** in a short while.

dentudo /den'tuðo/ *a.* toothy (person).

denuedo /de'nueðo/ *n. m.* bravery, courage.

denuesto /de'nuesto/ *n. m.* insult, offense.

denuncia /de'nunθia; de'nunsia/ *n. f.* denunciation; declaration; complaint.

denunciación /denunθia'θion; denunsia'sion/ *n. f.* denunciation.

denunciar /denun'θiar; denun'siar/ *v.* denounce.

deparar /depa'rar/ *v.* offer; grant.

departamento /departa'mento/ *n. m.* department, section.

departir /depar'tir/ *v.* talk, chat.

dependencia /depen'denθia; depen'densia/ *n. f.* dependence; branch office.

depender /depen'der/ *v.* depend.

dependiente /depen'diente/ *a. & m.* dependent; clerk.

depilar /depi'lar/ *v.* depilate, pluck.

depilatorio /depila'torio/ *a. & n.* depilatory.

depistar *v.* mislead, put off the track.

deplorable /deplo'raβle/ *a.* deplorable, wretched.

deplorablemente /deplora'ble'mente/ *adv.* deplorably.

deplorar /deplo'rar/ *v.* deplore.

deponer /depo'ner/ *v.* depose.

deportación /deporta'θion; deporta'sion/ *n. f.* deportation; exile.

deportar /depor'tar/ *v.* deport.

deporte /de'porte/ *n. m.* sport. —**deportivo,** *a.*

deposición /deposi'θion; deposi'sion/ *n. f.* assertion, deposition; removal; movement.

depositante /deposi'tante/ *n. m. & f.* depositor.

depósito /de'posito/ *n. m.* deposit. —**depositar,** *v.*

depravación /depraβa'θion; depraβa'sion/ *n. f.* depravation; depravity.

depravado /depra'βaðo/ *a.* depraved, wicked.

depravar /depra'βar/ *v.* deprave, corrupt, pervert.

depreciación /depreθia'θion; depresia'sion/ *n. f.* depreciation.

depreciar /depre'θiar; depre'siar/ *v.* depreciate.

depredación /depreða'θion; depreða'sion/ *n. f.* depredation.

depredar /depre'ðar/ *v.* pillage, depredate.

depresión /depre'sion/ *n. f.* depression.

depresivo /depre'siβo/ *a.* depressive.

deprimir /depri'mir/ *v.* depress.

depurar /depu'rar/ *v.* purify.

derecha /de'retʃa/ *n. f.* right (hand, side).

derechera /dere'tʃera/ *n. f.* shortcut.

derecho /de'retʃo/ *a.* **1.** right; straight. —*n.* **2.** *m.* right; (the) law. **derechos,** *Com.* duty.

derechos civiles /de'retʃos θi'βiles; de'retʃos si'βiles/ *n. m.pl.* civil rights.

derechos de aduana /de'retʃos de a'ðuana/ *n. m.pl.* customs duty.

derechura /dere'tʃura/ *n. f.* straightness.

derelicto /dere'likto/ *a.* abandoned, derelict.

deriva /de'riβa/ *n. f. Naut.* drift.

derivación /deriβa'θion; deriβa'sion/ *n. f.* derivation.

derivar /deri'βar/ *v.* derive.

dermatólogo /derma'tologo/ -**a** *n.* dermatologist, skin doctor.

derogar /dero'gar/ *v.* derogate; repeal, abrogate.

derramamiento /derrama'miento/ *n. m.* overflow.

derramar /derra'mar/ *v.* spill, pour, scatter.

derrame /de'rrame/ *n. m.* overflow; discharge.

derretir /derre'tir/ *v.* melt, dissolve.

derribar /derri'βar/ *v.* demolish, knock down; bowl over, floor, fell.

derrocamiento /derroka'miento/ *n. m.* overthrow.

derrocar /derro'kar/ *v.* overthrow; oust; demolish.

derrochar /derro'tʃar/ *v.* waste.

derroche /de'rrotʃe/ *n. m.* waste.

derrota /de'rrota/ *n. f.* rout, defeat. —**derrotar,** *v.*

derrotismo /derro'tismo/ *n. m.* defeatism.

derrumbamiento /derrumba'miento/ **derrumbe** *m.* collapse; landslide.

derrumbarse /derrum'βarse/ *v.* collapse, tumble.

derviche /der'βitʃe/ *n. m.* dervish.

desabotonar /desaβoto'nar/ *v.* unbutton.

desabrido /desa'βriðo/ *a.* insipid, tasteless.

desabrigar /desaβri'gar/ *v.* uncover.

desabrochar /desaβro'tʃar/ *v.* unbutton, unclasp.

desacato /desa'kato/ *n. m.* disrespect, lack of respect.

desacierto /desa'θierto; desa'sierto/ *n. m.* error.

desacobardar /desakoβar'ðar/ *v.* remove fear; embolden.

desacomodadamente /desakomo'ðaða'mente/ *adv.* inconveniently.

desacomodado /desakomo'ðaðo/ *a.* unemployed.

desacomodar /desakomo'ðar/ *v.* molest; inconvenience; dismiss.

desacomodo /desako'moðo/ *n. m.* loss of employment.

desaconsejar /desakonse'har/ v. dissuade (someone); advise against (something).

desacordadamente /desakorða-ða'mente/ adv. unadvisedly.

desacordar /desakor'ðar/ v. differ, disagree; be forgetful.

desacorde /desa'korðe/ a. discordant.

desacostumbradamente /desakostumbraða'mente/ adv. unusually.

desacostumbrado /desakostum-'braðo/ a. unusual, unaccustomed.

desacostumbrar /desakostum'brar/ v. give up a habit or custom.

desacreditar /desakreði'tar/ v. discredit.

desacuerdo /desa'kuerðo/ n. m. disagreement.

desadeudar /desaðeu'ðar/ v. pay one's debts.

desadormecer /desaðorme'θer; desaðorme'ser/ v. waken, rouse.

desadornar /desaðor'nar/ v. divest of ornament.

desadvertidamente /desaðßertiða'mente/ adv. inadvertently.

desadvertido /desaðßer'tiðo/ a. imprudent.

desadvertimiento /desaðßerti-'miento/ n. m. imprudence, rashness.

desadvertir /desaðßer'tir/ v. act imprudently.

desafección /desafek'θion; desafek-'sion/ n. f. disaffection.

desafecto /desa'fekto/ a. disaffected.

desafiar /desa'fiar/ v. defy; challenge.

desafinar /desafi'nar/ v. be out of tune.

desafío /desa'fio/ n. m. defiance; challenge.

desaforar /desafo'rar/ v. infringe one's rights; be outrageous.

desafortunado /desafortu'naðo/ a. unfortunate.

desafuero /desa'fuero/ n. m. violation of the law; outrage.

desagraciado /desagra'θiaðo; desagra'siaðo/ a. graceless.

desagradable /desagra'ðaßle/ a. disagreeable, unpleasant.

desagradablemente /desagra-ðaßle'mente/ adv. disagreeably.

desagradecido /desagraðe'θiðo; desagraðe'siðo/ a. ungrateful.

desagradecimiento /desagraðe-θi'miento; desagraðesimiento/ n. m. ingratitude.

desagrado /desa'graðo/ n. m. displeasure.

desagraviar /desagra'ßiar/ v. make amends.

desagregar /desagre'gar/ v. separate, disintegrate.

desagriar /desa'griar/ v. mollify, appease.

desaguadero /desagua'ðero/ n. m. drain, outlet; cesspool; sink.

desaguador /desagua'ðor/ n. m. water pipe.

desaguar /desa'guar/ v. drain.

desaguisado /desagi'saðo/ n. m. offense; injury.

desahogadamente /desaogaða-'mente/ adv. impudently; brazenly.

desahogado /desao'gaðo/ a. impudent, brazen; cheeky.

desahogar /desao'gar/ v. relieve.

desahogo /desa'ogo/ n. m. relief; nerve, cheek.

desahuciar /desau'θiar; desau'siar/ v. give up hope for; despair of.

desairado /desai'raðo/ a. graceless.

desaire /des'aire/ n. m. slight; scorn. —desairar, v.

desajustar /desahus'tar/ v. mismatch, misfit; make unfit.

desalar /desa'lar/ v. hurry, hasten.

desalentar /desalen'tar/ v. make out of breath; discourage.

desaliento /desa'liento/ n. m. discouragement.

desaliñar /desali'ɲar/ v. disarrange; make untidy.

desaliño /desa'liɲo/ n. m. slovenliness, untidiness.

desalivar /desali'ßar/ v. remove saliva from.

desalmadamente /desalmaða-'mente/ adv. mercilessly.

desalmado /desal'maðo/ a. merciless.

desalojamiento /desaloha'miento/ n. m. displacement; dislodging.

desalojar /desalo'har/ v. dislodge.

desalquilado /desalki'laðo/ a. vacant, unrented.

desamar /desa'mar/ v. cease loving.

desamasado /desama'saðo/ a. dissolved, disunited, undone.

desamistarse /desamis'tarse/ v. quarrel, disagree.

desamor /desa'mor/ n. m. disaffection, dislike; hatred.

desamorado /desamo'raðo/ a. cruel; harsh; rude.

desamparador /desampara'ðor/ n. m. deserter.

desamparar /desampa'rar/ v. desert, abandon.

desamparo /desam'paro/ n. m. desertion, abandonment.

desamueblado /desamue'ßlaðo/ a. unfurnished.

desamueblar /desamue'ßlar/ v. remove furniture from.

desandrajado /desandra'haðo/ a. shabby, ragged.

desanimadamente /desanimaða-'mente/ adv. in a discouraged manner; spiritlessly.

desanimar /desani'mar/ v. dishearten, discourage.

desánimo /des'animo/ n. m. discouragement.

desanudar /desanu'ðar/ v. untie; loosen; disentangle.

desapacible /desapa'θißle; desapa'sißle/ a. rough, harsh; unpleasant.

desaparecer /desapare'θer; desapare'ser/ v. disappear.

desaparición /desapari'θion; desapari'sion/ n. f. disappearance.

desapasionadamente /desapasionaða'mente/ adv. dispassionately.

desapasionado /desapasio'naðo/ a. dispassionate.

desapego /desa'pego/ n. m. impartiality.

desapercibido /desaperθi'ßiðo; desapersi'ßiðo/ a. unnoticed; unprepared.

desapiadado /desapia'ðaðo/ a. merciless, cruel.

desaplicación /desaplika'θion; desaplika'sion/ n. f. indolence, laziness; negligence.

desaplicado /desapli'kaðo/ a. indolent, lazy; negligent.

desaposesionar /desaposesio'nar/ v. dispossess.

desapreciar /desapre'θiar; desapre'siar/ v. depreciate.

desapretador /desapreta'ðor/ n. m. screwdriver.

desapretar /desapre'tar/ v. loosen; relieve, ease.

desaprisionar /desaprisio'nar/ v. set free, release.

desaprobación /desaproßa'θion; desaproßa'sion/ n. f. disapproval.

desaprobar /desapro'ßar/ v. disapprove.

desaprovechado /desaproße'tʃaðo/ a. useless, profitless; backward.

desaprovechar /desaproße'tʃar/ v. waste; be backward.

desarbolar /desarßo'lar/ v. unmast.

desarmado /desar'maðo/ a. disarmed, defenseless.

desarmar /desar'mar/ v. disarm.

desarme /de'sarme/ n. m. disarmament.

desarraigado /desarrai'gaðo/ a. rootless.

desarraigar /desarrai'gar/ v. uproot; eradicate; expel.

desarreglar /desarre'glar/ v. disarrange, mess up.

desarrollar /desarro'ʎar; desarro'yar/ v. develop.

desarrollo /desa'rroʎo; des'arroyo/ n. m. development.

desarropar /desarro'par/ v. undress; uncover.

desarrugar /desarru'gar/ v. remove wrinkles from.

desaseado /desase'aðo/ a. dirty; disorderly.

desasear /desase'ar/ v. make dirty or disorderly.

desaseo /desa'seo/ n. m. dirtiness; disorder.

desasir /desa'sir/ v. loosen; disengage.

desasociable /desaso'θiaßle; desaso'siaßle/ a. unsociable.

desasosegar /desasose'gar/ v. disturb.

desasosiego /desaso'siego/ n. m. uneasiness.

desastrado /desas'traðo/ a. ragged, wretched.

desastre /de'sastre/ n. m. disaster.

desastroso /desas'troso/ a. disastrous.

desatar /desa'tar/ v. untie, undo.

desatención /desaten'θion; desaten'sion/ n. f. inattention; disrespect; rudeness.

desatender /desaten'der/ v. ignore; disregard.

desatentado /desaten'taðo/ a. inconsiderate; imprudent.

desatinado /desati'naðo/ a. foolish; insane, wild.

desatino /desa'tino/ n. m. blunder. —desatinar, v.

desatornillar /desatorni'ʎar; desatorni'yar/ v. unscrew.

desautorizado /desautori'θaðo; desautori'saðo/ a. unauthorized.

desautorizar /desautori'θar; desautori'sar/ v. deprive of authority.

desavenencia /desaße'nenθia; desaße'nensia/ n. f. disagreement, discord.

desaventajado /desaßenta'haðo/ a. disadvantageous.

desayuno /desa'yuno/ n. m. breakfast. —desayunar, v.

desazón /desa'θon; desa'son/ n. f. insipidity; uneasiness.

desazonado /desaθo'naðo; desaso'naðo/ a. insipid; uneasy.

desbandada /desßan'daða/ n. f. disbanding.

desbandarse /desßan'darse/ v. disband.

desbarajuste /desßara'huste/ n. m. disorder, confusion.

desbaratar /desßara'tar/ v. destroy.

desbastar /desßas'tar/ v. plane, smoothen.

desbocado /desßo'kaðo/ a. foul-spoken, indecent.

desbocarse /desßo'karse/ v. use obscene language.

desbordamiento /desßorða'miento/ n. m. overflow; flood.

desbordar /desßor'ðar/ v. overflow.

desbrozar /desßro'θar; desßro'sar/ v. clear away rubbish.

descabal /deska'ßal/ a. incomplete.

descabalar /deskaßa'lar/ v. render incomplete; impair.

descabellado /deskaße'ʎaðo; deskaße'yaðo/ a. absurd, preposterous.

descabezar /deskaße'θar; deskaße'sar/ v. behead.

descaecimiento /deskaeθi'miento; deskaesi'miento/ n. m. weakness; dejection.

descafeinado /deskafei'naðo/ a. decaffeinated.

descalabrar /deskala'ßrar/ v. injure, wound (esp. the head).

descalabro /deska'laßro/ n. m. accident, misfortune.

descalzarse /deskal'θarse; deskal'sarse/ v. take off one's shoes.

descalzo /des'kalθo; des'kalso/ a. shoeless; barefoot.

descaminado /deskami'naðo/ a. wrong, misguided.

descaminar /deskami'nar/ v. mislead; lead into error.

descamisado /deskami'saðo/ a. shirtless; shabby.

descansillo /deskan'siʎo; deskan'siyo/ n. m. landing (of stairs).

descanso /des'kanso/ n. m. rest. —descansar, v.

descarado /deska'raðo/ a. saucy, fresh.

descarga /des'karga/ n. f. discharge.

descargar /deskar'gar/ v. discharge, unload, dump.

descargo /des'kargo/ n. m. unloading; acquittal.

descarnar /deskar'nar/ v. skin.

descaro /des'karo/ n. m. gall, effrontery.

descarriar /deska'rriar/ v. lead or go astray.

descarrilamiento /deskarrila-'miento/ n. m. derailment.

descarrilar /deskarri'lar/ v. derail.

descartar /deskar'tar/ v. discard.

descascarar /deskaska'rar/ v. peel; boast, brag.

descendencia /desθen'denθia; dessen'densia/ n. f. descent, origin; progeny.

descender /desθen'der; dessen'der/ v. descend.

descendiente /desθen'diente; dessen'diente/ n. m. & f. descendant.

descendimiento /desθendi'miento; dessendi'miento/ n. m. descent.

descenso /des'θenso; des'senso/ n. m. descent.

descentralización /desθentra-liθa'θion; dessentralisa'sion/ n. f. decentralization.

descifrar /desθi'frar; dessi'frar/ v. decipher, puzzle out.

descoco /des'koko/ n. m. boldness, brazenness.

descolgar /deskol'gar/ v. take down.

descollar /desko'ʎar; desko'yar/ v. stand out; excel.

descolorar /deskolo'rar/ v. discolor.

descolorido /deskolo'riðo/ a. pale, faded.

descomedido /deskome'ðiðo/ a. disproportionate; rude.

descomedirse /deskome'ðirse/ v. be rude.

descomponer /deskompo'ner/ v. decompose; break down, get out of order.

descomposición /deskomposi'θion; deskomposi'sion/ n. f. discomposure; disorder, confusion.

descompuesto /deskom'puesto/ a. impudent, rude.

descomulgar /deskomul'gar/ v. excommunicate.

descomunal /deskomu'nal/ a. extraordinary, huge.

desconcertar /deskonθer'tar; deskonser'tar/ v. disconcert, baffle.

desconcierto /deskon'θierto; deskon'sierto/ n. m. confusion, disarray.

desconectar /deskonek'tar/ v. disconnect.

desconfiado /deskon'fiaðo/ a. distrustful.

desconfianza /deskon'fianθa; deskon'fiansa/ n. f. distrust.

desconfiar /deskon'fiar/ v. distrust, mistrust; suspect.

descongelar /deskonge'lar/ v. defrost.

descongestionante /deskongestio-'nante/ n. m. decongestant.

desconocer /deskono'θer; deskono-'ser/ v. ignore, fail to recognize.

desconocido /deskono'θiðo; deskono-'siðo/ -da n. stranger.

desconocimiento /deskonoθi'miento; deskonosi'miento/ n. m. ingratitude; ignorance.

desconsejado /deskonse'haðo/ a. imprudent, ill advised, rash.

desconsolado /deskonso'laðo/ *a.* disconsolate, wretched.

desconsuelo /deskon'suelo/ *n. m.* grief.

descontar /deskon'tar/ *v.* discount, subtract.

descontentar /deskonten'tar/ *v.* dissatisfy.

descontento /deskon'tento/ *n. m.* discontent.

descontinuar /deskonti'nuar/ *v.* discontinue.

desconvenir /deskombe'nir/ *v.* disagree.

descorazonar /deskoraθo'nar; deskoraso'nar/ *v.* dishearten.

descorchar /deskor'tʃar/ *v.* uncork.

descortés /deskor'tes/ *a.* discourteous, impolite, rude.

descortesía /deskorte'sia/ *n. f.* discourtesy, rudeness.

descortezar /deskorte'θar; deskor;te'sar/ *v.* peel.

descoyuntar /deskoyun'tar/ *v.* dislocate.

descrédito /des'kreðito/ *n. m.* discredit.

describir /deskri'βir/ *v.* describe.

descripción /deskrip'θion; deskrip'sion/ *n. f.* description.

descriptivo /deskrip'tiβo/ *a.* descriptive.

descuartizar /deskuarti'θar; deskuarti'sar/ *v.* dismember, disjoint.

descubridor /deskuβri'ðor/ **-ra** *n.* discoverer.

descubrimiento /deskuβri'miento/ *n. m.* discovery.

descubrir /desku'βrir/ *v.* discover; uncover; disclose.

descubrirse /desku'βrirse/ *v.* take off one's hat.

descuento /des'kuento/ *n. m.* discount.

descuidado /deskui'ðaðo/ *a.* reckless, careless; slack.

descuido /des'kuiðo/ *n. m.* neglect. **—descuidar,** *v.*

desde /'desðe/ *prep.* since; from. **d. luego,** of course.

desdén /des'ðen/ *n. m.* disdain. **—desdeñar,** *v.*

desdeñoso /desðe'ɲoso/ *a.* contemptuous, disdainful, scornful.

desdicha /des'ðitʃa/ *n. f.* misfortune.

deseable /dese'aβle/ *a.* desirable.

desear /dese'ar/ *v.* desire, wish.

desecar /dese'kar/ *v.* dry, desiccate.

desechable /dese'tʃaβle/ *a.* disposable.

desechar /dese'tʃar/ *v.* scrap, reject.

desecho /de'setʃo/ *n. m.* remainder, residue; (*pl.*) waste.

desembalar /desemba'lar/ *v.* unpack.

desembarazado /desembara'θaðo; desembara'saðo/ *a.* free; unrestrained.

desembarazar /desembara'θar; desembara'sar/ *v.* free; extricate; unburden.

desembarcar /desembar'kar/ *v.* disembark, go ashore.

desembocar /desembo'kar/ *v.* flow into.

desembolsar /desembol'sar/ *v.* disburse; expend.

desembolso /desem'bolso/ *n. m.* disbursement.

desemejante /deseme'hante/ *a.* unlike, dissimilar.

desempacar /desempa'kar/ *v.* unpack.

desempeñar /desempe'ɲar/ *v.* carry out; redeem.

desempeño /desem'peɲo/ *n. m.* fulfillment.

desencajar /desenka'har/ *v.* disjoint; disturb.

desencantar /desenkan'tar/ *v.* disillusion.

desencanto /desen'kanto/ *n. m.* disillusion.

desencarcelar /desenkarθe'lar; desenkarse'lar/ *v.* set free; release.

desenchufar /desentʃu'far/ *v.* unplug.

desenfadado /desenfa'ðaðo/ *a.* free; unembarrassed; spacious.

desenfado /desen'faðo/ *n. m.* freedom; ease; calmness.

desenfocado /desenfo'kaðo/ *a.* out of focus.

desengaño /deseŋ'gaɲo/ *m.* disillusion. **—desengañar** *v.*

desenlace /desen'laθe; desen'lase/ *n. m.* outcome, conclusion.

desenredar /desenre'ðar/ *v.* disentangle.

desensartar /desensar'tar/ *v.* unthread (pearls).

desentenderse /desenten'derse/ *v.* overlook; avoid noticing.

desenterrar /desente'rrar/ *v.* disinter, exhume.

desenvainar /desembai'nar/ *v.* unsheath.

desenvoltura /desembol'tura/ *n. f.* confidence; impudence, boldness.

desenvolver /desembol'βer/ *v.* evolve, unfold.

deseo /de'seo/ *n. m.* wish, desire, urge.

deseoso /dese'oso/ *a.* desirous.

deserción /deser'θion; deser'sion/ *n. f.* desertion.

desertar /deser'tar/ *v.* desert.

desertor /deser'tor/ **-ra** *n.* deserter.

desesperación /desespera'θion; desespera'sion/ *n. f.* despair, desperation.

desesperado /desespe'raðo/ *a.* desperate; hopeless.

desesperar /desespe'rar/ *v.* despair.

desfachatez /desfatʃa'teθ; desfatʃa'tes/ *n. f.* cheek (gall).

desfalcar /desfal'kar/ *v.* embezzle.

desfase horario /des'fase o'rario/ *n. m.* jet lag.

desfavorable /desfaβo'raβle/ *a.* unfavorable.

desfigurar /desfigu'rar/ *v.* disfigure, mar.

desfiladero /desfila'ðero/ *n. m.* defile.

desfile /des'file/ *n. m.* parade. **—desfilar,** *v.*

desfile de modas /des'file de 'moðas/ fashion show.

desgaire /des'gaire/ *n. m.* slovenliness.

desgana /des'gana/ *n. f.* lack of appetite; unwillingness; repugnance.

desgarrar /desga'rrar/ *v.* tear, lacerate.

desgastar /desgas'tar/ *v.* wear away; waste; erode.

desgaste /des'gaste/ *n. m.* wear; erosion.

desgracia /des'graθia; des'grasia/ *n. f.* misfortune.

desgraciado /desgra'θiaðo; desgra'siaðo/ *a.* unfortunate.

desgranar /desgra'nar/ *v.* shell.

desgreñar /desgre'ɲar/ *v.* dishevel.

deshacer /desa'θer; desa'ser/ *v.* undo, take apart, destroy.

deshacerse de /desa'θerse de; desa'serse de/ *v.* get rid of, dispose of.

deshecho /des'etʃo/ *a.* undone; wasted.

deshelar /dese'lar/ *v.* thaw; melt.

desheredamiento /desereða'miento/ *n. m.* disinheriting.

desheredar /desere'ðar/ *v.* disinherit.

deshielo /des'ielo/ *n. m.* thaw, melting.

deshinchar /desin'tʃar/ *v.* reduce a swelling.

deshojarse /deso'harse/ *v.* shed (leaves).

deshonestidad /desonesti'ðað/ *n. f.* dishonesty.

deshonesto /deso'nesto/ *a.* dishonest.

deshonra /de'sonra/ *n. f.* dishonor.

deshonrar /deson'rar/ *v.* disgrace; dishonor.

deshonroso /deson'roso/ *a.* dishonorable.

desierto /de'sierto/ *n. m.* desert, wilderness.

designar /desig'nar/ *v.* appoint, name.

designio /de'signio/ *n. m.* purpose, intent.

desigual /desi'gual/ *a.* uneven, unequal.

desigualdad /desigual'dað/ *n. f.* inequality.

desilusión /desilu'sion/ *n. f.* disappointment.

desinfección /desinfek'θion; desinfek'sion/ *n. f.* disinfection.

desinfectar /desinfek'tar/ *v.* disinfect.

desintegrar /desinte'grar/ *v.* disintegrate, zap.

desinterés /desinte'res/ *n. m.* indifference.

desinteresado /desintere'saðo/ *a.* disinterested, unselfish.

desistir /desis'tir/ *v.* desist, stop.

desleal /desle'al/ *a.* disloyal.

deslealtad /desleal'tað/ *n. f.* disloyalty.

desleir /desle'ir/ *v.* dilute, dissolve.

desligar /desli'gar/ *v.* untie, loosen; free, release.

deslindar /deslin'dar/ *v.* make the boundaries of.

deslinde /des'linde/ *n. m.* demarcation.

desliz /des'liθ; des'lis/ *n. m.* slip; false step; weakness.

deslizarse /desli'θarse; desli'sarse/ *v.* slide; slip; glide; coast.

deslumbramiento /deslumbra'miento/ *n. m.* dazzling glare; confusion.

deslumbrar /deslumb'rar/ *v.* dazzle; glare.

deslustre /des'lustre/ *n. m.* tarnish. **—deslustrar,** *v.*

desmán /des'man/ *n. m.* mishap; misbehavior; excess.

desmantelar /desmante'lar/ *v.* dismantle.

desmañado /desma'ɲaðo/ *a.* awkward, clumsy.

desmaquillarse /desmaki'ʎarse; desmaki'yarse/ *v.* remove one's makeup.

desmayar /desma'yar/ *v.* depress, dishearten.

desmayo /des'mayo/ *n. m.* faint. **—desmayarse,** *v.*

desmejorar /desmeho'rar/ *v.* make worse; decline.

desmembrar /desmem'brar/ *v.* dismember.

desmemoria /desme'moria/ *n. f.* forgetfulness.

desmemoriado /desmemo'riaðo/ *a.* forgetful.

desmentir /desmen'tir/ *v.* contradict, disprove.

desmenuzable /desmenu'θaβle; desmenu'saβle/ *a.* crisp, crumbly.

desmenuzar /desmenu'θar; desmenu'sar/ *v.* crumble, break into bits.

desmesurado /desmesu'raðo/ *a.* excessive.

desmobilizar /desmoβili'θar; desmoβili'sar/ *v.* demobilize.

desmonetización /desmonetiθa'θion; desmonetisa'sion/ *n. f.* demonetization.

desmonetizar /desmoneti'θar; desmoneti'sar/ *v.* demonetize.

desmontado /desmon'taðo/ *a.* dismounted.

desmontar /desmon'tar/ *v.* dismantle.

desmontarse /desmon'tarse/ *v.* dismount.

desmoralización /desmoraliθa'θion; desmoralisa'sion/ *n. f.* demoralization.

desmoralizar /desmorali'θar; desmorali'sar/ *v.* demoralize.

desmoronar /desmoro'nar/ *v.* crumble, decay.

desmovilizar /desmoβili'θar; desmoβili'sar/ *v.* demobilize.

desnaturalización /desnaturaliθa'θion; desnaturalisa'sion/ *n. f.* denaturalization.

desnaturalizar /desnaturali'θar; desnaturali'sar/ *v.* denaturalize.

desnegamiento /desnega'miento/ *n. m.* denial, contradiction.

desnervar /desner'βar/ *v.* enervate.

desnivel /desni'βel/ *n. m.* unevenness or difference in elevation.

desnudamente /desnuða'mente/ *adv.* nakedly.

desnudar /desnu'ðar/ *v.* undress.

desnudez /desnu'ðeθ; desnu'ðes/ *n. f.* bareness, nudity.

desnudo /des'nuðo/ *a.* bare, naked.

desnutrición /desnutri'θion; desnutri'sion/ *n. f.* malnutrition.

desobedecer /desoβeðe'θer; desoβeðe'ser/ *v.* disobey.

desobediencia /desoβeðien'θia; desoβeðien'sia/ *n. f.* disobedience.

desobediente /desoβe'ðiente/ *a.* disobedient.

desobedientemente /desoβeðiente'mente/ *adv.* disobediently.

desobligar /desoβli'gar/ *v.* release from obligation; offend.

desocupado /desoku'paðo/ *a.* idle, not busy; vacant.

desocupar /desoku'par/ *v.* vacate.

desolación /desola'θion; desola'sion/ *n. f.* desolation; ruin.

desolado /deso'laðo/ *a.* desolate. **—desolar,** *v.*

desollar /deso'ʎar; deso'yar/ *v.* skin.

desorden /de'sorðen/ *n. m.* disorder.

desordenar /desorðe'nar/ *v.* disarrange.

desorganización /desorganiθa'θion; desorganisa'sion/ *n. f.* disorganization.

desorganizar /desorgani'θar; desorgani'sar/ *v.* disorganize.

despabilado /despaβi'laðo/ *a.* vigilant, watchful; lively.

despachar /despa'tʃar/ *v.* dispatch, ship, send.

despacho /despa'tʃo/ *n. m.* shipment; dispatch, promptness; office.

despacio /des'paθio; des'pasio/ *adv.* slowly.

desparpajo /despar'paho/ *n. m.* glibness; fluency of speech.

desparramar /desparra'mar/ *v.* scatter.

despavorido /despaβo'riðo/ *a.* terrified.

despecho /des'petʃo/ *n. m.* spite.

despedazar /despeða'θar; despeða'sar/ *v.* tear up.

despedida /despe'ðiða/ *n. f.* farewell; leave-taking; discharge.

despedir /despe'ðir/ *v.* dismiss, discharge; see off.

despedirse de /despe'ðirse de/ *v.* say good-bye to, take leave of.

despegar /despe'gar/ *v.* unglue; separate; *Aero.* take off.

despego /des'pego/ *n. m.* indifference; disinterest.

despejar /despe'har/ *v.* clear, clear up.

despejo /des'peho/ *n. m.* sprightliness; clarity; without obstruction.

despensa /des'pensa/ *n. f.* pantry.

despensero /despen'sero/ *n. m.* butler.

despeñar /despe'ɲar/ *v.* throw down.

desperdicio /desper'ðiθio; desper'ðisio/ *n. m.* waste. **—desperdiciar,** *v.*

despertador /desperta'ðor/ *n. m.* alarm clock.

despertar /desper'tar/ *v.* wake, wake up.

despesar /despe'sar/ *n. m.* dislike.

despicar /despi'kar/ *v.* satisfy.

despidida /despi'ðiða/ *n. f.* gutter.

despierto /des'pierto/ *a.* awake; alert, wide-awake.

despilfarrado /despilfa'rraðo/ *a.* wasteful, extravagant.

despilfarrar /despilfa'rrar/ *v.* waste, squander.

despilfarro /despil'farro/ *n. m.* waste, extravagance.

despique /des'pike/ *n. m.* revenge.

despistar /despis'tar/ *v.* mislead, put off the track.

desplazamiento /desplaθa'miento; desplasa'miento/ *n. m.* displacement.

desplegar /desple'gar/ *v.* display; unfold.

desplome /des'plome/ *n. m.* collapse. —**desplomarse,** *v.*

desplumar /desplu'mar/ *v.* defeather, pluck.

despoblar /despo'βlar/ *v.* depopulate.

despojar /despo'har/ *v.* strip; despoil, plunder.

despojo /des'poho/ *n. m.* plunder, spoils; (*pl.*) remains, debris.

desposado /despo'saðo/ *a.* newly married.

desposar /despo'sar/ *v.* marry.

desposeer /despose'er/ *v.* dispossess.

déspota /'despota/ *n. m. & f.* despot.

despótico /des'potiko/ *a.* despotic.

despotismo /despo'tismo/ *n. m.* despotism, tyranny.

despreciable /despre'θiaβle; despre-'siaβle/ *a.* contemptible.

despreciar /despre'θiar; despre'siar/ *v.* spurn, despise, scorn.

desprecio /des'preθio; des'presio/ *n. m.* scorn, contempt.

desprender /despren'der/ *v.* detach, unfasten.

desprenderse /despren'derse/ *v.* loosen, come apart. **d. de,** part with.

desprendido /despren'diðo/ *a.* disinterested.

despreocupado /despreoku'paðo/ *a.* unconcerned; unprejudiced.

desprevenido /despreβe'niðo/ *a.* unprepared, unready.

desproporción /despropor'θion; despropor'sion/ *n. f.* disproportion.

despropósito /despro'posito/ *n. m.* nonsense.

desprovisto /despro'βisto/ *a.* devoid.

después /des'pues/ *adv.* afterwards, later; then, next. **d. de, d. que,** after.

despuntar /despun'tar/ *v.* blunt; remove the point of.

desquiciar /deski'θiar; deski'siar/ *v.* unhinge; disturb, unsettle.

desquitar /deski'tar/ *v.* get revenge, retaliate.

desquite /des'kite/ *n. m.* revenge, retaliation.

desrazonable /desraθo'naβle; desraso'naβle/ *a.* unreasonable.

destacamento /destaka'mento/ *n. m.* Mil. detachment.

destacarse /desta'karse/ *v.* stand out, be prominent.

destajero /desta'hero/ **-a** *n.* **destajista,** *m. & f.* pieceworker.

destapar /desta'par/ *v.* uncover.

destello /des'teʎo; deste'yo/ *n. m.* sparkle, gleam.

destemplar /destem'plar/ *v. Mus.* untune; disturb, upset.

desteñir /deste'ɲir/ *v.* fade, discolor.

desterrado /deste'rraðo/ **-da** *n.* exile.

desterrar /deste'rrar/ *v.* banish, exile.

destetar /deste'tar/ *v.* wean.

destierro /des'tierro/ *n. m.* banishment, exile.

destilación /destila'θion; destila-'sion/ *n. f.* distillation.

destilar /desti'lar/ *v.* distill.

destilería /destile'ria/ *n. f.* distillery.

destilería de petróleo /destile'ria de pe'troleo/ oil refinery.

destinación /destina'θion; destina-'sion/ *n. f.* destination.

destinar /desti'nar/ *v.* destine, intend.

destinatario /destina'tario/ **-ria** *n.* addressee (mail); payee (money).

destino /des'tino/ *n. m.* destiny, fate; destination.

destitución /destitu'θion; destitu'sion/ *n. f.* dismissal; abandonment.

destituido /desti'tuiðo/ *a.* destitute.

destorcer /destor'θer; destor'ser/ *v.* undo, straighten out.

destornillado /destorni'ʎaðo; destorni'yaðo/ *a.* reckless, careless.

destornillador /destorni'ʎaðor; destorni'yaðor/ *n. m.* screwdriver.

destraillar /destrai'ʎar; destrai'yar/ *v.* unleash; set loose.

destral /des'tral/ *n. m.* hatchet.

destreza /des'treθa; des'tresa/ *n. f.* cleverness; dexterity, skill.

destripar /destri'par/ *v.* eviscerate, disembowel.

destrísimo /des'trisimo/ *a.* extremely dexterous.

destronamiento /destrona'miento/ *n. m.* dethronement.

destronar /destro'nar/ *v.* dethrone.

destrozador /destroθa'ðor; destrosa'ðor/ *n. m.* destroyer, wrecker.

destrozar /destro'θar; destro'sar/ *v.* destroy, wreck.

destrozo /des'troθo; des'troso/ *n. m.* destruction, ruin.

destrucción /destruk'θion; destruk-'sion/ *n. f.* destruction.

destructibilidad /destruktiβili'ðað/ *n. f.* destructibility.

destructible /destruk'tiβle/ *a.* destructible.

destructivamente /destruktiβa-'mente/ *adv.* destructively.

destructivo /destruk'tiβo/ *a.* destructive.

destruir /destru'ir/ *v.* destroy; wipe out.

desuello /desue'ʎo; desue'yo/ *n. m.* impudence.

desunión /desu'nion/ *n. f.* disunion; discord; separation.

desunir /desu'nir/ *v.* disconnect, sever.

desusadamente /desusaða'mente/ *adv.* unusually.

desusado /desu'saðo/ *a.* archaic; obsolete.

desuso /de'suso/ *n. m.* disuse.

desvalido /des'βaliðo/ *a.* helpless; destitute.

desvalijador /desβaliha'ðor/ *n. m.* highwayman.

desván /des'βan/ *n. m.* attic.

desvanecerse /desβane'θerse; desβane'serse/ *v.* vanish; faint.

desvariado /desβa'riaðo/ *a.* delirious; disorderly.

desvarío /desβa'rio/ *n. m.* raving. —**desvariar,** *v.*

desvedado /desβe'ðaðo/ *a.* free; unrestrained.

desveladamente /desβelaða'mente/ *adv.* watchfully, alertly.

desvelado /desβe'laðo/ *a.* watchful; alert.

desvelar /desβe'lar/ *v.* be watchful; keep awake.

desvelo /des'βelo/ *n. m.* vigilance; uneasiness; insomnia.

desventaja /desβen'taha/ *n. f.* disadvantage.

desventar /desβen'tar/ *v.* let air out of.

desventura /desβen'tura/ *n. f.* misfortune.

desventurado /desβentu'raðo/ *a.* unhappy; unlucky.

desvergonzado /desβergon'θaðo; desβergonsaðo/ *a.* shameless, brazen.

desvergüenza /desβer'guenθa; desβer'guensa/ *n. f.* shamelessness.

desvestir /desβes'tir/ *v.* undress.

desviación /desβia'θion; desβia'sion/ *n. f.* deviation.

desviado /des'βiaðo/ *a.* deviant; remote.

desviar /des'βiar/ *v.* divert; deviate, detour.

desvío /des'βio/ *n. m.* detour; side track; indifference.

desvirtuar /desβir'tuar/ *v.* decrease the value of.

deszumar /desθu'mar; dessu'mar/ *v.* remove the juice from.

detalle /de'taʎe; de'taye/ *n. m.* detail. —**detallar,** *v.*

detective /de'tektiβe/ *n. m. & f.* detective.

detención /deten'θion; deten'sion/ *n. f.* detention, arrest.

detenedor /detene'ðor/ **-ra** *n.* stopper; catch.

detener /dete'ner/ *v.* detain, stop; arrest.

detenidamente /deteniða'mente/ *adv.* carefully, slowly.

detenido /dete'niðo/ *adv.* stingy; thorough.

detergente /deter'hente/ *a.* detergent.

deterioración /deteriora'θion; deteriora'sion/ *n. f.* deterioration.

deteriorar /deterio'rar/ *v.* deteriorate.

determinable /determi'naβle/ *a.* determinable.

determinación /determina'θion; determina'sion/ *n. f.* determination.

determinar /determi'nar/ *v.* determine, settle, decide.

determinismo /determi'nismo/ *n. m.* determinism.

determinista /determi'nista/ *n. & a.* determinist.

detestable /detes'taβle/ *a.* detestable, hateful.

detestablemente /detestaβle-'mente/ *adv.* detestably, hatefully, abhorrently.

detestación /detesta'θion; detesta-'sion/ *n. f.* detestation, hatefulness.

detestar /detes'tar/ *v.* detest.

detonación /detona'θion; detona-'sion/ *n. f.* detonation.

detonar /deto'nar/ *v.* detonate, explode.

detracción /detrak'θion; detrak'sion/ *n. f.* detraction, defamation.

detractar /detrak'tar/ *v.* detract, defame, vilify.

detraer /detra'er/ *v.* detract.

detrás /de'tras/ *adv.* behind; in back.

detrimento /detri'mento/ *n. m.* detriment, damage.

deuda /'deuða/ *n. f.* debt.

deudo /'deuðo/ **-da** *n.* relative, kin.

deudor /deu'ðor/ **-ra** *n.* debtor.

Deuteronomio /deutero'nomio/ *n. m.* Deuteronomy.

devalar /deβa'lar/ *v.* drift off course.

devanar /deβa'nar/ *v.* to wind, as on a spool.

devanear /deβane'ar/ *v.* talk deliriously, rave.

devaneo /deβa'neo/ *n. m.* frivolity; idle pursuit; delirium.

devastación /deβasta'θion; deβasta-'sion/ *n. f.* devastation, ruin, havoc.

devastador /deβasta'ðor/ *a.* devastating.

devastar /deβas'tar/ *v.* devastate.

devenir /deβe'nir/ *v.* happen, occur; become.

devoción /deβo'θion; deβo'sion/ *n. f.* devotion.

devocionario /deβoθio'nario; deβosio'nario/ *n. m.* prayer book.

devocionero /deβoθio'nero; deβosio'nero/ *a.* devotional.

devolver /deβol'βer/ *v.* return, give back.

devorar /deβo'rar/ *v.* devour.

devotamente /deβota'mente/ *adv.* devotedly, devoutly, piously.

devoto /de'βoto/ *a.* devout; devoted.

deyección /deiek'θion; deiek'sion/ *n. f.* depression, dejection.

día /'dia/ *n. m.* day. **buenos días,** good morning.

diabetes /dia'βetes/ *n. f.* diabetes.

diabético /dia'βetiko/ *a.* diabetic.

diablear /diaβle'ar/ *v.* play pranks.

diablo /'diaβlo/ *n. m.* devil.

diablura /dia'βlura/ *n. f.* mischief.

diabólicamente /diaβolika'mente/ *adv.* diabolically.

diabólico /dia'βoliko/ *a.* diabolic, devilish.

diaconato /diako'nato/ *n. m.* deaconship.

diaconía /diako'nia/ *n. f.* deaconry.

diácono /'diakono/ *n. m.* deacon.

diacrítico /dia'kritiko/ *a.* diacritic.

diadema /dia'ðema/ *n. f.* diadem; crown.

diáfano /'diafano/ *a.* transparent.

diafragma /dia'fragma/ *n. m.* diaphragm.

diagnosticar /diagnosti'kar/ *v.* diagnose.

diagonal /diago'nal/ *n. f.* diagonal.

diagonalmente /diagonal'mente/ *adv.* diagonally.

diagrama /dia'grama/ *n. m.* diagram.

dialectal /dialek'tal/ *a.* dialectal.

dialéctico /dia'lektiko/ *a.* dialectic.

dialecto /dia'lekto/ *n. m.* dialect.

diálogo /'dialogo/ *n. m.* dialogue.

diamante /dia'mante/ *n. m.* diamond.

diamantista /diaman'tista/ *n. m. & f.* diamond cutter; jeweler.

diametral /diame'tral/ *a.* diametric.

diametralmente /diametral'mente/ *adv.* diametrically.

diámetro /'diametro/ *n. m.* diameter.

diana /'diana/ *n. f.* reveille; dartboard.

diapasón /diapa'son/ *n. m.* standard pitch; tuning fork.

diaplejía /diaple'hia/ *n. f.* paralysis.

diariamente /diaria'mente/ *adv.* daily.

diario /'diario/ *a. & m.* daily; daily paper; diary; journal.

diarrea /dia'rrea/ *n. f.* diarrhea.

diatriba /dia'triβa/ *n. f.* diatribe, harangue.

dibujo /di'βuho/ *n. m.* drawing, sketch. —**dibujar,** *v.*

dicción /dik'θion; dik'sion/ *n. f.* diction.

diccionario /dikθio'nario; diksio'nario/ *n. m.* dictionary.

diccionarista /dikθiona'rista; diksiona'rista/ *n. m. & f.* lexicographer.

dicha /'ditʃa/ *n. f.* happiness.

dicho /'ditʃo/ *n. m.* saying.

dichoso /di'tʃoso/ *a.* happy; fortunate.

diciembre /di'θiembre; di'siembre/ *n. m.* December.

dicotomía /dikoto'mia/ *n. f.* dichotomy.

dictado /dik'taðo/ *n. m.* dictation.

dictador /dikta'ðor/ **-ra** *n.* dictator.

dictadura /dikta'ðura/ *n. f.* dictatorship.

dictamen /dik'tamen/ *n. m.* dictate.

dictar /dik'tar/ *v.* dictate; direct.

dictatorial /diktato'rial/ **dictatorio** *a.* dictatorial.

didáctico /di'ðaktiko/ *a.* didactic.

diecinueve /dieθi'nueβe; diesi'nueβe/ *a. & pron.* nineteen.

dieciocho /die'θiotʃo; die'siotʃo/ *a. & pron.* eighteen.

dieciseis /dieθi'seis; diesi'seis/ *a. & pron.* sixteen.

diecisiete /dieθi'siete; diesi'siete/ *a. & pron.* seventeen.

diente /'diente/ *n. m.* tooth.

diestramente /diestra'mente/ *adv.* skillfully, ably; ingeniously.

diestro /'diestro/ *a.* dexterous, skillful; clever.

dieta /'dieta/ *n. f.* diet; allowance.

dietética /die'tetika/ *n. f.* dietetics.

dietético /die'tetiko/ *a.* **1.** dietetic; dietary. —*n.* **2. -ca.** dietician.

diez /dieθ; dies/ *a. & pron.* ten.

diezmal /dieθ'mal; dies'mal/ *a.* decimal.

diezmar /dieθ'mar; dies'mar/ *v.* decimate.

difamación /difama'θion; difama'sion/ *n. f.* defamation, smear.

difamar /difa'mar/ *v.* defame, smear, libel.

difamatorio /difama'torio/ *a.* defamatory.

diferencia /dife'renθia; dife'rensia/ *n. f.* difference.

diferencial /diferen'θial; diferen'sial/ *a. & f.* differential.

diferenciar /diferen'θiar; diferen'siar/ *v.* differentiate, distinguish.

diferente /dife'rente/ *a.* different.

diferentemente /diferente'mente/ *adv.* differently.

diferir /dife'rir/ *v.* differ; defer, put off.

difícil /di'fiθil; di'fisil/ *a.* difficult, hard.

difícilmente /difiθil'mente; difisil'mente/ *adv.* with difficulty or hardship.

dificultad /difikul'taδ/ *n. f.* difficulty.

dificultar /difikul'tar/ *v.* make difficult.

dificultoso /difikul'toso/ *a.* difficult, hard.

difidencia /difi'δenθia; difi'δensia/ *n. f.* diffidence.

difidente /difi'δente/ *a.* diffident.

difteria /dif'teria/ *n. f.* diphtheria.

difundir /difun'dir/ *v.* diffuse, spread.

difunto /di'funto/ *a.* **1.** deceased, dead, late. —*n.* **2. -ta,** deceased person.

difusamente /difusa'mente/ *adv.* diffusely.

difusión /difu'sion/ *n. f.* diffusion, spread.

digerible /dihe'riβle/ *a.* digestible.

digerir /dihe'rir/ *v.* digest.

digestible /dihes'tiβle/ *a.* digestible.

digestión /dihes'tion/ *n. f.* digestion.

digestivo /dihes'tiβo/ *a.* digestive.

digesto /di'hesto/ *n. m.* digest or code of laws.

digitado /dihi'taδo/ *a.* digitate.

digital /dihi'tal/ *a.* **1.** digital. —*n.* **2.** *f.* foxglove, digitalis.

dignación /digna'θion; digna'sion/ *f.* condescension; deigning.

dignamente /digna'mente/ *adv.* with dignity.

dignarse /dig'narse/ *v.* condescend, deign.

dignatario /digna'tario/ **-ra** *n.* dignitary.

dignidad /digni'δaδ/ *n. f.* dignity.

dignificar /dignifi'kar/ *v.* dignify.

digno /'digno/ *a.* worthy; dignified.

digresión /digre'sion/ *n. f.* digression.

digresivo /digre'siβo/ *a.* digressive.

dij, dije /dih; 'dihe/ *n. m.* trinket, piece of jewelry.

dilación /dila'θion; dila'sion/ *n. f.* delay.

dilapidación /dilapiδa'θion; dilapi-'δasion/ *n. f.* dilapidation.

dilapidado /dilapi'δaδo/ *a.* dilapidated.

dilatación /dilata'θion; dilata'sion/ *n. f.* dilatation, enlargement.

dilatar /dila'tar/ *v.* dilate; delay; expand.

dilatoria /dila'toria/ *n. f.* delay.

dilatorio /dila'torio/ *a.* dilatory.

dilecto /di'lekto/ *a.* loved.

dilema /di'lema/ *n. m.* dilemma.

diligencia /dili'henθia; dili'hensia/ *n. f.* diligence, industriousness.

diligente /dili'hente/ *a.* diligent, industrious.

diligentemente /dilihente'mente/ *adv.* diligently.

dilogía /dilo'hia/ *n. f.* ambiguous meaning.

dilución /dilu'θion; dilu'sion/ *n. f.* dilution.

diluir /di'luir/ *v.* dilute.

diluvial /dilu'βial/ *a.* diluvial.

diluvio /di'luβio/ *n. m.* flood, deluge.

dimensión /dimen'sion/ *n. f.* dimension; measurement.

diminución /diminu'θion; diminu-'sion/ *n. f.* diminution.

diminuto /dimi'nuto/ **diminutivo** *a.* diminutive, little.

dimisión /dimi'sion/ *n. f.* resignation.

dimitir /dimi'tir/ *v.* resign.

Dinamarca /dina'marka/ *n. f.* Denmark.

dinamarqués /dinamar'kes/ **-esa** *a. & n.* Danish, Dane.

dinámico /di'namiko/ *a.* dynamic.

dinamita /dina'mita/ *n. f.* dynamite.

dinamitero /dinami'tero/ **-ra** *n.* dynamiter.

dínamo /'dinamo/ *n. m.* dynamo.

dinasta /di'nasta/ *n. m.* dynast, king, monarch.

dinastía /dinas'tia/ *n. f.* dynasty.

dinástico /di'nastiko/ *a.* dynastic.

dinero /di'nero/ *n. m.* money, currency.

dinosauro /dino'sauro/ *n. m.* dinosaur.

diócesis /'dioθesis; 'diosesis/ *n. f.* diocese.

Dios /dios/ *n. m.* God.

dios -sa *n.* god, goddess.

diploma /di'ploma/ *n. m.* diploma.

diplomacia /diplo'maθia; diplo'masia/ *n. f.* diplomacy.

diplomado /diplo'maδo/ **-da** *n.* graduate.

diplomarse /diplo'marse/ *v.* graduate (from a school).

diplomática /diplo'matika/ *n. f.* diplomacy.

diplomático /diplo'matiko/ **-ca** *a. & n.* diplomat; diplomatic.

dipsomanía /dipsoma'nia/ *n. f.* dipsomania.

diptongo /dip'tongo/ *n. m.* diphthong.

diputación /diputa'θion; diputa'sion/ *n. f.* deputation, delegation.

diputado /dipu'taδo/ **-da** *n.* deputy; delegate.

diputar /dipu'tar/ *v.* depute, delegate; empower.

dique /'dike/ *n. m.* dike; dam.

dirección /direk'θion; direk'sion/ *n. f.* direction; address; guidance; *Com.* management.

directamente /direkta'mente/ *adv.* directly.

directo /di'rekto/ *a.* direct.

director /direk'tor/ **-ra** *n.* director; manager.

directorio /direk'torio/ *n. m.* directory.

dirigente /diri'hente/ *a.* directing, controlling, managing.

dirigible /diri'hiβle/ *n. m.* dirigible.

dirigir /diri'hir/ *v.* direct; lead; manage.

dirigirse a /diri'hirse a/ *v.* address; approach, turn to; head for.

dirruir /di'rruir/ *v.* destroy, devastate.

disanto /di'santo/ *n. m.* holy day.

discantar /diskan'tar/ *v.* sing (esp. in counterpoint); discuss.

disceptación /disθepta'θion; dissepta'sion/ *n. f.* argument, quarrel.

disceptar /disθep'tar; dissep'tar/ *v.* argue, quarrel.

discernimiento /disθerni'miento; disserni'miento/ *n. m.* discernment.

discernir /disθer'nir; disser'nir/ *v.* discern.

disciplina /disθi'plina; dissi'plina/ *n. f.* discipline.

disciplinable /disθipli'naβle; dissipli-'naβle/ *a.* disciplinable.

disciplinar /disθipli'nar; dissipli'nar/ *v.* discipline, train, teach.

discípulo /dis'θipulo; dis'sipulo/ **-la** *n.* disciple, follower; pupil.

disco /'disko/ *n. m.* disk; (phonograph) record.

disco compacto /'disko kom'pakto/ compact disk.

disco duro /'disko 'duro/ hard disk.

disco flexible /'disko flek'siβle/ floppy disk.

discontinuación /diskontinua'θion;

**diskontinua'sion/ *n. f.* discontinuation.

discontinuar /diskonti'nuar/ *v.* discontinue, break off, cease.

discordancia /diskor'δanθia; diskor-'δansia/ *n. f.* discordance.

discordar /diskor'δar/ *v.* disagree, conflict.

discordia /dis'korδia/ *n. f.* discord.

discoteca /disko'teka/ *n. f.* disco, discotheque.

discreción /diskre'θion; diskre'sion/ *n. f.* discretion.

discrecional /diskreθio'nal; diskresio'nal/ *a.* optional.

discrecionalmente /diskreθio-nal'mente; diskresional'mente/ *adv.* optionally.

discrepancia /diskre'panθia; diskre-'pansia/ *n. f.* discrepancy.

discretamente /diskreta'mente/ *adv.* discreetly.

discreto /dis'kreto/ *a.* discreet.

discrimen /dis'krimen/ *n. m.* risk, hazard.

discriminación /diskrimina'θion; diskrimina'sion/ *n. f.* discrimination.

discriminar /diskrimi'nar/ *v.* discriminate.

disculpa /dis'kulpa/ *n. f.* excuse; apology.

disculpar /diskul'par/ *v.* excuse; exonerate.

disculparse /diskul'parse/ *v.* apologize.

discurrir /disku'rrir/ *v.* roam; flow; think; plan.

discursante /diskur'sante/ *n.* lecturer, speaker.

discursivo /diskur'siβo/ *a.* discursive.

discurso /dis'kurso/ *n. m.* speech, talk.

discusión /disku'sion/ *n. f.* discussion.

discutible /disku'tiβle/ *a.* debatable.

discutir /disku'tir/ *v.* discuss; debate; contest.

disecación /diseka'θion; diseka'sion/ *n. f.* dissection.

disecar /dise'kar/ *v.* dissect.

disección /disek'θion; disek'sion/ *n. f.* dissection.

diseminación /disemina'θion; disemina'sion/ *n. f.* dissemination.

diseminar /disemi'nar/ *v.* disseminate, spread.

disensión /disen'sion/ *n. f.* dissension; dissent.

disenso /di'senso/ *n. m.* dissent.

disentería /disente'ria/ *n. f.* dysentery.

disentir /disen'tir/ *v.* disagree, dissent.

diseñador /diseɲa'δor/ **-ra** *n.* designer.

diseño /di'seɲo/ *n. m.* design. —**diseñar**, *v.*

disertación /diserta'θion; diserta-'sion/ *n. f.* dissertation.

disforme /dis'forme/ *a.* deformed, monstrous, ugly.

disformidad /disformi'δaδ/ *n. f.* deformity.

disfraz /dis'fraθ; dis'fras/ *n. m.* disguise. —**disfrazar**, *v.*

disfrutar /disfru'tar/ *v.* enjoy.

disfrute /dis'frute/ *n. m.* enjoyment.

disgustar /disgus'tar/ *v.* displease; disappoint.

disgusto /dis'gusto/ *n. m.* displeasure; disappointment.

disidencia /disi'δenθia; disi'δensia/ *n. f.* dissidence.

disidente /disi'δente/ *a. & n.* dissident.

disímil /di'simil/ *a.* unlike.

disimilitud /disimili'tuδ/ *n. f.* dissimilarity.

disimulación /disimula'θion; disimula'sion/ *n. f.* dissimulation.

disimulado /disimu'laδo/ *a.* dissembling, feigning; sly.

disimular /disimu'lar/ *v.* hide; dissemble.

disimulo /di'simulo/ *n. m.* pretense.

disipación /disipa'θion; disipa'sion/ *n. f.* dissipation.

disipado /disi'paδo/ *a.* dissipated; wasted; scattered.

disipar /disi'par/ *v.* waste; scatter.

dislexia /dis'leksia/ *n. f.* dyslexia.

disléxico /dis'leksiko/ *a.* dyslexic.

dislocación /disloka'θion; disloka-'sion/ *n. f.* dislocation.

dislocar /dislo'kar/ *v.* dislocate; displace.

disminuir /dismi'nuir/ *v.* diminish, lessen, reduce.

disociación /disoθia'θion; disosia-'sion/ *n. f.* dissociation.

disociar /diso'θiar; diso'siar/ *v.* dissociate.

disolubilidad /disoluβili'δaδ/ *n. f.* dissolubility.

disoluble /diso'luβle/ *a.* dissoluble.

disolución /disolu'θion; disolu'sion/ *n. f.* dissolution.

disolutamente /disoluta'mente/ *adv.* dissolutely.

disoluto /diso'luto/ *a.* dissolute.

disolver /disol'βer/ *v.* dissolve.

disonancia /diso'nanθia; diso'nansia/ *n. f.* dissonance; discord.

disonante /diso'nante/ *a.* dissonant; discordant.

disonar /diso'nar/ *v.* be discordant; clash in sound.

dísono /di'sono/ *a.* dissonant.

dispar /dis'par/ *a.* unlike.

disparadamente /disparaδa'mente/ *adv.* hastily, hurriedly.

disparar /dispa'rar/ *v.* shoot, fire (a weapon).

disparatado /dispara'taδo/ *a.* nonsensical.

disparatar /dispara'tar/ *v.* talk nonsense.

disparate /dispa'rate/ *n. m.* nonsense, tall tale.

disparejo /dispa'reho/ *a.* uneven, unequal.

disparidad /dispari'δaδ/ *n. f.* disparity.

disparo /dis'paro/ *n. m.* shot.

dispendio /dis'pendio/ *n. m.* extravagance.

dispendioso /dispen'dioso/ *a.* expensive; extravagant.

dispensa /dis'pensa/ **dispensación** *n. f.* dispensation.

dispensable /dispen'saβle/ *a.* dispensable; excusable.

dispensar /dispen'sar/ *v.* dispense, excuse; grant.

dispensario /dispen'sario/ *n. m.* dispensary.

dispepsia /dis'pepsia/ *n. f.* dyspepsia.

dispéptico /dis'peptiko/ *a.* dyspeptic.

dispersar /disper'sar/ *v.* scatter; dispel; disband.

dispersión /disper'sion/ *n. f.* dispersion, dispersal.

disperso /dis'perso/ *a.* dispersed.

displicente /displi'θente; displi'sente/ *a.* unpleasant.

disponer /dispo'ner/ *v.* dispose. **d. de,** have at one's disposal.

disponible /dispo'niβle/ *a.* available.

disposición /disposi'θion; disposi-'sion/ *n. f.* disposition; disposal.

dispuesto /dis'puesto/ *a.* disposed, inclined; attractive.

disputa /dis'puta/ *n. f.* dispute, argument.

disputable /dispu'taβle/ *a.* disputable.

disputador /disputa'δor/ **-ra** *n.* disputant.

disputar /dispu'tar/ *v.* argue; dispute.

disquete /dis'kete/ *n. m.* diskette.

disquetera /diske'tera/ *n. f.* disk drive.

disquisición /diskisi'θion; diskisi-'sion/ *n. f.* disquisition.

distancia /dis'tanθia; dis'tansia/ *n. f.* distance.

distante /dis'tante/ *a.* distant.

distantemente /distante'mente/ adv. distantly.

distar /dis'tar/ v. be distant, be far.

distender /disten'der/ v. distend, swell, enlarge.

distensión /disten'sion/ n. f. distension, swelling.

dístico /'distiko/ n. m. couplet.

distinción /distin'θion; distin'sion/ n. f. distinction, difference.

distingo /dis'tiŋgo/ n. m. restriction.

distinguible /distiŋ'ɡwiβle/ a. distinguishable.

distinguido /distiŋ'ɡwiðo/ a. distinguished, prominent.

distinguir /distiŋ'ɡwir/ v. distinguish; make out, spot.

distintamente /distinta'mente/ adv. distinctly, clearly; differently.

distintivo /distin'tiβo/ a. distinctive.

distintivo del país /distin'tiβo del pa'is/ country code.

distinto /dis'tinto/ a. distinct; different.

distracción /distrak'θion; distrak'sion/ n. f. distraction, pastime; absent-mindedness.

distraer /distra'er/ v. distract.

distraídamente /distraiða'mente/ adv. absent-mindedly, distractedly.

distraído /distra'iðo/ a. absent-minded; distracted.

distribución /distriβu'θion; distriβu'sion/ n. f. distribution.

distribuidor /distriβui'ðor/ -ra n. distributor.

distribuir /distri'βuir/ v. distribute.

distributivo /distriβu'tiβo/ a. distributive.

distributor /distriβu'tor/ n. m. distributor.

distrito /dis'trito/ n. m. district.

disturbar /distur'βar/ v. disturb, trouble.

disturbio /dis'turβio/ n. m. disturbance, outbreak; turmoil.

disuadir /disua'ðir/ v. dissuade.

disuasión /disua'sion/ n. f. dissuasion; deterrence.

disuasivo /disua'siβo/ a. dissuasive.

disyunción /disyun'θion; disyun'sion/ n. f. disjunction.

ditirambo /diti'rambo/ n. m. dithyramb.

diurno /'diurno/ a. diurnal.

diva /'diβa/ n. f. diva, prima donna.

divagación /diβaga'θion; diβaga'sion/ n. f. digression.

divagar /diβa'ɡar/ v. digress, ramble.

diván /di'βan/ n. m. couch.

divergencia /diβer'henθia; diβer'hensia/ n. f. divergence.

divergente /diβer'hente/ a. divergent, differing.

divergir /diβer'hir/ v. diverge.

diversamente /diβersa'mente/ adv. diversely.

diversidad /diβersi'ðað/ n. f. diversity.

diversificar /diβersifi'kar/ v. diversify, vary.

diversión /diβer'sion/ n. f. diversion, pastime.

diverso /di'βerso/ a. diverse, different; (pl.) various, several.

divertido /diβer'tiðo/ a. humorous, amusing.

divertimiento /diβerti'miento/ n. m. diversion; amusement.

divertir /diβer'tir/ v. entertain, amuse.

divertirse /diβer'tirse/ v. enjoy oneself, have a good time.

dividendo /diβi'ðendo/ n. m. dividend.

dividadero /diβiði'ðero/ a. to be divided.

dividido /diβi'ðiðo/ a. divided.

dividir /diβi'ðir/ v. divide; separate.

divieso /di'βieso/ n. m. Med. boil.

divinamente /diβina'mente/ adv. divinely.

divinidad /diβini'ðað/ n. f. divinity.

divinizar /diβini'θar; diβini'sar/ v. deify.

divino /di'βino/ a. divine; heavenly.

divisa /di'βisa/ n. f. badge, emblem.

divisar /diβi'sar/ v. sight, make out.

divisibilidad /diβisiβili'ðað/ n. f. divisibility.

divisible /diβi'siβle/ a. divisible.

división /diβi'sion/ n. f. division.

divisivo /diβi'siβo/ a. divisive.

divo /'diβo/ n. m. movie star.

divorcio /di'βorθio; di'βorsio/ n. m. divorce. —divorciar, v.

divulgable /diβul'ɡaβle/ a. divulgable.

divulgación /diβulɡa'θion; diβulɡa'sion/ n. f. divulgation.

divulgar /diβul'ɡar/ v. divulge, reveal.

dobladamente /doβlaða'mente/ adv. doubly.

dobladillo /doβla'ðiʎo; doβla'ðiyo/ n. m. hem of a skirt or dress.

dobladura /doβla'ðura/ n. f. fold; bend.

doblar /do'βlar/ v. fold; bend.

doble /'doβle/ a. double.

doblegable /doβle'ɡaβle/ a. flexible, foldable.

doblegar /doβle'ɡar/ v. fold, bend; yield.

doblez /do'βleθ; do'βles/ n. m. fold; duplicity.

doblón /do'βlon/ n. m. doubloon.

doce /'doθe; 'dose/ a. & pron. twelve.

docena /do'θena; do'sena/ n. f. dozen.

docente /do'θente; do'sente/ a. educational.

dócil /'doθil; 'dosil/ a. docile.

docilidad /doθili'ðað; dosili'ðað/ n. f. docility, tractableness.

dócilmente /doθil'mente; dosil'mente/ adv. docilely, meekly.

doctamente /dokta'mente/ adv. learnedly, profoundly.

docto /'dokto/ a. learned, expert.

doctor /dok'tor/ -ra n. doctor.

doctorado /dokto'raðo/ n. m. doctorate.

doctoral /dokto'ral/ a. doctoral.

doctrina /dok'trina/ n. f. doctrine.

doctrinador /doktrina'ðor/ -ra n. teacher.

doctrinal /doktri'nal/ n. m. doctrinal.

doctrinar /doktri'nar/ v. teach.

documentación /dokumenta'θion; dokumenta'sion/ n. f. documentation.

documental /dokumen'tal/ a. documentary.

documento /doku'mento/ n. m. document.

dogal /do'ɡal/ n. m. noose.

dogma /'doɡma/ n. m. dogma.

dogmáticamente /doɡmatika'mente/ adv. dogmatically.

dogmático /doɡ'matiko/ n. m. dogmatic.

dogmatismo /doɡma'tismo/ n. m. dogmatism.

dogmatista /doɡma'tista/ n. m. & f. dogmatist.

dogo /'doɡo/ n. m. bulldog.

dolar /'dolar/ v. cut, chop, hew.

dólar n. m. dollar.

dolencia /do'lenθia; do'lensia/ n. f. pain; disease.

doler /do'ler/ v. ache, hurt, be sore.

doliente /do'liente/ a. ill; aching.

dolor /do'lor/ n. m. pain; grief, sorrow, woe.

dolor de cabeza /do'lor de ka'βeθa; do'lor de ka'βesa/ headache.

dolor de espalda /do'lor de es'palda/ backache.

dolor de estómago /do'lor de es'tomaɡo/ stomachache.

dolorido /dolo'riðo/ a. painful, sorrowful.

dolorosamente /dolorosa'mente/ adv. painfully, sorrowfully.

doloroso /dolo'roso/ a. painful, sorrowful.

dolosamente /dolosa'mente/ adv. deceitfully.

doloso /do'loso/ a. deceitful.

domable /do'maβle/ a. that can be tamed or managed.

domar /do'mar/ v. tame; subdue.

dombo /'dombo/ n. m. dome.

domesticable /domesti'kaβle/ a. that can be domesticated.

domesticación /domestika'θion; domestika'sion/ n. f. domestication.

domésticamente /domestika'mente/ adv. domestically.

domesticar /domesti'kar/ v. tame, domesticate.

domesticidad /domestiθi'ðað; domestisi'ðað/ n. f. domesticity.

doméstico /do'mestiko/ a. domestic.

domicilio /domi'θilio; domi'silio/ n. m. dwelling, home, residence, domicile.

dominación /domina'θion; domina'sion/ n. f. domination.

dominador /domina'ðor/ a. dominating.

dominante /domi'nante/ a. dominant.

dominar /domi'nar/ v. rule, dominate; master.

dómine /'domine/ n. m. teacher.

domingo /do'miŋgo/ n. m. Sunday.

dominio /do'minio/ n. m. domain; rule; power.

dominó /domi'no/ n. m. domino.

domo /'domo/ n. m. dome.

Don /don/ title used before a man's first name.

don n. m. gift.

donación /dona'θion; dona'sion/ n. f. donation.

donador /dona'ðor/ -ra n. giver, donor.

donaire /do'naire/ n. m. grace.

donairosamente /donairosa'mente/ adv. gracefully.

donairoso /donai'roso/ a. graceful.

donante /do'nante/ n. giver, donor.

donar /do'nar/ v. donate.

donativo /dona'tiβo/ n. m. donation, contribution; gift.

doncella /don'θeʎa; don'seya/ n. f. lass; maid.

donde /'donde/ **dónde** conj. & adv. where.

dondequiera /donde'kiera/ adv. wherever, anywhere.

donosamente /donosa'mente/ adv. gracefully; wittily.

donoso /do'noso/ a. graceful; witty.

donosura /dono'sura/ n. f. gracefulness; wittiness.

Doña /'doɲa/ title used before a lady's first name.

dopar /do'par/ v. drug, dope.

dorado /do'raðo/ a. gilded.

dorador /dora'ðor/ -ra n. gilder.

dorar /do'rar/ v. gild.

dórico /'doriko/ a. Doric.

dormidero /dormi'ðero/ a. sleep-inducing; soporific.

dormido /dor'miðo/ a. asleep.

dormir /dor'mir/ v. sleep.

dormirse /dor'mirse/ v. fall asleep, go to sleep.

dormitar /dormi'tar/ v. doze.

dormitorio /dormi'torio/ n. m. dormitory; bedroom.

dorsal /dor'sal/ a. dorsal.

dorso /'dorso/ n. m. spine.

dos /dos/ a. & pron. two. **los d.,** both.

dosañal /dosa'nal/ a. biennial.

doscientos /dos'θientos; dos'sientos/ a. & pron. two hundred.

dosel /do'sel/ n. m. canopy; platform; dais.

dosificación /dosifika'θion; dosifika'sion/ n. f. dosage.

dosis /'dosis/ n. f. dose.

dotación /dota'θion; dota'sion/ n. f. endowment; Naut. crew.

dotador /dota'ðor/ -ra n. donor.

dotar /do'tar/ v. endow; give a dowry to.

dote /'dote/ n. f. dowry; (pl.) talents.

dragaminas /draɡa'minas/ n. m. mine sweeper.

dragar /dra'ɡar/ v. dredge; sweep.

dragón /dra'ɡon/ n. m. dragon; dragoon.

dragonear /draɡone'ar/ v. pretend to be.

drama /'drama/ n. m. drama; play.

dramática /dra'matika/ n. f. drama, dramatic art.

dramáticamente /dramatika'mente/ adv. dramatically.

dramático /dra'matiko/ a. dramatic.

dramatizar /dramati'θar; dramati'sar/ v. dramatize.

dramaturgo /drama'turɡo/ -ga n. playwright, dramatist.

drástico /'drastiko/ a. drastic.

drenaje /dre'nahe/ n. m. drainage.

dríada /'driaða/ n. f. dryad.

dril /dril/ n. m. denim.

driza /'driθa; 'drisa/ n. f. halyard.

droga /'droɡa/ n. f. drug.

drogadicto /droɡa'ðikto/ -ta n. drug addict.

droguería /droɡe'ria/ n. f. drugstore.

droguero /dro'ɡero/ n. m. druggist.

dromedario /drome'ðario/ n. m. dromedary.

druida /'druiða/ n. m. & f. Druid.

dualidad /duali'ðað/ n. f. duality.

dubitable /duβi'taβle/ a. doubtful.

dubitación /duβita'θion; duβita'sion/ n. f. doubt.

ducado /du'kaðo/ n. m. duchy.

ducal /du'kal/ a. ducal.

ducha /'dutʃa/ n. f. shower (bath).

ducharse /du'tʃarse/ v. take a shower.

dúctil /'duktil/ a. ductile.

ductilidad /duktili'ðað/ n. f. ductility.

duda /'duða/ n. f. doubt.

dudable /du'ðaβle/ a. doubtful.

dudar /du'ðar/ v. doubt; hesitate; question.

dudosamente /duðosa'mente/ adv. doubtfully.

dudoso /du'ðoso/ a. dubious; doubtful.

duela /'duela/ n. f. stave.

duelista /due'lista/ n. m. & f. duelist.

duelo /'duelo/ n. m. duel; grief; mourning.

duende /'duende/ n. m. elf, hobgoblin.

dueño /'dueɲo/ -ña n. owner; landlord -lady; master, mistress.

dulce /'dulθe; dulse/ a. **1.** sweet. **agua d.,** fresh water. —n. **2.** m. piece of candy; (pl.) candy.

dulcedumbre /dulθe'ðumbre; dulse'ðumbre/ n. f. sweetness.

dulcemente /dulθe'mente; dulse'mente/ adv. sweetly.

dulcería /dulθe'ria; dulse'ria/ n. f. confectionery; candy shop.

dulcificar /dulθifi'kar; dulsifi'kar/ v. sweeten.

dulzura /dul'θura; dul'sura/ n. f. sweetness; mildness.

duna /'duna/ n. f. dune.

dúo /'duo/ n. m. duo, duet.

duodenal /duoðe'nal/ a. duodenal.

duplicación /duplika'θion; duplika'sion/ n. f. duplication; doubling.

duplicadamente /duplikaða'mente/ adv. doubly.

duplicado /dupli'kaðo/ a. & m. duplicate.

duplicar /dupli'kar/ v. double, duplicate, repeat.

duplicidad /dupliθi'ðað; duplisi'ðað/ n. f. duplicity.

duplo /'duplo/ a. double.

duque /'duke/ n. m. duke.

duquesa /du'kesa/ n. f. duchess.

durabilidad /duraβili'ðað/ n. f. durability.

durable /du'raβle/ a. durable.

duración /dura'θion; dura'sion/ n. f. duration.

duradero /dura'ðero/ *a.* lasting, durable.

duramente /dura'mente/ *adv.* harshly, roughly.

durante /du'rante/ *prep.* during.

durar /du'rar/ *v.* last.

durazno /du'raθno; du'rasno/ *n. m.* peach; peach tree.

dureza /du'reθa; du'resa/ *n. f.* hardness.

durmiente /dur'miente/ *a.* sleeping.

duro /'duro/ *a.* hard; stiff; stern; stale.

dux /duks/ *n. m.* doge.

E

e /e/ *conj.* and.

ebanista /eβa'nista/ *n. m. & f.* cabinetmaker.

ebanizar /eβani'θar; eβani'sar/ *v.* give an ebony finish to.

ébano /'eβano/ *n. m.* ebony.

ebonita /eβo'nita/ *n. f.* ebonite.

ebrio /'eβrio/ *a.* drunken, inebriated.

ebullición /eβuʎi'θion; eβuyi'sion/ *n. f.* boiling.

echada /e'tʃaða/ *n. f.* throw.

echadillo /etʃa'ðiʎo; etʃa'ðiyo/ *n. m.* foundling; orphan.

echar /e'tʃar/ *v.* throw, toss; pour. **e. a,** start to. **e. a perder,** spoil, ruin. **e. de menos,** miss.

echarse /e'tʃarse/ *v.* lie down.

eclecticismo /eklekti'θismo; eklekti'sismo/ *n. m.* eclecticism.

ecléctico /e'klektiko/ *n. & a.* eclectic.

eclesiástico /ekle'siastiko/ *a. & m.* ecclesiastic.

eclipse /e'klipse/ *n. m.* eclipse. —**eclipsar,** *v.*

écloga /'ekloga/ *n. f.* eclogue.

eco /'eko/ *n. m.* echo.

ecología /ekolo'hia/ *n. f.* ecology.

ecológico /eko'lohiko/ *n. f.* ecological.

ecologista /ekolo'hista/ *n. m. & f.* ecologist.

economía /ekono'mia/ *n. f.* economy; thrift; economics. **e. política,** political economy.

económicamente /ekonomika'mente/ *adv.* economically.

económico /eko'nomiko/ *a.* economic; economical, thrifty; inexpensive.

economista /ekono'mista/ *n. m. & f.* economist.

economizar /ekonomi'θar; ekonomi'sar/ *v.* save, economize.

ecuación /ekua'θion; ekua'sion/ *n. f.* equation.

ecuador /ekua'ðor/ *n. m.* equator.

ecuanimidad /ekuanimi'ðað/ *n. f.* equanimity.

ecuatorial /ekuato'rial/ *a.* equatorial.

ecuatoriano /ekuato'riano/ **-na** *a. & n.* Ecuadorian.

ecuestre /e'kuestre/ *a.* equestrian.

ecuménico. /eku'meniko/ *a.* ecumenical.

edad /e'ðað/ *n. f.* age.

edecán /eðe'kan/ *n. m.* aide-de-camp.

Edén /e'ðen/ *n. m.* Eden.

edición /eði'θion; eði'sion/ *n. f.* edition; issue.

edicto /e'ðikto/ *n. m.* edict, decree.

edificación /eðifika'θion; eðifika'sion/ *n. f.* construction; edification.

edificador /eðifika'ðor/ *n.* constructor; builder.

edificar /eðifi'kar/ *v.* build.

edificio /eði'fiθio; eði'fisio/ *n. m.* edifice, building.

editar /eði'tar/ *v.* publish, issue; edit.

editor /eði'tor/ *n. m.* publisher; editor.

editorial /eðito'rial/ *n. m.* editorial; publishing house.

edredón /eðre'ðon/ *n. m.* quilt.

educación /eðuka'θion; eðuka'sion/ *n. f.* upbringing, breeding; education.

educado /eðu'kaðo/ *a.* well-mannered; educated.

educador /eðuka'ðor/ **-ra** *n.* educator.

educar /eðu'kar/ *v.* educate; bring up; train.

educativo /eðuka'tiβo/ *a.* educational.

educción /eðuk'θion; eðuk'sion/ *n. f.* deduction.

educir /eðu'θir; eðu'sir/ *v.* educe.

efectivamente /efektiβa'mente/ *adv.* actually, really.

efectivo /efek'tiβo/ *a.* effective; actual, real. **en e.,** *Com.* in cash.

efecto /e'fekto/ *n. m.* effect.

efecto invernáculo /e'fekto imber'nakulo/ greenhouse effect.

efectuar /efek'tuar/ *v.* effect; cash.

eferente /efe'rente/ *a.* efferent.

efervescencia /eferβes'θenθia; eferβes'sensia/ *n. f.* effervescence; zeal.

eficacia /efi'kaθia; efi'kasia/ *n. f.* efficacy.

eficaz /efi'kaθ; efi'kas/ *a.* efficient, effective.

eficazmente /efikaθ'mente; efikas'mente/ *adv.* efficaciously.

eficiencia /efi'θienθia; efi'siensia/ *n. f.* efficiency.

eficiente /efi'θiente; efi'siente/ *a.* efficient.

efigie /e'fihie/ *n. f.* effigy.

efímera /efi'mera/ *n. f.* mayfly.

efímero /e'fimero/ *a.* ephemeral, passing.

efluvio /e'fluβio/ *n. m.* effluvium.

efundir /efun'dir/ *v.* effuse; pour out.

efusión /efu'sion/ *n. f.* effusion.

egipcio /e'hipθio; e'hipsio/ **-cia** *a. & n.* Egyptian.

Egipto /e'hipto/ *n. m.* Egypt.

egoísmo /ego'ismo/ *n. m.* egoism, egotism, selfishness.

egoísta /ego'ista/ *a. & n.* selfish, egoistic; egoist.

egotismo /ego'tismo/ *n. m.* egotism.

egotista /ego'tista/ *n. m. & f.* egotist.

egreso /e'greso/ *n. m.* expense, outlay.

eje /'ehe/ *n. m.* axis; axle.

ejecución /eheku'θion; eheku'sion/ *n. f.* execution; performance; enforcement.

ejecutar /eheku'tar/ *v.* execute; enforce; carry out.

ejecutivo /eheku''tiβo/ **-va** *a. & n.* executive.

ejecutor /eheku'tor/ **-ra** *n.* executor.

ejemplar /ehem'plar/ *a.* **1.** exemplary. —*n.* **2.** *m.* copy.

ejemplificación /ehemplifika'θion; ehemplifika'sion/ *n. f.* exemplification.

ejemplificar /ehemplifi'kar/ *v.* illustrate.

ejemplo /e'hemplo/ *n. m.* example.

ejercer /eher'θer; eher'ser/ *v.* exert; practice.

ejercicio /eher'θiθio; eher'sisio/ *n. m.* exercise, drill. —**ejercitar,** *v.*

ejercitación /eherθita'θion; ehersita'sion/ *n. f.* exercise, training, drill.

ejercitar /eherθi'tar; ehersi'tar/ *v.* exercise, train, drill.

ejército /e'herθito; e'hersito/ *n. m.* army.

ejotes /e'hotes/ *n. m.pl.* string beans.

el /el/ *art. & pron.* the; the one.

él *pron.* he, him; it.

elaboración /elaβora'θion; elaβora'sion/ *n. f.* elaboration; working up.

elaborado /elaβo'raðo/ *a.* elaborate.

elaborador /elaβora'ðor/ *n. m.* manufacturer, maker.

elaborar /elaβo'rar/ *v.* elaborate; manufacture; brew.

elación /ela'θion; ela'sion/ *n. f.* elation; magnanimity; turgid style.

elasticidad /elastiθi'ðað; elastisi'ðað/ *n. f.* elasticity.

elástico /e'lastiko/ *n. m.* elastic.

elección /elek'θion; elek'sion/ *n. f.* election; option, choice.

electivo /elek'tiβo/ *a.* elective.

electo /e'lekto/ *a.* elected, chosen, appointed.

electorado /elekto'raðo/ *n. m.* electorate.

electoral /elekto'ral/ *a.* electoral.

electricidad /elektriθi'ðað; elektrisi'ðað/ *n. f.* electricity.

electricista /elektri'θista; elektri'sista/ *n. m. & f.* electrician.

eléctrico /e'lektriko/ *a.* electric.

electrización /elektriθa'θion; elektrisa'sion/ *n. f.* electrification.

electrocardiograma /e,lektrokarðio'grama/ *n. m.* electrocardiogram.

electrocución /elektroku'θion; elektroku'sion/ *n. f.* electrocution.

electrocutar /elektroku'tar/ *v.* electrocute.

electrodo /elek'troðo/ *n. m.* electrode.

electrodoméstico /e,lektroðo'mestiko/ *n. m.* electrical appliance, home appliance.

electroimán /elektroi'man/ *n. m.* electromagnet.

electrólisis /elek'trolisis/ *n. f.* electrolysis.

electrólito /elek'trolito/ *n. m.* electrolyte.

electrón /elek'tron/ *n. m.* electron.

electrónico /elek'troniko/ *a.* electronic.

elefante /ele'fante/ *n. m.* elephant.

elegancia /ele'ganθia; ele'gansia/ *n. f.* elegance.

elegante /ele'gante/ *a.* elegant, smart, stylish, fine.

elegantemente /elegante'mente/ *adv.* elegantly.

elegía /ele'hia/ *n. f.* elegy.

elegibilidad /elehiβili'ðað/ *n. f.* eligibility.

elegible /ele'hiβle/ *a.* eligible.

elegir /ele'hir/ *v.* select, choose; elect.

elemental /elemen'tal/ *a.* elementary.

elementalmente /elemental'mente/ *adv.* elementally; fundamentally.

elemento /ele'mento/ *n. m.* element.

elepé /ele'pe/ *n. m.* long-playing (record), LP.

elevación /eleβa'θion; eleβa'sion/ *n. f.* elevation; height.

elevador /eleβa'ðor/ *n. m.* elevator.

elevamiento /eleβa'miento/ *n. m.* elevation.

elevar /ele'βar/ *v.* elevate; erect, raise.

elidir /eli'ðir/ *v.* elide.

eliminación /elimina'θion; elimina'sion/ *n. f.* elimination.

eliminar /elimi'nar/ *v.* eliminate.

elipse /e'lipse/ *n. f.* ellipse.

elipsis /e'lipsis/ *n. f.* ellipsis.

elíptico /e'liptiko/ *a.* elliptic.

ella /'eʎa; 'eya/ *pron.* she, her; it.

ello /'eʎo; 'eyo/ *pron.* it.

ellos /'eʎos; 'eyos/ **-as** *pron. pl.* they, them.

elocuencia /elo'kuenθia; elo'kuensia/ *n. f.* eloquence.

elocuente /elo'kuente/ *a.* eloquent.

elocuentemente /elokuente'mente/ *adv.* eloquently.

elogio /e'lohio/ *n. m.* praise, compliment. —**elogiar,** *v.*

elucidación /eluθiða'θion; elusiða'sion/ *n. f.* elucidation.

elucidar /eluθi'ðar; elusi'ðar/ *v.* elucidate.

eludir /elu'ðir/ *v.* elude.

emanar /ema'nar/ *v.* emanate, stem.

emancipación /emanθipa'θion; emansipa'sion/ *n. f.* emancipation; freeing.

emancipador /emanθipa'ðor; emansipa'ðor/ **-ra** *n.* emancipator.

emancipar /emanθi'par; emansi'par/ *v.* emancipate; free.

embajada /emba'haða/ *n. f.* embassy; legation; *Colloq.* errand.

embajador /embaha'ðor/ **-ra** *n.* ambassador.

embalar /emba'lar/ *v.* pack, bale.

emblaldosado /embaldo'saðo/ *n. m.* tile floor.

embalsamador /embalsama'ðor/ *n. m.* embalmer.

embalsamar /embalsa'mar/ *v.* embalm.

embarazada /embara'θaða; embara'saða/ *a.* pregnant.

embarazadamente /embaraθaða'mente; embarasaða'mente/ *adv.* embarrassedly.

embarazar /embara'θar; embara'sar/ *v.* make pregnant; embarrass.

embarazo /emba'raθo; emba'raso/ *n. m.* embarrassment; pregnancy.

embarbascado /embarβas'kaðo/ *a.* difficult; complicated.

embarcación /embarka'θion; embarka'sion/ *n. f.* boat, ship; embarkation.

embarcadero /embarka'ðero/ *n. m.* wharf, pier, dock.

embarcador /embarka'ðor/ *n. m.* shipper, loader, stevedore.

embarcar /embar'kar/ *v.* embark, board ship.

embarcarse /embar'karse/ *v.* embark; sail.

embargador /embarga'ðor/ *n. m.* one who impedes; one who orders an embargo.

embargante /embar'gante/ *a.* impeding, hindering.

embargar /embar'gar/ *v.* impede, restrain; *Leg.* seize, embargo.

embargo /em'bargo/ *n. m.* seizure, embargo. **sin e.,** however, nevertheless.

embarnizar /embarni'θar; embarni'sar/ *v.* varnish.

embarque /em'barke/ *n. m.* shipment.

embarrador /embarra'ðor/ **-ra** *n.* plasterer.

embarrancar /embarran'kar/ *v.* get stuck in mud; *Naut.* run aground.

embarrar /emba'rrar/ *v.* plaster; besmear with mud.

embasamiento /embasa'miento/ *n. m.* foundation of a building.

embastecer /embaste'θer; embaste'ser/ *v.* get fat.

embaucador /embauka'ðor/ **-ra** *n.* impostor.

embaucar /embau'kar/ *v.* deceive, trick, hoax.

embaular /embau'lar/ *v.* pack in a trunk.

embausamiento /embausa'miento/ *n. m.* amazement.

embebecer /embeβe'θer; embeβe'ser/ *v.* amaze, astonish; entertain.

embeber /embe'βer/ *v.* absorb; incorporate; saturate.

embelecador /embeleka'ðor/ **-ra** *n.* impostor.

embeleco /embe'leko/ *n. m.* fraud, perpetration.

embeleñar /embele'ɲar/ *v.* fascinate, charm.

embelesamiento /embelesa'miento/ *n. m.* rapture.

embelesar /embele'sar/ *v.* fascinate, charm.

embeleso /embe'leso/ *n. m.* rapture, bliss.

embellecer /embeʎe'θer; embeye'ser/ *v.* beautify, embellish.

embestida /embes'tiða/ *n. f.* violent assault; attack.

emblandecer /emblande'θer; emblande'ser/ *v.* soften; moisten; move to pity.

emblema /em'blema/ *n. m.* emblem.

emblemático /emble'matiko/ *a.* emblematic.

embocadura /emboka'ðura/ *n. f.* narrow entrance; mouth of a river.

embocar /embo'kar/ *v.* eat hastily; gorge.

embolia /em'bolia/ *n. f.* embolism.

émbolo /'embolo/ *n. m.* piston.

embolsar /embol'sar/ *v.* pocket.

embonar /embo'nar/ *v.* improve, fix, repair.

emborrachador /emborratʃaˈðor/ a. intoxicating.

emborrachar /emborraˈtʃar/ v. get drunk.

emboscada /embosˈkaða/ n. f. ambush.

emboscar /embosˈkar/ v. put or lie in ambush.

embotado /emboˈtaðo/ a. blunt, dull (edged). —**embotar,** v.

embotadura /embotaˈðura/ n. f. bluntness; dullness.

embotellamiento /emboteʎaˈmiento; emboteyaˈmiento/ n. m. bottling (liquids); traffic jam.

embotellar /emboteˈʎar; emboteˈyar/ v. put in bottles.

embozado /emboˈθaðo; emboˈsaðo/ v. muzzled; muffled.

embozar /emboˈθar; emboˈsar/ v. muzzle; muffle.

embozo /emˈboθo; emˈboso/ n. m. muffler.

embrague /emˈbrage/ n. m. Auto. clutch.

embravecer /embraβeˈθer; embraβeˈser/ v. be or make angry.

embriagado /embriaˈgaðo/ a. drunken, intoxicated.

embriagar /embriaˈgar/ v. intoxicate.

embriaguez /embriaˈgeθ; embriaˈges/ n. f. drunkenness.

embrión /emˈbrion/ n. m. embryo.

embrionario /embrioˈnario/ a. embryonic.

embrochado /embroˈtʃaðo/ a. embroidered.

embrollo /emˈbroʎo; emˈbroyo/ n. m. muddle. —**embrollar,** v.

embromar /embroˈmar/ v. tease; joke.

embuchado /embuˈtʃaðo/ n. m. pork sausage.

embudo /emˈbuðo/ n. m. funnel.

embuste /emˈbuste/ n. m. lie, fib.

embustear /embusteˈar/ v. lie, fib.

embustero /embusˈtero/ **-ra** n. liar.

embutir /embuˈtir/ v. stuff, cram.

emergencia /emerˈhenθia; emerˈhensia/ n. f. emergency.

emérito /eˈmerito/ a. emeritus.

emético /eˈmetiko/ n. m. & a. emetic.

emigración /emigraˈθion; emigraˈsion/ n. f. emigration.

emigrante /emiˈgrante/ a. & n. emigrant.

emigrar /emiˈgrar/ v. emigrate.

eminencia /emiˈnenθia; emiˈnensia/ n. f. eminence, height.

eminente /emiˈnente/ a. eminent.

emisario /emiˈsario/ **-ria** n. emissary, spy; outlet.

emisión /emiˈsion/ n. f. issue; emission.

emisor /emiˈsor/ n. m. radio transmitter.

emitir /emiˈtir/ v. emit.

emoción /emoˈθion; emoˈsion/ n. f. feeling, emotion, thrill.

emocional /emoˈθional; emoˈsional/ a. emotional.

emocionante /emoθioˈnante; emosioˈnante/ a. exciting.

emocionar /emoθioˈnar; emosioˈnar/ v. touch, move, excite.

emolumento /emoluˈmento/ n. m. emolument; perquisite.

empacar /empaˈkar/ v. pack.

empacho /emˈpatʃo/ n. m. shyness, timidity; embarrassment.

empadronamiento /empaðronaˈmiento/ n. m. census; list of taxpayers.

empalizada /empaliˈθaða; empaliˈsaða/ n. f. palisade, stockade.

empanada /empaˈnaða/ n. f. meat pie.

empañar /empaˈɲar/ v. blur; soil, sully.

empapar /empaˈpar/ v. soak.

empapelado /empapeˈlaðo/ n. m. wallpaper.

empapelar /empapeˈlar/ v. wallpaper.

empaque /emˈpake/ n. m. packing; appearance, mien.

empaquetar /empakeˈtar/ v. pack, package.

emparedado /empareˈðaðo/ n. m. sandwich.

emparejarse /empareˈharse/ v. match, pair off; level, even off.

emparentado /emparenˈtaðo/ a. related by marriage.

emparrado /empaˈrraðo/ n. m. arbor.

empastadura /empastaˈðura/ n. f. (dental) filling.

empastar /empasˈtar/ v. fill (a tooth); paste.

empate /emˈpate/ n. m. tie, draw. —**empatarse,** v.

empecer /empeˈθer; empeˈser/ v. hurt, harm, injure; prevent.

empedernir /empeðerˈnir/ v. harden.

empeine /emˈpeine/ n. m. groin; instep; hoof.

empellar /empeˈʎar; empeˈyar/ v. shove, jostle.

empellón /empeˈʎon; empeˈyon/ n. m. hard push, shove.

empeñar /empeˈɲar/ v. pledge; pawn.

empeñarse en /empeˈɲarse en/ v. persist in, be bent on.

empeño /emˈpeɲo/ n. m. persistence; pledge; pawning.

empeoramiento /empeoraˈmiento/ n. m. deterioration.

empeorar /empeoˈrar/ v. get worse.

emperador /emperaˈðor/ n. m. emperor.

emperatriz /emperaˈtriθ; emperaˈtris/ n. f. empress.

empernar /emperˈnar/ v. bolt.

empero /emˈpero/ conj. however; but.

emperramiento /emperraˈmiento/ n. m. stubbornness.

empezar /empeˈθar; empeˈsar/ v. begin, start.

empinado /empiˈnaðo/ a. steep.

empinar /empiˈnar/ v. raise; exalt.

empíreo /emˈpireo/ a. celestial, heavenly; divine.

empíricamente /empirikaˈmente/ adv. empirically.

empírico /emˈpiriko/ a. empirical.

empirismo /empiˈrismo/ n. m. empiricism.

emplastarse /emplasˈtarse/ v. get smeared.

emplasto /emˈplasto/ n. m. salve.

emplazamiento /emplaθaˈmiento; emplasaˈmiento/ n. m. court summons.

emplazar /emplaˈθar; emplaˈsar/ v. summon to court.

empleado /empleˈaðo/ **-da** n. employee.

emplear /empleˈar/ v. employ; use.

empleo /emˈpleo/ n. m. employment, job; use.

empobrecer /empoβreˈθer; empoβreˈser/ v. impoverish.

empobrecimiento /empoβreθiˈmiento; empoβresiˈmiento/ n. m. impoverishment.

empollador /empoʎaˈðor; empoyaˈðor/ n. m. incubator.

empollar /empoˈʎar; empoˈyar/ v. hatch.

empolvado /empolˈβaðo/ a. dusty.

empolvar /empolˈβar/ v. powder.

emporcar /emporˈkar/ v. soil, make dirty.

emporio /emˈporio/ n. m. emporium.

emprendedor /emprendeˈðor/ a. enterprising.

emprender /emprenˈder/ v. undertake.

empreñar /empreˈɲar/ v. make pregnant; beget.

empresa /emˈpresa/ n. f. enterprise, undertaking; company.

empresario /empreˈsario/ **-ria** n. businessperson; impresario.

empréstito /emˈprestito/ n. m. loan.

empujón /empuˈhon/ n. m. push; shove. —**empujar,** v.

empuñar /empuˈɲar/ v. grasp, seize; wield.

emulación /emulaˈθion; emulaˈsion/ n. f. emulation; envy; rivalry.

emulador /emulaˈðor/ n. m. emulator; rival.

émulo /ˈemulo/ a. rival. —**emular,** v.

emulsión /emulˈsion/ n. f. emulsion.

emulsionar /emulsioˈnar/ v. emulsify.

en /en/ prep. in, on, at.

enaguas /eˈnaguas/ n. f.pl. petticoat; skirt.

enajenable /enaheˈnaβle/ a. alienable.

enajenación /enahenaˈθion; enahenaˈsion/ n. f. alienation; derangement, insanity.

enajenar /enaheˈnar/ v. alienate.

enamoradamente /enamoraðaˈmente/ adv. lovingly.

enamorado /enamoˈraðo/ a. in love.

enamorador /enamoraˈðor/ n. m. wooer; suitor; lover.

enamorarse /enamoˈrarse/ v. fall in love.

enano /eˈnano/ **-na** n. midget; dwarf.

enardecer /enarðeˈθer; enarðeˈser/ v. inflame.

enastado /enasˈtaðo/ a. horned.

encabestrar /enkaβesˈtrar/ v. halter.

encabezado /enkaβeˈθaðo; enkaβeˈsaðo/ n. m. headline.

encabezamiento /enkaβeθaˈmiento; enkaβesaˈmiento/ n. m. title; census; tax roll.

encabezar /enkaβeˈθar; enkaβeˈsar/ v. head.

encachar /enkaˈtʃar/ v. hide.

encadenamiento /enkaðenaˈmiento/ n. m. connection, linkage.

encadenar /enkaðeˈnar/ v. chain; link, connect.

encajar /enkaˈhar/ v. fit in, insert.

encaje /enˈkahe/ n. m. lace.

encalar /enkaˈlar/ v. whitewash.

encallarse /enkaˈʎarse; enkaˈyarse/ v. be stranded.

encallecido /enkaʎeˈθiðo; enkayeˈsiðo/ a. hardened; calloused.

encalvecer /enkalβeˈθer; enkalβeˈser/ v. lose one's hair.

encaminar /enkamiˈnar/ v. guide; direct; be on the way to.

encandilar /enkandiˈlar/ v. dazzle; daze.

encantación /enkantaˈθion; enkantaˈsion/ n. f. incantation.

encantado /enkanˈtaðo/ a. charmed, fascinated, enchanted.

encantador /enkantaˈðor/ a. charming, delightful.

encante /enˈkante/ n. m. public auction.

encanto /enˈkanto/ n. m. charm, delight. —**encantar,** v.

encapillado /enkapiˈʎaðo; enkapiˈyaðo/ n. m. clothes one is wearing.

encapotar /enkapoˈtar/ v. cover, cloak; muffle.

encaprichamiento /enkapritʃaˈmiento/ n. m. infatuation.

encaramarse /enkaraˈmarse/ v. perch; climb.

encararse con /enkaˈrarse kon/ v. face.

encarcelación /enkarθelaˈθion; enkarselaˈsion/ n. f. imprisonment.

encarcelar /enkarθeˈlar; enkareˈlar/ v. jail, imprison.

encarecer /enkareˈθer; enkareˈser/ v. recommend; extol.

encarecidamente /enkareθiðaˈmente; enkaresiðaˈmente/ adv. extremely; ardently.

encargado /enkarˈgaðo/ **-da** n. agent; attorney; representative.

encargar /enkarˈgar/ v. entrust; order.

encargarse /enkarˈgarse/ v. take charge, be in charge.

encargo /enˈkargo/ n. m. errand; assignment; Com. order.

encarnación /enkarnaˈθion; enkarnaˈsion/ n. f. incarnation.

encarnado /enkarˈnaðo/ a. red.

encarnar /enkarˈnar/ v. embody.

encarnecer /enkarneˈθer; enkarneˈser/ v. grow fat or heavy.

encarnizado /enkarniˈθaðo; enkarniˈsaðo/ a. bloody, fierce.

encarrilar /enkarriˈlar/ v. set right; put on the track.

encartar /enkarˈtar/ v. ban, outlaw; summon.

encastar /enkasˈtar/ v. improve by crossbreeding.

encastillar /enkastiˈʎar; enkastiˈyar/ v. be obstinate or unyielding.

encatarrado /enkataˈrraðo/ a. suffering from a cold.

encausar /enkauˈsar/ v. prosecute; take legal action against.

encauzar /enkauˈθar; enkauˈsar/ v. channel; direct.

encefalitis /enθefaˈlitis; ensefaˈlitis/ n. f. encephalitis.

encelamiento /enθelaˈmiento; enselaˈmiento/ n. m. envy, jealousy.

encelar /enθeˈlar; enseˈlar/ v. make jealous.

encenagar /enθenaˈgar; ensenaˈgar/ v. wallow in mud.

encendedor /enθendeˈðor; ensendeˈðor/ n. m. lighter.

encender /enθenˈder; ensenˈder/ v. light; set fire to, kindle; turn on.

encendido /enθenˈdiðo; ensenˈdiðo/ n. m. ignition.

encerado /enθeˈraðo; enseˈraðo/ n. m. oilcloth; tarpaulin.

encerar /enθeˈrar; enseˈrar/ v. wax.

encerrar /enθeˈrrar; enseˈrrar/ v. enclose; confine, shut in.

enchapado /entʃaˈpaðo/ n. m. veneer.

enchufe /enˈtʃufe/ n. m. Elec. plug, socket.

encía /enˈθia; enˈsia/ n. f. gum.

encíclico /enˈθikliko; enˈsikliko/ a. **1.** encyclic. —n. **2.** f. encyclical.

enciclopedia /enθikloˈpeðia; ensikloˈpeðia/ n. f. encyclopedia.

enciclopédico /enθikloˈpeðiko; ensikloˈpeðiko/ a. encyclopedic.

encierro /enˈθierro; enˈsierro/ n. m. confinement; enclosure.

encima /enˈθima; enˈsima/ adv. on top. **e. de,** on. **por e. de,** above.

encina /enˈθina; enˈsina/ n. f. oak.

encinta /enˈθinta; enˈsinta/ a. pregnant.

enclavar /enklaˈβar/ v. nail.

enclenque /enˈklenke/ a. frail, weak, sickly.

encogerse /enkoˈherse/ v. shrink. **e. de hombros,** shrug the shoulders.

encogido /enkoˈhiðo/ a. shy, bashful, timid.

encojar /enkoˈhar/ v. make or become lame; cripple.

encolar /enkoˈlar/ v. glue, paste, stick.

encolerizar /enkoleriˈθar; enkoleriˈsar/ v. make or become angry.

encomendar /enkomenˈdar/ v. commend; recommend.

encomiar /enkoˈmiar/ v. praise, laud, extol.

encomienda /enkoˈmienda/ n. f. commission, charge; (postal) package.

encomio /enˈkomio/ n. m. encomium, eulogy.

enconar /enkoˈnar/ v. irritate, annoy, anger.

encono /enˈkono/ n. m. rancor, resentment.

enconoso /enkoˈnoso/ a. rancorous, resentful.

encontrado /enkonˈtraðo/ a. opposite.

encontrar /enkonˈtrar/ v. find; meet.

encorajar /enkoraˈhar/ v. encourage; incite.

encornar /enkorˈnar/ v. gore.

encorralar /enkorraˈlar/ v. corral.

encorvadura /enkorβaˈðura/ n. f. bend, curvature.

encorvar /enkor'βar/ v. arch, bend.
encorvarse /enkor'βarse/ v. stoop.
encrucijada /enkruθi'haða; enkrusi-'haða/ n. f. crossroads.
encuadrar /enkuað'rar/ v. frame.
encubierta /enku'βierta/ a. **1.** secret, fraudulent. —n. **2.** f. fraud.
encubrir /enkuβ'rir/ v. hide, conceal.
encuentro /en'kuentro/ n. m. encounter; match, bout.
encurtido /enkur'tiðo/ n. m. pickle.
endeble /en'deβle/ a. rail, weak, sickly.
enderezar /endere'θar; endere'sar/ v. straighten; redress.
endeudarse /endeu'ðarse/ v. get into debt.
endiablado /endia'βlaðo/ a. devilish.
endibia /en'diβia/ n. f. endive.
endiosar /endio'sar/ v. deify.
endorso /en'dorso/ **endoso** n. m. endorsement.
endosador /endosa'ðor/ **-ra** n. endorser.
endosar /endo'sar/ v. endorse.
endosatario /endosa'tario/ **-ria** n. endorsee.
endulzar /endul'θar; endul'sar/ v. sweeten; soothe.
endurar /endu'rar/ v. harden.
endurecer /endure'θer; endure'ser/ v. harden.
enemigo /ene'migo/ **-ga** n. foe, enemy.
enemistad /enemis'tað/ n. f. enmity.
éneo /'eneo/ a. brass.
energía /ener'hia/ n. f. energy.
energía nuclear /ener'hia nukle'ar/ atomic energy, nuclear energy.
energía vital /ener'hia bi'tal/ élan vital, vitality.
enérgicamente /e'nerhikamente/ adv. energetically.
enérgico /e'nerhiko/ a. forceful; energetic.
enero /e'nero/ n. m. January.
enervación /enerβa'θion; enerβa-'sion/ n. f. enervation.
enfadado /enfa'ðaðo/ a. angry.
enfadar /enfa'ðar/ v. anger, vex.
enfado /en'faðo/ n. m. anger, vexation.
énfasis /'enfasis/ n. m. or f. emphasis, stress.
enfáticamente /en'fatikamente/ adv. emphatically.
enfático /en'fatiko/ a. emphatic.
enfermar /enfer'mar/ v. make ill; fall ill.
enfermedad /enferme'ðað/ n. f. illness, sickness, disease.
enfermera /enfer'mera/ n. f. nurse.
enfermería /enferme'ria/ n. f. sanatorium.
enfermo /en'fermo/ **-ma** a. & n. ill, sick; sickly; patient.
enfilar /enfi'lar/ v. line up; put in a row.
enflaquecer /enflake'θer; enflake-'ser/ v. make thin; grow thin.
enfoque /en'foke/ n. m. focus. —enfocar, v.
enfrascamiento /enfraska'miento/ n. m. entanglement.
enfrascar /enfras'kar/ v. bottle; entangle oneself.
enfrenar /enfre'nar/ v. bridle, curb; restrain.
enfrentamiento /enfrenta'miento/ n. m. clash, confrontation.
enfrente /en'frente/ adv. across, opposite; in front.
enfriadera /enfria'ðera/ n. f. icebox; cooler.
enfriar /enf'riar/ v. chill, cool.
enfurecer /enfure'θer; enfure'ser/ v. infuriate, enrage.
engalanar /eŋgala'nar/ v. adorn, trim.
enganchar /eŋgan'tʃar/ v. hook, hitch, attach.
engañar /eŋga'ɲar/ v. deceive, cheat.

engaño /eŋ'gaɲo/ n. m. deceit; delusion.
engañoso /eŋga'ɲoso/ a. deceitful.
engarce /eŋ'garθe; eŋgarse/ n. connection, link.
engastar /eŋgas'tar/ v. to put (gems) in a setting.
engaste /eŋ'gaste/ n. m. setting.
engatusar /eŋgatu'sar/ v. deceive, trick.
engendrar /enhen'drar/ v. engender, beget, produce.
engendro /en'hendro/ n. m. fetus, embryo.
englobar /eŋglo'βar/ v. include.
engolfar /eŋgol'far/ v. be deeply absorbed.
engolosinar /eŋgolosi'nar/ v. allure, charm, entice.
engomar /eŋgo'mar/ v. gum.
engordador /eŋgor'ðaðor/ a. fattening.
engordar /eŋgor'ðar/ v. fatten; grow fat.
engranaje /eŋgra'nahe/ n. m. Mech. gear.
engranar /eŋgra'nar/ v. gear; mesh together.
engrandecer /eŋgrande'θer; eŋgrande'ser/ v. increase, enlarge; exalt; exaggerate.
engrasación /eŋgrasa'θion; eŋgrasa-'sion/ n. f. lubrication.
engrasar /eŋgra'sar/ v. grease, lubricate.
engreído /eŋgre'iðo/ a. conceited.
engreimiento /eŋgrei'miento/ n. m. conceit.
engullidor /eŋguʎi'ðor; eŋguyi'ðor/ **-ra** n. devourer.
engullir /eŋgu'ʎir; eŋgu'yir/ v. devour.
enhebrar /ene'βrar/ v. thread.
enhestadura /enesta'ðura/ n. f. raising.
enhestar /enes'tar/ v. raise, erect, set up.
enhiesto /en'iesto/ a. erect, upright.
enhorabuena /enora'βuena/ n. f. congratulations.
enigma /e'nigma/ n. m. enigma, puzzle.
enigmáticamente /enigmatika'mente/ adv. enigmatically.
enigmático /enig'matiko/ a. enigmatic.
enjabonar /enhaβo'nar/ v. soap, lather.
enjalbegar /enhalβe'gar/ v. whitewash.
enjambradera /enhambra'ðera/ n. f. queen bee.
enjambre /en'hambre/ n. m. swarm. —enjambrar, v.
enjaular /enhau'lar/ v. cage, coop up.
enjebe /en'heβe/ n. m. lye.
enjuagar /enhua'gar/ v. rinse.
enjuague bucal /en'huage bu'kal/ n. m. mouthwash.
enjugar /enhu'gar/ v. wipe, dry off.
enjutez /enhu'teθ; enhu'tes/ n. f. dryness.
enjuto /en'huto/ a. dried; lean, thin.
enlace /en'laθe; en'lase/ n. m. attachment; involvement; connection.
enladrillador /enlaðriʎa'ðor; enlaðri-ya'ðor/ **-ra** n. bricklayer.
enlardar /enlar'ðar/ v. baste.
enlatado /enla'taðo/ **-da** a. canned (food).
enlatar /enla'tar/ v. can (food).
enlazar /enla'θar; enla'sar/ v. lace; join, connect; wed.
enlodar /enlo'ðar/ v. cover with mud.
enloquecer /enloke'θer; enloke'ser/ v. go insane; drive crazy.
enloquecimiento /enlokeθi'miento; enlokesi'miento/ n. m. insanity.
enlustrecer /enlustre'θer; enlustre-'ser/ v. polish, brighten.
enmarañar /emara'ɲar/ v. entangle.
enmendación /emenda'θion; emen-da'sion/ n. f. emendation.

enmendador /emenda'ðor/ **-ra** n. emender, reviser.
enmendar /emen'dar/ v. amend, correct.
enmienda /e'mienda/ n. f. amendment; correction.
enmohecer /emoe'θer; emoe'ser/ v. rust; mold.
enmohecido /emoe'θiðo; emoe'siðo/ a. rusty; moldy.
enmudecer /emuðe'θer; emuðe'ser/ v. silence; become silent.
ennegrecer /ennegre'θer; ennegre-'ser/ v. blacken.
ennoblecer /ennoβle'θer; ennoβle-'ser/ v. ennoble.
enodio /e'noðio/ n. m. young deer.
enojado /eno'haðo/ a. angry, cross.
enojarse /eno'harse/ v. get angry.
enojo /e'noho/ n. m. anger. —enojar, v.
enojosamente /enohosa'mente/ adv. angrily.
enorme /e'norme/ a. enormous, huge.
enormemente /enorme'mente/ adv. enormously; hugely.
enormidad /enormi'ðað/ n. f. enormity; hugeness.
enraizar /enrai'θar; enrai'sar/ v. take root, sprout.
enramada /enra'maða/ n. f. bower.
enredadera /enreða'ðera/ n. f. climbing plant.
enredado /enre'ðaðo/ a. entangled, snarled.
enredar /enre'ðar/ v. entangle, snarl; mess up.
enredo /en'reðo/ n. m. tangle, entanglement.
enriquecer /enrike'θer; enrike'ser/ v. enrich.
enrojecerse /enrohe'θerse; enrohe-'serse/ v. color; blush.
enrollar /enro'ʎar; enro'yar/ v. wind, coil, roll up.
enromar /enro'mar/ v. make dull, blunt.
enronquecimiento /enronkeθi-'miento; enronkesi'miento/ n. m. hoarseness.
enroscar /enros'kar/ v. twist, curl, wind.
ensacar /ensa'kar/ v. put in a bag.
ensalada /ensa'laða/ n. f. salad.
ensaladera /ensala'ðera/ n. f. salad bowl.
ensalmo /en'salmo/ n. m. charm, enchantment.
ensalzamiento /ensalθa'miento; en-salsa'miento/ n. m. praise.
ensalzar /ensal'θar; ensal'sar/ v. praise, laud, extol.
ensamblar /ensam'blar/ v. join; unite; connect.
ensanchamiento /ensantʃa'miento/ n. m. widening, expansion, extension.
ensanchar /ensan'tʃar/ v. widen, expand, extend.
ensangrentado /ensaŋgren'taðo/ a. bloody; bloodshot.
ensañar /ensa'ɲar/ v. enrage, infuriate; rage.
ensayar /ensa'yar/ v. try out; rehearse.
ensayista /ensa'yista/ n. m. & f. essayist.
ensayo /ensa'yo/ n. m. attempt; trial; rehearsal.
ensenada /ense'naða/ n. f. cove.
enseña /en'seɲa/ n. f. ensign, standard.
enseñador /enseɲa'ðor/ **-ra** n. teacher.
enseñanza /enseɲanθa; enseɲansa/ n. f. education; teaching.
enseñar /ense'ɲar/ v. teach, train; show.
enseres /en'seres/ n. m.pl. household goods.
ensilaje /ensi'lahe/ n. m. ensilage.
ensillar /ensi'ʎar; ensi'yar/ v. saddle.
ensordecedor /ensorðeθe'ðor; ensor-ðese'ðor/ a. deafening.

ensordecer /ensorðe'θer; ensorðe-'ser/ v. deafen.
ensordecimiento /ensorðeθi'miento; ensorðesi'miento/ n. m. deafness.
ensuciar /ensu'θiar; ensu'siar/ v. dirty, muddy, soil.
ensueño /en'sueɲo/ n. m. illusion, dream.
entablar /enta'βlar/ v. board up; initiate, begin.
entallador /entaʎa'ðor; entaya'ðor/ n. m. sculptor, carver.
entapizar /entapi'θar; entapi'sar/ v. upholster.
ente /'ente/ n. m. being.
entenada /ente'naða/ n. f. stepdaughter.
entenado /ente'naðo/ n. m. stepson.
entender /enten'der/ v. understand.
entendimiento /entendi'miento/ n. m. understanding.
entenebrecer /enteneβre'θer; ente-neβre'ser/ v. darken.
enterado /ente'raðo/ a. aware, informed.
enteramente /entera'mente/ adv. entirely, completely.
enterar /ente'rar/ v. inform.
enterarse /ente'rarse/ v. find out.
entereza /ente'reθa; ente'resa/ n. f. entirety; integrity; firmness.
entero /en'tero/ a. entire, whole, total.
enterramiento /enterra'miento/ n. m. burial, interment.
enterrar /ente'rrar/ v. bury.
entestado /entes'taðo/ a. stubborn, willful.
entibiar /enti'βiar/ v. to cool; moderate.
entidad /enti'ðað/ n. f. entity.
entierro /en'tierro/ n. m. interment, burial.
entonación /entona'θion; en-tona'sion/ n. f. intonation.
entonamiento /entona'miento/ n. m. intonation.
entonar /ento'nar/ v. chant; harmonize.
entonces /en'tonθes; entonses/ adv. then.
entono /en'tono/ n. m. intonation; arrogance; affectation.
entortadura /entorta'ðura/ n. f. crookedness.
entortar /entor'tar/ v. make crooked; bend.
entrada /en'traða/ n. f. entrance; admission, admittance.
entrambos /en'trambos/ a. & pron. both.
entrante /en'trante/ a. coming, next.
entrañable /entra'ɲaβle/ a. affectionate.
entrañas /en'traɲas/ n. f.pl. entrails, bowels; womb.
entrar /en'trar/ v. enter, go in, come in.
entre /'entre/ prep. among; between.
entreabierto /entrea'βierto/ a. ajar, half-open.
entreabrir /entrea'βrir/ v. set ajar.
entreacto /entre'akto/ n. m. intermission.
entrecejo /entre'θeho; entre'seho/ n. m. frown; space between the eyebrows.
entrecuesto /entre'kuesto/ n. m. spine, backbone.
entredicho /entre'ðitʃo/ n. m. prohibition.
entrega /en'trega/ n. f. delivery.
entregar /entre'gar/ v. deliver, hand; hand over.
entrelazar /entrela'θar; entrela'sar/ v. intertwine, entwine.
entremedias /entre'meðias/ adv. meanwhile; halfway.
entremés /entre'mes/ n. m. side dish.
entremeterse /entreme'terse/ v. meddle, intrude.
entremetido /entreme'tiðo/ **-da** n. meddler.

entrenador /entrena'ðor/ **-ra** *n.* coach. —**entrenar**, *v.*
entrenarse /entre'narse/ *v.* train.
entrepalado /entrepa'laðo/ *a.* variegated; spotted.
entrerenglonar /entrereŋglo'nar/ *v.* interline.
entresacar /entresa'kar/ *v.* select, choose; sift.
entresuelo /entre'suelo/ *n. m.* mezzanine.
entretanto /entre'tanto/ *adv.* meanwhile.
entretenedor /entretene'ðor/ **-ra** *n.* entertainer.
entretener /entrete'ner/ *v.* entertain, amuse; delay.
entretenimiento /entreteni'miento/ *n. m.* entertainment, amusement.
entrevista /entre'βista/ *n. f.* interview. —**entrevistar**, *v.*
entrevistador /entreβista'ðor/ **-ra** *n.* interviewer.
entristecedor /entristeθe'ðor; entriste'ðor/ *a.* sad.
entristecer /entriste'θer; entriste'ser/ *v.* sadden.
entronar /entro'nar/ *v.* enthrone.
entroncar /entron'kar/ *v.* be related or connected.
entronización /entroniθa'θion; entronisa'sion/ *n. f.* enthronement.
entronque /entron'ke/ *n. m.* relationship; connection.
entumecer /entume'θer; entume'ser/ *v.* become or be numb; swell.
entusiasmado /entusias'maðo/ *a.* enthusiastic.
entusiasmo /entu'siasmo/ *n. m.* enthusiasm.
entusiasta /entu'siasta/ *n. m. & f.* enthusiast.
entusiástico /entu'siastiko/ *a.* enthusiastic.
enumeración /enumera'θion; enumera'sion/ *n. f.* enumeration.
enumerar /enume'rar/ *v.* enumerate.
enunciación /enunθia'θion; enunsia'sion/ *n. f.* enunciation; statement.
enunciar /enun'θiar; enun'siar/ *v.* enunciate.
envainar /embai'nar/ *v.* sheathe.
envalentonar /embalento'nar/ *v.* encourage, embolden.
envanecimiento /embaneθimiento; embanesi'miento/ *n. m.* conceit, vanity.
envasar /emba'sar/ *v.* put in a container; bottle.
envase /em'base/ *n. m.* container.
envejecer /embehe'θer; embehe'ser/ *v.* age, grow old.
envejecimiento /embeheθi'miento; embehesi'miento/ *n. m.* oldness, aging.
envenenar /embene'nar/ *v.* poison.
envés /em'bes/ *n. m.* wrong side; back.
envestir /embes'tir/ *v.* put in office; invest.
enviada /em'biaða/ *n. f.* shipment.
enviado /em'biaðo/ **-da** *n.* envoy.
enviar /em'biar/ *v.* send; ship.
envidia /em'biðia/ *n. f.* envy. —**envidiar**, *v.*
envidiable /embi'ðiaβle/ *a.* enviable.
envidioso /embi'ðioso/ *a.* envious.
envilecer /embile'θer; embile'ser/ *v.* vilify, debase, disgrace.
envío /em'bio/ *n. m.* shipment.
envión /em'bion/ *n. m.* shove.
envoltura /embol'tura/ *n. f.* wrapping.
envolver /embol'βer/ *v.* wrap, wrap up.
enyesar /enye'sar/ *v.* plaster.
enyugar /enyu'gar/ *v.* yoke.
eperlano /eper'lano/ *n. m.* smelt (fish).
épica /'epika/ *n. f.* epic.
épico /'epiko/ *a.* epic.
epicureísmo /epikure'ismo/ *n. m.* epicureanism.

epicúreo /epi'kureo/ *n. & a.* epicurean.
epidemia /epi'ðemia/ *n. f.* epidemic.
epidémico /epi'ðemiko/ *a.* epidemic.
epidermis /epi'ðermis/ *n. f.* epidermis.
epigrama /epi'grama/ *n. m.* epigram.
epigramático /epigra'matiko/ **-ca** *a.* epigrammatic.
epilepsia /epi'lepsia/ *n. f.* epilepsy.
epiléptico /epi'leptiko/ **-ca** *n. & a.* epileptic.
epílogo /e'pilogo/ *n. m.* epilogue.
episcopado /episko'paðo/ *n. m.* bishopric; episcopate.
episcopal /episko'pal/ *a.* episcopal.
episódico /epi'soðiko/ *a.* episodic.
episodio /epi'soðio/ *n. m.* episode.
epístola /e'pistola/ *n. f.* epistle, letter.
epitafio /epi'tafio/ *n. m.* epitaph.
epitomadamente /epitomaða'mente/ *adv.* concisely.
epitomar /epito'mar/ *v.* epitomize, summarize.
época /'epoka/ *n. f.* epoch, age.
epopeya /epo'peya/ *n. f.* epic.
epsomita /epso'mita/ *n. f.* Epsom salts.
equidad /eki'ðað/ *n. f.* equity.
equilibrado /ekili'βraðo/ *a.* stable.
equilibrio /eki'liβrio/ *n. m.* equilibrium, balance.
equinoccio /eki'nokθio; ekinoksio/ *n. m.* equinox.
equipaje /eki'pahe/ *n. m.* luggage, baggage. **e. de mano**, luggage.
equipar /eki'par/ *v.* equip.
equiparar /ekipa'rar/ *v.* compare.
equipo /e'kipo/ *n. m.* equipment; team.
equitación /ekita'θion; ekita'sion/ *f.* horsemanship; horseback riding, riding.
equitativo /ekita'tiβo/ *a.* fair, equitable.
equivalencia /ekiβa'lenθia; ekiβa'lensia/ *n. f.* equivalence.
equivalente /ekiβa'lente/ *a.* equivalent.
equivaler /ekiβa'ler/ *v.* equal, be equivalent.
equivocación /ekiβoka'θion; ekiβoka'sion/ *n. f.* mistake.
equivocado /ekiβo'kaðo/ *a.* wrong, mistaken.
equivocarse /ekiβo'karse/ *v.* make a mistake, be wrong.
equívoco /e'kiβoko/ *a.* equivocal, ambiguous.
era /'era/ *n. f.* era, age.
erario /e'rario/ *n. m.* exchequer.
erección /erek'θion; erek'sion/ *n. f.* erection; elevation.
eremita /ere'mita/ *n. m.* hermit.
erguir /er'gir/ *v.* erect; straighten up.
erigir /eri'hir/ *v.* erect, build.
erisipela /erisi'pela/ *n. f.* erysipelas.
erizado /eri'θaðo; eri'saðo/ *a.* bristly.
erizarse /eri'θarse; eri'sarse/ *v.* bristle.
erizo /e'riθo; e'riso/ *n. m.* hedgehog; sea urchin.
ermita /er'mita/ *n. f.* hermitage.
ermitaño /ermi'taɲo/ *n. m.* hermit.
erogación /eroga'θion; eroga'sion/ *n. f.* expenditure. —**erogar**, *v.*
erosión /ero'sion/ *n. f.* erosion.
erótico /e'rotiko/ *a.* erotic.
erradicación /erraðika'θion; erraðika'sion/ *n. f.* eradication.
erradicar /erraði'kar/ *v.* eradicate.
errado /e'rraðo/ *a.* mistaken, erroneous.
errante /e'rrante/ *a.* wandering, roving.
errar /e'rrar/ *v.* be mistaken.
errata /e'rrata/ *n. f.* erratum.
errático /e'rratiko/ *a.* erratic.
erróneamente /erronea'mente/ *adv.* erroneously.
erróneo /e'rroneo/ *a.* erroneous.
error /e'rror/ *n. m.* error, mistake.

eructo /e'rukto/ *n. m.* belch. —**eructar**, *v.*
erudición /eruði'θion; eruði'sion/ *n. f.* scholarship, learning.
eruditamente /eruðita'mente/ *adv.* learnedly.
erudito /eru'ðito/ **-ta** *n.* **1.** scholar. —*a.* **2.** scholarly.
erupción /erup'θion; erup'sion/ *n. f.* eruption; rash.
eruptivo /erup'tiβo/ *a.* eruptive.
esbozo /es'βoθo; es'βoso/ *n. m.* outline, sketch. —**esbozar**, *v.*
escabechar /eskaβe't∫ar/ *v.* pickle; preserve.
escabeche /eska'βet∫e/ *n. m.* brine.
escabel /eska'βel/ *n. m.* small stool or bench.
escabroso /eska'βroso/ *a.* rough, irregular; craggy; rude.
escabullirse /eskaβu'ʎirse; eskaβu'yirse/ *v.* steal away, sneak away.
escala /es'kala/ *n. f.* scale; ladder. **hacer e.**, to make a stop.
escalada /eska'laða/ *n. f.* escalation.
escalador /eskala'ðor/ **-ra** *n.* climber.
escalar /eska'lar/ *v.* climb; scale.
escaldar /eskal'dar/ *v.* scald.
escalera /eska'lera/ *n. f.* stairs, staircase; ladder.
escalfado /eskal'faðo/ *a.* poached.
escalofriado /eskalo'friaðo/ *a.* chilled.
escalofrío /eskalo'frio/ *n. m.* chill.
escalón /eska'lon/ *n. m.* step.
escalonar /eskalo'nar/ *v.* space out, stagger.
escaloña /eska'loɲa/ *n. f.* scallion.
escalpar /eskal'par/ *v.* scalp.
escalpelo /eskal'pelo/ *n. m.* scalpel.
escama /es'kama/ *n. f.* (fish) scale. —**escamar**, *v.*
escamondar /eskamon'dar/ *v.* trim, cut; prune.
escampada /eskam'paða/ *n. f.* break in the rain, clear spell.
escandalizar /eskandali'θar; eskandali'sar/ *v.* shock, scandalize.
escandalizativo /eskandaliθa'tiβo; eskandalisa'tiβo/ *a.* scandalous.
escándalo /es'kandalo/ *n. m.* scandal.
escandaloso /eskanda'loso/ *a.* scandalous; disgraceful.
escandinavo /eskandi'naβo/ **-va** *n. & a.* Scandinavian.
escandir /eskan'dir/ *v.* scan.
escanear /eskane'ar/ *v.* scan (on a computer).
escáner /es'kaner/ *v.* scanner (of a computer).
escanilla /eska'niʎa; eska'niya/ *n. f.* cradle.
escañuelo /eska'ɲuelo/ *n. m.* small footstool.
escapada /eska'paða/ *n. f.* escapade.
escapar /eska'par/ *v.* escape.
escaparate /eskapa'rate/ *n. m.* shop window, store window.
escape /es'kape/ *n. m.* escape; *Auto.* exhaust.
escápula /es'kapula/ *n. f.* scapula.
escarabajo /eskara'βaho/ *n. m.* black beetle; scarab.
escaramucear /eskaramuθe'ar; eskaramuse'ar/ *v.* skirmish; dispute.
escarbadientes /eskarβa'ðientes/ *m.* toothpick.
escarbar /eskar'βar/ *v.* scratch; poke.
escarcha /es'kart∫a/ *n. f.* frost.
escardar /eskar'ðar/ *v.* weed.
escarlata /eskar'lata/ *n. f.* scarlet.
escarlatina /eskarla'tina/ *n. f.* scarlet fever.
escarmentar /eskarmen'tar/ *v.* correct severely.
escarnecedor /eskarneθe'ðor; eskarneseðor/ **-ra** *n.* scoffer; mocker.
escarnecer /eskarne'θer; eskarne'ser/ *v.* mock, make fun of.
escarola /eska'rola/ *n. f.* endive.
escarpa /es'karpa/ *n. f.* escarpment.

escarpado /eskar'paðo/ *a.* **1.** steep. —*n.* **2.** *m.* bluff.
escasamente /eskasa'mente/ *adv.* scarcely; sparingly; barely.
escasear /eskase'ar/ *v.* be scarce.
escasez /eska'seθ; eska'ses/ *n. f.* shortage, scarcity.
escaso /es'kaso/ *a.* scant; scarce.
escatimar /eskati'mar/ *v.* be stingy, skimp; save.
escatimoso /eskati'moso/ *a.* malicious; sly, cunning.
escena /es'θena; es'sena/ *n. f.* scene; stage.
escenario /esθe'nario; esse'nario/ *n. m.* stage (of theater); scenario.
escénico /es'θeniko; es'seniko/ *a.* scenic.
escépticamente /esθeptika'mente; esseptika'mente/ *adv.* skeptically.
escepticismo /esθepti'θismo; essepti'sismo/ *n. m.* skepticism.
escéptico /es'θeptiko; es'septiko/ **-ca** *a. & n.* skeptic; skeptical.
esclarecer /esklare'θer; esklare'ser/ *v.* clear up.
esclavitud /esklaβi'tuð/ *n. f.* slavery; bondage.
esclavizar /esklaβi'θar; esklaβi'sar/ *v.* enslave.
esclavo /es'klaβo/ **-va** *n.* slave.
escoba /es'koβa/ *n. f.* broom.
escocés /esko'θes; esko'ses/ **-esa** *a. & n.* Scotch, Scottish; Scot.
Escocia /es'koðia; eskosia/ *n. f.* Scotland.
escofinar /eskofi'nar/ *v.* rasp.
escoger /esko'her/ *v.* choose, select.
escogido /esko'hiðo/ *a.* chosen, selected.
escogimiento /eskohi'miento/ *n. m.* choice.
escolar /esko'lar/ *a.* **1.** scholastic, (of) school. —*n.* **2.** *m.& f.* student.
escolasticismo /eskolasti'θismo; eskolasti'sismo/ *n. m.* scholasticism.
escollo /es'koʎo; es'koyo/ *n. m.* reef.
escolta /es'kolta/ *n. f.* escort. —**escoltar**, *v.*
escombro /es'kombro/ *n. m.* mackerel.
escombros /es'kombros/ *n. m.pl.* debris, rubbish.
esconce /es'konθe; es'konse/ *n. m.* corner.
escondedero /eskonde'ðero/ *n. m.* hiding place.
esconder /eskon'der/ *v.* hide, conceal.
escondidamente /eskondiða'mente/ *adv.* secretly.
escondimiento /eskondi'miento/ *n. m.* concealment.
escondrijo /eskon'driho/ *n. m.* hiding place.
escopeta /esko'peta/ *n. f.* shotgun.
escopetazo /eskope'taθo; eskope'taso/ *n. m.* gunshot.
escoplo /es'koplo/ *n. m.* chisel.
escorbuto /eskor'βuto/ *n. m.* scurvy.
escorpena /eskor'pena/ *n. f.* grouper.
escorpión /eskor'pion/ *n. m.* scorpion.
escorzón /eskor'θon; eskor'son/ *n. m.* toad.
escotado /esko'taðo/ *a.* low-cut, with a low neckline.
escote /es'kote/ *n. m.* low neckline.
escribiente /eskri'βiente/ *n. m. & f.* clerk.
escribir /eskri'βir/ *v.* write.
escritor /eskri'tor/ **-ra** *n.* writer, author.
escritorio /eskri'torio/ *n. m.* desk.
escritura /eskri'tura/ *n. f.* writing, handwriting.
escrófula /es'krofula/ *n. f.* scrofula.
escroto /es'kroto/ *n. m.* scrotum.
escrúpulo /es'krupulo/ *n. m.* scruple.
escrupuloso /eskrupu'loso/ *a.* scrupulous.
escrutinio /eskru'tinio/ *n. m.* scrutiny; examination.

escuadra /es'kuaðra/ *n. f.* squad; fleet.

escuadrón /eskuað'ron/ *n. m.* squadron.

escualidez /eskuali'ðeθ; eskuali'ðes/ *n. f.* squalor; poverty; emaciation.

escuálido /es'kualiðo/ *a.* squalid.

escualo /es'kualo/ *n. m.* shark.

escuchar /esku'tʃar/ *v.* listen; listen to.

escudero /esku'ðero/ *n. m.* squire.

escudo /es'kuðo/ *n. m.* shield; protection; coin of certain countries.

escuela /es'kuela/ *n. f.* school.

escuela nocturna /es'kuela nok'turna/ night school.

escuela por correspondencia /es'kuela por korrespon'denθia; es'kuela por korrespon'densia/ correspondence school.

escuerzo /es'kuerθo; es'kuerso/ *n. m.* toad.

esculpir /eskul'pir/ *v.* carve, sculpture.

escultor /eskul'tor/ **-ra** *n.* sculptor.

escultura /eskul'tura/ *n. f.* sculpture.

escupidera /eskupi'ðera/ *n. f.* cuspidor.

escupir /esku'pir/ *v.* spit.

escurridero /eskurri'ðero/ *n. m.* drain board.

escurridor /eskurri'ðor/ *n. m.* colander, strainer.

escurrir /esku'rrir/ *v.* drain off; wring out.

escurrirse /esku'rrirse/ *v.* slip; sneak away.

ese /'ese/ **esa** *dem. a.* that.

ése, ésa *dem. pron.* that (one).

esencia /e'senθia; e'sensia/ *n. f.* essence; perfume.

esencial /esen'θial; esen'sial/ *a.* essential.

esencialmente /esenθial'mente; esensial'mente/ *adv.* essentially.

esfera /es'fera/ *n. f.* sphere.

esfinge /es'finhe/ *n. f.* sphinx.

esforzar /esfor'θar; esfor'sar/ *v.* strengthen.

esforzarse /esfor'θarse; esfor'sarse/ *v.* strive, exert oneself.

esfuerzo /es'fuerθo; es'fuerso/ *n. m.* effort, attempt; vigor.

esgrima /es'grima/ *n. f.* fencing.

esguince /es'ginθe; es'ginse/ *n. m.* sprain.

eslabón /esla'βon/ *n. m.* link (of a chain).

eslabonar /eslaβo'nar/ *v.* link, join, connect.

eslavo /es'laβo/ **-va** *a. & n.* Slavic; Slav.

esmalte /es'malte/ *n. m.* enamel, polish. —**esmaltar,** *v.*

esmerado /esme'raðo/ *a.* careful, thorough.

esmeralda /esme'ralda/ *n. f.* emerald.

esmerarse /esme'rarse/ *v.* take pains, do one's best.

esmeril /es'meril/ *n. m.* emery.

eso /'eso/ *dem. pron.* that.

esófago /e'sofago/ *n. m.* esophagus.

esotérico /eso'teriko/ *a.* esoteric.

espacial /espa'θial; espa'sial/ *a.* spatial.

espacio /es'paθio; es'pasio/ *n. m.* space. —**espaciar,** *v.*

espaciosidad /espaθiosi'ðað; espasiosi'ðað/ *n. f.* spaciousness.

espacioso /espa'θioso; espa'sioso/ *a.* spacious.

espada /es'paða/ *n. f.* sword; spade (in cards).

espadarte /espa'ðarte/ *n. m.* swordfish.

espaguetis /espa'getis/ *n. m.pl.* spaghetti.

espalda /es'palda/ *n. f.* back.

espaldera /espal'dera/ *n. f.* espalier.

espantar /espan'tar/ *v.* frighten, scare; scare away.

espanto /es'panto/ *n. m.* fright.

espantoso /espan'toso/ *a.* frightening, frightful.

España /es'paɲa/ *n. f.* Spain.

español /espa'ɲol/ **-ola** *a. & n.* Spanish; Spaniard.

esparcir /espar'θir; espar'sir/ *v.* scatter, disperse.

espárrago /es'parrago/ *n. m.* asparagus.

espartano /espar'tano/ **-na** *n. & a.* Spartan.

espasmo /es'pasmo/ *n. m.* spasm.

espasmódico /espas'moðiko/ *a.* spasmodic.

espata /es'pata/ *n. f.* spathe.

espato /es'pato/ *n. m.* spar (mineral).

espátula /es'patula/ *n. f.* spatula.

especia /es'peθia; es'pesia/ *n. f.* spice. —**especiar,** *v.*

especial /espe'θial; espe'sial/ *a.* special, especial.

especialidad /espeθiali'ðað; espesiali'ðað/ *n. f.* specialty.

especialista /espeθia'lista; espesia'lista/ *n. m. & f.* specialist.

especialización /espeθialiθa'θion; espesialisa'sion/ *n. f.* specialization.

especialmente /espeθial'mente; espesial'mente/ *adv.* especially.

especie /es'peθie; es'pesie/ *n. f.* species; sort.

especiería /espeθie'ria; espesie'ria/ *n. f.* grocery store; spice store.

especiero /espe'θiero; espe'siero/ **-ra** *n.* spice dealer; spice box.

especificar /espeθifi'kar; espesifi'kar/ *v.* specify.

específico /espe'θifiko; espe'sifiko/ *a.* specific.

espécimen /es'peθimen; es'pesimen/ *n. m.* specimen.

especioso /espe'θioso; espe'sioso/ *a.* neat; polished; specious.

espectacular /espektaku'lar/ *a.* spectacular.

espectáculo /espek'takulo/ *n. m.* spectacle, show.

espectador /espekta'ðor/ **-ra** *n.* spectator.

espectro /es'pektro/ *n. m.* specter, ghost.

especulación /espekula'θion; espekula'sion/ *n. f.* speculation.

especulador /espekula'ðor/ **-ra** *n.* speculator.

especular /espeku'lar/ *v.* speculate.

especulativo /espekula'tiβo/ *a.* speculative.

espejo /es'peho/ *n. m.* mirror.

espelunca /espe'lunka/ *n. f.* dark cave, cavern.

espera /es'pera/ *n. f.* wait.

esperanza /espe'ranθa; espe'ransa/ *n. f.* hope, expectation.

esperar /espe'rar/ *v.* hope; expect; wait, wait for, watch for.

espesar /espe'sar/ *v.* thicken.

espeso /es'peso/ *a.* thick, dense, bushy.

espesor /espe'sor/ *n. m.* thickness, density.

espía /es'pia/ *n. m. & f.* spy. —**espiar,** *v.*

espigón /espi'gon/ *n. m.* bee sting.

espina /es'pina/ *n. f.* thorn.

espinaca /espi'naka/ *n. f.* spinach.

espina dorsal /es'pina dor'sal/ spine.

espinal /espi'nal/ *a.* spinal.

espinazo /espi'naθo; espi'naso/ *n. m.* backbone.

espineta /espi'neta/ *n. f.* spinet.

espino /es'pino/ *n. m.* briar.

espinoso /espi'noso/ *a.* spiny, thorny.

espión /es'pion/ *n. m.* spy.

espionaje /espio'nahe/ *n. m.* espionage.

espiral /espi'ral/ *a. & m.* spiral.

espirar /espi'rar/ *v.* expire; breathe, exhale.

espíritu /es'piritu/ *n. m.* spirit.

espiritual /espiri'tual/ *a.* spiritual.

espiritualidad /espirituali'ðað/ *n. f.* spirituality.

espiritualmente /espiritual'mente/ *adv.* spiritually.

espita /es'pita/ *n. f.* faucet, spigot.

espléndido /es'plendiðo/ *a.* splendid.

esplendor /esplen'dor/ *n. m.* splendor.

espolear /espole'ar/ *v.* incite, urge on.

espoleta /espo'leta/ *n. f.* wishbone.

esponja /es'ponha/ *n. f.* sponge.

esponjoso /espon'hoso/ *a.* spongy.

esponsales /espon'sales/ *n. m.pl.* engagement, betrothal.

esponsalicio /esponsa'liθio; esponsa'lisio/ *a.* nuptial.

espontáneamente /espontanea'mente/ *adv.* spontaneously.

espontaneidad /espontanei'ðað/ *n. f.* spontaneity.

espontáneo /espon'taneo/ *a.* spontaneous.

espora /es'pora/ *n. f.* spore.

esporádico /espo'raðiko/ *a.* sporadic.

esposa /es'posa/ *n. f.* wife.

esposar /espo'sar/ *v.* shackle; handcuff.

esposo /es'poso/ *n. m.* husband.

espuela /es'puela/ *n. f.* spur. —**espolear,** *v.*

espuma /es'puma/ *n. f.* foam. —**espumar,** *v.*

espumadera /espuma'ðera/ *n. f.* whisk; skimmer.

espumajear /espumahe'ar/ *v.* foam at the mouth.

espumajo /espu'maho/ *n. m.* foam.

espumar /espu'mar/ *v.* foam, froth; skim.

espumoso /espu'moso/ *a.* foamy; sparkling (wine).

espurio /es'purio/ *a.* spurious.

esputar /espu'tar/ *v.* spit, expectorate.

esputo /es'puto/ *n. m.* spit, saliva.

esquela /es'kela/ *n. f.* note.

esqueleto /eske'leto/ *n. m.* skeleton.

esquema /es'kema/ *n. m.* scheme; diagram.

esquero /es'kero/ *n. m.* leather sack, leather pouch.

esquiar /es'kiar/ *v.* ski.

esquiciar /eski'θiar; eski'siar/ *v.* outline, sketch.

esquicio /es'kiθio; es'kisio/ *n. m.* rough sketch, rough outline.

esquife /es'kife/ *n. m.* skiff.

esquilar /eski'lar/ *v.* fleece, shear.

esquilmo /es'kilmo/ *n. m.* harvest.

esquimal /eski'mal/ *n. & a.* Eskimo.

esquina /es'kina/ *n. f.* corner.

esquivar /eski'βar/ *v.* evade, shun.

estabilidad /estaβili'ðað/ *n. f.* stability.

estable /es'taβle/ *a.* stable.

establecedor /estaβleθe'ðor; estaβlese'ðor/ *n. m.* founder, originator.

establecer /estaβle'θer; estaβle'ser/ *v.* establish, set up.

establecimiento /estaβleθi'miento; estaβlesi'miento/ *n. m.* establishment.

establero /estaβ'lero/ *n. m.* groom.

establo /es'taβlo/ *n. m.* stable.

estaca /es'taka/ *n. f.* stake.

estación /esta'θion; esta'sion/ *n. f.* station; season.

estacionamiento /estaθiona'miento; estasiona'miento/ *n. m.* parking; parking lot; parking space.

estacionar /estaθio'nar; estasio'nar/ *v.* station; park (a vehicle).

estacionario /estaθio'nario; estasio'nario/ *a.* stationary.

estación de servicio /esta'θion de ser'βiθio; esta'sion de ser'βisio/ service station.

estación de trabajo /esta'θion de tra'βaho; esta'sion de tra'βaho/ work station.

estadista /esta'ðista/ *n. m. & f.* statesman.

estadística /esta'ðistika/ *n. f.* statistics.

estadístico /esta'ðistiko/ *a.* statistical.

estado /es'taðo/ *n. m.* state; condition; status.

Estados Unidos /es'taðos u'niðos/ *n. m.pl.* United States.

estafa /es'tafa/ *n. f.* swindle, fake. —**estafar,** *v.*

estafeta /esta'feta/ *n. f.* post office.

estagnación /estagna'θion; estagna'sion/ *n. f.* stagnation.

estallar /esta'ʎar; esta'yar/ *v.* explode; burst; break out.

estallido /esta'ʎiðo; esta'yiðo/ *n. m.* crash; crack; explosion.

estampa /es'tampa/ *n. f.* stamp. —**estampar,** *v.*

estampado /estam'paðo/ *n. m.* printed cotton cloth.

estampida /estam'piða/ *n. f.* stampede.

estampilla /estam'piʎa; estam'piya/ *n. f.* (postage) stamp.

estancado /estan'kaðo/ *a.* stagnant.

estancar /estan'kar/ *v.* stanch, stop, check.

estancia /es'tanθia; es'tansia/ *n. f.* stay; (*S.A.*) small farm.

estanciero /estan'θiero; estan'siero/ **-ra** *n.* small farmer.

estandarte /estan'darte/ *n. m.* banner.

estanque /es'tanke/ *n. m.* pool; pond.

estante /es'tante/ *n. m.* shelf.

estaño /es'taɲo/ *n. m.* tin. —**estañar,** *v.*

estar /es'tar/ *v.* be; stand; look.

estática /es'tatika/ *n. f.* static.

estático /es'tatiko/ *a.* static.

estatua /es'tatua/ *n. f.* statue.

estatura /esta'tura/ *n. f.* stature.

estatuto /esta'tuto/ *n. m.* statute, law.

este /'este/ *n. m.* east.

este, esta *dem. a.* this.

éste, ésta *dem. pron.* this (one); the latter.

estelar /este'lar/ *a.* stellar.

estenografía /estenogra'fia/ *n. f.* stenography.

estenógrafo /este'nografo/ **-fa** *n.* stenographer.

estera /es'tera/ *n. f.* mat, matting.

estereofónico /estereo'foniko/ *a.* stereophonic.

estéril /es'teril/ *a.* barren; sterile.

esterilidad /esterili'ðað/ *n. f.* sterility, fruitlessness.

esterilizar /esterili'θar; esterili'sar/ *v.* sterilize.

esternón /ester'non/ *n. m.* breastbone.

estética /es'tetika/ *n. f.* esthetics.

estético /es'tetiko/ *a.* esthetic.

estetoscopio /esteto'skopio/ *n. m.* stethoscope.

estibador /estiβa'ðor/ *n. m.* stevedore.

estiércol /es'tierkol/ *n. m.* dung, manure.

estigma /es'tigma/ *n. m.* stigma; disgrace.

estilarse /esti'larse/ *v.* be in fashion, be in vogue.

estilo /es'tilo/ *n. m.* style; sort.

estilográfica /estilo'grafika/ *n. f.* (fountain) pen.

estima /es'tima/ *n. f.* esteem.

estimable /esti'maβle/ *a.* estimable, worthy.

estimación /estima'θion; estima'sion/ *n. f.* estimation.

estimar /esti'mar/ *v.* esteem; value; estimate; gauge.

estimular /estimu'lar/ *v.* stimulate.

estímulo /es'timulo/ *n. m.* stimulus.

estío /es'tio/ *n. m.* summer.

estipulación /estipula'θion; estipula'sion/ *n. f.* stipulation.

estipular /estipu'lar/ *v.* stipulate.

estirar /esti'rar/ *v.* stretch.

estirpe /es'tirpe/ *n. m.* stock, lineage.

esto /'esto/ *dem. pron.* this.
estocada /esto'kaða/ *n. f.* stab, thrust.
estofado /esto'faðo/ *n. m.* stew. —**estofar,** *v.*
estoicismo /estoi'θismo; estoi'sismo/ *n. m.* stoicism.
estoico /es'toiko/ *n.* & *a.* stoic.
estómago /es'tomago/ *n. m.* stomach.
estorbar /estor'βar/ *v.* bother, hinder, interfere with.
estorbo /es'torβo/ *n. m.* hindrance.
estornudo /estor'nuðo/ *n. m.* sneeze. —**estornudar,** *v.*
estrabismo /estra'βismo/ *n. m.* strabismus.
estrago /es'trago/ *n. m.* devastation, havoc.
estrangulación /estranɡula'θion; estranɡula'sion/ *n. f.* strangulation.
estrangular /estranɡu'lar/ *v.* strangle.
estraperlista /estraper'lista/ *n. m.* & *f.* black marketeer.
estraperlo /estra'perlo/ *n. m.* black market.
estratagema /estrata'hema/ *n. f.* stratagem.
estrategia /estra'tehia/ *n. f.* strategy.
estratégico /estra'tehiko/ *a.* strategic.
estrato /es'trato/ *n. m.* stratum.
estrechar /estre'tʃar/ *v.* tighten; narrow.
estrechez /estre'tʃeθ; estre'tʃes/ *n. f.* narrowness; tightness.
estrecho /es'tretʃo/ *a.* **1.** narrow, tight. —*n.* **2.** *m.* strait.
estregar /estre'gar/ *v.* scour, scrub.
estrella /es'treʎa; es'treya/ *n. f.* star.
estrellamar /estreʎa'mar; estreya'mar/ *n. f.* starfish.
estrellar /estre'ʎar; estre'yar/ *v.* shatter, smash.
estremecimiento /estremeθi'miento; estremesi'miento/ *n. m.* shudder. —**estremecerse,** *v.*
estrenar /estre'nar/ *v.* wear for the first time; open (a play).
estreno /es'treno/ *n. m.* debut, first performance.
estrenuo /es'trenuo/ *a.* strenuous.
estreñido /estre'ɲiðo/ **-da** *a.* constipated.
estreñimiento /estreɲi'miento/ *n. m.* constipation.
estreñir /estre'ɲir/ *v.* constipate.
estrépito /es'trepito/ *n. m.* din.
estreptococo /estrepto'koko/ *n. m.* streptococcus.
estría /es'tria/ *n. f.* groove.
estribillo /estri'βiʎo; estri'βiyo/ *n. m.* refrain.
estribo /es'triβo/ *n. m.* stirrup.
estribor /estri'βor/ *n. m.* starboard.
estrictamente /estrikta'mente/ *adv.* strictly.
estrictez /estrik'teθ; estrik'tes/ *n. f.* strictness.
estricto /es'trikto/ *a.* strict.
estrofa /es'trofa/ *n. f.* stanza.
estropajo /estro'paho/ *n. m.* mop.
estropear /estrope'ar/ *v.* cripple, damage, spoil.
estructura /estruk'tura/ *n. f.* structure.
estructural /estruktu'ral/ *a.* structural.
estruendo /es'truendo/ *n. m.* din, clatter.
estuario /es'tuario/ *n. m.* estuary.
estuco /es'tuko/ *n. m.* stucco.
estudiante /estu'ðiante/ **-ta** *n.* student.
estudiar /estu'ðiar/ *v.* study.
estudio /es'tuðio/ *n. m.* study; studio.
estudioso /estu'ðioso/ *a.* studious.
estufa /es'tufa/ *n. f.* stove.
estufa de aire /es'tufa de 'aire/ fan heater.
estulto /es'tulto/ *a.* foolish.

estupendo /estu'pendo/ *a.* wonderful, grand, fine.
estupidez /estupi'ðeθ; estupi'ðes/ *n. f.* stupidity.
estúpido /es'tupiðo/ *a.* stupid.
estupor /estu'por/ *n. m.* stupor.
estuque /es'tuke/ *n. m.* stucco.
esturión /estu'rion/ *n. m.* sturgeon.
etapa /e'tapa/ *n. f.* stage.
éter /'eter/ *n. m.* ether.
etéreo /e'tereo/ *a.* ethereal.
eternal /eter'nal/ *a.* eternal.
eternidad /eterni'ðað/ *n. f.* eternity.
eterno /e'terno/ *a.* eternal.
ética /'etika/ *n. f.* ethics.
ético /'etiko/ *a.* ethical.
etimología /etimolo'hia/ *n. f.* etymology.
etiqueta /eti'keta/ *n. f.* etiquette; tag, label.
étnico /'etniko/ *a.* ethnic.
etrusco /e'trusko/ **-ca** *n.* & *a.* Etruscan.
eucaristía /eukaris'tia/ *n. f.* Eucharist.
eufemismo /eufe'mismo/ *n. m.* euphemism.
eufonía /eufo'nia/ *n. f.* euphony.
Europa /eu'ropa/ *n. f.* Europe.
europeo /euro'peo/ **-pea** *a.* & *n.* European.
eutanasia /euta'nasia/ *n. f.* euthanasia.
evacuación /eβakua'θion; eβakua'sion/ *n. f.* evacuation.
evacuar /eβa'kuar/ *v.* evacuate.
evadir /eβa'ðir/ *v.* evade.
evangélico /eβan'heliko/ *a.* evangelical.
evangelio /eβan'helio/ *n. m.* gospel.
evangelista /eβanhe'lista/ *n. m.* evangelist.
evaporación /eβapora'θion; eβapora'sion/ *n. f.* evaporation.
evaporarse /eβapo'rarse/ *v.* evaporate.
evasión /eβa'sion, eβa'siβa/ *n. f.* evasion.
evasivamente /eβasiβa'mente/ *adv.* evasively.
evasivo /eβa'siβo/ *a.* evasive.
evento /e'βento/ *n. m.* event, occurrence.
eventual /eβen'tual/ *a.* eventual.
eventualidad /eβentuali'ðað/ *n. f.* eventuality.
evicción /eβik'θion; eβik'sion/ *n. f.* eviction.
evidencia /eβi'ðenθia; eβiðensia/ *n. f.* evidence.
evidenciar /eβiðen'θiar; eβiðen'siar/ *v.* prove, show.
evidente /eβi'ðente/ *a.* evident.
evitación /eβita'θion; eβita'sion/ *n. f.* avoidance.
evitar /eβi'tar/ *v.* avoid, shun.
evocación /eβoka'θion; eβoka'sion/ *n. f.* evocation.
evocar /eβo'kar/ *v.* evoke.
evolución /eβolu'θion; eβolu'sion/ *n. f.* evolution.
exacerbar /eksaθer'βar; eksaser'βar/ *v.* irritate deeply; exacerbate.
exactamente /eksakta'mente/ *adv.* exactly.
exactitud /eksakti'tuð/ *n. f.* precision, accuracy.
exacto /ek'sakto/ *a.* exact, accurate.
exageración /eksahera'θion; eksahera'sion/ *n. f.* exaggeration.
exagerar /eksahe'rar/ *v.* exaggerate.
exaltación /eksalta'θion; eksalta'sion/ *n. f.* exaltation.
exaltamiento /eksalta'miento/ *n. m.* exaltation.
exaltar /eksal'tar/ *v.* exalt.
examen /ek'samen/ *n. m.* test, examination.
examen de ingreso /ek'samen de iŋ'greso/ entrance examination.
examinar /eksami'nar/ *v.* test, examine.

exánime /eksa'nime/ *a.* spiritless, weak.
exasperación /eksaspera'θion; eksaspera'sion/ *n. f.* exasperation.
exasperar /eksaspe'rar/ *v.* exasperate.
excavación /ekskaβa'θion; ekskaβa'sion/ *n. f.* excavation.
excavar /ekska'βar/ *v.* excavate.
exceder /eksθe'ðer; eksse'ðer/ *v.* exceed, surpass; outrun.
excelencia /eksθe'lenθia; eksse'lensia/ *n. f.* excellence.
excelente /eksθe'lente; eksse'lente/ *a.* excellent.
excéntrico /ek'θentriko; eks'sentriko/ *a.* eccentric.
excepción /eksθep'θion; ekssep'sion/ *n. f.* exception.
excepcional /eksθepθio'nal; ekssepsio'nal/ *a.* exceptional.
excepto /eks'θepto; eks'septo/ *prep.* except, except for.
exceptuar /eksθep'tuar; ekssep'tuar/ *v.* except.
excesivamente /eksθesiβa'mente; ekssesiβa'mente/ *adv.* excessively.
excesivo /eksθe'siβo; eksse'siβo/ *a.* excessive.
exceso /eks'θeso; eks'seso/ *n. m.* excess.
excitabilidad /eksθitaβili'ðað; ekssitaβili'ðað/ *n. f.* excitability.
excitación /eksθita'θion; ekssita'sion/ *n. f.* excitement.
excitar /eksθi'tar; ekssi'tar/ *v.* excite.
exclamación /eksklama'θion; eksklama'sion/ *n. f.* exclamation.
exclamar /ekskla'mar/ *v.* exclaim.
excluir /eksk'luir/ *v.* exclude, bar, shut out.
exclusión /eksklu'sion/ *n. f.* exclusion.
exclusivamente /eksklusiβa'mente/ *adv.* exclusively.
exclusivo /eksklu'siβo/ *a.* exclusive.
excomulgar /ekskomul'gar/ *v.* excommunicate.
excomunión /ekskomu'nion/ *n. f.* excommunication.
excreción /ekskre'θion; ekskre'sion/ *n. f.* excretion.
excremento /ekskre'mento/ *n. m.* excrement.
excretar /ekskre'tar/ *v.* excrete.
exculpar /ekskul'par/ *v.* exonerate.
excursión /ekskur'sion/ *n. f.* excursion.
excursionista /ekskursio'nista/ *n. m.* & *f.* excursionist; tourist.
excusa /eks'kusa/ *n. f.* excuse. —**excusar,** *v.*
excusado /eksku'saðo/ *n. m.* toilet.
excusarse /eksku'sarse/ *v.* apologize.
exención /eksen'θion; eksen'sion/ *n. f.* exemption.
exento /ek'sento/ *a.* exempt. —**exentar,** *v.*
exhalación /eksala'θion; eksala'sion/ *n. f.* exhalation.
exhalar /eksa'lar/ *v.* exhale, breathe out.
exhausto /ek'sausto/ *a.* exhausted.
exhibición /eksiβi'θion; eksiβi'sion/ *n. f.* exhibit, exhibition.
exhibir /eksi'βir/ *v.* exhibit, display.
exhortación /eksorta'θion; eksorta'sion/ *n. f.* exhortation.
exhortar /eksor'tar/ *v.* exhort, admonish.
exhumación /eksuma'θion; eksuma'sion/ *n. f.* exhumation.
exhumar /eksu'mar/ *v.* exhume.
exigencia /eksi'henθia; eksi'hensia/ *n. f.* requirement, demand.
exigente /eksi'hente/ *a.* exacting, demanding.
exigir /eksi'hir/ *v.* require, exact, demand.
eximir /eksi'mir/ *v.* exempt.
existencia /eksis'tenθia; eksis'tensia/ *n. f.* existence; *Econ.* supply.
existente /eksis'tente/ *a.* existent.

existir /eksis'tir/ *v.* exist.
éxito /'eksito/ *n. m.* success.
éxodo /'eksoðo/ *n. m.* exodus.
exoneración /eksonera'θion; eksonera'sion/ *n. f.* exoneration.
exonerar /eksone'rar/ *v.* exonerate, acquit.
exorar /ekso'rar/ *v.* beg, implore.
exorbitancia /eksorβi'tanθia; eksorβi'tansia/ *n. f.* exorbitance.
exorbitante /eksorβi'tante/ *a.* exorbitant.
exorcismo /eksor'θismo; eksor'sismo/ *n. m.* exorcism.
exornar /eksor'nar/ *v.* adorn, decorate.
exótico /ek'sotiko/ *a.* exotic.
expansibilidad /ekspansiβili'ðað/ *n. f.* expansibility.
expansión /ekspan'sion/ *n. f.* expansion.
expansivo /ekspan'siβo/ *a.* expansive; effusive.
expatriación /ekspatria'θion; ekspatria'sion/ *n. f.* expatriation.
expatriar /ekspa'triar/ *v.* expatriate.
expectación /ekspekta'θion; ekspekta'sion/ *n. f.* expectation.
expectorar /ekspekto'rar/ *v.* expectorate.
expedición /ekspeði'θion; ekspeði'sion/ *n. f.* expedition.
expediente /ekspe'ðiente/ *n. m.* expedient; means.
expedir /ekspe'ðir/ *v.* send off, ship; expedite.
expeditivo /ekspeði'tiβo/ *a.* speedy, prompt.
expedito /ekspe'ðito/ *a.* speedy, prompt.
expeler /ekspe'ler/ *v.* expel, eject.
expendedor /ekspende'ðor/ **-ra** *n.* dealer.
expender /ekspen'der/ *v.* expend.
expensas /ek'spensas/ *n. f.pl.* expenses, costs.
experiencia /ekspe'rienθia; ekspe'riensia/ *n. f.* experience.
experimentado /eksperimen'taðo/ *a.* experienced.
experimental /eksperimen'tal/ *a.* experimental.
experimentar /eksperimen'tar/ *v.* experience.
experimento /eksperi'mento/ *n. m.* experiment.
expertamente /eksperta'mente/ *adv.* expertly.
experto /ek'sperto/ **-ta** *a.* & *n.* expert.
expiación /ekspia'θion; ekspia'sion/ *n. f.* atonement.
expiar /eks'piar/ *v.* atone for.
expiración /ekspira'θion; ekspira'sion/ *n. f.* expiration.
expirar /ekspi'rar/ *v.* expire.
explanación /eksplana'θion; eksplana'sion/ *n. f.* explanation.
explanar /ekspla'nar/ *v.* make level.
expletivo /eksple'tiβo/ *n.* & *a.* expletive.
explicable /ekspli'kaβle/ *a.* explicable.
explicación /eksplika'θion; eksplika'sion/ *n. f.* explanation.
explicar /ekspli'kar/ *v.* explain.
explicativo /eksplika'tiβo/ *a.* explanatory.
explícitamente /ekspliθita'mente; eksplisita'mente/ *adv.* explicitly.
explícito /eks'pliθito; eksplisito/ *adj.* explicit.
exploración /eksplora'θion; eksplorasion/ *n. f.* exploration.
explorador /eksplora'ðor/ **-ra** *n.* explorer; scout.
explorar /eksplo'rar/ *v.* explore; scout.
exploratorio /eksplora'torio/ *a.* exploratory.
explosión /eksplo'sion/ *n. f.* explosion; outburst.

explosivo /eksplo'siβo/ *a. & m.* explosive.

explotación /eksplota'θion; eksplota'sion/ *n. f.* exploitation.

explotar /eksplo'tar/ *v.* exploit.

exponer /ekspo'ner/ *v.* expose; set forth.

exportación /eksporta'θion; eksporta'sion/ *n. f.* exportation; export.

exportador /eksporta'ðor/ **-ra** *n.* exporter.

exportar /ekspor'tar/ *v.* export.

exposición /eksposi'θion; eksposi'sion/ *n. f.* exhibit; exposition; exposure.

expósito /eks'posito/ **-ta** *n.* foundling; orphan.

expresado /ekspre'saðo/ *a.* aforesaid.

expresamente /ekspresa'mente/ *adv.* clearly, explicitly.

expresar /ekspre'sar/ *v.* express.

expresión /ekspre'sion/ *n. f.* expression.

expresivo /ekspre'siβo/ *a.* expressive; affectionate.

expreso /eks'preso/ *a. & m.* express.

exprimidera de naranjas /eksprimi'ðera de na'ranhas/ *n. f.* orange squeezer.

exprimir /ekspri'mir/ *v.* squeeze.

expropiación /ekspropia'θion; ekspropia'sion/ *n. f.* expropriation.

expropiar /ekspro'piar/ *v.* expropriate.

expulsar /ekspul'sar/ *v.* expel, eject; evict.

expulsión /ekspul'sion/ *n. f.* expulsion.

expurgación /ekspurga'θion; ekspurga'sion/ *n. f.* expurgation.

expurgar /ekspur'gar/ *v.* expurgate.

exquisitamente /ekskisita'mente/ *adv.* exquisitely.

exquisito /eks'kisito/ *a.* exquisite.

éxtasis /'ekstasis/ *n. m.* ecstasy.

extemporáneo /ekstempo'raneo/ *a.* extemporaneous, impromptu.

extender /eksten'der/ *v.* extend; spread; widen; stretch.

extensamente /ekstensa'mente/ *adv.* extensively.

extensión /eksten'sion/ *n. f.* extension, spread, expanse.

extenso /eks'tenso/ *a.* extensive, widespread.

extenuación /ekstenua'θion; ekstenua'sion/ *n. f.* weakening; emaciation.

extenuar /ekste'nuar/ *v.* extenuate.

exterior /ekste'rior/ *a. & m.* exterior; foreign.

exterminar /ekstermi'nar/ *v.* exterminate.

exterminio /ekster'minio/ *n. m.* extermination, ruin.

extinción /ekstin'θion; ekstin'sion/ *n. f.* extinction.

extinguir /ekstiŋ'guir/ *v.* extinguish.

extinto /eks'tinto/ *a.* extinct.

extintor /ekstin'tor/ *n. m.* fire extinguisher.

extirpar /ekstir'par/ *v.* eradicate.

extorsión /ekstor'sion/ *n. f.* extortion.

extra /'ekstra/ *n.* extra.

extracción /ekstrak'θion; ekstrak'sion/ *n. f.* extraction.

extractar /ekstrak'tar/ *v.* summarize.

extracto /eks'trakto/ *n. m.* extract; summary.

extradición /ekstraði'θion; ekstraði'sion/ *n. f.* extradition.

extraer /ekstra'er/ *v.* extract.

extranjero /ekstran'hero/ **-ra** *n.* **1.** foreign. —*n.* **2.** foreigner; stranger.

extrañar /ekstra'ɲar/ *v.* surprise; miss.

extraño /eks'traɲo/ *a.* strange, queer.

extraordinariamente /ɛkstraorðinaria'mente/ *adv.* extraordinarily.

extraordinario /ekstraorði'nario/ *a.* extraordinary.

extravagancia /ekstraβa'ganθia; ekstraβa'gansia/ *n. f.* extravagance.

extravagante /ekstraβa'gante/ *a.* extravagant.

extraviado /ekstra'βiaðo/ *a.* lost, misplaced.

extraviarse /ekstra'βiarse/ *v.* stray, get lost.

extravío /ekstra'βio/ *n. m.* misplacement; aberration, deviation.

extremadamente /ekstremaða'mente/ *adv.* extremely.

extremado /ekstre'maðo/ *a.* extreme.

extremaunción /ekstremaun'θion; ekstremaun'sion/ *n. f.* extreme unction.

extremidad /ekstremi'ðað/ *n. f.* extremity.

extremista /ekstre'mista/ *n. & a.* extremist.

extremo /eks'tremo/ *a. & m.* extreme, end.

extrínseco /ekstrin'seko/ *a.* extrinsic.

exuberancia /eksuβe'ranθia; eksuβeransia/ *n. f.* exuberance.

exuberante /eksuβe'rante/ *a.* exuberant.

exudación /eksuða'θion; eksuða'sion/ *n. f.* exudation.

exudar /eksu'ðar/ *v.* exude, ooze.

exultación /eksulta'θion; eksulta'sion/ *n. f.* exultation.

eyaculación /eyakula'θion; eyakula'sion/ *n. f.* ejaculation.

eyacular /eyaku'lar/ *v.* ejaculate.

eyección /eyek'θion; eyek'sion/ *n. f.* ejection.

eyectar /eyek'tar/ *v.* eject.

F

fábrica /'faβrika/ *n. f.* factory.

fabricación /faβrika'θion; faβrika'sion/ *n. f.* manufacture, manufacturing.

fabricante /faβri'kante/ *n. m. & f.* manufacturer, maker.

fabricar /faβri'kar/ *v.* manufacture, make.

fabril /fa'βril/ *a.* manufacturing, industrial.

fábula /'faβula/ *n. f.* fable, myth.

fabuloso /faβu'loso/ *a.* fabulous.

facción /fak'θion; fak'sion/ *n. f.* faction, party; (*pl.*) features.

faccioso /fak'θioso; fak'sioso/ *a.* factious.

fachada /fa'tʃaða/ *n. f.* façade, front.

fácil /'faθil; 'fasil/ *a.* easy.

facilidad /faθili'ðað; fasili'ðað/ *n. f.* facility, ease.

facilitar /faθili'tar; fasili'tar/ *v.* facilitate, make easy.

fácilmente /,faθil'mente/ ,fasil'mente/ *adv.* easily.

facsímile /fak'simile/ *n. m.* facsimile.

factible /fak'tiβle/ *a.* feasible.

factor /fak'tor/ *n. m.* factor.

factótum /fak'totum/ *n. m.* factotum; jack of all trades.

factura /fak'tura/ *n. f.* invoice, bill.

facturar /faktu'rar/ *v.* bill; check (baggage).

facultad /fakulta'ð/ *n. f.* faculty; ability.

facultativo /fakulta'tiβo/ *a.* optional.

faena /fa'ena/ *n. f.* task; work.

faisán /fai'san/ *n. m.* pheasant.

faja /'faha/ *n. f.* band; sash; zone.

falacia /fa'laθia; fa'lasia/ *n. f.* fallacy; deceitfulness.

falda /'falda/ *n. f.* skirt; lap.

falibilidad /faliβili'ðað/ *n. f.* fallibility.

falla /'faʎa; faya/ *n. f.* failure; fault.

fallar /fa'ʎar; fa'yar/ *v.* fail.

fallecer /faʎe'θer; faye'ser/ *v.* pass away, die.

fallo /'faʎo; 'fayo/ *n. m.* verdict; shortcoming.

falsear /false'ar/ *v.* falsify, counterfeit; forge.

falsedad /false'ðað/ *n. f.* falsehood; lie; falseness.

falsificación /falsifika'θion; falsifika'sion/ *n. f.* falsification; forgery.

falsificar /falsifi'kar/ *v.* falsify, counterfeit, forge.

falso /'falso/ *a.* false; wrong.

falta /'falta/ *n. f.* error, mistake; fault; lack. **hacer f.,** to be lacking, to be necessary. **sin f.,** without fail.

faltar /fal'tar/ *v.* be lacking, be missing; be absent.

faltriquera /faltri'kera/ *n. f.* pocket.

fama /'fama/ *n. f.* fame; reputation; glory.

familia /fa'milia/ *n. f.* family; household.

familiar /fami'liar/ *a.* familiar; domestic; (of) family.

familiaridad /familiari'ðað/ *n. f.* familiarity, intimacy.

familiarizar /familiari'θar; familiari'sar/ *v.* familiarize, acquaint.

famoso /fa'moso/ *a.* famous.

fanal /fa'nal/ *n. m.* lighthouse; lantern, lamp.

fanático /fa'natiko/ **-ca** *a. & n.* fanatic.

fanatismo /fana'tismo/ *n. m.* fanaticism.

fanfarria /fan'farria/ *n. f.* bluster. —**fanfarrear,** *v.*

fango /'faŋgo/ *n. m.* mud.

fantasía /fanta'sia/ *n. f.* fantasy; fancy, whim.

fantasma /fan'tasma/ *n. m.* phantom; ghost.

fantástico /fan'tastiko/ *a.* fantastic.

faquín /fa'kin/ *n. m.* porter.

faquir /fa'kir/ *n. m.* fakir.

farallón /fara'ʎon; fara'yon/ *n. m.* cliff.

Faraón /fara'on/ *n. m.* Pharaoh.

fardel /far'ðel/ *n. m.* bag; package.

fardo /far'ðo/ *n. m.* bundle.

farináceo /fari'naθeo; fari'naseo/ *a.* farinaceous.

faringe /fa'rinhe/ *n. f.* pharynx.

fariseo /fari'seo/ *n. m.* pharisee, hypocrite.

farmacéutico /farma'θeutiko; farma'seutiko/ **-ca** *a.* **1.** pharmaceutical. —*n.* **2.** pharmacist.

farmacia /far'maθia; far'masia/ *n. f.* pharmacy.

faro /'faro/ *n. m.* beacon; lighthouse; headlight.

farol /fa'rol/ *n. m.* lantern; (street) light, street lamp.

farra /'farra/ *n. f.* spree.

fárrago /'farrago/ *n. m.* medley; hodgepodge.

farsa /'farsa/ *n. f.* farce.

fascinación /fasθina'θion; fassina'sion/ *n. f.* fascination.

fascinar /fasθi'nar; fassi'nar/ *v.* fascinate, bewitch.

fase /'fase/ *n. f.* phase.

fastidiar /fasti'ðiar/ *v.* disgust; irk, annoy.

fastidio /fasti'ðio/ *n. m.* disgust; annoyance.

fastidioso /fasti'ðioso/ *a.* annoying; tedious.

fasto /'fasto/ *a.* happy, fortunate.

fatal /fa'tal/ *a.* fatal.

fatalidad /fatali'ðað/ *n. f.* fate; calamity, bad luck.

fatalismo /fata'lismo/ *n. m.* fatalism.

fatalista /fata'lista/ *n. & a.* fatalist.

fatiga /fa'tiga/ *n. f.* fatigue. —**fatigar,** *v.*

fauna /'fauna/ *n. f.* fauna.

fauno /'fauno/ *n. m.* faun.

favor /fa'βor/ *n. m.* favor; behalf. **por f.,** please.

¡Favor! Puh-lease!

favorable /faβo'raβle/ *a.* favorable.

favorablemente /faβoraβle'mente/ *adv.* favorably.

favorecer /faβore'θer; faβore'ser/ *v.* favor; flatter.

favoritismo /faβori'tismo/ *n. m.* favoritism.

favorito /faβo'rito/ **-ta** *a. & n.* favorite.

fax /faks/ *n. m.* fax.

faz /faθ/ *n. f.* face.

fe /fe/ *n. f.* faith.

fealdad /feal'dað/ *n. f.* ugliness, homeliness.

febrero /fe'βrero/ *n. m.* February.

febril /fe'βril/ *a.* feverish.

fecha /'fetʃa/ *n. f.* date. —**fechar,** *v.*

fecha de caducidad /'fetʃa de kaðuθi'ðað; 'fetʃa de kaðusi'ðað/ expiration date.

fécula /'fekula/ *n. f.* starch.

fecundar /fekun'dar/ *v.* fertilize.

fecundidad /fekundi'ðað/ *n. f.* fecundity, fertility.

fecundo /fe'kundo/ *a.* fecund, fertile.

federación /feðera'θion; feðera'sion/ *n. f.* federation.

federal /feðe'ral/ *a.* federal.

felicidad /feliθi'ðað; felisi'ðað/ *n. f.* happiness; bliss.

felicitación /feliθita'θion; felisita'sion/ *n. f.* congratulation.

felicitar /feliθi'tar; felisi'tar/ *v.* congratulate.

feligrés /feli'gres/ **-esa** *n.* parishioner.

feliz /fe'liθ; fe'lis/ *a.* happy; fortunate.

felón /fe'lon/ *n. m.* felon.

felonía /felo'nia/ *n. f.* felony.

felpa /'felpa/ *n. f.* plush.

felpudo /fel'puðo/ *n. m.* doormat.

femenino /feme'nino/ *a.* feminine.

feminismo /femi'nismo/ *n. m.* feminism.

feminista /femi'nista/ *n. m. & f.* feminist.

fenecer /fene'θer; fene'ser/ *v.* conclude; die.

fénix /'feniks/ *n. m.* phoenix; model.

fenomenal /fenome'nal/ *a.* phenomenal.

fenómeno /fe'nomeno/ *n. m.* phenomenon.

feo /'feo/ *a.* ugly, homely.

feracidad /feraθi'ðað; ferasi'ðað/ *n. f.* feracity, fertility.

feraz /'feraθ; 'feras/ *a.* fertile, fruitful; copious.

feria /'feria/ *n. f.* fair; market.

feriado /fe'riaðo/ *a.* **día f.,** holiday.

fermentación /fermenta'θion; fermenta'sion/ *n. f.* fermentation.

fermento /fer'mento/ *n. m.* ferment. —**fermentar,** *v.*

ferocidad /feroθi'ðað; ferosi'ðað/ *n. f.* ferocity, fierceness.

feroz /fe'roθ; fe'ros/ *a.* ferocious, fierce.

férreo /'ferreo/ *a.* of iron.

ferrería /ferre'ria/ *n. f.* ironworks.

ferretería /ferrete'ria/ *n. f.* hardware; hardware store.

ferrocarril /ferroka'rril/ *n. m.* railroad.

fértil /'fertil/ *a.* fertile.

fertilidad /fertili'ðað/ *n. f.* fertility.

fertilizar /fertili'θar; fertili'sar/ *v.* fertilize.

férvido /'ferβiðo/ *a.* fervid, ardent.

ferviente /fer'βiente/ *a.* fervent.

fervor /fer'βor/ *n. m.* fervor, zeal.

fervoroso /ferβo'roso/ *a.* zealous, eager.

festejar /feste'har/ *v.* entertain, fete.

festejo /feste'ho/ *n. m.* feast.

festín /fes'tin/ *n. m.* feast.

festividad /festiβi'ðað/ *n. f.* festivity.

festivo /fes'tiβo/ *a.* festive.

fétido /'fetiðo/ *adj.* fetid.

feudal /feu'ðal/ *a.* feudal.

feudo /'feuðo/ *n. m.* fief; manor.

fiado /'fiaðo, al/ *adj.* on trust, on credit.

fiambrera /fiam'brera/ *n. f.* lunch box.

fianza /'fianθa; 'fiansa/ *n. f.* bail.

fiar /fi'ar/ *v.* trust, sell on credit; give credit.

fiarse de /'fiarse de/ *v.* trust (in), rely on.

fiasco /'fiasko/ *n. m.* fiasco.
fibra /'fiβra/ *n. f.* fiber; vigor.
fibroso /fi'βroso/ *a.* fibrous.
ficción /fik'θion; fik'sion/ *n. f.* fiction.
ficha /'fitʃa/ *n. f.* slip, index card; chip.
fichero /fi'tʃero/ *n. m.* computer file, filing cabinet, card catalog.
ficticio /fik'tiθio; fik'tisio/ *a.* fictitious.
fidedigno /fiðe'ðigno/ *a.* trustworthy.
fideicomisario /fiðeikomi'sario/ **-ria** *n.* trustee.
fideicomiso /fiðeiko'miso/ *n. m.* trust.
fidelidad /fiðeli'ðað/ *n. f.* fidelity.
fideo /fi'ðeo/ *n. m.* noodle.
fiebre /'fieβre/ *n. f.* fever.
fiebre del heno /'fieβre del 'eno/ hayfever.
fiel /fiel/ *a.* faithful.
fieltro /'fieltro/ *n. m.* felt.
fiera /'fiera/ *n. f.* wild animal.
fiereza /fie'reθa; fie'resa/ *n. f.* fierceness, wildness.
fiero /'fiero/ *a.* fierce; wild.
fiesta /'fiesta/ *n. f.* festival, feast; party.
figura /fi'gura/ *n. f.* figure. **—figurar,** *v.*
figurarse /figu'rarse/ *v.* imagine.
figurón /figu'ron/ *n. m.* dummy.
fijar /fi'har/ *v.* fix; set, establish; post.
fijarse en /fi'harse en/ *v.* notice.
fijeza /fi'heθa; fi'hesa/ *n. f.* firmness.
fijo /'fiho/ *a.* fixed, stationary, permanent, set.
fila /'fila/ *n. f.* row, rank, file, line.
filantropía /filantro'pia/ *n. f.* philanthropy.
filatelia /fila'telia/ *n. f.* philately, stamp collecting.
filete /fi'lete/ *n. m.* fillet; steak.
film /film/ *n. m.* film. **—filmar,** *v.*
filo /'filo/ *n. m.* (cutting) edge.
filón /fi'lon/ *n. m.* vein (of ore).
filosofía /filoso'fia/ *n. f.* philosophy.
filosófico /filo'sofiko/ *a.* philosophical.
filósofo /fi'losofo/ **-fa** *n.* philosopher.
filtro /'filtro/ *n. m.* filter. **—filtrar,** *v.*
fin /fin/ *n. m.* end, purpose, goal. **a f. de que,** in order that. **en f.,** in short. **por f.,** finally, at last.
final /fi'nal/ *a.* **1.** final. **—***n.* **2.** *m.* end.
finalidad /finali'ðað/ *n. f.* finality.
finalmente /final'mente/ *adv.* at last.
financiero /finan'θiero; finan'siero/ **-ra** *a.* **1.** financial. **—***n.* **2.** financier.
finca /'finka/ *n. f.* real estate; estate; farm.
finés /fi'nes/ **-esa** *a.* & *n.* Finnish; Finn.
fineza /fi'neθa; fi'nesa/ *n. f.* courtesy, politeness; fineness.
fingimiento /finhi'miento/ *n. m.* pretense.
fingir /fin'hir/ *v.* feign, pretend.
fino /'fino/ *a.* fine; polite, courteous.
firma /'firma/ *n. f.* signature; *Com.* firm.
firmamento /firma'mento/ *n. m.* firmament, heavens.
firmar /fir'mar/ *v.* sign.
firme /'firme/ *a.* firm, fast, steady, sound.
firmemente /firme'mente/ *adv.* firmly.
firmeza /fir'meθa; fir'mesa/ *n. f.* firmness.
fisco /'fisko/ *n. m.* exchequer, treasury.
física /'fisika/ *n. f.* physics.
físico /'fisiko/ **-ca** *a.* & *n.* physical; physicist.
fisiología /fisiolo'hia/ *n. f.* physiology.
fláccido /'flakθiðo; 'flaksiðo/ *a.* flaccid, soft.
flaco /'flako/ *a.* thin, gaunt.
flagelación /flahela'θion; flahela'sion/ *n. f.* flagellation.
flagelar /flahe'lar/ *v.* flagellate, whip.
flagrancia /fla'granθia; fla'gransia/ *n. f.* flagrancy.
flagrante /fla'grante/ *a.* flagrant.
flama /'flama/ *n. f.* flame; ardor, zeal.
flamante /fla'mante/ *a.* flaming.
flamenco /fla'menko/ *n. m.* flamingo.
flan /flan/ *n. m.* custard.
flanco /'flanko/ *n. m.* side; *Mil.* flank.
flanquear /flanke'ar/ *v.* flank.
flaqueza /fla'keθa; fla'kesa/ *n. f.* thinness; weakness.
flauta /'flauta/ *n. f.* flute.
flautín /flau'tin/ *n. m.* piccolo.
flautista /flau'tista/ *n. m.* & *f.* flutist, piper.
flecha /'fletʃa/ *n. f.* arrow.
flechazo /fle'tʃaθo; fle'tʃaso/ *n. m.* love at first sight.
flechero /fle'tʃero/ **-ra** *n.* archer.
fleco /'fleko/ *n. m.* fringe; flounce.
flema /'flema/ *n. f.* phlegm.
flemático /fle'matiko/ *a.* phlegmatic.
flequillo /fle'kiʎo; fle'kiyo/ *n. m.* fringe; bangs (of hair).
flete /'flete/ *n. m.* freight. **—fletar,** *v.*
flexibilidad /fleksiβili'ðað/ *n. f.* flexibility.
flexible /fle'ksiβle/ *a.* flexible, pliable.
flirtear /flirte'ar/ *v.* flirt.
flojo /'floho/ *a.* limp; loose, flabby, slack.
flor /flor/ *n. f.* flower; compliment.
flora /'flora/ *n. f.* flora.
floral /flo'ral/ *a.* floral.
florecer /flore'θer; flore'ser/ *v.* flower, bloom; flourish.
floreo /flo'reo/ *n. m.* flourish.
florero /flo'rero/ *n. m.* flower pot; vase.
floresta /flo'resta/ *n. f.* forest.
florido /flo'riðo/ *a.* flowery; flowering.
florista /flo'rista/ *n. m.* & *f.* florist.
flota /'flota/ *n. f.* fleet.
flotante /flo'tante/ *a.* floating.
flotar /flo'tar/ *v.* float.
flotilla /flo'tiʎa; flo'tiya/ *n. f.* flotilla, fleet.
fluctuación /fluktua'θion; fluktua'sion/ *n. f.* fluctuation.
fluctuar /fluktu'ar/ *v.* fluctuate.
fluente /'fluente/ *a.* fluent; flowing.
fluidez /flui'ðeθ; flui'ðes/ *n. f.* fluency.
flúido /'fluiðo/ *a.* & *m.* fluid, liquid.
fluir /flu'ir/ *v.* flow.
flujo /'fluho/ *n. m.* flow, flux.
fluor /'fluor/ *n. m.* fluorine.
fluorescencia /fluores'θenθia; fluores'sensia/ *n. f.* fluorescence.
fluorescente /fluores'θente; fluores'sente/ *a.* fluorescent.
fobia /'foβia/ *n. f.* phobia.
foca /'foka/ *n. f.* seal.
foco /'foko/ *n. m.* focus, center; floodlight.
fogata /fo'gata/ *n. f.* bonfire.
fogón /fo'gon/ *n. m.* hearth, fireplace.
fogosidad /fogosi'ðað/ *n. f.* vehemence, ardor.
fogoso /fo'goso/ *a.* vehement, ardent.
folclore /fol'klore/ *n. m.* folklore.
follaje /fo'ʎahe; fo'yahe/ *n. m.* foliage.
folleto /fo'ʎeto; fo'yeto/ *n. m.* pamphlet, booklet.
follón /fo'ʎon; fo'yon/ *n. m.* mess, chaos.
fomentar /fomen'tar/ *v.* develop, promote, further, foster.
fomento /fo'mento/ *n. m.* fomentation.
fonda /'fonda/ *n. f.* eating house, inn.
fondo /'fondo/ *n. m.* bottom; back (part); background; (*pl.*) funds; finances. **a f.,** thoroughly.
fonética /fo'netika/ *n. f.* phonetics.
fonético /fo'netiko/ *a.* phonetic.
fonógrafo /fo'nografo/ *n. m.* phonograph.
fontanero /fonta'nero/ **-era** *n.* plumber.
forastero /foras'tero/ **-ra** *a.* **1.** foreign, exotic. **—***n.* **2.** stranger.
forjar /for'har/ *v.* forge.
forma /'forma/ *n. f.* form, shape. **—formar,** *v.*
formación /forma'θion; forma'sion/ *n. f.* formation.
formal /for'mal/ *a.* formal.
formaldehido /formalde'iðo/ *n. m.* formaldehyde.
formalidad /formali'ðað/ *n. f.* formality.
formalizar /formali'θar; formali'sar/ *v.* finalize; formulate.
formidable /formi'ðaβle/ *a.* formidable.
formidablemente /formiðaβle'mente/ *adv.* formidably.
formón /for'mon/ *n. m.* chisel.
fórmula /'formula/ *n. f.* formula.
formular /formu'lar/ *v.* formulate, draw up.
formulario /formu'lario/ *n. m.* form.
foro /'foro/ *n. m.* forum.
forrado /fo'rraðo/ *a.* stuffed; *Colloq.* filthy rich.
forraje /fo'rrahe/ *n. m.* forage, fodder.
forrar /fo'rrar/ *v.* line.
forro /'forro/ *n. m.* lining; condom.
fortalecer /fortale'θer; fortale'ser/ *v.* fortify.
fortaleza /forta'leθa; forta'lesa/ *n. f.* fort, fortress; fortitude.
fortificación /fortifika'θion; fortifika'sion/ *n. f.* fortification.
fortitud /forti'tuð/ *n. f.* fortitude.
fortuitamente /fortuita'mente/ *adv.* fortuitously.
fortuito /for'tuito/ *a.* fortuitous.
fortuna /for'tuna/ *n. f.* fortune; luck.
forúnculo /fo'runkulo/ *n. m.* boil.
forzar /for'θar; for'sar/ *v.* force, compel, coerce.
forzosamente /forθosa'mente; forsosa'mente/ *adv.* compulsorily; forcibly.
forzoso /for'θoso; for'soso/ *a.* compulsory; necessary. **paro f.,** unemployment.
forzudo /for'θuðo; for'suðo/ *a.* powerful, vigorous.
fosa /'fosa/ *n. f.* grave; pit.
fósforo /'fosforo/ *n. m.* match; phosphorus.
fósil /'fosil/ *n. m.* fossil.
foso /'foso/ *n. m.* ditch, trench; moat.
fotocopia /foto'kopia/ *n. f.* photocopy.
fotocopiadora /fotokopia'ðora/ *n. f.* photocopier.
fotografía /fotogra'fia/ *n. f.* photograph; photography. **—fotografiar,** *v.*
frac /frak/ *n. m.* dress coat.
fracasar /fraka'sar/ *v.* fail.
fracaso /fra'kaso/ *n. m.* failure.
fracción /frak'θion; frak'sion/ *n. f.* fraction.
fractura /frak'tura/ *n. f.* fracture, break.
fragancia /fra'ganθia; fra'gansia/ *n. f.* fragrance; perfume; aroma.
fragante /fra'gante/ *a.* fragrant.
frágil /'frahil/ *a.* fragile, breakable.
fragilidad /frahili'ðað/ *n. f.* fragility.
fragmentario /fragmen'tario/ *a.* fragmentary.
fragmento /frag'mento/ *n. m.* fragment, bit.
fragor /fra'gor/ *n. m.* noise, clamor.
fragoso /fra'goso/ *a.* noisy.
fragua /'fragua/ *n. f.* forge. **—fraguar,** *v.*
fraile /'fraile/ *n. m.* monk.
frambuesa /fram'buesa/ *n. f.* raspberry.
francamente /franka'mente/ *adv.* frankly, candidly.
francés /fran'θes; fran'ses/ **-esa** *a.* & *n.* French; Frenchman, Frenchwoman.
Francia /'franθia; 'fransia/ *n. f.* France.
franco /'franko/ *a.* frank.
franela /fra'nela/ *n. f.* flannel.
frangible /fraŋ'giβle/ *a.* breakable.
franqueo /fran'keo/ *n. m.* postage.
franqueza /fran'keθa; fran'kesa/ *n. f.* frankness.
franquicia /fran'kiθia; fran'kisia/ *n. f.* franchise.
frasco /'frasko/ *n. m.* flask, bottle.
frase /'frase/ *n. f.* phrase; sentence.
fraseología /fraseolo'hia/ *n. f.* phraseology; style.
fraternal /frater'nal/ *a.* fraternal, brotherly.
fraternidad /fraterni'ðað/ *n. f.* fraternity, brotherhood.
fraude /'frauðe/ *n. m.* fraud.
fraudulento /frauðu'lento/ *a.* fraudulent.
frazada /fra'θaða; fra'saða/ *n. f.* blanket.
frecuencia /fre'kuenθia; fre'kuensia/ *n. f.* frequency.
frecuente /fre'kuente/ *a.* frequent.
frecuentemente /frekuente'mente/ *adv.* frequently, often.
fregadero /frega'ðero/ *n. m.* sink.
fregadura /frega'ðura/ *n. f.* scouring, scrubbing.
fregar /fre'gar/ *v.* scour, scrub, mop.
fregona /fre'gona/ *n. f.* mop.
freír /fre'ir/ *v.* fry.
fréjol /'frehol/ *n. m.* kidney bean.
frenazo /fre'naθo; fre'naso/ *n. m.* sudden braking, slamming on the brakes.
frenesí /frene'si/ *n. m.* frenzy.
frenéticamente /fre'netikamente/ *adv.* frantically.
frenético /fre'netiko/ *a.* frantic, frenzied.
freno /'freno/ *n. m.* brake. **—frenar,** *v.*
freno de auxilio /'freno de auk'silio/ emergency brake.
freno de mano /'freno de 'mano/ hand brake.
frente /'frente/ *n.* **1.** *f.* forehead. **2.** *m.* front. **en f., al f.,** opposite, across. **f. a,** in front of.
fresa /'fresa/ *n. f.* strawberry.
fresca /'freska/ *n. f.* fresh, cool air.
fresco /'fresko/ *a.* fresh; cool; crisp.
frescura /fres'kura/ *n. f.* coolness, freshness.
fresno /'fresno/ *n. m.* ash tree.
fresquería /freske'ria/ *n. f.* soda fountain.
friabilidad /friaβili'ðað/ *n. f.* brittleness.
friable /'friaβle/ *a.* brittle.
frialdad /frial'dað/ *n. f.* coldness.
fríamente /fria'mente/ *adv.* coldly; coolly.
fricandó /'frikando/ *n. m.* fricandeau.
fricar /fri'kar/ *v.* rub together.
fricción /frik'θion; frik'sion/ *n. f.* friction.
friccionar /frikθio'nar; friksio'nar/ *v.* rub.
friega /'friega/ *n. f.* friction; massage.
frigidez /frihi'ðeθ; frihi'ðes/ *n. f.* frigidity.
frígido /'frihiðo/ *a.* frigid.
frijol /fri'hol/ *n. m.* bean.
frío /'frio/ *a.* & *n.* cold. **tener f.,** to be cold, feel cold. **hacer f.,** to be cold (weather).
friolento /frio'lento/ **friolero** *a.* chilly; sensitive to cold.
friolera /frio'lera/ *n. f.* trifle, trinket.
friso /'friso/ *n. m.* frieze.
fritillas /fri'tiʎas; fri'tiyas/ *n. f.pl.* fritters.
frito /'frito/ *a.* fried.
fritura /fri'tura/ *n. f.* fritter.
frívolamente /'friβolamente/ *adv.* frivolously.
frivolidad /friβoli'ðað/ *n. f.* frivolity.
frívolo /'friβolo/ *a.* frivolous.
frondoso /fron'doso/ *a.* leafy.
frontera /fron'tera/ *n. f.* frontier; border.
frotar /fro'tar/ *v.* rub.

fructífero /fruk'tifero/ *a.* fruitful.
fructificar /fruktifi'kar/ *v.* bear fruit.
fructuosamente /fruktuosa'mente/ *adv.* fruitfully.
fructuoso /fruk'tuoso/ *a.* fruitful.
frugal /fru'gal/ *a.* frugal; thrifty.
frugalidad /frugali'ðað/ *n. f.* frugality; thrift.
frugalmente /frugal'mente/ *adv.* frugally, thriftily.
fruncir /frun'θir; frun'sir/ *v.* gather, contract. **f. el entrecejo,** frown.
fruslería /frusle'ria/ *n. f.* trinket.
frustrar /frus'trar/ *v.* frustrate, thwart.
fruta /'fruta/ *n. f.* fruit.
frutería /frute'ria/ *n. f.* fruit store.
fruto /'fruto/ *n. m.* fruit; product; profit.
fucsia /'fuksia/ *n. f.* fuchsia.
fuego /'fuego/ *n. m.* fire.
fuelle /'fueʎe; 'fueye/ *n. m.* bellows.
fuente /'fuente/ *n. f.* fountain; source; platter.
fuera /'fuera/ *adv.* without, outside.
fuero /'fuero/ *n. m.* statute.
fuerte /'fuerte/ *a.* **1.** strong; loud. —*n.* **2.** *m.* fort.
fuertemente /fuerte'mente/ *adv.* strongly; loudly.
fuerza /'fuerθa; 'fuersa/ *n. f.* force, strength.
fuga /'fuga/ *n. f.* flight, escape.
fugarse /fu'garse/ *v.* flee, escape.
fugaz /fu'gaθ; fu'gas/ *a.* fugitive, passing.
fugitivo /fuhi'tiβo/ **-va** *a. & n.* fugitive.
fulano /fu'lano/ **-na** Mr., Mrs. so-and-so.
fulcro /'fulkro/ *n. m.* fulcrum.
fulgor /ful'gor/ *n. m.* gleam, glow. —**fulgurar,** *v.*
fulminante /fulmi'nante/ *a.* explosive.
fumador /fuma'ðor/ **-ra** *n.* smoker.
fumar /fu'mar/ *v.* smoke.
fumigación /fumiga'θion; fumiga'sion/ *n. f.* fumigation.
fumigador /fumiga'ðor/ **-ra** *n.* fumigator.
fumigar /fumi'gar/ *v.* fumigate.
fumoso /fu'moso/ *a.* smoky.
función /fun'θion; fun'sion/ *n. f.* function; performance, show.
funcionar /funθio'nar; funsio'nar/ *v.* function; work, run.
funcionario /funθio'nario; funsio'nario/ **-ria** *n.* official, functionary.
funda /'funda/ *n. f.* case, sheath, slipcover.
fundación /funda'θion; funda'sion/ *n. f.* foundation.
fundador /funda'ðor/ **-ra** *n.* founder.
fundamental /funda'mental/ *a.* fundamental, basic.
fundamentalmente /fundamental'mente/ *adv.* fundamentally.
fundamento /funda'mento/ *n. m.* base, basis, foundation.
fundar /fun'dar/ *v.* found, establish.
fundición /fundi'θion; fundi'sion/ *n. f.* foundry; melting; meltdown.
fundir /fun'dir/ *v.* fuse; smelt.
fúnebre /'funeβre/ *a.* dismal.
funeral /fune'ral/ *n. m.* funeral.
funeraria /fune'raria/ *n. f.* funeral home, funeral parlor.
funestamente /funesta'mente/ *adv.* sadly.
fungo /'fungo/ *n. m.* fungus.
furente /fu'rente/ *a.* furious, enraged.
furgoneta /furgo'neta/ *n. f.* van.
furia /'furia/ *n. f.* fury.
furiosamente /furiosa'mente/ *adv.* furiously.
furioso /fu'rioso/ *a.* furious.
furor /fu'ror/ *n. m.* furor; fury.
furtivamente /furtiβa'mente/ *adv.* furtively.
furtivo /fur'tiβo/ *a.* furtive, sly.
furúnculo /fu'runkulo/ *n. m.* boil.
fusibilidad /fusiβili'ðað/ *n. f.* fusibility.

fusible /fu'siβle/ *n. m.* fuse.
fusil /fu'sil/ *n. m.* rifle, gun.
fusilar /fusi'lar/ *v.* shoot, execute.
fusión /fu'sion/ *n. f.* fusion; merger.
fusionar /fusio'nar/ *v.* unite, fuse, merge.
fútbol /'futβol/ *n. m.* football, soccer.
fútil /'futil/ *a.* trivial.
futilidad /futili'ðað/ *n. f.* triviality.
futuro /fu'turo/ *a. & m.* future.
futurología /futurolo'hia/ *n. f.* futurology.

G

gabán /ga'βan/ *n. m.* overcoat.
gabardina /gaβar'ðina/ *n. f.* raincoat.
gabinete /gaβi'nete/ *n. m.* closet; cabinet; study.
gacela /ga'θela; ga'sela/ *n. f.* gazelle.
gaceta /ga'θeta; ga'seta/ *n. f.* gazette, newspaper.
gacetilla /gaθe'tiʎa; gase'tiya/ *n. f.* personal news section of a newspaper.
gaélico /ga'eliko/ *a.* Gaelic.
gafas /'gafas/ *n. f.pl.* eyeglasses.
gaguear /gage'ar/ *v.* stutter, stammer.
gaita /'gaita/ *n. f.* bagpipes.
gaje /'gahe/ *n. m.* salary; fee.
gala /'gala/ *n. f.* gala, ceremony; (*pl.*) regalia. **tener a g.,** be proud of.
galán /ga'lan/ *n. m.* gallant.
galano /ga'lano/ *a.* stylishly dressed; elegant.
galante /ga'lante/ *a.* gallant.
galantería /galante'ria/ *n. f.* gallantry, compliment.
galápago /ga'lapago/ *n. m.* freshwater turtle.
galardón /galar'ðon/ *n. m.* prize; reward.
gáleo /'galeo/ *n. m.* swordfish.
galera /ga'lera/ *n. f.* wagon; shed; galley.
galería /gale'ria/ *n. f.* gallery, *Theat.* balcony.
galés /'gales/ **-esa** *a. & n.* Welsh; Welshman, Welshwoman.
galgo /'galgo/ *n. m.* greyhound.
galillo /ga'liʎo; ga'liyo/ *n. m.* uvula.
galimatías /galima'tias/ *n. m.* gibberish.
gallardete /gaʎar'ðete; gayar'ðete/ *n. m.* pennant.
galleta /ga'ʎeta; ga'yeta/ *n. f.* cracker.
gallina /ga'ʎina; ga'yina/ *n. f.* hen.
gallinero /gaʎi'nero; gayi'nero/ *n. m.* chicken coop.
gallo /ga'ʎo; ga'yo/ *n. m.* rooster.
galocha /ga'lotʃa/ *n. f.* galosh.
galón /ga'lon/ *n. m.* gallon; *Mil.* stripe.
galope /ga'lope/ *n. m.* gallop. —**galopar,** *v.*
galopín /galo'pin/ *n. m.* ragamuffin, urchin (child).
gamba /'gamba/ *n. f.* prawn.
gamberro /gam'βerro/ **-ra** *n.* hooligan.
gambito /gam'bito/ *n. m.* gambit.
gamuza /ga'muθa; ga'musa/ *n. f.* chamois.
gana /'gana/ *n. f.* desire, wish, mind (to). **de buena g.,** willingly. **tener ganas de,** to feel like.
ganado /ga'naðo/ *n. m.* cattle.
ganador /gana'ðor/ **-ra** *n.* winner.
ganancia /ga'nanθia; ga'nansia/ *n. f.* gain, profit; (*pl.*) earnings.
ganapán /gana'pan/ *n. m.* drudge.
ganar /ga'nar/ *v.* earn; win; beat.
ganchillo /gan'tʃiʎo; gan'tʃiyo/ *n. m.* crochet work.
gancho /'gantʃo/ *n. m.* hook, hanger, clip, hairpin.
gandul /gan'dul/ **-la** *n.* idler, tramp, hobo.
ganga /'ganga/ *n. f.* bargain.
gangrena /gan'grena/ *n. f.* gangrene.
gansarón /gansa'ron/ *n. m.* gosling.

ganso /'ganso/ *n. m.* goose.
garabato /gara'βato/ *n. m.* hook; scrawl, scribble.
garaje /ga'rahe/ *n. m.* garage.
garantía /garan'tia/ *n. f.* guarantee; collateral, security.
garantizar /garanti'θar; garanti'sar/ *v.* guarantee, secure, pledge.
garbanzo /gar'βanθo; gar'βanso/ *n. m.* chickpea.
garbo /'garβo/ *n. m.* grace.
garboso /gar'βoso/ *a.* graceful, sprightly.
gardenia /gar'ðenia/ *n. f.* gardenia.
garfa /'garfa/ *n. f.* claw, talon.
garganta /gar'ganta/ *n. f.* throat.
gárgara /'gargara/ *n. f.* gargle. —**gargarizar,** *v.*
garita /ga'rita/ *n. f.* sentry box.
garito /ga'rito/ *n. m.* gambling house.
garlopa /gar'lopa/ *n. f.* carpenter's plane.
garra /'garra/ *n. f.* claw.
garrafa /ga'rrafa/ *n. f.* decanter, carafe.
garrideza /garri'ðeθa; garri'ðesa/ *n. f.* elegance, handsomeness.
garrido /ga'rriðo/ *a.* elegant, handsome.
garrote /ga'rrote/ *n. m.* club, cudgel.
garrotillo /garro'tiʎo; garro'tiyo/ *n. m.* croup.
garrudo /ga'rruðo/ *a.* powerful, brawny.
garza /'garθa; 'garsa/ *n. f.* heron.
gas /gas/ *n. m.* gas.
gasa /'gasa/ *n. f.* gauze.
gaseosa /gase'osa/ *n. f.* carbonated water.
gaseoso /gase'oso/ *a.* gaseous.
gasolina /gaso'lina/ *n. f.* gasoline.
gasolinera /gasoli'nera/ *n. f.* gas station.
gastar /gas'tar/ *v.* spend; use up, wear out; waste.
gastritis /gas'tritis/ *n. f.* gastritis.
gastrómano /gas'tromano/ *n. m.* glutton.
gastrónomo /gas'tronomo/ **-ma** *n.* gourmet, epicure, gastronome.
gatear /gate'ar/ *v.* creep.
gatillo /ga'tiʎo; ga'tiyo/ *n. m.* trigger.
gato /'gato/ **-ta** *n.* cat.
gaucho /'gautʃo/ *n. m.* Argentine cowboy.
gaveta /ga'βeta/ *n. f.* drawer.
gavilla /ga'βiʎa; ga'βiya/ *n. f.* sheaf.
gaviota /ga'βiota/ *n. f.* seagull.
gayo /'gayo/ *a.* merry, gay.
gayola /ga'yola/ *n. f.* cage; *Colloq.* prison.
gazapera /gaθa'pera; gasa'pera/ *n. f.* rabbit warren.
gazapo /ga'θapo; ga'sapo/ *n. m.* rabbit.
gazmoñada /gaθmo'ɲaða; gasmo'ɲaða/ *n. f.* prudishness.
gazmoño /gaθ'moɲo; gas'moɲo/ *n. m.* prude.
gaznate /gaθ'nate; gas'nate/ *n. m.* windpipe.
gazpacho /gaθ'patʃo; gas'patʃo/ *n. m.* cold tomato soup; gazpacho.
gelatina /hela'tina/ *n. f.* gelatine.
gemelo /he'melo/ **-la** *n.* twin.
gemelos /he'melos/ *n. m.pl.* cuff links; opera glasses; **-as,** twins.
gemido /he'miðo/ *n. m.* moan, groan, wail. —**gemir,** *v.*
genciana /hen'θiana; hen'siana/ *n. f.* gentian.
genealogía /henealo'hia/ *n. f.* genealogy, pedigree.
generación /henera'θion; henera'sion/ *n. f.* generation.
generador /henera'ðor/ *n. m.* generator.
general /hene'ral/ *a. & m.* general.
generalidad /henerali'ðað/ *n. f.* generality.
generalización /heneraliθa'θion; heneralisa'sion/ *n. f.* generalization.

generalizar /henerali'θar; henerali'sar/ *v.* generalize.
generalmente /heneral'mente/ *adv.* generally.
género /'henero/ *n.* **1.** *m.* gender; kind. **2.** (*pl.*) goods, material.
generosidad /henerosi'ðað/ *n. f.* generosity.
generoso /hene'roso/ *a.* generous.
génesis /'henesis/ *n. m.* genesis.
genético /he'netiko/ *a.* genetic.
genial /he'nial/ *a.* genial; brilliant.
genio /'henio/ *n. m.* genius; temper; disposition.
genitivo /heni'tiβo/ *n. m.* genitive.
genocidio /heno'θiðio; heno'siðio/ *n. m.* genocide.
gente /'hente/ *n. f.* people, folk.
gentil /hen'til/ *a.* gracious; graceful.
gentileza /henti'leθa; henti'lesa/ *n. f.* grace, graciousness.
gentío /hen'tio/ *n. m.* mob, crowd.
genuino /he'nuino/ *a.* genuine.
geografía /heogra'fia/ *n. f.* geography.
geográfico /heo'grafiko/ *a.* geographical.
geométrico /heo'metriko/ *a.* geometric.
geranio /he'ranio/ *n. m.* geranium.
gerencia /he'renθia; he'rensia/ *n. f.* management.
gerente /he'rente/ *n. m. & f.* manager, director.
germen /'hermen/ *n. m.* germ.
germinar /hermi'nar/ *v.* germinate.
gerundio /he'rundio/ *n. m.* gerund.
gesticulación /hestikula'θion; hestikula'sion/ *n. f.* gesticulation.
gesticular /hestiku'lar/ *v.* gesticulate, gesture.
gestión /hes'tion/ *n. f.* conduct; effort; action.
gesto /'hesto/ *n. m.* gesture, facial expression.
gigante /hi'gante/ *a. & n.* gigantic, giant.
gigantesco /higan'tesko/ *a.* gigantic, huge.
gilipollas /gili'poʎas; gili'poyas/ *n. m. & f. Colloq.* fool, idiot.
gimnasio /him'nasio/ *n. m.* gymnasium.
gimnástica /him'nastika/ *n. f.* gymnastics.
gimotear /himote'ar/ *v.* whine.
ginebra /hi'neβra/ *n. f.* gin.
ginecólogo /hine'kologo/ **-ga** gynecologist.
gira /'hira/ *n. f.* tour, trip.
girado /hi'raðo/ **-da** *n. Com.* drawee.
girador /hira'ðor/ **-ra** *n. Com.* drawer.
girar /hi'rar/ *v.* revolve, turn, spin, whirl.
giratorio /hira'torio/ *a.* rotary, revolving.
giro /'hiro/ *n. m.* whirl, turn, spin; *Com.* draft. **g. postal,** money order.
gitano /hi'tano/ **-na** *a. & n.* Gypsy.
glacial /gla'θial; gla'sial/ *a.* glacial, icy.
glaciar /gla'θiar; gla'siar/ *n. m.* glacier.
gladiador /glaðia'ðor/ *n. m.* gladiator.
glándula /'glandula/ *n. f.* gland.
glándula endocrina /'glandula endo'krina/ endocrine gland.
glándula pituitaria /'glandula pitui'taria/ pituitary gland.
glándula prostática /'glandula pros'tatika/ prostate gland.
glasé /gla'se/ *n. m.* glacé.
glicerina /gliθe'rina; glise'rina/ *n. f.* glycerine.
globo /'gloβo/ *n. m.* globe; balloon.
gloria /'gloria/ *n. f.* glory.
glorieta /glo'rieta/ *n. f.* bower.
glorificación /glorifika'θion; glorifika'sion/ *n. f.* glorification.
glorificar /glorifi'kar/ *v.* glorify.
glorioso /glo'rioso/ *a.* glorious.

glosa /'glosa/ n. f. gloss. **—glosar,** v.

glosario /glo'sario/ n. m. glossary.

glotón /glo'ton/ **-ona** a. & n. gluttonous; glutton.

glucosa /glu'kosa/ n. f. glucose.

gluten /'gluten/ n. m. gluten; glue.

gobernación /goβerna'θion; goβerna'sion/ n. f. government.

gobernador /goβerna'ðor/ **-ra** n. governor.

gobernalle /goβer'naʎe; goβer'naye/ n. m. rudder, tiller, helm.

gobernante /goβer'nante/ n. m. & f. ruler.

gobernar /goβer'nar/ v. govern.

gobierno /go'βierno/ n. m. government.

goce /'goθe; 'gose/ n. m. enjoyment.

gola /'gola/ n. f. throat.

golf /golf/ n. m. golf.

golfista /gol'fista/ n. m. & f. golfer.

golfo /'golfo/ n. m. gulf.

gollete /go'ʎete; go'yete/ n. m. upper portion of one's throat.

golondrina /golon'drina/ n. f. swallow.

golosina /golo'sina/ n. f. delicacy.

goloso /go'loso/ a. sweet-toothed.

golpe /'golpe/ n. m. blow, stroke. **de g.,** suddenly.

golpear /golpe'ar/ v. strike, beat, pound.

goma /'goma/ n. f. rubber; gum; glue; eraser.

góndola /'gondola/ n. f. gondola.

gordo /'gorðo/ a. fat.

gordura /gor'ðura/ n. f. fatness.

gorila /go'rila/ n. m. gorilla.

gorja /'gorha/ n. f. gorge.

gorjeo /gor'heo/ n. m. warble, chirp. **—gorjear,** v.

gorrión /go'rrion/ n. m. sparrow.

gorro /'gorro/ n. m. cap.

gota /'gota/ n. f. drop (of liquid).

gotear /gote'ar/ v. drip, leak.

goteo /go'teo/ n. m. leak.

gotera /go'tera/ n. f. leak; gutter.

gótico /'gotiko/ a. Gothic.

gozar /go'θar; go'sar/ v. enjoy.

gozne /'goθne; 'gosne/ n. m. hinge.

gozo /'goθo; 'goso/ n. m. enjoyment, delight, joy.

gozoso /go'θoso; go'soso/ a. joyful, joyous.

grabado /gra'βaðo/ n. **1.** m. engraving, cut, print. **—a. 2.** recorded.

grabador /graβa'ðor/ n. m. engraver.

grabadora /graβa'ðora/ n. f. tape recorder.

grabar /gra'βar/ v. engrave; record.

gracia /'graθia; 'grasia/ n. f. grace; wit, charm. **hacer g.,** to amuse, strike as funny. **tener g.,** to be funny, to be witty.

gracias /'graθias; 'grasias/ n. f.pl. thanks, thank you.

gracioso /gra'θioso; gra'sioso/ a. witty, funny.

grada /'graða/ n. f. step.

gradación /graða'θion; graða'sion/ n. f. gradation.

grado /'graðo/ n. m. grade; rank; degree.

graduado /gra'ðuaðo/ **-da** n. graduate.

gradual /gra'ðual/ a. gradual.

graduar /gra'ðuar/ v. grade; graduate.

gráfico /'grafiko/ a. graphic, vivid.

grafito /gra'fito/ n. m. graphite.

grajo /'graho/ n. m. jackdaw.

gramática /gra'matika/ n. f. grammar.

gramo /'gramo/ n. m. gram.

gran /gran/ **grande** a. big, large; great.

granada /gra'naða/ n. f. grenade; pomegranate.

granar /gra'nar/ v. seed.

grandes almacenes /'grandes alma'θenes; 'grandes alma'senes/ n. m.pl. department store.

grandeza /gran'deθa; gran'desa/ n. f. greatness.

grandiosidad /grandiosi'ðað/ n. f. grandeur.

grandioso /gran'dioso/ a. grand, magnificent.

grandor /gran'dor/ n. m. size.

granero /gra'nero/ n. m. barn; granary.

granito /gra'nito/ n. m. granite.

granizada /grani'θaða; grani'saða/ n. f. hailstorm.

granizo /gra'niθo; gra'niso/ n. m. hail. **—granizar,** v.

granja /'granha/ n. f. grange; farm; farmhouse.

granjear /granhe'ar/ v. earn, gain; get.

granjero /gran'hero/ **-era** n. farmer.

grano /'grano/ n. m. grain; kernel.

granuja /gra'nuha/ n. m. waif, urchin.

grapa /'grapa/ n. f. clamp, clip.

grapadora /grapa'ðora/ n. f. stapler.

grasa /'grasa/ n. f. grease, fat.

grasiento /gra'siento/ a. greasy.

gratificación /gratifika'θion; gratifika'sion/ n. f. gratification; reward; tip.

gratificar /gratifi'kar/ v. gratify; reward; tip.

gratis /'gratis/ adv. gratis, free.

gratitud /grati'tuð/ n. f. gratitude.

grato /'grato/ a. grateful; pleasant.

gratuito /gra'tuito/ a. gratuitous; free.

gravamen /gra'βamen/ n. m. tax; burden; obligation.

grave /'graβe/ a. grave, serious, severe.

gravedad /graβe'ðað/ n. f. gravity, seriousness.

gravitación /graβita'θion; graβita'sion/ n. f. gravitation.

gravitar /graβi'tar/ v. gravitate.

gravoso /gra'βoso/ a. burdensome.

graznido /gra'θniðo; gras'niðo/ n. m. croak. **—graznar,** v.

Grecia /'greθia; 'gresia/ n. f. Greece.

greco /'greko/ **-ca** a. & n. Greek.

greda /'greða/ n. f. clay.

gresca /'greska/ n. f. revelry; quarrel.

griego /'griego/ **-ga** a. & n. Greek.

grieta /'grieta/ n. f. opening; crevice, crack.

grifo /'grifo/ n. m. faucet.

grillo /'griʎo; 'griyo/ n. m. cricket.

grima /'grima/ n. f. fright.

gringo /'gringo/ **-ga** n. foreigner (usually North American).

gripa /'gripa/ **gripe** n. f. grippe.

gris /gris/ a. gray.

grito /'grito/ n. m. shout, scream, cry. **—gritar,** v.

grosella /gro'seʎa; gro'seya/ n. f. currant.

grosería /grose'ria/ n. f. grossness; coarseness.

grosero /gro'sero/ a. coarse, vulgar; discourteous.

grotesco /gro'tesko/ a. grotesque.

grúa /'grua/ n. f. crane; tow truck.

gruesa /'gruesa/ n. f. gross.

grueso /'grueso/ a. **1.** bulky; stout; coarse, thick. **—n. 2.** m. bulk.

grulla /'gruʎa/ n. f. crane.

gruñido /gru'niðo/ n. m. growl, snarl, mutter. **—gruñir,** v.

grupo /'grupo/ n. m. group, party.

gruta /'gruta/ n. f. cavern.

guacamol /guaka'mol/ **guacamole** n. m. avocado sauce; guacamole.

guadaña /gua'ðaɲa/ n. f. scythe. **—guadañar,** v.

guagua /'guagua/ n. f. (S.A.) baby; (Carib.) bus.

gualdo /'gualdo/ n. m. yellow, golden.

guano /'guano/ n. m. guano (fertilizer).

guante /'guante/ n. m. glove.

guantera /guan'tera/ n. f. glove compartment.

guapo /'guapo/ a. handsome.

guarda /'guarða/ n. m. or f. guard.

guardabarros /guarða'βarros/ n. m. fender.

guardacostas /guarða'kostas/ n. m. revenue ship.

guardaespaldas /,guarðaes'paldas/ n. m. & f. bodyguard.

guardameta /guarða'meta/ n. m. & f. goalkeeper.

guardar /guar'ðar/ v. keep, store, put away; guard.

guardarropa /guarða'rropa/ n. f. coat room.

guardarse de /guar'ðarse de/ v. beware of, avoid.

guardia /'guarðia/ n. **1.** f. guard; watch. **—n. 2.** m. policeman.

guardián /guar'ðian/ **-na** n. guardian, keeper, watchman.

guardilla /guar'ðiʎa; guar'ðiya/ n. f. attic.

guarida /gua'riða/ n. f. den.

guarismo /gua'rismo/ n. m. number, figure.

guarnecer /guarne'θer; guarne'ser/ v. adorn.

guarnición /guarni'θion; guarni'sion/ n. f. garrison; trimming.

guasa /'guasa/ n. f. joke, jest.

guayaba /gua'yaβa/ n. f. guava.

gubernativo /guβerna'tiβo/ a. governmental.

guerra /'gerra/ n. f. war.

guerrero /ge'rrero/ **-ra** n. warrior.

guía /'gia/ n. **1.** m. & f. guide. **2.** f. guidebook, directory.

guiar /giar/ v. guide; steer, drive.

guija /'giha/ n. f. pebble.

guillotina /giʎo'tina; giyo'tina/ n. f. guillotine.

guindar /gin'dar/ v. hang.

guinga /'ginga/ n. f. gingham.

guiñada /gi'ɲaða/ n. f., **guiño,** m. wink. **—guiñar,** v.

guión /gi'on/ n. m. dash, hyphen; script.

guirnalda /gir'nalda/ n. f. garland, wreath.

guisa /'gisa/ n. f. guise, manner.

guisado /gi'saðo/ n. m. stew.

guisante /gi'sante/ n. m. pea.

guisar /gi'sar/ v. cook.

guiso /'giso/ n. m. stew.

guita /'gita/ n. f. twine.

guitarra /gi'tarra/ n. f. guitar.

guitarrista /gita'rrista/ n. m. & f. guitarist.

gula /'gula/ n. f. gluttony.

gurú /gu'ru/ n. m. guru.

gusano /gu'sano/ n. m. worm, caterpillar.

gustar /gus'tar/ v. please; taste.

gustillo /gus'tiʎo; gus'tiyo/ n. m. aftertaste, slight pleasure.

gusto /'gusto/ n. m. pleasure; taste; liking.

gustoso /gus'toso/ a. pleasant; tasteful.

gutural /gutu'ral/ a. guttural.

H

haba /'aβa/ n. f. bean.

habanera /aβa'nera/ n. f. Cuban dance melody.

haber /a'βer/ v. have. **h. de,** be to, be supposed to.

haberes /a'βeres/ n. m.pl. property; worldly goods.

habichuela /aβi'tʃuela/ n. f. bean.

hábil /'aβil/ a. skillful; capable; clever.

habilidad /aβili'ðað/ n. f. ability; skill; talent.

habilidoso /aβili'ðoso/ a. able, skillful, talented.

habilitado /aβili'taðo/ **-da** n. paymaster.

habilitar /aβili'tar/ v. qualify; supply, equip.

hábilmente /'aβilmente/ adv. ably.

habitación /aβita'θion; aβita'sion/ n. f. dwelling; room. **h. individual,** single room.

habitante /aβi'tante/ n. m. & f. inhabitant.

habitar /aβi'tar/ v. inhabit; dwell.

hábito /'aβito/ n. m. habit; custom.

habitual /aβi'tual/ a. habitual.

habituar /aβi'tuar/ v. accustom, habituate.

habla /'aβla/ n. f. speech.

hablador /aβla'ðor/ a. talkative.

hablar /a'βlar/ v. talk, speak.

haca /'aka/ n. f. pony.

hacedor /aθe'ðor; ase'ðor/ n. m. maker.

hacendado /aθen'daðo; asen'daðo/ **-da** n. hacienda owner; farmer.

hacendoso /aθen'doso; asen'doso/ a. industrious.

hacer /a'θer; a'ser/ v. do; make. **hace dos años,** etc., two years ago, etc.

hacerse /a'θerse; a'serse/ v. become, get to be.

hacha /'atʃa/ n. f. ax, hatchet.

hacia /'aθia; 'asia/ prep. toward.

hacienda /a'θienda; a'sienda/ n. f. property; estate; ranch; farm; Govt. treasury.

hada /'aða/ n. f. fairy.

hado /'aðo/ n. m. fate.

halagar /ala'gar/ v. flatter.

halar /a'lar/ v. haul, pull.

halcón /al'kon/ n. m. hawk, falcon.

haleche /a'letʃe/ n. m. anchovy.

hallado /a'ʎaðo; a'yaðo/ a. found. **bien h.,** welcome. **mal h.,** uneasy.

hallar /a'ʎar; a'yar/ v. find, locate.

hallarse /a'ʎarse; a'yarse/ v. be located; happen to be.

hallazgo /a'ʎaθgo; a'yasgo/ n. m. find, thing found.

hamaca /a'maka/ n. f. hammock.

hambre /'ambre/ n. f. hunger. **tener h., estar con h.,** to be hungry.

hambrear /ambre'ar/ v. hunger; starve.

hambriento /am'briento/ a. starving, hungry.

hamburguesa /ambur'gesa/ n. f. beefburger, hamburger.

haragán /ara'gan/ **-na** n. idler, lazy person.

haraganear /aragane'ar/ v. loiter.

harapo /a'rapo/ n. m. rag, tatter.

haraposo /ara'poso/ a. ragged, shabby.

harén /a'ren/ n. m. harem.

harina /a'rina/ n. f. flour, meal.

harnero /ar'nero/ n. m. sieve.

hartar /ar'tar/ v. satiate.

harto /'arto/ a. stuffed; fed up.

hartura /ar'tura/ n. f. superabundance, glut.

hasta /'asta/ prep. **1.** until, till; as far as, up to. **h. luego,** good-bye, so long. **—adv. 2.** even.

hastío /as'tio/ n. m. distaste, loathing.

hato /'ato/ n. m. herd.

hay /ai/ v. there is, there are. **h. que,** it is necessary to. **no h. de qué,** you're welcome, don't mention it.

haya /'aya/ n. f. beech tree.

haz /aθ/ n. m. bundle, sheaf; face.

hazaña /a'θaɲa; a'saɲa/ n. f. deed; exploit, feat.

hebdomadario /eβðoma'ðario/ a. weekly.

hebilla /e'βiʎa; e'βiya/ n. f. buckle.

hebra /'eβra/ n. f. thread, string.

hebreo /e'βreo/ **-rea** a. & n. Hebrew.

hechicero /etʃi'θero; etʃi'sero/ **-ra** n. wizard, witch.

hechizar /etʃi'θar; etʃi'sar/ v. bewitch.

hechizo /e'tʃiθo; e'tʃiso/ n. m. spell.

hecho /'etʃo/ n. m. fact; act; deed.

hechura /e'tʃura/ n. f. workmanship; make.

hediondez /eðion'deθ; eðion'des/ n. f. stench.

hégira /'ehira/ n. f. hegira.

helada /e'laða/ n. f. frost.

heladería /elaðe'ria/ n. f. ice-cream parlor.

helado /e'laðo/ n. m. ice cream.

helar /e'lar/ *v.* freeze.

helecho /e'letʃo/ *n. m.* fern.

hélice /'eliθe; 'elise/ *n. f.* propeller; helix.

helicóptero /eli'koptero/ *n. m.* helicopter.

helio /'elio/ *n. m.* helium.

hembra /'embra/ *n. f.* female.

hemisferio /emis'ferio/ *n. m.* hemisphere.

hemoglobina /emoglo'βina/ *n. f.* hemoglobin.

hemorragia /emo'rrahia/ *n. f.* hemorrhage.

hemorragia nasal /emo'rrahia na'sal/ nosebleed.

henchir /en'tʃir/ *v.* stuff.

hendedura /ende'ðura/ *n. f.* crevice, crack.

hendido /en'diðo/ *a.* cloven, cleft (lip).

heno /'eno/ *n. m.* hay.

hepática /e'patika/ *n. f.* liverwort.

hepatitis /epa'titis/ *n. f.* hepatitis.

heraldo /e'raldo/ *n. m.* herald.

herbáceo /er'βaθeo; er'βaseo/ *a.* herbaceous.

herbívoro /er'βiβoro/ *a.* herbivorous.

heredar /ere'ðar/ *v.* inherit.

heredero /ere'ðero/ **-ra** *n.* heir; successor.

hereditario /ereði'tario/ *a.* hereditary.

hereje /e'rehe/ *n. m. & f.* heretic.

herejía /ere'hia/ *n. f.* heresy.

herencia /e'renθia; e'rensia/ *n. f.* inheritance; heritage.

herético /e'retiko/ *a.* heretical.

herida /e'riða/ *n. f.* wound, injury.

herir /e'rir/ *v.* wound, injure.

hermafrodita /ermafro'ðita/ *a. & n.* hermaphrodite.

hermana /er'mana/ *n. f.* sister.

hermano /er'mano/ *n. m.* brother.

hermético /er'metiko/ *a.* airtight.

hermoso /er'moso/ *a.* beautiful, handsome.

hermosura /ermo'sura/ *n. f.* beauty.

hernia /'ernia/ *n. f.* hernia, rupture.

héroe /'eroe/ *n. m.* hero.

heroico /e'roiko/ *a.* heroic.

heroína /ero'ina/ *n. f.* heroine.

heroísmo /ero'ismo/ *n. m.* heroism.

herradura /erra'ðura/ *n. f.* horseshoe.

herramienta /erra'mienta/ *n. f.* tool; implement.

herrería /erre'ria/ *n. f.* blacksmith's shop.

herrero /e'rrero/ *n. m.* blacksmith.

herrumbre /e'rrumbre/ *n. f.* rust.

hertzio /'ertθio; 'ertsio/ *n. m.* hertz.

hervir /er'βir/ *v.* boil.

hesitación /esita'θion; esita'sion/ *n. f.* hesitation.

heterogéneo /etero'heneo/ *a.* heterogeneous.

heterosexual /eterosek'sual/ *a.* heterosexual.

hexagonal /eksago'nal/ *a.* hexagonal.

hexágono /e'ksagono/ *n. m.* hexagon.

hez /eθ; es/ *n. f.* dregs, sediment.

híbrido /'iβriðo/ **-da** *n. & a.* hybrid.

hidalgo /i'ðalgo/ **-ga** *a. & n.* noble.

hidalguía /iðal'gia/ *n. f.* nobility; generosity.

hidráulico /i'ðrauliko/ *a.* hydraulic.

hidroavión /iðroa'βion/ *n. m.* seaplane, hydroplane.

hidrofobia /iðro'foβia/ *n. f.* rabies.

hidrógeno /i'ðroheno/ *n. m.* hydrogen.

hidropesía /iðrope'sia/ *n. f.* dropsy.

hiedra /'ieðra/ *n. f.* ivy.

hiel /iel/ *n. f.* gall.

hielo /'ielo/ *n. m.* ice.

hiena /'iena/ *n. f.* hyena.

hierba /'ierβa/ *n. f.* grass; herb; marijuana.

hierbabuena /ierβa'βuena/ *n. f.* mint.

hierro /'ierro/ *n. m.* iron.

hígado /'igaðo/ *n. m.* liver.

higiene /i'hiene/ *n. f.* hygiene.

higiénico /i'hieniko/ *a.* sanitary, hygienic.

higo /'igo/ *n. m.* fig.

higuera /i'gera/ *n. f.* fig tree.

hija /'iha/ *n. f.* daughter.

hija adoptiva /'iha aðop'tiβa/ adopted daughter.

hijastro /i'hastro/ **-tra** *n.* stepchild.

hijo /'iho/ *n. m.* son.

hijo adoptivo /'iho aðop'tiβo/ *n. m.* adopted child, adopted son.

hila /'ila/ *n. f.* line.

hilandero /ilan'dero/ **-ra** *n.* spinner.

hilar /i'lar/ *v.* spin.

hilera /i'lera/ *n. f.* row, line, tier.

hilo /'ilo/ *n. m.* thread; string; wire; linen.

himno /'imno/ *n. m.* hymn.

hincar /in'kar/ *v.* drive, thrust; sink into.

hincarse /in'karse/ *v.* kneel.

hinchar /in'tʃar/ *v.* swell.

hindú /in'du/ *n. & a.* Hindu.

hinojo /i'noho/ *n. m.* knee.

hiperenlace /iperen'laθe, iperen'lase/ *n. m.* hyperlink.

hipermercado /ipermer'kaðo/ *n. m.* hypermarket.

hipertexto /iper'teksto/ *n. m.* hypertext.

hipnótico /ip'notiko/ *a.* hypnotic.

hipnotismo /ipno'tismo/ *n. m.* hypnotism.

hipnotista /ipno'tista/ *n. m. & f.* hypnotist.

hipnotizar /ipnoti'θar; ipnoti'sar/ *v.* hypnotize.

hipo /'ipo/ *n. m.* hiccough.

hipocresía /ipokre'sia/ *n. f.* hypocrisy.

hipócrita /i'pokrita/ *a. & n.* hypocritical; hypocrite.

hipódromo /i'poðromo/ *n. m.* race track.

hipoteca /ipo'teka/ *n. f.* mortgage. —**hipotecar**, *v.*

hipótesis /i'potesis/ *n. f.* hypothesis.

hirsuto /ir'suto/ *a.* hairy, hirsute.

hispano /is'pano/ *a.* Hispanic, Spanish American.

Hispanoamérica /ispanoa'merika/ *f.* Spanish America.

hispanoamericano /ispanoameri'kano/ **-na** *a. & n.* Spanish American.

histerectomía /isterekto'mia/ *n. f.* hysterectomy.

histeria /is'teria/ *n. f.* hysteria.

histérico /is'teriko/ *a.* hysterical.

historia /is'toria/ *n. f.* history; story.

historiador /istoria'ðor/ **-ra** *n.* historian.

histórico /is'toriko/ *a.* historic, historical.

histrión /is'trion/ *n. m.* actor.

hocico /o'θiko; o'siko/ *n. m.* snout, muzzle.

hogar /o'gar/ *n. m.* hearth; home.

hoguera /o'gera/ *n. f.* bonfire, blaze.

hoja /'oha/ *n. f.* leaf; sheet (of paper); pane; blade.

hoja de cálculo /'oha de 'kalkulo/ spreadsheet.

hoja de inscripción /'oha de inskrip'θion; 'oha de inskrip'sion/ entry blank.

hoja de pedidos /'oha de pe'ðiðos/ order blank.

hoja informativa /'oha informa'tiβa/ newsletter.

hojalata /oha'lata/ *n. f.* tin.

hojalatero /ohala'tero/ **-ra** *n.* tinsmith.

hojear /ohe'ar/ *v.* scan, skim through.

hola /'ola/ *interj.* hello.

Holanda /o'landa/ *n. f.* Holland, Netherlands.

holandés /olan'des/ **-esa** *a. & n.* Dutch; Hollander.

holganza /ol'ganθa; ol'gansa/ *n. f.* leisure; diversion.

holgazán /olga'θan; olga'san/ **-ana** *a.*

1. idle, lazy. —*n.* 2. *m.* idler, loiterer, tramp.

holgazanear /olgaθane'ar; olgasane'ar/ *v.* idle, loiter.

hollín /o'ʎin; o'yin/ *n. m.* soot.

holografía /ologra'fia/ *n. f.* holography.

holograma /olo'grama/ *n. m.* hologram.

hombre /'ombre/ *n. m.* man.

hombría /om'βria/ *n. f.* manliness.

hombro /'ombro/ *n. m.* shoulder.

hombruno /om'bruno/ *a.* mannish, masculine (woman).

homenaje /ome'nahe/ *n. m.* homage.

homeópata /ome'opata/ *n. m.* homeopath.

homicidio /omi'θiðio; omi'siðio/ *n. m.* homicide.

homilía /omi'lia/ *n. f.* homily.

homosexual /omose'ksual/ *a.* homosexual, gay.

honda /'onda/ *n. f.* sling.

hondo /'ondo/ *a.* deep.

hondonada /ondo'naða/ *n. f.* ravine.

hondura /on'dura/ *n. f.* depth.

honestidad /onesti'ðað/ *n. f.* modesty, unpretentiousness.

honesto /o'nesto/ *a.* honest; pure; just.

hongo /'oŋgo/ *n. m.* fungus; mushroom.

honor /o'nor/ *n. m.* honor.

honorable /ono'raβle/ *a.* honorable.

honorario /ono'rario/ *a.* 1. honorary. —*n.* 2. *m.* honorarium, fee.

honorífico /ono'rifiko/ *a.* honorary.

honra /'onra/ *n. f.* honor. —**honrar**, *v.*

honradez /onra'ðeθ; onra'ðes/ *n. f.* honesty.

honrado /on'raðo/ *a.* honest, honorable.

hora /'ora/ *n. f.* hour; time (of day).

horadar /ora'ðar/ *v.* perforate.

hora punta /'ora 'punta/ rush hour.

horario /o'rario/ *n. m.* timetable, schedule.

horca /'orka/ *n. f.* gallows; pitchfork.

horda /'orða/ *n. f.* horde.

horizontal /oriθon'tal; orison'tal/ *a.* horizontal.

horizonte /ori'θonte; ori'sonte/ *n. m.* horizon.

hormiga /or'miga/ *n. f.* ant.

hormiguear /ormige'ar/ *v.* itch.

hormiguero /ormi'gero/ *n. m.* ant hill.

hornero /or'nero/ **-ra** *n.* baker.

hornillo /or'niʎo; or'nijo/ *n. m.* stove.

horno /'orno/ *n. m.* oven; kiln.

horóscopo /o'roskopo/ *n. m.* horoscope.

horrendo /o'rrendo/ *a.* dreadful, horrendous.

horrible /o'rriβle/ *a.* horrible, hideous, awful.

hórrido /'orriðo/ *a.* horrid.

horror /o'rror/ *n. m.* horror.

horrorizar /orrori'θar; orrori'sar/ *v.* horrify.

horroroso /orro'roso/ *a.* horrible, frightful.

hortelano /orte'lano/ *n. m.* horticulturist.

hospedaje /ospe'ðahe/ *n. m.* lodging.

hospedar /ospe'ðar/ *v.* give or take lodgings.

hospital /ospi'tal/ *n. m.* hospital.

hospitalario /ospita'lario/ *a.* hospitable.

hospitalidad /ospitali'ðað/ *n. f.* hospitality.

hospitalmente /ospital'mente/ *adv.* hospitably.

hostia /'ostia/ *n. f.* host; *Colloq.* hit, blow.

hostil /os'til/ *a.* hostile.

hostilidad /ostili'ðað/ *n. f.* hostility.

hotel /o'tel/ *n. m.* hotel.

hoy /oi/ *adv.* today. **h. día, h. en día,** nowadays.

hoya /'oya/ *n. f.* dale, valley.

hoyo /'oyo/ *n. m.* pit, hole.

hoyuelo /o'yuelo/ *n. m.* dimple.

hoz /oθ; os/ *n. f.* sickle.

hucha /'utʃa/ *n. f.* chest, money box; savings.

hueco /'ueko/ *a.* 1. hollow, empty. —*n.* 2. *m.* hole, hollow.

huelga /'uelga/ *n. f.* strike.

huelgista /uel'hista/ *n. m. & f.* striker.

huella /'ueʎa; 'ueya/ *n. f.* track, trace; footprint.

huérfano /'uerfano/ **-na** *a. & n.* orphan.

huero /'uero/ *a.* empty.

huerta /'uerta/ *n. f.* (vegetable) garden.

huerto /'uerto/ *n. m.* orchard.

hueso /'ueso/ *n. m.* bone; fruit pit.

huésped /'uespeð/ *n. m. & f.* guest.

huesudo /ue'suðo/ *a.* bony.

huevo /'ueβo/ *n. m.* egg.

huída /'uiða/ *n. f.* flight, escape.

huir /uir/ *v.* flee.

hule /'ule/ *n. m.* oilcloth.

humanidad /umani'ðað/ *n. f.* humanity, mankind; humaneness.

humanista /uma'nista/ *n. m. & f.* humanist.

humanitario /umani'tario/ *a.* humane.

humano /u'mano/ *a.* human; humane.

humareda /uma'reða/ *n. f.* dense cloud of smoke.

humear /ume'ar/ *v.* emit smoke or steam.

humedad /ume'ðað/ *n. f.* humidity, moisture, dampness.

humedecer /umeðe'θer; umeðe'ser/ *v.* moisten, dampen.

húmedo /'umeðo/ *a.* humid, moist, damp.

humildad /umil'dað/ *n. f.* humility, meekness.

humilde /u'milde/ *a.* humble, meek.

humillación /umiʎa'θion; umiya'sion/ *n. f.* humiliation.

humillar /umi'ʎar; umi'yar/ *v.* humiliate.

humo /'umo/ *n. m.* smoke; (*pl.*) airs, affectation.

humor /u'mor/ *n. m.* humor, mood.

humorista /umo'rista/ *n. m. & f.* humorist.

hundimiento /undi'miento/ *n. m.* collapse.

hundir /un'dir/ *v.* sink; collapse.

húngaro /'uŋgaro/ **-ra** *a. & n.* Hungarian.

Hungría /uŋ'gria/ *n. f.* Hungary.

huracán /ura'kan/ *n. m.* hurricane.

huraño /u'raɲo/ *a.* shy, bashful.

hurgar /ur'gar/ *v.* stir.

hurón /u'ron/ *n. m.* ferret.

hurtadillas /urta'ðiʎas; urta'ðiyas/ *n. f.pl.* **a h.,** on the sly.

hurtador /urta'ðor/ **-ra** *n.* thief.

hurtar /ur'tar/ *v.* steal, rob of; hide.

hurtarse /ur'tarse/ *v.* hide; withdraw.

husmear /usme'ar/ *v.* scent, smell.

huso /'uso/ *n. m.* spindle; bobbin.

huso horario /'uso o'rario/ time zone.

I

ibérico /i'βeriko/ *a.* Iberian.

iberoamericano /iβeroameri'kano/ **-na** *a. & n.* Latin American.

ida /'iða/ *n. f.* departure; trip out. **i. y vuelta,** round trip.

idea /i'ðea/ *n. f.* idea.

ideal /i'ðeal/ *a. & m.* ideal.

idealismo /iðea'lismo/ *n. m.* idealism.

idealista /iðea'lista/ *n. m. & f.* idealist.

idear /iðe'ar/ *v.* plan, conceive.

idéntico /i'ðentiko/ *a.* identical.

identidad /iðenti'ðað/ *n. f.* identity; identification.

identificar /iðentifi'kar/ v. identify.

idilio /i'ðilio/ n. m. idyll.

idioma /i'ðioma/ n. m. language.

idiota /i'ðiota/ a. & n. idiotic; idiot.

idiotismo /iðio'tismo/ n. m. idiom; idiocy.

idolatrar /iðola'trar/ v. idolize, adore.

ídolo /'iðolo/ n. m. idol.

idóneo /i'ðoneo/ a. suitable, fit, apt.

iglesia /i'glesia/ n. f. church.

ignición /igni'θion; igni'sion/ n. f. ignition.

ignominia /igno'minia/ n. f. ignominy, shame.

ignominioso /ignomi'nioso/ a. ignominious, shameful.

ignorancia /igno'ranθia; igno'ransia/ n. f. ignorance.

ignorante /igno'rante/ a. ignorant.

ignorar /igno'rar/ v. be ignorant of, not know.

ignoto /ig'noto/ a. unknown.

igual /i'gual/ a. equal; the same; (pl.) alike. m. equal.

igualar /igua'lar/ v. equal; equalize; match.

igualdad /igual'dað/ n. f. equality; sameness.

ijada /i'haða/ n. f. flank (of an animal).

ilegal /ile'gal/ a. illegal.

ilegítimo /ile'hitimo/ a. illegitimate.

ileso /i'leso/ a. unharmed.

ilícito /i'liθito; i'lisito/ a. illicit, unlawful.

iluminación /ilumina'θion; ilumina'sion/ n. f. illumination.

iluminar /ilumi'nar/ v. illuminate.

ilusión /ilu'sion/ n. f. illusion.

ilusión de óptica /ilu'sion de 'optika/ optical illusion.

ilusorio /ilu'sorio/ a. illusive.

ilustración /ilustra'θion; ilustra'sion/ n. f. illustration; learning.

ilustrador /ilustra'ðor/ **-ra** n. illustrator.

ilustrar /ilus'trar/ v. illustrate.

ilustre /i'lustre/ a. illustrious, honorable, distinguished.

imagen /i'mahen/ n. f. image.

imaginación /imahina'θion; imahina'sion/ n. f. imagination.

imaginar /imahi'nar/ v. imagine.

imaginario /imahi'nario/ a. imaginary.

imaginativo /imahina'tiβo/ a. imaginative.

imán /i'man/ n. m. magnet; imam.

imbécil /im'beθil; im'besil/ a. & n. imbecile; stupid, foolish; fool.

imbuir /im'buir/ v. imbue, instil.

imitación /imita'θion; imita'sion/ n. f. imitation.

imitador /imita'ðor/ **-ra** n. imitator.

imitar /imi'tar/ v. imitate.

impaciencia /impa'θienθia; impa'siensia/ n. f. impatience.

impaciente /impa'θiente; impa'siente/ a. impatient.

impar /im'par/ a. unequal, uneven, odd.

imparcial /impar'θial; impar'sial/ a. impartial.

impasible /impa'siβle/ a. impassive, unmoved.

impávido /im'paβiðo/ adj. fearless, intrepid.

impedimento /impeði'mento/ n. m. impediment, obstacle.

impedir /impe'ðir/ v. impede, hinder, stop, obstruct.

impeler /impe'ler/ v. impel; incite.

impensado /impen'saðo/ a. unexpected.

imperar /impe'rar/ v. reign; prevail.

imperativo /impera'tiβo/ a. imperative.

imperceptible /imperθep'tiβle; impersep'tiβle/ a. imperceptible.

imperdible /imper'ðiβle/ n. m. safety pin.

imperecedero /impereθe'ðero; imperese'ðero/ a. imperishable.

imperfecto /imper'fekto/ a. imperfect, faulty.

imperial /impe'rial/ a. imperial.

imperialismo /imperia'lismo/ n. m. imperialism.

impericia /impe'riθia; impe'risia/ n. f. inexperience.

imperio /im'perio/ n. m. empire.

imperioso /impe'rioso/ a. imperious, domineering.

impermeable /imperme'aβle/ a. waterproof. m. raincoat.

impersonal /imperso'nal/ a. impersonal.

impertinencia /impertinen'θia; impertinen'sia/ n. f. impertinence.

ímpetu /'impetu/ n. m. impulse; impetus.

impetuoso /impe'tuoso/ a. impetuous.

impiedad /impie'ðað/ n. f. impiety.

impío /im'pio/ a. impious.

implacable /impla'kaβle/ a. implacable, unrelenting.

implicar /impli'kar/ v. implicate, involve.

implorar /implo'rar/ v. implore.

imponente /impo'nente/ a. impressive.

imponer /impo'ner/ v. impose.

impopular /impopu'lar/ a. unpopular.

importación /importa'θion; importa'sion/ n. f. importation, importing.

importador /importa'ðor/ **-ra** n. importer.

importancia /impor'tanθia; impor'tansia/ n. f. importance.

importante /impor'tante/ a. important.

importar /impor'tar/ v. be important, matter; import.

importe /im'porte/ n. m. value; amount.

importunar /importu'nar/ v. beg, importune.

imposibilidad /imposiβili'ðað/ n. f. impossibility.

imposibilitado /imposiβili'taðo/ a. helpless.

imposible /impo'siβle/ a. impossible.

imposición /imposi'θion; imposi'sion/ n. f. imposition.

impostor /impos'tor/ **-ra** n. imposter, faker.

impotencia /impo'tenθia; impo'tensia/ n. f. impotence.

impotente /impo'tente/ a. impotent.

imprecar /impre'kar/ v. curse.

impreciso /impre'θiso; impre'siso/ adj. inexact.

impregnar /impreg'nar/ v. impregnate.

imprenta /im'prenta/ n. f. press; printing house.

imprescindible /impresθin'diβle; impressin'diβle/ a. essential.

impresión /impre'sion/ n. f. impression.

impresionable /impresio'naβle/ a. impressionable.

impresionar /impresio'nar/ v. impress.

impresor /impre'sor/ n. m. printer.

imprevisión /impreβi'sion/ n. f. oversight; thoughtlessness.

imprevisto /impre'βisto/ a. unexpected, unforeseen.

imprimir /impri'mir/ v. print; imprint.

improbable /impro'βaβle/ a. improbable.

improbo /im'proβo/ a. dishonest.

improductivo /improðuk'tiβo/ a. unproductive.

improperio /impro'perio/ n. m. insult.

impropio /im'propio/ a. improper.

improvisación /improβisa'θion; improβisa'sion/ n. f. improvisation.

improvisar /improβi'sar/ v. improvise.

improviso /impro'βiso; impro'βisto/ a. unforeseen.

imprudencia /impru'ðenθia; impru'ðensia/ n. f. imprudence.

imprudente /impru'ðente/ a. imprudent, reckless.

impuesto /im'puesto/ n. m. tax.

impuesto sobre la renta /im'puesto soβre la 'rrenta/ income tax.

impulsar /impul'sar/ v. prompt, impel.

impulsivo /impul'siβo/ a. impulsive.

impulso /im'pulso/ n. m. impulse.

impureza /impu'reθa; impu'resa/ n. f. impurity.

impuro /im'puro/ a. impure.

imputación /imputa'θion; imputa'sion/ n. f. imputation.

imputar /impu'tar/ v. impute, attribute.

inaccesible /inakθe'siβle; inakse'siβle/ a. inaccessible.

inacción /inak'θion; inak'sion/ n. f. inaction; inactivity.

inaceptable /inaθep'taβle; inasep'taβle/ a. unacceptable.

inactivo /inak'tiβo/ a. inactive; sluggish.

inadecuado /inaðe'kuaðo/ a. inadequate.

inadvertencia /inaðβer'tenθia; inaðβer'tensia/ n. f. oversight.

inadvertido /inaðβer'tiðo/ a. inadvertent, careless; unnoticed.

inagotable /inago'taβle/ a. inexhaustible.

inalterado /inalte'raðo/ a. unchanged.

inanición /inani'θion; inani'sion/ n. f. starvation.

inanimado /inani'maðo/ adj. inanimate.

inapetencia /inape'tenθia; inape'tensia/ n. f. lack of appetite.

inaplicable /inapli'kaβle/ a. inapplicable; unfit.

inaudito /inau'ðito/ a. unheard of.

inauguración /inaugura'θion; inaugura'sion/ n. f. inauguration.

inaugurar /inaugu'rar/ v. inaugurate, open.

incandescente /inkandes'θente; inkandes'sente/ a. incandescent.

incansable /inkan'saβle/ a. tireless.

incapacidad /inkapaθi'ðað; inkapasi'ðað/ n. f. incapacity.

incapacitar /inkapaθi'tar; inkapasi'tar/ v. incapacitate.

incapaz /inka'paθ; inka'pas/ a. incapable.

incauto /in'kauto/ a. unwary.

incendiar /inθen'diar; insen'diar/ v. set on fire.

incendio /in'θendio; in'sendio/ n. m. fire; conflagration.

incertidumbre /inθerti'ðumbre; inserti'ðumbre/ n. f. uncertainty, suspense.

incesante /inθe'sante; inse'sante/ a. continual, incessant.

incidente /inθi'ðente; insi'ðente/ n. m. incident, event.

incienso /in'θienso; in'sienso/ n. m. incense.

incierto /in'θierto; in'sierto/ a. uncertain, doubtful.

incinerar /inθine'rar; insine'rar/ v. incinerate; cremate.

incisión /inθi'sion; insi'sion/ n. f. incision, cut.

incitamiento /inθita'miento; insita'miento/ n. m. incitement, motivation.

incitar /inθi'tar; insi'tar/ v. incite, instigate.

incivil /inθi'βil; insi'βil/ a. impolite, rude.

inclemencia /inkle'menθia; inkle'mensia/ n. f. inclemency.

inclemente /inkle'mente/ a. inclement, merciless.

inclinación /inklina'θion; inklina'sion/ n. f. inclination, bent; slope.

inclinar /inkli'nar/ v. incline; influence.

inclinarse /inkli'narse/ v. slope; lean, bend over; bow.

incluir /in'kluir/ v. include; enclose.

inclusivo /inklu'siβo/ a. inclusive.

incluso /in'kluso/ prep. including.

incógnito /in'kognito/ a. unknown.

incoherente /inkoe'rente/ a. incoherent.

incombustible /inkombus'tiβle/ a. fireproof.

incomible /inko'miβle/ a. inedible.

incomodar /inkomo'ðar/ v. disturb, bother, inconvenience.

incomodidad /inkomoði'ðað/ n. f. inconvenience.

incómodo /in'komoðo/ n. m. uncomfortable; cumbersome; inconvenient.

incomparable /inkompa'raβle/ a. incomparable.

incompatible /inkompa'tiβle/ a. incompatible.

incompetencia /inkompe'tenθia; inkompe'tensia/ n. f. incompetence.

incompetente /inkompe'tente/ a. incompetent.

incompleto /inkom'pleto/ a. incomplete.

incondicional /inkondiθio'nal; inkondisio'nal/ a. unconditional.

inconexo /inkone'kso/ a. incoherent; unconnected.

incongruente /inkoŋgru'ente/ a. incongruous.

inconsciencia /inkon'sθienθia; inkon'ssiensia/ n. f. unconsciousness.

inconsciente /inkon'sθiente; inkons'siente/ a. unconscious.

inconsecuencia /inkonse'kuenθia; inkonse'kuensia/ n. f. inconsistency.

inconsecuente /inkonse'kuente/ a. inconsistent.

inconsiderado /inkonsiðe'raðo/ a. inconsiderate.

inconstancia /inkons'tanθia; inkons'tansia/ n. f. changeableness.

inconstante /inkons'tante/ a. changeable.

inconveniencia /inkombe'nienθia; inkombe'niensia/ n. f. inconvenience; unsuitability.

inconveniente /inkombe'niente/ a. unsuitable. m. disadvantage; objection.

incorporar /inkorpo'rar/ v. incorporate, embody.

incorporarse /inkorpo'rarse/ v. sit up.

incorrecto /inko'rrekto/ a. incorrect, wrong.

incredulidad /inkreðuli'ðað/ n. f. incredulity.

incrédulo /in'kreðulo/ a. incredulous.

increíble /inkre'iβle/ a. incredible.

incremento /inkre'mento/ n. m. increase.

incubadora /inkuβa'ðora/ n. f. incubator.

incubar /inku'βar/ v. hatch.

inculto /in'kulto/ a. uncultivated.

incumplimento de contrato /inkumpli'mento de kon'trato/ n. m. breach of contract.

incurable /inku'raβle/ a. incurable.

incurrir /inku'rrir/ v. incur.

indagación /indaga'θion; indaga'sion/ n. f. investigation, inquiry.

indagador /indaga'ðor/ **-ra** n. investigator.

indagar /inda'gar/ v. investigate, inquire into.

indebido /inde'βiðo/ a. undue.

indecencia /inde'θenθia; inde'sensia/ n. f. indecency.

indecente /inde'θente; inde'sente/ a. indecent.

indeciso /inde'θiso; inde'siso/ a. undecided.

indefenso /inde'fenso/ a. defenseless.

indefinido /indefi'niðo/ a. indefinite; undefined.

indeleble /inde'leβle/ a. indelible.

indemnización de despido /indem-

niθa'θion de des'piðo; indemnisa'sion de des'piðo/ *n. f.* severance pay.
indemnizar /indemni'θar; indemni'sar/ *v.* indemnify.
independencia /indepen'denθia; independ'ensia/ *n. f.* independence.
independiente /indepen'diente/ *a.* independent.
indesmallable /indesma'ʎaβle; indesma'yaβle/ *a.* runproof.
India /'india/ *n. f.* India.
indicación /indika'θion; indika'sion/ *n. f.* indication.
indicar /indi'kar/ *v.* indicate, point out.
indicativo /indika'tiβo/ *a.* & *m.* indicative.
índice /'indiθe; 'indise/ *n. m.* index; forefinger.
índice de materias /'indiθe de ma'terias; 'indise de ma'terias/ table of contents.
indicio /in'diθio; in'disio/ *n. m.* hint, clue.
indiferencia /indife'renθia; indife'rensia/ *n. f.* indifference.
indiferente /indife'rente/ *a.* indifferent.
indígena /in'dihena/ *a.* & *n.* native.
indigente /indi'hente/ *a.* indigent, poor.
indignación /indigna'θion; indigna'sion/ *n. f.* indignation.
indignado /indig'naðo/ *a.* indignant, incensed.
indignar /indig'nar/ *v.* incense.
indigno /in'digno/ *a.* unworthy.
indio /'indio/ **-dia** *a.* & *n.* Indian.
indirecto /indi'rekto/ *a.* indirect.
indiscreción /indiskre'θion; indiskre'sion/ *n. f.* indiscretion.
indiscreto /indis'kreto/ *a.* indiscreet.
indiscutible /indisku'tiβle/ *a.* unquestionable.
indispensable /indispen'saβle/ *a.* indispensable.
indisposición /indisposi'θion; indisposi'sion/ *n. f.* indisposition, ailment; reluctance.
indistinto /indis'tinto/ *a.* indistinct, unclear.
individual /indiβi'ðual/ *a.* individual.
individualidad /indiβiðuali'ðað/ *n. f.* individuality.
individuo /indi'βiðuo/ *a.* & *m.* individual.
indócil /in'doθil; in'dosil/ *a.* headstrong, unruly.
índole /'indole/ *n. f.* nature, character, disposition.
indolencia /indo'lenθia; indo'lensia/ *n. f.* indolence.
indolente /indo'lente/ *a.* indolent.
indómito /in'domito/ *a.* untamed, wild; unruly.
inducir /indu'θir; indu'sir/ *v.* induce, persuade.
indudable /indu'ðaβle/ *a.* certain, indubitable.
indulgencia /indul'henθia; indul'hensia/ *n. f.* indulgence.
indulgente /indul'hente/ *a.* indulgent.
indultar /indul'tar/ *v.* free; pardon.
industria /in'dustria/ *n. f.* industry.
industrial /indus'trial/ *a.* industrial.
industrioso /indus'trioso/ *a.* industrious.
inédito /i'neðito/ *a.* unpublished.
ineficaz /inefi'kaθ; inefi'kas/ *a.* inefficient.
inepto /i'nepto/ *a.* incompetent.
inequívoco /ine'kiβoko/ *a.* unmistakable.
inercia /i'nerθia; i'nersia/ *n. f.* inertia.
inerte /i'nerte/ *a.* inert.
inesperado /inespe'raðo/ *a.* unexpected.
inestable /ines'taβle/ *a.* unstable.
inevitable /ineβi'taβle/ *a.* inevitable.
inexacto /ine'ksakto/ *a.* inexact.
inexperto /ineks'perto/ *a.* unskilled.
inexplicable /inekspli'kaβle/ *a.* inexplicable, unexplainable.
infalible /infa'liβle/ *a.* infallible.
infame /in'fame/ *a.* infamous, bad.
infamia /in'famia/ *n. f.* infamy.
infancia /in'fanθia; in'fansia/ *n. f.* infancy; childhood.
infante /in'fante/ **-ta** *n.* infant.
infantería /infante'ria/ *n. f.* infantry.
infantil /infan'til/ *a.* infantile, childish.
infarto (de miocardio) /in'farto de mio'karðio/ *n. m.* heart attack.
infatigable /infati'gaβle/ *a.* untiring.
infausto /in'fausto/ *a.* unlucky.
infección /infek'θion; infek'sion/ *n. f.* infection.
infeccioso /infek'θioso; infek'sioso/ *a.* infectious.
infectar /infek'tar/ *v.* infect.
infeliz /infe'liθ; infe'lis/ *a.* unhappy, miserable.
inferior /infe'rior/ *a.* inferior; lower.
inferir /infe'rir/ *v.* infer; inflict.
infernal /infer'nal/ *a.* infernal.
infestar /infes'tar/ *v.* infest.
infiel /in'fiel/ *a.* unfaithful.
infierno /in'fierno/ *n. m.* hell.
infiltrar /infil'trar/ *v.* infiltrate.
infinidad /infini'ðað/ *n. f.* infinity.
infinito /infi'nito/ *a.* infinite.
inflación /infla'θion; infla'sion/ *n. f.* inflation.
inflamable /infla'maβle/ *a.* flammable.
inflamación /inflama'θion; inflama'sion/ *n. f.* inflammation.
inflamar /infla'mar/ *v.* inflame, set on fire.
inflar /in'flar/ *v.* inflate, pump up, puff up.
inflexible /infle'ksiβle/ *a.* inflexible, rigid.
inflexión /infle'ksion/ *n. f.* inflection.
infligir /infli'hir/ *v.* inflict.
influencia /influ'enθia; influ'ensia/ *n. f.* influence.
influenza /in'fluenθa; in'fluensa/ *n. f.* influenza, flu.
influir /in'fluir/ *v.* influence, sway.
influyente /influ'yente/ *a.* influential.
información /informa'θion; informa'sion/ *n. f.* information.
informal /infor'mal/ *a.* informal.
informar /infor'mar/ *v.* inform; report.
informática /infor'matika/ *n. f.* computer science; information technology.
informe /in'forme/ *n. m.* report; (*pl.*) information, data.
infortunio /infor'tunio/ *n. m.* misfortune.
infracción /infrak'θion; infrak'sion/ *n. f.* violation.
infracetructura /infraθetruk'tura; infrasetruk'tura/ *n. f.* infrastructure.
infrascrito /infras'krito/ **-ta** *n.* signer, undersigned.
infringir /infrin'hir/ *v.* infringe, violate.
infructuoso /infruk'tuoso/ *a.* fruitless.
infundir /infun'dir/ *v.* instil, inspire with.
ingeniería /inhenie'ria/ *n. f.* engineering.
ingeniero /inhe'niero/ **-ra** *n.* engineer.
ingenio /in'henio/ *n. m.* wit; talent.
ingeniosidad /inheniosi'ðað/ *n. f.* ingenuity.
ingenioso /inhe'nioso/ *a.* witty; ingenious.
ingenuidad /inhenui'ðað/ *n. f.* candor; naïveté.
ingenuo /in'henuo/ *a.* ingenuous, naïve, candid.
Inglaterra /iŋgla'terra/ *n. f.* England.
ingle /'iŋgle/ *n. f.* groin.
inglés /iŋ'gles/ **-esa** *a.* & *n.* English; Englishman; Englishwoman.
ingratitud /iŋgrati'tuð/ *n. f.* ingratitude.
ingrato /iŋ'grato/ *a.* ungrateful.
ingravidez /iŋgraβi'ðeθ; iŋgraβi'ðes/ *n. f.* weightlessness.
ingrávido /iŋ'graβiðo/ *a.* weightless.
ingrediente /iŋgre'ðiente/ *n. m.* ingredient.
ingresar en /iŋgre'sar en/ *v.* enter; join.
ingreso /iŋ'greso/ *n. m.* entrance; (*pl.*) earnings, income.
inhábil /in'aβil/ *a.* unskilled; incapable.
inhabilitar /inaβili'tar/ *v.* disqualify.
inherente /ine'rente/ *a.* inherent.
inhibir /ini'βir/ *v.* inhibit.
inhumano /inu'mano/ *a.* cruel, inhuman.
iniciador /iniθia'ðor; inisia'ðor/ **-ra** *n.* initiator.
inicial /ini'θial; ini'sial/ *a.* initial.
iniciar /ini'θiar; ini'siar/ *v.* initiate, begin.
iniciativa /iniθia'tiβa; inisia'tiβa/ *n. f.* initiative.
inicuo /ini'kuo/ *a.* wicked.
iniquidad /iniki'ðað/ *n. f.* iniquity; sin.
injuria /in'huria/ *n. f.* insult. —**injuriar,** *v.*
injusticia /inhus'tiθia; inhus'tisia/ *n. f.* injustice.
injusto /in'husto/ *a.* unjust, unfair.
inmaculado /imaku'laðo/ *a.* immaculate; pure.
inmediato /ime'ðiato/ *a.* immediate.
inmensidad /imensi'ðað/ *n. f.* immensity.
inmenso /i'menso/ *a.* immense.
inmersión /imer'sion/ *n. f.* immersion.
inmigración /imigra'θion; imigra'sion/ *n. f.* immigration.
inmigrante /imi'grante/ *a.* & *n.* immigrant.
inmigrar /imi'grar/ *v.* immigrate.
inminente /imi'nente/ *a.* imminent.
inmoderado /imoðe'raðo/ *a.* immoderate.
inmodesto /imo'ðesto/ *a.* immodest.
inmoral /imo'ral/ *a.* immoral.
inmoralidad /imorali'ðað/ *n. f.* immorality.
inmortal /imor'tal/ *a.* immortal.
inmortalidad /imortali'ðað/ *n. f.* immortality.
inmóvil /i'moβil/ *a.* immobile, motionless.
inmundicia /imun'diθia; imun'disia/ *n. f.* dirt, filth.
inmune /i'mune/ *a.* immune; exempt.
inmunidad /imuni'ðað/ *n. f.* immunity.
innato /in'nato/ *a.* innate, inborn.
innecesario /inneθe'sario; innese'sario/ *a.* unnecessary, needless.
innegable /inne'gaβle/ *a.* undeniable.
innoble /in'noβle/ *a.* ignoble.
innocuo /inno'kuo/ *a.* innocuous.
innovación /innoβa'θion; innoβa'sion/ *n. f.* innovation.
innumerable /innume'raβle/ *a.* innumerable, countless.
inocencia /ino'θenθia; ino'sensia/ *n. f.* innocence.
inocentada /inoθen'taða; inosen'taða/ *n. f.* practical joke.
inocente /ino'θente; ino'sente/ *a.* innocent.
inocular /inoku'lar/ *v.* inoculate.
inodoro /ino'ðoro/ *n. m.* toilet.
inofensivo /inofen'siβo/ *a.* inoffensive, harmless.
inolvidable /inolβi'ðaβle/ *a.* unforgettable.
inoportuno /inopor'tuno/ *a.* inopportune.
inoxidable /inoksi'ðaβle/ *a.* stainless.
inquietante /inkie'tante/ *a.* disturbing, worrisome, worrying, upsetting.
inquietar /inkie'tar/ *v.* disturb, worry, trouble.
inquieto /in'kieto/ *a.* anxious, uneasy, worried; restless.
inquietud /inkie'tuð/ *n. f.* concern, anxiety, worry; restlessness.
inquilino /inki'lino/ **-na** *n.* occupant, tenant.
inquirir /inki'rir/ *v.* inquire into, investigate.
inquisición /inkisi'θion; inkisi'sion/ *n. f.* inquisition, investigation.
insaciable /insa'θiaβle; insa'siaβle/ *a.* insatiable.
insalubre /insa'luβre/ *a.* unhealthy.
insano /in'sano/ *a.* insane.
inscribir /inskri'βir/ *v.* inscribe; record.
inscribirse /inskri'βirse/ *v.* register, enroll.
inscripción /inskrip'θion; inskrip'sion/ *n. f.* inscription; registration.
insecticida /insekti'θiða; insekti'siða/ *n. m.* insecticide.
insecto /in'sekto/ *n. m.* insect.
inseguro /inse'guro/ *a.* unsure, uncertain; insecure, unsafe.
insensato /insen'sato/ *a.* stupid, senseless.
insensible /insen'siβle/ *a.* unfeeling, heartless.
inseparable /insepa'raβle/ *a.* inseparable.
inserción /inser'θion; inser'sion/ *n. f.* insertion.
insertar /inser'tar/ *v.* insert.
inservible /inser'βiβle/ *a.* useless.
insidioso /insi'ðioso/ *a.* insidious, crafty.
insigne /in'signe/ *a.* famous, noted.
insignia /in'signia/ *n. f.* insignia, badge.
insignificante /insignifi'kante/ *a.* insignificant, negligible.
insincero /insin'θero; insin'sero/ *a.* insincere.
insinuación /insinua'θion; insin;ua'sion/ *n. f.* insinuation; hint.
insinuar /insi'nuar/ *v.* insinuate, suggest, hint.
insipidez /insipi'ðeθ; insipi'ðes/ *n. f.* insipidity.
insípido /in'sipiðo/ *a.* insipid.
insistencia /insis'tenθia; insis'tensia/ *n. f.* insistence.
insistente /insis'tente/ *a.* insistent.
insistir /insis'tir/ *v.* insist.
insolación /insola'θion; insola'sion/ *n. f.* sunstroke.
insolencia /inso'lenθia; inso'lensia/ *n. f.* insolence.
insolente /inso'lente/ *a.* insolent.
insólito /in'solito/ *a.* unusual.
insolvente /insol'βente/ *a.* insolvent.
insomnio /in'somnio/ *n. m.* insomnia.
insonorizado /insonori'θaðo; insonori'saðo/ *a.* soundproof.
insonorizar /insonori'θar; insonori'sar/ *v.* soundproof.
insoportable /insopor'taβle/ *a.* unbearable.
inspección /inspek'θion; inspek'sion/ *n. f.* inspection.
inspeccionar /inspekθio'nar; inspeksio'nar/ *v.* inspect, examine.
inspector /inspek'tor/ **-ra** *n.* inspector.
inspiración /inspira'θion; inspira'sion/ *n. f.* inspiration.
inspirar /inspi'rar/ *v.* inspire.
instalación /instala'θion; instala'sion/ *n. f.* installation, fixture.
instalar /insta'lar/ *v.* install, set up.
instantánea /instan'tanea/ *n. f.* snapshot.
instantáneo /instan'taneo/ *a.* instantaneous.
instante /ins'tante/ *a.* & *m.* instant. **al i.,** at once.
instar /ins'tar/ *v.* coax, urge.
instigar /insti'gar/ *v.* instigate, urge.
instintivo /instin'tiβo/ *a.* instinctive.
instinto /ins'tinto/ *n. m.* instinct. **por i.,** by instinct, instinctively.
institución /institu'θion; institu'sion/ *n. f.* institution.

instituto /insti'tuto/ *n. m.* institute. —**instituir,** *v.*
institutriz /institu'triθ; institu'tris/ *n. f.* governess.
instrucción /instruk'θion; instruk'sion/ *n. f.* instruction; education.
instructivo /instruk'tiβo/ *a.* instructive.
instructor /instruk'tor/ **-ra** *n.* instructor.
instruir /ins'truir/ *v.* instruct, teach.
instrumento /instru'mento/ *n. m.* instrument.
insuficiente /insufi'θiente; insufi'siente/ *a.* insufficient.
insufrible /insu'friβle/ *a.* intolerable.
insular /insu'lar/ *a.* island, insular.
insulto /in'sulto/ *n. m.* insult. —**insultar,** *v.*
insuperable /insupe'raβle/ *a.* insuperable.
insurgente /insur'hente/ *n.* & *a.* insurgent, rebel.
insurrección /insurrek'θion; insurrek'sion/ *n. f.* insurrection, revolt.
insurrecto /insu'rrekto/ **-ta** *a.* & *n.* insurgent.
intacto /in'takto/ *a.* intact.
integral /inte'gral/ *a.* integral.
integridad /integri'ðað/ *n. f.* integrity; entirety.
íntegro /'integro/ *a.* entire; upright.
intelecto /inte'lekto/ *n. m.* intellect.
intelectual /intelek'tual/ *a.* & *n.* intellectual.
inteligencia /inteli'henθia; inteli'hensia/ *n. f.* intelligence.
inteligente /inteli'hente/ *a.* intelligent.
inteligible /inteli'hiβle/ *a.* intelligible.
intemperie /intem'perie/ *n. f.* bad weather.
intención /inten'θion; inten'sion/ *n. f.* intention.
intendente /inten'dente/ *n. m.* manager.
intensidad /intensi'ðað/ *n. f.* intensity.
intensificar /intensifi'kar/ *v.* intensify.
intensivo /inten'siβo/ *a.* intensive.
intenso /in'tenso/ *a.* intense.
intentar /inten'tar/ *v.* attempt, try.
intento /in'tento/ *n. m.* intent; attempt.
intercambiable /interkam'biaβle/ *a.* interchangeable.
intercambiar /interkam'βiar/ *v.* exchange, interchange.
interceptar /interθep'tar; intersep'tar/ *v.* intercept.
intercesión /interθe'sion; interse'sion/ *n. f.* intercession.
interés /inte'res/ *n. m.* interest; concern; appeal.
interesante /intere'sante/ *a.* interesting.
interesar /intere'sar/ *v.* interest, appeal to.
interfaz /inter'faθ; inter'fas/ *n. f.* interface.
interferencia /interfe'renθia; interfe'rensia/ *n. f.* interference.
interino /inte'rino/ *a.* temporary.
interior /inte'rior/ *a.* **1.** interior, inner. —*n.* **2.** *m.* interior.
interjección /interhek'θion; interhek'sion/ *n. f.* interjection.
intermedio /inter'meðio/ *a.* **1.** intermediate. —*n.* **2.** *m.* intermediary; intermission.
interminable /intermi'naβle/ *a.* interminable, endless.
intermisión /intermi'sion/ *n. f.* intermission.
intermitente /intermi'tente/ *a.* intermittent.
internacional /internaθio'nal; internasio'nal/ *a.* international.
internarse en /inter'narse en/ *v.* enter into, go into.
Internet, el /inter'net/ *n. m.* the Internet.
interno /in'terno/ *a.* internal.
interpelar /interpe'lar/ *v.* ask questions; implore.
interponer /interpo'ner/ *v.* interpose.
interpretación /interpreta'θion; interpreta'sion/ *n. f.* interpretation.
interpretar /interpre'tar/ *v.* interpret; construe.
intérprete /in'terprete/ *n. m.* & *f.* interpreter; performer.
interrogación /interroga'θion; interroga'sion/ *n. f.* interrogation.
interrogar /interro'gar/ *v.* question, interrogate.
interrogativo /interroga'tiβo/ *a.* interrogative.
interrumpir /interrum'pir/ *v.* interrupt.
interrupción /interrup'θion; interrup'sion/ *n. f.* interruption.
intersección /intersek'θion; intersek'sion/ *n. f.* intersection.
intervalo /inter'βalo/ *n. m.* interval.
intervención /interβen'θion; interβen'sion/ *n. f.* intervention.
intervenir /interβe'nir/ *v.* intervene, interfere.
intestino /intes'tino/ *n. m.* intestine.
intimación /intima'θion; intima'sion/ *n. f.* intimation, hint.
intimar /inti'mar/ *v.* suggest, hint.
intimidad /intimi'ðað/ *n. f.* intimacy.
intimidar /intimi'ðar/ *v.* intimidate.
íntimo /'intimo/ **-ma** *a.* & *n.* intimate.
intolerable /intole'raβle/ *a.* intolerable.
intolerancia /intole'ranθia; intole'ransia/ *n. f.* intolerance, bigotry.
intolerante /intole'rante/ *a.* intolerant.
intoxicación alimenticia /intoksika'θion alimen'tiθia; intoksika'sion alimen'tisia/ *n. f.* food poisoning.
intranquilo /intran'kilo/ *a.* uneasy.
intravenoso /intraβe'noso/ *a.* intravenous.
intrepidez /intrepi'ðeθ; intrepi'ðes/ *n. f.* daring.
intrépido /in'trepiðo/ *a.* intrepid.
intriga /in'triga/ *n. f.* intrigue, plot, scheme. —**intrigar,** *v.*
intrincado /intrin'kaðo/ *a.* intricate, involved; impenetrable.
introducción /introðuk'θion; introðuk'sion/ *n. f.* introduction.
introducir /introðu'θir; introðu'sir/ *v.* introduce.
intruso /in'truso/ **-sa** *n.* intruder.
intuición /intui'θion; intui'sion/ *n. f.* intuition.
inundación /inunda'θion; inunda'sion/ *n. f.* flood. —**inundar,** *v.*
inútil /i'nutil/ *a.* useless.
invadir /imba'ðir/ *v.* invade.
inválido /im'baliðo/ **-da** *a.* & *n.* invalid.
invariable /imba'riaβle/ *a.* constant.
invasión /imba'sion/ *n. f.* invasion.
invasor /imba'sor/ **-ra** *n.* invader.
invencible /imben'θiβle; imben'siβle/ *a.* invincible.
invención /imben'θion; imben'sion/ *n. f.* invention.
inventar /imben'tar/ *v.* invent; devise.
inventario /imben'tario/ *n. m.* inventory.
inventivo /imben'tiβo/ *a.* inventive.
invento /im'bento/ *n. m.* invention.
inventor /imben'tor/ **-ra** *n.* inventor.
invernáculo /imber'nakulo/ *n. m.* greenhouse.
invernal /imber'nal/ *a.* wintry.
inverosímil /imbero'simil/ *a.* improbable, unlikely.
inversión /imber'sion/ *n. f.* inversion; *Com.* investment.
inverso /im'berso/ *a.* inverse, reverse.
inversor /imber'sor/ **-ra** *n.* investor.
invertir /imber'tir/ *v.* invert; reverse; *Com.* invest.
investigación /imbestiga'θion; imbestiga'sion/ *n. f.* investigation.
investigador /imbestiga'ðor/ **-ra** *n.* investigator; researcher.
investigar /imbesti'gar/ *v.* investigate.
invierno /im'bierno/ *n. m.* winter.
invisible /imbi'siβle/ *a.* invisible.
invitación /imbita'θion; imbita'sion/ *n. f.* invitation.
invitar /imbi'tar/ *v.* invite.
invocar /imbo'kar/ *v.* invoke.
involuntario /imbolun'tario/ *a.* involuntary.
inyección /inyek'θion; inyek'sion/ *n. f.* injection.
inyectar /inyek'tar/ *v.* inject.
ir /ir/ *v.* go. **irse,** go away, leave.
ira /'ira/ *n. f.* anger, ire.
iracundo /ira'kundo/ *a.* wrathful, irate.
iris /'iris/ *n. m.* iris. **arco i.,** rainbow.
Irlanda /ir'landa/ *n. f.* Ireland.
irlandés /irlan'des/ **-esa** *a.* & *n.* Irish; Irishman, Irishwoman.
ironía /iro'nia/ *n. f.* irony.
irónico /i'roniko/ *a.* ironical.
irracional /irraθio'nal; irrasio'nal/ *a.* irrational; insane.
irradiación /irraðia'θion; irraðia'sion/ *n. f.* irradiation.
irradiar /irra'ðiar/ *v.* radiate.
irrazonable /irraθo'naβle; irraso'naβle/ *a.* unreasonable.
irregular /irregu'lar/ *a.* irregular.
irreligioso /irreli'hioso/ *a.* irreligious.
irremediable /irreme'ðiaβle/ *a.* irremediable, hopeless.
irresistible /irresis'tiβle/ *a.* irresistible.
irresoluto /irreso'luto/ *a.* irresolute, wavering.
irrespetuoso /irrespe'tuoso/ *a.* disrespectful.
irreverencia /irreβe'renθia; irreβe'rensia/ *n. f.* irreverence.
irreverente /irreβe'rente/ *adj.* irreverent.
irrigación /irriga'θion; irriga'sion/ *n. f.* irrigation.
irrigar /irri'gar/ *v.* irrigate.
irritación /irrita'θion; irrita'sion/ *n. f.* irritation.
irritar /irri'tar/ *v.* irritate.
irrupción /irrup'θion; irrup'sion/ *n. f.* raid, attack.
isla /'isla/ *n. f.* island.
isleño /is'leɲo/ **-ña** *n.* islander.
israelita /israe'lita/ *n.* & *a.* Israelite.
Italia /i'talia/ *n. f.* Italy.
italiano /ita'liano/ **-na** *a.* & *n.* Italian.
itinerario /itine'rario/ *n. m.* itinerary; timetable.
IVA, *abbrev.* **(impuesto sobre el valor añadido)** VAT (value-added tax).
izar /i'θar; i'sar/ *v.* hoist.
izquierda /iθ'kierða; is'kierða/ *n. f.* left (hand, side).
izquierdista /iθkier'ðista; is'kierðista/ *n.* & *a.* leftist.
izquierdo /iθ'kierðo; is'kierðo/ *a.* left.

J

jabalí /haβa'li/ *n. m.* wild boar.
jabón /ha'βon/ *n. m.* soap. **j. en polvo,** soap powder.
jabonar /haβo'nar/ *v.* soap.
jaca /'haka/ *n. f.* nag.
jacinto /ha'θinto; ha'sinto/ *n. m.* hyacinth.
jactancia /hak'tanθia; hak'tansia/ *n. f.* boast. —**jactarse,** *v.*
jactancioso /haktan'θioso; haktan'sioso/ *a.* boastful.
jadear /haðe'ar/ *v.* pant, puff.
jaez /ha'eθ; ha'es/ *n. m.* harness; kind.
jalar /ha'lar/ *v.* haul, pull.
jalea /ha'lea/ *n. f.* jelly.
jaleo /ha'leo/ *n. m.* row, uproar; hassle.
jamás /ha'mas/ *adv.* never, ever.
jamón /ha'mon/ *n. m.* ham.
Japón /ha'pon/ *n. m.* Japan.
japonés /hapo'nes/ **-esa** *a.* & *n.* Japanese.
jaqueca /ha'keka/ *n. f.* headache.
jarabe /ha'raβe/ *n. m.* syrup.
jaranear /harane'ar/ *v.* jest; carouse.
jardín /har'ðin/ *n. m.* garden.
jardín de infancia /har'ðin de in'fanθia; har'ðin de in'fansia/ nursery school.
jardinero /harði'nero/ **-ra** *n.* gardener.
jarra /'harra/ *n. f.* jar; pitcher.
jarro /'harro/ *n. m.* jug, pitcher.
jaspe /'haspe/ *n. m.* jasper.
jaula /'haula/ *n. f.* cage; coop.
jauría /hau'ria/ *n. f.* pack of hounds.
jazmín /haθ'min; has'min/ *n. m.* jasmine.
jefatura /hefa'tura/ *n. f.* headquarters.
jefe /'hefe/ **-fa** *n.* chief, boss.
jefe de comedor /'hefe de kome'ðor/ headwaiter.
jefe de sala /'hefe de 'sala/ maître d'.
jefe de taller /'hefe de ta'ʎer; 'hefe de ta'yer/ foreman.
Jehová /heo'βa/ *n. m.* Jehovah.
jengibre /hen'hiβre/ *n. m.* ginger.
jerez /he'reθ; he'res/ *n. m.* sherry.
jerga /'herga/ *n. f.* slang.
jergón /her'gon/ *n. m.* straw mattress.
jerigonza /heri'gonθa; heri'gonsa/ *n. f.* jargon.
jeringa /he'riŋga/ *n. f.* syringe.
jeringar /heriŋ'gar/ *v.* inject; annoy.
jeroglífico /hero'glifiko/ *n. m.* hieroglyph.
jersey /her'sei/ *n. m.* pullover; **j. de cuello alto,** turtleneck sweater.
Jerusalén /herusa'len/ *n. m.* Jerusalem.
jesuita /he'suita/ *n. m.* Jesuit.
Jesús /he'sus/ *n. m.* Jesus.
jeta /'heta/ *n. f.* snout.
jícara /'hikara/ *n. f.* cup.
jinete /hi'nete/ **-ta** *n.* horseman.
jingoísmo /hiŋgo'ismo/ *n. m.* jingoism.
jingoísta /hiŋgo'ista/ *n.* & *a.* jingoist.
jira /'hira/ *n. f.* picnic; outing.
jirafa /hi'rafa/ *n. f.* giraffe.
jiu-jitsu /hiu'hitsu/ *n. m.* jujitsu.
jocundo /ho'kundo/ *a.* jovial.
jornada /hor'naða/ *n. f.* journey; day's work.
jornal /hor'nal/ *n. m.* day's wage.
jornalero /horna'lero/ *n. m.* day laborer, workman.
joroba /ho'roβa/ *n. f.* hump.
jorobado /horo'βaðo/ *a.* humpbacked.
joven /'hoβen/ *a.* **1.** young. —*n.* **2.** *m.* & *f.* young person.
jovial /ho'βial/ *a.* jovial, jolly.
jovialidad /hoβiali'ðað/ *n. f.* joviality.
joya /'hoia/ *n. f.* jewel, gem.
joyas de fantasía /'hoias de fanta'sia/ *n. f.pl.* costume jewelry.
joyelero /hoie'lero/ *n. m.* jewel box.
joyería /hoie'ria/ *n. f.* jewelry; jewelry store.
joyero /ho'iero/ *n. m.* jeweler; jewel case.
juanete /hua'nete/ *n. m.* bunion.
jubilación /huβila'θion; huβila'sion/ *n. f.* retirement; pension.
jubilar /huβi'lar/ *v.* retire, pension.
jubileo /huβi'leo/ *n. m.* jubilee, public festivity.
júbilo /'huβilo/ *n. m.* glee, rejoicing.
jubiloso /huβi'loso/ *a.* joyful, gay.
judaico /hu'ðaiko/ *a.* Jewish.
judaísmo /huða'ismo/ *n. m.* Judaism.
judía /hu'ðia/ *n. f.* bean, string bean.
judicial /huði'θial; huði'sial/ *a.* judicial.
judío /hu'ðio/ **-día** *a.* & *n.* Jewish; Jew.
juego /'huego/ *n. m.* game; play;

gambling; set. **j. de damas,** checkers. **j. limpio,** fair play.
Juegos Olímpicos /huegos o'limpikos/ *n. m.pl.* Olympic Games.
juerga /'huerga/ *n. f.* spree.
jueves /'hueβes/ *n. m.* Thursday.
juez /hueθ; hues/ *n. m.* judge.
jugador /huga'ðor/ **-ra** *n.* player.
jugar /hu'gar/ *v.* play; gamble.
juglar /hug'lar/ *n. m.* minstrel.
jugo /'hugo/ *n. m.* juice. **j. de naranja,** orange juice.
jugoso /hu'goso/ *a.* juicy.
juguete /hu'gete/ *n. m.* toy, plaything.
juguetear /hugete'ar/ *v.* trifle.
juguetón /huge'ton/ *a.* playful.
juicio /'huiθio; 'huisio/ *n. m.* sense, wisdom, judgment; sanity; trial.
juicioso /hui'θioso; hui'sioso/ *a.* wise, judicious.
julio /'hulio/ *n. m.* July.
jumento /hu'mento/ *n. m.* donkey.
junco /'hunko/ *n. m.* reed, rush.
jungla /'huŋgla/ *n. f.* jungle.
junio /'hunio/ *n. m.* June.
junípero /hu'nipero/ *n. m.* juniper.
junquillo /hun'kiʎo; hun'kiyo/ *n. m.* jonquil.
junta /'hunta/ *n. f.* board, council; joint, coupling.
juntamente /hunta'mente/ *adv.* jointly.
juntar /hun'tar/ *v.* join; connect; assemble.
junto /'hunto/ *a.* together. **j. a,** next to.
juntura /hun'tura/ *n. f.* joint, juncture.
jurado /hu'raðo/ *n. m.* jury.
juramento /hura'mento/ *n. m.* oath.
jurar /hu'rar/ *v.* swear.
jurisconsulto /huriskon'sulto/ *n. m.* jurist.
jurisdicción /hurisðik'θion; hurisðik'sion/ *n. f.* jurisdiction; territory.
jurisprudencia /hurispru'ðenθia; hurispru'ðensia/ *n. f.* jurisprudence.
justa /'husta/ *n. f.* joust. **—justar,** *v.*
justicia /hus'tiθia; hus'tisia/ *n. f.* justice, equity.
justiciero /husti'θiero; husti'siero/ *a.* just.
justificación /hustifika'θion; hustifika'sion/ *n. f.* justification.
justificadamente /hustifikaða'mente/ *adv.* justifiably.
justificar /hustifi'kar/ *v.* justify, warrant.
justo /'husto/ *a.* right; exact; just; righteous.
juvenil /huβe'nil/ *a.* youthful.
juventud /huβen'tuð/ *n. f.* youth.
juzgado /huθ'gaðo; hus'gaðo/ *n. m.* court.
juzgar /huθ'gar; hus'gar/ *v.* judge, estimate.

K

káiser /'kaiser/ *n. m.* kaiser.
karate /ka'rate/ *n. m.* karate.
kepis /'kepis/ *n. m.* military cap.
kerosena /kero'sena/ *n. f.* kerosene.
kilo /'kilo/ **kilogramo** *n. m.* kilogram.
kilohercio /kilo'erθio; kilo'ersio/ *n. m.* kilohertz.
kilolitro /kilo'litro/ *n. m.* kiloliter.
kilometraje /kilome'trahe/ *n. m.* mileage.
kilómetro /ki'lometro/ *n. m.* kilometer.
kiosco /'kiosko/ *n. m.* newsstand; pavilion.

L

la /la/ *art. & pron.* **1.** the; the one. *—pron.* **2.** her, it, you; (*pl.*) them, you.
laberinto /laβe'rinto/ *n. m.* labyrinth, maze.
labia /'laβia/ *n. f.* eloquence, fluency.
labio /'laβio/ *n. m.* lip.
labor /la'βor/ *n. f.* labor, work.
laborar /laβo'rar/ *v.* work; till.
laboratorio /laβora'torio/ *n. m.* laboratory.
laborioso /laβo'rioso/ *a.* industrious.
labrador /laβra'ðor/ *n. m.* farmer.
labranza /la'βranθa; la'βransa/ *n. f.* farming; farmland.
labrar /la'βrar/ *v.* work, till.
labriego /la'βriego/ **-ga** *n.* peasant.
laca /'laka/ *n. f.* shellac.
lacio /'laθio; 'lasio/ *a.* withered; limp; straight.
lactar /lak'tar/ *v.* nurse, suckle.
lácteo /'lakteo/ *a.* milky.
ladear /laðe'ar/ *v.* tilt, tip; sway.
ladera /la'ðera/ *n. f.* slope.
ladino /la'ðino/ *a.* cunning, crafty.
lado /'laðo/ *n. m.* side. **al l. de,** beside. **de l.,** sideways.
ladra /'laðra/ *n. f.* barking. **—ladrar,** *v.*
ladrillo /la'ðriʎo; la'ðriyo/ *n. m.* brick.
ladrón /la'ðron/ **-ona** *n.* thief, robber.
lagarto /la'garto/ *n. m.* lizard; (Mex.) alligator.
lago /'lago/ *n. m.* lake.
lágrima /'lagrima/ *n. f.* tear.
lagrimear /lagrime'ar/ *v.* weep, cry.
laguna /la'guna/ *n. f.* lagoon; gap.
laico /'laiko/ *a.* lay.
laja /'laha/ *n. f.* stone slab.
lamentable /lamen'taβle/ *a.* lamentable.
lamentación /lamenta'θion; lamenta'sion/ *n. f.* lamentation.
lamentar /lamen'tar/ *v.* lament; wail; regret, be sorry.
lamento /la'mento/ *n. m.* lament, wail.
lamer /la'mer/ *v.* lick; lap.
lámina /'lamina/ *n. f.* print, illustration.
lámpara /'lampara/ *n. f.* lamp.
lampiño /lam'piɲo/ *a.* beardless.
lana /'lana/ *n. f.* wool.
lanar /la'nar/ *a.* woolen.
lance /'lanθe; 'lanse/ *n. m.* throw; episode; quarrel.
lancha /'lantʃa/ *n. f.* launch; small boat.
lanchón /lan'tʃon/ *n. m.* barge.
langosta /laŋ'gosta/ *n. f.* lobster; locust.
langostino /laŋgos'tino/ *n. m.* king prawn.
languidecer /laŋguiðe'θer; laŋguiðe'ser/ *v.* languish, pine.
languidez /laŋgui'ðeθ; laŋgui'ðes/ *n. f.* languidness.
lánguido /'laŋguiðo/ *a.* languid.
lanza /'lanθa; 'lansa/ *n. f.* lance, spear.
lanzada /lan'θaða; lan'saða/ *n. f.* thrust, throw.
lanzar /lan'θar; lan'sar/ *v.* hurl; launch.
lañar /la'ɲar/ *v.* cramp; clamp.
lapicero /lapi'θero; lapi'sero/ *n. m.* mechanical pencil.
lápida /'lapiða/ *n. f.* stone; tombstone.
lápiz /'lapiθ; 'lapis/ *n. m.* pencil; crayon.
lápiz de ojos /'lapiθ de 'ohos; 'lapis de 'ohos/ *n. m.* eyeliner.
lapso /'lapso/ *n. m.* lapse.
lardo /'larðo/ *n. m.* lard.
largar /lar'gar/ *v.* loosen; free.
largo /'largo/ *a.* **1.** long. **a lo l. de,** along. *—n.* **2.** *m.* length.
largometraje /largome'trahe/ *n. m.* feature film.
largor /lar'gor/ *n. m.* length.
largueza /lar'geθa; lar'gesa/ *n. f.* generosity; length.
largura /lar'gura/ *n. f.* length.
laringe /la'rinhe/ *n. f.* larynx.
larva /'larβa/ *n. f.* larva.
lascivia /las'θiβia; las'siβia/ *n. f.* lasciviousness.
lascivo /las'θiβo; las'siβo/ *a.* lascivious.
láser /'laser/ *n. m.* laser.
laso /'laso/ *a.* weary.
lástima /'lastima/ *n. f.* pity. **ser l.,** to be a pity, to be too bad.
lastimar /lasti'mar/ *v.* hurt, injure.
lastimoso /lasti'moso/ *a.* pitiful.
lastre /'lastre/ *n. m.* ballast. **—lastrar,** *v.*
lata /'lata/ *n. f.* tin can; tin (plate); *Colloq.* annoyance, bore.
latente /la'tente/ *a.* latent.
lateral /late'ral/ *a.* lateral, side.
latigazo /lati'gaθo; lati'gaso/ *n. m.* lash, whipping.
látigo /'latigo/ *n. m.* whip.
latín /la'tin/ *n. m.* Latin (language).
latino /la'tino/ *a.* Latin.
latir /la'tir/ *v.* beat, pulsate.
latitud /lati'tuð/ *n. f.* latitude.
latón /la'ton/ *n. m.* brass.
laúd /la'uð/ *n. m.* lute.
laudable /lau'ðaβle/ *a.* laudable.
láudano /'lauðano/ *n. m.* laudanum.
laurel /lau'rel/ *n. m.* laurel.
lava /'laβa/ *n. f.* lava.
lavabo /la'βaβo/ **lavamanos** *n. m.* washroom, lavatory.
lavadora /laβa'ðora/ *n. f.* washing machine.
lavandera /laβan'dera/ *n. f.* washerwoman, laundress.
lavandería /laβande'ria/ *f.* laundry; laundromat.
lavaplatos /laβa'platos/ *n.* **1.** *m.* dishwasher (machine). *—n.* **2.** *m. & f.* dishwasher (person).
lavar /la'βar/ *v.* wash.
lavatorio /laβa'torio/ *n. m.* lavatory.
laya /'laia/ *n. f.* spade. **—layar,** *v.*
lazar /la'θar; la'sar/ *v.* lasso.
lazareto /laθa'reto; lasa'reto/ *n. m.* isolation hospital; quarantine station.
lazo /'laθo; 'laso/ *n. m.* tie, knot; bow; loop.
le /le/ *pron.* him, her, you; (*pl.*) them, you.
leal /le'al/ *a.* loyal.
lealtad /leal'tað/ *n. f.* loyalty.
lebrel /le'βrel/ *n. m.* greyhound.
lección /lek'θion; lek'sion/ *n. f.* lesson.
leche /'letʃe/ *n. f.* milk.
lechería /letʃe'ria/ *n. f.* dairy.
lechero /le'tʃero/ *n. m.* milkman.
lecho /'letʃo/ *n. m.* bed; couch.
lechón /le'tʃon/ *n. m.* pig.
lechoso /le'tʃoso/ *a.* milky.
lechuga /le'tʃuga/ *n. f.* lettuce.
lechuza /le'tʃuθa; le'tʃusa/ *n. f.* owl.
lecito /le'θito; le'sito/ *n. m.* yolk.
lector /lek'tor/ **-ra** *n.* reader.
lectura /lek'tura/ *n. f.* reading.
leer /le'er/ *v.* read.
legación /lega'θion; lega'sion/ *n. f.* legation.
legado /le'gaðo/ *n. m.* bequest.
legal /le'gal/ *a.* legal, lawful.
legalizar /legali'θar; legali'sar/ *v.* legalize.
legar /le'gar/ *v.* bequeath, leave, will.
legible /le'hiβle/ *a.* legible.
legión /le'hion/ *n. f.* legion.
legislación /lehisla'θion; lehisla'sion/ *n. f.* legislation.
legislador /lehisla'ðor/ **-ra** *n.* legislator.
legislar /lehis'lar/ *v.* legislate.
legislativo /lehisla'tiβo/ *a.* legislative.
legislatura /lehisla'tura/ *n. f.* legislature.
legítimo /le'hitimo/ *a.* legitimate.
lego /'lego/ *n. m.* layman.
legua /'legua/ *n. f.* league (measure).
legumbre /le'gumbre/ *n. f.* vegetable.
lejano /le'hano/ *a.* distant, far-off.
lejía /le'hia/ *n. f.* lye.
lejos /'lehos/ *adv.* far. **a lo l.,** in the distance.
lelo /'lelo/ *a.* stupid, foolish.
lema /'lema/ *n. m.* theme; slogan.
lengua /'leŋgua/ *n. f.* tongue; language.
lenguado /leŋ'guaðo/ *n. m.* sole, flounder.
lenguaje /leŋ'guahe/ *n. m.* speech; language.
lenguaraz /leŋgua'raθ; leŋgua'ras/ *a.* talkative.
lente /'lente/ *n.* **1.** *m. or f.* lens. **2.** *m.pl.* eyeglasses.
lenteja /len'teha/ *n. f.* lentil.
lentilla /len'tiʎa; len'tiya/ *n. f.* contact lens.
lentitud /lenti'tuð/ *n. f.* slowness.
lento /'lento/ *a.* slow.
leña /'leɲa/ *n. f.* wood, firewood.
león /le'on/ *n. m.* lion.
leopardo /leo'parðo/ *n. m.* leopard.
lerdo /'lerðo/ *a.* dull-witted.
lesbiana /les'βiana/ *n. f.* lesbian.
lesión /le'sion/ *n. f.* wound; damage.
letanía /leta'nia/ *n. f.* litany.
letárgico /le'tarhiko/ *a.* lethargic.
letargo /le'targo/ *n. m.* lethargy.
letra /'letra/ *n. f.* letter (of alphabet); print; words (of a song).
letrado /le'traðo/ *a.* **1.** learned. *—n.* **2.** *m.* lawyer.
letrero /le'trero/ *n. m.* sign, poster.
leva /'leβa/ *n. f. Mil.* draft.
levadura /leβa'ðura/ *n. f.* yeast, leavening, baking powder.
levantador /leβanta'ðor/ *n. m.* lifter; rebel, mutineer.
levantar /leβan'tar/ *v.* raise, lift.
levantarse /leβan'tarse/ *v.* rise, get up; stand up.
levar /le'βar/ *v.* weigh (anchor).
leve /'leβe/ *a.* slight, light.
levita /le'βita/ *n. f.* frock coat.
léxico /'leksiko/ *n. m.* lexicon, dictionary.
ley /lei/ *n. f.* law, statute.
leyenda /le'ienda/ *n. f.* legend.
lezna /'leθna; 'lesna/ *n. f.* awl.
libación /liβa'θion; liβa'sion/ *n. f.* libation.
libelo /li'βelo/ *n. m.* libel.
libélula /li'βelula/ *n. f.* dragonfly.
liberación /liβera'θion; liβera'sion/ *n. f.* liberation, release.
liberal /liβe'ral/ *a.* liberal.
libertad /liβer'tað/ *n. f.* freedom.
libertador /liβerta'ðor/ **-ra** *n.* liberator.
libertar /liβer'tar/ *v.* free, liberate.
libertinaje /liβerti'nahe/ *n. m.* licentiousness.
libertino /liβer'tino/ **-na** *n.* libertine.
libídine /li'βiðine/ *n. f.* licentiousness; lust.
libidinoso /liβiði'noso/ *a.* lustful.
libra /'liβra/ *n. f.* pound.
libranza /li'βranθa; li'βransa/ *n. f.* draft, bill of exchange.
librar /li'βrar/ *v.* free, rid.
libre /'liβre/ *a.* free, unoccupied.
librería /liβre'ria/ *n. f.* bookstore.
librero /li'βrero/ **-ra** *n.* bookseller.
libreta /li'βreta/ *n. f.* notebook; booklet.
libreto /li'βreto/ *n. m.* libretto.
libro /'liβro/ *n. m.* book.
libro de texto /'liβro de 'teksto/ textbook.
licencia /li'θenθia; li'sensia/ *n. f.* permission, license, leave; furlough. **l. de armas,** gun permit.
licenciado /liθen'θiaðo; lisen'siaðo/ **-da** *n.* graduate.
licencioso /liθen'θioso; lisen'sioso/ *a.* licentious.
lícito /'liθito; 'lisito/ *a.* lawful.
licor /li'kor/ *n. m.* liquor.
licuadora /likua'ðora/ *n. f.* blender (for food).
lid /lið/ *n. f.* fight. **—lidiar,** *v.*
líder /'liðer/ *n. m. & f.* leader.
liebre /'lieβre/ *n. f.* hare.
lienzo /'lienθo; 'lienso/ *n. m.* linen.

liga /'liga/ *n. f.* league, confederacy; garter.
ligadura /liga'ðura/ *n. f.* ligature.
ligar /li'gar/ *v.* tie, bind, join.
ligero /li'hero/ *a.* light; fast, nimble.
ligustro /li'gustro/ *n. m.* privet.
lija /'liha/ *n. f.* sandpaper.
lijar /li'har/ *v.* sandpaper.
lima /'lima/ *n. f.* file; lime.
limbo /'limbo/ *n. m.* limbo.
limitación /limita'θion; limita'sion/ *n. f.* limitation.
límite /'limite/ *n. m.* limit. —**limitar,** *v.*
limo /'limo/ *n. m.* slime.
limón /li'mon/ *n. m.* lemon.
limonada /limo'naða/ *n. f.* lemonade.
limonero /limo'nero/ *n. m.* lemon tree.
limosna /li'mosna/ *n. f.* alms.
limosnero /limos'nero/ **-ra** *n.* beggar.
limpiabotas /limpia'βotas/ *n. m.* bootblack.
limpiadientes /limpia'ðientes/ *n. m.* toothpick.
limpiar /lim'piar/ *v.* clean, wash, wipe.
límpido /'limpiðo/ *a.* limpid, clear.
limpieza /lim'pieθa; lim'piesa/ *n. f.* cleanliness.
limpio /'limpio/ *n. m.* clean.
limusina /limu'sina/ *n. f.* limousine.
linaje /li'nahe/ *n. m.* lineage, ancestry.
linaza /li'naθa; li'nasa/ *n. f.* linseed.
lince /'linθe; 'linse/ *a.* sharp-sighted, observing.
linchamiento /lintʃa'miento/ *n. m.* lynching.
linchar /lin'tʃar/ *v.* lynch.
lindar /lin'dar/ *v.* border, bound.
linde /'linde/ *n. m.* boundary; landmark.
lindero /lin'dero/ *n. m.* boundary.
lindo /'lindo/ *a.* pretty, lovely, nice.
línea /'linea/ *n. f.* line.
línea de puntos /'linea de 'puntos/ dotted line.
lineal /line'al/ *a.* lineal.
linfa /'linfa/ *n. f.* lymph.
lingüista /liŋ'guista/ *n. m.* & *f.* linguist.
lingüístico /liŋ'guistiko/ *a.* linguistic.
linimento /lini'mento/ *n. m.* liniment.
lino /'lino/ *n. m.* linen; flax.
linóleo /li'noleo/ *n. m.* linoleum.
linterna /lin'terna/ *n. f.* lantern; flashlight.
lío /'lio/ *n. m.* pack, bundle; mess, scrape; hassle.
liquidación /likiða'θion; likiða'sion/ *n. f.* liquidation.
liquidar /liki'ðar/ *v.* liquidate; settle up.
líquido /'likiðo/ *a.* & *m.* liquid.
lira /'lira/ *n. f.* lyre.
lírico /'liriko/ *a.* lyric.
lirio /'lirio/ *n. m.* lily.
lirismo /li'rismo/ *n. m.* lyricism.
lis /lis/ *n. f.* lily.
lisiar /li'siar/ *v.* cripple, lame.
liso /'liso/ *a.* smooth, even.
lisonja /li'sonha/ *n. f.* flattery.
lisonjear /lisonhe'ar/ *v.* flatter.
lisonjero /lison'hero/ **-ra** *n.* flatterer.
lista /'lista/ *n. f.* list; stripe; menu.
lista negra /'lista 'negra/ blacklist.
listar /lis'tar/ *v.* list; put on a list.
listo /'listo/ *a.* ready; smart, clever.
listón /lis'ton/ *n. m.* ribbon.
litera /li'tera/ *n. f.* litter, bunk, berth.
literal /lite'ral/ *a.* literal.
literario /lite'rario/ *a.* literary.
literato /lite'rato/ *n. m.* literary person, writer.
literatura /litera'tura/ *n. f.* literature.
litigación /litiga'θion; litiga'sion/ *n. f.* litigation.
litigio /li'tihio/ *n. m.* litigation; lawsuit.
litoral /lito'ral/ *n. m.* coast.
litro /'litro/ *n. m.* liter.
liturgia /li'turhia/ *n. f.* liturgy.
liviano /li'βiano/ *a.* light (in weight).
lívido /'liβiðo/ *a.* livid.
llaga /'ʎaga; 'yaga/ *n. f.* sore.
llama /'ʎama; 'yama/ *n. f.* flame; llama.
llamada /ʎa'maða; ya'maða/ *n. f.* call; knock. —**llamar,** *v.*
llamarse /ʎa'marse; ya'marse/ *v.* be called, be named. **se llama...** etc., his name is... etc.
llamativo /ʎama'tiβo; yama'tiβo/ *a.* gaudy, showy.
llamear /ʎame'ar; yame'ar/ *v.* blaze.
llaneza /ʎa'neθa; ya'nesa/ *n. f.* simplicity.
llano /'ʎano; 'yano/ *a.* **1.** flat, level; plain. —*n.* **2.** *m.* plain.
llanta /'ʎanta; 'yanta/ *n. f.* tire.
llanto /'ʎanto; 'yanto/ *n. m.* crying, weeping.
llanura /ʎa'nura; ya'nura/ *n. f.* prairie, plain.
llave /'ʎaβe; 'yaβe/ *n. f.* key; wrench; faucet; *Elec.* switch. **ll. inglesa,** monkey wrench.
llegada /ʎe'gaða; ye'gaða/ *n. f.* arrival.
llegar /ʎe'gar; ye'gar/ *v.* arrive; reach. **ll. a ser,** become, come to be.
llenar /ʎe'nar; ye'nar/ *v.* fill.
lleno /'ʎeno; 'yeno/ *a.* full.
llenura /ʎe'nura; ye'nura/ *n. f.* abundance.
llevadero /ʎeβa'ðero; yeβa'ðero/ *a.* tolerable.
llevar /ʎe'βar; ye'βar/ *v.* take, carry, bear; wear (clothes); **ll. a cabo,** carry out.
llevarse /ʎe'βarse; ye'βarse/ *v.* take away, run away with. **ll. bien,** get along well.
llorar /ʎo'rar; yo'rar/ *v.* cry, weep.
lloroso /ʎo'roso; yo'roso/ *a.* sorrowful, tearful.
llover /ʎo'βer; yo'βer/ *v.* rain.
llovido /ʎo'βiðo; yo'βiðo/ *n. m.* stowaway.
llovizna /ʎo'βiθna; yo'βisna/ *n. f.* drizzle, sprinkle. —**lloviznar,** *v.*
lluvia /'ʎuβia; 'yuβia/ *n. f.* rain.
lluvia ácida /'ʎuβia 'aθiða; 'yuβia 'asiða/ acid rain.
lluvioso /ʎu'βioso; yu'βioso/ *a.* rainy.
lo /lo/ *pron.* the; him, it, you; (*pl.*) them, you.
loar /lo'ar/ *v.* praise, laud.
lobina /lo'βina/ *n. f.* striped bass.
lobo /'loβo/ *n. m.* wolf.
lóbrego /'loβrego/ *a.* murky; dismal.
local /lo'kal/ *a.* **1.** local. —*n.* **2.** *m.* site.
localidad /lokali'ðað/ *n. f.* locality, location; seat (in theater).
localizar /lokali'θar; lokali'sar/ *v.* localize.
loción /lo'θion; lo'sion/ *n. f.* lotion.
loco /'loko/ **-ca** *a.* **1.** crazy, insane, mad. —*n.* **2.** lunatic.
locomotora /lokomo'tora/ *n. f.* locomotive.
locuaz /lo'kuaθ; lo'kuas/ *a.* loquacious.
locución /loku'θion; loku'sion/ *n. f.* locution, expression.
locura /lo'kura/ *n. f.* folly; madness, insanity.
lodo /'loðo/ *n. m.* mud.
lodoso /lo'ðoso/ *a.* muddy.
lógica /'lohika/ *n. f.* logic.
lógico /'lohiko/ *a.* logical.
lograr /lo'grar/ *v.* achieve; succeed in.
logro /'logro/ *n. m.* accomplishment.
lombriz /lom'βriθ; lom'βris/ *n. f.* earthworm.
lomo /'lomo/ *n. m.* loin; back (of an animal).
lona /'lona/ *n. f.* canvas, tarpaulin.
longevidad /lonheβi'ðað/ *n. f.* longevity.
longitud /lonhi'tuð/ *n. f.* longitude; length.
lonja /'lonha/ *n. f.* shop; market.
lontananza /lonta'nanθa; lonta'nansa/ *n. f.* distance.
loro /'loro/ *n. m.* parrot.
losa /'losa/ *n. f.* slab.
lote /'lote/ *n. m.* lot, share.
lotería /lote'ria/ *n. f.* lottery.
loza /'loθa; 'losa/ *n. f.* china, crockery.
lozanía /loθa'nia; losa'nia/ *n. f.* freshness, vigor.
lozano /lo'θano; lo'sano/ *a.* fresh, spirited.
lubricación /luβrika'θion; luβrika'sion/ *n. f.* lubrication.
lubricar /luβri'kar/ *v.* lubricate.
lucero /lu'θero; lu'sero/ *n. m.* (bright) star.
lucha /'lutʃa/ *n. f.* fight, struggle; wrestling. —**luchar,** *v.*
luchador /lutʃa'ðor/ **-ra** *n.* fighter, wrestler.
lúcido /lu'θiðo; lu'siðo/ *a.* lucid, clear.
luciente /lu'θiente; lu'siente/ *a.* shining, bright.
luciérnaga /lu'θiernaga; lu'siernaga/ *n. f.* firefly.
lucimiento /luθi'miento; lusi'miento/ *n. m.* success; splendor.
lucir /lu'θir; lu'sir/ *v.* shine, sparkle; show off.
lucrativo /lukra'tiβo/ *a.* lucrative, profitable.
luego /'luego/ *adv.* right away; afterwards, next. **l. que,** as soon as. **desde l.,** of course. **hasta l.,** good-bye, so long.
lugar /lu'gar/ *n. m.* place, spot; space, room.
lúgubre /'luguβre/ *a.* gloomy; dismal.
lujo /'luho/ *n. m.* luxury. **de l.,** deluxe.
lujoso /lu'hoso/ *a.* luxurious.
lumbre /'lumbre/ *n. f.* fire; light.
luminoso /lumi'noso/ *a.* luminous.
luna /'luna/ *n. f.* moon.
lunar /lu'nar/ *n. m.* beauty mark, mole; polka dot.
lunático /lu'natiko/ **-ca** *a.* & *n.* lunatic.
lunes /'lunes/ *n. m.* Monday.
luneta /lu'neta/ *n. f. Theat.* orchestra seat.
lupa /'lupa/ *n. f.* magnifying glass.
lustre /'lustre/ *n. m.* polish, shine. —**lustrar,** *v.*
lustroso /lus'troso/ *a.* shiny.
luto /'luto/ *n. m.* mourning.
luz /luθ; lus/ *n. f.* light. **dar a l.,** give birth to.

M

maca /'maka/ *n. f.* blemish, flaw.
macaco /ma'kako/ *a.* ugly, horrid.
macareno /maka'reno/ *a.* boasting.
macarrones /maka'rrones/ *n. m.pl.* macaroni.
macear /maθe'ar; mase'ar/ *v.* molest, push around.
macedonia de frutas /maθe'ðonia de 'frutas; mase'ðonia de 'frutas/ *n. f.* fruit salad.
maceta /ma'θeta; ma'seta/ *n. f.* vase; mallet.
machacar /matʃa'kar/ *v.* pound; crush.
machina /ma'tʃina/ *n. f.* derrick.
machista /ma'tʃista/ *a.* macho.
macho /'matʃo/ *n. m.* male.
machucho /ma'tʃutʃo/ *a.* mature, wise.
macizo /ma'θiθo; ma'siso/ *a.* **1.** solid. —*n.* **2.** *m.* bulk; flower bed.
macular /maku'lar/ *v.* stain.
madera /ma'ðera/ *n. f.* lumber; wood.
madero /ma'ðero/ *n. m.* beam, timber.
madrastra /ma'ðrastra/ *n. f.* stepmother.
madre /'maðre/ *n. f.* mother. **m. política,** mother-in-law.
madreperla /maðre'perla/ *n. f.* mother-of-pearl.
madriguera /maðri'gera/ *n. f.* burrow; lair, den.
madrina /ma'ðrina/ *n. f.* godmother.
madroncillo /maðron'θiʎo; maðron'siyo/ *n. m.* strawberry.
madrugada /maðru'gaða/ *n. f.* daybreak.
madrugar /maðru'gar/ *v.* get up early.
madurar /maðu'rar/ *v.* ripen.
madurez /maðu'reθ; maðu'res/ *n. f.* maturity.
maduro /ma'ðuro/ *a.* ripe; mature.
maestría /maes'tria/ *n. f.* mastery; master's degree.
maestro /ma'estro/ *n. m.* master; teacher.
mafia /'mafia/ *n. f.* mafia.
maganto /ma'ganto/ *a.* lethargic, dull.
magia /'mahia/ *n. f.* magic.
mágico /'mahiko/ *a.* & *m.* magic; magician.
magistrado /mahis'traðo/ *n. m.* magistrate.
magnánimo /mag'nanimo/ *a.* magnanimous.
magnético /mag'netiko/ *a.* magnetic.
magnetismo /magne'tismo/ *n. m.* magnetism.
magnetófono /magne'tofono/ *n. m.* tape recorder.
magnificar /magnifi'kar/ *v.* magnify.
magnificencia /magnifi'θenθia; magnifi'sensia/ *n. f.* magnificence.
magnífico /mag'nifiko/ *a.* magnificent.
magnitud /magni'tuð/ *n. f.* magnitude.
magno /'magno/ *a.* great, grand.
magnolia /mag'nolia/ *n. f.* magnolia.
mago /'mago/ *n. m.* magician; wizard.
magosto /ma'gosto/ *n. m.* chestnut roast; picnic fire for roasting chestnuts.
magro /'magro/ *a.* meager; thin.
magullar /magu'ʎar; magu'yar/ *v.* bruise.
mahometano /maome'tano/ *n.* & *a.* Mohammedan.
mahometismo /maome'tismo/ *n. m.* Mohammedanism.
maíz /ma'iθ; ma'is/ *n. m.* corn.
majadero /maha'ðero/ **-ra** *a.* & *n.* foolish; fool.
majar /ma'har/ *v.* mash.
majestad /mahes'tað/ *n. f.* majesty.
majestuoso /mahes'tuoso/ *a.* majestic.
mal /mal/ *adv.* **1.** badly; wrong. —*n.* **2.** *m.* evil, ill; illness.
mala /'mala/ *n. f.* mail.
malacate /mala'kate/ *n. m.* hoist.
malandanza /malan'danθa; malan'dansa/ *n. f.* misfortune.
malaventura /malaβen'tura/ *n. f.* misfortune.
malcomido /malko'miðo/ *a.* underfed; malnourished.
malcontento /malkon'tento/ *a.* dissatisfied.
maldad /mal'dað/ *n. f.* badness; wickedness.
maldecir /malde'θir; malde'sir/ *v.* curse, damn.
maldición /maldi'θion; maldi'sion/ *n. f.* curse.
maldito /mal'dito/ *a.* accursed, damned.
malecón /male'kon/ *n. m.* embankment.
maledicencia /maleði'θenθia; maleði'sensia/ *n. f.* slander.
maleficio /male'fiθio; male'fisio/ *n. m.* spell, charm.
malestar /males'tar/ *n. m.* indisposition.
maleta /ma'leta/ *n. f.* suitcase, valise.
malévolo /ma'leβolo/ *a.* malevolent.
maleza /ma'leθa; ma'lesa/ *n. f.* weeds; underbrush.
malgastar /malgas'tar/ *v.* squander.
malhechor /male'tʃor/ **-ra** *n.* malefactor, evildoer.
malhumorado /malumo'raðo/ *a.* morose, ill-humored.

malicia /ma'liθia; ma'lisia/ *n. f.* malice.

maliciar /mali'θiar; mali'siar/ *v.* suspect.

malicioso /mali'θioso; mali'sioso/ *a.* malicious.

maligno /ma'ligno/ *a.* malignant, evil.

malla /'maʎa; 'maya/ *n. f.* mesh, net.

mallas /'maʎas; 'mayas/ *n. f.pl.* leotard.

mallete /ma'ʎete; ma'yete/ *n. m.* mallet.

malo /'malo/ *a.* bad; evil, wicked; naughty; ill.

malograr /malo'grar/ *v.* miss, lose.

malparto /mal'parto/ *n. m.* abortion, miscarriage.

malquerencia /malke'renθia; malke-'rensia/ *n. f.* hatred.

malquerer /malke'rer/ *v.* dislike; bear ill will.

malsano /mal'sano/ *a.* unhealthy; unwholesome.

malsín /mal'sin/ *n. m.* malicious gossip.

malta /'malta/ *n. f.* malt.

maltratar /maltra'tar/ *v.* mistreat.

malvado /mal'βaðo/ **-da** *a.* **1.** wicked. —*n.* **2.** villain.

malversar /malβer'sar/ *v.* embezzle.

malvís /mal'βis/ *n. m.* redwing.

mamá /'mama/ *n. f.* mama, mother.

mamar /ma'mar/ *v.* suckle; suck.

mamífero /ma'mifero/ *n. m.* mammal.

mampara /mam'para/ *n. f.* screen.

mampostería /mamposte'ria/ *n. f.* masonry.

mamut /ma'mut/ *n. m.* mammoth.

manada /ma'naða/ *n. f.* flock, herd, drove.

manantial /manan'tial/ *n. m.* spring (of water).

manar /ma'nar/ *v.* gush, flow out.

mancebo /man'θeβo; man'seβo/ *n. m.* young man.

mancha /'mantʃa/ *n. f.* stain, smear, blemish, spot. —**manchar,** *v.*

mancilla /man'θiʎa; man'siya/ *n. f.* stain; blemish.

manco /'manko/ *a.* armless; one-armed.

mandadero /manda'ðero/ *n. m.* messenger.

mandado /man'daðo/ *n. m.* order, command.

mandamiento /manda'miento/ *n. m.* commandment; command.

mandar /man'dar/ *v.* send; order, command.

mandatario /manda'tario/ *n. m.* attorney; representative.

mandato /man'dato/ *n. m.* mandate, command.

mandíbula /man'diβula/ *n. f.* jaw; jawbone.

mando /'mando/ *n. m.* command, order; leadership.

mando a distancia /'mando a dis'tanθia; 'mando a dis'tansia/ remote control.

mandón /man'don/ *a.* domineering.

mandril /man'dril/ *n. m.* baboon.

manejar /mane'har/ *v.* handle, manage; drive (a car).

manejo /ma'neho/ *n. m.* management; horsemanship.

manera /ma'nera/ *n. f.* way, manner, means. **de m. que,** so, as a result.

manga /'maŋga/ *n. f.* sleeve.

mangana /maŋ'gana/ *n. f.* lariat, lasso.

manganeso /maŋga'neso/ *n. m.* manganese.

mango /'maŋgo/ *n. m.* handle; mango (fruit).

mangosta /maŋ'gosta/ *n. f.* mongoose.

manguera /maŋ'guera/ *n. f.* hose.

manguito /maŋ'guito/ *n. m.* muff.

maní /ma'ni/ *n. m.* peanut.

manía /ma'nia/ *n. f.* mania, madness; hobby.

maníaco /ma'niako/ **-ca, maniático -ca** *a. & n.* maniac.

manicomio /mani'komio/ *n. m.* insane asylum.

manicura /mani'kura/ *n. f.* manicure.

manifactura /manifak'tura/ *n. f.* manufacture.

manifestación /manifesta'θion; manifesta'sion/ *n. f.* manifestation.

manifestar /manifes'tar/ *v.* manifest, show.

manifiesto /mani'fiesto/ *a. & m.* manifest.

manija /ma'niha/ *n. f.* handle; crank.

maniobra /ma'nioβra/ *n. f.* maneuver. —**maniobrar,** *v.*

manipulación /manipula'θion; manipula'sion/ *n. f.* manipulation.

manipular /manipu'lar/ *v.* manipulate.

maniquí /mani'ki/ *n. m.* mannequin.

manivela /mani'βela/ *n. f. Mech.* crank.

manjar /man'har/ *n. m.* food, dish.

manlieve /man'lieβe/ *n. m.* swindle.

mano /'mano/ *n. f.* hand.

manojo /ma'noho/ *n. m.* handful; bunch.

manómetro /ma'nometro/ *n. m.* gauge.

manopla /ma'nopla/ *n. f.* gauntlet.

manosear /manose'ar/ *v.* handle, feel, touch.

manotada /mano'taða/ *n. f.* slap, smack. —**manotear,** *v.*

mansedumbre /manse'ðumbre/ *n. f.* meekness, tameness.

mansión /man'sion/ *n. f.* mansion; abode.

manso /'manso/ *a.* tame, gentle.

manta /'manta/ *n. f.* blanket.

manteca /man'teka/ *n. f.* fat, lard; butter.

mantecado /mante'kaðo/ *n. m.* ice cream.

mantecoso /mante'koso/ *a.* buttery.

mantel /man'tel/ *n. m.* tablecloth.

mantener /mante'ner/ *v.* maintain, keep; sustain; support.

mantenimiento /manteni'miento/ *n. m.* maintenance.

mantequera /mante'kera/ *n. f.* butter dish; churn.

mantequilla /mante'kiʎa; mante'ki-ya/ *n. f.* butter.

mantilla /man'tiʎa; man'tiya/ *n. f.* mantilla; baby clothes.

mantillo /man'tiʎo; man'tiyo/ *n. m.* humus; manure.

manto /'manto/ *n. m.* mantle, cloak.

manual /ma'nual/ *a. & m.* manual.

manubrio /ma'nuβrio/ *n. m.* handle; crank.

manufacturar /manufaktu'rar/ *v.* manufacture; make.

manuscrito /manus'krito/ *n. m.* manuscript.

manzana /man'θana; man'sana/ *n. f.* apple; block (of street).

manzanilla /manθa'niʎa; mansa'niya/ *n. f.* dry sherry.

manzano /man'θano; man'sano/ *n. m.* apple tree.

maña /'maɲa/ *n. f.* skill; cunning; trick.

mañana /ma'ɲana/ *adv.* **1.** tomorrow. —*n.* **2.** *f.* morning.

mañanear /maɲane'ar/ *v.* rise early in the morning.

mañero /ma'ɲero/ *a.* clever; skillful; lazy.

mapa /'mapa/ *n. m.* map, chart.

mapache /ma'patʃe/ *n. m.* raccoon.

mapurito /mapu'rito/ *n. m.* skunk.

máquina /'makina/ *n. f.* machine. **m. de coser,** sewing machine. **m. de lavar,** washing machine.

maquinación /makina'θion; makina-'sion/ *n. f.* machination; plot.

maquinador /makina'ðor/ **-ra** *n.* plotter, schemer.

maquinal /maki'nal/ *a.* mechanical.

maquinar /maki'nar/ *v.* scheme, plot.

maquinaria /maki'naria/ *n. f.* machinery.

maquinista /maki'nista/ *n. m.* machinist; engineer.

mar /mar/ *n. m. or f.* sea.

marabú /mara'βu/ *n. m.* marabou.

maraña /ma'raɲa/ *n. f.* tangle; maze; snarl; plot.

maravilla /mara'βiʎa; mara'βiya/ *n. f.* marvel, wonder. —**maravillarse,** *v.*

maravilloso /maraβi'ʎoso; maraβi-'yoso/ *a.* marvelous, wonderful.

marbete /mar'βete/ *n. m.* tag, label; check.

marca /'marka/ *n. f.* mark, sign; brand, make.

marcador /marka'ðor/ *n. m.* highlighter.

marcapáginas /marka'pahinas/ *n. m.* bookmark.

marcar /mar'kar/ *v.* mark; observe, note.

marcha /'martʃa/ *n. f.* march; progress. —**marchar,** *v.*

marchante /mar'tʃante/ *n. m.* merchant; customer.

marcharse /mar'tʃarse/ *v.* go away, depart.

marchitable /martʃi'taβle/ *a.* perishable.

marchitar /martʃi'tar/ *v.* fade, wilt, wither.

marchito /mar'tʃito/ *a.* faded, withered.

marcial /mar'θial; mar'sial/ *a.* martial.

marco /'marko/ *n. m.* frame.

marea /ma'rea/ *n. f.* tide.

mareado /mare'aðo/ *a.* seasick.

marearse /mare'arse/ *v.* get dizzy; be seasick.

mareo /ma'reo/ *n. m.* dizziness; seasickness.

marfil /mar'fil/ *n. m.* ivory.

margarita /marga'rita/ *n. f.* pearl; daisy.

margen /'marhen/ *n. m. or f.* margin, edge, rim.

marido /ma'riðo/ *n. m.* husband.

marijuana /mari'huana/ *n. f.* marijuana.

marimacha /mari'matʃa/ *n. f.* lesbian.

marimacho /mari'matʃo/ *n. m.* mannish woman.

marimba /ma'rimba/ *n. f.* marimba.

marina /ma'rina/ *n. f.* navy; seascape.

marinero /mari'nero/ *n. m.* sailor, seaman.

marino /ma'rino/ *a. & m.* marine, (of) sea; mariner, seaman.

marión /ma'rion/ *n. m.* sturgeon.

mariposa /mari'posa/ *n. f.* butterfly.

mariquita /mari'kita/ *n. f.* ladybird.

mariscal /maris'kal/ *n. m.* marshal.

marisco /ma'risko/ *n. m.* shellfish; mollusk.

marital /mari'tal/ *a.* marital.

marítimo /ma'ritimo/ *a.* maritime.

marmita /mar'mita/ *n. f.* pot, kettle.

mármol /'marmol/ *n. m.* marble.

marmóreo /mar'moreo/ *a.* marble.

maroma /ma'roma/ *n. f.* rope.

marqués /mar'kes/ *n. m.* marquis.

marquesa /mar'kesa/ *n. f.* marquise.

Marruecos /ma'rruekos/ *n. m.* Morocco.

Marte /'marte/ *n. m.* Mars.

martes /'martes/ *n. m.* Tuesday.

martillo /mar'tiʎo; mar'tiyo/ *n. m.* hammer. —**martillar,** *v.*

mártir /'martir/ *n. m. & f.* martyr.

martirio /mar'tirio/ *n. m.* martyrdom.

martirizar /martiri'θar; martiri'sar/ *v.* martyrize.

marzo /'marθo; 'marso/ *n. m.* March.

mas /mas/ *conj.* but.

más /mas/ *a. & adv.* more, most; plus. **no m.,** only; no more.

masa /'masa/ *n. f.* mass; dough.

masaje /ma'sahe/ *n. m.* massage.

mascar /mas'kar/ *v.* chew.

máscara /'maskara/ *n. f.* mask.

mascarada /maska'raða/ *n. f.* masquerade.

mascota /mas'kota/ *n. f.* mascot; good-luck charm.

masculino /masku'lino/ *a.* masculine.

mascullar /masku'ʎar; masku'yar/ *v.* mumble.

masón /ma'son/ *n. m.* Freemason.

masticar /masti'kar/ *v.* chew.

mástil /'mastil/ *n. m.* mast; post.

mastín /mas'tin/ *n. m.* mastiff.

mastín danés /mas'tin da'nes/ Great Dane.

mastuerzo /mas'tuerθo; mas'tuerso/ *n. m.* fool; ninny.

mata /'mata/ *n. f.* plant; bush.

matadero /mata'ðero/ *n. m.* slaughterhouse.

matador /mata'ðor/ **-ra** *n.* matador.

matafuego /mata'fuego/ *n. m.* fire extinguisher.

matanza /ma'tanθa; ma'tansa/ *n. f.* killing, bloodshed, slaughter.

matar /ma'tar/ *v.* kill, slay; slaughter.

matasanos /mata'sanos/ *n. m.* quack.

mate /'mate/ *n. m.* checkmate; Paraguayan tea.

matemáticas /mate'matikas/ *n. f.pl.* mathematics.

matemático /mate'matiko/ *a.* mathematical.

materia /ma'teria/ *n. f.* material; subject (matter).

material /mate'rial/ *a. & m.* material.

materialismo /materia'lismo/ *n. m.* materialism.

materializar /materiali'θar; materiali'sar/ *v.* materialize.

maternal /mater'nal/ **materno** *a.* maternal.

maternidad /materni'ðað/ *n. f.* maternity; maternity hospital.

matiné /mati'ne/ *n. f.* matinee.

matiz /ma'tiθ; ma'tis/ *n. m.* hue, shade.

matizar /mati'θar; mati'sar/ *v.* blend; tint.

matón /ma'ton/ *n. m.* bully.

matorral /mato'rral/ *n. m.* thicket.

matoso /ma'toso/ *a.* weedy.

matraca /ma'traka/ *n. f.* rattle. —**matraquear,** *v.*

matrícula /ma'trikula/ *n. f.* registration; tuition.

matricularse /matriku'larse/ *v.* enroll, register.

matrimonio /matri'monio/ *n. m.* matrimony, marriage; married couple.

matriz /ma'triθ; ma'tris/ *n. f.* womb; *Mech.* die, mold.

matrona /ma'trona/ *n. f.* matron.

maullar /mau'ʎar; mau'yar/ *v.* mew.

máxima /'maksima/ *n. f.* maxim.

máxime /'maksime/ *a.* principally.

máximo /'maksimo/ *a. & m.* maximum.

maya /'maya/ *n. f.* daisy.

mayo /'mayo/ *n. m.* May.

mayonesa /mayo'nesa/ *n. f.* mayonnaise.

mayor /ma'yor/ *a.* larger, largest; greater, greatest; elder, eldest, senior. **m. de edad,** major, of age. **al por m.,** at wholesale. *m.* major.

mayoral /mayo'ral/ *n. m.* head shepherd; boss; foreman.

mayordomo /mayor'ðomo/ *n. m.* manager; butler, steward.

mayoría /mayo'ria/ *n. f.* majority, bulk.

mayorista /mayo'rista/ *n. m. & f.* wholesaler.

mayúscula /ma'yuskula/ *n. f.* capital letter, upper-case letter.

mazmorra /maθ'morra; mas'morra/ *n. f.* dungeon.

mazorca /ma'θorka; ma'sorka/ *n. f.* ear of corn.

me /me/ *pron.* me; myself.

mecánico /me'kaniko/ **-ca** *a. & n.* mechanical; mechanic.

mecanismo /meka'nismo/ *n. m.* mechanism.

mecanizar /mekani'θar; mekani'sar/ *v.* mechanize.

mecanografía /mekanogra'fia/ *n. f.* typewriting.

mecanógrafo /meka'nografo/ **-fa** *n.* typist.

mecedor /meθe'ðor; mese'ðor/ *n. m.* swing.

mecedora /meθe'ðora; mese'ðora/ *n. f.* rocking chair.

mecer /me'θer; me'ser/ *v.* rock; swing, sway.

mecha /'metʃa/ *n. f.* wick; fuse.

mechón /me'tʃon/ *n. m.* lock (of hair).

medalla /me'ðaʎa; me'ðaya/ *n. f.* medal.

médano /'meðano/ *n. m.* sand dune.

media /'meðia/ *n. f.* stocking.

mediación /meðia'θion; meðia'sion/ *n. f.* mediation.

mediador /meðia'ðor/ **-ra** *n.* mediator.

mediados /me'ðiaðos/ *n. m.pl.* **a m. de,** about the middle of (a period of time).

medianero /meðia'nero/ *n. m.* mediator.

medianía /meðia'nia/ *n. f.* mediocrity.

mediano /me'ðiano/ *a.* medium; moderate; mediocre.

medianoche /meðia'notʃe/ *n. f.* midnight.

mediante /me'ðiante/ *prep.* by means of.

mediar /me'ðiar/ *v.* mediate.

medicamento /meðika'mento/ *n. m.* medicine, drug.

medicastro /meði'kastro/ *n. m.* quack.

medicina /meði'θina; meði'sina/ *n. f.* medicine.

medicinar /meðiθi'nar; meðisi'nar/ *v.* treat (as a doctor).

médico /'meðiko/ *a.* **1.** medical. —*n.* **2.** *m. & f.* doctor, physician.

medida /me'ðiða/ *n. f.* measure, step.

medidor /meði'ðor/ *n. m.* meter.

medieval /meðie'βal/ *a.* medieval.

medio /'meðio/ *a.* **1.** half; mid, middle of. —*n.* **2.** *m.* middle; means.

mediocre /me'ðiokre/ *a.* mediocre.

mediocridad /meðiokri'ðað/ *n. f.* mediocrity.

mediodía /meðio'ðia/ *n. m.* midday, noon.

medir /me'ðir/ *v.* measure, gauge.

meditación /meðita'θion; meðita'sion/ *n. f.* meditation.

meditar /meði'tar/ *v.* meditate.

mediterráneo /meðite'rraneo/ *a.* Mediterranean.

medrar /me'ðrar/ *v.* thrive; grow.

medroso /me'ðroso/ *a.* fearful, cowardly.

megáfono /me'gafono/ *n. m.* megaphone.

megahercio /mega'erθio; mega'ersio/ *n. f.* megahertz.

mejicano /mehi'kano/ **-na** *a. & n.* Mexican.

mejilla /me'hiʎa; me'hiya/ *n. f.* cheek.

mejillón /mehi'ʎon; mehi'yon/ *n. m.* mussel.

mejor /me'hor/ *a. & adv.* better; best. **a lo m.,** perhaps.

mejora /me'hora/ *n. f.,* **mejoramiento,** *m.* improvement.

mejorar /meho'rar/ *v.* improve, better.

mejoría /meho'ria/ *n. f.* improvement; superiority.

melancolía /melanko'lia/ *n. f.* melancholy.

melancólico /melan'koliko/ *a.* melancholy.

melaza /me'laθa; me'lasa/ *n. f.* molasses.

melena /me'lena/ *n. f.* mane; long or loose hair.

melenudo /mele'nuðo/ **-da** *a.* long-haired.

melindroso /melin'droso/ *a.* fussy.

mella /'meʎa; 'meya/ *n. f.* notch; dent. —**mellar,** *v.*

mellizo /me'ʎiθo; me'yiso/ **-za** *n. & a.* twin.

melocotón /meloko'ton/ *n. m.* peach.

melodía /melo'ðia/ *n. f.* melody.

melodioso /melo'ðioso/ *a.* melodious.

melón /me'lon/ *n. m.* melon.

meloso /me'loso/ *a.* like honey.

membrana /mem'brana/ *n. f.* membrane.

membrete /mem'brete/ *n. m.* memorandum; letterhead.

membrillo /mem'briʎo; mem'briyo/ *n. m.* quince.

membrudo /mem'bruðo/ *a.* strong, muscular.

memorable /memo'raβle/ *a.* memorable.

memorándum /memo'randum/ *n. m.* memorandum; notebook.

memoria /me'moria/ *n. f.* memory; memoir; memorandum.

mención /men'θion; men'sion/ *n. f.* mention. —**mencionar,** *v.*

mendigar /mendi'gar/ *v.* beg (for alms).

mendigo /men'digo/ **-a** *n.* beggar.

mendrugo /men'drugo/ *n. m.* (hard) crust, chunk.

menear /mene'ar/ *v.* shake, wag; stir.

menester /menes'ter/ *n. m.* need, want; duty, task. **ser m.,** to be necessary.

menesteroso /meneste'roso/ *a.* needy.

mengua /'meŋgua/ *n. f.* decrease; lack; poverty.

menguar /meŋ'guar/ *v.* abate, decrease.

meningitis /meniŋ'gitis/ *n. f.* meningitis.

menopausia /meno'pausia/ *n. f.* menopause.

menor /me'nor/ *a.* smaller, smallest; lesser, least; younger, youngest, junior. *m.* **de edad,** minor, under age. **al por m.,** at retail.

menos /'menos/ *a. & adv.* less, least; minus. **a m. que,** unless. **echar de m.,** to miss.

menospreciar /menospre'θiar; menospre'siar/ *v.* cheapen; despise; slight.

mensaje /men'sahe/ *n. m.* message.

mensajero /mensa'hero/ **-ra** *n.* messenger.

menstruar /menstru'ar/ *v.* menstruate.

mensual /men'sual/ *a.* monthly.

mensualidad /mensuali'ðað/ *n. f.* monthly income or allowance; monthly payment.

menta /'menta/ *n. f.* mint, peppermint.

mentado /men'taðo/ *a.* famous.

mental /men'tal/ *a.* mental.

mentalidad /mentali'ðað/ *n. f.* mentality.

menta romana /'menta rro'mana/ spearmint.

mente /'mente/ *n. f.* mind.

mentecato /mente'kato/ *a.* foolish, stupid.

mentir /men'tir/ *v.* lie, tell a lie.

mentira /men'tira/ *n. f.* lie, falsehood. **parece m.,** it seems impossible.

mentiroso /menti'roso/ *a.* lying, untruthful.

mentol /'mentol/ *n. m.* menthol.

menú /me'nu/ *n. m.* menu.

menudeo /menu'ðeo/ *n. m.* retail.

menudo /menu'ðo/ *a.* small, minute. **a m.,** often.

meñique /me'ɲike/ *a.* tiny.

meple /'meple/ *n. m.* maple.

merca /'merka/ *n. f.* purchase.

mercader /merka'ðer/ *n. m.* merchant.

mercaderías /merkaðe'rias/ *n. f.pl.* merchandise, commodities.

mercado /mer'kaðo/ *n. m.* market.

Mercado Común /mer'kaðo ko'mun/ Common Market.

mercado negro /mer'kaðo 'negro/ black market.

mercancía /merkan'θia; merkan'sia/ *n. f.* merchandise; (*pl.*) wares.

mercante /mer'kante/ *a.* merchant.

mercantil /merkan'til/ *a.* mercantile.

merced /mer'θeð; mer'seð/ *n. f.* mercy, grace.

mercenario /merθe'nario; merse'nario/ **-ria** *a. & n.* mercenary.

mercurio /mer'kurio/ *n. m.* mercury.

merecedor /mereθe'ðor; merese'ðor/ *a.* worthy.

merecer /mere'θer; mere'ser/ *v.* merit, deserve.

merecimiento /mereθi'miento; meresi'miento/ *n. m.* merit.

merendar /meren'dar/ *v.* eat lunch; snack.

merendero /meren'dero/ *n. m.* lunchroom.

meridional /meriðio'nal/ *a.* southern.

merienda /me'rienda/ *n. f.* midday meal, lunch; afternoon snack.

mérito /'merito/ *n. m.* merit, worth.

meritorio /meri'torio/ *a.* meritorious.

merla /'merla/ *n. f.* blackbird.

merluza /mer'luθa; mer'lusa/ *n. f.* haddock.

mermelada /merme'laða/ *n. f.* marmalade.

mero /'mero/ *a.* mere.

merodeador /meroðea'ðor/ **-ra** *n.* prowler.

mes /'mes/ *n. m.* month.

mesa /'mesa/ *n. f.* table.

meseta /me'seta/ *n. f.* plateau.

mesón /me'son/ *n. m.* inn.

mesonero /meso'nero/ **-ra** *n.* innkeeper.

mestizo /mes'tiθo; mes'tiso/ **-za** *a. & n.* half-breed.

meta /'meta/ *n. f.* goal, objective.

metabolismo /metaβo'lismo/ *n. m.* metabolism.

metafísica /meta'fisika/ *n. f.* metaphysics.

metáfora /me'tafora/ *n. f.* metaphor.

metal /me'tal/ *n. m.* metal.

metálico /me'taliko/ *a.* metallic.

metalurgia /metalur'hia/ *n. f.* metallurgy.

meteoro /mete'oro/ *n. m.* meteor.

meteorología /meteorolo'hia/ *n. f.* meteorology.

meter /me'ter/ *v.* put (in).

meterse /me'terse/ *v.* interfere, meddle; go into.

metódico /me'toðiko/ *a.* methodic.

método /'metoðo/ *n. m.* method, approach.

metralla /me'traʎa; me'traya/ *n. f.* shrapnel.

métrico /'metriko/ *a.* metric.

metro /'metro/ *n. m.* meter (measure); subway.

metrópoli /me'tropoli/ *n. f.* metropolis.

mexicano /meksi'kano/ **-na** *a. & n.* Mexican.

mezcla /'meθkla; 'meskla/ *n. f.* mixture; blend.

mezclar /meθ'klar; mes'klar/ *v.* mix; blend.

mezcolanza /meθko'lanθa; mesko'lansa/ *n. f.* mixture; hodgepodge.

mezquino /meθ'kino; mes'kino/ *a.* stingy; petty.

mezquita /meθ'kita; mes'kita/ *n. f.* mosque.

mi /'mi/ *a.* my.

mí /'mi/ *pron.* me; myself.

microbio /mi'kroβio/ *n. m.* microbe, germ.

microbús /mikro'βus/ *n. m.* minibus.

microchip /mikro'tʃip/ *n. m.* microchip.

microficha /mikro'fitʃa/ *n. f.* microfiche.

micrófono /mi'krofono/ *n. m.* microphone.

microforma /mikro'forma/ *n. f.* microform.

microscópico /mikros'kopiko/ *a.* microscopic.

microscopio /mikros'kopio/ *n. m.* microscope.

microtaxi /mikro'taksi/ *n. m.* minicab.

miedo /'mieðo/ *n. m.* fear. **tener m.,** fear, be afraid.

miedoso /mie'ðoso/ *a.* fearful.

miel /miel/ *n. f.* honey.

miembro /mi'embro/ *n. m. & f.* member; limb.

mientras /'mientras/ *conj.* while. **m. tanto,** meanwhile. **m. más... más,** the more... the more.

miércoles /'mierkoles/ *n. m.* Wednesday.

miércoles de ceniza /'mierkoles de θe'niθa; 'mierkoles de se'nisa/ Ash Wednesday.

miga /'miga/ **migaja** *n. f.* scrap; crumb.

migración /migra'θion; migra'sion/ *n. f.* migration.

migratorio /migra'torio/ *a.* migratory.

mil /mil/ *a. & pron.* thousand.

milagro /mi'lagro/ *n. m.* miracle.

milagroso /mila'groso/ *a.* miraculous.

milicia /mi'liθia; mi'lisia/ *n. f.* militia.

militante /mili'tante/ *a.* militant.

militar /mili'tar/ *a.* **1.** military. —*n.* **2.** *m.* military man.

militarismo /milita'rismo/ *n. m.* militarism.

milla /'miʎa; 'miya/ *n. f.* mile.

millar /mi'ʎar; mi'yar/ *n. m.* (a) thousand.

millón /mi'ʎon; mi'yon/ *n. m.* million.

millonario /miʎo'nario; miyo'nario/ **-ria** *n.* millionaire.

mimar /mi'mar/ *v.* pamper, spoil (a child).

mimbre /'mimbre/ *n. m.* willow; wicker.

mímico /'mimiko/ *a.* mimic.

mimo /'mimo/ *n. m.* mime, mimic.

mina /'mina/ *n. f.* mine. —**minar,** *v.*

mineral /mine'ral/ *a. & m.* mineral.

minero /mi'nero/ **-ra** *n.* miner.

miniatura /minia'tura/ *n. f.* miniature.

miniaturizar /miniaturi'θar; miniaturi'sar/ *v.* miniaturize.

mínimo /'minimo/ *a. & m.* minimum.

ministerio /minis'terio/ *n. m.* ministry; cabinet.

ministro /mi'nistro/ **-a** *n. Govt.* minister, secretary.

minoría /mino'ria/ *n. f.* minority.

minoridad /minori'ðað/ *n. f.* minority (of age).

minucioso /minu'θioso; minu'sioso/ *a.* minute; thorough.

minué /mi'nue/ *n. m.* minuet.

minúscula /mi'nuskula/ *n. f.* lowercase letter, small letter.

minuta /mi'nuta/ *n. f.* draft.

mío /'mio/ *a.* mine.

miopía /mio'pia/ *n. f.* myopia.

mira /'mira/ *n. f.* gunsight.

mirada /mi'raða/ *n. f.* look; gaze, glance.

miramiento /mira'miento/ *n. m.* consideration; respect.

mirar /mi'rar/ *v.* look, look at; watch. **m. a,** face.

miríada /mi'riaða/ *n. f.* myriad.

mirlo /'mirlo/ *n. m.* blackbird.

mirón /mi'ron/ **-ona** *n.* bystander, observer.

mirra /'mirra/ *n. f.* myrrh.

mirto /'mirto/ *n. m.* myrtle.

misa /'misa/ *n. f.* mass, church service.

misceláneo /misθe'laneo; misse'laneo/ *a.* miscellaneous.

miserable /mise'raβle/ *a.* miserable, wretched.

miseria /mi'seria/ *n. f.* misery.

misericordia /miseri'korðia/ *n. f.* mercy.

misericordioso /miserikor'ðioso/ *a.* merciful.

misión /mi'sion/ *n. f.* assignment; mission.

misionario /misio'nario/ **-ria, misionero -ra** *n.* missionary.

mismo /'mismo/ *a. & pron.* **1.** same; -self, -selves. —*adv.* **2.** right, exactly.

misterio /mis'terio/ *n. m.* mystery.

misterioso /miste'rioso/ *a.* mysterious, weird.

místico /'mistiko/ **-ca** *a. & n.* mystical, mystic.

mitad /mi'tað/ *n. f.* half.

mítico /'mitiko/ *a.* mythical.

mitigar /miti'gar/ *v.* mitigate.

mitin /'mitin/ *n. m.* meeting; rally.

mito /'mito/ *n. m.* myth.

mitón /mi'ton/ *n. m.* mitten.

mitra /'mitra/ *n. f.* miter (bishop's).

mixto /'miksto/ *a.* mixed.

mixtura /miks'tura/ *n. f.* mixture.

mobiliario /moβi'liario/ *n. m.* household goods.

mocasín /moka'sin/ *n. m.* moccasin.

mocedad /moθe'ðað; mose'ðað/ *n. f.* youthfulness.

mochila /mo'tʃila/ *n. f.* knapsack, backpack.

mocho /'motʃo/ *a.* cropped, trimmed, shorn.

moción /mo'θion; mo'sion/ *n. f.* motion.

mocoso /mo'koso/ **-sa** *n.* brat.

moda /'moða/ *n. f.* mode, fashion, style.

modales /mo'ðales/ *n. m.pl.* manners.

modelo /mo'ðelo/ *n. m.* model, pattern.

módem /'moðem/ *n. m.* modem.

moderación /moðera'θion; moðera'sion/ *n. f.* moderation.

moderado /moðe'raðo/ *a.* moderate. —**moderar,** *v.*

modernizar /moðerni'θar; moðerni'sar/ *v.* modernize.

moderno /mo'ðerno/ *a.* modern.

modestia /mo'ðestia/ *n. f.* modesty.

modesto /mo'ðesto/ *a.* modest.

módico /'moðiko/ *a.* reasonable, moderate.

modificación /moðifi'kaθion; moðifika'sion/ *n. f.* modification.

modificar /moðifi'kar/ *v.* modify.

modismo /mo'ðismo/ *n. m. Gram.* idiom.

modista /mo'ðista/ *n. f.* dressmaker; milliner.

modo /'moðo/ *n. m.* way, means.

modular /moðu'lar/ *v.* modulate.

mofarse /mo'farse/ *v.* scoff, sneer.

mofletudo /mofle'tuðo/ *a.* fat-cheeked.

mohín /mo'in/ *n. m.* grimace.

moho /'moo/ *n. m.* mold, mildew.

mohoso /mo'oso/ *a.* moldy.

mojar /mo'har/ *v.* wet.

mojón /mo'hon/ *n. m.* landmark; heap.

molde /'molde/ *n. m.* mold, form.

molécula /mo'lekula/ *n. f.* molecule.

moler /mo'ler/ *v.* grind, mill.

molestar /moles'tar/ *v.* molest, bother, disturb, annoy, trouble.

molestia /mo'lestia/ *n. f.* bother, annoyance, trouble; hassle.

molesto /mo'lesto/ *a.* bothersome; annoyed; uncomfortable.

molicie /mo'liθie; mo'lisie/ *n. f.* softness.

molinero /moli'nero/ *n. m.* miller.

molino /mo'lino/ *n. m.* mill. **m. de viento,** windmill.

mollera /mo'ʎera; mo'yera/ *n. f.* top of the head.

molusco /mo'lusko/ *n. m.* mollusk.

momentáneo /momen'taneo/ *a.* momentary.

momento /mo'mento/ *n. m.* moment.

mona /'mona/ *n. f.* female monkey.

monarca /mo'narka/ *n. m. & f.* monarch.

monarquía /monar'kia/ *n. f.* monarchy.

monarquista /monar'kista/ *n. & a.* monarchist.

monasterio /mona'sterio/ *n. m.* monastery.

mondadientes /monda'ðientes/ *n. m.* toothpick.

moneda /mo'neða/ *n. f.* coin; money.

monetario /mone'tario/ *a.* monetary.

monición /moni'θion; moni'sion/ *n. m.* warning.

monigote /moni'gote/ *n. m.* puppet.

monja /'monha/ *n. f.* nun.

monje /'monhe/ *n. m.* monk.

mono /'mono/ **-na** *a.* **1.** *Colloq.* cute. —*n.* **2.** *m. & f.* monkey.

monólogo /mo'nologo/ *n. m.* monologue.

monopatín /monopa'tin/ *n. m.* skateboard.

monopolio /mono'polio/ *n. m.* monopoly.

monopolizar /monopoli'θar; monopoli'sar/ *v.* monopolize.

monosílabo /mono'silaβo/ *n. m.* monosyllable.

monotonía /monoto'nia/ *n. f.* monotony.

monótono /mo'notono/ *a.* monotonous, dreary.

monstruo /'monstruo/ *n. m.* monster.

monstruosidad /monstruosi'ðað/ *n. f.* monstrosity.

monstruoso /mon'struoso/ *a.* monstrous.

monta /'monta/ *n. f.* amount; price.

montaña /mon'tapa/ *n. f.* mountain.

montañoso /monta'ɲoso/ *a.* mountainous.

montar /mon'tar/ *v.* mount, climb; amount; *Mech.* assemble. **m. a caballo,** ride horseback.

montaraz /monta'raθ; monta'ras/ *a.* wild, barbaric.

monte /'monte/ *n. m.* mountain; forest.

montón /mon'ton/ *n. m.* heap, pile.

montuoso /mon'tuoso/ *a.* mountainous.

montura /mon'tura/ *n. f.* mount; saddle.

monumental /monumen'tal/ *a.* monumental.

monumento /monu'mento/ *n. m.* monument.

mora /'mora/ *n. f.* blackberry.

morada /mo'raða/ *n. f.* residence, dwelling.

morado /mo'raðo/ *a.* purple.

moral /mo'ral/ *a.* **1.** moral. —*n.* **2.** *f.* morale.

moraleja /mora'leha/ *n. f.* moral.

moralidad /morali'ðað/ *n. f.* morality, morals.

moralista /mora'lista/ *n. m. & f.* moralist.

morar /mo'rar/ *v.* dwell, live, reside.

mórbido /'morβiðo/ *a.* morbid.

mordaz /mor'ðaθ; mor'ðas/ *a.* caustic; sarcastic.

mordedura /morðe'ðura/ *n. f.* bite.

morder /mor'ðer/ *v.* bite.

moreno /mo'reno/ **-na** *a. & n.* brown; dark-skinned; dark-haired, brunette.

morfina /mor'fina/ *n. f.* morphine.

moribundo /mori'βundo/ *a.* dying.

morir /mo'rir/ *v.* die.

morisco /mo'risko/ **-ca, moro -ra** *a. & n.* Moorish; Moor.

morriña /mo'rriɲa/ *n. f.* sadness.

morro /'morro/ *n. m.* bluff; snout.

mortaja /mor'taha/ *n. f.* shroud.

mortal /mor'tal/ *a. & n.* mortal.

mortalidad /mortali'ðað/ *n. f.* mortality.

mortero /mor'tero/ *n. m.* mortar.

mortífero /mor'tifero/ *a.* fatal, deadly.

mortificar /mortifi'kar/ *v.* mortify.

mortuorio /mor'tuorio/ *a.* funereal.

mosaico /mo'saiko/ *a. & m.* mosaic.

mosca /'moska/ *n. f.* fly.

mosquito /mos'kito/ *n. m.* mosquito.

mostacho /mos'tatʃo/ *n. m.* mustache.

mostaza /mos'taθa; mos'tasa/ *n. f.* mustard.

mostrador /mostra'ðor/ *n. m.* counter; showcase.

mostrar /mos'trar/ *v.* show, display.

mote /'mote/ *n. m.* nickname; alias.

motel /mo'tel/ *n. m.* motel.

motín /mo'tin/ *n. m.* mutiny; riot.

motivo /mo'tiβo/ *n. m.* motive, reason.

motocicleta /motoθi'kleta; motosi'kleta/ *n. f.* motorcycle.

motociclista /motoθi'klista; motosi'klista/ *n. m. & f.* motorcyclist.

motor /mo'tor/ *n. m.* motor.

motorista /moto'rista/ *n. m. & f.* motorist.

movedizo /moβe'ðiθo; moβe'ðiso/ *a.* movable, shaky.

mover /mo'βer/ *v.* move; stir.

movible /mo'βiβle/ *a.* movable.

móvil /'moβil/ *a.* mobile.

movilización /moβiliθa'θion; moβilisa'sion/ *n. f.* mobilization.

movilizar /moβili'θar; moβili'sar/ *v.* mobilize.

movimiento /moβi'miento/ *n. m.* movement, motion.

mozo /'moθo; 'moso/ *n. m.* boy; servant, waiter, porter.

muaré /mua're/ *n. m.* moiré.

muchacha /mu'tʃatʃa/ *n. f.* girl, youngster; maid (servant).

muchachez /mutʃa'tʃeθ; mutʃa'tʃes/ *n. m.* boyhood, girlhood.

muchacho /mu'tʃatʃo/ *n. m.* boy; youngster.

muchedumbre /mutʃe'ðumbre/ *n. f.* crowd, mob.

mucho /'mutʃo/ *a.* **1.** much, many. —*adv.* **2.** much.

mucoso /mu'koso/ *a.* mucous.

muda /'muða/ *n. f.* change.

mudanza /mu'ðanθa; muðansa/ *n. f.* change; change of residence.

mudar /mu'ðar/ *v.* change, shift.

mudarse /mu'ðarse/ *v.* change residence, move.

mudo /'muðo/ **-da** *a. & n.* mute.

mueble /'mueβle/ *n. m.* piece of furniture; (*pl.*) furniture.

mueca /'mueka/ *n. f.* grimace.

muela /'muela/ *n. f.* (back) tooth.

muelle /'mueʎe; 'mueye/ *n. m.* pier, wharf; *Mech.* spring.

muerte /'muerte/ *n. f.* death.

muerto /'muerto/ **-ta** *a.* **1.** dead. —*n.* **2.** dead person.

muesca /'mueska/ *n. f.* notch; groove.

muestra /'muestra/ *n. f.* sample, specimen; sign.

mugido /mu'hiðo/ *n. m.* lowing; mooing.

mugir /mu'hir/ *v.* low, moo.

mugre /'mugre/ *n. f.* filth, dirt.

mugriento /mu'griento/ *a.* dirty.

mujer /mu'her/ *f.* woman; wife. **m. de la limpieza,** cleaning lady, charwoman.

mujeril /muhe'ril/ *a.* womanly, feminine.

mula /'mula/ *n. f.* mule.

mulato /mu'lato/ **-ta** *a. & n.* mulatto.

muleta /mu'leta/ *n. f.* crutch; prop.

mulo /'mulo/ **-la** *n. m.* mule.

multa /'multa/ *n. f.* fine, penalty.

multicolor /multiko'lor/ *a.* many-colored.

multinacional /multinaθio'nal; multinasio'nal/ *a.* multinational.

múltiple /'multiple/ *a.* multiple.

multiplicación /multiplika'θion; multiplika'sion/ *n. f.* multiplication.

multiplicar /multipli'kar/ *v.* multiply.

multiplicidad /multipliθi'ðað; multiplisi'ðað/ *n. f.* multiplicity.

multitud /multi'tuð/ *n. f.* multitude, crowd.

mundanal /munda'nal, mun'dano/ *a.* worldly.

mundano /mun'dano/ *a.* worldly, mundane.

mundial /mun'dial/ *a.* worldwide; (of the) world.

mundo /'mundo/ *n. m.* world.

munición /muni'θion; muni'sion/ *n. f.* ammunition.

municipal /muniθi'pal; munisi'pal/ *a.* municipal.

municipio /muni'θipio; muni'sipio/ *n. m.* city hall.

muñeca /mu'ɲeka/ *n. f.* doll; wrist.

muñeco /mu'ɲeko/ *n. m.* doll; puppet.

mural /mu'ral/ *a. & m.* mural.

muralla /mu'raʎa; mu'raya/ *n. f.* wall.

murciélago /mur'θielago; mur'sielago/ *n. m.* bat.

murga /'murga/ *n. f.* musical band.

murmullo /mur'muʎo; mur'muyo/ *n. m.* murmur; rustle.

murmurar /murmu'rar/ *v.* murmur; rustle; grumble.

musa /'musa/ *n. f.* muse.

muscular /musku'lar/ *a.* muscular.

músculo /'muskulo/ *n. m.* muscle.

muselina /muse'lina/ *n. f.* muslin.

museo /mu'seo/ *n. m.* museum.

música /'musika/ *n. f.* music.

musical /musi'kal/ *a.* musical.

músico /'musiko/ **-ca** *a. & n.* musical; musician.

muslo /'muslo/ *n. m.* thigh.

mustio /'mustio/ *a.* sad.

musulmano /musul'mano/ **-na** *a. & n.* Muslim.

muta /'muta/ *n. f.* pack of hounds.

mutabilidad /mutaβili'ðað/ *n. f.* mutability.

mutación /muta'θion; muta'sion/ *n. f.* mutation.

mutilación /mutila'θion; mutila'sion/ *n. f.* mutilation.

mutilar /muti'lar/ *v.* mutilate; mangle.

mutuo /'mutuo/ *a.* mutual.

muy /'mui/ *adv.* very.

N Ñ

nabo /'naβo/ *n. m.* turnip.

nácar /'nakar/ *n. m.* mother-of-pearl.

nacarado /naka'raðo, na'kareo/ *a.* pearly.

nacer /na'θer; na'ser/ *v.* be born.

naciente /na'θiente; na'siente/ *a.* rising; nascent.

nacimiento /naθi'miento; nasi'miento/ *n. m.* birth.

nación /na'θion; na'sion/ *n. f.* nation.

nacional /naθio'nal; nasio'nal/ *a.* national.

nacionalidad /naθionali'ðað; nasionali'ðað/ *n. f.* nationality.

nacionalismo /naθiona'lismo; nasiona'lismo/ *n. m.* nationalism.

nacionalista /naθiona'lista; nasiona'lista/ *n. & a.* nationalist.

nacionalización /naθionaliθa'θion; nasionalisa'sion/ *n. f.* nationalization.

nacionalizar /naθionali'θar; nasionali'sar/ *v.* nationalize.

Naciones Unidas /na'θiones u'niðas; na'siones u'niðas/ *n. f.pl.* United Nations.

nada /'naða/ *pron.* **1.** nothing; anything. **de n.,** you're welcome. —*adv.* **2.** at all.

nadador /naða'ðor/ **-ra** *n.* swimmer.

nadar /na'ðar/ *v.* swim.

nadie /'naðie/ *pron.* no one, nobody; anyone, anybody.

nafta /'nafta/ *n. f.* naphtha.

naipe /'naipe/ *n. m.* (playing) card.
naranja /na'ranha/ *n. f.* orange.
naranjada /naran'haða/ *n. f.* orangeade.
naranjo /na'ranho/ *n. m.* orange tree.
narciso /nar'θiso; nar'siso/ *n. m.* daffodil; narcissus.
narcótico /nar'kotiko/ *a.* & *m.* narcotic.
nardo /'narðo/ *n. m.* spikenard.
nariz /na'riθ; na'ris/ *n. f.* nose; (*pl.*) nostrils.
narración /narra'θion; narra'sion/ *n. f.* account.
narrador /narra'ðor/ **-ra** *n.* narrator.
narrar /na'rrar/ *v.* narrate.
narrativa /narra'tiβa/ *n. f.* narrative.
nata /'nata/ *n. f.* cream.
nata batida /'nata ba'tiða/ whipped cream.
natación /nata'θion; nata'sion/ *n. f.* swimming.
natal /na'tal/ *a.* native; natal.
natalicio /nata'liθio; nata'lisio/ *n. m.* birthday.
natalidad /natali'ðað/ *n. f.* birth rate.
natillas /na'tiʎas; na'tiyas/ *n. f.pl.* custard.
nativo /na'tiβo/ *a.* native; innate.
natural /natu'ral/ *a.* **1.** natural. —*n.* **2.** *m.* & *f.* native. **3.** *m.* nature, disposition.
naturaleza /natura'leθa; natura'lesa/ *n. f.* nature.
naturalidad /naturali'ðað/ *n. f.* naturalness; nationality.
naturalista /natura'lista/ *a.* & *n.* naturalistic; naturalist.
naturalización /naturaliθa'θion; naturalisa'sion/ *n. f.* naturalization.
naturalizar /naturali'θar; naturali'sar/ *v.* naturalize.
naufragar /naufra'gar/ *v.* be shipwrecked; fail.
naufragio /nau'frahio/ *n. m.* shipwreck; disaster.
náufrago /'naufrago/ **-ga** *a.* & *n.* shipwrecked (person).
náusea /'nausea/ *n. f.* nausea.
nausear /nause'ar/ *v.* feel nauseous.
náutico /'nautiko/ *a.* nautical.
navaja /na'βaha/ *n. f.* razor; pen knife.
naval /na'βal/ *a.* naval.
navasca /na'βaska/ *n. f.* blizzard, snowstorm.
nave /'naβe/ *n. f.* ship.
nave espacial /'naβe espa'θial; 'naβe es'pasial/ spaceship.
navegable /naβe'gaβle/ *a.* navigable.
navegación /naβega'θion; naβega'sion/ *n. f.* navigation.
navegador /naβega'ðor/ **-ra** *n.* navigator.
navegante /naβe'gante/ *n. m.* & *f.* navigator.
navegar /naβe'gar/ *v.* sail; navigate.
Navidad /naβi'ðað/ *n. f.* Christmas.
navío /na'βio/ *n. m.* ship.
neblina /ne'βlina/ *n. f.* mist, fog.
nebuloso /neβu'loso/ *a.* misty; nebulous.
necedad /neθe'ðað; nese'ðað/ *n. f.* stupidity; nonsense.
necesario /neθe'sario; nese'sario/ *a.* necessary.
necesidad /neθesi'ðað; nesesi'ðað/ *n. f.* necessity, need, want.
necesitado /neθesi'taðo; nesesi'taðo/ *a.* needy, poor.
necesitar /neθesi'tar; nesesi'tar/ *v.* need.
necio /'neθio; 'nesio/ **-cia** *a.* **1.** stupid, silly. —*n.* **2.** fool.
néctar /'nektar/ *n. m.* nectar.
nectarina /nekta'rina/ *n. f.* nectarine.
nefando /ne'fando/ *a.* nefarious.
nefasto /ne'fasto/ *a.* unlucky, ill-fated.
negable /ne'gaβle/ *a.* deniable.
negación /nega'θion; nega'sion/ *n. f.* denial, negation.
negar /ne'gar/ *v.* deny.
negarse /ne'garse/ *v.* refuse, decline.
negativa /nega'tiβa/ *n. f.* negative, refusal.
negativamente /negatiβa'mente/ *adv.* negatively.
negativo /nega'tiβo/ *a.* negative.
negligencia /negli'henθia; negli'hensia/ *n. f.* negligence, neglect.
negligente /negli'hente/ *a.* negligent.
negociación /negoθia'θion; negosia'sion/ *n. f.* negotiation, deal.
negociador /negoθia'ðor; negosia'ðor/ **-ra** *n.* negotiator.
negociante /nego'θiante; nego'siante/ **-ta** *n.* businessperson.
negociar /nego'θiar; nego'siar/ *v.* negotiate, trade.
negocio /ne'goθio; ne'gosio/ *n. m.* trade; business.
negro /'negro/ **-gra** *a.* **1.** black. —*n.* **2.** *m.* Black.
nene /'nene/ **-na** *n.* baby.
neo /'neo/ **neón** *n. m.* neon.
nervio /'nerβio/ *n. m.* nerve.
nerviosamente /nerβiosa'mente/ *adv.* nervously.
nervioso /ner'βioso/ *a.* nervous.
nesciencia /nesθien'θia; nessien'sia/ *n. f.* ignorance.
nesciente /nes'θiente; nes'siente/ *a.* ignorant.
neto /'neto/ *a.* net.
neumático /neu'matiko/ *a.* **1.** pneumatic. —*n.* **2.** *m.* (pneumatic) tire.
neumático de recambio /neu'matiko de rre'kambio/ spare tire.
neumonía /neumo'nia/ *n. f.* pneumonia.
neurótico /neu'rotiko/ *a.* neurotic.
neutral /neu'tral/ *a.* neutral.
neutralidad /neutrali'ðað/ *n. f.* neutrality.
neutro /'neutro/ *a.* neuter; neutral.
neutrón /neu'tron/ *n. m.* neutron.
nevada /ne'βaða/ *n. f.* snowfall.
nevado /ne'βaðo/ *a.* snow-white; snow-capped.
nevar /ne'βar/ *v.* snow.
nevera /ne'βera/ *n. f.* icebox.
nevoso /ne'βoso/ *a.* snowy.
ni /ni/ *conj.* **1.** nor. **ni... ni,** neither... nor. —*adv.* **2.** not even.
nicho /'nitʃo/ *n. m.* recess; niche.
nido /'niðo/ *n. m.* nest.
niebla /'nieβla/ *n. f.* fog; mist.
nieto /'nieto/ **-ta** *n.* grandchild.
nieve /'nieβe/ *n. f.* snow.
nilón /ni'lon/ *n. m.* nylon.
nimio /'nimio/ *adj.* stingy.
ninfa /'ninfa/ *n. f.* nymph.
ningún /niŋ'gun/ **-no -na** *a.* & *pron.* no, none, neither (one); any, either (one).
niñera /ni'ɲera/ *n. f.* nursemaid, nanny.
niñez /ni'ɲeθ; ni'ɲes/ *n. f.* childhood.
niño /'niɲo/ **-ña 1.** *a.* **1.** young; childish; childlike. —*n.* **2.** child.
níquel /'nikel/ *n. m.* nickel.
niquelado /nike'laðo/ *a.* nickel-plated.
nítido /'nitiðo/ *a.* neat, clean, bright.
nitrato /ni'trato/ *n. m.* nitrate.
nitro /'nitro/ *n. m.* niter.
nitrógeno /ni'troheno/ *n. m.* nitrogen.
nivel /ni'βel/ *n. m.* level; grade. —**nivelar,** *v.*
no /no/ *adv.* **1.** not. **no más,** only. —*interj.* **2.** no.
noble /'noβle/ *a.* & *m.* noble; nobleman.
nobleza /no'βleθa; no'βlesa/ *n. f.* nobility; nobleness.
noche /'notʃe/ *n. f.* night; evening.
Nochebuena /notʃe'βuena/ *n. f.* Christmas Eve.
noción /no'θion; no'sion/ *n. f.* notion, idea.
nocivo /no'θiβo; no'siβo/ *a.* harmful.
noctiluca /nokti'luka/ *n. f.* glowworm.
nocturno /nok'turno/ *a.* nocturnal.
nodriza /no'ðriθa; no'ðrisa/ *n. f.* wet nurse.
no fumador /no fuma'ðor/ **-ra** *n. m.* & *f.* nonsmoker.
nogal /no'gal/ *n. m.* walnut.
nombradía /nom'βraðia/ *n. f.* fame.
nombramiento /nombra'miento/ *n. m.* appointment, nomination.
nombrar /nom'βrar/ *v.* name, appoint, nominate; mention.
nombre /'nombre/ *n. m.* name; noun.
nombre y apellidos /'nombre i ape'ʎiðos; 'nombre i ape'yiðos/ (person's) full name.
nómina /'nomina/ *n. f.* list; payroll.
nominación /nomina'θion; nomina'sion/ *n. f.* nomination.
nominal /nomi'nal/ *a.* nominal.
nominar /nomi'nar/ *v.* nominate.
non /non/ *a.* uneven, odd.
nonada /no'naða/ *n. f.* trifle.
nordeste /nor'ðeste/ *n. m.* northeast.
nórdico /'norðiko/ *a.* Nordic; northerly.
norma /'norma/ *n. f.* norm, standard.
normal /nor'mal/ *a.* normal, standard.
normalidad /normali'ðað/ *n. f.* normality.
normalizar /normali'θar; normali'sar/ *v.* normalize; standardize.
noroeste /noro'este/ *n. m.* northwest.
norte /'norte/ *n. m.* north.
norteamericano /norteameri'kano/ **-na** *a.* & *n.* North American.
Noruega /no'ruega/ *n. f.* Norway.
noruego /no'ruego/ **-ga** *a.* & *n.* Norwegian.
nos /nos/ *pron.* us; ourselves.
nosotros /no'sotros, no'sotras/ **-as** *pron.* we, us; ourselves.
nostalgia /nos'talhia/ *n. f.* nostalgia, homesickness.
nostálgico /nos'talhiko/ *a.* nostalgic.
nota /'nota/ *n. f.* note; grade, mark.
notable /no'taβle/ *a.* notable, remarkable.
notación /nota'θion; nota'sion/ *n. f.* notation; note.
notar /no'tar/ *v.* note, notice.
notario /no'tario/ **-ria** *n.* notary.
noticia /no'tiθia; no'tisia/ *n. f.* notice; piece of news; (*pl.*) news.
noticia de última hora /no'tiθia de 'ultima 'ora; no'tisia de 'ultima 'ora/ news flash.
notificación /notifika'θion; notifika'sion/ *n. f.* notification.
notificación de reclutamiento /notifika'θion de rrekluta'miento; notifika'sion de rrekluta'miento/ draft notice.
notificar /notifi'kar/ *v.* notify.
notorio /no'torio/ *a.* well-known.
novato /no'βato/ **-ta** *n.* novice.
novecientos /noβe'θientos; noβe'sientos/ *a.* & *pron.* nine hundred.
novedad /noβe'ðað/ *n. f.* novelty; piece of news.
novel /no'βel/ *a.* new; inexperienced.
novela /no'βela/ *n. f.* novel.
novelista /noβe'lista/ *n. m.* & *f.* novelist.
novena /no'βena/ *n. f.* novena.
noveno /no'βeno/ *a.* ninth.
noventa /no'βenta/ *a.* & *pron.* ninety.
novia /'noβia/ *n. f.* bride; sweetheart; fiancée.
noviazgo /no'βiaθgo; no'βiasgo/ *n. m.* engagement.
novicio /no'βiθio; no'βisio/ **-cia** *n.* novice, beginner.
noviembre /no'βiembre/ *n. m.* November.
novilla /no'βiʎa; no'βiya/ *n. f.* heifer.
novio /'noβio/ *n. m.* bridegroom; sweetheart; fiancé.
nube /'nuβe/ *n. f.* cloud.
núbil /'nuβil/ *a.* marriageable.
nublado /nu'βlaðo/ *a.* cloudy.
nuclear /nukle'ar/ *a.* nuclear.
núcleo /'nukleo/ *n. m.* nucleus.
nudo /'nuðo/ *n. m.* knot.
nuera /'nuera/ *n. f.* daughter-in-law.
nuestro /'nuestro/ *a.* our, ours.
nueva /'nueβa/ *n. f.* news.
nueve /'nueβe/ *a.* & *pron.* nine.
nuevo /'nueβo/ *a.* new. **de n.,** again, anew.
nuez /nueθ; nues/ *n. f.* nut; walnut.
nulidad /nuli'ðað/ *n. f.* nonentity; nullity.
nulo /'nulo/ *a.* null, void.
numeración /numera'θion; numera'sion/ *n. f.* numeration.
numerar /nume'rar/ *v.* number.
numérico /nu'meriko/ *a.* numerical.
número /'numero/ *n. m.* number; size (of shoe, etc.) **n. impar,** odd number. **n. par,** even number.
numeroso /nume'roso/ *a.* numerous.
numismática /numis'matika/ *n. f.* numismatics.
nunca /'nunka/ *adv.* never; ever.
nupcial /nup'θial; nup'sial/ *a.* nuptial.
nupcias /'nupθias; 'nupsias/ *n. f.pl.* nuptials, wedding.
nutrición /nutri'θion; nutri'sion/ *n. f.* nutrition.
nutrimento /nutri'mento/ *n. m.* nourishment.
nutrir /nu'trir/ *v.* nourish.
nutritivo /nutri'tiβo/ *a.* nutritious.
nylon /'nilon/ *n. m.* nylon.
ñame /'ɲame/ *n. m.* yam.
ñapa /'ɲapa/ *n. f.* something extra.
ñoñeria /ɲoɲe'ria/ *n. f.* dotage.
ñoño /'ɲoɲo/ *a.* feeble-minded, senile.

O

o /o/ *conj.* or. **o... o,** either... or.
oasis /o'asis/ *n. m.* oasis.
obedecer /oβeðe'θer; oβeðe'ser/ *v.* obey, mind.
obediencia /oβe'ðienθia; oβe'ðiensia/ *n. f.* obedience.
obediente /oβe'ðiente/ *a.* obedient.
obelisco /oβe'lisko/ *n. m.* obelisk.
obertura /oβer'tura/ *n. f.* overture.
obeso /o'βeso/ *a.* obese.
obispo /o'βispo/ *n. m.* bishop.
obituario /oβi'tuario/ *n. m.* obituary.
objeción /oβhe'θion; oβhe'sion/ *n. f.* objection.
objetivo /oβhe'tiβo/ *a.* & *m.* objective.
objeto /oβ'heto/ *n. m.* object. —**objetar,** *v.*
objetor de conciencia /oβhe'tor de kon'θienθia; oβhe'tor de kon'siensia/ *n. m.* conscientious objector.
oblicuo /o'βlikuo/ *a.* oblique.
obligación /oβliga'θion; oβliga'sion/ *n. f.* obligation, duty.
obligar /oβli'gar/ *v.* oblige, require, compel; obligate.
obligatorio /oβliga'torio/ *a.* obligatory, compulsory.
oblongo /o'βloŋgo/ *a.* oblong.
oboe /o'βoe/ *n. m.* oboe.
obra /'oβra/ *n. f.* work. —**obrar,** *v.*
obrero /o'βrero/ **-ra** *n.* worker, laborer.
obscenidad /oβsθeni'ðað; oβsseni'ðað/ *n. f.* obscenity.
obsceno /oβs'θeno; oβs'seno/ *a.* obscene.
obscurecer /oβskure'θer; oβskure'ser/ *v.* obscure; darken.
obscuridad /oβskuri'ðað/ *n. f.* obscurity; darkness.
obscuro /oβs'kuro/ *a.* obscure; dark.
obsequiar /oβse'kiar/ *v.* court; make presents to, fete.
obsequio /oβ'sekio/ *n. m.* obsequiousness; gift; attention.
observación /oβserβa'θion; oβserβa'sion/ *n. f.* observation.
observador /oβserβa'ðor/ **-ra** *n.* observer.
observancia /oβser'βanθia; oβser'βansia/ *n. f.* observance.
observar /oβser'βar/ *v.* observe, watch.

observatorio /oβserβa'torio/ *n. m.* observatory.

obsesión /oβse'sion/ *n. f.* obsession.

obstáculo /oβs'takulo/ *n. m.* obstacle.

obstante /oβs'tante/ *adv.* **no o.,** however, yet, nevertheless.

obstar /oβs'tar/ *v.* hinder, obstruct.

obstetricia /oβste'triθia; oβste'trisia/ *n. f.* obstetrics.

obstinación /oβstina'θion; oβstina'sion/ *n. f.* obstinacy.

obstinado /oβsti'naðo/ *a.* obstinate, stubborn.

obstinarse /oβsti'narse/ *v.* persist, insist.

obstrucción /oβstruk'θion; oβstruk'sion/ *n. f.* obstruction.

obstruir /oβs'truir/ *v.* obstruct, clog, block.

obtener /oβte'ner/ *v.* obtain, get, secure.

obtuso /oβ'tuso/ *a.* obtuse.

obvio /'oββio/ *a.* obvious.

ocasión /oka'sion/ *n. f.* occasion; opportunity, chance. **de o.,** secondhand.

ocasional /okasio'nal/ *a.* occasional.

ocasionalmente /okasional'mente/ *adv.* occasionally.

ocasionar /okasio'nar/ *v.* cause, occasion.

occidental /okθiðen'tal; oksiðen'tal/ *a.* western.

occidente /okθi'ðente; oksi'ðente/ *n. m.* west.

océano /o'θeano; o'seano/ *n. m.* ocean.

Océano Atlántico /o'θeano a'tlantiko; o'seano a'tlantiko/ Atlantic Ocean.

Océano Pacífico /o'θeano pa'θifiko; o'seano pa'sifiko/ Pacific Ocean.

ocelote /oθe'lote; ose'lote/ *n. m.* ocelot.

ochenta /o'tʃenta/ *a. & pron.* eighty.

ocho /'otʃo/ *a. & pron.* eight.

ochocientos /otʃo'θientos; otʃo'sientos/ *a. & pron.* eight hundred.

ocio /'oθio; 'osio/ *n. m.* idleness, leisure.

ociosidad /oθiosi'ðað; osiosi'ðað/ *n. f.* idleness, laziness.

ocioso /o'θioso; o'sioso/ *a.* idle, lazy.

ocre /'okre/ *n. m.* ochre.

octagonal /oktago'nal/ *a.* octagonal.

octava /ok'taβa/ *n. f.* octave.

octavo /ok'taβo/ *a.* eighth.

octubre /ok'tuβre/ *n. m.* October.

oculista /oku'lista/ *n. m. & f.* oculist.

ocultación /okulta'θion; okulta'sion/ *n. f.* concealment.

ocultar /okul'tar/ *v.* hide, conceal.

oculto /o'kulto/ *a.* hidden.

ocupación /okupa'θion; okupa'sion/ *n. f.* occupation.

ocupado /oku'paðo/ *a.* occupied; busy.

ocupante /oku'pante/ *n. m. & f.* occupant.

ocupar /oku'par/ *v.* occupy.

ocuparse de /oku'parse de/ *v.* take care of, take charge of.

ocurrencia /oku'rrenθia; oku'rrensia/ *n. f.* occurrence; witticism.

ocurrente /oku'rrente/ *a.* witty.

ocurrir /oku'rrir/ *v.* occur, happen.

oda /'oða/ *n. f.* ode.

odio /'oðio/ *n. m.* hate. **—odiar,** *v.*

odiosidad /oðiosi'ðað/ *n. f.* odiousness; hatred.

odioso /o'ðioso/ *a.* obnoxious, odious.

odisea /oði'sea/ *n. f.* odyssey.

OEA, *abbr.* (Organización de los Estados Americanos). OAS (Organization of American States).

oeste /o'este/ *n. m.* west.

ofender /ofen'der/ *v.* offend, wrong.

ofenderse /ofen'derse/ *v.* be offended, take offense.

ofensa /o'fensa/ *n. f.* offense.

ofensiva /ofen'siβa/ *n. f.* offensive.

ofensivo /ofen'siβo/ *a.* offensive.

ofensor /ofen'sor/ **-ra** *n.* offender.

oferta /o'ferta/ *n. f.* offer, proposal.

ofertorio /ofer'torio/ *n. m.* offertory.

oficial /ofi'θial; ofi'sial/ *a. & m.* official; officer.

oficialmente /ofiθial'mente; ofisial'mente/ *adv.* officially.

oficiar /ofi'θiar; ofi'siar/ *v.* officiate.

oficina /ofi'θina; ofi'sina/ *n. f.* office.

oficio /o'fiθio; o'fisio/ *n. m.* office; trade; church service.

oficioso /ofi'θioso; ofi'sioso/ *a.* officious.

ofrecer /ofre'θer; ofre'ser/ *v.* offer.

ofrecimiento /ofreθi'miento; ofresi'miento/ *n. m.* offer, offering. **o. de presentación,** introductory offer.

ofrenda /o'frenda/ *n. f.* offering.

oftalmía /oftal'mia/ *n. f.* ophthalmia.

ofuscamiento /ofuska'miento/ *n. m.* obfuscation; bewilderment.

ofuscar /ofus'kar/ *v.* obfuscate; bewilder.

ogro /'ogro/ *n. m.* ogre.

oído /o'iðo/ *n. m.* ear; hearing.

oír /o'ir/ *v.* hear; listen.

ojal /o'hal/ *n. m.* buttonhole.

ojalá /oha'la/ *interj.* expressing wish or hope. **o. que...** would that...

ojeada /ohe'aða/ *n. f.* glance; peep; look.

ojear /ohe'ar/ *v.* eye, look at, glance at, stare at.

ojeriza /ohe'riθa; ohe'risa/ *n. f.* spite; grudge.

ojiva /o'hiβa/ *n. f.* pointed arch, ogive.

ojo /'oho/ *n. m.* eye. **¡Ojo!** Look out!

ola /'ola/ *n. f.* wave.

olaje /o'lahe/ *n. m.* surge of waves.

oleada /ole'aða/ *n. f.* swell.

oleo /'oleo/ *n. m.* oil; holy oil; extreme unction.

oleoducto /oleo'ðukto/ *n. m.* pipeline.

oleomargarina /oleomarga'rina/ *n. f.* oleomargarine.

oleoso /ole'oso/ *a.* oily.

oler /o'ler/ *v.* smell.

olfatear /olfate'ar/ *v.* smell.

olfato /ol'fato/ *n. m.* scent, smell.

oliva /o'liβa/ *n. f.* olive.

olivar /oli'βar/ *n. m.* olive grove.

olivo /o'liβo/ *n. m.* olive tree.

olla /'oʎa; 'oya/ *n. f.* pot, kettle. **o. podrida,** stew.

olmo /'olmo/ *n. m.* elm.

olor /o'lor/ *n. m.* odor, smell, scent.

oloroso /olo'roso/ *a.* fragrant, scented.

olvidadizo /olβiða'ðiθo; olβiða'ðiso/ *a.* forgetful.

olvidar /olβi'ðar/ *v.* forget.

olvido /ol'βiðo/ *n. m.* omission; forgetfulness.

ombligo /om'βligo/ *n. m.* navel.

ominar /omi'nar/ *v.* foretell.

ominoso /omi'noso/ *a.* ominous.

omisión /omi'sion/ *n. f.* omission.

omitir /omi'tir/ *v.* omit, leave out.

ómnibus /'omniβus/ *n. m.* bus.

omnipotencia /omnipo'tenθia; omnipo'tensia/ *n. f.* omnipotence.

omnipotente /omnipo'tente/ *a.* almighty.

omnipresencia /omnipre'senθia; omnipre'sensia/ *n. f.* omnipresence.

omnisciencia /omnis'θienθia; omnis'siensia/ *n. f.* omniscience.

omnívoro /om'niβoro/ *a.* omnivorous.

omóplato /omo'plato/ *n. m.* shoulder blade.

once /'onθe; 'onse/ *a. & pron.* eleven.

onda /'onda/ *n. f.* wave, ripple.

ondear /onde'ar/ *v.* ripple.

ondulación /ondula'θion; ondula'sion/ *n. f.* wave, undulation.

ondular /ondu'lar/ *v.* undulate, ripple.

onza /'onθa; 'onsa/ *n. f.* ounce.

opaco /o'pako/ *a.* opaque.

ópalo /'opalo/ *n. m.* opal.

opción /op'θion; op'sion/ *n. f.* option.

ópera /'opera/ *n. f.* opera.

operación /opera'θion; opera'sion/ *n. f.* operation.

operar /ope'rar/ *v.* operate; operate on.

operario /ope'rario/ **-ria** *n.* operator; (skilled) worker.

operarse /ope'rarse/ *v.* have an operation.

operativo /opera'tiβo/ *a.* operative.

opereta /ope'reta/ *n. f.* operetta.

opiato /o'piato/ *n. m.* opiate.

opinar /opi'nar/ *v.* opine.

opinión /opi'nion/ *n. f.* opinion, view.

opio /'opio/ *n. m.* opium.

oponer /opo'ner/ *v.* oppose.

Oporto /o'porto/ *n. m.* port (wine).

oportunidad /oportuni'ðað/ *n. f.* opportunity.

oportunismo /oportu'nismo/ *n. m.* opportunism.

oportunista /oportu'nista/ *n. & a.* opportunist.

oportuno /opor'tuno/ *a.* opportune, expedient.

oposición /oposi'θion; oposi'sion/ *n. f.* opposition.

opresión /opre'sion/ *n. f.* oppression.

opresivo /opre'siβo/ *a.* oppressive.

oprimir /opri'mir/ *v.* oppress.

oprobio /o'proβio/ *n. m.* infamy.

optar /op'tar/ *v.* select, choose.

óptica /'optika/ *n. f.* optics.

óptico /'optiko/ *a.* optic.

optimismo /opti'mismo/ *n. m.* optimism.

optimista /opti'mista/ *a. & n.* optimistic; optimist.

óptimo /'optimo/ *a.* best.

opuesto /o'puesto/ *a.* opposite; opposed.

opugnar /opug'nar/ *v.* attack.

opulencia /opu'lenθia; opu'lensia/ *n. f.* opulence, wealth.

opulento /opu'lento/ *a.* opulent, wealthy.

oración /ora'θion; ora'sion/ *n. f.* sentence; prayer; oration.

oráculo /o'rakulo/ *n. m.* oracle.

orador /ora'ðor/ **-ra** *n.* orator, speaker.

oral /o'ral/ *a.* oral.

orangután /oraŋgu'tan/ *n. m.* orangutan.

orar /o'rar/ *v.* pray.

oratoria /ora'toria/ *n. f.* oratory.

oratorio /ora'torio/ *a.* oratorical.

orbe /'orβe/ *n. m.* orb; globe.

órbita /'orβita/ *n. f.* orbit.

orden /'orðen/ *n. m. or f.* order.

ordenador /orðena'ðor/ *n. m.* computer; regulator.

ordenador de sobremesa /orðena'ðor de soβre'mesa/ desktop computer.

ordenador doméstico /orðena'ðor do'mestiko/ home computer.

ordenanza /orðe'nanθa; orðe'nansa/ *n. f.* ordinance.

ordenar /orðe'nar/ *v.* order; put in order; ordain.

ordeñar /orðe'ɲar/ *v.* milk.

ordinal /orði'nal/ *a. & m.* ordinal.

ordinario /orði'nario/ *a.* ordinary; common, usual.

oreja /o'reha/ *n. f.* ear.

orejera /ore'hera/ *n. f.* earmuff.

orfanato /orfa'nato/ *n. m.* orphanage.

organdí /organ'di/ *n. m.* organdy.

orgánico /or'ganiko/ *a.* organic.

organigrama /organi'grama/ *n. m.* flow chart.

organismo /orga'nismo/ *n. m.* organism.

organista /orga'nista/ *n. m. & f.* organist.

organización /organiθa'θion; organisa'sion/ *n. f.* organization.

organizar /organi'θar; organi'sar/ *v.* organize.

órgano /'organo/ *n. m.* organ.

orgía /or'hia/ *n. f.* orgy, revel.

orgullo /or'guʎo; or'guyo/ *n. m.* pride.

orgulloso /orgu'ʎoso; orgu'yoso/ *a.* proud.

orientación /orienta'θion; orienta'sion/ *n. f.* orientation.

oriental /orien'tal/ *a.* Oriental; eastern.

orientar /orien'tar/ *v.* orient.

oriente /o'riente/ *n. m.* orient, east.

orificación /orifika'θion; orifika'sion/ *n. f.* gold filling (for tooth).

origen /o'rihen/ *n. m.* origin; parentage, descent.

original /orihi'nal/ *a.* original.

originalidad /orihinali'ðað/ *n. f.* originality.

originalmente /orihinal'mente/ *adv.* originally.

originar /orihi'nar/ *v.* originate.

orilla /o'riʎa; o'riya/ *n. f.* shore; bank; edge.

orín /o'rin/ *n. m.* rust.

orina /o'rina/ *n. f.* urine.

orinar /ori'nar/ *v.* urinate.

orines /o'rines/ *n. m.pl.* urine.

oriol /o'riol/ *n. m.* oriole.

orla /'orla/ *n. f.* border; edging.

ornado /or'naðo/ *a.* ornate.

ornamentación /ornamenta'θion; ornamenta'sion/ *n. f.* ornamentation.

ornamento /orna'mento/ *n. m.* ornament. **—ornamentar,** *v.*

ornar /or'nar/ *v.* ornament, adorn.

oro /'oro/ *n. m.* gold.

oropel /oro'pel/ *n. m.* tinsel.

orquesta /or'kesta/ *n. f.* orchestra.

ortiga /or'tiga/ *n. f.* nettle.

ortodoxo /orto'ðokso/ *a.* orthodox.

ortografía /ortogra'fia/ *n. f.* orthography, spelling.

ortóptero /or'toptero/ *a.* orthopterous.

oruga /o'ruga/ *n. f.* caterpillar.

orzuelo /or'θuelo; or'suelo/ *n. m.* sty.

os /os/ *pron.* you (*pl.*); yourselves.

osadía /osa'ðia/ *n. f.* daring.

osar /o'sar/ *v.* dare.

oscilación /osθila'θion; ossila'sion/ *n. f.* oscillation.

oscilar /osθi'lar; ossi'lar/ *v.* oscillate, rock.

ósculo /'oskulo/ *n. m.* kiss.

oscurecer /oskure'θer; oskure'ser/ **oscuridad, oscuro =** obscur-.

oso /'oso/ **osa** *n.* bear.

oso de felpa /'oso de 'felpa/ teddy bear.

ostentación /ostenta'θion; ostenta'sion/ *n. f.* ostentation, showiness.

ostentar /osten'tar/ *v.* show off.

ostentoso /osten'toso/ *a.* ostentatious, flashy.

ostra /'ostra/ *n. f.* oyster.

ostracismo /ostra'θismo; ostra'sismo/ *n. m.* ostracism.

otalgia /o'talhia/ *n. f.* earache.

otero /o'tero/ *n. m.* hill, knoll.

otoño /o'toɲo/ *n. m.* autumn, fall.

otorgar /otor'gar/ *v.* grant, award.

otro /'otro/ *a. & pron.* other, another. **o. vez,** again. **el uno al o.,** one another, each other.

ovación /oβa'θion; oβa'sion/ *n. f.* ovation.

oval /o'βal/ **ovalado** *a.* oval.

óvalo /'oβalo/ *n. m.* oval.

ovario /o'βario/ *n. m.* ovary.

oveja /o'βeha/ *n. f.* sheep.

ovejero /oβe'hero/ *n. m.* sheep dog.

ovillo /o'βiʎo; o'βiyo/ *n. m.* ball of yarn.

OVNI /'oβni/ *abbr.* (objeto volador no identificado) UFO (unidentified flying object).

oxidación /oksiða'θion; oksiða'sion/ *n. f.* oxidation.

oxidar /oksi'ðar/ *v.* oxidize; rust.

óxido /'oksiðo/ *n. m.* oxide.

oxígeno /ok'siheno/ *n. m.* oxygen.

oyente /o'iente/ *n. m. & f.* hearer; (*pl.*) audience.

ozono /o'θono; o'sono/ *n. m.* ozone.

P

pabellón /paβe'ʎon; paβe'yon/ *n. m.* pavilion. **p. de deportes,** sports center.

pabilo /pa'βilo/ *n. m.* wick.

paciencia /pa'θienθia; pa'siensia/ *n. f.* patience.

paciente /pa'θiente; pa'siente/ *a. & n.* patient.

pacificar /paθifi'kar; pasifi'kar/ *v.* pacify.

pacífico /pa'θifiko; pa'sifiko/ *a.* pacific.

pacifismo /paθi'fismo; pasi'fismo/ *m.* pacifism.

pacifista /paθi'fista; pasi'fista/ *n. & a.* pacifist.

pacto /'pakto/ *n. m.* pact, treaty.

padecer /paðe'θer; paðe'ser/ *v.* suffer. **p. del corazón,** have heart trouble.

padrastro /pa'ðrastro/ *n. m.* stepfather.

padre /'paðre/ *n. m.* father; priest; (*pl.*) parents.

padrenuestro /paðre'nuestro/ *n. m.* paternoster, Lord's Prayer.

padrino /pa'ðrino/ *n. m.* godfather; sponsor.

paella /pa'eʎa; pa'eya/ *n. f.* dish of rice with meat or chicken.

paga /'paga/ *n. f.* pay, wages. **p. extra** bonus.

pagadero /paga'ðero/ *a.* payable.

pagador /paga'ðor/ **-ra** *n.* payer.

paganismo /paga'nismo/ *n. m.* paganism.

pagano /pa'gano/ **-na** *a. & n.* heathen, pagan.

pagar /pa'gar/ *v.* pay, pay for. **p. en metálico,** pay cash.

página /'pahina/ *n. f.* page.

pago /'pago/ *n. m.* pay, payment.

país /pa'is/ *n. m.* country, nation.

paisaje /pai'sahe/ *n. m.* landscape, scenery, countryside.

paisano /pai'sano/ **-na** *n.* countryman; compatriot; civilian.

paja /'paha/ *n. f.* straw.

pajar /pa'har/ *n. m.* barn.

pajarita /paha'rita/ *n. f.* bow tie.

pájaro /'paharo/ *n. m.* bird.

paje /'pahe/ *n. m.* page (person).

pala /'pala/ *n. f.* shovel, spade.

palabra /pa'laβra/ *n. f.* word.

palabrero /pala'βrero/ *a.* talkative, wordy.

palabrista /pala'βrista/ *n. m. & f.* talkative person.

palacio /pa'laθio; pa'lasio/ *n. m.* palace.

paladar /pala'ðar/ *n. m.* palate.

paladear /palaðe'ar/ *v.* taste; relish.

palanca /pa'lanka/ *n. f.* lever. **p. de cambio,** gearshift.

palangana /palaŋ'gana/ *n. f.* washbasin.

palco /'palko/ *n. m.* theater box.

palenque /pa'lenke/ *n. m.* palisade.

paleta /pa'leta/ *n. f.* mat, pallet.

paletilla /pale'tiʎa; pale'tiya/ *n. f.* shoulder blade.

palidecer /paliðe'θer; paliðe'ser/ *v.* turn pale.

palidez /pali'ðeθ; pali'ðes/ *n. f.* paleness.

pálido /'paliðo/ *a.* pale.

paliza /pa'liθa; pa'lisa/ *n. f.* beating.

palizada /pali'θaða; pali'saða/ *n. m.* palisade.

palma /'palma/ **palmera** *n. f.* palm (tree).

palmada /pal'maða/ *n. f.* slap, clap.

palmear /palme'ar/ *v.* applaud.

palo /'palo/ *n. m.* pole, stick; suit (in cards); *Naut.* mast.

paloma /pa'loma/ *n. f.* dove, pigeon.

palpar /pal'par/ *v.* touch, feel.

palpitación /palpita'θion; palpita'sion/ *n. f.* palpitation.

palpitar /palpi'tar/ *v.* palpitate.

paludismo /palu'ðismo/ *n. m.* malaria.

pampa /'pampa/ *n. f.* (*S.A.*) prairie, plain.

pan /pan/ *n. m.* bread; loaf. **p. de centeno,** rye bread.

pana /'pana/ *n. f.* corduroy.

panacea /pana'θea; pana'sea/ *n. f.* panacea.

panadería /panaðe'ria/ *n. f.* bakery.

panadero /pana'ðero/ **-ra** *n.* baker.

panameño /pana'meɲo/ **-ña** *a. & n.* Panamanian, of Panama.

panamericano /panameri'kano/ *a.* Pan-American.

páncreas /'pankreas/ *n. m.* pancreas.

pandeo /pan'deo/ *n. m.* bulge.

pandilla /pan'diʎa; pan'diya/ *n. f.* band, gang.

panecillo /pane'θiʎo; pane'siyo/ *n. m.* roll, muffin.

panegírico /pane'hiriko/ *n. m.* panegyric.

pánico /'paniko/ *n. m.* panic.

panocha /pa'notʃa/ *n. f.* ear of corn.

panorama /pano'rama/ *n. m.* panorama.

panorámico /pano'ramiko/ *a.* panoramic.

pantalla /pan'taʎa; pan'taya/ *n. f.* (movie) screen; lamp shade.

pantalones /panta'lones/ *n. m.pl.* trousers, pants.

pantano /pan'tano/ *n. m.* bog, marsh, swamp.

pantanoso /panta'noso/ *a.* swampy, marshy.

pantera /pan'tera/ *n. f.* panther.

pantomima /panto'mima/ *n. f.* pantomime.

pantorrilla /panto'rriʎa; panto'rriya/ *n. f.* calf (of body).

panza /'panθa; 'pansa/ *n. f.* belly, paunch.

pañal /pa'ɲal/ *n. m.* diaper.

paño /'paɲo/ *n. m.* piece of cloth.

pañuelo /pa'ɲuelo/ *n. m.* handkerchief.

Papa /'papa/ *n. m.* Pope.

papa *n. f.* potato.

papá *n. m.* papa, father.

papado /pa'paðo/ *n. m.* papacy.

papagayo /papa'gaio/ *n. m.* parrot.

papal /pa'pal/ *a.* papal.

Papá Noel /pa'pa no'el/ *n. m.* Santa Claus.

papel /pa'pel/ *n. m.* paper; role, part.

papel crespón /pa'pel kres'pon/ crepe paper.

papel de aluminio /pa'pel de alu'minio/ aluminum foil.

papel de escribir /pa'pel de eskri'βir/ writing paper.

papel de estaño /pa'pel de es'taɲo/ tin foil.

papel de lija /pa'pel de 'liha/ sandpaper.

papelera /pape'lera/ *n. f.* file cabinet; wastepaper basket.

papelería /papele'ria/ *n. f.* stationery store.

papel moneda /pa'pel mo'neða/ paper money.

paperas /pa'peras/ *n. f.pl.* mumps.

paquete /pa'kete/ *n. m.* package.

par /par/ *a.* **1.** even, equal. —*n.* **2.** *m.* pair; equal, peer. **abierto de p. en p.,** wide open.

para /'para/ *prep.* for; in order to. **p. que,** in order that. **estar p.,** to be about to.

parabién /para'βien/ *n. m.* congratulation.

parabrisa /para'βrisa/ *n. m.* windshield.

paracaídas /paraka'iðas/ *n. m.* parachute.

parachoques /para'tʃokes/ *n. m. Auto.* bumper.

parada /pa'raða/ *n. f.* stop, halt; stopover; parade.

paradero /para'ðero/ *n. m.* whereabouts; stopping place.

paradigma /para'ðigma/ *n. m.* paradigm.

paradoja /para'ðoha/ *n. f.* paradox.

parafina /para'fina/ *n. f.* paraffin.

parafrasear /parafrase'ar/ *v.* paraphrase.

paraguas /pa'raguas/ *n. m.* umbrella.

paraguayano /paragua'yano/ **-na** *n. & a.* Paraguayan.

paraíso /para'iso/ *n. m.* paradise.

paralelo /para'lelo/ *a. & m.* parallel.

parálisis /pa'ralisis/ *n. f.* paralysis.

paralizar /parali'θar; parali'sar/ *v.* paralyze.

paramédico /para'meðiko/ *n. m.* paramedic.

parámetro /pa'rametro/ *n. m.* parameter.

parapeto /para'peto/ *n. m.* parapet.

parar /pa'rar/ *v.* stop, stem, ward off; stay.

pararse /pa'rarse/ *v.* stop; stand up.

parasítico /para'sitiko/ *a.* parasitic.

parásito /pa'rasito/ *n. m.* parasite.

parcela /par'θela; par'sela/ *n. f.* plot of ground.

parcial /par'θial; par'sial/ *a.* partial.

parcialidad /parθiali'ðað; parsiali'ðað/ *n. f.* partiality; bias.

parcialmente /parθial'mente; parsial'mente/ *adv.* partially.

pardo /'parðo/ *a.* brown.

parear /pare'ar/ *v.* pair; match; mate.

parecer /pare'θer; pare'ser/ *n.* **1.** *m.* opinion. —*v.* **2.** seem, appear, look.

parecerse /pare'θerse; pare'serse/ *v.* look alike. **p. a,** look like.

parecido /pare'θiðo; pare'siðo/ *a.* similar.

pared /pa'reð/ *n. f.* wall.

pareja /pa'reha/ *n. f.* pair, couple; (dancing) partner.

parentela /paren'tela/ *n. f.* kinfolk.

parentesco /paren'tesko/ *n. m.* parentage, lineage; kin.

paréntesis /pa'rentesis/ *n. m.* parenthesis.

paria /'paria/ *n. m.* outcast, pariah.

paricipante /pariθi'pante; parisi'pante/ *n. m. & f.* participant.

paridad /pari'ðað/ *n. f.* parity.

pariente /pa'riente/ *n. m. & f.* relative.

parir /pa'rir/ *v.* give birth.

parisiense /pari'siense/ *n. & a.* Parisian.

parlamentario /parlamen'tario/ *a.* parliamentary.

parlamento /parla'mento/ *n. m.* parliament.

paro /'paro/ *n. m.* stoppage; strike. **p. forzoso,** unemployment.

parodia /pa'roðia/ *n. f.* parody.

parodista /paro'ðista/ *n. m. & f.* parodist.

paroxismo /parok'sismo/ *n. m.* paroxysm.

párpado /'parpaðo/ *n. m.* eyelid.

parque /'parke/ *n. m.* park.

parquímetro /par'kimetro/ *n. m.* parking meter.

parra /'parra/ *n. f.* grapevine.

párrafo /'parrafo/ *n. m.* paragraph.

parranda /pa'rranda/ *n. f.* spree.

parrandear /parrande'ar/ *v.* carouse.

parrilla /pa'rriʎa; pa'rriya/ *n. f.* grill; grillroom.

párroco /'parroko/ *n. m.* parish priest.

parroquia /pa'rrokia/ *n. f.* parish.

parroquial /parro'kial/ *a.* parochial.

parsimonia /parsi'monia/ *n. f.* economy, thrift.

parsimonioso /parsimo'nioso/ *a.* economical, thrifty.

parte /'parte/ *n. f.* part. **de p. de,** on behalf of. **alguna p.,** somewhere. **por otra p.,** on the other hand. **dar p. a,** to notify.

partera /par'tera/ *n. f.* midwife.

partición /parti'θion; parti'sion/ *n. f.* distribution.

participación /partiθipa'θion; partisipa'sion/ *n. f.* participation.

participar /partiθi'par; partisi'par/ *v.* participate; announce.

participio /parti'θipio; parti'sipio/ *n. m.* participle.

partícula /par'tikula/ *n. f.* particle.

particular /partiku'lar/ *a.* **1.** particular; private. —*n.* **2.** *m.* particular; detail; individual.

particularmente /partikular'mente/ *adv.* particularly.

partida /par'tiða/ *n. f.* departure; *Mil.* party; (sport) game.

partida de defunción /par'tiða de defun'θion; par'tiða de defun'sion/ death certificate.

partida de matrimonio /par'tiða de matri'monio/ marriage certificate.

partida de nacimiento /par'tiða de naθi'miento; par'tiða de nasi'miento/ birth certificate.

partidario /parti'ðario/ **-ria** *n.* partisan.

partido /par'tiðo/ *n. m.* side, party, faction; game, match.

partir /par'tir/ *v.* leave, depart; part, cleave, split.

parto /'parto/ *n. m.* delivery, childbirth.

pasa /'pasa/ *n. f.* raisin.

pasado /pa'saðo/ *a.* **1.** past; last. —*n.* **2.** *m.* past.

pasaje /pa'sahe/ *n. m.* passage, fare.

pasajero /pasa'hero/ **-ra** *a.* **1.** passing, transient. —*n.* **2.** *m.* passenger.

pasamano /pasa'mano/ *n. m.* banister.

pasaporte /pasa'porte/ *n. m.* passport.

pasar /pa'sar/ *v.* pass; happen; spend (time). **p. por alto,** overlook. **p. lista,** call the roll. **p. sin,** do without.

pasatiempo /pasa'tiempo/ *n. m.* pastime; hobby.

pascua /'paskua/ *n. f.* religious holiday; (*pl.*) Christmas (season). **P. Florida,** Easter.

pase de modelos /'pase de mo'ðelos/ *n. m.* fashion show.

paseo /pa'seo/ *n. m.* walk, stroll; drive. —**pasear,** *v.*

pasillo /pa'siʎo; pa'siyo/ *n. m.* aisle; hallway.

pasión /pa'sion/ *n. f.* passion.

pasivo /pa'siβo/ *a.* passive.

pasmar /pas'mar/ *v.* astonish, astound, stun.

pasmo /'pasmo/ *n. m.* spasm; wonder.

paso /'paso/ *n. m.* **1.** dried (fruit). —*n.* **2.** *m.* pace, step; (mountain) pass.

paso cebra /'paso 'θeβra; 'paso 'seβra/ crosswalk.

paso de ganso /'paso de 'ganso/ goose step.

paso de peatones /'paso de pea'tones/ pedestrian crossing.

pasta /'pasta/ *n. f.* paste; batter; plastic.

pasta dentífrica /'pasta den'tifrika/ toothpaste.

pastar /pas'tar/ *v.* graze.

pastel /pas'tel/ *n. m.* pastry; pie.

pastelería /pastele'ria/ *n. f.* pastry; pastry shop.

pasteurización /pasteuriθa'θion; pasteurisa'sion/ *n. f.* pasteurization.

pasteurizar /pasteuri'θar; pasteuri'sar/ *v.* pasteurize.

pastilla /pas'tiʎa; pas'tiya/ *n. f.* tablet, lozenge, coughdrop.

pasto /'pasto/ *n. m.* pasture; grass.

pastor /pas'tor/ *n. m.* pastor; shepherd.

pastorear /pastore'ar/ *v.* pasture, tend (a flock).

pastrón /pas'tron/ *n. m.* pastrami.

pastura /pas'tura/ *n. f.* pasture.

pata /'pata/ *n. f.* foot (of animal).

patada /pa'taða/ *n. f.* kick.

patán /pa'tan/ *n. m.* boor.

patanada /pata'naða/ *n. f.* rudeness.
patata /pa'tata/ *n. f.* potato. **p. asada,** baked potato.
patear /pate'ar/ *v.* stamp, tramp, kick.
patente /pa'tente/ *a. & m.* patent. —**patentar,** *v.*
paternal /pater'nal/ **paterno** *a.* paternal.
paternidad /paterni'ðað/ *n. f.* paternity, fatherhood.
patético /pa'tetiko/ *a.* pathetic.
patíbulo /pa'tiβulo/ *n. m.* scaffold; gallows.
patín /pa'tin/ *n. m.* skate. —**patinar,** *v.*
patín de ruedas /pa'tin de 'rrueðas/ roller skate.
patio /'patio/ *n. m.* yard, court, patio.
pato /'pato/ *n. m.* duck.
patria /'patria/ *n. f.* native land.
patriarca /pa'triarka/ *n. m. & f.* patriarch.
patrimonio /patri'monio/ *n. m.* inheritance.
patriota /pa'triota/ *n. m. & f.* patriot.
patriótico /pa'triotiko/ *a.* patriotic.
patriotismo /patrio'tismo/ *n. m.* patriotism.
patrocinar /patroθi'nar/ patrosi'nar/ *v.* patronize, sponsor.
patrón /pa'tron/ **-ona** *n.* patron; boss; (dress) pattern.
patrulla /pa'truʎa/ pa'truya/ *n. f.* patrol. —**patrullar,** *v.*
paulatino /paula'tino/ *a.* gradual.
pausa /'pausa/ *n. f.* pause. —**pausar,** *v.*
pausa para el café /'pausa 'para el ka'fe/ coffee break.
pauta /'pauta/ *n. f.* guideline.
pavesa /pa'βesa/ *n. f.* spark, cinder.
pavimentar /paβimen'tar/ *v.* pave.
pavimento /paβi'mento/ *n. m.* pavement.
pavo /'paβo/ *n. m.* turkey. **p. real,** peacock.
pavor /pa'βor/ *n. m.* terror.
payaso /pa'iaso/ **-sa** *n.* clown.
paz /paθ/ pas/ *n. f.* peace.
peatón /pea'ton/ **-na** *n.* pedestrian.
peca /'peka/ *n. f.* freckle.
pecado /pe'kaðo/ *n. m.* sin. —**pecar,** *v.*
pecador /peka'ðor/ **-ra** *a. & n.* sinful; sinner.
pecera /pe'θera; pe'sera/ *n. f.* aquarium, fishbowl.
pechera /pe'tʃera/ *n. f.* shirt front.
pecho /'petʃo/ *n. m.* chest; breast; bosom.
pechuga /pe'tʃuga/ *n. f.* breast (of fowl).
pecoso /pe'koso/ *a.* freckled, freckly.
peculiar /peku'liar/ *a.* peculiar.
peculiaridad /pekuliari'ðað/ *n. f.* peculiarity.
pedagogía /peðago'hia/ *n. f.* pedagogy.
pedagogo /peða'gogo/ **-ga** *n.* pedagogue, teacher.
pedal /pe'ðal/ *n. m.* pedal.
pedantesco /peðan'tesko/ *a.* pedantic.
pedazo /pe'ðaθo; pe'ðaso/ *n. m.* piece.
pedernal /peðer'nal/ *n. m.* flint.
pedestal /peðes'tal/ *n. m.* pedestal.
pediatra /pe'ðiatra/ *n. m. & f.* pediatrician.
pediatría /peðia'tria/ *n. f.* pediatrics.
pedicuro /peði'kuro/ *n. m.* chiropodist.
pedir /pe'ðir/ *v.* ask, ask for, request; apply for; order.
pedo /'pedo/ *n. m.* fart; intoxication.
pedregoso /peðre'goso/ *a.* rocky.
pegajoso /pega'hoso/ *a.* sticky.
pegamento /pega'mento/ *n. m.* glue.
pegar /pe'gar/ *v.* beat, strike; adhere, fasten, stick.
peinado /pei'naðo/ *n. m.* coiffure; hairdo.

peine /'peine/ *n. m.* comb. —**peinar,** *v.*
peineta /pei'neta/ *n. f.* (ornamental) comb.
pelagra /pe'lagra/ *n. f.* pellagra.
pelar /pe'lar/ *v.* skin, pare, peel.
pelea /pe'lea/ *n. f.* fight, row. —**pelearse,** *v.*
pelícano /pe'likano/ *n. m.* pelican.
película /pe'likula/ *n. f.* movie, motion picture, film. **p. de terror** horror film.
peligrar /peli'grar/ *v.* be in danger.
peligro /pe'ligro/ *n. m.* peril, danger.
peligroso /peli'groso/ *a.* perilous, dangerous.
pelirrojo /peli'rroho/ **-ja** *a. & n.* redhead.
pellejo /pe'ʎeho; pe'yeho/ *n. m.* skin; peel (of fruit).
pellizco /pe'ʎiθko; pe'yisko/ *n. m.* pinch. —**pellizcar,** *v.*
pelo /'pelo/ *n. m.* hair.
pelota /pe'lota/ *n. f.* ball.
peltre /'peltre/ *n. m.* pewter.
peluca /pe'luka/ *n. f.* wig.
peludo /pe'luðo/ *a.* hairy.
peluquería /peluke'ria/ *n. f.* hairdresser's shop, beauty parlor.
peluquero /pelu'kero/ **-ra** *n.* hairdresser.
pena /'pena/ *n. f.* pain, grief, trouble, woe; penalty. **valer la p.,** to be worthwhile.
penacho /pe'natʃo/ *n. m.* plume.
penalidad /penali'ðað/ *n. f.* trouble; penalty.
pender /pen'der/ *v.* hang, dangle; be pending.
pendiente /pen'diente/ *a.* **1.** hanging; pending. —*n.* **2.** *m.* incline, slope; earring, pendant.
pendón /pen'don/ *n. m.* pennant, flag.
penetración /penetra'θion; penetra-'sion/ *n. f.* penetration.
penetrar /pene'trar/ *v.* penetrate, pierce.
penicilina /peniθi'lina; penisi'lina/ *n. f.* penicillin.
península /pe'ninsula/ *n. f.* peninsula.
penitencia /peni'tenθia; peni'tensia/ *n. f.* penitence, penance.
penitenciaría /penitenθia'ria; penitensia'ria/ *n. f.* penitentiary.
penoso /pe'noso/ *a.* painful, troublesome, grievous, distressing.
pensador /pensa'ðor/ **-ra** *n.* thinker.
pensamiento /pensa'miento/ *n. m.* thought.
pensar /pen'sar/ *v.* think; intend, plan.
pensativo /pensa'tiβo/ *a.* pensive, thoughtful.
pensión /pen'sion/ *n. f.* pension; boardinghouse.
pensionista /pensio'nista/ *n. m. & f.* boarder.
pentagonal /pentago'nal/ *a.* pentagonal.
penúltimo /pe'nultimo/ *a.* next-to-the-last, last but one, penultimate.
penuria /pe'nuria/ *n. f.* penury, poverty.
peña /'pena/ *n. f.* rock.
peñascoso /penas'koso/ *a.* rocky.
peñón /pe'non/ *n. m.* rock, crag.
Peñón de Gibraltar /pe'non de hiβral'tar/ Rock of Gibraltar.
peón /pe'on/ *n. m.* unskilled laborer; infantryman.
peonada /peo'naða/ *n. f.* group of laborers.
peonía /peo'nia/ *n. f.* peony.
peor /pe'or/ *a.* worse, worst.
pepino /pe'pino/ *n. m.* cucumber.
pepita /pe'pita/ *n. f.* seed (in fruit).
pequeñez /peke'neθ; peke'nes/ *n. f.* smallness; trifle.
pequeño /pe'keno/ **-ña** *a.* **1.** small, little, short, slight. —*n.* **2.** child.
pera /'pera/ *n. f.* pear.

peral /pe'ral/ *n. m.* pear tree.
perca /'perka/ *n. f.* perch (fish).
percal /per'kal/ *n. m.* calico, percale.
percance /per'kanθe; per'kanse/ *n. m.* mishap, snag, hitch.
percepción /perθep'θion; persep-'sion/ *n. f.* perception.
perceptivo /perθep'tiβo; persep'tiβo/ *a.* perceptive.
percha /'pertʃa/ *n. f.* perch; clothes hanger, rack.
percibir /perθi'βir; persi'βir/ *v.* perceive, sense; collect.
perder /per'ðer/ *v.* lose; miss; waste. **echar a p.,** spoil. **p. el conocimiento,** lose consciousness.
perdición /perði'θion; perði'sion/ *n. f.* perdition, downfall.
pérdida /'perðiða/ *n. f.* loss.
perdiz /per'ðiθ; per'ðis/ *n. f.* partridge.
perdón /per'ðon/ *n. m.* pardon, forgiveness.
perdonar /perðo'nar/ *v.* forgive, pardon; spare.
perdurable /perðu'raβle/ *a.* enduring, everlasting.
perdurar /perðu'rar/ *v.* endure, last.
perecedero /pereθe'ðero; perese-'ðero/ *a.* perishable.
perecer /pere'θer; pere'ser/ *v.* perish.
peregrinación /peregrina'θion; peregrina'sion/ *n. f.* peregrination; pilgrimage.
peregrino /pere'grino/ **-na** *n.* pilgrim.
perejil /pere'hil/ *n. m.* parsley.
perenne /pe'renne/ *a.* perennial.
pereza /pe'reθa; pe'resa/ *n. f.* laziness.
perezoso /pere'θoso; pere'soso/ *a.* lazy, sluggish.
perfección /perfek'θion; perfek'sion/ *n. f.* perfection.
perfeccionar /perfekθio'nar; perfeksio'nar/ *v.* perfect.
perfeccionista /perfekθio'nista; perfeksio'nista/ *a. & n.* perfectionist.
perfectamente /perfekta'mente/ *adv.* perfectly.
perfecto /per'fekto/ *a.* perfect.
perfidia /per'fiðia/ *n. f.* falseness, perfidy.
pérfido /'perfiðo/ *a.* perfidious.
perfil /per'fil/ *n. m.* profile.
perforación /perfora'θion; perfora-'sion/ *n. f.* perforation.
perforar /perfo'rar/ *v.* pierce, perforate.
perfume /per'fume/ *n. m.* perfume, scent. —**perfumar,** *v.*
pergamino /perga'mino/ *n. m.* parchment.
pericia /pe'riθia; pe'risia/ *n. f.* skill, expertness.
perico /pe'riko/ *n. m.* parakeet.
perímetro /pe'rimetro/ *n. m.* perimeter.
periódico /pe'rioðiko/ *a.* **1.** periodic. —*n.* **2.** *m.* newspaper.
periodista /perio'ðista/ *n. m. & f.* journalist.
período /pe'rioðo/ *n. m.* period.
periscopio /peris'kopio/ *n. m.* periscope.
perito /pe'rito/ **-ta** *a. & n.* experienced; expert, connoisseur.
perjudicar /perhuði'kar/ *v.* damage, hurt; impair.
perjudicial /perhuði'θial; perhuði-'sial/ *a.* harmful, injurious.
perjuicio /per'huiθio; per'huisio/ *n. m.* injury, damage.
perjurar /perhu'rar/ *v.* commit perjury.
perjurio /per'hurio/ *n. m.* perjury.
perla /'perla/ *n. f.* pearl.
permanecer /permane'θer; permane-'ser/ *v.* remain, stay.
permanencia /perma'nenθia; perma-'nensia/ *n. f.* permanence; stay.
permanente /perma'nente/ *a.* permanent.

permiso /per'miso/ *n. m.* permission; permit; furlough.
permitir /permi'tir/ *v.* permit, enable, let, allow.
permuta /per'muta/ *n. f.* exchange, barter.
pernicioso /perni'θioso; perni'sioso/ *a.* pernicious.
perno /'perno/ *n. m.* bolt.
pero /'pero/ *conj.* but.
peróxido /pe'roksiðo/ *n. m.* peroxide.
perpendicular /perpendiku'lar/ *n. m. & a.* perpendicular.
perpetración /perpetra'θion; perpetra'sion/ *n. f.* perpetration.
perpetrar /perpe'trar/ *v.* perpetrate.
perpetuar /perpe'tuar/ *v.* perpetuate.
perpetuidad /perpetui'ðað/ *n. f.* perpetuity.
perpetuo /per'petuo/ *a.* perpetual.
perplejo /per'pleho/ *a.* perplexed, puzzled.
perrito caliente /pe'rrito ka'liente/ *n. m.* hot dog.
perro /'perro/ **-rra** *n.* dog.
persecución /perseku'θion; perseku-'sion/ *n. f.* persecution.
perseguir /perse'gir/ *v.* pursue; persecute.
perseverancia /perseβe'ranθia; perseβe'ransia/ *n. f.* perseverance.
perseverar /perseβe'rar/ *v.* persevere.
persiana /per'siana/ *n. f.* shutter, Venetian blind.
persistente /persis'tente/ *a.* persistent.
persistir /persis'tir/ *v.* persist.
persona /per'sona/ *n. f.* person.
personaje /perso'nahe/ *n. m.* personage; *Theat.* character.
personal /perso'nal/ *a.* **1.** personal. —*n.* **2.** *m.* personnel, staff.
personalidad /personali'ðað/ *n. f.* personality.
personalmente /personal'mente/ *adv.* personally.
perspectiva /perspek'tiβa/ *n. f.* perspective; prospect.
perspicaz /perspi'kaθ; perspi'kas/ *a.* perspicacious, acute.
persuadir /persua'ðir/ *v.* persuade.
persuasión /persua'sion/ *n. f.* persuasion.
persuasivo /persua'siβo/ *a.* persuasive.
pertenecer /pertene'θer; pertene'ser/ *v.* pertain; belong.
pertinencia /perti'nenθia; perti'nensia/ *n. f.* pertinence.
pertinente /perti'nente/ *a.* pertinent; relevant.
perturbar /pertur'βar/ *v.* perturb, disturb.
peruano /pe'ruano/ **-na** *a. & n.* Peruvian.
perversidad /perβersi'ðað/ *n. f.* perversity.
perverso /per'βerso/ *a.* perverse.
pesadez /pesa'ðeθ; pesa'ðes/ *n. f.* dullness.
pesadilla /pesa'ðiʎa; pesa'ðiya/ *n. f.* nightmare.
pesado /pe'saðo/ *a.* heavy; dull, dreary, boring.
pésame /'pesame/ *n. m.* condolence.
pesar /pe'sar/ *n. m.* sorrow; regret. **a p. de,** in spite of. *v.* weigh.
pesca /'peska/ *n. f.* fishing; catch (of fish).
pescadería /peskaðe'ria/ *n. f.* fish store.
pescado /pes'kaðo/ *n. m.* fish. —**pescar,** *v.*
pescador /peska'ðor/ *n. m.* fisherman.
pesebre /pe'seβre/ *n. m.* stall, manger; crib.
peseta /pe'seta/ *n. f.* peseta (monetary unit).
pesimismo /pesi'mismo/ *n. m.* pessimism.
pesimista /pesi'mista/ *a. & n.* pessimistic; pessimist.

pésimo /'pesimo/ *a.* awful, terrible, very bad.

peso /'peso/ *n. m.* weight; load; peso (monetary unit).

pesquera /pes'kera/ *n. f.* fishery.

pesquisa /pes'kisa/ *n. f.* investigation.

pestaña /pes'taɲa/ *n. f.* eyelash.

pestañeo /pesta'ɲeo/ *n. m.* wink, blink. —**pestañear,** *v.*

peste /'peste/ *n. f.* plague.

pesticida /pesti'θiða; pesti'siða/ *n. m.* pesticide.

pestilencia /pesti'lenθia; pesti'lensia/ *n. f.* pestilence.

pétalo /'petalo/ *n. m.* petal.

petardo /pe'tarðo/ *n. m.* firecracker.

petición /peti'θion; peti'sion/ *n. f.* petition.

petirrojo /peti'rroho/ *n. m.* robin.

petrel /pe'trel/ *n. m.* petrel.

pétreo /'petreo/ *a.* rocky.

petrificar /petrifi'kar/ *v.* petrify.

petróleo /pe'troleo/ *n. m.* petroleum.

petrolero /petro'lero/ *n. m.* oil tanker.

petunia /pe'tunia/ *n. f.* petunia.

pez /peθ; pes/ *n.* **1.** *m.* fish (in the water). —*n.* **2.** *f.* pitch, tar.

pezuña /pe'θuɲa; pe'suɲa/ *n. f.* hoof.

piadoso /pia'ðoso/ *a.* pious; merciful.

pianista /pia'nista/ *n. m. & f.* pianist.

piano /'piano/ *n. m.* piano.

picadero /pika'ðero/ *n. m.* riding school.

picadura /pika'ðura/ *n. f.* sting, bite, prick.

picamaderos /pikama'ðeros/ *n. m.* woodpecker.

picante /pi'kante/ *a.* hot, spicy.

picaporte /pika'porte/ *n. m.* latch.

picar /pi'kar/ *v.* sting, bite, prick; itch; chop up, grind up.

pícaro /'pikaro/ **-ra** *a.* **1.** knavish, mischievous. —*n.* **2.** rogue, rascal.

picarse /pi'karse/ *v.* be offended, piqued.

picazón /pika'θon; pika'son/ *n. f.* itch.

pícea /'piθea; 'pisea/ *n. f.* spruce.

pichón /pi't ʃon/ *n. m.* pigeon, squab.

pico /'piko/ *n. m.* peak; pick; beak; spout; small amount.

picotazo /piko'taθo; piko'taso/ *n. m.* peck. —**picotear,** *v.*

pictórico /pik'toriko/ *a.* pictorial.

pie /pie/ *n. m.* foot. **al p. de la letra,** literally; thoroughly.

piedad /pie'ðað/ *n. f.* piety; pity; mercy.

piedra /'pieðra/ *n. f.* stone.

piel /piel/ *n. f.* skin, hide; fur.

pienso /'pienso/ *n. m.* fodder.

pierna /'pierna/ *n. f.* leg.

pieza /'pieθa; 'piesa/ *n. f.* piece; room; *Theat.* play.

pijama /pi'hama/ *n. m. or m.pl.* pajamas.

pila /'pila/ *n. f.* pile, stack; battery; sink.

pilar /pi'lar/ *n. m.* pillar, column.

píldora /'pildora/ *n. f.* pill.

pillo /'piʎo; 'piyo/ **-a** *n.* thief; rascal.

piloto /pi'loto/ *n. m. & f.* pilot.

pimentón /pimen'ton/ *n. m.* paprika.

pimienta /pi'mienta/ *n. f.* pepper (spice).

pimiento /pi'miento/ *n. m.* pepper (vegetable).

pináculo /pi'nakulo/ *n. m.* pinnacle.

pincel /pin'θel; pin'sel/ *n. m.* (artist's) brush.

pinchadiscos /pintʃa'ðiskos/ *m. & f.* disk jockey.

pinchazo /pin'tʃaθo; pin'tʃaso/ *n. m.* puncture; prick. —**pinchar,** *v.*

pingajo /piŋ'gaho/ *n. m.* rag, tatter.

pino /'pino/ *n. m.* pine.

pinta /'pinta/ *n. f.* pint.

pintar /pin'tar/ *v.* paint; portray, depict.

pintor /pin'tor/ **-ra** *n.* painter.

pintoresco /pinto'resko/ *a.* picturesque.

pintura /pin'tura/ *n. f.* paint; painting.

pinzas /'pinθas; 'pinsas/ *n. f.pl.* pincers, tweezers; claws.

piña /'piɲa/ *n. f.* pineapple.

pío /'pio/ *a.* pious; merciful.

piojo /'pioho/ *n. m.* louse.

pionero /pio'nero/ **-ra** *n.* pioneer.

pipa /'pipa/ *n. f.* tobacco pipe.

pique /'pike/ *n. m.* resentment, pique. **echar a p.,** sink (ship).

pira /'pira/ *n. f.* pyre.

piragua /pi'ragua/ *n. f.* canoe.

piragüismo /pira'guismo/ *n. m.* canoeing.

piragüista /pira'guista/ *n. m. & f.* canoeist.

pirámide /pi'ramiðe/ *n. f.* pyramid.

pirata /pi'rata/ *n. m. & f.* pirate. **p. de aviones,** hijacker.

pisada /pi'saða/ *n. f.* tread, step. —**pisar,** *v.*

pisapapeles /pisapa'peles/ *n. m.* paperweight.

piscina /pis'θina; pis'sina/ *n. f.* fishpond; swimming pool.

piso /'piso/ *n. m.* floor.

pista /'pista/ *n. f.* trace, clue, track; racetrack.

pista de tenis /'pista de 'tenis/ tennis court.

pistola /pis'tola/ *n. f.* pistol.

pistón /pis'ton/ *n. m.* piston.

pitillo /pi'tiʎo; pi'tiyo/ *n. m.* cigarette.

pito /'pito/ *n. m.* whistle. —**pitar,** *v.*

pizarra /pi'θarra; pi'sarra/ *n. f.* slate; blackboard.

pizca /'piθka; 'piska/ *n. f.* bit, speck; pinch.

pizza /'piθθa; 'pissa/ *n. f.* pizza.

placentero /plaθen'tero; plasen'tero/ *a.* pleasant.

placer /pla'θer; pla'ser/ *n.* **1.** *m.* pleasure. —*v.* **2.** please.

plácido /'plaθiðo; 'plasiðo/ *a.* placid.

plaga /'plaga/ *n. f.* plague, scourge.

plagio /'plahio/ *n. m.* plagiarism; *(S.A.)* kidnapping.

plan /plan/ *n. m.* plan. —**planear,** *v.*

plancha /'plantʃa/ *n. f.* plate; slab, flatiron.

planchar /plan'tʃar/ *v.* iron, press.

planeta /pla'neta/ *n. m.* planet.

planificación /planifika'θion; planifika'sion/ *n. f.* planning.

planificar /planifi'kar/ *v.* plan.

plano /'plano/ *a.* **1.** level, flat. —*n.* **2.** *m.* plan; plane.

planta /'planta/ *n. f.* plant; sole (of foot).

planta baja /'planta 'baha/ *n. f.* ground floor.

plantación /planta'θion; planta'sion/ *n. f.* plantation.

plantar /plan'tar/ *v.* plant.

plantear /plante'ar/ *v.* pose, present.

plantel /plan'tel/ *n. m.* educational institution; *Agr.* nursery.

plasma /'plasma/ *n. m.* plasma.

plástico /'plastiko/ *a. & m.* plastic.

plata /'plata/ *n. f.* silver; *Colloq.* money.

plataforma /plata'forma/ *n. f.* platform.

plátano /'platano/ *n. m.* plantain; banana.

platel /pla'tel/ *n. m.* platter.

plática /'platika/ *n. f.* chat, talk. —**platicar,** *v.*

platillo /pla'tiʎo; pla'tiyo/ *n. m.* saucer.

platillo volante /pla'tiʎo bo'lante; pla'tiyo bo'lante/ flying saucer.

plato /'plato/ *n. m.* plate, dish.

playa /'plaia/ *n. f.* beach, shore.

plaza /'plaθa; 'plasa/ *n. f.* square. **p. de toros,** bullring.

plazo /'plaθo; 'plaso/ *n. m.* term, deadline; installment.

plebe /'pleβe/ *n. f.* common people; masses.

plebiscito /pleβis'θito; pleβis'sito/ *n. m.* plebiscite.

plegable /ple'gaβle/ *a.* foldable, folding.

plegadura /plega'ðura/ *n. f.* fold, pleat. —**plegar,** *v.*

pleito /'pleito/ *n. m.* lawsuit; dispute.

plenitud /pleni'tuð/ *n. f.* fullness; abundance.

pleno /'pleno/ *a.* full. **en pleno...** in the middle of...

pliego /'pliego/ *n. m.* sheet of paper.

pliegue /'pliege/ *n. m.* fold, pleat, crease.

plomería /plome'ria/ *n. f.* plumbing.

plomero /plo'mero/ *n. m.* plumber.

plomizo /plo'miθo; plo'miso/ *a.* leaden.

plomo /'plomo/ *n. m.* lead; fuse.

pluma /'pluma/ *n. f.* feather; (writing) pen.

pluma estiglográfica /'pluma estiglo'grafika/ fountain pen.

plumafuente /pluma'fuente/ *n. f.* fountain pen.

plumaje /plu'mahe/ *n. m.* plumage.

plumero /plu'mero/ *n. m.* feather duster; plume.

plumoso /plu'moso/ *a.* feathery.

plural /plu'ral/ *a. & m.* plural.

pluriempleo /pluriem'pleo/ *n. m.* moonlighting.

PNB, *abbr.* (producto nacional bruto), GNP (gross national product).

población /poβla'θion; poβla'sion/ *n. f.* population; town.

poblador /poβla'ðor/ **-ra** *n.* settler.

poblar /po'βlar/ *v.* populate; settle.

pobre /'poβre/ *a. & n.* poor; poor person.

pobreza /po'βreθa; po'βresa/ *n. f.* poverty, need.

pocilga /po'θilga; po'silga/ *n. f.* pigpen.

poción /po'θion; po'sion/ *n. f.* drink; potion.

poco /'poko/ *a. & adv.* **1.** little, not much, *(pl.)* few. **por p.,** almost, nearly. —*n.* **2.** *m.* **un p. (de),** a little, a bit (of).

poder /po'ðer/ *n.* **1.** *m.* power. —*v.* **2.** be able to, can; be possible, may, might. **no p. menos de,** not be able to help.

poder adquisitivo /po'ðer aðkisi'tiβo/ purchasing power.

poderío /poðe'rio/ *n. m.* power, might.

poderoso /poðe'roso/ *a.* powerful, mighty, potent.

podrido /po'ðriðo/ *a.* rotten.

poema /po'ema/ *n. m.* poem.

poesía /poe'sia/ *n. f.* poetry; poem.

poeta /po'eta/ *n. m. & f.* poet.

poético /po'etiko/ *a.* poetic.

polaco /po'lako/ **-ca** *a. & n.* Polish; Pole.

polar /po'lar/ *a.* polar.

polaridad /polari'ðað/ *n. f.* polarity.

polea /po'lea/ *n. f.* pulley.

polen /'polen/ *n. m.* pollen.

policía /poli'θia; poli'sia/ *n.* **1.** *f.* police. —*n.* **2.** *m.* policeman.

polideportivo /poliðepor'tiβo/ *n. m.* sports center.

poliéster /poli'ester/ *n. m.* polyester.

poligamia /poli'gamia/ *n. f.* polygamy.

poligloto /poli'gloto/ **-ta** *n.* polyglot.

polígono industrial /po'ligono indus'trial/ *n. m.* industrial park.

polilla /po'liʎa; po'liya/ *n. f.* moth.

política /po'litika/ *n. f.* politics; policy.

político /po'litiko/ **-ca** *a. & n.* politic; political; politician.

póliza /'poliθa; 'polisa/ *n. f.* (insurance) policy; permit, ticket.

polizonte /poli'θonte; poli'sonte/ *n. m.* policeman.

pollada /po'ʎaða; po'yaða/ *n. f.* brood.

pollería /poʎe'ria; poye'ria/ *n. f.* poultry shop.

pollino /po'ʎino; po'yino/ *n. m.* donkey.

pollo /'poʎo; 'poyo/ *n. m.* chicken.

polo /'polo/ *n. m.* pole; polo; popsicle.

polonés /polo'nes/ *a.* Polish.

Polonia /po'lonia/ *n. f.* Poland.

polvera /pol'βera/ *n. f.* powder box; powder puff.

polvo /'polβo/ *n. m.* powder; dust.

pólvora /'polβora/ *n. f.* gunpowder.

pompa /'pompa/ *n. f.* pomp.

pomposo /pom'poso/ *a.* pompous.

pómulo /'pomulo/ *n. m.* cheekbone.

ponche /'pontʃe/ *n. m.* punch (beverage).

ponchera /pon'tʃera/ *n. f.* punch bowl.

ponderar /ponde'rar/ *v.* ponder.

ponderoso /ponde'roso/ *a.* ponderous.

poner /po'ner/ *v.* put, set, lay, place.

ponerse /po'nerse/ *v.* put on; become, get; set (sun). **p. a,** start to.

poniente /po'niente/ *n. m.* west.

pontífice /pon'tifiθe; pon'tifise/ *n. m.* pontiff.

popa /'popa/ *n. f.* stern.

popular /popu'lar/ *a.* popular.

popularidad /populari'ðað/ *n. f.* popularity.

populazo /popu'laθo; popu'laso/ *n. m.* populace; masses.

por /por/ *prep.* by, through, because of; via; for. **p. qué,** why?

porcelana /porθe'lana; porse'lana/ *n. f.* porcelain, chinaware.

porcentaje /porθen'tahe; porsen'tahe/ *n. m.* percentage.

porche /'portʃe/ *n. m.* porch; portico.

porción /por'θion; por'sion/ *n. f.* portion, lot.

porfiar /por'fiar/ *v.* persist; argue.

pormenor /porme'nor/ *n. m.* detail.

pornografía /pornogra'fia/ *n. f.* pornography.

poro /'poro/ *n. m.* pore.

poroso /po'roso/ *a.* porous.

porque /'porke/ *conj.* because.

porqué *n. m.* reason, motive.

porra /'porra/ *n. f.* stick, club.

porrazo /po'rraθo; po'rraso/ *n. m.* blow.

porro /'porro/ *n. m. Colloq.* joint (marijuana).

portaaviones /portaa'βiones/ *n. m.* aircraft carrier.

portador /porta'ðor/ **-ra** *n.* bearer.

portal /por'tal/ *n. m.* portal.

portar /por'tar/ *v.* carry.

portarse /por'tarse/ *v.* behave, act.

portátil /por'tatil/ *a.* portable.

portavoz /porta'βoθ; porta'βos/ *n.* **1.** *m.* megaphone. **2.** *m. & f.* spokesperson.

porte /'porte/ *n. m.* bearing; behavior; postage.

portero /por'tero/ *n. m.* porter; janitor.

pórtico /'portiko/ *n. m.* porch.

portorriqueño /portorri'keɲo/ **-ña** *n. & a.* Puerto Rican.

portugués /portu'ges/ **-esa** *a. & n.* Portuguese.

posada /po'saða/ *n. f.* lodge, inn.

posar /po'sar/ *v.* pose.

posdata /pos'ðata/ *n. f.* postscript.

poseer /pose'er/ *v.* possess, own.

posesión /pose'sion/ *n. f.* possession.

posibilidad /posiβili'ðað/ *n. f.* possibility.

posible /po'siβle/ *a.* possible.

posiblemente /posiβle'mente/ *adv.* possibly.

posición /posi'θion; posi'sion/ *n. f.* position, stand.

positivo /posi'tiβo/ *a.* positive.

posponer /pospo'ner/ *v.* postpone.

postal /pos'tal/ *a.* postal; postcard.

poste /'poste/ *n. m.* post, pillar.

posteridad /posteri'ðað/ *n. f.* posterity.

posterior /poste'rior/ *a.* posterior, rear.

postizo /pos'tiθo; pos'tiso/ *a.* false, artificial.

postrado /pos'traðo/ *a.* prostrate. —**postrar,** *v.*

postre /'postre/ *n. m.* dessert.

póstumo /'postumo/ *a.* posthumous.

postura /pos'tura/ *n. f.* posture, pose; bet.

potable /po'taβle/ *a.* drinkable.

potaje /po'tahe/ *n. m.* porridge; pot stew.

potasa /po'tasa/ *n. f.* potash.

potasio /po'tasio/ *n. m.* potassium.

pote /'pote/ *n. m.* pot, jar.

potencia /po'tenθia; po'tensia/ *n. f.* potency, power.

potencial /poten'θial; poten'sial/ *a. & m.* potential.

potentado /poten'taðo/ *n. m.* potentate.

potente /po'tente/ *a.* potent, powerful.

potestad /potes'taθ/ *n. f.* power.

potro /'potro/ *n. m.* colt.

pozo /'poθo; 'poso/ *n. m.* well.

práctica /'praktika/ *n. f.* practice. —**practicar,** *v.*

práctico /'praktiko/ *a.* practical.

pradera /pra'ðera/ *n. f.* prairie, meadow.

prado /'praðo/ *n. m.* meadow; lawn.

pragmatismo /pragma'tismo/ *n. m.* pragmatism.

preámbulo /pre'ambulo/ *n. m.* preamble.

precario /pre'kario/ *a.* precarious.

precaución /prekau'θion; prekau'sion/ *n. f.* precaution.

precaverse /preka'βerse/ *v.* beware.

precavido /preka'βiðo/ *a.* cautious, guarded, wary.

precedencia /preθe'ðenθia; prese'ðensia/ *n. f.* precedence, priority.

precedente /preθe'ðente; prese'ðente/ *a. & m.* preceding; precedent.

preceder /preθe'ðer; prese'ðer/ *v.* precede.

precepto /pre'θepto; pre'septo/ *n. m.* precept.

preciar /pre'θiar; pre'siar/ *v.* value, prize.

preciarse de /pre'θiarse de; pre'siarse de/ *v.* take pride in.

precio /'preθio; 'presio/ *n. m.* price. **p. del billete de avión** air fare. **p. del cubierto** cover charge.

precioso /pre'θioso; pre'sioso/ *a.* precious; beautiful, gorgeous.

precipicio /preθi'piθio; presi'pisio/ *n. m.* precipice, cliff.

precipitación /preθipita'θion; presipita'sion/ *n. f.* precipitation.

precipitar /preθipi'tar; presipi'tar/ *v.* precipitate, rush; throw headlong.

precipitoso /preθipi'toso; presipi'toso/ *a.* precipitous; rash.

precisar /preθi'sar; presi'sar/ *v.* fix, specify; be necessary.

precisión /preθi'sion; presi'sion/ *n. f.* precision; necessity.

preciso /pre'θiso; pre'siso/ *a.* precise; necessary.

precocidad /prekoθi'ðaθ; prekosi'ðaθ/ *n. f.* precocity.

precocinado /prekoθi'naðo; prekosi'naðo/ *a.* precooked, ready-cooked.

precoz /pre'koθ; pre'kos/ *a.* precocious.

precursor /prekur'sor/ **-ra** *n.* **1.** preceding. —*n.* **2.** precursor, forerunner.

predecesor /preðeθe'sor; preðese'sor/ **-ra** *a. & n.* predecessor.

predecir /preðe'θir; preðe'sir/ *v.* predict, foretell.

predicación /preðika'θion; preðika'sion/ *n. f.* sermon.

predicador /preðika'ðor/ **-ra** *n.* preacher.

predicar /preði'kar/ *v.* preach.

predicción /preðik'θion; preðik'sion/ *n. f.* prediction.

predilecto /preði'lekto/ *a.* favorite, preferred.

predisponer /preðispo'ner/ *v.* predispose.

predisposición /preðisposi'θion; preðisposi'sion/ *n. f.* predisposition; bias.

predominante /preðomi'nante/ *a.* prevailing, prevalent, predominant.

predominar /preðomi'nar/ *v.* prevail, predominate.

predominio /preðo'minio/ *n. m.* predominance, sway.

prefacio /pre'faθio; pre'fasio/ *n. m.* preface.

preferencia /prefe'renθia; prefe'rensia/ *n. f.* preference.

preferentemente /preferente'mente/ *adv.* preferably.

preferible /prefe'riβle/ *a.* preferable.

preferir /prefe'rir/ *v.* prefer.

prefijo /pre'fiho/ *n. m.* prefix; area code, dialing code. —**prefijar,** *v.*

pregón /pre'gon/ *n. m.* proclamation; street cry.

pregonar /prego'nar/ *v.* proclaim; cry out.

pregunta /pre'gunta/ *n. f.* question, inquiry. **hacer una p.,** to ask a question.

preguntar /pregun'tar/ *v.* ask, inquire.

preguntarse /pregun'tarse/ *v.* wonder.

prehistórico /preis'toriko/ *a.* prehistoric.

prejuicio /pre'huiθio; pre'huisio/ *n. m.* prejudice.

prelacía /prela'θia; prela'sia/ *n. f.* prelacy.

preliminar /prelimi'nar/ *a. & m.* preliminary.

preludio /pre'luðio/ *n. m.* prelude.

prematuro /prema'turo/ *a.* premature.

premeditación /premeðita'θion; premeðita'sion/ *n. f.* premeditation.

premeditar /premeði'tar/ *v.* premeditate.

premiar /pre'miar/ *v.* reward; award a prize to.

premio /'premio/ *n. m.* prize, award; reward. **p. de consuelo,** consolation prize.

premisa /pre'misa/ *n. f.* premise.

premura /pre'mura/ *n. f.* pressure; urgency.

prenda /'prenda/ *n. f.* jewel; (personal) quality. **p. de vestir,** garment.

prender /pren'der/ *v.* seize, arrest, catch; pin, clip. **p. fuego a,** set fire to.

prensa /'prensa/ *n. f.* printing press; (the) press.

prensar /pren'sar/ *v.* press, compress.

preñado /pre'ɲaðo/ *a.* pregnant.

preocupación /preokupa'θion; preokupa'sion/ *n. f.* worry, preoccupation.

preocupar /preoku'par/ *v.* worry, preoccupy.

preparación /prepara'θion; prepara'sion/ *n. f.* preparation.

preparar /prepa'rar/ *v.* prepare.

preparativo /prepara'tiβo/ *n. m.* preparation.

preparatorio /prepara'torio/ *n. m.* preparatory.

preponderante /preponde'rante/ *a.* preponderant.

preposición /preposi'θion; preposi'sion/ *n. f.* preposition.

prerrogativa /prerroga'tiβa/ *n. f.* prerogative, privilege.

presa /'presa/ *n. f.* capture; (water) dam.

presagiar /presa'hiar/ *v.* presage, forebode.

presbiteriano /presβite'riano/ **-na** *n. & a.* Presbyterian.

presbítero /pres'βitero/ *n. m.* priest.

prescindir de /presθin'dir de; pressin'dir de/ *v.* dispense with; omit.

prescribir /preskri'βir/ *v.* prescribe.

prescripción /preskrip'θion; preskrip'sion/ *n. f.* prescription.

presencia /pre'senθia; pre'sensia/ *n. f.* presence.

presenciar /presen'θiar; presen'siar/ *v.* witness, be present at.

presentable /presen'taβle/ *a.* presentable.

presentación /presenta'θion; presenta'sion/ *n. f.* presentation; introduction.

presentar /presen'tar/ *v.* present; introduce.

presente /pre'sente/ *a. & m.* present.

presentimiento /presenti'miento/ *n. m.* premonition.

preservación /preserβa'θion; preserβa'sion/ *n. f.* preservation.

preservar /preser'βar/ *v.* preserve, keep.

preservativo /preserβa'tiβo/ *a. & m.* preservative; condom.

presidencia /presi'ðenθia; presi'ðensia/ *n. f.* presidency.

presidencial /presiðen'θial; presiðen'sial/ *a.* presidential.

presidente /presi'ðente/ **-ta** *n.* president.

presidiario /presi'ðiario/ **-ria** *n. m. & f.* prisoner.

presidio /pre'siðio/ *n. m.* prison; garrison.

presidir /presi'ðir/ *v.* preside.

presión /pre'sion/ *n. f.* pressure.

presión arterial /pre'sion arte'rial/ blood pressure.

preso /'preso/ **-sa** *n.* prisoner.

presta /'presta/ *n. f.* mint (plant).

prestador /presta'ðor/ **-ra** *n.* lender.

prestamista /presta'mista/ *n. m. & f.* money lender.

préstamo /'prestamo/ *n. m.* loan.

prestar /pres'tar/ *v.* lend.

presteza /pres'teθa; pres'tesa/ *n. f.* haste, promptness.

prestidigitación /prestiðihita'θion; prestiðihita'sion/ *n. f.* sleight of hand.

prestigio /pres'tihio/ *n. m.* prestige.

presto /'presto/ *a.* **1.** quick, prompt; ready. —*adv.* **2.** quickly; at once.

presumido /presu'miðo/ *a.* conceited, presumptuous.

presumir /presu'mir/ *v.* presume; boast; claim; be conceited.

presunción /presun'θion; presun'sion/ *n. f.* presumption; conceit.

presunto /pre'sunto/ *a.* presumed; prospective.

presuntuoso /presun'tuoso/ *a.* presumptuous.

presupuesto /presu'puesto/ *n. m.* premise; budget.

pretender /preten'der/ *v.* pretend; intend; aspire.

pretendiente /preten'diente/ *n. m.* suitor; pretender (to throne).

pretensión /preten'sion/ *n. f.* pretension; claim.

pretérito /pre'terito/ *a. & m.* preterit, past (tense).

pretexto /pre'teksto/ *n. m.* pretext.

prevalecer /preβale'θer; preβale'ser/ *v.* prevail.

prevención /preβen'θion; preβen'sion/ *n. f.* prevention.

prevenir /preβe'nir/ *v.* prevent; forewarn; prearrange.

preventivo /preβen'tiβo/ *a.* preventive.

prever /pre'βer/ *v.* foresee.

previamente /preβia'mente/ *adv.* previously.

previo /'preβio/ *a.* previous.

previsible /preβi'siβle/ *a.* predictable.

previsión /preβi'sion/ *n. f.* foresight. **p. social,** social security.

prieto /'prieto/ *a.* blackish, very dark.

primacía /prima'θia; prima'sia/ *n. f.* primacy.

primario /pri'mario/ *a.* primary.

primavera /prima'βera/ *n. f.* spring (season).

primero /pri'mero/ *a. & adv.* first.

primitivo /primi'tiβo/ *a.* primitive.

primo /'primo/ **-ma** *n.* cousin.

primor /pri'mor/ *n. m.* beauty; excellence; lovely thing.

primoroso /primo'roso/ *a.* exquisite, elegant; graceful.

princesa /prin'θesa; prin'sesa/ *n. f.* princess.

principal /prinθi'pal; prinsi'pal/ *a.* **1.** principal, main. —*n.* **2.** *m.* chief, head, principal.

principalmente /prinθipal'mente; prinsipal'mente/ *adv.* principally.

príncipe /'prinθipe; 'prinsipe/ *n. m.* prince.

Príncipe Azul /'prinθipe a'θul; 'prinsipe a'sul/ Prince Charming.

principiar /prinθi'piar; prinsi'piar/ *v.* begin, initiate.

principio /prin'θipio; prin'sipio/ *n. m.* beginning, start; principle.

pringado /priŋ'gaðo/ *n. m.* low-life, loser.

prioridad /priori'ðaθ/ *n. f.* priority.

prisa /'prisa/ *n. f.* hurry, haste. **darse p.,** hurry, hasten. **tener p.,** be in a hurry.

prisión /pri'sion/ *n. f.* prison; imprisonment.

prisionero /prisio'nero/ **-ra** *n.* captive, prisoner.

prisma /'prisma/ *n. m.* prism.

prismático /pris'matiko/ *a.* prismatic.

privación /priβa'θion; priβa'sion/ *n. f.* privation, want.

privado /pri'βaðo/ *a.* private, secret; deprived.

privar /pri'βar/ *v.* deprive.

privilegio /priβi'lehio/ *n. m.* privilege.

pro /pro/ *n. m. or f.* benefit, advantage. **en p. de,** in behalf of. **en p. y en contra,** pro and con.

proa /'proa/ *n. f.* prow, bow.

probabilidad /proβaβili'ðaθ/ *n. f.* probability.

probable /pro'βaβle/ *a.* probable, likely.

probablemente /proβaβle'mente/ *adv.* probably.

probador /proβa'ðor/ *n. m.* fitting room.

probar /pro'βar/ *v.* try, sample; taste; test; prove.

probarse /pro'βarse/ *v.* try on.

probidad /proβi'ðaθ/ *n. f.* honesty, integrity.

problema /pro'βlema/ *n. m.* problem.

probo /'proβo/ *a.* honest.

procaz /pro'kaθ; pro'kas/ *a.* impudent, saucy.

proceder /proθe'ðer; prose'ðer/ *v.* proceed.

procedimiento /proθeði'miento; proseði'miento/ *n. m.* procedure.

procesar /proθe'sar; prose'sar/ *v.* prosecute; sue; process.

procesión /proθe'sion; prose'sion/ *n. f.* procession.

proceso /pro'θeso; pro'seso/ *n. m.* process; (court) trial.

proclama /pro'klama/ **proclamación** *n. f.* proclamation.

proclamar /prokla'mar/ *v.* proclaim.

procreación /prokrea'θion; prokrea'sion/ *n. f.* procreation.

procrear /prokre'ar/ *v.* procreate.

procurar /proku'rar/ *v.* try; see to it; get, procure.

prodigalidad /proðigali'ðaθ/ *n. f.* prodigality.

prodigar /proði'gar/ *v.* lavish; squander, waste.

prodigio /pro'ðihio/ *n. m.* prodigy.

pródigo /'proðigo/ *a.* prodigal; profuse; lavish.

producción /proðuk'θion; proðuk'sion/ *n. f.* production.

producir /proðu'θir; proðu'sir/ *v.* produce.

productivo /proðuk'tiβo/ *a.* productive.

producto /pro'ðukto/ *n. m.* product.
producto nacional bruto /pro'ðukto naθio'nal 'bruto; pro'ðukto nasio'nal 'bruto/ gross national product.
proeza /pro'eθa; pro'esa/ *n. f.* prowess.
profanación /profana'θion; profana-'sion/ *n. f.* profanation.
profanar /profa'nar/ *v.* defile, desecrate.
profanidad /profani'ðað/ *n. f.* profanity.
profano /pro'fano/ *a.* profane.
profecía /profe'θia; profe'sia/ *n. f.* prophecy.
proferir /profe'rir/ *v.* utter, express.
profesar /profe'sar/ *v.* profess.
profesión /profe'sion/ *n. f.* profession.
profesional /profesio'nal/ *a.* professional.
profesor /profe'sor/ **-ra** *n.* professor, teacher.
profeta /pro'feta/ *n. m.* prophet.
profético /pro'fetiko/ *a.* prophetic.
profetizar /profeti'θar; profeti'sar/ *v.* prophesy.
proficiente /profi'θiente; profi'siente/ *a.* proficient.
profundamente /profunda'mente/ *adv.* profoundly, deeply.
profundidad /profundi'ðað/ *n. f.* profundity, depth.
profundizar /profundi'θar; profundi'sar/ *v.* deepen.
profundo /pro'fundo/ *a.* profound, deep.
profuso /pro'fuso/ *a.* profuse.
progenie /pro'henie/ *n. f.* progeny, offspring.
programa /pro'grama/ *n. m.* program; schedule.
programador /programa'ðor/ **-ra** *n.* (computer) programmer.
progresar /progre'sar/ *v.* progress, advance.
progresión /progre'sion/ *n. f.* progression.
progresista /progre'sista/ **progresivo** *a.* progressive.
progreso /pro'greso/ *n. m.* progress.
prohibición /proiβi'θion; proiβi'sion/ *n. f.* prohibition.
prohibir /proi'βir/ *v.* prohibit, forbid.
prohibitivo /proiβi'tiβo, proiβi'torio/ *a.* prohibitive.
prole /'prole/ *n. f.* progeny.
proletariado /proleta'riaðo/ *n. m.* proletariat.
proliferación /prolifera'θion; prolifera'sion/ *n. f.* proliferation.
prolijo /pro'liho/ *a.* prolix, tedious; long-winded.
prólogo /'prologo/ *n. m.* prologue; preface.
prolongar /proloŋ'gar/ *v.* prolong.
promedio /pro'meðio/ *n. m.* average.
promesa /pro'mesa/ *n. f.* promise.
prometer /prome'ter/ *v.* promise.
prometido /prome'tiðo/ *a.* promised; engaged (to marry).
prominencia /promi'nenθia; promi'nensia/ *n. f.* prominence.
promiscuamente /promiskua'mente/ *adv.* promiscuously.
promiscuo /pro'miskuo/ *a.* promiscuous.
promisorio /promi'sorio/ *a.* promissory.
promoción /promo'θion; promo'sion/ *n. f.* promotion.
promocionar /promoθio'nar; promosio'nar/ *v.* advertise, promote.
promover /promo'βer/ *v.* promote, further.
promulgación /promulga'θion; promulga'sion/ *n. f.* promulgation.
promulgar /promul'gar/ *v.* promulgate.
pronombre /pro'nombre/ *n. m.* pronoun.
pronosticación /pronostika'θion;

pronosticación /pronostika'sion/ *n. f.* prediction, forecast.
pronosticar /pronosti'kar/ *v.* predict, forecast.
pronóstico /pro'nostiko/ *n. m.* prediction.
prontamente /pronta'mente/ *adv.* promptly.
prontitud /pronti'tuð/ *n. f.* promptness.
pronto /'pronto/ *a.* **1.** prompt; ready. —*adv.* **2.** soon; quickly. **de p.,** abruptly.
pronunciación /pronunθia'θion; pronunsia'sion/ *n. f.* pronunciation.
pronunciar /pronun'θiar; pronun'siar/ *v.* pronounce.
propagación /propaga'θion; propaga'sion/ *n. f.* propagation.
propaganda /propa'ganda/ *n. f.* propaganda.
propagandista /propagan'dista/ *n. m. & f.* propagandist.
propagar /propa'gar/ *v.* propagate.
propicio /pro'piθio; pro'pisio/ *a.* propitious, auspicious, favorable.
propiedad /propie'ðað/ *n. f.* property.
propietario /propie'tario/ **-ria** *n.* proprietor; owner; landlord, landlady.
propina /pro'pina/ *n. f.* gratuity, tip.
propio /'propio/ *a.* proper, suitable; typical; (one's) own; -self.
proponer /propo'ner/ *v.* propose.
proporción /propor'θion; propor'sion/ *n. f.* proportion.
proporcionado /proporθio'naðo; proporsio'naðo/ *a.* proportionate.
proporcionar /proporθio'nar; proporsio'nar/ *v.* provide with, supply, afford.
proposición /proposi'θion; proposi'sion/ *n. f.* proposition, offer; proposal.
propósito /pro'posito/ *n. m.* purpose; plan; **a p.,** by the way, apropos; on purpose.
propuesta /pro'puesta/ *n. f.* proposal, motion.
prorrata /pro'rrata/ *n. f.* quota.
prórroga /'prorroga/ *n. f.* renewal, extension.
prorrogar /prorro'gar/ *v.* renew, extend.
prosa /'prosa/ *n. f.* prose.
prosaico /pro'saiko/ *a.* prosaic.
proscribir /proskri'βir/ *v.* prohibit, proscribe, ban.
prosecución /proseku'θion; proseku'sion/ *n. f.* prosecution.
proseguir /prose'gir/ *v.* pursue; proceed, go on.
prosélito /pro'selito/ **-ta** *n.* proselyte.
prospecto /pros'pekto/ *n. m.* prospectus.
prosperar /prospe'rar/ *v.* prosper, thrive, flourish.
prosperidad /prosperi'ðað/ *n. f.* prosperity.
próspero /'prospero/ *a.* prosperous, successful.
prosternado /proster'naðo/ *a.* prostrate.
prostitución /prostitu'θion; prostitu'sion/ *n. f.* prostitution.
prostituir /prosti'tuir/ *v.* prostitute; debase.
prostituta /prosti'tuta/ *n. f.* prostitute.
protagonista /protago'nista/ *n. m. & f.* protagonist, hero, heroine.
protección /protek'θion; protek'sion/ *n. f.* protection.
protector /protek'tor/ **-ra** *a. & n.* protective; protector.
proteger /prote'her/ *v.* protect, safeguard. **p. contra escritura,** write-protect (diskette).
protegido /prote'hiðo/ **-da** *n.* **1.** protégé. —*a.* **2.** protected. **p. contra escritura,** write-protected.
proteína /prote'ina/ *n. f.* protein.
protesta /pro'testa/ *n. f.* protest. —**protestar,** *v.*

protestante /protes'tante/ *a. & n.* Protestant.
protocolo /proto'kolo/ *n. m.* protocol.
protuberancia /protuβe'ranθia; protuβe'ransia/ *n. f.* protuberance, lump.
protuberante /protuβe'rante/ *a.* bulging.
provecho /pro'βetʃo/ *n. m.* profit, gain, benefit. **¡Buen provecho!** May you enjoy your meal!
provechoso /proβe'tʃoso/ *a.* beneficial, advantageous, profitable.
proveer /proβe'er/ *v.* provide, furnish.
provenir de /proβe'nir de/ *v.* originate in, be due to, come from.
proverbial /proβer'βial/ *a.* proverbial.
proverbio /pro'βerβio/ *n. m.* proverb.
providencia /proβi'ðenθia; proβi'ðensia/ *n. f.* providence.
providente /proβi'ðente/ *a.* provident.
provincia /pro'βinθia; pro'βinsia/ *n. f.* province.
provincial /proβin'θial; proβin'sial/ *a.* provincial.
provinciano /proβin'θiano; proβin'siano/ **-na** *a. & n.* provincial.
provisión /proβi'sion/ *n. f.* provision, supply, stock.
provisional /proβisio'nal/ *a.* provisional.
provocación /proβoka'θion; proβoka'sion/ *n. f.* provocation.
provocador /proβoka'ðor/ **-ra** *n.* provoker.
provocar /proβo'kar/ *v.* provoke, excite.
provocativo /proβoka'tiβo/ *a.* provocative.
proximidad /proksimi'ðað/ *n. f.* proximity, vicinity.
próximo /'proksimo/ *a.* next; near.
proyección /proiek'θion; proiek'sion/ *n. f.* projection.
proyectar /proiek'tar/ *v.* plan, project.
proyectil /proyek'til/ *n. m.* projectile, missile, shell.
proyecto /pro'iekto/ *n. m.* plan, project, scheme.
proyector /proiek'tor/ *n. m.* projector.
prudencia /pru'ðenθia; pru'ðensia/ *n. f.* prudence.
prudente /pru'ðente/ *a.* prudent.
prueba /'prueβa/ *n. f.* proof; trial; test.
psicoanálisis /psikoa'nalisis/ *n. m.* psychoanalysis.
psicoanalista /psikoana'lista/ *n. m. & f.* psychoanalyst.
psicodélico /psiko'ðeliko/ *a.* psychedelic.
psicología /psikolo'hia/ *n. f.* psychology.
psicológico /psiko'lohiko/ *a.* psychological.
psicólogo /psi'kologo/ **-ga** *n.* psychologist.
psiquiatra /psi'kiatra/ *n. m. & f.* psychiatrist.
psiquiatría /psikia'tria/ *n. f.* psychiatry.
publicación /puβlika'θion; puβlika'sion/ *n. f.* publication.
publicar /puβli'kar/ *v.* publish.
publicidad /puβliθi'ðað; puβlisi'ðað/ *n. f.* publicity.
publicista /puβli'θista; puβli'sista/ *n. m. & f.* publicity agent.
público /'puβliko/ *a. & m.* public.
puchero /pu'tʃero/ *n. m.* pot.
pudiente /pu'ðiente/ *a.* powerful; wealthy.
pudín /pu'ðin/ *n. m.* pudding.
pudor /pu'ðor/ *n. m.* modesty.
pudoroso /puðo'roso/ *a.* modest.
pudrirse /pu'ðrirse/ *v.* rot.
pueblo /'pueβlo/ *n. m.* town, village; (the) people.
puente /'puente/ *n. m.* bridge.

puente para peatones /'puente para pea'tones/ *n. m.* footbridge.
puerco /'puerko/ **-ca** *n.* pig.
puericultura /puerikul'tura/ *n. f.* pediatrics.
pueril /pue'ril/ *a.* childish.
puerilidad /puerili'ðað/ *n. f.* puerility.
puerta /'puerta/ *n. f.* door; gate.
puerta giratoria /'puerta hira'toria/ revolving door.
puerta principal /'puerta prinθi'pal; 'puerta prinsi'pal/ front door.
puerto /'puerto/ *n. m.* port, harbor.
puertorriqueño /puertorri'keno/ **-ña** *a. & n.* Puerto Rican.
pues /pues/ *adv.* **1.** well... —*conj.* **2.** as, since, for.
puesto /'puesto/ *n. m.* appointment, post, job; place; stand. **p. que,** since.
pugilato /puhi'lato/ *n. m.* boxing.
pugna /'pugna/ *n. f.* conflict.
pugnacidad /pugnaθi'ðað; pugnasi'ðað/ *n. f.* pugnacity.
pugnar /pug'nar/ *v.* fight; oppose.
pulcritud /pulkri'tuð/ *n. f.* neatness; exquisitness.
pulga /'pulga/ *n. f.* flea.
pulgada /pul'gaða/ *n. f.* inch.
pulgar /pul'gar/ *n. m.* thumb.
pulir /pu'lir/ *v.* polish; beautify.
pulmón /pul'mon/ *n. m.* lung.
pulmonía /pulmo'nia/ *n. f.* pneumonia.
pulpa /'pulpa/ *n. f.* pulp.
púlpito /'pulpito/ *n. m.* pulpit.
pulque /'pulke/ *n. m.* pulque (fermented maguey juice).
pulsación /pulsa'θion; pulsa'sion/ *n. f.* pulsation, beat.
pulsar /pul'sar/ *v.* pulsate, beat.
pulsera /pul'sera/ *n. f.* wristband; bracelet.
pulso /'pulso/ *n. m.* pulse.
pulverizar /pulβeri'θar; pulβeri'sar/ *v.* pulverize.
puma /'puma/ *n. m.* puma.
pundonor /pundo'nor/ *n. m.* point of honor.
punta /'punta/ *n. f.* point, tip, end.
puntada /pun'taða/ *n. f.* stitch.
puntapié /punta'pie/ *n. m.* kick.
puntería /punte'ria/ *n. f.* (marksman's) aim.
puntiagudo /puntia'guðo/ *a.* sharp-pointed.
puntillas /pun'tiʎas; pun'tiyas/ *n. f.pl.* **de p., en p.,** on tiptoe.
punto /'punto/ *n. m.* point; period; spot, dot. **dos puntos,** *Punct.* colon. **a p. de,** about to; at present. **p. de,** instantly.
punto de admiración /'punto de aðmira'θion; 'punto de aðmira'sion/ exclamation mark.
punto de congelación /'punto de koŋgela'θion; 'punto de koŋgela'sion/ freezing point.
punto de ebullición /'punto de eβuʎi'θion; 'punto de eβuyi'sion/ boiling point.
punto de vista /'punto de 'bista/ point of view, viewpoint.
puntuación /puntua'θion; puntua'sion/ *n. f.* punctuation.
puntual /pun'tual/ *a.* punctual, prompt.
puntuar /pun'tuar/ *v.* punctuate.
puñada /pu'naða/ *n. f.* punch.
puñado /pu'naðo/ *n. m.* handful.
puñal /pu'nal/ *n. m.* dagger.
puñalada /puna'laða/ *n. f.* stab.
puñetazo /pune'taθo; pune'taso/ *n. m.* punch, fist blow.
puño /'puno/ *n. m.* fist; cuff; handle.
pupila /pu'pila/ *n. f.* pupil (of eye).
pupitre /pu'pitre/ *n. m.* writing desk, school desk.
pureza /pu'reθa; pu'resa/ *n. f.* purity; chastity.
purgante /pur'gante/ *n. m.* laxative.
purgar /pur'gar/ *v.* purge, cleanse.
purgatorio /purga'torio/ *n. m.* purgatory.
puridad /puri'ðað/ *n. f.* secrecy.

purificación /purifika'θion; purifika-'sion/ *n. f.* purification.
purificar /purifi'kar/ *v.* purify.
purismo /pu'rismo/ *n. m.* purism.
purista /pu'rista/ *n. m. & f.* purist.
puritanismo /purita'nismo/ *n. m.* puritanism.
puro /'puro/ *a.* **1.** pure. —*n.* **2.** *m.* cigar.
púrpura /'purpura/ *n. f.* purple.
purpúreo /pur'pureo/ *a.* purple.
purulencia /puru'lenθia; puru'lensia/ *n. f.* purulence.
purulento /puru'lento/ *a.* purulent.
pus /pus/ *n. m.* pus.
pusilánime /pusi'lanime/ *a.* pusillanimous.
puta /'puta/ **-to** *n.* prostitute.
putrefacción /putrefak'θion; putrefak'sion/ *n. f.* putrefaction, rot.
putrefacto /putre'fakto/ *a.* putrid, rotten.
pútrido /'putriðo/ *a.* putrid.
puya /'puya/ *n. f.* goad.

Q

que /ke/ *rel. pron.* **1.** who, whom; that, which. —*conj.* **2.** than.
qué *a. & pron.* what. **por q., para q.,** why? *adv.* how.
quebrada /ke'βraða/ *n. f.* ravine, gully, gulch; stream.
quebradizo /keβra'ðiθo; keβra'ðiso/ *a.* fragile, brittle.
quebraley /keβra'lei/ *n. m. & f.* lawbreaker, outlaw.
quebrar /ke'βrar/ *v.* break.
queda /'keða/ *n. f.* curfew.
quedar /ke'ðar/ *v.* remain, be located; be left. **q. bien a,** be becoming to.
quedarse /ke'ðarse/ *v.* stay, remain. **q. con,** keep, hold on to; remain with.
quedo /'keðo/ *a.* quiet; gentle.
quehacer /kea'θer; kea'ser/ *n. m.* task; chore.
queja /'keha/ *n. f.* complaint.
quejarse /ke'harse/ *v.* complain, grumble.
quejido /ke'hiðo/ *n. m.* moan.
quejoso /ke'hoso/ *a.* complaining.
quema /'kema/ *n. f.* burning.
quemadura /kema'ðura/ *n. f.* burn.
quemar /ke'mar/ *v.* burn.
querella /ke'reʎa; ke'reya/ *n. f.* quarrel; complaint.
querencia /ke'renθia; ke'rensia/ *n. f.* affection, liking.
querer /ke'rer/ *v.* want, wish; will; love (a person). **q. decir,** mean. **sin q.,** without meaning to; unwillingly.
querido /ke'riðo/ *a.* dear, loved, beloved.
quesería /kese'ria/ *n. f.* dairy.
queso /'keso/ *n. m.* cheese.
queso crema /'keso 'krema/ cream cheese.
quetzal /ket'θal; ket'sal/ *n. m.* quetzal.
quiche /'kitʃe/ *n. f.* quiche.
quiebra /'kieβra/ *n. f.* break, fracture; damage; bankruptcy.
quien /kien/ *rel. pron.* who, whom.
quién *interrog. pron.* who, whom.
quienquiera /kien'kiera/ *pron.* whoever, whomever.
quietamente /kieta'mente/ *adv.* quietly.
quieto /'kieto/ *a.* quiet, still.
quietud /kie'tuð/ *n. f.* quiet, quietude.
quijada /ki'haða/ *n. f.* jaw.
quijotesco /kiho'tesko/ *a.* quixotic.
quilate /ki'late/ *n. m.* carat.
quilla /'kiʎa; 'kiya/ *n. f.* keel.
quimera /ki'mera/ *n. f.* chimera; vision; quarrel.
química /'kimika/ *n. f.* chemistry.
químico /'kimiko/ **-ca** *a. & n.* chemical; chemist.

quimoterapia /kimote'rapia/ *n. f.* chemotherapy.
quincalla /kin'kaʎa; kin'kaya/ *n. f.* (computer) hardware.
quincallería /kinkaʎe'ria; kinkaye-'ria/ *n. f.* hardware store.
quince /'kinθe; 'kinse/ *a. & pron.* fifteen.
quinientos /ki'nientos/ *a. & pron.* five hundred.
quinina /ki'nina/ *n. f.* quinine.
quintana /kin'tana/ *n. f.* country home.
quinto /'kinto/ *a.* fifth.
quirúrgico /ki'rurhiko/ *a.* surgical.
quiste /'kiste/ *n. m.* cyst.
quitamanchas /kita'mantʃas/ *n. m.* stain remover.
quitanieves /kita'nieβes/ *n. m.* snowplow.
quitar /ki'tar/ *v.* take away, remove.
quitarse /ki'tarse/ *v.* take off; get rid of.
quitasol /kita'sol/ *n. m.* parasol, umbrella.
quitasueño /kita'sueɲo/ *n. m. Colloq.* nightmare; worry.
quizá /ki'θa; ki'sa/ **quizás** *adv.* perhaps, maybe.
quórum /'korum/ *n. m.* quorum.

R

rábano /'rraβano/ *n. m.* radish.
rabí /rra'βi/ **rabino** *n. m.* rabbi.
rabia /'rraβia/ *n. f.* rage; grudge; rabies.
rabiar /rra'βiar/ *v.* rage, be furious.
rabieta /rra'βieta/ *n. f.* tantrum.
rabioso /rra'βioso/ *a.* furious; rabid.
rabo /'rraβo/ *n. m.* tail.
racha /'rratʃa/ *n. f.* streak.
racimo /rra'θimo; rra'simo/ *n. m.* bunch, cluster.
ración /rra'θion; rra'sion/ *n. f.* ration. —*racionar, v.*
racionabilidad /rraθionaβili'ðað; rrasionaβili'ðað/ *n. f.* rationality.
racional /rraθio'nal; rrasio'nal/ *a.* rational.
racionalismo /rraθiona'lismo; rrasiona'lismo/ *n. m.* rationalism.
racionalmente /rraθional'mente; rrasional'mente/ *adv.* rationally.
radar /rra'ðar/ *n. m.* radar.
radiación /rraðia'θion; rraðia'sion/ *n. f.* radiation.
radiador /rraðia'ðor/ *n. m.* radiator.
radiante /rra'ðiante/ *a.* radiant.
radical /rraði'kal/ *a. & n.* radical.
radicalismo /rraðika'lismo/ *n. m.* radicalism.
radicoso /rraði'koso/ *a.* radical.
radio /'rraðio/ *n. m. or f.* radio.
radioactividad /rraðioaktiβi'ðað/ *n. f.* radioactivity.
radioactivo /rraðioak'tiβo/ *a.* radioactive.
radiocasete /rraðioka'sete/ *n. m.* radio cassette.
radiodifundir /rraðioðifun'dir/ *v.* broadcast.
radiodifusión /rraðioðifu'sion/ *n. f.* (radio) broadcasting.
radiografía /rraðiogra'fia/ *n. f.* X-ray.
radiografiar /rraðiogra'fiar/ *v.* X-ray.
ráfaga /'rrafaga/ *n. f.* gust (of wind).
raíz /rra'iθ; rra'is/ *n. f.* root.
raja /'rraha/ *n. f.* rip; split, crack. —*rajar, v.*
ralea /rra'lea/ *n. f.* stock, breed.
ralo /'rralo/ *a.* thin, scattered.
rama /'rrama/ *n. f.* branch, bough.
ramillete /rrami'ʎete; rrami'yete/ *n. m.* bouquet.
ramo /'rramo/ *n. m.* branch, bough; bouquet.
ramonear /rramone'ar/ *v.* browse.
rampa /'rrampa/ *n. f.* ramp.
rana /'rrana/ *n. f.* frog.

ranchero /rran'tʃero/ **-ra** *n.* small farmer.
rancho /'rrantʃo/ *n. m.* ranch.
rancidez /rranθi'ðeθ; rransi'ðes/ *n. f.* rancidity.
rancio /'rranθio; 'rransio/ *a.* rancid, rank, stale, sour.
rango /'rrango/ *n. m.* rank.
ranúnculo /rra'nunkulo/ *n. m.* ranunculus; buttercup.
ranura /rra'nura/ *n. f.* slot.
ranura de expansión /rra'nura de ekspan'sion/ expansion slot.
rapacidad /rrapaθi'ðað; rrapasi'ðað/ *n. f.* rapacity.
rapaz /rra'paθ; rra'pas/ *a.* **1.** rapacious. —*n.* **2.** *m.* young boy.
rapé /'rrape/ *n. m.* snuff.
rápidamente /rrapiða'mente/ *adv.* rapidly.
rapidez /rrapi'ðeθ; rrapi'ðes/ *n. f.* rapidity, speed.
rápido /'rrapiðo/ *a.* **1.** rapid, fast, speedy. —*n.* **2.** *m.* express (train).
rapiña /rra'piɲa/ *n. f.* robbery, plundering.
rapsodia /rrap'soðia/ *n. f.* rhapsody.
rapto /'rrapto/ *n. m.* kidnapping.
raquero /rra'kero/ **-ra** *n.* beachcomber.
raqueta /rra'keta/ *n. f.* (tennis) racket.
rareza /rra'reθa; rra'resa/ *n. f.* rarity; freak.
raridad /rrari'ðað/ *n. f.* rarity.
raro /'rraro/ *a.* rare, strange, unusual, odd, queer.
rasar /rra'sar/ *v.* skim.
rascacielos /rraska'θielos; rraska'sielos/ *n. m.* skyscraper.
rascar /rras'kar/ *v.* scrape; scratch.
rasgadura /rrasga'ðura/ *n. f.* tear, rip. —*rasgar, v.*
rasgo /'rrasgo/ *n. m.* trait.
rasgón /rras'gon/ *n. m.* tear.
rasguño /rras'guɲo/ *n. m.* scratch. —*rasguñar, v.*
raso /'rraso/ *a.* **1.** plain. **soldado r.,** *Mil.* private. —*n.* **2.** *m.* satin.
raspar /rras'par/ *v.* scrape; erase.
rastra /'rrastra/ *n. f.* trail, track. —*rastrear, v.*
rastrillar /rrastri'ʎar; rrastri'yar/ *v.* rake.
rastro /'rrastro/ *n. m.* track, trail, trace; rake; flea market.
rata /'rrata/ *n. f.* rat.
ratificación /rratifika'θion; rratifika-'sion/ *n. f.* ratification.
ratificar /rratifi'kar/ *v.* ratify.
rato /'rrato/ *n. m.* while, spell, short time.
ratón /rra'ton/ *n. m.* mouse.
ratonera /rrato'nera/ *n. f.* mousetrap.
raya /'rraya/ *n. f.* dash, line, streak, stripe.
rayar /rra'yar/ *v.* rule, stripe; scratch; cross out.
rayo /'rrayo/ *n. m.* lightning bolt; ray; flash.
rayón /rra'yon/ *n. m.* rayon.
raza /'rraθa; 'rrasa/ *n. f.* race; breed, stock.
razón /rra'θon; rra'son/ *n. f.* reason; ratio. **a r. de,** at the rate of. **tener r.,** to be right.
razonable /rraθo'naβle; rraso'naβle/ *a.* reasonable, sensible.
razonamiento /rraθona'miento; rrasona'miento/ *n. m.* argument.
razonar /rraθo'nar; rraso'nar/ *v.* reason.
reacción /rreak'θion; rreak'sion/ *n. f.* reaction.
reaccionar /rreakθio'nar; rreaksio-'nar/ *v.* react.
reaccionario /rreakθio'nario; rreaksio'nario/ **-ria** *a. & n.* reactionary.
reacondicionar /rreakondiθio'nar; rreakondisio'nar/ *v.* recondition.
reactivo /rreak'tiβo/ *a. & m.* reactive; *Chem.* reagent.
reactor /rreak'tor/ *n. m.* reactor.

real /rre'al/ *a.* royal, regal; real, actual.
realdad /rreal'dað/ *n. f.* royal authority.
realeza /rrea'leθa; rrea'lesa/ *n. f.* royalty.
realidad /rreali'ðað/ *n. f.* reality.
realidad virtual /rreali'ðað βir'tual/ virtual reality.
realista /rrea'lista/ *a. & n.* realistic; realist.
realización /rrealiθa'θion; rrealisa-'sion/ *n. f.* achievement, accomplishment.
realizar /rreali'θar; rreali'sar/ *v.* accomplish; fulfill; effect; *Com.* realize.
realmente /rreal'mente/ *adv.* in reality, really.
realzar /rreal'θar; rreal'sar/ *v.* enhance.
reata /rre'ata/ *n. f.* rope; lasso, lariat.
rebaja /rre'βaha/ *n. f.* reduction.
rebajar /rreβa'har/ *v.* cheapen; reduce (in price); lower.
rebanada /rreβa'naða/ *n. f.* slice. —*rebanar, v.*
rebaño /rre'βaɲo/ *n. m.* flock, herd.
rebato /rre'βato/ *n. m.* alarm; sudden attack.
rebelarse /rreβe'larse/ *v.* rebel, revolt.
rebelde /rre'βelde/ *a. & n.* rebellious; rebel.
rebelión /rreβe'lion/ *n. f.* rebellion, revolt.
reborde /rre'βorðe/ *n. m.* border.
rebotar /rreβo'tar/ *v.* rebound.
rebozo /rre'βoθo; rre'βoso/ *n. m.* shawl.
rebuscar /rreβus'kar/ *v.* search thoroughly.
rebuznar /rreβuθ'nar; rreβus'nar/ *v.* bray.
recado /rre'kaðo/ *n. m.* message; errand.
recaída /rreka'iða/ *n. f.* relapse. —*recaer, v.*
recalcar /rrekal'kar/ *v.* stress, emphasize.
recalentar /rrekalen'tar/ *v.* reheat.
recámara /rre'kamara/ *n. f.* (Mex.) bedroom.
recapitulación /rrekapitula'θion; rrekapitula'sion/ *n. f.* recapitulation.
recapitular /rrekapitu'lar/ *v.* recapitulate.
recatado /rreka'taðo/ *n. m.* coy; prudent.
recaudador /rrekauða'ðor/ **-ra** *n.* tax collector.
recelar /rreθe'lar; rrese'lar/ *v.* fear, distrust.
receloso /rreθe'loso; rrese'loso/ *a.* distrustful.
recepción /rreθep'θion; rresep'sion/ *n. f.* reception.
recepcionista /rreθepθio'nista; rresepsio'nista/ *n. m. & f.* desk clerk.
receptáculo /rreθep'takulo; rresep-'takulo/ *n. m.* receptacle.
receptividad /rreθeptiβi'ðað; rresep-tiβi'ðað/ *n. f.* receptivity.
receptivo /rreθep'tiβo; rresep'tiβo/ *a.* receptive.
receptor /rreθep'tor; rresep'tor/ *n. m.* receiver.
receta /rre'θeta; rre'seta/ *n. f.* recipe; prescription.
recetar /rreθe'tar; rrese'tar/ *v.* prescribe.
rechazar /rretʃa'θar; rretʃa'sar/ *v.* reject, spurn, discard.
rechinar /rretʃi'nar/ *v.* chatter.
recibimiento /rreθiβi'miento; rresiβi'miento/ *n. m.* reception; welcome; anteroom.
recibir /rreθi'βir; rresi'βir/ *v.* receive.
recibo /rre'θiβo; rre'siβo/ *n. m.* receipt.
reciclaje /reθi'klahe; resi'klahe/ *n. m.* recycling.
reciclar /reθi'klar; rresi'klar/ *v.* recycle.

recidiva /rreθi'ðiβa; rresi'ðiβa/ *n. f.* relapse.

recién /rre'θien; rre'sien/ *adv.* recently, newly, just.

reciente /rre'θiente; rre'siente/ *a.* recent.

recinto /rre'θinto; rre'sinto/ *n. m.* enclosure.

recipiente /rreθi'piente; rresi'piente/ *n. m.* recipient.

reciprocación /rreθiproka'θion; rresiproka'sion/ *n. f.* reciprocation.

recíprocamente /rreθiproka'mente; rresiproka'mente/ *adv.* reciprocally.

reciprocar /rreθipro'kar; rresipro'kar/ *v.* reciprocate.

reciprocidad /rreθiproθi'ðað; rresiprosi'ðað/ *n. f.* reciprocity.

recitación /rreθita'θion; rresita'sion/ *n. f.* recitation.

recitar /rreθi'tar; rresi'tar/ *v.* recite.

reclamación /rreklama'θion; rreklama'sion/ *n. f.* claim; complaint.

reclamar /rrekla'mar/ *v.* claim; complain.

reclamo /rre'klamo/ *n. m.* claim; advertisement, advertising; decoy.

reclinar /rrekli'nar/ *v.* recline, repose, lean.

recluta /rre'kluta/ *n. m. & f.* recruit.

reclutar /rreklu'tar/ *v.* recruit, draft.

recobrar /rreko'βrar/ *v.* recover, salvage, regain.

recobro /rre'koβro/ *n. m.* recovery.

recoger /rreko'her/ *v.* gather; collect; pick up. **r. el conocimiento,** regain consciousness.

recogerse /rreko'herse/ *v.* retire (for night).

recolectar /rrekolek'tar/ *v.* gather, assemble; harvest.

recomendación /rrekomenda'θion; rrekomenda'sion/ *n. f.* recommendation; commendation.

recomendar /rrekomen'dar/ *v.* recommend; commend.

recompensa /rrekom'pensa/ *n. f.* recompense; compensation.

recompensar /rrekompen'sar/ *v.* reward; compensate.

reconciliación /rrekonθilia'θion; rrekonsilia'sion/ *n. f.* reconciliation.

reconciliar /rrekonθi'liar; rrekonsi'liar/ *v.* reconcile.

reconocer /rrekono'θer; rrekono'ser/ *v.* recognize; acknowledge; inspect, examine; *Mil.* reconnoiter.

reconocimiento /rrekonoθi'miento; rrekonosi'miento/ *n. m.* recognition; appreciation, gratitude.

reconstituir /rrekonsti'tuir/ *v.* reconstitute.

reconstruir /rrekons'truir/ *v.* reconstruct, rebuild.

record /'rrekorð/ *n. m.* (sports) record.

recordar /rrekor'ðar/ *v.* recall, recollect; remind.

recorrer /rreko'rrer/ *v.* go over; read over; cover (distance).

recorte /rre'korte/ *n. m.* clipping, cutting.

recostarse /rrekos'tarse/ *v.* recline, lean back, rest.

recreación /rrekrea'θion; rrekrea'sion/ *n. f.* recreation.

recreo /rre'kreo/ *n. m.* recreation.

recriminación /rrekrimina'θion; rrekrimina'sion/ *n. f.* recrimination.

rectangular /rrektaŋgu'lar/ *a.* rectangular.

rectángulo /rrek'taŋgulo/ *n. m.* rectangle.

rectificación /rrektifika'θion; rrektifika'sion/ *n. f.* rectification.

rectificar /rrektifi'kar/ *v.* rectify.

recto /'rrekto/ *a.* straight; just, fair. **ángulo r.,** right angle.

recuento /rre'kuento/ *n. m.* recount.

recuerdo /rre'kuerðo/ *n. m.* memory; souvenir; remembrance; (*pl.*) regards.

reculada /rreku'laða/ *n. f.* recoil. —**recular,** *v.*

recuperación /rrekupera'θion; rrekupera'sion/ *n. f.* recuperation.

recuperar /rrekupe'rar/ *v.* recuperate.

recurrir /rreku'rrir/ *v.* revert; resort, have recourse.

recurso /rre'kurso/ *n. m.* resource; recourse.

red /rreð/ *n. f.* net; trap. **r. local** local area network.

redacción /rreðak'θion; rreðak'sion/ *n. f.* (editorial) staff; composition (of written material).

redactar /rreðak'tar/ *v.* draft, draw up; edit.

redactor /rreðak'tor/ **-ra** *n.* editor.

redada /rre'ðaða/ *n. f.* netful, catch, haul.

redargución /rreðargu'θion; rreðargu'sion/ *n. f.* retort. —**redargüir,** *v.*

redención /rreðen'θion; rreðen'sion/ *n. f.* redemption, salvation.

redentor /rreðen'tor/ *n. m.* redeemer.

redimir /rreði'mir/ *v.* redeem.

redoblante /rreðo'βlante/ *n. m.* snare drum; snare dummer.

redonda /rre'ðonda/ *n. f.* neighborhood, vicinity.

redondo /rre'ðondo/ *a.* round, circular.

reducción /rreðuk'θion; rreðuk'sion/ *n. f.* reduction.

reducir /rreðu'θir; rreðu'sir/ *v.* reduce.

reembolso /rreem'βolso/ *n. m.* refund. —**reembolsar,** *v.*

reemplazar /rreempla'θar; rreempla'sar/ *v.* replace, supersede.

reencarnación /rreenkarna'θion; rreenkarna'sion/ *n. f.* reincarnation.

reexaminar /rreeksami'nar/ *v.* reexamine.

reexpedir /rreekspe'ðir/ *v.* forward (mail).

referencia /rrefe'renθia; rrefe'rensia/ *n. f.* reference.

referéndum /rrefe'rendum/ *n. m.* referendum.

referir /rrefe'rir/ *v.* relate, report on.

referirse /rrefe'rirse/ *v.* refer.

refinamiento /rrefina'miento/ *n. m.* refinement.

refinar /rrefi'nar/ *v.* refine.

refinería /rrefine'ria/ *n. f.* refinery.

reflejar /rrefle'har/ *v.* reflect; think, ponder.

reflejo /rre'fleho/ *n. m.* reflection; glare.

reflexión /rreflek'sion/ *n. f.* reflection, thought.

reflexionar /rrefleksio'nar/ *v.* reflect, think.

reflujo /rre'fluho/ *n. m.* ebb; ebb tide.

reforma /rre'forma/ *n. f.* reform. —**reformar,** *v.*

reformación /rreforma'θion; rreforma'sion/ *n. f.* reformation.

reformador /rreforma'ðor/ **-ra** *n.* reformer.

reforma tributaria /rre'forma triβu'taria/ tax reform.

reforzar /rrefor'θar; rrefor'sar/ *v.* reinforce, strengthen; encourage.

refractario /rrefrak'tario/ *a.* refractory.

refrán /rre'fran/ *n. m.* proverb, saying.

refrenar /rrefre'nar/ *v.* curb, rein; restrain.

refrescar /rrefres'kar/ *v.* refresh, freshen, cool.

refresco /rre'fresko/ *n. m.* refreshment; cold drink.

refrigeración /rrefrihera'θion; rrefrihera'sion/ *n. f.* refrigeration.

refrigerador /rrefrihera'ðor/ *n. m.* refrigerator.

refrigerar /rrefrihe'rar/ *v.* refrigerate.

refuerzo /rre'fuerθo; rre'fuerso/ *n. m.* reinforcement.

refugiado /rrefu'hiaðo/ **-da** refugee.

refugiarse /rrefu'hiarse/ *v.* take refuge.

refugio /rre'fuhio/ *n. m.* refuge, asylum, shelter.

refulgencia /rreful'henθia; rreful'hensia/ *n. f.* refulgence.

refulgente /rreful'hente/ *a.* refulgent.

refulgir /rreful'hir/ *v.* shine.

refunfuñar /rrefunfu'ɲar/ *v.* mutter, grumble, growl.

refutación /rrefuta'θion; rrefuta'sion/ *n. f.* refutation; rebuttal.

refutar /rrefu'tar/ *v.* refute.

regadera /rrega'ðera/ *n. f.* watering can.

regadizo /rrega'ðiθo; rrega'ðiso/ *a.* irrigable.

regadura /rrega'ðura/ *n. f.* irrigation.

regalar /rrega'lar/ *v.* give (a gift), give away.

regaliz /rrega'liθ; rrega'lis/ *n. m.* licorice.

regalo /rre'galo/ *n. m.* gift, present, **con r.,** in luxury.

regañar /rrega'ɲar/ *v.* reprove; scold.

regaño /rre'gaɲo/ *n. m.* reprimand; scolding.

regar /rre'gar/ *v.* water, irrigate.

regatear /rregate'ar/ *v.* haggle.

regateo /rrega'teo/ *n. m.* bargaining, haggling.

regazo /rre'gaθo; rre'gaso/ *n. m.* lap.

regencia /rre'henθia; rre'hensia/ *n. f.* regency.

regeneración /rrehenera'θion; rrehenera'sion/ *n. f.* regeneration.

regenerar /rrehene'rar/ *v.* regenerate.

regente /rre'hente/ **-ta** *a. & n.* regent.

régimen /'rrehimen/ *n. m.* regime; diet.

regimentar /rrehimen'tar/ *v.* regiment.

regimiento /rrehi'miento/ *n. m.* regiment.

región /rre'hion/ *n. f.* region.

regional /rrehio'nal/ *a.* regional, sectional.

regir /rre'hir/ *v.* rule; be in effect.

registrar /rrehis'trar/ *v.* register; record; search.

registro /rre'histro/ *n. m.* register; record; search.

regla /'rregla/ *n. f.* rule, regulation. **en r.,** in order.

reglamento /rregla'mento/ *n. m.* code of regulations.

regocijarse /rregoθi'harse; rregosi'harse/ *v.* rejoice, exult.

regocijo /rrego'θiho; rrego'siho/ *n. m.* rejoicing; merriment, joy.

regordete /rregor'ðete/ *a.* chubby, plump.

regresar /rregre'sar/ *v.* go back, return.

regresión /rregre'sion/ *n. f.* regression.

regresivo /rregre'siβo/ *a.* regressive.

regreso /rre'greso/ *n. m.* return.

regulación /rregula'θion; rregula'sion/ *n. f.* regulation.

regular /rregu'lar/ *a.* **1.** regular; fair, middling. —*v.* **2.** regulate.

regularidad /rregulari'ðað/ *n. f.* regularity.

regularmente /rregular'mente/ *adv.* regularly.

rehabilitación /rreaβilita'θion; rreaβilita'sion/ *n. f.* rehabilitation.

rehabilitar /rreaβili'tar/ *v.* rehabilitate.

rehén /rre'en/ *n. m.* hostage.

rehogar /rreo'gar/ *v.* brown.

rehusar /rreu'sar/ *v.* refuse; decline.

reina /'rreina/ *n. f.* queen.

reinado /rrei'naðo/ *n. m.* reign. —**reinar,** *v.*

reino /'rreino/ *n. m.* kingdom; realm; reign.

reír /rre'ir/ *v.* laugh.

reiteración /rreitera'θion; rreitera'sion/ *n. f.* reiteration.

reiterar /rreite'rar/ *v.* reiterate.

reja /'rreha/ *n. f.* grating, grillwork.

relación /rrela'θion; rrela'sion/ *n. f.* relation; account, report.

relacionar /rrelaθio'nar; rrelasio'nar/ *v.* relate, connect.

relajamiento /rrelaha'miento/ *n. m.* laxity, laxness.

relajar /rrela'har/ *v.* relax, slacken.

relámpago /rre'lampago/ *n. m.* lightning; flash (of lightning).

relatador /rrelata'ðor/ **-ra** *n.* teller.

relatar /rrela'tar/ *v.* relate, recount.

relativamente /rrelatiβa'mente/ *adv.* relatively.

relatividad /rrelatiβi'ðað/ *n. f.* relativity.

relativo /rrela'tiβo/ *a.* relative.

relato /rre'lato/ *n. m.* account, story.

relegación /rrelega'θion; rrelega'sion/ *n. f.* relegation.

relegar /rrele'gar/ *v.* relegate.

relevar /rrele'βar/ *v.* relieve.

relicario /rreli'kario/ *n. m.* reliquary; locket.

relieve /rre'lieβe/ *n. m.* (sculpture) relief.

religión /rreli'hion/ *n. f.* religion.

religiosidad /rrelihiosi'ðað/ *n. f.* religiosity.

religioso /rreli'hioso/ **-sa** *a.* **1.** religious. —*n.* **2.** *m.* member of a religious order.

reliquia /rre'likia/ *n. f.* relic.

rellenar /rreʎe'nar; rreye'nar/ *v.* refill; fill up, stuff.

relleno /rre'ʎeno; rre'yeno/ *n. m.* filling; stuffing.

reloj /rre'loh/ *n. m.* clock; watch.

reloj de pulsera /rre'loh de pul'sera/ wrist watch.

relojería /rrelohe'ria/ *n. f.* watchmaker's shop.

relojero /rrelo'hero/ **-ra** *n.* watchmaker.

relucir /rrelu'θir; rrelu'sir/ *v.* glow, shine; excel.

relumbrar /rrelum'βrar/ *v.* glitter, sparkle.

remache /rre'matʃe/ *n. m.* rivet. —**remachar,** *v.*

remar /rre'mar/ *v.* row (a boat).

rematado /rrema'taðo/ *a.* finished; sold.

remate /rre'mate/ *n. m.* end, finish; auction. **de r.,** utterly.

remedador /rremeða'ðor/ **-ra** *n.* imitator.

remedar /rreme'ðar/ *v.* imitate.

remedio /rre'meðio/ *n. m.* remedy. —**remediar,** *v.*

remendar /rremen'dar/ *v.* mend, patch.

remesa /rre'mesa/ *n. f.* shipment; remittance.

remiendo /rre'miendo/ *n. m.* patch.

remilgado /rremil'gaðo/ *a.* prudish; affected.

reminiscencia /rreminis'θenθia; rreminis'sensia/ *n. f.* reminiscence.

remitir /rremi'tir/ *v.* remit.

remo /'rremo/ *n. m.* oar.

remolacha /rremo'latʃa/ *n. f.* beet.

remolcador /rremolka'ðor/ *n. m.* tug (boat); tow truck.

remolino /rremo'lino/ *n. m.* whirl; whirlpool; whirlwind.

remolque /rre'molke/ *n. m.* tow. —**remolcar,** *v.*

remontar /rremon'tar/ *v.* ascend, go up.

remontarse /rremon'tarse/ *v.* get excited; soar. **r. a,** date from; go back to (in time).

remordimiento /rremorði'miento/ *n. m.* remorse.

remotamente /rremota'mente/ *adv.* remotely.

remoto /rre'moto/ *a.* remote.

remover /rremo'βer/ *v.* remove; stir; shake; loosen.

rempujar /rrempu'har/ *v.* jostle.

remuneración /rremunera'θion; rremunera'sion/ *n. f.* remuneration.

remunerar /rremune'rar/ v. remunerate.

renacido /rrena'θiðo; rrena'siðo/ a. reborn, born-again.

renacimiento /rrenaθi'miento; rrenasi'miento/ n. m. rebirth; renaissance.

rencor /rren'kor/ n. m. rancor, bitterness, animosity; grudge.

rencoroso /rrenko'roso/ a. rancorous, bitter.

rendición /rrendi'θion; rrendi'sion/ n. f. surrender.

rendido /rren'diðo/ a. weary, worn out.

rendir /rren'dir/ v. yield; surrender, give up; win over.

renegado /rrene'gaðo/ **-da** n. renegade.

renglón /rreŋ'glon/ n. m. line; Com. item.

reno /'rreno/ n. m. reindeer.

renombre /rre'nombre/ n. m. renown.

renovación /rrenoβa'θion; rrenoβa'sion/ f. renovation, renewal.

renovar /rreno'βar/ v. renew; renovate.

renta /'rrenta/ n. f. income; rent.

rentar /rren'tar/ v. yield; rent.

renuencia /rre'nuenθia; rre'nuensia/ n. f. reluctance.

renuente /rre'nuente/ a. reluctant.

renuncia /rre'nunθia; rre'nunsia/ n. f. resignation; renunciation.

renunciar /rrenun'θiar; rrenun'siar/ v. resign; renounce, give up.

reñir /rre'ɲir/ v. scold, berate; quarrel, wrangle.

reo /'rreo/ a. & n. criminal; convict.

reorganizar /rreorgani'θar; rreorgani'sar/ v. reorganize.

reparación /rrepara'θion; rrepara'sion/ n. f. reparation, atonement; repair.

reparar /rrepa'rar/ v. repair; mend; stop, stay over. **r. en**, notice; consider.

reparo /rre'paro/ n. m. repair; remark; difficulty; objection.

repartición /rreparti'θion; rreparti'sion/ n. f., **repartimiento, reparto,** m. division, distribution.

repartir /rrepar'tir/ v. divide, apportion, distribute; Theat. cast.

repaso /rre'paso/ n. m. review. —**repasar,** v.

repatriación /rrepatria'θion; rrepatria'sion/ n. f. repatriation.

repatriar /rrepa'triar/ v. repatriate.

repeler /rrepe'ler/ v. repel.

repente /rre'pente/ n. m. **de r.,** suddenly; unexpectedly.

repentinamente /rrepentina'mente/ adv. suddenly.

repentino /rrepen'tino/ a. sudden.

repercusión /rreperku'sion/ n. f. repercussion.

repertorio /rreper'torio/ n. m. repertoire.

repetición /rrepeti'θion; rrepeti'sion/ n. f. repetition; action replay.

repetidamente /rrepetiða'mente/ adv. repeatedly.

repetir /rrepe'tir/ v. repeat.

repisa /rre'pisa/ n. f. shelf.

réplica /'rreplika/ n. f. reply; objection; replica.

replicar /rrepli'kar/ v. reply; answer back.

repollo /rre'poʎo; rre'poyo/ n. m. cabbage.

reponer /rrepo'ner/ v. replace; repair.

reponerse /rrepo'nerse/ v. recover, get well.

reporte /rre'porte/ n. m. report; news.

repórter /rre'porter/ **reportero -ra** n. reporter.

reposado /rrepo'saðo/ a. tranquil, peaceful, quiet.

reposo /rre'poso/ n. m. repose, rest. —**reposar,** v.

reposte /rre'poste/ n. f. pantry.

represalia /rrepre'salia/ n. f. reprisal.

representación /rrepresenta'θion; rrepresenta'sion/ n. f. representation; Theat. performance.

representante /rrepresen'tante/ n. m. & f. representative, agent.

representar /rrepresen'tar/ v. represent; depict; Theat. perform.

representativo /rrepresenta'tiβo/ a. representative.

represión /rrepre'sion/ n. f. repression.

represivo /rrepre'siβo/ a. repressive.

reprimenda /rrepri'menda/ n. f. reprimand.

reprimir /rrepri'mir/ v. repress, quell.

reproche /rre'protʃe/ n. m. reproach. —**reprochar,** v.

reproducción /rreproðuk'θion; rreproðuk'sion/ n. f. reproduction.

reproducir /rreproðu'θir; rreproðu'sir/ v. reproduce.

reptil /rrep'til/ n. m. reptile.

república /rre'puβlika/ n. f. republic.

republicano /rrepuβli'kano/ **-na** a. & n. republican.

repudiación /rrepuðia'θion; rrepuðia'sion/ n. f. repudiation.

repudiar /rrepu'ðiar/ v. repudiate; disown.

repuesto /rre'puesto/ n. m. spare part. **de r.,** spare.

repugnancia /rrepug'nanθia; rrepug'nansia/ n. f. repugnance.

repugnante /rrepug'nante/ a. disgusting, repugnant, repulsive, revolting.

repugnar /rrepug'nar/ v. disgust.

repulsa /rre'pulsa/ n. f. refusal; repulse.

repulsivo /rrepul'siβo/ a. repulsive.

reputación /rreputa'θion; rreputa'sion/ n. f. reputation.

reputar /rrepu'tar/ v. repute; appreciate.

requerir /rreke'rir/ v. require.

requesón /rreke'son/ n. m. cottage cheese.

requisición /rrekisi'θion; rrekisi'sion/ n. f. requisition.

requisito /rreki'sito/ n. m. requisite, requirement.

res /rres/ n. f. head of cattle.

resaca /rre'saka/ n. f. hangover.

resbalar /rresβa'lar/ v. slide; slip.

resbaloso /rresβa'loso/ a. slippery.

rescate /rres'kate/ n. m. rescue; ransom. —**rescatar,** v.

rescindir /rresθin'dir; rressin'dir/ v. rescind.

resentimiento /rresenti'miento/ n. m. resentment.

resentirse /rresen'tirse/ v. resent.

reserva /rre'serβa/ n. f. reserve. —**reservar,** v.

reservación /rreserβa'θion; rreserβa'sion/ n. f. reservation.

resfriado /rres'friaðo/ n. m. Med. cold.

resfriarse /rres'friarse/ v. catch cold.

resguardar /rresguar'ðar/ v. guard, protect.

residencia /rresi'ðenθia; rresi'ðensia/ n. f. residence; seat, headquarters.

residente /rresi'ðente/ a. & n. resident.

residir /rresi'ðir/ v. reside.

residuo /rre'siðuo/ n. m. remainder.

resignación /rresigna'θion; rresigna'sion/ n. f. resignation.

resignar /rresig'nar/ v. resign.

resina /rre'sina/ n. f. resin; rosin.

resistencia /rresis'tenθia; rresis'tensia/ n. f. resistance.

resistir /rresis'tir/ v. resist; endure.

resolución /rresolu'θion; rresolu'sion/ n. f. resolution.

resolutivamente /rresolutiβa'mente/ adv. resolutely.

resolver /rresol'βer/ v. resolve; solve.

resonante /rreso'nante/ a. resonant.

resonar /rreso'nar/ v. resound.

resorte /rre'sorte/ n. m. Mech. spring.

respaldar /rrespal'dar/ v. endorse; back.

respaldo /rres'paldo/ n. m. back (of a seat).

respectivo /rrespek'tiβo/ a. respective.

respecto /rres'pekto/ n. m. relation, proportion; **r. a,** concerning, regarding.

respetabilidad /rrespetaβili'ðað/ n. f. respectability.

respetable /rrespe'taβle/ a. respectable.

respeto /rres'peto/ n. m. respect. —**respetar,** v.

respetuosamente /rrespetuosa'mente/ adv. respectfully.

respetuoso /rrespe'tuoso/ a. respectful.

respiración /rrespira'θion; rrespira'sion/ n. f. respiration, breath.

respirar /rrespi'rar/ v. breathe.

resplandeciente /rresplande'θiente; rresplande'siente/ a. resplendent.

resplandor /rresplan'dor/ n. m. brightness, glitter.

responder /rrespon'der/ v. respond, answer.

responsabilidad /rresponsaβili'ðað/ n. f. responsibility.

responsable /rrespon'saβle/ a. responsible.

respuesta /rres'puesta/ n. f. answer, response, reply.

resquicio /rres'kiθio; rres'kisio/ n. m. crack, slit.

resta /'rresta/ n. f. subtraction; remainder.

restablecer /rrestaβle'θer; rrestaβle'ser/ v. restore; reestablish.

restablecerse /rrestaβle'θerse; rrestaβle'serse/ v. recover, get well.

restar /rres'tar/ v. remain; subtract.

restauración /rrestaura'θion; rrestaura'sion/ n. f. restoration.

restaurante /rrestau'rante/ n. m. restaurant.

restaurar /rrestau'rar/ v. restore.

restitución /rrestitu'θion; rrestitu'sion/ n. f. restitution.

restituir /rresti'tuir/ v. restore, give back.

resto /'rresto/ n. m. remainder, rest; (pl.) remains.

restorán /rresto'ran/ n. m. restaurant.

restregar /rrestre'gar/ v. rub hard; scrub.

restricción /rrestrik'θion; rrestrik'sion/ n. f. restriction.

restrictivo /rrestrik'tiβo/ a. restrictive.

restringir /rrestriŋ'gir/ v. restrict, curtail.

resucitar /rresuθi'tar; rresusi'tar/ v. revive, resuscitate.

resuelto /rre'suelto/ a. resolute.

resultado /rresul'taðo/ n. m. result.

resultar /rresul'tar/ v. result; turn out; ensue.

resumen /rre'sumen/ n. m. résumé, summary, **en r.,** in brief.

resumir /rresu'mir/ v. sum up.

resurgir /rresur'hir/ v. resurge, reappear.

resurrección /rresurrek'θion; rresurrek'sion/ n. f. resurrection.

retaguardia /rreta'guarðia/ n. f. rear guard.

retal /rre'tal/ n. m. remnant.

retardar /rretar'ðar/ v. retard, slow.

retardo /rre'tarðo/ n. m. delay.

retención /rreten'θion; rreten'sion/ n. f. retention.

retener /rrete'ner/ v. retain, keep; withhold.

reticencia /rreti'θenθia; rreti'sensia/ n. f. reticence.

reticente /rreti'θente; rreti'sente/ a. reticent.

retirada /rreti'raða/ n. f. retreat, retirement.

retirar /rreti'rar/ v. retire, retreat, withdraw.

retiro /rre'tiro/ n. m. retirement.

retorcer /rretor'θer; rretor'ser/ v. wring.

retórica /rre'torika/ n. f. rhetoric.

retórico /rre'toriko/ a. rhetorical.

retorno /rre'torno/ n. m. return.

retozo /rre'toθo; rre'toso/ n. m. frolic, romp. —**retozar,** v.

retozón /rreto'θon; rreto'son/ a. frisky.

retracción /rretrak'θion; rretrak'sion/ n. f. retraction.

retractar /rretrak'tar/ v. retract.

retrasar /rretra'sar/ v. delay, set back.

retrasarse /rretra'sarse/ v. be slow.

retraso /rre'traso/ n. m. delay, lag, slowness.

retratar /rretra'tar/ v. portray; photograph.

retrato /rre'trato/ n. m. portrait; picture, photograph.

retreta /rre'treta/ n. f. Mil. retreat.

retrete /rre'trete/ n. m. toilet.

retribución /rretriβu'θion; rretriβu'sion/ n. f. retribution.

retroactivo /rretroak'tiβo/ a. retroactive.

retroalimentación /rretroalimenta'θion; rretroalimenta'sion/ n. f. feedback.

retroceder /rretroθe'ðer; rretrose'ðer/ v. recede, go back, draw back, back up.

retumbar /rretum'βar/ v. resound, rumble.

reumático /rreu'matiko/ a. rheumatic.

reumatismo /rreuma'tismo/ n. m. rheumatism.

reunión /rreu'nion/ n. f. gathering, meeting, party; reunion.

reunir /rreu'nir/ v. gather, collect, bring together.

reunirse /rreu'nirse/ v. meet, assemble, get together.

reutilizar /rreutili'zar/ v. reuse.

revelación /rreβela'θion; rreβela'sion/ n. f. revelation.

revelar /rreβe'lar/ v. reveal; betray; Phot. develop.

reventa /rre'βenta/ n. f. resale.

reventar /rreβen'tar/ v. burst; split apart.

reventón /rreβen'ton/ n. m. blowout (of tire).

reverencia /rreβeren'θia; rreβeren'sia/ n. f. reverence.

reverendo /rreβe'rendo/ a. reverend.

reverente /rreβe'rente/ a. reverent.

revertir /rreβer'tir/ v. revert.

revés /rre'βes/ n. m. reverse; back, wrong side. **al r.,** just the opposite; inside out.

revisar /rreβi'sar/ v. revise; review.

revisión /rreβi'sion/ n. f. revision.

revista /rre'βista/ n. f. magazine, periodical; review.

revivir /rreβi'βir/ v. revive.

revocación /rreβoka'θion; rreβoka'sion/ n. f. revocation.

revocar /rreβo'kar/ v. revoke, reverse.

revolotear /rreβolote'ar/ v. hover.

revolución /rreβolu'θion; rreβolu'sion/ n. f. revolution.

revolucionario /rreβoluθio'nario; rreβolusio'nario/ **-ria** a. & n. revolutionary.

revolver /rreβol'βer/ v. revolve; stir, agitate.

revólver /rre'βolβer/ n. m. revolver, pistol.

revuelta /rre'βuelta/ n. f. revolt; turn.

rey /rrei/ n. m. king.

reyerta /rre'yerta/ n. f. quarrel, wrangle.

rezar /rre'θar; rre'sar/ v. pray.

rezongar /rreθoŋ'gar; rresoŋ'gar/ v. grumble; mutter.

ría /'rria/ n. f. estuary.

riachuelo /rria'tʃuelo/ n. m. creek.

riba /'rriβa/ n. f. embankment.

rico /'rriko/ a. rich, wealthy; delicious.

ridículamente /rriˈðikulamente/ adv. ridiculously.

ridiculizar /rriðikuliˈθar; rriðikuliˈsar/ v. ridicule.

ridículo /rriˈðikulo/ a. & m. ridiculous; ridicule.

riego /ˈrriego/ n. m. irrigation.

rienda /ˈrrienda/ n. f. rein.

riesgo /ˈrriesgo/ n. m. risk, gamble.

rifa /ˈrrifa/ n. f. raffle; lottery; scuffle.

rifle /ˈrrifle/ n. m. rifle.

rígidamente /ˈrrihiðamente/ adv. rigidly.

rigidez /rrihiˈðeθ; rrihiˈðes/ n. f. rigidity.

rígido /ˈrrihiðo/ a. rigid, stiff.

rigor /rriˈgor/ n. m. rigor.

riguroso /rriguˈroso/ a. rigorous, strict.

rima /ˈrrima/ n. f. rhyme. —**rimar,** v.

rimel /rriˈmel/ n. f. mascara.

rincón /rrinˈkon/ n. m. corner, nook.

rinoceronte /rrinoθeˈronte; rrinoseˈronte/ n. m. rhinoceros.

riña /ˈrriɲa/ n. f. quarrel, feud.

riñón /rriˈɲon/ n. m. kidney.

río /ˈrrio/ n. m. river. **r. abajo** downstream, downriver. **r. arriba,** upstream, upriver.

ripio /ˈrripio/ n. m. debris.

riqueza /rriˈkeθa; rriˈkesa/ n. f. wealth.

risa /ˈrrisa/ n. f. laugh; laughter.

risco /ˈrrisko/ n. m. cliff.

risibilidad /rrisiβiliˈðað/ n. f. risibility.

risotada /rrisoˈtaða/ n. f. peal of laughter.

risueño /rriˈsueɲo/ a. cheerful, smiling.

rítmico /ˈrritmiko/ a. rhythmical.

ritmo /ˈrritmo/ n. m. rhythm.

rito /ˈrrito/ n. m. rite.

ritual /rriˈtual/ a. & m. ritual.

rivalidad /rriβaliˈðað/ n. f. rivalry.

rivera /rriˈβera/ n. f. brook.

rizado /rriˈθaðo; rriˈsaðo/ a. curly.

rizo /ˈrriθo; ˈrriso/ n. m. curl. —**rizar,** v.

robar /rroˈβar/ v. rob, steal.

roble /ˈrroβle/ n. m. oak.

roblón /rroˈβlon/ n. m. rivet. —**roblar,** v.

robo /ˈrroβo/ n. m. robbery, theft.

robustamente /rroβustaˈmente/ adv. robustly.

robusto /rroˈβusto/ a. robust.

roca /ˈrroka/ n. f. rock; cliff.

rociada /rroˈθiaða; rroˈsiaða/ n. f. spray, sprinkle. —**rociar,** v.

rocío /rroˈθio; ˈrrosio/ n. m. dew.

rocoso /rroˈkoso/ a. rocky.

rodar /rroˈðar/ v. roll; roam.

rodear /rroðeˈar/ v. surround, encircle.

rodeo /rroˈðeo/ n. m. turn, winding; roundup.

rodilla /rroˈðiʎa; rroˈðiya/ n. f. knee.

rodillo /rroˈðiʎo; rroˈðiyo/ n. m. roller.

rodio /ˈrroðio/ n. m. rhodium.

rododendro /rroðoˈðendro/ n. m. rhododendron.

roedor /rroeˈðor/ n. m. rodent.

roer /rroˈer/ v. gnaw.

rogación /rrogaˈθion; rrogaˈsion/ n. f. request, entreaty.

rogar /rroˈgar/ v. beg, plead with, supplicate.

rojizo /rroˈhiθo; rroˈhiso/ a. reddish.

rojo /ˈrroho/ a. red.

rollizo /rroˈʎiθo; rroˈyiso/ a. chubby.

rollo /ˈrroʎo; ˈrroyo/ n. m. roll; coil.

romadizo /rromaˈðiθo; rromaˈðiso/ n. m. head cold.

romance /rroˈmanθe; rroˈmanse/ n. m. romance; ballad.

románico /rroˈmaniko/ a. Romance.

romano /rroˈmano/ **-na** a. & n. Roman.

romántico /rroˈmantiko/ a. romantic.

romería /rromeˈria/ n. f. pilgrimage; picnic.

romero /rroˈmero/ **-ra** n. pilgrim.

rompecabezas /rrompekaˈβeθas; rrompekaˈβesas/ n. m. puzzle (pastime).

romper /rromˈper/ v. break, smash, shatter; sever; tear.

rompible /rromˈpiβle/ a. breakable.

ron /rron/ n. m. rum.

roncar /rronˈkar/ v. snore.

ronco /ˈrronko/ a. hoarse.

ronda /ˈrronda/ n. f. round.

rondar /rronˈdar/ v. prowl.

ronquido /rronˈkiðo/ n. m. snore.

ronronear /rronroneˈar/ v. purr.

ronzal /rronˈθal; rronˈsal/ n. m. halter.

roña /ˈrroɲa/ n. f. scab; filth.

ropa /ˈrropa/ n. f. clothes, clothing. **r. blanca,** linen. **r. interior,** underwear.

ropa de marca /ˈrropa de ˈmarka/ designer clothing.

ropero /rroˈpero/ n. m. closet.

rosa /ˈrrosa/ n. f. rose. **r. náutica,** compass.

rosado /rroˈsaðo/ a. pink, rosy.

rosal /rroˈsal/ n. m. rose bush.

rosario /rroˈsario/ n. m. rosary.

rosbif /rrosˈβif/ n. m. roast beef.

rosca /ˈrroska/ n. f. thread (of screw).

róseo /ˈrroseo/ a. rosy.

rostro /ˈrrostro/ n. m. face, countenance.

rota /ˈrrota/ n. f. defeat; Naut. course.

rotación /rrotaˈθion; rrotaˈsion/ n. f. rotation.

rotatorio /rrotaˈtorio/ a. rotary.

rótula /ˈrrotula/ n. f. kneecap.

rotulador /rrotulaˈðor/ n. m. felt-tipped pen.

rótulo /ˈrrotulo/ n. m. label. —**rotular,** v.

rotundo /rroˈtundo/ a. round; sonorous.

rotura /rroˈtura/ n. f. break, fracture, rupture.

rozar /rroˈθar; rroˈsar/ v. rub against, chafe; graze.

rubí /rruˈβi/ n. m. ruby.

rubio /ˈrruβio/ **-bia** a. & n. blond.

rubor /rruˈβor/ n. m. blush; bashfulness.

rúbrica /ˈrruβrika/ n. f. caption; scroll.

rucho /ˈrrutʃo/ n. m. donkey.

rudeza /rruˈðeθa; rruˈðesa/ n. f. rudeness; roughness.

rudimentario /rruðimenˈtario/ a. rudimentary.

rudimento /rruðiˈmento/ n. m. rudiment.

rudo /ˈrruðo/ a. rude, rough.

rueda /ˈrrueða/ n. f. wheel.

rueda de feria /ˈrrueða de ˈferia/ Ferris wheel.

ruego /ˈrruego/ n. m. plea; entreaty.

rufián /rruˈfian/ n. m. ruffian.

rufo /ˈrrufo/ a. sandy haired.

rugir /rruˈhir/ v. bellow, roar.

rugoso /rruˈgoso/ a. wrinkled.

ruibarbo /rruiˈβarβo/ n. m. rhubarb.

ruido /ˈrruiðo/ n. m. noise.

ruidoso /rruiˈðoso/ a. noisy.

ruina /ˈrruina/ n. f. ruin, wreck.

ruinar /rruiˈnar/ v. ruin, destroy.

ruinoso /rruiˈnoso/ a. ruinous.

ruiseñor /rruiseˈɲor/ n. m. nightingale.

ruleta /rruˈleta/ n. f. roulette.

rumba /ˈrrumba/ n. f. rumba (dance or music).

rumbo /ˈrrumbo/ n. m. course, direction.

rumor /rruˈmor/ n. m. rumor; murmur.

runrún /rrunˈrun/ n. m. rumor.

ruptura /rrupˈtura/ n. f. rupture, break.

rural /rruˈral/ a. rural.

Rusia /ˈrrusia/ n. f. Russia.

ruso /ˈrruso/ **-sa** a. & n. Russian.

rústico /ˈrrustiko/ **-ca** a. & n. rustic. **en r.,** paperback f.

ruta /ˈrruta/ n. f. route.

rutina /rruˈtina/ n. f. routine.

rutinario /rrutiˈnario/ a. routine.

S

sábado /ˈsaβaðo/ n. m. Saturday.

sábalo /ˈsaβalo/ n. m. shad.

sábana /saˈβana/ n. f. sheet.

sabañon /saˈβaɲon/ n. m. chilblain.

saber /saˈβer/ v. **1.** m. knowledge. —v. **2.** know; learn, find out; know how to; taste. **a s.,** namely, to wit.

sabiduría /saβiðuˈria/ n. f. wisdom; learning.

sabio /ˈsaβio/ **-a** a. **1.** wise; scholarly. —n. **2.** sage; scholar.

sable /ˈsaβle/ n. m. saber.

sabor /saˈβor/ n. m. flavor, taste, savor.

saborear /saβoreˈar/ v. savor, relish.

sabotaje /saβoˈtahe/ n. m. sabotage.

sabroso /saˈβroso/ a. savory, tasty.

sabueso /saˈβueso/ n. m. hound.

sacacorchos /sakaˈkortʃos/ n. m. corkscrew.

sacapuntas /sakaˈpuntas/ n. f. pencil sharpener.

sacar /saˈkar/ v. draw out; take out; take.

sacerdocio /saθerˈðoθio; saserˈðosio/ n. m. priesthood.

sacerdote /saθerˈðote; saserˈðote/ n. m. priest.

saciar /saˈθiar; saˈsiar/ v. satiate.

saco /ˈsako/ n. m. sack, bag, pouch; suit coat, jacket.

sacramento /sakraˈmento/ n. m. sacrament.

sacrificio /sakriˈfiθio; sakriˈfisio/ n. m. sacrifice. —**sacrificar,** v.

sacrilegio /sakriˈlehio/ n. m. sacrilege.

sacristán /sakrisˈtan/ n. m. sexton.

sacro /ˈsakro/ a. sacred, holy.

sacrosanto /sakroˈsanto/ a. sacrosanct.

sacudir /sakuˈðir/ v. shake, jerk, jolt.

sádico /ˈsaðiko/ a. sadistic.

sadismo /saˈðismo/ n. m. sadism.

sagacidad /sagaθiˈðað; sagasiˈðað/ n. f. sagacity.

sagaz /saˈgaθ; saˈgas/ a. sagacious, sage.

sagrado /saˈgraðo/ a. sacred, holy.

sal /sal/ n. f. salt; Colloq. wit.

sala /ˈsala/ n. f. room; living room, parlor; hall, auditorium.

salado /saˈlaðo/ a. salted, salty; Colloq. witty.

salar /saˈlar/ v. salt; steep in brine.

salario /saˈlario/ n. m. salary, wages.

salchicha /salˈtʃitʃa/ n. f. sausage.

sal de la Higuera /sal de la iˈgera/ Epsom salts.

saldo /ˈsaldo/ n. m. remainder, balance; (bargain) sale.

saldo acreedor /ˈsaldo akreeˈðor/ credit balance.

saldo deudor /ˈsaldo deuˈðor/ debit balance.

salero /saˈlero/ n. m. salt shaker.

salida /saˈliða/ n. f. exit, outlet; departure.

salida de urgencia /saˈliða de urˈhenθia; saˈliða de urˈhensia/ emergency exit, fire exit.

salir /saˈlir/ v. go out, come out; set out, leave, start; turn out, result.

salirse de /saˈlirse de/ v. get out of. **s. con la suya,** have one's own way.

salitre /saˈlitre/ n. m. saltpeter.

saliva /saˈliβa/ n. f. saliva.

salmo /ˈsalmo/ n. m. psalm.

salmón /salˈmon/ n. m. salmon.

salmonete /salmoˈnete/ n. m. red mullet.

salmuera /salˈmuera/ n. f. pickle; brine.

salobre /saˈloβre/ a. salty.

salón /saˈlon/ n. m. parlor, living room; hall. **s. de baile,** dance hall. **s. de belleza** beauty parlor.

salpicar /salpiˈkar/ v. spatter, splash.

salpullido /salpuˈʎiðo; salpuˈyiðo/ n. m. rash.

salsa /ˈsalsa/ n. f. sauce; gravy.

saltamontes /saltaˈmontes/ n. m. grasshopper.

salteador /salteaˈðor/ n. m. highwayman.

saltear /salteˈar/ v. hold up, rob; sauté.

salto /ˈsalto/ n. m. jump, leap, spring. —**saltar,** v.

saltón /salˈton/ n. m. grasshopper.

salubre /saˈluβre/ a. salubrious, healthful.

salubridad /saluβriˈðað/ n. f. health.

salud /saˈluð/ n. f. health.

saludable /saluˈðaβle/ a. healthful, wholesome.

saludar /saluˈðar/ v. greet; salute.

saludo /saˈluðo/ n. m. greeting; salutation; salute.

salutación /salutaˈθion; salutaˈsion/ n. f. salutation.

salva /ˈsalβa/ n. f. salvo.

salvación /salβaˈθion; salβaˈsion/ n. f. salvation; deliverance.

salvador /salβaˈðor/ **-ra** n. savior; rescuer.

salvaguardia /salβaˈguarðia/ n. m. safeguard.

salvaje /salˈβahe/ a. & n. savage, wild (person).

salvamento /salβaˈmento/ n. m. salvation; rescue.

salvar /salˈβar/ v. save; salvage; rescue; jump over.

salvavidas /salβaˈβiðas/ n. m. life preserver.

salvia /ˈsalβia/ n. f. sage (plant).

salvo /ˈsalβo/ a. **1.** safe. —prep. **2.** except, save (for). **s. que,** unless.

San /san/ title. Saint.

sanar /saˈnar/ v. heal, cure.

sanatorio /sanaˈtorio/ n. m. sanatorium.

sanción /sanˈθion; sanˈsion/ n. f. sanction. —**sancionar,** v.

sancochar /sankoˈtʃar/ v. parboil.

sandalia /sanˈdalia/ n. f. sandal.

sandez /sanˈdeθ; sanˈdes/ n. f. stupidity.

sandía /sanˈdia/ n. f. watermelon.

saneamiento /saneaˈmiento/ n. m. sanitation.

sangrar /sanˈgrar/ v. bleed.

sangre /ˈsangre/ n. f. blood.

sangriento /sanˈgriento/ a. bloody.

sanguinario /sangiˈnario/ a. bloodthirsty.

sanidad /saniˈðað/ n. f. health.

sanitario /saniˈtario/ a. sanitary.

sano /ˈsano/ a. healthy, sound, sane; healthful, wholesome.

santidad /santiˈðað/ n. f. sanctity, holiness.

santificar /santifiˈkar/ v. sanctify.

santo /ˈsanto/ **-ta** a. **1.** holy, saintly. —n. **2.** m. saint.

Santo -ta title. Saint.

santuario /sanˈtuario/ n. m. sanctuary, shrine.

saña /ˈsaɲa/ n. f. rage, anger.

sapiente /saˈpiente/ a. wise.

sapo /ˈsapo/ n. m. toad.

saquear /sakeˈar/ v. sack; ransack; plunder.

sarampión /saramˈpion/ n. m. measles.

sarape /saˈrape/ n. m. (Mex.) woven blanket; shawl.

sarcasmo /sarˈkasmo/ n. m. sarcasm.

sarcástico /sarˈkastiko/ a. sarcastic.

sardina /sarˈðina/ n. f. sardine.

sargento /sarˈhento/ n. m. sergeant.

sarna /ˈsarna/ n. f. itch.

sartén /sarˈten/ n. f. frying pan.

sastre /ˈsastre/ n. m. tailor.

satánico /saˈtaniko/ a. satanic.

satélite /saˈtelite/ n. m. satellite.

sátira /'satira/ n. f. satire.

satírico /sa'tiriko/ a. & m. satirical; satirist.

satirizar /satiri'θar; satiri'sar/ v. satirize.

sátiro /'satiro/ n. m. satyr.

satisfacción /satisfak'θion; satisfak'sion/ n. f. satisfaction.

satisfacer /satisfa'θer; satisfa'ser/ v. satisfy.

satisfactorio /satisfak'torio/ a. satisfactory.

saturación /satura'θion; satura'sion/ n. f. saturation.

saturar /satu'rar/ v. saturate.

sauce /'sauθe; 'sause/ n. m. willow.

sauna /'sauna/ n. f. sauna.

savia /'saβia/ n. f. sap.

saxofón /sakso'fon/ **saxófono** n. m. saxophone.

saya /'saya/ n. f. skirt.

sazón /sa'θon; sa'son/ n. f. season; seasoning. **a la s.,** at that time.

sazonar /saθo'nar; saso'nar/ v. flavor, season.

se /se/ pron. -self, -selves.

seca /'seka/ n. f. drought.

secador /seka'ðor/ **secador de pelo** n. m. hair dryer.

secante /se'kante/ a. **papel s.,** blotting paper.

secar /se'kar/ v. dry.

sección /sek'θion; sek'sion/ n. f. section.

seco /'seko/ a. dry; curt.

secreción /sekre'θion; sekre'sion/ n. f. secretion.

secretar /sekre'tar/ v. secrete.

secretaría /sekreta'ria/ n. f. secretary's office; secretariat.

secretario /sekre'tario/ **-ra** n. secretary.

secreto /se'kreto/ a. & m. secret.

secta /'sekta/ n. f. denomination; sect.

secuela /se'kuela/ n. f. result; sequel.

secuestrar /sekues'trar/ v. abduct, kidnap; hijack.

secuestro /se'kuestro/ n. m. abduction, kidnapping.

secular /seku'lar/ a. secular.

secundario /sekun'dario/ a. secondary.

sed /seð/ n. f. thirst. **tener s., estar con s.,** to be thirsty.

seda /'seða/ n. f. silk.

sedar /se'ðar/ v. quiet, allay.

sedativo /seða'tiβo/ a. & m. sedative.

sede /'seðe/ n. f. seat, headquarters.

sedentario /seðen'tario/ a. sedentary.

sedición /seði'θion; seði'sion/ n. f. sedition.

sedicioso /seði'θioso; seði'sioso/ a. seditious.

sediento /se'ðiento/ a. thirsty.

sedimento /seði'mento/ n. m. sediment.

sedoso /se'ðoso/ a. silky.

seducir /seðu'θir; seðu'sir/ v. seduce.

seductivo /seðuk'tiβo/ a. seductive, alluring.

segar /se'gar/ v. reap, harvest; mow.

seglar /seg'lar/ n. m. & f. layman, laywoman.

segmento /seg'mento/ n. m. segment.

segregar /segre'gar/ v. segregate.

seguida /se'giða/ n. f. succession. **en s.,** right away, at once.

seguido /se'giðo/ a. consecutive.

seguir /se'gir/ v. follow; continue, keep on, go on.

según /se'gun/ prep. **1.** according to. —conj. **2.** as.

segundo /se'gundo/ a. & m. second. —**segundar,** v.

seguridad /seguri'ðað/ n. f. safety, security; assurance.

seguro /se'guro/ a. **1.** safe, secure; sure, certain. —n. **2.** m. insurance.

seis /seis/ a. & pron. six.

seiscientos /seis'θientos; seis'sientos/ a. & pron. six hundred.

selección /selek'θion; selek'sion/ n. f. selection, choice.

seleccionar /selekθio'nar; seleksio'nar/ v. select, choose.

selecto /se'lekto/ a. select, choice, elite.

sello /'seʎo; 'seyo/ n. m. seal; stamp. —**sellar,** v.

selva /'selβa/ n. f. forest; jungle.

selvoso /sel'βoso/ a. sylvan.

semáforo /se'maforo/ n. m. semaphore; traffic light.

semana /se'mana/ n. f. week.

semana inglesa /se'mana iŋ'glesa/ five-day work week.

semanal /sema'nal/ a. weekly.

semana laboral /se'mana laβo'ral/ work week.

semántica /se'mantika/ n. f. semantics.

semblante /sem'βlante/ n. m. look, expression.

sembrado /sem'βraðo/ n. m. sown field.

sembrar /sem'βrar/ v. sow, seed.

semejante /seme'hante/ a. **1.** like, similar; such (a). —n. **2.** m. fellow man.

semejanza /seme'hanθa; seme'hansa/ n. f. similarity, likeness.

semejar /seme'har/ v. resemble.

semilla /se'miʎa; se'miya/ n. f. seed.

seminario /semi'nario/ n. m. seminary.

sémola /'semola/ n. f. semolina.

senado /se'naðo/ n. m. senate.

senador /sena'ðor/ **-ra** n. senator.

sencillez /senθi'ʎeθ; sensi'yes/ n. f. simplicity; naturalness.

sencillo /sen'θiʎo; sen'siyo/ a. simple, natural; single.

senda /'senda/ n. f. **sendero,** m. path, footpath.

senectud /senek'tuð/ n. f. old age.

senil /se'nil/ a. senile.

seno /'seno/ n. m. breast, bosom.

sensación /sensa'θion; sensa'sion/ n. f. sensation.

sensacional /sensaθio'nal; sensasio'nal/ a. sensational.

sensato /sen'sato/ a. sensible, wise.

sensibilidad /sensiβili'ðað/ n. f. sensibility; sensitiveness.

sensible /sen'siβle/ a. sensitive; emotional.

sensitivo /sensi'tiβo/ a. sensitive.

sensual /sen'sual/ a. sensual.

sensualidad /sensuali'ðað/ n. f. sensuality.

sentar /sen'tar/ v. seat. **s. bien,** fit well, be becoming.

sentarse /sen'tarse/ v. sit, sit down.

sentencia /sen'tenθia; sen'tensia/ n. f. (court) sentence.

sentidamente /sentiða'mente/ adv. feelingly.

sentido /sen'tiðo/ n. m. meaning, sense; consciousness.

sentido común /sen'tiðo ko'mun/ common sense.

sentimental /sentimen'tal/ a. sentimental.

sentimiento /senti'miento/ n. m. sentiment, feeling.

sentir /sen'tir/ v. feel, sense; hear; regret, be sorry.

seña /'seɲa/ n. f. sign, indication; (pl.) address.

señal /se'ɲal/ n. f. sign, signal; mark.

señalar /seɲa'lar/ v. designate, point out; mark.

señal de marcar /se'ɲal de mar'kar/ dial tone.

señor /se'ɲor/ n. m. gentleman; lord; (title) Mr., Sir.

señora /se'ɲora/ n. f. lady; wife; (title) Mrs., Madam.

señora de la limpieza /se'ɲora de la lim'pieθa; se'ɲora de la lim'piesa/ cleaning woman.

señorita /seɲo'rita/ n. f. young lady; (title) Miss.

separación /separa'θion; separa'sion/ n. f. separation, parting.

separadamente /separaða'mente/ adv. separately.

separado /sepa'raðo/ a. separate; separated. —**separar,** v.

septentrional /septentrio'nal/ a. northern.

septiembre /sep'tiembre/ n. m. September.

séptimo /'septimo/ a. seventh.

sepulcro /se'pulkro/ n. m. sepulcher.

sepultar /sepul'tar/ v. bury, entomb.

sepultura /sepul'tura/ n. f. grave.

sequedad /seke'ðað/ n. f. dryness.

sequía /se'kia/ n. f. drought.

ser /ser/ v. be.

serenata /sere'nata/ n. f. serenade.

serenidad /sereni'ðað/ n. f. serenity.

sereno /se'reno/ a. **1.** serene, calm. —n. **2.** m. dew; watchman.

ser humano /ser u'mano/ n. human being.

serie /'serie/ n. f. series, sequence.

seriedad /serie'ðað/ n. f. seriousness.

serio /'serio/ a. serious. **en s.,** seriously.

sermón /ser'mon/ n. m. sermon.

seroso /se'roso/ a. watery.

serpiente /ser'piente/ n. f. serpent, snake.

serpiente de cascabel /ser'piente de kaska'βel/ rattlesnake.

serrano /se'rrano/ **-na** n. mountaineer.

serrar /se'rrar/ v. saw.

serrín /se'rrin/ n. m. sawdust.

servicial /serβi'θial; serβi'sial/ a. helpful, of service.

servicio /ser'βiθio; ser'βisio/ n. m. service; toilet.

servidor /serβi'ðor/ **-ra** n. servant.

servidumbre /serβi'ðumbre/ n. f. bondage; staff of servants.

servil /ser'βil/ a. servile, menial.

servilleta /serβi'ʎeta; serβi'yeta/ n. f. napkin.

servir /ser'βir/ v. serve. **s. para,** be good for.

servirse /ser'βirse/ v. help oneself.

sesenta /se'senta/ a. & pron. sixty.

sesgo /'sesgo/ n. m. slant. —**sesgar,** v.

sesión /se'sion/ n. f. session; sitting.

seso /'seso/ n. m. brain.

seta /'seta/ n. f. mushroom.

setecientos /sete'θientos; sete'sientos/ a. & pron. seven hundred.

setenta /se'tenta/ a. & pron. seventy.

seto /'seto/ n. m. hedge.

severamente /seβera'mente/ adv. severely.

severidad /seβeri'ðað/ n. f. severity.

severo /se'βero/ a. severe, strict, stern.

sexismo /sek'sismo/ n. m. sexism.

sexista /sek'sista/ a. & n. sexist.

sexo /'sekso/ n. m. sex.

sexto /'seksto/ a. sixth.

sexual /sek'sual/ a. sexual.

si /si/ conj. if; whether.

sí pron. **1.** -self, -selves. —interj. **2.** yes.

sico-. See **psicoanálisis, psicología,** etc.

sicómoro /siko'moro/ n. m. sycamore.

SIDA /'siða/ n. m. AIDS.

sidra /'siðra/ n. f. cider.

siempre /'siempre/ adv. always. **para s.,** forever. **s. que,** whenever; provided that.

sierra /'sierra/ n. f. saw; mountain range.

siervo /'sierβo/ **-va** n. slave; serf.

siesta /'siesta/ n. f. (afternoon) nap.

siete /'siete/ a. & pron. seven.

sifón /si'fon/ n. m. siphon; siphon bottle.

siglo /'siglo/ n. m. century.

signatura /signa'tura/ n. f. Mus. signature.

significación /signifika'θion; signifika'sion/ n. f. significance.

significado /signifi'kaðo/ n. m. meaning.

significante /signifi'kante/ a. significant.

significar /signifi'kar/ v. signify, mean.

significativo /signifika'tiβo/ a. significant.

signo /'signo/ n. m. sign, symbol; mark.

siguiente /si'giente/ a. following, next.

sílaba /'silaβa/ n. f. syllable.

silbar /sil'βar/ v. whistle; hiss, boo.

silbato /sil'βato/ **silbido** n. m. whistle.

silencio /si'lenθio; si'lensio/ n. m. silence, stillness.

silenciosamente /silenθiosa'mente; silensiosa'mente/ a. silently.

silencioso /silen'θioso; silen'sioso/ a. silent, still.

silicato /sili'kato/ n. m. silicate.

silicio /si'liθio; si'lisio/ n. m. silicon.

silla /'siʎa; 'siya/ n. f. chair; saddle.

sillón /si'ʎon; si'yon/ n. m. armchair.

silueta /si'lueta/ n. f. silhouette.

silvestre /sil'βestre/ a. wild, uncultivated. **fauna s.,** wildlife.

sima /'sima/ n. f. chasm; cavern.

simbólico /sim'boliko/ a. symbolic.

símbolo /'simbolo/ n. m. symbol.

simetría /sime'tria/ n. f. symmetry.

simétrico /si'metriko/ a. symmetrical.

símil /'simil/ **similar** a. similar, alike.

similitud /simili'tuð/ n. f. similarity.

simpatía /simpa'tia/ n. f. congeniality; friendly feeling.

simpático /sim'patiko/ a. likeable, nice, congenial.

simple /'simple/ a. simple.

simpleza /sim'pleθa; sim'plesa/ n. f. silliness; trifle.

simplicidad /simpliθi'ðað; simplisi'ðað/ n. f. simplicity.

simplificación /simplifika'θion; simplifika'sion/ n. f. simplification.

simplificar /simplifi'kar/ v. simplify.

simular /simu'lar/ v. simulate.

simultáneo /simul'taneo/ a. simultaneous.

sin /sin/ prep. without. **s. sentido,** meaningless.

sinagoga /sina'goga/ n. f. synagogue.

sinceridad /sinθeri'ðað; sinseri'ðað/ n. f. sincerity.

sincero /sin'θero; sin'sero/ a. sincere.

sincronizar /sinkroni'θar; sinkroni'sar/ v. synchronize.

sindicato /sindi'kato/ n. m. syndicate; labor union.

síndrome /'sindrome/ n. m. syndrome.

sinfonía /sinfo'nia/ n. f. symphony.

sinfónico /sin'foniko/ a. symphonic.

singular /singu'lar/ a. & m. singular.

siniestro /si'niestro/ a. sinister, ominous.

sino /'sino/ conj. but.

sinónimo /si'nonimo/ n. m. synonym.

sinrazón /sinra'θon; sinra'son/ n. f. wrong, injustice.

sinsabor /sinsa'βor/ n. m. displeasure, distaste; trouble.

sintaxis /sin'taksis/ n. f. syntax.

síntesis /'sintesis/ n. f. synthesis.

sintético /sin'tetiko/ a. synthetic.

síntoma /'sintoma/ n. m. symptom.

siquiera /si'kiera/ adv. **ni s.,** not even.

sirena /si'rena/ n. f. siren.

sirviente /sir'βiente/ **-ta** n. servant.

sistema /sis'tema/ n. m. system.

sistemático /siste'matiko/ a. systematic.

sistematizar /sistemati'θar; sistemati'sar/ v. systematize.

sitiar /si'tiar/ v. besiege.

sitio /'sitio/ n. m. site, location, place, spot.

situación /situa'θion; situa'sion/ *n. f.* situation; location.
situar /si'tuar/ *v.* situate; locate.
smoking /'smokiŋg/ *n. m.* tuxedo, dinner jacket.
so /so/ *prep.* under.
soba /'soβa/ *n. f.* massage. **—sobar,** *v.*
sobaco /so'βako/ *n. m.* armpit.
sobaquero /soβa'kero/ *n. f.* armhole.
soberano /soβe'rano/ **-na** *a. & n.* sovereign.
soberbia /so'βerβia/ *n. f.* arrogance.
soberbio /so'βerβio/ *a.* superb; arrogant.
soborno /so'βorno/ *n. m.* bribe. **—sobornar,** *v.*
sobra /'soβra/ *n. f.* excess, surplus. **de sobra,** to spare.
sobrado /so'βraðo/ *n. m.* attic.
sobrante /so'βrante/ *a. & m.* surplus.
sobras /'soβras/ *n. f.pl.* leftovers.
sobre /'soβre/ *prep.* **1.** about; above, over. **—***n.* **2.** *m.* envelope.
sobrecama /soβre'kama/ *n. f.* bedspread.
sobrecargo /soβre'kargo/ *n. m.* supercargo.
sobredicho /soβre'ðitʃo/ *a.* aforesaid.
sobredosis /soβre'ðosis/ *n. f.* overdose.
sobrehumano /soβreu'mano/ *a.* superhuman.
sobrenatural /soβrenatu'ral/ *a.* supernatural, weird.
sobrepasar /soβrepa'sar/ *v.* surpass.
sobresalir /soβresa'lir/ *v.* excel.
sobretodo /soβre'toðo/ *n. m.* overcoat.
sobrevivir /soβreβi'βir/ *v.* survive, outlive.
sobriedad /soβrie'ðað/ *n. f.* sobriety; moderation.
sobrina /so'βrina/ *n. f.* niece.
sobrino /so'βrino/ *n. m.* nephew.
sobrio /'soβrio/ *a.* sober, temperate.
socarrén /soka'rren/ *n. m.* eaves.
sociable /so'θiaβle; so'siaβle/ *a.* sociable.
social /so'θial; so'sial/ *a.* social.
socialismo /soθia'lismo; sosia'lismo/ *n. m.* socialism.
socialista /soθia'lista; sosia'lista/ *a. & n.* socialist.
sociedad /soθie'ðað; sosie'ðað/ *n. f.* society; association.
sociedad de consumo /soθie'ðað de kon'sumo; sosie'ðað de kon'sumo/ consumer society.
socio /'soθio; 'sosio/ **-cia** *n.* associate, partner; member.
sociología /soθiolo'hia; sosiolo'hia/ *n. f.* sociology.
sociológico /soθio'lohiko; sosio'lohiko/ *a.* sociological.
sociólogo /so'θiologo; so'siologo/ **-ga** *n.* sociologist.
socorrista /soko'rrista/ *n. m. & f.* lifeguard.
socorro /so'korro/ *n. m.* help, aid. **—socorrer,** *v.*
soda /'soða/ *n. f.* soda.
sodio /'soðio/ *n. m.* sodium.
soez /so'eθ; so'es/ *a.* vulgar.
sofá /so'fa/ *n. m.* sofa, couch.
sofisma /so'fisma/ *n. m.* sophism.
sofista /so'fista/ *n. m. & f.* sophist.
sofocación /sofoka'θion; sofoka'sion/ *n. f.* suffocation.
sofocar /sofo'kar/ *v.* smother, suffocate, stifle, choke.
sofrito /so'frito/ *n. m.* sauce of sautéed tomatoes, peppers, onions, and garlic.
software /'sofθwer/ *n. m.* software.
soga /'soga/ *n. f.* rope.
soja /'soha/ *n. f.* soya.
sol /sol/ *n. m.* sun.
solada /so'laða/ *n. f.* dregs.
solanera /sola'nera/ *n. f.* sunburn.
solapa /so'lapa/ *n. f.* lapel.
solar /so'lar/ *a.* **1.** solar. **—***n.* **2.** *m.* building lot.
solaz /so'laθ; so'las/ *n. m.* solace, comfort. **—solazar,** *v.*
soldado /sol'daðo/ *n. m.* soldier.
soldar /sol'dar/ *v.* solder, weld.
soledad /sole'ðað/ *n. f.* solitude, privacy.
solemne /so'lemne/ *a.* solemn.
solemnemente /solemne'mente/ *adv.* solemnly.
solemnidad /solemni'ðað/ *n. f.* solemnity.
soler /so'ler/ *v.* be in the habit of.
solicitador /soliθita'ðor; solisita'ðor/ **-ra** *n.* applicant, petitioner.
solicitar /soliθi'tar; solisi'tar/ *v.* solicit; apply for.
solícito /so'liθito; so'lisito/ *a.* solicitous.
solicitud /soliθi'tuð; solisi'tuð/ *n. f.* solicitude; application.
sólidamente /soliða'mente/ *adv.* solidly.
solidaridad /soliðari'ðað/ *n. f.* solidarity.
solidez /soli'ðeθ; soli'ðes/ *n. f.* solidity.
solidificar /soliðifi'kar/ *v.* solidify.
sólido /'soliðo/ *a. & m.* solid.
soliloquio /soli'lokio/ *n. m.* soliloquy.
solitario /soli'tario/ *a.* solitary, lone.
sollozo /so'ʎoθo; so'yoso/ *n. m.* sob. **—sollozar,** *v.*
solo /'solo/ *a.* **1.** only; single; alone; lonely. **a solas,** alone. **—***n.* **2.** *m. Mus.* solo.
sólo *adv.* only, just.
solomillo /solo'miʎo; solo'miyo/ *n. m.* sirloin.
soltar /sol'tar/ *v.* release; loosen.
soltero /sol'tero/ **-ra** *a. & n.* single, unmarried (person).
soltura /sol'tura/ *n. f.* poise, ease, facility.
solubilidad /soluβili'ðað/ *n. f.* solubility.
solución /solu'θion; solu'sion/ *n. f.* solution.
solucionar /soluθio'nar; solusio'nar/ *v.* solve, settle.
solvente /sol'βente/ *a.* solvent.
sombra /'sombra/ *n. f.* shade; shadow. **—sombrear,** *v.*
sombra de ojos /'sombra de 'ohos/ eye shadow.
sombrerera /sombre'rera/ *n. f.* hatbox.
sombrero /som'βrero/ *n. m.* hat.
sombrilla /som'βriʎa; som'βriya/ *n. f.* parasol.
sombrío /som'βrio/ *a.* somber, bleak, gloomy.
sombroso /som'βroso/ *a.* very shady.
someter /some'ter/ *v.* subject; submit.
somnífero /som'nifero/ *n. m.* speeping pill.
somnolencia /somno'lenθia; somno'lensia/ *n. f.* drowsiness.
son /son/ *n. m.* sound. **—sonar,** *v.*
sonata /so'nata/ *n. f.* sonata.
sondar /son'dar/ *v.* sound, fathom.
sonido /so'niðo/ *n. m.* sound.
sonoridad /sonori'ðað/ *n. f.* sonority.
sonoro /so'noro/ *a.* sonorous.
sonrisa /son'risa/ *n. f.* smile. **—sonreír,** *v.*
sonrojo /son'roho/ *n. m.* flush, blush. **—sonrojarse,** *v.*
soñador /soɲa'ðor/ **-ra** *a. & n.* dreamy; dreamer.
soñar /so'ɲar/ *v.* dream.
soñoliento /soɲo'liento/ *a.* sleepy.
sopa /'sopa/ *n. f.* soup.
soplar /so'plar/ *v.* blow.
soplete /so'plete/ *n. m.* blowtorch.
soplo /'soplo/ *n. m.* breath; puff, gust.
soportar /sopor'tar/ *v.* abide, bear, stand.
soprano /so'prano/ *n. m. & f.* soprano.
sorbete /sor'βete/ *n. m.* sherbet.
sorbo /'sorβo/ *n. m.* sip. **—sorber,** *v.*
sordera /sor'ðera/ *n. f.* deafness.
sórdidamente /sorðiða'mente/ *adv.* sordidly.
sordidez /sorði'ðeθ; sorði'ðes/ *n. f.* sordidness.
sórdido /'sorðiðo/ *a.* sordid.
sordo /'sorðo/ *a.* deaf; muffled, dull.
sordomudo /sorðo'muðo/ **-da** *a. & n.* deaf-mute.
sorpresa /sor'presa/ *n. f.* surprise. **—sorprender,** *v.*
sorteo /sor'teo/ *n. m.* drawing lots; raffle.
sortija /sor'tiha/ *n. f.* ring.
sosa /'sosa/ *n. f. Chem.* soda.
soso /'soso/ *a.* dull, insipid, tasteless.
sospecha /sos'petʃa/ *n. f.* suspicion.
sospechar /sospe'tʃar/ *v.* suspect.
sospechoso /sospe'tʃoso/ *a.* suspicious.
sostén /sos'ten/ *n. m.* bra, brassiere; support.
sostener /soste'ner/ *v.* hold, support; maintain.
sostenimiento /sosteni'miento/ *n. m.* sustenance.
sota /'sota/ *n. f.* jack (in cards).
sótano /'sotano/ *n. m.* basement, cellar.
soto /'soto/ *n. m.* grove.
soviet /so'βiet/ *n. m.* soviet.
soya /'soya/ *n. f.* soybean.
su /su/ *a.* his, her, its, their, your.
suave /'suaβe/ *a.* smooth; gentle, soft, mild.
suavidad /suaβi'ðað/ *n. f.* smoothness; gentleness, softness, mildness.
suavizar /suaβi'θar; suaβi'sar/ *v.* soften.
subalterno /suβal'terno/ **-na** *a. & n.* subordinate.
subasta /su'βasta/ *n. f.* auction.
subcampeón /suβkampe'on/ **-na** *n.* runner-up.
subconsciencia /suβkons'θienθia; suβkons'siensia/ *n. f.* subconscious.
súbdito /'suβðito/ **-ta** *n.* subject.
subestimar /suβesti'mar/ *v.* underestimate.
subida /su'βiða/ *n. f.* ascent, rise.
subilla /su'βiʎa; su'βiya/ *n. f.* awl.
subir /su'βir/ *v.* rise, climb, ascend, mount. **s. a,** amount to.
súbito /'suβito/ *a.* sudden.
subjetivo /suβhe'tiβo/ *a.* subjective.
subjuntivo /suβhun'tiβo/ *a. & m.* subjunctive.
sublimación /suβlima'θion; suβlima'sion/ *n. f.* sublimation.
sublimar /suβli'mar/ *v.* elevate; sublimate.
sublime /su'βlime/ *a.* sublime.
submarinismo /suβmari'nismo/ *n. m.* scuba diving.
submarino /suβma'rino/ *a. & m.* submarine.
subordinación /suβorðina'θion; suβorðina'sion/ *n. f.* subordination.
subordinado /suβorði'naðo/ **-da** *a. & n.* subordinate. **—subordinar,** *v.*
subrayar /suβra'yar/ *v.* underline.
subscribirse /suβskri'βirse/ *v.* subscribe; sign one's name.
subscripción /suβskrip'θion; suβskrip'sion/ *n. f.* subscription.
subsecuente /suβse'kuente/ *a.* subsequent.
subsidiario /suβsi'ðiario/ *a.* subsidiary.
subsiguiente /suβsi'giente/ *a.* subsequent.
substancia /suβs'tanθia; suβs'tansia/ *n. f.* substance.
substancial /suβs'tanθial; suβs'tansial/ *a.* substantial.
substantivo /suβstan'tiβo/ *n. m.* substantive, noun.
substitución /suβstitu'θion; suβstitu'sion/ *n. f.* substitution.
substituir /suβsti'tuir/ *v.* replace; substitute.
substitutivo /suβstitu'tiβo/ *a.* substitute.
substituto /suβsti'tuto/ **-ta** *n.* substitute.
substraer /suβstra'er/ *v.* subtract.
subsuelo /suβ'suelo/ *n. m.* subsoil.
subterfugio /suβter'fuhio/ *n. m.* subterfuge.
subterráneo /suβte'rraneo/ *a.* **1.** subterranean, underground. **—***n.* **2.** *m.* place underground; subway.
subtítulo /suβ'titulo/ *n. m.* subtitle.
suburbio /su'βurβio/ *n. m.* suburb.
subvención /suββen'θion; suββen'sion/ *n. f.* subsidy, grant.
subversión /suββer'sion/ *n. f.* subversion.
subversivo /suββer'siβo/ *a.* subversive.
subvertir /suββer'tir/ *v.* subvert.
subyugación /suβyuga'θion; suβyuga'sion/ *n. f.* subjugation.
subyugar /suβyu'gar/ *v.* subjugate, quell.
succión /suk'θion; suk'sion/ *n. f.* suction.
suceder /suθe'ðer; suse'ðer/ *v.* happen, occur, befall. **s. a,** succeed, follow.
sucesión /suθe'sion; suse'sion/ *n. f.* succession.
sucesivo /suθe'siβo; suse'siβo/ *a.* successive. **en lo s.,** in the future.
suceso /su'θeso; su'seso/ *n. m.* event.
sucesor /suθe'sor; suse'sor/ **-ra** *n.* successor.
suciedad /suθie'ðað; susie'ðað/ *n. f.* filth, dirt.
sucio /'suθio; 'susio/ *a.* filthy, dirty.
suculento /suku'lento/ *a.* succulent.
sucumbir /sukum'βir/ *v.* succumb.
sud /suð/ *n. m.* south.
sudadera /suða'ðera/ *n. f.* sweatshirt.
Sudáfrica /su'ðafrika/ *n. f.* South Africa.
sudafricano /suðafri'kano/ **-na** *a. & n.* South African.
sudamericano /suðameri'kano/ **-na** *a. & n.* South American.
sudar /su'ðar/ *v.* perspire, sweat.
sudeste /su'ðeste/ *n. m.* southeast.
sudoeste /suðo'este/ *n. m.* southwest.
sudor /su'ðor/ *n. m.* perspiration, sweat.
Suecia /'sueθia; 'suesia/ *n. f.* Sweden.
sueco /'sueko/ **-ca** *a. & n.* Swedish; Swede.
suegra /'suegra/ *n. f.* mother-in-law.
suegro /'suegro/ *n. m.* father-in-law.
suela /'suela/ *n. f.* sole.
sueldo /'sueldo/ *n. m.* salary, wages.
suelo /'suelo/ *n. m.* soil; floor; ground.
suelto /'suelto/ *a.* **1.** loose; free; odd, separate. **—***n.* **2.** loose change.
sueño /'sueɲo/ *n. m.* sleep; sleepiness; dream. **tener s.,** to be sleepy.
suero /'suero/ *n. m.* serum.
suerte /'suerte/ *n. f.* luck; chance; lot.
suéter /'sueter/ *n. m.* sweater.
suficiente /sufi'θiente; sufi'siente/ *a.* sufficient.
sufragio /su'frahio/ *n. m.* suffrage.
sufrimiento /sufri'miento/ *n. m.* suffering, agony.
sufrir /su'frir/ *v.* suffer; undergo; endure.
sugerencia /suhe'renθia; suhe'rensia/ *n. f.* suggestion.
sugerir /suhe'rir/ *v.* suggest.
sugestión /suhes'tion/ *n. f.* suggestion.
sugestionar /suhestio'nar/ *v.* influence; hypnotize.
suicida /sui'θiða; sui'siða/ *n. m. & f.* suicide (person).
suicidarse /suiθi'ðarse; suisi'ðarse/ *v.* commit suicide.
suicidio /sui'θiðio; sui'siðio/ *n. m.* (act of) suicide.
Suiza /'suiθa; 'suisa/ *n. f.* Switzerland.
suizo /'suiθo; 'suiso/ **-za** *a. & n.* Swiss.

sujeción /suhe'θion; suhe'sion/ n. f. subjection.

sujetador /suheta'ðor/ n. m. bra, brassiere.

sujetapapeles /su'hetapa'peles/ n. m. paper clip.

sujetar /suhe'tar/ v. hold, fasten, clip.

sujeto /su'heto/ a. **1.** subject, liable. —n. **2.** m. Gram. subject.

sulfato /sul'fato/ n. m. sulfate.

sulfuro /sul'furo/ n. m. sulfide.

sultán /sul'tan/ n. m. sultan.

suma /'suma/ n. f. sum, amount. **en s.,** in short. **s. global,** lump sum.

sumar /su'mar/ v. add up.

sumaria /su'maria/ n. f. indictment.

sumario /su'mario/ a. & m. summary.

sumergir /sumer'hir/ v. submerge.

sumersión /sumer'sion/ n. f. submersion.

sumisión /sumi'sion/ n. f. submission.

sumiso /su'miso/ a. submissive.

sumo /'sumo/ a. great, high, utmost.

suntuoso /sun'tuoso/ a. sumptuous.

superar /supe'rar/ v. overcome, surpass.

superficial /superfi'θial; superfi'sial/ a. superficial, shallow.

superficie /super'fiθie; super'fisie/ n. f. surface.

superfluo /su'perfluo/ a. superfluous.

superhombre /super'ombre/ n. m. superman.

superintendente /superinten'dente/ n. m. & f. superintendent.

superior /supe'rior/ a. **1.** superior; upper, higher. —n. **2.** m. superior.

superioridad /superiori'ðað/ n. f. superiority.

superlativo /superla'tiβo/ n. m. & a. superlative.

superstición /supersti'θion; supersti'sion/ n. f. superstition.

supersticioso /supersti'θioso; supersti'sioso/ a. superstitious.

supervisar /superβi'sar/ v. supervise.

supervivencia /superβi'βenθia; superβi'βensia/ n. f. survival.

suplantar /suplan'tar/ v. supplant.

suplementario /suplemen'tario/ a. supplementary.

suplemento /suple'mento/ n. m. supplement. —**suplementar,** v.

suplente /su'plente/ a. & n. substitute.

súplica /'suplika/ n. f. request, entreaty, plea.

suplicación /suplika'θion; suplika'sion/ n. f. supplication; request, entreaty.

suplicar /supli'kar/ v. request, entreat; implore.

suplicio /su'pliθio; su'plisio/ n. m. torture, ordeal.

suplir /su'plir/ v. supply.

suponer /supo'ner/ v. suppose, presume, assume.

suposición /suposi'θion; suposi'sion/ n. f. supposition, assumption.

supositorio /suposi'torio/ n. m. suppository.

supremacía /suprema'θia; suprema'sia/ n. f. supremacy.

supremo /su'premo/ a. supreme.

supresión /supre'sion/ n. f. suppression.

suprimir /supri'mir/ v. suppress; abolish.

supuesto /su'puesto/ a. supposed. **por s.,** of course.

sur /sur/ n. m. south.

surco /'surko/ n. m. furrow. —**surcar,** v.

surgir /sur'hir/ v. arise; appear suddenly.

surtido /sur'tiðo/ n. m. assortment; supply, stock.

surtir /sur'tir/ v. furnish, supply.

susceptibilidad /susθeptiβili'ðað; susseptiβili'ðað/ n. f. susceptibility.

susceptible /susθep'tiβle; sussep-'tiβle/ a. susceptible.

suscitar /susθi'tar; sussi'tar/ v. stir up.

suscri- = subscri-

suspender /suspen'der/ v. withhold; suspend; fail (in a course).

suspensión /suspen'sion/ n. f. suspension.

suspenso /sus'penso/ n. m. failing grade. **en s.,** in suspense.

suspicacia /suspi'kaθia; suspi'kasia/ n. f. suspicion, distrust.

suspicaz /suspi'kaθ; suspi'kas/ a. suspicious.

suspicazmente /suspika'θ'mente; suspikas'mente/ adv. suspiciously.

suspiro /sus'piro/ n. m. sigh. —**suspirar,** v.

sustan- = substan-

sustentar /susten'tar/ v. sustain, support.

sustento /sus'tento/ n. m. sustenance, support, living.

susti- = substi-

susto /'susto/ n. m. fright, scare.

sustraer /sustra'er/ = substraer.

susurro /su'surro/ n. m. rustle; whisper. —**susurrar,** v.

sutil /'sutil/ a. subtle.

sutileza /suti'leθa, sutili'ðað; suti'lesa, sutili'ðað/ **sutilidad** n. f. subtlety.

sutura /su'tura/ n. f. suture.

suyo /'suyo/ a. his, hers, theirs, yours.

T

tabaco /ta'βako/ n. m. tobacco.

tábano /'taβano/ n. m. horsefly.

tabaquería /taβake'ria/ n. f. tobacco shop.

taberna /ta'βerna/ n. f. tavern, bar.

tabernáculo /taβer'nakulo/ n. m. tabernacle.

tabique /ta'βike/ n. m. dividing wall, partition.

tabla /'taβla/ n. f. board, plank; table, list. **t. de planchar,** ironing board.

tablado /ta'βlaðo/ n. m. stage, platform.

tablero /ta'βlero/ n. m. panel.

tableta /ta'βleta/ n. f. tablet.

tablilla /ta'βliʎa; ta'βliya/ n. f. bulletin board.

tabú /ta'βu/ n. m. taboo.

tabular /taβu'lar/ a. tabular.

tacaño /ta'kaɲo/ a. stingy.

tacha /'tatʃa/ n. f. fault, defect.

tachar /ta'tʃar/ v. find fault with; cross out.

tachuela /ta'tʃuela/ n. f. tack.

tácitamente /'taθitamente; 'tasitamente/ adv. tacitly.

tácito /'taθito; 'tasito/ a. tacit.

taciturno /taθi'turno; tasi'turno/ a. taciturn.

taco /'tako/ n. m. heel (of shoe); billiard cue.

tacón /ta'kon/ n. m. heel (of shoe).

táctico /'taktiko/ a. tactical.

tacto /'takto/ n. m. (sense of) touch; tact.

tafetán /tafe'tan/ n. m. taffeta.

taimado /tai'maðo/ a. sly.

tajada /ta'haða/ n. cut, slice. —**tajar,** v.

tajea /ta'hea/ n. f. channel.

tal /tal/ a. such. **con t. que,** provided that. **t. vez,** perhaps.

taladrar /tala'ðrar/ v. drill.

taladro /ta'laðro/ n. m. Mech. drill.

talante /ta'lante/ n. m. humor, disposition.

talco /'talko/ n. m. talc.

talega /ta'lega/ n. f. bag, sack.

talento /ta'lento/ n. m. talent.

talla /'taʎa; 'taya/ n. f. engraving; stature; size (of suit).

tallador /taʎa'ðor; taya'ðor/ **-ra** n. engraver; dealer (at cards).

talle /'taʎe; 'taye/ n. m. figure; waist; fit.

taller /ta'ʎer; ta'yer/ n. m. workshop, factory.

tallo /'taʎo; 'tayo/ n. m. stem, stalk.

talón /ta'lon/ n. m. heel (of foot); (baggage) check, stub.

tamal /ta'mal/ n. m. tamale.

tamaño /ta'maɲo/ n. m. size.

tambalear /tambale'ar/ v. stagger, totter.

también /tam'bien/ adv. also, too.

tambor /tam'bor/ n. m. drum.

tamiz /ta'miθ; ta'mis/ n. m. sieve, sifter.

tampoco /tam'poko/ adv. neither, either.

tan /tan/ adv. so.

tanda /'tanda/ n. f. turn, relay.

tándem /'tandem/ n. m. tandem; pair.

tangencia /taŋ'genθia; taŋ'gensia/ n. f. tangency.

tangible /taŋ'giβle/ a. tangible.

tango /'taŋgo/ n. m. tango (dance or music).

tanque /'tanke/ n. m. tank.

tanteo /tan'teo/ n. m. estimate. —**tantear,** v.

tanto /'tanto/ a. & pron. **1.** so much, so many; as much, as many. **entre t., mientras t.,** meanwhile. **por lo t.,** therefore. **un t.,** somewhat, a bit. —n. **2.** m. point (in games) **3.** (pl.) score. **estar al t.,** to be up to date.

tañer /ta'ɲer/ v. play (an instrument); ring (bells).

tapa /'tapa/ n. f. cap, cover; snack served in a bar. —**tapar,** v.

tapadero /tapa'ðero/ n. m. stopper, lid.

tápara /'tapara/ n. f. caper.

tapete /ta'pete/ n. m. small rug, mat, cover.

tapia /'tapia/ n. f. wall.

tapicería /tapiθe'ria; tapise'ria/ n. f. tapestry.

tapioca /ta'pioka/ n. f. tapioca.

tapiz /ta'piθ; ta'pis/ n. m. tapestry; carpet.

tapizado (de pared) /tapi'θaðo de pa'reð tapi'saðo de pa'reð/ n. m. (wall) covering.

tapón /ta'pon/ n. m. plug; cork.

taquigrafía /takigra'fia/ n. f. shorthand.

taquilla /ta'kiʎa; ta'kiya/ n. f. ticket office; box office; ticket window.

tara /'tara/ n. f. hang-up.

tarántula /ta'rantula/ n. f. tarantula.

tararear /tarare'ar/ v. hum.

tardanza /tar'ðanθa; tar'ðansa/ n. f. delay; lateness.

tardar /tar'ðar/ v. delay; be late; take (of time). **a más t.,** at the latest.

tarde /'tarðe/ adv. **1.** late. —n. **2.** f. afternoon.

tardío /tar'ðio/ a. late, belated.

tarea /ta'rea/ n. f. task, assignment.

tarifa /ta'rifa/ n. f. rate; tariff; price list.

tarjeta /tar'heta/ n. f. card.

tarjeta bancaria /tar'heta ban'karia/ bank card.

tarjeta de crédito /tar'heta de 'kreðito/ credit card.

tarjeta de embarque /tar'heta de em'βarke/ boarding pass.

tarta /'tarta/ n. f. tart.

tartamudear /tartamuðe'ar/ v. stammer, falter.

tasa /'tasa/ n. f. rate.

tasación /tasa'θion; tasa'sion/ n. f. valuation.

tasar /ta'sar/ v. assess, appraise.

tasca /'taska/ n. f. bar, pub.

tasugo /ta'sugo/ n. m. badger.

tatuar /tatu'ar/ v. tattoo.

tautología /tautolo'hia/ n. f. tautology.

taxi /'taksi/ **taxímetro** n. m. taxi.

taxista /tak'sista/ n. m. & f. taxi driver.

taxonomía /taksono'mia/ n. f. taxonomy.

taza /'taθa; 'tasa/ n. f. cup.

te /te/ pron. you; yourself.

té n. m. tea.

team /tim/ n. m. team.

teátrico /te'atriko/ a. theatrical.

teatro /te'atro/ n. m. theater.

tebeo /te'βeo/ n. m. comic book.

techo /'tetʃo/ n. m. roof. —**techar,** v.

tecla /'tekla/ n. f. key (of a piano, etc.).

teclado /te'klaðo/ n. m. keyboard.

teclado numérico /te'klaðo nu'meriko/ numeric keypad.

técnica /'teknika/ n. f. technique.

técnicamente /'teknikamente/ adv. technically.

técnico /'tekniko/ a. **1.** technical; —m. **2.** repairman, technician.

tecnología /teknolo'hia/ n. f. technology.

tedio /'teðio/ n. m. tedium, boredom.

tedioso /te'ðioso/ a. tedious.

teísmo /te'ismo/ n. m. theism.

teja /'teha/ n. f. tile.

tejado /te'haðo/ n. m. roof.

tejano /te'hano/ **-na** a. & n. Texan.

tejanos /te'hanos/ n. m.pl. jeans.

tejer /te'her/ v. weave; knit.

tejido /te'hiðo/ n. m. fabric; weaving.

tejón /te'hon/ n. m. badger.

tela /'tela/ n. f. cloth, fabric, web. **t. metálica,** screen; screening. **t. vaquera,** denim.

telar /te'lar/ n. m. loom.

telaraña /tela'raɲa/ n. f. cobweb, spiderweb.

telefonista /telefo'nista/ n. m. & f. (telephone) operator.

teléfono /te'lefono/ n. m. telephone. —**telefonear,** v.

teléfono gratuito /te'lefono gra'tuito/ toll-free number.

teléfono público /te'lefono 'puβliko/ pay phone, public telephone.

teléfono rojo /te'lefono 'rroho/ hotline.

telégrafo /te'legrafo/ n. m. telegraph. —**telegrafiar,** v.

telegrama /tele'grama/ n. m. telegram.

telescopio /teles'kopio/ n. m. telescope.

televisión /teleβi'sion/ n. f. television.

telón /te'lon/ n. m. Theat. curtain.

telurio /te'lurio/ n. m. tellurium.

tema /'tema/ n. m. theme, subject.

temblar /tem'blar/ v. tremble, quake; shake, shiver.

temblor /tem'blor/ n. m. tremor; shiver.

temer /te'mer/ v. fear, be afraid of, dread.

temerario /teme'rario/ a. rash.

temeridad /temeri'ðað/ n. f. temerity.

temerosamente /temerosa'mente/ adv. timorously.

temeroso /teme'roso/ a. fearful.

temor /te'mor/ n. m. fear.

témpano /'tempano/ n. m. kettledrum; iceberg.

temperamento /tempera'mento/ n. m. temperament.

temperancia /tempe'ranθia; tempe'ransia/ n. f. temperance.

temperatura /tempera'tura/ n. f. temperature.

tempestad /tempes'tað/ n. f. tempest, storm.

tempestuoso /tempes'tuoso/ a. tempestuous, stormy.

templado /tem'plaðo/ a. temperate, mild, moderate.

templanza /tem'planθa; tem'plansa/ n. f. temperance; mildness.

templar /tem'plar/ v. temper; tune (an instrument).

templo /'templo/ n. m. temple.

temporada /tempo'raða/ n. f. season, time, spell.

temporal /tempo'ral/ **temporáneo** *a.* temporary.
temprano /tem'prano/ *a. & adv.* early.
tenacidad /tenaθi'ðað; tenasi'ðað/ *n. f.* tenacity.
tenaz /te'naθ; te'nas/ *a.* tenacious, stubborn.
tenazmente /tenaθ'mente; tenas'mente/ *adv.* tenaciously.
tendencia /ten'denθia; tendensia/ *n. f.* tendency, trend.
tender /ten'der/ *v.* stretch, stretch out.
tendero /ten'dero/ **-ra** *n.* shopkeeper, storekeeper.
tendón /ten'don/ *n. m.* tendon, sinew.
tenebrosidad /teneβrosi'ðað/ *n. f.* gloom.
tenebroso /tene'βroso/ *a.* dark, gloomy.
tenedor /tene'ðor/ *n.* **1.** *m. & f.* keeper; holder. **2.** *m.* fork.
tener /te'ner/ *v.* have; own; hold. **t. que,** have to, must.
teniente /te'niente/ *n. m.* lieutenant.
tenis /'tenis/ *n. m.* tennis; (*pl.*) sneakers.
tenor /te'nor/ *n. m.* tenor.
tensión /ten'sion/ *n. f.* tension, stress, strain.
tenso /'tenso/ *a.* tense.
tentación /tenta'θion; tenta'sion/ *n. f.* temptation.
tentáculo /ten'takulo/ *n. m.* tentacle.
tentador /tenta'ðor/ *a.* alluring, tempting.
tentar /ten'tar/ *v.* tempt, lure; grope, probe.
tentativa /tenta'tiβa/ *n. f.* attempt.
tentativo /tenta'tiβo/ *a.* tentative.
teñir /te'ɲir/ *v.* tint, dye.
teología /teolo'hia/ *n. f.* theology.
teológico /teo'lohiko/ *a.* theological.
teoría /teo'ria/ *n. f.* theory.
teórico /te'oriko/ *a.* theoretical.
terapéutico /tera'peutiko/ *a.* therapeutic.
tercero /ter'θero; ter'sero/ *a.* third.
tercio /'terθio; 'tersio/ *n. m.* third.
terciopelo /terθio'pelo; tersio'pelo/ *n. m.* velvet.
terco /'terko/ *a.* obstinate, stubborn.
termal /ter'mal/ *a.* thermal.
terminación /termina'θion; termina'sion/ *n. f.* termination; completion.
terminal aérea /termi'nal 'airea/ *n. f.* air terminal.
terminar /termi'nar/ *v.* terminate, finish.
término /'termino/ *n. m.* term; end.
terminología /terminolo'hia/ *n. f.* terminology.
termómetro /ter'mometro/ *n. m.* thermometer.
termos /'termos/ *n. m.* thermos.
termostato /ter'mostato/ *n. m.* thermostat.
ternero /ter'nero/ **-ra** *n.* calf.
ternura /ter'nura/ *n. f.* tenderness.
terquedad /terke'ðað/ *n. f.* stubbornness.
terraza /te'rraθa; te'rrasa/ *n. f.* terrace.
terremoto /terre'moto/ *n. m.* earthquake.
terreno /te'rreno/ *a.* **1.** earthly, terrestrial. **—***n.* **2.** *m.* ground, terrain; lot, plot.
terrible /te'rriβle/ *a.* terrible, awful.
terrífico /te'rrifiko/ *a.* terrifying.
territorio /terri'torio/ *n. m.* territory.
terrón /te'rron/ *n. m.* clod, lump; mound.
terror /te'rror/ *n. m.* terror.
terso /'terso/ *a.* smooth, glossy; terse.
tertulia /ter'tulia/ *n. f.* social gathering, party.
tesis /'tesis/ *n. f.* thesis.
tesorería /tesore'ria/ *n. f.* treasury.
tesorero /teso'rero/ **-ra** *n.* treasurer.
tesoro /te'soro/ *n. m.* treasure.
testamento /testa'mento/ *n. m.* will, testament.
testarudo /testa'ruðo/ *a.* stubborn.
testificar /testifi'kar/ *v.* testify.
testigo /tes'tigo/ *n. m. & f.* witness.
testimonial /testimo'nial/ *a.* testimonal.
testimonio /testi'monio/ *n. m.* testimony.
teta /'teta/ *n. f.* teat.
tetera /te'tera/ *n. f.* teapot.
tétrico /'tetriko/ *a.* sad; gloomy.
texto /'teksto/ *n. m.* text.
textura /teks'tura/ *n. f.* texture.
tez /teθ; tes/ *n. f.* complexion.
ti /ti/ *pron.* you; yourself.
tía /'tia/ *n. f.* aunt.
tibio /'tiβio/ *a.* lukewarm.
tiburón /tiβu'ron/ *n. m.* shark.
tiemblo /'tiemblo/ *n. m.* aspen.
tiempo /'tiempo/ *n. m.* time; weather; *Gram.* tense.
tienda /'tienda/ *n. f.* shop, store; tent.
tientas /'tientas/ *n. f.pl.* **andar a t.,** to grope (in the dark).
tierno /'tierno/ *a.* tender.
tierra /'tierra/ *n. f.* land; ground; earth, dirt, soil.
tieso /'tieso/ *a.* taut, stiff, hard, strong.
tiesto /'tiesto/ *n. m.* flower pot.
tiesura /tie'sura/ *n. f.* stiffness; harshness.
tifo /'tifo/ *n. m.* typhus.
tifoideo /tifoi'ðeo/ *n. m.* typhoid fever.
tigre /'tigre/ *n. m.* tiger.
tijeras /ti'heras/ *n. f.pl.* scissors.
tila /'tila/ *n. f.* linden.
timbre /'timbre/ *n. m.* seal, stamp; tone; (electric) bell.
tímidamente /'timiðamente/ *adv.* timidly.
timidez /timi'ðeθ; timi'ðes/ *n. f.* timidity.
tímido /'timiðo/ *a.* timid, shy.
timón /ti'mon/ *n. m.* rudder, helm.
tímpano /'timpano/ *n. m.* kettledrum; eardrum.
tina /'tina/ *n. f.* tub, vat.
tinaja /ti'naha/ *n. f.* jar.
tinta /'tinta/ *n. f.* ink.
tinte /'tinte/ *n. m.* tint, shade.
tintero /tin'tero/ *n. m.* inkwell.
tinto /'tinto/ *a.* wine-colored; red (of wine).
tintorería /tintore'ria/ *n. f.* dry cleaning shop.
tintorero /tinto'rero/ **-ra** *n.* dyer; dry cleaner.
tintura /tin'tura/ *n. f.* tincture; dye.
tiñoso /ti'ɲoso/ *a.* scabby; stingy.
tío /'tio/ *n. m.* uncle.
tíovivo /tio'βiβo/ *n. m.* merry-go-round.
típico /'tipiko/ *a.* typical.
tipo /'tipo/ *n. m.* type, sort; (interest) rate; *Colloq.* guy, fellow.
tipo de cambio /'tipo de 'kambio/ exchange rate.
tipo de interés /'tipo de inte'res/ interest rate.
tira /'tira/ *n. f.* strip.
tirabuzón /tiraβu'θon; tiraβu'son/ *n. m.* corkscrew.
tirada /ti'raða/ *n. f.* edition.
tirado /ti'raðo/ **-da** *a.* dirt-cheap.
tiranía /tira'nia/ *n. f.* tyranny.
tiránico /ti'raniko/ *n. m.* tyrannical.
tirano /ti'rano/ **-na** *n.* tyrant.
tirante /ti'rante/ *a.* **1.** tight, taut; tense. **—***n.* **2.** *m.pl.* suspenders.
tirar /ti'rar/ *v.* throw; draw; pull; fire (a weapon).
tiritar /tiri'tar/ *v.* shiver.
tiro /'tiro/ *n. m.* throw; shot.
tirón /ti'ron/ *n. m.* pull. **de un t.,** at a stretch, at one stroke.
tísico /'tisiko/ *n. & a.* consumptive.
tisis /'tisis/ *n. f.* consumption, tuberculosis.
titanio /ti'tanio/ *n. m.* titanium.
títere /'titere/ *n. m.* puppet.
titilación /titila'θion; titila'sion/ *n. f.* twinkle.
titubear /tituβe'ar/ *v.* stagger; totter; waver.
titulado /titu'laðo/ *a.* entitled; so-called.
titular /titu'lar/ *a.* **1.** titular. **—***v.* **2.** entitle.
título /'titulo/ *n. m.* title, headline.
tiza /'tiθa; 'tisa/ *n. f.* chalk.
tiznar /tiθ'nar; tis'nar/ *v.* smudge; stain.
toalla /to'aʎa; to'aya/ *n. f.* towel. **t. sanitaria,** sanitary napkin.
toalleta /toa'ʎeta; toa'yeta/ *n. f.* small towel.
tobillo /to'βiʎo; to'βiyo/ *n. m.* ankle.
tobogán /toβo'gan/ *n. m.* toboggan.
tocadiscos /toka'ðiskos/ *n. m.* record player.
tocadiscos compacto /toka'ðiskos kom'pakto/ **tocadiscos digital** CD player.
tocado /to'kaðo/ *n. m.* hairdo.
tocador /toka'ðor/ *n. m.* boudoir; dressing table.
tocante /to'kante/ *a.* touching. **t. a,** concerning, relative to.
tocar /to'kar/ *v.* touch; play (an instrument). **t. a uno,** be one's turn; be up to one.
tocayo /to'kayo/ **-ya** *n.* namesake.
tocino /to'θino; to'sino/ *n. m.* bacon.
tocólogo /to'kologo/ **-ga** *n.* obstetrician.
todavía /toða'βia/ *adv.* yet, still.
todo /'toðo/ *a.* **1.** all, whole. **todos los,** every. **—***pron.* **2.** all, everything. **con t.,** still, however. **del t.,** wholly; at all.
todopoderoso /toðopoðe'roso/ *a.* almighty.
toldo /'toldo/ *n. m.* awning.
tolerancia /tole'ranθia; tole'ransia/ *n. f.* tolerance.
tolerante /tole'rante/ *a.* tolerant.
tolerar /tole'rar/ *v.* tolerate.
toma /'toma/ *n. f.* taking, capture, seizure.
tomaína /to'maina/ *n. f.* ptomaine.
tomar /to'mar/ *v.* take; drink. **t. el sol,** sunbathe.
tomate /to'mate/ *n. m.* tomato.
tomillo /to'miʎo; to'miyo/ *n. m.* thyme.
tomo /'tomo/ *n. m.* volume.
tonada /to'naða/ *n. f.* tune.
tonel /to'nel/ *n. m.* barrel, cask.
tonelada /tone'laða/ *n. f.* ton.
tonelaje /tone'lahe/ *n. m.* tonnage.
tónico /'toniko/ *a. & m.* tonic.
tono /'tono/ *n. m.* tone, pitch, shade. **darse t.,** to put on airs.
tonsila /ton'sila/ *n. f.* tonsil.
tonsilitis /tonsi'litis/ *n. f.* tonsilitis.
tontería /tonte'ria/ *n. f.* nonsense, foolishness.
tontifútbol /tonti'futβol/ *n. m.* excessively defensive strategy (in soccer).
tonto /'tonto/ **-ta** *a. & n.* foolish, silly; fool.
topacio /to'paθio; to'pasio/ *n. m.* topaz.
topar /to'par/ *v.* run into. **t. con,** come upon.
tópico /'topiko/ *a.* **1.** topical. **—***n.* **2.** *m.* cliché.
topo /'topo/ *n. m.* mole (animal).
toque /'toke/ *n. m.* touch.
tórax /'toraks/ *n. m.* thorax.
torbellino /torβe'ʎino; torβe'yino/ *n. m.* whirlwind.
torcer /tor'θer; tor'ser/ *v.* twist; wind; distort.
toreador /torea'ðor/ **-a** *n.* toreador.
torero /to'rero/ **-ra** *n.* bullfighter.
torio /'torio/ *n. m.* thorium.
tormenta /tor'menta/ *n. f.* storm.
tormento /tor'mento/ *n. m.* torment.
tornado /tor'naðo/ *n. m.* tornado.
tornar /tor'nar/ *v.* return; turn.
tornarse en /tor'narse en/ *v.* turn into, become.
torneo /tor'neo/ *n. m.* tournament.
tornillo /tor'niʎo; tor'niyo/ *n. m.* screw.
toro /'toro/ *n. m.* bull.
toronja /to'ronha/ *n. f.* grapefruit.
torpe /'torpe/ *a.* awkward, clumsy; sluggish.
torpedero /torpe'ðero/ *n. m.* torpedo boat.
torpedo /tor'peðo/ *n. m.* torpedo.
torre /'torre/ *n. f.* tower.
torre de mando /'torre de 'mando/ control tower.
torrente /to'rrente/ *n. m.* torrent.
tórrido /'torriðo/ *a.* torrid.
torta /'torta/ *n. f.* cake; loaf.
tortilla /tor'tiʎa; tor'tiya/ *n. f.* omelet; (Mex.) tortilla, pancake.
tórtola /'tortola/ *n. f.* dove.
tortuga /tor'tuga/ *n. f.* turtle.
tortuoso /tor'tuoso/ *a.* tortuous.
tortura /tor'tura/ *n. f.* torture. **—torturar,** *v.*
tos /tos/ *n. m.* cough. **—toser,** *v.*
tosco /'tosko/ *a.* coarse, rough, uncouth.
tosquedad /toske'ðað/ *n. f.* coarseness, roughness.
tostador /tosta'ðor/ *n. m.* toaster.
tostar /'tostar/ *v.* toast; tan.
total /to'tal/ *a. & m.* total.
totalidad /totali'ðað/ *n. f.* totality, entirety, whole.
totalitario /totali'tario/ *a.* totalitarian.
totalmente /total'mente/ *adv.* totally; entirely.
tótem /'totem/ *n. m.* totem.
tóxico /'toksiko/ *a.* toxic.
toxicómano /toksi'komano/ **-na** *n. m. & f.* drug addict.
trabajador /traβaha'ðor/ **-ra** *a.* **1.** hardworking. **—***n.* **2.** worker.
trabajo /tra'βaho/ *n. m.* work; labor. **—trabajar,** *v.*
trabar /tra'βar/ *v.* fasten, shackle; grasp; strike up.
tracción /trak'θion; trak'sion/ *n. f.* traction.
tracto /'trakto/ *n. m.* tract.
tractor /trak'tor/ *n. m.* tractor.
tradición /traði'θion; traði'sion/ *n. f.* tradition.
tradicional /traðiθio'nal; traðisio'nal/ *a.* traditional.
traducción /traðuk'θion; traðuk'sion/ *n. f.* translation.
traducir /traðu'θir; traðu'sir/ *v.* translate.
traductor /traðuk'tor/ **-ra** *n.* translator.
traer /tra'er/ *v.* bring; carry; wear.
tráfico /'trafiko/ *n. m.* traffic. **—traficar,** *v.*
tragaperras /traga'perras/ *n. f.* slot machine, one-armed bandit.
tragar /tra'gar/ *v.* swallow.
tragedia /tra'heðia/ *n. f.* tragedy.
trágicamente /'trahikamente/ *adv.* tragically.
trágico /'trahiko/ **-ca** *a.* **1.** tragic. **—***n.* **2.** tragedian.
trago /'trago/ *n. m.* swallow; drink.
traición /trai'θion; trai'sion/ *n. f.* treason, betrayal.
traicionar /traiθio'nar; traisio'nar/ *v.* betray.
traidor /trai'ðor/ **-ra** *a. & n.* traitorous; traitor.
traje /'trahe/ *n. m.* suit; dress; garb, apparel.
traje de baño /'trahe de 'baɲo/ bathing suit.
trama /'trama/ *v.* plot (of a story).
tramador /trama'ðor/ **-ra** *n.* weaver; plotter.
tramar /tra'mar/ *v.* weave; plot, scheme.
trámite /'tramite/ *n. m.* (business) deal, transaction.

tramo /'tramo/ *n. m.* span, stretch, section.

trampa /'trampa/ *n. f.* trap, snare.

trampista /tram'pista/ *n. m. & f.* cheater; swindler.

trance /'tranθe; 'transe/ *n. m.* critical moment or stage. **a todo t.,** at any cost.

tranco /'tranko/ *n. m.* stride.

tranquilidad /trankili'ðað/ *n. f.* tranquility, calm, quiet.

tranquilizante /trankili'θante; tran-kili'sante/ *n. m.* tranquilizer.

tranquilizar /trankili'θar; trankili'sar/ *v.* quiet, calm down.

tranquilo /tran'kilo/ *a.* tranquil, calm.

transacción /transak'θion; trans-ak'sion/ *n. f.* transaction.

transbordador /transβorða'ðor/ *n. m.* ferry.

transbordador espacial /trans-βorða'ðor espa'θial; transβorða'ðor espa'sial/ space, shuttle.

transcribir /transkri'βir/ *v.* transcribe.

transcripción /transkrip'θion; trans-krip'sion/ *n. f.* transcription.

transcurrir /transku'rrir/ *v.* elapse.

transeúnte /tran'seunte/ *a. & n.* transient; passerby.

transexual /transek'sual/ *a.* transsexual.

transferencia /transfe'renθia; trans-fe'rensia/ *n. f.* transference.

transferir /transfe'rir/ *v.* transfer.

transformación /transforma'θion; transforma'sion/ *n. f.* transformation.

transformar /transfor'mar/ *v.* transform.

transfusión /transfu'sion/ *n. f.* transfusion.

transgresión /transgre'sion/ *n. f.* transgression.

transgresor /transgre'sor/ **-ra** *n.* transgressor.

transición /transi'θion; transi'sion/ *n. f.* transition.

transigir /transi'hir/ *v.* compromise, settle; agree.

transistor /transis'tor/ *n. m.* transistor.

transitivo /transi'tiβo/ *a.* transitive.

tránsito /'transito/ *n. m.* transit, passage.

transitorio /transi'torio/ *a.* transitory.

transmisión /transmi'sion/ *n. f.* transmission; broadcast.

transmisora /transmi'sora/ *n. f.* broadcasting station.

transmitir /transmi'tir/ *v.* transmit; broadcast.

transparencia /transpa'renθia; trans-pa'rensia/ *n. f.* transparency.

transparente /transpa'rente/ *a.* **1.** transparent. —*n.* **2.** *m.* (window) shade.

transportación /transporta'θion; transporta'sion/ *n. f.* transportation.

transportar /transpor'tar/ *v.* transport, convey.

transporte /trans'porte/ *n. m.* transportation; transport.

tranvía /tram'bia/ *n. m.* streetcar, trolley.

trapacero /trapa'θero; trapa'sero/ **-ra** *n.* cheat; swindler.

trapo /'trapo/ *n. m.* rag.

tráquea /'trakea/ *n. f.* trachea.

tras /tras/ *prep.* after; behind.

trasegar /trase'gar/ *v.* upset, overturn.

trasero /tra'sero/ *a.* rear, back.

traslado /tras'laðo/ *n. m.* transfer. —**trasladar,** *v.*

traslapo /tras'lapo/ *n. m.* overlap. —**traslapar,** *v.*

trasnochar /trasno'tʃar/ *v.* stay up all night.

traspalar /traspa'lar/ *v.* shovel.

traspasar /traspa'sar/ *v.* go beyond; cross; violate; pierce.

trasquilar /traski'lar/ *v.* shear; clip.

trastornar /trastor'nar/ *v.* overturn, overthrow, upset.

trastorno /tras'torno/ *m.* overthrow; upheaval.

trasvasar /trasβa'sar/ *v.* download; download.

tratado /tra'taðo/ *n. m.* treaty; treatise.

tratamiento /trata'miento/ *n. m.* treatment.

tratar /tra'tar/ *v.* treat, handle. **t. de,** deal with; try to; call (a name).

tratarse de /tra'tarse de/ *v.* be a question of.

trato /'trato/ *n. m.* treatment; manners; *Com.* deal.

través /tra'βes/ *adv.* **a t. de,** through, across. **de t.,** sideways.

travesía /traβe'sia/ *n. f.* crossing, voyage.

travesti /tra'βesti/ *n. m.* transvestite.

travestido /traβes'tiðo/ *a.* disguised.

travesura /traβe'sura/ *n. f.* prank; mischief.

travieso /tra'βieso/ *a.* naughty, mischievous.

trayectoria /trayek'toria/ *n. f.* trajectory.

trazar /tra'θar; tra'sar/ *v.* plan, devise; trace; draw.

trazo /'traθo; 'traso/ *n.* plan, outline; line, stroke.

trébol /'treβol/ *n. m.* clover.

trece /'treθe; 'trese/ *a. & pron.* thirteen.

trecho /'tretʃo/ *n. m.* space, distance, stretch.

tregua /'tregua/ *n. f.* truce; respite, lull.

treinta /'treinta/ *a. & pron.* thirty.

tremendo /tre'mendo/ *a.* tremendous.

tremer /tre'mer/ *v.* tremble.

tren /tren/ *n. m.* train.

trenza /'trenθa; 'trensa/ *n. f.* braid. —**trenzar,** *v.*

trepar /tre'par/ *v.* climb, mount.

trepidación /trepiða'θion; trepi-ða'sion/ *n. f.* trepidation.

tres /tres/ *a. & pron.* three.

trescientos /tres'θientos; tres'sien-tos/ *a. & pron.* three hundred.

triángulo /tri'angulo/ *n. m.* triangle.

triar /triar/ *v.* sort, separate.

tribu /'triβu/ *n. f.* tribe.

tribulación /triβula'θion; triβula-'sion/ *n. f.* tribulation.

tribuna /tri'βuna/ *n. f.* rostrum, stand; (*pl.*) grandstand.

tribunal /triβu'nal/ *n. m.* court, tribunal.

tributario /triβu'tario/ *a. & m.* tributary.

tributo /tri'βuto/ *n. m.* tribute.

triciclo /tri'θiklo; tri'siklo/ *n. m.* tricycle.

trigo /'trigo/ *n. m.* wheat.

trigonometría /trigonome'tria/ *n. f.* trigonometry.

trigueño /tri'geɲo/ *a.* swarthy, dark.

trilogía /trilo'hia/ *n. f.* trilogy.

trimestral /trimes'tral/ *a.* quarterly.

trinchar /trin'tʃar/ *v.* carve (meat).

trinchera /trin'tʃera/ *n. f.* trench, ditch.

trineo /tri'neo/ *n. m.* sled; sleigh.

trinidad /trini'ðað/ *n. f.* trinity.

tripa /'tripa/ *n. f.* tripe, entrails.

triple /'triple/ *a.* triple. —**triplicar,** *v.*

trípode /'tripoðe/ *n. m.* tripod.

tripulación /tripula'θion; tripula-'sion/ *n. f.* crew.

tripulante /tripu'lante/ *m & f.* crew member.

tripular /tripu'lar/ *v.* man.

triste /'triste/ *a.* sad, sorrowful; dreary.

tristemente /triste'mente/ *adv.* sadly.

tristeza /tris'teθa; tris'tesa/ *n. f.* sadness; gloom.

triunfal /triun'fal/ *a.* triumphal.

triunfante /triun'fante/ *a.* triumphant.

triunfo /'triunfo/ *n. m.* triumph; trump. —**triunfar,** *v.*

trivial /tri'βial/ *a.* trivial, commonplace.

trivialidad /triβiali'ðað/ *n. f.* triviality.

trocar /tro'kar/ *v.* exchange, switch; barter.

trofeo /tro'feo/ *n. m.* trophy.

trombón /trom'bon/ *n. m.* trombone.

trompa /'trompa/ **trompeta** *n. f.* trumpet, horn.

tronada /tro'naða/ *n. f.* thunderstorm.

tronar /tro'nar/ *v.* thunder.

tronco /'tronko/ *n. m.* trunk, stump.

trono /'trono/ *n. m.* throne.

tropa /'tropa/ *n. f.* troop.

tropel /tro'pel/ *n. m.* crowd, throng.

tropezar /trope'θar; trope'sar/ *v.* trip, stumble. **t. con,** come upon, run into.

trópico /'tropiko/ *a. & m.* tropical; tropics.

tropiezo /tro'pieθo; tro'pieso/ *n. m.* stumble; obstacle; slip, error.

trote /'trote/ *n. m.* trot. —**trotar,** *v.*

trovador /troβa'ðor/ *n. m.* troubadour.

trozo /'troθo; 'troso/ *n. m.* piece, portion, fragment; selection, passage.

trucha /'trutʃa/ *n. f.* trout.

trueco /'trueko/ **trueque** *n. m.* exchange, barter.

trueno /'trueno/ *n. m.* thunder.

trufa /'trufa/ *n. f.* truffle.

tu /tu/ *a.* your.

tú *pron.* you.

tuberculosis /tuβerku'losis/ *n. f.* tuberculosis.

tubo /'tuβo/ *n. m.* tube, pipe.

tubo de ensayo /'tuβo de en'sayo/ test tube.

tubo de escape /'tuβo de es'kape/ exhaust pipe.

tuerca /'tuerka/ *n. f. Mech.* nut.

tulipán /tuli'pan/ *n. m.* tulip.

tumba /'tumba/ *n. f.* tomb, grave.

tumbar /tum'bar/ *v.* knock down.

tumbarse /tum'βarse/ *v.* lie down.

tumbo /'tumbo/ *n. m.* tumble; somersault.

tumbona /tum'βona/ *n. f.* deck chair.

tumor /tu'mor/ *n. m.* tumor; growth.

tumulto /tu'multo/ *n. m.* tumult, commotion.

tumultuoso /tumul'tuoso/ *a.* tumultuous, boisterous.

tunante /tu'nante/ *n. m.* rascal, rogue.

tunda /'tunda/ *n. f.* spanking, whipping.

túnel /'tunel/ *n. m.* tunnel.

túnel del Canal de la Mancha /'tunel del ka'nal de la 'mantʃa/ Channel Tunnel, Chunnel.

tungsteno /tuŋgs'teno/ *n. m.* tungsten.

túnica /'tunika/ *n. f.* tunic, robe.

tupir /tu'pir/ *v.* pack tight, stuff; stop up.

turbación /turβa'θion; turβa'sion/ *n. f.* confusion, turmoil.

turbamulta /turβa'multa/ *n. f.* mob, disorderly crowd.

turbar /tur'βar/ *v.* disturb, upset; embarrass.

turbina /tur'βina/ *n. f.* turbine.

turbio /'turβio/ *a.* turbid; muddy.

turco /'turko/ **-ca** *a. & n.* Turkish; Turk.

turismo /tu'rismo/ *n. m.* touring, (foreign) travel, tourism.

turista /tu'rista/ *n. m. & f.* tourist.

turno /'turno/ *n. m.* turn; (work) shift.

turquesa /tur'kesa/ *n. f.* turquoise.

Turquía /tur'kia/ *n. f.* Turkey.

turrón /tu'rron/ *n. m.* nougat.

tusa /'tusa/ *n. f.* corncob; corn.

tutear /tute'ar/ *v.* use the pronoun **tú,** etc., in addressing a person.

tutela /tu'tela/ *n. f.* guardianship; aegis.

tutor /tu'tor/ **-ra** *n.* tutor; guardian.

tuyo /'tuyo/ *a.* your, yours.

U

u /u/ *conj.* or.

ubre /'uβre/ *n. f.* udder.

Ucrania /u'krania/ *n. f.* Ukraine.

ucranio /u'kranio/ **-ia** *a. & n.* Ukrainian.

ufano /u'fano/ *a.* proud, haughty.

úlcera /'ulθera; 'ulsera/ *n. f.* ulcer.

ulterior /ulte'rior/ *a.* ulterior.

último /'ultimo/ *a.* last, final; ultimate; latest. **por ú.,** finally. **ú. minuto,** last minute, eleventh hour.

ultraje /ul'trahe/ *n. m.* outrage. —**ultrajar,** *v.*

ultrasónico /ultra'soniko/ *a.* ultrasonic.

umbral /um'βral/ *n. m.* threshold.

umbroso /um'broso/ *a.* shady.

un /un/ **una** *art. & a.* a, an; one; (*pl.*) some.

unánime /u'nanime/ *a.* unanimous.

unanimidad /unanimi'ðað/ *n. f.* unanimity.

unción /un'θion; un'sion/ *n. f.* unction.

ungüento /uŋ'guento/ *n. m.* ointment, salve.

único /'uniko/ *a.* only, sole; unique.

unicornio /uni'kornio/ *n. m.* unicorn.

unidad /uni'ðað/ *n. f.* unit; unity.

unidad de cuidados intensivos /uni'ðað de kui'ðaðos inten'siβos/ **unidad de vigilancia intensiva** intensive-care unit.

unidad de disco /uni'ðað de 'disko/ disk drive.

unificar /unifi'kar/ *v.* unify.

uniforme /uni'forme/ *a. & m.* uniform.

uniformidad /uniformi'ðað/ *n. f.* uniformity.

unión /u'nion/ *n. f.* union; joining.

unir /u'nir/ *v.* unite, join.

universal /uniβer'sal/ *a.* universal.

universalidad /uniβersali'ðað/ *n. f.* universality.

universidad /uniβersi'ðað/ *n. f.* university; college.

universo /uni'βerso/ *n. m.* universe.

uno /'uno/ **una** *pron.* one; (*pl.*) some.

untar /un'tar/ *v.* spread; grease; anoint.

uña /'uɲa/ *n. f.* fingernail.

urbanidad /urβani'ðað/ *n. f.* urbanity; good breeding.

urbanismo /urβa'nismo/ *n. m.* city planning.

urbano /ur'βano/ *a.* urban; urbane; well-bred.

urbe /'urβe/ *n. f.* large city.

urgencia /ur'henθia; ur'hensia/ *n. f.* urgency.

urgente /ur'hente/ *a.* urgent, pressing. **entrega u.,** special delivery.

urgir /ur'hir/ *v.* be urgent.

urna /'urna/ *n. f.* urn; ballot box; (*pl.*) polls.

urraca /u'rraka/ *n. f.* magpie.

usanza /u'sanθa; usansa/ *n. f.* usage, custom.

usar /u'sar/ *v.* use; wear.

uso /'uso/ *n. m.* use; usage; wear.

usted /us'teð/ *pron.* you.

usual /u'sual/ *a.* usual.

usualmente /usual'mente/ *adv.* usually.

usura /u'sura/ *n. f.* usury.

usurero /usu'rero/ **-ra** *n.* usurer.

usurpación /usurpa'θion; usur-pa'sion/ *n. f.* usurpation.

usurpar /usur'par/ *v.* usurp.

utensilio /uten'silio/ *n. m.* utensil.

útero /'utero/ *n. m.* uterus.

útil /'util/ *a.* useful, handy.

utilidad /utili'ðað/ *n. f.* utility, usefulness.
utilizar /utili'θar; utili'sar/ *v.* use, utilize.
útilmente /util'mente/ *adv.* usefully.
utópico /u'topiko/ *a.* utopian.
uva /'uβa/ *n. f.* grape.

V

vaca /'baka/ *n. f.* cow; beef.
vacaciones /baka'θiones; baka'siones/ *n. f.pl.* vacation, holidays.
vacancia /ba'kanθia; ba'kansia/ *n. f.* vacancy.
vacante /ba'kante/ *a.* **1.** vacant. —*n.* **2.** *f.* vacancy.
vaciar /ba'θiar; ba'siar/ *v.* empty; pour out.
vacilación /baθila'θion; basila'sion/ *n. f.* vacillation, hesitation.
vacilante /baθi'lante; basi'lante/ *a.* vacillating.
vacilar /baθi'lar; basi'lar/ *v.* falter, hesitate; waver; stagger.
vacío /ba'θio; ba'sio/ *a.* **1.** empty. —*n.* **2.** *m.* void, empty space.
vacuna /ba'kuna/ *n. f.* vaccine.
vacunación /bakuna'θion; bakuna'sion/ *n. f.* vaccination.
vacunar /baku'nar/ *v.* vaccinate.
vacuo /'bakuo/ *a.* **1.** empty, vacant. —*n.* **2.** *m.* vacuum.
vadear /baðe'ar/ *v.* wade through, ford.
vado /'baðo/ *n. m.* ford.
vagabundo /baga'βundo/ **-da** *a.* & *n.* vagabond.
vagar /ba'gar/ *v.* wander, rove, roam; loiter.
vago /'bago/ **-ga** *a.* **1.** vague, hazy; wandering, vagrant. —*n.* **2.** vagrant, tramp.
vagón /ba'gon/ *n. m.* railroad car.
vahído /ba'iðo/ *n. m.* dizziness.
vaina /'baina/ *n. f.* sheath; pod.
vainilla /bai'niʎa; bai'niya/ *n. f.* vanilla.
vaivén /bai'βen/ *n. m.* vibration, sway.
vajilla /ba'hiʎa; ba'hiya/ *n. f.* (dinner) dishes.
valentía /balen'tia/ *n. f.* valor, courage.
valer /ba'ler/ *n.* **1.** *m.* worth. —*v.* **2.** be worth.
valerse de /ba'lerse de/ *v.* make use of, avail oneself of.
valía /ba'lia/ *n. f.* value.
validez /bali'ðeθ; bali'ðes/ *n. f.* validity.
válido /ba'liðo/ *a.* valid.
valiente /ba'liente/ *a.* valiant, brave, courageous.
valija /ba'liha/ *n. f.* valise.
valioso /ba'lioso/ *a.* valuable.
valla /'baʎa; 'baya/ *n. f.* fence, barrier.
valle /'baʎe; 'baye/ *n. m.* valley.
valor /ba'lor/ *n. m.* value, worth; bravery, valor; (*pl.*, *Com.*) securities.
valoración /balora'θion; balora'sion/ *n. f.* appraisal.
valorar /balo'rar/ *v.* value, appraise.
vals /bals/ *n. m.* waltz.
valsar /bal'sar/ *v.* waltz.
valuación /balua'θion; balua'sion/ *n. f.* valuation.
valuar /balu'ar/ *v.* value; rate.
válvula /'balβula/ *n. f.* valve.
válvula de seguridad /'balβula de seguri'ðað/ safety valve.
vandalismo /banda'lismo/ *n. m.* vandalism.
vándalo /'bandalo/ **-la** *n.* vandal.
vanidad /bani'ðað/ *n. f.* vanity.
vanidoso /bani'ðoso/ *a.* vain, conceited.
vano /'bano/ *a.* vain; inane.
vapor /ba'por/ *n. m.* vapor; steam; steamer, steamship.
vaquero /ba'kero/ **-ra** *n.* cowboy.
vara /'bara/ *n. f.* wand, stick, switch.
varadero /bara'ðero/ *n. m.* shipyard.
varar /ba'rar/ *v.* launch; be stranded; run aground.
variable /ba'riaβle/ *a.* variable.
variación /baria'θion; baria'sion/ *n. f.* variation.
variar /ba'riar/ *v.* vary.
varicela /bari'θela; bari'sela/ *n. f.* chicken pox.
variedad /barie'ðað/ *n. f.* variety.
varios /'barios/ *a.* & *pron. pl.* various; several.
variz /ba'riθ; ba'ris/ *n. f.* varicose vein.
varón /ba'ron/ *n. m.* man; male.
varonil /baro'nil/ *a.* manly, virile.
vasallo /ba'saʎo; ba'sayo/ *n. m.* vassal.
vasectomía /basekto'mia/ *n. f.* vasectomy.
vasija /ba'siha/ *n. f.* bowl, container (for liquids).
vaso /'baso/ *n. m.* water glass; vase. **v. de papel,** paper cup.
vástago /'bastago/ *n. m.* bud, shoot; twig; offspring.
vasto /'basto/ *a.* vast.
vecindad /beθin'dað; besin'dað/ *n. f.* **vecindario,** *m.* neighborhood, vicinity.
vecino /be'θino; be'sino/ **-na** *a.* & *n.* neighboring; neighbor.
vedar /be'ðar/ *v.* forbid; impede.
vega /'bega/ *n. f.* meadow.
vegetación /beheta'θion; beheta'sion/ *n. f.* vegetation.
vegetal /behe'tal/ *n. m.* vegetable.
vehemente /bee'mente/ *a.* vehement.
vehículo /be'ikulo/ *n. m.* vehicle; conveyance.
veinte /'beinte/ *a.* & *pron.* twenty.
vejez /be'heθ; be'hes/ *n. f.* old age.
vejiga /be'higa/ *n. f.* bladder.
vela /'bela/ *n. f.* vigil, watch; candle; sail.
velar /be'lar/ *v.* stay up, sit up; watch over.
vellón /be'ʎon; be'yon/ *n. m.* fleece.
velloso /be'ʎoso; be'yoso/ *a.* hairy; fuzzy.
velludo /be'ʎuðo; be'yuðo/ *a.* downy.
velo /'belo/ *n. m.* veil.
velocidad /beloθi'ðað; belosi'ðað/ *n. f.* velocity, speed; rate. **v. máxima,** speed limit.
velomotor /belomo'tor/ *n. m.* motorbike, moped.
veloz /be'loθ; be'los/ *a.* speedy, fast, swift.
vena /'bena/ *n. f.* vein.
venado /be'naðo/ *n. m.* deer.
vencedor /benθe'ðor; bense'ðor/ **-ra** *n.* victor.
vencer /ben'θer; ben'ser/ *v.* defeat, overcome, conquer; *Com.* become due, expire.
vencimiento /benθi'miento; bensi'miento/ *n. m.* defeat; expiration.
venda /'benda/ *n. f.* **vendaje,** *m.* bandage. —**vendar,** *v.*
vendedor /bende'ðor/ **-ra** *n.* seller, trader; sales clerk.
vender /ben'der/ *v.* sell.
vendimia /ben'dimia/ *n. f.* vintage; grape harvest.
Venecia /be'neθia; be'nesia/ *n. f.* Venice.
veneciano /bene'θiano; bene'siano/ **-na** *a.* & *n.* Venetian.
veneno /be'neno/ *n. m.* poison.
venenoso /bene'noso/ *a.* poisonous.
veneración /benera'θion; benera'sion/ *n. f.* veneration.
venerar /bene'rar/ *v.* venerate, revere.
venero /be'nero/ *n. m.* spring; origin.
véneto /'beneto/ *a.* Venetian.
venezolano /beneθo'lano; beneso'lano/ **-na** *a.* & *n.* Venezuelan.
vengador /beŋga'ðor/ **-ra** *n.* avenger.
venganza /beŋ'ganθa; beŋ'gansa/ *n. f.* vengeance, revenge.
vengar /beŋ'gar/ *v.* avenge.
venida /be'niða/ *n. f.* arrival, advent, coming.
venidero /beni'ðero/ *a.* future; coming.
venir /be'nir/ *v.* come.
venta /'benta/ *n. f.* sale; sales.
ventaja /ben'taha/ *n. f.* advantage; profit.
ventajoso /benta'hoso/ *a.* advantageous; profitable.
ventana /ben'tana/ *n. f.* window.
ventero /ben'tero/ **-ra** *n.* innkeeper.
ventilación /bentila'θion; bentila'sion/ *n. m.* ventilation.
ventilador /bentila'ðor/ *n. m.* ventilator, fan.
ventilar /benti'lar/ *v.* ventilate, air.
ventisquero /bentis'kero/ *n. m.* snowdrift; glacier.
ventoso /ben'toso/ *a.* windy.
ventura /ben'tura/ *n. f.* venture; happiness; luck.
ver /ber/ *v.* see. **tener que v. con,** have to do with.
vera /'bera/ *n. f.* edge.
veracidad /beraθi'ðað; berasi'ðað/ *n. f.* truthfulness, veracity.
verano /be'rano/ *n. m.* summer. —**veranear,** *v.*
veras /'beras/ *n. f.pl.* **de v.,** really, truly.
veraz /be'raθ; be'ras/ *a.* truthful.
verbigracia /berβi'graθia; berβi'grasia/ *adv.* for example.
verbo /'berβo/ *n. m.* verb.
verboso /ber'βoso/ *a.* verbose.
verdad /ber'ðað/ *n. f.* truth. **ser v.,** to be true.
verdadero /berða'ðero/ *a.* true, real.
verde /'berðe/ *a.* green; risqué, off-color.
verdor /ber'ðor/ *n. m.* greenness, verdure.
verdugo /ber'ðugo/ *n. m.* hangman.
verdura /ber'ðura/ *n. f.* verdure, vegetation; (*pl.*) vegetables.
vereda /be'reða/ *n. f.* path.
veredicto /bere'ðikto/ *n. m.* verdict.
vergonzoso /bergon'θoso; bergon'soso/ *a.* shameful, embarrassing; shy, bashful.
vergüenza /ber'guenθa; ber'guensa/ *n. f.* shame; disgrace; embarrassment.
verificar /berifi'kar/ *v.* verify, check.
verja /'berha/ *n. f.* grating, railing.
verosímil /bero'simil/ *a.* likely, plausible.
verraco /be'rrako/ *n. m.* boar.
verruga /be'rruga/ *n. f.* wart.
versátil /ber'satil/ *a.* versatile.
verse /'berse/ *v.* look, appear.
versión /ber'sion/ *n. f.* version.
verso /'berso/ *n. m.* verse, stanza; line (of poetry).
verter /ber'ter/ *v.* pour, spill; shed; empty.
vertical /berti'kal/ *a.* vertical.
vertiente /ber'tiente/ *n. f.* slope; watershed.
vertiginoso /bertihi'noso/ *a.* dizzy.
vértigo /'bertigo/ *n. m.* vertigo, dizziness.
vestíbulo /bes'tiβulo/ *n. m.* vestibule, lobby.
vestido /bes'tiðo/ *n. m.* dress; clothing.
vestigio /bes'tihio/ *n. m.* vestige, trace.
vestir /bes'tir/ *v.* dress, clothe.
veterano /bete'rano/ **-na** *a.* & *n.* veteran.
veterinario /beteri'nario/ **-ria** *a.* **1.** veterinary. —*n.* **2.** veterinarian.
veto /'beto/ *n. m.* veto.
vetusto /be'tusto/ *a.* ancient, very old.
vez /beθ; bes/ *n. f.* time; turn. **tal v.,** perhaps. **a la v.,** at the same time. **en v. de,** instead of. **una v.,** once. **otra v.,** again.
vía /'bia/ *n. f.* track; route, way.
viaducto /bia'ðukto/ *n. m.* viaduct.
viajante /bia'hante/ *a.* & *n.* traveling; traveler.
viajar /bia'har/ *v.* travel; journey; tour.
viaje /'biahe/ *n. m.* trip, journey, voyage; (*pl.*) travels.
viaje de estudios /'biahe de es'tuðios/ field trip.
viajero /bia'hero/ **-ra** *n.* traveler; passenger.
viaje todo incluido /'biahe 'toðo in'kluiðo/ package tour.
viandas /'biandas/ *n. f.pl.* victuals, food.
víbora /'biβora/ *n. f.* viper.
vibración /biβra'θion; biβra'sion/ *n. f.* vibration.
vibrar /bi'βrar/ *v.* vibrate.
vicepresidente /biθepresi'ðente; bisepresi'ðente/ **-ta** *n.* vice president.
vicio /'biθio; 'bisio/ *n. m.* vice.
vicioso /bi'θioso; bi'sioso/ *a.* vicious; licentious.
víctima /'biktima/ *n. f.* victim.
victoria /bik'toria/ *n. f.* victory.
victorioso /bikto'rioso/ *a.* victorious.
vid /bið/ *n. f.* grapevine.
vida /'biða/ *n. f.* life; living.
vídeo /bi'ðeo/ *n. m.* videotape.
videocámara /biðeo'kamara/ *n. f.* video camera.
videodisco /biðeo'ðisko/ *n. m.* videodisc.
videojuego /biðeo'huego/ *n. m.* video game.
vidrio /'biðrio/ *n. m.* glass.
viejo /'bieho/ **-ja** *a.* & *n.* old; old person.
viento /'biento/ *n. m.* wind. **hacer v.,** to be windy.
vientre /'bientre/ *n. m.* belly.
viernes /'biernes/ *n. m.* Friday.
viga /'biga/ *n. f.* beam, rafter.
vigente /bi'hente/ *a.* in effect (prices, etc.).
vigilante /bihi'lante/ *a.* & *m.* vigilant, watchful; watchman.
vigilante nocturno /bihi'lante nok'turno/ night watchman.
vigilar /bihi'lar/ *v.* guard, watch over.
vigilia /bi'hilia/ *n. f.* vigil, watchfulness; *Relig.* fast.
vigor /bi'gor/ *n. m.* vigor. **en v.,** in effect, in force.
vil /bil/ *a.* vile, low, contemptible.
vileza /bi'leθa; bi'lesa/ *n. f.* baseness; vileness.
villa /'biʎa; 'biya/ *n. f.* town; country house.
villancico /biʎan'θiko; biyan'siko/ *n. m.* Christmas carol.
villanía /biʎa'nia; biya'nia/ *n. f.* villainy.
villano /bi'ʎano; bi'yano/ *n. m.* boor.
vinagre /bi'nagre/ *n. m.* vinegar.
vinagrera /bina'grera/ *n. f.* cruet.
vínculo /'binkulo/ *n. m.* link. —**vincular,** *v.*
vindicar /bindi'kar/ *v.* vindicate.
vino /'bino/ *n. m.* wine.
viña /'biɲa/ *n. f.* vineyard.
violación /biola'θion; biola'sion/ *n. f.* violation; rape.
violador /biola'ðor/ **-ra** *n. m.* & *f.* rapist.
violar /bio'lar/ *v.* violate; rape.
violencia /bio'lenθia; bio'lensia/ *n. f.* violence.
violento /bio'lento/ *a.* violent; impulsive.
violeta /bio'leta/ *n. f.* violet.
violín /bio'lin/ *n. m.* violin.
violón /bio'lon/ *n. m.* bass viol.
virar /bi'rar/ *v.* veer, change course.
virgen /bir'hen/ *n. f.* virgin.
viril /bi'ril/ *a.* virile, manly.
virilidad /birili'ðað/ *n. f.* virility, manhood.
virtual /bir'tual/ *a.* virtual.
virtud /bir'tuð/ *n. f.* virtue; efficacy, power.
virtuoso /bir'tuoso/ *a.* virtuous.
viruela /bi'ruela/ *n. f.* smallpox.

viruelas locas /bi'ruelas 'lokas/ *n. f.pl.* chicken pox.

virus /'birus/ *n. m.* virus.

visa /'bisa/ *n. f.* visa.

visaje /bi'sahe/ *n. m.* grimace.

visera /bi'sera/ *n. f.* visor.

visible /bi'siβle/ *a.* visible.

visión /bi'sion/ *n. f.* vision.

visionario /bisio'nario/ **-ria** *a. & n.* visionary.

visita /bi'sita/ *n. f.* visit; *m. & f.* visitor, caller. **v. con guía, v. explicada, v. programada,** guided tour.

visitación /bisita'θion; bisita'sion/ *n. f.* visitation.

visitante /bisi'tante/ *a. & n.* visiting; visitor.

visitar /bisi'tar/ *v.* visit; inspect, examine.

vislumbrar /bislum'βrar/ *v.* glimpse.

vislumbre /bis'lumbre/ *n. f.* glimpse.

viso /'biso/ *n. m.* looks; outlook.

víspera /'bispera/ *n. f.* eve, day before.

vista /'bista/ *n. f.* view; scene; sight.

vista de pájaro /'bista de 'paharo/ bird's-eye view.

vistazo /bis'taθo; bis'taso/ *n. m.* glance, glimpse.

vistoso /bis'toso/ *a.* beautiful; showy.

visual /bi'sual/ *a.* visual.

vital /bi'tal/ *a.* vital.

vitalidad /bitali'ðað/ *n. f.* vitality.

vitamina /bita'mina/ *n. f.* vitamin.

vitando /bi'tando/ *a.* hateful.

vituperar /bitupe'rar/ *v.* vituperate; revile.

viuda /'biuða/ *n. f.* widow.

viudo /'biuðo/ *n. m.* widower.

vivaz /bi'βaθ; bi'βas/ *a.* vivacious, buoyant; clever.

víveres /'biβeres/ *n. m.pl.* provisions.

viveza /bi'βeθa; bi'βesa/ *n. f.* animation, liveliness.

vívido /bi'βiðo/ *a.* vivid, bright.

vivienda /bi'βienda/ *n. f.* (living) quarters, dwelling.

vivificar /biβifi'kar/ *v.* vivify, enliven.

vivir /bi'βir/ *v.* live.

vivo /'biβo/ *a.* live, alive, living; vivid; animated, brisk.

vocablo /bo'kaβlo/ *n. m.* word.

vocabulario /bokaβu'lario/ *n. m.* vocabulary.

vocación /boka'θion; boka'sion/ *n. f.* vocation, calling.

vocal /bo'kal/ *a.* **1.** vocal. —*n.* **2.** *f.* vowel.

vocear /boθe'ar; bose'ar/ *v.* vociferate.

vodca /'boðka/ *n. m.* vodka.

vodevil /boðe'βil/ *n. m.* vaudeville.

volante /bo'lante/ *a.* **1.** flying. —*n.* **2.** *m.* memorandum; (steering) wheel.

volar /bo'lar/ *v.* fly; explode.

volcán /bol'kan/ *n. m.* volcano.

volcar /bol'kar/ *v.* upset, capsize.

voltaje /bol'tahe/ *n. m.* voltage.

voltear /bolte'ar/ *v.* turn, whirl; overturn.

voltio /'boltio/ *n. m.* volt.

volumen /bo'lumen/ *n. m.* volume.

voluminoso /bolumi'noso/ *a.* voluminous.

voluntad /bolun'tað/ *n. f.* will. **buena v.** goodwill.

voluntario /bolun'tario/ **-ria** *a. & n.* voluntary; volunteer.

voluntarioso /bolunta'rioso/ *a.* willful.

volver /bol'βer/ *v.* turn; return, go back, come back. **v. a hacer** (etc.), do (etc.) again.

volverse /bol'βerse/ *v.* turn around; turn, become.

vómito /'bomito/ *n. m.* vomit. —**vomitar,** *v.*

voracidad /boraθi'ðað; borasi'ðað/ *n. f.* voracity; greed.

voraz /bo'raθ; bo'ras/ *a.* greedy, ravenous.

vórtice /'bortiθe; 'bortise/ *n. m.* whirlpool.

vosotros /bo'sotros, bo'sotras/ **-as** *pron.pl.* you; yourselves.

votación /bota'θion; bota'sion/ *n. f.* voting; vote.

voto /'boto/ *n. m.* vote; vow. —**votar,** *v.*

voz /boθ; bos/ *n. f.* voice; word. **a voces,** by shouting. **en v. alta,** aloud.

vuelco /'buelko/ *n. m.* upset.

vuelo /'buelo/ *n. m.* flight. **v. libre,** hang gliding.

vuelo chárter /'buelo 'tʃarter/ charter flight.

vuelo regular /'buelo rregu'lar/ scheduled flight.

vuelta /'buelta/ *n. f.* turn, bend; return. **a la v. de,** around. **dar una v.,** to take a walk.

vuestro /'buestro/ *a.* your, yours.

vulgar /bul'gar/ *a.* vulgar, common.

vulgaridad /bulgari'ðað/ *n. f.* vulgarity.

vulgo /'bulgo/ *n. m.* (the) masses, (the) common people.

vulnerable /bulne'raβle/ *a.* vulnerable.

Y Z

y /i/ *conj.* and.

ya /ya/ *adv.* already; now; at once. **y. no,** no longer, any more. **y. que,** since.

yacer /ya'θer; ya'ser/ *v.* lie.

yacimiento /yaθi'miento; yasi'miento/ *n. m.* deposit.

yanqui /'yanki/ *a. & n.* North American.

yate /'yate/ *n. m.* yacht.

yegua /'yegua/ *n. f.* mare.

yelmo /'yelmo/ *n. m.* helmet.

yema /'yema/ *n. f.* yolk (of an egg).

yerba /'yerβa/ *n. f.* grass; herb.

yerno /'yerno/ *n. m.* son-in-law.

yerro /'yerro/ *n. m.* error, mistake.

yeso /'yeso/ *n. m.* plaster.

yídish /'yiðis/ *n. m.* Yiddish.

yo /yo/ *pron.* I.

yodo /'yoðo/ *n. m.* iodine.

yoduro /jo'ðuro/ *n. m.* iodide.

yonqui /'yonki/ *m. & f. Colloq.* drug addict, junkie.

yugo /'yugo/ *n. m.* yoke.

yunque /'yunke/ *n. m.* anvil.

yunta /'yunta/ *n. f.* team (of animals).

zafarse /θa'farse; sa'farse/ *v.* run away, escape. **z. de,** get rid of.

zafio /'θafio; 'safio/ *a.* coarse, uncivil.

zafiro /θa'firo; sa'firo/ *n. m.* sapphire.

zaguán /θa'guan; sa'guan/ *n. m.* vestibule, hall.

zalamero /θala'mero; sala'mero/ **-ra** *n.* flatterer, wheedler.

zambullir /θambu'ʎir; sambu'yir/ *v.* plunge, dive.

zampar /θam'par; sam'par/ *v. Colloq.* gobble down, wolf down.

zanahoria /θana'oria; sana'oria/ *n. f.* carrot.

zanja /'θanha; 'sanha/ *n. f.* ditch, trench.

zapatería /θapate'ria; sapate'ria/ *n. f.* shoe store; shoemaker's shop.

zapatero /θapa'tero; sapa'tero/ *n. m.* shoemaker.

zapato /θa'pato; sa'pato/ *n. m.* shoe.

zar /θar; sar/ *n. m.* czar.

zaraza /θa'raθa; sa'rasa/ *n. f.* calico; chintz.

zarza /'θarθa; 'sarsa/ *n. f.* bramble.

zarzuela /θar'θuela; sar'suela/ *n. f.* musical comedy.

zodíaco /θo'ðiako; so'ðiako/ *n. m.* zodiac.

zona /'θona; 'sona/ *n. f.* zone.

zoología /θoolo'hia; soolo'hia/ *n. f.* zoology.

zoológico /θoo'lohiko; soo'lohiko/ *a.* zoological.

zorro /'θorro; 'sorro/ **-rra** *n.* fox.

zozobra /θo'θoβra; so'soβra/ *n. f.* worry, anxiety; capsizing.

zozobrar /θoθo'βrar; soso'βrar/ *v.* capsize; worry.

zumba /'θumba; 'sumba/ *n. f.* spanking.

zumbido /θum'βiðo; sum'βiðo/ *n. m.* buzz, hum. —**zumbar,** *v.*

zumo /'θumo; 'sumo/ *n. m.* juice. **z. de naranja,** orange juice.

zurcir /θur'θir; sur'sir/ *v.* darn, mend.

zurdo /'θurðo; 'surðo/ *a.* left-handed.

zurrar /θu'rrar; su'rrar/ *v.* flog, drub.

English–Spanish

inglés–español

A

a /ə, *when stressed* ā/ *art.* un, una.

abacus /ˈæbəkəs/ *n.* ábaco *m.*

abandon /əˈbændən/ *n.* **1.** desenfreno, abandono *m.* —*v.* **2.** abandonar, desamparar.

abandoned /əˈbændənd/ *a.* abandonado.

abandonment /əˈbændənmənt/ *n.* abandono, desamparo *m.*

abase /əˈbeis/ *v.* degradar, humillar.

abasement /əˈbeismənt/ *n.* degradación, humillación *f.*

abash /əˈbæʃ/ *v.* avergonzar.

abate /əˈbeit/ *v.* menguar, moderarse.

abatement /əˈbeitmənt/ *n.* disminución *f.*

abbess /ˈæbɪs/ *n.* abadesa *f.*

abbey /ˈæbi/ *n.* abadía *f.*

abbot /ˈæbət/ *n.* abad *m.*

abbreviate /əˈbriviˌeit/ *v.* abreviar.

abbreviation /əˌbriviˈeiʃən/ *n.* abreviatura *f.*

abdicate /ˈæbdɪˌkeit/ *v.* abdicar.

abdication /ˌæbdɪˈkeiʃən/ *n.* abdicación *f.*

abdomen /ˈæbdəmən/ *n.* abdomen *m.*

abdominal /æbˈdɒmənl̩/ *a.* abdominal.

abduct /æbˈdʌkt/ *v.* secuestrar.

abduction /æbˈdʌkʃən/ *n.* secuestración *f.*

abductor /æbˈdʌktər/ *n.* secuestrador -ra.

aberrant /əˈbɛrənt, ˈæbər-/ *a.* aberrante.

aberration /ˌæbəˈreiʃən/ *n.* aberración *f.*

abet /əˈbɛt/ *v.* apoyar, favorecer.

abetment /əˈbɛtmənt/ *n.* apoyo *m.*

abettor /əˈbɛtər/ *n.* cómplice *m.* & *f.*

abeyance /əˈbeiəns/ *n.* suspensión *f.*

abhor /æbˈhɔr/ *v.* abominar, odiar.

abhorrence /æbˈhɔrəns/ *n.* detestación *f.*; aborrecimiento *m.*

abhorrent /æbˈhɔrənt/ *a.* detestable, aborrecible.

abide /əˈbaid/ *v.* soportar. **to a. by,** cumplir con.

abiding /əˈbaidɪŋ/ *a.* perdurable.

ability /əˈbɪlɪti/ *n.* habilidad *f.*

abject /ˈæbdʒɛkt/ *a.* abyecto; desanimado.

abjuration /ˌæbdʒəˈreiʃən/ *n.* renuncia *f.*

abjure /æbˈdʒʊr/ *v.* renunciar.

ablative /ˈæblətɪv/ *a.* & *n.* *Gram.* ablativo *m.*

ablaze /əˈbleiz/ *a.* en llamas.

able /ˈeibəl/ *a.* capaz; competente. **to be a.,** poder.

able-bodied /ˈeibəl ˈbɒdid/ *a.* robusto.

ablution /əˈbluʃən/ *n.* ablución *f.*

ably /ˈeibli/ *adv.* hábilmente.

abnegate /ˈæbnɪˌgeit/ *v.* repudiar; negar.

abnegation /ˌæbnɪˈgeiʃən/ *n.* abnegación; repudiación *f.*

abnormal /æbˈnɔrməl/ *a.* anormal.

abnormality /ˌæbnɔrˈmælɪti/ *n.* anormalidad, deformidad *f.*

abnormally /æbˈnɔrməli/ *adv.* anormalmente.

aboard /əˈbɔrd/ *adv.* a bordo.

abode /əˈboud/ *n.* residencia *f.*

abolish /əˈbɒlɪʃ/ *v.* suprimir.

abolishment /əˈbɒlɪʃmənt/ *n.* abolición *f.*

abolition /ˌæbəˈlɪʃən/ *n.* abolición *f.*

abominable /əˈbɒmənəbəl/ *a.* abominable.

abominate /əˈbɒməˌneit/ *v.* abominar, detestar.

abomination /əˌbɒməˈneiʃən/ *n.* abominación *f.*

aboriginal /ˌæbəˈrɪdʒənl̩/ *a.* & *n.* aborigen *f.*

abortion /əˈbɔrʃən/ *n.* aborto *m.*

abortive /əˈbɔrtɪv/ *a.* abortivo.

abound /əˈbaund/ *v.* abundar.

about /əˈbaut/ *adv.* **1.** como. **about to,** para; a punto de. —*prep.* **2.** de, sobre, acerca de.

about-face /əˈbautˌfeis, əˈbautˈfeis/ *n. Mil.* media vuelta.

above /əˈbʌv/ *adv.* **1.** arriba. —*prep.* **2.** sobre; por encima de.

aboveboard /əˈbʌvˌbɔrd/ *a.* & *adv.* sincero, franco.

abrasion /əˈbreiʒən/ *n.* raspadura *f.*; *Med.* abrasión *f.*

abrasive /əˈbreisɪv/ *a.* raspante. *n.* abrasivo *m.*

abreast /əˈbrɛst/ *adv.* de frente.

abridge /əˈbrɪdʒ/ *v.* abreviar.

abridgment /əˈbrɪdʒmənt/ *n.* abreviación *f.*; compendio *m.*

abroad /əˈbrɔd/ *adv.* en el extranjero, al extranjero.

abrogate /ˈæbrəˌgeit/ *v.* abrogar, revocar.

abrogation /ˌæbrəˈgeiʃən/ *n.* abrogación, revocación *f.*

abrupt /əˈbrʌpt/ *a.* repentino; brusco.

abruptly /əˈbrʌptli/ *adv.* bruscamente, precipitadamente.

abruptness /əˈbrʌptnɪs/ *n.* precipitación; brusquedad *f.*

abscess /ˈæbsɛs/ *n.* absceso *m.*

abscond /æbˈskɒnd/ *v.* fugarse.

absence /ˈæbsəns/ *n.* ausencia, falta *f.*

absent /ˈæbsənt/ *a.* ausente.

absentee /ˌæbsənˈti/ *a.* & *n.* ausente *m.* & *f.*

absent-minded /ˈæbsənt ˈmaindɪd/ *a.* distraído.

absinthe /ˈæbsɪnθ/ *n.* absenta *f.*

absolute /ˈæbsəˌlut/ *a.* absoluto.

absolutely /ˌæbsəˈlutli/ *adv.* absolutamente.

absoluteness /ˌæbsəˈlutnɪs/ *n.* absolutismo *m.*

absolution /ˌæbsəˈluʃən/ *n.* absolución *f.*

absolutism /ˈæbsəluˌtɪzəm/ *n.* absolutismo, despotismo *m.*

absolve /æbˈzɒlv/ *v.* absolver.

absorb /æbˈsɔrb/ *v.* absorber; preocupar.

absorbed /æbˈsɔrbd/ *a.* absorbido; absorto.

absorbent /æbˈsɔrbənt/ *a.* absorbente.

absorbent cotton algodón hidrófilo *m.*

absorbing /æbˈsɔrbɪŋ/ *a.* interesante.

absorption /æbˈsɔrpʃən/ *n.* absorción; preocupación *f.*

abstain /æbˈstein/ *v.* abstenerse.

abstemious /æbˈstimiəs/ *a.* abstemio, sobrio.

abstinence /ˈæbstənəns/ *n.* abstinencia *f.*

abstract /*a, v* æbˈstrækt, ˈæbstrækt; *n* ˈæbstrækt/ *a.* **1.** abstracto. —*n.* **2.** resumen *m.* —*v.* **3.** abstraer.

abstracted /æbˈstræktɪd/ *a.* distraído.

abstraction /æbˈstrækʃən/ *n.* abstracción *f.*

abstruse /æbˈstrus/ *a.* abstruso.

absurd /æbˈsɜrd/ *a.* absurdo, ridículo.

absurdity /æbˈsɜrdɪti/ *n.* absurdo *m.*

absurdly /æbˈsɜrdli/ *adv.* absurdamente.

abundance /əˈbʌndəns/ *n.* abundancia *f.*

abundant /əˈbʌndənt/ *a.* abundante.

abundantly /əˈbʌndəntli/ *adv.* abundantemente.

abuse /*n* əˈbyus; *v* əˈbyuz/ *n.* **1.** abuso *m.* —*v.* **2.** abusar de; maltratar.

abusive /əˈbyusɪv/ *a.* abusivo.

abusively /əˈbyusɪvli/ *adv.* abusivamente, ofensivamente.

abutment /əˈbʌtmənt/ *n.* (building) estribo, contrafuerte *m.*

abut (on) /əˈbʌt/ *v.* terminar (en); lindar (con).

abyss /əˈbɪs/ *n.* abismo *m.*

Abyssinian /ˌæbəˈsɪniən/ *a.* & *n.* abisinio -nia.

acacia /əˈkeiʃə/ *n.* acacia *f.*

academic /ˌækəˈdɛmɪk/ *a.* académico.

academy /əˈkædəmi/ *n.* academia *f.*

acanthus /əˈkænθəs/ *n. Bot.* acanto *m.*

accede /ækˈsid/ *v.* acceder; consentir.

accelerate /ækˈsɛləˌreit/ *v.* acelerar.

acceleration /ækˌsɛləˈreiʃən/ *n.* aceleración *f.*

accelerator /ækˈsɛləˌreitər/ *n. Auto.* acelerador *m.*

accent /ˈæksɛnt/ *n.* **1.** acento *m.* —*v.* **2.** acentuar.

accentuate /ækˈsɛntʃuˌeit/ *v.* acentuar.

accept /ækˈsɛpt/ *v.* aceptar.

acceptability /ækˌsɛptəˈbɪlɪti/ *n.* aceptabilidad *f.*

acceptable /ækˈsɛptəbəl/ *a.* aceptable.

acceptably /ækˈsɛptəbli/ *adv.* aceptablemente.

acceptance /ækˈsɛptəns/ *n.* aceptación *f.*

access /ˈæksɛs/ *n.* acceso *m.*, entrada *f.*

accessible /ækˈsɛsəbəl/ *a.* accesible.

accessory /ækˈsɛsəri/ *a.* **1.** accesorio. —*n.* **2.** cómplice *m.* & *f.*

accident /ˈæksɪdənt/ *n.* accidente *m.* **by a.,** por casualidad.

accidental /ˌæksɪˈdɛntl̩/ *a.* accidental.

accidentally /ˌæksɪˈdɛntl̩i/ *adv.* accidentalmente, casualmente.

acclaim /əˈkleim/ *v.* aclamar.

acclamation /ˌækləˈmeiʃən/ *n.* aclamación *f.*

acclimate /ˈækləˌmeit/ *v.* aclimatar.

acclivity /əˈklɪvɪti/ *n.* subida *f.*

accolade /ˈækəˌleid/ *n.* acolada *f.*

accommodate /əˈkɒməˌdeit/ *v.* acomodar.

accommodating /əˈkɒməˌdeitɪŋ/ *a.* bondadoso, complaciente.

accommodation /əˌkɒməˈdeiʃən/ *n.* servicio *m.*; *(pl.)* alojamiento *m.*

accompaniment /əˈkʌmpənɪmənt/ *n.* acompañamiento *m.*

accompanist /əˈkʌmpənɪst/ *n.* acompañante *m.* & *f.*

accompany /əˈkʌmpəni/ *v.* acompañar.

accomplice /əˈkɒmplɪs/ *n.* cómplice *m.* & *f.*

accomplish /əˈkɒmplɪʃ/ *v.* llevar a cabo; realizar.

accomplished /əˈkɒmplɪʃt/ *a.* acabado, cumplido; culto.

accomplishment /əˈkɒmplɪʃmənt/ *n.* realización *f.*; logro *m.*

accord /əˈkɔrd/ *n.* **1.** acuerdo *m.* —*v.* **2.** otorgar.

accordance /əˈkɔrdn̩s/ *n.*: **in a. with,** de acuerdo con.

accordingly /əˈkɔrdɪŋli/ *adv.* en conformidad.

according to /əˈkɔrdɪŋ/ *prep.* según.

accordion /əˈkɔrdiən/ *n.* acordeón *m.*

accost /əˈkɔst/ *v.* dirigirse a.

account /əˈkaunt/ *n.* **1.** relato *m.*; *Com.* cuenta *f.* **on a. of,** a causa de. **on no a.,** de ninguna manera. —*v.* **2.** **a. for,** explicar.

accountable /əˈkauntəbəl/ *a.* responsable.

accountant /əˈkauntn̩t/ *n.* contador -ra.

accounting /əˈkauntɪŋ/ *n.* contabilidad *f.*

accouter /əˈkutər/ *v.* equipar, ataviar.

accouterments /əˈkutərmənts/ *n.* equipo, atavío *m.*

accredit /əˈkrɛdɪt/ *v.* acreditar.

accretion /əˈkriʃən/ *n.* aumento *m.*

accrual /əˈkruəl/ *n.* aumento, incremento *m.*

accrue /əˈkru/ *v.* provenir; acumularse.

accumulate /əˈkyumyəˌleit/ *v.* acumular.

accumulation /əˌkyumyəˈleiʃən/ *n.* acumulación *f.*

accumulative /əˈkyumyəˌleitɪv/ *a.* acumulativo.

accumulator /əˈkyumyəˌleitər/ *n.* acumulador *m.*

accuracy /ˈækyərəsi/ *n.* exactitud, precisión *f.*

accurate /ˈækyərɪt/ *a.* exacto.

accursed /əˈkɜrsɪd, əˈkɜrst/ *a.* maldito.

accusation /ˌækyʊˈzeiʃən/ *n.* acusación *f.*, cargo *m.*

accusative /əˈkyuzətɪv/ *a.* & *n.* acusativo *m.*

accuse /əˈkyuz/ *v.* acusar.

accused /əˈkyuzd/ *a.* & *n.* acusado -da, procesado -da.

accuser /əˈkyuzər/ *n.* acusador -ra.

accustom /əˈkʌstəm/ *v.* acostumbrar.

accustomed /əˈkʌstəmd/ *a.* acostumbrado.

ace /eis/ *a.* **1.** sobresaliente. —*n.* **2.** as *m.*

acerbity /əˈsɜrbɪti/ *n.* acerbidad, amargura *f.*

acetate /ˈæsɪˌteit/ *n. Chem.* acetato *m.*

acetic /əˈsitɪk/ *a.* acético.

acetylene /əˈsɛtl̩ˌin/ *a.* **1.** acetilénico. —*n.* **2.** *Chem.* acetileno *m.*

ache /eik/ *n.* **1.** dolor *m.* —*v.* **2.** doler.

achieve /əˈtʃiv/ *v.* lograr, llevar a cabo.

achievement /əˈtʃivmənt/ *n.* realización *f.*; hecho notable *m.*

acid /ˈæsɪd/ *a.* & *n.* ácido *m.*

acidify /əˈsɪdəˌfai/ *v.* acidificar.

acidity /əˈsɪdɪti/ *n.* acidez *f.*

acidosis /ˌæsɪˈdousɪs/ *n.* *Med.* acidismo *m.*

acid rain lluvia ácida *f.*

acid test prueba decisiva.

acidulous /əˈsɪdʒələs/ *a.* agrio, acídulo.

acknowledge /ækˈnɒlɪdʒ/ *v.* admitir; (receipt) acusar.

acme /ˈækmi/ *n.* apogeo, colmo *m.*

acne /ˈækni/ *n. Med.* acné *m.* & *f.*

acolyte /ˈækəˌlait/ *n.* acólito *m.*

acorn /ˈeikɔrn/ *n.* bellota *f.*

acoustics /əˈkustɪks/ *n.* acústica *f.*

acquaint /əˈkweint/ *v.* familiarizar. **to be acquainted with,** conocer.

acquaintance /əˈkweintn̩s/ *n.* conocimiento *m.*; (person known) conocido -da. **to make the a. of,** conocer.

acquiesce /ˌækwiˈɛs/ *v.* consentir.

acquiescence /ˌækwiˈɛsəns/ *n.* consentimiento *m.*

acquire /əˈkwaiᵊr/ *v.* adquirir.

acquirement /əˈkwaiᵊrmənt/ *n.* adquisición *f.*; *(pl.)* conocimientos *m.pl.*

acquisition /ˌækwəˈzɪʃən/ *n.* adquisición *f.*

acquisitive /əˈkwɪzɪtɪv/ *a.* adquisitivo.

acquit /əˈkwɪt/ *v.* exonerar, absolver.

acquittal /əˈkwɪtl̩/ *n.* absolución *f.*

acre /ˈeikər/ *n.* acre *m.*

acreage /ˈeikərɪdʒ/ número de acres.

acrid /ˈækrɪd/ *a.* acre, punzante.

acrimonious /ˌækrəˈmouniəs/ *a.* acrimonioso, mordaz.

acrimony /ˈækrəˌmouni/ *n.* acrimonia, aspereza *f.*

acrobat /ˈækrəˌbæt/ *n.* acróbata *m.* & *f.*

acrobatic /ˌækrəˈbætɪk/ *a.* acrobático.

across /əˈkrɔs/ *adv.* **1.** a través, al otro lado. —*prep.* **2.** al otro lado de, a través de.

acrostic /əˈkrɔstɪk/ *n.* acróstico *m.*

act /ækt/ *n.* **1.** acción *f.*; acto *m.* —*v.* **2.** actuar, portarse. **act as,** hacer de. **act on,** decidir sobre.

acting /ˈæktɪŋ/ *a.* **1.** interino. —*n.* **2.** acción *f.*; *Theat.* representación *f.*

actinism /ˈæktəˌnɪzəm/ *n.* actinismo *m.*

actinium /ækˈtɪniəm/ *n. Chem.* actinio *m.*

action /ˈækʃən/ *n.* acción *f.* **take a.,** tomar medidas.

action replay /ˈriˌplei/ repetición *f.*

activate /ˈæktəˌveit/ *v.* activar.

activation /ˌæktəˈveiʃən/ *n.* activación *f.*
activator /ˈæktəˌveitər/ *n. Chem.* activador *m.*
active /ˈæktɪv/ *a.* activo.
activity /ækˈtɪvɪti/ *n.* actividad *f.*
actor /ˈæktər/ *n.* actor *m.*
actress /ˈæktrɪs/ *n.* actriz *f.*
actual /ˈæktʃuəl/ *a.* real, efectivo.
actuality /ˌæktʃuˈælɪti/ *n.* realidad, actualidad *f.*
actually /ˈæktʃuəli/ *adv.* en realidad.
actuary /ˈæktʃuˌɛri/ *n.* actuario *m.*
actuate /ˈæktʃuˌeit/ *v.* impulsar, mover.
acumen /əˈkyumən/ *n.* cacumen *m.*, perspicacia *f.*
acupuncture /ˈækyʊˌpʌŋktʃər/ *n.* acupuntura *f.*
acute /əˈkyut/ *a.* agudo; perspicaz.
acutely /əˈkyutli/ *adv.* agudamente.
acuteness /əˈkyutnɪs/ *n.* agudeza *f.*
adage /ˈædɪdʒ/ *n.* refrán, proverbio *m.*
adamant /ˈædəmənt/ *a.* firme.
Adam's apple /ˈædəmz/ nuez de la garganta.
adapt /əˈdæpt/ *v.* adaptar.
adaptability /əˌdæptəˈbɪlɪti/ *n.* adaptabilidad *f.*
adaptable /əˈdæptəbəl/ *a.* adaptable.
adaptation /ˌædəpˈteiʃən/ *n.* adaptación *f.*
adapter /əˈdæptər/ *n. Elec.* adaptador *m.*; *Mech.* ajustador *m.*
adaptive /əˈdæptɪv/ *a.* adaptable, acomodable.
add /æd/ *v.* agregar, añadir. **a. up,** sumar.
adder /ˈædər/ *n.* víbora; serpiente *f.*
addict /ˈædɪkt/ *n.* adicto -ta; (fan) aficionado -da.
addition /əˈdɪʃən/ *n.* adición *f.* **in a. to,** además de.
additional /əˈdɪʃənl̩/ *a.* adicional.
addle /ˈædl̩/ *v.* confundir.
address /*n* əˈdrɛs, ˈædrɛs; *v* əˈdrɛs/ *n.* **1.** dirección *f.*; señas *f.pl.*; (speech) discurso. **—***v.* **2.** dirigirse a.
addressee /ˌædrɛˈsi/ *n.* destinatario -ia.
adduce /əˈdus/ *v.* aducir.
adenoid /ˈædn̩ˌɔid/ *a.* adenoidea.
adept /əˈdɛpt/ *a.* adepto.
adeptly /əˈdɛptli/ *adv.* diestramente.
adeptness /əˈdɛptnɪs/ *n.* destreza *f.*
adequacy /ˈædɪkwəsi/ *n.* suficiencia *f.*
adequate /ˈædɪkwɪt/ *a.* adecuado.
adequately /ˈædɪkwɪtli/ *adv.* adecuadamente.
adhere /ædˈhɪər/ *v.* adherirse, pegarse.
adherence /ædˈhɪərəns/ *n.* adhesión *f.*; apego *m.*
adherent /ædˈhɪərənt/ *n.* adherente *m.*, partidario -ria.
adhesion /ædˈhiʒən/ *n.* adhesión *f.*
adhesive /ædˈhisɪv/ *a.* adhesivo. **a. tape,** esparadrapo *m.*
adhesiveness /ædˈhisɪvnɪs/ *n.* adhesividad *f.*
adieu /əˈdu/ *interj.* **1.** adiós. **—***n.* **2.** despedida *f.*
adjacent /əˈdʒeisənt/ *a.* adyacente.
adjective /ˈædʒɪktɪv/ *n.* adjetivo *m.*
adjoin /əˈdʒɔin/ *v.* lindar (con).
adjoining /əˈdʒɔinɪŋ/ *a.* contiguo.
adjourn /əˈdʒɜrn/ *v.* suspender, levantar.
adjournment /əˈdʒɜrnmənt/ *n.* suspensión *f.*; *Leg.* espera *f.*
adjunct /ˈædʒʌŋkt/ *n.* adjunto *m.*; *Gram.* atributo *m.*
adjust /əˈdʒʌst/ *v.* ajustar, acomodar; arreglar.
adjuster /əˈdʒʌstər/ *n.* ajustador -ra.
adjustment /əˈdʒʌstmənt/ *n.* ajuste; arreglo *m.*
adjutant /ˈædʒətənt/ *n. Mil.* ayudante *m.*
administer /ædˈmɪnəstər/ *v.* administrar.
administration /ædˌmɪnəˈstreiʃən/ *n.* administración *f.*; gobierno *m.*
administrative /ædˈmɪnəˌstreitɪv/ *a.* administrativo.
administrator /ædˈmɪnəˌstreitər/ *n.* administrador -ra.
admirable /ˈædmərəbəl/ *a.* admirable.
admirably /ˈædmərəbli/ *adv.* admirablemente.
admiral /ˈædmərəl/ *n.* almirante *m.*
admiralty /ˈædmərəlti/ *n.* Ministerio de Marina.
admiration /ˌædməˈreiʃən/ *n.* admiración *f.*
admire /ædˈmaiᵊr/ *v.* admirar.
admirer /ædˈmaiᵊrər/ *n.* admirador -ra; enamorado -da.
admiringly /ædˈmaiᵊrɪŋli/ *adv.* admirativamente.
admissible /ædˈmɪsəbəl/ *a.* admisible, aceptable.
admission /ædˈmɪʃən/ *n.* admisión; entrada *f.*
admit /ædˈmɪt/ *v.* admitir.
admittance /ædˈmɪtn̩s/ *n.* entrada *f.*
admittedly /ædˈmɪtɪdli/ *adv.* reconocidamente.
admixture /ædˈmɪkstʃər/ *n.* mezcla *f.*
admonish /ædˈmɒnɪʃ/ *v.* amonestar.
admonition /ˌædməˈnɪʃən/ *n.* admonición *f.*
adolescence /ˌædl̩ˈɛsəns/ *n.* adolescencia *f.*
adolescent /ˌædl̩ˈɛsənt/ *n.* & *a.* adolescente.
adopt /əˈdɒpt/ *v.* adoptar.
adopted child /əˈdɒptɪd/ hija adoptiva *f.*, hijo adoptivo *m.*
adoption /əˈdɒpʃən/ *n.* adopción *f.*
adorable /əˈdɔrəbəl/ *a.* adorable.
adoration /ˌædəˈreiʃən/ *n.* adoración *f.*
adore /əˈdɔr/ *v.* adorar.
adorn /əˈdɔrn/ *v.* adornar.
adornment /əˈdɔrnmənt/ *n.* adorno *m.*
adrenalin /əˈdrɛnl̩ɪn/ *n.* adrenalina *f.*
adrift /əˈdrɪft/ *adv.* a la ventura.
adroit /əˈdrɔit/ *a.* diestro.
adulate /ˈædʒəˌleit/ *v.* adular.
adulation /ˌædʒəˈleiʃən/ *n.* adulación *f.*
adult /əˈdʌlt/ *a.* & *n.* adulto -a.
adulterant /əˈdʌltərənt/ *a.* & *n.* adulterante *m.*
adulterate /əˈdʌltəˌreit/ *v.* adulterar.
adulterer /əˈdʌltərər/ *n.* adúltero -ra.
adulteress /əˈdʌltərɪs/ *n.* adúltera *f.*
adultery /əˈdʌltəri/ *n.* adulterio *m.*
advance /ædˈvæns/ *n.* **1.** avance; adelanto *m.* **in a.,** de antemano, antes. **—***v.* **2.** avanzar, adelantar.
advanced /ædˈvænst/ *a.* avanzado, adelantado.
advancement /ædˈvænsmənt/ *n.* adelantamiento *m.*; promoción *f.*
advantage /ædˈvæntɪdʒ/ *n.* ventaja *f.* **take a. of,** aprovecharse de.
advantageous /ˌædvənˈteidʒəs/ *a.* provechoso, ventajoso.
advantageously /ˌædvənˈteidʒəsli/ *adv.* ventajosamente.
advent /ˈædvɛnt/ *n.* venida, llegada *f.*
adventitious /ˌædvənˈtɪʃəs/ *a.* adventicio, espontáneo.
adventure /ædˈvɛntʃər/ *n.* aventura *f.*
adventurer /ædˈvɛntʃərər/ *n.* aventurero -ra.
adventurous /ædˈvɛntʃərəs/ *a.* aventurero, intrépido.
adventurously /ædˈvɛntʃərəsli/ *adv.* arriesgadamente.
adverb /ˈædvɜrb/ *n.* adverbio *m.*
adverbial /ædˈvɜrbiəl/ *a.* adverbial.
adversary /ˈædvərˌsɛri/ *n.* adversario -a.
adverse /ædˈvɜrs/ *a.* adverso.
adversely /ædˈvɜrsli/ *adv.* adversamente.
adversity /ædˈvɜrsɪti/ *n.* adversidad *f.*
advert /ædˈvɜrt/ *v.* hacer referencia a.
advertise /ˈædvərˌtaiz/ *v.* avisar, anunciar; (promote) promocionar.
advertisement /ˌædvərˈtaizmənt, ædˈvɜrtɪsmənt/ *n.* aviso, anuncio *m.*
advertiser /ˈædvərˌtaizər/ *n.* anunciante *m.* & *f.*, avisador -ra.
advertising /ˈædvərˌtaizɪŋ/ *n.* publicidad *f.*
advice /ædˈvais/ *n.* consejos *m.pl.*
advisability /ædˌvaizəˈbɪlɪti/ *n.* prudencia, propiedad *f.*
advisable /ædˈvaizəbəl/ *a.* aconsejable, prudente.
advisably /ædˈvaizəbli/ *adv.* prudentemente.
advise /ædˈvaiz/ *v.* aconsejar. **a. against,** desaconsejar.
advisedly /ædˈvaizɪdli/ *adv.* avisadamente, prudentemente.
advisement /ædˈvaizmənt/ *n.* consideración *f.*; **take under a.,** someter a estudio.
adviser /ædˈvaizər/ *n.* consejero -ra.
advocacy /ˈædvəkəsi/ *n.* abogacía; defensa *f.*
advocate /*n* ˈædvəkɪt; *v* -ˌkeit/ *n.* **1.** abogado -da. **—***v.* **2.** apoyar.
aegis /ˈidʒɪs/ *n.* amparo *m.*
aerate /ˈɛəreit/ *v.* airear, ventilar.
aeration /ˌɛəˈreiʃən/ *n.* aeración, ventilación *f.*
aerial /ˈɛəriəl/ *a.* aéreo.
aerie /ˈɛəri/ *n.* nido de águila.
aeronautics /ˌɛərəˈnɔtɪks/ *n.* aeronáutica *f.*
aerosol bomb /ˈɛərəˌsɔl/ bomba insecticida.
afar /əˈfɑr/ *adv.* lejos. **from a.,** de lejos, desde lejos.
affability /ˌæfəˈbɪlɪti/ *n.* afabilidad, amabilidad *f.*
affable /ˈæfəbəl/ *a.* afable.
affably /ˈæfəbli/ *adv.* afablemente.
affair /əˈfɛər/ *n.* asunto *m.* **love a.,** aventura amorosa.
affect /əˈfɛkt/ *v.* afectar; (emotionally) conmover.
affectation /ˌæfɛkˈteiʃən/ *n.* afectación *f.*
affected /əˈfɛktɪd/ *a.* artificioso.
affecting /əˈfɛktɪŋ/ *a.* conmovedor.
affection /əˈfɛkʃən/ *n.* cariño *m.*
affectionate /əˈfɛkʃənɪt/ *a.* afectuoso, cariñoso.
affectionately /əˈfɛkʃənɪtli/ *adv.* afectuosamente, con cariño.
affiance /əˈfaiəns/ *v.* dar palabra de casamiento; **become affianced,** comprometerse.
affidavit /ˌæfɪˈdeivɪt/ *n. Leg.* declaración, deposición *f.*
affiliate /*n* əˈfɪliˌɪt; *v* əˈfɪliˌeit/ *n.* **1.** afiliado -da. **—***v.* **2.** afiliar.
affiliation /əˌfɪliˈeiʃən/ *n.* afiliación *f.*
affinity /əˈfɪnɪti/ *n.* afinidad *f.*
affirm /əˈfɜrm/ *v.* afirmar.
affirmation /ˌæfərˈmeiʃən/ *n.* afirmación, aserción *f.*
affirmative /əˈfɜrmətɪv/ *n.* **1.** afirmativa *f.* **—***a.* **2.** afirmativo.
affirmatively /əˈfɜrmətɪvli/ *adv.* afirmativamente, aseveradamente.
affix /*n* ˈæfɪks; *v* əˈfɪks/ *n.* **1.** *Gram.* afijo *m.* **—***v.* **2.** fijar, pegar, poner.
afflict /əˈflɪkt/ *v.* afligir.
affliction /əˈflɪkʃən/ *n.* aflicción *f.*; mal *m.*
affluence /ˈæfluəns/ *n.* abundancia, opulencia *f.*
affluent /ˈæfluənt/ *a.* opulento, afluente.
afford /əˈfɔrd/ *v.* proporcionar. **be able to a.,** tener con que comprar.
affordable /əˈfɔrdəbəl/ *a.* asequible.
affront /əˈfrʌnt/ *n.* **1.** afrenta *f.* **—***v.* **2.** afrentar, insultar.
afield /əˈfild/ *adv.* lejos de casa; lejos del camino; lejos del asunto.
afire /əˈfaiᵊr/ *adv.* ardiendo.
afloat /əˈflout/ *adv. Naut.* a flote.
aforementioned /əˈfɔrˌmɛnʃənd/ *a.* dicho, susodicho.
afraid /əˈfreid/ *a.* **to be a.,** tener miedo, temer.
African /ˈæfrɪkən/ *n.* & *a.* africano -na.
aft /æft/ *adv. Naut.* a popa, en popa.
after /ˈæftər/ *prep.* **1.** después de. **—***conj.* **2.** después que.
aftermath /ˈæftərˌmæθ/ *n.* resultados *m.pl.*, consecuencias *f.pl.*
afternoon /ˌæftərˈnun/ *n.* tarde *f.* **good a.,** buenas tardes.
aftertaste /ˈæftərˌteist/ *n.* gustillo *m.*
afterthought /ˈæftərˌθɔt/ *n.* idea tardía.
afterward(s) /ˈæftərwərdz/ *adv.* después.
again /əˈgɛn/ *adv.* otra vez, de nuevo. **to do a.,** volver a hacer.
against /əˈgɛnst/ *prep.* contra; en contra de.
agape /əˈgeip/ *adv.* con la boca abierta.
agate /ˈægɪt/ *n.* ágata *f.*
age /eidʒ/ *n.* **1.** edad *f.* **of a.,** mayor de edad. **old a.,** vejez *f.* **—***v.* **2.** envejecer.
aged /eidʒd; ˈeidʒɪd/ *a.* viejo, anciano, añejo.
ageism /ˈeidʒɪzəm/ *n.* discriminación contra las personas de edad.
ageless /ˈeidʒlɪs/ *a.* sempiterno.
agency /ˈeidʒənsi/ *n.* agencia *f.*
agenda /əˈdʒɛndə/ *n.* agenda *f.*, orden *m.*
agent /ˈeidʒənt/ *n.* agente; representante *m.* & *f.*
agglutinate /əˈglutn̩ˌeit/ *v.* aglutinar.
agglutination /əˌglutn̩ˈeiʃən/ *n.* aglutinación *f.*
aggrandize /əˈgrændaiz/ *v.* agrandar; elevar.
aggrandizement /əˈgrændɪzmənt/ *n.* engrandecimiento *m.*
aggravate /ˈægrəˌveit/ *v.* agravar; irritar.
aggravation /ˌægrəˈveiʃən/ *n.* agravamiento; empeoramiento *m.*
aggregate /ˈægrɪgɪt, -ˌgeit/ *a.* & *n.* agregado *m.*
aggregation /ˌægrɪˈgeiʃən/ *n.* agregación *f.*
aggression /əˈgrɛʃən/ *n.* agresión *f.*
aggressive /əˈgrɛsɪv/ *a.* agresivo.
aggressively /əˈgrɛsɪvli/ *adv.* agresivamente.
aggressiveness /əˈgrɛsɪvnɪs/ *n.* agresividad *f.*
aggressor /əˈgrɛsər/ *n.* agresor -ra.
aghast /əˈgæst/ *a.* horrorizado.
agile /ˈædʒəl/ *a.* ágil.
agility /əˈdʒɪlɪti/ *n.* agilidad, ligereza, prontitud *f.*
agitate /ˈædʒɪˌteit/ *v.* agitar.
agitation /ˌædʒɪˈteiʃən/ *n.* agitación *f.*
agitator /ˈædʒɪˌteitər/ *n.* agitador -ra.
agnostic /ægˈnɒstɪk/ *a.* & *n.* agnóstico -ca.
ago /əˈgou/ *adv.* hace. **two days a.,** hace dos días.
agonized /ˈægəˌnaizd/ *a.* angustioso.
agony /ˈægəni/ *n.* sufrimiento *m.*; angustia *f.*
agrarian /əˈgrɛəriən/ *a.* agrario.
agree /əˈgri/ *v.* estar de acuerdo; convenir. **a. with one,** sentar bien.
agreeable /əˈgriəbəl/ *a.* agradable.
agreeably /əˈgriəbli/ *adv.* agradablemente.
agreement /əˈgrimənt/ *n.* acuerdo *m.*
agriculture /ˈægrɪˌkʌltʃər/ *n.* agricultura *f.*
ahead /əˈhɛd/ *adv.* adelante.
aid /eid/ *n.* **1.** ayuda *f.* **—***v.* **2.** ayudar.
aide /eid/ *n.* ayudante -ta.
AIDS /eidz/ *n.* SIDA *m.*
ailing /ˈeilɪŋ/ *adj.* enfermo.
ailment /ˈeilmənt/ *n.* enfermedad *f.*
aim /eim/ *n.* **1.** puntería *f.*; (purpose) propósito *m.* **—***v.* **2.** apuntar.
aimless /ˈeimlɪs/ *a.* sin objeto.
air /ɛər/ *n.* **1.** aire *m.* **by a.** por avión. **—***v.* **2.** ventilar, airear.

airbag /ˈɛərˌbæg/ *n.* (in automobiles) saco de aire *m.*

air-conditioned /ˈɛər kənˌdɪʃənd/ *a.* con aire acondicionado.

air-conditioning /ɛər kənˌdɪʃənɪŋ/ acondicionamiento del aire.

aircraft /ˈɛərˌkræft/ *n.* avión *m.*

aircraft carrier portaaviones *m.*

airfare /ˈɛərˌfɛər/ *n.* precio del billete de avión *m.*

airing /ˈɛərɪŋ/ *n.* ventilación *f.*

airline /ˈɛərˌlain/ *n.* línea aérea *f.*

airliner /ˈɛərˌlainər/ *n.* avión de pasajeros.

airmail /ˈɛərˌmeil/ *n.* correo aéreo.

airplane /ˈɛərˌplein/ *n.* avión, aeroplano *m.*

air pollution contaminación atmosférica, contaminación del aire.

airport /ˈɛərˌpɔrt/ *n.* aeropuerto *m.*

air pressure presión atmosférica.

air raid ataque aéreo.

airsick /ˈɛərˌsɪk/ *a.* mareado.

air terminal terminal aérea *f.*

airtight /ˈɛərˌtait/ *a.* hermético.

air traffic controller controlador aéreo *m.*

aisle /ail/ *n.* pasillo *m.*

ajar /əˈdʒɑr/ *a.* entreabierto.

akin /əˈkɪn/ *a.* emparentado, semejante.

alacrity /əˈlækrɪti/ *n.* alacridad, presteza *f.*

alarm /əˈlɑrm/ *n.* **1.** alarma *f.* —*v.* **2.** alarmar.

alarmist /əˈlɑrmɪst/ *n.* alarmista *m.* & *f.*

albino /ælˈbainou/ *n.* albino -na.

album /ˈælbəm/ *n.* álbum *m.*

alcohol /ˈælkəˌhɔl/ *n.* alcohol *m.*

alcoholic /ˌælkəˈhɔlɪk/ *a.* alcohólico.

alcove /ˈælkouv/ *n.* alcoba *f.*

ale /eil/ *n.* cerveza inglesa.

alert /əˈlɜrt/ *n.* **1.** alarma *f.* **on the a.,** alerta, sobre aviso. —*a.* **2.** listo, vivo. —*v.* **3.** poner sobre aviso.

alfalfa /ælˈfælfə/ *n.* alfalfa *f.*

algebra /ˈældʒəbrə/ *n.* álgebra *f.*

alias /ˈeiliəs/ *n.* alias *m.*

alibi /ˈæləˌbai/ *n.* excusa *f.*; *Leg.* coartada *f.*

alien /ˈeiliən/ *a.* **1.** ajeno, extranjero. —*n.* **2.** extranjero -ra.

alienate /ˈeiliəˌneit/ *v.* enajenar.

alight /əˈlait/ *v.* bajar, apearse.

align /əˈlain/ *v.* alinear.

alike /əˈlaik/ *a.* **1.** semejante, igual. —*adv.* **2.** del mismo modo, igualmente.

alimentary canal /ˌæləˈmɛntəri/ *n.* tubo digestivo *m.*

alive /əˈlaiv/ *a.* vivo; animado.

alkali /ˈælkəˌlai/ *n.* *Chem.* álcali, cali *m.*

alkaline /ˈælkəˌlain/ *a.* alcalino.

all /ɔl/ *a.* & *pron.* todo. **not at a.,** de ninguna manera, nada.

allay /əˈlei/ *v.* aquietar.

allegation /ˌælɪˈgeiʃən/ *n.* alegación *f.*

allege /əˈlɛdʒ/ *v.* alegar; pretender.

allegiance /əˈlidʒəns/ *n.* lealtad *f.*; (to country) homenaje *m.*

allegory /ˈæləˌgɔri/ *n.* alegoría *f.*

allergy /ˈælərdʒi/ *n.* alergia *f.*

alleviate /əˈliviˌeit/ *v.* aliviar.

alley /ˈæli/ *n.* callejón *m.* **bowling a.,** bolera *f.*, boliche *m.*

alliance /əˈlaiəns/ *n.* alianza *f.*

allied /ˈælaid/ *a.* aliado.

alligator /ˈælɪˌgeitər/ *n.* caimán *m.*; (Mex.) lagarto *m.* **a. pear,** aguacate *m.*

allocate /ˈæləˌkeit/ *v.* colocar, asignar.

allot /əˈlɒt/ *v.* asignar.

allotment /əˈlɒtmənt/ *n.* lote, porción *f.*

allow /əˈlau/ *v.* permitir, dejar.

allowance /əˈlauəns/ *n.* abono *m.*; dieta *f.* **make a. for,** tener en cuenta.

alloy /ˈælɔi/ *n.* mezcla *f.*; (metal) aleación *f.*

all right está bien.

allude /əˈlud/ *v.* aludir.

allure /əˈlʊr/ *n.* **1.** atracción *f.* —*v.* **2.** atraer, tentar.

alluring /əˈlʊrɪŋ/ *a.* tentador, seductivo.

allusion /əˈluʒən/ *n.* alusión *f.*

ally /*n* ˈælai, *v* əˈlai/ *n.* **1.** aliado -da. —*v.* **2.** aliar.

almanac /ˈɔlməˌnæk/ *n.* almanaque *m.*

almighty /ɔlˈmaiti/ *a.* todopoderoso.

almond /ˈɑmənd/ *n.* almendra *f.*

almost /ˈɔlmoust/ *adv.* casi.

alms /ɑmz/ *n.* limosna *f.*

aloft /əˈlɔft/ *adv.* arriba, en alto.

alone /əˈloun/ *adv.* solo, a solas. **to leave a.,** dejar en paz.

along /əˈlɔŋ/ *prep.* por; a lo largo de. **a. with,** junto con.

alongside /əˈlɔŋˈsaid/ *adv.* **1.** al lado. —*prep.* **2.** junto a.

aloof /əˈluf/ *a.* apartado.

aloud /əˈlaud/ *adv.* en voz alta.

alpaca /ælˈpækə/ *n.* alpaca *f.*

alphabet /ˈælfəˌbɛt/ *n.* alfabeto *m.*

alphabetical /ˌælfəˈbɛtɪkəl/ *a.* alfabético.

alphabetize /ˈælfəbɪˌtaiz/ *v.* alfabetizar.

already /ɔlˈrɛdi/ *adv.* ya.

also /ˈɔlsou/ *adv.* también.

altar /ˈɔltər/ *n.* altar *m.*

alter /ˈɔltər/ *v.* alterar.

alteration /ˌɔltəˈreiʃən/ *n.* alteración *f.*

alternate /*a*, *n* ˈɔltərnɪt; *v* -ˌneit/ *a.* **1.** alterno. —*n.* **2.** substituto -ta. —*v.* **3.** alternar.

alternative /ɔlˈtɜrnətɪv/ *a.* **1.** alternativo. —*n.* **2.** alternativa *f.*

although /ɔlˈðou/ *conj.* aunque.

altitude /ˈæltɪˌtud/ *n.* altura *f.*

alto /ˈæltou/ *n.* contralto *m.*

altogether /ˌɔltəˈgɛðər/ *adv.* en junto; enteramente.

altruism /ˈæltruˌɪzəm/ *n.* altruismo *m.*

alum /ˈæləm/ *n.* alumbre *m.*

aluminum /əˈlumənəm/ *n.* aluminio *m.*

aluminum foil papel de aluminio *m.*

always /ˈɔlweiz/ *adv.* siempre.

amalgam /əˈmælgəm/ *n.* amalgama *f.*

amalgamate /əˈmælgəˌmeit/ *v.* amalgamar.

amass /əˈmæs/ *v.* amontonar.

amateur /ˈæməˌtʃʊr/ *n.* aficionado -da.

amaze /əˈmeiz/ *v.* asombrar; sorprender.

amazement /əˈmeizmənt/ *n.* asombro *m.*

amazing /əˈmeizɪŋ/ *a.* asombroso, pasmoso.

ambassador /æmˈbæsədər/ *n.* embajador -ra.

amber /ˈæmbər/ *a.* **1.** ambarino. —*n.* **2.** ámbar *m.*

ambidextrous /ˌæmbɪˈdɛkstrəs/ *a.* ambidextro.

ambiguity /ˌæmbɪˈgyuɪti/ *n.* ambigüedad *f.*

ambiguous /æmˈbɪgyuəs/ *a.* ambiguo.

ambition /æmˈbɪʃən/ *n.* ambición *f.*

ambitious /æmˈbɪʃəs/ *a.* ambicioso.

ambulance /ˈæmbyələns/ *n.* ambulancia *f.*

ambush /ˈæmbʊʃ/ *n.* **1.** emboscada *f.* —*v.* **2.** acechar.

ameliorate /əˈmilyəˌreit/ *v.* mejorar.

amenable /əˈminəbəl/ *a.* tratable, dócil.

amend /əˈmɛnd/ *v.* enmendar.

amendment /əˈmɛndmənt/ *n.* enmienda *f.*

amenity /əˈmɛnɪti/ *n.* amenidad *f.*

American /əˈmɛrɪkən/ *a.* & *n.* americano -na, norteamericano -na.

amethyst /ˈæməθɪst/ *n.* amatista *f.*

amiable /ˈeimiəbəl/ *a.* amable.

amicable /ˈæmɪkəbəl/ *a.* amigable.

amid /əˈmɪd/ *prep.* entre, en medio de.

amidships /əˈmɪdˌʃɪps/ *adv.* *Naut.* en medio del navío.

amiss /əˈmɪs/ *adv.* mal. **to take a.,** llevar a mal.

amity /ˈæmɪti/ *n.* amistad, armonía *f.*

ammonia /əˈmounyə/ *n.* amoníaco *m.*

ammunition /ˌæmyəˈnɪʃən/ *n.* municiones *f.pl.*

amnesia /æmˈniʒə/ *n.* amnesia *f.*

amnesty /ˈæmnəsti/ *n.* amnistía *f.*, indulto *m.*

amniocentesis /ˌæmniousɛnˈtisɪs/ *n.* amniocéntesis *f.*

amoeba /əˈmibə/ *n.* amiba *f.*

among /əˈmʌŋ/ *prep.* entre.

amoral /eiˈmɔrəl/ *a.* amoral.

amorous /ˈæmərəs/ *a.* amoroso.

amorphous /əˈmɔrfəs/ *a.* amorfo.

amortize /ˈæmərˌtaiz/ *v.* *Com.* amortizar.

amount /əˈmaunt/ *n.* **1.** cantidad, suma *f.* —*v.* **2. a. to,** subir a.

ampere /ˈæmpɪər/ *n.* *Elec.* amperio *m.*

amphibian /æmˈfɪbiən/ *a.* & *n.* anfibio *m.*

amphitheater /ˈæmfəˌθiətər/ *n.* anfiteatro, circo *m.*

ample /ˈæmpəl/ *a.* amplio; suficiente.

amplify /ˈæmpləˌfai/ *v.* amplificar.

amputate /ˈæmpyʊˌteit/ *v.* amputar.

amuse /əˈmyuz/ *v.* entretener, divertir.

amusement /əˈmyuzmənt/ *n.* diversión *f.*

an /ən, *when stressed* æn/ *art.* un, una.

anachronism /əˈnækrəˌnɪzəm/ *n.* anacronismo, *m.*

analogous /əˈnæləgəs/ *a.* análogo, parecido.

analogy /əˈnælədʒi/ *n.* analogía *f.*

analysis /əˈnæləsɪs/ *n.* análisis *m.*

analyst /ˈænl̩ɪst/ *n.* analista *m.* & *f.*

analytic /ˌænl̩ˈɪtɪk/ *a.* analítico.

analyze /ˈænl̩ˌaiz/ *v.* analizar.

anarchy /ˈænərki/ *n.* anarquía *f.*

anatomy /əˈnætəmi/ *n.* anatomía *f.*

ancestor /ˈænsɛstər/ *n.* antepasado *m.*

ancestral /ænˈsɛstrəl/ *a.* de los antepasados, hereditario.

ancestry /ˈænsɛstri/ *n.* linaje, abolengo *m.*

anchor /ˈæŋkər/ *n.* **1.** ancla *f.* **weigh a.,** levar el ancla. —*v.* **2.** anclar.

anchorage /ˈæŋkərɪdʒ/ *n.* *Naut.* ancladero, anclaje *m.*

anchovy /ˈæntʃouvi/ *n.* anchoa *f.*

ancient /ˈeinʃənt/ *a.* & *n.* antiguo -ua.

and /ænd, ənd/ *conj.* y, (before *i-*, *hi-*) e.

anecdote /ˈænɪkˌdout/ *n.* anécdota *f.*

anemia /əˈnimiə/ *n.* *Med.* anemia *f.*

anesthetic /ˌænəsˈθɛtɪk/ *n.* anestesia *f.*

anew /əˈnu/ *adv.* de nuevo.

angel /ˈeindʒəl/ *n.* ángel *m.*

anger /ˈæŋgər/ *n.* **1.** ira *f.*, enojo *m.* —*v.* **2.** enfadar, enojar.

angle /ˈæŋgəl/ *n.* ángulo *m.*

angry /ˈæŋgri/ *a.* enojado, enfadado.

anguish /ˈæŋgwɪʃ/ *n.* angustia *f.*

angular /ˈæŋgyələr/ *a.* angular.

aniline /ˈænl̩ɪn/ *n.* *Chem.* anilina *f.*

animal /ˈænəməl/ *a.* & *n.* animal *m.*

animate /*v* ˈænəˌmeit; *a* -mɪt/ *v.* **1.** animar. —*a.* **2.** animado.

animated /ˈænəˌmeitɪd/ *a.* vivo, animado.

animation /ˌænəˈmeiʃən/ *n.* animación, viveza *f.*

animosity /ˌænəˈmɒsɪti/ *n.* rencor *m.*

anise /ˈænɪs/ *n.* anís *m.*

ankle /ˈæŋkəl/ *n.* tobillo *m.*

annals /ˈænl̩z/ *n.pl.* anales *m.pl.*

annex /*n* ˈænɛks; *v* əˈnɛks, ˈænɛks/ *n.* **1.** anexo *m.*, adición *f.* —*v.* **2.** anexar.

annexation /ˌænɪkˈseiʃən/ *n.* anexión, adición *f.*

annihilate /əˈnaiəˌleit/ *v.* aniquilar, destruir.

anniversary /ˌænəˈvɜrsəri/ *n.* aniversario *m.*

annotate /ˈænəˌteit/ *v.* anotar.

annotation /ˌænəˈteiʃən/ *n.* anotación *f.*, apunte *m.*

announce /əˈnauns/ *v.* anunciar.

announcement /əˈnaunsmənt/ *n.* anuncio, aviso *m.*

announcer /əˈnaunsər/ *n.* anunciador -ra; (radio) locutor -ra.

annoy /əˈnɔi/ *v.* molestar.

annoyance /əˈnɔiəns/ *n.* molestia, incomodidad *f.*

annual /ˈænyuəl/ *a.* anual.

annuity /əˈnuɪti/ *n.* anualidad, pensión *f.*

annul /əˈnʌl/ *v.* anular, invalidar.

anode /ˈænoud/ *n.* *Elec.* ánodo *m.*

anoint /əˈnɔint/ *v.* untar; *Relig.* ungir.

anomalous /əˈnɒmələs/ *a.* anómalo, irregular.

anonymous /əˈnɒnəməs/ *a.* anónimo.

anorexia /ˌænəˈrɛksiə/ *n.* anorexia *f.*

another /əˈnʌðər/ *a.* & *pron.* otro.

answer /ˈænsər, ˈɑn-/ *n.* **1.** contestación, respuesta *f.* —*v.* **2.** contestar, responder. **a. for,** ser responsable de.

answerable /ˈænsərəbəl/ *a.* discutible, refutable.

answering machine /ˈænsərɪŋ/ contestador automático *m.*

ant /ænt/ *n.* hormiga *f.*

antacid /æntˈæsɪd/ *a.* & *n.* antiácido *m.*

antagonism /ænˈtægəˌnɪzəm/ *n.* antagonismo *m.*

antagonist /ænˈtægənɪst/ *n.* antagonista *m.* & *f.*

antagonistic /ænˌtægəˈnɪstɪk/ *a.* antagónico, hostil.

antagonize /ænˈtægəˌnaiz/ *v.* contrariar.

antarctic /æntˈɑrktɪk/ *a.* & *n.* antártico *m.*

antecedent /ˌæntəˈsidn̩t/ *a.* & *n.* antecedente *m.*

antedate /ˈæntɪˌdeit/ *v.* antedatar.

antelope /ˈæntl̩ˌoup/ *n.* antílope *m.*, gacela *f.*

antenna /ænˈtɛnə/ *n.* antena *f.*

antepenultimate /ˌæntipɪˈnʌltəmɪt/ *a.* antepenúltimo.

anterior /ænˈtɪəriər/ *a.* anterior.

anteroom /ˈæntiˌrum/ *n.* antecámara *f.*

anthem /ˈænθəm/ *n.* himno *m.*; (religious) antífona *f.*

anthology /ænˈθɒlədʒi/ *n.* antología *f.*

anthracite /ˈænθrəˌsait/ *n.* antracita *f.*

anthrax /ˈænθræks/ *n.* *Med.* ántrax *m.*

anthropology /ˌænθrəˈpɒlədʒi/ *n.* antropología *f.*

antiaircraft /ˌæntiˈɛərˌkræft, ˌæntai-/ *a.* antiaéreo.

antibody /ˈæntɪˌbɒdi/ *n.* anticuerpo *m.*

anticipate /ænˈtɪsəˌpeit/ *v.* esperar, anticipar.

anticipation /ænˌtɪsəˈpeiʃən/ *n.* anticipación *f.*

anticlerical /ˌæntiˈklɛrɪkəl, ˌæntai-/ *a.* anticlerical.

anticlimax /ˌæntiˈklaimæks, ˌæntai-/ *n.* anticlímax *m.*

antidote /ˈæntɪˌdout/ *n.* antídoto *m.*

antifreeze /ˈæntɪˌfriz/ *n.* anticongelante *m.*

antihistamine /ˌæntiˈhɪstəˌmin, -mɪn, ˌæntai-/ *n.* antihistamínico *m.*

antimony /ˈæntəˌmouni/ *n.* antimonio *m.*

antinuclear /ˌæntiˈnukliər, æntai-/ *a.* antinuclear.

antipathy /ænˈtɪpəθi/ *n.* antipatía *f.*

antiquated /ˈæntɪˌkweitɪd/ *a.* anticuado.

antique /ænˈtik/ *a.* **1.** antiguo. —*n.* **2.** antigüedad *f.*

antiquity /ænˈtɪkwɪti/ *n.* antigüedad *f.*

antiseptic /ˌæntəˈsɛptɪk/ *a.* & *n.* antiséptico *m.*

antisocial /ˌæntiˈsouʃəl, ˌæntai-/ *a.* antisocial.

antitoxin /ˌæntɪ'tɒksɪn/ n. Med. antitoxina f.

antler /'æntlər/ n. asta f.

anvil /'ænvɪl/ n. yunque m.

anxiety /æŋ'zaɪɪti/ n. ansia, ansiedad f.

anxious /'æŋkʃəs, 'æŋʃəs/ a. inquieto, ansioso.

any /'ɛni/ a. alguno; (at all) cualquiera; (after not) ninguno.

anybody /'ɛni,bɒdi/ pron. alguien; (at all) cualquiera; (after not) nadie.

anyhow /'ɛni,haʊ/ adv. de todos modos; en todo caso.

anyone /'ɛni,wʌn/ pron. = anybody.

anything /'ɛni,θɪŋ/ pron. algo; (at all) cualquier cosa; (after not) nada.

anyway /'ɛni,weɪ/ adv. = anyhow.

anywhere /'ɛni,wɛər/ adv. en alguna parte; (at all) dondequiera; (after not) en ninguna parte.

apart /ə'part/ adv. aparte. **to take a.,** deshacer.

apartheid /ə'partheɪt, -haɪt/ n. apartheid m.

apartment /ə'partmənt/ n. apartamento, piso m.

apartment house casa de pisos f.

apathetic /ˌæpə'θɛtɪk/ a. apático.

apathy /'æpəθi/ n. apatía f.

ape /eɪp/ n. **1.** mono -na. —v. **2.** imitar.

aperture /'æpərtʃər/ n. abertura f.

apex /'eɪpɛks/ n. ápice m.

aphorism /'æfə,rɪzəm/ n. aforismo m.

apiary /'eɪpi,ɛri/ n. colmenario, abejar m.

apiece /ə'pis/ adv. por persona; cada uno.

apologetic /ə,pɒlə'dʒɛtɪk/ a. apologético.

apologist /ə'pɒlədʒɪst/ n. apologista m. & f.

apologize /ə'pɒlə,dʒaɪz/ v. excusarse, disculparse.

apology /ə'pɒlədʒi/ n. excusa; apología f.

apoplectic /ˌæpə'plɛktɪk/ a. apoplético.

apoplexy /'æpə,plɛksi/ n. apoplejía f.

apostate /ə'pɒsteɪt/ n. apóstata m. & f.

apostle /ə'pɒsəl/ n. apóstol m.

apostolic /ˌæpə'stɒlɪk/ a. apostólico.

appall /ə'pɔl/ v. horrorizar; consternar.

apparatus /ˌæpə'rætəs/ n. aparato m.

apparel /ə'pærəl/ n. ropa f.

apparent /ə'pærənt/ a. aparente; claro.

apparition /ˌæpə'rɪʃən/ n. aparición f.; fantasma m.

appeal /ə'pil/ n. **1.** súplica f.; interés m.; Leg. apelación f. —v. **2.** apelar, suplicar; interesar.

appear /ə'pɪər/ v. aparecer, asomar; (seem) parecer; Leg. comparecer.

appearance /ə'pɪərəns/ n. apariencia f., aspecto m.; aparición f.

appease /ə'piz/ v. aplacar, apaciguar.

appeasement /ə'pizmənt/ n. apaciguamiento m.

appeaser /ə'pizər/ n. apaciguador -ra, pacificador -ra.

appellant /ə'pɛlənt/ n. apelante, demandante m. & f.

appellate /ə'pɛlɪt/ a. Leg. de apelación.

appendage /ə'pɛndɪdʒ/ n. añadidura f.

appendectomy /ˌæpən'dɛktəmi/ n. apendectomía f.

appendicitis /ə,pɛndə'saɪtɪs/ n. apendicitis f.

appendix /ə'pɛndɪks/ n. apéndice m.

appetite /'æpɪ,taɪt/ n. apetito m.

appetizer /'æpɪ,taɪzər/ n. aperitivo m.

appetizing /'æpɪ,taɪzɪŋ/ a. apetitoso.

applaud /ə'plɔd/ v. aplaudir.

applause /ə'plɔz/ n. aplauso m.

apple /'æpəl/ n. manzana f. **a. tree,** manzano m.

applesauce /'æpəl,sɔs/ n. compota de manzana.

appliance /ə'plaɪəns/ n. aparato m.

applicable /'æplɪkəbəl/ a. aplicable.

applicant /'æplɪkənt/ n. suplicante m. & f.; candidato -ta.

application /ˌæplɪ'keɪʃən/ n. solicitud f., (computer) programa m.

applied /ə'plaɪd/ a. aplicado. **a. for,** pedido.

appliqué /ˌæplɪ'keɪ/ n. (sewing) aplicación f.

apply /ə'plaɪ/ v. aplicar. **a. for,** solicitar, pedir.

appoint /ə'pɔɪnt/ v. nombrar.

appointment /ə'pɔɪntmənt/ n. nombramiento m.; puesto m.

apportion /ə'pɔrʃən/ v. repartir.

apposition /ˌæpə'zɪʃən/ n. Gram. aposición f.

appraisal /ə'preɪzəl/ n. valoración f.

appraise /ə'preɪz/ v. evaluar; tasar; estimar.

appreciable /ə'priʃiəbəl/ a. apreciable; notable.

appreciate /ə'priʃi,eɪt/ v. apreciar, estimar.

appreciation /ə,priʃi'eɪʃən/ n. aprecio; reconocimiento m.

apprehend /ˌæprɪ'hɛnd/ v. prender, capturar.

apprehension /ˌæprɪ'hɛnʃən/ n. aprensión f.; detención f.

apprehensive /ˌæprɪ'hɛnsɪv/ a. aprensivo.

apprentice /ə'prɛntɪs/ n. aprendiz -iza.

apprenticeship /ə'prɛntɪs,ʃɪp/ n. aprendizaje m.

apprise /ə'praɪz/ v. informar.

approach /ə'proʊtʃ/ n. **1.** acceso; método m. —v. **2.** acercarse.

approachable /ə'proʊtʃəbəl/ a. accesible.

approbation /ˌæprə'beɪʃən/ n. aprobación f.

appropriate /a ə'proʊpriɪt; v -,eɪt/ a. **1.** apropiado. —v. **2.** apropiar.

appropriation /ə,proʊpri'eɪʃən/ n. apropiación f.

approval /ə'pruvəl/ n. aprobación f.

approve /ə'pruv/ v. aprobar.

approximate /a ə'prɒksəmɪt; v -,meɪt/ a. **1.** aproximado. —v. **2.** aproximar.

approximately /ə'prɒksəmɪtli/ adv. aproximadamente.

approximation /ə,prɒksə'meɪʃən/ n. aproximación f.

appurtenance /ə'pɜrtṇəns/ n. dependencia f.

apricot /'æprɪ,kɒt/ n. albaricoque, damasco m.

April /'eɪprəl/ n. abril m.

apron /'eɪprən/ n. delantal m.

apropos /ˌæprə'poʊ/ adv. a propósito.

apt /æpt/ a. apto; capaz.

aptitude /'æptɪ,tud/ n. aptitud; facilidad f.

aquarium /ə'kwɛəriəm/ n. acuario m., pecera f.

aquatic /ə'kwætɪk/ a. acuático.

aqueduct /'ækwɪ,dʌkt/ n. acueducto m.

aqueous /'ækwiəs/ a. ácueo, acuoso, aguoso.

aquiline /'ækwə,laɪn/ a. aquilino, aguileño.

Arab /'ærəb/ a. & n. árabe m. & f.

arable /'ærəbəl/ a. cultivable.

arbitrary /'arbɪ,trɛri/ a. arbitrario.

arbitrate /'arbɪ,treɪt/ v. arbitrar.

arbitration /ˌarbɪ'treɪʃən/ n. arbitraje m., arbitración f.

arbitrator /'arbɪ,treɪtər/ n. arbitrador m.

arbor /'arbər/ n. emparrado m.

arboreal /ar'bɔriəl/ a. arbóreo.

arc /ark/ n. arco m.

arch /artʃ/ n. **1.** arco m. —v. **2.** arquear, encorvar.

archaeology /ˌarki'ɒlədʒi/ n. arqueología f.

archaic /ar'keɪɪk/ a. arcaico.

archbishop /artʃ'bɪʃəp/ n. arzobispo m.

archdiocese /ˌartʃ'daɪə,sis, -sɪs/ n. archidiócesis f.

archduke /artʃ'duk/ n. archiduque m.

archer /'artʃər/ n. arquero m.

archery /'artʃəri/ n. ballestería f.

archipelago /ˌarkə'pɛlə,goʊ/ n. archipiélago m.

architect /'arkɪ,tɛkt/ n. arquitecto -ta.

architectural /ˌarkɪ'tɛktʃərəl/ a. arquitectural.

architecture /'arkɪ,tɛktʃər/ n. arquitectura f.

archive /'arkaɪv/ n. archivo m.

archway /'artʃ,weɪ/ n. arcada f.

arctic /'arktɪk, 'artɪk/ a. ártico.

ardent /'ardṇt/ a. ardiente.

ardor /'ardər/ n. ardor m., pasión f.

arduous /'ardʒuəs/ a. arduo, difícil.

area /'ɛəriə/ n. área; extensión f.

area code prefijo m.

arena /ə'rinə/ n. arena f.

argue /'argyu/ v. disputar; sostener.

argument /'argyəmənt/ n. disputa f.; razonamiento m.

argumentative /ˌargyə'mɛntətɪv/ a. argumentoso.

aria /'ariə/ n. aria f.

arid /'ærɪd/ a. árido, seco.

arise /ə'raɪz/ v. surgir; alzarse.

aristocracy /ˌærə'stɒkrəsi/ n. aristocracia f.

aristocrat /ə'rɪstə,kræt/ n. aristócrata m.

aristocratic /ə,rɪstə'krætɪk/ a. aristocrático.

arithmetic /ə'rɪθmətɪk/ n. aritmética f.

ark /ark/ n. arca f.

arm /arm/ n. **1.** brazo m.; (weapon) arma f. —v. **2.** armar.

armament /'arməmənt/ n. armamento m.

armchair /'arm,tʃɛər/ n. sillón m., butaca f.

armed forces /armd 'fɔrsɪz/ fuerzas militares.

armful /'arm,fʊl/ n. brazada f.

armhole /'arm,hoʊl/ n. (sew.) sobaquera f.

armistice /'arməstɪs/ n. armisticio m.

armor /'armər/ n. armadura f., blindaje m.

armored /'armərd/ a. blindado.

armory /'arməri/ n. armería f., arsenal m.

armpit /'arm,pɪt/ n. axila f., sobaco m.

army /'armi/ n. ejército m.

arnica /'arnɪkə/ n. árnica f.

aroma /ə'roʊmə/ n. fragancia f.

aromatic /ˌærə'mætɪk/ a. aromático.

around /ə'raʊnd/ prep. alrededor de, a la vuelta de; cerca de. **a. here,** por aquí.

arouse /ə'raʊz/ v. despertar; excitar.

arraign /ə'reɪn/ v. Leg. procesar criminalmente.

arrange /ə'reɪndʒ/ v. arreglar; concertar; Mus. adaptar.

arrangement /ə'reɪndʒmənt/ n. arreglo; orden m.

array /ə'reɪ/ n. **1.** orden; adorno m. —v. **2.** adornar.

arrears /ə'rɪərz/ n. atrasos m.pl.

arrest /ə'rɛst/ n. **1.** detención f. —v. **2.** detener, arrestar.

arrival /ə'raɪvəl/ n. llegada f.

arrive /ə'raɪv/ v. llegar.

arrogance /'ærəgəns/ n. arrogancia f.

arrogant /'ærəgənt/ a. arrogante.

arrogate /'ærə,geɪt/ v. arrogarse, usurpar.

arrow /'æroʊ/ n. flecha f.

arrowhead /'æroʊ,hɛd/ n. punta de flecha f.

arsenal /'arsənəl/ n. arsenal m.

arsenic /'arsənɪk/ n. arsénico m.

arson /'arsən/ n. incendio premeditado.

art /art/ arte m. (f. in pl.); (skill) maña f.

arterial /ar'tɪəriəl/ a. arterial.

arteriosclerosis /ar,tɪəriousklə-'rousɪs/ n. arteriosclerosis f.

artery /'artəri/ n. arteria f.

artesian well /ar'tiʒən/ pozo artesiano.

artful /'artfəl/ a. astuto.

arthritis /ar'θraɪtɪs/ n. artritis f.

artichoke /'artɪ,tʃoʊk/ n. alcachofa f.

article /'artɪkəl/ n. artículo m.

articulate /ar'tɪkyə,leɪt/ v. articular.

articulation /ar,tɪkyə'leɪʃən/ n. articulación f.

artifice /'artəfɪs/ n. artificio m.

artificial /ˌartə'fɪʃəl/ a. artificial.

artificially /ˌartə'fɪʃəli/ adv. artificialmente.

artillery /ar'tɪləri/ n. artillería f.

artisan /'artəzən/ n. artesano -na.

artist /'artɪst/ n. artista m. & f.

artistic /ar'tɪstɪk/ a. artístico.

artistry /'artɪstri/ n. arte m. & f.

artless /'artlɪs/ a. natural, cándido.

as /æz/ adv. & conj. como; **as... as** tan... como.

asbestos /æs'bɛstəs/ n. asbesto m.

ascend /ə'sɛnd/ v. ascender.

ascendancy /ə'sɛndənsi/ n. ascendiente m.

ascendant /ə'sɛndənt/ a. ascendente.

ascent /ə'sɛnt/ n. subida f., ascenso m.

ascertain /ˌæsər'teɪn/ v. averiguar.

ascetic /ə'sɛtɪk/ a. **1.** ascético. —n. **2.** asceta m. & f.

ascribe /ə'skraɪb/ v. atribuir.

ash /æʃ/ n. ceniza f.

ashamed /ə'ʃeɪmd/ a. avergonzado.

ashen /'æʃən/ a. pálido.

ashore /ə'ʃɔr/ adv. a tierra. **go a.,** desembarcar.

ashtray /'æʃ,treɪ/ n. cenicero m.

Ash Wednesday miércoles de ceniza m.

Asiatic /ˌeɪʒi'ætɪk/ a. & n. asiático -ca.

aside /ə'saɪd/ adv. al lado. **a. from,** aparte de.

ask /æsk/ v. preguntar; invitar; (request) pedir. **a. for,** pedir. **a. a question,** hacer una pregunta.

askance /ə'skæns/ adv. de soslayo; con recelo.

asleep /ə'slip/ a. dormido. **to fall a.,** dormirse.

asparagus /ə'spærəgəs/ n. espárrago m.

aspect /'æspɛkt/ n. aspecto m., apariencia f.

asperity /ə'spɛrɪti/ n. aspereza f.

aspersion /ə'spɜrʒən/ n. calumnia f.

asphalt /'æsfɔlt/ n. asfalto m.

asphyxia /æs'fɪksiə/ n. asfixia f.

asphyxiate /æs'fɪksi,eɪt/ v. asfixiar, sofocar.

aspirant /'æspərənt/ a. & n. aspirante m. & f.

aspirate /'æspə,reɪt/ v. aspirar.

aspiration /ˌæspə'reɪʃən/ n. aspiración f.

aspirator /'æspə,reɪtər/ n. aspirador m.

aspire /ə'spaɪər/ v. aspirar. **a. to,** ambicionar.

aspirin /'æspərɪn/ n. aspirina f.

ass /æs/ n. asno, burro m.

assail /ə'seɪl/ v. asaltar, acometer.

assailant /ə'seɪlənt/ n. asaltador -ra.

assassin /ə'sæsɪn/ n. asesino -na.

assassinate /ə'sæsə,neɪt/ v. asesinar.

assassination /ə,sæsə'neɪʃən/ n. asesinato m.

assault /ə'sɔlt/ n. **1.** asalto m. —v. **2.** asaltar, atacar.

assay /'æseɪ/ v. examinar; ensayar.

assemblage /ə'sɛmblɪdʒ/ n. asamblea f.

assemble /ə'sɛmbəl/ v. juntar, convocar; (mechanism) montar.

assembly /ə'sɛmbli/ *n.* asamblea, concurrencia *f.*

assent /ə'sɛnt/ *n.* **1.** asentimiento *m.* —*v.* **2.** asentir, convenir.

assert /ə'sɜrt/ *v.* afirmar, aseverar. **a. oneself,** hacerse sentir.

assertion /ə'sɜrʃən/ *n.* aserción, aseveración *f.*

assertive /ə'sɜrtɪv/ *a.* asertivo.

assess /ə'sɛs/ *v.* tasar, evaluar.

assessor /ə'sɛsər/ *n.* asesor -ra.

asset /'æsɛt/ *n.* ventaja *f.* **assets,** *Com.* capital *m.*

asseverate /ə'sɛvəˌreit/ *v.* aseverar, afirmar.

asseveration /əˌsɛvə'reiʃən/ *n.* aseveración *f.*

assiduous /ə'sɪdʒuəs/ *a.* asiduo.

assiduously /ə'sɪdʒuəsli/ *adv.* asiduamente.

assign /ə'sain/ *v.* asignar; destinar.

assignable /ə'sainəbəl/ *a.* asignable, transferible.

assignation /ˌæsɪg'neiʃən/ *n.* asignación *f.*

assignment /ə'sainmənt/ *n.* misión; tarea *f.*

assimilate /ə'sɪməˌleit/ *v.* asimilar.

assimilation /əˌsɪmə'leiʃən/ *n.* asimilación *f.*

assimilative /ə'sɪmələtɪv/ *a.* asimilativo.

assist /ə'sɪst/ *v.* ayudar, auxiliar.

assistance /ə'sɪstəns/ *n.* ayuda *f.*, auxilio *m.*

assistant /ə'sɪstənt/ *n.* ayudante -ta, asistente -ta.

associate /*n* ə'sousiɪt; *v* -siˌeit/ *n.* **1.** socio -cia. —*v.* **2.** asociar.

association /əˌsousi'eiʃən/ *n.* asociación; sociedad *f.*

assonance /'æsənəns/ *n.* asonancia *f.*

assort /ə'sɔrt/ *v.* surtir con variedad.

assorted /ə'sɔrtɪd/ *a.* variado, surtido.

assortment /ə'sɔrtmənt/ *n.* surtido *m.*

assuage /ə'sweidʒ/ *v.* mitigar, aliviar.

assume /ə'sum/ *v.* suponer; asumir.

assuming /ə'sumɪŋ/ *a.* presuntuoso. **a. that,** dado que.

assumption /ə'sʌmpʃən/ *n.* suposición; *Relig.* asunción *f.*

assurance /ə'ʃʊrəns/ *n.* seguridad; confianza *f.*; garantía *f.*

assure /ə'ʃʊr/ *v.* asegurar; dar confianza.

assured /ə'ʃʊrd/ *a.* **1.** seguro. —*a.* & *n.* **2.** *Com.* asegurado -da.

assuredly /ə'ʃʊrɪdli/ *adv.* ciertamente.

aster /'æstər/ *n.* aster *f.*

asterisk /'æstərɪsk/ *n.* asterisco *m.*

astern /ə'stɜrn/ *adv. Naut.* a popa.

asteroid /'æstəˌrɔid/ *n.* asteroide *m.*

asthma /'æzmə/ *n. Med.* asma *f.*

astigmatism /ə'stɪgməˌtɪzəm/ *n.* astigmatismo *m.*

astir /ə'stɜr/ *adv.* en movimiento.

astonish /ə'stɒnɪʃ/ *v.* asombrar, pasmar.

astonishment /ə'stɒnɪʃmənt/ *n.* asombro *m.*, sorpresa *f.*

astound /ə'staund/ *v.* pasmar, sorprender.

astral /'æstrəl/ *a.* astral, estelar.

astray /ə'strei/ *a.* desviado.

astride /ə'straid/ *adv.* a horcajadas.

astringent /ə'strɪndʒənt/ *a.* & *n.* astringente *m.*

astrology /ə'strɒlədʒi/ *n.* astrología *f.*

astronaut /'æstrəˌnɔt/ *n.* astronauta *m.* & *f.*

astronomy /ə'strɒnəmi/ *n.* astronomía *f.*

astute /ə'stut/ *a.* astuto; agudo.

asunder /ə'sʌndər/ *adv.* en dos.

asylum /ə'sailəm/ *n.* asilo, refugio *m.*

asymmetry /ei'sɪmɪtri/ *n.* asimetría *f.*

at /æt/ *prep.* a, en; cerca de.

ataxia /ə'tæksiə/ *n. Med.* ataxia *f.*

atheist /'eiθiɪst/ *n.* ateo -tea.

athlete /'æθlit/ *n.* atleta *m.* & *f.*

athletic /æθ'lɛtɪk/ *a.* atlético.

athletics /æθ'lɛtɪks/ *n.* atletismo *m.*, deportes *m.pl.*

athwart /ə'θwɔrt/ *prep.* a través de.

Atlantic /æt'læntɪk/ *a.* **1.** atlántico. —*n.* **2.** Atlántico *m.*

Atlantic Ocean Océano Atlántico *m.*

atlas /'ætləs/ *n.* atlas *m.*

atmosphere /'ætməsˌfɪər/ *n.* atmósfera *f.*; *Fig.* ambiente *m.*

atmospheric /ˌætməs'fɛrɪk/ *a.* atmosférico.

atoll /'ætɔl/ *n.* atolón *m.*

atom /'ætəm/ *n.* átomo *m.*

atomic /ə'tɒmɪk/ *a.* atómico.

atomic bomb bomba atómica *f.*

atomic energy energía atómica, energía nuclear *f.*

atomic theory teoría atómica. *f.*

atomic weight peso atómico *m.*

atonal /ei'tounl̩/ *a. Mus.* atonal.

atone /ə'toun/ *v.* expiar, compensar.

atonement /ə'tounmənt/ *n.* expiación; reparación *f.*

atrocious /ə'trouʃəs/ *a.* atroz.

atrocity /ə'trɒsɪti/ *n.* atrocidad *f.*

atrophy /'ætrəfi/ *n.* **1.** *Med.* atrofia *f.* —*v.* **2.** atrofiar.

atropine /'ætrəˌpin, -pɪn/ *n.* atropina *f.*

attach /ə'tætʃ/ *v.* juntar; prender; (hook) enganchar; *Fig.* atribuir.

attaché /ætæ'ʃei/ *n.* agregado -da.

attachment /ə'tætʃmənt/ enlace *m.*; accesorio *m.*; (emotional) afecto, cariño *m.*

attack /ə'tæk/ *n.* **1.** ataque *m.* —*v.* **2.** atacar.

attacker /ə'tækər/ *n.* asaltador -ra.

attain /ə'tein/ *v.* lograr, alcanzar.

attainable /ə'teinəbəl/ *a.* accesible, realizable.

attainment /ə'teinmənt/ *n.* logro; *(pl.)* dotes *f.pl.*

attempt /ə'tɛmpt/ *n.* **1.** ensayo; esfuerzo *m.*; tentativa *f.* —*v.* **2.** ensayar, intentar.

attend /ə'tɛnd/ *v.* atender; (a meeting) asistir a.

attendance /ə'tɛndəns/ *n.* asistencia; presencia *f.*

attendant /ə'tɛndənt/ *a.* **1.** concomitante. —*n.* **2.** servidor -ra.

attention /ə'tɛnʃən/ *n.* atención *f.*; obsequio *m.* **to pay a. to,** hacer caso a.

attentive /ə'tɛntɪv/ *a.* atento.

attentively /ə'tɛntɪvli/ *adv.* atentamente.

attenuate /ə'tɛnyuˌeit/ *v.* atenuar, adelgazar.

attest /ə'tɛst/ *v.* confirmar, atestiguar.

attic /'ætɪk/ *n.* desván *m.*, guardilla *f.*

attire /ə'taiᵊr/ *n.* **1.** traje *m.* —*v.* **2.** vestir.

attitude /'ætɪˌtud/ *n.* actitud *f.*, ademán *m.*

attorney /ə'tɜrni/ *n.* abogado -da, apoderado -da.

attract /ə'trækt/ *v.* atraer. **a. attention,** llamar la atención.

attraction /ə'trækʃən/ *n.* atracción *f.*, atractivo *m.*

attractive /ə'træktɪv/ *a.* atractivo; simpático.

attributable /ə'trɪbyʊtəbəl/ *a.* atribuible, imputable.

attribute /*n* 'ætrəˌbyut; *v* ə'trɪbyut/ *n.* **1.** atributo *m.* —*v.* **2.** atribuir.

attrition /ə'trɪʃən/ *n.* roce, desgaste *m.*; atrición *f.*

attune /ə'tun/ *v.* armonizar.

auction /'ɔkʃən/ *n.* subasta *f.*, *S.A.* venduta *f.*

auctioneer /ˌɔkʃə'nɪər/ *n.* subastador -ra, *S.A.* martillero -ra.

audacious /ɔ'deiʃəs/ *a.* audaz.

audacity /ɔ'dæsɪti/ *n.* audacia *f.*

audible /'ɔdəbəl/ *a.* audible.

audience /'ɔdiəns/ *n.* auditorio, público *m.*; entrevista *f.*

audiovisual /ˌɔdiou'vɪʒuəl/ *a.* audiovisual.

audit /'ɔdɪt/ *n.* **1.** revisión de cuentas *f.* —*v.* **2.** revisar cuentas.

audition /ɔ'dɪʃən/ *n.* audición *f.*

auditor /'ɔdɪtər/ *n.* interventor -ora, revisor -ora.

auditorium /ˌɔdɪ'tɔriəm/ *n.* sala *f.*; teatro *m.*

auditory /'ɔdɪˌtɔri/ *a.* & *n.* auditorio *m.*

augment /ɔg'mɛnt/ *v.* aumentar.

augur /'ɔgər/ *v.* augurar, pronosticar.

August /'ɔgəst/ *n.* agosto *m.*

aunt /ænt, ɑnt/ *n.* tía *f.*

auspice /'ɔspɪs/ *n.* auspicio *m.*

auspicious /ɔ'spɪʃəs/ *a.* favorable; propicio.

austere /ɔ'stɪər/ *a.* austero.

austerity /ɔ'stɛrɪti/ *n.* austeridad, severidad *f.*

Austrian /'ɔstriən/ *a.* & *n.* austríaco -ca.

authentic /ɔ'θɛntɪk/ *a.* auténtico.

authenticate /ɔ'θɛntɪˌkeit/ *v.* autenticar.

authenticity /ˌɔθɛn'tɪsɪti/ *n.* autenticidad *f.*

author /'ɔθər/ *n.* autor -ra, escritor -ra.

authoritarian /əˌθɔrɪ'tɛəriən/ *a.* & *n.* autoritario -ria.

authoritative /ə'θɔrɪˌteitɪv/ *a.* autoritativo; autorizado.

authoritatively /ə'θɔrɪˌteitɪvli/ *adv.* autoritativamente.

authority /ə'θɔrɪti/ *n.* autoridad *f.*

authorization /ˌɔθərə'zeiʃən/ *n.* autorización *f.*

authorize /'ɔθəˌraiz/ *v.* autorizar.

auto /'ɔtou/ *n.* auto, automóvil *m.*

autobiography /ˌɔtəbai'ɒgrəfi/ *n.* autobiografía *f.*

autocracy /ɔ'tɒkrəsi/ *n.* autocracia *f.*

autocrat /'ɔtəˌkræt/ *n.* autócrata *m.* & *f.*

autograph /'ɔtəˌgræf/ *n.* autógrafo *m.*

automatic /ˌɔtə'mætɪk/ *a.* automático.

automatically /ˌɔtə'mætɪkəli/ *adv.* automáticamente.

automobile /ˌɔtəmə'bil/ *n.* automóvil, coche *m.*

automotive /ˌɔtə'moutɪv/ *a.* automotriz.

autonomy /ɔ'tɒnəmi/ *n.* autonomía *f.*

autopsy /'ɔtɒpsi/ *n.* autopsia *f.*

autumn /'ɔtəm/ *n.* otoño *m.*

auxiliary /ɔg'zɪlyəri/ *a.* auxiliar.

avail /ə'veil/ *n.* **1. of no a.,** en vano. —*v.* **2. a. oneself of,** aprovecharse.

available /ə'veiləbəl/ *a.* disponible.

avalanche /'ævəˌlæntʃ/ *n.* alud *m.*

avarice /'ævərɪs/ *n.* avaricia, codicia *f.*

avariciously /ˌævə'rɪʃəsli/ *adv.* avaramente.

avenge /ə'vɛndʒ/ *v.* vengar.

avenger /ə'vɛndʒər/ *n.* vengador -ra.

avenue /'ævəˌnu/ *n.* avenida *f.*

average /'ævərɪdʒ/ *a.* **1.** medio; común. —*n.* **2.** promedio, término medio *m.* —*v.* **3.** calcular el promedio.

averse /ə'vɜrs/ *a.* **to be a. to,** tener antipatía a, opuesto a.

aversion /ə'vɜrʒən/ *n.* aversión *f.*

avert /ə'vɜrt/ *v.* desviar; impedir.

aviary /'eiviˌɛri/ *n.* pajarera, avería *f.*

aviation /ˌeivi'eiʃən/ *n.* aviación *f.*

aviator /'eiviˌeitər/ *n.* aviador -ra.

aviatrix /ˌeivi'eitrɪks/ *n.* aviatriz *f.*

avid /'ævɪd/ *a.* ávido.

avocado /ˌævə'kɑdou, ˌɑvə-/ *n.* aguacate *m.*

avocation /ˌævə'keiʃən/ *n.* pasatiempo *f.*

avoid /ə'vɔid/ *v.* evitar.

avoidable /ə'vɔidəbəl/ *a.* evitable.

avoidance /ə'vɔidn̩s/ *n.* evitación *f.*; *Leg.* anulación *f.*

avow /ə'vau/ *v.* declarar; admitir.

avowal /ə'vauəl/ *n.* admisión *f.*

avowed /ə'vaud/ *a.* reconocido; admitido.

avowedly /ə'vauɪdli/ *adv.* reconocidamente; confesadamente.

await /ə'weit/ *v.* esperar, aguardar.

awake /ə'weik/ *a.* despierto.

awaken /ə'weikən/ *v.* despertar.

award /ə'wɔrd/ *n.* **1.** premio *m.* —*v.* **2.** otorgar.

aware /ə'wɛər/ *a.* enterado, consciente.

awash /ə'wɒʃ/ *a.* & *adv. Naut.* a flor de agua.

away /ə'wei/ *adv.* (see under verb: **go away, put away, take away,** etc.)

awe /ɔ/ *n.* pavor *m.*

awesome /'ɔsəm/ *a.* pavoroso; aterrador.

awful /'ɔfəl/ *a.* horrible, terrible, muy malo, pésimo.

awhile /ə'wail/ *adv.* por un rato.

awkward /'ɔkwərd/ *a.* torpe, desmañado; *Fig.* delicado, embarazoso.

awning /'ɔnɪŋ/ *n.* toldo *m.*

awry /ə'rai/ *a.* oblicuo, torcido.

ax /æks/ *n.* hacha *f.*

axiom /'æksiəm/ *n.* axioma *m.*

axis /'æksɪs/ *n.* eje *m.*

axle /'æksəl/ *n.* eje *m.*

ayatollah /ˌɑyə'toulə/ *n.* ayatolá *m.*

azure /'æʒər/ *a.* azul.

B

babble /'bæbəl/ *n.* **1.** balbuceo, murmullo *m.* —*v.* **2.** balbucear.

babbler /'bæblər/ *n.* hablador -ra, charlador -ra.

baboon /bæ'bun/ *n.* mandril *m.*

baby /'beibi/ *n.* nene, bebé *m.*

baby carriage cochecito de niño *m.*

babyish /'beibiɪʃ/ *a.* infantil.

baby squid /skwɪd/ chipirón *m.*

bachelor /'bætʃələr/ *n.* soltero *m.*

bacillus /bə'sɪləs/ *n.* bacilo, microbio *m.*

back /bæk/ *adv.* **1.** atrás. **to be b.,** estar de vuelta. **b. of,** detrás de. —*n.* **2.** espalda *f.*; (of animal) lomo *m.*

backache /'bækˌeik/ *n.* dolor de espalda *m.*

backbone /'bækˌboun/ *n.* espinazo *m.*; *Fig.* firmeza *f.*

backer /'bækər/ *n.* sostenedor -ra.

background /'bækˌgraund/ *n.* fondo *m.* antecedentes *m.pl.*

backing /'bækɪŋ/ *n.* apoyo *m.*, garantía *f.*

backlash /'bækˌlæʃ/ *n.* repercusión negativa.

backlog /'bækˌlɔg/ *n.* atrasos *m.pl.*

backpack /'bækˌpæk/ *n.* mochila *f.*

back seat asiento trasero *m.*

backstage /'bæk'steidʒ/ *n.* entre bastidores *m.*

backup /'bækˌʌp/ *n.* copia de seguridad *f.*

backward /'bækwərd/ *a.* **1.** atrasado. —*adv.* **2.** hacia atrás.

backwardness /'bækwərdnɪs/ *n.* atraso *m.*

backwater /'bækˌwɔtər/ *n.* parte de río estancada *f.*

backwoods /'bæk'wʊdz/ *n.* región del monte apartada *f.*

bacon /'beikən/ *n.* tocino *m.*

bacteria /bæk'tɪəriə/ *n.* bacterias *f.pl.*

bacteriologist /ˌbæktɪəri'ɒlədʒɪst/ *n.* bacteriólogo -a.

bacteriology /ˌbæktɪəri'ɒlədʒi/ *n.* bacteriología *f.*

bad /bæd/ *a.* malo.

badge /bædʒ/ *n.* insignia, divisa *f.*

badger /'bædʒər/ *n.* **1.** tejón *m.* —*v.* **2.** atormentar.

badly /'bædli/ *adv.* mal.

badness /'bædnɪs/ *n.* maldad *f.*

bad-tempered /'bæd'tɛmpərd/ *a.* de mal humor.

baffle /'bæfəl/ *v.* desconcertar.

bafflement /'bæfəlmənt/ *n.* contrariedad; confusión *f.*

bag /bæg/ *n.* **1.** saco *m.;* bolsa *f.* **—***v.* **2.** ensacar, cazar.

baggage /ˈbægɪdʒ/ *n.* equipaje *m.* **b. check,** talón *m.*

baggage cart (airport) carrillo para llevar equipaje.

baggy /ˈbægi/ *a.* abotagado; bolsudo; hinchado.

bagpipe /ˈbægˌpaip/ *n.* gaita *f.*

bail /beil/ *n.* **1.** fianza *f.* **—***v.* **2.** desaguar.

bailiff /ˈbeilɪf/ *n.* alguacil *m.*

bait /beit/ *n.* **1.** cebo *m.* **—***v.* **2.** cebar.

bake /beik/ *v.* cocer en horno.

baked potato /beikt/ patata asada *f.*

baker /ˈbeikər/ *n.* panadero -ra, hornero -ra.

bakery /ˈbeikəri, ˈbeikri/ *n.* panadería *f.*

baking /ˈbeikɪŋ/ *n.* hornada *f.* **b. powder,** levadura *f.*

balance /ˈbæləns/ *n.* balanza *f.;* equilibrio *m.; Com.* saldo *m.*

balcony /ˈbælkəni/ *n.* balcón *m.; Theat.* galería *f.*

bald /bɔld/ *a.* calvo.

baldness /ˈbɔldnɪs/ *n.* calvicie *f.*

bale /beil/ *n.* **1.** bala *f.* **—***v.* **2.** embalar.

balk /bɔk/ *v.* frustrar; rebelarse.

Balkans /ˈbɔlkənz/ *n.pl.* Balcanes *m.pl.*

balky /ˈbɔki/ *a.* rebelón.

ball /bɔl/ *n.* bola, pelota *f.;* (dance) baile *m.*

ballad /ˈbæləd/ *n.* romance, *m.;* balada *f.*

ballast /ˈbæləst/ *n.* **1.** lastre *m.* **—***v.* **2.** lastrar.

ball bearing cojinete de bolas *m.*

ballerina /ˌbæləˈrinə/ *n.* bailarina *f.*

ballet /bæˈlei/ *n.* danza *f.;* ballet *m.*

ballistics /bəˈlɪstɪks/ *n.* balística *f.*

balloon /bəˈlun/ *n.* globo *m.* **b. tire,** neumático de balón.

ballot /ˈbælət/ *n.* **1.** balota *f.,* voto *m.* **—***v.* **2.** balotar, votar.

ballpoint pen /ˈbɔlˌpɔint/ bolígrafo *m.*

ballroom /ˈbɔlˌrum/ *n.* salón de baile *m.*

balm /bɑm/ *n.* bálsamo; ungüento *m.*

balmy /ˈbɑmi/ *a.* fragante; reparador; calmante.

balsa /ˈbɔlsə/ *n.* balsa *f.*

balsam /ˈbɔlsəm/ *n.* bálsamo *m.*

balustrade /ˈbæləˌstreid/ *n.* barandilla *f.*

bamboo /bæmˈbu/ *n.* bambú *m.,* caña *f.*

ban /bɑn/ *n.* **1.** prohibición *f.* **—***v.* **2.** prohibir; proscribir.

banal /bəˈnæl/ *a.* trivial; vulgar.

banana /bəˈnænə/ *n.* banana *f.,* cambur *m.* **b. tree,** banano, plátano *m.*

band /bænd/ *n.* **1.** banda *f.;* (of men) banda, cuadrilla, partida *f.* **—***v.* **2.** asociarse.

bandage /ˈbændɪdʒ/ *n.* **1.** vendaje *m.* **—***v.* **2.** vendar.

bandanna /bænˈdænə/ *n.* pañuelo (grande) *m.;* bandana *f.*

bandbox /ˈbændˌbɒks/ *n.* caja de cartón.

bandit /ˈbændɪt/ *n.* bandido -da.

bandmaster /ˈbændˌmæstər/ *n.* director de una banda musical *m.*

bandstand /ˈbændˌstænd/ *n.* kiosco de música.

bang /bæŋ/ *interj.* **1.** ¡pum! **—***n.* **2.** ruido de un golpe. **—***v.* **3.** golpear ruidosamente.

banish /ˈbænɪʃ/ *v.* desterrar.

banishment /ˈbænɪʃmənt/ *n.* destierro *m.*

banister /ˈbænəstər/ *n.* pasamanos *m.pl.*

bank /bæŋk/ *n.* **1.** banco *m.;* (of a river) margen *f.* **—***v.* **2.** depositar.

bank account cuenta bancaria *f.*

bankbook /ˈbæŋkˌbʊk/ *n.* libreta de depósitos *f.*

bank card tarjeta bancaria *f.*

banker /ˈbæŋkər/ *n.* banquero -ra.

banking /ˈbæŋkɪŋ/ *a.* bancaria. *n.* banca *f.*

bank note billete de banco *m.*

bankrupt /ˈbæŋkrʌpt/ *a.* insolvente.

bankruptcy /ˈbæŋkrʌptsi/ *n.* bancarrota *f.*

banner /ˈbænər/ *n.* bandera *f.;* estandarte *m.*

banquet /ˈbæŋkwɪt/ *n.* banquete *m.*

banter /ˈbæntər/ *n.* **1.** choteo *m.;* zumba; burla *f.* **—***v.* **2.** chotear; zumbar; burlarse.

baptism /ˈbæptɪzəm/ *n.* bautismo, bautizo *m.*

baptismal /bæpˈtɪzməl/ *a.* bautismal.

Baptist /ˈbæptɪst/ *n.* bautista *m.* & *f.*

baptize /bæpˈtaiz, ˈbæptaiz/ *v.* bautizar.

bar /bɑr/ *n.* **1.** barra *f.;* obstáculo *m.;* (tavern) taberna *f.,* bar *m.* **—***v.* **2.** barrear; prohibir, excluir.

barbarian /bɑrˈbɛəriən/ *a.* bárbaro. *n.* bárbaro -ra.

barbarism /ˈbɑrbəˌrɪzəm/ *n.* barbarismo *m.,* barbarie *f.*

barbarous /ˈbɑrbərəs/ *a.* bárbaro, cruel.

barbecue /ˈbɑrbɪˌkyu/ *n.* animal asado entero; (Mex.) barbacoa *f.*

barber /ˈbɑrbər/ *n.* barbero *m.* **b. shop,** barbería *f.*

barbiturate /bɑrˈbɪtʃərɪt/ *n.* barbitúrico *m.*

bar code código de barras *m.*

bare /bɛər/ *a.* **1.** desnudo; descubierto. **—***v.* **2.** desnudar; descubrir.

bareback /ˈbɛərˌbæk/ *adv.* sin silla.

barefoot(ed) /ˈbɛərˌfʊtɪd/ *a.* descalzo.

barely /ˈbɛərli/ *adv.* escasamente, apenas.

bareness /ˈbɛərnɪs/ *n.* desnudez *f.;* pobreza *f.*

bargain /ˈbɑrgən/ *n.* **1.** ganga *f.,* compra ventajosa *f.;* contrato *m.* **—***v.* **2.** regatear; negociar.

barge /bɑrdʒ/ *n.* lanchón *m.,* barcaza *f.*

baritone /ˈbærɪˌtoun/ *n.* barítono *m.*

barium /ˈbɛəriəm/ *n.* bario *m.*

bark /bɑrk/ *n.* **1.** corteza *f.;* (of dog) ladrido *f.* **—***v.* **2.** ladrar.

barley /ˈbɑrli/ *n.* cebada *f.*

barn /bɑrn/ *n.* granero *m.*

barnacle /ˈbɑrnəkəl/ *n.* lapa *f.*

barnyard /ˈbɑrnˌyɑrd/ *n.* corral *m.*

barometer /bəˈrɒmɪtər/ *n.* barómetro *m.*

barometric /ˌbærəˈmɛtrɪk/ *a.* barométrico.

baron /ˈbærən/ *n.* barón *m.*

baroness /ˈbærənɪs/ *n.* baronesa *f.*

baronial /bəˈrouniəl/ *a.* baronial.

baroque /bəˈrouk/ *a.* barroco.

barracks /ˈbærəks/ *n.* cuartel *m.*

barrage /bəˈrɑʒ/ *n.* cortina de fuego *f.*

barred /bɑrd/ *a.* excluído; prohibido.

barrel /ˈbærəl/ *n.* barril *m.;* (of gun) cañón *m.*

barren /ˈbærən/ *a.* estéril.

barrenness /ˈbærənˌnɪs/ *n.* esterilidad *f.*

barricade /ˈbærɪˌkeid/ *n.* barricada, barrera *f.*

barrier /ˈbæriər/ *n.* barrera *f.;* obstáculo *m.*

barroom /ˈbɑrˌrum, -ˌrʊm/ *n.* cantina *f.*

bartender /ˈbɑrˌtɛndər/ *n.* tabernero; cantinero *m.*

barter /ˈbɑrtər/ *n.* **1.** cambio, trueque *m.* **—***v.* **2.** cambiar, trocar.

base /beis/ *a.* **1.** bajo, vil. **—***n.* **2.** base *f.* **—***v.* **3.** basar.

baseball /ˈbeisˌbɔl/ *n.* béisbol *m.*

baseboard /ˈbeisˌbɔrd/ *n.* tabla de resguardo.

basement /ˈbeismənt/ *n.* sótano *m.*

baseness /ˈbeisnɪs/ *n.* bajeza, vileza *f.*

bashful /ˈbæʃfəl/ *a.* vergonzoso, tímido.

bashfully /ˈbæʃfəli/ *adv.* tímidamente; vergonzosamente.

bashfulness /ˈbæʃfəlnɪs/ *n.* vergüenza; timidez *f.*

basic /ˈbeisɪk/ *a.* fundamental, básico.

basin /ˈbeisən/ *n.* bacía *f.;* (of river) cuenca *f.*

basis /ˈbeisɪs/ *n.* base *f.*

bask /bæsk/ *v.* tomar el sol.

basket /ˈbæskɪt/ *n.* cesta, canasta *f.*

bass /bæs; beis/ *n.* (fish) lobina *f.; Mus.* bajo profundo *m.* **b. viol.** violón *m.*

bassinet /ˌbæsəˈnɛt/ *n.* bacinete *m.*

bassoon /bæˈsun/ *n.* bajón *m.*

bastard /ˈbæstərd/ *a.* & *n.* bastardo -da; hijo -a natural.

baste /beist/ *v.* (sew) bastear; (cooking) pringar.

bat /bæt/ *n.* **1.** (animal) murciélago *m.;* (baseball) bate *m.* **—***v.* **2.** batear.

batch /bætʃ/ *n.* cantidad de cosas.

bath /bæθ/ *n.* baño *m.*

bathe /beið/ *v.* bañar, bañarse.

bather /ˈbeiðər/ *n.* bañista *m.* & *f.*

bathing resort /ˈbeiðɪŋ/ balneario *m.*

bathing suit /ˈbeiðɪŋ/ traje de baño.

bathrobe /ˈbæθˌroub/ *n.* bata de baño *f.*

bathroom /ˈbæθˌrum, -ˌrʊm/ *n.* cuarto de baño.

bathtub /ˈbæθˌtʌb/ *n.* bañera *f.*

baton /bəˈtɒn/ *n.* bastón *m.; Mus.* batuta *f.*

battalion /bəˈtælyən/ *n.* batallón *m.*

batter /ˈbætər/ *n.* **1.** (cooking) batido *m.;* (baseball) voleador *m.* **—***v.* **2.** batir; derribar.

battery /ˈbætəri/ *n.* batería; *Elec.* pila *f.*

batting /ˈbætɪŋ/ *n.* agramaje, moldeaje *m.*

battle /ˈbætl̩/ *n.* **1.** batalla *f.;* combate *m.* **—***v.* **2.** batallar.

battlefield /ˈbætl̩ˌfild/ *n.* campo de batalla.

battleship /ˈbætl̩ˌʃɪp/ *n.* acorazado *m.*

bauxite /ˈbɔksait, ˈbouzait/ *n.* bauxita *f.*

bawl /bɔl/ *v.* gritar; vocear.

bay /bei/ *n.* bahía *f.* *v.* aullar.

bayonet /ˈbeiənɛt/ *n.* bayoneta *f.*

bazaar /bəˈzɑr/ *n.* bazar *m.,* feria *f.*

BC *abbr.* (**before Christ**) a.C. (antes de Cristo).

be /bi/ *v.* ser; estar. (See **hacer; hay; tener** in Sp.-Eng. section.)

beach /bitʃ/ *n.* playa *f.*

beachcomber /ˈbitʃˌkoumər/ *n.* raquero -ra *m.* & *f.*

beacon /ˈbikən/ *n.* faro *m.*

bead /bid/ *n.* cuenta *f.; pl. Relig.* rosario *m.*

beading /ˈbidɪŋ/ *n.* abalorio *m.*

beady /ˈbidi/ *a.* globuloso; burbujoso.

beak /bik/ *n.* pico *m.*

beaker /ˈbikər/ *n.* vaso con pico *m.*

beam /bim/ *n.* viga *f.;* (of wood) madero *m.;* (of light) rayo *m.*

beaming /ˈbimɪŋ/ *a.* radiante.

bean /bin/ *n.* haba, habichuela *f.,* frijol *m.*

bear /bɛər/ *n.* **1.** oso -sa. **—***v.* **2.** llevar; (endure) aguantar.

bearable /ˈbɛərəbəl/ *a.* sufrible; soportable.

beard /bɪərd/ *n.* barba *f.*

bearded /ˈbɪərdɪd/ *a.* barbado; barbudo.

beardless /ˈbɪərdlɪs/ *a.* lampiño; imberbe.

bearer /ˈbɛərər/ *n.* portador -ra.

bearing /ˈbɛərɪŋ/ *n.* porte, aguante *m.*

bearskin /ˈbɛərˌskɪn/ *n.* piel de oso *f.*

beast /bist/ *n.* bestia *f.;* bruto -ta.

beat /bit/ *v.* golpear; batir; pulsar; (in games) ganar, vencer.

beaten /ˈbitn̩/ *a.* vencido; batido.

beatify /biˈætəˌfai/ *v.* beatificar.

beating /ˈbitɪŋ/ *n.* paliza *f.*

beau /bou/ *n.* novio *m.*

beautiful /ˈbyutəfəl/ *a.* hermoso, bello.

beautifully /ˈbyutəfəli/ *adv.* bellamente.

beautify /ˈbyutəˌfai/ *v.* embellecer.

beauty /ˈbyuti/ *n.* hermosura, belleza *f.* **b. parlor,** salón de belleza.

beaver /ˈbivər/ *n.* castor *m.*

becalm /bɪˈkɑm/ *v.* calmar; sosegar; encalmarse.

because /bɪˈkɔz/ *conj.* porque. **b. of,** a causa de.

beckon /ˈbɛkən/ *v.* hacer señas.

become /bɪˈkʌm/ *v.* hacerse; ponerse.

becoming /bɪˈkʌmɪŋ/ *a.* propio, correcto; **be b.,** quedar bien, sentar bien.

bed /bɛd/ *n.* cama *f.;* lecho *m.;* (of river) cauce *m.*

bedbug /ˈbɛdˌbʌg/ *n.* chinche *m.*

bedclothes /ˈbɛdˌklouz, -ˌklouðz/ *n.* ropa de cama *f.*

bedding /ˈbɛdɪŋ/ *n.* colchones *m.pl.*

bedfellow /ˈbɛdˌfɛlou/ *n.* compañero -ra de cama.

bedizen /bɪˈdaizən, -ˈdɪzən/ *v.* adornar; aderezar.

bedridden /ˈbɛdˌrɪdn̩/ *a.* postrado (en cama).

bedrock /ˈbɛdˌrɒk/ *n.* (mining) lecho de roca *m.; Fig.* fundamento *m.*

bedroom /ˈbɛdˌrum/ *n.* alcoba *f.;* (Mex.) recámara *f.*

bedside /ˈbɛdˌsaid/ *n.* al lado de una cama *m.*

bedspread /ˈbɛdˌsprɛd/ *n.* cubrecama, sobrecama *f.*

bedstead /ˈbɛdˌstɛd/ *n.* armadura de cama *f.*

bedtime /ˈbɛdˌtaim/ *n.* hora de acostarse.

bee /bi/ *n.* abeja *f.*

beef /bif/ *n.* carne de vaca.

beefburger /ˈbifˌbɜrgər/ *n.* hamburguesa *f.*

beefsteak /ˈbifˌsteik/ *n.* bistec, bisté *m.*

beehive /ˈbiˌhaiv/ *n.* colmena *f.*

beer /bɪər/ *n.* cerveza *f.*

beeswax /ˈbizˌwæks/ *n.* cera de abejas.

beet /bit/ *n.* remolacha *f.;* (Mex.) betabel *m.*

beetle /ˈbitl̩/ *n.* escarabajo *m.*

befall /bɪˈfɔl/ *v.* suceder, sobrevenir.

befitting /bɪˈfɪtɪŋ/ *a.* conveniente; propio; digno.

before /bɪˈfɔr/ *adv.* antes. *prep.* antes de; (in front of) delante de. *conj.* antes que.

beforehand /bɪˈfɔrˌhænd/ *adv.* de antemano.

befriend /bɪˈfrɛnd/ *v.* amparar.

befuddle /bɪˈfʌdl̩/ *v.* confundir; aturdir.

beg /bɛg/ *v.* rogar, suplicar; (for alms) mendigar.

beget /bɪˈgɛt/ *v.* engendrar; producir.

beggar /ˈbɛgər/ *n.* mendigo -ga; *S.A.* limosnero -ra.

beggarly /ˈbɛgərli/ *a.* pobre, miserable.

begin /bɪˈgɪn/ *v.* empezar, comenzar, principiar.

beginner /bɪˈgɪnər/ *n.* principiante -ta.

beginning /bɪˈgɪnɪŋ/ *n.* principio, comienzo *m.*

begrudge /bɪˈgrʌdʒ/ *v.* envidiar.

behalf /bɪˈhæf/ *n.:* **in, on b. of,** a favor de, en pro de.

behave /bɪˈheiv/ *v.* portarse, comportarse.

behavior /bɪˈheivyər/ *n.* conducta *f.;* comportamiento *m.*

behead /bɪˈhɛd/ *v.* decapitar.

behind /bɪˈhaind/ *adv.* atrás, detrás. *prep.* detrás de.

behold /bɪˈhould/ *v.* contemplar.

beige /beiʒ/ *a.* beige.

being /ˈbiɪŋ/ *n.* existencia *f.;* (person) ser *m.*

bejewel /bɪ'dʒuəl/ v. adornar con joyas.
belated /bɪ'leitɪd/ a. atrasado, tardío.
belch /bɛltʃ/ n. **1.** eructo m. —v. **2.** vomitar; eructar.
belfry /'bɛlfri/ n. campanario m.
Belgian /'bɛldʒən/ a. & n. belga m. & f.
Belgium /'bɛldʒəm/ n. Bélgica f.
belie /bɪ'lai/ v. desmentir.
belief /bɪ'lif/ n. creencia f.; parecer m.
believable /bɪ'livəbəl/ a. creíble.
believe /bɪ'liv/ v. creer.
believer /bɪ'livər/ n. creyente m. & f.
belittle /bɪ'lɪtl/ v. dar poca importancia a.
bell /bɛl/ n. campana f.; (of house) campanilla f.; (electric) timbre m.
bellboy /'bɛl,bɔi/ n. mozo, botones m.
bellicose /'bɛlɪ,kous/ a. guerrero.
belligerence /bə'lɪdʒərəns/ n. beligerancia f.
belligerent /bə'lɪdʒərənt/ a. & n. beligerante m. & f.
belligerently /bə'lɪdʒərəntli/ adv. belicosamente.
bellow /'bɛlou/ v. bramar, rugir.
bellows /'bɛlouz/ n. fuelle m.
belly /'bɛli/ n. vientre m.; panza, barriga f.
belong /bɪ'lɔŋ/ v. pertenecer.
belongings /bɪ'lɔŋɪŋz/ n. propiedad f.
beloved /bɪ'lʌvɪd/ a. querido, amado.
below /bɪ'lou/ adv. **1.** debajo, abajo. —prep. **2.** debajo de.
belt /bɛlt/ n. cinturón m.
bench /bɛntʃ/ n. banco m.
bend /bɛnd/ n. vuelta; curva f. v. encorvar, doblar.
beneath /bɪ'niθ/ adv. **1.** debajo, abajo. —prep. **2.** debajo de.
benediction /,bɛnɪ'dɪkʃən/ n. bendición f.
benefactor /'bɛnə,fæktər/ n. bienhechor -ra.
benefactress /'bɛnə,fæktrɪs/ n. bienhechora f.
beneficial /,bɛnə'fɪʃəl/ a. provechoso, beneficioso.
beneficiary /,bɛnə'fɪʃi,ɛri/ n. beneficiario -ria, beneficiado -da.
benefit /'bɛnəfɪt/ n. **1.** provecho, beneficio m. —v. **2.** beneficiar.
benevolence /bə'nɛvələns/ n. benevolencia f.
benevolent /bə'nɛvələnt/ a. benévolo.
benevolently /bə'nɛvələntli/ adv. benignamente.
benign /bɪ'nain/ bɪ'nɪgnənt/ a. benigno.
benignity /bɪ'nɪgnɪti/ n. benignidad; bondad f.
bent /bɛnt/ a. **1.** encorvado. **b. on**, resuelto a. —n. **2.** inclinación f.
benzene /'bɛnzin, bɛn'zin/ n. benceno m.
bequeath /bɪ'kwið/ v. legar.
bequest /bɪ'kwɛst/ n. legado m.
berate /bɪ'reit/ v. reñir, regañar.
bereave /bɪ'riv/ v. despojar; desolar.
bereavement /bɪ'rivmənt/ n. privación f.; despojo m.; (mourning) luto m.
berry /'bɛri/ n. baya f.
berth /bɜrθ/ n. camarote m.; Naut. litera f.; (for vessel) amarradero m.
beseech /bɪ'sitʃ/ v. suplicar; implorar.
beseechingly /bɪ'sitʃɪŋli/ adv. suplicantemente.
beset /bɪ'sɛt/ v. acosar; rodear.
beside /bɪ'said/ prep. al lado de.
besides /bɪ'saidz/ adv. además, por otra parte.
besiege /bɪ'sidʒ/ v. sitiar; asediar.
besieged /bɪ'sidʒd/ a. sitiado.
besieger /bɪ'sidʒər/ n. sitiador -ra.
besmirch /bɪ'smɜrtʃ/ v. manchar; deshonrar.
best /bɛst/ a. & adv. mejor. **at b.,** a lo más.

bestial /'bɛstʃəl/ a. bestial; brutal.
bestir /bɪ'stɜr/ v. incitar; intrigar.
best man n. padrino de boda.
bestow /bɪ'stou/ v. conferir.
bestowal /bɪ'stouəl/ n. dádiva; presentación f.
bet /bɛt/ n. **1.** apuesta f. —v. **2.** apostar.
betoken /bɪ'toukən/ v. presagiar, anunciar.
betray /bɪ'trei/ v. traicionar; revelar.
betrayal /bɪ'treiəl/ n. traición f.
betroth /bɪ'trouð/ v. contraer esponsales; prometerse.
betrothal /bɪ'trouðəl/ n. esponsales m.pl.
better /'bɛtər/ a. & adv. **1.** mejor. —v. **2.** mejorar.
between /bɪ'twin/ prep. entre, en medio de.
bevel /'bɛvəl/ n. **1.** cartabón m. —v. **2.** cortar al sesgo.
beverage /'bɛvərɪdʒ/ n. bebida f.; (cold) refresco m.
bewail /bɪ'weil/ v. llorar; lamentar.
beware /bɪ'wɛər/ v. guardarse, precaverse.
bewilder /bɪ'wɪldər/ v. aturdir.
bewildered /bɪ'wɪldərd/ a. descarriado.
bewildering /bɪ'wɪldərɪŋ/ a. aturdente.
bewilderment /bɪ'wɪldərmənt/ n. aturdimiento m.; perplejidad f.
bewitch /bɪ'wɪtʃ/ v. hechizar; embrujar.
beyond /bi'ɒnd/ prep. más allá de.
biannual /bai'ænyuəl/ a. semianual; semestral.
bias /'baiəs/ n. **1.** parcialidad f.; prejuicio m. **on the b.,** al sesgo. —v. **2.** predisponer, influir.
bib /bɪb/ n. babador m.
Bible /'baibəl/ n. Biblia f.
Biblical /'bɪblɪkəl/ a. bíblico.
bibliography /,bɪbli'ɒgrəfi/ n. bibliografía f.
bicarbonate /bai'kɑrbənɪt/ n. bicarbonato m.
bicentennial /,baisɛn'tɛniəl/ a. & n. bicentenario m.
biceps /'baisɛps/ n. bíceps m.
bicker /'bɪkər/ v. altercar.
bicycle /'baisɪkəl/ n. bicicleta f.
bicyclist /'baisɪklɪst/ n. biciclista m. & f.
bid /bɪd/ n. **1.** proposición, oferta f. —v. **2.** mandar; ofrecer.
bidder /'bɪdər/ n. postor -ra.
bide /baid/ v. aguardar; esperar.
bier /bɪər/ n. ataúd m.
bifocal /bai'foukəl/ a. bifocal.
big /bɪg/ a. grande.
bigamist /'bɪgəmɪst/ n. bígamo -ma.
bigamy /'bɪgəmi/ n. bigamia f.
bigot /'bɪgət/ n. persona intolerante.
bigotry /'bɪgətri/ n. intolerancia f.
bikini /bɪ'kini/ n. bikini m.
bilateral /bai'lætərəl/ a. bilateral.
bile /bail/ n. bilis f.
bilingual /bai'lɪŋgwəl/ a. bilingüe.
bilingualism /bai'lɪŋgwə,lɪzəm/ n. bilingüismo m.
bilious /'bɪlyəs/ a. bilioso.
bill /bɪl/ **1.** n. cuenta, factura f.; (money) billete m.; (of bird) pico m. —v. **2.** facturar.
billboard /'bɪl,bɔrd/ n. cartelera f.
billet /'bɪlɪt/ n. **1.** billete m.; Mil. boleta f. —v. **2.** aposentar.
billfold /'bɪl,fould/ n. cartera f.
billiard balls /'bɪlyərd bɔlz/ bolas de billar.
billiards /'bɪlyərdz/ n. billar m.
billion /'bɪlyən/ n. billón m.
bill of health n. certificado de sanidad.
bill of lading /'leidɪŋ/ n. conocimiento de embarque.
bill of sale n. escritura de venta.
billow /'bɪlou/ n. ola; oleada f.
bimetallic /,baimə'tælɪk/ a. bimetálico.

bimonthly /bai'mʌnθli/ a. & adv. bimestral.
bin /bɪn/ n. hucha f.; depósito m.
bind /baind/ v. atar; obligar; (book) encuadernar.
bindery /'baindəri/ n. taller de encuadernación m.
binding /'baindɪŋ/ n. encuadernación f.
bingo /'bɪŋgou/ n. bingo m.
binocular /bə'nɒkyələr/ a. binocular. n.pl. gemelos m.pl.
biochemistry /,baiou'kɛməstri/ n. bioquímica f.
biodegradable /,baioudɪ'greidəbəl/ a. biodegradable.
biofeedback /,baiou'fid,bæk/ n. biofeedback.
biographer /bai'ɒgrəfər/ n. biógrafo -fa.
biographical /,baiə'græfɪkəl/ a. biográfico.
biography /bai'ɒgrəfi/ n. biografía f.
biological /,baiə'lɒdʒɪkəl/ a. biológico.
biologically /,baiə'lɒdʒɪkəli/ adv. biológicamente.
biology /bai'ɒlədʒi/ n. biología f.
bipartisan /bai'pɑrtəzən/ a. bipartito.
biped /'baiped/ n. bípedo m.
bird /bɜrd/ n. pájaro m.; ave f.
birdie /'bɜrdi/ n. (golf) uno bajo par m.
bird of prey n. ave de rapiña f.
bird's-eye view /'bɜrdz,ai/ n. vista de pájaro f.
birth /bɜrθ/ n. nacimiento m. **give b. to,** dar a luz.
birth certificate partida de nacimiento f.
birth control n. contracepción f.
birthday /'bɜrθ,dei/ n. cumpleaños m.
birthmark /'bɜrθ,mɑrk/ n. marca de nacimiento f.
birthplace /'bɜrθ,pleis/ n. natalicio m.
birth rate n. natalidad f.
birthright /'bɜrθ,rait/ n. primogenitura f.
biscuit /'bɪskɪt/ n. bizcocho m.
bisect /bai'sɛkt/ v. bisecar.
bishop /'bɪʃəp/ n. obispo m.; (chess) alfil m.
bishopric /'bɪʃəprɪk/ n. obispado m.
bismuth /'bɪzməθ/ n. bismuto m.
bison /'baisən/ n. bisonte m.
bit /bɪt/ n. pedacito m.; Mech. taladro m.; (for horse) bocado m.; (computer) bit m.
bitch /bɪtʃ/ n. perra f.
bite /bait/ n. **1.** bocado m.; picada f. —v. **2.** morder; picar.
biting /'baitɪŋ/ a. penetrante; mordaz.
bitter /'bɪtər/ a. amargo.
bitterly /'bɪtərli/ adv. amargamente; agriamente.
bitterness /'bɪtərnɪs/ n. amargura f.; rencor m.
bivouac /'bɪvu,æk/ n. **1.** vivaque m. —v. **2.** vivaquear.
biweekly /bai'wikli/ a. quincenal.
black /blæk/ a. negro.
Black /blæk/ n. (person) negro -gra; persona de color.
blackberry /'blæk,bɛri/ n. mora f.
blackbird /'blæk,bɜrd/ n. mirlo m.
blackboard /'blæk,bɔrd/ n. pizarra f.
blacken /'blækən/ v. ennegrecer.
black eye n. ojo amoratado.
blackguard /'blægərd/ n. tunante; pillo m.
blacklist /'blæk,lɪst/ n. lista negra f.
blackmail /'blæk,meil/ n. **1.** chantaje m. —v. **2.** amenazar con chantaje, chantajear.
black market mercado negro, estraperlo m.
black marketeer /,mɑrkɪ'tir/ estraperlista mf.
blackout /'blæk,aut/ n. oscurecimiento, apagamiento m.

blacksmith /'blæk,smɪθ/ n. herrero -ra.
bladder /'blædər/ n. vejiga f.
blade /bleid/ n. (sword) hoja f.; (oar) pala f.; (grass) brizna f.
blame /bleim/ v. culpar, echar la culpa a.
blameless /'bleimlɪs/ a. inculpable.
blanch /blæntʃ/ v. blanquear; escaldar.
bland /blænd/ a. blando.
blank /blæŋk/ a. & n. en blanco.
blanket /'blæŋkɪt/ n. manta f.; cobertor m.
blare /blɛər/ n. sonido de trompeta. v. sonar como trompeta.
blaspheme /blæs'fim/ v. blasfemar.
blasphemer /blæs'fimər/ n. blasfemo -ma, blasfemador -ra.
blasphemous /'blæsfəməs/ a. blasfemo, impío.
blasphemy /'blæsfəmi/ n. blasfemia f.
blast /blæst/ n. **1.** barreno m.; (wind) ráfaga f. —v. **2.** barrenar.
blatant /'bleitnt/ a. bramante; descarado.
blaze /bleiz/ n. **1.** llama, hoguera f. —v. **2.** encenderse en llama.
blazing /'bleizɪŋ/ a. flameante.
bleach /blitʃ/ n. **1.** lejía, blanqueador. —v. **2.** blanquear.
bleachers /'blitʃərz/ n. asientos al aire libre.
bleak /blik/ a. frío y sombrío.
bleakness /'bliknɪs/ n. desolación f.
bleed /blid/ v. sangrar.
blemish /'blɛmɪʃ/ n. **1.** mancha f.; lunar m. —v. **2.** manchar.
blend /blɛnd/ n. **1.** mezcla f. —v. **2.** mezclar, combinar.
blended /'blɛndɪd/ a. mezclado.
blender /'blɛndər/ n. (for food) licuadora f.
bless /blɛs/ v. bendecir.
blessed /'blɛsɪd/ a. bendito.
blessing /'blɛsɪŋ/ n. bendición f.
blight /blait/ n. **1.** plaga f.; tizón m. —v. **2.** atizonar.
blind /blaind/ a. ciego.
blindfold /'blaind,fould/ v. vendar los ojos.
blinding /'blaindɪŋ/ a. deslumbrante; ofuscante.
blindly /'blaindli/ adv. ciegamente.
blindness /'blaindnɪs/ n. ceguedad, ceguera f.
blink /blɪŋk/ n. **1.** guiñada f. —v. **2.** guiñar.
bliss /blɪs/ n. felicidad f.
blissful /'blɪsfəl/ a. dichoso; bienaventurado.
blissfully /'blɪsfəli/ adv. felizmente.
blister /'blɪstər/ n. ampolla f.
blithe /blaið/ a. alegre; jovial; gozoso.
blizzard /'blɪzərd/ n. nevasca f.
bloat /blout/ v. hinchar.
bloc /blɒk/ n. grupo (político); bloc.
block /blɒk/ n. **1.** bloque m.; (street) manzana, cuadra f. —v. **2.** bloquear.
blockade /blɒ'keid/ n. **1.** bloqueo m. —v. **2.** bloquear.
blond /blɒnd/ a. & n. rubio -ia.
blood /blʌd/ n. sangre f.; parentesco, linaje m.
bloodhound /'blʌd,haund/ n. sabueso m.
bloodless /'blʌdlɪs/ a. exangüe; desangrado.
blood poisoning /'pɔizənɪŋ/ envenenamiento de sangre.
blood pressure presión arterial.
bloodshed /'blʌd,ʃɛd/ n. matanza f.
bloodthirsty /'blʌd,θɜrsti/ a. cruel, sanguinario.
bloody /'blʌdi/ a. ensangrentado, sangriento.
bloom /blum/ n. **1.** flor f. —v. **2.** florecer.
blooming /'blumɪŋ/ a. lozano; fresco; floreciente.
blossom /'blɒsəm/ n. **1.** flor f. —v. **2.** florecer.

blot /blɒt/ n. **1.** mancha f. —v. **2.** manchar.

blotch /blɒtʃ/ n. **1.** mancha, roncha f. —v. **2.** manchar.

blotter /blɒtər/ n. papel secante.

blouse /blaus/ n. blusa f.

blow /blou/ n. **1.** golpe m.; Fig. chasco m. —v. **2.** soplar.

blowout /blou,aut/ n. reventón de neumático m.

blubber /blʌbər/ n. grasa de ballena.

bludgeon /blʌdʒən/ n. porra f. v. apalear.

blue /blu/ a. azul; triste, melancólico.

bluebird /blu,bərd/ n. azulejo m.

blue jeans jeans; vaqueros m.pl.

blueprint /blu,prɪnt/ n. heliografía f.

bluff /blʌf/ n. risco m. v. alardear; baladronar.

bluing /bluɪŋ/ n. añil m.

blunder /blʌndər/ n. **1.** desatino m. —v. **2.** desatinar.

blunderer /blʌndərər/ n. desatinado -da.

blunt /blʌnt/ a. embotado; descortés. v. embotar.

bluntly /blʌntli/ a. bruscamente.

bluntness /blʌntnɪs/ n. grosería f.; brusquedad.

blur /blɜr/ n. **1.** trazo confuso. —v. **2.** hacer indistinto.

blush /blʌʃ/ n. **1.** rubor, sonrojo m. —v. **2.** sonrojarse.

bluster /blʌstər/ n. **1.** fanfarria f. —v. **2.** fanfarrear.

boar /bɔr/ n. verraco m. **wild b.,** jabalí.

board /bɔrd/ n. **1.** tabla; Govt. consejo m.; junta f. **b. and room,** cuarto y comida, casa y comida. —v. **2.** (ship) abordar.

boarder /bɔrdər/ n. pensionista m. & f.

boardinghouse /bɔrdɪŋ/ n. pensión f., casa de huéspedes.

boarding pass /bɔrdɪŋ/ boleto de embarque m., tarjeta de embarque f.

boast /boust/ n. **1.** jactancia f. v. jactarse.

boaster /boustər/ n. fanfarrón -na.

boastful /boustfəl/ a. jactancioso.

boastfulness /boustfəlnɪs/ n. jactancia f.

boat /bout/ n. barco, buque, bote m.

boathouse /bout,haus/ n. casilla de botes f.

boatswain /bousən/ n. contramaestre m.

bob /bɒb/ v. menear.

bobbin /bɒbɪn/ n. bobina f.

bobby pin /bɒbi/ n. gancho m., horquilla.

bodice /bɒdɪs/ n. corpiño m.

bodily /bɒdl͡i/ a. corporal.

body /bɒdi/ n. cuerpo m.

body builder culturista mf.

body building culturismo m.

bodyguard /bɒdi,gard/ n. guardaespaldas.

bog /bɒg/ n. pantano m.

bogey /bougi/ n. (golf) uno sobre par m.

Bohemian /bou'himiən/ a. & n. bohemio -mia.

boil /bɔil/ n. **1.** hervor m.; Med. divieso m. —v. **2.** hervir.

boiler /bɔilər/ n. marmita; caldera f.

boiling point /bɔilɪŋ/ punto de ebullición m.

boisterous /bɔistərəs/ a. tumultuoso.

boisterously /bɔistərəsli/ adv. tumultuosamente.

bold /bould/ a. atrevido, audaz.

boldface /bould,feis/ n. (type) letra negra.

boldly /bouldli/ adv. audazmente; descaradamente.

boldness /bouldnɪs/ n. atrevimiento m.; osadía f.

Bolivian /bou'lɪviən/ a. & n. boliviano -na.

bologna /bə'louni/ n. salchicha f., mortadela.

bolster /boulstər/ n. **1.** travesero, cojín m. —v. **2.** apoyar, sostener.

bolt /boult/ n. perno m.; (of door) cerrojo m.; (lightning) rayo m. v. acerrojar.

bomb /bɒm/ n. **1.** bomba f. —v. **2.** bombardear.

bombard /bɒm'bard/ v. bombardear.

bombardier /,bɒmbər'dɪər/ n. bombardero -ra.

bombardment /bɒm'bardmənt/ n. bombardeo m.

bomber /bɒmər/ n. avión de bombardeo.

bombproof /bɒm,pruf/ a. a prueba de granadas.

bombshell /bɒm,ʃɛl/ n. bomba f.

bonbon /bɒn,bɒn/ n. dulce, bombón m.

bond /bɒnd/ n. lazo m.; Com. bono f.

bondage /bɒndɪdʒ/ n. esclavitud, servidumbre f.

bonded /bɒndɪd/ a. garantizado.

bone /boun/ n. hueso m.

boneless /bounlɪs/ a. sin huesos.

bonfire /bɒn,faɪər/ n. hoguera, fogata f.

bonnet /bɒnɪt/ n. gorra f.

bonus /bounəs/ n. sobrepaga f.

bony /bouni/ a. huesudo.

boo /bu/ v. abuchear.

book /bʊk/ n. libro m.

bookbinder /bʊk,baɪndər/ n. encuadernador -ora.

bookcase /bʊk,keis/ n. armario para libros.

bookkeeper /bʊk,kipər/ n. tenedor -ra de libros.

bookkeeping /bʊk,kipɪŋ/ n. contabilidad f.

booklet /bʊklɪt/ n. folleto m., libreta f.

bookmark /bʊk,mark/ n. marcapáginas m.

bookseller /bʊk,sɛlər/ n. librero -ra.

bookstore /bʊk,stɔr/ n. librería f.

boom /bum/ n. Naut. botalón m.; prosperidad repentina.

boon /bun/ n. dádiva f.

boor /bʊr/ n. patán, rústico m.

boorish /bʊrɪʃ/ a. villano.

boost /bust/ n. **1.** alza; ayuda f. —v. **2.** levantar, alzar; fomentar.

booster /bustər/ n. fomentador m.

boot /but/ n. bota f.

bootblack /but,blæk/ n. limpiabotas m.

booth /buθ/ n. cabaña; casilla f.

booty /buti/ n. botín m.

border /bɔrdər/ n. **1.** borde m.; frontera f. —v. **2. b. on,** lindar con.

borderline /bɔrdər,laɪn/ a. marginal. n. margen m.

bore /bɔr/ n. lata f.; persona pesada. v. aburrir, fastidiar; Mech. taladrar.

boredom /bɔrdəm/ n. aburrimiento m.

boric acid /bɔrɪk/ n. ácido bórico m.

boring /bɔrɪŋ/ a. aburrido, pesado.

born /bɔrn/ a. nacido. **be born,** nacer.

born-again /bɔrn ə'gɛn/ a. renacido.

borrow /bɒrou/ v. pedir prestado.

bosom /bʊzəm/ v. seno, pecho m.

boss /bɒs/ n. jefe, patrón m.

botany /bɒtni/ n. botánica f.

both /bouθ/ pron. & a. ambos, los dos.

bother /bɒðər/ n. molestia f. v. molestar, incomodar.

bothersome /bɒðərsəm/ a. molesto.

bottle /bɒtl/ n. **1.** botella f. —v. **2.** embotellar.

bottling /bɒtlɪŋ/ n. embotellamiento m.

bottom /bɒtəm/ n. fondo m.

boudoir /budwar/ n. tocador m.

bough /bau/ n. rama f.

boulder /bouldər/ n. canto rodado.

boulevard /bulə,vard/ n. bulevar m.

bounce /bauns/ n. **1.** brinco m. —v. **2.** brincar; hacer saltar.

bound /baund/ n. **1.** salto m. —v. **2.** limitar.

boundary /baundəri/ n. límite, lindero m.

bouquet /bou'kei, bu-/ n. ramillete de flores.

bourgeois /bʊr'ʒwa/ a. & n. burgués -esa.

bout /baut/ n. encuentro; combate m.

bow /bau/ n bau, bou; v bau/ n. **1.** saludo m.; (of ship) proa f.; (archery) arco m.; (ribbon) lazo m. —v. **2.** saludar, inclinar.

bowels /bauəlz/ n. intestinos m.pl.; entrañas f.pl.

bowl /boul/ n. **1.** vasija f.; platón m. —v. **2.** jugar a los bolos. **b. over,** derribar.

bowlegged /bou,lɛgɪd/ a. perniabierto.

bowling /boulɪŋ/ n. bolos m.pl.

bow tie /bou/ pajarita f.

box /bɒks/ n. **1.** caja f.; Theat. palco m. —v. **2.** (sports) boxear.

boxcar /bɒks,kar/ n. vagón m.

boxer /bɒksər/ n. boxeador -ra, pugilista m. & f.

boxing /bɒksɪŋ/ n. boxeo m.

box office n. taquilla f.

boy /bɔi/ n. muchacho, chico, niño m.

boycott /bɔikɒt/ n. **1.** boicoteo m. —v. **2.** boicotear.

boyhood /bɔihʊd/ n. muchachez f.

boyish /bɔiɪʃ/ a. pueril.

boyishly /bɔiɪʃli/ adv. puerilmente.

bra /bra/ n. sujetador, sostén m.

brace /breis/ n. **1.** grapón m.; pl. tirantes m.pl. —v. **2.** reforzar.

bracelet /breislɪt/ n. brazalete m., pulsera f.

bracket /brækɪt/ n. ménsula f.

brag /bræg/ v. jactarse.

braggart /brægərt/ a. **1.** jactancioso. —n. **2.** jaque m.

braid /breid/ n. **1.** trenza f. —v. **2.** trenzar.

brain /brein/ n. cerebro, seso m.

brainy /breini/ a. sesudo, inteligente.

brake /breik/ n. **1.** freno m. —v. **2.** frenar.

bran /bræn/ n. salvado m.

branch /bræntʃ, brantʃ/ n. ramo m.; (of tree) rama f.

brand /brænd/ n. marca f.

brandish /brændɪʃ/ v. blandir.

brand-new /bræn'nu/ a. enteramente nuevo.

brandy /brændi/ n. aguardiente, coñac m.

brash /bræʃ/ a. impetuoso.

brass /bræs/ n. bronce, latón m.

brassiere /brə'zɪər/ n. corpiño, sujetador, sostén m.

brat /bræt/ n. mocoso m.

bravado /brə'vadou/ n. bravata f.

brave /breiv/ a. valiente.

bravery /breivəri/ n. valor m.

brawl /brɔl/ n. alboroto m. v. alborotar.

brawn /brɔn/ n. músculo m.

bray /brei/ v. rebuznar.

brazen /breizən/ a. desvergonzado.

Brazil /brə'zɪl/ n. Brasil m.

Brazilian /brə'zɪlyən/ a. & n. brasileño -ña.

breach /britʃ/ n. rotura; infracción f.

breach of contract incumplimiento de contrato m.

bread /brɛd/ n. pan m.

breadth /brɛdθ/ n. anchura f.

break /breik/ n. **1.** rotura; pausa f. —v. **2.** quebrar, romper.

breakable /breikəbəl/ a. rompible, frágil.

breakage /breikɪdʒ/ n. rotura f., destrozo m.

breakfast /brɛkfəst/ n. **1.** desayuno, almuerzo m. —v. **2.** desayunar, almorzar.

breakneck /breik,nɛk/ a. rápido, precipitado, atropellado.

breast /brɛst/ n. (of human) pecho, seno m.; (of fowl) pechuga f.

breastbone /brɛst,boun/ n. esternón m.

breath /brɛθ/ n. aliento; soplo m.

breathe /brið/ v. respirar.

breathless /brɛθlɪs/ a. desalentado.

breathlessly /brɛθlɪsli/ adv. jadeantemente, intensamente.

bred /brɛd/ a. criado; educado.

breeches /britʃiz/ n.pl. calzones; pantalones, m.pl.

breed /brid/ n. **1.** raza f. —v. **2.** engendrar; criar.

breeder /bridər/ n. criador -ra.

breeding /bridɪŋ/ n. cría f.

breeze /briz/ n. brisa f.

breezy /brizi/ a.: **it is b.,** hace brisa.

brevity /brɛvɪti/ n. brevedad f.

brew /bru/ v. fraguar; elaborar.

brewer /bruər/ n. cervecero -ra.

brewery /bruəri/ n. cervecería f.

bribe /braib/ n. **1.** soborno, cohecho m. —v. **2.** sobornar, cohechar.

briber /braibər/ n. sobornador -ra.

bribery /braibəri/ n. soborno, cohecho m.

brick /brik/ n. ladrillo m.

bricklayer /brik,leiər/ n. albañil m.

bridal /braidl/ a. nupcial.

bride /braid/ n. novia f.

bridegroom /braid,grum/ n. novio m.

bridesmaid /braidz,meid/ n. madrina de boda.

bridge /bridʒ/ n. puente m.

bridged /bridʒd/ a. conectado.

bridgehead /bridʒ,hɛd/ n. Mil. cabeza de puente.

bridle /braidl/ n. brida f.

brief /brif/ a. breve.

briefcase /brif,keis/ n. maletín m.

briefly /brifli/ adv. brevemente.

briefness /brifnɪs/ n. brevedad f.

brier /braiər/ n. zarza f.

brig /brig/ n. bergantín m.

brigade /brɪ'geid/ n. brigada f.

bright /brait/ a. claro, brillante.

brighten /braitn/ v. abrillantar; alegrar.

brightness /braitnɪs/ n. resplandor m.

brilliance /brɪlyəns/ n. brillantez f.

brilliant /brɪlyənt/ a. brillante.

brim /brim/ n. borde m.; (of hat) ala f.

brine /brain/ n. escabeche, m. salmuera f.

bring /brɪŋ/ v. traer. **b. about,** efectuar, llevar a cabo.

brink /brɪŋk/ n. borde m.

briny /braini/ a. salado.

brisk /brisk/ a. vivo; enérgico.

briskly /briskli/ adv. vivamente.

briskness /brisknɪs/ n. viveza f.

bristle /brisəl/ n. cerda f.

bristly /brisli/ a. hirsuto.

Britain /britn/ n. **Great B.,** Gran Bretaña f.

British /britɪʃ/ a. británico.

British Empire imperio británico m.

British Isles /ailz/ islas británicas f.

Briton /britn/ n. inglés m.

brittle /britl/ a. quebradizo, frágil.

broad /brɔd/ a. ancho.

broadcast /brɔd,kæst/ n. **1.** radiodifusión f. —v. **2.** radiodifundir.

broadcaster /brɔd,kæstər/ n. locutor -ra.

broadcloth /brɔd,klɔθ/ n. paño fino.

broaden /brɔdn/ v. ensanchar.

broadly /brɔdli/ adv. ampliamente.

broadminded /brɔd'maindɪd/ a. tolerante, liberal.

brocade /brou'keid/ n. brocado m.

brocaded /brou'keidɪd/ a. espolinado.

broccoli /brɒkəli/ n. brécol m.

broil /brɔil/ v. asar.

broiler /brɔilər/ n. parrilla f.

broken /broukən/ a. roto, quebrado.

broken-hearted /broukən'hartɪd/ a. angustiado.

broker /'broukər/ n. corredor -ra, bolsista m. & f.

brokerage /'broukərıdʒ/ n. corretaje m.

bronchial /'brɒŋkiəl/ a. bronquial.

bronchitis /brɒŋ'kaitıs/ n. bronquitis f.

bronze /brɒnz/ n. bronce m.

brooch /broutʃ/ n. broche m.

brood /brud/ n. **1.** cría, progenie f. —v. **2.** empollar; cobijar.

brook /brʊk/ n. arroyo m., quebrada f.

broom /brum/ n. escoba f.

broomstick /'brum,stık/ n. palo de escoba.

broth /brɔθ/ n. caldo m.

brothel /'brɒθəl/ n. burdel m.

brother /'brʌðər/ n. hermano m.

brotherhood /'brʌðər,hʊd/ n. fraternidad f.

brother-in-law /'brʌðər ın ,lɔ/ n. cuñado m.

brotherly /'brʌðərli/ a. fraternal.

brow /brau/ n. ceja; frente f.

brown /braun/ a. pardo, moreno; marrón. v. rehogar.

brown sugar azúcar moreno m.

browse /brauz/ v. curiosear; ramonear.

browser /'brauzər/ n. (Internet) nagegador m., visualizador m., visor m.

bruise /bruz/ n. **1.** contusión f. —v. **2.** magullar.

brunette /bru'nɛt/ a. & n. moreno -na, trigueño -ña.

brush /brʌʃ/ n. **1.** cepillo m.; brocha f. —v. **2.** cepillar.

brushwood /'brʌʃ,wʊd/ n. matorral m.

brusque /brʌsk/ a. brusco.

brusquely /'brʌskli/ adv. bruscamente.

brutal /'brutl/ a. brutal.

brutality /bru'tælıti/ n. brutalidad f.

brutalize /'brutl,aiz/ v. embrutecer.

brute /brut/ n. bruto -ta, bestia f.

bubble /'bʌbəl/ n. ampolla f.

bucket /'bʌkıt/ n. cubo m.

buckle /'bʌkəl/ n. hebilla f.

buckram /'bʌkrəm/ n. bucarán m.

bucksaw /'bʌk'sɔ/ n. sierra de bastidor.

buckshot /'bʌk,ʃɒt/ n. posta f.

buckwheat /'bʌk,wit/ n. trigo sarraceno.

bud /bʌd/ n. **1.** brote m. —v. **2.** brotar.

budding /'bʌdıŋ/ a. en capullo.

budge /bʌdʒ/ v. moverse.

budget /'bʌdʒıt/ n. presupuesto m.

buffalo /'bʌfə,lou/ n. búfalo m.

buffer /'bʌfər/ n. parachoques m.

buffet /bə'fei/ n. bufet m.; (furniture) aparador m.

buffoon /bə'fun/ n. bufón m.

bug /bʌg/ n. insecto m.; (computer) error m.

bugle /'byugəl/ n. clarín m.; corneta f.

build /bıld/ v. construir.

builder /'bıldər/ n. constructor -ra.

building /'bıldıŋ/ n. edificio m.

bulb /bʌlb/ n. bulbo m.; (of lamp) bombilla, ampolla f.

bulge /bʌldʒ/ n. abultamiento m. v. abultar.

bulging /'bʌldʒıŋ/ a. protuberante.

bulimia /bu'limiə/ n. bulimia f.

bulk /bʌlk/ n. masa f.; grueso m.; mayoría f.

bulkhead /'bʌlk,hɛd/ n. frontón m.

bulky /'bʌlki/ a. grueso, abultado.

bull /bʊl/ n. toro m.

bulldog /'bʊl,dɔg/ n. perro de presa.

bullet /'bʊlıt/ n. bala f.

bulletin /'bʊlıtın/ n. boletín m.

bulletproof /'bʊlıt,pruf/ a. a prueba de bala.

bullfight /'bʊl,fait/ n. corrida de toros.

bullfighter /'bʊl,faitər/ n. torero -ra.

bullfinch /'bʊl,fıntʃ/ n. pinzón real m.

bully /'bʊli/ n. **1.** rufián m. —v. **2.** bravear.

bulwark /'bʊlwərk/ n. baluarte m.

bum /bʌm/ n. holgazán m.

bump /bʌmp/ n. **1.** golpe, choque m. —v. **2. b. into,** chocar contra.

bumper /'bʌmpər/ n. parachoques m.

bun /bʌn/ n. bollo m.

bunch /bʌntʃ/ n. racimo; montón m.

bundle /'bʌndl/ n. **1.** bulto m. —v. **2. b. up,** abrigar.

bungalow /'bʌŋgə,lou/ n. casa de un solo piso.

bungle /'bʌŋgəl/ v. estropear.

bunion /'bʌnyən/ n. juanete m.

bunk /bʌŋk/ n. litera f.

bunny /'bʌni/ n. conejito -ta.

bunting /'bʌntıŋ/ n. lanilla; banderas f.

buoy /'bui/ n. boya f.

buoyant /'bɔiənt/ a. boyante; vivaz.

burden /'bərdn/ n. **1.** carga f. —v. **2.** cargar.

burdensome /'bərdnsəm/ a. gravoso.

bureau /'byʊrou/ n. (furniture) cómoda f.; departamento m.

burglar /'bərglər/ n. ladrón -ona.

burglarize /'bərglə,raiz/ v. robar.

burglary /'bərgləri/ n. robo m.

burial /'bɛriəl/ n. entierro m.

burlap /'bərlæp/ n. arpillera f.

burly /'bərli/ a. corpulento.

burn /bərn/ v. quemar; arder.

burner /'bərnər/ n. mechero m.

burning /'bərnıŋ/ a. ardiente.

burnish /'bərnıʃ/ v. pulir; acicalar.

burrow /'bərou/ v. minar; horadar.

burst /bərst/ v. reventar.

bury /'bɛri/ v. enterrar.

bus /bʌs/ n. autobús m.

bush /bʊʃ/ n. arbusto m.

bushy /'bʊʃi/ a. matoso; peludo.

business /'bıznıs/ n. negocios m.pl.; comercio m.

businesslike /'bıznıs,laik/ a. directo, práctico.

businessman /'bıznıs,mæn/ n. hombre de negocios, comerciante m.

businesswoman /'bıznıs,wʊmən/ n. mujer de negocios.

bust /bʌst/ n. busto; pecho m.

bustle /'bʌsəl/ n. bullicio m.; animación f.

busy /'bızi/ a. ocupado, atareado.

busybody /'bızi,bɒdi/ n. entremetido -da.

but /bʌt/ conj. pero; sino.

butcher /'bʊtʃər/ n. carnicero -ra.

butchery /'bʊtʃəri/ n. carnicería; matanza f.

butler /'bʌtlər/ n. mayordomo m.

butt /bʌt/ n. punta f.; cabo extremo m.

butter /'bʌtər/ n. manteca, mantequilla f.

buttercup /'bʌtər,kʌp/ n. ranúnculo m.

butterfat /'bʌtər,fæt/ n. mantequilla f.

butterfly /'bʌtər,flai/ n. mariposa f.

buttermilk /'bʌtər,mılk/ n. suero (de leche) m.

button /'bʌtn/ n. botón m.

buttonhole /'bʌtn,houl/ n. ojal m.

buttress /'bʌtrıs/ n. sostén; refuerzo m.

buxom /'bʌksəm/ a. regordete.

buy /bai/ v. comprar.

buyer /'baiər/ n. comprador -ra.

buzz /bʌz/ n. **1.** zumbido m. —v. **2.** zumbar.

buzzard /'bʌzərd/ n. gallinazo m.

buzzer /'bʌzər/ n. zumbador m.; timbre m.

buzz saw n. sierra circular f.

by /bai/ prep. por; (near) cerca de, al lado de; (time) para.

by-and-by /,baiən'bai/ adv. pronto; luego.

bygone /'bai,gɒn/ a. pasado.

bylaw /'bai,lɔ/ n. estatuto, reglamento m.

bypass /'bai,pæs/ n. desvío m.

byproduct /'bai,prɒdəkt/ n. subproducto m.

bystander /'bai,stændər/ n. espectador -ra; mirón -na.

byte /bait/ n. en teoría de la información: ocho bits, byte m.

byway /'bai,wei/ n. camino desviado m.

C

cab /kæb/ n. taxi, coche de alquiler m.

cabaret /,kæbə'rei/ n. cabaret m.

cabbage /'kæbıdʒ/ n. repollo m.

cabin /'kæbın/ n. cabaña f.

cabinet /'kæbənıt/ n. gabinete; ministerio m.

cabinetmaker /'kæbənıt,meikər/ n. ebanista m.

cable /'keibəl/ n. cable m.

cablegram /'keibəl,græm/ n. cablegrama m.

cache /kæʃ/ n. escondite m.

cackle /'kækəl/ n. charla f.; cacareo m. v. cacarear.

cacophony /kə'kɒfəni/ n. cacofonía f.

cactus /'kæktəs/ n. cacto m.

cad /kæd/ n. persona vil.

cadaver /kə'dævər/ n. cadáver m.

cadaverous /kə'dævərəs/ a. cadavérico.

caddie /'kædi/ n. (golf) ayudante m. & f.

cadence /'keidns/ n. cadencia f.

cadet /kə'dɛt/ n. cadete m.

cadmium /'kædmiəm/ n. cadmio m.

cadre /'kædri, 'kɑdrei/ n. núcleo; Mil. cuadro m.

café /kæ'fei/ n. café m., cantina f.

cafeteria /,kæfı'tıəriə/ n. cafetería f.

caffeine /kæ'fin/ n. cafeína f.

cage /keidʒ/ n. jaula f. v. enjaular.

caged /keidʒd/ a. enjaulado.

caisson /'keisɒn, -sən/ n. arcón m.; Mil. furgón m.

cajole /kə'dʒoul/ v. lisonjear; adular.

cake /keik/ n. torta f.; bizcocho m.

calamitous /kə'læmıtəs/ a. calamitoso.

calamity /kə'læmıti/ n. calamidad f.

calcify /'kælsə,fai/ v. calcificar.

calcium /'kælsiəm/ n. calcio m.

calculable /'kælkyələbəl/ a. calculable.

calculate /'kælkyə,leit/ v. calcular.

calculating /'kælkyə,leitıŋ/ a. interesado.

calculation /,kælkyə'leiʃən/ n. calculación f.; cálculo m.

calculus /'kælkyələs/ n. cálculo m.

caldron /'kɔldrən/ n. caldera f.

calendar /'kæləndər/ n. calendario m.

calf /kæf/ n. ternero m. (animal); pantorrilla f. (of the body).

calfskin /'kæf,skın/ n. piel de becerro.

caliber /'kælıbər/ n. calibre m.

calico /'kælı,kou/ n. calicó m.

caliper /'kæləpər/ n. calibrador m.

calisthenics /,kæləs'θɛnıks/ n. calistenia, gimnasia f.

calk /kɔk/ v. calafatear; rellenar.

calker /'kɔkər/ n. calafate -ta.

call /kɔl/ n. **1.** llamada f. —v. **2.** llamar.

calligraphy /kə'lıgrəfi/ n. caligrafía f.

calling /'kɔlıŋ/ n. vocación f.

calling card tarjeta (de visita) f.

callously /'kæləsli/ adv. insensiblemente.

callow /'kælou/ a. sin experiencia.

callus /'kæləs/ n. callo m.

calm /kɑm/ a. **1.** tranquilo, calmado. —n. **2.** calma f. —v. **3.** calmar.

calmly /'kɑmli/ adv. serenamente.

calmness /'kɑmnıs/ n. calma f.

caloric /kə'lɔrık/ a. calórico.

calorie /'kæləri/ n. caloría f.

calorimeter /,kælə'rımıtər/ n. calorímetro m.

calumniate /kə'lʌmni,eit/ v. calumniar.

calumny /'kæləmni/ n. calumnia f.

Calvary /'kælvəri/ n. Calvario m.

calve /kæv/ v. parir (la vaca).

calyx /'keilıks/ n. cáliz m.

camaraderie /,kɑmə'rɑdəri/ n. compañerismo m., compadrería f.

cambric /'keimbrık/ n. batista f.

camcorder /'kæm,kɔrdər/ n. videocámara f.

camel /'kæməl/ n. camello -lla.

camellia /kə'milyə/ n. camelia f.

camel's hair /'kæməlz/ pelo de camello.

cameo /'kæmi,ou/ n. camafeo m.

camera /'kæmərə/ n. cámara f.

camouflage /'kæmə,flɑʒ/ n. camuflaje m.

camouflaging /'kæmə,flɑʒıŋ/ n. simulacro, disfraz m.

camp /kæmp/ n. **1.** campamento m. —v. **2.** acampar.

campaign /kæm'pein/ n. campaña f.

camper /'kæmpər/ n. acampado m.

campfire /'kæmp,faiər/ n. fogata de campamento.

camphor /'kæmfər/ n. alcanfor m.

camphor ball bola de alcanfor.

campus /'kæmpəs/ n. campo de colegio (o universidad), campus m.

can /kæn/ v. (be able) poder.

can /kæn/ n. **1.** lata f. —v. **2.** conservar en latas, enlatar.

Canada /'kænədə/ n. Canadá m.

Canadian /kə'neidiən/ a. & n. canadiense.

canal /kə'næl/ n. canal m.

canalize /'kænl,aiz/ v. canalizar.

canard /kə'nɑrd/ n. embuste m.

canary /kə'nɛəri/ n. canario -ria.

cancel /'kænsəl/ v. cancelar.

cancellation /,kænsə'leiʃən/ n. cancelación f.

cancer /'kænsər/ n. cáncer m.

candelabrum /,kændl'ɑbrəm/ n. candelabro m.

candid /'kændıd/ a. cándido, sincero.

candidacy /'kændıdəsi/ n. candidatura f.

candidate /'kændı,deit/ n. candidato -ta.

candidly /'kændıdli/ adv. cándidamente.

candidness /'kændıdnıs/ n. candidez; sinceridad f.

candied /'kændid/ a. garapiñado.

candle /'kændl/ n. vela f.

candlestick /'kændl,stık/ n. candelero m.

candor /'kændər/ n. candor m.; sinceridad f.

candy /'kændi/ n. dulces m.pl.

cane /kein/ n. caña f.; (for walking) bastón m.

canine /'keinain/ a. canino.

canister /'kænəstər/ n. frasco m.; lata f.

canker /'kæŋkər/ n. llaga; úlcera f.

cankerworm /'kæŋkər,wɜrm/ n. oruga f.

canned /kænd/ a. envasado, enlatado.

canner /'kænər/ n. envasador m.

cannery /'kænəri/ n. fábrica de conservas alimenticias f.

cannibal /'kænəbəl/ n. caníbal m. & f.

cannon /'kænən/ n. cañón m.

cannonade /,kænə'neid/ n. cañoneo m.

cannoneer /,kænə'nıər/ n. cañonero -ra.

canny /'kæni/ a. sagaz; prudente.

canoe /kə'nu/ n. canoa, piragua f.

canoeing /kə'nuıŋ/ n. piragüismo m.

canoeist /kə'nuıst/ n. piragüista m. & f.

canon /'kænən/ n. canon m.; Relig. canónigo m.

canonical /kə'nɒnıkəl/ a. canónico.

canonize /'kænə,naiz/ v. canonizar.

can opener /'oupənər/ abrelatas m.

canopy /'kænəpi/ n. dosel m.

cant /kænt/ *n.* hipocresía *f.*
cantaloupe /ˈkæntḷˌoup/ *n.* melón *m.*
canteen /kænˈtin/ *n.* cantina *f.*
canter /ˈkæntər/ *n.* **1.** medio galope *m.* —*v.* **2.** galopar.
cantonment /kænˈtɒnmənt/ *n. Mil.* acuartelamiento *m.*
canvas /ˈkænvəs/ *n.* lona *f.*
canyon /ˈkænyən/ *n.* cañón, desfiladero *m.*
cap /kæp/ *n.* **1.** tapa *f.*; (headwear) gorro *m.* —*v.* **2.** tapar.
capability /ˌkeipəˈbɪlɪti/ *n.* capacidad *f.*
capable /ˈkeipəbəl/ *a.* capaz.
capably /ˈkeipəbli/ *adv.* hábilmente.
capacious /kəˈpeiʃəs/ *a.* espacioso.
capacity /kəˈpæsɪti/ *n.* capacidad *f.*
cape /keip/ *n.* capa *f.*, *Geog.* cabo *m.*
caper /ˈkeipər/ *n.* zapateta *f.*; *Bot.* alcaparra *f.*
capillary /ˈkæpəˌlɛri/ *a.* capilar.
capital /ˈkæpɪtḷ/ *n.* capital *m.*; *Govt.* capital *f.*
capitalism /ˈkæpɪtḷˌɪzəm/ *n.* capitalismo *m.*
capitalist /ˈkæpɪtḷɪst/ *n.* capitalista *m.* & *f.*
capitalistic /ˌkæpɪtḷˈɪstɪk/ *a.* capitalista.
capitalization /ˌkæpɪtḷəˈzeiʃən/ *n.* capitalización *f.*
capitalize /ˈkæpɪtḷˌaiz/ *v.* capitalizar.
capital letter *n.* mayúscula *f.*
capitulate /kəˈpɪtʃəˌleit/ *v.* capitular.
capon /ˈkeipɒn/ *n.* capón *m.*
caprice /kəˈpris/ *n.* capricho *m.*
capricious /kəˈprɪʃəs/ *a.* caprichoso.
capriciously /kəˈprɪʃəsli/ *adv.* caprichosamente.
capriciousness /kəˈprɪʃəsnɪs/ *n.* capricho *m.*
capsize /ˈkæpsaiz/ *v.* zozobrar, volcar.
capsule /ˈkæpsəl/ *n.* cápsula *f.*
captain /ˈkæptən/ *n.* capitán -tana.
caption /ˈkæpʃən/ *n.* título *m.*; (motion pictures) subtítulo *m.*
captious /ˈkæpʃəs/ *a.* capcioso.
captivate /ˈkæptəˌveit/ *v.* cautivar.
captivating /ˈkæptəˌveitɪŋ/ *a.* encantador.
captive /ˈkæptɪv/ *n.* cautivo -va, prisionero -ra.
captivity /kæpˈtɪvɪti/ *n.* cautividad *f.*
captor /ˈkæptər/ *n.* apresador -ra.
capture /ˈkæptʃər/ *n.* **1.** captura *f.* —*v.* **2.** capturar.
car /kɑr/ *n.* coche, carro *m.*; (of train) vagón, coche *m.* **baggage c.,** vagón de equipajes. **parlor c.,** coche salón.
carafe /kəˈræf/ *n.* garrafa *f.*
caramel /ˈkærəməl/ *n.* caramelo *m.*
carat /ˈkærət/ *n.* quilate *m.*
caravan /ˈkærəˌvæn/ *n.* caravana *f.*
caraway /ˈkærəˌwei/ *n.* alcaravea *f.*
carbide /ˈkɑrbaid/ *n.* carburo *m.*
carbine /ˈkɑrbin/ *n.* carabina *f.*
carbohydrate /ˌkɑrbouˈhaidreit/ *n.* hidrato de carbono.
carbon /ˈkɑrbən/ *n.* carbón *m.*
carbon dioxide /daiˈɒksaid/ anhídrido carbónico.
carbon monoxide /mɒnˈɒksaid/ monóxido de carbono.
carbon paper papel carbón *m.*
carbuncle /ˈkɑrbʌŋkəl/ *n.* carbúnculo *m.*
carburetor /ˈkɑrbəˌreitər/ *n.* carburador *m.*
carcinogenic /ˌkɑrsənəˈdʒɛnɪk/ *a.* carcinogénico.
card /kɑrd/ *n.* tarjeta *f.* **playing c.,** naipe *m.*
cardboard /ˈkɑrdˌbɔrd/ *n.* cartón *m.*
cardiac /ˈkɑrdiˌæk/ *a.* cardíaco.
cardigan /ˈkɑrdɪgən/ *n.* chaqueta de punto.
cardinal /ˈkɑrdṇl/ *a.* **1.** cardinal. —*n.* **2.** cardenal *m.*
cardiologist /ˌkɑrdiˈɒlədʒɪst/ *n.* cardiólogo, -ga *m.* & *f.*
care /kɛər/ *n.* **1.** cuidado. —*v.* **2. c. for,** cuidar.
careen /kəˈrin/ *v.* carenar; echarse de costado.
career /kəˈrɪər/ *n.* carrera *f.*
carefree /ˈkɛərˌfri/ *a.* descuidado.
careful /ˈkɛərfəl/ *a.* cuidadoso. **be. c.,** tener cuidado.
carefully /ˈkɛərfəli/ *adv.* cuidadosamente.
carefulness /ˈkɛərfəlnɪs/ *n.* esmero; cuidado *m.*; cautela *f.*
careless /ˈkɛərlɪs/ *a.* descuidado.
carelessly /ˈkɛərlɪsli/ *adv.* descuidadamente; negligentemente.
carelessness /ˈkɛərlɪsnɪs/ *n.* descuido *m.*
caress /kəˈrɛs/ *n.* **1.** caricia *f.* —*v.* **2.** acariciar.
caretaker /ˈkɛərˌteikər/ *n.* guardián -ana.
cargo /ˈkɑrgou/ *n.* carga *f.*
caricature /ˈkærɪkətʃər/ *n.* caricatura *f.*
caricaturist /ˈkærɪkəˌtʃʊrɪst/ *n.* caricaturista *m.* & *f.*
caries /ˈkɛəriz/ *n.* caries *f.*
carjacking /ˈkɑrˌdʒækɪŋ/ *n.* robo de coche *m.*
carload /ˈkɑrˌloud/ *a.* furgonada, vagonada.
carnal /ˈkɑrnḷ/ *a.* carnal.
carnation /kɑrˈneiʃən/ *n.* clavel *m.*
carnival /ˈkɑrnəvəl/ *n.* carnaval *m.*
carnivorous /kɑrˈnɪvərəs/ *a.* carnívoro.
carol /ˈkærəl/ *n.* villancico *m.*
carouse /kəˈrauz/ *v.* parrandear.
carpenter /ˈkɑrpəntər/ *n.* carpintero -ra.
carpet /ˈkɑrpɪt/ *n.* alfombra *f.*
carpeting /ˈkɑrpɪtɪŋ/ *n.* alfombrado *m.*
car pool /ˈkɑrˌpul/ uso habitual, por varias personas, de un automóvil perteneciente a una de ellas.
carriage /ˈkærɪdʒ/ *n.* carruaje; (bearing) porte *m.*
carrier /ˈkæriər/ *n.* portador -ra.
carrier pigeon paloma mensajera.
carrot /ˈkærət/ *n.* zanahoria *f.*
carrousel /ˌkærəˈsɛl/ *n.* volantín, carrusel *m.*
carry /ˈkæri/ *v.* llevar, cargar. **c. out,** cumplir, llevar a cabo.
cart /kɑrt/ *n.* carreta *f.*
cartage /ˈkɑrtɪdʒ/ *n.* acarreo, carretaje *m.*
cartel /kɑrˈtɛl/ *n.* cartel *m.*
cartilage /ˈkɑrtḷɪdʒ/ *n.* cartílago *m.*
carton /ˈkɑrtṇ/ *n.* caja de cartón.
cartoon /kɑrˈtun/ *n.* caricatura *f.*
cartoonist /kɑrˈtunɪst/ *n.* caricaturista *m.* & *f.*
cartridge /ˈkɑrtrɪdʒ/ *n.* cartucho *m.*
carve /kɑrv/ *v.* esculpir; (meat) trinchar.
carver /ˈkɑrvər/ *n.* tallador -ra; grabador -ra.
carving /ˈkɑrvɪŋ/ *n.* entalladura *f.*; arte de trinchar. **c. knife,** trinchante *m.*
cascade /kæsˈkeid/ *n.* cascada *f.*
case /keis/ *n.* caso *m.*; (box) caja *f.* **in any c.,** sea como sea.
cash /kæʃ/ *n.* **1.** dinero contante. —*v.* **2.** efectuar, cambiar.
cashier /kæˈʃɪər/ *n.* cajero -ra.
cashmere /ˈkæʒmɪər/ *n.* casimir *m.*
casino /kəˈsinou/ *n.* casino *m.*
cask /kæsk/ *n.* barril *m.*
casket /ˈkæskɪt/ *n.* ataúd *m.*
casserole /ˈkæsəˌroul/ *n.* cacerola *f.*
cassette /kəˈsɛt/ *n.* cassette *m.*, cartucho *m.*
cast /kæst/ *n.* **1.** *Theat.* reparto de papeles. —*v.* **2.** echar; *Theat.* repartir.
castanet /ˌkæstəˈnɛt/ *n.* castañuela *f.*
castaway /ˈkæstəˌwei/ *n.* náufrago -ga.
caste /kæst/ *n.* casta *f.*
caster /ˈkæstər/ *n.* tirador *m.*
castigate /ˈkæstɪˌgeit/ *v.* castigar.
Castilian /kæˈstɪlyən/ *a.* castellano.
cast iron *n.* hierro colado *m.*
castle /ˈkæsəl/ *n.* castillo *m.*
castoff /ˈkæstˌɔf/ *a.* descartado.
casual /ˈkæʒuəl/ *a.* casual.
casually /ˈkæʒuəli/ *adv.* casualmente.
casualness /ˈkæʒuəlnɪs/ *n.* casualidad *f.*
casualty /ˈkæʒuəlti/ *n.* víctima *f.*; *Mil.* baja *f.*
cat /kæt/ *n.* gato -ta.
cataclysm /ˈkætəˌklɪzəm/ *n.* cataclismo *m.*
catacomb /ˈkætəˌkoum/ *n.* catacumba *f.*
catalogue /ˈkætḷˌɔg/ *n.* catálogo *m.*
catapult /ˈkætəˌpʌlt/ *n.* catapulta *f.*
cataract /ˈkætəˌrækt/ *n.* catarata *f.*
catarrh /kəˈtɑr/ *n.* catarro *m.*
catastrophe /kəˈtæstrəfi/ *n.* catástrofe *f.*
catch /kætʃ/ *v.* alcanzar, atrapar, coger.
catchy /ˈkætʃi/ *a.* contagioso.
catechism /ˈkætɪˌkɪzəm/ *n.* catequismo *m.*
catechize /ˈkætɪˌkaiz/ *v.* catequizar.
categorical /ˌkætɪˈgɔrɪkəl/ *a.* categórico.
category /ˈkætɪˌgɔri/ *n.* categoría *f.*
cater /ˈkeitər/ *v.* abastecer; proveer. **c. to,** complacer.
caterpillar /ˈkætəˌpɪlər/ *n.* gusano *m.*
catgut /ˈkætˌgʌt/ *n.* cuerda (de tripa).
catharsis /kəˈθɑrsɪs/ *n.* catarsis, purga *f.*
cathartic /kəˈθɑrtɪk/ *a.* **1.** catártico; purgante. —*n.* **2.** purgante *m.*
cathedral /kəˈθidrəl/ *n.* catedral *f.*
cathode /ˈkæθoud/ *n.* cátodo *m.*
Catholic /ˈkæθəlɪk/ *a.* católico & *n.* católico -ca.
Catholicism /kəˈθɒləˌsɪzəm/ *n.* catolicismo *m.*
catnap /ˈkætˌnæp/ *n.* siesta corta.
catsup /ˈkætsəp, ˈkɛtʃəp/ *n.* salsa de tomate.
cattle /ˈkætḷ/ *n.* ganado *m.*
cattleman /ˈkætḷmən, -ˌmæn/ *n.* ganadero *m.*
cauliflower /ˈkɔləˌflauər/ *n.* coliflor *m.*
causation /kɔˈzeiʃən/ *n.* causalidad *f.*
cause /kɔz/ *n.* causa *f.*
causeway /ˈkɔzˌwei/ *n.* calzada elevada *f.*; terraplén *m.*
caustic /ˈkɔstɪk/ *a.* cáustico.
cauterize /ˈkɔtəˌraiz/ *v.* cauterizar.
cautery /ˈkɔtəri/ *n.* cauterio *m.*
caution /ˈkɔʃən/ *n.* cautela *f.*
cautious /ˈkɔʃəs/ *a.* cauteloso.
cavalcade /ˌkævəlˈkeid/ *n.* cabalgata *f.*
cavalier /ˌkævəˈlɪər/ *n.* caballero *m.*
cavalry /ˈkævəlri/ *n.* caballería *f.*
cave /keiv/ **cavern** *n.* caverna, gruta *f.*
cave-in /ˈkeiv ˌɪn/ *n.* hundimiento *m.*
caviar /ˈkæviˌɑr/ *n.* caviar *m.*
cavity /ˈkævɪti/ *n.* hueco *m.*
cayman /ˈkeimən/ *n.* caimán *m.*
CD player tocadiscos compacto, tocadiscos digital *m.*
cease /sis/ *v.* cesar.
ceaseless /ˈsislɪs/ *a.* incesante.
cedar /ˈsidər/ *n.* cedro *m.*
cede /sid/ *v.* ceder.
ceiling /ˈsilɪŋ/ *n.* techo; cielo *m.*
celebrant /ˈsɛləbrənt/ *n.* celebrante -ta.
celebrate /ˈsɛləˌbreit/ *v.* celebrar.
celebration /ˌsɛləˈbreiʃən/ *n.* celebración *f.*
celebrity /səˈlɛbrɪti/ *n.* celebridad.
celerity /səˈlɛrɪti/ *n.* celeridad; prontitud *f.*
celery /ˈsɛləri/ *n.* apio *m.*
celestial /səˈlɛstʃəl/ *a.* celeste.
celibacy /ˈsɛləbəsi/ *n.* celibato -ta.
celibate /ˈsɛləbɪt/ *a.* & *n.* célibe *m.* & *f.*
cell /sɛl/ *n.* celda *f.*; *Biol.* célula *f.*
cellar /ˈsɛlər/ *n.* sótano *m.*
cellist /ˈtʃɛlɪst/ *a.* celista *m.* & *f.*
cello /ˈtʃɛlou/ *n.* violonchelo *m.*
cellophane /ˈsɛləˌfein/ *n.* celofán *m.*
cellular /ˈsɛlyələr/ *a.* celular.
cellular phone /foun/ teléfono móvil *m.*
celluloid /ˈsɛlyəˌlɔid/ *n.* celuloide *m.*
cellulose /ˈsɛlyəˌlous/ *a.* **1.** celuloso. —*n.* **2.** celulosa *f.*
Celtic /ˈkɛltɪk, ˈsɛl-/ *a.* céltico.
cement /sɪˈmɛnt/ *n.* cemento *m.*
cemetery /ˈsɛmɪˌtɛri/ *n.* cementerio *m.*; campo santo *m.*
censor /ˈsɛnsər/ *n.* censor -ra.
censorious /sɛnˈsɔriəs/ *a.* severo; crítico.
censorship /ˈsɛnsərˌʃɪp/ *n.* censura *f.*
censure /ˈsɛnʃər/ *n.* **1.** censura *f.* —*v.* **2.** censurar.
census /ˈsɛnsəs/ *n.* censo *m.*
cent /sɛnt/ *n.* centavo, céntimo *m.*
centenary /sɛnˈtɛnəri/ *a.* & *n.* centenario *m.*
centennial /sɛnˈtɛniəl/ *a.* & *n.* centenario *m.*
center /ˈsɛntər/ *n.* centro *m.*
centerfold /ˈsɛntərˌfould/ *n.* página central desplegable en una revista.
centerpiece /ˈsɛntərˌpis/ *n.* centro de mesa.
centigrade /ˈsɛntɪˌgreid/ *a.* centígrado.
centigrade thermometer termómetro centígrado.
central /ˈsɛntrəl/ *a.* central.
Central American *a.* & *n.* centroamericano -na.
centralize /ˈsɛntrəˌlaiz/ *v.* centralizar.
century /ˈsɛntʃəri/ *n.* siglo *m.*
century plant maguey *m.*
ceramic /səˈræmɪk/ *a.* cerámico.
ceramics /səˈræmɪks/ *n.* cerámica *f.*
cereal /ˈsɪəriəl/ *n.* cereal *m.*
cerebral /səˈribrəl/ *a.* cerebral.
ceremonial /ˌsɛrəˈmouniəl/ *a.* ceremonial.
ceremonious /ˌsɛrəˈmouniəs/ *a.* ceremonioso.
ceremony /ˈsɛrəˌmouni/ *n.* ceremonia *f.*
certain /ˈsɜrtṇ/ *a.* cierto, seguro.
certainly /ˈsɜrtṇli/ *adv.* sin duda, seguramente.
certainty /ˈsɜrtṇti/ *n.* certeza *f.*
certificate /sərˈtɪfɪkɪt/ *n.* certificado *m.*
certification /ˌsɜrtəfɪˈkeiʃən, sərˌtɪfə-/ *n.* certificación *f.*
certified /ˈsɜrtəˌfaid/ *a.* certificado.
certify /ˈsɜrtəˌfai/ *v.* certificar.
certitude /ˈsɜrtɪˌtyud/ *n.* certeza *f.*
cessation /sɛˈseiʃən/ *n.* cesación, descontinuación *f.*
cession /ˈsɛʃən/ *n.* cesión *f.*
chafe /tʃeif/ *v.* irritar.
chafing dish /ˈtʃeifɪŋ/ *n.* escalfador *m.*
chagrin /ʃəˈgrɪn/ *n.* disgusto *m.*
chain /tʃein/ *n.* **1.** cadena *f.* —*v.* **2.** encadenar.
chair /tʃɛər/ *n.* silla *f.*
chairman /ˈtʃɛərmən/ *n.* presidente -ta.
chairperson /ˈtʃɛərˌpɜrsən/ *n.* presidente -ta; persona que preside.
chalk /tʃɔk/ *n.* tiza *f.*
challenge /ˈtʃælɪndʒ/ *n.* **1.** desafío *m.* —*v.* **2.** desafiar.
challenger /ˈtʃælɪndʒər/ *n.* desafiador -ra.
chamber /ˈtʃeimbər/ *n.* cámara *f.*
chamberlain /ˈtʃeimbərlɪn/ *n.* camarero *m.*
chambermaid /ˈtʃeimbərˌmeid/ *n.* camarera *f.*
chameleon /kəˈmiliən/ *n.* camaleón *m.*
chamois /ˈʃæmi/ *n.* gamuza *f.*
champagne /ʃæmˈpein/ *n.* champán *m.*, champaña *f.*
champion /ˈtʃæmpiən/ *n.* **1.** campeón -na —*v.* **2.** defender.
championship /ˈtʃæmpiənˌʃɪp/ *n.* campeonato *m.*

chance /tʃæns/ *n.* oportunidad, ocasión *f.* **by c.,** por casualidad, por acaso. **take a c.,** aventurarse.
chancel /ˈtʃænsəl/ *n.* antealtar *m.*
chancellery /ˈtʃænsələri/ *n.* cancillería *f.*
chancellor /ˈtʃænsələr/ *n.* canciller *m.*
chandelier /ˌʃændḷˈɪər/ *n.* araña de luces.
change /tʃeindʒ/ *n.* **1.** cambio; (from a bill) moneda *f.* —*v.* **2.** cambiar.
changeability /ˌtʃeindʒəˈbɪlɪti/ *n.* mutabilidad *f.*
changeable /ˈtʃeindʒəbəl/ *a.* variable, inconstante.
changer /ˈtʃeindʒər/ *n.* cambiador -ra.
channel /ˈtʃænl/ *n.* **1.** canal *m.* —*v.* **2.** encauzar.
Channel Tunnel túnel del Canal de la Mancha *m.*
chant /tʃænt/ *n.* **1.** canto llano *m.* —*v.* **2.** cantar.
chaos /ˈkeiɒs/ *n.* caos *m.*
chaotic /keiˈɒtɪk/ *a.* caótico.
chap /tʃæp/ *n.* **1.** *Colloq.* tipo *m.* —*v.* **2.** rajar.
chapel /ˈtʃæpəl/ *n.* capilla *f.*
chaperon /ˈʃæpəˌroun/ *n.* acompañante -ta de señorita.
chaplain /ˈtʃæplɪn/ *n.* capellán *m.*
chapter /ˈtʃæptər/ *n.* capítulo *m.*
char /tʃɑr/ *v.* carbonizar.
character /ˈkærɪktər/ *n.* carácter *m.*
characteristic /ˌkærɪktəˈrɪstɪk/ *a.* **1.** característico. —*n.* **2.** característica *f.*
characterization /ˌkærɪktərəˈzeiʃən/ *n.* caracterización *f.*
characterize /ˈkærɪktəˌraiz/ *v.* caracterizar.
charcoal /ˈtʃɑrˌkoul/ *n.* carbón leña.
charge /tʃɑrdʒ/ *n.* **1.** acusación *f.*; ataque *m.* —*v.* **2.** cargar; acusar; atacar.
chariot /ˈtʃæriət/ *n.* carroza *f.*
charisma /kəˈrɪzmə/ *n.* carisma *m.*
charitable /ˈtʃærɪtəbəl/ *a.* caritativo.
charitableness /ˈtʃærɪtəbəlnɪs/ *n.* caridad *f.*
charitably /ˈtʃærɪtəbli/ *adv.* caritativamente.
charity /ˈtʃærɪti/ *n.* caridad *f.*; (alms) limosna *f.*
charlatan /ˈʃɑrlətn̩/ *n.* charlatán -na.
charlatanism /ˈʃarlətn̩ˌɪzəm/ *n.* charlatanería *f.*
charm /tʃɑrm/ *n.* **1.** encanto *m.*; (witchcraft) hechizo *m.* —*v.* **2.** encantar; hechizar.
charming /ˈtʃɑrmɪŋ/ *a.* encantador.
charred /tʃɑrd/ *a.* carbonizado.
chart /tʃɑrt/ *n.* tabla, esquema *f.*
charter /ˈtʃɑrtər/ *n.* **1.** carta *f.* —*v.* **2.** alquilar.
charter flight vuelo chárter *m.*
charwoman /ˈtʃɑrˌwʊmən/ *n.* mujer de la limpieza *f.*
chase /tʃeis/ *n.* **1.** caza *f.* —*v.* **2.** cazar; perseguir.
chaser /ˈtʃeisər/ *n.* perseguidor -ra.
chasm /ˈkæzəm/ *n.* abismo *m.*
chassis /ˈtʃæsi/ *n.* chasis *m.*
chaste /tʃeist/ *a.* casto.
chasten /ˈtʃeisən/ *v.* corregir, castigar.
chastise /tʃæsˈtaiz/ *v.* castigar.
chastisement /tʃæsˈtaizmənt/ *n.* castigo *m.*
chastity /ˈtʃæstɪti/ *n.* castidad, pureza *f.*
chat /tʃæt/ *n.* **1.** plática, charla *f.* —*v.* **2.** platicar, charlar.
chateau /ʃæˈtou/ *n.* castillo *m.*
chattels /ˈtʃætəlz/ *n.pl.* bienes *m.*
chatter /ˈtʃætər/ *v.* **1.** cotorrear; (teeth) rechinar. —*n.* **2.** cotorreo *m.*
chatterbox /ˈtʃætˌər bɒks/ *n.* charlador -ra.
chauffeur /ˈʃoufər/ *n.* chofer *m.*
cheap /tʃip/ *a.* barato.
cheapen /ˈtʃipən/ *v.* rebajar, menospreciar.
cheaply /ˈtʃipli/ *adv.* barato.
cheapness /ˈtʃipnɪs/ *n.* baratura *f.*
cheat /tʃit/ *v.* engañar.
cheater /ˈtʃitər/ *n.* engañador -ra.
check /tʃɛk/ *n.* **1.** verificación *f.*; (bank) cheque *m.*; (restaurant) cuenta *f.*; (chess) jaque *m.* —*v.* **2.** verificar.
checkers /ˈtʃɛkərz/ *n.* juego de damas.
checkmate /ˈtʃɛkˌmeit/ *v.* dar mate.
checkout counter /ˈtʃɛkˌaut/ caja *f.*
cheek /tʃik/ *n.* mejilla *f.* (of face), desfachatez *f.* (gall).
cheekbone /ˈtʃikˌboun/ *n.* pómulo *m.*
cheeky /ˈtʃiki/ *a.* fresco, descarado, chulo.
cheer /tʃɪər/ *n.* **1.** alegría *f.*; aplauso *m.* —*v.* **2.** alegrar; aplaudir.
cheerful /ˈtʃɪərfəl/ *a.* alegre.
cheerfully /ˈtʃɪərfəli/ *adv.* alegremente.
cheerfulness /ˈtʃɪərfəlnɪs/ *n.* alegría *f.*
cheerless /ˈtʃɪərlɪs/ *a.* triste.
cheery /ˈtʃɪəri/ *a.* alegre.
cheese /tʃiz/ *n.* queso *m.* **cottage c.,** requesón *m.*
chef /ʃɛf/ *n.* cocinero en jefe.
chemical /ˈkɛmɪkəl/ *a.* **1.** químico. —*n.* **2.** reactivo *m.*
chemically /ˈkɛmɪkli/ *adv.* químicamente.
chemist /ˈkɛmɪst/ *n.* químico -ca.
chemistry /ˈkɛməstri/ *n.* química *f.*
chemotherapy /ˌkimouˈθɛrəpi/ *n.* quimioterapia *f.*
chenille /ʃəˈnil/ *n.* felpilla *f.*
cherish /ˈtʃɛrɪʃ/ *v.* apreciar.
cherry /ˈtʃɛri/ *n.* cereza *f.*
cherub /ˈtʃɛrəb/ *n.* querubín *m.*
chess /tʃɛs/ *n.* ajedrez *m.*
chest /tʃɛst/ *n.* arca *f.*; (physiology) pecho *m.*
chestnut /ˈtʃɛsˌnʌt/ *n.* castaña *f.*
chevron /ˈʃɛvrən/ *n.* sardineta *f.*
chew /tʃu/ *v.* mascar, masticar.
chewer /ˈtʃuər/ *n.* mascador -ra.
chic /ʃik/ *a.* elegante, paquete.
chicanery /ʃɪˈkeinəri/ *n.* trampería *f.*
chick /tʃɪk/ *n.* pollito -ta.
chicken /ˈtʃɪkən/ *n.* pollo *m.*, gallina *f.*
chicken-hearted /ˈtʃɪkən ˈhɑrtɪd/ *a.* cobarde.
chicken pox /pɒks/ viruelas locas, varicela *f.*
chicle /ˈtʃɪkəl/ *n.* chicle *m.*
chicory /ˈtʃɪkəri/ *n.* achicoria *f.*
chide /tʃaid/ *v.* regañar, reprender.
chief /tʃif/ *a.* **1.** principal. —*n.* **2.** jefe -fa.
chiefly /ˈtʃifli/ *adv.* principalmente, mayormente.
chieftain /ˈtʃiftən/ *n.* caudillo *m.*; (Indian c.) cacique *m.*
chiffon /ʃɪˈfɒn/ *n.* chifón *m.*, gasa *f.*
chilblain /ˈtʃɪlblein/ *n.* sabañón *m.*
child /tʃaild/ *n.* niño -ña; hijo -ja.
childbirth /ˈtʃaildˌbɜrθ/ *n.* parto *m.*
childhood /ˈtʃaildhʊd/ *n.* niñez *f.*
childish /ˈtʃaildɪʃ/ *a.* pueril.
childishness /ˈtʃaildɪʃnɪs/ *n.* puerilidad *f.*
childless /ˈtʃaildlɪs/ *a.* sin hijos.
childlike /ˈtʃaildˌlaik/ *a.* infantil.
Chilean /ˈtʃɪliən/ *a.* & *n.* chileno -na.
chili /ˈtʃɪli/ *n.* chile, ají *m.*
chill /tʃɪl/ *n.* **1.** frío; escalofrío *m.* —*v.* **2.** enfriar.
chilliness /ˈtʃɪlinɪs/ *n.* frialdad *f.*
chilly /ˈtʃɪli/ *a.* frío; friolento.
chimes /tʃaimz/ *n.* juego de campanas.
chimney /ˈtʃɪmni/ *n.* chimenea *f.*
chimpanzee /ˌtʃɪmpænˈzi, tʃɪmˈpænzi/ *n.* chimpancé *m.*
chin /tʃɪn/ *n.* barba *f.*
china /ˈtʃainə/ *n.* loza *f.*
chinchilla /tʃɪnˈtʃɪlə/ *n.* chinchilla *f.*
Chinese /tʃaiˈniz/ *a.* & *n.* chino -na.
chink /tʃɪŋk/ *n.* grieta *f.*
chintz /tʃɪnts/ *n.* zaraza *f.*
chip /tʃɪp/ *n.* **1.** astilla *f.* —*v.* **2.** astillar.
chiropodist /kɪˈrɒpədɪst/ *n.* pedicuro -ra.
chiropractor /ˈkairəˌpræktər/ *n.* quiropráctico -ca.
chirp /tʃɜrp/ *n.* **1.** chirrido *m.* —*v.* **2.** chirriar, piar.
chisel /ˈtʃɪzəl/ *n.* **1.** cincel *m.* —*v.* **2.** cincelar, talar.
chivalrous /ˈʃɪvəlrəs/ *a.* caballeroso.
chivalry /ˈʃɪvəlri/ *n.* caballería *f.*
chive /tʃaiv/ *n.* cebollino *m.*
chloride /ˈklɔraid/ *n.* cloruro *m.*
chlorine /ˈklɔrin/ *n.* cloro *m.*
chloroform /ˈklɔrəˌfɔrm/ *n.* cloroformo *m.*
chlorophyll /ˈklɔrəfɪl/ *n.* clorofila *f.*
chock-full /ˈtʃɒkˈfʊl/ *a.* repleto, colmado.
chocolate /ˈtʃɔkəlɪt/ *n.* chocolate *m.*
choice /tʃɔis/ *a.* **1.** selecto, escogido. —*n.* **2.** selección *f.*; escogimiento *m.*
choir /kwaiᵊr/ *n.* coro *m.*
choke /tʃouk/ *v.* sofocar, ahogar.
cholera /ˈkɒlərə/ *n.* cólera *f.*
choleric /ˈkɒlərɪk/ *a.* colérico, irascible.
cholesterol /kəˈlɛstəˌroul/ *n.* colesterol *m.*
choose /tʃuz/ *v.* elegir, escoger.
chop /tʃɒp/ *n.* **1.** chuleta, costilla *f.* —*v.* **2.** tajar; cortar.
chopper /ˈtʃɒpər/ *n.* tajador -ra.
choppy /ˈtʃɒpi/ *a.* agitado.
choral /ˈkɔrəl/ *a.* coral.
chord /kɔrd/ *n.* cuerda *f.*; acorde *m.*
chore /tʃɔr/ *n.* tarea *f.*, quehacer *m.*
choreography /ˌkɔriˈɒgrəfi, ˌkour-/ *n.* coreografía *f.*
chorister /ˈkɔrəstər/ *n.* corista *m.*
chorus /ˈkɔrəs/ *n.* coro *m.*
christen /ˈkrɪsən/ *v.* bautizar.
Christendom /ˈkrɪsəndəm/ *n.* cristiandad *f.*
Christian /ˈkrɪsʃən/ *a.* & *n.* cristiano -na.
Christianity /ˌkrɪsʃiˈænɪti/ *n.* cristianismo *m.*
Christmas /ˈkrɪsməs/ *n.* Navidad, Pascua *f.* **Merry C.,** felices Pascuas. **C. Eve,** Nochebuena *f.*
chromatic /krouˈmætɪk/ *a.* cromático.
chromium /ˈkroumiəm/ *n.* cromo *m.*
chromosome /ˈkrouməˌsoum/ *n.* cromosoma *m.*
chronic /ˈkrɒnɪk/ *a.* crónico.
chronicle /ˈkrɒnɪkəl/ *n.* crónica *f.*
chronological /ˌkrɒnḷˈɒdʒɪkəl/ *a.* cronológico.
chronology /krəˈnɒlədʒi/ *n.* cronología *f.*
chrysalis /ˈkrɪsəlɪs/ *n.* crisálida *f.*
chrysanthemum /krɪˈsænθəməm/ *n.* crisantemo *m.*
chubby /ˈtʃʌbi/ *a.* regordete, rollizo.
chuck /tʃʌk/ *v.* (cluck) cloquear; (throw) echar, tirar.
chuckle /ˈtʃʌkəl/ *v.* reír entre dientes.
chum /tʃʌm/ *n.* amigo -ga; compinche *m.*
chummy /ˈtʃʌmi/ *a.* íntimo.
chunk /tʃʌŋk/ *n.* trozo *m.*
chunky /ˈtʃʌŋki/ *a.* fornido, trabado.
Chunnel /ˈtʃʌnl/ *n.* túnel del Canal de la Mancha *m.*
church /tʃɜrtʃ/ *n.* iglesia *f.*
churchman /ˈtʃɜrtʃmən/ *n.* eclesiástico *m.*
churchyard /ˈtʃɜrtʃˌyɑrd/ *n.* cementerio *m.*
churn /tʃɜrn/ *n.* **1.** mantequera *f.* —*v.* **2.** agitar, revolver.
chute /ʃut/ *n.* conducto; canal *m.*
cicada /sɪˈkeidə/ *n.* cigarra, chicharra *f.*
cider /ˈsaidər/ *n.* sidra *f.*
cigar /sɪˈgɑr/ *n.* cigarro, puro *m.*
cigarette /ˌsɪgəˈrɛt/ *n.* cigarrillo, cigarro, pitillo *m.* **c. case,** cigarrillera *f.* **c. lighter,** encendedor *m.*
cinchona /sɪŋˈkounə/ *n.* cinchona *f.*
cinder /ˈsɪndər/ *n.* ceniza *f.*
cinema /ˈsɪnəmə/ *n.* cine *m.*
cinnamon /ˈsɪnəmən/ *n.* canela *f.*
cipher /ˈsaifər/ *n.* cifra *f.*
circle /ˈsɜrkəl/ *n.* círculo *m.*
circuit /ˈsɜrkɪt/ *n.* circuito *m.*
circuitous /sərˈkyuɪtəs/ *a.* tortuoso.
circuitously /sərˈkyuɪtəsli/ *adv.* tortuosamente.
circular /ˈsɜrkyələr/ *a.* circular, redondo.
circularize /ˈsɜrkyələˌraiz/ *v.* hacer circular.
circulate /ˈsɜrkyəˌleit/ *v.* circular.
circulation /ˌsɜrkyəˈleiʃən/ *n.* circulación *f.*
circulator /ˈsɜrkyəˌleitər/ *n.* diseminador -ra.
circulatory /ˈsɜrkyələˌtɔri/ *a.* circulatorio.
circumcise /ˈsɜrkəmˌsaiz/ *v.* circuncidar.
circumcision /ˌsɜrkəmˈsɪʒən/ *n.* circuncisión *f.*
circumference /sərˈkʌmfərəns/ *n.* circunferencia *f.*
circumlocution /ˌsɜrkəmlouˈkyuʃən/ *n.* circunlocución *f.*
circumscribe /ˈsɜrkəmˌskraib/ *v.* circunscribir; limitar.
circumspect /ˈsɜrkəmˌspɛkt/ *a.* discreto.
circumstance /ˈsɜrkəmˌstæns/ *n.* circunstancia *f.*
circumstantial /ˌsɜrkəmˈstænʃəl/ *a.* circunstancial, indirecto.
circumstantially /ˌsɜrkəmˈstænʃəli/ *adv.* minuciosamente.
circumvent /ˌsɜrkəmˈvɛnt/ *v.* evadir, evitar.
circumvention /ˌsɜrkəmˈvɛnʃən/ *n.* trampa *f.*
circus /ˈsɜrkəs/ *n.* circo *m.*
cirrhosis /sɪˈrousɪs/ *n.* cirrosis *f.*
cistern /ˈsɪstərn/ *n.* cisterna *f.*
citadel /ˈsɪtədl/ *n.* ciudadela *f.*
citation /saiˈteiʃən/ *n.* citación *f.*
cite /sait/ *v.* citar.
citizen /ˈsɪtəzən/ *n.* ciudadano -na.
citizenship /ˈsɪtəzənˌʃɪp/ *n.* ciudadanía *f.*
citric /ˈsɪtrɪk/ *a.* cítrico.
city /ˈsɪti/ *n.* ciudad *f.*
city hall ayuntamiento, municipio *m.*
city planning urbanismo *m.*
civic /ˈsɪvɪk/ *a.* cívico.
civics /ˈsɪvɪks/ *n.* ciencia del gobierno civil.
civil /ˈsɪvəl/ *a.* civil; cortés.
civilian /sɪˈvɪlyən/ *a.* & *n.* civil *m.* & *f.*
civility /sɪˈvɪlɪti/ *n.* cortesía *f.*
civilization /ˌsɪvələˈzeiʃən/ *n.* civilización *f.*
civilize /ˈsɪvəˌlaiz/ *v.* civilizar.
civil rights /raits/ derechos civiles *m. pl.*
civil service *n.* servicio civil oficial *m.*
civil war *n.* guerra civil *f.*
clabber /ˈklæbər/ *n.* **1.** cuajo *m.* —*v.* **2.** cuajarse.
clad /klæd/ *a.* vestido.
claim /kleim/ *n.* **1.** demanda; pretensión *f.* —*v.* **2.** demandar, reclamar.
claimant /ˈkleimənt/ *n.* reclamante -ta.
clairvoyance /klɛərˈvɔiəns/ *n.* clarividencia *f.*
clairvoyant /klɛərˈvɔiənt/ *a.* clarividente.
clam /klæm/ *n.* almeja *f.*
clamber /ˈklæmbər/ *v.* trepar.
clamor /ˈklæmər/ *n.* **1.** clamor *m.* —*v.* **2.** clamar.
clamorous /ˈklæmərəs/ *a.* clamoroso.
clamp /klæmp/ *n.* **1.** prensa de sujeción *f.* —*v.* **2.** asegurar, sujetar.
clan /klæn/ *n.* tribu *f.*, clan *m.*
clandestine /klænˈdɛstɪn/ *a.* clandestino.
clandestinely /klænˈdɛstɪnli/ *adv.* clandestinamente.
clangor /ˈklæŋər, ˈklæŋgər/ *n.* estruendo *m.*, estrépito *m.*

clannish /'klænɪʃ/ a. unido; exclusivista.

clap /klæp/ v. aplaudir.

clapboard /'klæbərd, 'klæp,bɔrd/ n. chilla f.

claque /klæk/ n. claque f.

claret /'klærɪt/ n. clarete m.

clarification /,klærəfə'keiʃən/ n. clarificación f.

clarify /'klærə,fai/ v. clarificar.

clarinet /,klærə'nɛt/ n. clarinete m.

clarinetist /,klærə'nɛtɪst/ n. clarinetista m. & f.

clarity /'klærɪti/ n. claridad f.

clash /klæʃ/ n. **1.** choque, enfrentamiento m. —v. **2.** chocar.

clasp /klæsp/ n. **1.** broche m. —v. **2.** abrochar.

class /klæs/ n. clase f.

classic, /'klæsɪk/ classical a. clásico.

classicism /'klæsə,sɪzəm/ n. clasicismo m.

classifiable /'klæsə,faiəbəl/ a. clasificable, calificable.

classification /,klæsəfɪ'keiʃən/ n. clasificación f.

classify /'klæsə,fai/ v. clasificar.

classmate /'klæs,meit/ n. compañero -ra de clase.

classroom /'klæs,rum, -,rʊm/ n. sala de clase.

clatter /'klætər/ n. **1.** alboroto m. —v. **2.** alborotar.

clause /klɔz/ n. cláusula f.

claustrophobia /,klɔstrə'foubiə/ n. claustrofobia f.

claw /klɔ/ n. garra f.

clay /klei/ n. arcilla f.; barro m.

clean /klin/ a. **1.** limpio. —v. **2.** limpiar.

cleaner /'klinər/ n. limpiador -ra.

cleaning lady, cleaning woman /'klinɪŋ/ señora de la limpieza, mujer de la limpieza f.

cleanliness /'klɛnlinɪs/ n. limpieza f.

cleanse /klɛnz/ v. limpiar, purificar.

cleanser /'klɛnzər/ n. limpiador m., purificador m.

clear /klɪər/ a. claro.

clearance /'klɪərəns/ n. espacio libre. **c. sale,** venta de liquidación.

clearing /'klɪərɪŋ/ n. despejo m.; desmonte m.

clearly /'klɪərli/ adv. claramente, evidentemente.

clearness /'klɪərnɪs/ n. claridad f.

cleavage /'klivɪdʒ/ n. resquebradura f.

cleaver /'klivər/ n. partidor m., hacha f.

clef /klɛf/ n. clave, llave f.

clemency /'klɛmənsi/ n. clemencia f.

clench /klɛntʃ/ v. agarrar.

clergy /'klɜrdʒi/ n. clero m.

clergyman /'klɜrdʒimən/ n. clérigo m.

clerical /'klɛrɪkəl/ a. clerical. **c. work,** trabajo de oficina.

clericalism /'klɛrɪkə,lɪzəm/ n. clericalismo m.

clerk /klɜrk/ n. dependiente, escribiente m.

clerkship /'klɜrkʃɪp/ n. escribanía f., secretaría f.

clever /'klɛvər/ a. diestro, hábil.

cleverly /'klɛvərli/ adv. diestramente, hábilmente.

cleverness /'klɛvərnɪs/ n. destreza f.

cliché /kli'ʃei/ n. tópico m.

client /'klaiənt/ n. cliente -ta.

clientele /,klaiən'tɛl/ n. clientela f.

cliff /klɪf/ n. precipicio, risco m.

climate /'klaimɪt/ n. clima m.

climatic /klai'mætɪk/ a. climático.

climax /'klaimæks/ n. colmo m., culminación f.

climb /klaim/ v. escalar; subir.

climber /'klaimər/ n. trepador -ra, escalador -ra; Bot. enredadera f.

climbing plant /'klaimɪŋ/ enredadera f.

clinch /klɪntʃ/ v. afirmar.

cling /klɪŋ/ v. pegarse.

clinic /'klɪnɪk/ n. clínica f.

clinical /'klɪnɪkəl/ a. clínico.

clinically /'klɪnɪkəli/ adv. clínicamente.

clip /klɪp/ n. **1.** grapa f. **paper c.,** gancho m. —v. **2.** prender; (shear) trasquilar.

clipper /'klɪpər/ n. recortador m.; Aero. clíper m.

clipping /'klɪpɪŋ/ n. recorte m.

clique /klik/ n. camarilla f., compadraje m.

cloak /klouk/ n. capa f., manto m.

clock /klɒk/ n. reloj m. **alarm c.,** despertador m.

clod /klɒd/ n. terrón m.; césped m.

clog /klɒg/ v. obstruir.

cloister /'klɔistər/ n. claustro m.

clone /kloun/ n. clon m. & f. v. clonar.

close /a, adv. klous; v klouz/ a. **1.** cercano. —adv. **2.** cerca. **c. to,** cerca de. —v. **3.** cerrar; tapar.

closely /'klousli/ adv. (near) de cerca; (tight) estrechamente; (care) cuidadosamente.

closeness /'klousnɪs/ n. contigüidad f., apretamiento m.; (airless) falta de ventilación f.

closet /'klɒzɪt/ n. gabinete m. **clothes c.,** ropero m.

clot /klɒt/ n. **1.** coágulo f. —v. **2.** coagularse.

cloth /klɔθ/ n. paño m.; tela f.

clothe /klouð/ v. vestir.

clothes /klouz/ n. ropa f.

clothing /'klouðɪŋ/ n. vestidos m., ropa f.

cloud /klaud/ n. nube f.

cloudburst /'klaud,bɜrst/ n. chaparrón m.

cloudiness /'klaudinɪs/ n. nebulosidad f.; obscuridad f.

cloudless /'klaudlɪs/ a. despejado, sin nubes.

cloudy /'klaudi/ a. nublado.

clove /klouv/ n. clavo m.

clover /'klouvər/ n. trébol m.

clown /klaun/ n. bufón -na, payaso -sa.

clownish /'klaunɪʃ/ a. grosero; bufonesco.

cloy /klɔi/ v. saciar, empalagar.

club /klʌb/ n. **1.** porra f.; (social) círculo, club m.; (cards) basto m. —v. **2.** golpear con una porra.

clubfoot /'klʌb,fʊt/ n. pateta m., pie zambo m.

clue /klu/ n. seña, pista f.

clump /klʌmp/ n. grupo m., masa f.

clumsiness /'klʌmzinɪs/ n. tosquedad f.; desmaña f.

clumsy /'klʌmzi/ a. torpe, desmañado.

cluster /'klʌstər/ n. **1.** grupo m.; (fruit) racimo m. —v. **2.** agrupar.

clutch /klʌtʃ/ n. **1.** Auto. embrague m. —v. **2.** agarrar.

clutter /'klʌtər/ n. **1.** confusión f. —v. **2.** poner en desorden.

coach /koutʃ/ n. **1.** coche, vagón m.; coche ordinario; (sports) entrenador m. —v. **2.** entrenar.

coachman /'koutʃmən/ n. cochero -ra.

coagulate /kou'ægyə,leit/ v. coagular.

coagulation /kou,ægyə'leiʃən/ n. coagulación f.

coal /koul/ n. carbón m.

coalesce /,kouə'lɛs/ v. unirse, soldarse.

coalition /,kouə'lɪʃən/ n. coalición f.

coal oil n. petróleo m.

coal tar n. alquitrán m.

coarse /kɔrs/ a. grosero, burdo; (material) tosco, grueso.

coarsen /'kɔrsən/ v. vulgarizar.

coarseness /'kɔrsnɪs/ n. grosería, tosquedad f.

coast /koust/ n. **1.** costa f., litoral m. —v. **2.** deslizarse.

coastal /'koustl/ a. costanero.

coast guard guardacostas m. & f.

coat /kout/ n. **1.** saco m., chaqueta f.; (paint) capa f. —v. **2.** cubrir.

coat of arms /ɑrmz/ n. escudo m.

coax /kouks/ v. instar.

cobalt /'koubɔlt/ n. cobalto m.

cobbler /'kɒblər/ n. zapatero -ra.

cobblestone /'kɒbəl,stoun/ n. guijarro m.

cobra /'koubrə/ n. cobra f.

cobweb /'kɒb,wɛb/ n. telaraña f.

cocaine /kou'kein/ n. cocaína f.

cock /kɒk/ n. (rooster) gallo m.; (water, etc.) llave f.; (gun) martillo m.

cockfight /'kɒk,fait/ n. riña de gallos f.

cockpit /'kɒk,pɪt/ n. gallera f.; reñidero de gallos m.; Aero. cabina f.

cockroach /'kɒk,routʃ/ n. cucaracha f.

cocktail /'kɒk,teil/ n. cóctel m.

cocky /'kɒki/ a. confiado, atrevido.

cocoa /'koukou/ n. cacao m.

coconut /'koukə,nʌt/ n. coco m.

cocoon /kə'kun/ n. capullo m.

cod /kɒd/ n. bacalao m.

code /koud/ n. código m.; clave f.

codeine /'koudin/ n. codeína f.

codfish /'kɒd,fɪʃ/ n. bacalao m.

codify /'kɒdə,fai/ v. compilar.

cod-liver oil /'kɒd 'lɪvər/ aceite de hígado de bacalao m.

coeducation /,kouɛdʒu'keiʃən/ n. coeducación f.

coequal /kou'ikwəl/ a. mutuamente igual.

coerce /kou'ɜrs/ v. forzar.

coercion /kou'ɜrʃən/ n. coerción f.

coercive /kou'ɜrsɪv/ a. coercitivo.

coexist /,kouɪg'zɪst/ v. coexistir.

coffee /'kɔfi/ n. café m. **c. plantation,** cafetal m. **c. shop,** café m.

coffee break pausa para el café m.

coffer /'kɔfər/ n. cofre m.

coffin /'kɔfɪn/ n. ataúd m.

cog /kɒg/ n. diente de rueda m.

cogent /'koudʒənt/ a. convincente.

cogitate /'kɒdʒɪ,teit/ v. pensar, reflexionar.

cognizance /'kɒgnəzəns/ n. conocimiento m., comprensión f.

cognizant /'kɒgnəzənt/ a. conocedor, informado.

cogwheel /'kɒg,wil/ n. rueda dentada f.

cohere /kou'hɪər/ v. pegarse.

coherent /kou'hɪərənt/ a. coherente.

cohesion /kou'hiʒən/ n. cohesión f.

cohesive /kou'hisɪv/ a. cohesivo.

cohort /'kouhɔrt/ n. cohorte f.

coiffure /kwɑ'fyʊr/ n. peinado, tocado m.

coil /kɔil/ n. **1.** rollo m.; Naut. adujada f. —v. **2.** enrollar.

coin /kɔin/ n. moneda f.

coinage /'kɔinɪdʒ/ n. sistema monetario m.

coincide /,kouɪn'said/ v. coincidir.

coincidence /kou'ɪnsɪdəns/ n. coincidencia; casualidad f.

coincident /kou'ɪnsɪdənt/ a. coincidente.

coincidental /kou,ɪnsɪ'dɛntl/ a. coincidental.

coincidentally /kou,ɪnsɪ'dɛntli/ adv. coincidentalmente, al mismo tiempo.

colander /'kɒləndər/ n. colador m.

cold /kould/ a. & n. frío -a; Med. resfriado m. **to be c.,** tener frío; (weather) hacer frío.

coldly /'kouldli/ adv. fríamente.

coldness /'kouldnɪs/ n. frialdad f.

collaborate /kə'læbə,reit/ v. colaborar.

collaboration /kə,læbə'reiʃən/ n. colaboración f.

collaborator /kə'læbə,reitər/ n. colaborador -ra.

collapse /kə'læps/ n. **1.** desplome m.; Med. colapso m. —v. **2.** desplomarse.

collar /'kɒlər/ n. cuello m.

collarbone /'kɒlər,boun/ n. clavícula f.

collate /kou'leit/ v. comparar.

collateral /kə'lætərəl/ a. **1.** colateral. —n. **2.** garantía f.

collation /kə'leiʃən/ n. comparación f.; (food) colación f., merienda f.

colleague /'kɒlig/ n. colega m. & f.

collect /'kɒlɛkt/ v. cobrar; recoger; coleccionar.

collection /kə'lɛkʃən/ n. colección f.

collective /kə'lɛktɪv/ a. colectivo.

collectively /kə'lɛktɪvli/ adv. colectivamente, en masa.

collector /kə'lɛktər/ n. colector -ra; coleccionista m. & f.

college /'kɒlɪdʒ/ n. colegio m.; universidad f.

collegiate /kə'lidʒɪt/ a. colegiado m.

collide /kə'laid/ v. chocar.

collision /kə'lɪʒən/ n. choque m.

colloquial /kə'loukwiəl/ a. familiar.

colloquially /kə'loukwiəli/ adv. familiarmente.

colloquy /'kɒləkwi/ n. conversación f., coloquio m.

collusion /kə'luʒən/ n. colusión f., connivencia f.

Cologne /kə'loun/ n. Colonia f.

Colombian /kə'lʌmbiən/ a. & n. colombiano -na.

colon /'koulən/ n. colon m.; Punct. dos puntos.

colonel /'kɜrnl/ n. coronel m.

colonial /kə'louniəl/ a. colonial.

colonist /'kɒlənɪst/ n. colono -na.

colonization /,kɒlənə'zeiʃən/ n. colonización f.

colonize /'kɒlə,naiz/ v. colonizar.

colony /'kɒləni/ n. colonia f.

color /'kʌlər/ n. **1.** color; colorido m. —v. **2.** colorar; colorir.

coloration /,kʌlə'reiʃən/ n. colorido m.

colored /'kʌlərd/ a. de color.

colorful /'kʌlərfəl/ a. vívido.

colorless /'kʌlərlɪs/ a. descolorido, sin color.

colossal /kə'lɒsəl/ a. colosal.

colt /koult/ n. potro m.

column /'kɒləm/ n. columna f.

coma /'koumə/ n. coma m.

comb /koum/ n. **1.** peine m. —v. **2.** peinar.

combat /n 'kɒmbæt; v kəm'bæt/ n. **1.** combate m. —v. **2.** combatir.

combatant /kəm'bætnt/ n. combatiente -ta.

combative /kəm'bætɪv/ a. combativo.

combination /,kɒmbə'neiʃən/ n. combinación f.

combine /kəm'bain/ v. combinar.

combustible /kəm'bʌstəbəl/ a. & n. combustible m.

combustion /kəm'bʌstʃən/ n. combustión f.

come /kʌm/ v. venir. **c. back,** volver. **c. in,** entrar. **c. out,** salir. **c. up,** subir. **c. upon,** encontrarse con.

comedian /kə'midiən/ n. cómico -ca.

comedienne /kə,midi'ɛn/ n. cómica f., actriz f.

comedy /'kɒmɪdi/ n. comedia f.

comet /'kɒmɪt/ n. cometa m.

comfort /'kʌmfərt/ n. **1.** confort m.; solaz m. —v. **2.** confortar; solazar.

comfortable /'kʌmftəbəl/ a. cómodo.

comfortably /'kʌmftəbli/ adv. cómodamente.

comforter /'kʌmfərtər/ n. colcha f.

comfortingly /'kʌmfərtɪŋli/ adv. confortantemente.

comfortless /'kʌmfərtlɪs/ a. sin consuelo; sin comodidades.

comic /'kɒmɪk/ **comical** a. cómico.

comic book n. tebeo m.

coming /'kʌmɪŋ/ n. **1.** venida f., llegada f. —a. **2.** próximo, que viene, entrante.

comma /'kɒmə/ n. coma f.

command /kə'mænd/ n. **1.** mando m. —v. **2.** mandar.

commandeer /,kɒmən'dɪər/ v. reclutir forzosamente, expropiar.

commander /kə'mændər/ *n.* comandante -ta.

commander in chief *n.* generalísimo, jefe supremo.

commandment /kə'mændmənt/ *n.* mandato; mandamiento *m.*

commemorate /kə'mɛmə,reit/ *v.* conmemorar.

commemoration /kə,mɛmə'reiʃən/ *n.* conmemoración *f.*

commemorative /kə'mɛmə,reitiv/ *a.* conmemorativo.

commence /kə'mɛns/ *v.* comenzar, principiar.

commencement /kə'mɛnsmənt/ *n.* comienzo *m.*; graduación *f.*

commend /kə'mɛnd/ *v.* encomendar; elogiar.

commendable /kə'mɛndəbəl/ *a.* recomendable.

commendably /kə'mɛndəbli/ *adv.* loablemente.

commendation /,kɒmən'deiʃən/ *n.* recomendación *f.*; elogio *m.*

commensurate /kə'mɛnsərit/ *a.* proporcionado.

comment /'kɒmɛnt/ *n.* **1.** comentario *m.* —*v.* **2.** comentar.

commentary /'kɒmən,tɛri/ *n.* comentario *m.*

commentator /'kɒmən,teitər/ *n.* comentador -ra.

commerce /'kɒmɚs/ *n.* comercio *m.*

commercial /kə'mɚʃəl/ *a.* comercial.

commercialism /kə'mɚʃə,lizəm/ *n.* comercialismo *m.*

commercialize /kə'mɚʃə,laiz/ *v.* mercantilizar, explotar.

commercially /kə'mɚʃəli/ *a. & adv.* comercialmente.

commiserate /kə'mizə,reit/ *v.* compadecerse.

commissary /'kɒmə,sɛri/ *n.* comisario *m.*

commission /kə'miʃən/ *n.* **1.** comisión *f.* —*v.* **2.** comisionar.

commissioner /kə'miʃənər/ *n.* comisario -ria.

commit /kə'mit/ *v.* cometer.

commitment /kə'mitmənt/ *n.* compromiso *m.*

committee /kə'miti/ *n.* comité *m.*

commodious /kə'moudiəs/ *a.* cómodo.

commodity /kə'mɒditi/ *n.* mercadería *f.*

common /'kɒmən/ *a.* común; ordinario.

commonly /'kɒmənli/ *adv.* comúnmente, vulgarmente.

Common Market Mercado Común *m.*

commonplace /'kɒmən,pleis/ *a.* trivial, banal.

common sense sentido común *m.*

commonwealth /'kɒmən,wɛlθ/ *n.* estado *m.*; nación *f.*

commotion /kə'mouʃən/ *n.* tumulto *m.*

communal /kə'myunḷ/ *a.* comunal, público.

commune /'kɒmyun/ *n.* **1.** distrito municipal *m.*; comuna *f.* —*v.* **2.** conversar.

communicable /kə'myunikəbəl/ *a.* comunicable; *Med.* transmisible.

communicate /kə'myuni,keit/ *v.* comunicar.

communication /kə,myuni'keiʃən/ *n.* comunicación *f.*

communicative /kə'myuni,keitiv/ *a.* comunicativo.

communion /kə'myunyən/ *n.* comunión *f.* **take c.,** comulgar.

communiqué /kə,myuni'kei/ *n.* comunicación *f.*

communism /'kɒmyə,nizəm/ *n.* comunismo *m.*

communist /'kɒmyənist/ *n.* comunista *m. & f.*

communistic /,kɒmyə'nistik/ *a.* comunístico.

community /kə'myuniti/ *n.* comunidad *f.*

commutation /,kɒmyə'teiʃən/ *n.* conmutación *f.*

commuter /kə'myutər/ *n.* empleado que viaja diariamente desde su domicilio hasta la ciudad donde trabaja.

compact /*a* kəm'pækt; *n* 'kɒmpækt/ *a.* **1.** compacto. —*n.* **2.** pacto *m.*; (lady's) polvera *f.*

compact disk disco compacto *m.*

companion /kəm'pænyən/ *n.* compañero -ra.

companionable /kəm'pænyənəbəl/ *a.* sociable.

companionship /kəm'pænyən,ʃip/ *n.* compañerismo *m.*

company /'kʌmpəni/ *n.* compañía *f.*

comparable /'kɒmpərəbəl/ *a.* comparable.

comparative /kəm'pærətiv/ *a.* comparativo.

comparatively /kəm'pærətivli/ *a.* relativamente.

compare /kəm'pɛər/ *v.* comparar.

comparison /kəm'pærəsən/ *n.* comparación *f.*

compartment /kəm'pɑrtmənt/ *n.* compartimiento *m.*

compass /'kʌmpəs/ *n.* compás *m.*; *Naut.* brújula *f.*

compassion /kəm'pæʃən/ *n.* compasión *f.*

compassionate /kəm'pæʃənit/ *a.* compasivo.

compassionately /kəm'pæʃənitli/ *adv.* compasivamente.

compatible /kəm'pætəbəl/ *a.* compatible.

compatriot /kəm'peitriət/ *n.* patriota *m. & f.*

compel /kəm'pɛl/ *v.* obligar.

compensate /'kɒmpən,seit/ *v.* compensar.

compensation /,kɒmpən'seiʃən/ *n.* compensación *f.*

compensatory /kəm'pɛnsə,tɔri/ *a.* compensatorio.

compete /kəm'pit/ *v.* competir.

competence /'kɒmpitəns/ *n.* competencia *f.*

competent /'kɒmpitənt/ *a.* competente, capaz.

competently /'kɒmpitəntli/ *adv.* competentemente.

competition /,kɒmpi'tiʃən/ *n.* concurrencia *f.*; concurso *m.*

competitive /kəm'pɛtitiv/ *a.* competidor.

competitor /kəm'pɛtitər/ *n.* competidor -ra.

compile /kəm'pail/ *v.* compilar.

complacency /kəm'pleisənsi/ *n.* complacencia *f.*

complacent /kəm'pleisənt/ *a.* complaciente.

complacently /kəm'pleisəntli/ *adv.* complacientemente.

complain /kəm'plein/ *v.* quejarse.

complaint /kəm'pleint/ *n.* queja *f.*

complement /'kɒmpləmənt/ *n.* complemento *m.*

complete /kəm'plit/ *a.* **1.** completo —*v.* **2.** completar.

completely /kəm'plitli/ *adv.* completamente, enteramente.

completeness /kəm'plitnis/ *n.* integridad *f.*

completion /kəm'pliʃən/ *n.* terminación *f.*

complex /kəm'plɛks/ *a.* complejo.

complexion /kəm'plɛkʃən/ *n.* tez *f.*

complexity /kəm'plɛksiti/ *n.* complejidad *f.*

compliance /kəm'plaiəns/ *n.* consentimiento *m.* **in c. with,** de acuerdo con.

compliant /kəm'plaiənt/ *a.* dócil; complaciente.

complicate /'kɒmpli,keit/ *v.* complicar.

complicated /'kɒmpli,keitid/ *a.* complicado.

complication /,kɒmpli'keiʃən/ *n.* complicación *f.*

complicity /kəm'plisiti/ *n.* complicidad *f.*

compliment /*n* 'kɒmpləmənt; *v* -,mɛnt/ *n.* **1.** elogio *m.* *Fig.* —*v.* **2.** felicitar; echar flores.

complimentary /,kɒmplə'mɛntəri/ *a.* galante, obsequioso, regaloso.

comply /kəm'plai/ *v.* cumplir.

component /kəm'pounənt/ *a. & n.* componente *m.*

comport /kəm'pɔrt/ *v.* portarse.

compose /kəm'pouz/ *v.* componer.

composed /kəm'pouzd/ *a.* tranquilo; (made up) compuesto.

composer /kəm'pouzər/ *n.* compositor -ra.

composite /kəm'pɒzit/ *a.* compuesto.

composition /,kɒmpə'ziʃən/ *n.* composición *f.*

composure /kəm'pouʒər/ *n.* serenidad *f.*; calma *f.*

compote /'kɒmpout/ *n.* compota *f.*

compound /'kɒmpaund/ *a. & n.* compuesto *m.*

comprehend /,kɒmpri'hɛnd/ *v.* comprender.

comprehensible /,kɒmpri'hɛnsəbəl/ *a.* comprensible.

comprehension /,kɒmpri'hɛnʃən/ *n.* comprensión *f.*

comprehensive /,kɒmpri'hɛnsiv/ *a.* comprensivo.

compress /*n* 'kɒmprɛs; *v* kəm'prɛs/ *n.* **1.** cabezal *m.* —*v.* **2.** comprimir.

compressed /kəm'prɛst/ *a.* comprimido.

compression /kəm'prɛʃən/ *n.* presión *f.*

compressor /kəm'prɛsər/ *n.* compresor *m.*

comprise /kəm'praiz/ *v.* comprender; abarcar.

compromise /'kɒmprə,maiz/ *n.* **1.** compromiso *m.* —*v.* **2.** comprometer.

compromiser /'kɒmprə,maizər/ *n.* compromisario *m.*

compulsion /kəm'pʌlʃən/ *n.* compulsión *f.*

compulsive /kəm'pʌlsiv/ *a.* compulsivo.

compulsory /kəm'pʌlsəri/ *a.* obligatorio.

compunction /kəm'pʌŋkʃən/ *n.* punción *f.*; escrúpulo *m.*

computation /,kɒmpyu'teiʃən/ *n.* computación *f.*

compute /kəm'pyut/ *v.* computar, calcular.

computer /kəm'pyutər/ *n.* computadora *f.*, ordenador *m.*

computerize /kəm'pyutə,raiz/ *v.* procesar en computadora, computerizar.

computer programmer /'prougræmər/ programador -ra de ordenadores.

computer science informática *f.*

comrade /'kɒmræd/ *n.* camarada *m. & f.*; compañero -ra.

comradeship /'kɒmræd,ʃip/ *n.* camaradería *f.*

concave /kɒn'keiv/ *a.* cóncavo.

conceal /kən'sil/ *v.* ocultar, esconder.

concealment /kən'silmənt/ *n.* ocultación *f.*

concede /kən'sid/ *v.* conceder.

conceit /kən'sit/ *n.* amor propio; engreimiento *m.*

conceited /kən'sitid/ *a.* engreído.

conceivable /kən'sivəbəl/ *a.* concebible.

conceive /kən'siv/ *v.* concebir.

concentrate /'kɒnsən,treit/ *v.* concentrar.

concentration /,kɒnsən'treiʃən/ *n.* concentración *f.*

concentration camp campo de concentración *m.*

concept /'kɒnsɛpt/ *n.* concepto *m.*

conception /kən'sɛpʃən/ *n.* concepción *f.*; concepto *m.*

concern /kən'sɚn/ *n.* **1.** interés *m.*; inquietud *f.*; *Com.* negocio *m.* —*v.* **2.** concernir.

concerning /kən'sɚniŋ/ *prep.* respecto a.

concert /'kɒnsɚt/ *n.* concierto *m.*

concerted /kən'sɚtid/ *a.* convenido.

concession /kən'sɛʃən/ *n.* concesión *f.*

conciliate /kən'sili,eit/ *v.* conciliar.

conciliation /kən,sili'eiʃən/ *n.* conciliación *f.*

conciliator /kən'sili,eitər/ *n.* conciliador -ra.

conciliatory /kən'silia,tɔri/ *a.* conciliatorio.

concise /kən'sais/ *a.* conciso.

concisely /kən'saisli/ *adv.* concisamente.

conciseness /kən'saisnis/ *n.* concisión *f.*

conclave /'kɒnkleiv/ *n.* conclave *m.*

conclude /kən'klud/ *v.* concluir.

conclusion /kən'kluʒən/ *n.* conclusión *f.*

conclusive /kən'klusiv/ *a.* conclusivo, decisivo.

conclusively /kən'klusivli/ *adv.* concluyentemente.

concoct /kɒn'kɒkt/ *v.* confeccionar.

concomitant /kɒn'kɒmitənt/ *n. & a.* concomitante *m.*

concord /'kɒnkɔrd/ *n.* concordia *f.*

concordat /kɒn'kɔrdæt/ *n.* concordato *m.*

concourse /'kɒnkɔrs/ *n.* concurso *m.*; confluencia *f.*

concrete /'kɒnkrit/ *a.* concreto.

concretely /kɒn'kritli/ *adv.* concretamente.

concubine /'kɒŋkyə,bain/ *n.* concubina, amiga *f.*

concur /kən'kɚ/ *v.* concurrir.

concurrence /kən'kɚəns/ *n.* concurrencia *f.*; casualidad *f.*

concurrent /kən'kɚənt/ *a.* concurrente.

concussion /kən'kʌʃən/ *n.* concusión *f.*; (c. of the brain) conmoción cerebral *f.*

condemn /kən'dɛm/ *v.* condenar.

condemnable /kən'dɛmnəbəl/ *a.* culpable, condenable.

condemnation /,kɒndɛm'neiʃən/ *n.* condenación *f.*

condensation /,kɒndɛn'seiʃən/ *n.* condensación *f.*

condense /kən'dɛns/ *v.* condensar.

condenser /kən'dɛnsər/ *n.* condensador *m.*

condescend /,kɒndə'sɛnd/ *v.* condescender.

condescension /,kɒndə'sɛnʃən/ *n.* condescendencia *f.*

condiment /'kɒndəmənt/ *n.* condimento *m.*

condition /kən'diʃən/ *n.* **1.** condición *f.*; estado *m.* —*v.* **2.** acondicionar.

conditional /kən'diʃənḷ/ *a.* condicional.

conditionally /kən'diʃənḷi/ *adv.* condicionalmente.

condole /kən'doul/ *v.* condolerse.

condolence /kən'douləns/ *n.* pésame *m.*

condom /'kɒndəm/ *n.* forro, preservativo *m.*

condominium /,kɒndə'miniəm/ *n.* condominio *m.*

condone /kən'doun/ *v.* condonar.

conducive /kən'dusiv, -'dyu-/ *a.* conducente.

conduct /*n* 'kɒndʌkt; *v* kən'dʌkt/ *n.* **1.** conducta *f.* —*v.* **2.** conducir.

conductivity /,kɒndʌk'tiviti/ *n.* conductividad *f.*

conductor /kən'dʌktər/ *n.* conductor *m.*

conduit /'kɒnduit/ *n.* caño *m.*, canal *f.*; conducto *m.*

cone /koun/ *n.* cono *m.* **ice-cream c.,** barquillo de helado.

confection /kən'fɛkʃən/ *n.* confitura *f.*

confectioner /kən'fɛkʃənər/ *n.* confitero -ra.

confectionery /kənˈfɛkʃəˌnɛri/ n. dulcería f.

confederacy /kənˈfɛdərəsi/ n. federación f.

confederate / kənˈfɛdərɪt/ a. & n. confederado m.

confederation /kənˌfɛdəˈreiʃən/ n. confederación f.

confer /kənˈfɜr/ v. conferenciar; conferir.

conference /ˈkɒnfərəns/ n. conferencia f.; congreso m.

confess /kənˈfɛs/ v. confesar.

confession /kənˈfɛʃən/ n. confesión f.

confessional /kənˈfɛʃənḷ/ n. 1. confesionario m. —a. 2. confesional.

confessor /kənˈfɛsər/ n. confesor m.

confetti /kənˈfɛti/ n. confetti m.

confidant /ˈkɒnfɪˌdænt/ **confidante** n. confidente m. & f.

confide /kənˈfaid/ v. confiar.

confidence /ˈkɒnfɪdəns/ n. confianza f.

confident /ˈkɒnfɪdənt/ a. confiado; cierto.

confidential /ˌkɒnfɪˈdɛnʃəl/ a. confidencial.

confidentially /ˌkɒnfɪˈdɛnʃəli/ adv. confidencialmente, en secreto.

confidently /ˈkɒnfɪdəntli/ adv. confiadamente.

confine /kənˈfain/ n. 1. confín m. —v. 2. confinar; encerrar.

confirm /kənˈfɜrm/ v. confirmar.

confirmation /ˌkɒnfərˈmeiʃən/ n. confirmación f.

confiscate /ˈkɒnfəˌskeit/ v. confiscar.

confiscation /ˌkɒnfəˈskeiʃən/ n. confiscación f.

conflagration /ˌkɒnfləˈgreiʃən/ n. incendio m.

conflict /n ˈkɒnflɪkt; v kənˈflɪkt/ n. 1. conflicto m. —v. 2. oponerse; estar en conflicto.

conform /kənˈfɔrm/ v. conformar.

conformation /ˌkɒnfərˈmeiʃən/ n. conformación f.

conformer /kənˈfɔrmər/ n. conformista m. & f.

conformist /kənˈfɔrmɪst/ n. conformista m. & f.

conformity /kənˈfɔrmɪti/ n. conformidad f.

confound /kɒnˈfaund/ v. confundir.

confront /kənˈfrʌnt/ v. confrontar.

confrontation /ˌkɒnfrənˈteiʃən/ n. enfrentamiento m.

confuse /kənˈfyuz/ v. confundir.

confusion /kənˈfyuʒən/ n. confusión f.

congeal /kənˈdʒil/ v. congelar, helar.

congealment /kənˈdʒilmənt/ n. congelación f.

congenial /kənˈdʒinyəl/ a. congenial.

congenital /kənˈdʒɛnɪtḷ/ a. congénito.

congenitally /kənˈdʒɛnɪtḷi/ adv. congenitalmente.

congestion /kənˈdʒɛstʃən/ n. congestión f.

conglomerate /v kənˈglɒməˌreit; a, n kənˈglɒmərɪt/ v. 1. conglomerar. —a. & n. 2. conglomerado.

conglomeration /kənˌglɒməˈreiʃən/ n. conglomeración f.

congratulate /kənˈgrætʃəˌleit/ v. felicitar.

congratulation /kənˌgrætʃəˈleiʃən/ n. felicitación f.

congratulatory /kənˈgrætʃələˌtɔri/ a. congratulatorio.

congregate /ˈkɒŋgrɪˌgeit/ v. congregar.

congregation /ˌkɒŋgrɪˈgeiʃən/ n. congregación f.

congress /ˈkɒŋgrɪs/ n. congreso m.

conic /ˈkɒnɪk/ n. 1. cónica f. —a. 2. cónico.

conjecture /kənˈdʒɛktʃər/ n. 1. conjetura f. —v. 2. conjeturar.

conjugal /ˈkɒndʒəgəl/ a. conyugal, matrimonial.

conjugate /ˈkɒndʒəˌgeit/ v. conjugar.

conjugation /ˌkɒndʒəˈgeiʃən/ n. conjugación f.

conjunction /kənˈdʒʌŋkʃən/ n. conjunción f.

conjunctive /kənˈdʒʌŋktɪv/ n. 1. Gram. conjunción f. —a. 2. conjuntivo.

conjunctivitis /kənˌdʒʌŋktəˈvaitɪs/ n. conjuntivitis f.

conjure /ˈkɒndʒər/ v. conjurar.

connect /kəˈnɛkt/ v. juntar; relacionar.

connection /kəˈnɛkʃən/ n. conexión f.

connivance /kəˈnaivəns/ n. consentimiento m.

connive /kəˈnaiv/ v. disimular.

connoisseur /ˌkɒnəˈsɜr/ n. perito -ta.

connotation /ˌkɒnəˈteiʃən/ n. connotación f.

connote /kəˈnout/ v. connotar.

connubial /kəˈnubiəl/ a. conyugal.

conquer /ˈkɒŋkər/ v. conquistar.

conquerable /ˈkɒŋkərəbəl/ a. conquistable, vencible.

conqueror /ˈkɒŋkərər/ n. conquistador -ra.

conquest /ˈkɒnkwɛst/ n. conquista f.

conscience /ˈkɒnʃəns/ n. conciencia f.

conscientious /ˌkɒnʃiˈɛnʃəs/ a. concienzudo.

conscientiously /ˌkɒnʃiˈɛnʃəsli/ adv. escrupulosamente.

conscientious objector /ɒbˈdʒɛktər/ objetor de conciencia m.

conscious /ˈkɒnʃəs/ a. consciente.

consciously /ˈkɒnʃəsli/ adv. con conocimiento.

consciousness /ˈkɒnʃəsnɪs/ n. conciencia f.

conscript /n ˈkɒnskrɪpt; v kənˈskrɪpt/ n. 1. conscripto m., recluta m. —v. 2. reclutar, alistar.

conscription /kənˈskrɪpʃən/ n. conscripción f., alistamiento m.

consecrate /ˈkɒnsɪˌkreit/ v. consagrar.

consecration /ˌkɒnsɪˈkreiʃən/ n. consagración f.

consecutive /kənˈsɛkyətɪv/ a. consecutivo, seguido.

consecutively /kənˈsɛkyətɪvli/ adv. consecutivamente, de seguida.

consensus /kənˈsɛnsəs/ n. consenso m., acuerdo general m.

consent /kənˈsɛnt/ n. 1. consentimiento m. —v. 2. consentir.

consequence /ˈkɒnsɪˌkwɛns/ n. consecuencia f.

consequent /ˈkɒnsɪˌkwɛnt/ a. consiguiente.

consequential /ˌkɒnsɪˈkwɛnʃəl/ a. importante.

consequently /ˈkɒnsɪˌkwɛntli/ adv. por lo tanto, por consiguiente.

conservation /ˌkɒnsərˈveiʃən/ n. conservación f.

conservatism /kənˈsɜrvəˌtɪzəm/ n. conservatismo m.

conservative /kənˈsɜrvətɪv/ a. conservador, conservativo.

conservatory /kənˈsɜrvəˌtɔri/ (plants) invernáculo m.; (school) conservatorio m.

conserve /kənˈsɜrv/ v. conservar.

consider /kənˈsɪdər/ v. considerar. **C. it done!** ¡Dalo por hecho!

considerable /kənˈsɪdərəbəl/ a. considerable.

considerably /kənˈsɪdərəbli/ adv. considerablemente.

considerate /kənˈsɪdərɪt/ a. considerado.

considerately /kənˈsɪdərɪtli/ adv. consideradamente.

consideration /kənˌsɪdəˈreiʃən/ n. consideración f.

considering /kənˈsɪdərɪŋ/ prep. visto que, en vista de.

consign /kənˈsain/ v. consignar.

consignment /kənˈsainmənt/ n. consignación f., envío m.

consist /kənˈsɪst/ v. consistir.

consistency /kənˈsɪstənsi/ n. consistencia f.

consistent /kənˈsɪstənt/ a. consistente.

consolation /ˌkɒnsəˈleiʃən/ n. consolación f.

consolation prize premio de consuelo m.

console /ˈkɒnsoul/ v. consolar.

consolidate /kənˈsɒlɪˌdeit/ v. consolidar.

consommé /ˌkɒnsəˈmei/ n. caldo m.

consonant /ˈkɒnsənənt/ n. consonante f.

consort /n ˈkɒnsɔrt, v kənˈsɔrt/ n. 1. cónyuge m. & f.; socio. —v. 2. asociarse.

conspicuous /kənˈspɪkyuəs/ a. conspicuo.

conspicuously /kənˈspɪkyuəsli/ adv. visiblemente, llamativamente.

conspicuousness /kənˈspɪkyuəsnɪs/ n. visibilidad f.; evidencia f.; fama f.

conspiracy /kənˈspɪrəsi/ n. conspiración f.; complot m.

conspirator /kənˈspɪrətər/ n. conspirador -ra.

conspire /kənˈspaiər/ v. conspirar.

conspirer /kənˈspaiərər/ n. conspirante m. & f.

constancy /ˈkɒnstənsi/ n. constancia f., lealtad f.

constant /ˈkɒnstənt/ a. constante.

constantly /ˈkɒnstəntli/ adv. constantemente, de continuo.

constellation /ˌkɒnstəˈleiʃən/ n. constelación f.

consternation /ˌkɒnstərˈneiʃən/ n. consternación f.

constipate /ˈkɒnstəˌpeit/ v. estreñir.

constipated /ˈkɒnstəˌpeitɪd/ a. estreñido, m.

constipation /ˌkɒnstəˈpeiʃən/ n. estreñimiento, m.

constituency /kənˈstɪtʃuənsi/ n. distrito electoral m.

constituent /kənˈstɪtʃuənt/ a. 1. constituyente. —n. 2. elector m.

constitute /ˈkɒnstɪˌtut/ v. constituir.

constitution /ˌkɒnstɪˈtuʃən/ n. constitución f.

constitutional /ˌkɒnstɪˈtuʃənḷ/ a. constitucional.

constrain /kənˈstrein/ v. constreñir.

constraint /kənˈstreint/ n. constreñimiento m., compulsión f.

constrict /kənˈstrɪkt/ v. apretar, estrechar.

construct /kənˈstrʌkt/ v. construir.

construction /kənˈstrʌkʃən/ n. construcción f.

constructive /kənˈstrʌktɪv/ a. constructivo.

constructively /kənˈstrʌktɪvli/ adv. constructivamente; por deducción.

constructor /kənˈstrʌktər/ n. constructor m.

construe /kənˈstru/ v. interpretar.

consul /ˈkɒnsəl/ n. cónsul m.

consular /ˈkɒnsələr/ a. consular.

consulate /ˈkɒnsəlɪt/ n. consulado m.

consult /kənˈsʌlt/ v. consultar.

consultant /kənˈsʌltənt/ n. consultor -ora.

consultation /ˌkɒnsəlˈteiʃən/ n. consulta f.

consume /kənˈsum/ v. consumir.

consumer /kənˈsuˈmər/ n. consumidor -ra.

consumer society sociedad de consumo f.

consummation /ˌkɒnsəˈmeiʃən/ n. consumación f.

consumption /kənˈsʌmpʃən/ n. consumo m.; Med. tisis.

consumptive /kənˈsʌmptɪv/ n. 1. tísico m. —a. 2. consuntivo.

contact /ˈkɒntækt/ n. 1. contacto m. —v. 2. ponerse en contacto con.

contact lens lentilla f.

contagion /kənˈteidʒən/ n. contagio m.

contagious /kənˈteidʒəs/ a. contagioso.

contain /kənˈtein/ v. contener.

container /kənˈteinər/ n. envase m.

contaminate /kənˈtæməˌneit/ v. contaminar.

contemplate /ˈkɒntəmˌpleit/ v. contemplar.

contemplation /ˌkɒntəmˈpleiʃən/ n. contemplación f.

contemplative /kənˈtɛmplətɪv/ a. contemplativo.

contemporary /kənˈtɛmpəˌrɛri/ n. & a. contemporáneo -nea.

contempt /kənˈtɛmpt/ n. desprecio m.

contemptible /kənˈtɛmptəbəl/ a. vil, despreciable.

contemptuous /kənˈtɛmptʃuəs/ a. desdeñoso.

contemptuously /kənˈtɛmptʃuəsli/ adv. desdeñosamente.

contend /kənˈtɛnd/ v. contender; competir.

contender /kənˈtɛndər/ n. competidor -ra.

content /a, v kənˈtɛnt; n ˈkɒntɛnt/ a. 1. contento. —n. 2. contenido m. —v. 3. contentar.

contented /kənˈtɛntɪd/ a. contento.

contention /kənˈtɛnʃən/ n. contención f.

contentment /kənˈtɛntmənt/ n. contentamiento m.

contest /n ˈkɒntɛst; v kənˈtɛst/ n. 1. concurso m. —v. 2. disputar.

contestable /kənˈtɛstəbəl/ a. contestable.

context /ˈkɒntɛkst/ n. contexto m.

contiguous /kənˈtɪgyuəs/ a. contiguo.

continence /ˈkɒntṇəns/ n. continencia f., castidad f.

continent /ˈkɒntṇənt/ n. continente m.

continental /ˌkɒntṇˈɛntḷ/ a. continental.

contingency /kənˈtɪndʒənsi/ n. eventualidad f., casualidad f.

contingent /kənˈtɪndʒənt/ a. contingente.

continual /kənˈtɪnyuəl/ a. continuo.

continuation /kənˌtɪnyuˈeiʃən/ n. continuación f.

continue /kənˈtɪnyu/ v. continuar.

continuity /ˌkɒntṇˈuiti/ n. continuidad f.

continuous /kənˈtɪnyuəs/ a. continuo.

continuously /kənˈtɪnyuəsli/ adv. continuamente.

contour /ˈkɒntur/ n. contorno m.

contraband /ˈkɒntrəˌbænd/ n. contrabando m.

contraception /ˌkɒntrəˈsɛpʃən/ n. contracepción f.

contraceptive /ˌkɒntrəˈsɛptɪv/ n. & a. anticeptivo m.

contract /n ˈkɒntrækt; v kənˈtrækt/ n. 1. contrato m. —v. 2. contraer.

contraction /kənˈtrækʃən/ n. contracción f.

contractor /ˈkɒntræktər/ n. contratista m. & f.

contradict /ˌkɒntrəˈdɪkt/ v. contradecir.

contradiction /ˌkɒntrəˈdɪkʃən/ n. contradicción f.

contradictory /ˌkɒntrəˈdɪktəri/ a. contradictorio.

contralto /kənˈtræltou/ n. contralto m.

contrary /ˈkɒntrɛri/ a. & n. contrario -ria.

contrast /n ˈkɒntræst; v kənˈtræst/ n. 1. contraste m. —v. 2. contrastar.

contribute /kənˈtrɪbyut/ v. contribuir.

contribution /ˌkɒntrəˈbyuʃən/ n. contribución f.

contributor /kənˈtrɪbyətər/ n. contribuidor -ra.

contributory /kənˈtrɪbyəˌtɔri/ a. contribuyente.

contrite /kən'trait/ *a.* contrito.
contrition /kən'trɪʃən/ *n.* contrición *f.*
contrivance /kən'traivəns/ *n.* aparato *m.*; estratagema *f.*
contrive /kən'traiv/ *v.* inventar, tramar; darse maña.
control /kən'troul/ *n.* **1.** control *m.* —*v.* **2.** controlar.
controllable /kən'trouləbəl/ *a.* controlable, dominable.
controller /kən'troulər/ *n.* interventor -ra; contralor -ra.
control tower torre de mando *f.*
controversial /ˌkɒntrə'vɜrʃəl/ *a.* contencioso.
controversy /'kɒntrə,vɜrsi/ *n.* controversia *f.*
contusion /kən'tuʒən/ *n.* contusión *f.*
convalesce /ˌkɒnvə'lɛs/ *v.* convalecer.
convalescence /ˌkɒnvə'lɛsəns/ *n.* convalecencia *f.*
convalescent /ˌkɒnvə'lɛsənt/ *n.* convaleciente *m. & f.*
convalescent home clínica de reposo *f.*
convene /kən'vin/ *v.* juntarse; convocar.
convenience /kən'vinyəns/ *n.* comodidad *f.*
convenient /kən'vinyənt/ *a.* cómodo; oportuno.
conveniently /kən'vinyəntli/ *adv.* cómodamente.
convent /'kɒnvɛnt/ *n.* convento *m.*
convention /kən'vɛnʃən/ *n.* convención *f.*
conventional /kən'vɛnʃənl/ *a.* convencional.
conventionally /kən'vɛnʃənli/ *adv.* convencionalmente.
converge /kən'vɜrdʒ/ *v.* convergir.
convergence /kən'vɜrdʒəns/ *n.* convergencia *f.*
convergent /kən'vɜrdʒənt/ *a.* convergente.
conversant /kən'vɜrsənt/ *a.* versado; entendido (de).
conversation /ˌkɒnvər'seiʃən/ *n.* conversación, plática *f.*
conversational /ˌkɒnvər'seiʃənl/ *a.* de conversación.
conversationalist /ˌkɒnvər'seiʃənlɪst/ *n.* conversador -ra.
converse /kən'vɜrs/ *v.* conversar.
conversely /kən'vɜrsli/ *adv.* a la inversa.
convert /n 'kɒnvɜrt; v kən'vɜrt/ *n.* **1.** convertido da-. —*v.* **2.** convertir.
converter /kən'vɜrtər/ *n.* convertidor *m.*
convertible /kən'vɜrtəbəl/ *a.* convertible.
convex /kɒn'vɛks/ *a.* convexo.
convey /kən'vei/ *v.* transportar; comunicar.
conveyance /kən'veiəns/ *n.* transporte; vehículo *m.*
conveyor /kən'veiər/ *n.* conductor *m.*; Mech. transportador *m.*
conveyor belt correa transportadora *f.*
convict /n 'kɒnvɪkt; v kən'vɪkt/ *n.* **1.** reo *m.* —*v.* **2.** declarar culpable.
conviction /kən'vɪkʃən/ *n.* convicción *f.*
convince /kən'vɪns/ *v.* convencer.
convincing /kən'vɪnsɪŋ/ *a.* convincente.
convivial /kən'vɪviəl/ *a.* convival.
convocation /ˌkɒnvə'keiʃən/ *n.* convocación; asamblea *f.*
convoke /kən'vouk/ *v.* convocar, citar.
convoy /'kɒnvɔi/ *n.* convoy *m.*; escolta *f.*
convulse /kən'vʌls/ *v.* convulsionar; agitar violentamente.
convulsion /kən'vʌlʃən/ *n.* convulsión *f.*
convulsive /kən'vʌlsɪv/ *a.* convulsivo.

cook /kʊk/ *n.* **1.** cocinero -ra. —*v.* **2.** cocinar, cocer.
cookbook /'kʊk,bʊk/ *n.* libro de cocina *m.*
cookie /'kʊki/ *n.* galleta dulce *f.*
cool /kul/ *a.* **1.** fresco. —*v.* **2.** refrescar.
cooler /'kulər/ *n.* enfriadera *f.*
coolness /'kulnɪs/ *n.* frescura *f.*
coop /kup/ *n.* **1.** jaula *f.* **chicken c.,** gallinero *m.* —*v.* **2.** enjaular.
cooperate /kou'ɒpə,reit/ *v.* cooperar.
cooperation /kou,ɒpə'reiʃən/ *n.* cooperación *f.*
cooperative /kou'ɒpərətɪv/ *a.* cooperativo.
cooperatively /kou'ɒpərətɪvli/ *adv.* cooperativamente.
coordinate /kou'ɔrdn,eit/ *v.* coordinar.
coordination /kou,ɔrdn'eiʃən/ *n.* coordinación *f.*
coordinator /kou'ɔrdn,eitər/ *n.* coordinador -ra.
cope /koup/ *v.* contender. **c. with,** superar, hacer frente a.
copier /'kɒpiər/ *n.* copiadora *f.*
copious /'koupiəs/ *a.* copioso, abundante.
copiously /'koupiəsli/ *adv.* copiosamente.
copiousness /'koupiəsnɪs/ *n.* abundancia *f.*
copper /'kɒpər/ *n.* cobre *m.*
copy /'kɒpi/ *n.* **1.** copia *f.*; ejemplar *m.* —*v.* **2.** copiar.
copyist /'kɒpiɪst/ *n.* copista *m. & f.*
copyright /'kɒpi,rait/ *n.* derechos de propiedad literaria *m.pl.*
coquetry /'koukɪtri/ *n.* coquetería *f.*
coquette /kou'kɛt/ *n.* coqueta *f.*
coral /'kɔrəl/ *n.* coral *m.*
cord /kɔrd/ *n.* cuerda *f.*
cordial /'kɔrdʒəl/ *a.* cordial.
cordiality /kɔr'dʒælɪti/ *n.* cordialidad *f.*
cordially /'kɔrdʒəli/ *adv.* cordialmente.
cordon off /'kɔrdn/ *v.* acordonar.
cordovan /'kɔrdəvən/ *n.* cordobán *m.*
corduroy /'kɔrdə,rɔi/ *n.* pana *f.*
core /kɔr/ *n.* corazón; centro *m.*
cork /kɔrk/ *n.* corcho *m.*
corkscrew /'kɔrk,skru/ *n.* tirabuzón *m.*
corn /kɔrn/ *n.* maíz *m.*
cornea /'kɔrniə/ *n.* córnea *f.*
corned beef /kɔrnd/ carne acecinada *f.*
corner /'kɔrnər/ *n.* rincón *m.*; (of street) esquina *f.*
cornet /kɔr'nɛt/ *n.* corneta *f.*
cornetist /kɔr'nɛtɪst/ *n.* cornetín *m.*
cornice /'kɔrnɪs/ *n.* cornisa *f.*
cornstarch /'kɔrn,startʃ/ *n.* maicena *f.*
corollary /'kɔrə,lɛri/ *n.* corolario *m.*
coronary /'kɔrə,nɛri/ *a.* coronario.
coronation /ˌkɔrə'neiʃən/ *n.* coronación *f.*
corporal /'kɔrpərəl/ *a.* **1.** corpóreo. —*n.* **2.** cabo *m.*
corporate /'kɔrpərɪt/ *a.* corporativo.
corporation /ˌkɔrpə'reiʃən/ *n.* corporación *f.*
corps /kɔr/ *n.* cuerpo *m.*
corpse /kɔrps/ *n.* cadáver *m.*
corpulent /'kɔrpyələnt/ *a.* corpulento.
corpuscle /'kɔrpəsəl/ *n.* corpúsculo *m.*
corral /kə'ræl/ *n.* **1.** corral. —*v.* **2.** acorralar.
correct /kə'rɛkt/ *a.* **1.** correcto. —*v.* **2.** corregir.
correction /kə'rɛkʃən/ *n.* corrección; enmienda *f.*
corrective /kə'rɛktɪv/ *n. & a.* correctivo.
correctly /kə'rɛktli/ *adv.* correctamente.
correctness /kə'rɛktnɪs/ *n.* exactitud *f.*

correlate /'kɔrə,leit/ *v.* correlacionar.
correlation /ˌkɔrə'leiʃən/ *n.* correlación *f.*
correspond /ˌkɔrə'spɒnd/ *v.* corresponder.
correspondence /ˌkɔrə'spɒndəns/ *n.* correspondencia *f.*
correspondence course curso por correspondencia *m.*
correspondence school escuela por correspondencia *f.*
correspondent /ˌkɔrə'spɒndənt/ *a. & n.* correspondiente *m. & f.*
corresponding /ˌkɔrə'spɒndɪŋ/ *a.* correspondiente.
corridor /'kɔridər/ *n.* corredor, pasillo *m.*
corroborate /kə'rɒbə,reit/ *v.* corroborar.
corroboration /kə,rɒbə'reiʃən/ *n.* corroboración *f.*
corroborative /kə'rɒbə,reitɪv/ *a.* corroborante.
corrode /kə'roud/ *v.* corroer.
corrosion /kə'rouʒən/ *n.* corrosión *f.*
corrugate /'kɔrə,geit/ *v.* arrugar; ondular.
corrupt /kə'rʌpt/ *a.* **1.** corrompido. —*v.* **2.** corromper.
corruptible /kə'rʌptəbəl/ *a.* corruptible.
corruption /kə'rʌpʃən/ *n.* corrupción *f.*
corruptive /kə'rʌptɪv/ *a.* corruptivo.
corset /'kɔrsɪt/ *n.* corsé *m.*, (girdle) faja *f.*
cortege /kɔr'tɛʒ/ *n.* comitiva *f.*, séquito *m.*
corvette /kɔr'vɛt/ *n.* corbeta *f.*
cosmetic /kɒz'mɛtɪk/ *a. & n.* cosmético *m.*
cosmic /'kɒzmɪk/ *a.* cósmico.
cosmonaut /'kɒzmə,nɔt/ *n.* cosmonauta *m. & f.*
cosmopolitan /ˌkɒzmə'pɒlɪtn/ *a. & n.* cosmopolita *m. & f.*
cosmos /'kɒzməs/ *n.* cosmos *m.*
cost /kɔst/ *n.* **1.** coste *m.*; costa *f.* —*v.* **2.** costar.
Costa Rican /'kɒstə'rikən/ *a. & n.* costarricense *m. & f.*
costly /'kɔstli/ *a.* costoso, caro.
costume /'kɒstum/ *n.* traje; disfraz *m.*
costume jewelry bisutería *f.*, joyas de fantasía *f.pl.*
cot /kɒt/ *n.* catre *m.*
coterie /'koutəri/ *n.* camarilla *f.*
cotillion /kə'tɪlyən/ *n.* cotillón *m.*
cottage /'kɒtɪdʒ/ *n.* casita *f.*
cottage cheese requesón *m.*
cotton /'kɒtn/ *n.* algodón *m.*
cottonseed /'kɒtn,sid/ *n.* semilla del algodón *f.*
couch /kautʃ/ *n.* sofá *m.*
cougar /'kugər/ *n.* puma *m.*
cough /kɔf/ *n.* **1.** tos *f.* —*v.* **2.** toser.
council /'kaunsəl/ *n.* consejo, concilio *m.*
counsel /'kaunsəl/ *n.* **1.** consejo; (law) abogado -da. —*v.* **2.** aconsejar. **to keep one's c.,** no decir nada.
counselor /'kaunsələr/ *n.* consejero -ra; (law) abogado -da.
count /kaunt/ *n.* **1.** cuenta *f.*; (title) conde *m.* —*v.* **2.** contar.
countenance /'kauntnəns/ *n.* **1.** aspecto *m.*; cara *f.* —*v.* **2.** aprobar.
counter /'kauntər/ *adv.* **1. c. to,** contra, en contra de. —*n.* **2.** mostrador *m.*
counteract /ˌkauntər'ækt/ *v.* contrarrestar.
counteraction /ˌkauntər'ækʃən/ *n.* neutralización *f.*
counterbalance /'kauntər,bæləns/ *n.* **1.** contrapeso *m.* —*v.* **2.** contrapesar.
counterfeit /'kauntər,fɪt/ *a.* **1.** falsificado. —*v.* **2.** falsear.
countermand /ˌkauntər'mænd/ *v.* contramandar.
counteroffensive /ˌkauntərə'fɛnsɪv/ *n.* contraofensiva *f.*

counterpart /'kauntər,part/ *n.* contraparte *f.*
counterproductive /ˌkauntərprə'dʌktɪv/ *a.* contraproducente.
countess /'kauntɪs/ *n.* condesa *f.*
countless /'kauntlɪs/ *a.* innumerable.
country /'kʌntri/ *n.* campo *m.*; Pol. país *m.*; (homeland) patria *f.*
country code distintivo del país *m.*
countryman /'kʌntrimən/ *n.* paisano *m.* **fellow c.,** compatriota *m.*
countryside /'kʌntri,said/ *n.* campo, paisaje *m.*
county /'kaunti/ *n.* condado *m.*
coupé /kup/ *n.* cupé *m.*
couple /'kʌpəl/ *n.* **1.** par *m.* —*v.* **2.** unir.
coupon /'kupɒn/ *n.* cupón, talón *m.*
courage /'kɜridʒ/ *n.* valor *m.*
courageous /kə'reidʒəs/ *a.* valiente.
course /kɔrs/ *n.* curso *m.* **of c.,** por supuesto, desde luego.
court /kɔrt/ *n.* **1.** corte *f.*; cortejo *m.*; (of law) tribunal *m.* —*v.* **2.** cortejar.
courteous /'kɜrtiəs/ *a.* cortés.
courtesy /'kɜrtəsi/ *n.* cortesía *f.*
courthouse /'kɔrt,haus/ *n.* palacio de justicia *m.*, tribunal *m.*
courtier /'kɔrtiər/ *n.* cortesano *m.*
courtly /'kɔrtli/ *a.* cortés, galante.
courtroom /'kɔrt,rum, -,rʊm/ *n.* sala de justicia *f.*
courtship /'kɔrtʃɪp/ *n.* cortejo *m.*
courtyard /'kɔrt,yard/ *n.* patio *m.*
cousin /'kʌzən/ *n.* primo -ma.
covenant /'kʌvənənt/ *n.* contrato, convenio *m.*
cover /'kʌvər/ *n.* **1.** cubierta, tapa *f.* —*v.* **2.** cubrir, tapar.
cover charge precio del cubierto *m.*
covet /'kʌvɪt/ *v.* ambicionar, suspirar por.
covetous /'kʌvɪtəs/ *a.* codicioso.
cow /kau/ *n.* vaca *f.*
coward /'kauərd/ *n.* cobarde *m. & f.*
cowardice /'kauərdɪs/ *n.* cobardía *f.*
cowardly /'kauərdli/ *a.* cobarde.
cowboy /'kau,bɔi/ *n.* vaquero, gaucho *m.*
cower /'kauər/ *v.* agacharse (de miedo).
cowhide /'kau,haid/ *n.* cuero *m.*
coy /kɔi/ *a.* recatado, modesto.
coyote /kai'outi/ *n.* coyote *m.*
cozy /'kouzi/ *a.* cómodo y agradable.
crab /kræb/ *n.* cangrejo *m.*
crab apple *n.* manzana silvestre *f.*
crack /kræk/ *n.* **1.** hendedura *f.*; (noise) crujido *m.* —*v.* **2.** hender; crujir.
cracker /'krækər/ *n.* galleta *f.*
cradle /'kreidl/ *n.* cuna *f.*
craft /kræft/ *n.* arte *m.*
craftsman /'kræftsmən/ *n.* artesano -na.
craftsmanship /'kræftsmən,ʃip/ *n.* artesanía *f.*
crafty /'kræfti/ *a.* ladino.
crag /kræg/ *n.* despeñadero *m.*; peña *f.*
cram /kræm/ *v.* rellenar, hartar.
cramp /kræmp/ *n.* calambre *m.*
cranberry /'kræn,bɛri/ *n.* arándano *m.*
crane /krein/ *n.* (bird) grulla *f.*; Mech. grúa *f.*
cranium /'kreiniəm/ *n.* cráneo *m.*
crank /kræŋk/ *n.* Mech. manivela *f.*
cranky /'kræŋki/ *a.* chiflado, caprichoso.
crash /kræʃ/ *n.* **1.** choque; estallido *m.* —*v.* **2.** estallar.
crate /kreit/ *n.* canasto *m.*
crater /'kreitər/ *n.* cráter *m.*
crave /kreiv/ *v.* desear; anhelar.
craven /'kreivən/ *a.* cobarde.
craving /'kreivɪŋ/ *n.* sed *m.*, anhelo *m.*
crawl /krɔl/ *v.* andar a gatas, arrastrarse.
crayon /'kreiɒn/ *n.* creyón; lápiz *m.*
crazy /'kreizi/ *a.* loco.

creak /krik/ v. crujir.
creaky /'kriki/ a. crujiente.
cream /krim/ n. crema f.
cream cheese queso crema m.
creamery /'krimǝri/ n. lechería f.
creamy /'krimi/ a. cremoso.
crease /kris/ n. **1.** pliegue m. —v. **2.** plegar.
create /kri'eit/ v. crear.
creation /kri'eiʃǝn/ n. creación f.
creative /kri'eitɪv/ a. creativo, creador.
creator /kri'eitǝr/ n. creador -ra.
creature /'kritʃǝr/ n. criatura f.
credence /'kridns/ n. creencia f.
credentials /krɪ'dɛnʃǝlz/ n. credenciales f.pl.
credibility /,krɛdǝ'bɪliti/ n. credibilidad f.
credible /'krɛdǝbǝl/ a. creíble.
credit /'krɛdɪt/ n. **1.** crédito m. **on c.,** al fiado. —v. **2.** Com. abonar.
creditable /'krɛdɪtǝbǝl/ a. fidedigno.
credit balance saldo acreedor.
credit card n. tarjeta de crédito f.
creditor /'krɛdɪtǝr/ n. acreedor -ra.
credit union banco cooperativo m.
credo /'kridou/ n. credo m.
credulity /krǝ'duliti/ n. credulidad f.
credulous /'krɛdʒǝlǝs/ a. crédulo.
creed /krid/ n. credo m.
creek /krik/ n. riachuelo m.
creep /krip/ v. gatear.
cremate /'krimeit/ v. incinerar.
crematory /'krimǝ,tɔri/ n. crematorio m.
creosote /'kriǝ,sout/ n. creosota f.
crepe /kreip/ n. crespón m.
crepe paper papel crespón m.
crescent /'krɛsǝnt/ a. & n. creciente f.
crest /krɛst/ n. cresta; cima f.; (heraldry) timbre m.
cretonne /krɪ'tɒn/ n. cretona f.
crevice /'krɛvɪs/ n. grieta f.
crew /kru/ n. tripulación f.
crew member tripulante m. & f.
crib /krɪb/ n. pesebre m.; cuna.
cricket /'krɪkɪt/ n. grillo m.
crime /kraim/ n. crimen m.
criminal /'krɪmǝnl/ a. & n. criminal m. & f.
criminologist /,krɪmǝ'nɒlǝdʒɪst/ n. criminólogo -ga, criminalista m. & f.
criminology /,krɪmǝ'nɒlǝdʒi/ n. criminología f.
crimson /'krɪmzǝn, -sǝn/ a. & n. carmesí m.
cringe /krɪndʒ/ v. encogerse, temblar.
cripple /'krɪpǝl/ n. **1.** lisiado -da. —v. **2.** estropear, lisiar.
crisis /'kraisɪs/ n. crisis f.
crisp /krɪsp/ a. crespo, fresco.
crispness /'krɪspnɪs/ n. encrespadura f.
crisscross /'krɪs,krɔs/ a. entrelazado.
criterion /krai'tɪǝriǝn/ n. criterio m.
critic /'krɪtɪk/ n. crítico -ca.
critical /'krɪtɪkǝl/ a. crítico.
criticism /'krɪtǝ,sɪzǝm/ n. crítica; censura f.
criticize /'krɪtǝ,saiz/ v. criticar; censurar.
critique /krɪ'tik/ n. crítica f.
croak /krouk/ n. **1.** graznido m. —v. **2.** graznar.
crochet /krou'ʃei/ n. **1.** crochet m. —v. **2.** hacer crochet.
crochet work ganchillo m.
crock /krɒk/ n. cazuela f.; olla de barro.
crockery /'krɒkǝri/ n. loza f.
crocodile /'krɒkǝ,dail/ n. cocodrilo m.
crony /'krouni/ n. compinche m.
crooked /'krʊkɪd/ a. encorvado; deshonesto.
croon /krun/ v. canturrear.
crop /krɒp/ n. cosecha f.
croquet /krou'kei/ n. juego de croquet m.
croquette /krou'kɛt/ n. croqueta f.
cross /krɔs/ a. **1.** enojado, mal hu-

morado. —n. **2.** cruz f. —v. **3.** cruzar, atravesar.
crossbreed /'krɔs,brid/ n. **1.** mestizo m. —v. **2.** cruzar (animales o plantas).
cross-examine /'krɔs ɪg,zæmɪn/ v. interrogar.
cross-eyed /'krɔs ,aid/ a. bizco.
cross-fertilization /'krɔs ,fɛrtlǝ'zeiʃǝn/ n. alogamia f.
crossing /'krɔsɪŋ/ **crossroads** n. cruce m.
cross section corte transversal m.
crosswalk /'krɔs,wɔk/ n. paso cebra m.
crossword puzzle /'krɔs ,wɜrd/ crucigrama m.
crotch /krɒtʃ/ n. bifurcación f.; Anat. bragadura f.
crouch /krautʃ/ v. agacharse.
croup /krup/ n. Med. crup m.
croupier /'krupiǝr/ n. crupié m. & f.
crow /krou/ n. cuervo m.
crowd /kraud/ n. **1.** muchedumbre f.; tropel m. —v. **2.** apretar.
crowded /'kraudɪd/ a. lleno de gente.
crown /kraun/ n. **1.** corona f. —v. **2.** coronar.
crown prince príncipe heredero m.
crucial /'kruʃǝl/ a. crucial.
crucible /'krusǝbǝl/ n. crisol m.
crucifix /'krusǝfɪks/ n. crucifijo m.
crucifixion /,krusǝ'fɪkʃǝn/ n. crucifixión f.
crucify /'krusǝ,fai/ v. crucificar.
crude /krud/ a. crudo; (oil) bruto.
crudeness /'krudnɪs/ a. crudeza.
cruel /'kruǝl/ a. cruel.
cruelty /'kruǝlti/ n. crueldad f.
cruet /'kruɪt/ n. vinagrera f.
cruise /kruz/ n. **1.** viaje por mar. —v. **2.** navegar.
cruiser /'kruzǝr/ n. crucero m.
crumb /krʌm/ n. miga; migaja f.
crumble /'krʌmbǝl/ v. desmigajar; desmoronar.
crumple /'krʌmpǝl/ v. arrugar; encogerse.
crusade /kru'seid/ n. cruzada f.
crusader /kru'seidǝr/ n. cruzado m.
crush /krʌʃ/ v. aplastar.
crust /krʌst/ n. costra; corteza f.
crustacean /krʌ'steiʃǝn/ n. crustáceo m.
crutch /krʌtʃ/ n. muleta f.
cry /krai/ n. **1.** grito m. —v. **2.** gritar; (weep) llorar.
cryosurgery /,kraiou'sɜrdʒǝri/ n. criocirugía f.
crypt /krɪpt/ n. gruta f., cripta f.
cryptic /'krɪptɪk/ a. secreto.
cryptography /krɪp'tɒgrǝfi/ n. criptografía f.
crystal /'krɪstl/ n. cristal m.
crystalline /'krɪstlɪn/ a. cristalino, transparente.
crystallize /'krɪstl,aiz/ v. cristalizar.
cub /kʌb/ n. cachorro m.
Cuban /'kyubǝn/ n. & a. cubano -na.
cube /kyub/ n. cubo m.
cubic /'kyubɪk/ a. cúbico.
cubicle /'kyubɪkǝl/ n. cubículo m.
cubic measure medida de capacidad f.
cubism /'kyubɪzǝm/ n. cubismo m.
cuckoo /'kuku/ n. cuco m.
cucumber /'kyukʌmbǝr/ n. pepino m.
cuddle /'kʌdl/ v. abrazar.
cudgel /'kʌdʒǝl/ n. palo m.
cue /kyu/ n. apunte m.; (billiards) taco m.
cuff /kʌf/ n. puño de camisa. **c. links,** gemelos.
cuisine /kwɪ'zin/ n. arte culinario m.
culinary /'kyulǝ,nɛri/ a. culinario.
culminate /'kʌlmǝ,neit/ v. culminar.
culmination /,kʌlmǝ'neiʃǝn/ n. culminación f.
culpable /'kʌlpǝbǝl/ a. culpable.
culprit /'kʌlprɪt/ n. criminal; delincuente m. & f.
cult /kʌlt/ n. culto m.

cultivate /'kʌltǝ,veit/ v. cultivar.
cultivated /'kʌltǝ,veitɪd/ a. cultivado.
cultivation /,kʌltǝ'veiʃǝn/ n. cultivo m.; cultivación f.
cultivator /'kʌltǝ,veitǝr/ n. cultivador -ra.
cultural /'kʌltʃǝrǝl/ a. cultural.
culture /'kʌltʃǝr/ n. cultura f.
cultured /'kʌltʃǝrd/ a. culto.
cumbersome /'kʌmbǝrsǝm/ a. pesado, incómodo.
cumulative /'kyumyǝlǝtɪv/ a. acumulativo.
cunning /'kʌnɪŋ/ a. **1.** astuto. —n. **2.** astucia f.
cup /kʌp/ n. taza, jícara f.
cupboard /'kʌbǝrd/ n. armario, aparador m.
cupidity /kyu'pɪditi/ n. avaricia f.
curable /'kyurǝbǝl/ a. curable.
curator /kyu'reitǝr/ n. guardián -ana.
curb /kɜrb/ n. **1.** freno m. —v. **2.** refrenar.
curd /kɜrd/ n. cuajada f.
curdle /'kɜrdl/ v. cuajarse, coagularse.
cure /kyur/ n. **1.** remedio m. —v. **2.** curar, sanar.
curfew /'kɜrfyu/ n. toque de queda m.
curio /'kyuri,ou/ n. objeto curioso.
curiosity /,kyuri'ɒsiti/ n. curiosidad f.
curious /'kyuriǝs/ a. curioso.
curl /kɜrl/ n. **1.** rizo m. —v. **2.** rizar.
curly /'kɜrli/ a. rizado.
currant /'kɜrǝnt/ n. grosella f.
currency /'kɜrǝnsi/ n. circulación f.; dinero m.
current /'kɜrǝnt/ a. & n. corriente f.
current events /ɪ'vɛnts/ actualidades f.pl.
currently /'kɜrǝntli/ adv. corrientemente.
curriculum /kǝ'rɪkyǝlǝm/ n. plan de estudio m.
curse /kɜrs/ n. **1.** maldición f. —v. **2.** maldecir.
cursor /'kɜrsǝr/ n. cursor m.
cursory /'kɜrsǝri/ a. sumario.
curt /kɜrt/ a. brusco.
curtail /kǝr'teil/ v. reducir; restringir.
curtain /'kɜrtn/ n. cortina f.; Theat. telón m.
curtsy /'kɜrtsi/ n. **1.** reverencia f. —v. **2.** hacer una reverencia.
curvature /'kɜrvǝtʃǝr/ n. curvatura f.
curve /kɜrv/ n. **1.** curva f. —v. **2.** encorvar.
cushion /'kuʃǝn/ n. cojín m.; almohada f.
cuspidor /'kʌspɪ,dɔr/ n. escupidera f.
custard /'kʌstǝrd/ n. flan m.; natillas f.pl.
custodian /kʌ'stoudiǝn/ n. custodio m.
custody /'kʌstǝdi/ n. custodia f.
custom /'kʌstǝm/ n. costumbre f.
customary /'kʌstǝ,mɛri/ a. acostumbrado, usual.
customer /'kʌstǝmǝr/ n. cliente m. & f.
customhouse /'kʌstǝm,haus/ n. aduana f.
customs duty /'kʌstǝmz/ derechos de aduana m.pl.
customs officer /'kʌstǝmz/ agente de aduana m. & f.
cut /kʌt/ n. **1.** corte m.; cortada f.; tajada f.; (printing) grabado m. —v. **2.** cortar; tajar.
cute /kyut/ a. mono, lindo.
cut glass cristal tallado m.
cuticle /'kyutɪkǝl/ n. cutícula f.
cutlery /'kʌtlǝri/ n. cuchillería f.
cutlet /'kʌtlɪt/ n. chuleta f.
cutter /'kʌtǝr/ n. cortador -ra; Naut. cúter m.
cutthroat /'kʌt,θrout/ n. asesino -na.
cyberpunk /'saibǝr,pʌŋk/ n. ciberpunk m. & f.
cyberspace /'saibǝr,speis/ n. ciberespacio m.
cyclamate /'saiklǝ,meit, 'sɪklǝ-/ n. ciclamato m.

cycle /'saikǝl/ n. ciclo m.
cyclist /'saiklɪst/ n. ciclista m. & f.
cyclone /'saikloun/ n. ciclón, huracán m.
cyclotron /'saiklǝ,trɒn, 'sɪklǝ-/ n. ciclotrón m.
cylinder /'sɪlɪndǝr/ n. cilindro m.
cylindrical /sɪ'lɪndrɪkǝl/ a. cilíndrico.
cymbal /'sɪmbǝl/ n. címbalo m.
cynic /'sɪnɪk/ n. cínico -ca.
cynical /'sɪnɪkǝl/ a. cínico.
cynicism /'sɪnǝ,sɪzǝm/ n. cinismo m.
cypress /'saiprǝs/ n. ciprés m. **c. nut,** piñuela f.
cyst /sɪst/ n. quiste m.

D

dad /dæd/ n. papá m., papito m.
daffodil /'dæfǝdɪl/ n. narciso m.
dagger /'dægǝr/ n. puñal m.
dahlia /'dælyǝ/ n. dalia f.
daily /'deili/ a. diario, cotidiano.
daintiness /'deintinɪs/ n. delicadeza f.
dainty /'deinti/ a. delicado.
dairy /'dɛǝri/ n. lechería, quesería f.
dais /'deiɪs/ n. tablado m.
daisy /'deizi/ n. margarita f.
dale /deil/ n. valle m.
dally /'dæli/ v. holgar; perder el tiempo.
dam /dæm/ n. presa f.; dique m.
damage /'dæmɪdʒ/ n. **1.** daño m. —v. **2.** dañar.
damask /'dæmǝsk/ n. damasco m.
damn /dæm/ v. condenar.
damnation /dæm'neiʃǝn/ n. condenación f.
damp /dæmp/ a. húmedo.
dampen /'dæmpǝn/ v. humedecer.
dampness /'dæmpnɪs/ n. humedad f.
damsel /'dæmzǝl/ n. doncella f.
dance /dæns/ n. **1.** baile m.; danza f. —v. **2.** bailar.
dance hall salón de baile m.
dancer /'dænsǝr/ n. bailador -ra; (professional) bailarín -na.
dancing /'dænsɪŋ/ n. baile m.
dandelion /'dændl,aiǝn/ n. amargón m.
dandruff /'dændrǝf/ n. caspa f.
dandy /'dændi/ n. petimetre m.
danger /'deindʒǝr/ n. peligro m.
dangerous /'deindʒǝrǝs/ a. peligroso.
dangle /'dæŋgǝl/ v. colgar.
Danish /'deinɪʃ/ a. & n. danés -sa; dinamarqués -sa.
dapper /'dæpǝr/ a. gallardo.
dare /dɛǝr/ v. atreverse, osar.
daredevil /'dɛǝr,dɛvǝl/ n. atrevido m., -da f.
daring /'dɛǝrɪŋ/ a. **1.** atrevido. —n. **2.** osadía f.
dark /dɑrk/ a. **1.** obscuro; moreno. —n. **2.** obscuridad f.
darken /'dɑrkǝn/ v. obscurecer.
darkness /'dɑrknɪs/ n. obscuridad f.
darkroom /'dɑrk,rum, -,rʊm/ n. cámara obscura f.
darling /'dɑrlɪŋ/ a. & n. querido -da, amado -da.
darn /dɑrn/ v. zurcir.
darning needle /'dɑrnɪŋ/ aguja de zurcir m.
dart /dɑrt/ n. dardo m.
dartboard /'dɑrt,bɔrd/ n. diana f.
dash /dæʃ/ n. arranque m.; Punct. guión m.
data /'deitǝ/ n. datos m.
database /'deitǝbeis/ n. base de datos m.
data processing /'prɒsɛsɪŋ/ proceso de datos m.
date /deit/ n. fecha f.; (engagement) cita f.; (fruit) dátil m.
daughter /'dɔtǝr/ n. hija f.
daughter-in-law /'dɔ,tǝr ɪn lɔ/ n. nuera f.
daunt /dɔnt, dɑnt/ v. intimidar.
dauntless /'dɔntlɪs/ a. intrépido.

davenport /'dævən,pɔrt/ n. sofá m.

dawn /dɔn/ n. **1.** alba, madrugada f. —v. **2.** amanecer.

day /dei/ n. día m. **good d.,** buenos días.

daybreak /'dei,breik/ n. alba, madrugada f.

daydream /'dei,drim/ n. fantasía f.

daylight /'dei,lait/ n. luz del día.

daze /deiz/ v. aturdir.

dazzle /'dæzəl/ v. deslumbrar.

deacon /'dikən/ n. diácono m.

dead /dɛd/ a. muerto.

deaden /'dɛdn/ v. amortecer.

dead end atolladero m. (impasse); callejón sin salida m. (street).

deadline /'dɛd,lain/ n. fecha límite f.

deadlock /'dɛd,lɒk/ n. paro m.

deadly /'dɛdli/ a. mortal.

deaf /dɛf/ a. sordo.

deafen /'dɛfən/ v. ensordecer.

deafening /'dɛfənɪŋ/ a. ensordecedor.

deaf-mute /'dɛf 'myut/ n. sordomudo -da.

deafness /'dɛfnɪs/ n. sordera f.

deal /dil/ n. **1.** trato m.; negociación f. **a great d., a good d.,** mucho. —v. **2.** tratar; negociar.

dealer /'dilər/ n. comerciante m., (at cards) tallador -ra.

dean /din/ n. decano -na.

dear /dɪər/ a. querido; caro.

dearth /dɜrθ/ n. escasez f.

death /dɛθ/ n. muerte f.

death certificate partida de defunción f.

deathless /'dɛθlɪs/ a. inmortal.

debacle /də'bakəl/ n. desastre m.

debase /dɪ'beis/ v. degradar.

debatable /dɪ'beitəbəl/ a. discutible.

debate /dɪ'beit/ n. **1.** debate m. —v. **2.** disputar, deliberar.

debauch /dɪ'bɔtʃ/ v. corromper.

debilitate /dɪ'bɪlɪ,teit/ v. debilitar.

debit /'dɛbɪt/ n. débito m.

debit balance saldo deudor m.

debonair /,dɛbə'nɛər/ a. cortés; alegre, vivo.

debris /dei'bri/ n. escombros m.pl.

debt /dɛt/ n. deuda f. **get into d.** endeudarse.

debtor /'dɛtər/ n. deudor -ra.

debug /di'bʌg/ v. depurar, limpiar.

debunk /dɪ'bʌŋk/ v. desacreditar; desenmascarar.

debut /dei'byu/ n. debut, estreno m.

debutante /'dɛbyʊ,tɑnt/ n. debutante f.

decade /'dɛkeid/ n. década f.

decadence /'dɛkədəns/ n. decadencia f.

decadent /'dɛkədənt/ a. decadente.

decaffeinated /di'kæfɪ,neitɪd/ a. descafeinado.

decalcomania /dɪ,kælkə'meiniə/ n. calcomanía f.

decanter /dɪ'kæntər/ n. garrafa f.

decapitate /dɪ'kæpɪ,teit/ v. descabezar.

decay /dɪ'kei/ n. **1.** descaecimiento m.; (dental) caries f. —v. **2.** decaer; (dental) cariarse.

deceased /dɪ'sist/ a. muerto, difunto.

deceit /dɪ'sit/ n. engaño m.

deceitful /dɪ'sitfəl/ a. engañoso.

deceive /dɪ'siv/ v. engañar.

December /dɪ'sɛmbər/ n. diciembre m.

decency /'disənsi/ n. decencia f.; decoro m.

decent /'disənt/ a. decente.

decentralize /di'sɛntrə,laiz/ v. descentralizar.

deception /dɪ'sɛpʃən/ n. decepción f.

deceptive /dɪ'sɛptɪv/ a. deceptivo.

decibel /'dɛsə,bɛl/ n. decibelio m.

decide /dɪ'said/ v. decidir.

decimal /'dɛsəməl/ a. decimal.

decipher /dɪ'saifər/ v. descifrar.

decision /dɪ'sɪʒən/ n. decisión f.

decisive /dɪ'saisɪv/ a. decisivo.

deck /dɛk/ n. cubierta f.

deck chair tumbona f.

declamation /,dɛklə'meiʃən/ n. declamación f.

declaration /,dɛklə'reiʃən/ n. declaración f.

declarative /dɪ'klærətɪv/ a. declarativo.

declare /dɪ'klɛər/ v. declarar.

declension /dɪ'klɛnʃən/ n. declinación f.

decline /dɪ'klain/ n. **1.** decadencia f. —v. **2.** decaer; negarse; Gram. declinar.

decompose /,dikəm'pouz/ v. descomponer.

decongestant /,dikən'dʒɛstənt/ n. descongestionante m.

decorate /'dɛkə,reit/ v. decorar, adornar.

decoration /,dɛkə'reiʃən/ n. decoración f.

decorative /'dɛkərətɪv/ a. decorativo.

decorator /'dɛkə,reitər/ n. decorador -ra.

decorous /'dɛkərəs/ a. correcto.

decorum /dɪ'kɔrəm/ n. decoro m.

decrease /dɪ'kris/ v. disminuir.

decree /dɪ'kri/ n. decreto m.

decrepit /dɪ'krɛpɪt/ a. decrépito.

decry /dɪ'krai/ v. desacreditar.

dedicate /'dɛdɪ,keit/ v. dedicar; consagrar.

dedication /,dɛdɪ'keiʃən/ n. dedicación; dedicatoria f.

deduce /dɪ'dus/ v. deducir.

deduction /dɪ'dʌkʃən/ n. rebaja; deducción f.

deductive /dɪ'dʌktɪv/ a. deductivo.

deed /did/ n. acción; hazaña f.

deem /dim/ v. estimar.

deep /dip/ a. hondo, profundo.

deepen /'dipən/ v. profundizar, ahondar.

deep freeze congelación f.

deeply /'dipli/ adv. profundamente.

deer /dɪər/ n. venado, ciervo m.

deface /dɪ'feis/ v. mutilar.

defamation /,dɛfə'meiʃən/ n. calumnia f.

defame /dɪ'feim/ v. difamar.

default /dɪ'fɔlt/ n. **1.** defecto m. —v. **2.** faltar.

defeat /dɪ'fit/ n. **1.** derrota f. —v. **2.** derrotar.

defeatism /dɪ'fitɪzəm/ n. derrotismo m.

defect /'difɛkt, dɪ'fɛkt/ n. defecto m.

defective /dɪ'fɛktɪv/ a. defectivo.

defend /dɪ'fɛnd/ v. defender.

defendant /dɪ'fɛndənt/ n. acusado -da.

defender /dɪ'fɛndər/ n. defensor -ra.

defense /dɪ'fɛns/ n. defensa f.

defensive /dɪ'fɛnsɪv/ a. defensivo.

defer /dɪ'fɜr/ v. aplazar; deferir.

deference /'dɛfərəns/ n. deferencia f.

defiance /dɪ'faiəns/ n. desafío m.

defiant /dɪ'faiənt/ a. desafiador.

deficiency /dɪ'fɪʃənsi/ n. defecto m.

deficient /dɪ'fɪʃənt/ a. deficiente.

deficit /'dɛfəsɪt/ n. déficit, descubierto m.

defile /dɪ'fail/ n. **1.** desfiladero m. —v. **2.** profanar.

define /dɪ'fain/ v. definir.

definite /'dɛfənɪt/ a. exacto; definitivo.

definitely /'dɛfənɪtli/ adv. definitivamente.

definition /,dɛfə'nɪʃən/ n. definición f.

definitive /dɪ'fɪnɪtɪv/ a. definitivo.

deflation /dɪ'fleiʃən/ n. desinflación f.

deflect /dɪ'flɛkt/ v. desviar.

deform /dɪ'fɔrm/ v. deformar.

deformity /dɪ'fɔrmɪti/ n. deformidad f.

defraud /dɪ'frɔd/ v. defraudar.

defray /dɪ'frei/ v. costear.

defrost /dɪ'frɔst/ v. descongelar.

deft /dɛft/ a. diestro.

defy /dɪ'fai/ v. desafiar.

degenerate /a dɪ'dʒɛnərɪt; v -,reit/ a. **1.** degenerado. —v. **2.** degenerar.

degeneration /dɪ,dʒɛnə'reiʃən/ n. degeneración f.

degradation /,dɛgrɪ'deiʃən/ n. degradación f.

degrade /dɪ'greid/ v. degradar.

degree /dɪ'gri/ n. grado m.

deign /dein/ v. condescender.

deity /'diɪti/ n. deidad f.

dejected /dɪ'dʒɛktɪd/ a. abatido.

dejection /dɪ'dʒɛkʃən/ n. tristeza f.

delay /dɪ'lei/ n. **1.** retardo m., demora f. —v. **2.** tardar, demorar.

delegate /n 'dɛlɪgɪt; v -,geit/ n. **1.** delegado -da. —v. **2.** delegar.

delegation /,dɛlɪ'geiʃən/ n. delegación f.

delete /dɪ'lit/ v. suprimir, tachar.

deliberate /a dɪ'lɪbərɪt; v -ə,reit/ a. **1.** premeditado. —v. **2.** deliberar.

deliberately /dɪ'lɪbərɪtli/ adv. deliberadamente.

deliberation /dɪ,lɪbə'reiʃən/ n. deliberación f.

deliberative /dɪ'lɪbərətɪv/ a. deliberativo.

delicacy /'dɛlɪkəsi/ n. delicadeza f.

delicate /'dɛlɪkɪt/ a. delicado.

delicious /dɪ'lɪʃəs/ a. delicioso.

delight /dɪ'lait/ n. deleite m.

delightful /dɪ'laitfəl/ a. deleitoso.

delinquency /dɪ'lɪŋkwənsi/ a. delincuencia f.

delinquent /dɪ'lɪŋkwənt/ a. & n. delincuente. m. & f.

delirious /dɪ'lɪəriəs/ a. delirante.

deliver /dɪ'lɪvər/ v. entregar.

deliverance /dɪ'lɪvərəns/ n. liberación; salvación f.

delivery /dɪ'lɪvəri/ n. entrega f.; Med. parto m.

delude /dɪ'lud/ v. engañar.

deluge /'dɛlyudʒ/ n. inundación f.

delusion /dɪ'luʒən/ n. decepción f.; engaño m.

delve /dɛlv/ v. cavar, sondear.

demagogue /'dɛmə,gɒg/ n. demagogo -ga.

demand /dɪ'mænd/ n. **1.** demanda f. —v. **2.** demandar; exigir.

demarcation /,dimɑr'keiʃən/ n. demarcación f.

demeanor /dɪ'minər/ n. conducta f.

demented /dɪ'mɛntɪd/ a. demente, loco.

demilitarize /di'mɪlɪtə,raiz/ v. desmilitarizar.

demobilize /di'moubə,laiz/ v. desmovilizar.

democracy /dɪ'mɒkrəsi/ n. democracia f.

democrat /'dɛmə,kræt/ n. demócrata m. & f.

democratic /,dɛmə'krætɪk/ a. democrático.

demolish /dɪ'mɒlɪʃ/ v. demoler.

demon /'dimən/ n. demonio m.

demonstrate /'dɛmən,streit/ v. demostrar.

demonstration /,dɛmən'streiʃən/ n. demostración f.

demonstrative /də'mɒnstrətɪv/ a. demostrativo.

demoralize /dɪ'mɔrə,laiz, -'mɒr-/ v. desmoralizar.

demure /dɪ'myʊr/ a. modesto, serio.

den /dɛn/ n. madriguera, caverna f.

denature /di'neitʃər/ v. alterar.

denial /dɪ'naiəl/ n. negación f.

denim /'dɛnəm/ n. dril, tela vaquera f.

Denmark /'dɛnmɑrk/ n. Dinamarca f.

denomination /dɪ,nɒmə'neiʃən/ n. denominación; secta f.

denote /dɪ'nout/ v. denotar.

denounce /dɪ'nauns/ v. denunciar.

dense /dɛns/ a. denso, espeso; estúpido.

density /'dɛnsɪti/ n. densidad f.

dent /dɛnt/ n. **1.** abolladura f. —v. **2.** abollar.

dental /'dɛntl/ a. dental.

dentist /'dɛntɪst/ n. dentista m. & f.

dentistry /'dɛntəstri/ n. odontología f.

denture /'dɛntʃər/ n. dentadura f.

denunciation /dɪ,nʌnsi'eiʃən/ n. denunciación f.

deny /dɪ'nai/ v. negar, rehusar.

deodorant /di'oudərənt/ n. desodorante m.

depart /dɪ'pɑrt/ v. partir; irse, marcharse.

department /dɪ'pɑrtmənt/ n. departamento m.

departmental /dɪ,pɑrt'mɛntl/ a. departamental.

department store grandes almacenes m.pl.

departure /dɪ'pɑrtʃər/ n. salida; desviación f.

depend /dɪ'pɛnd/ v. depender.

dependability /dɪ,pɛndə'bɪlɪti/ n. confiabilidad f.

dependable /dɪ'pɛndəbəl/ a. confiable.

dependence /dɪ'pɛndəns/ n. dependencia f.

dependent /dɪ'pɛndənt/ a. & n. dependiente m. & f.

depict /dɪ'pɪkt/ v. pintar; representar.

deplete /dɪ'plit/ v. agotar.

deplorable /dɪ'plɔrəbəl/ a. deplorable.

deplore /dɪ'plɔr/ v. deplorar.

deport /dɪ'pɔrt/ v. deportar.

deportation /,dipɔr'teiʃən/ n. deportación f.

deportment /dɪ'pɔrtmənt/ n. conducta f.

depose /dɪ'pouz/ v. deponer.

deposit /dɪ'pɒzɪt/ n. **1.** depósito m. (of money); yacimiento (of ore, etc.) m. —v. **2.** depositar.

depositor /dɪ'pɒzɪtər/ n. depositante m. & f.

depot /'dipou/ n. depósito m.; (railway) estación f.

depravity /dɪ'prævɪti/ n. depravación f.

deprecate /'dɛprɪ,keit/ v. deprecar.

depreciate /dɪ'priʃi,eit/ v. depreciar.

depreciation /dɪ,priʃi'eiʃən/ n. depreciación f.

depredation /,dɛprə'deiʃən/ n. predación f.

depress /dɪ'prɛs/ v. deprimir; desanimar.

depression /dɪ'prɛʃən/ n. depresión f.

deprive /dɪ'praiv/ v. privar.

depth /dɛpθ/ n. profundidad, hondura f.

depth charge carga de profundidad f.

deputy /'dɛpyəti/ n. diputado -da.

deride /dɪ'raid/ v. burlar.

derision /dɪ'rɪʒən/ n. burla f.

derivation /,dɛrə'veiʃən/ n. derivación f.

derivative /dɪ'rɪvətɪv/ a. derivativo.

derive /dɪ'raiv/ v. derivar.

dermatologist /,dɜrmə'tɒlədʒɪst/ n. dermatólogo -ga.

derogatory /dɪ'rɒgə,tɔri/ a. derogatorio.

derrick /'dɛrɪk/ n. grúa f.

descend /dɪ'sɛnd/ v. descender, bajar.

descendant /dɪ'sɛndənt/ n. descendiente m. & f.

descent /dɪ'sɛnt/ n. descenso m.; origen m.

describe /dɪ'skraib/ v. describir.

description /dɪ'skrɪpʃən/ n. descripción f.

descriptive /dɪ'skrɪptɪv/ a. descriptivo.

desecrate /'dɛsɪ,kreit/ v. profanar.

desert /n 'dɛzərt; v dɪ'zɜrt/ n. **1.** desierto m. —v. **2.** abandonar.

deserter /dɪ'zɜrtər/ n. desertor -ra.

desertion /dɪ'zɜrʃən/ n. deserción f.

deserve /dɪ'zɜrv/ v. merecer.

design /dɪ'zain/ n. **1.** diseño m. —v. **2.** diseñar.

designate /'dɛzɪg,neit/ v. señalar, apuntar; designar.

designation /,dɛzɪg'neiʃən/ n. designación f.

designer /dɪ'zainər/ n. diseñador -ra; (technical) proyectista m. & f.

designer clothes, designer clothing ropa de marca f.

desirability /dɪ,zaiᵊrə'bɪliti/ n. conveniencia f.

desirable /dɪ'zaiᵊrəbəl/ a. deseable.

desire /dɪ'zaiᵊr/ n. **1.** deseo m. —v. **2.** desear.

desirous /dɪ'zaiᵊrəs/ a. deseoso.

desist /dɪ'sɪst/ v. desistir.

desk /dɛsk/ n. escritorio m.

desk clerk recepcionista m. & f.

desktop computer /'dɛsk,tɒp/ computadora de sobremesa f., ordenador de sobremesa m.

desolate /a 'dɛsəlɪt; v -,leit/ a. **1.** desolado. —v. **2.** desolar.

desolation /,dɛsə'leiʃən/ n. desolación, ruina f.

despair /dɪ'spɛər/ n. **1.** desesperación f. —v. **2.** desesperar.

despatch /dɪ'spætʃ/ **dispatch** n. **1.** despacho m.; prontitud f. —v. **2.** despachar.

desperado /,dɛspə'rɑdou/ n. bandido m.

desperate /'dɛspərɪt/ a. desesperado.

desperation /,dɛspə'reiʃən/ n. desesperación f.

despicable /'dɛspɪkəbəl/ a. vil.

despise /dɪ'spaiz/ v. despreciar.

despite /dɪ'spait/ prep. a pesar de.

despondent /dɪ'spɒndənt/ a. abatido; desanimado.

despot /'dɛspət/ n. déspota m. & f.

despotic /dɛs'pɒtɪk/ a. despótico.

dessert /dɪ'zɜrt/ n. postre m.

destination /,dɛstə'neiʃən/ n. destinación f.

destine /'dɛstɪn/ v. destinar.

destiny /'dɛstəni/ n. destino m.

destitute /'dɛstɪ,tut/ a. destituído, indigente.

destitution /,dɛstɪ'tuʃən/ n. destitución f.

destroy /dɪ'strɔi/ v. destrozar, destruir.

destroyer /dɪ'strɔiər/ n. destruidor -ra; (naval) destructor m.

destruction /dɪ'strʌkʃən/ n. destrucción f.

destructive /dɪ'strʌktɪv/ a. destructivo.

desultory /'dɛsəl,tɔri/ a. inconexo; casual.

detach /dɪ'tætʃ/ v. separar, desprender.

detachment /dɪ'tætʃmənt/ n. Mil. destacamento; desprendimiento f.

detail /dɪ'teil/ n. **1.** detalle m. —v. **2.** detallar.

detain /dɪ'tein/ v. detener.

detect /dɪ'tɛkt/ v. descubrir.

detection /dɪ'tɛkʃən/ n. detección f.

detective /dɪ'tɛktɪv/ n. detective m. & f.

deténte /dei'tɑnt/ n. distensión f.; Pol. deténte.

detention /dɪ'tɛnʃən/ n. detención; cautividad f.

deter /dɪ'tɜr/ v. disuadir.

detergent /dɪ'tɜrdʒənt/ n. & a. detergente m.

deteriorate /dɪ'tɪəriə,reit/ v. deteriorar.

deterioration /dɪ,tɪəriə'reiʃən/ n. deterioración f.

determination /dɪ,tɜrmə'neiʃən/ n. determinación f.

determine /dɪ'tɜrmɪn/ v. determinar.

deterrence /dɪ'tɛrəns/ n. disuasión f.

detest /dɪ'tɛst/ v. detestar.

detonate /'dɛtn,eit/ v. detonar.

detour /'ditʊr/ n. desvío m. v. desviar.

detract /dɪ'trækt/ v. disminuir.

detriment /'dɛtrəmənt/ n. detrimento m., daño m.

detrimental /,dɛtrə'mɛntl/ a. dañoso.

devaluate /di'vælyu,eit/ v. depreciar.

devastate /'dɛvə,steit/ v. devastar.

develop /dɪ'vɛləp/ v. desarrollar; Phot. revelar.

developing nation /dɪ'vɛləpɪŋ/ nación en desarrollo.

development /dɪ'vɛləpmənt/ n. desarrollo m.

deviate /'divi,eit/ v. desviar.

deviation /,divi'eiʃən/ n. desviación f.

device /dɪ'vais/ n. aparato; artificio m.

devil /'dɛvəl/ n. diablo, demonio m.

devious /'diviəs/ a. desviado.

devise /dɪ'vaiz/ v. inventar.

devoid /dɪ'vɔid/ a. desprovisto.

devote /dɪ'vout/ v. dedicar, consagrar.

devoted /dɪ'voutɪd/ a. devoto.

devotee /,dɛvə'ti/ n. aficionado -da.

devotion /dɪ'vouʃən/ n. devoción f.

devour /dɪ'vaur/ v. devorar.

devout /dɪ'vaut/ a. devoto.

dew /du/ n. rocío, sereno m.

dexterity /dɛk'stɛrɪti/ n. destreza f.

dexterous /'dɛkstrəs/ a. diestro.

diabetes /,daiə'bitɪs/ n. diabetes f.

diabolic /,daiə'bɒlɪk/ a. diabólico.

diadem /'daiə,dɛm/ n. diadema f.

diagnose /'daiəg,nous/ v. diagnosticar.

diagnosis /,daiəg'nousɪs/ n. diagnóstico m.

diagonal /dai'ægənl/ n. diagonal f.

diagram /'daiə,græm/ n. diagrama m.

dial /'daiəl/ n. **1.** cuadrante m., carátula f. —v. **2. dial up** marcar.

dialect /'daiə,lɛkt/ n. dialecto m.

dialing code /'daiəlɪŋ/ prefijo m.

dialogue /'daiə,lɔg/ n. diálogo m.

dial tone señal de marcar f.

diameter /dai'æmɪtər/ n. diámetro m.

diamond /'daimənd/ n. diamante, brillante m.

diaper /'daipər/ n. pañal m.

diarrhea /,daiə'riə/ n. diarrea f.

diary /'daiəri/ n. diario m.

diathermy /'daiə,θɜrmi/ n. diatermia f.

dice /dais/ n. dados m.pl.

dictate /'dɪkteit/ n. **1.** mandato m. —v. **2.** dictar.

dictation /dɪk'teiʃən/ n. dictado m.

dictator /'dɪkteitər/ n. dictador -ra.

dictatorship /dɪk'teitər,ʃɪp/ n. dictadura f.

diction /'dɪkʃən/ n. dicción f.

dictionary /'dɪkʃə,nɛri/ n. diccionario m.

die /dai/ n. **1.** matriz f.; (game) dado m. —v. **2.** morir.

diet /'daiɪt/ n. dieta f.

dietary /'daiɪ,tɛri/ a. dietético.

dietitian /,daiɪ'tɪʃən/ n. & a. dietético -ca.

differ /'dɪfər/ v. diferir.

difference /'dɪfərəns/ n. diferencia f. **to make no d.,** no importar.

different /'dɪfərənt/ a. diferente, distinto.

differential /,dɪfə'rɛnʃəl/ n. diferencial f.

differentiate /,dɪfə'rɛnʃi,eit/ v. diferenciar.

difficult /'dɪfɪ,kʌlt/ a. difícil.

difficulty /'dɪfɪ,kʌlti/ n. dificultad f.

diffident /'dɪfɪdənt/ a. tímido.

diffuse /dɪ'fyuz/ v. difundir.

diffusion /dɪ'fyuʒən/ n. difusión f.

dig /dɪg/ v. cavar.

digest /n 'daidʒɛst; v dɪ'dʒɛst, dai-/ n. **1.** extracto m. —v. **2.** digerir.

digestible /dɪ'dʒɛstəbəl, dai-/ a. digerible.

digestion /dɪ'dʒɛstʃən, dai-/ n. digestión f.

digestive /dɪ'dʒɛstɪv, dai-/ a. digestivo.

digital /'dɪdʒɪtl/ a. digital.

digitalis /,dɪdʒɪ'tælɪs/ n. digital f.

dignified /'dɪgnə,faid/ a. digno.

dignify /'dɪgnə,fai/ v. dignificar.

dignitary /'dɪgnɪ,tɛri/ n. dignatario -ria.

dignity /'dɪgnɪti/ n. dignidad f.

digress /dɪ'grɛs, dai-/ v. divagar.

digression /dɪ'grɛʃən, dai-/ n. digresión f.

dike /daik/ n. dique m.

dilapidated /dɪ'læpɪ,deitɪd/ a. dilapidado.

dilapidation /dɪ,læpə'deiʃən/ n. dilapidación f.

dilate /dai'leit/ v. dilatar.

dilatory /'dɪlə,tɔri/ a. dilatorio.

dilemma /dɪ'lɛmə/ n. dilema m.

dilettante /'dɪlɪ,tɑnt/ n. diletante m. & f.

diligence /'dɪlɪdʒəns/ n. diligencia f.

diligent /'dɪlɪdʒənt/ a. diligente, aplicado.

dilute /dɪ'lut, dai-/ v. diluir.

dim /dɪm/ a. **1.** oscuro. —v. **2.** oscurecer.

dimension /dɪ'mɛnʃən/ n. dimensión f.

diminish /dɪ'mɪnɪʃ/ v. disminuir.

diminution /,dɪmə'nuʃən/ n. disminución f.

diminutive /dɪ'mɪnyətɪv/ a. diminutivo.

dimness /'dɪmnɪs/ n. oscuridad f.

dimple /'dɪmpəl/ n. hoyuelo m.

din /dɪn/ n. alboroto, estrépito m.

dine /dain/ v. comer, cenar.

diner /'dainər/ n. coche comedor m.

dingy /'dɪndʒi/ a. deslucido, deslustrado.

dining room /'dainɪŋ/ comedor m.

dinner /'dɪnər/ n. comida, cena f.

dinosaur /'dainə,sɔr/ n. dinosauro m.

diocese /'daiəsɪs/ n. diócesis f.

dip /dɪp/ v. sumergir, hundir.

diphtheria /dɪf'θɪəriə/ n. difteria f.

diploma /dɪ'ploumə/ n. diploma m.

diplomacy /dɪ'plouməsi/ n. diplomacia f.

diplomat /'dɪplə,mæt/ n. diplomático -ca.

diplomatic /,dɪplə'mætɪk/ a. diplomático.

dipper /'dɪpər/ n. cucharón m.

dire /daiᵊr/ a. horrendo.

direct /dɪ'rɛkt, dai-/ a. **1.** directo. —v. **2.** dirigir.

direction /dɪ'rɛkʃən, 'dai-/ n. dirección f.

directive /dɪ'rɛktɪv, dai-/ n. directiva f.

directly /dɪ'rɛktli, dai-/ adv. directamente.

director /dɪ'rɛktər, dai-/ n. director -ra.

directory /dɪ'rɛktəri, dai-/ n. directorio m., guía f.

dirigible /'dɪrɪdʒəbəl/ n. dirigible m.

dirt /dɜrt/ n. basura f.; (earth) tierra f.

dirt-cheap /'dɜrt 'tʃip/ a. tirado.

dirty /'dɜrti/ a. sucio.

dis /dis/ v. Colloq. ofender, faltar al respeto.

disability /,dɪsə'bɪliti/ n. inhabilidad f.

disable /dɪs'eibəl/ v. incapacitar.

disabuse /,dɪsə'byuz/ v. desengañar.

disadvantage /,dɪsəd'væntɪdʒ/ n. desventaja f.

disagree /,dɪsə'gri/ v. desconvenir; disentir.

disagreeable /,dɪsə'griəbəl/ a. desagradable.

disagreement /,dɪsə'grimənt/ n. desacuerdo m.

disappear /,dɪsə'pɪər/ v. desaparecer.

disappearance /,dɪsə'pɪərəns/ n. desaparición f.

disappoint /,dɪsə'pɔint/ v. disgustar, desilusionar.

disappointment /,dɪsə'pɔintmənt/ n. disgusto m., desilusión f.

disapproval /,dɪsə'pruvəl/ n. desaprobación f.

disapprove /,dɪsə'pruv/ v. desaprobar.

disarm /dɪs'ɑrm/ v. desarmar.

disarmament /dɪs'ɑrməmənt/ n. desarme m.

disarrange /,dɪsə'reindʒ/ v. desordenar; desarreglar.

disaster /dɪ'zæstər/ n. desastre m.

disastrous /dɪ'zæstrəs/ a. desastroso.

disavow /,dɪsə'vau/ v. repudiar.

disavowal /,dɪsə'vauəl/ n. repudiación f.

disband /dɪs'bænd/ v. dispersarse.

disbelieve /,dɪsbɪ'liv/ v. descreer.

disburse /dɪs'bɜrs/ v. desembolsar, pagar.

discard /dɪ'skɑrd/ v. descartar.

discern /dɪ'sɜrn/ v. discernir.

discerning /dɪ'sɜrnɪŋ/ a. discernidor, perspicaz.

discernment /dɪ'sɜrnmənt/ n. discernimiento m.

discharge /dɪs'tʃɑrdʒ/ v. descargar; despedir.

disciple /dɪ'saipəl/ n. discípulo -la.

disciplinary /'dɪsəplə,nɛri/ a. disciplinario.

discipline /'dɪsəplɪn/ n. disciplina f.

disclaim /dɪs'kleim/ v. repudiar.

disclaimer /dɪs'kleimər/ n. negación f.

disclose /dɪ'sklouz/ v. revelar.

disclosure /dɪ'sklouʒər/ n. revelación f.

disco /'dɪskou/ n. discoteca f.

discolor /dɪs'kʌlər/ v. descolorar.

discomfort /dɪs'kʌmfərt/ n. incomodidad f.

disconcert /,dɪskən'sɜrt/ v. desconcertar.

disconnect /,dɪskə'nɛkt/ v. desunir; desconectar.

disconnected /,dɪskə'nɛktɪd/ a. desunido.

disconsolate /dɪs'kɒnsəlɪt/ a. desconsolado.

discontent /,dɪskən'tɛnt/ n. descontento m.

discontented /,dɪskən'tɛntɪd/ a. descontento.

discontinue /,dɪskən'tɪnyu/ v. descontinuar.

discord /'dɪskɔrd/ n. discordia f.

discordant /dɪs'kɔrdənt/ a. disonante.

discotheque /'dɪskə,tɛk/ n. discoteca f.

discount /'dɪskaunt/ n. descuento m.

discourage /dɪ'skɜrɪdʒ/ v. desalentar, desanimar.

discouragement /dɪ'skɜrɪdʒmənt/ n. desaliento, desánimo m.

discourse /'dɪskɔrs/ n. discurso m.

discourteous /dɪs'kɜrtiəs/ a. descortés.

discourtesy /dɪs'kɜrtəsi/ n. descortesía f.

discover /dɪ'skʌvər/ v. descubrir.

discoverer /dɪ'skʌvərər/ n. descubridor -ra.

discovery /dɪ'skʌvəri/ n. descubrimiento m.

discreet /dɪ'skrit/ a. discreto.

discrepancy /dɪ'skrɛpənsi/ n. discrepancia f.

discretion /dɪ'skrɛʃən/ n. discreción f.

discriminate /dɪ'skrɪm,əneit/ v. distinguir. **d. against** discriminar contra.

discrimination /dɪ,skrɪmə'neiʃən/ n. discernimiento m.; discriminación f.

discuss /dɪ'skʌs/ v. discutir.

discussion /dɪ'skʌʃən/ n. discusión f.

disdain /dɪs'dein/ n. **1.** desdén m. —v. **2.** desdeñar.

disdainful /dɪs'deinfəl/ a. desdeñoso.

disease /dɪ'ziz/ n. enfermedad f., mal m.

disembark /,dɪsɛm'bɑrk/ v. desembarcar.

disentangle /ˌdɪsɛn'tæŋgəl/ v. desenredar.

disfigure /dɪs'fɪgyər/ v. desfigurar.

disgrace /dɪs'greis/ n. **1.** vergüenza; deshonra f. —v. **2.** deshonrar.

disgraceful /dɪs'greisfəl/ a. vergonzoso.

disguise /dɪs'gaiz/ n. **1.** disfraz m. —v. **2.** disfrazar.

disgust /dɪs'gʌst/ n. **1.** repugnancia —v. **2.** fastidiar; repugnar.

dish /dɪʃ/ n. plato m.

dishearten /dɪs'hɑrtn/ v. desanimar; descorazonar.

dishonest /dɪs'ɒnɪst/ a. deshonesto.

dishonesty /dɪs'ɒnɒsti/ n. deshonestidad f.

dishonor /dɪs'ɒnər/ n. **1.** deshonra f. —v. **2.** deshonrar.

dishonorable /dɪs'ɒnərəbəl/ a. deshonroso.

dishwasher /'dɪʃˌwɒʃər/ n. lavaplatos m.

disillusion /ˌdɪsɪ'luʒən/ n. **1.** desengaño m. —v. **2.** desengañar.

disinfect /ˌdɪsɪn'fɛkt/ v. desinfectar.

disinfectant /ˌdɪsɪn'fɛktənt/ n. desinfectante m.

disinherit /ˌdɪsɪn'hɛrɪt/ v. desheredar.

disintegrate /dɪs'ɪntəˌgreit/ v. desintegrar.

disinterested /dɪs'ɪntəˌrɛstɪd, -trɪstɪd/ a. desinteresado.

disk /dɪsk/ n. disco m.

disk drive disquetera f.

diskette /dɪ'skɛt/ n. disquete m.

disk jockey pinchadiscos m. & f.

dislike /dɪs'laik/ n. **1.** antipatía f. —v. **2.** no gustar de.

dislocate /'dɪslouˌkeit/ v. dislocar.

dislodge /dɪs'lɒdʒ/ v. desalojar; desprender.

disloyal /dɪs'lɔiəl/ a. desleal; infiel.

disloyalty /dɪs'lɔiəlti/ n. deslealtad f.

dismal /'dɪzməl/ a. lúgubre.

dismantle /dɪs'mæntl/ v. desmantelar, desmontar.

dismay /dɪs'mei/ n. **1.** consternación f. —v. **2.** consternar.

dismiss /dɪs'mɪs/ v. despedir.

dismissal /dɪs'mɪsəl/ n. despedida f.

dismount /dɪs'maunt/ v. apearse, desmontarse.

disobedience /ˌdɪsə'bidiəns/ n. desobediencia f.

disobedient /ˌdɪsə'bidiənt/ a. desobediente.

disobey /ˌdɪsə'bei/ v. desobedecer.

disorder /dɪs'ɔrdər/ n. desorden m.

disorderly /dɪs'ɔrdərli/ a. desarreglado, desordenado.

disown /dɪs'oun/ v. repudiar.

dispassionate /dɪs'pæʃənɪt/ a. desapasionado; templado.

dispatch /dɪs'pætʃ/ n. **1.** despacho m. —v. **2.** despachar.

dispel /dɪs'pɛl/ v. dispersar.

dispensary /dɪ'spɛnsəri/ n. dispensario m.

dispensation /ˌdɪspən'seiʃən/ n. dispensación f.

dispense /dɪ'spɛns/ v. dispensar.

dispersal /dɪ'spɜrsəl/ n. dispersión f.

disperse /dɪ'spɜrs/ v. dispersar.

displace /dɪs'pleis/ v. dislocar.

display /dɪs'plei/ n. **1.** despliegue m.; exhibición f. —v. **2.** desplegar, exhibir.

displease /dɪs'pliz/ v. disgustar; ofender.

displeasure /dɪs'plɛʒər/ n. disgusto, sinsabor m.

disposable /dɪ'spouzəbəl/ a. disponible; desechable.

disposal /dɪ'spouzəl/ n. disposición f.

dispose /dɪ'spouz/ v. disponer.

disposition /ˌdɪspə'zɪʃən/ n. disposición f.; índole f., genio m.

dispossess /ˌdɪspə'zɛs/ v. desposeer.

disproportionate /ˌdɪsprə'pɔrʃənɪt/ a. desproporcionado.

disprove /dɪs'pruv/ v. confutar.

dispute /dɪ'spyut/ n. **1.** disputa f. —v. **2.** disputar.

disqualify /dɪs'kwɒləˌfai/ v. inhabilitar.

disregard /ˌdɪsrɪ'gɑrd/ n. **1.** desatención f. —v. **2.** desatender.

disrepair /ˌdɪsrɪ'pɛər/ n. descompostura f.

disreputable /dɪs'rɛpyətəbəl/ a. desacreditado.

disrespect /ˌdɪsrɪ'spɛkt/ n. falta de respeto, f., desacato m.

disrespectful /ˌdɪsrɪ'spɛktfəl/ a. irrespetuoso.

disrobe /dɪs'roub/ v. desvestir.

disrupt /dɪs'rʌpt/ v. romper; desbaratar.

dissatisfaction /ˌdɪssætɪs'fækʃən/ n. descontento m.

dissatisfy /dɪs'sætɪsˌfai/ v. descontentar.

dissect /dɪ'sɛkt/ v. disecar.

dissemble /dɪ'sɛmbəl/ v. disimular.

disseminate /dɪ'sɛməˌneit/ v. diseminar.

dissension /dɪ'sɛnʃən/ n. disensión f.

dissent /dɪ'sɛnt/ n. **1.** disensión f. —v. **2.** disentir.

dissertation /ˌdɪsər'teiʃən/ n. disertación f.

dissimilar /dɪ'sɪmələr/ a. desemejante.

dissipate /'dɪsəˌpeit/ v. disipar.

dissipation /ˌdɪsə'peiʃən/ n. disipación f.; libertinaje m.

dissolute /'dɪsəˌlut/ a. disoluto.

dissolution /ˌdɪsə'luʃən/ n. disolución f.

dissolve /dɪ'zɒlv/ v. disolver; derretirse.

dissonant /'dɪsənənt/ a. disonante.

dissuade /dɪ'sweid/ v. disuadir.

distance /'dɪstəns/ n. distancia f. **at a d., in the d.,** a lo lejos.

distant /'dɪstənt/ a. distante, lejano.

distaste /dɪs'teist/ n. disgusto, sinsabor m.

distasteful /dɪs'teistfəl/ a. desagradable.

distill /dɪ'stɪl/ v. destilar.

distillation /ˌdɪstl'eiʃən/ n. destilación f.

distillery /dɪ'stɪləri/ n. destilería f.

distinct /dɪ'stɪŋkt/ a. distinto.

distinction /dɪ'stɪŋkʃən/ n. distinción f.

distinctive /dɪ'stɪŋktɪv/ a. distintivo; característico.

distinctly /dɪ'stɪŋktli/ adv. distintamente.

distinguish /dɪ'stɪŋgwɪʃ/ v. distinguir.

distinguished /dɪ'stɪŋgwɪʃt/ a. distinguido.

distort /dɪ'stɔrt/ v. falsear; torcer.

distract /dɪ'strækt/ v. distraer.

distraction /dɪ'strækʃən/ n. distracción f.

distraught /dɪ'strɔt/ a. aturrullado; demente.

distress /dɪ'strɛs/ n. **1.** dolor m. —v. **2.** afligir.

distressing /dɪ'strɛsɪŋ/ a. penoso.

distribute /dɪ'strɪbyut/ v. distribuir.

distribution /ˌdɪstrə'byuʃən/ n. distribución f.; reparto m.

distributor /dɪ'strɪbyətər/ n. distribuidor -ra.

district /'dɪstrɪkt/ n. distrito m.

distrust /dɪs'trʌst/ n. **1.** desconfianza f. —v. **2.** desconfiar.

distrustful /dɪs'trʌstfəl/ a. desconfiado; sospechoso.

disturb /dɪ'stɜrb/ v. incomodar; inquietar.

disturbance /dɪ'stɜrbəns/ n. disturbio m.

disturbing /dɪ'stɜrbɪŋ/ a. inquietante.

ditch /dɪtʃ/ n. zanja f.; foso m.

divan /dɪ'væn/ n. diván m.

dive /daiv/ n. **1.** clavado m.; Colloq. leonera f. —v. **2.** echar un clavado; bucear.

diver /'daivər/ n. buzo m.

diverge /dɪ'vɜrdʒ/ v. divergir.

divergence /dɪ'vɜrdʒəns/ n. divergencia f.

divergent /dɪ'vɜrdʒənt/ a. divergente.

diverse /dɪ'vɜrs/ a. diverso.

diversion /dɪ'vɜrʒən/ n. diversión f.; pasatiempo m.

diversity /dɪ'vɜrsɪti/ n. diversidad f.

divert /dɪ'vɜrt/ v. desviar; divertir.

divest /dɪ'vɛst/ v. desnudar, despojar.

divide /dɪ'vaid/ v. dividir.

dividend /'dɪvɪˌdɛnd/ n. dividendo m.

divine /dɪ'vain/ a. divino.

divinity /dɪ'vɪnɪti/ n. divinidad f.

division /dɪ'vɪʒən/ n. división f.

divorce /dɪ'vɔrs/ n. **1.** divorcio m. —v. **2.** divorciar.

divorcee /dɪvɔr'sei/ n. divorciado -da.

divulge /dɪ'vʌldʒ/ v. divulgar, revelar.

dizziness /'dɪzɪnɪs/ n. vértigo, mareo m.

dizzy /'dɪzi/ a. mareado.

DNA abbr. (deoxyribonucleic acid) ADN (ácido deoxirribonucleico) m.

do /du/ v. hacer.

docile /'dɒsəl/ a. dócil.

dock /dɒk/ n. **1.** muelle m. **dry d.,** astillero m. —v. **2.** entrar en muelle.

doctor /'dɒktər/ n. médico m.; doctor -ra.

doctorate /'dɒktərɪt/ n. doctorado m.

doctrine /'dɒktrɪn/ n. doctrina f.

document /'dɒkyəmənt/ n. documento m.

documentary /ˌdɒkyə'mɛntəri/ a. documental.

documentation /ˌdɒkyəmɛn'teiʃən/ n. documentación f.

dodge /dɒdʒ/ n. **1.** evasión f. —v. **2.** evadir.

dodgem /'dɒdʒɪm/ n. coche de choque m.

doe /dou/ n. gama f.

dog /dɔg/ n. perro -a.

dogma /'dɔgmə/ n. dogma m.

dogmatic /dɔg'mætɪk/ a. dogmático.

dogmatism /'dɔgməˌtɪzəm/ n. dogmatismo m.

doily /'dɔili/ n. servilletita f.

doleful /'doulfəl/ a. triste.

doll /dɒl/ n. muñeca -co.

dollar /'dɒlər/ n. dólar m.

dolorous /'doulərəs/ a. lastimoso.

dolphin /'dɒlfɪn/ n. delfín m.

domain /dou'mein/ n. dominio m.

dome /doum/ n. domo m.

domestic /də'mɛstɪk/ a. doméstico.

domesticate /də'mɛstɪˌkeit/ v. domesticar.

domicile /'dɒməˌsail/ n. domicilio m.

dominance /'dɒmənəns/ n. dominación f.

dominant /'dɒmənənt/ a. dominante.

dominate /'dɒməˌneit/ v. dominar.

domination /ˌdɒmə'neiʃən/ n. dominación f.

domineer /ˌdɒmə'nɪər/ v. dominar.

domineering /ˌdɒmə'nɪərɪŋ/ a. tiránico, mandón.

dominion /də'mɪnyən/ n. dominio; territorio m.

domino /'dɒməˌnou/ n. dominó m.

donate /'douneit/ v. donar; contribuir.

donation /dou'neiʃən/ n. donación f.

donkey /'dɒŋki/ n. asno, burro m.

doom /dum/ n. **1.** perdición, ruina f. —v. **2.** perder, ruinar.

door /dɔr/ n. puerta f.

doorman /'dɔrˌmæn, -mən/ n. portero m.

doormat /'dɔrˌmæt/ n. felpudo m.

doorway /'dɔrˌwei/ n. entrada f.

dope /doup/ n. Colloq. narcótico m.; idiota m.

dormant /'dɔrmənt/ a. durmiente; inactivo.

dormitory /'dɔrmɪˌtɔri/ n. dormitorio m.

dosage /'dousɪdʒ/ n. dosificación f.

dose /dous/ n. dosis f.

dot /dɒt/ n. punto m.

dotted line /'dɒtɪd/ línea de puntos f.

double /'dʌbəl/ a. **1.** doble. —v. **2.** duplicar.

double bass /beis/ contrabajo m.

double-breasted /'dʌbəl 'brɛstɪd/ a. cruzado.

double-cross /'dʌbəl 'krɔs/ v. traicionar.

doubly /'dʌbli/ adv. doblemente.

doubt /daut/ n. **1.** duda f. —v. **2.** dudar.

doubtful /'dautfəl/ a. dudoso, incierto.

doubtless /'dautlɪs/ a. **1.** indudable. —adv. **2.** sin duda.

dough /dou/ n. pasta, masa f.

doughnut /'dounət, -ˌnʌt/ n. buñuelo m.

dove /dʌv/ n. paloma f.

dowager /'dauədʒər/ n. viuda (con título) f.

down /daun/ adv. **1.** abajo. —prep. **2. d. the street,** etc. calle abajo, etc.

downcast /'daunˌkæst/ a. cabizbajo.

downfall /'daunˌfɔl/ n. ruina, perdición f.

downhearted /'daun'hɑrtɪd/ a. descorazonado.

download /'daunˌloud/ v. bajar, descargar.

downpour /'daunˌpɔr/ n. chaparrón m.

downright /'daunˌrait/ a. absoluto, completo.

downriver /'daun'rɪvər/ adv. aguas abajo, río abajo.

downstairs /'daun'stɛərz/ adv. **1.** abajo. —n. **2.** primer piso.

downstream /'daun'strim/ adv. aguas abajo, río abajo.

downtown /'daun'taun/ adv. al centro, en el centro.

downward /'daunwərd/ a. **1.** descendente. —adv. **2.** hacia abajo.

dowry /'dauri/ n. dote f.

doze /douz/ v. dormitar.

dozen /'dʌzən/ n. docena f.

draft /dræft/ n. **1.** dibujo m.; Com. giro m.; Mil. conscripción f. —v. **2.** dibujar; Mil. reclutar.

draftee /dræf'ti/ n. conscripto m.

draft notice notificación de reclutamiento f.

drag /dræg/ v. arrastrar.

dragon /'drægən/ n. dragón m.

drain /drein/ n. **1.** desaguadero m. —v. **2.** desaguar.

drainage /'dreinɪdʒ/ n. drenaje m.

drain board escurridero m.

drama /'drɑmə, 'dræmə/ n. drama m.

dramatic /drə'mætɪk/ a. dramático.

dramatics /drə'mætɪks/ n. dramática f.

dramatist /'dræmətɪst, 'drɑmə-/ n. dramaturgo -ga.

dramatize /'dræməˌtaiz, 'drɑmə-/ v. dramatizar.

drape /dreip/ n. cortinas f.pl. v. vestir; adornar.

drapery /'dreipəri/ n. colgaduras f.pl.; ropaje m.

drastic /'dræstɪk/ a. drástico.

draw /drɔ/ v. dibujar; atraer. **d. up,** formular.

drawback /'drɔˌbæk/ n. desventaja f.

drawer /drɔr/ n. cajón m.

drawing /'drɔɪŋ/ n. dibujo m.; rifa f.

dread /drɛd/ n. **1.** terror m. —v. **2.** temer.

dreadful /'drɛdfəl/ a. terrible.

dreadfully /'drɛdfəli/ adv. horrendamente.

dream /drim/ n. **1.** sueño, ensueño m. —v. **2.** soñar.

dreamer /'drimər/ n. soñador -ra; visionario -ia.

dreamy /'drimi/ a. soñador, contemplativo.

dreary /'drɪəri/ a. monótono y pesado.

dredge /dredʒ/ n. **1.** rastra f. —v. **2.** rastrear.

dregs /dregz/ n. sedimento m.

drench /drentʃ/ v. mojar.

dress /dres/ n. **1.** vestido; traje m. —v. **2.** vestir.

dresser /'dresər/ n. (furniture) tocador.

dressing /'dresɪŋ/ n. Med. curación f.; (cookery) relleno m., salsa f.

dressing gown bata f.

dressing table tocador m.

dressmaker /'dres,meikər/ n. modista m. & f.

drift /drɪft/ n. **1.** tendencia f.; Naut. deriva f. —v. **2.** Naut. derivar; (snow) amontonarse.

drill /drɪl/ n. **1.** ejercicio m.; Mech. taladro m. —v. **2.** Mech. taladrar.

drink /drɪŋk/ n. **1.** bebida f. —v. **2.** beber, tomar.

drinkable /'drɪŋkəbəl/ a. potable, bebible.

drip /drɪp/ v. gotear.

drive /draiv/ n. **1.** paseo m. —v. **2.** impeler; Auto. guiar, conducir.

drive-in (movie theater) /'draiv ,ɪn/ n. autocine, autocinema m.

driver /'draivər/ n. conductor -ra; chofer m. **d.'s license,** permiso de conducir.

driveway /'draiv,wei/ n. entrada para coches.

drizzle /'drɪzəl/ n. **1.** llovizna f. —v. **2.** lloviznar.

dromedary /'dromɪ,deri/ n. dromedario m.

droop /drup/ v. inclinarse.

drop /drop/ n. **1.** gota f. —v. **2.** soltar; dejar caer.

dropout /'drop,aut/ n. joven que abandona sus estudios.

dropper /'dropər/ n. cuentagotas f.

dropsy /'dropsi/ n. hidropesía f.

drought /draut/ n. sequía f.

drove /drouv/ n. manada f.

drown /draun/ v. ahogar.

drowse /drauz/ v. adormecer.

drowsiness /'drauzinɪs/ n. somnolencia f.

drowsy /'drauzi/ a. soñoliento.

drudge /drʌdʒ/ n. ganapán m.

drudgery /'drʌdʒəri/ n. trabajo penoso.

drug /drʌg/ n. **1.** droga f. —v. **2.** narcotizar.

drug addict drogadicto -ta, toxicómano -na m. & f.

druggist /'drʌgɪst/ n. farmacéutico -ca, boticario -ria.

drugstore /'drʌg,stɔr/ n. farmacia, botica, droguería f.

drum /drʌm/ n. tambor m.

drummer /'drʌmər/ n. tambor m.

drumstick /'drʌm,stɪk/ n. palillo m.; Leg. pierna f.

drunk /drʌŋk/ a. & n. borracho, -a.

drunkard /'drʌŋkərd/ n. borrachón m.

drunken /'drʌŋkən/ a. borracho; ebrio.

drunkenness /'drʌŋkənnɪs/ n. embriaguez f.

dry /drai/ a. **1.** seco, árido. —v. **2.** secar.

dry cell n. pila seca f.

dry cleaner tintorero -ra.

dryness /'drainɪs/ n. sequedad f.

dual /'duəl/ a. doble.

dubious /'dubiəs/ a. dudoso.

duchess /'dʌtʃɪs/ n. duquesa f.

duck /dʌk/ n. **1.** pato m. —v. **2.** zambullir; (avoid) esquivar.

duct /dʌkt/ n. canal m.

due /du/ a. **1.** debido; Com. vencido. —n. **2. dues** cuota f.

duel /'duəl/ n. duelo f.

duelist /'duəlɪst/ n. duelista m.

duet /du'et/ n. dúo m.

duke /duk/ n. duque m.

dull /dʌl/ a. apagado, desteñido; sin punta; Fig. pesado, soso.

dullness /'dʌlnɪs/ n. estupidez; pesadez f.; deslustre m.

duly /'duli/ adv. debidamente.

dumb /dʌm/ a. mudo; Colloq. estúpido.

dumbwaiter /'dʌm,weitər/ n. montaplatos m.

dumfound /dʌm'faund/ v. confundir.

dummy /'dʌmi/ n. maniquí m.

dump /dʌmp/ n. **1.** depósito m. —v. **2.** descargar.

dune /dun/ n. duna f.

dungeon /'dʌndʒən/ n. calabozo m.

dunk /dʌŋk/ v. mojar.

dupe /dup/ v. engañar.

duplicate /a, n 'duplɪkɪt; v -,keit/ a. & n. **1.** duplicado m. —v. **2.** duplicar.

duplication /,duplɪ'keiʃən/ n. duplicación f.

duplicity /du'plɪsiti/ n. duplicidad f.

durability /,durə'bɪliti/ n. durabilidad f.

durable /'durəbəl/ a. durable, duradero.

duration /dʊ'reiʃən/ n. duración f.

duress /dʊ'res/ n. compulsión f.; encierro m.

during /'dʊrɪŋ/ prep. durante.

dusk /dʌsk/ n. crepúsculo m.

dusky /'dʌski/ a. oscuro; moreno.

dust /dʌst/ n. **1.** polvo m. —v. **2.** polvorear; despolvorear.

dusty /'dʌsti/ a. empolvado.

Dutch /dʌtʃ/ a. holandés -sa.

dutiful /'dutəfəl/ a. respetuoso.

dutifully /'dutəfəli/ adv. respetuosamente, obedientemente.

duty /'duti/ n. deber m.; Com. derechos m.pl.

duty-free /'duti 'fri/ a. libre de derechos.

dwarf /dwɔrf/ n. **1.** enano -na. —v. **2.** achicar.

dwell /dwel/ v. habitar, residir. **d. on,** espaciarse en.

dwelling /'dwelɪŋ/ n. morada, casa f.

dwindle /'dwɪndl/ v. disminuirse.

dye /dai/ n. **1.** tintura f. —v. **2.** teñir.

dyer /'daiər/ n. tintorero -ra.

dynamic /dai'næmɪk/ a. dinámico.

dynamite /'dainə,mait/ n. dinamita f.

dynamo /'dainə,mou/ n. dínamo f.

dynasty /'dainəsti/ n. dinastía f.

dysentery /'dɪsən,teri/ n. disentería f.

dyslexia /dɪs'leksiə/ n. dislexia f.

dyslexic /dɪs'leksɪk/ a. disléxico.

dyspepsia /dɪs'pepʃə/ n. dispepsia f.

E

each /itʃ/ a. **1.** cada. —pron. **2.** cada uno -na. **e. other,** el uno al otro.

eager /'igər/ a. ansioso.

eagerly /'igərli/ adv. ansiosamente.

eagerness /'igərnɪs/ n. ansia f.

eagle /'igəl/ n. águila f.

ear /ɪər/ n. oído m.; (outer) oreja f.; (of corn) mazorca f.

earache /'ɪər,eik/ n. dolor de oído m.

earl /ɜrl/ n. conde m.

early /'ɜrli/ a. & adv. temprano.

earn /ɜrn/ v. ganar.

earnest /'ɜrnɪst/ a. serio.

earnestly /'ɜrnɪstli/ adv. seriamente.

earnings /'ɜrnɪŋz/ n. ganancias f.pl.; Com. ingresos m.pl.

earphone /'ɪər,foun/ n. auricular m.

earring /'ɪər,rɪŋ/ n. pendiente, arete m.

earth /ɜrθ/ n. tierra f.

earthquake /'ɜrθ,kweik/ n. terremoto m.

ease /iz/ n. **1.** reposo m.; facilidad f. —v. **2.** aliviar.

easel /'izəl/ n. caballete m.

easily /'izəli/ adv. fácilmente.

east /ist/ n. oriente, este m.

Easter /'istər/ n. Pascua Florida.

eastern /'istərn/ a. oriental.

eastward /'istwərd/ adv. hacia el este.

easy /'izi/ a. fácil.

eat /it/ v. comer.

eau de Cologne /'ou də kə'loun/ colonia f.

eaves /ivz/ n. socarrén m.

ebb /eb/ n. **1.** menguante f. —v. **2.** menguar.

ebony /'ebəni/ n. ébano m.

eccentric /ɪk'sentrɪk/ a. excéntrico.

eccentricity /,eksən'trɪsiti/ n. excentricidad f.

ecclesiastic /ɪ,klizi'æstɪk/ a. & n. eclesiástico.

echelon /'eʃə,lɒn/ n. escalón m.

echo /'ekou/ n. eco m.

eclipse /ɪ'klɪps/ n. **1.** eclipse m. —v. **2.** eclipsar.

ecological /,ekə'lɒdʒɪkəl/ a. ecológico.

ecology /ɪ'kɒlədʒi/ n. ecología f.

economic /,ekə'nɒmɪk, ,ikə-/ a. económico.

economical /,ekə'nɒmɪkəl, ,ikə-/ a. económico.

economics /,ekə'nɒmɪks, ,ikə-/ n. economía política.

economist /ɪ'kɒnəmɪst/ n. economista m. & f.

economize /ɪ'kɒnə,maiz/ v. economizar.

economy /ɪ'kɒnəmi/ n. economía f.

ecstasy /'ekstəsi/ n. éxtasis m.

Ecuadorian /,ekwə'dɔriən/ a. & n. ecuatoriano -na.

ecumenical /,ekyu'menɪkəl/ a. ecuménico.

eczema /'eksəmə/ n. eczema f.

eddy /'edi/ n. **1.** remolino m. —v. **2.** remolinar.

edge /edʒ/ n. **1.** filo; borde m. —v. **2. e. one's way,** abrirse paso.

edible /'edəbəl/ a. comestible.

edict /'idɪkt/ n. edicto m.

edifice /'edəfɪs/ n. edificio m.

edify /'edə,fai/ v. edificar.

edition /ɪ'dɪʃən/ n. edición f.

editor /'edɪtər/ n. redactor -ra.

editorial /,edɪ'tɔriəl/ a. editorial m. **e. board,** consejo de redacción m. **e. staff,** redacción f.

educate /'edʒʊ,keit/ v. educar.

education /,edʒʊ'keiʃən/ n. instrucción; enseñanza f.

educational /,edʒʊ'keiʃənl/ a. educativo.

educator /'edʒʊ,keitər/ n. educador -ra, pedagogo -ga.

eel /il/ n. anguila f.

efface /ɪ'feis/ v. tachar.

effect /ɪ'fekt/ n. **1.** efecto m. **in e.,** en vigor. —v. **2.** efectuar, realizar.

effective /ɪ'fektɪv/ a. eficaz; efectivo; en vigor.

effectively /ɪ'fektɪvli/ adv. eficazmente.

effectiveness /ɪ'fektɪvnɪs/ n. efectividad f.

effectual /ɪ'fektʃuəl/ a. eficaz.

effeminate /ɪ'femənɪt/ a. afeminado.

efficacy /'efɪkəsi/ n. eficacia f.

efficiency /ɪ'fɪʃənsi/ n. eficiencia f.

efficient /ɪ'fɪʃənt/ a. eficaz.

efficiently /ɪ'fɪʃəntli/ adv. eficazmente.

effigy /'efɪdʒi/ n. efigie f.

effort /'efərt/ n. esfuerzo m.

effrontery /ɪ'frʌntəri/ n. impudencia f.

effusive /ɪ'fyusɪv/ a. efusivo.

egg /eg/ n. huevo m. **fried e.,** huevo frito. **soft-boiled e.,** h. pasado por agua. **scrambled eggs,** huevos revueltos.

eggplant /'eg,plænt/ n. berenjena f.

egg white clara de huevo f.

egoism /'igou,ɪzəm/ **egotism** egoísmo m.

egoist /'igouɪst/ **egotist** n. egoísta m. & f.

egotism /'igə,tɪzəm/ n. egotismo m.

egotist /'igotɪst/ n. egotista m. & f.

Egypt /'idʒɪpt/ n. Egipto m.

Egyptian /ɪ'dʒɪpʃən/ a. & n. egipcio -ia.

eight /eit/ a. & pron. ocho.

eighteen /'ei'tin/ a. & pron. dieciocho.

eighth /eitθ, eiθ/ a. octavo.

eightieth /'eitiɪθ/ a. octogésimo m.

eighty /'eiti/ a. & pron. ochenta.

either /'iðər/ a. & pron. **1.** cualquiera de los dos. —adv. **2.** tampoco. —conj. **3. either... or,** o... o.

ejaculate /ɪ'dʒækyə,leit/ v. exclamar; eyacular.

ejaculation /ɪ,dʒækyə'leiʃən/ n. eyaculación f.

eject /ɪ'dʒekt/ v. expeler; eyectar.

ejection /ɪ'dʒekʃən/ n. expulsión f.; eyección f.

elaborate /a ɪ'læbərɪt; v -ə,reit/ a. **1.** elaborado. —v. **2.** elaborar; ampliar.

elapse /ɪ'læps/ v. transcurrir; pasar.

elastic /ɪ'læstɪk/ a. & n. elástico m.

elasticity /ɪlæ'stɪsiti/ n. elasticidad f.

elate /ɪ'leit/ v. exaltar.

elation /ɪ'leiʃən/ n. exaltación f.

elbow /'elbou/ n. codo m.

elder /'eldər/ a. **1.** mayor. —n. **2.** anciano -na.

elderly /'eldərli/ a. de edad.

eldest /'eldɪst/ a. mayor.

elect /ɪ'lekt/ v. elegir.

election /ɪ'lekʃən/ n. elección f.

elective /ɪ'lektɪv/ a. electivo.

electorate /ɪ'lektərɪt/ n. electorado m.

electric /ɪ'lektrɪk/ **electrical** a. eléctrico.

electrician /ɪlek'trɪʃən/ n. electricista m. & f.

electricity /ɪlek'trɪsiti/ n. electricidad f.

electrocardiogram /ɪ,lektrou'kardiə,græm/ n. electrocardiograma m.

electrocute /ɪ'lektrə,kyut/ v. electrocutar.

electrode /ɪ'lektroud/ n. electrodo m.

electrolysis /ɪlek'trɒləsɪs/ n. electrólisis f.

electron /ɪ'lektrɒn/ n. electrón m.

electronic /ɪlek'trɒnɪk/ a. electrónico.

electronics /ɪlek'trɒnɪks/ n. electrónica f.

elegance /'elɪgəns/ n. elegancia f.

elegant /'elɪgənt/ a. elegante.

elegy /'elɪdʒi/ n. elegía f.

element /'eləmənt/ n. elemento m.

elemental /,elə'mentl/ a. elemental.

elementary /,elə'mentəri/ a. elemental.

elephant /'eləfənt/ n. elefante -ta.

elevate /'elə,veit/ v. elevar.

elevation /,elə'veiʃən/ n. elevación f.

elevator /'elə,veitər/ n. ascensor m.

eleven /ɪ'levən/ a. & pron. once.

eleventh /ɪ'levənθ/ a. undécimo.

eleventh hour último minuto m.

elf /elf/ n. duende m.

elicit /ɪ'lɪsɪt/ v. sacar; despertar.

eligibility /,elɪdʒə'bɪliti/ n. elegibilidad f.

eligible /'elɪdʒəbəl/ a. elegible.

eliminate /ɪ'lɪmə,neit/ v. eliminar.

elimination /ɪ,lɪmə'neiʃən/ n. eliminación f.

elixir /ɪ'lɪksər/ n. elixir m.

elk /elk/ n. alce m., anta m.

elm /elm/ n. olmo m.

elocution /,elə'kyuʃən/ n. elocución f.

elongate /ɪ'lɔŋgeit/ v. alargar.

elope /ɪ'loup/ v. fugarse.

eloquence /'eləkwəns/ n. elocuencia f.

eloquent /'eləkwənt/ a. elocuente.

eloquently /'eləkwəntli/ adv. elocuentemente.

else /els/ adv. más. **someone e.,** otra persona. **something e.,** otra cosa. **or e.,** de otro modo.

elsewhere /'els,wer/ adv. en otra parte.

elucidate /ɪ'lusɪ,deit/ v. elucidar.
elude /ɪ'lud/ v. eludir.
elusive /ɪ'lusɪv/ a. evasivo.
emaciated /ɪ'meiʃi,eitɪd/ a. demacrado, enflaquecido.
e-mail /'i,meil/ n. correo electrónico m.
emanate /'ɛmə,neit/ v. emanar.
emancipate /ɪ'mænsə,peit/ v. emancipar.
emancipation /ɪ,mænsə'peiʃən/ n. emancipación f.
emancipator /ɪ'mænsə,peitər/ n. libertador -ra.
embalm /ɛm'bɑm/ v. embalsamar.
embankment /ɛm'bæŋkmənt/ n. malecón, dique m.
embargo /ɛm'bɑrgou/ n. embargo m.
embark /ɛm'bɑrk/ v. embarcar.
embarrass /ɛm'bærəs/ v. avergonzar; turbar.
embarrassing /ɛm'bærəsɪŋ/ a. penoso, vergonzoso.
embarrassment /ɛm'bærəsmənt/ n. turbación f.; vergüenza f.
embassy /'ɛmbəsi/ n. embajada f.
embellish /ɛm'bɛlɪʃ/ v. hermosear, embellecer.
embellishment /ɛm'bɛlɪʃmənt/ n. embellecimiento m.
embezzle /ɛm'bɛzəl/ v. desfalcar, malversar.
emblem /'ɛmbləm/ n. emblema m.
embody /ɛm'bɒdi/ v. incorporar; personificar.
embrace /ɛm'breis/ n. 1. abrazo m. —v. 2. abrazar.
embroider /ɛm'brɔidər/ v. bordar.
embroidery /ɛm'brɔidəri, -dri/ n. bordado m.
embryo /'ɛmbri,ou/ n. embrión m.
embryonic /,ɛmbri'ɒnɪk/ a. embrionario.
emerald /'ɛmərəld/ n. esmeralda f.
emerge /ɪ'mɜrdʒ/ v. salir.
emergency /ɪ'mɜrdʒənsi/ n. emergencia f.
emergency brake freno de auxilio m.
emergency exit salida de urgencia f.
emergency landing aterrizaje forzoso m.
emergent /ɪ'mɜrdʒənt/ a. emergente.
emery /'ɛməri/ n. esmeril m.
emetic /ɪ'mɛtɪk/ n. emético m.
emigrant /'ɛmɪgrənt/ a. & n. emigrante m. & f.
emigrate /'ɛmɪ,greit/ v. emigrar.
emigration /,ɛmə'greiʃən/ n. emigración f.
eminence /'ɛmənəns/ n. altura; eminencia f.
eminent /'ɛmənənt/ a. eminente.
emissary /'ɛmə,sɛri/ n. emisario m.
emission /ɪ'mɪʃən/ n. emisión f.
emit /ɪ'mɪt/ v. emitir.
emolument /ɪ'mɒlyəmənt/ n. emolumento m.
emotion /ɪ'mouʃən/ n. emoción f.
emotional /ɪ'mouʃṇl/ a. emocional; sentimental.
emperor /'ɛmpərər/ n. emperador m.
emphasis /'ɛmfəsɪs/ n. énfasis m. or f.
emphasize /'ɛmfə,saiz/ v. acentuar, recalcar.
emphatic /ɛm'fætɪk/ a. enfático.
empire /'ɛmpaiər/ n. imperio m.
empirical /ɛm'pɪrɪkəl/ a. empírico.
employ /ɛm'plɔi/ v. emplear.
employee /ɛm'plɔii/ n. empleado -da.
employer /ɛm'plɔiər/ n. patrón -ona.
employment /ɛm'plɔimənt/ n. empleo m.
employment agency agencia de colocaciones f.
empower /ɛm'pauər/ v. autorizar.
emptiness /'ɛmptɪnɪs/ n. vaciedad; futilidad f.
empty /'ɛmpti/ a. 1. vacío. —v. 2. vaciar.
emulate /'ɛmyə,leit/ v. emular.
emulsion /ɪ'mʌlʃən/ n. emulsión f.

enable /ɛn'eibəl/ v. capacitar; permitir.
enact /ɛn'ækt/ v. promulgar, decretar.
enactment /ɛn'æktmənt/ n. ley f., estatuto m.
enamel /ɪ'næməl/ n. 1. esmalte m. —v. 2. esmaltar.
enamored /ɪ'næmərd/ a. enamorado.
enchant /ɛn'tʃænt/ v. encantar.
enchantment /ɛn'tʃæntmənt/ n. encanto m.
encircle /ɛn'sɜrkəl/ v. circundar.
enclose /ɛn'klouz/ v. encerrar. **enclosed**, (in letter) adjunto.
enclosure /ɛn'klouʒər/ n. recinto m.; (in letter) incluso m.
encompass /ɛn'kʌmpəs/ v. circundar.
encounter /ɛn'kauntər/ n. 1. encuentro m. —v. 2. encontrar.
encourage /ɛn'kɜridʒ/ v. animar.
encouragement /ɛn'kɜridʒmənt/ n. estímulo m.
encroach /ɛn'kroutʃ/ v. usurpar; meterse.
encryption /ɛn'krɪpʃən/ n. encriptación f., cifrado m.
encyclical /ɛn'sɪklɪkəl/ n. encíclica f.
encyclopedia /ɛn,saiklə'pidiə/ n. enciclopedia f.
end /ɛnd/ n. 1. fin, término, cabo; extremo; (aim) propósito m. —v. 2. acabar; terminar.
endanger /ɛn'deindʒər/ v. poner en peligro.
endear /ɛn'diər/ v. hacer querer.
endeavor /ɛn'dɛvər/ n. 1. esfuerzo m. —v. 2. esforzarse.
ending /'ɛndɪŋ/ n. conclusión f.
endless /'ɛndlɪs/ a. sin fin.
endocrine gland /'ɛndəkrɪn/ glándula endocrina f.
endorse /ɛn'dɔrs/ v. endosar; apoyar.
endorsement /ɛn'dɔrsmənt/ n. endoso m.
endow /ɛn'dau/ v. dotar, fundar.
endowment /ɛn'daumənt/ n. dotación f., fundación f.
endurance /ɛn'durəns/ n. resistencia f.
endure /ɛn'dur/ v. soportar, resistir, aguantar.
enema /'ɛnəmə/ n. enema; lavativa f.
enemy /'ɛnəmi/ n. enemigo -ga.
energetic /,ɛnər'dʒɛtɪk/ a. enérgico.
energy /'ɛnərdʒi/ n. energía f.
enervate /'ɛnər,veit/ v. enervar.
enervation /,ɛnər'veiʃən/ n. enervación f.
enfold /ɛn'fould/ v. envolver.
enforce /ɛn'fɔrs/ v. ejecutar.
enforcement /ɛn'fɔrsmənt/ n. ejecución f.
engage /ɛn'geidʒ/ v. emplear; ocupar.
engaged /ɛn'geidʒd/ a. (to marry) prometido.
engagement /ɛn'geidʒmənt/ n. combate; compromiso; contrato m.; cita f.
engine /'ɛndʒən/ n. máquina f. (railroad) locomotora f.
engineer /,ɛndʒə'niər/ n. ingeniero -ra; maquinista m.
engineering /,ɛndʒə'niərɪŋ/ n. ingeniería f.
England /'ɪŋglənd/ n. Inglaterra f.
English /'ɪŋglɪʃ/ a. & n. inglés -esa.
English Channel Canal de la Mancha m.
Englishman /'ɪŋglɪʃmən/ n. inglés m.
Englishwoman /'ɪŋglɪʃ,wumən/ n. inglesa f.
engrave /ɛn'greiv/ v. grabar.
engraver /ɛn'greivər/ n. grabador m.
engraving /ɛn'greivɪŋ/ n. grabado m.
engross /ɛn'grous/ v. absorber.
enhance /ɛn'hæns/ v. aumentar en valor; realzar.
enigma /ə'nɪgmə/ n. enigma m.
enigmatic /,ɛnɪg'mætɪk/ a. enigmático.
enjoy /ɛn'dʒɔi/ v. gozar de; disfrutar de. **e. oneself**, divertirse.
enjoyable /ɛn'dʒɔiəbəl/ a. agradable.
enjoyment /ɛn'dʒɔimənt/ n. goce m.

enlarge /ɛn'lɑrdʒ/ v. agrandar; ampliar.
enlargement /ɛn'lɑrdʒmənt/ n. ensanchamiento m., ampliación f.
enlarger /ɛn'lɑrdʒər/ n. amplificador m.
enlighten /ɛn'laitṇ/ v. informar.
enlightenment /ɛn'laitṇmənt/ n. esclarecimiento m.; cultura f.
enlist /ɛn'lɪst/ v. reclutar; alistarse.
enlistment /ɛn'lɪstmənt/ n. alistamiento m.
enliven /ɛn'laivən/ v. avivar.
enmesh /ɛn'mɛʃ/ v. entrampar.
enmity /'ɛnmɪti/ n. enemistad f.
enormity /ɪ'nɔrmɪti/ v. enormidad f.
enormous /ɪ'nɔrməs/ a. enorme.
enough /ɪ'nʌf/ a. & adv. bastante. **to be e.**, bastar.
enrage /ɛn'reidʒ/ v. enfurecer.
enrich /ɛn'rɪtʃ/ v. enriquecer.
enroll /ɛn'roul/ v. registrar; matricularse.
enrollment /ɛn'roulmənt/ n. matriculación f.
ensign /'ɛnsən/ n. bandera f.; (naval) subteniente m.
enslave /ɛn'sleiv/ v. esclavizar.
ensue /ɛn'su/ v. seguir, resultar.
entail /ɛn'teil/ v. acarrear, ocasionar.
entangle /ɛn'tæŋgəl/ v. enredar.
enter /'ɛntər/ v. entrar.
enterprise /'ɛntər,praiz/ n. empresa f.
enterprising /'ɛntər,praizɪŋ/ a. emprendedor.
entertain /,ɛntər'tein/ v. entretener; divertir.
entertainment /,ɛntər'teinmənt/ n. entretenimiento m.; diversión f.
enthrall /ɛn'θrɔl/ v. esclavizar; cautivar.
enthusiasm /ɛn'θuzi,æzəm/ n. entusiasmo m.
enthusiast /ɛn'θuzi,æst, -ɪst/ n. entusiasta m. & f.
enthusiastic /ɛn,θuzi'æstɪk/ a. entusiasmado.
entice /ɛn'tais/ v. inducir.
entire /ɛn'taiər/ a. entero.
entirely /ɛn'taiərli/ adv. enteramente.
entirety /ɛn'taiərti/ n. totalidad f.
entitle /ɛn'taitḷ/ v. autorizar; (book) titular.
entity /'ɛntɪti/ n. entidad f.
entrails /'ɛntreilz/ n. entrañas f.pl.
entrance /'ɛntrəns/ n. entrada f.
entrance examination examen de ingreso m.
entrant /'ɛntrənt/ n. competidor -ra.
entreat /ɛn'trit/ v. rogar, suplicar.
entreaty /ɛn'triti/ n. ruego m., súplica f.
entrench /ɛn'trɛntʃ/ v. atrincherar.
entrust /ɛn'trʌst/ v. confiar.
entry /'ɛntri/ n. entrada f.; Com. partida f.
entry blank hoja de inscripción f.
enumerate /ɪ'numə,reit/ v. enumerar.
enumeration /ɪ,numə'reiʃən/ n. enumeración f.
enunciate /ɪ'nʌnsi,eit/ v. enunciar.
enunciation /ɪ,nʌnsi'eiʃən/ n. enunciación f.
envelop /ɛn'vɛləp/ v. envolver.
envelope /'ɛnvə,loup/ n. sobre m.; cubierta f.
enviable /'ɛnviəbəl/ a. envidiable.
envious /'ɛnviəs/ a. envidioso.
environment /ɛn'vairənmənt/ n. ambiente m.
environmentalist /ɛn,vairən'mɛntḷɪst/ n. ambientalista, ecologista m. & f.
environmental protection /ɛn,vairən'mɛntəl/ protección del ambiente.
environs /ɛn'vairənz/ n. alrededores m.
envoy /'ɛnvɔi/ n. enviado m.
envy /'ɛnvi/ n. 1. envidia f. —v. 2. envidiar.
eon /'iən/ n. eón m.

ephemeral /ɪ'fɛmərəl/ a. efímero.
epic /'ɛpɪk/ a. 1. épico. —n. 2. epopeya f.
epicure /'ɛpɪ,kyur/ n. epicúreo m.
epidemic /,ɛpɪ'dɛmɪk/ a. 1. epidémico. —n. 2. epidemia f.
epidermis /,ɛpɪ'dɜrmɪs/ n. epidermis f.
epigram /'ɛpɪ,græm/ n. epigrama m.
epilepsy /'ɛpə,lɛpsi/ n. epilepsia f.
epilogue /'ɛpə,lɔg/ n. epílogo m.
episode /'ɛpə,soud/ n. episodio m.
epistle /ɪ'pɪsəl/ n. epístola f.
epitaph /'ɛpɪ,tæf/ n. epitafio m.
epithet /'ɛpə,θɛt/ n. epíteto m.
epitome /ɪ'pɪtəmi/ n. epítome f.
epoch /'ɛpək/ n. época, era f.
Epsom salts /'ɛpsəm/ n.pl. sal de la Higuera f.
equal /'ikwəl/ a. & n. 1. igual m. —v. 2. igualar; equivaler.
equality /ɪ'kwɒlɪti/ n. igualdad f.
equalize /'ikwə,laiz/ v. igualar.
equanimity /,ikwə'nɪmɪti/ n. ecuanimidad f.
equate /ɪ'kweit/ v. igualar.
equation /ɪ'kweiʒən/ n. ecuación f.
equator /ɪ'kweitər/ n. ecuador m.
equatorial /,ikwə'tɔriəl/ a. ecuatorial.
equestrian /ɪ'kwɛstriən/ n. 1. jinete m. —a. 2. ecuestre.
equilibrium /,ikwə'lɪbriəm/ n. equilibrio m.
equinox /'ikwə,nɒks/ n. equinoccio m.
equip /ɪ'kwɪp/ v. equipar.
equipment /ɪ'kwɪpmənt/ n. equipo m.
equitable /'ɛkwɪtəbəl/ a. equitativo.
equity /'ɛkwɪti/ n. equidad, justicia f.
equivalent /ɪ'kwɪvələnt/ a. & n. equivalente m.
equivocal /ɪ'kwɪvəkəl/ a. equívoco, ambiguo.
era /'iərə, 'ɛrə/ n. era, época, edad f.
eradicate /ɪ'rædɪ,keit/ v. extirpar.
erase /ɪ'reis/ v. borrar.
eraser /ɪ'reisər/ n. borrador m.
erasure /ɪ'reiʃər/ n. borradura f.
erect /ɪ'rɛkt/ a. 1. derecho, erguido. —v. 2. erigir.
erection /ɪ'rɛkʃən/ **erectness** n. erección f.
ermine /'ɜrmɪn/ n. armiño m.
erode /ɪ'roud/ v. corroer.
erosion /ɪ'rouʒən/ n. erosión f.
erotic /ɪ'rɒtɪk/ a. erótico.
err /ɜr, ɛr/ v. equivocarse.
errand /'ɛrənd/ n. encargo, recado m.
errant /'ɛrənt/ a. errante.
erratic /ɪ'rætɪk/ a. errático.
erroneous /ə'rouniəs/ a. erróneo.
error /'ɛrər/ n. error m.
erudite /'ɛryu,dait/ a. erudito.
erudition /,ɛryu'dɪʃən/ n. erudición f.
eruption /ɪ'rʌpʃən/ n. erupción, irrupción f.
erysipelas /,ɛrə'sɪpələs/ n. erisipela f.
escalate /'ɛskə,leit/ v. escalar; intensificarse.
escalator /'ɛskə,leitər/ n. escalera mecánica f.
escapade /'ɛskə,peid/ n. escapada; correría f.
escape /ɪ'skeip/ n. 1. fuga, huída f. **fire e.**, escalera de salvamento. —v. 2. escapar; fugarse.
eschew /ɛs'tʃu/ v. evadir.
escort /n 'ɛskɔrt; v ɪ'skɔrt/ n. 1. escolta f. —v. 2. escoltar.
escrow /'ɛskrou/ n. plica f.
escutcheon /ɪ'skʌtʃən/ n. escudo de armas m.
esophagus /ɪ'sɒfəgəs/ n. esófago m.
esoteric /,ɛsə'tɛrɪk/ a. esotérico.
especially /ɪ'spɛʃəli/ adv. especialmente.
espionage /'ɛspiə,nɑʒ/ n. espionaje m.
espresso /ɛ'sprɛsou/ n. café exprés, m.
essay /'ɛsei/ n. ensayo m.

essayist /ˈɛseiɪst/ *n.* ensayista *m. & f.*

essence /ˈɛsəns/ *n.* esencia *f.;* perfume *m.*

essential /əˈsɛntʃəl/ *a.* esencial.

essentially /əˈsɛntʃəli/ *adv.* esencialmente.

establish /ɪˈstæblɪʃ/ *v.* establecer.

establishment /ɪˈstæblɪʃmənt/ *n.* establecimiento *m.*

estate /ɪˈsteit/ *n.* estado *m.;* hacienda *f.;* bienes *m.pl.*

esteem /ɪˈstim/ *n.* **1.** estima *f.* —*v.* **2.** estimar.

estimable /ˈɛstəməbəl/ *a.* estimable.

estimate /*n* ˈɛstəˌmɪt; *v* -ˌmeit/ *n.* **1.** cálculo; presupuesto *m.* —*v.* **2.** estimar.

estimation /ˌɛstəˈmeiʃən/ *n.* estimación *f.;* cálculo *m.*

estrange /ɪˈstreindʒ/ *v.* extrañar; enajenar.

estuary /ˈɛstʃuˌɛri/ *n.* estuario *m.*

etch /ɛtʃ/ *v.* grabar al agua fuerte.

etching /ˈɛtʃɪŋ/ *n.* aguafuerte.

eternal /ɪˈtɜrnl/ *a.* eterno.

eternity /ɪˈtɜrnɪti/ *n.* eternidad *f.*

ether /ˈiθər/ *n.* éter *m.*

ethereal /ɪˈθɪəriəl/ *a.* etéreo.

ethical /ˈɛθɪkəl/ *a.* ético.

ethics /ˈɛθɪks/ *n.* ética *f.*

ethnic /ˈɛθnɪk/ *a.* étnico.

etiquette /ˈɛtɪkɪt/ *n.* etiqueta *f.*

etymology /ˌɛtəˈmɒlədʒi/ *n.* etimología *f.*

eucalyptus /ˌyukəˈlɪptəs/ *n.* eucalipto *m.*

eugenic /yuˈdʒɛnɪk/ *a.* eugenésico.

eugenics /yuˈdʒɛnɪks/ *n.* eugenesia *f.*

eulogize /ˈyuləˌdʒaiz/ *v.* elogiar.

eulogy /ˈyulədʒi/ *n.* elogio *m.*

eunuch /ˈyunək/ *n.* eunuco *m.*

euphonious /yuˈfouniəs/ *a.* eufónico.

Europe /ˈyʊrəp/ *n.* Europa *f.*

European /ˌyʊrəˈpiən/ *a. & n.* europeo -pea.

euthanasia /ˌyuθəˈneiʒə, -ʒiə, -ziə/ *n.* eutanasia *f.*

evacuate /ɪˈvækyuˌeit/ *v.* evacuar.

evade /ɪˈveid/ *v.* evadir.

evaluate /ɪˈvælyuˌeit/ *v.* evaluar.

evaluation /ɪˌvælyuˈeiʃən/ *n.* valoración *f.*

evangelist /ɪˈvændʒəlɪst/ *n.* evangelista *m. & f.*

evaporate /ɪˈvæpəˌreit/ *v.* evaporarse.

evaporation /ɪˌvæpəˈreiʃən/ *n.* evaporación *f.*

evasion /ɪˈveiʒən/ *n.* evasión *f.*

evasive /ɪˈveisɪv/ *a.* evasivo.

eve /iv/ *n.* víspera *f.*

even /ˈivən/ *a.* **1.** llano; igual. —*adv.* **2.** aun; hasta. **not e.,** ni siquiera.

evening /ˈivnɪŋ/ *n.* noche, tarde *f.* **good e.!** ¡buenas tardes! ¡buenas noches!

evening class clase nocturna *f.*

evenness /ˈivənnɪs/ *n.* uniformidad *f.*

even number número par *m.*

event /ɪˈvɛnt/ *n.* acontecimiento, suceso *m.*

eventful /ɪˈvɛntfəl/ *a.* memorable.

eventual /ɪˈvɛntʃuəl/ *a.* eventual.

ever /ˈɛvər/ *adv.* alguna vez; (after *not*) nunca. **e. since,** desde que.

everlasting /ˌɛvərˈlæstɪŋ/ *a.* eterno.

every /ˈɛvri/ *a.* cada, todos los.

everybody /ˈɛvriˌbɒdi, -ˌbʌdi/ *pron.* todo el mundo; cada uno.

everyday /ˈɛvriˌdei/ *a.* ordinario, de cada día.

everyone /ˈɛvriˌwʌn/ *pron.* todo el mundo; cada uno; cada cual.

everything /ˈɛvriˌθɪŋ/ *pron.* todo *m.*

everywhere /ˈɛvriˌwɛər/ *adv.* por todas partes, en todas partes.

evict /ɪˈvɪkt/ *v.* expulsar.

eviction /ɪˈvɪkʃən/ *n.* evicción *f.*

evidence /ˈɛvɪdəns/ *n.* evidencia *f.*

evident /ˈɛvɪdənt/ *a.* evidente.

evidently /ˈɛvɪdəntli/ *adv.* evidentemente.

evil /ˈivəl/ *a.* **1.** malo; maligno. —*n.* **2.** mal *m.*

evince /ɪˈvɪns/ *v.* revelar.

evoke /ɪˈvouk/ *v.* evocar.

evolution /ˌɛvəˈluʃən/ *n.* evolución *f.*

evolve /ɪˈvɒlv/ *v.* desenvolver; desarrollar.

ewe /yu/ *v.* oveja *f.*

exact /ɪgˈzækt/ *a.* **1.** exacto. —*v.* **2.** exigir.

exacting /ɪgˈzæktɪŋ/ *a.* exigente.

exactly /ɪgˈzæktli/ *adv.* exactamente.

exaggerate /ɪgˈzædʒəˌreit/ *v.* exagerar.

exaggeration /ɪgˌzædʒəˈreiʃən/ *n.* exageración *f.*

exalt /ɪgˈzɔlt/ *v.* exaltar.

exaltation /ˌɛgzɔlˈteiʃən/ *n.* exaltación *f.*

examination /ɪgˌzæməˈneiʃən/ *n.* examen *m.;* (legal) interrogatorio *m.*

examine /ɪgˈzæmɪn/ *v.* examinar.

example /ɪgˈzæmpəl/ *n.* ejemplo *m.*

exasperate /ɪgˈzæspəˌreit/ *v.* exasperar.

exasperation /ɪgˌzæspəˈreiʃən/ *n.* exasperación *f.*

excavate /ˈɛkskəˌveit/ *v.* excavar, cavar.

exceed /ɪkˈsid/ *v.* exceder.

exceedingly /ɪkˈsidɪŋli/ *adv.* sumamente, extremadamente.

excel /ɪkˈsɛl/ *v.* sobresalir.

excellence /ˈɛksələns/ *n.* excelencia *f.*

Excellency /ˈɛksələnsi/ *n.* (title) Excelencia *f.*

excellent /ˈɛksələnt/ *a.* excelente.

except /ɪkˈsɛpt/ *prep.* **1.** salvo, excepto. —*v.* **2.** exceptuar.

exception /ɪkˈsɛpʃən/ *n.* excepción *f.*

exceptional /ɪkˈsɛpʃənl/ *a.* excepcional.

excerpt /ˈɛksɜrpt/ *n.* extracto.

excess /ɪkˈsɛs, ˈɛksɛs/ *n.* exceso *m.*

excessive /ɪkˈsɛsɪv/ *a.* excesivo.

exchange /ɪksˈtʃeindʒ/ *n.* **1.** cambio; canje *m.* **stock e.,** bolsa *f.* **telephone e.,** central telefónica. —*v.* **2.** cambiar, canjear, intercambiar.

exchangeable /ɪksˈtʃeindʒəbəl/ *a.* cambiable.

exchange rate tipo de cambio *m.*

excise /*n* ˈɛksaiz; *v* ɪkˈsaiz/ *n.* **1.** sisa *f.* —*v.* **2.** extirpar.

excite /ɪkˈsait/ *v.* agitar; provocar; emocionar.

excitement /ɪkˈsaitmənt/ *n.* agitación, conmoción *f.*

exciting /ɪkˈsaitɪŋ/ *a.* emocionante.

exclaim /ɪkˈskleim/ *v.* exclamar.

exclamation /ˌɛkskləˈmeiʃən/ *n.* exclamación *f.*

exclamation mark punto de admiración *m.*

exclude /ɪkˈsklud/ *v.* excluir.

exclusion /ɪkˈskluʒən/ *n.* exclusión *f.*

exclusive /ɪkˈsklusɪv/ *a.* exclusivo.

excommunicate /ˌɛkskəˈmyunɪˌkeit/ *v.* excomulgar, descomulgar.

excommunication /ˌɛkskəˌmyunɪˈkeiʃən/ *n.* excomunión *f.*

excrement /ˈɛkskrəmənt/ *n.* excremento *m.*

excruciating /ɪkˈskruʃiˌeitɪŋ/ *a.* penosísimo.

exculpate /ˈɛkskʌlˌpeit/ *v.* exculpar.

excursion /ɪkˈskɜrʒən/ *n.* excursión, jira *f.*

excuse /*n* ɪkˈskyus; *v* ɪkˈskyuz/ *n.* **1.** excusa *f.* —*v.* **2.** excusar, perdonar, disculpar; dispensar.

execrable /ˈɛksɪkrəbəl/ *a.* execrable.

execute /ˈɛksɪˌkyut/ *v.* ejecutar.

execution /ˌɛksɪˈkyuʃən/ *n.* ejecución *f.*

executioner /ˌɛksɪˈkyuʃənər/ *n.* verdugo *m.*

executive /ɪgˈzɛkyətɪv/ *a. & n.* ejecutivo -va.

executor /ɪgˈzɛkyətər/ *n.* testamentario *m.*

exemplary /ɪgˈzɛmpləri/ *a.* ejemplar.

exemplify /ɪgˈzɛmpləˌfai/ *v.* ejemplificar.

exempt /ɪgˈzɛmpt/ *a.* **1.** exento. —*v.* **2.** exentar.

exercise /ˈɛksərˌsaiz/ *n.* **1.** ejercicio *m.* —*v.* **2.** ejercitar.

exert /ɪgˈzɜrt/ *v.* esforzar.

exertion /ɪgˈzɜrʃən/ *n.* esfuerzo *m.*

exhale /ɛksˈheil/ *v.* exhalar.

exhaust /ɪgˈzɔst/ *n.* **1.** *Auto.* escape *m.* —*v.* **2.** agotar.

exhaustion /ɪgˈzɔstʃən/ *n.* agotamiento *m.*

exhaustive /ɪgˈzɔstɪv/ *a.* exhaustivo.

exhaust pipe tubo de escape *m.*

exhibit /ɪgˈzɪbɪt/ *n.* **1.** exhibición, exposición *f.* —*v.* **2.** exhibir.

exhibition /ˌɛksəˈbɪʃən/ *n.* exhibición *f.*

exhilarate /ɪgˈzɪləˌreit/ *v.* alegrar; estimular.

exhort /ɪgˈzɔrt/ *v.* exhortar.

exhortation /ˌɛgzɔrˈteiʃən/ *n.* exhortación *f.*

exhume /ɪgˈzum/ *v.* exhumar.

exigency /ˈɛksɪdʒənsi/ *n.* exigencia *f.,* urgencia *f.*

exile /ˈɛgzail/ *n.* **1.** destierro *m.,* (person) desterrado *m.* —*v.* **2.** desterrar.

exist /ɪgˈzɪst/ *v.* existir.

existence /ɪgˈzɪstəns/ *n.* existencia *f.*

existent /ɪgˈzɪstənt/ *a.* existente.

exit /ˈɛgzɪt, ˈɛksɪt/ *n.* salida *f.*

exodus /ˈɛksədəs/ *n.* éxodo *m.*

exonerate /ɪgˈzɒnəˌreit/ *v.* exonerar.

exorbitant /ɪgˈzɔrbɪtənt/ *a.* exorbitante.

exorcise /ˈɛksɔrˌsaiz/ *v.* exorcizar.

exotic /ɪgˈzɒtɪk/ *a.* exótico.

expand /ɪkˈspænd/ *v.* dilatar; ensanchar.

expanse /ɪkˈspæns/ *n.* espacio *m.;* extensión *f.*

expansion /ɪkˈspænʃən/ *n.* expansión *f.*

expansion slot ranura de expansión *f.*

expansive /ɪkˈspænsɪv/ *a.* expansivo.

expatiate /ɪkˈspeiʃiˌeit/ *v.* espaciarse.

expatriate /*n,* *a* ɛksˈpeitriɪt; *v* ɛksˈpeitriˌeit/ *n. & a.* **1.** expatriado *m.* —*v.* **2.** expatriar.

expect /ɪkˈspɛkt/ *v.* esperar; contar con.

expectancy /ɪkˈspɛktənsi/ *n.* esperanza *f.*

expectation /ˌɛkspɛkˈteiʃən/ *n.* esperanza *f.*

expectorate /ɪkˈspɛktəˌreit/ *v.* expectorar.

expediency /ɪkˈspidiənsi/ *n.* conveniencia *f.*

expedient /ɪkˈspidiənt/ *a.* **1.** oportuno. —*n.* **2.** expediente *m.*

expedite /ˈɛkspɪˌdait/ *v.* acelerar, despachar.

expedition /ˌɛkspɪˈdɪʃən/ *n.* expedición *f.*

expel /ɪkˈspɛl/ *v.* expeler; expulsar.

expend /ɪkˈspɛnd/ *v.* desembolsar, expender.

expenditure /ɪkˈspɛndɪtʃər/ *n.* desembolso; gasto *m.*

expense /ɪkˈspɛns/ *n.* gasto *m.;* costa *f.*

expensive /ɪkˈspɛnsɪv/ *a.* caro, costoso.

expensively /ɪkˈspɛnsɪvli/ *adv.* costosamente.

experience /ɪkˈspɪəriəns/ *n.* **1.** experiencia *f.* —*v.* **2.** experimentar.

experienced /ɪkˈspɪəriənst/ *a.* experimentado, perito.

experiment /*n* ɪkˈspɛrəmənt; *v* -ˌmɛnt/ *n.* **1.** experimento *m.* —*v.* **2.** experimentar.

experimental /ɪkˌspɛrəˈmɛntl/ *a.* experimental.

expert /ˈɛkspɜrt/ *a. & n.* experto -ta.

expertise /ˌɛkspərˈtiz/ *n.* pericia *f.*

expiate /ˈɛkspiˌeit/ *v.* expiar.

expiration /ˌɛkspəˈreiʃən/ *n.* expiración *f.*

expiration date fecha de caducidad *f.*

expire /ɪkˈspaiᵊr/ *v.* expirar; *Com.* vencerse.

explain /ɪkˈsplein/ *v.* explicar.

explanation /ˌɛkspləˈneiʃən/ *n.* explicación *f.*

explanatory /ɪkˈsplænəˌtɔri/ *a.* explicativo.

expletive /ˈɛksplɪtɪv/ *n.* **1.** interjección *f.* —*a.* **2.** expletivo.

explicit /ɪkˈsplɪsɪt/ *a.* explícito, claro.

explode /ɪkˈsploud/ *v.* estallar, volar; refutar.

exploit /ɪkˈsplɔit/ *n.* **1.** hazaña *f.* —*v.* **2.** explotar.

exploitation /ˌɛksplɔiˈteiʃən/ *n.* explotación *f.*

exploration /ˌɛkspləˈreiʃən/ *n.* exploración *f.*

exploratory /ɪkˈsplɔrəˌtɔri/ *a.* exploratorio.

explore /ɪkˈsplɔr/ *v.* explorar.

explorer /ɪkˈsplɔrər/ *n.* explorador -ra.

explosion /ɪkˈsplouʒən/ *n.* explosión *f.*

explosive /ɪkˈsplousɪv/ *a.* explosivo.

export /*n* ˈɛkspɔrt; *v* ɪkˈspɔrt/ *n.* **1.** exportación *f.* —*v.* **2.** exportar.

exportation /ˌɛkspɔrˈteiʃən/ *n.* exportación *f.*

expose /ɪkˈspouz/ *v.* exponer; descubrir.

exposition /ˌɛkspəˈzɪʃən/ *n.* exposición *f.*

expository /ɪkˈspɒzɪˌtɔri/ *a.* expositivo.

expostulate /ɪkˈspɒstʃəˌleit/ *v.* altercar.

exposure /ɪkˈspouʒər/ *n.* exposición *f.*

expound /ɪkˈspaund/ *v.* exponer, explicar.

express /ɪkˈsprɛs/ *a. & n.* **1.** expreso *m.* **e. company,** compañía de porteo. —*v.* **2.** expresar.

expression /ɪkˈsprɛʃən/ *n.* expresión *f.*

expressive /ɪkˈsprɛsɪv/ *a.* expresivo.

expressly /ɪkˈsprɛsli/ *adv.* expresamente.

expressman /ɪkˈsprɛsmən, -ˌmæn/ *n.* empresario de expresos *m.*

expressway /ɪkˈsprɛsˌwei/ *n.* autopista *f.*

expropriate /ɛksˈproupriˌeit/ *v.* expropriar.

expulsion /ɪkˈspʌlʃən/ *n.* expulsión *f.*

expunge /ɪkˈspʌndʒ/ *v.* borrar, expurgar.

expurgate /ˈɛkspərˌgeit/ *v.* expurgar.

exquisite /ɪkˈskwɪzɪt/ *a.* exquisito.

extant /ˈɛkstənt/ *a.* existente.

extemporaneous /ɪkˌstɛmpəˈreiniəs/ *a.* improvisado.

extend /ɪkˈstɛnd/ *v.* extender.

extension /ɪkˈstɛnʃən/ *n.* extensión *f.*

extensive /ɪkˈstɛnsɪv/ *a.* extenso.

extensively /ɪkˈstɛnsɪvli/ *adv.* extensamente.

extent /ɪkˈstɛnt/ *n.* extensión *f.;* grado *m.* **to a certain e.,** hasta cierto punto.

extenuate /ɪkˈstɛnyuˌeit/ *v.* extenuar.

exterior /ɪkˈstɪəriər/ *a. & n.* exterior *m.*

exterminate /ɪkˈstɜrməˌneit/ *v.* exterminar.

extermination /ɪkˌstɜrməˈneiʃən/ *n.* exterminio *m.*

external /ɪkˈstɜrnl/ *a.* externo, exterior.

extinct /ɪkˈstɪŋkt/ *a.* extinto.

extinction /ɪkˈstɪŋkʃən/ *n.* extinción *f.*

extinguish /ɪkˈstɪŋgwɪʃ/ *v.* extinguir, apagar.

extol /ɪkˈstoul/ *v.* alabar.

extort /ɪkˈstɔrt/ *v.* exigir dinero sin derecho.

extortion /ɪkˈstɔrʃən/ *n.* extorsión *f.*

extra /ˈɛkstrə/ *a.* **1.** extraordinario;

adicional. —*n.* **2.** (newspaper) extra *m.*

extract /*n* 'ɛkstrækt; *v* ɪk'strækt/ *n.* **1.** extracto *m.* —*v.* **2.** extraer.

extraction /ɪk'strækʃən/ *n.* extracción *f.*

extraneous /ɪk'streiniəs/ *a.* extraño; ajeno.

extraordinary /ɪk'strɔrdṇˌɛri/ *a.* extraordinario.

extravagance /ɪk'strævəgəns/ *n.* extravagancia *f.*

extravagant /ɪk'strævəgənt/ *a.* extravagante.

extreme /ɪk'strim/ *a.* & *n.* extremo *m.*

extremity /ɪk'strɛmɪti/ *n.* extremidad *f.*

extricate /'ɛkstrɪˌkeit/ *v.* desenredar.

exuberant /ɪg'zubərənt/ *a.* exuberante.

exude /ɪg'zud/ *v.* exudar.

exult /ɪg'zʌlt/ *v.* regocijarse.

exultant /ɪg'zʌltṇt/ *a.* triunfante.

eye /ai/ *n.* **1.** ojo *m.* —*v.* **2.** ojear.

eyeball /'aiˌbɔl/ *n.* globo del ojo.

eyebrow /'aiˌbrau/ *n.* ceja *f.*

eyeglasses /'aiˌglæsɪz/ *n.* lentes *m.pl.*

eyelash /'aiˌlæʃ/ *n.* pestaña *f.*

eyelid /'aiˌlɪd/ *n.* párpado *m.*

eyeliner /'aiˌlainər/ *n.* lápiz de ojos *m.*

eye shadow *n.* sombra de ojos *f.*

eyesight /'aiˌsait/ *n.* vista *f.*

F

fable /'feibəl/ *n.* fábula; ficción *f.*

fabric /'fæbrɪk/ *n.* tejido *m.*, tela *f.*

fabricate /'fæbrɪˌkeit/ *v.* fabricar.

fabulous /'fæbyələs/ *a.* fabuloso.

façade /fə'sɑd/ *n.* fachada *f.*

face /feis/ *n.* **1.** cara *f.* **make faces,** hacer muecas. —*v.* **2.** encararse con. **f. the street,** dar a la calle.

facet /'fæsɪt/ *n.* faceta *f.*

facetious /fə'siʃəs/ *a.* chistoso.

facial /'feiʃəl/ *n.* **1.** masaje facial *m.* —*a.* **2.** facial.

facile /'fæsɪl/ *a.* fácil.

facilitate /fə'sɪlɪˌteit/ *v.* facilitar.

facility /fə'sɪlɪti/ *n.* facilidad *f.*

facsimile /fæk'sɪməli/ *n.* facsímile *m.*

fact /fækt/ *n.* hecho *m.* **in f.,** en realidad.

faction /'fækʃən/ *n.* facción *f.*

factor /'fæktər/ *n.* factor *m.*

factory /'fæktəri/ *n.* fábrica *f.*

factual /'fæktʃuəl/ *a.* verdadero.

faculty /'fækəlti/ *n.* facultad *f.*

fad /fæd/ *n.* boga; novedad *f.*

fade /feid/ *v.* desteñirse; (flowers) marchitarse.

fail /feil/ *n.* **1. without f.,** sin falla. —*v.* **2.** fallar; fracasar. **not to f. to,** no dejar de.

failure /'feilyər/ *n.* fracaso *m.*

faint /feint/ *a.* **1.** débil; vago; pálido. —*n.* **2.** desmayo *m.* —*v.* **3.** desmayarse.

faintly /'feintli/ *adv.* débilmente; indistintamente.

fair /fɛər/ *a.* **1.** razonable, justo; (hair) rubio; (weather) bueno. —*n.* **2.** feria *f.*

fairly /'fɛərli/ *adv.* imparcialmente; regularmente; claramente; bellamente.

fairness /'fɛərnɪs/ *n.* justicia *f.*

fair play juego limpio *m.*

fairway /'fɛərˌwei/ *n.* (golf) calle *f.*

fairy /'fɛəri/ *n.* hada *f.*, duende *m.*

faith /feiθ/ *n.* fe; confianza *f.*

faithful /'feiθfəl/ *a.* fiel.

fake /feik/ *a.* **1.** falso; postizo. —*n.* **2.** imitación; estafa *f.* —*v.* **3.** imitar; fingir.

faker /'feikər/ *n.* imitador *m.*; farsante *m.*

falcon /'fɔlkən/ *n.* halcón *m.*

fall /fɔl/ *n.* **1.** caída; catarata *f.*; (season) otoño *m.*; (in price) baja *f.* —*v.* **2.** caer; bajar. **f. asleep,** dormirse; **f. in love,** enamorarse.

fallacious /fə'leiʃəs/ *a.* falaz.

fallacy /'fæləsi/ *n.* falacia *f.*

fallible /'fæləbəl/ *a.* falible.

fallout /'fɔlˌaut/ *n.* lluvia radiactiva, polvillo radiactivo.

fallow /'fælou/ *a.* sin cultivar; barbecho.

false /fɔls/ *a.* falso; postizo.

falsehood /'fɔlshʊd/ *n.* falsedad; mentira *f.*

falseness /'fɔlsnɪs/ *n.* falsedad, perfidia *f.*

false teeth /tiθ/ dentadura postiza *f.*

falsetto /fɔl'sɛtou/ *n.* falsete *m.*

falsification /ˌfɔlsəfɪ'keiʃən/ *n.* falsificación *f.*

falsify /'fɔlsəfai/ *v.* falsificar.

falter /'fɔltər/ *v.* vacilar; (in speech) tartamudear.

fame /feim/ *n.* fama *f.*

familiar /fə'mɪlyər/ *a.* familiar; conocido. **be f. with,** estar familiarizado con.

familiarity /fəˌmɪli'ærɪti/ *n.* familiaridad *f.*

familiarize /fə'mɪlyəˌraiz/ *v.* familiarizar.

family /'fæməli/ *n.* familia; especie *f.*

family name apellido *m.*

family tree árbol genealógico *m.*

famine /'fæmɪn/ *n.* hambre; carestía *f.*

famished /'fæmɪʃt/ *a.* hambriento.

famous /'feiməs/ *a.* famoso, célebre.

fan /fæn/ *n.* abanico; ventilador *m.* (sports) aficionado -da.

fanatic /fə'nætɪk/ *a.* & *n.* fanático -ca.

fanatical /fə'nætɪkəl/ *a.* fanático.

fanaticism /fə'nætəˌsɪzəm/ *n.* fanatismo *m.*

fanciful /'fænsɪfəl/ *a.* caprichoso; fantástico.

fancy /'fænsi/ *a.* **1.** fino, elegante. **f. foods,** novedades *f.pl.* —*n.* **2.** fantasía *f.*; capricho *m.* —*v.* **3.** imaginar.

fanfare /'fænfɛər/ *n.* fanfarria *f.*

fang /fæŋ/ *n.* colmillo *m.*

fan heater estufa de aire *f.*

fantastic /fæn'tæstɪk/ *a.* fantástico.

fantasy /'fæntəsi/ *n.* fantasía *f.*

FAQ /fæk/ *n.* (Frequently Asked Questions) preguntas más frecuentes *f.pl.*

far /fɑr/ *a.* **1.** lejano, distante. —*adv.* **2.** lejos. **how f.,** a qué distancia. **as f. as,** hasta. **so f., thus f.,** hasta aquí.

farce /fɑrs/ *n.* farsa *f.*

fare /fɛər/ *n.* pasaje *m.*

farewell /ˌfɛər'wɛl/ *n.* **1.** despedida *f.* **to say f.** despedirse. —*interj.* **2.** ¡adiós!

farfetched /'fɑr'fɛtʃt/ *a.* forzado, inverosímil.

farm /fɑrm/ *n.* **1.** granja; hacienda *f.* —*v.* **2.** cultivar, labrar la tierra.

farmer /'fɑrmər/ *n.* labrador, agricultor *m.*

farmhouse /'fɑrmˌhaus/ *n.* hacienda, alquería *f.*

farming /'fɑrmɪŋ/ *n.* agricultura *f.*; cultivo *m.*

fart /fɑrt/ *n. Colloq.* pedo *m.*

fascinate /'fæsəˌneit/ *v.* fascinar, embelesar.

fascination /ˌfæsə'neiʃən/ *n.* fascinación *f.*

fascism /'fæʃˌɪzəm/ *n.* fascismo *m.*

fashion /'fæʃən/ *n.* **1.** moda; costumbre; guisa *f.* **be in f.,** estilarse. —*v.* **2.** formar.

fashionable /'fæʃənəbəl/ *a.* de moda, en boga.

fashion show desfile de modas, pase de modelos *m.*

fast /fæst/ *a.* **1.** rápido, veloz; (watch) adelantado; (color) firme. —*adv.* **2.** ligero, de prisa. —*n.* **3.** ayuno *m.* —*v.* **4.** ayunar.

fasten /'fæsən/ *v.* afirmar; atar; fijar.

fastener /'fæsənər/ *n.* asegurador *m.*

fastidious /fæ'stɪdiəs/ *a.* melindroso.

fat /fæt/ *a.* **1.** gordo. —*n.* **2.** grasa, manteca *f.*

fatal /'feitḷ/ *a.* fatal.

fatality /fei'tælɪti/ *n.* fatalidad *f.*

fatally /'feitḷi/ *adv.* fatalmente.

fate /feit/ *n.* destino *m.*; suerte *f.*

fateful /'feitfəl/ *a.* fatal; ominoso.

father /'fɑðər/ *n.* padre *m.*

fatherhood /'fɑðərˌhʊd/ *n.* paternidad *f.*

father-in-law /'fɑˌðər ɪn lɔ/ *n.* suegro *m.*

fatherland /'fɑðərˌlænd/ *n.* patria *f.*

fatherly /'fɑðərli/ *a.* **1.** paternal. —*adv.* **2.** paternalmente.

fathom /'fæðəm/ *n.* **1.** braza *f.* —*v.* **2.** sondar; *Fig.* penetrar en.

fatigue /fə'tig/ *n.* **1.** fatiga *f.*, cansancio *m.* —*v.* **2.** fatigar, cansar.

fatten /'fætṇ/ *v.* engordar, cebar.

faucet /'fɔsɪt/ *n.* grifo *m.*, llave *f.*

fault /fɔlt/ *n.* culpa *f.*; defecto *m.* **at f.,** culpable.

faultless /'fɔltlɪs/ *a.* sin tacha, perfecto.

faultlessly /'fɔltlɪsli/ *adv.* perfectamente.

faulty /'fɔlti/ *a.* defectuoso, imperfecto.

fauna /'fɔnə/ *n.* fauna *f.*

favor /'feivər/ *n.* **1.** favor *m.* —*v.* **2.** favorecer.

favorable /'feivərəbəl/ *a.* favorable.

favorite /'feivərɪt/ *a.* & *n.* favorito -ta.

favoritism /'feivərɪˌtɪzəm/ *n.* favoritismo *m.*

fawn /fɔn/ *n.* **1.** cervato *m.* —*v.* **2.** halagar, adular.

fax /fæks/ *n.* **1.** fax *m.* —*v.* **2.** mandar un fax.

faze /feiz/ *v.* desconcertar.

fear /fɪər/ *n.* **1.** miedo, temor *m.* —*v.* **2.** temer.

fearful /'fɪərfəl/ *a.* temeroso, medroso.

fearless /'fɪərlɪs/ *a.* intrépido; sin temor.

fearlessness /'fɪərlɪsnɪs/ *n.* intrepidez *f.*

feasible /'fizəbəl/ *a.* factible.

feast /fist/ *n.* banquete *m.*; fiesta *f.*

feat /fit/ *n.* hazaña *f.*; hecho *m.*

feather /'fɛðər/ *n.* pluma *f.*

feature /'fitʃər/ *n.* **1.** facción *f.*; rasgo *m.*; (movies) película principal *f.*, largometraje *m.* —*v.* **2.** presentar como atracción especial.

February /'fɛbruˌɛri, 'fɛbyu-/ *n.* febrero *m.*

federal /'fɛdərəl/ *a.* federal.

federation /ˌfɛdə'reiʃən/ *n.* confederación, federación *f.*

fee /fi/ *n.* honorarios *m.pl.*

feeble /'fibəl/ *a.* débil.

feeble-minded /'fibəl 'maindɪd/ *a.* imbécil.

feebleness /'fibəlnɪs/ *a.* debilidad *f.*

feed /fid/ *n.* **1.** pasto *m.* —*v.* **2.** alimentar; dar de comer. **fed up with,** harto de.

feedback /'fidˌbæk/ *n.* feedback *m.*, retroalimentación *f.*

feel /fil/ *n.* **1.** sensación *f.* —*v.* **2.** sentir; palpar. **f. like,** tener ganas de.

feeling /'filɪŋ/ *n.* sensación; sentimiento.

feign /fein/ *v.* fingir.

felicitate /fɪ'lɪsɪˌteit/ *v.* felicitar.

felicitous /fɪ'lɪsɪtəs/ *a.* feliz.

felicity /fɪ'lɪsɪti/ *n.* felicidad *f.*, dicha *f.*

feline /'filain/ *a.* felino.

fellow /'fɛlou/ *n.* compañero; socio *m.*; *Colloq.* tipo *m.*

fellowship /'fɛlouˌʃɪp/ *n.* compañerismo; (for study) beca *f.*

felon /'fɛlən/ *n.* reo *m.* & *f.*, felón -ona.

felony /'fɛləni/ *n.* felonía *f.*

felt /fɛlt/ *n.* fieltro *m.*

felt-tipped pen /'fɛlt ˌtɪpt/ rotulador *m.*

female /'fimeil/ *a.* & *n.* hembra *f.*

feminine /'fɛmənɪn/ *a.* femenino.

feminist /'fɛmənɪst/ *a.* & *n.* feminista *m.* & *f.*

fence /fɛns/ *n.* **1.** cerca *f.* —*v.* **2.** cercar.

fender /'fɛndər/ *n.* guardabarros *m.pl.*

ferment /*n* 'fɜrmɛnt; *v* fər'mɛnt/ *n.* **1.** fermento *m.*; *Fig.* agitación *f.* —*v.* **2.** fermentar.

fermentation /ˌfɜrmɛn'teiʃən/ *n.* fermentación *f.*

fern /fɜrn/ *n.* helecho *m.*

ferocious /fə'rouʃəs/ *a.* feroz, fiero.

ferociously /fə'rouʃəsli/ *adv.* ferozmente.

ferocity /fə'rɒsɪti/ *n.* ferocidad, fiereza *f.*

Ferris wheel /'fɛrɪs/ rueda de feria *f.*

ferry /'fɛri/ *n.* transbordador *m.*, barca de transporte.

fertile /'fɜrtḷ/ *a.* fecundo; (land) fértil.

fertility /fər'tɪlɪti/ *n.* fertilidad *f.*

fertilization /ˌfɜrtḷə'zeiʃən/ *n.* fertilización *f.*

fertilize /'fɜrtḷˌaiz/ *v.* fertilizar, abonar.

fertilizer /'fɜrtḷˌaizər/ *n.* abono *m.*

fervency /'fɜrvənsi/ *n.* ardor *m.*

fervent /'fɜrvənt/ *a.* fervoroso.

fervently /'fɜrvəntli/ *adv.* fervorosamente.

fervid /'fɜrvɪd/ *a.* férvido.

fervor /'fɜrvər/ *n.* fervor *m.*

fester /'fɛstər/ *v.* ulcerarse.

festival /'fɛstəvəl/ *n.* fiesta *f.*

festive /'fɛstɪv/ *a.* festivo.

festivity /fɛ'stɪvɪti/ *n.* festividad *f.*

festoon /fɛ'stun/ *n.* **1.** festón *m.* —*v.* **2.** festonear.

fetch /fɛtʃ/ *v.* ir por; traer.

fete /feit/ *n.* **1.** fiesta *f.* —*v.* **2.** festejar.

fetid /'fɛtɪd/ *a.* fétido.

fetish /'fɛtɪʃ/ *n.* fetiche *m.*

fetter /'fɛtər/ *n.* **1.** grillete *m.* —*v.* **2.** engrillar.

fetus /'fitəs/ *n.* feto *m.*

feud /fyud/ *n.* riña *f.*

feudal /'fyudḷ/ *a.* feudal.

feudalism /'fyudḷˌɪzəm/ *n.* feudalismo *m.*

fever /'fivər/ *n.* fiebre *f.*

feverish /'fivərɪʃ/ *a.* febril.

feverishly /'fivərɪʃli/ *adv.* febrilmente.

few /fyu/ *a.* pocos. **a. f.,** algunos, unos cuantos.

fiancé, fiancée /ˌfiɑn'sei/ *n.* novio -via.

fiasco /fi'æskou/ *n.* fiasco *m.*

fiat /'fiɑt/ *n.* fiat *m.*, orden *f.*

fib /fɪb/ *n.* **1.** mentira *f.* —*v.* **2.** mentir.

fiber /'faibər/ *n.* fibra *f.*

fibrous /'faibrəs/ *a.* fibroso.

fickle /'fɪkəl/ *a.* caprichoso.

fickleness /'fɪkəlnɪs/ *n.* inconstancia *f.*

fiction /'fɪkʃən/ *n.* ficción *f.*; (literature) novelas *f.pl.*

fictitious /fɪk'tɪʃəs/ *a.* ficticio.

fidelity /fɪ'dɛlɪti/ *n.* fidelidad *f.*

fidget /'fɪdʒɪt/ *v.* inquietar.

field /fild/ *n.* campo *m.*

field trip viaje de estudios *m.*

fiend /find/ *n.* demonio *m.*

fiendish /'findɪʃ/ *a.* diabólico, malvado.

fierce /fɪərs/ *a.* fiero, feroz.

fiery /'faiəri/ *a.* ardiente.

fiesta /fi'ɛstə/ *n.* fiesta *f.*

fife /faif/ *n.* pífano *m.*

fifteen /'fɪf'tin/ *a.* & *pron.* quince.

fifteenth /'fɪf'tinθ/ *n.* & *a.* décimoquinto.

fifth /fɪfθ/ *a.* quinto.

fifty /'fɪfti/ *a.* & *pron.* cincuenta.

fig /fɪg/ *n.* higo *m.* **f. tree,** higuera *f.*

fight /fait/ *n.* **1.** lucha, pelea *f.* —*v.* **2.** luchar, pelear.

fighter /'faitər/ *n.* peleador -ra, luchador -ra.

figment /'fɪgmənt/ n. invención f.
figurative /'fɪgyərətɪv/ a. metafórico.
figuratively /'fɪgyərətɪvli/ adv. figuradamente.
figure /'fɪgyər/ n. **1.** figura; cifra f. —v. **2.** figurar; calcular.
filament /'fɪləmənt/ n. filamento m.
file /fail/ n. **1.** archivo m.; (instrument) lima f.; (row) fila f. —v. **2.** archivar; limar.
file cabinet archivador m.
filial /'fɪliəl/ a. filial.
filigree /'fɪləˌgri/ n. filigrana f.
fill /fɪl/ v. llenar.
fillet /'fɪlɪt/ n. filete m.
filling /'fɪlɪŋ/ n. relleno m.; (dental) empastadura f. **f. station,** gasolinera f.
film /fɪlm/ n. **1.** película f., film m. —v. **2.** filmar.
filter /'fɪltər/ n. **1.** filtro m. —v. **2.** filtrar.
filth /fɪlθ/ n. suciedad, mugre f.
filthy /'fɪlθi/ a. sucio.
fin /fɪn/ n. aleta f.
final /'fainəl/ a. **1.** final, último. —n. **2.** examen final. **finals** (sports) final f.
finalist /'fainlɪst/ n. finalista m. & f.
finally /'fainli/ adv. finalmente.
finances /fɪ'nænsəz/ n. recursos, fondos m.pl.
financial /fɪ'nænʃəl/ a. financiero.
financier /ˌfɪnən'sɪər, ˌfainən-/ n. financiero -ra.
find /faind/ n. **1.** hallazgo m. —v. **2.** hallar; encontrar. **f. out,** averiguar, enterarse, saber.
fine /fain/ a. **1.** fino; bueno. —adv. **2.** muy bien. —n. **3.** multa f. —v. **4.** multar.
fine arts /arts/ bellas artes f.pl.
finery /'fainəri/ n. gala f., adorno m.
finesse /fɪ'nɛs/ n. **1.** artificio m. —v. **2.** valerse de artificio.
finger /'fɪŋgər/ n. dedo m.
finger bowl n. enjuagatorio m.
fingernail /'fɪŋgərˌneɪl/ n. uña f.
fingerprint /'fɪŋgərˌprɪnt/ n. **1.** impresión digital f. —v. **2.** tomar las impresiones digitales.
finicky /'fɪnɪki/ a. melindroso.
finish /'fɪnɪʃ/ n. **1.** conclusión f. —v. **2.** acabar, terminar.
finished /'fɪnɪʃt/ a. acabado.
finite /'fainait/ a. finito.
fir /fɜr/ n. abeto m.
fire /faiᵊr/ n. **1.** fuego; incendio m. —v. **2.** disparar, tirar; Colloq. despedir.
fire alarm n. alarma de incendio f.
firearm /'faiᵊrˌarm/ n. arma de fuego.
firecracker /'faiᵊrˌkrækər/ n. triquitraque m., buscapiés m., petardo m.
fire engine bomba de incendios f.
fire escape escalera de incendios f.
fire exit salida de urgencia f.
fire extinguisher /ɪk'stɪŋgwɪʃər/ matafuego m.
firefly /'faiᵊrˌflai/ n. luciérnaga f.
fireman /'faiᵊrmən/ n. bombero m.; (railway) fogonero m.
fireplace /'faiᵊrˌpleis/ n. hogar, fogón m.
fireproof /'faiᵊrˌpruf/ a. incombustible.
fireside /'faiᵊrˌsaid/ n. hogar, fogón m.
fireworks /'faiᵊrˌwɜrks/ n. fuegos artificiales.
firm /fɜrm/ a. **1.** firme. —n. **2.** firma, empresa f.
firmness /'fɜrmnɪs/ n. firmeza f.
first /fɜrst/ a. & adv. primero. **at f.,** al principio.
first aid primeros auxilios.
first-class /'fɜrst 'klæs/ a. de primera clase.
fiscal /'fɪskəl/ a. fiscal.
fish /fɪʃ/ n. **1.** (food) pescado m.; (alive) pez m. —v. **2.** pescar.
fisherman /'fɪʃərmən/ n. pescador m.
fishhook /'fɪʃˌhʊk/ n. anzuelo m.

fishing /'fɪʃɪŋ/ n. pesca f. **go f.,** ir de pesca.
fishmonger /'fɪʃˌmʌŋgər/ n. pescadero m.
fish store pescadería f.
fission /'fɪʃən/ n. fisión f.
fissure /'fɪʃər/ n. grieta f., quebradura f.; fisura.
fist /fɪst/ n. puño m.
fit /fɪt/ a. **1.** capaz; justo. —n. **2.** corte, talle m.; Med. convulsión f. —v. **3.** caber; quedar bien, sentar bien.
fitful /'fɪtfəl/ a. espasmódico; caprichoso.
fitness /'fɪtnɪs/ n. aptitud; conveniencia f.
fitting /'fɪtɪŋ/ a. **1.** conveniente. **be f.,** convenir. —n. **2.** ajuste m.
fitting room probador m.
five /faiv/ a. & pron. cinco.
five-day work week /faiv 'dei/ semana inglesa f.
fix /fɪks/ n. **1.** apuro m. —v. **2.** fijar; arreglar; componer, reparar.
fixation /fɪk'seiʃən/ n. fijación f.; fijeza f.
fixed /fɪkst/ a. fijo.
fixture /'fɪkstʃər/ n. instalación; guarnición f.
flabby /'flæbi/ a. flojo.
flaccid /'flæksɪd, 'flæsɪd/ a. flojo; flácido.
flag /flæg/ n. bandera f.
flagellant /'flædʒələnt/ n. & a. flagelante m.
flagon /'flægən/ n. frasco m.
flagrant /'fleigrənt/ a. flagrante.
flagrantly /'fleigrəntli/ adv. notoriamente.
flair /flɛər/ n. aptitud especial f.
flake /fleik/ n. **1.** escama f.; copo de nieve. —v. **2.** romperse en láminas.
flamboyant /flæm'bɔiənt/ a. flamante, llamativo.
flame /fleim/ n. **1.** llama f. —v. **2.** llamear.
flaming /'fleimɪŋ/ a. llameante, flamante.
flamingo /flə'mɪŋgou/ n. flamenco m.
flammable /'flæməbəl/ a. inflamable.
flank /flæŋk/ n. **1.** ijada f.; Mil. flanco m. —v. **2.** flanquear.
flannel /'flænl/ n. franela f.
flap /flæp/ n. **1.** cartera f. —v. **2.** aletear; sacudirse.
flare /flɛər/ n. **1.** llamarada f. —v. **2.** brillar; Fig. enojarse.
flash /flæʃ/ n. **1.** resplandor m.; (lightning) rayo, relámpago m.; Fig. instante m. —v. **2.** brillar.
flashcube /'flæʃˌkyub/ n. cubo de flash m.
flashlight /'flæʃˌlait/ n. linterna (eléctrica).
flashy /'flæʃi/ a. ostentoso.
flask /flæsk/ n. frasco m.
flat /flæt/ a. **1.** llano; (tire) desinflado. —n. **2.** llanura f.; apartamento m.
flatness /'flætnɪs/ n. llanura f.
flatten /'flætn/ v. aplastar, allanar; abatir.
flatter /'flætər/ v. adular, lisonjear.
flatterer /'flætərər/ n. lisonjero -ra; zalamero -ra.
flattery /'flætəri/ n. adulación, lisonja f.
flaunt /flɔnt/ v. ostentar.
flavor /'fleivər/ n. **1.** sabor m. —v. **2.** sazonar.
flavoring /'fleivərɪŋ/ n. condimento m.
flaw /flɔ/ n. defecto m.
flax /flæks/ n. lino m.
flay /flei/ v. despellejar; excoriar.
flea /fli/ n. pulga f.
flea market rastro m.
fleck /flɛk/ n. **1.** mancha f. —v. **2.** varetear.
flee /fli/ v. huir.
fleece /flis/ n. **1.** vellón m. —v. **2.** esquilar.

fleet /flit/ a. **1.** veloz. —n. **2.** flota f.
fleeting /'flitɪŋ/ a. fugaz, pasajero.
flesh /flɛʃ/ n. carne f.
fleshy /'flɛʃi/ a. gordo; carnoso.
flex /flɛks/ n. **1.** doblez m. —v. **2.** doblar.
flexibility /ˌflɛksə'bɪlɪti/ n. flexibilidad f.
flexible /'flɛksəbəl/ a. flexible.
flier /'flaiər/ n. aviador -ra.
flight /flait/ n. vuelo m.; fuga f.
flight attendant n. azafata f.; ayudante de vuelo m.
flimsy /'flɪmzi/ a. débil.
flinch /flɪntʃ/ v. acobardarse.
fling /flɪŋ/ v. lanzar.
flint /flɪnt/ n. pedernal m.
flip /flɪp/ v. lanzar.
flippant /'flɪpənt/ a. impertinente.
flippantly /'flɪpəntli/ adv. impertinentemente.
flirt /flɜrt/ n. **1.** coqueta f. —v. **2.** coquetear, flirtear.
flirtation /flɜr'teiʃən/ n. coqueteo m.
float /flout/ v. flotar.
flock /flɒk/ n. **1.** rebaño m. —v. **2.** congregarse.
flog /flɒg/ v. azotar.
flood /flʌd/ n. **1.** inundación f. —v. **2.** inundar.
floor /flɔr/ n. **1.** suelo, piso m. —v. **2.** derribar.
floppy disk /'flɒpi/ floppy m., disquete, m.
floral /'flɔrəl/ a. floral.
florid /'flɔrɪd/ a. florido.
florist /'flɔrɪst/ n. florista m. & f.
flounce /flauns/ n. **1.** (sewing) volante m. —v. **2.** pernear.
flounder /'flaundər/ n. rodaballo m.
flour /flauᵊr/ n. harina f.
flourish /'flɜrɪʃ/ n. **1.** Mus. floreo m. —v. **2.** florecer; prosperar; blandir.
flow /flou/ n. **1.** flujo m. —v. **2.** fluir.
flow chart organigrama m.
flower /'flauər/ n. **1.** flor f. —v. **2.** florecer.
flowerpot /'flauər,pɒt/ n. maceta f.
flowery /'flauəri/ a. florido.
fluctuate /'flʌktʃuˌeit/ v. fluctuar.
fluctuation /ˌflʌktʃu'eiʃən/ n. fluctuación f.
flue /flu/ n. humero m.
fluency /'fluənsi/ n. fluidez f.
fluent /'fluənt/ a. fluido; competente.
fluffy /'flʌfi/ a. velloso.
fluid /'fluɪd/ a. & n. fluido m.
fluidity /flu'ɪdɪti/ n. fluidez f.
fluoroscope /'flurəˌskoup/ n. fluoroscopio m.
flurry /'flɜri/ n. agitación f.
flush /flʌʃ/ a. **1.** bien provisto. —n. **2.** sonrojo m. —v. **3.** limpiar con un chorro de agua; sonrojarse.
flute /flut/ n. flauta f.
flutter /'flʌtər/ n. **1.** agitación f. —v. **2.** agitarse.
flux /flʌks/ n. flujo m.
fly /flai/ n. **1.** mosca f. —v. **2.** volar.
flying saucer /'flaiɪŋ/ platillo volante m.
foam /foum/ n. **1.** espuma f. —v. **2.** espumar.
focal /'foukəl/ a. focal.
focus /'foukəs/ n. **1.** enfoque m. —v. **2.** enfocar.
fodder /'fɒdər/ n. forraje m., pienso m.
foe /fou/ n. adversario -ria, enemigo -ga.
fog /fɒg/ n. niebla f.
foggy /'fɒgi/ a. brumoso.
foil /fɔil/ v. frustrar.
foist /fɔist/ v. imponer.
fold /fould/ n. **1.** pliegue m. —v. **2.** doblar, plegar.
foldable /'fouldəbəl/ a. plegable.
folder /'fouldər/ n. circular m.; (for filing) carpeta f.
folding /'fouldɪŋ/ a. plegable.
foliage /'fouliɪdʒ/ n. follaje m.
folio /'fouliˌou/ n. infolio; folio m.

folklore /'foukˌlɔr/ n. folklore m.
folks /fouks/ n. gente; familia f.
follicle /'fɒlɪkəl/ n. folículo m.
follow /'fɒlou/ v. seguir.
follower /'fɒlouər/ n. partidario -ria.
folly /'fɒli/ n. locura f.
foment /fou'mɛnt/ v. fomentar.
fond /fɒnd/ a. cariñoso, tierno. **be f. of,** ser aficionado a.
fondle /'fɒndl/ v. acariciar.
fondly /'fɒndli/ adv. tiernamente.
fondness /'fɒndnɪs/ n. afición f.; cariño m.
food /fud/ n. alimento m.; comida f.
foodie /'fudi/ n. Colloq. gastrónomo -ma, gourmet m. & f.
food poisoning /'pɔizənɪŋ/ intoxicación alimenticia f.
foodstuffs /'fudˌstʌfs/ n.pl. comestibles, víveres m.pl.
fool /ful/ **1.** tonto -ta; bobo -ba; bufón -ona. —v. **2.** engañar.
foolhardy /'fulˌhardi/ a. temerario.
foolish /'fulɪʃ/ a. bobo, tonto, majadero.
foolproof /'fulˌpruf/ a. seguro.
foot /fʊt/ n. pie m.
footage /'fʊtɪdʒ/ n. longitud en pies.
football /'fʊtˌbɔl/ n. fútbol, balompié m.
footbridge /'fʊtˌbrɪdʒ/ n. puente para peatones m.
foothold /'fʊtˌhould/ n. posición establecida.
footing /'fʊtɪŋ/ n. base f., fundamento m.
footlights /'fʊtˌlaits/ n.pl. luces del proscenio.
footnote /'fʊtˌnout/ n. nota al pie de una página.
footpath /'fʊtˌpæθ/ n. sendero m.
footprint /'fʊtˌprɪnt/ n. huella f.
footstep /'fʊtˌstɛp/ n. paso m.
footstool /'fʊtˌstul/ n. escañuelo m., banqueta f.
fop /fɒp/ n. petimetre m.
for /fɔr; unstressed fər/ prep. **1.** para; por. **as f.,** en cuanto a. **what f.,** ¿para qué? —conj. **2.** porque, pues.
forage /'fɔrɪdʒ/ n. **1.** forraje m. —v. **2.** forrajear.
foray /'fɔrei/ n. correría f.
forbear /'fɔrˌbɛər/ v. cesar; abstenerse.
forbearance /fɔr'bɛərəns/ n. paciencia f.
forbid /fər'bɪd/ v. prohibir.
forbidding /fər'bɪdɪŋ/ a. repugnante.
force /fɔrs/ n. **1.** fuerza f. —v. **2.** forzar.
forced landing /fɔrst/ aterrizaje forzoso m.
forceful /'fɔrsfəl/ a. fuerte; enérgico.
forcible /'fɔrsəbəl/ a. a la fuerza; enérgico.
ford /fɔrd/ n. **1.** vado m. —v. **2.** vadear.
fore /fɔr/ a. **1.** delantero. —n. **2.** delantera f.
fore and aft de popa a proa.
forearm /'fɔrˌarm/ n. antebrazo m.
forebears /'fɔrˌbɛərz/ n.pl. antepasados m.pl.
forebode /fɔr'boud/ v. presagiar.
foreboding /fɔr'boudɪŋ/ n. presentimiento m.
forecast /'fɔrˌkæst/ n. **1.** pronóstico m.; profecía f. —v. **2.** pronosticar.
forecastle /'fouksəl/ n. Naut. castillo de proa.
forefathers /'fɔrˌfaðərz/ n. antepasados m.pl.
forefinger /'fɔrˌfɪŋgər/ n. índice m.
forego /fɔr'gou/ v. renunciar.
foregone /fɔr'gɔn/ a. predeterminado.
foreground /'fɔrˌgraund/ n. primer plano m.
forehead /'fɔrɪd/ n. frente f.
foreign /'fɔrɪn/ a. extranjero.
foreign aid n. ayuda exterior f.
foreigner /'fɔrənər/ n. extranjero -ra; forastero -ra.

foreleg /'fɔr,lɛg/ n. pierna delantera.
foreman /'fɔrmən/ n. capataz, jefe de taller m.
foremost /'fɔr,moust/ a. **1.** primero. —adv. **2.** en primer lugar.
forenoon /'fɔr,nun/ n. mañana f.
forensic /fə'rɛnsɪk/ a. forense.
forerunner /'fɔr,rʌnər/ n. precursor -ra.
foresee /fɔr'si/ v. prever.
foreshadow /fɔr'ʃædou/ v. prefigurar, anunciar.
foresight /'fɔr,sait/ n. previsión f.
forest /'fɔrɪst/ n. bosque m.; selva f.
forestall /fɔr'stɔl/ v. anticipar; prevenir.
forester /'fɔrəstər/ n. silvicultor -ra; guardamontes m.pl. & f.pl.
forestry /'fɔrəstri/ n. silvicultura f.
foretell /fɔr'tɛl/ v. predecir.
forever /fɔr'ɛvər/ adv. por siempre, para siempre.
forevermore /fɔr,ɛvər'mɔr/ adv. siempre.
forewarn /fɔr'wɔrn/ v. advertir, avisar.
foreword /'fɔr,wərd/ n. prefacio m.
forfeit /'fɔrfɪt/ n. **1.** prenda; multa f. —v. **2.** perder.
forfeiture /'fɔrfɪtʃər/ n. decomiso m., multa f.; pérdida f.
forgather /fɔr'gæðər/ v. reunirse.
forge /fɔrdʒ/ n. **1.** fragua f. —v. **2.** forjar; falsear.
forger /'fɔrdʒər/ n. forjador -ra; falsificador -ra.
forgery /'fɔrdʒəri/ n. falsificación f.
forget /fər'gɛt/ v. olvidar.
forgetful /fər'gɛtfəl/ a. olvidadizo.
forgive /fər'gɪv/ v. perdonar.
forgiveness /fər'gɪvnɪs/ n. perdón m.
fork /fɔrk/ n. **1.** tenedor m.; bifurcación f. —v. **2.** bifurcarse.
forlorn /fɔr'lɔrn/ a. triste.
form /fɔrm/ n. **1.** forma f.; (document) formulario m. —v. **2.** formar.
formal /'fɔrməl/ a. formal; ceremonioso. **f. dance,** baile de etiqueta. **f. dress,** traje de etiqueta.
formality /fɔr'mælɪti/ n. formalidad f.
formally /'fɔrməli/ adv. formalmente.
format /'fɔrmæt/ n. formato m.
formation /fɔr'meiʃən/ n. formación f.
formative /'fɔrmətɪv/ a. formativo.
formatting /'fɔrmætɪŋ/ n. formateo m.
former /'fɔrmər/ a. anterior; antiguo. **the f.,** aquél.
formerly /'fɔrmərli/ adv. antiguamente.
formidable /'fɔrmɪdəbəl/ a. formidable.
formless /'fɔrmlɪs/ a. sin forma.
formula /'fɔrmyələ/ n. fórmula f.
formulate /'fɔrmyə,leit/ v. formular.
formulation /,fɔrmyə'leiʃən/ n. formulación f.; expresión f.
forsake /fɔr'seik/ v. abandonar.
fort /fɔrt/ n. fortaleza f.; fuerte m.
forte /'fɔrtei/ a. & adv. Mus. forte; fuerte.
forth /fɔrθ/ adv. adelante. **back and f.,** de aquí allá. **and so f.,** etcétera.
forthcoming /'fɔrθ'kʌmɪŋ/ a. futuro, próximo.
forthright /'fɔrθ,rait/ a. franco.
forthwith /,fɔrθ'wɪθ/ adv. inmediatamente.
fortification /,fɔrtəfɪ'keiʃən/ n. fortificación f.
fortify /'fɔrtə,fai/ v. fortificar.
fortissimo /fɔr'tɪsə,mou/ a. & adv. Mus. fortísimo.
fortitude /'fɔrtɪ,tud/ n. fortaleza; fortitud f.
fortnight /'fɔrt,nait/ n. quincena f.
fortress /'fɔrtrɪs/ n. fuerte m., fortaleza f.
fortuitous /fɔr'tuɪtəs/ a. fortuito.
fortunate /'fɔrtʃənɪt/ a. afortunado.
fortune /'fɔrtʃən/ n. fortuna; suerte f.

fortune-teller /'fɔrtʃən ,tɛlər/ n. sortílego -ga, adivino -na.
forty /'fɔrti/ a. & pron. cuarenta.
forum /'fɔrəm/ n. foro m.
forward /'fɔrwərd/ a. **1.** delantero; atrevido. —adv. **2.** adelante. —v. **3.** trasmitir, reexpedir.
foster /'fɔstər/ n. **1. f. child,** hijo adoptivo. —v. **2.** fomentar; criar.
foul /faul/ a. sucio; impuro.
found /faund/ v. fundar.
foundation /faun'deiʃən/ n. fundación f.; (of building) cimientos m.pl.
founder /'faundər/ n. **1.** fundador -ra. —v. **2.** irse a pique.
foundry /'faundri/ n. fundición f.
fountain /'fauntn̩/ n. fuente f.
fountain pen pluma estilográfica, plumafuente f.
four /fɔr/ a. & pron. cuatro.
fourteen /'fɔr'tin/ a. & pron. catorce.
fourth /fɔrθ/ a. & n. cuarto m.
fowl /faul/ n. ave f.
fox /fɒks/ n. zorro -rra.
fox-trot /'fɒks,trɒt/ n. foxtrot m.
foxy /'fɒksi/ a. astuto.
foyer /'fɔiər/ n. salón de entrada.
fracas /freikəs, 'fræksəs/ n. riña f.
fraction /'frækʃən/ n. fracción f.
fracture /'fræktʃər/ n. **1.** fractura, rotura f. —v. **2.** fracturar, romper.
fragile /'frædʒəl/ a. frágil.
fragment /'frægmənt/ n. fragmento, trozo m.
fragmentary /'frægmən,tɛri/ a. fragmentario.
fragrance /'freigrəns/ n. fragancia f.
fragrant /'freigrənt/ a. fragante.
frail /freil/ a. débil, frágil.
frailty /'freilti/ n. debilidad, fragilidad f.
frame /freim/ n. **1.** marco; armazón; cuadro; cuerpo m. —v. **2.** fabricar; formar; encuadrar.
frame-up /'freim ,ʌp/ n. Colloq. conspiración f.
framework /'freim,wərk/ n. armazón m.
France /fræns/ n. Francia f.
franchise /'fræntʃaiz/ n. franquicia f.
frank /fræŋk/ a. **1.** franco. —n. **2.** carta franca. —v. **3.** franquear.
frankfurter /'fræŋkfərtər/ n. salchicha f.
frankly /'fræŋkli/ adv. francamente.
frankness /'fræŋknɪs/ n. franqueza f.
frantic /'fræntɪk/ a. frenético.
fraternal /frə'tərnl̩/ a. fraternal.
fraternity /frə'tərnɪti/ n. fraternidad f.
fraternization /,frætərnə'zeiʃən/ n. fraternización f.
fraternize /'frætər,naiz/ v. confraternizar.
fratricide /'frætrɪ,said/ n. fratricida m. & f.; fratricidio m.
fraud /frɔd/ n. fraude m.
fraudulent /'frɔdʒələnt/ a. fraudulento.
fraudulently /'frɔdʒələntli/ adv. fraudulentamente.
fraught /frɔt/ a. cargado.
freak /frik/ n. rareza f.; monstruosidad.
freckle /'frɛkəl/ n. peca f.
freckled /'frɛkəld/ a. pecoso.
free /fri/ a. **1.** libre; gratis. —v. **2.** libertar, librar.
freedom /'fridəm/ n. libertad f.
freeze /friz/ v. helar, congelar.
freezer /'frizər/ n. heladora f.
freezing point /'frizɪŋ/ punto de congelación m.
freight /freit/ n. **1.** carga f.; flete m. —v. **2.** cargar; fletar.
freighter /'freitər/ n. Naut. fletador m.
French /frɛntʃ/ a. & n. francés -esa.
Frenchman /'frɛntʃmən/ n. francés m.
Frenchwoman /'frɛntʃ,wumən/ n. francesa f.
frenzied /'frɛnzid/ a. frenético.

frenzy /'frɛnzi/ n. frenesí m.
frequency /'frikwənsi/ n. frecuencia f.
frequency modulation /,mɒdʒə-'leiʃən/ modulación de frequencia.
frequent /'frikwənt/ a. frecuente.
frequently /'frikwəntli/ adv. frecuentemente.
fresco /'frɛskou/ n. fresco.
fresh /frɛʃ/ a. fresco. **f. water,** agua dulce.
freshen /'frɛʃən/ v. refrescar.
freshness /'frɛʃnɪs/ n. frescura f.
fret /frɛt/ v. quejarse, irritarse; Mus. traste m.
fretful /'frɛtfəl/ a. irritable.
fretfully /'frɛtfəli/ adv. de mala gana.
fretfulness /'frɛtfəlnɪs/ n. mal humor.
friar /'fraiər/ n. fraile m.
fricassee /,frɪkə'si/ n. fricasé m.
friction /'frɪkʃən/ n. fricción f.
Friday /'fraidei/ n. viernes m. **Good F.,** Viernes Santo m.
fried /fraid/ a. frito.
friend /frɛnd/ n. amigo -ga.
friendless /'frɛndlɪs/ a. sin amigos.
friendliness /'frɛndlinɪs/ n. amistad f.
friendly /'frɛndli/ a. amistoso.
friendship /'frɛndʃɪp/ n. amistad f.
fright /frait/ n. susto m.
frighten /'fraitn̩/ v. asustar, espantar.
frightful /'fraitfəl/ a. espantoso.
frigid /'frɪdʒɪd/ a. frígido; frío.
frill /frɪl/ n. (sewing) lechuga f.
fringe /frɪndʒ/ n. fleco; borde m.
frisky /'frɪski/ a. retozón.
fritter /'frɪtər/ n. fritura f.
frivolity /frɪ'vɒlɪti/ n. frivolidad f.
frivolous /'frɪvələs/ a. frívolo.
frivolousness /'frɪvələsnɪs/ n. frivolidad f.
frock /frɒk/ n. vestido de mujer. **f. coat,** levita f.
frog /frɒg/ n. rana f.
frolic /'frɒlɪk/ n. **1.** retozo m. —v. **2.** retozar.
from /frʌm, unstressed frəm/ prep. de; desde.
front /frʌnt/ n. frente; (of building) fachada f. **in f. of,** delante de.
frontal /'frʌntl̩/ a. frontal.
front door puerta principal f.
frontier /frʌn'tiər/ n. frontera f.
front seat asiento delantero m.
frost /frɔst/ n. helada, escarcha f.
frosty /'frɔsti/ a. helado.
froth /frɔθ/ n. espuma f.
frown /fraun/ n. **1.** ceño m. —v. **2.** fruncir el entrecejo.
frowzy /'frauzi/ a. desaliñado.
frozen /'frouzən/ a. helado; congelado.
fructify /'frʌktə,fai/ v. fructificar.
frugal /'frugəl/ a. frugal.
frugality /fru'gælɪti/ n. frugalidad f.
fruit /frut/ n. fruta f.; (benefits) frutos m.pl. **f. tree,** árbol frutal.
fruitful /'frutfəl/ a. productivo.
fruition /fru'ɪʃən/ n. fruición f.
fruitless /'frutlɪs/ a. inútil, en vano.
fruit salad macedonia de frutas f.
fruit store frutería f.
frustrate /'frʌstreit/ v. frustrar.
frustration /frʌ'streiʃən/ n. frustración f.
fry /frai/ v. freír.
fuel /'fyuəl/ n. combustible m.
fugitive /'fyudʒɪtɪv/ a. & n. fugitivo -va.
fugue /fyug/ n. fuga f.
fulcrum /'fulkrəm/ n. fulcro m.
fulfill /ful'fɪl/ v. cumplir.
fulfillment /ful'fɪlmənt/ n. cumplimiento m.; realización f.
full /ful/ a. lleno; completo; pleno.
full name nombre y apellidos.
fullness /'fulnɪs/ n. plenitud f.
fulminate /'fʌlmə,neit/ v. volar; fulminar.

fulmination /,fʌlmə'neiʃən/ n. fulminación; detonación f.
fumble /'fʌmbəl/ v. chapucear.
fume /fyum/ n. **1.** humo m. —v. **2.** humear.
fumigate /'fyumɪ,geit/ v. fumigar.
fumigator /'fyumɪ,geitər/ n. fumigador m.
fun /fʌn/ n. diversión f. **to make f. of,** burlarse de. **to have f.,** divertirse.
function /'fʌŋkʃən/ n. **1.** función f. —v. **2.** funcionar.
functional /'fʌŋkʃənl̩/ a. funcional.
fund /fʌnd/ n. fondo m.
fundamental /,fʌndə'mɛntl̩/ a. fundamental.
funeral /'fyunərəl/ n. funeral m.
funeral home, funeral parlor funeraria f.
fungus /'fʌŋgəs/ n. hongo m.
funnel /'fʌnl̩/ n. embudo m.; (of ship) chimenea f.
funny /'fʌni/ a. divertido, gracioso. **to be f.,** tener gracia.
fur /fər/ n. piel f.
furious /'fyuriəs/ a. furioso.
furlough /'fərlou/ n. permiso m.
furnace /'fərnɪs/ n. horno m.
furnish /'fərnɪʃ/ v. surtir, proveer; (a house) amueblar.
furniture /'fərnɪtʃər/ n. muebles m.pl.
furrow /'fərou/ n. **1.** surco m. —v. **2.** surcar.
further /'fərðər/ a. & adv. **1.** más. —v. **2.** adelantar, fomentar.
furthermore /'fərðər,mɔr/ adv. además.
fury /'fyuri/ n. furor m.; furia f.
fuse /fyuz/ n. **1.** fusible m. —v. **2.** fundir.
fuss /fʌs/ n. **1.** alboroto m. —v. **2.** preocuparse por pequeñeces.
fussy /'fʌsi/ a. melindroso.
futile /'fyutl̩/ a. fútil.
future /'fyutʃər/ a. **1.** futuro. —n. **2.** porvenir m.
futurology /,fyutʃə'rɒlədʒi/ n. futurología f.
fuzzy logic /'fʌzi/ lógica matizada f.
FYI abbr. (For Your Information) para su información.

G

gag /gæg/ n. chiste m.; mordaza f.
gaiety /'geiɪti/ n. alegría f.
gain /gein/ n. **1.** ganancia f. —v. **2.** ganar.
gait /geit/ n. paso m.
gale /geil/ n. ventarrón m.
gall /gɔl/ n. hiel f.; Fig. amargura f.; descaro m.
gallant /'gælənt, gə'lænt, -'lɑnt/ a. **1.** galante. —n. **2.** galán m.
gallery /'gæləri/ n. galería f.; Theat. paraíso m.
gallon /'gælən/ n. galón m.
gallop /'gæləp/ n. **1.** galope m. —v. **2.** galopar.
gallows /'gælouz/ n. horca f.
gamble /'gæmbəl/ n. **1.** riesgo m. —v. **2.** jugar, aventurar.
game /geim/ n. juego m.; (match) partida f.; (hunting) caza f.
gang /gæŋ/ n. cuadrilla; pandilla f.
gangster /'gæŋstər/ n. rufián m.
gap /gæp/ n. raja f.
gape /geip/ v. boquear.
garage /gə'rɑʒ/ n. garaje m.
garbage /'gɑrbɪdʒ/ n. basura f.
garden /'gɑrdn̩/ n. jardín m.; (vegetable) huerta f.
gardener /'gɑrdnər/ n. jardinero -ra.
gargle /'gɑrgəl/ n. **1.** gárgara f. —v. **2.** gargarizar.
garland /'gɑrlənd/ n. guirnalda f.
garlic /'gɑrlɪk/ n. ajo m.
garment /'gɑrmənt/ n. prenda de vestir.
garrison /'gærəsən/ n. guarnición f.

garter /ˈgɑrtər/ *n.* liga *f.;* ataderas *f.pl.*

gas /gæs/ *n.* gas *m.*

gasohol /ˈgæsəˌhɔl, -ˌhɒl/ *n.* gasohol *m.*

gasoline /ˌgæsəˈlin/ *n.* gasolina *f.*

gasp /gæsp/ *n.* **1.** boqueada *f.* —*v.* **2.** boquear.

gas station gasolinera *f.*

gate /geit/ *n.* puerta; entrada; verja *f.*

gather /ˈgæðər/ *v.* recoger; inferir; reunir.

gaudy /ˈgɔdi/ *a.* brillante; llamativo.

gauge /geidʒ/ *n.* **1.** manómetro, indicador *m.* —*v.* **2.** medir; estimar.

gaunt /gɔnt/ *a.* flaco.

gauze /gɔz/ *n.* gasa *f.*

gay /gei/ *a.* **1.** alegre; homosexual. —*n.* **2.** homosexual.

gaze /geiz/ *n.* **1.** mirada *f.* —*v.* **2.** mirar con fijeza.

gear /gɪər/ *n.* engranaje *m.* **in g.,** en juego.

gearshift /ˈgɪərˌʃɪft/ *n.* palanca de cambio *f.*

gem /dʒɛm/ *n.* joya *f.*

gender /ˈdʒɛndər/ *n.* género *m.*

general /ˈdʒɛnərəl/ *a.* & *n.* general *m.*

generality /ˌdʒɛnəˈrælɪti/ *n.* generalidad *f.*

generalize /ˈdʒɛnərəˌlaiz/ *v.* generalizar.

generation /ˌdʒɛnəˈreiʃən/ *n.* generación *f.*

generator /ˈdʒɛnəˌreitər/ *n.* generador *m.*

generosity /ˌdʒɛnəˈrɒsɪti/ *n.* generosidad *f.*

generous /ˈdʒɛnərəs/ *a.* generoso.

genetic /dʒəˈnɛtɪk/ *a.* genético.

genial /ˈdʒinyəl/ *a.* genial.

genius /ˈdʒinyəs/ *n.* genio *m.*

genocide /ˈdʒɛnəˌsaid/ *n.* genocidio *m.*

gentle /ˈdʒɛntl̩/ *a.* suave; manso; benigno.

gentleman /ˈdʒɛntl̩mən/ *n.* señor; caballero *m.*

gentleness /ˈdʒɛntl̩nɪs/ *n.* suavidad *f.*

genuine /ˈdʒɛnyuɪn/ *a.* genuino.

genuineness /ˈdʒɛnyuɪnɪs/ *n.* pureza *f.*

geographical /ˌdʒiəˈgræfɪkəl/ *a.* geográfico.

geography /dʒiˈɒgrəfi/ *n.* geografía *f.*

geometric /ˌdʒiəˈmɛtrɪk/ *a.* geométrico.

geranium /dʒəˈreiniəm/ *n.* geranio *m.*

germ /dʒɜrm/ *n.* germen; microbio *m.*

German /ˈdʒɜrmən/ *a.* & *n.* alemán -mana.

Germany /ˈdʒɜrməni/ *n.* Alemania *f.*

gesticulate /dʒɛˈstɪkyəˌleit/ *v.* gesticular.

gesture /ˈdʒɛstʃər/ *n.* **1.** gesto *m.* —*v.* **2.** gesticular, hacer gestos.

get /gɛt/ *v.* obtener; conseguir; (become) ponerse. **go and g.,** ir a buscar; **g. away,** irse; escaparse; **g. together,** reunirse; **g. on,** subirse; **g. off,** bajarse; **g. up,** levantarse; **g. there,** llegar.

ghastly /ˈgæstli/ *a.* pálido; espantoso.

ghost /goust/ *n.* espectro, fantasma *m.*

giant /ˈdʒaiənt/ *n.* gigante *m.*

gibberish /ˈdʒɪbərɪʃ/ *n.* galimatías, *m.*

gift /gɪft/ *n.* regalo, don; talento *m.*

gigabyte /ˈgɪgəˌbait, ˈdʒɪg-/ *n.* giga *m.*

gild /gɪld/ *v.* dorar.

gin /dʒɪn/ *n.* ginebra *f.*

ginger /ˈdʒɪndʒər/ *n.* jengibre *m.*

gingerbread /ˈdʒɪndʒərˌbrɛd/ *n.* pan de jengibre.

gingham /ˈgɪŋəm/ *n.* guinga *f.*

gird /gɜrd/ *v.* ceñir.

girdle /ˈgɜrdl̩/ *n.* faja *f.*

girl /gɜrl/ *n.* muchacha, niña, chica *f.*

give /gɪv/ *v.* dar; regalar. **g. back,** devolver. **g. up,** rendirse; renunciar.

giver /ˈgɪvər/ *n.* dador -ra; donador -ra.

glacier /ˈgleiʃər/ *n.* glaciar; ventisquero *m.*

glad /glæd/ *a.* alegre, contento. **be g.,** alegrarse.

gladly /ˈglædli/ *adj.* con mucho gusto.

gladness /ˈglædnɪs/ *n.* alegría *f.;* placer *m.*

glamor /ˈglæmər/ *n.* encanto *m.;* elegancia *f.*

glamorous /ˈglæmərəs/ *a.* encantador; elegante.

glamour /ˈglæmər/ *n.* encanto *m.;* elegancia *f.*

glance /glæns/ *n.* **1.** vistazo *m.,* ojeada *f.* —*v.* **2.** ojear.

gland /glænd/ *n.* glándula *f.*

glare /glɛər/ *n.* **1.** reflejo; brillo *m.* —*v.* **2.** deslumbrar; echar miradas indignadas.

glass /glæs/ *n.* vidrio; vaso *m.;* **(eyeglasses),** lentes, anteojos *m.pl.*

gleam /glim/ *n.* **1.** fulgor *m.* —*v.* **2.** fulgurar.

glee /gli/ *n.* alegría *f.;* júbilo *m.*

glide /glaid/ *v.* deslizarse.

glimpse /glɪmps/ *n.* **1.** vislumbre, vistazo *m.* —*v.* **2.** vislumbrar, ojear.

glisten /ˈglɪsən/ *n.* **1.** brillo *m.* —*v.* **2.** brillar.

glitter /ˈglɪtər/ *n.* **1.** resplandor *m.* —*v.* **2.** brillar.

globe /gloub/ *n.* globo; orbe *m.*

gloom /glum/ *n.* oscuridad; tristeza *f.*

gloomy /ˈglumi/ *a.* oscuro; sombrío, triste.

glorify /ˈglɔrəˌfai/ *v.* glorificar.

glorious /ˈglɔriəs/ *a.* glorioso.

glory /ˈglɔri/ *n.* gloria, fama *f.*

glossary /ˈglɒsəri/ *n.* glosario *m.*

glove /glʌv/ *n.* guante *m.*

glove compartment guantera *f.*

glow /glou/ *n.* **1.** fulgor *m.* —*v.* **2.** relucir; arder.

glucose /ˈglukous/ *f.* glucosa.

glue /glu/ *n.* **1.** cola *f.,* pegamento *m.* —*v.* **2.** encolar, pegar.

glum /glʌm/ *a.* de mal humor.

glutton /ˈglʌtn̩/ *n.* glotón -ona.

gnaw /nɔ/ *v.* roer.

GNP (*abbr.* **gross national product**), PNB (producto nacional bruto).

go /gou/ *v.* ir, irse. **g. away,** irse, marcharse. **g. back,** volver, regresar. **g. down,** bajar. **g. in,** entrar. **g. on,** seguir. **g. out,** salir. **g. up,** subir.

goal /goul/ *n.* meta *f.;* objeto *m.*

goalkeeper /ˈgoulˌkipər/ *n.* guardameta *mf.*

goat /gout/ *n.* cabra *f.*

goblet /ˈgɒblɪt/ *n.* copa *f.*

God /gɒd/ *n.* Dios *m.*

gold /gould/ *n.* oro *m.*

golden /ˈgouldən/ *a.* áureo.

gold-plated /ˈgould ˌpleitɪd/ *a.* chapado en oro.

golf /gɒlf/ *n.* golf *m.*

golf course campo de golf *m.*

golfer /ˈgɒlfər/ *n.* golfista *m.* & *f.*

good /gʊd/ *a.* **1.** bueno. —*n.* **2.** bienes *m.pl.; Com.* géneros *m.pl.*

good-bye /ˌgʊdˈbai/ *n.* **1.** adiós *m.* —*interj.* **2.** ¡adiós!, ¡hasta la vista!, ¡hasta luego! **say g. to,** despedirse de.

goodness /ˈgʊdnɪs/ *n.* bondad *f.*

goodwill /ˈgʊdˈwɪl/ *n.* buena voluntad. *f.*

goose /gus/ *n.* ganso *m.*

gooseberry /ˈgusˌbɛri/ *n.* uva crespa *f.*

gooseneck /ˈgusˌnɛk/ *n.* **1.** cuello de cisne *m.* —*a.* **2.** curvo.

goose step /ˈgusˌstɛp/ paso de ganso *m.*

gore /gɔr/ *n.* **1.** sangre *f.* —*v.* **2.** acornear.

gorge /gɔrdʒ/ *n.* **1.** gorja *f.* —*v.* **2.** engullir.

gorgeous /ˈgɔrdʒəs/ *a.* magnífico; precioso.

gorilla /gəˈrɪlə/ *n.* gorila *m.*

gory /ˈgɔri/ *a.* sangriento.

gosling /ˈgɒzlɪŋ/ *n.* gansarón *m.*

gospel /ˈgɒspəl/ *n.* evangelio *m.*

gossamer /ˈgɒsəmər/ *n.* **1.** telaraña *f.* —*a.* **2.** delgado.

gossip /ˈgɒsəp/ *n.* **1.** chisme *m.* —*v.* **2.** chismear.

Gothic /ˈgɒθɪk/ *a.* gótico.

gouge /gaudʒ/ *n.* **1.** gubia *f.* —*v.* **2.** escoplear.

gourd /gɔrd/ *n.* calabaza *f.*

gourmand /gʊrˈmɑnd/ *n.* glotón *m.*

gourmet /gʊrˈmei/ *a.* gastrónomo -ma.

govern /ˈgʌvərn/ *v.* gobernar.

governess /ˈgʌvərnɪs/ *n.* aya, institutriz *f.*

government /ˈgʌvərnmənt, -ərmənt/ *n.* gobierno *m.*

governmental /ˌgʌvərnˈmɛntl̩, ˌgʌvər-/ *a.* gubernamental.

governor /ˈgʌvərnər/ *n.* gobernador -ra.

governorship /ˈgʌvərnərˌʃɪp/ *n.* gobernatura *f.*

gown /gaun/ *n.* vestido *m.* **dressing g.,** bata *f.*

grab /græb/ *v.* agarrar, arrebatar.

grace /greis/ *n.* gracia; gentileza; merced *f.*

graceful /ˈgreisfəl/ *a.* agraciado.

graceless /ˈgreislɪs/ *a.* réprobo; torpe.

gracious /ˈgreiʃəs/ *a.* gentil, cortés.

grackle /ˈgrækəl/ *n.* grajo *m.*

grade /greid/ *n.* **1.** grado; nivel *m.;* pendiente; nota; calidad *f.* —*v.* **2.** graduar.

grade crossing *n.* paso a nivel *m.*

gradual /ˈgrædʒuəl/ *a.* gradual, paulatino.

gradually /ˈgrædʒuəli/ *adv.* gradualmente.

graduate /*n* ˈgrædʒuɪt; *v* -ˌeit/ *n.* **1.** graduado -da, diplomado -da. —*v.* **2.** graduar; diplomarse.

graft /græft/ *n.* **1.** injerto *m.;* soborno público. —*v.* **2.** injertar.

graham /ˈgreiəm/ *a.* centeno; acemita.

grail /greil/ *n.* grial *m.*

grain /grein/ *n.* grano; cereal *m.*

grain alcohol *n.* alcohol de madera *m.*

gram /græm/ *n.* gramo *m.*

grammar /ˈgræmər/ *n.* gramática *f.*

grammarian /grəˈmɛəriən/ *n.* gramático -ca.

grammar school *n.* escuela elemental *f.*

grammatical /grəˈmætɪkəl/ *a.* gramatical.

gramophone /ˈgræməˌfoun/ *n.* gramófono *m.*

granary /ˈgreinəri/ *n.* granero *m.*

grand /grænd/ *a.* grande, ilustre; estupendo.

grandchild /ˈgrænˌtʃaild/ *n.* nieto -ta.

granddaughter /ˈgrænˌdɔtər/ *n.* nieta *f.*

grandee /grænˈdi/ *n.* noble *m.*

grandeur /ˈgrændʒər/ *n.* grandeza *f.*

grandfather /ˈgrænˌfɑðər/ *n.* abuelo *m.*

grandiloquent /grænˈdɪləkwənt/ *a.* grandílocuo.

grandiose /ˈgrændiˌous/ *a.* grandioso.

grand jury jurado de acusación, jurado de juicio *m.*

grandly /ˈgrændli/ *adv.* grandiosamente.

grandmother /ˈgrænˌmʌðər/ *n.* abuela *f.*

grand opera ópera grande *f.*

grandparents /ˈgrændˌpɛərənts/ *n.* abuelos *m.pl.*

grandson /ˈgrænˌsʌn/ *n.* nieto *m.*

grandstand /ˈgrænˌstænd/ *n.* andanada *f.,* tribuna *f.*

grange /greindʒ/ *n.* granja *f.*

granger /ˈgreindʒər/ *n.* labriego *m.*

granite /ˈgrænɪt/ *n.* granito *m.*

granny /ˈgræni/ *n.* abuelita *f.*

grant /grænt/ *n.* **1.** concesión; subvención *f.* —*v.* **2.** otorgar; conceder; conferir. **take for granted,** tomar por cierto.

granular /ˈgrænyələr/ *a.* granular.

granulate /ˈgrænyəˌleit/ *v.* granular.

granulation /ˌgrænyəˈleiʃən/ *n.* granulación *f.*

granule /ˈgrænyul/ *n.* gránulo *m.*

grape /greip/ *n.* uva *f.*

grapefruit /ˈgreipˌfrut/ *n.* toronja *f.*

grape harvest vendimia *f.*

grapeshot /ˈgreipˌʃɒt/ *n.* metralla *f.*

grapevine /ˈgreipˌvain/ *n.* vid; parra *f.*

graph /græf/ *n.* gráfica *f.*

graphic /ˈgræfɪk/ *a.* gráfico.

graphite /ˈgræfait/ *n.* grafito *m.*

graphology /græˈfɒlədʒi/ *n.* grafología *f.*

grapple /ˈgræpəl/ *v.* agarrar.

grasp /græsp/ *n.* **1.** puño; poder; conocimiento *m.* —*v.* **2.** empuñar, agarrar; comprender.

grasping /ˈgræspɪŋ/ *a.* codicioso.

grass /græs/ *n.* hierba *f.;* (marijuana) marijuana *f.*

grasshopper /ˈgræsˌhɒpər/ *n.* saltamontes *m.*

grassy /ˈgræsi/ *a.* herboso.

grate /greit/ *n.* reja *f.*

grateful /ˈgreitfəl/ *a.* agradecido.

gratify /ˈgrætəˌfai/ *v.* satisfacer.

grating /ˈgreitɪŋ/ *n.* **1.** enrejado *m.* —*a.* **2.** discordante.

gratis /ˈgrætɪs/ *adv.* & *a.* gratis.

gratitude /ˈgrætɪˌtud/ *n.* agradecimiento *m.*

gratuitous /grəˈtuɪtəs/ *adj.* gratuito.

gratuity /grəˈtuɪti/ *n.* propina *f.*

grave /greiv/ *a.* **1.** grave. —*n.* **2.** sepultura; tumba *f.*

gravel /ˈgrævəl/ *n.* cascajo *m.*

gravely /ˈgreivli/ *adv.* gravemente.

gravestone /ˈgreivˌstoun/ *n.* lápida sepulcral *f.*

graveyard /ˈgreivˌyɑrd/ *n.* cementerio *m.*

gravitate /ˈgrævɪˌteit/ *v.* gravitar.

gravitation /ˌgrævɪˈteiʃən/ *n.* gravitación *f.*

gravity /ˈgrævɪti/ *n.* gravedad; seriedad *f.*

gravure /grəˈvyʊr/ *n.* fotograbado *m.*

gravy /ˈgreivi/ *n.* salsa *f.*

gray /grei/ *a.* gris; (hair) cano.

grayish /ˈgreiɪʃ/ *a.* pardusco.

gray matter substancia gris *f.*

graze /greiz/ *v.* rozar; (cattle) pastar.

grazing /ˈgreizɪŋ/ *a.* pastando.

grease /gris/ *n.* **1.** grasa *f.* —*v.* **2.** engrasar.

greasy /ˈgrisi/ *a.* grasiento.

great /greit/ *a.* grande, ilustre; estupendo.

Great Dane /dein/ mastín danés *m.*

great-grandfather /ˌgreit ˈgrænˌfɑðər/ *n.* bisabuelo.

great-grandmother /ˌgreit ˈgrænˌmʌðər/ *f.* bisabuela.

greatness /ˈgreitnɪs/ *n.* grandeza *f.*

Greece /gris/ *n.* Grecia *f.*

greed /grid/ **greediness** *n.* codicia, voracidad *f.*

greedy /ˈgridi/ *a.* voraz.

Greek /grik/ *a.* & *n.* griego -ga.

green /grin/ *a.* & *n.* verde *m.* **greens,** *n.* verduras *f.pl.*

greenery /ˈgrinəri/ *n.* verdor *m.*

greenhouse /ˈgrinˌhaus/ *n.* invernáculo *m.*

greenhouse effect *n.* efecto invernáculo *m.*

greet /grit/ *v.* saludar.

greeting /ˈgritɪŋ/ *n.* saludo *m.*

gregarious /grɪˈgɛəriəs/ *a.* gregario; sociable.

grenade /grɪˈneid/ *n.* granada; bomba *f.*

greyhound /ˈgreiˌhaund/ *n.* galgo *m.*

grid /grɪd/ *n.* parrilla *f.*

griddle /ˈgrɪdl̩/ *n.* tortera *f.*

griddlecake /ˈgrɪdl̩ˌkeik/ *n.* tortita de harina *f.*

gridiron /'grɪd,aɪərn/ *n.* parrilla *f.*; campo de fútbol *m.*
grief /grif/ *n.* dolor *m.*; pena *f.*
grievance /'grivəns/ *n.* pesar; agravio *m.*
grieve /griv/ *v.* afligir.
grievous /'grivəs/ *a.* penoso.
grill /grɪl/ *n.* 1. parrilla *f.* —*v.* 2. asar a la parrilla.
grillroom /'grɪl,rum, -,rʊm/ *n.* parrilla *f.*
grim /grɪm/ *a.* ceñudo.
grimace /'grɪməs/ *n.* 1. mueca *f.* —*v.* 2. hacer muecas.
grime /graɪm/ *n.* mugre *f.*
grimy /'graɪmi/ *a.* sucio; mugroso.
grin /grɪn/ *n.* 1. sonrisa *f.* —*v.* 2. sonreír.
grind /graɪnd/ *v.* moler; afilar.
grindstone /'graɪnd,stoun/ *n.* amoladera *f.*
gringo /'grɪŋgou/ *n.* gringo; yanqui *m.*
grip /grɪp/ *n.* 1. maleta *f.* —*v.* 2. agarrar.
gripe /graɪp/ *v.* 1. agarrar. —*n.* 2. asimiento *m.*, opresión *f.*
grippe /grɪp/ *n.* gripe *f.*
grisly /'grɪzli/ *a.* espantoso.
grist /grɪst/ *n.* molienda *f.*
gristle /'grɪsəl/ *n.* cartílago *m.*
grit /grɪt/ *n.* arena *f.*; entereza *f.*
grizzled /'grɪzəld/ *a.* tordillo.
groan /groun/ *n.* 1. gemido *m.* —*v.* 2. gemir.
grocer /'grousər/ *n.* abacero *m.*
grocery /'grousəri/ *n.* tienda de comestibles, abacería; (Carib.) bodega *f.*
grog /grɒg/ *n.* brebaje *m.*
groggy /'grɒgi/ *a.* medio borracho; vacilante.
groin /grɔin/ *n.* ingle *f.*
groom /grum/ *n.* (of horses) establero; (at wedding) novio *m.*
groove /gruv/ *n.* 1. estría *f.* —*v.* 2. acanalar.
grope /group/ *v.* tentar; andar a tientas.
gross /grous/ *a.* 1. grueso; grosero. —*n.* 2. gruesa *f.*
grossly /'grousli/ *adv.* groseramente.
gross national product producto nacional bruto *m.*
grossness /'grousnɪs/ *n.* grosería *f.*
grotesque /grou'tɛsk/ *a.* grotesco.
grotto /'grɒtou/ *n.* gruta *f.*
grouch /grautʃ/ *n.* gruñón; descontento *m.*
ground /graund/ *n.* tierra *f.*; terreno; suelo; campo; fundamento *m.*
ground floor planta baja *f.*
groundhog /'graund,hɒg/ *n.* marmota *f.*
groundless /'graundlɪs/ *a.* infundado.
groundwork /'graund,wɜrk/ *n.* base *f.*, fundamento *m.*
group /grup/ *n.* 1. grupo *m.* —*v.* 2. agrupar.
groupie /'grupi/ *n.* persona aficionada que acompaña a un grupo de música moderna.
grouse /graus/ *v.* quejarse.
grove /grouv/ *n.* arboleda *f.*
grovel /'grɒvəl/ *v.* rebajarse; envilecerse.
grow /grou/ *v.* crecer; cultivar.
growl /graul/ *n.* 1. gruñido *m.* —*v.* 2. gruñir.
grown /groun/ *a.* crecido; desarrollado.
grownup /'groun,ʌp/ *n.* adulto -ta.
growth /grouθ/ *n.* crecimiento *m.*; vegetación *f.*; *Med.* tumor *m.*
grub /grʌb/ *n.* gorgojo *m.*, larva *f.*
grubby /'grʌbi/ *a.* gorgojoso, mugriento.
grudge /grʌdʒ/ *n.* rencor *m.* **bear a g.,** guardar rencor.
gruel /'gruəl/ *n.* 1. atole *m.* —*v.* 2. agotar.
gruesome /'grusəm/ *a.* horripilante.
gruff /grʌf/ *a.* ceñudo.

grumble /'grʌmbəl/ *v.* quejarse.
grumpy /'grʌmpi/ *a.* gruñón; quejoso.
grunt /grʌnt/ *v.* gruñir.
guarantee /,gærən'ti/ *n.* 1. garantía *f.* —*v.* 2. garantizar.
guarantor /'gærən,tɔr/ *n.* fiador -ra.
guaranty /'gærən,ti/ *n.* garantía *f.*
guard /gard/ *n.* 1. guardia *m.* & *f.* —*v.* 2. vigilar.
guarded /'gardɪd/ *a.* cauteloso.
guardhouse /'gard,haus/ *n.* prisión militar *f.*
guardian /'gardiən/ *n.* guardián -ana.
guardianship /'gardiən,ʃɪp/ *n.* tutela *f.*
guardsman /'gardzmən/ *n.* centinela *m.*
guava /'gwavə/ *n.* guayaba *f.*
gubernatorial /,gubərnə'tɔriəl/ *a.* gubernativo.
guerrilla /gə'rɪlə/ *n.* guerrilla *f.*; guerrillero, -ra.
guess /gɛs/ *n.* 1. conjetura *f.* —*v.* 2. adivinar; *Colloq.* creer.
guesswork /'gɛs,wɜrk/ *n.* conjetura *f.*
guest /gɛst/ *n.* huésped *m.* & *f.*
guest room alcoba de huéspedes *f.*, alcoba de respeto *f.*, cuarto para invitados *m.*
guffaw /gʌ'fɔ/ *n.* risotada *f.*
guidance /'gaɪdns/ *n.* dirección *f.*
guide /gaɪd/ *n.* 1. guía *m.* & *f.* —*v.* 2. guiar.
guidebook /'gaɪd,bʊk/ *n.* guía *f.*
guided tour /'gaɪdɪd/ visita explicada, visita programada, visita con guía *f.*
guideline /'gaɪd,laɪn/ *n.* pauta *f.*
guidepost /'gaɪd,poust/ *n.* poste indicador *m.*
guild /gɪld/ *n.* gremio *m.*
guile /gaɪl/ *n.* engaño *m.*
guillotine /'gɪlə,tin/ *n.* 1. guillotina *f.* —*v.* 2. guillotinar.
guilt /gɪlt/ *n.* culpa *f.*
guiltily /'gɪltəli/ *adv.* culpablemente.
guiltless /'gɪltlɪs/ *a.* inocente.
guilty /'gɪlti/ *a.* culpable.
guinea fowl /'gɪni/ gallina de Guinea *f.*
guinea pig /'gɪni/ cobayo *m.*, conejillo de Indias *m.*
guise /gaɪz/ *n.* modo *m.*
guitar /gɪ'tar/ *n.* guitarra *f.*
guitarist /gɪ'tarɪst/ *n.* guitarrista *m.* & *f.*
gulch /gʌltʃ/ *n.* quebrada *f.*
gulf /gʌlf/ *n.* golfo *m.*
gull /gʌl/ *n.* gaviota *f.*
gullet /'gʌlɪt/ *n.* esófago *m.*; zanja *f.*
gullible /'gʌləbəl/ *a.* crédulo.
gully /'gʌli/ *n.* barranca *f.*
gulp /gʌlp/ *n.* 1. trago *m.* —*v.* 2. tragar.
gum /gʌm/ *n.* 1. goma *f.*; *Anat.* encía *f.* **chewing g.,** chicle *m.* —*v.* 2. engomar.
gumbo /'gʌmbou/ *n.* quimbombó *m.*
gummy /'gʌmi/ *a.* gomoso.
gun /gʌn/ *n.* fusil, revólver *m.*
gunboat /'gʌn,bout/ *n.* cañonero *m.*
gunman /'gʌnmən/ *n.* bandido *m.*
gunner /'gʌnər/ *n.* artillero *m.*
gun permit licencia de armas *f.*
gunpowder /'gʌn,paudər/ *n.* pólvora *f.*
gunshot /'gʌn,ʃɒt/ *n.* escopetazo *m.*
gunwale /'gʌnl/ *n.* borda *f.*
gurgle /'gɜrgəl/ *n.* 1. gorgoteo *m.* —*v.* 2. gorgotear.
guru /'guru, gu'ru/ *n.* gurú *m.*
gush /gʌʃ/ *n.* 1. chorro *m.* —*v.* 2. brotar, chorrear.
gusher /'gʌʃər/ *n.* pozo de petróleo *m.*
gust /gʌst/ *n.* soplo *m.*; ráfaga *f.*
gustatory /'gʌstə,tɔri/ *a.* gustativo.
gusto /'gʌstou/ *n.* gusto; placer *m.*
gusty /'gʌsti/ *a.* borrascoso.
gut /gʌt/ *n.* intestino *m.*, tripa *f.*
gutter /'gʌtər/ *n.* canal; zanja *f.*
guttural /'gʌtərəl/ *a.* gutural.

guy /gaɪ/ *n.* tipo *m.*
guzzle /'gʌzəl/ *v.* engullir; tragar.
gym /dʒɪm/ *n.* gimnasio *m.*
gymnasium /gɪm'naziəm/ *n.* gimnasio *m.*
gymnast /'dʒɪmnæst/ *n.* gimnasta *m.* & *f.*
gymnastic /dʒɪm'næstɪk/ *a.* gimnástico.
gymnastics /dʒɪm'næstɪks/ *n.* gimnasia *f.*
gynecologist /,gaɪnɪ'kɒlədʒɪst/ *n.* ginecólogo, -ga *m.* & *f.*
gynecology /,gaɪnɪ'kɒlədʒi/ *n.* ginecología *f.*
gypsum /'dʒɪpsəm/ *n.* yeso *m.*
Gypsy /'dʒɪpsi/ *a.* & *n.* gitano -na.
gyrate /'dʒaɪreɪt/ *v.* girar.
gyroscope /'dʒaɪrə,skoup/ *n.* giroscopio *m.*

H

habeas corpus /'heibiəs 'kɔrpəs/ habeas corpus *m.*
haberdasher /'hæbər,dæʃər/ *n.* camisero *m.*
haberdashery /'hæbər,dæʃəri/ *n.* camisería *f.*
habiliment /hə'bɪləmənt/ *n.* vestuario *m.*
habit /'hæbɪt/ *n.* costumbre *f.*, hábito *m.* **be in the h. of,** estar acostumbrado a; soler.
habitable /'hæbɪtəbəl/ *a.* habitable.
habitat /'hæbɪ,tæt/ *n.* habitación *f.*, ambiente *m.*
habitation /,hæbɪ'teiʃən/ *n.* habitación *f.*
habitual /hə'bɪtʃuəl/ *a.* habitual.
habituate /hə'bɪtʃu,eit/ *v.* habituar.
habitué /hə'bɪtʃu,ei/ *n.* parroquiano *m.*
hack /hæk/ *n.* 1. coche de alquiler. —*v.* 2. tajar.
hacker /'hækər/ *n.* pirata *m.* & *f.*
hackneyed /'hæknid/ *a.* trillado.
hacksaw /'hæk,sɔ/ *n.* sierra para cortar metal *f.*
haddock /'hædək/ *n.* merluza *f.*
haft /hæft/ *n.* mango *m.*
hag /hæg/ *n.* bruja *f.*
haggard /'hægərd/ *a.* trasnochado.
haggle /'hægəl/ *v.* regatear.
hail /heil/ *n.* 1. granizo; (greeting) saludo *m.* —*v.* 2. granizar; saludar.
Hail Mary /'mɛəri/ Ave María *f.*
hailstone /'heil,stoun/ *n.* piedra de granizo *f.*
hailstorm /'heil,stɔrm/ *n.* granizada *f.*
hair /hɛər/ *n.* pelo; cabello *m.*
haircut /'hɛər,kʌt/ *n.* corte de pelo.
hairdo /'hɛər,du/ *n.* peinado *m.*
hairdresser /'hɛər,drɛsər/ *n.* peluquero *m.*
hair dryer /'draiər/ secador de pelo, secador *m.*
hairpin /'hɛər,pɪn/ *n.* horquilla *f.*; gancho *m.*
hair's-breadth /'hɛərz,brɛdθ/ *n.* ancho de un pelo *m.*
hairspray /'hɛərsprei/ *n.* aerosol para cabello.
hairy /'hɛəri/ *a.* peludo.
halcyon /'hælsiən/ *n.* 1. alcedón *m.* —*a.* 2. tranquilo.
hale /heil/ *a.* sano.
half /hæf/ *a.* 1. medio. —*n.* 2. mitad *f.*
half-and-half /'hæf ən 'hæf/ *a.* mitad y mitad.
half-baked /'hæf 'beikt/ *a.* medio crudo.
half-breed /'hæf ,brid/ *n.* mestizo *m.*
half brother *n.* medio hermano *m.*
half-hearted /'hæf'hartɪd/ *a.* sin entusiasmo.
half-mast /'hæf 'mæst/ *a.* & *n.* media asta *m.*
halfpenny /'heipəni/ *n.* medio penique *m.*
halfway /'hæf'wei/ *adv.* a medio camino.

half-wit /'hæf ,wɪt/ *n.* bobo *m.*
halibut /'hæləbət/ *n.* hipogloso *m.*
hall /hɔl/ *n.* corredor *m.*; (for assembling) sala *f.* **city h.,** ayuntamiento *m.*
hallmark /'hɔl,mark/ *n.* marca del contraste *f.*
hallow /'hælou/ *v.* consagrar.
Halloween /,hælə'win/ *n.* víspera de Todos los Santos *f.*
hallucination /hə,lusə'neiʃən/ *n.* alucinación *f.*
hallway /'hɔl,wei/ *n.* pasadizo *m.*
halo /'heilou/ *n.* halo *m.*; corona *f.*
halt /hɔlt/ *a.* 1. cojo. —*n.* 2. parada *f.* —*v.* 3. parar. —*interj.* 4. ¡alto!
halter /'hɔltər/ *n.* cabestro *m.*
halve /hæv/ *v.* dividir en dos partes.
halyard /'hælyərd/ *n.* driza *f.*
ham /hæm/ *n.* jamón *m.*
hamburger /'hæm,bɜrgər/ *n.* albóndiga *f.*
hamlet /'hæmlɪt/ *n.* aldea *f.*
hammer /'hæmər/ *n.* 1. martillo *m.* —*v.* 2. martillar.
hammock /'hæmək/ *n.* hamaca *f.*
hamper /'hæmpər/ *n.* canasta *f.*, cesto *m.*
hamstring /'hæm,strɪŋ/ *n.* 1. tendón de la corva *m.* —*v.* 2. desjarretar.
hand /hænd/ *n.* 1. mano *f.* **on the other h.,** en cambio. —*v.* 2. pasar. **h. over,** entregar.
handbag /'hænd,bæg/ *n.* cartera *f.*
handball /'hænd,bɔl/ *n.* pelota *f.*
handbook /'hænd,bʊk/ *n.* manual *m.*
handbrake /'hændbreik/ *n.* freno de mano *m.*
handcuff /'hænd,kʌf/ *n.* esposa *v.* esposar.
handful /'hændfʊl/ *n.* puñado *m.*
handicap /'hændi,kæp/ *n.* desventaja *f.*
handicraft /'hændi,kræft/ *n.* artífice *m.*; destreza manual.
handiwork /'hændi,wɜrk/ *n.* artefacto *m.*
handkerchief /'hæŋkərtʃɪf/ *n.* pañuelo *m.*
handle /'hændl/ *n.* 1. mango *m.* —*v.* 2. manejar.
hand luggage equipaje de mano *m.*
handmade /'hænd'meid/ *a.* hecho a mano.
handmaid /'hænd,meid/ *n.* criada de mano, sirvienta *f.*
hand organ organillo *m.*
handsome /'hænsəm/ *a.* guapo; hermoso.
hand-to-hand /'hænd tə 'hænd/ *adv.* de mano a mano.
handwriting /'hænd,raitɪŋ/ *n.* escritura *f.*
handy /'hændi/ *a.* diestro; útil; a la mano.
hang /hæŋ/ *v.* colgar; ahorcar.
hangar /'hæŋər/ *n.* hangar *m.*
hangdog /'hæŋ,dɒg/ *a.* & *n.* camastrón *m.*
hanger /'hæŋər/ *n.* colgador, gancho *m.*
hanger-on /'hæŋər 'ɒn/ *n.* dependiente; mogollón *m.*
hang glider /'glaidər/ aparato para vuelo libre, delta, ala delta *f.*
hanging /'hæŋɪŋ/ *n.* 1. ahorcadura *f.* —*a.* 2. colgante.
hangman /'hæŋmən/ *n.* verdugo *m.*
hangnail /'hæŋ,neil/ *n.* padrastro *m.*
hang out *v.* enarbolar.
hangover /'hæŋ,ouvər/ *n.* resaca *f.*
hangup /'hæŋʌp/ *n.* tara (psicológica) *f.*
hank /hæŋk/ *n.* madeja *f.*
hanker /'hæŋkər/ *v.* ansiar; apetecer.
haphazard. /hæp'hæzərd/ *a.* casual.
happen /'hæpən/ *v.* acontecer, suceder, pasar.
happening /'hæpənɪŋ/ *n.* acontecimiento *m.*
happiness /'hæpɪnɪs/ *n.* felicidad; dicha *f.*
happy /'hæpi/ *a.* feliz; contento; dichoso.

happy-go-lucky /ˈhæpi gou ˈlʌki/ *a. & n.* descuidado *m.*
harakiri /ˈhɑrəˈkɪəri/ *n.* harakiri (suicidio japonés) *m.*
harangue /həˈræŋ/ *n.* **1.** arenga *f.* —*v.* **2.** arengar.
harass /həˈræs/ *v.* acosar; atormentar.
harbinger /ˈhɑrbɪndʒər/ *n.* presagio *m.*
harbor /ˈhɑrbər/ *n.* **1.** puerto; albergue *m.* —*v.* **2.** abrigar.
hard /hɑrd/ *a.* **1.** duro; difícil. —*adv.* **2.** mucho.
hard coal antracita *m.*
hard disk disco duro *m.*
harden /ˈhɑrdn̩/ *v.* endurecer.
hard-headed /ˈhɑrd ˈhɛdɪd/ *a.* terco.
hard-hearted /ˈhɑrdˈhɑrtɪd/ *a.* empedernido.
hardiness /ˈhɑrdinɪs/ *n.* vigor *m.*
hardly /ˈhɑrdli/ *adv.* apenas.
hardness /ˈhɑrdnɪs/ *n.* dureza; dificultad *f.*
hardship /ˈhɑrdʃɪp/ *n.* penalidad *f.*; trabajo *m.*
hardware /ˈhɑrdˌwɛər/ *n.* hardware *m.*; (computer) quincalla *f.*
hardwood /ˈhɑrdˌwʊd/ *n.* madera dura *f.*
hardy /ˈhɑrdi/ *a.* fuerte, robusto.
hare /hɛər/ *n.* liebre *f.*
harebrained /ˈhɛərˌbreind/ *a.* tolondro.
harelip /ˈhɛərˌlɪp/ *n.* **1.** labio leporino *m.* —*a.* **2.** labihendido.
harem /ˈhɛərəm/ *n.* harén *m.*
hark /hɑrk/ *v.* escuchar; atender.
Harlequin /ˈhɑrləkwɪn/ *n.* arlequín *m.*
harlot /ˈhɑrlət/ *n.* ramera *f.*
harm /hɑrm/ *n.* **1.** mal, daño; perjuicio *m.* —*v.* **2.** dañar.
harmful /ˈhɑrmfəl/ *a.* dañoso.
harmless /ˈhɑrmlɪs/ *a.* inocente.
harmonic /hɑrˈmɒnɪk/ *n.* armónico *m.*
harmonica /hɑrˈmɒnɪkə/ *n.* armónica *f.*
harmonious /hɑrˈmouniəs/ *a.* armonioso.
harmonize /ˈhɑrməˌnaiz/ *v.* armonizar.
harmony /ˈhɑrməni/ *n.* armonía *f.*
harness /ˈhɑrnɪs/ *n.* arnés *m.*
harp /hɑrp/ *n.* arpa *f.*
harpoon /hɑrˈpun/ *n.* arpón *m.*
harridan /ˈhɑrɪdn̩/ *n.* vieja regañona *f.*
harrow /ˈhærou/ *n.* **1.** rastro *m.*; grada *f.* —*v.* **2.** gradar.
harry /ˈhæri/ *v.* acosar.
harsh /hɑrʃ/ *a.* áspero.
harshness /ˈhɑrʃnɪs/ *n.* aspereza *f.*
harvest /ˈhɑrvɪst/ *n.* **1.** cosecha *f.* —*v.* **2.** cosechar.
hash /hæʃ/ *n.* picadillo *m.*
hashish /ˈhæʃiʃ/ *n.* haxis *m.*
hasn't /ˈhæzənt/ *v.* no tiene (neg. + tener).
hassle /ˈhæsəl/ *n.* lío *m.*, molestia *f.*; controversia *f.*
hassock /ˈhæsək/ *n.* cojín *m.*
haste /heist/ *n.* prisa *f.*
hasten /ˈheisən/ *v.* apresurarse, darse prisa.
hasty /ˈheisti/ *a.* apresurado.
hat /hæt/ *n.* sombrero *m.*
hat box /ˈhætˌbɒks/ sombrerera *f.*
hatch /hætʃ/ *n.* **1.** *Naut.* cuartel *m.* —*v.* **2.** incubar; *Fig.* tramar.
hatchery /ˈhætʃəri/ *n.* criadero *m.*
hatchet /ˈhætʃɪt/ *n.* hacha pequeña.
hate /heit/ *n.* **1.** odio *m.* —*v.* **2.** odiar, detestar.
hateful /ˈheitfəl/ *a.* detestable.
hatred /ˈheitrɪd/ *n.* odio *m.*
haughtiness /ˈhɔtinɪs/ *n.* arrogancia *f.*
haughty /ˈhɔti/ *a.* altivo.
haul /hɔl/ *n.* **1.** (fishery) redada *f.* —*v.* **2.** tirar, halar.
haunch /hɔntʃ/ *n.* anca *f.*
haunt /hɔnt/ *n.* **1.** lugar frecuentado. —*v.* **2.** frecuentar, andar por.
have /hæv; *unstressed* həv, əv/ *v.* tener; haber.
haven /ˈheivən/ *n.* puerto; asilo *m.*
haven't /ˈhævənt/ *v.* no tiene (neg. + tener).
havoc /ˈhævək/ *n.* ruina *f.*
hawk /hɔk/ *n.* halcón *m.*
hawker /ˈhɔkər/ *n.* buhonero *m.*
hawser /ˈhɔzər/ *n.* cable *m.*
hawthorn /ˈhɔˌθɔrn/ *n.* espino *m.*
hay /hei/ *n.* heno *m.*
hay fever *n.* fiebre del heno *f.*
hayfield /ˈheifild/ *n.* henar *m.*
hayloft /ˈheiˌlɔft/ *n.* henil *m.*
haystack /ˈheiˌstæk/ *n.* hacina de heno *f.*
hazard /ˈhæzərd/ *n.* **1.** azar *m.* —*v.* **2.** aventurar.
hazardous /ˈhæzərdəs/ *a.* peligroso.
haze /heiz/ *n.* niebla *f.*
hazel /ˈheizəl/ *n.* avellano *m.*
hazelnut /ˈheizəlˌnʌt/ avellana *f.*
hazy /ˈheizi/ *a.* brumoso.
he /hei/ *pron.* él *m.*
head /hɛd/ *n.* **1.** cabeza *f.*; jefe *m.* —*v.* **2.** dirigir; encabezar.
headache /ˈhɛdˌeik/ *n.* dolor de cabeza *m.*
headband /ˈhɛdˌbænd/ *n.* venda para cabeza *f.*
headfirst /ˈhɛdˈfɜrst/ *adv.* de cabeza.
headgear /ˈhɛdˌgɪər/ *n.* tocado *m.*
headlight /ˈhɛdˌlait/ *n.* linterna delantera *f.*, farol de tope *m.*
headline /ˈhɛdˌlain/ *n.* encabezado *m.*
headlong /ˈhɛdˌlɔŋ/ *a.* precipitoso.
head-on /ˈhɛd ˈɒn/ *adv.* de frente.
headphones /ˈhɛdˌfounz/ *n.pl.* auriculares *m.pl.*
headquarters /ˈhɛdˌkwɔrtərz/ *n.* jefatura *f.*; *Mil.* cuartel general.
headstone /ˈhɛdˌstoun/ *n.* lápida mortuoria *f.*
headstrong /ˈhɛdˌstrɔŋ/ *a.* terco.
headwaiter /ˈhɛdˈweitər/ jefe de comedor *m. & f.*
headwaters /ˈhɛdˌwɔtərz/ *n.* cabeceras *f.pl.*
headway /ˈhɛdˌwei/ *n.* avance *m.*, progreso *m.*
headwork /ˈhɛdˌwɜrk/ *n.* trabajo mental *m.*
heady /ˈhɛdi/ *a.* impetuoso.
heal /hil/ *v.* curar, sanar.
health /hɛlθ/ *n.* salud *f.*
healthful /ˈhɛlθfəl/ *a.* saludable.
healthy /ˈhɛlθi/ *a.* sano; salubre.
heap /hip/ *n.* montón *m.*
hear /hɪər/ *v.* oír. **h. from,** tener noticias de. **h. about, h. of,** oír hablar de.
hearing /ˈhɪərɪŋ/ *n.* oído *m.*
hearing aid audífono *m.*
hearsay /ˈhɪərˌsei/ *n.* rumor *m.*
hearse /hɜrs/ *n.* ataúd *m.*
heart /hɑrt/ *n.* corazón; ánimo *m.* **by h.,** de memoria. **have h. trouble** padecer del corazón.
heartache /ˈhɑrtˌeik/ *n.* angustia *f.*
heart attack ataque cardíaco, infarto, infarto de miocardio *m.*
heartbreak /ˈhɑrtˌbreik/ *n.* angustia *f.*; pesar *m.*
heartbroken /ˈhɑrtˌbroukən/ *a.* acongojado.
heartburn /ˈhɑrtˌbɜrn/ *n.* acedía *f.*, ardor de estómago *m.*
heartfelt /ˈhɑrtˌfɛlt/ *a.* sentido.
hearth /hɑrθ/ *n.* hogar *m.*, chimenea *f.*
heartless /ˈhɑrtlɪs/ *a.* empedernido.
heartsick /ˈhɑrtˌsɪk/ *a.* desconsolado.
heart-stricken /ˈhɑrt ˈstrɪkən/ *a.* afligido.
heart-to-heart /ˈhɑrt tə ˈhɑrt/ *adv.* franco; sincero.
hearty /ˈhɑrti/ *a.* cordial; vigoroso.
heat /hit/ *n.* **1.** calor; ardor *m.*; calefacción *f.* —*v.* **2.** calentar.
heated /ˈhitɪd/ *a.* acalorado.
heater /ˈhitər/ *n.* calentador *m.*
heath /hiθ/ *n.* matorral *m.*
heathen /ˈhiðən/ *a. & n.* pagano -na.
heather /ˈhɛðər/ *n.* brezo *m.*
heating /ˈhitɪŋ/ *n.* calefacción *f.*
heatstroke /ˈhitˌstrouk/ *n.* insolación *f.*
heat wave onda de calor *f.*
heave /hiv/ *v.* tirar.
heaven /ˈhɛvən/ *n.* cielo *m.*
heavenly /ˈhɛvənli/ *a.* divino.
heavy /ˈhɛvi/ *a.* pesado; oneroso.
Hebrew /ˈhibru/ *a. & n.* hebreo -ea.
hectic /ˈhɛktɪk/ *a.* turbulento.
hedge /hɛdʒ/ *n.* seto *m.*
hedgehog /ˈhɛdʒˌhɒg/ *n.* erizo *m.*
hedonism /ˈhidn̩ˌɪzəm/ *n.* hedonismo *m.*
heed /hid/ *n.* **1.** cuidado *m.* —*v.* **2.** atender.
heedless /ˈhidlɪs/ *a.* desatento; incauto.
heel /hil/ *n.* talón *m.*; (of shoe) tacón *m.*
heifer /ˈhɛfər/ *n.* novilla *f.*
height /hait/ *n.* altura *f.*
heighten /ˈhaitn̩/ *n.* elevar; exaltar.
heinous /ˈheinəs/ *a.* nefando.
heir /ɛər/ **heiress** *n.* heredero -ra.
helicopter /ˈhɛlɪˌkɒptər/ *n.* helicóptero *m.*
heliotrope /ˈhiliəˌtroup/ *n.* heliotropo *m.*
helium /ˈhiliəm/ *n.* helio *m.*
hell /hɛl/ *n.* infierno *m.*
Hellenism /ˈhɛləˌnɪzəm/ *n.* helenismo *m.*
hellish /ˈhɛlɪʃ/ *a.* infernal.
hello /hɛˈlou/ *interj.* ¡hola!; (on telephone) aló; bueno.
helm /hɛlm/ *n.* timón *m.*
helmet /ˈhɛlmɪt/ *n.* yelmo, casco *m.*
helmsman /ˈhɛlmzmən/ *n.* limonero *m.*
help /hɛlp/ *n.* **1.** ayuda *f.* **help!** ¡socorro! —*v.* **2.** ayudar. **h. oneself,** servirse. **can't help (but),** no poder menos de.
helper /ˈhɛlpər/ *n.* ayudante *m.*
helpful /ˈhɛlpfəl/ *a.* útil; servicial.
helpfulness /ˈhɛlpfəlnɪs/ *n.* utilidad *f.*
helpless /ˈhɛlplɪs/ *a.* imposibilitado.
hem /hɛm/ *n.* **1.** ribete *m.* —*v.* **2.** ribetear.
hemisphere /ˈhɛmɪˌsfɪər/ *n.* hemisferio *m.*
hemlock /ˈhɛmˌlɒk/ *n.* abeto *m.*
hemoglobin /ˈhiməˌgloubɪn/ *n.* hemoglobina *f.*
hemophilia /ˌhiməˈfɪliə/ *n.* hemofilia *f.*
hemorrhage /ˈhɛmərɪdʒ/ *n.* hemorragia *f.*
hemorrhoids /ˈhɛməˌrɔidz/ *n.* hemorroides *f.pl.*
hemp /hɛmp/ *n.* cáñamo *m.*
hemstitch /ˈhɛmˌstɪtʃ/ *n.* **1.** vainica *f.* —*v.* **2.** hacer una vainica.
hen /hɛn/ *n.* gallina *f.*
hence /hɛns/ *adv.* por lo tanto.
henceforth /ˌhɛnsˈfɔrθ/ *adv.* de aquí en adelante.
henchman /ˈhɛntʃmən/ *n.* paniaguado *m.*
henna /ˈhɛnə/ *n.* alheña *f.*
hepatitis /ˌhɛpəˈtaitɪs/ *n.* hepatitis *f.*
her /hɜr; *unstressed* hər, ər/ *a.* **1.** su. —*pron.* **2.** ella; la; le.
herald /ˈhɛrəld/ *n.* heraldo *m.*
heraldic /hɛˈrældɪk/ *a.* heráldico.
heraldry /ˈhɛrəldri/ *n.* heráldica *f.*
herb /ɜrb; *esp. Brit.* hɜrb/ *n.* yerba, hierba *f.*
herbaceous /hɜrˈbeiʃəs, ɜr-/ *a.* herbáceo.
herbarium /hɜrˈbɛəriəm, ɜr-/ *n.* herbario *m.*
herd /hɜrd/ *n.* **1.** hato, rebaño *m.* —*v.* **2.** reunir en hatos.
here /hɪər/ *adv.* aquí; acá.
hereafter /hɪərˈæftər/ *adv.* en lo futuro.
hereby /hɪərˈbai/ *adv.* por éstas, por la presente.
hereditary /həˈrɛdɪˌtɛri/ *a.* hereditario.
heredity /həˈrɛdɪti/ *n.* herencia *f.*
herein /hɪərˈɪn/ *adv.* aquí dentro; incluso.
heresy /ˈhɛrəsi/ *n.* herejía *f.*
heretic /ˈhɛrɪtɪk/ *a.* **1.** herético. —*n.* **2.** hereje *m. & f.*
heretical /həˈrɛtɪkəl/ *a.* herético.
heretofore /ˌhɪərtəˈfɔr/ *adv.* hasta ahora.
herewith /hɪərˈwɪθ/ *adv.* con esto, adjunto.
heritage /ˈhɛrɪtɪdʒ/ *n.* herencia *f.*
hermetic /hɜrˈmɛtɪk/ *a.* hermético.
hermit /ˈhɜrmɪt/ *n.* ermitaño *m.*
hernia /ˈhɜrniə/ *n.* hernia *f.*
hero /ˈhɪərou/ *n.* héroe *m.*
heroic /hɪˈrouɪk/ *a.* heroico.
heroically /hɪˈrouɪkəli/ *adv.* heroicamente.
heroin /ˈhɛrouɪn/ *n.* heroína *f.*
heroine /ˈhɛrouɪn/ *n.* heroína *f.*
heroism /ˈhɛrouˌɪzəm/ *n.* heroísmo *m.*
heron /ˈhɛrən/ *n.* garza *f.*
herring /ˈhɛrɪŋ/ *n.* arenque *m.*
hers /hɜrz/ *pron.* suyo, de ella.
herself /hərˈsɛlf/ *pron.* sí, sí misma, se. **she h.,** ella misma. **with h.,** consigo.
hertz /hɜrts/ *n.* hertzio *m.*
hesitancy /ˈhɛzɪtənsi/ *n.* hesitación *f.*
hesitant /ˈhɛzɪtənt/ *a.* indeciso.
hesitate /ˈhɛzɪˌteit/ *v.* vacilar.
hesitation /ˌhɛzɪˈteiʃən/ *n.* duda; vacilación *f.*
heterogeneous /ˌhɛtərəˈdʒiniəs/ *a.* heterogéneo.
heterosexual /ˌhɛtərəˈsɛkʃuəl/ *a.* heterosexual.
hexagon /ˈhɛksəˌgɒn/ *n.* hexágono *m.*
hibernate /ˈhaibərˌneit/ *v.* invernar.
hibernation /ˌhaibərˈneiʃən/ *n.* invernada *f.*
hibiscus /haiˈbɪskəs/ *n.* hibisco *m.*
hiccup /ˈhɪkʌp/ *n.* **1.** hipo *m.* —*v.* **2.** tener hipo.
hickory /ˈhɪkəri/ *n.* nogal americano *m.*
hidden /ˈhɪdn̩/ *a.* oculto; escondido.
hide /haid/ *n.* **1.** cuero *m.*; piel *f.* —*v.* **2.** esconder; ocultar.
hideous /ˈhɪdiəs/ *a.* horrible.
hide-out /ˈhaid ˌaut/ *n.* escondite *m.*
hiding place /ˈhaidɪŋ/ escondrijo *m.*
hierarchy /ˈhaiəˌrɑrki/ *n.* jerarquía *f.*
high /hai/ *a.* alto, elevado; (in price) caro.
highbrow /ˈhaiˌbrau/ *n.* erudito *m.*
highfalutin /ˌhaifəˈlutn̩/ *a.* pomposo, presumido.
high fidelity de alta fidelidad.
highlighter /ˈhaiˌlaitər/ *n.* marcador *m.*
highly /ˈhaili/ *adv.* altamente; sumamente.
high school escuela secundaria *f.*
highway /ˈhaiˌwei/ *n.* carretera *f.*; camino real *m.*
hijacker /ˈhaiˌdʒækər/ *n.* secuestrador, pirata de aviones *m.*
hike /haik/ *n.* caminata *f.*
hilarious /hɪˈlɛəriəs/ *a.* alegre, bullicioso.
hilarity /hɪˈlærɪti/ *n.* hilaridad *f.*
hill /hɪl/ *n.* colina *f.*; cerro *m.*; **down h.,** cuesta abajo. **up h.,** cuesta arriba.
hilly /ˈhɪli/ *a.* accidentado.
hilt /hɪlt/ *n.* puño *m.* **up to the h.,** a fondo.
him /hɪm/ *pron.* él; lo; le.
himself /hɪmˈsɛlf/ *pron.* sí, sí mismo; se. **he h.,** él mismo. **with h.,** consigo.
hinder /ˈhɪndər/ *v.* impedir.
hindmost /ˈhaindˌmoust/ *a.* último.
hindquarter /ˈhaindˌkwɔrtər/ *n.* cuarto trasero *m.*
hindrance /ˈhɪndrəns/ *n.* obstáculo *m.*
hinge /hɪndʒ/ *n.* **1.** gozne *m.* —*v.* **2.** engoznar. **h. on,** depender de.
hint /hɪnt/ *n.* **1.** insinuación *f.*; indicio *m.* —*v.* **2.** insinuar.

hip /hɪp/ *n.* cadera *f.*
hippopotamus /ˌhɪpəˈpɒtəməs/ *n.* hipopótamo *m.*
hire /haiᵊr/ *v.* alquilar.
his /hɪz; *unstressed* ɪz/ *a.* **1.** su. —*pron.* **2.** suyo, de él.
Hispanic /hɪˈspænɪk/ *a.* hispano.
hiss /hɪs/ *v.* silbar, sisear.
historian /hɪˈstɔriən/ *n.* historiador *m.*
historic /hɪˈstɔrɪk/ **historical** *a.* histórico.
history /ˈhɪstəri/ *n.* historia *f.*
histrionic /ˌhɪstriˈɒnɪk/ *a.* histriónico.
hit /hɪt/ *n.* **1.** golpe *m.*; *Colloq.* éxito *m.*; (Internet) hit *m.* —*v.* **2.** golpear.
hitch /hɪtʃ/ *v.* amarrar; enganchar.
hitchhike /ˈhɪtʃˌhaik/ *v.* hacer autostop.
hitchhiker /ˈhɪtʃˌhaikər/ *n.* autostopista *f.*
hitchhiking /ˈhɪtʃˌhaikɪŋ/ *n.* autostop *m.*
hither /ˈhɪðər/ *adv.* acá, hacia acá.
hitherto /ˈhɪðərˌtu/ *adv.* hasta ahora.
hive /haiv/ *n.* colmena *f.*
hives /haivz/ *n.* urticaria *f.*
hoard /hɔrd/ *n.* **1.** acumulación *f.* —*v.* **2.** acaparar; atesorar.
hoarse /hɔrs/ *a.* ronco.
hoax /houks/ *n.* **1.** engaño *m.* —*v.* **2.** engañar.
hobby /ˈhɒbi/ *n.* afición *f.*, pasatiempo *m.*
hobgoblin /ˈhɒbˌgɒblɪn/ *n.* trasgo *m.*
hobnob /ˈhɒbˌnɒb/ *v.* tener intimidad.
hobo /ˈhoubou/ *n.* vagabundo *m.*
hockey /ˈhɒki/ *n.* hockey *m.* **ice-h.,** hockey sobre hielo.
hod /hɒd/ *n.* esparavel *m.*
hodgepodge /ˈhɒdʒˌpɒdʒ/ *n.* baturrillo *m.*; mezcolanza *f.*
hoe /hou/ *n.* **1.** azada *f.* —*v.* **2.** cultivar con azada.
hog /hɔg/ *n.* cerdo, puerco *m.*
hoist /hɔist/ *n.* **1.** grúa *f.*, elevador *m.* —*v.* **2.** elevar, enarbolar.
hold /hould/ *n.* **1.** presa *f.*; agarro *m.*; *Naut.* bodega *f.* **to get h. of,** conseguir, apoderarse de. —*v.* **2.** tener; detener; sujetar; celebrar.
holder /ˈhouldər/ *n.* tenedor *m.* **cigarette h.,** boquilla *f.*
holdup /ˈhouldˌʌp/ *n.* salteamiento *m.*
hole /houl/ *n.* agujero; hoyo; hueco *m.*
holiday /ˈhɒlɪˌdei/ *n.* día de fiesta.
holiness /ˈhoulinɪs/ *n.* santidad *f.*
Holland /ˈhɒlənd/ *n.* Holanda *f.*
hollow /ˈhɒlou/ *a.* **1.** hueco. —*n.* **2.** cavidad *f.* —*v.* **3.** ahuecar; excavar.
holly /ˈhɒli/ *n.* acebo *m.*
hollyhock /ˈhɒliˌhɒk/ *n.* malva real *f.*
holocaust /ˈhɒləˌkɔst/ *n.* holocausto *m.*
hologram /ˈhɒləˌgræm/ *n.* holograma *m.*
holography /həˈlɒgrəfi/ *n.* holografía *f.*
holster /ˈhoulstər/ *n.* pistolera *f.*
holy /ˈhouli/ *a.* santo.
holy day disanto *m.*
Holy See Santa Sede *f.*
Holy Spirit Espíritu Santo *m.*
Holy Week Semana Santa *f.*
homage /ˈhɒmɪdʒ/ *n.* homenaje *m.*
home /houm/ *n.* casa, morada *f*; hogar *m.* **at h.,** en casa. **to go h.,** ir a casa.
home appliance electrodoméstica *m.*
home computer ordenador doméstico *m.*, computadora doméstica *f.*
homeland /ˈhoumˌlænd/ *n.* patria *f.*
homely /ˈhoumli/ *a.* feo; casero.
home rule *n.* autonomía *f.*
homesick /ˈhoumˌsɪk/ *a.* nostálgico.
homespun /ˈhoumˌspʌn/ *a.* casero; tocho.
homeward /ˈhoumwərd/ *adv.* hacia casa.
homework /ˈhoumˌwɜrk/ *n.* deberes *m.pl.*
homicide /ˈhɒməˌsaid/ *n.* homicida *m.* & *f.*
homily /ˈhɒməli/ *n.* homilía *f.*
homogeneous /ˌhouməˈdʒiniəs/ *a.* homogéneo.
homogenize /həˈmɒdʒəˌnaiz/ *v.* homogenezar.
homosexual /ˌhouməˈsɛkʃuəl/ *n.* & *a.* homosexual *m.*
Honduras /hɒnˈdʊrəs/ *n.* Honduras *f.*
hone /houn/ *n.* **1.** piedra de afilar *f.* —*v.* **2.** afilar.
honest /ˈɒnɪst/ *a.* honrado, honesto; sincero.
honestly /ˈɒnɪstli/ *adv.* honradamente; de veras.
honesty /ˈɒnəsti/ *n.* honradez, honestidad *f.*
honey /ˈhʌni/ *n.* miel *f.*
honeybee /ˈhʌniˌbi/ *n.* abeja obrera *f.*
honeymoon /ˈhʌniˌmun/ *n.* luna de miel.
honeysuckle /ˈhʌniˌsʌkəl/ *n.* madreselva *f.*
honor /ˈɒnər/ *n.* **1.** honra *f.*; honor *m.* —*v.* **2.** honrar.
honorable /ˈɒnərəbəl/ *a.* honorable; ilustre.
honorary /ˈɒnəˌrɛri/ *a.* honorario.
hood /hʊd/ *n.* capota; capucha *f.*; *Auto.* cubierta del motor.
hoodlum /ˈhudləm/ *n.* pillo *m.*, rufián *m.*
hoodwink /ˈhʊdˌwɪŋk/ *v.* engañar.
hoof /hʊf/ *n.* pezuña *f.*
hook /hʊk/ *n.* **1.** gancho *m.* —*v.* **2.** enganchar.
hooligan /ˈhulɪgən/ *n.* gamberro -rra.
hoop /hup/ *n.* cerco *m.*
hop /hɒp/ *n.* **1.** salto *m.* —*v.* **2.** saltar.
hope /houp/ *n.* **1.** esperanza *f.* —*v.* **2.** esperar.
hopeful /ˈhoupfəl/ *a.* lleno de esperanzas.
hopeless /ˈhouplɪs/ *a.* desesperado; sin remedio.
horde /hɔrd/ *n.* horda *f.*
horehound /ˈhɔrˌhaund/ *n.* marrubio *m.*
horizon /həˈraizən/ *n.* horizonte *m.*
horizontal /ˌhɔrəˈzɒntl̩/ *a.* horizontal.
hormone /ˈhɔrmoun/ *n.* hormón *m.*
horn /hɔrn/ *n.* cuerno *m.*; (music) trompa *f.*; *Auto.* bocina *f.*
hornet /ˈhɔrnɪt/ *n.* avispón *m.*
horny /ˈhɔrni/ *a.* córneo; calloso.
horoscope /ˈhɔrəˌskoup/ *n.* horóscopo *m.*
horrendous /həˈrɛndəs/ *a.* horrendo.
horrible /ˈhɔrəbəl/ *a.* horrible.
horrid /ˈhɔrɪd/ *a.* horrible.
horrify /ˈhɔrəˌfai/ *v.* horrorizar.
horror /ˈhɔrər/ *n.* horror *m.*
horror film película de terror *f.*
hors d'oeuvre /ɔr ˈdɜrv/ *n.* entremés *m.*
horse /hɔrs/ *n.* caballo *m.* **to ride a h.,** cabalgar.
horseback /ˈhɔrsˌbæk/ *n.* **on h.,** a caballo. **to ride h.,** montar a caballo.
horseback riding equitación *f.*
horsefly /ˈhɔrsˌflai/ *n.* tábano *m.*
horsehair /ˈhɔrsˌhɛər/ *n.* pelo de caballo *m.*; tela de crin *f.*
horseman /ˈhɔrsmən/ *n.* jinete *m.*
horsemanship /ˈhɔrsmənˌʃɪp/ *n.* manejo *m.*, equitación *f.*
horsepower /ˈhɔrsˌpauər/ *n.* caballo de fuerza *m.*
horse race carrera de caballos *f.*
horseradish /ˈhɔrsˌrædɪʃ/ *n.* rábano picante *m.*
horseshoe /ˈhɔrsˌʃu/ *n.* herradura *f.*
hortatory /ˈhɔrtəˌtɔri/ *a.* exhortatorio.
horticulture /ˈhɔrtɪˌkʌltʃər/ *n.* horticultura *f.*
hose /houz/ *n.* medias *f.pl.*; (garden) manguera *f.*
hosiery /ˈhouʒəri/ *n.* calcetería *f.*
hospitable /ˈhɒspɪtəbəl/ *a.* hospitalario.
hospital /ˈhɒspɪtl̩/ *n.* hospital *m.*
hospitality /ˌhɒspɪˈtælɪti/ *n.* hospitalidad *f.*
hospitalization /ˌhɒspɪtl̩ɪˈzeiʃən/ *n.* hospitalización *f.*
hospitalize /ˈhɒspɪtl̩ˌaiz/ *v.* hospitalizar.
host /houst/ *n.* anfitrión *m.*, dueño de la casa; *Relig.* hostia *f.*
hostage /ˈhɒstɪdʒ/ *n.* rehén *m.*
hostel /ˈhɒstl̩/ *n.* hostería *f.*
hostelry /ˈhɒstl̩ri/ *n.* fonda *f.*, parador *m.*
hostess /ˈhoustɪs/ *n.* anfitriona *f.*, dueña de la casa.
hostile /ˈhɒstl̩/ *a.* hostil.
hostility /hɒˈstɪlɪti/ *n.* hostilidad *f.*
hot /hɒt/ *a.* caliente; (sauce) picante. **to be h.,** tener calor; (weather) hacer calor.
hotbed /ˈhɒtˌbɛd/ *n.* estercolero *m.* *Fig.* foco *m.*
hot dog perrito caliente *m.*
hotel /houˈtɛl/ *n.* hotel *m.*
hotelier /ˌoutəlˈyei, ˌhoutl̩ˈɪər/ *n.* hotelero -ra.
hot-headed /ˈhɒt ˈhɛdɪd/ *a.* turbulento, alborotadizo.
hothouse /ˈhɒtˌhaus/ *n.* invernáculo *m.*
hot-water bottle /ˈhɒt ˈwɔtər/ bolsa de agua caliente *f.*
hound /haund/ *n.* **1.** sabueso *m.* —*v.* **2.** perseguir; seguir la pista.
hour /auᵊr/ *n.* hora *f.*
hourglass /ˈauᵊrˌglæs/ *n.* reloj de arena *m.*
hourly /ˈauᵊrli/ *a.* **1.** por horas. —*adv.* **2.** a cada hora.
house /*n* haus; *v* hauz/ *n.* **1.** casa *f.*; *Theat.* público *m.* —*v.* **2.** alojar, albergar.
housefly /ˈhausˌflai/ *n.* mosca ordinaria *f.*
household /ˈhausˌhould/ *n.* familia; casa *f.*
housekeeper /ˈhausˌkipər/ *n.* ama de llaves.
housemaid /ˈhausˌmeid/ *n.* criada *f.*, sirvienta *f.*
housewife /ˈhausˌwaif/ *n.* ama de casa.
housework /ˈhausˌwɜrk/ *n.* tareas domésticas.
hovel /ˈhʌvəl/ *n.* choza *f.*
hover /ˈhʌvər/ *v.* revolotear.
hovercraft /ˈhʌvərˌkræft/ *n.* aerodeslizador *m.*
how /hau/ *adv.* cómo. **h. much,** cuánto. **h. many,** cuántos. **h. far,** a qué distancia.
however /hauˈɛvər/ *adv.* como quiera; sin embargo.
howl /haul/ *n.* **1.** aullido *m.* —*v.* **2.** aullar.
HTML *abbr.* (HyperText Markup Language) Lenguaje de Marcado de Hipertexto *m.*
hub /hʌb/ *n.* centro *m.*; eje *m.* **h. of a wheel,** cubo de la rueda *m.*
hubbub /ˈhʌbʌb/ *n.* alboroto *m.*, bulla *f.*
hue /hyu/ *n.* matiz; color *m.*
hug /hʌg/ *n.* **1.** abrazo *m.* —*v.* **2.** abrazar.
huge /hyudʒ/ *a.* enorme.
hulk /hʌlk/ *n.* casco de buque *m.*
hull /hʌl/ *n.* **1.** cáscara *f.*; (naval) casco *m.* —*v.* **2.** decascarar.
hum /hʌm/ *n.* **1.** zumbido *m.* —*v.* **2.** tararear; zumbar.
human /ˈhyumən/ *a.* & *n.* humano -na.
human being ser humano *m.*
humane /hyuˈmein/ *a.* humano, humanitario.
humanism /ˈhyuməˌnɪzəm/ *n.* humanidad *f.*; benevolencia *f.*
humanitarian /hyuˌmænɪˈtɛəriən/ *a.* humanitario.
humanity /hyuˈmænɪti/ *n.* humanidad *f.*
humanly /ˈhyumənli/ *a.* humanamente.
humble /ˈhʌmbəl/ *a.* humilde.
humbug /ˈhʌmˌbʌg/ *n.* farsa *f.*, embaucador *m.*
humdrum /ˈhʌmˌdrʌm/ *a.* monótono.
humid /ˈhyumɪd/ *a.* húmedo.
humidity /hyuˈmɪdɪti/ *n.* humedad *f.*
humiliate /hyuˈmɪliˌeit/ *v.* humillar.
humiliation /hyuˌmɪliˈeiʃən/ *n.* mortificación *f.*; bochorno *m.*
humility /hyuˈmɪlɪti/ *n.* humildad *f.*
humor /ˈhyumər/ *n.* **1.** humor; capricho *m.* —*v.* **2.** complacer.
humorist /ˈhyumərɪst/ *n.* humorista *m.*
humorous /ˈhyumərəs/ *a.* divertido.
hump /hʌmp/ *n.* joroba *f.*
humpback /ˈhʌmpˌbæk/ *n.* jorobado *m.*
humus /ˈhyuməs/ *n.* humus *m.*
hunch /hʌntʃ/ *n.* giba *f.*; (idea) corazonada *f.*
hunchback /ˈhʌntʃˌbæk/ *n.* jorobado *m.*
hundred /ˈhʌndrɪd/ *a.* & *pron.* **1.** cien, ciento. **200,** doscientos. **300,** trescientos. **400,** cuatrocientos. **500,** quinientos. **600,** seiscientos. **700,** setecientos. **800,** ochocientos. **900,** novecientos. —*n.* **2.** centenar *m.*
hundredth /ˈhʌndrɪdθ/ *n.* & *a.* centésimo *m.*
Hungarian /hʌŋˈgɛəriən/ *a.* & *n.* húngaro -ra.
Hungary /ˈhʌŋgəri/ Hungría *f.*
hunger /ˈhʌŋgər/ *n.* hambre *f.*
hunger strike huelga de hambre *f.*
hungry /ˈhʌŋgri/ *a.* hambriento. **to be h.,** tener hambre.
hunt /hʌnt/ *n.* **1.** caza *f.* —*v.* **2.** cazar. **h. up,** buscar.
hunter /ˈhʌntər/ *n.* cazador *m.*
hunting /ˈhʌntɪŋ/ *n.* caza *f.* **to go h.,** ir de caza.
hurdle /ˈhɜrdl̩/ *n.* zarzo *m.*, valla *f.*; dificultad *f.*
hurl /hɜrl/ *v.* arrojar.
hurricane /ˈhɜrɪˌkein/ *n.* huracán *m.*
hurry /ˈhɜri/ *n.* **1.** prisa *f.* **to be in a h.,** tener prisa. —*v.* **2.** apresurar; darse prisa.
hurt /hɜrt/ *n.* **1.** daño, perjuicio *m.* —*v.* **2.** dañar; lastimar; doler; ofender.
hurtful /ˈhɜrtfəl/ *a.* perjudicial, dañino.
hurtle /ˈhɜrtl̩/ *v.* lanzar.
husband /ˈhʌzbənd/ *n.* marido, esposo *m.*
husk /hʌsk/ *n.* **1.** cáscara *f.* —*v.* **2.** descascarar.
husky /ˈhʌski/ *a.* fornido.
hustle /ˈhʌsəl/ *v.* empujar.
hustle and bustle ajetreo *m.*
hut /hʌt/ *n.* choza *f.*
hyacinth /ˈhaiəsɪnθ/ *n.* jacinto *m.*
hybrid /ˈhaibrɪd/ *a.* híbrido.
hydrangea /haiˈdreindʒə/ *n.* hortensia *f.*
hydraulic /haiˈdrɔlɪk/ *a.* hidráulico.
hydroelectric /ˌhaidrouɪˈlɛktrɪk/ *a.* hidroeléctrico.
hydrogen /ˈhaidrədʒən/ *n.* hidrógeno *m.*
hydrophobia /ˌhaidrəˈfoubiə/ *n.* hidrofobia. *f.*
hydroplane /ˈhaidrəˌplein/ *n.* hidroavión *m.*
hydrotherapy /ˌhaidrəˈθɛrəpi/ *n.* hidroterapia *f.*
hyena /haiˈinə/ *n.* hiena *f.*
hygiene /ˈhaidʒin/ *n.* higiene *f.*
hygienic /ˌhaidʒiˈɛnɪk/ *a.* higiénico.
hymn /hɪm/ *n.* himno *m.*
hymnal /ˈhɪmnl̩/ *n.* himnario *m.*
hype /haip/ *n.* *Colloq.* **1.** bomba publicitario *f.* —*v.* **2.** promocionar a bombo y platillo.
hypercritical /ˌhaipərˈkrɪtɪkəl/ *a.* hipercrítico.
hyperlink /ˈhaipərˌlɪŋk/ *n.* (Internet) hiperenlace *m.*
hypermarket /ˈhaipərˌmɑrkɪt/ *n.* hipermercado *m.*
hypertension /ˌhaipərˈtɛnʃən/ *n.* hipertensión *f.*

hypertext /'haipər,tɛkst/ n. (Internet) hipertexto m.
hyphen /'haifən/ n. guión m.
hyphenate /'haifə,neit/ v. separar con guión.
hypnosis /hip'nousis/ n. hipnosis f.
hypnotic /hip'nɒtik/ a. hipnótico.
hypnotism /'hipnə,tizəm/ n. hipnotismo m.
hypnotize /'hipnə,taiz/ v. hipnotizar.
hypochondria /,haipə'kɒndriə/ n. hipocondría f.
hypochondriac /,haipə'kɒndri,æk/ n. & a. hipocondríaco m.
hypocrisy /hi'pɒkrəsi/ n. hipocresía f.
hypocrite /'hipəkrit/ n. hipócrita m. & f.
hypocritical /,hipə'kritikəl/ a. hipócrita.
hypodermic /,haipə'dɜrmik/ a. hipodérmico.
hypotenuse /hai'pɒtn̩,us/ n. hipotenusa f.
hypothesis /hai'pɒθəsis/ n. hipótesis f.
hypothetical /,haipə'θɛtikəl/ a. hipotético.
hysterectomy /,histə'rɛktəmi/ n. histerectomía f.
hysteria /hi'stɛriə/ **hysterics** n. histeria f.
hysterical /hi'stɛrikəl/ a. histérico.

I

I /ai/ pron. yo.
iambic /ai'æmbik/ a. yámbico.
ice /ais/ n. hielo m.
iceberg /'aisbɜrg/ n. iceberg m.
icebox /'ais,bɒks/ n. refrigerador m.
ice cream helado, mantecado m.; **i.-c. cone**, barquillo de helado; **i.-c. parlor** heladería f.
ice cube cubito de hielo m.
ice skate patín de cuchilla m.
icon /'aikɒn/ n. icón m.
icy /'aisi/ a. helado; indiferente.
idea /ai'diə/ n. idea f.
ideal /ai'diəl/ a. ideal.
idealism /ai'diə,lizəm/ n. idealismo m.
idealist /ai'diəlist/ n. idealista m. & f.
idealistic /ai,diə'listik/ a. idealista.
idealize /ai'diə,laiz/ v. idealizar.
ideally /ai'diəli/ adv. idealmente.
identical /ai'dɛntikəl/ a. idéntico.
identifiable /ai,dɛnti'faiəbəl/ a. identificable.
identification /ai,dɛntəfi'keiʃən/ n. identificación f. **i. papers**, cédula de identidad f.
identify /ai'dɛntə,fai/ v. identificar.
identity /ai'dɛntiti/ n. identidad f.
ideology /,aidi'ɒlədʒi/ n. ideología f.
idiocy /'idiəsi/ n. idiotez f.
idiom /'idiəm/ n. modismo m.; idioma m.
idiot /'idiət/ n. idiota m. & f.
idiotic /,idi'ɒtik/ a. idiota, tonto.
idle /'aidl̩/ a. desocupado; perezoso.
idleness /'aidl̩nis/ n. ociosidad, pereza f.
idol /'aidl̩/ n. ídolo m.
idolatry /ai'dɒlətri/ n. idolatría f.
idolize /'aidl̩,aiz/ v. idolatrar.
idyl /'aidl̩/ n. idilio m.
idyllic /ai'dilik/ a. idílico.
if /if/ conj. si. **even if**, aunque.
ignite /ig'nait/ v. encender.
ignition /ig'niʃən/ n. ignición f.
ignoble /ig'noubəl/ a. innoble, indigno.
ignominious /,ignə'miniəs/ a. ignominioso.
ignoramus /,ignə'reiməs/ n. ignorante m.
ignorance /'ignərəns/ n. ignorancia f.
ignorant /'ignərənt/ a. ignorante. **to be i. of**, ignorar.
ignore /ig'nɔr/ v. desconocer, pasar por alto.

ill /il/ a. enfermo, malo.
illegal /i'ligəl/ a. ilegal.
illegible /i'lɛdʒəbəl/ a. ilegible.
illegibly /i'lɛdʒəbli/ a. ilegiblemente.
illegitimacy /,ili'dʒitəməsi/ n. ilegitimidad f.
illegitimate /,ili'dʒitəmit/ a. ilegítimo; desautorizado.
illicit /i'lisit/ a. ilícito.
illiteracy /i'litərəsi/ n. analfabetismo m.
illiterate /i'litərit/ a. & n. analfabeto -ta.
illness /'ilnis/ n. enfermedad, maldad f.
illogical /i'lɒdʒikəl/ a. ilógico.
illuminate /i'lumə,neit/ v. iluminar.
illumination /i,lumə'neiʃən/ n. iluminación f.
illusion /i'luʒən/ n. ilusión f.; ensueño m.
illusive /i'lusiv/ a. ilusivo.
illustrate /'ilə,streit/ v. ilustrar; ejemplificar.
illustration /,ilə'streiʃən/ n. ilustración f.; ejemplo; grabado m.
illustrative /i'lʌstrətiv/ a. ilustrativo.
illustrious /i'lʌstriəs/ a. ilustre.
ill will n. malevolencia f.
image /'imidʒ/ n. imagen, estatua f.
imagery /'imidʒri/ n. imaginación f.
imaginable /i'mædʒənəbəl/ a. imaginable.
imaginary /i'mædʒə,nɛri/ a. imaginario.
imagination /i,mædʒə'neiʃən/ n. imaginación f.
imaginative /i'mædʒənətiv/ a. imaginativo.
imagine /i'mædʒin/ v. imaginarse, figurarse.
imam /i'mɑm/ n. imán m.
imbecile /'imbəsil/ n. & a. imbécil m.
imitate /'imi,teit/ v. imitar.
imitation /,imi'teiʃən/ n. imitación f.
imitative /'imi,teitiv/ a. imitativo.
immaculate /i'mækyəlit/ a. inmaculado.
immanent /'imənənt/ a. inmanente.
immaterial /,imə'tiəriəl/ a. inmaterial; sin importancia.
immature /'imə'tʃur/ a. inmaturo.
immediate /i'midiit/ a. inmediato.
immediately /i'miditli/ adv. inmediatamente.
immense /i'mɛns/ a. inmenso.
immerse /i'mɜrs/ v. sumergir.
immigrant /'imigrənt/ n. & a. inmigrante m. & f.
immigrate /'imi,greit/ v. inmigrar.
imminent /'imənənt/ a. inminente.
immobile /i'moubəl/ a. inmóvil.
immoderate /i'mɒdərit/ a. inmoderado.
immodest /i'mɒdist/ a. inmodesto; atrevido.
immoral /i'mɔrəl/ a. inmoral.
immorality /,imə'ræliti/ n. inmoralidad f.
immorally /i'mɔrəli/ adv. licenciosamente.
immortal /i'mɔrtl̩/ a. inmortal.
immortality /,imɔr'tæliti/ n. inmortalidad f.
immortalize /i'mɔrtl̩,aiz/ v. inmortalizar.
immune /i'myun/ a. inmune.
immunity /i'myuniti/ n. inmunidad f.
immunize /'imyə,naiz/ v. inmunizar.
impact /'impækt/ n. impacto m.
impair /im'pɛər/ v. empeorar, perjudicar.
impale /im'peil/ v. empalar.
impart /im'pɑrt/ v. impartir, comunicar.
impartial /im'pɑrʃəl/ a. imparcial.
impatience /im'peiʃəns/ n. impaciencia f.
impatient /im'peiʃənt/ a. impaciente.
impede /im'pid/ v. impedir, estorbar.
impediment /im'pɛdəmənt/ n. impedimento m.
impel /im'pɛl/ v. impeler.

impenetrable /im'pɛnitrəbəl/ a. impenetrable.
impenitent /im'pɛnitənt/ n. & a. impenitente m.
imperative /im'pɛrətiv/ a. imperativo.
imperceptible /,impər'sɛptəbəl/ a. imperceptible.
imperfect /im'pɜrfikt/ a. imperfecto.
imperfection /,impər'fɛkʃən/ n. imperfección f.
imperial /im'piəriəl/ a. imperial.
imperialism /im'piəriə,lizəm/ n. imperialismo m.
imperious /im'piəriəs/ a. imperioso.
impersonal /im'pɜrsənl̩/ a. impersonal.
impersonate /im'pɜrsə,neit/ v. personificar; imitar.
impersonation /im,pɜrsə'neiʃən/ n. personificación f.; imitación f.
impertinence /im'pɜrtnəns/ n. impertinencia f.
impervious /im'pɜrviəs/ a. impermeable.
impetuous /im'pɛtʃuəs/ a. impetuoso.
impetus /'impitəs/ n. ímpetu m., impulso m.
impinge /im'pindʒ/ v. tropezar; infringir.
implacable /im'plækəbəl/ a. implacable.
implant /im'plænt/ v. implantar; inculcar.
implement /'impləmənt/ n. herramienta f.
implicate /'impli,keit/ v. implicar; embrollar.
implication /,impli'keiʃən/ n. inferencia f.; complicidad f.
implicit /im'plisit/ a. implícito.
implied /im'plaid/ a. implícito.
implore /im'plɔr/ v. implorar.
imply /im'plai/ v. significar; dar a entender.
impolite /,impə'lait/ a. descortés.
import /n. 'impɔrt; v. im'pɔrt/ n. **1.** importación f. —v. **2.** importar.
importance /im'pɔrtns/ n. importancia f.
important /im'pɔrtn̩t/ a. importante.
importation /,impɔr'teiʃən/ n. importación f.
importune /,impɔr'tun/ v. importunar.
impose /im'pouz/ v. imponer.
imposition /,impə'ziʃən/ n. imposición f.
impossibility /im,pɒsə'biliti/ n. imposibilidad f.
impossible /im'pɒsəbəl/ a. imposible.
impotence /'impətəns/ n. impotencia f.
impotent /'impətənt/ a. impotente.
impregnable /im'prɛgnəbəl/ a. impregnable.
impregnate /im'prɛgneit/ v. impregnar; fecundizar.
impresario /,imprə'sɑri,ou/ n. empresario m.
impress /im'prɛs/ v. impresionar.
impression /im'prɛʃən/ n. impresión f.
impressive /im'prɛsiv/ a. imponente.
imprison /im'prizən/ v. encarcelar.
imprisonment /im'prizənmənt/ n. prisión, encarcelación f.
improbable /im'prɒbəbəl/ a. improbable.
impromptu /im'prɒmptu/ a. extemporáneo.
improper /im'prɒpər/ a. impropio.
improve /im'pruv/ v. mejorar; progresar.
improvement /im'pruvmənt/ n. mejoramiento; progreso m.
improvise /'imprə,vaiz/ v. improvisar.
impudent /'impyədənt/ a. descarado.
impugn /im'pyun/ v. impugnar.
impulse /'impʌls/ n. impulso m.
impulsive /im'pʌlsiv/ a. impulsivo.

impunity /im'pyuniti/ n. impunidad f.
impure /im'pyur/ a. impuro.
impurity /im'pyuriti/ n. impureza f.; deshonestidad f.
impute /im'pyut/ v. imputar.
in /in/ prep. **1.** en; dentro de. —adv. **2.** adentro.
inadvertent /,inəd'vɜrtn̩t/ a. inadvertido.
inalienable /in'eilyənəbəl/ a. inalienable.
inane /i'nein/ a. mentecato.
inaugural /in'ɔgyərəl/ a. inaugural.
inaugurate /in'ɔgyə,reit/ v. inaugurar.
inauguration /in,ɔgyə'reiʃən/ n. inauguración f.
Inca /'iŋkə/ n. inca m.
incandescent /,inkən'dɛsənt/ a. incandescente.
incantation /,inkæn'teiʃən/ n. encantación f., conjuro m.
incapacitate /,inkə'pæsi,teit/ v. incapacitar.
incarcerate /in'kɑrsə,reit/ v. encarcelar.
incarnate /in'kɑrnit/ a. encarnado; personificado.
incarnation /,inkɑr'neiʃən/ n. encarnación f.
incendiary /in'sɛndi,ɛri/ a. incendiario.
incense /in'sɛns/ n. **1.** incienso m. —v. **2.** indignar.
incentive /in'sɛntiv/ n. incentivo m.
inception /in'sɛpʃən/ n. comienzo m.
incessant /in'sɛsənt/ a. incesante.
incest /'insɛst/ n. incesto m.
inch /intʃ/ n. pulgada f.
incidence /'insidəns/ n. incidencia f.
incident /'insidənt/ n. incidente m.
incidental /,insi'dɛntl̩/ a. incidental.
incidentally /,insi'dɛntl̩i/ adv. incidentalmente; entre paréntesis.
incinerate /in'sinə,reit/ v. incinerar.
incinerator /in'sinə,reitər/ n. incinerador m.
incipient /in'sipiənt/ a. incipiente.
incision /in'siʒən/ n. incisión f.; cortadura f.
incisive /in'saisiv/ a. incisivo; mordaz.
incisor /in'saizər/ n. incisivo m.
incite /in'sait/ v. incitar, instigar.
inclination /,inklə'neiʃən/ n. inclinación f.; declive m.
incline /n. 'inklain; v. in'klain/ n. **1.** pendiente m. —v. **2.** inclinar.
inclose /in'klouz/ v. incluir.
include /in'klud/ v. incluir, englobar.
including /in'kludiŋ/ prep. incluso.
inclusive /in'klusiv/ a. inclusivo.
incognito /,inkɒg'nitou/ n. & adv. incógnito m.
income /'inkʌm/ n. renta f.; ingresos m.pl.
income tax impuesto sobre la renta m.
incomparable /in'kɒmpərəbəl/ a. incomparable.
inconvenience /,inkən'vinyəns/ n. **1.** incomodidad f. —v. **2.** incomodar.
inconvenient /,inkən'vinyənt/ a. incómodo.
incorporate /in'kɔrpə,reit/ v. incorporar; dar cuerpo.
incorrigible /in'kɔridʒəbəl/ a. incorregible.
increase /in'kris/ v. crecer; aumentar.
incredible /in'krɛdəbəl/ a. increíble.
incredulity /,inkri'duliti/ n. incredulidad f.
incredulous /in'krɛdʒələs/ a. incrédulo.
increment /'inkrəmənt/ n. incremento m., aumento m.
incriminate /in'krimə,neit/ v. incriminar.
incrimination /in,krimə'neiʃən/ n. incriminación f.
incrust /in'krʌst/ v. incrustar.

incubator /'ɪnkyəˌbeitər/ n. incubadora f.

inculcate /ɪn'kʌlkeit/ v. inculcar.

incumbency /ɪn'kʌmbənsi/ n. incumbencia f.

incumbent /ɪn'kʌmbənt/ a. obligatorio; colocado sobre.

incur /ɪn'kɜr/ v. incurrir.

incurable /ɪn'kyurəbəl/ a. incurable.

indebted /ɪn'detɪd/ a. obligado; adeudado.

indeed /ɪn'did/ adv. verdaderamente, de veras. **no i.,** de ninguna manera.

indefatigable /ˌɪndɪ'fætɪgəbəl/ a. incansable.

indefinite /ɪn'defənɪt/ a. indefinido.

indefinitely /ɪn'defənɪtli/ adv. indefinidamente.

indelible /ɪn'deləbəl/ a. indeleble.

indemnify /ɪn'demnəˌfai/ v. indemnizar.

indemnity /ɪn'demnɪti/ n. indemnificación f.

indent /ɪn'dent/ n. **1.** diente f., mella f. —v. **2.** indentar, mellar.

indentation /ˌɪnden'teiʃən/ n. indentación f.

independence /ˌɪndɪ'pendəns/ n. independencia f.

independent /ˌɪndɪ'pendənt/ a. independiente.

in-depth /'ɪn 'depθ/ adj. en profundidad.

index /'ɪndeks/ n. índice m.; (of book) tabla f.

index card ficha f.

index finger dedo índice m.

India /'ɪndiə/ n. India f.

Indian /'ɪndiən/ a. & n. indio -dia.

indicate /'ɪndɪˌkeit/ v. indicar.

indication /ˌɪndɪ'keiʃən/ n. indicación f.

indicative /ɪn'dɪkətɪv/ a. & n. indicativo m.

indict /ɪn'dait/ v. encausar.

indictment /ɪn'daitmənt/ n. (law) sumaria; denuncia f.

indifference /ɪn'dɪfərəns/ n. indiferencia f.

indifferent /ɪn'dɪfərənt/ a. indiferente.

indigenous /ɪn'dɪdʒənəs/ a. indígena.

indigent /'ɪndɪdʒənt/ a. indigente, pobre.

indigestion /ˌɪndɪ'dʒestʃən/ n. indigestión f.

indignant /ɪn'dɪgnənt/ a. indignado.

indignation /ˌɪndɪg'neiʃən/ n. indignación f.

indignity /ɪn'dɪgnɪti/ n. indignidad f.

indirect /ˌɪndə'rekt/ a. indirecto.

indiscreet /ˌɪndɪ'skrit/ a. indiscreto.

indiscretion /ˌɪndɪ'skreʃən/ n. indiscreción f.

indiscriminate /ˌɪndɪ'skrɪmənɪt/ a. promiscuo.

indispensable /ˌɪndɪ'spensəbəl/ a. indispensable.

indisposed /ˌɪndɪ'spouzd/ a. indispuesto.

individual /ˌɪndə'vɪdʒuəl/ a. & n. individuo m.

individuality /ˌɪndəˌvɪdʒu'ælɪti/ n. individualidad f.

individually /ˌɪndə'vɪdʒuəli/ adv. individualmente.

indivisible /ˌɪndə'vɪzəbəl/ a. indivisible.

indoctrinate /ɪn'dɒktrəˌneit/ v. doctrinar, enseñar.

indolent /'ɪndlənt/ a. indolente.

indoor /'ɪnˌdɔr/ a. **1.** interior. **indoors** —adv. **2.** en casa; bajo techo.

indorse /ɪn'dɔrs/ v. endosar.

induce /ɪn'dus/ v. inducir, persuadir.

induct /ɪn'dʌkt/ v. instalar, iniciar.

induction /ɪn'dʌkʃən/ n. introducción f.; instalación f.

inductive /ɪn'dʌktɪv/ a. inductivo; introductor.

indulge /ɪn'dʌldʒ/ v. favorecer. **i. in,** entregarse a.

indulgence /ɪn'dʌldʒəns/ n. indulgencia f.

indulgent /ɪn'dʌldʒənt/ a. indulgente.

industrial /ɪn'dʌstriəl/ a. industrial.

industrialist /ɪn'dʌstriəlɪst/ n. industrial m.

industrial park polígono industrial m.

industrious /ɪn'dʌstriəs/ a. industrioso, trabajador.

industry /'ɪndəstri/ n. industria f.

inedible /ɪn'edəbəl/ a. incomible.

ineligible /ɪn'elɪdʒəbəl/ a. inelegible.

inept /ɪn'ept/ a. inepto.

inert /ɪn'ɜrt/ a. inerte.

inertia /ɪn'ɜrʃə/ n. inercia f.

inevitable /ɪn'evɪtəbəl/ a. inevitable.

inexpensive /ˌɪnɪk'spensɪv/ a. económico.

inexplicable /ɪn'eksplɪkəbəl/ a. inexplicable.

infallible /ɪn'fæləbəl/ a. infalible.

infamous /'ɪnfəməs/ a. infame.

infamy /'ɪnfəmi/ n. infamia f.

infancy /'ɪnfənsi/ n. infancia f.

infant /'ɪnfənt/ n. nene m.; criatura f.

infantile /'ɪnfən,tail/ a. infantil.

infantry /'ɪnfəntri/ n. infantería f.

infatuated /ɪn'fætʃuˌeitɪd/ a. infatuado.

infatuation /ɪnˌfætʃu'eiʃən/ n. encaprichamiento m.

infect /ɪn'fekt/ v. infectar.

infection /ɪn'fekʃən/ n. infección f.

infectious /ɪn'fekʃəs/ a. infeccioso.

infer /ɪn'fɜr/ v. inferir.

inference /'ɪnfərəns/ n. inferencia f.

inferior /ɪn'fɪəriər/ a. inferior.

infernal /ɪn'fɜrnl/ a. infernal.

inferno /ɪn'fɜrnou/ n. infierno m.

infest /ɪn'fest/ v. infestar.

infidel /'ɪnfɪdl/ n. **1.** infiel m. & f.; pagano -na. —a. **2.** infiel.

infidelity /ˌɪnfɪ'delɪti/ n. infidelidad f.

infiltrate /ɪn'fɪltreit/ v. infiltrar.

infinite /'ɪnfənɪt/ a. infinito.

infinitesimal /ˌɪnfɪnɪ'tesəməl/ a. infinitesimal.

infinitive /ɪn'fɪnɪtɪv/ n. & a. infinitivo m.

infinity /ɪn'fɪnɪti/ n. infinidad f.

infirm /ɪn'fɜrm/ a. enfermizo.

infirmary /ɪn'fɜrməri/ n. hospital m., enfermería f.

infirmity /ɪn'fɜrmɪti/ n. enfermedad f.

inflame /ɪn'fleim/ v. inflamar.

inflammable /ɪn'flæməbəl/ a. inflamable.

inflammation /ˌɪnflə'meiʃən/ n. inflamación f.

inflammatory /ɪn'flæməˌtɔri/ a. inflamante; Med. inflamatorio.

inflate /ɪn'fleit/ v. inflar.

inflation /ɪn'fleiʃən/ n. inflación f.

inflection /ɪn'flekʃən/ n. inflexión f.; (of the voice) modulación de la voz f.

inflict /ɪn'flɪkt/ v. infligir.

infliction /ɪn'flɪkʃən/ n. imposición f.

influence /'ɪnfluəns/ n. **1.** influencia f. —v. **2.** influir en.

influential /ˌɪnflu'enʃəl/ a. influyente.

influenza /ˌɪnflu'enzə/ n. gripe f.

influx /'ɪnˌflʌks/ n. afluencia f.

inform /ɪn'fɔrm/ v. informar. **i. oneself,** enterarse.

informal /ɪn'fɔrməl/ a. informal.

information /ˌɪnfər'meiʃən/ n. informaciones f.pl.

information technology n. informática f.

infrastructure /'ɪnfrəˌstrʌktʃər/ n. infraestructura f.

infringe /ɪn'frɪndʒ/ v. infringir.

infuriate /ɪn'fyuriˌeit/ v. enfurecer.

ingenious /ɪn'dʒinyəs/ a. ingenioso.

ingenuity /ˌɪndʒə'nuɪti/ n. ingeniosidad; destreza f.

ingredient /ɪn'gridiənt/ n. ingrediente m.

inhabit /ɪn'hæbɪt/ v. habitar.

inhabitant /ɪn'hæbɪtənt/ n. habitante m. & f.

inhale /ɪn'heil/ v. inhalar.

inherent /ɪn'hɪərənt/ a. inherente.

inherit /ɪn'herɪt/ v. heredar.

inheritance /ɪn'herɪtəns/ n. herencia f.

inhibit /ɪn'hɪbɪt/ v. inhibir.

inhibition /ˌɪnɪ'bɪʃən/ n. inhibición f.

inhuman /ɪn'hyumən/ a. inhumano.

inimical /ɪ'nɪmɪkəl/ a. hostil.

inimitable /ɪ'nɪmɪtəbəl/ a. inimitable.

iniquity /ɪ'nɪkwɪti/ n. iniquidad f.

initial /ɪ'nɪʃəl/ a. & n. inicial f.

initiate /ɪ'nɪʃiˌeit/ v. iniciar.

initiation /ɪˌnɪʃi'eiʃən/ n. iniciación f.

initiative /ɪ'nɪʃiətɪv/ n. iniciativa f.

inject /ɪn'dʒekt/ v. inyectar.

injection /ɪn'dʒekʃən/ n. inyección f.

injunction /ɪn'dʒʌŋkʃən/ n. mandato m.; (law) embargo m.

injure /'ɪndʒər/ v. herir; lastimar; ofender.

injurious /ɪn'dʒuriəs/ a. perjudicial.

injury /'ɪndʒəri/ n. herida; afrenta f.; perjuicio m.

injustice /ɪn'dʒʌstɪs/ n. injusticia f.

ink /ɪŋk/ n. tinta f.

inland /'ɪnlænd/ a. **1.** interior. —adv. **2.** tierra adentro.

inlet /'ɪnlet/ n. entrada f.; ensenada f.; estuario m.

inmate /'ɪnˌmeit/ n. residente m. & f.; (of a prison) preso -sa.

inn /ɪn/ n. posada f.; mesón m.

inner /'ɪnər/ a. interior. **i. tube,** cámara de aire.

innocence /'ɪnəsəns/ n. inocencia f.

innocent /'ɪnəsənt/ a. inocente.

innocuous /ɪ'nɒkyuəs/ a. innocuo.

innovation /ˌɪnə'veiʃən/ n. innovación f.

innuendo /ˌɪnyu'endou/ n. insinuación f.

innumerable /ɪ'numərəbəl/ a. innumerable.

inoculate /ɪ'nɒkyəˌleit/ v. inocular.

inoculation /ɪˌnɒkyə'leiʃən/ n. inoculación f.

input /'ɪnˌput/ n. aducto m., ingreso m., entrada f.

inquest /'ɪnkwest/ n. indagación f.

inquire /ɪn'kwaiər/ v. preguntar; inquirir.

inquiry /ɪn'kwaiəri/ n. pregunta; investigación f.

inquisition /ˌɪnkwə'zɪʃən/ n. escudriñamiento m.; (church) Inquisición f.

insane /ɪn'sein/ a. loco. **to go i.,** perder la razón; volverse loco.

insanity /ɪn'sænɪti/ n. locura f., demencia f.

inscribe /ɪn'skraib/ v. inscribir.

inscription /ɪn'skrɪpʃən/ n. inscripción; dedicatoria f.

insect /'ɪnsekt/ n. insecto m.

insecticide /ɪn'sektəˌsaid/ n. & a. insecticida m.

inseparable /ɪn'sepərəbəl/ a. inseparable.

insert /ɪn'sɜrt/ v. insertar, meter.

insertion /ɪn'sɜrʃən/ n. inserción f.

inside /ˌɪn'said/ a. & n. **1.** interior m. —adv. **2.** adentro, por dentro. **i. out,** al revés. —prep. **3.** dentro de.

insidious /ɪn'sɪdiəs/ a. insidioso.

insight /'ɪnˌsait/ n. perspicacia f.; comprensión f.

insignia /ɪn'sɪgniə/ n. insignias f.pl.

insignificance /ˌɪnsɪg'nɪfɪkəns/ n. insignificancia f.

insignificant /ˌɪnsɪg'nɪfɪkənt/ a. insignificante.

insinuate /ɪn'sɪnyuˌeit/ v. insinuar.

insinuation /ɪnˌsɪnyu'eiʃən/ n. insinuación f.

insipid /ɪn'sɪpɪd/ a. insípido.

insist /ɪn'sɪst/ v. insistir.

insistence /ɪn'sɪstəns/ n. insistencia f.

insistent /ɪn'sɪstənt/ a. insistente.

insolence /'ɪnsələns/ n. insolencia f.

insolent /'ɪnsələnt/ a. insolente.

insomnia /ɪn'sɒmniə/ n. insomnio m.

inspect /ɪn'spekt/ v. inspeccionar, examinar.

inspection /ɪn'spekʃən/ n. inspección f.

inspector /ɪn'spektər/ n. inspector -ora.

inspiration /ˌɪnspə'reiʃən/ n. inspiración f.

inspire /ɪn'spaiər/ v. inspirar.

install /ɪn'stɔl/ v. instalar.

installation /ˌɪnstə'leiʃən/ n. instalación f.

installment /ɪn'stɔlmənt/ n. plazo m.

instance /'ɪnstəns/ n. ocasión f. **for i.,** por ejemplo.

instant /'ɪnstənt/ a. & n. instante m.

instantaneous /ˌɪnstən'teiniəs/ a. instantáneo.

instant coffee café soluble m.

instantly /'ɪnstəntli/ adv. al instante.

instead /ɪn'sted/ adv. en lugar de eso. **i. of,** en vez de, en lugar de.

instigate /'ɪnstɪˌgeit/ v. instigar.

instill /ɪn'stɪl/ v. instilar.

instinct /'ɪnstɪŋkt/ n. instinto m. **by i.** por instinto.

instinctive /ɪn'stɪŋktɪv/ a. instintivo.

instinctively /ɪn'stɪŋktɪvli/ adv. por instinto.

institute /'ɪnstɪˌtut/ n. **1.** instituto m. —v. **2.** instituir.

institution /ˌɪnstɪ'tuʃən/ n. institución f.

instruct /ɪn'strʌkt/ v. instruir.

instruction /ɪn'strʌkʃən/ n. instrucción f.

instructive /ɪn'strʌktɪv/ a. instructivo.

instructor /ɪn'strʌktər/ n. instructor -ora.

instrument /'ɪnstrəmənt/ n. instrumento m.

instrumental /ˌɪnstrə'mentl/ a. instrumental.

insufficient /ˌɪnsə'fɪʃənt/ a. insuficiente.

insular /'ɪnsələr/ a. insular; estrecho de miras.

insulate /'ɪnsəˌleit/ v. aislar.

insulation /ˌɪnsə'leiʃən/ n. aislamiento m.

insulator /'ɪnsəˌleitər/ n. aislador m.

insulin /'ɪnsəlɪn/ n. insulina f.

insult /ɪn'sʌlt; -'sʌlt/ n. **1.** insulto m. —v. **2.** insultar.

insuperable /ɪn'supərəbəl/ a. insuperable.

insurance /ɪn'ʃurəns/ n. seguro m.

insure /ɪn'ʃur, -'ʃɜr/ v. asegurar.

insurgent /ɪn'sɜrdʒənt/ a. & n. insurgente m. & f.

insurrection /ˌɪnsə'rekʃən/ n. insurrección f.

intact /ɪn'tækt/ a. intacto.

intangible /ɪn'tændʒəbəl/ a. intangible, impalpable.

integral /'ɪntɪgrəl/ a. íntegro.

integrate /'ɪntɪˌgreit/ v. integrar.

integrity /ɪn'tegrɪti/ n. integridad f.

intellect /'ɪntlˌekt/ n. intelecto m.

intellectual /ˌɪntl'ektʃuəl/ a. & n. intelectual m. & f.

intelligence /ɪn'telɪdʒəns/ n. inteligencia f.

intelligence quotient /'kwouʃənt/ coeficiente intelectual m.

intelligent /ɪn'telɪdʒənt/ a. inteligente.

intelligible /ɪn'telɪdʒəbəl/ a. inteligible.

intend /ɪn'tend/ v. pensar; intentar; destinar.

intense /ɪn'tens/ a. intenso.

intensify /ɪn'tensəˌfai/ v. intensificar.

intensity /ɪn'tensɪti/ n. intensidad f.

intensive /ɪn'tensɪv/ a. intensivo.

intensive-care unit /ɪn'tensɪv'kɛər/ unidad de cuidados intensivos, unidad de vigilancia intensiva f.

intent /ɪn'tent/ n. intento m.

intention /ɪn'tɛnʃən/ *n.* intención *f.*

intentional /ɪn'tɛnʃənl̩/ *a.* intencional.

intercede /ˌɪntər'sid/ *v.* interceder.

intercept /ˌɪntər'sɛpt/ *v.* interceptar; detener.

interchange /ˌɪntər'tʃendʒ/ *v.* intercambiar.

interchangeable /ˌɪntər'tʃeindʒəbəl/ *a.* intercambiable.

intercourse /'ɪntərˌkɔrs/ *n.* tráfico *m.*; comunicación *f.*; coito *m.*

interest /'ɪntərɪst/ *n.* **1.** interés *m.* —*v.* **2.** interesar.

interesting /'ɪntərəstɪŋ/ *a.* interesante.

interest rate *n.* tipo de interés *m.*

interface /'ɪntərˌfeis/ *n.* interfaz.

interfere /ˌɪntər'fɪər/ *v.* entrometerse, intervenir. **i. with,** estorbar.

interference /ˌɪntər'fɪərəns/ *n.* intervención *f.*; obstáculo *m.*

interior /ɪn'tɪəriər/ *a.* interior.

interject /ˌɪntər'dʒɛkt/ *v.* interponer; intervenir.

interjection /ˌɪntər'dʒɛkʃən/ *n.* interjección *f.*; interposición *f.*

interlude /'ɪntərˌlud/ *n.* intervalo *m.*; *Theat.* intermedio *m.*; (music) interludio *m.*

intermediary /ˌɪntər'midiˌɛri/ *n.* intermediario -ria.

intermediate /ˌɪntər'midiˌeit/ *a.* intermedio.

interment /ɪn'tɜrmənt/ *n.* entierro.

intermission /ˌɪntər'mɪʃən/ *n.* intermisión *f.*; *Theat.* entreacto *m.*

intermittent /ˌɪntər'mɪtn̩t/ *a.* intermitente.

intern /ɪn'tɜrn/ *n.* **1.** interno -na, internado -da. —*v.* **2.** internar.

internal /ɪn'tɜrnl̩/ *a.* interno.

international /ˌɪntər'næʃənl̩/ *a.* internacional.

internationalism /ˌɪntər'næʃənl̩ˌɪzəm/ *n.* internacionalismo *m.*

Internet, the /'ɪntərˌnɛt/ *n.* el Internet *m.*

interpose /ˌɪntər'pouz/ *v.* interponer.

interpret /ɪn'tɜrprɪt/ *v.* interpretar.

interpretation /ɪnˌtɜrprɪ'teiʃən/ *n.* interpretación *f.*

interpreter /ɪn'tɜrprɪtər/ *n.* intérprete *m.* & *f.*

interrogate /ɪn'tɛrəˌgeit/ *v.* interrogar.

interrogation /ɪnˌtɛrə'geiʃən/ *n.* interrogación; pregunta *f.*

interrogative /ˌɪntə'rɒgətɪv/ *a.* interrogativo.

interrupt /ˌɪntə'rʌpt/ *v.* interrumpir.

interruption /ˌɪntə'rʌpʃən/ *n.* interrupción *f.*

intersect /ˌɪntər'sɛkt/ *v.* cortar.

intersection /ˌɪntər'sɛkʃən/ *n.* intersección *f.*; (street) bocacalle *f.*

intersperse /ˌɪntər'spɜrs/ *v.* entremezclar.

interval /'ɪntərvəl/ *n.* intervalo *m.*

intervene /ˌɪntər'vin/ *v.* intervenir.

intervention /ˌɪntər'vɛnʃən/ *n.* intervención *f.*

interview /'ɪntərˌvyu/ *n.* **1.** entrevista *f.* —*v.* **2.** entrevistar.

interviewer /'ɪntərˌvyuər/ *n.* entrevistador -ora *m.* & *f.*

intestine /ɪn'tɛstɪn/ *n.* intestino *m.*

intimacy /'ɪntəməsi/ *n.* intimidad; familiaridad *f.*

intimate /'ɪntəmɪt/ *a.* **1.** íntimo, familiar. —*n.* **2.** amigo -ga íntimo -ma. —*v.* **3.** insinuar.

intimidate /ɪn'tɪmɪˌdeit/ *v.* intimidar.

intimidation /ɪnˌtɪmɪ'deiʃən/ *n.* intimidación *f.*

into /'ɪntu; *unstressed* -tʊ, -tə/ *prep.* en, dentro de.

intonation /ˌɪntou'neiʃən/ *n.* entonación *f.*

intone /ɪn'toun/ *v.* entonar.

intoxicate /ɪn'tɒksɪˌkeit/ *v.* embriagar.

intoxication /ɪnˌtɒksɪ'keiʃən/ *n.* embriaguez *f.*

intravenous /ˌɪntrə'vinəs/ *a.* intravenoso.

intrepid /ɪn'trɛpɪd/ *a.* intrépido.

intricacy /'ɪntrɪkəsi/ *n.* complejidad *f.*; enredo *m.*

intricate /'ɪntrɪkɪt/ *a.* intrincado; complejo.

intrigue /ɪn'trig; *n. also* 'ɪntrig/ *n.* **1.** intriga *f.* —*v.* **2.** intrigar.

intrinsic /ɪn'trɪnsɪk/ *a.* intrínseco.

introduce /ˌɪntrə'dus/ *v.* introducir; (a person) presentar.

introduction /ˌɪntrə'dʌkʃən/ *n.* presentación; introducción *f.*

introductory /ˌɪntrə'dʌktəri/ *a.* introductor; preliminar. **i. offer,** ofrecimiento de presentación *m.*

introvert /'ɪntrəˌvɜrt/ *n.* & *a.* introvertido -da.

intrude /ɪn'trud/ *v.* entremeterse.

intruder /ɪn'trudər/ *n.* intruso -sa.

intuition /ˌɪntu'ɪʃən/ *n.* intuición *f.*

intuitive /ɪn'tuɪtɪv/ *a.* intuitivo.

inundate /'ɪnənˌdeit/ *v.* inundar.

invade /ɪn'veid/ *v.* invadir.

invader /ɪn'veidər/ *n.* invasor -ra.

invalid /ɪn'vælɪd/ *a.* & *n.* inválido -da.

invariable /ɪn'vɛəriəbəl/ *a.* invariable.

invasion /ɪn'veiʒən/ *n.* invasión *f.*

invective /ɪn'vɛktɪv/ *n.* **1.** invectiva *f.* —*a.* **2.** ultrajante.

inveigle /ɪn'veigəl/ *v.* seducir.

invent /ɪn'vɛnt/ *v.* inventar.

invention /ɪn'vɛnʃən/ *n.* invención *f.*

inventive /ɪn'vɛntɪv/ *a.* inventivo.

inventor /ɪn'vɛntər/ *n.* inventor -ra.

inventory /'ɪnvənˌtɔri/ *n.* inventario *m.*

invertebrate /ɪn'vɜrtəbrɪt/ *n.* & *a.* invertebrado *m.*

invest /ɪn'vɛst/ *v.* investir; *Com.* invertir.

investigate /ɪn'vɛstɪˌgeit/ *v.* investigar.

investigation /ɪnˌvɛstɪ'geiʃən/ *n.* investigación *f.*

investment /ɪn'vɛstmənt/ *n.* inversión *f.*

investor /ɪn'vɛstər/ *n.* inversor, -ra.

inveterate /ɪn'vɛtərɪt/ *a.* inveterado.

invidious /ɪn'vɪdiəs/ *a.* abominable, odioso, injusto.

invigorate /ɪn'vɪgəˌreit/ *v.* vigorizar, fortificar.

invincible /ɪn'vɪnsəbəl/ *a.* invencible.

invisible /ɪn'vɪzəbəl/ *a.* invisible.

invitation /ˌɪnvɪ'teiʃən/ *n.* invitación *f.*

invite /ɪn'vait/ *v.* invitar, convidar.

invocation /ˌɪnvə'keiʃən/ *n.* invocación *f.*

invoice /'ɪnvɔis/ *n.* factura *f.*

invoke /ɪn'vouk/ *v.* invocar.

involuntary /ɪn'vɒlənˌtɛri/ *a.* involuntario.

involve /ɪn'vɒlv/ *v.* envolver; implicar.

involved /ɪn'vɒlvd/ *a.* complicado.

invulnerable /ɪn'vʌlnərəbəl/ *a.* invulnerable.

inward /'ɪnwərd/ *adv.* hacia adentro.

inwardly /'ɪnwərdli/ *adv.* interiormente.

iodine /'aiəˌdain/ *n.* iodo *m.*

IQ *abbr.* CI (coeficiente intelectual) *m.*

irate /ai'reit/ *a.* encolerizado.

Ireland /'aiᵊrlənd/ *n.* Irlanda *f.*

iris /'airɪs/ *n.* *Anat.* iris *m.*; (botany) flor de lis *f.*

Irish /'airɪʃ/ *a.* irlandés.

irk /ɜrk/ *v.* fastidiar.

iron /'aiərn/ *n.* **1.** hierro *m.*; (appliance) plancha *f.* —*v.* **2.** planchar.

ironical /ai'rɒnɪkəl/ *a.* irónico.

ironing board /'aiərnɪŋ/ tabla de planchar *f.*

irony /'airəni/ *n.* ironía *f.*

irrational /ɪ'ræʃənl̩/ *a.* irracional; ilógico.

irregular /ɪ'rɛgyələr/ *a.* irregular.

irregularity /ɪˌrɛgyə'lærɪti/ *n.* irregularidad *f.*

irrelevant /ɪ'rɛləvənt/ *a.* ajeno.

irresistible /ˌɪrɪ'zɪstəbəl/ *a.* irresistible.

irresponsible /ˌɪrɪ'spɒnsəbəl/ *a.* irresponsable.

irreverent /ɪ'rɛvərənt/ *a.* irreverente.

irrevocable /ɪ'rɛvəkəbəl/ *a.* irrevocable.

irrigate /'ɪrɪˌgeit/ *v.* regar; *Med.* irrigar.

irrigation /ˌɪrɪ'geiʃən/ *n.* riego *m.*

irritability /ˌɪrɪtə'bɪlɪti/ *n.* irritabilidad *f.*

irritable /'ɪrɪtəbəl/ *a.* irritable.

irritant /'ɪrɪtn̩t/ *n.* & *a.* irritante *m.*

irritate /'ɪrɪˌteit/ *v.* irritar.

irritation /ˌɪrɪ'teiʃən/ *n.* irritación *f.*

island /'ailənd/ *n.* isla *f.*

isolate /'aisəˌleit/ *v.* aislar.

isolation /ˌaisə'leiʃən/ *n.* aislamiento *m.*

isosceles /ai'sɒsəˌliz/ *a.* isósceles.

issuance /'ɪʃuəns/ *n.* emisión *f.*; publicación *f.*

issue /'ɪʃu/ *n.* **1.** emisión; edición; progenie *f.*; número *m.*; punto en disputa. —*v.* **2.** emitir; publicar.

isthmus /'ɪsməs/ *n.* istmo *m.*

it /ɪt/ *pron.* ello; él, ella; lo, la.

Italian /ɪ'tælyən/ *a.* & *n.* italiano -na.

Italy /'ɪtl̩i/ *n.* Italia *f.*

itch /ɪtʃ/ *n.* **1.** picazón *f.* —*v.* **2.** picar.

item /'aitəm/ *n.* artículo; detalle *m.*; inserción *f.*; *Com.* renglón *m.*

itemize /'aitəˌmaiz/ *v.* detallar.

itinerant /ai'tɪnərənt/ *n.* **1.** viandante *m.* —*a.* **2.** ambulante.

itinerary /ai'tɪnəˌrɛri/ *n.* itinerario *m.*

its /ɪts/ *a.* su.

itself /ɪt'sɛlf/ *pron.* sí; se.

ivory /'aivəri/ *n.* marfil *m.*

ivy /'aivi/ *n.* hiedra *f.*

J

jab /dʒæb/ *n.* **1.** pinchazo *m.* —*v.* **2.** pinchar.

jack /dʒæk/ *n.* (for lifting) gato *m.*; (cards) sota *f.*

jackal /'dʒækəl/ *n.* chacal *m.*

jackass /'dʒækˌæs/ *n.* asno *m.*

jacket /'dʒækɪt/ *n.* chaqueta *f.*; saco *m.*

jack-of-all-trades /'dʒæk əv 'ɔl 'treidz/ *n.* estuche *m.*

jade /dʒeid/ *n.* (horse) rocín *m.*; (woman) picarona *f.*; (mineral) jade *m.*

jaded /'dʒeidɪd/ *a.* rendido.

jagged /'dʒægɪd/ *a.* mellado.

jaguar /'dʒægwɑr/ *n.* jaguar *m.*

jail /dʒeil/ *n.* cárcel *f.*

jailer /'dʒeilər/ *n.* carcelero *m.*

jam /dʒæm/ *n.* **1.** conserva *f.*; aprieto, apretón *m.* —*v.* **2.** apiñar, apretar; trabar.

janitor /'dʒænɪtər/ *n.* portero *m.*

January /'dʒænyuˌɛri/ *n.* enero *m.*

Japan /dʒə'pæn/ *n.* Japón *m.*

Japanese /ˌdʒæpə'niz/ *a.* & *n.* japonés -esa.

jar /dʒɑr/ *n.* **1.** jarro *m.* —*v.* **2.** chocar; agitar.

jargon /'dʒɑrgən/ *n.* jerga *f.*

jasmine /'dʒæzmɪn/ *n.* jazmín *m.*

jaundice /'dʒɔndɪs/ *n.* ictericia *f.*

jaunt /dʒɔnt/ *n.* paseo *m.*

javelin /'dʒævlɪn/ *n.* jabalina *f.*

jaw /dʒɔ/ *n.* quijada *f.*

jay /dʒei/ *n.* grajo *m.*

jazz /dʒæz/ *n.* jazz *m.*

jealous /'dʒɛləs/ *a.* celoso. **to be j.,** tener celos.

jealousy /'dʒɛləsi/ *n.* celos *m.pl.*

jeans /dʒinz/ *n.* vaqueros, tejanos *m.pl.*

jeer /dʒɪər/ *n.* **1.** burla *f.*, mofa *f.* —*v.* **2.** burlar, mofar.

jelly /'dʒɛli/ *n.* jalea *f.*

jellyfish /'dʒɛliˌfɪʃ/ *n.* aguamar *m.*

jeopardize /'dʒɛpərˌdaiz/ *v.* arriesgar.

jeopardy /'dʒɛpərdi/ *n.* riesgo *m.*

jerk /dʒɜrk/ *n.* **1.** sacudida *f.* —*v.* **2.** sacudir.

jerky /'dʒɜrki/ *a.* espasmódico.

Jerusalem /dʒɪ'rusələm/ *n.* Jerusalén *m.*

jest /dʒɛst/ *n.* **1.** broma *f.* —*v.* **2.** bromear.

jester /'dʒɛstər/ *n.* bufón -ona; burlón -ona.

Jesuit /'dʒɛʒuɪt/ *a.* & *n.* jesuita *m.*

Jesus Christ /'dʒizəs 'kraist/ *n.* Jesucristo *m.*

jet /dʒɛt/ *n.* chorro *m.*; (gas) mechero *m.*

jet lag *n.* defase horario *m.*, inadaptación horaria *f.*

jetsam /'dʒɛtsəm/ *n.* echazón *f.*

jettison /'dʒɛtəsən/ *v.* echar al mar.

jetty /'dʒɛti/ *n.* muelle *m.*

Jew /dʒu/ *n.* judío -día.

jewel /'dʒuəl/ *n.* joya *f.*

jeweler /'dʒuələr/ *n.* joyero -ra.

jewelry /'dʒuəlri/ *n.* joyas *f.pl.* **j. store,** joyería *f.*

Jewish /'dʒuɪʃ/ *a.* judío.

jib /dʒɪb/ *n.* *Naut.* foque *m.*

jiffy /'dʒɪfi/ *n.* instante *m.*

jig /dʒɪg/ *n.* jiga *f.* **j-saw,** sierra de vaivén *f.*

jilt /dʒɪlt/ *v.* dar calabazas.

jingle /'dʒɪŋgəl/ *n.* **1.** retintín *m.*; rima pueril *f.* —*v.* **2.** retiñir.

jinx /dʒɪŋks/ *n.* **1.** aojo *m.* —*v.* **2.** aojar.

jittery /'dʒɪtəri/ *a.* nervioso.

job /dʒɒb/ *n.* empleo *m.*

jobber /'dʒɒbər/ *n.* destajista *m.* & *f.*, corredor *m.*

jockey /'dʒɒki/ *n.* jockey *m.*

jocular /'dʒɒkyələr/ *a.* jocoso.

jog /dʒɒg/ *n.* empujoncito *m.* *v.* empujar; estimular. **j. along,** ir a un trote corto.

join /dʒɔin/ *v.* juntar; unir.

joiner /'dʒɔinər/ *n.* ebanista *m.*

joint /dʒɔint/ *n.* juntura *f.*

jointly /'dʒɔintli/ *adv.* conjuntamente.

joke /dʒouk/ *n.* **1.** broma, chanza *f.*; chiste *m.* —*v.* **2.** bromear.

joker /'dʒoukər/ *n.* bromista *m.* & *f.*; comodín *m.*

jolly /'dʒɒli/ *a.* alegre, jovial.

jolt /dʒoult/ *n.* **1.** sacudido *m.* —*v.* **2.** sacudir.

jonquil /'dʒɒŋkwɪl/ *n.* junquillo *m.*

jostle /'dʒɒsəl/ *v.* empujar.

journal /'dʒɜrnl̩/ *n.* diario *m.*; revista *f.*

journalism /'dʒɜrnl̩ˌɪzəm/ *n.* periodismo *m.*

journalist /'dʒɜrnl̩ɪst/ *n.* periodista *m.* & *f.*

journey /'dʒɜrni/ *n.* **1.** viaje *m.*; jornada *f.* —*v.* **2.** viajar.

journeyman /'dʒɜrnimən/ *n.* jornalero *m.*, oficial *m.*

jovial /'dʒouviəl/ *a.* jovial.

jowl /dʒaul/ *n.* carrillo *m.*

joy /dʒɔi/ *n.* alegría *f.*

joyful /'dʒɔifəl/ **joyous** *a.* alegre, gozoso.

jubilant /'dʒubələnt/ *a.* jubiloso.

jubilee /'dʒubəˌli/ *n.* jubileo *m.*

Judaism /'dʒudiˌɪzəm/ *n.* judaísmo *m.*

judge /dʒʌdʒ/ *n.* **1.** juez *m.* & *f.* —*v.* **2.** juzgar.

judgment /'dʒʌddʒmənt/ *n.* juicio *m.*

judicial /dʒu'dɪʃəl/ *a.* judicial.

judiciary /dʒu'dɪʃiˌɛri/ *a.* judiciario.

judicious /dʒu'dɪʃəs/ *a.* juicioso.

jug /dʒʌg/ *n.* jarro *m.*

juggle /'dʒʌgəl/ *v.* escamotear.

juice /dʒus/ *n.* jugo, zumo *m.*

juicy /'dʒusi/ *a.* jugoso.

July /dʒu'lai/ *n.* julio *m.*

jumble /'dʒʌmbəl/ *n.* **1.** revoltillo *m.* —*v.* **2.** arrebujar, revolver.

jump /dʒʌmp/ *n.* **1.** salto *m.* —*v.* **2.** saltar, brincar.

junction /'dʒʌŋkʃən/ n. confluencia f.; (railway) empalme m.
juncture /'dʒʌŋktʃər/ n. juntura f.; coyuntura f.
June /dʒun/ n. junio m.
jungle /'dʒʌŋgəl/ n. jungla, selva f.
junior /'dʒunyər/ a. menor; más joven. **Jr.**, hijo.
juniper /'dʒunəpər/ n. enebro m.
junk /dʒʌŋk/ n. basura f.
junket /'dʒʌŋkɪt/ n. **1.** leche cuajada f. —v. **2.** festejar.
junkie /'dʒʌŋki/ n. Colloq. yonqui m. & f., toxicómano -na.
junk mail n. porpaganda indeseada f., correo basura m.
jurisdiction /,dʒʊrɪs'dɪkʃən/ n. jurisdicción f.
jurisprudence /,dʒʊrɪs'prudns/ n. jurisprudencia f.
jurist /'dʒʊrɪst/ n. jurista m. & f.
juror /'dʒʊrər/ n. jurado -da.
jury /'dʒʊri/ n. jurado m.
just /dʒʌst/ a. **1.** justo; exacto. —adv. **2.** exactamente; (only) sólo. **j. now**, ahora mismo. **to have j.**, acabar de.
justice /'dʒʌstɪs/ n. justicia f.; (person) juez m. & f.
justifiable /'dʒʌstə,faiəbəl/ a. justificable.
justification /,dʒʌstəfɪ'keiʃən/ n. justificación f.
justify /'dʒʌstə,fai/ v. justificar.
jut /dʒʌt/ v. sobresalir.
jute /dʒut/ n. yute m.
juvenile /'dʒuvənəl/ a. juvenil.
juvenile delinquency delincuencia de menores, delincuencia juvenil f.

K

kaleidoscope /kə'laidə,skoup/ n. calidoscopio m.
kangaroo /,kæŋgə'ru/ n. canguro m.
karakul /'kærəkəl/ n. caracul m.
karat /'kærət/ n. quilate m.
karate /kə'rati/ n. karate m.
keel /kil/ n. **1.** quilla f. —v. **2. to k. over**, volcarse.
keen /kin/ a. agudo; penetrante.
keep /kip/ v. mantener, retener; guardar; preservar. **k. on**, seguir, continuar.
keeper /'kipər/ n. guardián m.
keepsake /'kip,seik/ n. recuerdo m.
keg /kɛg/ n. barrilito m.
kennel /'kɛnl/ n. perrera f.
kerchief /'kɜrtʃɪf/ n. pañuelo m.
kernel /'kɜrnl/ n. pepita f.; grano m.
kerosene /'kɛrə,sin/ n. kerosén m.
ketchup /'kɛtʃəp/ n. salsa de tomate f.
kettle /'kɛtl/ n. caldera, olla f.
kettledrum /'kɛtl,drʌm/ n. tímpano m.
key /ki/ n. llave f.; (music) clave f.; (piano) tecla f.
keyboard /'ki,bɔrd/ n. teclado m.
keyhole /'ki,houl/ n. bocallave f.
keypad /'ki,pæd/ n. teclado m.
khaki /'kæki/ a. caqui.
kick /kɪk/ n. **1.** patada f. —v. **2.** patear; Colloq. quejarse.
kid /kɪd/ n. **1.** cabrito m.; Colloq. niño -ña, chico -ca. —v. **2.** Colloq. bromear.
kidnap /'kɪdnæp/ v. secuestrar.
kidnaper /'kɪdnæpər/ n. secuestrador -ora.
kidnaping /'kɪdnæpɪŋ/ n. rapto, secuestro m.
kidney /'kɪdni/ n. riñón m.
kidney bean n. frijol m.
kill /kɪl/ v. matar.
killer /'kɪlər/ n. matador -ora.
killjoy /'kɪldʒɔi/ n. aguafiestas m. & f.
kiln /kɪl/ n. horno m.
kilogram /'kɪlə,græm/ n. kilogramo m.
kilohertz /'kɪlə,hɜrts/ n. kilohercio m.
kilometer /kɪ'lɒmɪtər/ n. kilómetro m.

kilowatt /'kɪlə,wɒt/ n. kilovatio m.
kin /kɪn/ n. parentesco m.; parientes m.pl.
kind /kaind/ a. **1.** bondadoso, amable. —n. **2.** género m.; clase f. **k. of**, algo, un poco.
kindergarten /'kɪndər,gɑrtn/ n. kindergarten m.
kindle /'kɪndl/ v. encender.
kindling /'kɪndlɪŋ/ n. encendimiento m. **k.-wood**, leña menuda f.
kindly /'kaindli/ a. bondadoso.
kindness /'kaindnɪs/ n. bondad f.
kindred /'kɪndrɪd/ n. parentesco m.
kinetic /kɪ'nɛtɪk/ a. cinético.
king /kɪŋ/ n. rey m.
kingdom /'kɪŋdəm/ n. reino m.
king prawn langostino m.
kink /kɪŋk/ n. retorcimiento m.
kinky /'kɪŋki/ a. Colloq. pervertidillo; (hair) rizado.
kiosk /'kiɒsk/ n. kiosco m.
kiss /kɪs/ n. **1.** beso m. —v. **2.** besar.
kitchen /'kɪtʃən/ n. cocina f.
kite /kait/ n. cometa f.
kitten /'kɪtn/ n. gatito -ta.
kleptomania /,klɛptə'meiniə/ n. cleptomanía f.
kleptomaniac /,klɛptə'meiniæk/ n. cleptómano -na.
klutz /klʌts/ n. Colloq. torpe, patoso -sa.
knack /næk/ n. don m., destreza f.
knapsack /'næp,sæk/ n. alforja f.
knead /nid/ v. amasar.
knee /ni/ n. rodilla f.
kneecap /'ni,kæp/ n. rodillera, rótula f.
kneel /nil/ v. arrodillarse.
knickers /'nɪkərz/ n. calzón corto m., pantalones m.pl.
knife /naif/ n. cuchillo m.
knight /nait/ n. caballero m.; (chess) caballo m.
knit /nɪt/ v. tejer.
knob /nɒb/ n. tirador m.
knock /nɒk/ n. **1.** golpe m.; llamada f. —v. **2.** golpear; tocar, llamar.
knot /nɒt/ n. **1.** nudo; lazo m. —v. **2.** anudar.
knotty /'nɒti/ a. nudoso.
know /nou/ v. saber; (a person) conocer.
knowledge /'nɒlɪdʒ/ n. conocimiento, saber m.
knuckle /'nʌkəl/ n. nudillo m. **k. bone**, jarrete m. **to k. under**, ceder a.
Koran /kə'ran/ n. Corán m.
Korea /kə'riə/ n. Corea f.
Korean /kə'riən/ a. & n. coreano.

L

label /'leibəl/ n. **1.** rótulo m. —v. **2.** rotular; designar.
labor /'leibər/ n. **1.** trabajo m.; la clase obrera. —v. **2.** trabajar.
laboratory /'læbrə,tɔri/ n. laboratorio m.
laborer /'leibərər/ n. trabajador, obrero m.
laborious /lə'bɔriəs/ a. laborioso, difícil.
labor union gremio obrero, sindicato m.
labyrinth /'læbərɪnθ/ n. laberinto m.
lace /leis/ n. **1.** encaje m.; (of shoe) lazo m. —v. **2.** amarrar.
lacerate /'læsə,reit/ v. lacerar, lastimar.
laceration /,læsə'reiʃən/ n. laceración f., desgarro m.
lack /læk/ n. **1.** falta f. **l. of respect**, desacato m. —v. **2.** faltar, carecer.
lackadaisical /,lækə'deizikəl/ a. indiferente; soñador.
laconic /lə'kɒnɪk/ a. lacónico.
lacquer /'lækər/ n. **1.** laca f., barniz m. —v. **2.** laquear, barnizar.
lactic /'læktɪk/ a. láctico.
lactose /'læktous/ n. lactosa f.
ladder /'lædər/ n. escalera f.

ladle /'leidl/ n. **1.** cucharón m. —v. **2.** servir con cucharón.
lady /'leidi/ n. señora, dama f.
ladybug /'leidi,bʌg/ n. mariquita f.
lag /læg/ n. **1.** retraso m. —v. **2.** quedarse atrás.
lagoon /lə'gun/ n. laguna f.
laid-back /'leid 'bæk/ a. de buen talante, ecuánime, pacífico.
laity /'leiɪti/ n. laicado m.
lake /leik/ n. lago m.
lamb /læm/ n. cordero m.
lame /leim/ a. **1.** cojo; estropeado. —v. **2.** estropear, lisiar; incapacitar.
lament /lə'mɛnt/ n. **1.** lamento m. —v. **2.** lamentar.
lamentable /lə'mɛntəbəl/ a. lamentable.
lamentation /,læmən'teiʃən/ n. lamento m.; lamentación f.
laminate /'læmə,neit/ a. laminado. v. laminar.
lamp /læmp/ n. lámpara f.
lampoon /læm'pun/ n. **1.** pasquín m. —v. **2.** pasquinar.
lance /læns/ n. **1.** lanza f. —v. **2.** Med. abrir.
land /lænd/ n. **1.** país m.; tierra f. **native l.**, patria f. —v. **2.** desembarcar; (plane) aterrizar.
landholder /'lænd,houldər/ n. hacendado -da.
landing /'lændɪŋ/ n. (of stairs) descanso, descansillo m.; (ship) desembarcadero m.; (airplane) aterrizaje m.
landlady /'lænd,leidi/ **landlord** n. propietario -ria.
landmark /'lænd,mɑrk/ n. mojón m., señal f.; rasgo sobresaliente m.
landscape /'lænd,skeip/ n. paisaje m.
landslide /'lænd,slaid/ n. derrumbe m.
lane /lein/ n. senda f.
language /'læŋgwɪdʒ/ n. lengua f., idioma; lenguaje m.
languid /'læŋgwɪd/ a. lánguido.
languish /'læŋgwɪʃ/ v. languidecer.
languor /'læŋgər/ n. languidez f.
lanky /'læŋki/ a. larguirucho; desgarbado.
lanolin /'lænlɪn/ n. lanolina f.
lantern /'læntərn/ n. linterna f.; farol m.
lap /læp/ n. **1.** regazo m.; falda f. —v. **2.** lamer.
lapel /lə'pɛl/ n. solapa f.
lapse /læps/ n. **1.** lapso m. —v. **2.** pasar; decaer; caer en error.
laptop computer /'læp,tɒp/ ordenador portátil m.
larceny /'lɑrsəni/ n. ratería f.
lard /lɑrd/ n. manteca de cerdo f.
large /lɑrdʒ/ a. grande.
largely /'lɑrdʒli/ adv. ampliamente; mayormente; muy.
largo /'lɑrgou/ n. & a. Mus. largo m.
lariat /'læriət/ n. lazo m.
lark /lɑrk/ n. (bird) alondra f.
larva /'lɑrvə/ n. larva f.
laryngitis /,lærən'dʒaitɪs/ n. laringitis f.
larynx /'lærɪŋks/ n. laringe f.
lascivious /lə'sɪviəs/ a. lascivo.
laser /'leizər/ n. láser m.
lash /læʃ/ n. **1.** azote, latigazo m. —v. **2.** azotar.
lass /læs/ n. doncella f.
lassitude /'læsɪ,tud/ n. lasitud f.
lasso /'læsou/ n. **1.** lazo m. —v. **2.** enlazar.
last /læst/ a. **1.** pasado; (final) último. **at l.**, por fin. **l. but one**, penúltimo. **l. but two**, antepenútimo. —v. **2.** durar.
lasting /'læstɪŋ/ a. duradero.
latch /lætʃ/ n. aldaba f.
late /leit/ a. **1.** tardío; (deceased) difunto. **to be l.**, llegar tarde. —adv. **2.** tarde.
lately /'leitli/ adv. recientemente.
latent /'leitnt/ a. latente.
lateral /'lætərəl/ a. lateral.
lather /'læðər/ n. **1.** espuma de jabón. —v. **2.** enjabonar.

Latin /'lætn/ n. latín m.
Latin America /ə'mɛrikə/ Hispanoamérica, América Latina f.
Latin American hispanoamericano -na.
latitude /'lætɪ,tud/ n. latitud f.
latrine /lə'trin/ n. letrina f.
latter /'lætər/ a. posterior. **the l.**, éste.
lattice /'lætɪs/ n. celosía f.
laud /lɔd/ v. loar.
laudable /'lɔdəbəl/ a. laudable.
laudanum /'lɔdnəm/ n. láudano m.
laudatory /'lɔdə,tori/ a. laudatorio.
laugh /læf/ n. **1.** risa, risotada f. —v. **2.** reír. **l. at**, reírse de.
laughable /'læfəbəl/ a. risible.
laughter /'læftər/ n. risa f.
launch /lɔntʃ/ n. **1.** Naut. lancha f. —v. **2.** lanzar.
launder /'lɔndər/ v. lavar y planchar la ropa.
laundry /'lɔndri/ n. lavandería f.
laundryman /'lɔndri,mæn/ n. lavandero -ra.
laureate /'lɔriɪt/ n. & a. laureado -da.
laurel /'lɔrəl/ n. laurel m.
lava /'lɑvə/ n. lava f.
lavatory /'lævə,tori/ n. lavatorio m.
lavender /'lævəndər/ n. lavándula f.
lavish /'lævɪʃ/ a. **1.** pródigo. —v. **2.** prodigar.
law /lɔ/ n. ley f.; derecho m.
lawful /'lɔfəl/ a. legal.
lawless /'lɔlɪs/ a. sin ley.
lawn /lɔn/ n. césped; prado m.
lawn mower /'mouər/ n. cortacésped m. & f.
lawsuit /'lɔ,sut/ n. pleito m.
lawyer /'lɔyər/ n. abogado m. & f.
lax /læks/ a. flojo, laxo.
laxative /'læksətɪv/ n. purgante m.
laxity /'læksɪti/ n. laxidad f.; flojedad f.
lay /lei/ v. **1.** secular. —v. **2.** poner.
layer /'leiər/ n. capa f.
layman /'leimən/ n. lego, seglar m.
lazy /'leizi/ a. perezoso.
lead /lɛd , lid/ n. **1.** plomo m.; Theat. papel principal. **to take the l.**, tomar la delantera. —v. **2.** conducir; dirigir.
leaden /'lɛdn/ a. plomizo; pesado; abatido.
leader /'lidər/ n. líder m. & f.; jefe m. & f.; director -ora.
leadership /'lidər,ʃɪp/ n. dirección f.
leaf /lif/ n. hoja f.
leaflet /'liflɪt/ n. Bot. hojilla f.; folleto m.
league /lig/ n. liga; (measure) legua f.
leak /lik/ n. **1.** escape; goteo m. —v. **2.** gotear; Naut. hacer agua.
leakage /'likɪdʒ/ n. goteo m., escape m., pérdida f.
leaky /'liki/ a. llovedizo, resquebrajado.
lean /lin/ a. **1.** flaco, magro. —v. **2.** apoyarse, arrimarse.
leap /lip/ n. **1.** salto m. —v. **2.** saltar.
leap year n. año bisiesto m.
learn /lɜrn/ v. aprender; saber.
learned /'lɜrnɪd/ a. erudito.
learning /'lɜrnɪŋ/ n. erudición f., instrucción f.
lease /lis/ n. **1.** arriendo m. —v. **2.** arrendar.
leash /liʃ/ n. **1.** correa f. —v. **2.** atraillar.
least /list/ a. menor; mínimo. **the l.**, lo menos. **at l.**, por lo menos.
leather /'lɛðər/ n. cuero m.
leathery /'lɛðəri/ a. coriáceo.
leave /liv/ n. **1.** licencia f. **to take l.**, despedirse. —v. **2.** dejar; (depart) salir, irse. **l. out**, omitir.
leaven /'lɛvən/ n. **1.** levadura f. —v. **2.** fermentar, imbuir.
lecherous /'lɛtʃərəs/ a. lujurioso.
lecture /'lɛktʃər/ n. conferencia f.
lecturer /'lɛktʃərər/ n. conferencista m. & f.; catedrático -ca.
ledge /lɛdʒ/ n. borde m.; capa f.
ledger /'lɛdʒər/ n. libro mayor m.

lee /li/ *n.* sotavento *m.*
leech /litʃ/ *n.* sanguijuela *f.*
leek /lik/ *n.* puerro *m.*
leer /lɪər/ *v.* mirar de soslayo.
leeward /'liwərd/ *a.* sotavento.
left /lɛft/ *a.* izquierdo. **the l.,** la izquierda. **to be left,** quedarse.
left-handed /'lɛft 'hændɪd/ *a.* zurdo.
leftist /'lɛftɪst/ *n.* izquierdista *m.* & *f.*
leftovers /'lɛftˌouvərz/ *n.* sobras *f.pl.*
leg /lɛg/ *n.* pierna *f.*
legacy /'lɛgəsi/ *n.* legado *m.*, herencia *f.*
legal /'ligəl/ *a.* legal.
legalize /'ligəˌlaiz/ *v.* legalizar.
legation /lɪ'geiʃən/ *n.* legación, embajada *f.*
legend /'lɛdʒənd/ *n.* leyenda *f.*
legendary /'lɛdʒənˌdɛri/ *a.* legendario.
legible /'lɛdʒəbəl/ *a.* legible.
legion /'lidʒən/ *n.* legión *f.*
legislate /'lɛdʒɪsˌleit/ *v.* legislar.
legislation /ˌlɛdʒɪs'leiʃən/ *n.* legislación *f.*
legislator /'lɛdʒɪsˌleitər/ *n.* legislador -ra.
legislature /'lɛdʒɪsˌleitʃər/ *n.* legislatura *f.*
legitimate /lɪ'dʒɪtəmɪt/ *a.* legítimo.
legume /'lɛgyum/ *n.* legumbre *f.*
leisure /'liʒər/ *n.* desocupación *f.*; horas libres.
leisurely /'liʒərli/ *a.* **1.** deliberado. —*adv.* **2.** despacio.
lemon /'lɛmən/ *n.* limón *m.*
lemonade /ˌlɛmə'neid/ *n.* limonada *f.*
lend /lɛnd/ *v.* prestar.
length /lɛŋkθ/ *n.* largo *m.*; duración *f.*
lengthen /'lɛŋkθən/ *v.* alargar.
lengthwise /'lɛŋkθˌwaiz/ *adv.* a lo largo.
lengthy /'lɛŋkθi/ *a.* largo.
lenient /'liniənt/ *a.* indulgente.
lens /lɛnz/ *n.* lente *m.* *or* *f.*
Lent /lɛnt/ *n.* cuaresma *f.*
Lenten /'lɛntn/ *a.* cuaresmal.
lentil /'lɛntɪl/ *n.* lenteja *f.*
leopard /'lɛpərd/ *n.* leopardo *m.*
leotard /'liəˌtɑrd/ *n.* mallas *f.pl.*
leper /'lɛpər/ *n.* leproso -sa.
leprosy /'lɛprəsi/ *n.* lepra *f.*
lesbian /'lɛzbiən/ *n.* lesbiana *f.*
lesion /'liʒən/ *n.* lesión *f.*
less /lɛs/ *a.* & *adv.* menos.
lessen /'lɛsən/ *v.* disminuir.
lesser /'lɛsər/ *a.* menor; más pequeño.
lesson /'lɛsən/ *n.* lección *f.*
lest /lɛst/ *conj.* para que no.
let /lɛt/ *v.* dejar; permitir; arrendar.
letdown /'lɛtˌdaun/ *n.* decepción *f.*
lethal /'liθəl/ *a.* letal.
lethargic /lə'θɑrdʒɪk/ *a.* letárgico.
lethargy /'lɛθərdʒi/ *n.* letargo *m.*
letter /'lɛtər/ *n.* carta; (of alphabet) letra *f.*
letterhead /'lɛtərˌhɛd/ *n.* membrete *m.*
lettuce /'lɛtɪs/ *n.* lechuga *f.*
leukemia /lu'kimiə/ *n.* leucemia *f.*
levee /'lɛvi, lɛ'vi/ *n.* recepción *f.*
level /'lɛvəl/ *a.* **1.** llano, nivelado. —*n.* **2.** nivel *m.*; llanura *f.* —*v.* **3.** allanar; nivelar.
lever /'lɛvər/ *n.* palanca *f.*
levity /'lɛvɪti/ *n.* levedad *f.*
levy /'lɛvi/ *n.* **1.** leva *f.* —*v.* **2.** imponer.
lewd /lud/ *a.* lascivo.
lexicon /'lɛksɪˌkɒn/ *n.* léxico *m.*
liability /ˌlaiə'bɪlɪti/ *n.* riesgo *m.*; obligación *f.*
liable /'laiəbəl/ *a.* sujeto; responsable.
liaison /li'eizən/ *n.* vinculación *f.*, enlace *m.*; concubinaje *m.*
liar /'laiər/ *n.* embustero -ra.
libel /'laibəl/ *n.* **1.** libelo *m.* —*v.* **2.** difamar.
libelous /'laibələs/ *a.* difamatorio.
liberal /'lɪbərəl/ *a.* liberal; generoso.
liberalism /'lɪbərəˌlɪzəm/ *n.* liberalismo *m.*
liberality /ˌlɪbə'rælɪti/ *n.* liberalidad *f.*
liberate /'lɪbəˌreit/ *v.* libertar.
liberty /'lɪbərti/ *n.* libertad *f.*
libidinous /lɪ'bɪdnəs/ *a.* libidinoso.
librarian /lai'brɛəriən/ *n.* bibliotecario -ria.
library /'laiˌbrɛri/ *n.* biblioteca *f.*
libretto /lɪ'brɛtou/ *n.* libreto *m.*
license /'laisəns/ *n.* licencia *f.*; permiso *m.*
licentious /lai'sɛnʃəs/ *a.* licencioso.
lick /lɪk/ *v.* lamer.
licorice /'lɪkərɪʃ, 'lɪkrɪʃ, 'lɪkərɪs/ *n.* regaliz *m.*
lid /lɪd/ *n.* tapa *f.*
lie /lai/ *n.* **1.** mentira *f.* —*v.* **2.** mentir. **l. down,** acostarse, echarse.
lieutenant /lu'tɛnənt/ *n.* teniente *m.*
life /laif/ *n.* vida *f.*
lifeboat /'laifˌbout/ *n.* bote salvavidas *m.*
life buoy boya *f.*
lifeguard /'laifˌgɑrd/ socorrista *m.* & *f.*
life insurance seguro de vida *m.*
life jacket chaleco salvavidas *m.*
lifeless /'laiflɪs/ *a.* sin vida.
life preserver /prɪ'zɜrvər/ salvavidas *m.*
lifestyle /'laifstail/ *n.* modo de vida *m.*
lift /lɪft/ *v.* levantar, alzar, elevar.
ligament /'lɪgəmənt/ *n.* ligamento *m.*
ligature /'lɪgətʃər/ *n.* ligadura *f.*
light /lait/ *a.* **1.** ligero; liviano; (in color) claro. —*n.* **2.** luz; candela *f.* —*v.* **3.** encender; iluminar.
light bulb bombilla *f.*
lighten /'laitn/ *v.* aligerar; aclarar; iluminar.
lighter /'laitər/ *n.* encendedor *m.*
lighthouse /'laitˌhaus/ *n.* faro *m.*
lightness /'laitnɪs/ *n.* ligereza; agilidad *f.*
lightning /'laitnɪŋ/ *n.* relámpago *m.*
like /laik/ *a.* **1.** semejante. —*prep.* **2.** como. —*v.* **3. I like...** me gusta, me gustan... **I should like,** quisiera.
likeable /'laikəbəl/ *a.* simpático, agradable.
likelihood /'laikliˌhʊd/ *n.* probabilidad *f.*
likely /'laikli/ *a.* probable; verosímil.
liken /'laikən/ *v.* comparar; asemejar.
likeness /'laiknɪs/ *n.* semejanza *f.*
likewise /'laikˌwaiz/ *adv.* igualmente.
lilac /'lailək/ *n.* lila *f.*
lilt /lɪlt/ *n.* **1.** cadencia alegre *f.* —*v.* **2.** cantar alegremente.
lily /'lɪli/ *n.* lirio *m.*
lily of the valley muguete *m.*
limb /lɪm/ *n.* rama *f.*
limber /'lɪmbər/ *a.* flexible. **to l. up,** ponerse flexible.
limbo /'lɪmbou/ *n.* limbo *m.*
lime /laim/ *n.* cal *f.*; (fruit) limoncito *m.*, lima *f.*
limestone /'laimˌstoun/ *n.* piedra caliza *f.*
limewater /'laimˌwɔtər/ *n.* agua de cal *f.*
limit /'lɪmɪt/ *n.* **1.** límite *m.* —*v.* **2.** limitar.
limitation /ˌlɪmɪ'teiʃən/ *n.* limitación *f.*
limitless /'lɪmɪtlɪs/ *a.* ilimitado.
limousine /'lɪməˌzin/ *n.* limusina *f.*
limp /lɪmp/ *n.* **1.** cojera *f.* —*a.* **2.** flojo. —*v.* **3.** cojear.
limpid /'lɪmpɪd/ *a.* límpido.
line /lain/ *n.* **1.** línea; fila; raya *f.*; (of print) renglón *m.* —*v.* **2.** forrar; rayar.
lineage /'lɪnɪdʒ/ *n.* linaje *m.*
lineal /'lɪniəl/ *a.* lineal.
linear /'lɪniər/ *a.* linear, longitudinal.
linen /'lɪnən/ *n.* lienzo, lino *m.*; ropa blanca.
liner /'lainər/ *n.* vapor *m.*
linger /'lɪŋgər/ *v.* demorarse.
lingerie /ˌlɑnʒə'rei/ *n.* ropa blanca *f.*
linguist /'lɪŋgwɪst/ *n.* lingüista *m.* & *f.*
linguistic /lɪŋ'gwɪstɪk/ *a.* lingüístico.
liniment /'lɪnəmənt/ *n.* linimento *m.*
lining /'lainɪŋ/ *n.* forro *m.*
link /lɪŋk/ *n.* **1.** eslabón; vínculo *m.* —*v.* **2.** vincular.
linoleum /lɪ'nouliəm/ *n.* linóleo *m.*
linseed /'lɪnˌsid/ *n.* linaza *f.*; simiente de lino *f.*
lint /lɪnt/ *n.* hilacha *f.*
lion /'laiən/ *n.* león *m.*
lip /lɪp/ *n.* labio *m.*
liposuction /'lɪpəˌsʌkʃən, 'laipə-/ *n.* liposucción *f.*
lipstick /'lɪpˌstɪk/ *n.* lápiz de labios.
liqueur /lɪ'kɜr/ *n.* licor *m.*
liquid /'lɪkwɪd/ *a.* & *n.* líquido *m.*
liquidate /'lɪkwɪˌdeit/ *v.* liquidar.
liquidation /ˌlɪkwɪ'deiʃən/ *n.* liquidación *f.*
liquor /'lɪkər/ *n.* licor *m.*
lisp /lɪsp/ *n.* **1.** ceceo *m.* —*v.* **2.** cecear.
list /lɪst/ *n.* **1.** lista *f.* —*v.* **2.** registrar.
listen (to) /'lɪsən/ *v.* escuchar.
listless /'lɪstlɪs/ *a.* indiferente.
litany /'lɪtni/ *n.* letanía *f.*
liter /'litər/ *n.* litro *m.*
literal /'lɪtərəl/ *a.* literal.
literary /'lɪtəˌrɛri/ *a.* literario.
literate /'lɪtərɪt/ *a.* alfabetizado.
literature /'lɪtərətʃər/ *n.* literatura *f.*
litigant /'lɪtɪgənt/ *n.* & *a.* litigante *m.* & *f.*
litigation /ˌlɪtɪ'geiʃən/ *n.* litigio, pleito *m.*
litter /'lɪtər/ *n.* **1.** litera *f.*; cama de paja. —*v.* **2.** poner en desorden.
little /'lɪtl/ *a.* pequeño; (quantity) poco.
little finger meñique *m.*
liturgical /lɪ'tɜrdʒɪkəl/ *a.* litúrgico.
liturgy /'lɪtərdʒi/ *n.* liturgia *f.*
live /*a* laiv; *v* lɪv/ *a.* **1.** vivo. —*v.* **2.** vivir.
livelihood /'laivliˌhʊd/ *n.* subsistencia *f.*
lively /'laivli/ *a.* vivo; rápido; animado.
liver /'lɪvər/ *n.* hígado *m.*
livery /'lɪvəri/ *n.* librea *f.*
livestock /'laivˌstɒk/ *n.* ganadería *f.*
livid /'lɪvɪd/ *a.* lívido.
living /'lɪvɪŋ/ *a.* **1.** vivo. —*n.* **2.** sustento *m.* **to earn (make) a living,** ganarse la vida.
living room salón *m.*
lizard /'lɪzərd/ *n.* lagarto *m.*, lagartija *f.*
llama /'lɑmə/ *n.* llama *f.*
load /loud/ *n.* **1.** carga *f.* —*v.* **2.** cargar.
loaf /louf/ *n.* **1.** pan *m.* —*v.* **2.** holgazanear.
loam /loum/ *n.* marga *f.*
loan /loun/ *n.* **1.** préstamo *m.* —*v.* **2.** prestar.
loathe /louð/ *v.* aborrecer, detestar.
loathsome /'louðsəm/ *a.* repugnante.
lobby /'lɒbi/ *n.* vestíbulo *m.*
lobe /loub/ *n.* lóbulo *m.*
lobster /'lɒbstər/ *n.* langosta *f.*
local /'loukəl/ *a.* local.
local area network red local *f.*
locale /lou'kæl/ *n.* localidad *f.*
locality /lou'kælɪti/ *n.* localidad *f.*, lugar *m.*
localize /'loukəˌlaiz/ *v.* localizar.
locate /'loukeit/ *v.* situar; hallar.
location /lou'keiʃən/ *n.* sitio *m.*; posición *f.*
lock /lɒk/ *n.* **1.** cerradura *f.*; (*pl.*) cabellos *m.pl.* —*v.* **2.** cerrar con llave.
locker /'lɒkər/ *n.* cajón *m.*; ropero *m.*
locket /'lɒkɪt/ *n.* guardapelo *m.*; medallón *m.*
lockjaw /'lɒkˌdʒɔ/ *n.* trismo *m.*
locksmith /'lɒkˌsmɪθ/ *n.* cerrajero -ra.
locomotive /ˌloukə'moutɪv/ *n.* locomotora *f.*
locust /'loukəst/ *n.* cigarra *f.*, saltamontes *m.*
locution /lou'kyuʃən/ *n.* locución *f.*
lode /loud/ *n.* filón *m.*, veta *f.*
lodge /lɒdʒ/ *n.* **1.** logia; (inn) posada *f.* —*v.* **2.** fijar; alojar, morar.
lodger /'lɒdʒər/ *n.* inquilino *m.*
lodging /'lɒdʒɪŋ/ *n.* alojamiento *m.*
loft /lɔft/ *n.* desván, sobrado *m.*
lofty /'lɔfti/ *a.* alto; altivo.
log /lɔg/ *n.* tronco de árbol; *Naut.* barquilla *f.*
loge /louʒ/ *n.* palco *m.*
logic /'lɒdʒɪk/ *n.* lógica *f.*
logical /'lɒdʒɪkəl/ *a.* lógico.
loin /lɔin/ *n.* lomo *m.*
loincloth /'lɔinˌklɔθ/ *n.* taparrabos *m.*
loiter /'lɔitər/ *v.* haraganear.
lone /loun/ *a.* solitario.
loneliness /'lounlinɪs/ *n.* soledad *f.*
lonely, /'lounli/ **lonesome** *a.* solo y triste.
lonesome /'lounsəm/ *a.* solitario, aislado.
long /lɔŋ/ *a.* **1.** largo. **a l. time,** mucho tiempo. —*adv.* **2.** mucho tiempo. **how l.,** cuánto tiempo. **no longer,** ya no. —*v.* **3. l. for,** anhelar.
long-distance call /'lɔŋ 'dɪstəns/ conferencia interurbana *f.*
longevity /lɒn'dʒɛvɪti/ *n.* longevidad *f.*
long-haired /'lɔŋ 'hɛərd/ *a.* melenudo.
longing /'lɔŋɪŋ/ *n.* anhelo *m.*
longitude /'lɒndʒɪˌtud/ *n.* longitud *m.*
look /lʊk/ *n.* **1.** mirada *f.*; aspecto *m.* —*v.* **2.** parecer; mirar. **l. at,** mirar. **l. for,** buscar. **l. like,** parecerse a. **l. out!,** ¡cuidado! **l. up,** buscar; ir a ver, venir a ver.
looking glass /'lʊkɪŋ/ espejo *m.*
loom /lum/ *n.* **1.** telar *m.* —*v.* **2.** asomar.
loop /lup/ *n.* vuelta *f.*
loophole /'lupˌhoul/ *n.* aspillera *f.*; *Fig.* callejuela, evasiva *f.*, efugio *m.*
loose /lus/ *a.* suelto; flojo.
loose change suelto *m.*
loosen /'lusən/ *v.* soltar; aflojar.
loot /lut/ *n.* **1.** botín *m.*, saqueo *m.* —*v.* **2.** saquear.
lopsided /'lɒp'saidɪd/ *a.* desequilibrado.
loquacious /lou'kweiʃəs/ *a.* locuaz.
lord /lɔrd/ *n.* señor *m.*; (Brit. title) lord *m.*
lordship /'lɔrdʃɪp/ *n.* señorío *m.*
lose /luz/ *v.* perder. **l. consciousness,** perder el concimiento.
loss /lɔs/ *n.* pérdida *f.*
lost /lɔst/ *a.* perdido.
lot /lɒt/ *n.* suerte *f.* **building l.,** solar *m.* **a lot (of), lots of,** mucho.
lotion /'louʃən/ *n.* loción *f.*
lottery /'lɒtəri/ *n.* lotería *f.*
loud /laud/ *a.* **1.** fuerte; ruidoso. —*adv.* **2.** alto.
loudspeaker /'laudˌspikər/ *n.* altavoz *m.*
lounge /laundʒ/ *n.* sofá *m.*; salón de fumar *m.*
louse /laus/ *n.* piojo *m.*
love /lʌv/ *n.* **1.** amor *m.* **in l.,** enamorado. **to fall in l.,** enamorarse. **l. at first sight,** flechazo *m.* —*v.* **2.** querer; amar; adorar.
lovely /'lʌvli/ *a.* hermoso.
lover /'lʌvər/ *n.* amante *m.* & *f.*
low /lou/ *a.* bajo; vil.
low-cut /'lou 'kʌt/ *a.* escotado.
lower /'louər/ *v.* bajar; (in price) rebajar.
lower-case letter /'louər 'keis/ minúscula *f.*
lowly /'louli/ *a.* humilde.
low neckline /'nɛkˌlain/ escote *m.*
loyal /'lɔiəl/ *a.* leal, fiel.
loyalist /'lɔiəlɪst/ *n.* lealista *m.* & *f.*
loyalty /'lɔiəlti/ *n.* lealtad *f.*
lozenge /'lɒzɪndʒ/ *n.* pastilla *f.*
lubricant /'lubrɪkənt/ *n.* lubricante *m.*
lubricate /'lubrɪˌkeit/ *v.* engrasar, lubricar.
lucid /'lusɪd/ *a.* claro, lúcido.

luck /lʌk/ *n.* suerte; fortuna *f.*
lucky /'lʌki/ *a.* afortunado. **to be l.,** tener suerte.
lucrative /'lukrətɪv/ *a.* lucrativo.
ludicrous /'ludɪkrəs/ *a.* ridículo.
luggage /'lʌgɪdʒ/ *n.* equipaje *m.*
lukewarm /'luk'wɔrm/ *a.* tibio.
lull /lʌl/ *n.* **1.** momento de calma. —*v.* **2.** calmar.
lullaby /'lʌlə,bai/ *n.* arrullo *m.*
lumbago /lʌm'beigou/ *n.* lumbago *m.*
lumber /'lʌmbər/ *n.* madera *f.*
luminous /'lumənəs/ *a.* luminoso.
lump /lʌmp/ *n.* protuberancia *f.;* (of sugar) terrón *m.*
lump sum suma global *f.*
lunacy /'lunəsi/ *n.* locura *f.*
lunar /'lunər/ *a.* lunar.
lunatic /'lunətɪk/ *a. & n.* loco -ca.
lunch, luncheon /lʌntʃ; 'lʌnteshən;/ *n.* **1.** merienda *f.,* almuerzo *m.* —*v.* **2.** merendar, almorzar.
lunch box /'lʌntʃ,bɒks/ fiambrera *f.*
lung /lʌŋ/ *n.* pulmón *m.*
lunge /lʌndʒ/ *n.* **1.** estocada, arremetida *f.* —*v.* **2.** dar un estocada, arremeter.
lure /lur/ *v.* atraer.
lurid /'lʊrɪd/ *a.* sensacional; espeluznante.
lurk /lɜrk/ *v.* esconderse; espiar.
luscious /'lʌʃəs/ *a.* sabroso, delicioso.
lust /lʌst/ *n.* sensualidad; codicia *f.*
luster /'lʌstər/ *n.* lustre *m.*
lustful /'lʌstfəl/ *a.* sensual, lascivo.
lusty /'lʌsti/ *a.* vigoroso.
lute /lut/ *n.* laúd *m.*
Lutheran /'luθərən/ *n. & a.* luterano -na.
luxuriant /lʌg'ʒʊriənt/ *a.* exuberante, frondoso.
luxurious /lʌg'ʒʊriəs/ *a.* lujoso.
luxury /'lʌkʃəri/ *n.* lujo *m.*
lying /'laiŋ/ *a.* mentiroso.
lymph /lɪmf/ *n.* linfa *f.*
lynch /lɪntʃ/ *v.* linchar.
lyre /laiᵊr/ *n.* lira *f.*
lyric /'lɪrɪk/ *a.* lírico.
lyricism /'lɪrə,sɪzəm/ *n.* lirismo *m.*

M

macabre /mə'kɑbrə/ *a.* macabro.
macaroni /,mækə'rouni/ *n.* macarrones *m.*
machine /mə'ʃin/ *n.* máquina *f.*
machine gun ametralladora *f.*
machinery /mə'ʃinəri/ *n.* maquinaria *f.*
machinist /mə'ʃinɪst/ *n.* maquinista *m. & f.,* mecánico *m.*
macho /'matʃou/ *n.* machista *m.*
mackerel /'mækərəl/ *n.* escombro *m.*
macro /'mækrou/ *n.* (computer) macro *m.*
mad /mæd/ *a.* loco; furioso.
madam /'mædəm/ *n.* señora *f.*
mafia /'mɑfiə/ *n.* mafia *f.*
magazine /,mægə'zin/ *n.* revista *f.*
magic /'mædʒɪk/ *a.* **1.** mágico. —*n.* **2.** magia *f.*
magician /mə'dʒɪʃən/ *n.* mágico *m.*
magistrate /'mædʒə,streit/ *n.* magistrado, -da.
magnanimous /mæg'nænəməs/ *a.* magnánimo.
magnate /'mægneit/ *n.* magnate *m.*
magnesium /mæg'niziəm/ *n.* magnesio *m.*
magnet /'mægnɪt/ *n.* imán *m.*
magnetic /mæg'netɪk/ *a.* magnético.
magnificence /mæg'nɪfəsəns/ *n.* magnificencia *f.*
magnificent /mæg'nɪfəsənt/ *a.* magnífico.
magnify /'mægnə,fai/ *v.* magnificar.
magnifying glass /'mægnə,faiŋ/ lupa *f.*
magnitude /'mægnɪ,tud/ *n.* magnitud *f.*
magpie /'mæg,pai/ *n.* hurraca *f.*

mahogany /mə'hɒgəni/ *n.* caoba *f.*
maid /meid/ *n.* criada *f.* **old m.,** solterona *f.*
maiden /'meidn/ *a.* soltera.
mail /meil/ *n.* **1.** correo *m.* **air m.,** correo aéreo. **by return m.,** a vuelta de correo. —*v.* **2.** echar al correo.
mailbox /'meil,bɒks/ *n.* buzón *m.*
mailman /'meil,mæn/ *n.* cartero *m.*
maim /meim/ *v.* mutilar.
main /mein/ *a.* principal.
mainframe /'mein,freim/ *n.* componente central de una computadora.
mainland /'mein,lænd/ *n.* continente *m.*
maintain /mein'tein/ *v.* mantener; sostener.
maintenance /'meintənəns/ *n.* mantenimiento; sustento *m.;* conservación *f.*
maître d' /,mei'tər di , ,meitrə, ,metrə/ *n.* jefe de sala *m. & f.*
maize /meiz/ *n.* maíz *m.*
majestic /mə'dʒestɪk/ *a.* majestuoso.
majesty /'mædʒəsti/ *n.* majestad *f.*
major /'meidʒər/ *a.* **1.** mayor. —*n.* **2.** *Mil.* comandante *m.;* (study) especialidad *f.*
majority /mə'dʒɔrɪti/ *n.* mayoría *f.*
make /meik/ *n.* **1.** marca *f.* —*v.* **2.** hacer; fabricar; (earn) ganar.
maker /'meikər/ *n.* fabricante *m.*
makeshift /'meik,ʃɪft/ *a.* provisional.
make-up /'meik,ʌp/ *n.* cosméticos *m.pl.*
malady /'mælədi/ *n.* mal *m.,* enfermedad *f.*
malaria /mə'lɛəriə/ *n.* paludismo *m.*
male /meil/ *a. & n.* macho *m.*
malevolent /mə'lɛvələnt/ *a.* malévolo.
malice /'mælɪs/ *n.* malicia *f.*
malicious /mə'lɪʃəs/ *a.* malicioso.
malign /mə'lain/ *v.* **1.** difamar. —*a.* **2.** maligno.
malignant /mə'lɪgnənt/ *a.* maligno.
malnutrition /,mælnu'trɪʃən/ *n.* desnutrición *f.*
malt /mɔlt/ *n.* malta *f.*
mammal /'mæməl/ *n.* mamífero *m.*
man /mæn/ *n.* hombre; varón *m. v.* tripular.
manage /'mænɪdʒ/ *v.* manejar; dirigir; administrar; arreglárselas. **m. to,** lograr.
management /'mænɪdʒmənt/ *n.* dirección, administración *f.*
manager /'mænɪdʒər/ *n.* director -ora.
mandate /'mændeit/ *n.* mandato *m.*
mandatory /'mændə,tɔri/ *a.* obligatorio.
mandolin /'mændlɪn/ *n.* mandolina *f.*
mane /mein/ *n.* crines *f.pl.*
maneuver /mə'nuvər/ *n.* **1.** maniobra *f.* —*v.* **2.** maniobrar.
manganese /'mæŋgə,nis, -,niz/ *n.* manganeso *m.*
manger /'meindʒər/ *n.* pesebre *m.*
mangle /'mæŋgəl/ *n.* **1.** rodillo, exprimidor *m.* —*v.* **2.** mutilar.
manhood /'mænhʊd/ *n.* virilidad *f.*
mania /'meiniə/ *n.* manía *f.*
maniac /'meini,æk/ *a. & n.* maniático -ca; maníaco -ca.
manicure /'mænɪ,kyʊr/ *n.* manicura *f.*
manifest /'mænə,fest/ *a. & n.* **1.** manifiesto *m.* —*v.* **2.** manifestar.
manifesto /,mænə'festou/ *n.* manifiesto *m.*
manifold /'mænə,fould/ *a.* **1.** muchos. —*n.* **2.** *Auto.* tubo múltiple.
manipulate /mə'nɪpyə,leit/ *v.* manipular.
mankind /'mæn'kaind/ *n.* humanidad *f.*
manly /'mænli/ *a.* varonil.
manner /'mænər/ *n.* manera *f.,* modo *m.* **manners,** modales *m.pl.*
mannerism /'mænə,rɪzəm/ *n.* manerismo *m.*
mansion /'mænʃən/ *n.* mansión *f.*

mantel /'mæntl/ *n.* manto de chimenea.
mantle /'mæntl/ *n.* manto *m.*
manual /'mænyuəl/ *a. & n.* manual *m.*
manufacture /,mænyə'fæktʃər/ *v.* fabricar.
manufacturer /,mænyə'fæktʃərər/ *n.* fabricante *m.*
manufacturing /,mænyə'fæktʃərɪŋ/ *n.* fabricación *f.*
manure /mə'nʊr/ *n.* abono, estiércol *m.*
manuscript /'mænyə,skrɪpt/ *n.* manuscrito *m.*
many /'meni/ *a.* muchos. **how m.,** cuántos. **so m.,** tantos. **too m.,** demasiados. **as m. as,** tantos como.
map /mæp/ *n.* mapa *m.*
maple /'meipəl/ *n.* arce *m.*
mar /mɑr/ *v.* estropear; desfigurar.
marble /'mɑrbəl/ *n.* mármol *m.*
march /mɑrtʃ/ *n.* **1.** marcha *f.* —*v.* **2.** marchar.
March /mɑrtʃ/ *n.* marzo *m.*
mare /mɛər/ *n.* yegua *f.*
margarine /'mɑrdʒərɪn/ *n.* margarina *f.*
margin /'mɑrdʒɪn/ *n.* margen *m.* or *f.*
marijuana /,mærə'wɑnə/ *n.* marijuana *f.*
marine /mə'rin/ *a.* **1.** marino. —*n.* **2.** soldado de marina.
mariner /'mærənər/ *n.* marinero *m.*
marionette /,mæriə'nɛt/ *n.* marioneta *f.*
marital /'mærɪtl/ *a.* marital.
maritime /'mærɪ,taim/ *a.* marítimo.
mark /mɑrk/ *n.* **1.** marca *f.* —*v.* **2.** marcar.
market /'mɑrkɪt/ *n.* mercado *m.* **meat m.,** carnicería *f.* **stock m.,** bolsa *f. v.* comercializar.
marmalade /'mɑrmə,leid/ *n.* mermelada *f.*
maroon /mə'run/ *a. & n.* color rojo oscuro. *v.* dejar abandonado.
marquis /'mɑrkwɪs/ *n.* marqués *m.*
marriage /'mærɪdʒ/ *n.* matrimonio *m.*
marriage certificate partida de matrimonio *f.*
married /'mærid/ *a.* casado. **to get m.,** casarse.
marrow /'mærou/ *n.* médula *f.;* substancia *f.*
marry /'mæri/ *v.* casarse con; casar.
marsh /mɑrʃ/ *n.* pantano *m.*
marshal /'mɑrʃəl/ *n.* mariscal *m.*
marshmallow /'mɑrʃ,mɛlou/ *n.* malvarisco *m.;* bombón de altea *m.*
martial /'mɑrʃəl/ *a.* marcial. **m. law,** gobierno militar.
martyr /'mɑrtər/ *n.* mártir *m. & f.*
martyrdom /'mɑrtərdəm/ *n.* martirio *m.*
marvel /'mɑrvəl/ *n.* **1.** maravilla *f.* —*v.* **2.** maravillarse.
marvelous /'mɑrvələs/ *a.* maravilloso.
mascara /mæ'skærə/ *n.* rimel *m.*
mascot /'mæskɒt/ *n.* mascota *f.*
masculine /'mæskyəlɪn/ *a.* masculino.
mash /mæʃ/ *v.* majar. **mashed potatoes,** puré de papas *m.*
mask /mæsk/ *n.* máscara *f.*
mason /'meisən/ *n.* albañil *m.*
masquerade /,mæskə'reid/ *n.* mascarada *f.*
mass /mæs/ *n.* masa *f.; Relig.* misa *f.* **to say m.,** cantar misa. **m. production,** producción en serie.
massacre /'mæsəkər/ *n.* **1.** carnicería, matanza *f.* —*v.* **2.** matar atrozmente, destrozar.
massage /mə'sɑʒ/ *n.* **1.** masaje *m.;* soba *f.* —*v.* **2.** sobar.
masseur /mə'sɜr/ *n.* masajista *m. & f.*
massive /'mæsɪv/ *a.* macizo, sólido.
mast /mæst/ *n.* palo, árbol *m.*
master /'mæstər/ *n.* **1.** amo; maestro *m.* —*v.* **2.** domar, dominar.

masterpiece /'mæstər,pis/ *n.* obra maestra *f.*
master's degree /'mæstərz/ maestría *f.*
mastery /'mæstəri/ *n.* maestría *f.*
mat /mæt/ *n.* **1.** estera; palleta *f.* —*v.* **2.** enredar.
match /mætʃ/ *n.* **1.** igual *m;* fósforo *m.;* (sport) partida, contienda *f.;* (marriage) noviazgo; casamiento. —*v.* **2.** ser igual a; igualar.
matchbox /'mætʃ,bɒks/ caja de cerillas, caja de fósforos *f.*
mate /meit/ *n.* **1.** consorte *m. & f.;* compañero -ra. —*v.* **2.** igualar; casar.
material /mə'tɪəriəl/ *a. & n.* material *m.* **raw materials,** materias primas.
materialism /mə'tɪəriə,lɪzəm/ *n.* materialismo *m.*
materialize /mə'tɪəriə,laiz/ *v.* materializar.
maternal /mə'tɜrnl/ *a.* materno.
maternity /mə'tɜrnɪti/ *n.* maternidad *f.*
maternity hospital maternidad *f.*
mathematical /,mæθə'mætɪkəl/ *a.* matemático.
mathematics /,mæθə'mætɪks/ *n.* matemáticas *f.pl.*
matinee /,mætn'ei/ *n.* matiné *f.*
matrimony /'mætrə,mouni/ *n.* matrimonio *m.*
matron /'meitrən/ *n.* matrona; directora *f.*
matter /'mætər/ *n.* **1.** materia *f.;* asunto *m.* **what's the m.?,** ¿qué pasa? —*v.* **2.** importar.
mattress /'mætrɪs/ *n.* colchón *m.*
mature /mə'tʃʊr/ *a.* **1.** maduro. —*v.* **2.** madurar.
maturity /mə'tʃʊrɪti/ *n.* madurez *f.*
maudlin /'mɔdlɪn/ *a.* sentimental en exceso; sensiblero.
maul /mɔl/ *v.* aporrear.
maxim /'mæksɪm/ *n.* máxima *f.*
maximum /'mæksəməm/ *a. & n.* máximo.
may /mei/ *v.* poder.
May /mei/ *n.* mayo *m.*
maybe /'meibi/ *adv.* quizá, quizás, tal vez.
mayonnaise /,meiə'neiz/ *n.* mayonesa *f.*
mayor /'meiər/ *n.* alcalde *m.* alcaldesa *f.*
maze /meiz/ *n.* laberinto *m.*
me /mi/ *pron.* mí; me. **with me,** conmigo.
meadow /'mɛdou/ *n.* prado *m.;* vega *f.*
meager /'migər/ *a.* magro; pobre.
meal /mil/ *n.* comida; (flour) harina *f.*
mean /min/ *a.* **1.** bajo; malo. —*n.* **2.** medio (see also **means**). —*v.* **3.** significar; querer decir.
meander /mi'ændər/ *v.* (river) serpentear; (person) deambular.
meaning /'miniŋ/ *n.* sentido, significado *m.*
meaningless /'miniŋlɪs/ *a.* sin sentido.
means /minz/ *n.pl.* medios, recursos *m.* **by all m.,** sin falta. **by no m.,** de ningún modo. **by m. of,** por medio de.
meanwhile /'min,wail/ *adv.* mientras tanto.
measles /'mizəlz/ *n.* sarampión *m.*
measure /'mɛʒər/ *n.* **1.** medida *f.;* (music) compás *m.* —*v.* **2.** medir.
measurement /'mɛʒərmənt/ *n.* medida, dimensión *f.*
meat /mit/ *n.* carne *f.*
mechanic /mə'kænɪk/ *n.* mecánico *m. & f.*
mechanical /mə'kænɪkəl/ *a.* mecánico.
mechanism /'mɛkə,nɪzəm/ *n.* mecanismo *m.*
mechanize /'mɛkə,naiz/ *v.* mecanizar.
medal /'mɛdl/ *n.* medalla *f.*

meddle /'mɛdl̩/ v. meterse, entremeterse.
mediate /'midi,eit/ v. mediar.
medical /'mɛdɪkəl/ a. médico.
medicine /'mɛdəsɪn/ n. medicina f.
medicine chest botiquín m.
medieval /,midi'ivəl/ a. medieval.
mediocre /,midi'oukər/ a. mediocre.
mediocrity /,midi'ɒkrɪti/ n. mediocridad f.
meditate /'mɛdɪ,teit/ v. meditar.
meditation /,mɛdɪ'teiʃən/ n. meditación f.
Mediterranean /,mɛdɪtə'reiniən/ a. Mediterráneo m.
medium /'midiəm/ a. **1.** mediano, medio. —n. **2.** medio m.
medley /'mɛdli/ n. mezcla f., ensalada f.
meek /mik/ a. manso; humilde.
meekness /'miknɪs/ n. modestia; humildad f.
meet /mit/ a. **1.** apropiado. —n. **2.** concurso m. —v. **3.** encontrar; reunirse; conocer.
meeting /'mitɪŋ/ n. reunión f.; mitin m.
megahertz /'mɛgə,hɜrts/ n. megahercio m.
megaphone /'mɛgə,foun/ n. megáfono m.
melancholy /'mɛlən,kɒli/ a. **1.** melancólico. —n. **2.** melancolía f.
mellow /'mɛlou/ a. suave; blando; maduro.
melodious /mə'loudiəs/ a. melodioso.
melodrama /'mɛlə,drɑmə/ n. melodrama m.
melody /'mɛlədi/ n. melodía f.
melon /'mɛlən/ n. melón m.
melt /mɛlt/ v. derretir.
meltdown /'mɛlt,daun/ n. fundición resultante de un accidente en un reactor nuclear.
member /'mɛmbər/ n. socio -ia; miembro m. **m. of the crew,** tripulante m. & f.
membership /'mɛmbər,ʃɪp/ n. número de miembros.
membrane /'mɛmbrein/ n. membrana f.
memento /mə'mɛntou/ n. recuerdo m.
memoir /'mɛmwɑr/ n. memoria f.
memorable /'mɛmərəbəl/ a. memorable.
memorandum /,mɛmə'rændəm/ n. memorándum, volante m.
memorial /mə'mɔriəl/ a. **1.** conmemorativo. —n. **2.** memorial m.
memorize /'mɛmə,raiz/ v. aprender de memoria.
memory /'mɛməri/ n. memoria f.; recuerdo m.
menace /'mɛnɪs/ n. **1.** amenaza f. —v. **2.** amenazar.
mend /mɛnd/ v. reparar, remendar.
menial /'miniəl/ a. **1.** servil. —n. **2.** sirviente -ta.
meningitis /,mɛnɪn'dʒaitɪs/ n. meningitis f.
menopause /'mɛnə,pɔz/ n. menopausia f.
menstruation /,mɛnstru'eiʃən/ n. menstruación f.
menswear /'mɛnz,wɛər/ n. ropa de caballeros f.
mental /'mɛntl̩/ a. mental.
mental disorder trastorno mental m.
mentality /mɛn'tælɪti/ n. mentalidad f.
menthol /'mɛnθɒl/ n. mentol m.
mention /'mɛnʃən/ n. **1.** mención f. —v. **2.** mencionar.
menu /'mɛnyu/ n. menú m., lista f.
mercantile /'mɜrkən,til/ a. mercantil.
mercenary /'mɜrsə,nɛri/ a. & n. mercenario -ria.
merchandise /'mɜrtʃən,daiz/ n. mercancía f.
merchant /'mɜrtʃənt/ a. **1.** mercante. —n. **2.** comerciante m.

merciful /'mɜrsɪfəl/ a. misericordioso, compasivo.
merciless /'mɜrsɪlɪs/ a. cruel, inhumano.
mercury /'mɜrkyəri/ n. mercurio m.
mercy /'mɜrsi/ n. misericordia; merced f.
mere /mɪər/ a. mero, puro.
merely /'mɪərli/ adv. solamente; simplemente.
merge /mɜrdʒ/ v. unir, combinar.
merger /'mɜrdʒər/ n. consolidación, fusión f.
meringue /mə'ræŋ/ n. merengue m.
merit /'mɛrɪt/ n. **1.** mérito m. —v. **2.** merecer.
meritorious /,mɛrɪ'tɔriəs/ a. meritorio.
mermaid /'mɜr,meid/ n. sirena f.
merriment /'mɛrɪmənt/ n. regocijo m.
merry /'mɛri/ a. alegre, festivo.
merry-go-round /'mɛri gou ,raund/ n. caballitos m. pl.; tiovivo m.
mesh /mɛʃ/ n. malla f.
mess /mɛs/ n. **1.** lío m.; confusión f.; Mil. salón comedor; rancho m. —v. **2.** **m. up,** ensuciar; enredar.
message /'mɛsɪdʒ/ n. mensaje, recado m.
messenger /'mɛsəndʒər/ n. mensajero -ra.
messy /'mɛsi/ a. confuso; desarreglado.
metabolism /mə'tæbə,lɪzəm/ n. metabolismo m.
metal /'mɛtl̩/ n. metal m.
metallic /mə'tælɪk/ a. metálico.
metaphysics /,mɛtə'fɪzɪks/ n. metafísica f.
meteor /'mitiər/ n. meteoro m.
meteorology /,mitiə'rɒlədʒi/ n. meteorología f.
meter /'mitər/ n. contador, medidor; (measure) metro m.
method /'mɛθəd/ n. método m.
meticulous /mə'tɪkyələs/ a. meticuloso.
metric /'mɛtrɪk/ a. métrico.
metropolis /mɪ'trɒpəlɪs/ n. metrópoli f.
metropolitan /,mɛtrə'pɒlɪtn̩/ a. metropolitano.
Mexican /'mɛksɪkən/ a. & n. mexicano -na.
Mexico /'mɛksɪ,kou/ n. México m.
mezzanine /'mɛzə,nin/ n. entresuelo m.
microbe /'maikroub/ n. microbio m.
microchip /'maikrou,tʃɪp/ n. microchip m.
microfiche /'maikrə,fiʃ/ n. microficha f.
microfilm /'maikrə,fɪlm/ n. microfilm m.
microform /'maikrə,fɔrm/ n. microforma f.
microphone /'maikrə,foun/ n. micrófono m.
microscope /'maikrə,skoup/ n. microscopio m.
microscopic /,maikrə'skɒpɪk/ a. microscópico.
mid /mɪd/ a. medio.
middle /'mɪdl̩/ a. & n. medio m. **in the m. of,** en medio de, a mediados de.
middle-aged /eidʒd/ a. de edad madura.
Middle East Medio Oriente m.
middle finger dedo corazón m.
midget /'mɪdʒɪt/ n. enano -na.
midnight /'mɪd,nait/ n. medianoche f.
midwife /'mɪd,waif/ n. comadrona, partera f.
might /mait/ n. poder m., fuerza f.
mighty /'maiti/ a. poderoso.
migraine /'maigrein/ n. migraña f.; jaqueca f.
migrate /'maigreit/ v. emigrar.
migration /mai'greiʃən/ n. emigración f.

migratory /'maigrə,tɔri/ a. migratorio.
mild /maild/ a. moderado, suave; templado.
mildew /'mɪl,du/ n. añublo m., moho m.
mile /mail/ n. milla f.
mileage /'mailɪdʒ/ n. kilometraje m.
militant /'mɪlɪtənt/ a. militante.
militarism /'mɪlɪtə,rɪzəm/ n. militarismo m.
military /'mɪlɪ,tɛri/ a. militar.
militia /mɪ'lɪʃə/ n. milicia f.
milk /mɪlk/ n. **1.** leche f. —v. **2.** ordeñar.
milk chocolate chocolate con leche m.
milkman /'mɪlk,mæn/ n. lechero m.
milk shake batido m.
milky /'mɪlki/ a. lácteo; lechoso.
mill /mɪl/ n. **1.** molino m.; fábrica f. —v. **2.** moler.
miller /'mɪlər/ n. molinero -ra.
millimeter /'mɪlə,mitər/ n. milímetro m.
milliner /'mɪlənər/ n. sombrerero -ra.
millinery /'mɪlə,nɛri/ n. sombrerería f.
million /'mɪlyən/ n. millón m.
millionaire /,mɪlyə'nɛər/ n. millonario -ria.
mimic /'mɪmɪk/ n. **1.** mimo -ma. —v. **2.** imitar.
mind /maind/ n. **1.** mente; opinión f. —v. **2.** obedecer. **never m.,** no se ocupe.
mindful /'maindfəl/ a. atento.
mine /main/ pron. **1.** mío. —n. **2.** mina f. —v. **3.** minar.
miner /'mainər/ n. minero m.
mineral /'mɪnərəl/ a. & n. mineral m.
mineral water agua mineral f.
mine sweeper /'main,swipər/ dragaminas f.
mingle /'mɪŋgəl/ v. mezclar.
miniature /'mɪniətʃər/ n. miniatura f.
miniaturize /'mɪniətʃə,raiz/ v. miniaturizar.
minibus /'mɪni,bʌs/ n. microbús m.
minicab /'mɪni,kæb/ n. microtaxi m.
minimize /'mɪnə,maiz/ v. menospreciar.
minimum /'mɪnəməm/ a. & n. mínimo m.
mining /'mainɪŋ/ n. minería f.
minister /'mɪnɪstər/ n. **1.** ministro -tra; Relig. pastor m. —v. **2.** ministrar.
ministry /'mɪnəstri/ n. ministerio m.
mink /mɪŋk/ n. visón m.; (fur) piel de visón m.
minor /'mainər/ a. **1.** menor. —n. **2.** menor de edad.
minority /mɪ'nɔriti/ n. minoría f.
minstrel /'mɪnstrəl/ n. juglar m.
mint /mɪnt/ n. **1.** menta f.; casa de moneda. —v. **2.** acuñar.
minus /'mainəs/ prep. menos.
minute /mai'nut/ a. **1.** minucioso. —n. **2.** minuto, momento m.
miracle /'mɪrəkəl/ n. milagro m.
miraculous /mɪ'rækyələs/ a. milagroso.
mirage /mɪ'rɑʒ/ n. espejismo m.
mire /maiər/ n. lodo m.
mirror /'mɪrər/ n. espejo m.
mirth /mɜrθ/ n. alegría; risa f.
misbehave /,mɪsbɪ'heiv/ v. portarse mal.
miscellaneous /,mɪsə'leiniəs/ a. misceláneo.
mischief /'mɪstʃɪf/ n. travesura, diablura f.
mischievous /'mɪstʃəvəs/ a. travieso, dañino.
miser /'maizər/ n. avaro -ra.
miserable /'mɪzərəbəl/ a. miserable; infeliz.
miserly /'maizərli/ a. avariento, tacaño.
misfortune /mɪs'fɔrtʃən/ n. desgracia f., infortunio, revés m.
misgiving /mɪs'gɪvɪŋ/ n. recelo m., desconfianza f.

mishap /'mɪshæp/ n. desgracia f., contratiempo m.
mislay /mɪs'lei/ v. perder.
mislead /mɪs'lid/ v. extraviar, despistar; pervertir.
misplaced /mɪs'pleist/ a. extraviado.
mispronounce /,mɪsprə'nouns/ v. pronunciar mal.
miss /mɪs/ n. **1.** señorita f. —v. **2.** perder; echar de menos, extrañar. **be missing,** faltar.
missile /'mɪsəl/ n. proyectil m.
mission /'mɪʃən/ n. misión f.
missionary /'mɪʃə,nɛri/ n. misionero -ra.
mist /mɪst/ n. niebla, bruma f.
mistake /mɪ'steik/ n. equivocación f.; error m. **to make a m.,** equivocarse.
mistaken /mɪ'steikən/ a. equivocado.
mister /'mɪstər/ n. señor m.
mistletoe /'mɪsəl,tou/ n. muérdago m.
mistreat /mɪs'trit/ v. maltratar.
mistress /'mɪstrɪs/ n. ama; señora; concubina f.
mistrust /mɪs'trʌst/ v. desconfiar; sospechar.
misty /'mɪsti/ a. nebuloso, brumoso.
misunderstand /,mɪsʌndər'stænd/ v. entender mal.
misuse /mɪs'yuz/ v. maltratar; abusar.
mite /mait/ n. pizca f., blanca f.
mitten /'mɪtn̩/ n. mitón, confortante m.
mix /mɪks/ v. mezclar. **m. up,** confundir.
mixer /'mɪksər/ (for food), n. batidora f.
mixture /'mɪkstʃər/ n. mezcla, mixtura f.
mix-up /'mɪks,ʌp/ n. confusión f.
moan /moun/ n. **1.** quejido, gemido m. —v. **2.** gemir.
mob /mɒb/ n. muchedumbre f.; gentío m.
mobilization /,moubələ'zeiʃən/ n. movilización f.
mobilize /'moubə,laiz/ v. movilizar.
mock /mɒk/ v. burlar.
mockery /'mɒkəri/ n. burla f.
mod /mɒd/ a. a la última; en boga.
mode /moud/ n. modo m.
model /'mɒdl̩/ n. **1.** modelo m. —v. **2.** modelar.
modem /'moudəm/ n. módem m.
moderate /a 'mɒdərɪt; v -ə,reit/ a. **1.** moderado. —v. **2.** moderar.
moderation /,mɒdə'reiʃən/ n. moderación; sobriedad f.
modern /'mɒdərn/ a. moderno.
modernize /'mɒdər,naiz/ v. modernizar.
modest /'mɒdɪst/ a. modesto.
modesty /'mɒdɪsti/ n. modestia f.
modify /'mɒdə,fai/ v. modificar.
modulate /'mɒdʒə,leit/ v. modular.
moist /mɔist/ a. húmedo.
moisten /'mɔisən/ v. humedecer.
moisture /'mɔistʃər/ n. humedad f.
moisturize /'mɔistʃə,raiz/ v. hidratar.
molar /'moulər/ n. molar m.
molasses /mə'læsɪz/ n. melaza f.
mold /mould/ n. **1.** molde; moho m. —v. **2.** moldar, formar; enmohecerse.
moldy /'mouldi/ a. mohoso.
mole /moulei/ n. lunar m.; (animal) topo m.
molecule /'mɒlɪ,kyul/ n. molécula f.
molest /mə'lɛst/ v. molestar.
mollify /'mɒlə,fai/ v. molificar.
moment /'moumənt/ n. momento m.
momentary /'moumən,tɛri/ a. momentáneo.
momentous /mou'mɛntəs/ a. importante.
monarch /'mɒnərk/ n. monarca m. & f.
monarchy /'mɒnərki/ n. monarquía f.
monastery /'mɒnə,stɛri/ n. monasterio m.
Monday /'mʌndei/ n. lunes m.
monetary /'mɒnɪ,tɛri/ a. monetario.

money /'mʌni/ *n.* dinero *m.* **m. order,** giro postal.
mongrel /'mʌŋgrəl/ *n.* **1.** mestizo *m.* —*a.* **2.** mestizo, cruzado.
monitor /'mɒnɪtər/ *n.* amonestador *m.*; (computer) consola *f.*, pantalla *f.*
monk /mʌŋk/ *n.* monje *m.*
monkey /'mʌŋki/ *n.* mono -na.
monocle /'mɒnəkəl/ *n.* monóculo *m.*
monologue /'mɒnə,lɔg/ *n.* monólogo *m.*
monopolize /mə'nɒpə,laiz/ *v.* monopolizar.
monopoly /mə'nɒpəli/ *n.* monopolio *m.*
monosyllable /'mɒnə,sɪləbəl/ *n.* monosílabo *m.*
monotone /'mɒnə,toun/ *n.* monotonía *f.*
monotonous /mə'nɒtn̩əs/ *a.* monótono.
monotony /mə'nɒtn̩i/ *n.* monotonía *f.*
monsoon /mɒn'sun/ *n.* monzón *m.*
monster /'mɒnstər/ *n.* monstruo *m.*
monstrosity /mɒn'strɒsɪti/ *n.* monstruosidad *f.*
monstrous /'mɒnstrəs/ *a.* monstruoso.
month /mʌnθ/ *n.* mes *m.*
monthly /'mʌnθli/ *a.* mensual.
monument /'mɒnyəmənt/ *n.* monumento *m.*
monumental /,mɒnyə'mɛntl̩/ *a.* monumental.
mood /mud/ *n.* humor *m.*; *Gram.* modo *m.*
moody /'mudi/ *a.* caprichoso, taciturno.
moon /mun/ *n.* luna *f.*
moonlight /'mun,lait/ *n.* luz de la luna.
moonlighting /'mun,laitɪŋ/ *n.* pluriempleo *m.*
moor /mʊr/ *n.* **1.** párano *m.* —*v.* **2.** anclar.
Moor /mʊr/ *n.* moro -ra.
mop /mɒp/ *n.* **1.** fregasuelos *m.*, fregona *f.*, (*S.A.*) trapeador *m.* —*v.* **2.** fregar, (*S.A.*) trapear.
moped /'mou,pɛd/ *n.* (vehicle) velomotor *m.*
moral /'mɔrəl/ *a.* **1.** moral. —*n.* **2.** moraleja *f.* **morals,** moralidad *f.*
morale /mə'ræl/ *n.* espíritu *m.*
moralist /'mɔrəlɪst/ *n.* moralista *m.* & *f.*
morality /mə'rælɪti/ *n.* moralidad, ética *f.*
morbid /'mɔrbɪd/ *a.* mórbido.
more /mɔr/ *a.* & *adv.* más. **m. and m.,** cada vez más.
moreover /mɔr'ouvər/ *adv.* además.
morgue /mɔrg/ *n.* necrocomio *m.*
morning /'mɔrnɪŋ/ *n.* mañana *f.* **good m.,** buenos días.
Morocco /mə'rɒkou/ *n.* Marruecos *m.*
morose /mə'rous/ *a.* malhumorado.
morphine /'mɔrfin/ *n.* morfina *f.*
morsel /'mɔrsəl/ *n.* bocado *m.*
mortal /'mɔrtl̩/ *a.* & *n.* mortal *m.* & *f.*
mortality /mɔr'tælɪti/ *n.* mortalidad *f.*
mortar /'mɔrtər/ *n.* mortero *m.*
mortgage /'mɔrgɪdʒ/ *n.* **1.** hipoteca *f.* —*v.* **2.** hipotecar.
mortify /'mɔrtə,fai/ *v.* mortificar.
mosaic /mou'zeiɪk/ *n.* & *a.* mosaico *m.*
mosque /mɒsk/ *n.* mezquita *f.*
mosquito /mə'skitou/ *n.* mosquito *m.*
moss /mɔs/ *n.* musgo *m.*
most /moust/ *a.* **1.** más. —*adv.* **2.** más; sumamente. —*pron.* **3. m. of,** la mayor parte de.
mostly /'moustli/ *adv.* principalmente; en su mayor parte.
motel /mou'tɛl/ *n.* motel *m.*
moth /mɔθ/ *n.* polilla *f.*
mother /'mʌðər/ *n.* madre *f.*
mother-in-law /'mʌðər ɪn ,lɔ/ *n.* suegra *f.*
motif /mou'tif/ *n.* tema *m.*
motion /'mouʃən/ *n.* **1.** moción *f.*; movimiento *m.* —*v.* **2.** hacer señas.
motionless /'mouʃənlɪs/ *a.* inmóvil.
motion picture película *f.*
motivate /'moutə,veit/ *v.* motivar.
motive /'moutɪv/ *n.* motivo *m.*
motor /'moutər/ *n.* motor *m.*
motorboat /'moutər,bout/ *n.* lancha motora *f.*, autobote, motorbote *m.*, gasolinera *f.*
motorcycle /'moutər,saikəl/ *n.* motocicleta *f.*
motorcyclist /'moutər,saiklɪst/ *n.* motociclista *m.* & *f.*
motorist /'moutərɪst/ *n.* motorista *m.* & *f.*
motto /'mɒtou/ *n.* lema *m.*
mound /maund/ *n.* terrón; montón *m.*
mount /maunt/ *n.* **1.** monte *m.*; (horse) montura *f.* —*v.* **2.** montar; subir.
mountain /'mauntn̩/ *n.* montaña *f.*
mountaineer /,mauntn̩'ɪər/ *n.* montañés *m.*
mountainous /'mauntn̩əs/ *a.* montañoso.
mourn /mɔrn/ *v.* lamentar, llorar; llevar luto.
mournful /'mɔrnfəl/ *a.* triste.
mourning /'mɔrnɪŋ/ *n.* luto; lamento *m.*
mouse /maus/ *n.* ratón, ratoncito *m.*
mouth /mauθ/ *n.* boca *f.*; (of river) desembocadura *f.*
mouthwash /'mauθ,wɔʃ/ *n.* enjuague bucal *m.*
movable /'muvəbəl/ *a.* movible, movedizo.
move /muv/ *n.* **1.** movimiento *m.*; mudanza *f.* —*v.* **2.** mover; mudarse; emocionar, conmover. **m. away,** quitar; alejarse; mudarse.
movement /'muvmənt/ *n.* movimiento *m.*
movie /'muvi/ *n.* película *f.* **m. theater, movies,** cine *m.*
moving /'muvɪŋ/ *a.* conmovedor; persuasivo.
mow /mou/ *v.* guadañar, segar.
Mr. /'mɪstər/ *title.* Señor (Sr.).
Mrs. /'mɪsəz/ *title.* Señora (Sra.).
much /mʌtʃ/ *a.* & *adv.* mucho. **how m.,** cuánto. **so m.,** tanto. **too m.,** demasiado. **as m. as,** tanto como.
mucilage /'myusəlɪdʒ/ *n.* mucílago *m.*
mucous /'myukəs/ *a.* mucoso.
mucous membrane *n.* membrana mucosa *f.*
mud /mʌd/ *n.* fango, lodo *m.*
muddy /'mʌdi/ *a.* **1.** lodoso; turbio. —*v.* **2.** ensuciar; enturbiar.
muff /mʌf/ *n.* manguito *m.*
muffin /'mʌfɪn/ *n.* panecillo *m.*
mug /mʌg/ *n.* cubilete *m.*
mugger /'mʌgər/ *n.* asaltante *m.* & *f.*
mulatto /mə'lætou/ *n.* mulato *m.*
mule /myul/ *n.* mula *f.*
mullah /'mʌlə/ *n.* mullah *m.*
multicultural /,mʌlti'kʌltʃərəl, ,mʌltai-/ *a.* multicultural.
multinational /,mʌlti'næʃənl̩, ,mʌltai-/ *a.* multinacional.
multiple /'mʌltəpəl/ *a.* múltiple.
multiplication /,mʌltəplɪ'keiʃən/ *n.* multiplicación *f.*
multiplicity /,mʌltə'plɪsɪti/ *n.* multiplicidad *f.*
multiply /'mʌltəpli/ *v.* multiplicar.
multitasking /,mʌlti'tæskɪŋ, ,mʌltai-/ *n.* multitarea *f.*
multitude /'mʌltɪ,tud/ *n.* multitud *f.*
mummy /'mʌmi/ *n.* momia *f.*
mumps /mʌmps/ *n.* paperas *f.pl.*
municipal /myu'nɪsəpəl/ *a.* municipal.
munificent /myu'nɪfəsənt/ *a.* munífico.
munitions /myu'nɪʃənz/ *n.* municiones *m.pl.*
mural /'myʊrəl/ *a.* & *n.* mural *m.*
murder /'mɜrdər/ *n.* **1.** asesinato; homicidio *m.* —*v.* **2.** asesinar.
murderer /'mɜrdərər/ *n.* asesino -na.
murmur /'mɜrmər/ *n.* **1.** murmullo *m.* —*v.* **2.** murmurar.
muscle /'mʌsəl/ *n.* músculo *m.*
muscular /'mʌskyələr/ *a.* muscular.
muse /myuz/ *n.* **1.** musa *f.* —*v.* **2.** meditar.
museum /myu'ziəm/ *n.* museo *m.*
mushroom /'mʌʃrum/ *n.* seta *f.*, hongo *m.*
music /'myuzɪk/ *n.* música *f.*
musical /'myuzɪkəl/ *a.* musical; melodioso.
musician /myu'zɪʃən/ *n.* músico -ca.
Muslim /'mʌzlɪm/ *a.* & *n.* musulmano.
muslin /'mʌzlɪn/ *n.* muselina *f.*; percal *m.*
mussel /'mʌsəl/ *n.* mejillón *m.*
must /mʌst/ *v.* deber; tener que.
mustache /'mʌstæʃ/ *n.* bigotes *m.pl.*
mustard /'mʌstərd/ *n.* mostaza *f.*
muster /'mʌstər/ *n.* **1.** *Mil.* revista *f.* —*v.* **2.** reunir, juntar.
mute /myut/ *a.* & *n.* mudo -da.
mutilate /'myutl̩,eit/ *v.* mutilar.
mutiny /'myutn̩i/ *n.* **1.** motín *m.* —*v.* **2.** amotinarse.
mutt /mʌt/ *n.* *Colloq.* chucho *m.*
mutter /'mʌtər/ *v.* refunfuñar, gruñir.
mutton /'mʌtn̩/ *n.* carnero *m.*
mutual /'myutʃuəl/ *a.* mutuo.
muzzle /'mʌzəl/ *n.* **1.** hocico *m.*; bozal *m.* —*v.* **2.** embozar.
my /mai/ *a.* mi.
myriad /'mɪriəd/ *n.* miríada *f.*
myrtle /'mɜrtl̩/ *n.* mirto *m.*
myself /mai'sɛlf/ *pron.* mí, mí mismo; me. **I m.,** yo mismo.
mysterious /mɪ'stɪəriəs/ *a.* misterioso.
mystery /'mɪstəri/ *n.* misterio *m.*
mystic /'mɪstɪk/ *a.* místico.
mystify /'mɪstə,fai/ *v.* confundir.
myth /mɪθ/ *n.* mito *m.*
mythical /'mɪθɪkəl/ *a.* mítico.
mythology /mɪ'θɒlədʒi/ *n.* mitología *f.*

N

nag /næg/ *n.* **1.** jaca *f.* —*v.* **2.** regañar; sermonear.
nail /neil/ *n.* **1.** clavo *m.*; (finger) uña *f.* **n. polish,** esmalte para las uñas. —*v.* **2.** clavar.
naïve /nɑ'iv/ *a.* ingenuo.
naked /'neikɪd/ *a.* desnudo.
name /neim/ *n.* **1.** nombre *m.*; reputación *f.* —*v.* **2.** nombrar, mencionar.
namely /'neimli/ *adv.* a saber; es decir.
namesake /'neim,seik/ *n.* tocayo *m.*
nanny /'næni/ *n.* niñera *f.*
nap /næp/ *n.* siesta *f.* **to take a n.,** echar una siesta.
naphtha /'næfθə, 'næp-/ *n.* nafta *f.*
napkin /'næpkɪn/ *n.* servilleta *f.*
narcissus /nɑr'sɪsəs/ *n.* narciso *m.*
narcotic /nɑr'kɒtɪk/ *a.* & *n.* narcótico *m.*
narrate /'næreit/ *v.* narrar.
narrative /'nærətɪv/ *a.* **1.** narrativo. —*n.* **2.** cuento, relato *m.*
narrow /'nærou/ *a.* estrecho, angosto. **n.-minded,** intolerante.
nasal /'neizəl/ *a.* nasal.
nasty /'næsti/ *a.* desagradable.
nation /'neiʃən/ *n.* nación *f.*
national /'næʃənl̩/ *a.* nacional.
nationalism /'næʃənl̩,ɪzəm/ *n.* nacionalismo *m.*
nationality /,næʃə'nælɪti/ *n.* nacionalidad *f.*
nationalization /,næʃənl̩ə'zeiʃən/ *n.* nacionalización *f.*
nationalize /'næʃənl̩,aiz, 'næʃnə,laiz/ *v.* nacionalizar.
native /'neitɪv/ *a.* **1.** nativo. —*n.* **2.** natural; indígena *m.* & *f.*
nativity /nə'tɪvɪti/ *n.* natividad *f.*
natural /'nætʃərəl/ *a.* natural.
naturalist /'nætʃərəlɪst/ *n.* naturalista *m.* & *f.*
naturalize /'nætʃərə,laiz/ *v.* naturalizar.
naturalness /,nætʃərəlnɪs/ *n.* naturalidad *f.*
nature /'neitʃər/ *n.* naturaleza *f.*; índole *f.*; humor *m.*
naughty /'nɔti/ *a.* travieso, desobediente.
nausea /'nɔziə, -ʒə/ *n.* náusea *f.*
nauseous /'nɔʃəs/ *a.* nauseoso.
nautical /'nɔtɪkəl/ *a.* náutico.
naval /'neivəl/ *a.* naval.
nave /neiv/ *n.* nave *f.*
navel /'neivəl/ *n.* ombligo *m.*
navigable /'nævɪgəbəl/ *a.* navegable.
navigate /'nævɪ,geit/ *v.* navegar.
navigation /,nævɪ'geiʃən/ *n.* navegación *f.*
navigator /'nævɪ,geitər/ *n.* navegante *m.* & *f.*
navy /'neivi/ *n.* marina *f.*
navy blue azul marino *m.*
near /nɪər/ *a.* **1.** cercano, próximo. —*adv.* **2.** cerca. —*prep.* **3.** cerca de.
nearby /'nɪər'bai/ *a.* **1.** cercano. —*adv.* **2.** cerca.
nearly /'nɪərli/ *adv.* casi.
nearsighted /'nɪər,saitɪd/ *a.* corto de vista.
neat /nit/ *a.* aseado; ordenado.
neatness /'nitnɪs/ *n.* aseo *m.*
nebulous /'nɛbyələs/ *a.* nebuloso.
necessary /'nɛsə,sɛri/ *a.* necesario.
necessity /nə'sɛsɪti/ *n.* necesidad *f.*
neck /nɛk/ *n.* cuello *m.*
necklace /'nɛklɪs/ *n.* collar *m.*
necktie /'nɛk,tai/ *n.* corbata *f.*
nectar /'nɛktər/ *n.* néctar *m.*
nectarine /,nɛktə'rin/ *n.* nectarina *f.*
need /nid/ *n.* **1.** necesidad; (poverty) pobreza *f.* —*v.* **2.** necesitar.
needle /'nidl̩/ *n.* aguja *f.*
needless /'nidlɪs/ *a.* innecesario, inútil.
needy /'nidi/ *a.* indigente, necesitado, pobre.
nefarious /nɪ'fɛəriəs/ *a.* nefario.
negative /'nɛgətɪv/ *a.* negativo. *n.* negativa *f.*
neglect /nɪ'glɛkt/ *n.* **1.** negligencia *f.*; descuido *m.* —*v.* **2.** descuidar.
negligee /,nɛglɪ'ʒei/ *n.* negligé *m.*, bata de casa *f.*
negligent /'nɛglɪdʒənt/ *a.* negligente, descuidado.
negligible /'nɛglɪdʒəbəl/ *a.* insignificante.
negotiate /nɪ'gouʃi,eit/ *v.* negociar.
negotiation /nɪ,gouʃi'eiʃən/ *n.* negociación *f.*
Negro /'nigrou/ *n.* negro -ra.
neighbor /'neibər/ *n.* vecino -na.
neighborhood /'neibər,hʊd/ *n.* vecindad *f.*
neither /'niðər, 'nai-/ *a.* & *pron.* **1.** ninguno de los dos. —*adv.* **2.** tampoco. —*conj.* **3. neither... nor,** ni... ni.
neon /'niɒn/ *n.* neón *m.* **n. light,** tubo neón *m.*
nephew /'nɛfyu/ *n.* sobrino *m.*
nerve /nɜrv/ *n.* nervio *m.*; *Colloq.* audacia *f.*
nervous /'nɜrvəs/ *a.* nervioso.
nervous breakdown /'breik,daun/ crisis nerviosa *f.*
nest /nɛst/ *n.* nido *m.*
net /nɛt/ *a.* **1.** neto. —*n.* **2.** red *f.* **hair n.,** albanega, redecilla *f.* *v.* redar; *Com.* ganar.
netiquette /'nɛtɪkɪt/ *n.* etiqueta de la red *f.*
netting /'nɛtɪŋ/ *n.* red *m.*; obra de malla *f.*
network /'nɛt,wɜrk/ *n.* (radio) red radiodifusora.
neuralgia /nʊ'rældʒə/ *n.* neuralgia *f.*
neurology /nʊ'rɒlədʒi/ *n.* neurología *f.*
neurotic /nʊ'rɒtɪk/ *a.* neurótico.

neutral /ˈnutrəl/ *a.* neutral.
neutrality /nuˈtrælɪti/ *n.* neutralidad *f.*
neutron /ˈnutrɒn/ *n.* neutrón *m.*
neutron bomb bomba de neutrones *f.*
never /ˈnɛvər/ *adv.* nunca, jamás; **n. mind,** no importa.
nevertheless /ˌnɛvərðəˈlɛs/ *adv.* no obstante, sin embargo.
new /nu/ *a.* nuevo.
newbie /ˈnubi/ *n. Colloq.* novato -ta, inexperto -ta.
news /nuz/ *n.* noticias *f.pl.*
newsboy /ˈnuzˌbɔi/ *n.* vendedor -ra de periódicos.
news bulletin boletín informativo *m.*
news flash *n.* noticia de última hora *f.*
newsgroup /ˈnuzˌgrup/ *n.* grupo de discusion *m.*
newsletter /ˈnuzˌlɛtər/ *n.* hoja informativa *f.*
newspaper /ˈnuzˌpeipər/ *n.* periódico *m.*
New Testament Nuevo Testamento *m.*
new year *n.* año nuevo *m.*
next /nɛkst/ *a.* **1.** próximo; siguiente; contiguo. **—***adv.* **2.** luego, después. **n. door,** al lado. **n. to,** al lado de.
next-to-the-last /ˈnɛkst tə ðə ˈlæst/ *a.* penúltimo.
nibble /ˈnɪbəl/ *v.* picar.
nice /nis/ *a.* simpático, agradable; amable; hermoso; exacto.
nick /nɪk/ *n.* muesca *f.*, picadura *f.* **in the n. of time,** a punto.
nickel /ˈnɪkəl/ *n.* níquel *m.*
nickname /ˈnɪkˌneim/ *n.* **1.** apodo, mote *m.* **—***v.* **2.** apodar.
nicotine /ˈnɪkəˌtin/ *n.* nicotina *f.*
niece /nis/ *n.* sobrina *f.*
niggardly /ˈnɪgərdli/ *a.* mezquino.
night /nait/ *n.* noche *f.* **good n.,** buenas noches. **last n.,** anoche. **n. club,** cabaret *m.*
nightclub /ˈnaitˌklʌb/ *n.* cabaret *m.*
nightclub owner cabaretero -ra *m. & f.*
nightgown /ˈnaitˌgaun/ *n.* camisa de dormir.
nightingale /ˈnaitn̩ˌgeil, ˈnaitɪŋ-/ *n.* ruiseñor *m.*
nightly /ˈnaitli/ *adv.* todas las noches.
nightmare /ˈnaitˌmɛər/ *n.* pesadilla *f.*
night school escuela nocturna *f.*
night watchman vigilante nocturno *m.*
nimble /ˈnɪmbəl/ *a.* ágil.
nine /nain/ *a. & pron.* nueve.
nineteen /ˈnainˈtin/ *a. & pron.* diecinueve.
ninety /ˈnainti/ *a. & pron.* noventa.
ninth /nainθ/ *a.* noveno.
nipple /ˈnɪpəl/ *n.* teta *f.*; pezón *m.*
nitrogen /ˈnaitrədʒən/ *n.* nitrógeno *m.*
no /nou/ *a.* **1.** ninguno. **no one,** nadie. **—***adv.* **2.** no.
nobility /nouˈbɪlɪti/ *n.* nobleza *f.*
noble /ˈnoubəl/ *a. & n.* noble *m.*
nobleman /ˈnoubəlmən/ *n.* noble *m.*
nobody /ˈnouˌbɒdi/ *pron.* nadie.
nocturnal /nɒkˈtɜrnl̩/ *a.* nocturno.
nocturne /ˈnɒktɜrn/ *n.* nocturno *m.*
nod /nɒd/ *n.* **1.** seña con la cabeza. **—***v.* **2.** inclinar la cabeza; (doze) dormitar.
no-frills /ˈnou ˈfrɪlz/ *a.* sin extras.
noise /nɔiz/ *n.* ruido *m.*
noiseless /ˈnɔizlɪs/ *a.* silencioso.
noisy /ˈnɔizi/ *a.* ruidoso.
nominal /ˈnɒmənl̩/ *a.* nominal.
nominate /ˈnɒməˌneit/ *v.* nombrar.
nomination /ˌnɒməˈneiʃən/ *n.* nombramiento *m.*, nominación *f.*
nominee /ˌnɒməˈni/ *n.* candidato -ta.
nonaligned /ˌnɒnəˈlaind/ (in political sense), *a.* no alineado.
nonchalant /ˌnɒnʃəˈlɑnt/ *a.* indiferente.
noncombatant /ˌnɒnkəmˈbætnt/ *n.* no combatiente *m.*
noncommittal /ˌnɒnkəˈmɪtl̩/ *a.* evasivo; reservado.
nondescript /ˌnɒndɪˈskrɪpt/ *a.* difícil de describir.
none /nʌn/ *pron.* ninguno.
nonentity /nɒnˈɛntɪti/ *n.* nulidad *f.*
nonpartisan /nɒnˈpɑrtəzən/ *a.* sin afiliación.
non-proliferation /ˌnɒnprəˌlɪfəˈreiʃən/ *n.* no proliferación *m.*
nonsense /ˈnɒnsɛns/ *n.* tontería *f.*
nonsmoker /nɒnˈsmoukər/ *n.* no fumador -dora.
noodle /ˈnudl̩/ *n.* fideo *m.*
noon /nun/ *n.* mediodía *m.*
noose /nus/ *n.* lazo corredizo *m.*; dogal *m.*
nor /nɔr; *unstressed* nər/ *conj.* ni.
normal /ˈnɔrməl/ *a.* normal.
north /nɔrθ/ *n.* norte *m.*
North America /əˈmɛrɪkə/ Norte América *f.*
North American *a. & n.* norteamericano -na.
northeast /ˌnɔrθˈist; *Naut.* ˌnɔr-/ *n.* nordeste *m.*
northern /ˈnɔrðərn/ *a.* septentrional.
North Pole *n.* Polo Norte *m.*
northwest /ˌnɔrθˈwɛst; *Naut.* ˌnɔr-/ *n.* noroeste *m.*
Norway /ˈnɔrwei/ *n.* Noruega *f.*
Norwegian /nɔrˈwidʒən/ *a. & n.* noruego -ga.
nose /nouz/ *n.* nariz *f.*
nosebleed /ˈnouzˌblid/ *n.* hemorragia nasal *f.*
nostalgia /nɒˈstældʒə/ *n.* nostalgia *f.*
nostril /ˈnɒstrəl/ *n.* ventana de la nariz; (pl.) narices *f.pl.*
not /nɒt/ *adv.* no. **n. at all,** de ninguna manera. **n. even,** ni siquiera.
notable /ˈnoutəbəl/ *a.* notable.
notary /ˈnoutəri/ *n.* notario *m.*
notation /nouˈteiʃən/ *a.* notación *f.*
notch /nɒtʃ/ *n.* muesca *f.*; corte *m.*
note /nout/ *n.* **1.** nota *f.*; apunte *m.* **—***v.* **2.** notar.
notebook /ˈnoutˌbʊk/ *n.* libreta *f.*, cuaderno *m.*
noted /ˈnoutɪd/ *a.* célebre.
notepaper /ˈnoutˌpeipər/ *n.* papel de notas *m.*
noteworthy /ˈnoutˌwɜrði/ *a.* notable.
nothing /ˈnʌθɪŋ/ *pron.* nada.
notice /ˈnoutɪs/ *n.* **1.** aviso *m.*; noticia *f.* **—***v.* **2.** observar, fijarse en.
noticeable /ˈnoutɪsəbəl/ *a.* notable.
notification /ˌnoutəfɪˈkeiʃən/ *n.* notificación *f.*
notify /ˈnoutəˌfai/ *v.* notificar.
notion /ˈnouʃən/ *n.* noción; idea *f.*; (pl.) novedades *f.pl.*
notoriety /ˌnoutəˈraiɪti/ *n.* notoriedad *f.*
notorious /nouˈtɔriəs/ *a.* notorio.
noun /naun/ *n.* nombre, sustantivo *m.*
nourish /ˈnɜrɪʃ/ *v.* nutrir, alimentar.
nourishment /ˈnɜrɪʃmənt/ *n.* nutrimento; alimento *m.*
novel /ˈnɒvəl/ *a.* **1.** nuevo, original. **—***n.* **2.** novela *f.*
novelist /ˈnɒvəlɪst/ *n.* novelista *m. & f.*
novelty /ˈnɒvəlti/ *n.* novedad *f.*
November /nouˈvɛmbər/ *n.* noviembre *m.*
novena /nouˈvinə/ *n.* novena *f.*
novice /ˈnɒvɪs/ *n.* novicio -cia, novato -ta.
novocaine /ˈnouvəˌkein/ *n.* novocaína *f.*
now /nau/ *adv.* ahora. **n. and then,** de vez en cuando. **by n.,** ya. **from n. on,** de ahora en adelante. **just n.,** ahorita. **right n.,** ahora mismo.
nowadays /ˈnauəˌdeiz/ *adv.* hoy día, hoy en día, actualmente.
nowhere /ˈnouˌwɛər/ *adv.* en ninguna parte.
nozzle /ˈnɒzəl/ *n.* boquilla *f.*
nuance /ˈnuɑns/ *n.* matiz *m.*
nuclear /ˈnukliər/ *a.* nuclear.
nuclear energy energía nuclear *f.*
nuclear warhead /ˈwɔrˌhɛd/ cabeza nuclear *f.*
nuclear waste desechos nucleares *m.pl.*
nucleus /ˈnukliəs/ *n.* núcleo *m.*
nude /nud/ *a.* desnudo.
nuisance /ˈnusəns/ *n.* molestia *f.*
nuke /nuk/ *n.* bomba atómica *f.*
nullify /ˈnʌləˌfai/ *v.* anular.
number /ˈnʌmbər/ *n.* **1.** número *m.*; cifra *f.* **license n.,** matrícula *f.* **—***v.* **2.** numerar, contar.
numeric /nuˈmɛrɪk/ **numerical** *a.* numérico.
numeric keypad /nuˈmɛrɪk/ teclado numérico *m.*
numerous /ˈnumərəs/ *a.* numeroso.
nun /nʌn/ *n.* monja *f.*
nuptial /ˈnʌpʃəl/ *a.* nupcial.
nurse /nɜrs/ *n.* **1.** enfermera *f.*; (child's) ama, niñera *f.* **—***v.* **2.** criar, alimentar, amamantar; cuidar.
nursery /ˈnɜrsəri/ *n.* cuarto destinado a los niños; *Agr.* plantel, criadero *m.*
nursery school jardín de infancia *m.*
nurture /ˈnɜrtʃər/ *v.* nutrir.
nut /nʌt/ *n.* nuez *f.*; *Mech.* tuerca *f.*
nutcracker /ˈnʌtˌkrækər/ *n.* cascanueces *m.*
nutrition /nuˈtrɪʃən/ *n.* nutrición *f.*
nutritious /nuˈtrɪʃəs/ *a.* nutritivo.
nylon /ˈnailɒn/ *n.* nilón *m.*
nymph /nɪmf/ *n.* ninfa *f.*

O

oak /ouk/ *n.* roble *m.*
oar /ɔr/ *n.* remo *m.*
OAS *abbr.* (Organization of American States) OEA (Organización de los Estados Americanos) *f.*
oasis /ouˈeisɪs/ *n.* oasis *m.*
oat /out/ *n.* avena *f.*
oath /ouθ/ *n.* juramento *m.*
oatmeal /ˈoutˌmil/ *n.* harina de avena *f.*
obedience /ouˈbidiəns/ *n.* obediencia *f.*
obedient /ouˈbidiənt/ *a.* obediente.
obese /ouˈbis/ *a.* obeso, gordo.
obey /ouˈbei/ *v.* obedecer.
obituary /ouˈbɪtʃuˌɛri/ *n.* obituario *m.*
object /*n* ˈɒbdʒɪkt; *v* əbˈdʒɛkt/ *n.* **1.** objeto *m.*; *Gram.* complemento *m.* **—***v.* **2.** oponerse; objetar.
objection /əbˈdʒɛkʃən/ *n.* objeción *f.*
objectionable /əbˈdʒɛkʃənəbəl/ *a.* censurable.
objective /əbˈdʒɛktɪv/ *a. & n.* objetivo *m.*
obligation /ˌɒblɪˈgeiʃən/ *n.* obligación *f.*
obligatory /əˈblɪgəˌtɔri/ *a.* obligatorio.
oblige /əˈblaidʒ/ *v.* obligar; complacer.
oblique /əˈblik/ *a.* oblicuo.
obliterate /əˈblɪtəˌreit/ *v.* borrar; destruir.
oblivion /əˈblɪviən/ *n.* olvido *m.*
oblong /ˈɒbˌlɔŋ/ *a.* oblongo.
obnoxious /əbˈnɒkʃəs/ *a.* ofensivo, odioso.
obscene /əbˈsin/ *a.* obsceno, indecente.
obscure /əbˈskyʊr/ *a.* **1.** obscuro. **—***v.* **2.** obscurecer.
observance /əbˈzɜrvəns/ *n.* observancia; ceremonia *f.*
observation /ˌɒbzɜrˈveiʃən/ *n.* observación *f.*
observatory /əbˈzɜrvəˌtɔri/ *n.* observatorio *m.*
observe /əbˈzɜrv/ *v.* observar; celebrar.
observer /əbˈzɜrvər/ *n.* observador -ra.
obsession /əbˈsɛʃən/ *n.* obsesión *f.*
obsolete /ˌɒbsəˈlit/ *a.* anticuado.
obstacle /ˈɒbstəkəl/ *n.* obstáculo *m.*
obstetrician /ˌɒbstɪˈtrɪʃən/ *n.* obstétrico -ca, tocólogo -ga *m. & f.*
obstinate /ˈɒbstənɪt/ *a.* obstinado, terco.
obstruct /əbˈstrʌkt/ *v.* obstruir, impedir.
obstruction /əbˈstrʌkʃən/ *n.* obstrucción *f.*
obtain /əbˈtein/ *v.* obtener, conseguir.
obtuse /əbˈtus/ *a.* obtuso.
obviate /ˈɒbviˌeit/ *v.* obviar.
obvious /ˈɒbviəs/ *a.* evidente, obvio.
occasion /əˈkeiʒən/ *n.* **1.** ocasión *f.* **—***v.* **2.** ocasionar.
occasional /əˈkeiʒənl̩/ *a.* ocasional.
occult /əˈkʌlt/ *a.* oculto.
occupant /ˈɒkyəpənt/ *n.* ocupante *m. & f.*; inquilino -na.
occupation /ˌɒkyəˈpeiʃən/ *n.* ocupación *f.*; empleo *m.*
occupy /ˈɒkyəˌpai/ *v.* ocupar; emplear.
occur /əˈkɜr/ *v.* ocurrir.
occurrence /əˈkɜrəns/ *n.* ocurrencia *f.*
ocean /ˈouʃən/ *n.* océano *m.*
o'clock /əˈklɒk/ **it's one o.,** es la una. **it's two o.,** son las dos, etc. **at... o.,** a las...
octagon /ˈɒktəˌgɒn/ *n.* octágono *m.*
octave /ˈɒktɪv/ *n.* octava *f.*
October /ɒkˈtoubər/ *n.* octubre *m.*
octopus /ˈɒktəpəs/ *n.* pulpo *m.*
oculist /ˈɒkyəlɪst/ *n.* oculista *m. & f.*
odd /ɒd/ *a.* impar; suelto; raro.
odd number número impar *m.*
odious /ˈoudiəs/ *a.* odioso.
odor /ˈoudər/ *n.* olor *m.*; fragancia *f.*
of /əv/ *prep.* de.
off /ɔf/ *adv.* (see under verb: **stop off, take off,** etc.)
offend /əˈfɛnd/ *v.* ofender.
offender /əˈfɛndər/ *n.* ofensor -ra; delincuente *m. & f.*
offense /əˈfɛns/ *n.* ofensa *f.*; crimen *m.*
offensive /əˈfɛnsɪv/ *a.* **1.** ofensivo. **—***n.* **2.** ofensiva *f.*
offer /ˈɔfər/ *n.* **1.** oferta *f.* **—***v.* **2.** ofrecer.
offering /ˈɔfərɪŋ/ *n.* oferta *f.*
office /ˈɔfɪs/ *n.* oficina *f.*; despacho *m.*; oficio, cargo *m.*
officer /ˈɔfəsər/ *n.* oficial *m. & f.* **police o.,** agente de policía *m. & f.*
official /əˈfɪʃəl/ *a.* **1.** oficial. **—***n.* **2.** oficial *m. & f.*, funcionario -ria.
officiate /əˈfɪʃiˌeit/ *v.* oficiar.
officious /əˈfɪʃəs/ *a.* oficioso.
offspring /ˈɔfˌsprɪŋ/ *n.* hijos *m.pl.*; progenie *f.*
often /ˈɔfən/ *adv.* muchas veces, a menudo. **how o.,** con qué frecuencia.
oil /ɔil/ *n.* **1.** aceite; óleo; petróleo *m.* **—***v.* **2.** aceitar; engrasar.
oil refinery /rɪˈfainəri/ destilería de petróleo *f.*
oil tanker /ˈtæŋkər/ petrolero *m.*
oily /ˈɔili/ *a.* aceitoso.
ointment /ˈɔintmənt/ *n.* ungüento *m.*
okay /ˈouˈkei, ˌouˈkei/ *adv.* bien; de acuerdo.
old /ould/ *a.* viejo; antiguo. **o. man, o. woman,** viejo -ja.
old-fashioned /ˈould ˈfæʃənd/ *a.* fuera de moda, anticuado.
Old Testament Antiguo Testamento *m.*
olive /ˈɒlɪv/ *n.* aceituna, oliva *f.*
ombudsman /ˈɒmbədzmən/ *n.* ombudsman *m.*
omelet /ˈɒmlɪt/ *n.* tortilla de huevos.
omen /ˈoumən/ *n.* agüero *m.*
ominous /ˈɒmənəs/ *a.* ominoso, siniestro.
omission /ouˈmɪʃən/ *n.* omisión *f.*; olvido *m.*
omit /ouˈmɪt/ *v.* omitir.
omnibus /ˈɒmnəˌbʌs/ *n.* ómnibus *m.*
omnipotent /ɒmˈnɪpətənt/ *a.* omnipotente.
on /ɒn/ *prep.* **1.** en, sobre, encima de. **—***adv.* **2.** adelante.

once /wʌns/ *adv.* una vez. **at o.,** en seguida. **o. in a while,** de vez en cuando.
one /wʌn/ *a. & pron.* uno -na.
one-armed bandit /ˈwʌn ˌɑrmd/ tragaperras *f.*
oneself /wʌnˈsɛlf/ *pron.* sí mismo -ma; se. **with o.,** consigo.
onion /ˈʌnyən/ *n.* cebolla *f.*
on-line /ˈɒn ˈlain/ *a.* conectado.
only /ˈounli/ *a.* **1.** único, solo. —*adv.* **2.** sólo, solamente.
onward /ˈɒnwərd/ *adv.* adelante.
opal /ˈoupəl/ *n.* ópalo *m.*
opaque /ouˈpeik/ *a.* opaco.
open /ˈoupən/ *a.* **1.** abierto; franco. **o. air,** aire libre. —*v.* **2.** abrir.
opening /ˈoupənɪŋ/ *n.* abertura *f.*
opera /ˈɒpərə/ *n.* ópera *f.* **o. glasses,** anteojos de ópera; gemelos *m.pl.*
operate /ˈɒpəˌreit/ *v.* operar.
operation /ˌɒpəˈreiʃən/ *n.* operación *f.* **to have an o.,** operarse, ser operado.
operative /ˈɒpərətɪv/ *a.* eficaz, operativo.
operator /ˈɒpəˌreitər/ *n.* operario -ria. **elevator o.,** ascensorista *m. & f.* **telephone o.,** telefonista *m. & f.*
operetta /ˌɒpəˈrɛtə/ *n.* opereta *f.*
ophthalmic /ɒfˈθælmɪk, ɒp-/ *a.* oftálmico.
opinion /əˈpɪnyən/ *n.* opinión *f.*
opponent /əˈpounənt/ *n.* antagonista *m. & f.*
opportunism /ˌɒpərˈtunɪzəm/ *n.* oportunismo *m.*
opportunity /ˌɒpərˈtunɪti/ *n.* ocasión, oportunidad *f.*
oppose /əˈpouz/ *v.* oponer.
opposite /ˈɒpəzɪt/ *a.* **1.** opuesto, contrario. —*prep.* **2.** al frente de. —*n.* **3.** contrario *m.*
opposition /ˌɒpəˈzɪʃən/ *n.* oposición *f.*
oppress /əˈprɛs/ *v.* oprimir.
oppression /əˈprɛʃən/ *n.* opresión *f.*
oppressive /əˈprɛsɪv/ *a.* opresivo.
optic /ˈɒptɪk/ *a.* óptico.
optical disc /ˈɒptɪkəl ˈdɪsk/ disco óptico *m.*
optical illusion /ˈɒptɪkəl/ ilusión de óptica *f.*
optician /ɒpˈtɪʃən/ *n.* óptico -ca.
optics /ˈɒptɪks/ *n.* óptica *f.*
optimism /ˈɒptəˌmɪzəm/ *n.* optimismo.
optimistic /ˌɒptəˈmɪstɪk/ *a.* optimista.
option /ˈɒpʃən/ *n.* opción, elección *f.*
optional /ˈɒpʃənl̩/ *a.* discrecional, facultativo.
optometry /ɒpˈtɒmɪtri/ *n.* optometría *f.*
opulent /ˈɒpyələnt/ *a.* opulento.
or /ɔr/ *conj.* o, (before *o-, ho-*) u.
oracle /ˈɔrəkəl/ *n.* oráculo *m.*
oral /ˈɔrəl/ *a.* oral, vocal.
orange /ˈɔrɪndʒ/ *n.* naranja *f.*
orange juice jugo de naranja, zumo de naranja *m.*
orange squeezer /ˈskwizər/ *n.* exprimidora de naranjas *f.*
oration /ɔˈreiʃən/ *n.* discurso *m.;* oración *f.*
orator /ˈɔrətər/ *n.* orador -ra.
oratory /ˈɔrəˌtɔri/ *n.* oratoria *f.;* (church) oratorio *m.*
orbit /ˈɔrbɪt/ *n.* órbita *f.*
orchard /ˈɔrtʃərd/ *n.* huerto *m.*
orchestra /ˈɔrkəstrə/ *n.* orquesta *f.* **o. seat,** butaca *f.*
orchid /ˈɔrkɪd/ *n.* orquídea *f.*
ordain /ɔrˈdein/ *v.* ordenar.
ordeal /ɔrˈdil/ *n.* prueba *f.*
order /ˈɔrdər/ *n.* orden, *m. or f.;* clase *f.; Com.* pedido *m.* **in o. that,** para que. *v.* ordenar; mandar; pedir.
order blank hoja de pedidos *f.*
orderly /ˈɔrdərli/ *a.* ordenado.
ordinance /ˈɔrdn̩əns/ *n.* ordenanza *f.*
ordinary /ˈɔrdn̩ˌɛri/ *a.* ordinario.
ordination /ˌɔrdn̩ˈeiʃən/ *n.* ordenación *f.*
ore /ɔr/ *n.* mineral *m.*
organ /ˈɔrgən/ *n.* órgano *m.*
organdy /ˈɔrgəndi/ *n.* organdí *m.*
organic /ɔrˈgænɪk/ *a.* orgánico.
organism /ˈɔrgəˌnɪzəm/ *n.* organismo *m.*
organist /ˈɔrgənɪst/ *n.* organista *m. & f.*
organization /ˌɔrgənəˈzeiʃən/ *n.* organización *f.*
organize /ˈɔrgəˌnaiz/ *v.* organizar.
orgy /ˈɔrdʒi/ *n.* orgía *f.*
orient /ˈɔriənt/ *n.* **1.** oriente *m.* —*v.* **2.** orientar.
Orient /ˈɔriənt/ *n.* Oriente *m.*
Oriental /ˌɔriˈɛntl̩/ *a.* oriental.
orientation /ˌɔriənˈteiʃən/ *n.* orientación *f.*
origin /ˈɔrɪdʒɪn/ *n.* origen *m.*
original /əˈrɪdʒənl̩/ *a. & n.* original *m.*
originality /əˌrɪdʒəˈnælɪti/ *n.* originalidad *f.*
ornament /*n* ˈɔrnəmənt; *v* -ˌmɛnt/ *n.* **1.** ornamento *m.* —*v.* **2.** ornamentar.
ornamental /ˌɔrnəˈmɛntl̩/ *a.* ornamental, decorativo.
ornate /ɔrˈneit/ *a.* ornado.
ornithology /ˌɔrnəˈθɒlədʒi/ *n.* ornitología *f.*
orphan /ˈɔrfən/ *a. & n.* huérfano -na.
orphanage /ˈɔrfənɪdʒ/ *n.* orfanato *m.*
orthodox /ˈɔrθəˌdɒks/ *a.* ortodoxo.
ostentation /ˌɒstɛnˈteiʃən/ *n.* ostentación *f.*
ostentatious /ˌɒstɛnˈteiʃəs/ *a.* ostentoso.
ostrich /ˈɔstrɪtʃ/ *n.* avestruz *f.*
other /ˈʌðər/ *a. & pron.* otro. **every o. day,** un día sí otro no.
otherwise /ˈʌðərˌwaiz/ *adv.* de otra manera.
ought /ɔt/ *v.* deber.
ounce /auns/ *n.* onza *f.*
our /auᵊr; *unstressed* ɑr/ **ours** *a. & pron.* nuestro.
ourselves /ɑrˈsɛlvz/ *pron.* nosotros -as; mismos -as; nos.
oust /aust/ *v.* desalojar.
ouster /ˈaustər/ *n.* desahucio *m.*
out /aut/ *adv.* **1.** fuera, afuera. **out of,** fuera de. —*prep.* **2.** por.
outbreak /ˈautˌbreik/ *n.* erupción *f.*
outcast /ˈautˌkæst/ *n.* paria *m. & f.*
outcome /ˈautˌkʌm/ *n.* resultado *m.*
outdoors /ˌautˈdɔrz/ *adv.* fuera de casa; al aire libre.
outer /ˈautər/ *a.* exterior, externo.
outfit /ˈautˌfɪt/ *n.* **1.** equipo; traje *m.* —*v.* **2.** equipar.
outgrowth /ˈautˌgrouθ/ *n.* resultado *m.*
outing /ˈautɪŋ/ *n.* paseo *m.*
outlaw /ˈautˌlɔ/ *n.* **1.** bandido *m.* —*v.* **2.** proscribir.
outlet /ˈautlɛt/ *n.* salida *f.*
outline /ˈautˌlain/ *n.* **1.** contorno; esbozo *m.;* silueta *f.* —*v.* **2.** esbozar.
outlive /ˌautˈlɪv/ *v.* sobrevivir.
out-of-court settlement /ˈautəvˌkɔrt/ arreglo pacífico *m.*
out-of-date /ˈaut əv ˈdeit/ *a.* anticuado.
out of focus *a.* desenfocado.
outpost /ˈautˌpoust/ *n.* puesto avanzado.
output /ˈautˌpʊt/ *n.* capacidad *f.;* producción *f.*
outrage /ˈautreidʒ/ *n.* **1.** ultraje *m.;* atrocidad *f.* —*v.* **2.** ultrajar.
outrageous /autˈreidʒəs/ *a.* atroz.
outrun /ˌautˈrʌn/ *v.* exceder.
outside /*a, prep, adv* ˌautˈsaid; *n* ˈautˈsaid/ *a. & n.* **1.** exterior *m.* —*adv.* **2.** afuera, por fuera. —*prep.* **3.** fuera de.
outskirt /ˈautˌskɜrt/ *n.* borde *m.*
outward /ˈautwərd/ *adv.* hacia afuera.
outwardly /ˈautwərdli/ *adv.* exteriormente.
oval /ˈouvəl/ *a.* **1.** oval, ovalado. —*n.* **2.** óvalo *m.*
ovary /ˈouvəri/ *n.* ovario *m.*
ovation /ouˈveiʃən/ *n.* ovación *f.*
oven /ˈʌvən/ *n.* horno *m.*
over /ˈouvər/ *prep.* **1.** sobre, encima de; por. —*adv.* **2. o. here,** aquí. **o. there,** allí, por allí. **to be o.,** estar terminado.
overcoat /ˈouvərˌkout/ *n.* abrigo, sobretodo *m.*
overcome /ˌouvərˈkʌm/ *v.* superar, vencer.
overdose /ˈouvərˌdous/ *n.* sobredosis *f.*
overdue /ˌouvərˈdu/ *a.* retrasado.
overflow /*n* ˈouvərˌflou; *v* ˌouvərˈflou/ *n.* **1.** inundación *f.* —*v.* **2.** inundar.
overhaul /ˌouvərˈhɔl/ *v.* repasar.
overhead /ˈouvərˈhɛd/ *adv.* arriba, en lo alto.
overkill /ˈouvərˌkɪl/ *n.* efecto mayor que el pretendido.
overlook /ˌouvərˈlʊk/ *v.* pasar por alto.
overnight /ˈouvərˈnait/ *adv.* **to stay or stop o.,** pasar la noche.
overpower /ˌouvərˈpauər/ *v.* vencer.
overrule /ˌouvərˈrul/ *v.* predominar.
overrun /ˌouvərˈrʌn/ *v.* invadir.
oversee /ˌouvərˈsi/ *v.* superentender.
oversight /ˈouvərˌsait/ *n.* descuido *m.*
overt /ouˈvɜrt/ *a.* abierto.
overtake /ˌouvərˈteik/ *v.* alcanzar.
overthrow /*n* ˈouvərˌθrou; *v* ˌouvərˈθrou/ *n.* **1.** trastorno *m.* —*v.* **2.** trastornar.
overture /ˈouvərtʃər/ *n. Mus.* obertura *f.*
overturn /ˌouvərˈtɜrn/ *v.* trastornar.
overview /ˈouvərˌvyu/ *n.* visión de conjunto *f.*
overweight /ˈouvərˌweit/ *a.* demasiado pesado.
overwhelm /ˌouvərˈwɛlm/ *v.* abrumar.
overwork /ˌouvərˈwɜrk/ *v.* trabajar demasiado.
owe /ou/ *v.* deber. **owing to,** debido a.
owl /aul/ *n.* búho *m.*, lechuza *f.*
own /oun/ *a.* **1.** propio. —*v.* **2.** poseer.
owner /ˈounər/ *n.* dueño -ña.
ox /ɒks/ *n.* buey *m.*
oxygen /ˈɒksɪdʒən/ *n.* oxígeno *m.*
oxygen tent tienda de oxígeno *f.*
oyster /ˈɔistər/ *n.* ostra *f.*

P

pace /peis/ *n.* **1.** paso *m.* —*v.* **2.** pasearse. **p. off,** medir a pasos.
pacific /pəˈsɪfɪk/ *a.* pacífico.
Pacific Ocean Océano Pacífico *m.*
pacifier /ˈpæsəˌfaiər/ *n.* pacificador *m.;* (baby p.) chupete *m.*
pacifism /ˈpæsəˌfɪzəm/ *n.* pacifismo *m.*
pacifist /ˈpæsəfɪst/ *n.* pacifista *m. & f.*
pacify /ˈpæsəˌfai/ *v.* pacificar.
pack /pæk/ *n.* **1.** fardo; paquete *m.;* (animals) muta *f.* **p. of cards,** baraja *f.* —*v.* **2.** empaquetar; (baggage) empacar.
package /ˈpækɪdʒ/ *n.* paquete, bulto *m.*
package tour viaje todo incluido *m.*
pact /pækt/ *n.* pacto *m.*
pad /pæd/ *n.* **1.** colchoncillo *m.* **p. of paper,** bloc de papel. —*v.* **2.** rellenar.
paddle /ˈpædl̩/ *n.* **1.** canalete *m.* —*v.* **2.** remar.
padlock /ˈpædˌlɒk/ *n.* candado *m.*
pagan /ˈpeigən/ *a. & n.* pagano -na.
page /peidʒ/ *n.* página *f.;* (boy) paje *m.*
pageant /ˈpædʒənt/ *n.* espectáculo *m.;* procesión *f.*
pail /peil/ *n.* cubo *m.*
pain /pein/ *n.* dolor *m.* **to take pains,** esmerarse.
painful /ˈpeinfəl/ *a.* doloroso; penoso.
pain killer /ˈpeinˌkɪlər/ analgésico *m.*
paint /peint/ *n.* **1.** pintura *f.* —*v.* **2.** pintar.
painter /ˈpeintər/ *n.* pintor -ra.
painting /ˈpeintɪŋ/ *n.* pintura *f.;* cuadro *m.*
pair /pɛər/ *n.* **1.** par *m.;* pareja *f.* —*v.* **2.** parear. **p. off,** emparejarse.
pajamas /pəˈdʒɑməz, -ˈdʒæməz/ *n.* pijama *m.*
palace /ˈpælɪs/ *n.* palacio *m.*
palatable /ˈpælətəbəl/ *a.* sabroso, agradable.
palate /ˈpælɪt/ *n.* paladar *m.*
palatial /pəˈleiʃəl/ *a.* palaciego, suntuoso.
pale /peil/ *a.* pálido. **to turn pale,** palidecer.
paleness /ˈpeilnɪs/ *n.* palidez *f.*
palette /ˈpælɪt/ *n.* paleta *f.*
pallbearer /ˈpɔlˌbɛərər/ *n.* portador del féretro, portaféretro *m.*
pallid /ˈpælɪd/ *a.* pálido.
palm /pɑm/ *n.* palma *f.* **p. tree,** palmera *f.*
palpitate /ˈpælpɪˌteit/ *v.* palpitar.
paltry /ˈpɔltri/ *a.* miserable.
pamper /ˈpæmpər/ *v.* mimar.
pamphlet /ˈpæmflɪt/ *n.* folleto *m.*
pan /pæn/ *n.* cacerola *f.*
panacea /ˌpænəˈsiə/ *n.* panacea *f.*
Pan-American /ˌpænəˈmɛrɪkən/ *a.* panamericano.
pane /pein/ *n.* hoja de vidrio *f.*, cuadro *m.*
panel /ˈpænl̩/ *n.* tablero *m.*
pang /pæŋ/ *n.* dolor; remordimiento *m.*
panic /ˈpænɪk/ *n.* pánico *m.*
panorama /ˌpænəˈræmə, -ˈrɑmə/ *n.* panorama *m.*
pant /pænt/ *v.* jadear.
panther /ˈpænθər/ *n.* pantera *f.*
pantomime /ˈpæntəˌmaim/ *n.* pantomima *f.;* mímica *f.*
pantry /ˈpæntri/ *n.* despensa *f.*
pants /pænts/ *n.* pantalones, *m.pl.*
panty hose /ˈpæntiˌhouz/ *n.* pantys, pantimedias *f.pl.* (medias hasta la cintura).
papal /ˈpeipəl/ *a.* papal.
paper /ˈpeipər/ *n.* papel; periódico; artículo *m.*
paperback /ˈpeipərˌbæk/ *n.* libro en rústica *m.*
paper clip sujetapapeles *m.*
paper cup vaso de papel *m.*
paper hanger /ˈpeipərˌhæŋər/ empapelador -ra.
paper money papel moneda *m.*
paperweight /ˈpeipərˌweit/ pisapapeles *m.*
papier-mâché /ˌpeipərməˈʃei, pɑˌpyei-/ *n.* cartón piedra *m.*
paprika /pæˈprikə, pə-, pɑ-, ˈpæprɪkə/ *n.* pimentón *m.*
par /pɑr/ *n.* paridad *f.; Com.* par *f.*
parable /ˈpærəbəl/ *n.* parábola *f.*
parachute /ˈpærəˌʃut/ *n.* paracaídas *m.*
parade /pəˈreid/ *n.* **1.** desfile *m.*, procesión *f.* —*v.* **2.** desfilar.
paradise /ˈpærəˌdais/ *n.* paraíso *m.*
paradox /ˈpærəˌdɒks/ *n.* paradoja *f.*
paraffin /ˈpærəfɪn/ *n.* parafina *f.*
paragraph /ˈpærəˌgræf/ *n.* párrafo *m.*
parakeet /ˈpærəˌkit/ *n.* perico *m.*
parallel /ˈpærəˌlɛl/ *a.* **1.** paralelo. —*v.* **2.** correr parejas con.
paralysis /pəˈræləsɪs/ *n.* parálisis *f.*
paralyze /ˈpærəˌlaiz/ *v.* paralizar.
paramedic /ˌpærəˈmɛdɪk/ *n.* paramédico -ca.
parameter /pəˈræmɪtər/ *n.* parámetro *m.*
paramount /ˈpærəˌmaunt/ *a.* supremo.
paraphrase /ˈpærəˌfreiz/ *n.* **1.** paráfrasis *f.* —*v.* **2.** parafrasear.
paraplegic /ˈpærəˈplidʒɪk/ *n.* parapléjico -ca.
parasite /ˈpærəˌsait/ *n.* parásito *m.*

parboil /'pɑr,bɔil/ v. sancochar.

parcel /'pɑrsəl/ n. paquete m. **p. of land,** lote de terreno.

parchment /'pɑrtʃmənt/ n. pergamino m.

pardon /'pɑrdn/ n. **1.** perdón m. —v. **2.** perdonar.

pare /pɛɑr/ v. pelar.

parentage /'pɛərəntidʒ, 'pær-/ n. origen m.; extracción f.

parenthesis /pə'rɛnθəsis/ n. paréntesis m.

parents /'pɛərənts/ n. padres m.pl.

parish /'pærɪʃ/ n. parroquia f.

Parisian /pə'rɪʒən, -'riʒən, -'rɪziən/ a. & n. parisiense m. & f.

parity /'pærɪti/ n. igualdad, paridad f.

park /pɑrk/ n. **1.** parque m. —v. **2.** estacionar.

parking lot /'pɑrkɪŋ/ n. estacionamiento, aparcamiento m.

parking meter /'pɑrkɪŋ/ parquímetro m.

parking space /'pɑrkɪŋ/ estacionamiento, aparcamiento m.

parkway /'pɑrk,wei/ n. bulevar m.; autopista f.

parley /'pɑrli/ n. conferencia f.; Mil. parlamento m.

parliament /'pɑrləmənt/ n. parlamento m.

parliamentary /,pɑrlə'mɛntəri, -tri; sometimes ,pɑrlyə-/ a. parlamentario.

parlor /'pɑrlər/ n. sala f., salón m.

parochial /pə'roukiəl/ a. parroquial.

parody /'pærədi/ n. **1.** parodia f. —v. **2.** parodiar.

parole /pə'roul/ n. **1.** palabra de honor f.; Mil. santo y seña. —v. **2.** poner en libertad bajo palabra.

paroxysm /'pærək,sizəm/ n. paroxismo m.

parrot /'pærət/ n. loro, papagayo m.

parsimony /'pɑrsə,mouni/ n. parsimonia f.

parsley /'pɑrsli/ n. perejil m.

parson /'pɑrsən/ n. párroco m.

part /pɑrt/ n. **1.** parte f.; Theat. papel m. —v. **2.** separarse, partirse. **p. with,** desprenderse de.

partake /pɑr'teik/ v. tomar parte.

partial /'pɑrʃəl/ a. parcial.

participant /pɑr'tɪsəpənt/ n. participante m. & f.

participate /pɑr'tɪsə,peit/ v. participar.

participation /pɑr,tɪsə'peiʃən/ n. participación f.

participle /'pɑrtə,sɪpəl, -səpəl/ n. participio m.

particle /'pɑrtɪkəl/ n. partícula f.

particular /pər'tɪkyələr/ a. & n. particular m.

parting /'pɑrtɪŋ/ n. despedida f.

partisan /'pɑrtəzən, -sən/ a. & n. partidario -ria.

partition /pɑr'tɪʃən, pər-/ n. tabique m. v. dividir, partir.

partly /'pɑrtli/ adv. en parte.

partner /'pɑrtnər/ n. socio -cia; compañero -ra.

partridge /'pɑrtrɪdʒ/ n. perdiz f.

party /'pɑrti/ n. tertulia, fiesta f.; grupo m.; (political) partido m.

pass /pæs/ n. **1.** pase; (mountain) paso m. —v. **2.** pasar. **p. away,** fallecer.

passable /'pæsəbəl/ a. transitable; regular.

passage /'pæsɪdʒ/ n. pasaje; (corridor) pasillo m.

passé /pæ'sei/ a. anticuado.

passenger /'pæsəndʒər/ n. pasajero -ra.

passenger ship buque de pasajeros m.

passerby /'pæsər'bai/ n. transeúnte m. & f.

passion /'pæʃən/ n. pasión f.

passionate /'pæʃənɪt/ a. apasionado.

passive /'pæsɪv/ a. pasivo.

passport /'pæsport/ n. pasaporte m.

password /'pæs,wɜrd/ n. código m., clave m., contraseña f.

past /pæst/ a. & n. **1.** pasado m. —prep. **2.** más allá de; después de.

paste /peist/ n. **1.** pasta f. —v. **2.** empastar; pegar.

pasteurize /'pæstʃə,raiz/ v. pasteurizar.

pastime /'pæs,taim/ n. pasatiempo m.; diversión f.

pastor /'pæstər/ n. pastor m.

pastrami /pə'strɑmi/ n. pastrón m.

pastry /'peistri/ n. pastelería f.

pasture /'pæstʃər/ n. **1.** pasto m.; pradera f. —v. **2.** pastar.

pat /pæt/ n. **1.** golpecillo m. **to stand p.,** mantenerse firme. —v. **2.** dar golpecillos.

patch /pætʃ/ n. **1.** remiendo m. —v. **2.** remendar.

patent /'pætnt/ a. & n. **1.** patente m. —v. **2.** patentar.

patent leather /'pætnt, 'pætn/ charol m.

paternal /pə'tɜrnl/ a. paterno, paternal.

paternity /pə'tɜrnɪti/ n. paternidad f.

path /pæθ/ n. senda f.

pathetic /pə'θɛtɪk/ a. patético.

pathology /pə'θɒlədʒi/ n. patología f.

pathos /'peiθɒs/ n. rasgo conmovedor m.

patience /'peiʃəns/ n. paciencia f.

patient /'peiʃənt/ a. **1.** paciente. —n. **2.** enfermo -ma, paciente m. & f.

patio /'pæti,ou/ n. patio m.

patriarch /'peitri,ɑrk/ n. patriarca m.

patriot /'peitriət/ n. patriota m. & f.

patriotic /,peitri'ɒtɪk/ a. patriótico.

patriotism /'peitriə,tɪzəm/ n. patriotismo m.

patrol /pə'troul/ n. **1.** patrulla f. —v. **2.** patrullar.

patrolman /pə'troulmən/ n. vigilante m.; patrullador m.

patron /'peitrən/ n. patrón m.

patronize /'peitrə,naiz/ v. condescender; patrocinar; ser cliente de.

pattern /'pætərn/ n. modelo m.

pauper /'pɔpər/ n. indigente m. & f.

pause /pɔz/ n. **1.** pausa f. —v. **2.** pausar.

pave /peiv/ v. pavimentar. **p. the way,** preparar el camino.

pavement /'peivmənt/ n. pavimento m.

pavilion /pə'vɪlyən/ n. pabellón m.

paw /pɔ/ n. **1.** pata f. —v. **2.** patear.

pawn /pɔn/ n. **1.** prenda f.; (chess) peón de ajedrez m. —v. **2.** empeñar.

pay /pei/ n. **1.** pago; sueldo, salario m.; —v. **2.** pagar. **p. back,** pagar; vengarse de. **p. cash,** pagar en metálico.

payee /pei'i/ n. destinatario -ria m. & f.

payment /'peimənt/ n. pago m.; recompensa f.

pay phone teléfono público m.

pea /pi/ n. guisante m.

peace /pis/ n. paz f.

peaceable /'pisəbəl/ a. pacífico.

peaceful /'pisfəl/ a. tranquilo.

peach /pitʃ/ n. durazno, melocotón m.

peacock /'pi,kɒk/ n. pavo real m.

peak /pik/ n. pico, cumbre; máximo m.

peal /pil/ n. repique; estruendo m. **p. of laughter,** risotada f.

peanut /'pi,nʌt/ n. maní, cacahuete m.

pear /pɛɑr/ n. pera f.

pearl /pɜrl/ n. perla f.

peasant /'pɛzənt/ n. campesino -na.

pebble /'pɛbəl/ n. guija f.

peck /pɛk/ n. **1.** picotazo m. —v. **2.** picotear.

peckish /'pɛkɪʃ/ a. tener un poco de hambre.

peculiar /pɪ'kyulyər/ a. peculiar.

pecuniary /pɪ'kyuni,ɛri/ a. pecuniario.

pedagogue /'pɛdə,gɒg/ n. pedagogo -ga.

pedagogy /'pɛdə,goudʒi, -,gɒdʒi/ n. pedagogía f.

pedal /'pɛdl/ n. pedal m.

pedant /'pɛdnt/ n. pedante m. & f.

peddler /'pɛdlər/ n. buhonero m.

pedestal /'pɛdəstl/ n. pedestal m.

pedestrian /pə'dɛstriən/ n. peatón -na.

pedestrian crossing paso de peatones m.

pediatrician /,pidiə'trɪʃən/ n. pediatra m. & f.

pediatrics /,pidi'ætrɪks/ n. puericultura f.

pedigree /'pɛdɪ,gri/ n. genealogía f.

peek /pik/ n. **1.** atisbo m. —v. **2.** atisbar.

peel /pil/ n. **1.** corteza f.; (fruit) pellejo m. —v. **2.** descortezar; pelar.

peep /pip/ n. **1.** ojeada f. —v. **2.** mirar, atisbar.

peer /pɪər/ n. **1.** par m. —v. **2.** mirar fijamente.

peg /pɛg/ n. clavija; estaquilla f.; gancho m.

pelt /pɛlt/ n. **1.** pellejo m. —v. **2.** apedrear; (rain) caer con fuerza.

pelvis /'pɛlvɪs/ n. pelvis f.

pen /pɛn/ n. pluma f.; corral m. **fountain p.,** pluma fuente.

penalty /'pɛnlti/ n. pena; multa f.; castigo m.

penance /'pɛnəns/ n. penitencia f. **to do p.,** penar.

penchant /'pɛntʃənt;/ n. propensión f.

pencil /'pɛnsəl/ n. lápiz m.

pencil sharpener /'ʃɑrpənər/ sacapuntas m.

pending /'pɛndɪŋ/ a. pendiente. **to be p.,** pender.

penetrate /'pɛnɪ,treit/ v. penetrar.

penetration /,pɛnɪ'treiʃən/ n. penetración f.

penicillin /,pɛnə'sɪlɪn/ n. penicilina f.

peninsula /pə'nɪnsələ, -'nɪnsyələ/ n. península f.

penitent /'pɛnɪtənt/ n. & a. penitente m. & f.

penknife /'pɛn,naif/ n. cortaplumas m.

penniless /'pɛnɪlɪs/ a. indigente.

penny /'pɛni/ n. penique m.

pension /'pɛnʃən/ n. pensión f.

pensive /'pɛnsɪv/ a. pensativo.

penultimate /pɪ'nʌltəmɪt/ a. penúltimo.

penury /'pɛnyəri/ n. penuria f.

people /'pipəl/ n. **1.** gente f.; (of a nation) pueblo m. —v. **2.** poblar.

pepper /'pɛpər/ n. pimienta f.; (plant) pimiento m.

per /pər; unstressed pər/ prep. por.

perambulator /pər'æmbyə,leitər/ n. cochecillo de niño m.

perceive /pər'siv/ v. percibir.

percent /pər'sɛnt/ adv. por ciento.

percentage /pər'sɛntɪdʒ/ n. porcentaje m.

perceptible /pər'sɛptəbəl/ a. perceptible.

perception /pər'sɛpʃən/ n. percepción f.

perch /pɜrtʃ/ n. percha f.; (fish) perca f.

perdition /pər'dɪʃən/ n. perdición f.

peremptory /pə'rɛmptəri/ a. perentorio, terminante.

perennial /pə'rɛniəl/ a. perenne.

perfect /a. 'pɜrfɪkt; v. pər'fɛkt/ a. **1.** perfecto. —v. **2.** perfeccionar.

perfection /pər'fɛkʃən/ n. perfección f.

perfectionist /pər'fɛkʃənɪst/ a. & n. perfeccionista m.

perforation /,pɜrfə'reiʃən/ n. perforación f.

perform /pər'fɔrm/ v. hacer; ejecutar; Theat. representar.

performance /pər'fɔrməns/ n. ejecución f.; Theat. representación f.

perfume /n. 'pɜrfyum; v. pər'fyum/ n. **1.** perfume m.; fragancia f. —v. **2.** perfumar.

perfunctory /pər'fʌŋktəri/ a. perfunctorio, superficial.

perhaps /pər'hæps/ adv. quizá, quizás, tal vez.

peril /'pɛrəl/ n. peligro m.

perilous /'pɛrələs/ a. peligroso.

perimeter /pə'rɪmɪtər/ n. perímetro m.

period /'pɪəriəd/ n. período m.; Punct. punto m.

periodic /,pɪəri'ɒdɪk/ a. periódico.

periodical /,pɪəri'ɒdɪkəl/ n. revista f.

periphery /pə'rɪfəri/ n. periferia f.

perish /'pɛrɪʃ/ v. perecer.

perishable /'pɛrɪʃəbəl/ a. perecedero.

perjury /'pɜrdʒəri/ n. perjurio m.

permanent /'pɜrmənənt/ a. permanente. **p. wave,** ondulado permanente.

permeate /'pɜrmi,eit/ v. penetrar.

permissible /pər'mɪsəbəl/ a. permisible.

permission /pər'mɪʃən/ n. permiso m.

permit /n. 'pɜrmɪt; v. pər'mɪt/ n. **1.** permiso m. —v. **2.** permitir.

pernicious /pər'nɪʃəs/ a. pernicioso.

perpendicular /,pɜrpən'dɪkyələr/ n. & a. perpendicular f.

perpetrate /'pɜrpɪ,treit/ v. perpetrar.

perpetual /pər'pɛtʃuəl/ a. perpetuo.

perplex /pər'plɛks/ v. confundir.

perplexity /pər'plɛksɪti/ n. perplejidad f.

persecute /'pɜrsɪ,kyut/ v. perseguir.

persecution /,pɜrsɪ'kyuʃən/ n. persecución f.

perseverance /,pɜrsə'vɪərəns/ n. perseverancia f.

persevere /,pɜrsə'vɪər/ v. perseverar.

persist /pər'sɪst/ v. persistir.

persistent /pər'sɪstənt/ a. persistente.

person /'pɜrsən/ n. persona f.

personage /'pɜrsənɪdʒ/ n. personaje m.

personal /'pɜrsənl/ a. personal.

personality /,pɜrsə'nælɪti/ n. personalidad f.

personnel /,pɜrsə'nɛl/ n. personal m.

perspective /pər'spɛktɪv/ n. perspectiva f.

perspiration /'pɜrspə'reiʃən/ n. sudor m.

perspire /pər'spaiᵊr/ v. sudar.

persuade /pər'sweid/ v. persuadir.

persuasive /pər'sweisɪv/ a. persuasivo.

pertain /pər'tein/ v. pertenecer.

pertinent /'pɜrtnənt/ a. pertinente.

perturb /pər'tɜrb/ v. perturbar.

peruse /pə'ruz/ v. leer con cuidado.

pervade /pər'veid/ v. penetrar; llenar.

perverse /pər'vɜrs/ a. perverso.

perversion /pər'vɜrʒən/ n. perversión f.

pessimism /'pɛsə,mɪzəm/ n. pesimismo m.

pester /'pɛstər/ v. molestar; fastidiar.

pesticide /'pɛstə,said/ n. pesticida m.

pestilence /'pɛstləns/ n. pestilencia f.

pet /pɛt/ n. **1.** favorito -ta; animal doméstico m. —v. **2.** mimar.

petal /'pɛtl/ n. pétalo m.

petition /pə'tɪʃən/ n. **1.** petición, súplica f. —v. **2.** pedir, suplicar.

petrify /'pɛtrə,fai/ v. petrificar.

petroleum /pə'trouliəm/ n. petróleo m.

petticoat /'pɛti,kout/ n. enagua f.

petty /'pɛti/ a. mezquino, insignificante.

petulant /'pɛtʃələnt/ a. quisquilloso.

pew /pyu/ n. banco de iglesia m.

pewter /'pyutər/ n. peltre m.

phantom /'fæntəm/ n. espectro, fantasma m.

pharmacist /'fɑrməsɪst/ n. farmacéutico -ca, boticario -ria.

pharmacy /'fɑrməsi/ n. farmacia, botica f.

phase /feiz/ n. fase f.

pheasant /'fɛzənt/ n. faisán m.

phenomenal /fɪ'nɒmənl̩/ *a.* fenomenal.
phenomenon /fɪ'nɒmə,nɒn/ *n.* fenómeno *f.*
philanthropy /fɪ'lænθrəpi/ *n.* filantropía *f.*
philately /fɪ'lætl̩i/ *n.* filatelia *f.*
philosopher /fɪ'lɒsəfər/ *n.* filósofo -fa.
philosophical /,fɪlə'sɒfɪkəl/ *a.* filosófico.
philosophy /fɪ'lɒsəfi/ *n.* filosofía *f.*
phlegm /flɛm/ *n.* flema *f.*
phlegmatic /flɛg'mætɪk/ *a.* flemático.
phobia /'foubiə/ *n.* fobia *f.*
phone /foun/ *n.* teléfono *m.*
phonetic /fə'nɛtɪk/ *a.* fonético.
phonograph /'founə,græf/ *n.* fonógrafo *m.*
phosphorus /'fɒsfərəs/ *n.* fósforo *m.*
photocopier /'foutə,kɒpiər/ *n.* fotocopiadora *f.*
photocopy /'foutə,kɒpi/ *n.* **1.** fotocopia *f.* —*v.* **2.** fotocopiar.
photoelectric /,foutouɪ'lɛktrɪk/ *a.* fotoeléctrico.
photogenic /,foutə'dʒɛnɪk/ *a.* fotogénico.
photograph /'foutə,græf/ *n.* **1.** fotografía *f.* —*v.* **2.** fotografiar; retratar.
photography /fə'tɒgrəfi/ *n.* fotografía *f.*
phrase /freiz/ *n.* **1.** frase *f.* —*v.* **2.** expresar.
physical /'fɪzɪkəl/ *a.* físico.
physician /fɪ'zɪʃən/ *n.* médico *m.* & *f.*
physics /'fɪzɪks/ *n.* física *f.*
physiology /,fɪzi'ɒlədʒi/ *n.* fisiología *f.*
physiotherapy /,fɪziou'θɛrəpi/ *n.* fisioterapia *f.*
physique /fɪ'zik/ *n.* físico *m.*
pianist /pi'ænɪst, 'piənɪst/ *n.* pianista *m.* & *f.*
piano /pi'ænou/ *n.* piano *m.*
picayune /,pɪkə'yun/ *a.* insignificante.
piccolo /'pɪkə,lou/ *n.* flautín *m.*
pick /pɪk/ *n.* **1.** pico *m.* —*v.* **2.** escoger. **p. up,** recoger.
picket /'pɪkɪt/ *n.* piquete *m.*
pickle /'pɪkəl/ *n.* **1.** salmuera *f.*; encurtido *m.* —*v.* **2.** escabechar.
pickpocket /'pɪk,pɒkɪt/ *n.* cortabolsas *m.* & *f.*
picnic /'pɪknɪk/ *n.* picnic *m.*
picture /'pɪktʃər/ *n.* **1.** cuadro; retrato *m.*; fotografía *f.*; (movie) película *f.* —*v.* **2.** imaginarse.
picturesque /,pɪktʃə'rɛsk/ *a.* pintoresco.
pie /pai/ *n.* pastel *m.*
piece /pis/ *n.* pedazo *m.*; pieza *f.*
pieceworker /'pis,wɜrkər/ *n.* destajero -ra, destajista *m.* & *f.*
pier /pɪər/ *n.* muelle *m.*
pierce /pɪərs/ *v.* perforar; pinchar; traspasar.
piety /'paiɪti/ *n.* piedad *f.*
pig /pɪg/ *n.* puerco, cerdo, lechón *m.*
pigeon /'pɪdʒən/ *n.* paloma *f.*
pigeonhole /'pɪdʒən,houl/ *n.* casilla *f.*
pigment /'pɪgmənt/ *n.* pigmento *m.*
pile /pail/ *n.* **1.** pila *f.*; montón *m.*; *Med.* hemorroides *f.pl.* —*v.* **2.** amontonar.
pilfer /'pɪlfər/ *v.* ratear.
pilgrim /'pɪlgrɪm/ *n.* peregrino -na, romero -ra.
pilgrimage /'pɪlgrəmɪdʒ/ *n.* romería *f.*
pill /pɪl/ *n.* píldora *f.*
pillage /'pɪlɪdʒ/ *n.* **1.** pillaje *m.* —*v.* **2.** pillar.
pillar /'pɪlər/ *n.* columna *f.*
pillow /'pɪlou/ *n.* almohada *f.*
pillowcase /'pɪlou,keis/ *n.* funda de almohada *f.*
pilot /'pailət/ *n.* **1.** piloto *m.* & *f.* —*v.* **2.** pilotar.
pimple /'pɪmpəl/ *n.* grano *m.*
pin /pɪn/ *n.* **1.** alfiler; broche *m.*; *Mech.* clavija *f.* —*v.* **2.** prender. **p. up,** fijar.
pinafore /'pɪnə,fɔr/ *n.* delantal (de niña) *m.*
pinch /pɪntʃ/ *n.* **1.** pellizco *m.* —*v.* **2.** pellizcar.
pine /pain/ *n.* **1.** pino *m.* —*v.* **2. p. away,** languidecer. **p. for,** anhelar.
pineapple /'pai,næpəl/ *n.* piña *f.*, ananás *m.pl.*
pink /pɪŋk/ *a.* rosado.
pinky /'pɪŋki/ *n.* meñique *m.*
pinnacle /'pɪnəkəl/ *n.* pináculo *m.*; cumbre *f.*
pint /paint/ *n.* pinta *f.*
pioneer /,paiə'nɪər/ *n.* pionero -ra.
pious /'paiəs/ *a.* piadoso.
pipe /paip/ *n.* pipa *f.*; tubo; (of organ) cañón *m.*
pipeline /'paip,lain/ *n.* oleoducto *m.*
piper /'paipər/ *n.* flautista *m.* & *f.*
piquant /'pikənt/ *a.* picante.
pirate /'pairət/ *n.* pirata *m.*
pistol /'pɪstl̩/ *n.* pistola *f.*
piston /'pɪstən/ *n.* émbolo, pistón *m.*
pit /pɪt/ *n.* hoyo *m.*; (fruit) hueso *m.*
pitch /pɪtʃ/ *n.* **1.** brea *f.*; grado de inclinación; (music) tono *m.*; —*v.* **2.** lanzar; (ship) cabecear.
pitchblende /'pɪtʃ,blɛnd/ *n.* pechblenda *f.*
pitcher /'pɪtʃər/ *n.* cántaro *m.*; (baseball) lanzador -ra.
pitchfork /'pɪtʃ,fɔrk/ *n.* horca *f.*; tridente *m.*
pitfall /'pɪt,fɔl/ *n.* trampa *f.*, hoya cubierta *f.*
pitiful /'pɪtɪfəl/ *a.* lastimoso.
pitiless /'pɪtɪlɪs/ *a.* cruel.
pituitary gland /pɪ'tuɪ,tɛri/ glándula pituitaria *f.*
pity /'pɪti/ *n.* **1.** compasión, piedad *f.* **to be a p.,** ser lástima. —*v.* **2.** compadecer.
pivot /'pɪvət/ *n.* **1.** espiga *f.*, pivote *m.*; punto de partida *m.* —*v.* **2.** girar sobre un pivote.
pizza /'pitsə/ *n.* pizza *f.*
placard /'plækɑrd/ *n.* **1.** cartel *m.* —*v.* **2.** fijar carteles.
placate /'pleikeit/ *v.* aplacar.
place /pleis/ *n.* **1.** lugar, sitio, puesto *m.* —*v.* **2.** colocar, poner.
placid /'plæsɪd/ *a.* plácido.
plagiarism /'pleidʒə,rɪzəm/ *n.* plagio *m.*
plague /pleig/ *n.* **1.** plaga, peste *f.* —*v.* **2.** atormentar.
plain /plein/ *a.* **1.** sencillo; puro; evidente. —*n.* **2.** llano *m.*
plaintiff /'pleintɪf/ *n.* demandante *m.* & *f.*
plan /plæn/ *n.* **1.** plan, propósito *m.* —*v.* **2.** planear; pensar; planificar. **p. on,** contar con.
plane /plein/ *n.* **1.** plano; (tool) cepillo *m.* —*v.* **2.** allanar; acepillar.
planet /'plænɪt/ *n.* planeta *m.*
planetarium /,plænɪ'tɛəriəm/ *n.* planetario *m.*
plank /plæŋk/ *n.* tablón *m.*
planning /'plænɪŋ/ *n.* planificación *f.*
plant /plænt/ *n.* **1.** mata, planta *f.* —*v.* **2.** sembrar, plantar.
plantation /plæn'teiʃən/ *n.* plantación *f.* **coffee p.,** cafetal *m.*
planter /'plæntər/ *n.* plantador; hacendado *m.*
plasma /'plæzmə/ *n.* plasma *m.*
plaster /'plæstər/ *n.* **1.** yeso; emplasto *m.* —*v.* **2.** enyesar; emplastar.
plastic /'plæstɪk/ *a.* plástico.
plate /pleit/ *n.* **1.** plato *m.*; plancha de metal. —*v.* **2.** planchear.
plateau /plæ'tou/ *n.* meseta *f.*
platform /'plætfɔrm/ *n.* plataforma *f.*
platinum /'plætn̩əm/ *n.* platino *m.*
platitude /'plætɪ,tud/ *n.* perogrullada *f.*
platter /'plætər/ *n.* fuente *f.*, platel *m.*
plaudit /'plɔdɪt/ *n.* aplauso *m.*
plausible /'plɔzəbəl/ *a.* plausible.
play /plei/ *n.* **1.** juego *m.*; *Theat.* pieza *f.* —*v.* **2.** jugar; (music) tocar; *Theat.* representar. **p. a part,** hacer un papel.
player /'pleiər/ *n.* jugador -ra; (music) músico -ca.; *Theat.* actor *m.*, actriz *f.*
playful /'pleifəl/ *a.* juguetón.
playground /'plei,graund/ *n.* campo de deportes; patio de recreo.
playmate /'plei,meit/. *n.* compañero -ra de juego.
playwright /'plei,rait/ *n.* dramaturgo -ga.
plea /pli/ *n.* ruego *m.*; súplica *f.*; (legal) declaración *f.*
plead /plid/ *v.* suplicar; declararse. **p. a case,** defender un pleito.
pleasant /'plɛzənt/ *a.* agradable.
please /pliz/ *v.* **1.** gustar, agradar. **Pleased to meet you,** Mucho gusto en conocer a Vd. —*adv.* **2.** por favor. **Please...** Haga el favor de..., Tenga la bondad de..., Sírvase...
pleasure /'plɛʒər/ *n.* gusto, placer *m.*
pleat /plit/ *n.* **1.** pliegue *m.* —*v.* **2.** plegar.
plebiscite /'plɛbə,sait/ *n.* plebiscito *m.*
pledge /plɛdʒ/ *n.* **1.** empeño *m.* —*v.* **2.** empeñar.
plentiful /'plɛntɪfəl/ *a.* abundante.
plenty /'plɛnti/ *n.* abundancia *f.* **p. of,** bastante. **p. more,** mucho más.
pleurisy /'plʊrəsi/ *n.* pleuritis *f.*
pliable, pliant /'plaiəbəl; 'plaiənt/ *a.* flexible.
pliers /'plaiərz/ *n.pl.* alicates *m.pl.*
plight /plait/ *n.* apuro, aprieto *m.*
plot /plɒt/ *n.* **1.** conspiración; (of a story) trama; (of land) parcela *f.* —*v.* **2.** conspirar; tramar.
plow /plau/ *n.* **1.** arado *m.* —*v.* **2.** arar.
pluck /plʌk/ *n.* **1.** valor *m.* —*v.* **2.** arrancar; desplumar.
plug /plʌg/ *n.* **1.** tapón; *Elec.* enchufe *m.* **spark p.,** bujía *f.* —*v.* **2.** tapar.
plum /plʌm/ *n.* ciruela *f.*
plumage /'plumɪdʒ/ *n.* plumaje *m.*
plumber /'plʌmər/ *n.* fontanero -era, plomero -era.
plume /plum/ *n.* pluma *f.*
plump /plʌmp/ *a.* regordete.
plunder /'plʌndər/ *n.* **1.** botín *m.*; despojos *m.pl.* —*v.* **2.** saquear.
plunge /plʌndʒ/ *v.* zambullir; precipitar.
plural /'plʊrəl/ *a.* & *n.* plural *m.*
plus /plʌs/ *prep.* más.
plutocrat /'plutə,kræt/ *n.* plutócrata *m.* & *f.*
pneumatic /nʊ'mætɪk/ *a.* neumático.
pneumonia /nʊ'mounyə/ *n.* pulmonía *f.*
poach /poutʃ/ *v.* (eggs) escalfar; invadir; cazar en vedado.
pocket /'pɒkɪt/ *n.* **1.** bolsillo *m.* —*v.* **2.** embolsar.
pocketbook /'pɒkɪt,bʊk/ *n.* cartera *f.*
podiatry /pə'daiətri/ *n.* podiatría *f.*
poem /'pouəm/ *n.* poema *m.*
poet /'pouɪt/ *n.* poeta *m.* & *f.*
poetic /pou'ɛtɪk/ *a.* poético.
poetry /'pouɪtri/ *n.* poesía *f.*
poignant /'pɔinyənt/ *a.* conmovedor.
point /pɔint/ *n.* **1.** punta *f.*; punto *m.* —*v.* **2.** apuntar. **p. out,** señalar.
pointed /'pɔintɪd/ *a.* puntiagudo; directo.
pointless /'pɔintlɪs/ *a.* inútil.
poise /pɔiz/ *n.* **1.** equilibrio *m.*; serenidad *f.* —*v.* **2.** equilibrar; estar suspendido.
poison /'pɔizən/ *n.* **1.** veneno *m.* —*v.* **2.** envenenar.
poisonous /'pɔizənəs/ *a.* venenoso.
poke /pouk/ *n.* **1.** empuje *m.*, hurgonada *f.* —*v.* **2.** picar; haronear.
Poland /'poulənd/ *n.* Polonia *f.*
polar /'poulər/ *a.* polar.
pole /poul/ *n.* palo; *Geog.* polo *m.*
polemical /pə'lɛmɪkəl/ *a.* polémico.
police /pə'lis/ *n.* policía *f.*
policeman /pə'lismən/ *n.* policía *m.*
policy /'pɒləsi/ *n.* política *f.* **insurance p.,** póliza de seguro.
Polish /'poulɪʃ/ *a.* & *n.* polaco -ca.
polish /'pɒlɪʃ/ *n.* **1.** lustre *m.* —*v.* **2.** pulir, lustrar.
polite /pə'lait/ *a.* cortés.
politic /'pɒlɪtɪk/ **political** *a.* político.
politician /,pɒlɪ'tɪʃən/ *n.* político -ca.
politics /'pɒlɪtɪks/ *n.* política *f.*
poll /poul/ *n.* encuesta *f.*; (pl.) urnas *f.pl.*
pollen /'pɒlən/ *n.* polen *m.*
pollute /pə'lut/ *v.* contaminar.
pollution /pə'luʃən/ *n.* contaminación *f.*
polo /'poulou/ *n.* polo *m.*
polyester /,pɒli'ɛstər/ *n.* poliéster *m.*
polygamy /pə'lɪgəmi/ *n.* poligamia *f.*
polygon /'pɒli,gɒn/ *n.* polígono *m.*
pomp /pɒmp/ *n.* pompa *f.*
pompous /'pɒmpəs/ *a.* pomposo.
poncho /'pɒntʃou/ *n.* poncho *m.*
pond /pɒnd/ *n.* charca *f.*
ponder /'pɒndər/ *v.* ponderar, meditar.
ponderous /'pɒndərəs/ *a.* ponderoso, pesado.
pontiff /'pɒntɪf/ *n.* pontífice *m.*
pontoon /pɒn'tun/ *n.* pontón *m.*
pony /'pouni/ *n.* caballito *m.*
ponytail /'pouni,teil/ *n.* cola de caballo *f.*
poodle /'pudl̩/ *n.* caniche *m.*
pool /pul/ *n.* charco *m.* **swimming p.,** piscina *f.*
poor /pʊr/ *a.* pobre; (not good) malo.
pop /pɒp/ *n.* chasquido *m.*
popcorn /'pɒp,kɔrn/ *n.* rosetas de maíz, palomitas de maíz *f.pl.*
pope /poup/ *n.* papa *m.*
poppy /'pɒpi/ *n.* amapola *f.*
popsicle /'pɒpsɪkəl/ *n.* polo *m.*
popular /'pɒpyələr/ *a.* popular.
popularity /,pɒpyə'lærɪti/ *n.* popularidad *f.*
population /,pɒpyə'leiʃən/ *n.* población *f.*
porcelain /'pɔrsəlɪn/ *n.* porcelana *f.*
porch /pɔrtʃ/ *n.* pórtico *m.*; galería *f.*
pore /pɔr/ *n.* poro *m.*
pork /pɔrk/ *n.* carne de puerco.
pornography /pɔr'nɒgrəfi/ *n.* pornografía *f.*
porous /'pɔrəs/ *a.* poroso, esponjoso.
port /pɔrt/ *n.* puerto; *Naut.* babor *m.* **p. wine,** oporto *m.*
portable /'pɔrtəbəl/ *a.* portátil.
portal /'pɔrtl̩/ *n.* portal *m.*
portend /pɔr'tɛnd/ *v.* pronosticar.
portent /'pɔrtɛnt/ *n.* presagio *m.*, portento *m.*
porter /'pɔrtər/ *n.* portero *m.*
portfolio /pɔrt'fouli,ou/ *n.* cartera *f.*
porthole /'pɔrt,houl/ *n.* porta *f.*
portion /'pɔrʃən/ *n.* porción *f.*
portly /'pɔrtli/ *a.* corpulento.
portrait /'pɔrtrɪt/ *n.* retrato *m.*
portray /pɔr'trei/ *v.* pintar.
Portugal /'pɔrtʃəgəl/ *n.* Portugal *m.*
Portuguese /,pɔrtʃə'giz/ *a.* & *n.* portugués -esa.
pose /pouz/ *n.* **1.** postura; actitud *f.* —*v.* **2.** posar. **p. as,** pretender ser.
position /pə'zɪʃən/ *n.* posición *f.*
positive /'pɒzɪtɪv/ *a.* positivo.
possess /pə'zɛs/ *v.* poseer.
possession /pə'zɛʃən/ *n.* posesión *f.*
possessive /pə'zɛsɪv/ *a.* posesivo.
possibility /,pɒsə'bɪlɪti/ *n.* posibilidad *f.*
possible /'pɒsəbəl/ *a.* posible.
post /poust/ *n.* **1.** poste; puesto *m.* —*v.* **2.** fijar; situar; echar al correo.
postage /'poustɪdʒ/ *n.* porte de correo. **p. stamp,** sello *m.*
postal /'poustl̩/ *a.* postal.
post card tarjeta postal.
poster /'poustər/ *n.* cartel, letrero *m.*
posterior /pɒ'stɪəriər/ *a.* posterior.
posterity /pɒ'stɛrɪti/ *n.* posteridad *f.*
postgraduate /poust'grædʒuɪt/ *a.* & *n.* postgraduado -da.

postmark /ˈpoustˌmɑrk/ *n.* matasellos *m.*
post office correos *m.pl.*
postpone /poustˈpoun/ *v.* posponer, aplazar.
postscript /ˈpoustˌskrɪpt/ *n.* posdata *f.*
posture /ˈpɒstʃər/ *n.* postura *f.*
pot /pɒt/ *n.* olla, marmita; (marijuana) marijuana, hierba *f.* **flower p.,** tiesto *m.*
potassium /pəˈtæsiəm/ *n.* potasio *m.*
potato /pəˈteitou/ *n.* patata, papa *f.* **sweet p.,** batata *f.*
potent /ˈpoutn̩t/ *a.* potente, poderoso.
potential /pəˈtɛnʃəl/ *a.* & *n.* potencial *f.*
potion /ˈpouʃən/ *n.* poción, pócima *f.*
pottery /ˈpɒtəri/ *n.* alfarería *f.*
pouch /pautʃ/ *n.* saco *m.*; bolsa *f.*
poultry /ˈpoultri/ *n.* aves de corral.
pound /paund/ *n.* **1.** libra *f.* —*v.* **2.** golpear.
pour /pɔr/ *v.* echar; verter; llover a cántaros.
poverty /ˈpɒvərti/ *n.* pobreza *f.*
powder /ˈpaudər/ *n.* **1.** polvo *m.*; (gun) pólvora *f.* —*v.* **2.** empolvar; pulverizar.
power /ˈpauər/ *n.* poder *m.*; potencia *f.*
powerful /ˈpauərfəl/ *a.* poderoso, fuerte.
powerless /ˈpauərlɪs/ *a.* impotente.
practical /ˈpræktɪkəl/ *a.* práctico.
practical joke inocentada *f.*
practically /ˈpræktɪkli/ *adv.* casi; prácticamente.
practice /ˈpræktɪs/ *n.* **1.** práctica; costumbre; clientela *f.* —*v.* **2.** practicar; ejercer.
practiced /ˈpræktɪst/ *a.* experto.
practitioner /prækˈtɪʃənər/ *n.* practicante *m.* & *f.*
pragmatic /prægˈmætɪk/ *a.* pragmático.
prairie /ˈprɛəri/ *n.* llanura; *S.A.* pampa *f.*
praise /preiz/ *n.* **1.** alabanza *f.* —*v.* **2.** alabar.
prank /præŋk/ *n.* travesura *f.*
prawn /prɒn/ *n.* gamba *f.*
pray /prei/ *v.* rezar; (beg) rogar.
prayer /ˈpreiər/ *n.* oración; súplica *f.*, ruego *m.*
preach /pritʃ/ *v.* predicar; sermonear.
preacher /ˈpritʃər/ *n.* predicador *m.*
preamble /ˈpriˌæmbəl/ *n.* preámbulo *m.*
precarious /prɪˈkɛəriəs/ *a.* precario.
precaution /prɪˈkɔʃən/ *n.* precaución *f.*
precede /prɪˈsid/ *v.* preceder, anteceder.
precedent /*n.* ˈprɛsɪdənt; *a.* prɪˈsidnt/ *n.* & *a.* precedente *m.*
precept /ˈprisɛpt/ *n.* precepto *m.*
precinct /ˈprisɪŋkt/ *n.* recinto *m.*
precious /ˈprɛʃəs/ *a.* precioso.
precipice /ˈprɛsəpɪs/ *n.* precipicio *m.*
precipitate /prɪˈsɪpɪˌteit/ *v.* precipitar.
precise /prɪˈsais/ *a.* preciso, exacto.
precision /prɪˈsɪʒən/ *n.* precisión *f.*
preclude /prɪˈklud/ *v.* evitar.
precocious /prɪˈkouʃəs/ *a.* precoz.
precooked /priˈkukt/ *a.* precocinado.
predatory /ˈprɛdəˌtɔri/ *a.* de rapiña, rapaz.
predecessor /ˈprɛdəˌsɛsər/ *n.* predecesor -ra, antecesor -ra.
predicament /prɪˈdɪkəmənt/ *n.* dificultad *f.*; apuro *m.*
predict /prɪˈdɪkt/ *v.* pronosticar, predecir.
predictable /prɪˈdɪktəbəl/ *a.* previsible.
predilection /ˌprɛdlˈɛkʃən/ *n.* predilección *f.*
predispose /ˌpridɪˈspouz/ *v.* predisponer.
predominant /prɪˈdɒmənənt/ *a.* predominante.
prefabricate /priˈfæbrɪˌkeit/ *v.* fabricar de antemano.
preface /ˈprɛfɪs/ *n.* prefacio *m.*
prefer /prɪˈfɜr/ *v.* preferir.
preferable /ˈprɛfərəbəl/ *a.* preferible.
preference /ˈprɛfərəns/ *n.* preferencia *f.*
prefix /ˈprifɪks/ *n.* **1.** prefijo *m.* —*v.* **2.** prefijar.
pregnant /ˈprɛgnənt/ *a.* preñada.
prehistoric /ˌprihɪˈstɔrɪk/ *a.* prehistórico.
prejudice /ˈprɛdʒədɪs/ *n.* prejuicio *m.*
prejudiced /ˈprɛdʒədɪst/ *a.* (*S.A.*) prejuiciado.
preliminary /prɪˈlɪməˌnɛri/ *a.* preliminar.
prelude /ˈprɛlyud/ *n.* preludio *m.*
premature /ˌpriməˈtʃʊr/ *a.* prematuro.
premeditate /prɪˈmɛdɪˌteit/ *v.* premeditar.
premier /prɪˈmɪər/ *n.* primer ministro.
première /prɪˈmɪər/ *n.* estreno *m.*
premise /ˈprɛmɪs/ *n.* premisa *f.*
premium /ˈprimiəm/ *n.* premio *m.*
premonition /ˌpriməˈnɪʃən/ *n.* presentimiento *m.*
prenatal /priˈneitl̩/ *a.* prenatal.
preparation /ˌprɛpəˈreiʃən/ *n.* preparativo *m.*; preparación *f.*
preparatory /prɪˈpærəˌtɔri/ *a.* preparatorio. **p. to,** antes de.
prepare /prɪˈpɛər/ *v.* preparar.
preponderant /prɪˈpɒndərənt/ *a.* preponderante.
preposition /ˌprɛpəˈzɪʃən/ *n.* preposición *f.*
preposterous /prɪˈpɒstərəs/ *a.* prepóstero, absurdo.
prerequisite /prɪˈrɛkwəzɪt/ *n.* requisito previo.
prerogative /prɪˈrɒgətɪv/ *n.* prerrogativa *f.*
prescribe /prɪˈskraib/ *v.* prescribir; *Med.* recetar.
prescription /prɪˈskrɪpʃən/ *n.* prescripción; *Med.* receta *f.*
presence /ˈprɛzəns/ *n.* presencia *f.*; porte *m.*
present /*a, n* ˈprɛzənt; *v* prɪˈzɛnt/ *a.* **1.** presente. **to be present at,** asistir a. —*n.* **2.** presente; (gift) regalo *m.* **at p.,** ahora, actualmente. **for the p.,** por ahora. —*v.* **3.** presentar.
presentable /prɪˈzɛntəbəl/ *a.* presentable.
presentation /ˌprɛzənˈteiʃən/ *n.* presentación; introducción *f.*; *Theat.* representación *f.*
presently /ˈprɛzəntli/ *adv.* luego; dentro de poco.
preservative /prɪˈzɜrvətɪv/ *a.* & *n.* preservativo *m.*
preserve /prɪˈzɜrv/ *n.* **1.** conserva *f.*; (hunting) vedado *m.* —*v.* **2.** preservar.
preside /prɪˈzaid/ *v.* presidir.
presidency /ˈprɛzɪdənsi/ *n.* presidencia *f.*
president /ˈprɛzɪdənt/ *n.* presidente -ta.
press /prɛs/ *n.* **1.** prensa *f.* —*v.* **2.** apretar; urgir; (clothes) planchar.
pressing /ˈprɛsɪŋ/ *a.* urgente.
pressure /ˈprɛʃər/ *n.* presión *f.*
pressure cooker /ˈkukər/ cocina de presión *f.*
prestige /prɛˈstiʒ/ *n.* prestigio *m.*
presume /prɪˈzum/ *v.* presumir, suponer.
presumptuous /prɪˈzʌmptʃuəs/ *a.* presuntuoso.
presuppose /ˌprisəˈpouz/ *v.* presuponer.
pretend /prɪˈtɛnd/ *v.* fingir. **p. to the throne,** aspirar al trono.
pretense /prɪˈtɛns, ˈpritɛns/ *n.* pretensión *f.*; fingimiento *m.*
pretension /prɪˈtɛnʃən/ *n.* pretensión *f.*
pretentious /prɪˈtɛnʃəs/ *a.* presumido.
pretext /ˈpritɛkst/ *n.* pretexto *m.*
pretty /ˈprɪti/ *a.* **1.** bonito, lindo. —*adv.* **2.** bastante.
prevail /prɪˈveil/ *v.* prevalecer.
prevailing /prɪˈveilɪŋ/ **prevalent** *a.* predominante.
prevent /prɪˈvɛnt/ *v.* impedir; evitar.
prevention /prɪˈvɛnʃən/ *n.* prevención *f.*
preventive /prɪˈvɛntɪv/ *a.* preventivo.
preview /ˈpriˌvyu/ *n.* vista anticipada *f.*
previous /ˈpriviəs/ *a.* anterior, previo.
prey /prei/ *n.* presa *f.*
price /prais/ *n.* precio *m.*
priceless /ˈpraislɪs/ *a.* sin precio.
prick /prɪk/ *n.* **1.** punzada *f.* —*v.* **2.** punzar.
pride /praid/ *n.* orgullo *m.*
priest /prist/ *n.* sacerdote, cura *m.*
prim /prɪm/ *a.* estirado, remilgado.
primary /ˈpraimɛri/ *a.* primario, principal.
prime /praim/ *a.* **1.** primero. —*n.* **2.** flor *f.* —*v.* **3.** alistar.
prime minister primer ministro *m.* & *f.*
primitive /ˈprɪmɪtɪv/ *a.* primitivo.
prince /prɪns/ *n.* príncipe *m.*
Prince Charming Príncipe Azul *m.*
princess /ˈprɪnsɪs/ *n.* princesa *f.*
principal /ˈprɪnsəpəl/ *a.* **1.** principal. —*n.* **2.** principal *m.* & *f.*; director -ra.
principle /ˈprɪnsəpəl/ *n.* principio *m.*
print /prɪnt/ *n.* **1.** letra de molde *f.*; (art) grabado *m.* —*v.* **2.** imprimir, estampar.
printer /ˈprɪntər/ *n.* impresora *f.*
printing /ˈprɪntɪŋ/ *n.* impresión; **p. office,** imprenta *f.*
printing press prensa *f.*
printout /ˈprɪntˌaut/ *n.* impreso producido por una computadora, impresión *f.*
priority /praiˈɔrɪti/ *n.* prioridad, precedencia *f.*
prism /ˈprɪzəm/ *n.* prisma *m.*
prison /ˈprɪzən/ *n.* prisión, cárcel *f.*
prisoner /ˈprɪzənər/ *n.* presidiario -ria, prisionero -ra, preso -sa.
pristine /ˈprɪstin/ *a.* inmaculado.
privacy /ˈpraivəsi/ *n.* soledad *f.*
private /ˈpraivɪt/ *a.* **1.** particular. —*n.* **2.** soldado raso. **in p.,** en particular.
privation /praiˈveiʃən/ *n.* privación *f.*
privet /ˈprɪvɪt/ *n.* ligustro *m.*
privilege /ˈprɪvəlɪdʒ/ *n.* privilegio *m.*
privy /ˈprɪvi/ *n.* letrina *f.*
prize /praiz/ *n.* **1.** premio *m.* —*v.* **2.** apreciar, estimar.
probability /ˌprɒbəˈbɪlɪti/ *n.* probabilidad *f.*
probable /ˈprɒbəbəl/ *a.* probable.
probate /ˈproubeit/ *a.* testamentario.
probation /prouˈbeiʃən/ *n.* prueba *f.*; probación *f.*; libertad condicional *f.*
probe /proub/ *n.* **1.** indagación *f.* —*v.* **2.** indagar; tentar.
probity /ˈproubɪti/ *n.* probidad *f.*
problem /ˈprɒbləm/ *n.* problema *m.*
procedure /prəˈsidʒər/ *n.* procedimiento *m.*
proceed /prəˈsid/ *v.* proceder; proseguir.
process /ˈprɒsɛs/ *n.* proceso *m.*
procession /prəˈsɛʃən/ *n.* procesión *f.*
proclaim /prouˈkleim/ *v.* proclamar, anunciar.
proclamation /ˌprɒkləˈmeiʃən/ *n.* proclamación *f.*; decreto *m.*
procrastinate /prouˈkræstəˌneit/ *v.* dilatar.
procure /prouˈkyʊr/ *v.* obtener, procurar.
prodigal /ˈprɒdɪgəl/ *n.* & *a.* pródigo -ga.
prodigy /ˈprɒdɪdʒi/ *n.* prodigio *m.*
produce /prəˈdus/ *v.* producir.
product /ˈprɒdəkt/ *n.* producto *m.*
production /prəˈdʌkʃən/ *n.* producción *f.*
productive /prəˈdʌktɪv/ *a.* productivo.
profane /prəˈfein/ *a.* **1.** profano. —*v.* **2.** profanar.
profanity /prəˈfænɪti/ *n.* profanidad *f.*
profess /prəˈfɛs/ *v.* profesar; declarar.
profession /prəˈfɛʃən/ *n.* profesión *f.*
professional /prəˈfɛʃənl/ *a.* & *n.* profesional *m.* & *f.*
professor /prəˈfɛsər/ *n.* profesor -ra; catedrático -ca.
proficient /prəˈfɪʃənt/ *a.* experto, proficiente.
profile /ˈproufail/ *n.* perfil *m.*
profit /ˈprɒfɪt/ *n.* **1.** provecho *m.*; ventaja *f.*; *Com.* ganancia *f.* —*v.* **2.** aprovechar; beneficiar.
profitable /ˈprɒfɪtəbəl/ *a.* provechoso, ventajoso, lucrativo.
profiteer /ˌprɒfɪˈtɪər/ *n.* **1.** explotador -ra. —*v.* **2.** explotar.
profound /prəˈfaund/ *a.* profundo, hondo.
profuse /prəˈfyus/ *a.* pródigo; profuso.
prognosis /prɒgˈnousɪs/ *n.* pronóstico *m.*
program /ˈprougræm/ *n.* programa *m.*
progress /*n.* ˈprɒgrɛs; *v.* prəˈgrɛs/ *n.* **1.** progresos *m.pl.* **in p.,** en marcha. —*v.* **2.** progresar; marchar.
progressive /prəˈgrɛsɪv/ *a.* progresivo; progresista.
prohibit /prouˈhɪbɪt/ *v.* prohibir.
prohibition /ˌprouəˈbɪʃən/ *n.* prohibición *f.*
prohibitive /prouˈhɪbɪtɪv/ *a.* prohibitivo.
project /*n.* ˈprɒdʒɛkt; *v.* prəˈdʒɛkt/ *n.* **1.** proyecto *m.* —*v.* **2.** proyectar.
projectile /prəˈdʒɛktɪl/ *n.* proyectil *m.*
projection /prəˈdʒɛkʃən/ *n.* proyección *f.*
projector /prəˈdʒɛktər/ *n.* proyector *m.*
proliferation /prəˌlɪfəˈreiʃən/ *n.* proliferación *f.*
prolific /prəˈlɪfɪk/ *a.* prolífico.
prologue /ˈproulɔg/ *n.* prólogo *m.*
prolong /prəˈlɔŋ/ *v.* prolongar.
prominent /ˈprɒmənənt/ *a.* prominente; eminente.
promiscuous /prəˈmɪskyuəs/ *a.* promiscuo.
promise /ˈprɒmɪs/ *n.* **1.** promesa *f.* —*v.* **2.** prometer.
promote /prəˈmout/ *v.* fomentar; estimular; adelantar; promocionar.
promotion /prəˈmouʃən/ *n.* promoción *f.*; adelanto *m.*
prompt /prɒmpt/ *a.* **1.** puntual. —*v.* **2.** impulsar; *Theat.* apuntar. —*adv.* **3.** pronto.
promulgate /ˈprɒməlˌgeit/ *v.* promulgar.
pronoun /ˈprouˌnaun/ *n.* pronombre *m.*
pronounce /prəˈnauns/ *v.* pronunciar.
pronunciation /prəˌnʌnsiˈeiʃən/ *n.* pronunciación *f.*
proof /pruf/ *n.* prueba *f.*
proof of purchase certificado de compra *m.*
proofread /ˈprufˌrid/ *v.* corregir pruebas.
prop /prɒp/ *n.* **1.** apoyo, *m.* —*v.* **2.** sostener.
propaganda /ˌprɒpəˈgændə/ *n.* propaganda *f.*
propagate /ˈprɒpəˌgeit/ *v.* propagar.
propel /prəˈpɛl/ *v.* propulsar.
propeller /prəˈpɛlər/ *n.* hélice *f.*
propensity /prəˈpɛnsɪti/ *n.* tendencia *f.*
proper /ˈprɒpər/ *a.* propio; correcto.
property /ˈprɒpərti/ *n.* propiedad *f.*
prophecy /ˈprɒfəsi/ *n.* profecía *f.*
prophesy /ˈprɒfəˌsai/ *v.* predecir, profetizar.
prophet /ˈprɒfɪt/ *n.* profeta *m.*
prophetic /prəˈfɛtɪk/ *a.* profético.
propitious /prəˈpɪʃəs/ *a.* propicio.

proponent /prə'pounənt/ n. & a. proponente m.

proportion /prə'pɔrʃən/ n. proporción f.

proportionate /prə'pɔrʃənɪt/ a. proporcionado.

proposal /prə'pouzəl/ n. propuesta; oferta f.; (marriage) declaración f.

propose /prə'pouz/ v. proponer; pensar; declararse.

proposition /ˌprɒpə'zɪʃən/ n. proposición f.

proprietor /prə'praɪtər/ n. propietario -ria, dueño -ña.

propriety /prə'praɪti/ n. corrección f., decoro m.

prosaic /prou'zeɪɪk/ a. prosaico.

proscribe /prou'skraɪb/ v. proscribir.

prose /prouz/ n. prosa f.

prosecute /'prɒsɪˌkyut/ v. acusar, procesar.

prospect /'prɒspɛkt/ n. perspectiva; esperanza f.

prospective /prə'spɛktɪv/ a. anticipado, presunto.

prosper /'prɒspər/ v. prosperar.

prosperity /prɒ'spɛrɪti/ n. prosperidad f.

prosperous /'prɒspərəs/ a. próspero.

prostate gland /'prɒsteɪt/ glándula prostática f.

prostitute /'prɒstɪˌtut/ n. **1.** prostituta f. —v. **2.** prostituir.

prostrate /'prɒstreɪt/ a. **1.** postrado. —v. **2.** postrar.

protect /prə'tɛkt/ v. proteger; amparar.

protection /prə'tɛkʃən/ n. protección f.; amparo m.

protective /prə'tɛktɪv/ a. protector.

protector /prə'tɛktər/ n. protector -ora.

protégé /'proutəˌʒeɪ/ n. protegido -da.

protein /'proutin, -tiɪn/ n. proteína f.

protest /n. 'proutɛst; v. prə'tɛst, 'proutɛst/ n. **1.** protesta f. —v. **2.** protestar.

Protestant /'prɒtəstənt/ a. & n. protestante m. & f.

protocol /'proutəˌkɔl/ n. protocolo m.

proton /'proutɒn/ n. protón m.

protract /prou'trækt/ v. alargar, demorar.

protrude /prou'trud/ v. salir fuera.

protuberance /prou'tubərəns/ n. protuberancia f.

proud /praud/ a. orgulloso.

prove /pruv/ v. comprobar.

proverb /'prɒvərb/ n. proverbio, refrán m.

provide /prə'vaɪd/ v. proporcionar; proveer.

provided /prə'vaɪdɪd/ conj. con tal que.

providence /'prɒvɪdəns/ n. providencia f.

province /'prɒvɪns/ n. provincia f.

provincial /prə'vɪnʃəl/ a. **1.** provincial. —n. **2.** provinciano -na.

provision /prə'vɪʒən/ n. **1.** provisión f.; (pl.) comestibles m.pl. —v. **2.** abastecer.

provocation /ˌprɒvə'keɪʃən/ n. provocación f.

provoke /prə'vouk/ v. provocar.

prowess /'prauɪs/ n. proeza f.

prowl /praul/ v. rondar.

prowler /'praulər/ n. merodeador -dora m. & f.

proximity /prɒk'sɪmɪti/ n. proximidad f.

proxy /'prɒksi/ n. delegado -da. **by p.,** mediante apoderado.

prudence /'prudəns/ n. prudencia f.

prudent /'prudnt/ a. prudente, cauteloso.

prune /prun/ n. ciruela pasa f.

pry /praɪ/ v. atisbar; curiosear; Mech. alzaprimar.

psalm /sɑm/ n. salmo m.

pseudonym /'sudnɪm/ n. seudónimo m.

psychedelic /ˌsaɪkɪ'dɛlɪk/ a. psiquedélico.

psychiatrist /sɪ'kaɪətrɪst, saɪ-/ n. psiquiatra m. & f.

psychiatry /sɪ'kaɪətri, saɪ-/ n. psiquiatría f.

psychoanalysis /ˌsaɪkouə'næləsɪs/ n. psicoanálisis m.

psychoanalyst /ˌsaɪkou'ænlɪst/ n. psicoanalista m. & f.

psychological /ˌsaɪkə'lɒdʒɪkəl/ a. psicológico.

psychology /saɪ'kɒlədʒi/ n. psicología f.

psychosis /saɪ'kousɪs/ n. psicosis f.

ptomaine /'toumeɪn/ n. tomaína f.

pub /pʌb/ n. bar m.

public /'pʌblɪk/ a. & n. público m.

publication /ˌpʌblɪ'keɪʃən/ n. publicación; revista f.

publicity /pʌ'blɪsɪti/ n. publicidad f.

publicity agent publicista m. & f.

publish /'pʌblɪʃ/ v. publicar.

publisher /'pʌblɪʃər/ n. editor -ora.

pudding /'pudɪŋ/ n. pudín m.

puddle /'pʌdl/ n. charco, lodazal m.

Puerto Rican /'pwɛrtə 'rikən, 'pɔr-/ a. & n. puertorriqueño -ña.

Puerto Rico /'pwɛr'tə rikou, 'pɔrtə/ Puerto Rico m.

puff /pʌf/ n. **1.** soplo m.; (of smoke) bocanada f. **powder p.,** polvera f. —v. **2.** jadear; echar bocanadas. **p. up,** hinchar; Fig. engreír.

pugnacious /pʌg'neɪʃəs/ a. pugnaz.

puh-lease! /pʌ 'liz/ ¡Favor!

pull /pul/ n. **1.** tirón f.; Colloq. influencia f. —v. **2.** tirar; halar.

pulley /'puli/ n. polea f., motón m.

pulmonary /'pʌlməˌnɛri/ a. pulmonar.

pulp /pʌlp/ n. pulpa; (of fruit) carne f.

pulpit /'pulpɪt, 'pʌl-/ n. púlpito m.

pulsar /'pʌlsɑr/ n. pulsar m.

pulsate /'pʌlseɪt/ v. pulsar.

pulse /pʌls/ n. pulso m.

pump /pʌmp/ n. **1.** bomba f. —v. **2.** bombear. **p. up,** inflar.

pumpkin /'pʌmpkɪn/ n. calabaza f.

pun /pʌn/ n. juego de palabras.

punch /pʌntʃ/ n. **1.** puñetazo; Mech. punzón; (beverage) ponche m. —v. **2.** dar puñetazos; punzar.

punch bowl ponchera f.

punctual /'pʌŋktʃuəl/ a. puntual.

punctuate /'pʌŋktʃuˌeɪt/ v. puntuar.

puncture /'pʌŋktʃər/ n. **1.** pinchazo m., perforación f. —v. **2.** pinchar, perforar.

pungent /'pʌndʒənt/ a. picante, pungente.

punish /'pʌnɪʃ/ v. castigar.

punishment /'pʌnɪʃmənt/ n. castigo m.

punitive /'pyunɪtɪv/ a. punitivo.

puny /'pyuni/ a. encanijado.

pupil /'pyupəl/ n. alumno -na; Anat. pupila f.

puppet /'pʌpɪt/ n. muñeco m.

puppy /'pʌpi/ n. perrito -ta.

purchase /'pɜrtʃəs/ n. **1.** compra f. —v. **2.** comprar.

purchasing power /'pɜrtʃəsɪŋ/ poder adquisitivo m.

pure /pyur/ a. puro.

purée /pyu'reɪ/ n. puré m.

purge /pɜrdʒ/ v. purgar.

purify /'pyurəˌfaɪ/ v. purificar.

puritanical /ˌpyurɪ'tænɪkəl/ a. puritano.

purity /'pyurɪti/ n. pureza f.

purple /'pɜrpəl/ a. **1.** purpúreo. —n. **2.** púrpura f.

purport /n. 'pɜrpɔrt; v. pər'pɔrt/ n. **1.** significación f. —v. **2.** significar.

purpose /'pɜrpəs/ n. propósito m. **on p.,** de propósito.

purr /pɜr/ v. ronronear.

purse /pɜrs/ n. bolsa f.

pursue /pər'su/ v. perseguir.

pursuit /pər'sut/ n. caza; busca; ocupación f. **p. plane,** avión de caza m.

push /puʃ/ n. **1.** empuje; impulso m. —v. **2.** empujar.

put /put/ v. poner, colocar. **p. away,** guardar. **p. in,** meter. **p. off,** dejar. **p. on,** ponerse. **p. out,** apagar. **p. up with,** aguantar.

putrid /'pyutrɪd/ a. podrido.

putt /pʌt/ n. (golf) golpe corto m.

puzzle /'pʌzəl/ n. **1.** enigma; rompecabezas m. —v. **2.** dejar perplejo. **p. out,** descifrar.

pyramid /'pɪrəmɪd/ n. pirámide f.

pyromania /ˌpaɪrə'meɪniə/ n. piromanía f.

Q

quack /kwæk/ n. **1.** (doctor) curandero -ra; (duck) graznido m. —v. **2.** graznar.

quadrangle /'kwɒd,ræŋgəl/ n. cuadrángulo m.

quadraphonic /ˌkwɒdrə'fɒnɪk/ a. cuatrifónico.

quadruped /'kwɒdruˌpɛd/ a. & n. cuadrúpedo m.

quail /kweɪl/ n. **1.** codorniz f. —v. **2.** descorazonarse.

quaint /kweɪnt/ a. curioso.

quake /kweɪk/ n. **1.** temblor m. —v. **2.** temblar.

qualification /ˌkwɒləfɪ'keɪʃən/ n. requisito m.; (pl.) preparaciones f.pl.

qualified /'kwɒləˌfaɪd/ a. calificado, competente; preparado.

qualify /'kwɒləˌfaɪ/ v. calificar, modificar; llenar los requisitos.

quality /'kwɒlɪti/ n. calidad f.

quandary /'kwɒndəri, -dri/ n. incertidumbre f.

quantity /'kwɒntɪti/ n. cantidad f.

quarantine /'kwɒrənˌtin, 'kwɒr-, ˌkwɒrən'tin, ˌkwɒr-/ n. cuarentena f.

quarrel /'kwɒrəl, 'kwɒr-/ n. **1.** riña, disputa f. —v. **2.** reñir, disputar.

quarry /'kwɒri, 'kwɒri/ n. cantera; (hunting) presa f.

quarter /'kwɔrtər/ n. cuarto m.; (pl.) vivienda f.

quarterly /'kwɔrtərli/ a. **1.** trimestral. —adv. **2.** por cuartos.

quartet /kwɔr'tɛt/ n. cuarteto m.

quartz /kwɔrts/ n. cuarzo m.

quasar /'kweɪzɑr/ n. cuasar m.

quaver /'kweɪvər/ v. temblar.

queen /kwin/ n. reina f.; (chess) dama f.

queer /kwɪər/ a. extraño, raro.

quell /kwɛl/ v. reprimir.

quench /kwɛntʃ/ v. apagar.

query /'kwɪəri/ n. **1.** pregunta f. —v. **2.** preguntar.

quest /kwɛst/ n. busca f.

question /'kwɛstʃən/ n. **1.** pregunta; cuestión f. **q. mark,** signo de interrogación. —v. **2.** preguntar; interrogar; dudar.

questionable /'kwɛstʃənəbəl/ a. dudoso.

questionnaire /ˌkwɛstʃə'nɛər/ n. cuestionario m.

quiche /kiʃ/ n. quiche f.

quick /kwɪk/ a. rápido.

quicken /'kwɪkən/ v. acelerar.

quicksand /'kwɪk,sænd/ n. arena movediza.

quiet /'kwaɪɪt/ a. **1.** quieto, tranquilo; callado. **be q., keep q.,** callarse. —n. **2.** calma; quietud f. —v. **3.** tranquilizar. **q. down,** callarse; calmarse.

quilt /kwɪlt/ n. colcha f.

quinine /'kwaɪnaɪn/ n. quinina f.

quintet /kwɪn'tɛt/ n. Mus. quinteto m.

quip /kwɪp/ n. **1.** pulla f. —v. **2.** echar pullas.

quit /kwɪt/ v. dejar; renunciar a. **q. doing** (etc.) dejar de hacer (etc.).

quite /kwaɪt/ adv. bastante; completamente. **not q.,** no precisamente; no completamente.

push /puʃ/ n. **1.** empuje; impulso m. —v. **2.** temblar.

quiver /'kwɪvər/ n. **1.** aljaba f.; temblor m. —v. **2.** temblar.

quixotic /kwɪk'sɒtɪk/ a. quijotesco.

quorum /'kwɔrəm/ n. quórum m.

quota /'kwoutə/ n. cuota f.

quotation /kwou'teɪʃən/ n. citación; Com. cotización f. **q. marks,** comillas f.pl.

quote /kwout/ v. citar; Com. cotizar.

R

rabbi /'ræbaɪ/ n. rabí, rabino m.

rabbit /'ræbɪt/ n. conejo m.

rabble /'ræbəl/ n. canalla f.

rabid /'ræbɪd/ a. rabioso.

rabies /'reɪbiz/ n. hidrofobia f.

race /reɪs/ n. **1.** raza; carrera f. —v. **2.** echar una carrera; correr de prisa.

race track /'reɪs,træk/ hipódromo m.

rack /ræk/ n. **1.** (cooking) pesebre m.; (clothing) colgador m. —v. **2.** atormentar.

racket /'rækɪt/ n. (noise) ruido m.; (tennis) raqueta f.; (graft) fraude organizado.

radar /'reɪdɑr/ n. radar m.

radiance /'reɪdiəns/ n. brillo m.

radiant /'reɪdiənt/ a. radiante.

radiate /'reɪdiˌeɪt/ v. irradiar.

radiation /ˌreɪdi'eɪʃən/ n. irradiación f.

radiator /'reɪdiˌeɪtər/ n. calorífero m.; Auto. radiador m.

radical /'rædɪkəl/ a. & n. radical m.

radio /'reɪdiˌou/ n. radio m. or f. **r. station,** estación radiodifusora f.

radioactive /ˌreɪdiou'æktɪv/ a. radioactivo.

radio cassette radiocasete m.

radish /'rædɪʃ/ n. rábano m.

radium /'reɪdiəm/ n. radio m.

radius /'reɪdiəs/ n. radio m.

raffle /'ræfəl/ n. **1.** rifa, lotería f. —v. **2.** rifar.

raft /ræft/ n. balsa f.

rafter /'ræftər/ n. viga f.

rag /ræg/ n. trapo m.

ragamuffin /'rægəˌmʌfɪn/ n. galopín m.

rage /reɪdʒ/ n. **1.** rabia f. —v. **2.** rabiar.

ragged /'rægɪd/ a. andrajoso; desigual.

raid /reɪd/ n. Mil. correría f.

rail /reɪl/ n. baranda f.; carril m. **by r.,** por ferrocarril.

railroad /'reɪl,roud/ n. ferrocarril m.

rain /reɪn/ n. **1.** lluvia f. —v. **2.** llover.

rainbow /'reɪn,bou/ n. arco iris m.

raincoat /'reɪn,kout/ n. impermeable m.; gabardina f.

rainfall /'reɪn,fɔl/ n. precipitación f.

rainy /'reɪni/ a. lluvioso.

raise /reɪz/ n. **1.** aumento m. —v. **2.** levantar; criar.

raisin /'reɪzɪn/ n. pasa f.

rake /reɪk/ n. **1.** rastro m. —v. **2.** rastrillar.

rally /'ræli/ n. **1.** reunión f. —v. **2.** reunirse.

ram /ræm/ n. carnero m.

ramble /'ræmbəl/ v. vagar.

ramp /ræmp/ n. rampa f.

rampart /'ræmpɑrt/ n. terraplén m.

ranch /ræntʃ/ n. rancho m.

rancid /'rænsɪd/ a. rancio.

rancor /'ræŋkər/ n. rencor m.

random /'rændəm/ a. fortuito. **at r.,** a la ventura.

range /reɪndʒ/ n. **1.** extensión f.; alcance m.; estufa; sierra f.; terreno de pasto. —v. **2.** recorrer; extenderse.

rank /ræŋk/ a. **1.** espeso; rancio. —n. **2.** fila f.; grado m. —v. **3.** clasificar.

ransack /'rænsæk/ v. saquear.

ransom /'rænsəm/ n. **1.** rescate m. —v. **2.** rescatar.

rap /ræp/ n. **1.** golpecito m. —v. **2.** golpear.

rapid /'ræpɪd/ a. rápido.

rapist /ˈreipɪst/ *n.* violador -dora *m. & f.*
rapport /ræˈpɔr/ *n.* armonía *f.*
rapture /ˈræptʃər/ *n.* éxtasis *m.*
rare /rɛər/ *a.* raro; (of food) a medio cocer.
rascal /ˈræskəl/ *n.* pícaro, bribón *m.*
rash /ræʃ/ *a.* **1.** temerario. —*n.* **2.** erupción *f.*
raspberry /ˈræzˌbɛri/ *n.* frambuesa *f.*
rat /ræt/ *n.* rata *f.*
rate /reit/ *n.* **1.** velocidad; tasa *f.*; precio *m.*; (of exchange; of interest) tipo *m.* **at any r.,** de todos modos. —*v.* **2.** valuar.
rather /ˈræðər/ *adv.* bastante; más bien, mejor dicho.
ratify /ˈrætəˌfai/ *v.* ratificar.
ratio /ˈreiʃou/ *n.* razón; proporción *f.*
ration /ˈræʃən, ˈreiʃən/ *n.* **1.** ración *f.* —*v.* **2.** racionar.
rational /ˈræʃənl̩/ *a.* racional.
rattle /ˈrætl̩/ *n.* **1.** ruido *m.*; matraca *f.* **r. snake,** culebra de cascabel, serpiente de cascabel *f.* —*v.* **2.** matraquear; rechinar.
raucous /ˈrɔkəs/ *a.* ronco.
ravage /ˈrævɪdʒ/ *v.* pillar; destruir; asolar.
rave /reiv/ *v.* delirar; entusiasmarse.
ravel /ˈrævəl/ *v.* deshilar.
raven /ˈreivən/ *n.* cuervo *m.*
ravenous /ˈrævənəs/ *a.* voraz.
raw /rɔ/ *a.* crudo; verde.
ray /rei/ *n.* rayo *m.*
rayon /ˈreiɒn/ *n.* rayón *m.*
razor /ˈreizər/ *n.* navaja de afeitar. **r. blade,** hoja de afeitar.
reach /ritʃ/ *n.* **1.** alcance *m.* —*v.* **2.** alcanzar.
react /riˈækt/ *v.* reaccionar.
reaction /riˈækʃən/ *n.* reacción *f.*
reactionary /riˈækʃəˌnɛri/ *a.* **1.** reaccionario. —*n.* **2.** *Pol.* retrógrado *m.*
read /rid/ *v.* leer.
reader /ˈridər/ *n.* lector -ra; libro de lectura *m.*
readily /ˈrɛdl̩i/ *adv.* fácilmente.
reading /ˈridɪŋ/ *n.* lectura *f.*
ready /ˈrɛdi/ *a.* listo, preparado; dispuesto.
ready-cooked /ˈrɛdi ˌkʊkt/ *a.* precocinado.
real /reiˈɑl/ *a.* verdadero; real.
real estate bienes inmuebles, *m.pl.*
real-estate agent /ˈriəl ɪˈsteit/ agente inmobiliario *m.*, agente inmobiliaria *f.*
realist /ˈriəlɪst/ *n.* realista *m. & f.*
realistic /ˌriəˈlɪstɪk/ *a.* realista.
reality /riˈælɪti/ *n.* realidad *f.*
realization /ˌriələˈzeiʃən/ *n.* comprensión; realización *f.*
realize /ˈriəˌlaiz/ *v.* darse cuenta de; realizar.
really /ˈriəli/ *adv.* de veras; en realidad.
realm /rɛlm/ *n.* reino; dominio *m.*
reap /rip/ *v.* segar, cosechar.
rear /rɪər/ *a.* **1.** posterior. —*n.* **2.** parte posterior. —*v.* **3.** criar; levantar.
reason /ˈrizən/ *n.* **1.** razón; causa *f.*; motivo *m.* —*v.* **2.** razonar.
reasonable /ˈrizənəbəl/ *a.* razonable.
reassure /ˌriəˈʃʊr/ *v.* calmar, tranquilizar.
rebate /ˈribeit/ *n.* rebaja *f.*
rebel /*n.* ˈrɛbəl; *v.* rɪˈbɛl/ *n.* **1.** rebelde *m. & f.* —*v.* **2.** rebelarse.
rebellion /rɪˈbɛlyən/ *n.* rebelión *f.*
rebellious /rɪˈbɛlyəs/ *a.* rebelde.
rebirth /riˈbɜrθ/ *n.* renacimiento *m.*
rebound /rɪˈbaund/ *v.* repercutir; resaltar.
rebuff /rɪˈbʌf/ *n.* **1.** repulsa *f.* —*v.* **2.** rechazar.
rebuke /rɪˈbyuk/ *n.* **1.** reprensión *f.* —*v.* **2.** reprender.
rebuttal /rɪˈbʌtl̩/ *n.* refutación *f.*
recalcitrant /rɪˈkælsɪtrənt/ *a.* recalcitrante.
recall /rɪˈkɔl/ *v.* recordar; acordarse de; hacer volver.
recapitulate /ˌrikəˈpɪtʃəˌleit/ *v.* recapitular.
recede /rɪˈsid/ *v.* retroceder.
receipt /rɪˈsit/ *n.* recibo *m.*; (com., pl.) ingresos *m.pl.*
receive /rɪˈsiv/ *v.* recibir.
receiver /rɪˈsivər/ *n.* receptor *m.*
recent /ˈrisənt/ *a.* reciente.
recently /ˈrisəntli/ *adv.* recién.
receptacle /rɪˈsɛptəkəl/ *n.* receptáculo *m.*
reception /rɪˈsɛpʃən/ *n.* acogida; recepción *f.*
receptionist /rɪˈsɛpʃənɪst/ *n.* recepcionista *m. & f.*
receptive /rɪˈsɛptɪv/ *a.* receptivo.
recess /rɪˈsɛs, ˈrisɛs/ *n.* nicho; retiro; recreo *m.*
recipe /ˈrɛsəpi/ *n.* receta *f.*
recipient /rɪˈsɪpiənt/ *n.* recibidor -ra, recipiente *m. & f.*
reciprocate /rɪˈsɪprəˌkeit/ *v.* corresponder; reciprocar.
recite /rɪˈsait/ *v.* recitar.
reckless /ˈrɛklɪs/ *a.* descuidado; imprudente.
reckon /ˈrɛkən/ *v.* contar; calcular.
reclaim /rɪˈkleim/ *v.* reformar; *Leg.* reclamar.
recline /rɪˈklain/ *v.* reclinar; recostar.
recognition /ˌrɛkəgˈnɪʃən/ *n.* reconocimiento *m.*
recognize /ˈrɛkəgˌnaiz/ *v.* reconocer.
recoil /*n.* ˈriˌkɔil; *v.* rɪˈkɔil/ *n.* **1.** culatada *f.* —*v.* **2.** recular.
recollect /ˌrɛkəˈlɛkt/ *v.* recordar, acordarse de.
recommend /ˌrɛkəˈmɛnd/ *v.* recomendar.
recommendation /ˌrɛkəmɛnˈdeiʃən/ *n.* recomendación *f.*
recompense /ˈrɛkəmˌpɛns/ *n.* **1.** recompensa *f.* —*v.* **2.** recompensar.
reconcile /ˈrɛkənˌsail/ *v.* reconciliar.
recondition /ˌrikənˈdɪʃən/ *v.* reacondicionar.
reconsider /ˌrikənˈsɪdər/ *v.* considerar de nuevo.
reconstruct /ˌrikənˈstrʌkt/ *v.* reconstruir.
record /*n.* ˈrɛkərd, *v.* rɪˈkɔrd/ *n.* **1.** registro; (sports) record *m.* **phonograph r.,** disco *m.* —*v.* **2.** registrar.
record player tocadiscos *m.*
recount /rɪˈkaunt/ *v.* relatar; contar.
recover /rɪˈkʌvər/ *v.* recobrar; restablecerse.
recovery /rɪˈkʌvəri/ *n.* recobro *m.*; recuperación *f.*
recruit /rɪˈkrut/ *n.* **1.** recluta *m.* —*v.* **2.** reclutar.
rectangle /ˈrɛkˌtæŋgəl/ *n.* rectángulo *m.*
rectify /ˈrɛktəˌfai/ *v.* rectificar.
recuperate /rɪˈkupəˌreit/ *v.* recuperar.
recur /rɪˈkɜr/ *v.* recurrir.
recycle /riˈsaikəl/ *v.* reciclar.
red /rɛd/ *a.* rojo, colorado.
redeem /rɪˈdim/ *v.* redimir, rescatar.
redemption /rɪˈdɛmpʃən/ *n.* redención *f.*
redhead /ˈrɛdˌhɛd/ *n.* pelirrojo -ja.
red mullet /ˈmʌlɪt/ salmonete *m.*
reduce /rɪˈdus/ *v.* reducir.
reduction /rɪˈdʌkʃən/ *n.* reducción *f.*
reed /rid/ *n.* caña *f.*, *S.A.* bejuco *m.*
reef /rif/ *n.* arrecife, escollo *m.*
reel /ril/ *n.* **1.** aspa *f.*, carrete *m.* —*v.* **2.** aspar.
refer /rɪˈfɜr/ *v.* referir.
referee /ˌrɛfəˈri/ *n.* árbitro *m. & f.*
reference /ˈrɛfərəns/ *n.* referencia *f.*
refill /*n.* ˈriˌfɪl; *v.* riˈfɪl/ *n.* **1.** relleno *m.* —*v.* **2.** rellenar.
refine /rɪˈfain/ *n.* refinar.
refinement /rɪˈfainmənt/ *n.* refinamiento *m.*; cultura *f.*
reflect /rɪˈflɛkt/ *v.* reflejar; reflexionar.
reflection /rɪˈflɛkʃən/ *n.* reflejo *m.*; reflexión *f.*
reflex /ˈriflɛks/ *a.* reflejo.
reform /rɪˈfɔrm/ *n.* **1.** reforma *f.* —*v.* **2.** reformar.
reformation /ˌrɛfərˈmeiʃən/ *n.* reformación *f.*
refractory /rɪˈfræktəri/ *a.* refractario.
refrain /rɪˈfrein/ *n.* **1.** estribillo *m.* —*v.* **2.** abstenerse.
refresh /rɪˈfrɛʃ/ *v.* refrescar.
refreshment /rɪˈfrɛʃmənt/ *n.* refresco *m.*
refrigerator /rɪˈfrɪdʒəˌreitər/ *n.* refrigerador *m.*
refuge /ˈrɛfyudʒ/ *n.* refugio *m.*
refugee /ˌrɛfyʊˈdʒi/ *n.* refugiado -da.
refund /*n* ˈrifʌnd; *v* riˈfʌnd/ *n.* **1.** reembolso *m.* —*v.* **2.** reembolsar.
refusal /rɪˈfyuzəl/ *n.* negativa *f.*
refuse /*n* ˈrɛfyus; *v* rɪˈfyuz/ *n.* **1.** basura *f.* —*v.* **2.** negarse, rehusar.
refute /rɪˈfyut/ *v.* refutar.
regain /riˈgein/ *v.* recobrar. **r. consciousness,** recobrar el conocimiento.
regal /ˈrigəl/ *a.* real.
regard /rɪˈgɑrd/ *n.* **1.** aprecio; respeto *m.* **with r. to,** con respecto a. —*v.* **2.** considerar; estimar.
regarding /rɪˈgɑrdɪŋ/ *prep.* en cuanto a, acerca de.
regardless (of) /rɪˈgɑrdlɪs/ a pesar de.
regent /ˈridʒənt/ *n.* regente *m. & f.*
regime /rəˈʒim, rei-/ *n.* régimen *m.*
regiment /*n.* ˈrɛdʒəmənt; *v.* -ˌmɛnt/ *n.* **1.** regimiento *m.* —*v.* **2.** regimentar.
region /ˈridʒən/ *n.* región *f.*
register /ˈrɛdʒəstər/ *n.* **1.** registro *m.* **cash r.,** caja registradora *f.* —*v.* **2.** registrar; matricularse; (a letter) certificar.
registration /ˌrɛdʒəˈstreiʃən/ *n.* registro *m.*; matrícula *f.*
regret /rɪˈgrɛt/ *n.* **1.** pena *f.* —*v.* **2.** sentir, lamentar.
regular /ˈrɛgyələr/ *a.* regular; ordinario.
regularity /ˌrɛgyəˈlærɪti/ *n.* regularidad *f.*
regulate /ˈrɛgyəˌleit/ *v.* regular.
regulation /ˌrɛgyəˈleiʃən/ *n.* regulación *f.*
regulator /ˈrɛgyəˌleitər/ *n.* regulador *m.*
rehabilitate /ˌrihəˈbɪlɪˌteit, ˌriə-/ *v.* rehabilitar.
rehearse /rɪˈhɜrs/ *v.* repasar; *Theat.* ensayar.
reheat /riˈhit/ *v.* recalentar.
reign /rein/ *n.* **1.** reino, reinado *m.* —*v.* **2.** reinar.
reimburse /ˌriɪmˈbɜrs/ *v.* reembolsar.
rein /rein/ *n.* **1.** rienda *f.* —*v.* **2.** refrenar.
reincarnation /ˌriɪnkɑrˈneiʃən/ *n.* reencarnación *f.*
reindeer /ˈreinˌdɪər/ *n.* reno *m.*
reinforce /ˌriɪnˈfɔrs, -ˈfours/ *v.* reforzar.
reinforcement /ˌriɪnˈfɔrsmənt, -ˈfours-/ *n.* refuerzo *m.*; armadura *f.*
reiterate /riˈɪtəˌreit/ *v.* reiterar.
reject /rɪˈdʒɛkt/ *v.* rechazar.
rejoice /rɪˈdʒɔis/ *v.* regocijarse.
rejoin /rɪˈdʒɔin/ *v.* reunirse con; replicar.
rejuvenate /rɪˈdʒuvəˌneit/ *v.* rejuvenecer.
relapse /*v.* rɪˈlæps; *n. also* ˈrilæps/ *v.* **1.** recaer. —*n.* **2.** recaída *f.*
relate /rɪˈleit/ *v.* relatar, contar; relacionar. **r. to,** llevarse bien con.
relation /rɪˈleiʃən/ *n.* relación *f.*; pariente *m. & f.*
relative /ˈrɛlətɪv/ *a.* **1.** relativo. —*n.* **2.** pariente *m. & f.*
relativity /ˌrɛləˈtɪvɪti/ *n.* relatividad *f.*
relax /rɪˈlæks/ *v.* descansar; relajar.
relay /ˈrilei; *v. also* rɪˈlei/ *n.* **1.** relevo *m.* —*v.* **2.** retransmitir.
release /rɪˈlis/ *n.* **1.** liberación *f.* —*v.* **2.** soltar.
relent /rɪˈlɛnt/ *v.* ceder.
relevant /ˈrɛləvənt/ *a.* pertinente.
reliability /rɪˌlaiəˈbɪlɪti/ *n.* veracidad *f.*
reliable /rɪˈlaiəbəl/ *a.* responsable; digno de confianza.
relic /ˈrɛlɪk/ *n.* reliquia *f.*
relief /rɪˈlif/ *n.* alivio; (sculpture) relieve *m.*
relieve /rɪˈliv/ *v.* aliviar.
religion /rɪˈlɪdʒən/ *n.* religión *f.*
religious /rɪˈlɪdʒəs/ *a.* religioso.
relinquish /rɪˈlɪŋkwɪʃ/ *v.* abandonar.
relish /ˈrɛlɪʃ/ *n.* **1.** sabor; condimento *m.* —*v.* **2.** saborear.
reluctant /rɪˈlʌktənt/ *a.* renuente.
rely /rɪˈlai/ *v.* **r. on,** confiar en; contar con; depender de.
remain /rɪˈmein/ *n.* **1.** (pl.) restos *m.pl.* —*v.* **2.** quedar, permanecer.
remainder /rɪˈmeindər/ *n.* resto *m.*
remark /rɪˈmɑrk/ *n.* **1.** observación *f.* —*v.* **2.** observar.
remarkable /rɪˈmɑrkəbəl/ *a.* notable.
remedial /rɪˈmidiəl/ *a.* reparador.
remedy /ˈrɛmɪdi/ *n.* **1.** remedio *m.* —*v.* **2.** remediar.
remember /rɪˈmɛmbər/ *v.* acordarse de, recordar.
remembrance /rɪˈmɛmbrəns/ *n.* recuerdo *m.*
remind /rɪˈmaind/ *v.* **r. of,** recordar.
reminisce /ˌrɛməˈnɪs/ *v.* pensar en o hablar de cosas pasadas.
remiss /rɪˈmɪs/ *a.* remiso; flojo.
remit /rɪˈmɪt/ *v.* remitir.
remorse /rɪˈmɔrs/ *n.* remordimiento *m.*
remote /rɪˈmout/ *a.* remoto.
remote control mando a distancia *m.*
removal /rɪˈmuvəl/ *n.* alejamiento *m.*; eliminación *f.*
remove /rɪˈmuv/ *v.* quitar; remover.
renaissance /ˌrɛnəˈsɑns/ *n.* renacimiento *m.*
rend /rɛnd/ *v.* hacer pedazos; separar.
render /ˈrɛndər/ *v.* dar; rendir; *Theat.* interpretar.
rendezvous /ˈrɑndəˌvu, -dei-/ *n.* cita *f.*
rendition /rɛnˈdɪʃən/ *n.* interpretación, rendición *f.*
renege /rɪˈnɪg, -ˈnɛg/ *v.* renunciar; faltar a su palabra, no cumplir una promesa.
renew /rɪˈnu, -ˈnyu/ *v.* renovar.
renewal /rɪˈnuəl, -ˈnyu-/ *n.* renovación; *Com.* prórroga *f.*
renounce /rɪˈnauns/ *v.* renunciar a.
renovate /ˈrɛnəˌveit/ *v.* renovar.
renown /rɪˈnaun/ *n.* renombre *m.*, fama *f.*
rent /rɛnt/ *n.* **1.** alquiler *m.* —*v.* **2.** arrendar, alquilar.
repair /rɪˈpɛər/ *n.* **1.** reparo *m.* —*v.* **2.** reparar.
repairman /rɪˈpɛərˌmæn/ *n.* técnico *m.*
repatriate /riˈpeitriˌeit/ *v.* repatriar.
repay /rɪˈpei/ *v.* pagar; devolver.
repeat /rɪˈpit/ *v.* repetir.
repel /rɪˈpɛl/ *v.* repeler, repulsar.
repent /ˈripənt, rɪˈpɛnt/ *v.* arrepentirse.
repentance /rɪˈpɛntns, -ˈpɛntəns/ *n.* arrepentimiento *m.*
repercussion /ˌripərˈkʌʃən, ˌrɛpər-/ *n.* repercusión *f.*
repertoire /ˈrɛpərˌtwɑr/ *n.* repertorio *m.*
repetition /ˌrɛpɪˈtɪʃən/ *n.* repetición *f.*
replace /rɪˈpleis/ *v.* reemplazar.
replenish /rɪˈplɛnɪʃ/ *v.* rellenar; surtir de nuevo.
reply /rɪˈplai/ *n.* **1.** respuesta *f.* —*v.* **2.** replicar; contestar.
report /rɪˈpɔrt, -ˈpourt/ *n.* **1.** informe *m.* —*v.* **2.** informar, contar; denunciar; presentarse.
reporter /rɪˈpɔrtər, -ˈpour-/ *n.* repórter *m. & f.*, reportero -ra.
repose /rɪˈpouz/ *n.* **1.** reposo *m.* —*v.* **2.** reposar; reclinar.

reprehensible /ˌrɛprɪˈhɛnsəbəl/ *a.* reprensible.
represent /ˌrɛprɪˈzɛnt/ *v.* representar.
representation /ˌrɛprɪzɛnˈteiʃən, -zən-/ *n.* representación *f.*
representative /ˌrɛprɪˈzɛntətɪv/ *a.* **1.** representativo. **—***n.* **2.** representante *m.* & *f.*
repress /rɪˈprɛs/ *v.* reprimir.
reprimand /ˈrɛprəˌmænd, -ˌmɑnd/ *n.* **1.** regaño *m.* **—***v.* **2.** regañar.
reprisal /rɪˈpraizəl/ *n.* represalia *f.*
reproach /rɪˈproutʃ/ *n.* **1.** reproche *m.* **—***v.* **2.** reprochar.
reproduce /ˌriprəˈdus, -ˈdyus/ *v.* reproducir.
reproduction /ˌriprəˈdʌkʃən/ *n.* reproducción *f.*
reproof /rɪˈpruf/ *n.* censura *f.*
reprove /rɪˈpruv/ *v.* censurar, regañar.
reptile /ˈrɛptɪl, -tail/ *n.* reptil *m.*
republic /rɪˈpʌblɪk/ *n.* república *f.*
republican /rɪˈpʌblɪkən/ *a.* & *n.* republicano -na.
repudiate /rɪˈpyudiˌeit/ *v.* repudiar.
repulsive /rɪˈpʌlsɪv/ *a.* repulsivo, repugnante.
reputation /ˌrɛpyəˈteiʃən/ *n.* reputación; fama *f.*
repute /rɪˈpyut/ *n.* **1.** reputación *f.* **—***v.* **2.** reputar.
request /rɪˈkwɛst/ *n.* **1.** súplica *f.*, ruego *m.* **—***v.* **2.** pedir; rogar, suplicar.
require /rɪˈkwaiᵊr/ *v.* requerir; exigir.
requirement /rɪˈkwaiᵊrmənt/ *n.* requisito *m.*
requisite /ˈrɛkwəzɪt/ *a.* **1.** necesario. **—***n.* **2.** requisito *m.*
requisition /ˌrɛkwəˈzɪʃən/ *n.* requisición *f.*
rescind /rɪˈsɪnd/ *v.* rescindir, anular.
rescue /ˈrɛskyu/ *n.* **1.** rescate *m.* **—***v.* **2.** rescatar.
research /rɪˈsɜrtʃ, ˈrisɜrtʃ/ *n.* investigación *f.*
researcher /rɪˈsɜrtʃər/ *n.* investigador -dora.
resemble /rɪˈzɛmbəl/ *v.* parecerse a, asemejarse a.
resent /rɪˈzɛnt/ *v.* resentirse de.
reservation /ˌrɛzərˈveiʃən/ *n.* reservación *f.*
reserve /rɪˈzɜrv/ *n.* **1.** reserva *f.* **—***v.* **2.** reservar.
reservoir /ˈrɛzərˌvwɑr, -ˌvwɔr, -ˌvɔr, ˈrɛzə-/ *n* depósito; tanque *m.*
reside /rɪˈzaid/ *v.* residir, morar.
residence /ˈrɛzɪdəns/ *n.* residencia, morada *f.*
resident /ˈrɛzɪdənt/ *n.* residente *m.* & *f.*
residue /ˈrɛzɪˌdu/ *n.* residuo *m.*
resign /rɪˈzain/ *v.* dimitir; resignar.
resignation /ˌrɛzɪgˈneiʃən/ *n.* dimisión; resignación *f.*
resist /rɪˈzɪst/ *v.* resistir.
resistance /rɪˈzɪstəns/ *n.* resistencia *f.*
resolute /ˈrɛzəˌlut/ *a.* resuelto.
resolution /ˌrɛzəˈluʃən/ *n.* resolución *f.*
resolve /rɪˈzɒlv/ *v.* resolver.
resonant /ˈrɛzənənt/ *a.* resonante.
resort /rɪˈzɔrt/ *n.* **1.** recurso; expediente *m.* **summer r.,** lugar de veraneo. **—***v.* **2.** acudir, recurrir.
resound /rɪˈzaund/ *v.* resonar.
resource /ˈrisɔrs/ *n.* recurso *m.*
respect /rɪˈspɛkt/ *n.* **1.** respeto *m.* **with r. to,** con respecto a. **—***v.* **2.** respetar.
respectable /rɪˈspɛktəbəl/ *a.* respetable.
respectful /rɪˈspɛktfəl/ *a.* respetuoso.
respective /rɪˈspɛktɪv/ *a.* respectivo.
respiration /ˌrɛspəˈreiʃən/ *n.* respiración *f.*
respite /ˈrɛspɪt/ *n.* pausa, tregua *f.*
respond /rɪˈspɒnd/ *v.* responder.
response /rɪˈspɒns/ *n.* respuesta *f.*
responsibility /rɪˌspɒnsəˈbɪlɪti/ *n.* responsabilidad *f.*
responsible /rɪˈspɒnsəbəl/ *a.* responsable.
responsive /rɪˈspɒnsɪv/ *a.* sensible a.
rest /rɛst/ *n.* **1.** descanso; reposo *m.*; (music) pausa *f.* **the r.,** el resto, lo demás; los demás. **—***v.* **2.** descansar; recostar.
restaurant /ˈrɛstərənt, -təˌrɑnt, -trɑnt/ *n.* restaurante *m.*
restful /ˈrɛstfəl/ *a.* tranquilo.
restitution /ˌrɛstɪˈtuʃən, -ˈtyu-/ *n.* restitución *f.*
restless /ˈrɛstlɪs/ *a.* inquieto.
restoration /ˌrɛstəˈreiʃən/ *n.* restauración *f.*
restore /rɪˈstɔr, -ˈstour/ *v.* restaurar.
restrain /rɪˈstrein/ *v.* refrenar.
restraint /rɪˈstreint/ *n.* limitación, restricción *f.*
restrict /rɪˈstrɪkt/ *v.* restringir, limitar.
rest room aseos *m.pl.*
result /rɪˈzʌlt/ *n.* **1.** resultado *m.* **—***v.* **2.** resultar.
resume /rɪˈzum/ *v.* reasumir; empezar de nuevo.
résumé /ˈrɛzʊˌmei/ *n.* resumen *m.*
resurgent /rɪˈsɜrdʒənt/ *a.* resurgente.
resurrect /ˌrɛzəˈrɛkt/ *v.* resucitar.
resuscitate /rɪˈsʌsɪˌteit/ *v.* resucitar.
retail /ˈriteil/ *n.* **at r.,** al por menor.
retain /rɪˈtein/ *v.* retener.
retaliate /rɪˈtæliˌeit/ *v.* vengarse.
retard /rɪˈtɑrd/ *v.* retardar.
retention /rɪˈtɛnʃən/ *n.* retención *f.*
reticent /ˈrɛtəsənt/ *a.* reticente.
retire /rɪˈtaiᵊr/ *v.* retirar.
retirement /rɪˈtaiᵊrmənt/ *n.* jubilación *f.*
retort /rɪˈtɔrt/ *n.* **1.** réplica; *Chem.* retorta *f.* **—***v.* **2.** replicar.
retreat /rɪˈtrit/ *n.* **1.** retiro *m.*; *Mil.* retirada, retreta *f.* **—***v.* **2.** retirarse.
retribution /ˌrɛtrəˈbyuʃən/ *n.* retribución *f.*
retrieve /rɪˈtriv/ *v.* recobrar.
return /rɪˈtɜrn/ *n.* **1.** vuelta *f.*, regreso; retorno *m.* **by r. mail,** a vuelta de correo. **—***v.* **2.** volver, regresar; devolver.
reunion /riˈyunyən/ *n.* reunión *f.*
rev /rɛv/ *n.* **1.** revolución *f.* **—***v.* **2.** (motor) acelerar.
reveal /rɪˈvil/ *v.* revelar.
revelation /ˌrɛvəˈleiʃən/ *n.* revelación *f.*
revenge /rɪˈvɛndʒ/ *n.* venganza *f.* **to get r.,** vengarse.
revenue /ˈrɛvənˌyu, -əˌnu/ *n.* renta *f.*
revere /rɪˈvɪər/ *v.* reverenciar, venerar.
reverence /ˈrɛvərəns, ˈrɛvrəns/ *n.* **1.** reverencia *f.* **—***v.* **2.** reverenciar.
reverend /ˈrɛvərənd, ˈrɛvrənd/ *a.* **1.** reverendo. **—***n.* **2.** pastor *m.*
reverent /ˈrɛvərənt, ˈrɛvrənt/ *a.* reverente.
reverse /rɪˈvɜrs/ *a.* **1.** inverso. **—***n.* **2.** revés, inverso *m.* **—***v.* **3.** invertir; revocar.
revert /rɪˈvɜrt/ *v.* revertir.
review /rɪˈvyu/ *n.* **1.** repaso *m.*; revista *f.* **—***v.* **2.** repasar; *Mil.* revistar.
revise /rɪˈvaiz/ *v.* revisar.
revision /rɪˈvɪʒən/ *n.* revisión *f.*
revival /rɪˈvaivəl/ *n.* reavivamiento *m.*
revive /rɪˈvaiv/ *v.* avivar; revivir, resucitar.
revoke /rɪˈvouk/ *v.* revocar.
revolt /rɪˈvoult/ *n.* **1.** rebelión *f.* **—***v.* **2.** rebelarse.
revolting /rɪˈvoultɪŋ/ *a.* repugnante.
revolution /ˌrɛvəˈluʃən/ *n.* revolución *f.*
revolutionary /ˌrɛvəˈluʃəˌnɛri/ *a.* & *n.* revolucionario -ria.
revolve /rɪˈvɒlv/ *v.* girar; dar vueltas.
revolver /rɪˈvɒlvər/ *n.* revólver *m.*
revolving door /rɪˈvɒlvɪŋ/ puerta giratoria *f.*
reward /rɪˈwɔrd/ *n.* **1.** pago *m.*; recompensa *f.* **—***v.* **2.** recompensar.
rhetoric /ˈrɛtərɪk/ *n.* retórica *f.*
rheumatism /ˈruməˌtɪzəm/ *n.* reumatismo *m.*
rhinoceros /raiˈnɒsərəs/ *n.* rinoceronte *m.*
rhubarb /ˈrubɑrb/ *n.* ruibarbo *m.*
rhyme /raim/ *n.* **1.** rima *f.* **—***v.* **2.** rimar.
rhythm /ˈrɪðəm/ *n.* ritmo *m.*
rhythmical /ˈrɪðmɪkəl/ *a.* rítmico.
rib /rɪb/ *n.* costilla *f.*
ribbon /ˈrɪbən/ *n.* cinta *f.*
rib cage caja torácica *f.*
rice /rais/ *n.* arroz *m.*
rich /rɪtʃ/ *a.* rico.
rid /rɪd/ *v.* librar. **get r. of,** deshacerse de, quitarse.
riddle /ˈrɪdl̩/ *n.* enigma; rompecabezas *m.*
ride /raid/ *n.* **1.** paseo (a caballo, en coche, etc.) *m.* **—***v.* **2.** cabalgar; ir en coche.
ridge /rɪdʒ/ *n.* cerro *m.*; arruga *f.*; (of a roof) caballete *m.*
ridicule /ˈrɪdɪˌkyul/ *n.* **1.** ridículo *m.* **—***v.* **2.** ridiculizar.
ridiculous /rɪˈdɪkyələs/ *a.* ridículo.
riding /ˈraidɪŋ/ *n.* equitación *f.*
riding school picadero *m.*
rifle /ˈraifəl/ *n.* **1.** fusil *m.* **—***v.* **2.** robar.
rig /rɪg/ *n.* **1.** aparejo *m.* **—***v.* **2.** aparejar.
right /rait/ *a.* **1.** derecho; correcto. **to be r.,** tener razón. **—***adv.* **2.** bien, correctamente. **r. here,** etc., aquí mismo, etc. **all r.,** está bien, muy bien. **—***n.* **3.** derecho *m.*; justicia *f.* **to the r.,** a la derecha. **—***v.* **4.** corregir; enderezar.
righteous /ˈraitʃəs/ *a.* justo.
rigid /ˈrɪdʒɪd/ *a.* rígido.
rigor /ˈrɪgər/ *n.* rigor *m.*
rigorous /ˈrɪgərəs/ *a.* riguroso.
rim /rɪm/ *n.* margen *m. or f.*; borde *m.*
ring /rɪŋ/ *n.* **1.** anillo *m.*; sortija *f.*; círculo; campaneo *m.* **—***v.* **2.** cercar; sonar; tocar.
ring finger dedo anular *m.*
rinse /rɪns/ *v.* enjuagar, lavar.
riot /ˈraiət/ *n.* motín; alboroto *m.*
rip /rɪp/ *n.* **1.** rasgadura *f.* **—***v.* **2.** rasgar; descoser.
ripe /raip/ *a.* maduro.
ripen /ˈraipən/ *v.* madurar.
ripoff /ˈrɪpˌɔf/ *n.* robo, atraco *m.*
ripple /ˈrɪpəl/ *n.* **1.** onda *f.* **—***v.* **2.** ondear.
rise /raiz/ *n.* **1.** subida *f.* **—***v.* **2.** ascender; levantarse; (moon) salir.
risk /rɪsk/ *n.* **1.** riesgo *m.* **—***v.* **2.** arriesgar.
rite /rait/ *n.* rito *m.*
ritual /ˈrɪtʃuəl/ *a.* & *n.* ritual *m.*
rival /ˈraivəl/ *n.* rival *m.* & *f.*
rivalry /ˈraivəlri/ *n.* rivalidad *f.*
river /ˈrɪvər/ *n.* río *m.*
rivet /ˈrɪvɪt/ *n.* **1.** remache, roblón *m.* **—***v.* **2.** remachar, roblar.
road /roud/ *n.* camino *m.*; carretera *f.*
roadside /ˈroudˌsaid/ *n.* borde de la carretera *m.*
roam /roum/ *v.* vagar.
roar /rɔr, rour/ *n.* **1.** rugido, bramido *m.* **—***v.* **2.** rugir, bramar.
roast /roust/ *n.* **1.** asado *m.* **—***v.* **2.** asar.
rob /rɒb/ *v.* robar.
robber /ˈrɒbər/ *n.* ladrón -na.
robbery /ˈrɒbəri/ *n.* robo *m.*
robe /roub/ *n.* manto *m.*
robin /ˈrɒbɪn/ *n.* petirrojo *m.*
robust /rouˈbʌst, ˈroubʌst/ *a.* robusto.
rock /rɒk/ *n.* **1.** roca, peña *f.*; (music) rock *m.*, música (de) rock *f.* **—***v.* **2.** mecer; oscilar.
rocker /ˈrɒkər/ *n.* mecedora *f.*
rocket /ˈrɒkɪt/ *n.* cohete *m.*
rocking chair /ˈrɒkɪŋ/ mecedora *f.*
Rock of Gibraltar /dʒɪˈbrɔltər/ Peñón de Gibraltar *m.*
rocky /ˈrɒki/ *a.* pedregoso.
rod /rɒd/ *n.* varilla *f.*
rodent /ˈroudnt/ *n.* roedor *m.*
rogue /roug/ *n.* bribón, pícaro *m.*
roguish /ˈrougɪʃ/ *a.* pícaro.
role /roul/ *n.* papel *m.*
roll /roul/ **1.** rollo *m.*; lista *f.*; panecillo *m.* **to call the r.,** pasar lista. **—***v.* **2.** rodar. **r. up,** enrollar. **r. up one's sleeves,** arremangarse.
roller /ˈroulər/ *n.* rodillo, cilindro *m.*
roller skate patín de ruedas *m.*
Roman /ˈroumən/ *a.* & *n.* romano -na.
romance /rouˈmæns, ˈroumæns/ *a.* **1.** románico. **—***n.* **2.** romance *m.*; amorío *m.*
romantic /rouˈmæntɪk/ *a.* romántico.
romp /rɒmp/ *v.* retozar; jugar.
roof /ruf, rʊf/ *n.* **1.** techo *m.*; **—***v.* **2.** techar.
room /rum, rʊm/ *n.* **1.** cuarto *m.*, habitación *f.*; lugar *m.* **—***v.* **2.** alojarse.
roommate /ˈrumˌmeit, ˈrʊm-/ *n.* compañero -ra de cuarto.
rooster /ˈrustər/ *n.* gallo *m.*
root /rut/ *n.* raíz *f.* **to take r.,** arraigar.
rootless /ˈrutlɪs/ *a.* desarraigado.
rope /roup/ *n.* cuerda, soga *f.*
rose /rouz/ *n.* rosa *f.*
rosy /ˈrouzi/ *a.* róseo, rosado.
rot /rɒt/ *n.* **1.** putrefacción *f.* **—***v.* **2.** pudrirse.
rotary /ˈroutəri/ *a.* giratorio; rotativo.
rotate /ˈrouteit/ *v.* girar; alternar.
rotation /rouˈteiʃən/ *n.* rotación *f.*
rotten /ˈrɒtn̩/ *a.* podrido.
rouge /ruʒ/ *n.* colorete *m.*
rough /rʌf/ *a.* áspero; rudo; grosero; aproximado.
round /raund/ *a.* **1.** redondo. **r. trip,** viaje de ida y vuelta. **—***n.* **2.** ronda *f.*; (boxing) asalto *m.*
rouse /rauz/ *v.* despertar.
rout /raut, rut/ *n.* **1.** derrota *f.* **—***v.* **2.** derrotar.
route /rut, raut/ *n.* ruta, vía *f.*
routine /ruˈtin/ *a.* **1.** rutinario. **—***n.* **2.** rutina *f.*
rove /rouv/ *v.* vagar.
rover /ˈrouvər/ *n.* vagabundo -da.
row /rou/ *n.* **1.** fila *f.* **—***v.* **2.** *Naut.* remar.
rowboat /ˈrouˌbout/ *n.* bote de remos.
rowdy /ˈraudi/ *a.* alborotado.
royal /ˈrɔiəl/ *a.* real.
royalty /ˈrɔiəlti/ *n.* realeza *f.*; (pl.) regalías *f.pl.*
rub /rʌb/ *v.* frotar. **r. against,** rozar. **r. out,** borrar.
rubber /ˈrʌbər/ *n.* goma *f.*; caucho *m.*; (pl.) chanclos *m.pl.*, zapatos de goma.
rubbish /ˈrʌbɪʃ/ *n.* basura *f.*; (nonsense) tonterías *f.pl.*
ruby /ˈrubi/ *n.* rubí *m.*
rudder /ˈrʌdər/ *n.* timón *m.*
ruddy /ˈrʌdi/ *a.* colorado.
rude /rud/ *a.* rudo; grosero; descortés.
rudiment /ˈrudəmənt/ *n.* rudimento *m.*
rudimentary /ˌrudəˈmɛntəri, -tri/ *a.* rudimentario.
rue /ru/ *v.* deplorar; lamentar.
ruffian /ˈrʌfiən, ˈrʌfyən/ *n.* rufián, bandolero *m.*
ruffle /ˈrʌfəl/ *n.* **1.** volante fruncido. **—***v.* **2.** fruncir; irritar.
rug /rʌg/ *n.* alfombra *f.*
rugged /ˈrʌgɪd/ *a.* áspero; robusto.
ruin /ˈruɪn/ *n.* **1.** ruina *f.* **—***v.* **2.** arruinar.
ruinous /ˈruənəs/ *a.* ruinoso.
rule /rul/ *n.* **1.** regla *f.* **as a r.,** por regla general. **—***v.* **2.** gobernar; mandar; rayar.
ruler /ˈrulər/ *n.* gobernante *m.* & *f.*; soberano -na; regla *f.*
rum /rʌm/ *n.* ron *m.*
rumble /ˈrʌmbəl/ *v.* retumbar.
rumor /ˈrumər/ *n.* rumor *m.*
rumpus /ˈrʌmpəs/ *n.* lío, jaleo, escandalo *m.*
run /rʌn/ *v.* correr; hacer correr. **r. away,** escaparse. **r. into,** chocar con.

runner /'rʌnər/ *n.* corredor -ra; mensajero -ra.

runner-up /'rʌnər 'ʌp/ *n.* subcampeón -ona.

runproof /'rʌnpruf/ *a.* indesmallable.

rupture /'rʌptʃər/ *n.* **1.** rotura; hernia *f.* —*v.* **2.** reventar.

rural /'rurəl/ *a.* rural, campestre.

rush /rʌʃ/ *n.* **1.** prisa *f.; Bot.* junco *m.* —*v.* **2.** ir de prisa.

rush hour hora punta *f.*

Russia /'rʌʃə/ *n.* Rusia *f.*

Russian /'rʌʃən/ *a. & n.* ruso -sa.

rust /rʌst/ *n.* **1.** herrumbre *f.* —*v.* **2.** aherrumbrarse.

rustic /'rʌstɪk/ *a.* rústico.

rustle /'rʌsəl/ *n.* **1.** susurro *m.* —*v.* **2.** susurrar.

rusty /'rʌsti/ *a.* mohoso.

rut /rʌt/ *n.* surco *m.*

ruthless /'ruθlɪs/ *a.* cruel, inhumano.

rye /rai/ *n.* centeno *m.*

rye bread pan de centeno *m.*

S

saber /'seibər/ *n.* sable *m.*

sable /'seibəl/ *n.* cebellina *f.*

sabotage /'sæbə,taʒ/ *n.* sabotaje *m.*

sachet /sæ'ʃei/ *n.* perfumador *m.*

sack /sæk/ *n.* **1.** saco *m.* —*v.* **2.** *Mil.* saquear.

sacred /'seikrɪd/ *a.* sagrado, santo.

sacrifice /'sækrə,fais/ *n.* **1.** sacrificio *m.* —*v.* **2.** sacrificar.

sacrilege /'sækrəlɪdʒ/ *n.* sacrilegio *m.*

sad /sæd/ *a.* triste.

saddle /'sædḷ/ *n.* **1.** silla de montar. —*v.* **2.** ensillar.

sadness /'sædnɪs/ *n.* tristeza *f.*

safe /seif/ *a.* **1.** seguro; salvo. —*n.* **2.** caja de caudales.

safeguard /'seif,gard/ *n.* **1.** salvaguardia *m.* —*v.* **2.** proteger, poner a salvo.

safety /'seifti/ *n.* seguridad, protección *f.*

safety belt cinturón de seguridad *m.*

safety pin imperdible *m.*

safety valve /vælv/ válvula de seguridad *f.*

sage /seidʒ/ *a.* **1.** sabio, sagaz. —*n.* **2.** sabio *m.; Bot.* salvia *f.*

sail /seil/ *n.* **1.** vela *f.*; paseo por mar. —*v.* **2.** navegar; embarcarse.

sailboat /'seil,bout/ *n.* barco de vela.

sailor /'seilər/ *n.* marinero *m.*

saint /seint/ *n.* santo -ta.

sake /seik/ *n.* **for the s. of,** por; por el bien de.

salad /'sæləd/ *n.* ensalada *f.* **s. bowl,** ensaladera *f.*

salad dressing aliño *m.*

salary /'sæləri/ *n.* sueldo, salario *m.*

sale /seil/ *n.* venta *f.*

salesman /'seilzmən/ *n.* vendedor *m.*; viajante de comercio.

sales tax /seilz/ impuesto sobre la venta.

saliva /sə'laivə/ *n.* saliva *f.*

salmon /'sæmən/ *n.* salmón *m.*

salt /sɔlt/ *a.* **1.** salado. —*n.* **2.** sal *f.* —*v.* **3.** salar.

salute /sə'lut/ *n.* **1.** saludo *m.* —*v.* **2.** saludar.

salvage /'sælvɪdʒ/ *v.* salvar; recobrar.

salvation /sæl'veiʃən/ *n.* salvación *f.*

salve /sælv/ *n.* emplasto, ungüento *m.*

same /seim/ *a. & pron.* mismo. **it's all the s.,** lo mismo da.

sample /'sæmpəl/ *n.* **1.** muestra *f.* —*v.* **2.** probar.

sanatorium /,sænə'tɔriəm/ *n.* sanatorio *m.*

sanctify /'sæŋktə,fai/ *v.* santificar.

sanction /'sæŋkʃən/ *n.* **1.** sanción *f.* —*v.* **2.** sancionar.

sanctity /'sæŋktɪti/ *n.* santidad *f.*

sanctuary /'sæŋktʃu,ɛri/ *n.* santuario, asilo *m.*

sand /sænd/ *n.* arena *f.*

sandal /'sændḷ/ *n.* sandalia *f.*

sandpaper /'sænd,peipər/ *n.* papel de lija *m.*

sandwich /'sændwɪtʃ, 'sæn-/ *n.* emparedado, sándwich *m.*

sandy /'sændi/ *a.* arenoso; (color) rufo.

sane /sein/ *a.* cuerdo; sano.

sanitary /'sænɪ,tɛri/ *a.* higiénico, sanitario. **s. napkin,** toalla sanitaria.

sanitation /,sænɪ'teiʃən/ *n.* saneamiento *m.*

sanity /'sænɪti/ *n.* cordura *f.*

Santa Claus /'sæntə klɔz/ Papá Noel *m.*

sap /sæp/ *n.* **1.** savia *f.; Colloq.* estúpido, bobo *m.* —*v.* **2.** agotar.

sapphire /'sæfaiər/ *n.* zafiro *m.*

sarcasm /'sarkæzəm/ *n.* sarcasmo *m.*

sardine /sar'din/ *n.* sardina *f.*

sash /sæʃ/ *n.* cinta *f.*

satellite /'sætḷ,ait/ *n.* satélite *m.*

satellite dish antena parabólica *f.*

satin /'sætn/ *n.* raso *m.*

satire /'sætaiər/ *n.* sátira *f.*

satisfaction /,sætɪs'fækʃən/ *n.* satisfacción; recompensa *f.*

satisfactory /,sætɪs'fæktəri/ *a.* satisfactorio.

satisfy /'sætɪs,fai/ *v.* satisfacer. **be satisfied that...,** estar convencido de que.

saturate /'sætʃə,reit/ *v.* saturar.

Saturday /'sætər,dei/ *n.* sábado *m.*

sauce /sɔs/ *n.* salsa; compota *f.*

saucer /'sɔsər/ *n.* platillo *m.*

saucy /'sɔsi/ *a.* descarado, insolente.

sauna /'sɔnə/ *n.* sauna *f.*

sausage /'sɔsɪdʒ/ *n.* salchicha *f.*

savage /'sævɪdʒ/ *a. & n.* salvaje *m. & f.*

save /seiv/ *v.* **1.** salvar; guardar; ahorrar, economizar. —*prep.* **2.** salvo, excepto.

savings /'seivɪŋz/ *n.* ahorros *m.pl.*

savings account cuenta de ahorros *m.*

savings bank caja de ahorros *f.*

savior /'seivyər/ *n.* salvador -ora.

savor /'seivər/ *n.* **1.** sabor *m.* —*v.* **2.** saborear.

savory /'seivəri/ *a.* sabroso.

saw /sɔ/ *n.* **1.** sierra *f.* —*v.* **2.** aserrar.

saxophone /'sæksə,foun/ *n.* saxofón, saxófono, *m.*

say /sei/ *v.* decir; recitar.

saying /'seiɪŋ/ *n.* dicho, refrán *m.*

scaffold /'skæfəld/ *n.* andamio; (gallows) patíbulo *m.*

scald /skɔld/ *v.* escaldar.

scale /skeil/ *n.* **1.** escala; (of fish) escama *f.*; (pl.) balanza *f.* —*v.* **2.** escalar; escamar.

scalp /skælp/ *n.* pericráneo *m. v.* escalpar.

scan /skæn/ *v.* hojear, repasar; (poetry) escandir; (computer) escanear, digitalizar.

scandal /'skændḷ/ *n.* escándalo *m.*

scanner /'skænər/ *n.* escáner *m.*

scant /skænt/ *a.* escaso.

scar /skar/ *n.* cicatriz *f.*

scarce /skɛərs/ *a.* escaso; raro.

scarcely /'skɛərsli/ *adv. & conj.* apenas.

scare /skɛər/ *n.* **1.** susto *m.* —*v.* **2.** asustar. **s. away,** espantar.

scarf /skarf/ *n.* pañueleta, bufanda *f.*

scarlet /'skarlɪt/ *a.* escarlata *f.*

scarlet fever escarlatina *f.*

scatter /'skætər/ *v.* esparcir; dispersar.

scavenger /'skævɪndʒər/ *n.* basurero *m.*

scenario /sɪ'nɛəri,ou, -'nar-/ *n.* escenario *m.*

scene /sin/ *n.* vista *f.*, paisaje *m.; Theat.* escena *f.* **behind the scenes,** entre bastidores.

scenery /'sinəri/ *n.* paisaje *m.; Theat.* decorado *m.*

scent /sɛnt/ *n.* **1.** olor, perfume;

(sense) olfato *m.* —*v.* **2.** perfumar; *Fig.* sospechar.

schedule /'skɛdʒul, -ʊl, -uəl/ *n.* **1.** programa, horario *m.* —*v.* **2.** fijar la hora para.

scheme /skim/ *n.* **1.** proyecto; esquema *m.* —*v.* **2.** intrigar.

scholar /'skɒlər/ *n.* erudito -ta; becado -da.

scholarship /'skɒlər,ʃɪp/ *n.* beca; erudición *f.*

school /skul/ *n.* **1.** escuela *f.*; colegio *m.*; (of fish) banco *m.* —*v.* **2.** enseñar.

sciatica /sai'ætɪkə/ *n.* ciática *f.*

science /'saiəns/ *n.* ciencia *f.*

science fiction ciencia ficción.

scientific /,saiən'tɪfɪk/ *a.* científico.

scientist /'saiəntɪst/ *n.* científico -ca.

scissors /'sɪzərz/ *n.* tijeras *f.pl.*

scoff /skɔf, skɒf/ *v.* mofarse, burlarse.

scold /skould/ *v.* regañar.

scoop /skup/ *n.* **1.** cucharón *m.*; cucharada *f.* —*v.* **2.** **s. out,** recoger, sacar.

scope /skoup/ *n.* alcance; campo *m.*

score /skɔr/ *n.* **1.** tantos *m.pl.*; (music) partitura *f.* —*v.* **2.** marcar, hacer tantos.

scorn /skɔrn/ *n.* **1.** desprecio *m.* —*v.* **2.** despreciar.

scornful /'skɔrnfəl/ *a.* desdeñoso.

Scotland /'skɒtlənd/ *n.* Escocia *f.*

Scottish /'skɒtɪʃ/ *a.* escocés.

scour /skauər/ *v.* fregar, estregar.

scourge /skɜrdʒ/ *n.* azote *m.*; plaga *f.*

scout /skaut/ *n.* **1.** explorador -ra. —*v.* **2.** explorar, reconocer.

scramble /'skræmbəl/ *n.* **1.** rebatiña *f.* —*v.* **2.** bregar. **scrambled eggs,** huevos revueltos.

scrap /skræp/ *n.* **1.** migaja *f.*; pedacito *m.; Colloq.* riña *f.* **s. metal,** hierro viejo *m.* **s. paper,** papel borrador. —*v.* **2.** desechar; *Colloq.* reñir.

scrapbook /'skræp,bʊk/ *n.* álbum de recortes *m.*

scrape /skreip/ *n.* **1.** lío, apuro *m.* —*v.* **2.** raspar; (feet) restregar.

scratch /skrætʃ/ *n.* **1.** rasguño *m.* —*v.* **2.** rasguñar; rayar.

scream /skrim/ *n.* **1.** grito, chillido *m.* —*v.* **2.** gritar, chillar.

screen /skrin/ *n.* biombo *m.*; (for window) tela metálica; (movie) pantalla *f.*

screw /skru/ *n.* **1.** tornillo *m.* —*v.* **2.** atornillar.

screwdriver /'skru,draivər/ *n.* destornillador *m.*

scribble /'skrɪbəl/ *v.* hacer garabatos.

scroll /skroul/ *n.* rúbrica *f.*; rollo de papel.

scroll bar *n.* barra de enrollar *f.*

scrub /skrʌb/ *v.* fregar, estregar.

scruple /'skrupəl/ *n.* escrúpulo *m.*

scrupulous /'skrupyələs/ *a.* escrupuloso.

scuba diving /'skubə 'daivɪŋ/ submarinismo *m.*

sculptor /'skʌlptər/ *n.* escultor -ra.

sculpture /'skʌlptʃər/ *n.* **1.** escultura *f.* —*v.* **2.** esculpir.

scythe /saið/ *n.* guadaña *f.*

sea /si/ *n.* mar *m.* or *f.*

seabed /'si,bɛd/ *n.* lecho marino *m.*

sea breeze brisa marina *f.*

seafood /'si,fud/ *n.* mariscos *m.pl.*

seal /sil/ *n.* **1.** sello *m.*; (animal) foca *f.* —*v.* **2.** sellar.

seam /sim/ *n.* costura *f.*

seamy /'simi/ *a.* sórdido.

seaplane /'si,plein/ *n.* hidroavión *m.*

seaport /'si,pɔrt/ *n.* puerto de mar.

search /sɜrtʃ/ *n.* **1.** registro *m.* **in s. of,** en busca de. —*v.* **2.** registrar. **s. for,** buscar.

search engine motor de búsqueda *m.*, buscador *m.*, indexador de información *m.*

seasick /'si,sɪk/ *a.* mareado. **to get s.,** marearse.

season /'sizən/ *n.* **1.** estación; sazón; temporada *f.* —*v.* **2.** sazonar.

seasoning /'sizəniŋ/ *n.* condimento *m.*

season ticket abono *m.*

seat /sit/ *n.* **1.** asiento *m.*; residencia, sede *f.; Theat.* localidad *f.* **s. belt,** cinturón de seguridad. —*v.* **2.** sentar. **be seated,** sentarse.

seaweed /'si,wid/ *n.* alga, alga marina *f.*

second /'sɛkənd/ *a. & n.* **1.** segundo *m.* —*v.* **2.** apoyar, segundar.

secondary /'sɛkən,dɛri/ *a.* secundario.

secret /'sikrɪt/ *a. & n.* secreto *m.*

secretary /'sɛkrɪ,tɛri/ *n.* secretario -ria; *Govt.* ministro -tra; (furniture) papelera *f.*

sect /sɛkt/ *n.* secta *f.*; partido *m.*

section /'sɛkʃən/ *n.* sección, parte *f.*

sectional /'sɛkʃənḷ/ *a.* regional, local.

secular /'sɛkyələr/ *a.* secular.

secure /sɪ'kyur/ *a.* **1.** seguro. —*v.* **2.** asegurar; obtener; *Fin.* garantizar.

security /sɪ'kyurɪti/ *n.* seguridad; garantía *f.*

sedative /'sɛdətɪv/ *a. & n.* sedativo *m.*

seduce /sɪ'dus/ *v.* seducir.

see /si/ *v.* ver; comprender. **s. off,** despedirse de. **s. to,** encargarse de.

seed /sid/ *n.* **1.** semilla *f.* —*v.* **2.** sembrar.

seek /sik/ *v.* buscar. **s. to,** tratar de.

seem /sim/ *v.* parecer.

seep /sip/ *v.* colarse.

segment /'sɛgmənt/ *n.* segmento *m.*

segregate /'sɛgrɪ,geit/ *v.* segregar.

seize /siz/ *v.* agarrar; apoderarse de.

seldom /'sɛldəm/ *adv.* rara vez.

select /sɪ'lɛkt/ *a.* **1.** escogido, selecto. —*v.* **2.** elegir, seleccionar.

selection /sɪ'lɛkʃən/ *n.* selección *f.*

selective /sɪ'lɛktɪv/ *a.* selectivo.

selfish /'sɛlfɪʃ/ *a.* egoísta.

selfishness /'sɛlfɪʃnɪs/ *n.* egoísmo *m.*

sell /sɛl/ *v.* vender.

semester /sɪ'mɛstər/ *n.* semestre *m.*

semicircle /'sɛmɪ,sɜrkəl/ *n.* semicírculo *m.*

semolina /,sɛmə'linə/ *n.* sémola *f.*

senate /'sɛnɪt/ *n.* senado *m.*

senator /'sɛnətər/ *n.* senador -ra.

send /sɛnd/ *v.* mandar, enviar; (a wire) poner. **s. away,** despedir. **s. back,** devolver. **s. for,** mandar buscar. **s. off,** expedir. **s. word,** mandar recado.

senile /'sinail/ *a.* senil.

senior /'sinyər/ *a.* mayor; más viejo. **Sr.,** padre.

senior citizen persona de edad avanzada.

sensation /sɛn'seiʃən/ *n.* sensación *f.*

sensational /sɛn'seiʃənḷ/ *a.* sensacional.

sense /sɛns/ *n.* **1.** sentido; juicio *m.* —*v.* **2.** percibir; sospechar.

sensible /'sɛnsəbəl/ *a.* sensato, razonable.

sensitive /'sɛnsɪtɪv/ *a.* sensible; sensitivo.

sensual /'sɛnʃuəl/ *a.* sensual.

sentence /'sɛntns/ *n.* **1.** frase; *Gram.* oración; *Leg.* sentencia *f.* —*v.* **2.** condenar.

sentiment /'sɛntəmənt/ *n.* sentimiento *m.*

sentimental /,sɛntə'mɛntḷ/ *a.* sentimental.

separate /*a.* 'sɛpərɪt; *v.* -,reit/ *a.* **1.** separado; suelto. —*v.* **2.** separar, dividir.

separation /,sɛpə'reiʃən/ *n.* separación *f.*

September /sɛp'tɛmbər/ *n.* septiembre *m.*

sequence /'sikwəns/ *n.* serie *f.* **in s.,** seguidos.

serenade /,sɛrə'neid/ *n.* **1.** serenata *f.* —*v.* **2.** dar serenata a.

serene /sə'rin/ *a.* sereno; tranquilo.

sergeant /'sardʒənt/ *n.* sargento *m.*

serial /ˈsɪəriəl/ a. en serie, de serie.

series /ˈsɪəriz/ n. serie f.

serious /ˈsɪəriəs/ a. serio; grave.

sermon /ˈsɜrmən/ n. sermón m.

serpent /ˈsɜrpənt/ n. serpiente f.

servant /ˈsɜrvənt/ n. criado -da; servidor -ra.

serve /sɜrv/ v. servir.

server /ˈsɜrvər/ n. servidor m.

service /ˈsɜrvɪs/ n. **1.** servicio m. **at the s. of,** a las órdenes de. **be of s.,** servir; ser útil. —v. **2.** Auto. reparar.

service station estación de servicio f.

session /ˈsɛʃən/ n. sesión f.

set /sɛt/ a. **1.** fijo. —n. **2.** colección f.; (of a game) juego; Mech. aparato; Theat. decorado m. —v. **3.** poner, colocar; fijar; (sun) ponerse. **s. forth,** exponer. **s. off, s. out,** salir. **s. up,** instalar; establecer.

settle /ˈsɛtl̩/ v. solucionar; arreglar; establecerse.

settlement /ˈsɛtl̩mənt/ n. caserío; arreglo; acuerdo m.

settler /ˈsɛtlər/ n. poblador -ra.

seven /ˈsɛvən/ a. & pron. siete.

seventeen /ˈsɛvənˈtin/ a. & pron. diecisiete.

seventh /ˈsɛvənθ/ a. séptimo.

seventy /ˈsɛvənti/ a. & pron. setenta.

sever /ˈsɛvər/ v. desunir; romper.

several /ˈsɛvərəl/ a. & pron. varios.

severance pay /ˈsɛvərəns/ indemnización de despido.

severe /səˈvɪər/ a. severo; grave.

severity /səˈvɛrɪti/ n. severidad f.

sew /sou/ v. coser.

sewer /ˈsuər/ n. cloaca f.

sewing /ˈsouɪŋ/ n. costura f.

sewing basket costurero m.

sewing machine máquina de coser f.

sex /sɛks/ n. sexo m.

sexism /ˈsɛksɪzəm/ n. sexismo m.

sexist /ˈsɛksɪst/ a. & n. sexista m. & f.

sexton /ˈsɛkstən/ n. sacristán m.

sexual /ˈsɛkʃuəl/ a. sexual.

shabby /ˈʃæbi/ a. haraposo, desaliñado.

shade /ʃeid/ n. **1.** sombra f.; tinte m.; (window) transparente m. —v. **2.** sombrear.

shadow /ˈʃædou/ n. sombra f.

shady /ˈʃeidi/ a. sombroso; sospechoso.

shaft /ʃæft/ n. (columna) fuste; Mech. asta f.

shake /ʃeik/ v. sacudir; agitar; temblar. **s. hands with,** dar la mano a.

shallow /ˈʃælou/ a. poco hondo; superficial.

shame /ʃeim/ n. **1.** vergüenza f. **be a s.,** ser una lástima. —v. **2.** avergonzar.

shameful /ˈʃeimfəl/ a. vergonzoso.

shampoo /ʃæmˈpu/ n. champú m.

shape /ʃeip/ n. **1.** forma f.; estado m. —v. **2.** formar.

share /ʃɛər/ n. **1.** parte; (stock) acción f. 2 —v. **2.** compartir.

shareholder /ˈʃɛərˌhouldər/ n. accionista m. & f.

shareware /ˈʃɛərˌwɛər/ n. programas compartidos m.pl.

shark /ʃɑrk/ n. tiburón m.

sharp /ʃɑrp/ a. agudo; (blade) afilado.

sharpen /ˈʃɑrpən/ v. aguzar; afilar.

shatter /ˈʃætər/ v. estrellar; hacer pedazos.

shave /ʃeiv/ n. **1.** afeitada f. —v. **2.** afeitarse.

shawl /ʃɔl/ n. rebozo, chal m.

she /ʃi/ pron. ella f.

sheaf /ʃif/ n. gavilla f.

shear /ʃɪər/ v. cizallar.

shears /ʃɪərz/ n. cizallas f.pl.

sheath /ʃiθ/ n. vaina f.

shed /ʃɛd/ n. **1.** cobertizo m. —v. **2.** arrojar, quitarse.

sheep /ʃip/ n. oveja f.

sheet /ʃit/ n. sábana; (of paper) hoja f.

shelf /ʃɛlf/ n. estante, m., repisa f.

shell /ʃɛl/ n. **1.** cáscara; (sea) concha f.; Mil. proyectil m. —v. **2.** desgranar; bombardear.

shellac /ʃəˈlæk/ n. laca f.

shelter /ˈʃɛltər/ n. **1.** albergue; refugio m. —v. **2.** albergar; amparar.

shepherd /ˈʃɛpərd/ n. pastor m.

sherry /ˈʃɛri/ n. jerez m.

shield /ʃild/ n. **1.** escudo m. —v. **2.** amparar.

shift /ʃɪft/ n. **1.** cambio; (work) turno m. —v. **2.** cambiar, mudar. **s. for oneself,** arreglárselas.

shine /ʃain/ n. **1.** brillo, lustre m. —v. **2.** brillar; (shoes) lustrar.

shiny /ˈʃaini/ a. brillante, lustroso.

ship /ʃɪp/ n. **1.** barco m., nave f. —v. **2.** embarcar; Com. enviar.

shipment /ˈʃɪpmənt/ n. envío; embarque m.

shirk /ʃɜrk/ v. faltar al deber.

shirt /ʃɜrt/ n. camisa f.

shiver /ˈʃɪvər/ n. **1.** temblor m. —v. **2.** temblar.

shock /ʃɒk/ n. **1.** choque m. —v. **2.** chocar.

shoe /ʃu/ n. zapato m.

shoelace /ˈʃuˌleis/ n. lazo m.; cordón de zapato.

shoemaker /ˈʃuˌmeikər/ n. zapatero m.

shoot /ʃut/ v. tirar; (gun) disparar. **s. away, s. off,** salir disparado.

shop /ʃɒp/ n. tienda f.

shopping /ˈʃɒpɪŋ/ n. **to go s.,** hacer compras, ir de compras.

shop window escaparate m.

shore /ʃɔr/ n. orilla; playa f.

short /ʃɔrt/ a. corto; breve; (in stature) pequeño, bajo. **a s. time,** poco tiempo. **in s.,** en suma.

shortage /ˈʃɔrtɪdʒ/ n. escasez; falta f.

shorten /ˈʃɔrtn̩/ v. acortar, abreviar.

shortly /ˈʃɔrtli/ adv. en breve, dentro de poco.

shorts /ʃɔrts/ n. calzoncillos m.pl.

shot /ʃɒt/ n. tiro, disparo m.

shoulder /ˈʃouldər/ n. **1.** hombro m. —v. **2.** asumir; cargar con.

shoulder blade n. omóplato m., paletilla f.

shout /ʃaut/ n. **1.** grito m. —v. **2.** gritar.

shove /ʃʌv/ n. **1.** empujón m. —v. **2.** empujar.

shovel /ˈʃʌvəl/ n. **1.** pala f. —v. **2.** traspalar.

show /ʃou/ n. **1.** ostentación f.; Theat. función f.; espectáculo m. —v. **2.** enseñar, mostrar; verse. **s. up,** destacarse; Colloq. asomar.

shower /ˈʃauər/ n. chubasco m.; (bath) ducha f. v. ducharse.

shrapnel /ˈʃræpnl̩/ n. metralla f.

shrewd /ʃrud/ a. astuto.

shriek /ʃrik/ n. **1.** chillido m. —v. **2.** chillar.

shrill /ʃrɪl/ a. chillón, agudo.

shrimp /ʃrɪmp/ n. camarón m.

shrine /ʃrain/ n. santuario m.

shrink /ʃrɪŋk/ v. encogerse, contraerse. **s. from,** huir de.

shroud /ʃraud/ n. **1.** mortaja f. —v. **2.** Fig. ocultar.

shrub /ʃrʌb/ n. arbusto m.

shudder /ˈʃʌdər/ n. **1.** estremecimiento m. —v. **2.** estremecerse.

shun /ʃʌn/ v. evitar, huir de.

shut /ʃʌt/ v. cerrar. **s. in,** encerrar. **s. up,** Colloq. callarse.

shutter /ˈʃʌtər/ n. persiana f.

shy /ʃai/ a. tímido, vergonzoso.

sick /sɪk/ a. enfermo. **s. of,** aburrido de, cansado de.

sickness /ˈsɪknɪs/ n. enfermedad f.

side /said/ n. **1.** lado; partido m.; parte f.; Anat. costado m. —v. **2. s. with,** ponerse del lado de.

sidewalk /ˈsaidˌwɔk/ n. acera, vereda f.

siege /sidʒ/ n. asedio m.

sieve /sɪv/ n. cedazo m.

sift /sɪft/ v. cerner.

sigh /sai/ n. **1.** suspiro m. —v. **2.** suspirar.

sight /sait/ n. **1.** vista f.; punto de interés m. **lose s. of,** perder de vista. —v. **2.** divisar.

sign /sain/ n. **1.** letrero; señal, seña f. —v. **2.** firmar. **s. up,** inscribirse.

signal /ˈsɪgnl̩/ n. **1.** señal f. —v. **2.** hacer señales.

signature /ˈsɪgnətʃər/ n. firma f.

significance /sɪgˈnɪfɪkəns/ n. significación f.

significant /sɪgˈnɪfɪkənt/ a. significativo.

significant other pareja m. & f.

signify /ˈsɪgnəˌfai/ v. significar.

silence /ˈsailəns/ n. **1.** silencio m. —v. **2.** hacer callar.

silent /ˈsailənt/ a. silencioso; callado.

silk /sɪlk/ n. seda f.

silken /ˈsɪlkən/ **silky** a. sedoso.

sill /sɪl/ n. umbral de puerta m., solera f.

silly /ˈsɪli/ a. necio, tonto.

silo /ˈsailou/ n. silo m.

silver /ˈsɪlvər/ n. plata f.

silver-plated /ˈsɪlvər ˈpleitɪd/ a. chapado en plata.

silverware /ˈsɪlvərˌwɛər/ n. vajilla de plata f.

similar /ˈsɪmələr/ a. semejante, parecido.

similarity /ˌsɪməˈlærɪti/ n. semejanza f.

simple /ˈsɪmpəl/ a. sencillo, simple.

simplicity /sɪmˈplɪsɪti/ n. sencillez f.

simplify /ˈsɪmpləˌfai/ v. simplificar.

simulate /ˈsɪmyəˌleit/ v. simular.

simultaneous /ˌsaiməlˈteiniəs/ a. simultáneo.

sin /sɪn/ n. **1.** pecado m. —v. **2.** pecar.

since /sɪns/ adv. **1.** desde entonces. —prep. **2.** desde. —conj. **3.** desde que; puesto que.

sincere /sɪnˈsɪər/ a. sincero.

sincerely /sɪnˈsɪərli/ adv. sinceramente.

sincerity /sɪnˈsɛrɪti/ n. sinceridad f.

sinew /ˈsɪnyu/ n. tendón m.

sinful /ˈsɪnfəl/ a. pecador.

sing /sɪŋ/ v. cantar.

singe /sɪndʒ/ v. chamuscar.

singer /ˈsɪŋər/ n. cantante m. & f.

single /ˈsɪŋgəl/ a. solo; (room) sencillo; (unmarried) soltero. **s. room,** habitación individual.

singular /ˈsɪŋgyələr/ a. & n. singular m.

sinister /ˈsɪnəstər/ a. siniestro.

sink /sɪŋk/ n. **1.** fregadero m. —v. **2.** hundir; Fig. abatir.

sinner /ˈsɪnər/ n. pecador -ra.

sinuous /ˈsɪnyuəs/ a. sinuoso.

sinus /ˈsainəs/ n. seno m.

sip /sɪp/ n. **1.** sorbo m. —v. **2.** sorber.

siphon /ˈsaifən/ n. sifón m.

sir /sɜr/ title. señor.

siren /ˈsairən/ n. sirena f.

sirloin /ˈsɜrlɔin/ n. solomillo m.

sisal /ˈsaisəl, ˈsɪsəl/ n. henequén m.

sister /ˈsɪstər/ n. hermana f.

sister-in-law /ˈsɪstərɪnˌlɔ/ n. cuñada f.

sit /sɪt/ v. sentarse; posar. **be sitting,** estar sentado. **s. down,** sentarse. **s. up,** incorporarse; quedar levantado.

site /sait/ n. sitio, local m.

sitting /ˈsɪtɪŋ/ n. sesión f. a. sentado.

situate /ˈsɪtʃuˌeit/ v. situar.

situation /ˌsɪtʃuˈeiʃən/ n. situación f.

sit-up /ˈsɪt ˌʌp/ n. abdominal m.

six /sɪks/ a. & pron. seis.

sixteen /ˈsɪksˈtin/ a. & pron. dieciseis.

sixth /sɪksθ/ a. sexto.

sixty /ˈsɪksti/ a. & pron. sesenta.

size /saiz/ n. tamaño; (of shoe, etc.) número m.; talla f.

sizing /ˈsaizɪŋ/ n. upreso m.; sisa, cola de retazo f.

skate /skeit/ n. **1.** patín m. —v. **2.** patinar.

skateboard /ˈskeitˌbɔrd/ n. monopatín m.

skein /skein/ n. madeja f.

skeleton /ˈskɛlɪtn̩/ n. esqueleto m.

skeptic /ˈskɛptɪk/ n. escéptico -ca.

skeptical /ˈskɛptɪkəl/ a. escéptico.

sketch /skɛtʃ/ n. **1.** esbozo m. —v. **2.** esbozar.

ski /ski/ n. **1.** esquí m. —v. **2.** esquiar.

skid /skɪd/ v. **1.** resbalar. —n. **2.** varadera f.

skill /skɪl/ n. destreza, habilidad f.

skillful /ˈskɪlfəl/ a. diestro, hábil.

skim /skɪm/ v. rasar; (milk) desnatar. **s. over, s. through,** hojear.

skin /skɪn/ n. **1.** piel; (of fruit) corteza f. —v. **2.** desollar.

skin doctor dermatólogo -ga m. & f.

skip /skɪp/ n. **1.** brinco m. —v. **2.** brincar. **s. over,** pasar por alto.

skirmish /ˈskɜrmɪʃ/ n. escaramuza f.

skirt /skɜrt/ n. falda f.

skull /skʌl/ n. cráneo m.

skunk /skʌŋk/ n. zorrillo m.

sky /skai/ n. cielo m.

skylight /ˈskaiˌlait/ n. tragaluz m.

skyscraper /ˈskaiˌskreipər/ n. rascacielos m.

slab /slæb/ n. tabla f.

slack /slæk/ a. flojo; descuidado.

slacken /ˈslækən/ v. relajar.

slacks /slæks/ n. pantalones flojos.

slam /slæm/ n. **1.** portazo m. —v. **2.** cerrar de golpe. **slamming on the brakes,** frenazo m.

slander /ˈslændər/ n. **1.** calumnia f. —v. **2.** calumniar.

slang /slæŋ/ n. jerga f.

slant /slænt/ n. **1.** sesgo m. —v. **2.** sesgar.

slap /slæp/ n. **1.** bofetada, palmada f. —v. **2.** dar una bofetada.

slash /slæʃ/ n. **1.** cuchillada f. —v. **2.** acuchillar.

slat /slæt/ n. **1.** tablilla f. —v. **2.** lanzar.

slate /sleit/ n. **1.** pizarra f.; lista de candidatos. —n. **2.** destinar.

slaughter /ˈslɔtər/ n. **1.** matanza f. —v. **2.** matar.

slave /sleiv/ n. esclavo -va.

slavery /ˈsleivəri/ n. esclavitud f.

Slavic /ˈslɑvɪk/ a. eslavo.

slay /slei/ v. matar, asesinar.

sled /slɛd/ n. trineo m.

sleek /slik/ a. liso y brillante.

sleep /slip/ n. **1.** sueño m. **to get much s.,** dormir mucho. —v. **2.** dormir.

sleeping car /ˈslipɪŋ/ coche cama.

sleeping pill /ˈslipɪŋ/ pastilla para dormir, somnífero m.

sleepy /ˈslipi/ a. soñoliento. **to be s.,** tener sueño.

sleet /slit/ n. **1.** cellisca f. —v. **2.** cellisquear.

sleeve /sliv/ n. manga f.

slender /ˈslɛndər/ a. delgado.

slice /slais/ n. **1.** rebanada; (of meat) tajada f. —v. **2.** rebanar; tajar.

slide /slaid/ v. resbalar, deslizarse.

slide rule regla de cálculo f.

slight /slait/ n. **1.** desaire m. —a. **2.** pequeño; leve. —v. **3.** desairar.

slim /slɪm/ a. delgado.

slime /slaim/ n. lama f.

sling /slɪŋ/ n. **1.** honda f.; Med. cabestrillo m. —v. **2.** tirar.

slink /slɪŋk/ v. escabullirse.

slip /slɪp/ n. **1.** imprudencia; (garment) combinación f.; (of paper) trozo m.; ficha f. —v. **2.** resbalar; deslizar. **s. up,** equivocarse.

slipper /ˈslɪpər/ n. chinela f.

slippery /ˈslɪpəri/ a. resbaloso.

slit /slɪt/ n. **1.** abertura f. —v. **2.** cortar.

slogan /ˈslougən/ n. lema m.

slope /sloup/ n. **1.** declive m. —v. **2.** inclinarse.

sloppy /ˈslɒpi/ a. desaliñado, chapucero.

slot /slɒt/ n. ranura f.

slot machine tragaperras *f.*
slouch /slautʃ/ *n.* **1.** patán *m.* —*v.* **2.** estar gacho.
slovenly /ˈslʌvənli/ *a.* desaliñado.
slow /slou/ *a.* **1.** lento; (watch) atrasado. —*v.* **2. s. down, s. up,** retardar; ir más despacio.
slowly /ˈslouli/ *adv.* despacio.
slowness /ˈslounɪs/ *n.* lentitud *f.*
sluggish /ˈslʌgɪʃ/ *a.* perezoso, inactivo.
slum /slʌm/ *n.* barrio bajo *m.*
slumber /ˈslʌmbər/ *v.* dormitar.
slur /slɜr/ *n.* **1.** estigma *m.* —*v.* **2.** menospreciar.
slush /slʌʃ/ *n.* fango *m.*
sly /slai/ *a.* taimado. **on the s.** a hurtadillas.
smack /smæk/ *n.* **1.** manotada *f.* —*v.* **2.** manotear.
small /smɔl/ *a.* pequeño.
small letter minúscula *f.*
smallpox /ˈsmɔlˌpɒks/ *n.* viruela *f.*
smart /smɑrt/ *a.* **1.** listo; elegante. —*v.* **2.** escocer.
smash /smæʃ/ *v.* aplastar; hacer pedazos.
smear /smɪər/ *n.* **1.** mancha; difamación *f.* —*v.* **2.** manchar; difamar.
smell /smɛl/ *n.* **1.** olor; (sense) olfato *m.* —*v.* **2.** oler.
smelt /smɛlt/ *n.* **1.** eperlano *m.* —*v.* **2.** fundir.
smile /smail/ *n.* **1.** sonrisa *f.* —*v.* **2.** sonreír.
smite /smait/ *v.* afligir; apenar.
smock /smɒk/ *n.* camisa de mujer *f.*
smoke /smouk/ *n.* **1.** humo *m.* —*v.* **2.** fumar; (food) ahumar.
smokestack /ˈsmoukˌstæk/ *n.* chimenea *f.*
smolder /ˈsmouldər/ *v.* arder sin llama.
smooth /smuð/ *a.* **1.** liso; suave; tranquilo. —*v.* **2.** alisar.
smother /ˈsmʌðər/ *v.* sofocar.
smug /smʌg/ *a.* presumido.
smuggle /ˈsmʌgəl/ *v.* pasar de contrabando.
snack /snæk/ *n.* bocadillo *m.*
snag /snæg/ *n.* nudo; obstáculo *m.*
snail /sneil/ *n.* caracol *m.*
snake /sneik/ *n.* culebra, serpiente *f.*
snap /snæp/ *n.* **1.** trueno *m.* —*v.* **2.** tronar; romper.
snapshot /ˈsnæpˌʃɒt/ *n.* instantánea *f.*
snare /snɛər/ *n.* trampa *f.*
snarl /snɑrl/ *n.* **1.** gruñido *m.* —*v.* **2.** gruñir; (hair) enredar.
snatch /snætʃ/ *v.* arrebatar.
sneak /snik/ *v.* ir, entrar, salir (etc.) a hurtadillas.
sneaker /ˈsnikər/ *n.* sujeto ruín *m.* zapatilla de tenis.
sneer /snɪər/ *n.* **1.** mofa *f.* —*v.* **2.** mofarse.
sneeze /sniz/ *n.* **1.** estornudo *m.* —*v.* **2.** estornudar.
snicker /ˈsnɪkər/ *n.* risita *m.*
snob /snɒb/ *n.* esnob *m.*
snore /snɔr/ *n.* **1.** ronquido *m.* —*v.* **2.** roncar.
snow /snou/ *n.* **1.** nieve *f.* —*v.* **2.** nevar.
snowball /ˈsnouˌbɔl/ *n.* bola de nieve *f.*
snowdrift /ˈsnouˌdrɪft/ *n.* ventisquero *m.*
snowplow /ˈsnouˌplau/ *n.* quitanieves *m.*
snowstorm /ˈsnouˌstɔrm/ *n.* nevasca *f.*
snub /snʌb/ *v.* desairar.
snug /snʌg/ *a.* abrigado y cómodo.
so /sou/ *adv.* **1.** así; (also) también. **so as to,** para. **so that,** para que. **so... as,** tan... como. **so... that,** tan... que. —*conj.* **2.** así es que.
soak /souk/ *v.* empapar.
soap /soup/ *n.* **1.** jabón *m.* —*v.* **2.** enjabonar.
soap powder jabón en polvo *m.*
soar /sɔr/ *v.* remontarse.
sob /sɒb/ *n.* **1.** sollozo *m.* —*v.* **2.** sollozar.
sober /ˈsoubər/ *a.* sobrio; pensativo.
sociable /ˈsouʃəbəl/ *a.* sociable.
social /ˈsouʃəl/ *a.* **1.** social. —*n.* **2.** tertulia *f.*
socialism /ˈsouʃəˌlɪzəm/ *n.* socialismo *m.*
socialist /ˈsouʃəlɪst/ *a.* & *n.* socialista *m.* & *f.*
society /səˈsaiɪti/ *n.* sociedad; compañía *f.*
sociological /ˌsousiəˈlɒdʒɪkəl/ *a.* sociológico.
sociologist /ˌsousiˌɒlədʒɪst/ *n.* sociólogo -ga *m.* & *f.*
sociology /ˌsousiˈɒlədʒi/ *n.* sociología *f.*
sock /sɒk/ *n.* **1.** calcetín; puñetazo *m.* —*v.* **2.** dar un puñetazo a.
socket /ˈsɒkɪt/ *n.* cuenca *f.*; *Elec.* enchufe *m.*
sod /sɒd/ *n.* césped *m.*
soda /ˈsoudə/ *n.* soda; *Chem.* sosa *f.*
sodium /ˈsoudiəm/ *n.* sodio *m.*
sofa /ˈsoufə/ *n.* sofá *m.*
soft /sɔft/ *a.* blando; fino; suave.
soft drink bebida no alcohólica.
soften /ˈsɔfən/ *v.* ablandar; suavizar.
software /ˈsɔftˌwɛər/ *n.* software *m.*, programa *m.*
soil /sɔil/ *n.* **1.** suelo *m.* —*v.* **2.** ensuciar.
sojourn /ˈsoudʒɜrn/ *n.* morada *f.*, estancia *f.*
solace /ˈsɒlɪs/ *n.* **1.** solaz *m.* —*v.* **2.** solazar.
solar /ˈsoulər/ *a.* solar.
solar system sistema solar *m.*
solder /ˈsɒdər/ *v.* **1.** soldar. —*n.* **2.** soldadura *f.*
soldier /ˈsouldʒər/ *n.* soldado *m.* & *f.*
sole /soul/ *n.* **1.** suela; (of foot) planta *f.*; (fish) lenguado *m.* —*a.* **2.** único.
solemn /ˈsɒləm/ *a.* solemne.
solemnity /səˈlɛmnɪti/ *n.* solemnidad *f.*
solicit /səˈlɪsɪt/ *v.* solicitar.
solicitous /səˈlɪsɪtəs/ *a.* solícito.
solid /ˈsɒlɪd/ *a.* & *n.* sólido *m.*
solidify /səˈlɪdəˌfai/ *v.* solidificar.
solidity /səˈlɪdɪti/ *n.* solidez *f.*
solitary /ˈsɒlɪˌtɛri/ *a.* solitario.
solitude /ˈsɒlɪˌtud/ *n.* soledad *f.*
solo /ˈsoulou/ *n.* solo *m.*
soloist /ˈsoulouɪst/ *n.* solista *m.* & *f.*
soluble /ˈsɒlyəbəl/ *a.* soluble.
solution /səˈluʃən/ *n.* solución *f.*
solve /sɒlv/ *v.* solucionar; resolver.
solvent /ˈsɒlvənt/ *a.* solvente.
somber /ˈsɒmbər/ *a.* sombrío.
some /sʌm; *unstressed* səm/ *a.* & *pron.* algo (de), un poco (de); alguno; (pl.) algunos, unos.
somebody, someone /ˈsʌmbɒdi; ˈsʌmˌwʌn/ *pron.* alguien.
somehow /ˈsʌmˌhau/ *adv.* de algún modo.
someone /ˈsʌmˌwʌn/ *n.* alguien o alguno.
somersault /ˈsʌmərˌsɔlt/ *n.* salto mortal *m.*
something /ˈsʌmˌθɪŋ/ *pron.* algo, alguna cosa.
sometime /ˈsʌmˌtaim/ *adv.* alguna vez.
sometimes /ˈsʌmˌtaimz/ *adv.* a veces, algunas veces.
somewhat /ˈsʌmˌwʌt/ *adv.* algo, un poco.
somewhere /ˈsʌmˌwɛər/ *adv.* en (*or* a) alguna parte.
son /sʌn/ *n.* hijo *m.*
song /sɔŋ/ *n.* canción *f.*
son-in-law /ˈsʌn ɪn ˌlɔ/ *n.* yerno *m.*
soon /sun/ *adv.* pronto. **as s. as possible,** cuanto antes. **sooner or later,** tarde o temprano. **no sooner... than,** apenas... cuando.
soot /sʊt/ *n.* hollín *m.*
soothe /suð/ *v.* calmar.
soothingly /ˈsuðɪŋli/ *adv.* tiernamente.
sophisticated /səˈfɪstɪˌkeitɪd/ *a.* sofisticado.
sophomore /ˈsɒfəˌmɔr/ *n.* estudiante de segundo año *m.*
soprano /səˈprænou/ *n.* soprano *m.* & *f.*
sorcery /ˈsɔrsəri/ *n.* encantamiento *m.*
sordid /ˈsɔrdɪd/ *a.* sórdido.
sore /sɔr/ *n.* **1.** llaga *f.* —*a.* **2.** lastimado; *Colloq.* enojado. **to be s.,** doler.
sorority /səˈrɔrɪti, -ˈrɒr-/ *n.* hermandad de mujeres *f.*
sorrow /ˈsɒrou/ *n.* pesar, dolor *m.*, aflicción *f.*
sorrowful /ˈsɒrəfəl/ *a.* doloroso; afligido.
sorry /ˈsɒri/ *a.* **to be s.,** sentir, lamentar. **to be s. for,** compadecer.
sort /sɔrt/ *n.* **1.** tipo *m.*; clase, especie *f.* **s. of,** algo, un poco. —*v.* **2.** clasificar.
soul /soul/ *n.* alma *f.*
sound /saund/ *a.* **1.** sano; razonable; firme. —*n.* **2.** sonido *m.* —*v.* **3.** sonar; parecer.
soundproof /ˈsaundˌpruf/ *a.* insonorizado. *v.* insonorizar.
soundtrack /ˈsaundˌtræk/ *n.* banda sonora *f.*
soup /sup/ *n.* sopa *f.*
sour /sauᵊr/ *a.* agrio; ácido; rancio.
source /sɔrs/ *n.* fuente; causa *f.*
south /sauθ/ *n.* sur *m.*
South Africa /ˈæfrɪkə/ Sudáfrica *f.*
South African *a.* & *n.* sudafricano.
South America /əˈmɛrɪkə/ Sud América, América del Sur.
South American *a.* & *n.* sudamericano -na.
southeast /ˌsauθˈist; *Naut.* ˌsau-/ *n.* sudeste *m.*
southern /ˈsʌðərn/ *a.* meridional.
South Pole *n.* Polo Sur *m.*
southwest /ˌsauθˈwɛst; *Naut.* ˌsau-/ *n.* sudoeste *m.*
souvenir /ˌsuvəˈnɪər/ *n.* recuerdo *m.*
sovereign /ˈsɒvrɪn/ *n.* soberano -na.
sovereignty /ˈsɒvrɪnti/ *n.* soberanía *f.*
Soviet Russia Rusia Soviética *f.*
sow /sau/ *n.* **1.** puerca *f.* —*v.* **2.** sembrar.
space /speis/ *n.* **1.** espacio *m.* —*v.* **2.** espaciar.
space out *v.* escalonar.
spaceship /ˈspeisˌʃɪp/ *n.* nave espacial, astronave *f.*
space shuttle /ˈʃʌtl/ transbordador espacial *m.*
spacious /ˈspeiʃəs/ *a.* espacioso.
spade /speid/ *n.* **1.** laya; (cards) espada *f.* —*v.* **2.** layar.
spaghetti /spəˈgɛti/ *n.* espaguetis *m.pl.*
Spain /spein/ *n.* España *f.*
span /spæn/ *n.* **1.** tramo *m.* —*v.* **2.** extenderse sobre.
Spaniard /ˈspænyərd/ *n.* español -ola.
Spanish /ˈspænɪʃ/ *a.* & *n.* español -ola.
spank /spæŋk/ *v.* pegar.
spanking /ˈspæŋkɪŋ/ *n.* tunda, zumba *f.*
spar /spɑr/ *v.* altercar.
spare /spɛər/ *a.* **1.** de repuesto. —*v.* **2.** perdonar; ahorrar; prestar. **have... to s.,** tener... de sobra.
spare tire neumático de recambio *m.*
spark /spɑrk/ *n.* chispa *f.*
sparkle /ˈspɑrkəl/ *n.* **1.** destello *m.* —*v.* **2.** chispear. **sparkling wine,** vino espumoso.
spark plug /ˈspɑrkˌplʌg/ *n.* bujía *f.*
sparrow /ˈspærou/ *n.* gorrión *m.*
sparse /spɑrs/ *a.* esparcido.
spasm /ˈspæzəm/ *n.* espasmo *m.*
spasmodic /spæzˈmɒdɪk/ *a.* espasmódico.
spatter /ˈspætər/ *v.* salpicar; manchar.
speak /spik/ *v.* hablar.
speaker /ˈspikər/ *n.* conferencista *m.* & *f.*
spear /spɪər/ *n.* lanza *f.*
spearmint /ˈspɪərˌmɪnt/ *n.* menta romana *f.*
special /ˈspɛʃəl/ *a.* especial. **s. delivery,** entrega inmediata, entrega urgente.
specialist /ˈspɛʃəlɪst/ *n.* especialista *m.* & *f.*
specialty /ˈspɛʃəlti/ *n.* especialidad *f.*
species /ˈspiʃiz, -siz/ *n.* especie *f.*
specific /spɪˈsɪfɪk/ *a.* específico.
specify /ˈspɛsəˌfai/ *v.* especificar.
specimen /ˈspɛsəmən/ *n.* espécimen *m.*; muestra *f.*
spectacle /ˈspɛktəkəl/ *n.* espectáculo *m.*; (pl.) lentes, anteojos *m.pl.*
spectacular /spɛkˈtækyələr/ *a.* espectacular, aparatoso.
spectator /ˈspɛkteitər/ *n.* espectador -ra.
spectrum /ˈspɛktrəm/ *n.* espectro *m.*
speculate /ˈspɛkyəˌleit/ *v.* especular.
speculation /ˌspɛkyəˈleiʃən/ *n.* especulación *f.*
speech /spitʃ/ *n.* habla *f.*; lenguaje; discurso *m.* **part of s.,** parte de la oración.
speechless /ˈspitʃlɪs/ *a.* mudo.
speed /spid/ *n.* **1.** velocidad; rapidez *f.* —*v.* **2. s. up,** acelerar, apresurar.
speed limit velocidad máxima *f.*
speedometer /spiˈdɒmɪtər/ *n.* velocímetro *m.*
speedy /ˈspidi/ *a.* veloz, rápido.
spell /spɛl/ *n.* **1.** hechizo; rato; *Med.* ataque *m.* —*v.* **2.** escribir; relevar.
spelling /ˈspɛlɪŋ/ *n.* ortografía *f.*
spend /spɛnd/ *v.* gastar; (time) pasar.
spendthrift /ˈspɛndˌθrɪft/ *a.* & *n.* pródigo; manirroto *m.*
sphere /sfɪər/ *n.* esfera *f.*
spice /spais/ *n.* **1.** especia *f.* —*v.* **2.** especiar.
spider /ˈspaidər/ *n.* araña *f.*
spider web telaraña *f.*
spike /spaik/ *n.* alcayata *f.*; punta *f.*, clavo *m.*
spill /spɪl/ *v.* derramar. *n.* caída *f.*, vuelco *m.*
spillway /ˈspɪlˌwei/ *n.* vertedero *m.*
spin /spɪn/ *v.* hilar; girar.
spinach /ˈspɪnɪtʃ/ *n.* espinaca *f.*
spine /spain/ *n.* espina dorsal *f.*
spinet /ˈspɪnɪt/ *n.* espineta *m.*
spinster /ˈspɪnstər/ *n.* solterona *f.*
spiral /ˈspairəl/ *a.* & *n.* espiral *f.*
spire /spaiᵊr/ *n.* caracol *m.*, espiral *f.*
spirit /ˈspɪrɪt/ *n.* espíritu; ánimo *m.*
spiritual /ˈspɪrɪtʃuəl/ *a.* espiritual.
spiritualism /ˈspɪrɪtʃuəˌlɪzəm/ *n.* espiritismo *m.*
spirituality /ˌspɪrɪtʃuˈælɪti/ *n.* espiritualidad *f.*
spit /spɪt/ *v.* escupir.
spite /spait/ *n.* despecho *m.* **in s. of,** a pesar de.
splash /splæʃ/ *n.* **1.** salpicadura *f.* —*v.* **2.** salpicar.
splendid /ˈsplɛndɪd/ *a.* espléndido.
splendor /ˈsplɛndər/ *n.* esplendor *m.*
splice /splais/ *v.* **1.** empalmar. —*n.* **2.** empalme *m.*
splint /splɪnt/ *n.* tablilla *f.*
splinter /ˈsplɪntər/ *n.* **1.** astilla *f.* —*v.* **2.** astillar.
split /splɪt/ *n.* **1.** división *f.* —*v.* **2.** dividir, romper en dos.
splurge /splɜrdʒ/ *v.* **1.** fachendear. —*n.* **2.** fachenda *f.*
spoil /spɔil/ *n.* **1.** (pl.) botín *m.* —*v.* **2.** echar a perder; (a child) mimar.
spoke /spouk/ *n.* rayo (de rueda) *m.*
spokesman /ˈspouksmən/ *n.* portavoz *m.* & *f.*
spokesperson /ˈspouksˌpɜrsən/ *n.* portavoz *m.* & *f.*
sponge /spʌndʒ/ *n.* esponja *f.*
sponsor /ˈspɒnsər/ *n.* **1.** patrocinador *m.* —*v.* **2.** patrocinar; costear.
spontaneity /ˌspɒntəˈniɪti, -ˈnei-/ *n.* espontaneidad *f.*

spontaneous /spɒn'teiniəs/ *a.* espontáneo.
spool /spul/ *n.* carrete *m.*
spoon /spun/ *n.* cuchara *f.*
spoonful /'spunful/ *n.* cucharada *f.*
sporadic /spə'rædɪk/ *a.* esporádico.
sport /spɔrt/ *n.* deporte *m.*
sport jacket chaqueta deportiva *f.*
sports center /spɔrts/ pabellón de deportes, polideportivo *m.*
sportsman /'spɔrtsmən/ *a.* **1.** deportivo. *—n.* **2.** deportista *m.* & *f.*
spot /spɒt/ *n.* **1.** mancha *f.;* lugar, punto *m.* *—v.* **2.** distinguir.
spouse /spaus/ *n.* esposo -sa.
spout /spaut/ *n.* **1.** chorro; (of teapot) pico *m.* *—v.* **2.** correr a chorro.
sprain /sprein/ *n.* **1.** torcedura *f.,* esguince *m.* *—v.* **2.** torcerse.
sprawl /sprɔl/ *v.* tenderse.
spray /sprei/ *n.* **1.** rociada *f.* *—v.* **2.** rociar.
spread /sprɛd/ *n.* **1.** propagación; extensión; (for bed) colcha *f.* *—v.* **2.** propagar; extender.
spreadsheet /'sprɛd,ʃit/ *n.* hoja de cálculo *f.*
spree /spri/ *n.* parranda *f.*
sprig /sprɪg/ *n.* ramita *f.*
sprightly /'spraitli/ *a.* garboso.
spring /sprɪŋ/ *n.* resorte, muelle *m.;* (season) primavera *f.;* (of water) manantial *m.*
springboard /'sprɪŋ,bɔrd/ *n.* trampolín *m.*
spring onion cebolleta *f.*
sprinkle /'sprɪŋkəl/ *v.* rociar; (rain) lloviznar.
sprint /sprɪnt/ *n.* carrera *f.*
sprout /spraut/ *n.* retoño *m.*
spry /sprai/ *a.* ágil.
spun /spʌn/ *a.* hilado.
spur /spɜr/ *n.* **1.** espuela *f.* **on the s. of the moment,** sin pensarlo. *—v.* **2.** espolear.
spurious /'spyʊriəs/ *a.* espurio.
spurn /spɜrn/ *v.* rechazar, despreciar.
spurt /spɜrt/ *n.* **1.** chorro *m.;* esfuerzo supremo. *—v.* **2.** salir en chorro.
spy /spai/ **1.** espía *m.* & *f.* *—v.* **2.** espiar.
squabble /'skwɒblɪŋ/ *n.* **1.** riña *f.* *—v.* **2.** reñir.
squad /skwɒd/ *n.* escuadra *f.*
squadron /'skwɒdrən/ *n.* escuadrón *m.*
squalid /'skwɒlɪd/ *a.* escuálido.
squall /skwɔl/ *n.* borrasca *f.*
squalor /'skwɒlər/ *n.* escualidez *f.*
squander /'skwɒndər/ *v.* malgastar.
square /skwɛər/ *a.* **1.** cuadrado. *—n.* **2.** cuadrado *m.;* plaza *f.*
square dance *n.* contradanza *f.*
squat /skwɒt/ *v.* agacharse.
squeak /skwik/ *n.* **1.** chirrido *m.* *—v.* **2.** chirriar.
squeamish /'skwimɪʃ/ *a.* escrupuloso.
squeeze /skwiz/ *n.* **1.** apretón *m.* *—v.* **2.** apretar; (fruit) exprimir.
squirrel /'skwɜrəl// *n.* ardilla *f.*
squirt /skwɜrt/ *n.* **1.** chisguete *m.* *—v.* **2.** jeringar.
stab /stæb/ *n.* **1.** puñalada *f.* *—v.* **2.** apuñalar.
stability /stə'bɪlɪti/ *n.* estabilidad *f.*
stabilize /'steibə,laiz/ *v.* estabilizar.
stable /'steibəl/ *a.* **1.** estable, equilibrado. *—n.* **2.** caballeriza *f.*
stack /stæk/ *n.* **1.** pila *f.* *—v.* **2.** apilar.
stadium /'steidiəm/ *n.* estadio *m.*
staff /stæf/ *n.* personal *m.* **editorial s.,** cuerpo de redacción. **general s.,** estado mayor.
stag /stæg/ *n.* ciervo *m.*
stage /steidʒ/ *n.* **1.** etapa; *Theat.* escena *f.* *—v.* **2.** representar.
stagflation /stæg'fleiʃən/ *n.* estagflación.
stagger /'stægər/ *v.* (teeter) tambalear; (space out) escalonar.
stagnant /'stægnənt/ *a.* estancado.
stagnate /'stægneit/ *v.* estancarse.
stain /stein/ *n.* **1.** mancha *f.* *—v.* **2.** manchar.
stainless steel /'steinlɪs/ acero inoxidable *m.*
staircase /'stɛər,keis/ **stairs** *n.* escalera *f.*
stake /steik/ *n.* estaca; (bet) apuesta *f.* **at s.,** en juego; en peligro.
stale /steil/ *a.* rancio.
stalemate /'steil,meit/ *n.* estancación *f.;* tablas *f.pl.*
stalk /stɔk/ *n.* caña *f.;* (of flower) tallo *m.* *v.* acechar.
stall /stɔl/ *n.* **1.** tenderete; (for horse) pesebre *m.* *—v.* **2.** demorar; (motor) atascar.
stallion /'stælyən/ *n.* *S.A.* garañón *m.*
stalwart /'stɔlwərt/ *a.* fornido.
stamina /'stæmənə/ *n.* vigor *m.*
stammer /'stæmər/ *v.* tartamudear.
stamp /stæmp/ *n.* **1.** sello *m.,* estampilla *f.* *—v.* **2.** sellar.
stamp collecting /kə'lɛktɪŋ/ filatelia *f.*
stampede /stæm'pid/ *n.* estampida *f.*
stand /stænd/ *n.* **1.** puesto *m.;* posición; (speaker's) tribuna; (furniture) mesita *f.* *—v.* **2.** estar; estar de pie; aguantar. **s. up,** pararse, levantarse.
standard /'stændərd/ *a.* **1.** normal, corriente. *—n.* **2.** norma *f.* **s. of living,** nivel de vida.
standardize /'stændər,daiz/ *v.* uniformar.
standing /'stændɪŋ/ *a.* fijo; establecido.
standpoint /'stænd,pɔint/ *n.* punto de vista *m.*
staple /'steipəl/ *n.* materia prima *f.;* grapa *f.*
stapler /'steiplər/ *n.* grapadora *f.*
star /stɑr/ *n.* estrella *f.*
starboard /'stɑrbərd/ *n.* estribor *m.*
starch /stɑrtʃ/ *n.* **1.** almidón *m.;* (in diet) fécula *f.* *—v.* **2.** almidonar.
stare /stɛər/ *v.* mirar fijamente.
stark /stɑrk/ *a.* **1.** severo. *—adv.* **2.** completamente.
start /stɑrt/ *n.* **1.** susto; principio *m.* *—v.* **2.** comenzar, empezar; salir; poner en marcha; causar.
startle /'stɑrtl̩/ *v.* asustar.
starvation /stɑr'veiʃən/ *n.* hambre *f.*
starve /stɑrv/ *v.* morir de hambre.
state /steit/ *n.* **1.** estado *m.* *—v.* **2.** declarar, decir.
statement /'steitmənt/ *n.* declaración *f.*
stateroom /'steit,rum/ *n.* camarote *m.*
statesman /'steitsmən/ *n.* estadista *m.*
static /'stætɪk/ *a.* **1.** estático. *—n.* **2.** estática *f.*
station /'steiʃən/ *n.* estación *f.*
stationary /'steiʃə,nɛri/ *a.* estacionario, fijo.
stationery /'steiʃə,nɛri/ *n.* papel de escribir.
statistics /stə'tɪstɪks/ *n.* estadística *f.*
statue /'stætʃu/ *n.* estatua *f.*
stature /'stætʃər/ *n.* estatura *f.*
status /'steitəs, 'stætəs/ *n.* condición, estado *m.*
statute /'stætʃut/ *n.* ley *f.*
staunch /stɔntʃ/ *a.* fiel; constante.
stay /stei/ *n.* **1.** estancia; visita *f.* *—v.* **2.** quedar, permanecer; parar, alojarse. **s. away,** ausentarse. **s. up,** velar.
steadfast /'stɛd,fæst/ *a.* inmutable.
steady /'stɛdi/ *a.* **1.** firme; permanente; regular. *—v.* **2.** sostener.
steak /steik/ *n.* biftec, bistec *m.*
steal /stil/ *v.* robar. **s. away,** escabullirse.
stealth /stɛlθ/ *n.* cautela *f.*
steam /stim/ *n.* vapor *m.*
steamboat /'stim,bout/ **steamer, steamship** *n.* vapor *m.*
steel /stil/ *n.* **1.** acero *m.* *—v.* **2. s. oneself,** fortalecerse.
steep /stip/ *a.* escarpado, empinado.
steeple /'stipəl/ *n.* campanario *m.*
steer /stɪər/ *n.* **1.** buey *m.* *—v.* **2.** guiar, manejar.
stellar /'stɛlər/ *a.* astral.
stem /stɛm/ *n.* **1.** tallo *m.* *—v.* **2.** parar. **s. from,** emanar de.
stencil /'stɛnsəl/ *n.* **1.** estarcido. *—v.* **2.** estarcir.
stenographer /stə'nɒgrəfər/ *n.* estenógrafo -fa.
stenography /stə'nɒgrəfi/ *n.* taquigrafía *f.*
step /stɛp/ *n.* **1.** paso *m.;* medida *f.;* (stairs) escalón *m.* *—v.* **2.** pisar. **s. back,** retirarse.
stepladder /'stɛp,lædər/ *n.* escalera de mano *f.*
stereophonic /,stɛriə'fɒnɪk/ *a.* estereofónico.
stereotype /'stɛriə,taip/ *n.* **1.** estereotipo *m.* *—v.* **2.** estereotipar.
sterile /'stɛrɪl/ *a.* estéril.
sterilize /'stɛrə,laiz/ *v.* esterilizar.
sterling /'stɜrlɪŋ/ *a.* esterlina, genuino.
stern /stɜrn/ *n.* **1.** popa *f.* *—a.* **2.** duro, severo.
stethoscope /'stɛθə,skoup/ *n.* estetoscopio *m.*
stevedore /'stivɪ,dɔr/ *n.* estibador *m.*
stew /stu/ *n.* **1.** guisado *m.* *—v.* **2.** estofar.
steward /'stuərd/ *n.* camarero.
stewardess /'stuərdɪs/ *n.* azafata *f.,* aeromoza *f.*
stick /stɪk/ *n.* **1.** palo, bastón *m.* *—v.* **2.** pegar; (put) poner, meter.
sticky /'stɪki/ *a.* pegajoso.
stiff /stɪf/ *a.* tieso; duro.
stiffness /'stɪfnɪs/ *n.* tiesura *f.*
stifle /'staifəl/ *v.* sofocar; *Fig.* suprimir.
stigma /'stɪgmə/ *n.* estigma *m.*
still /stɪl/ *a.* **1.** quieto; silencioso. **to keep s.,** quedarse quieto. *—adv.* **2.** todavía, aún; no obstante. *—n.* **3.** alambique *m.*
stillborn /'stɪl,bɔrn/ *n.* & *a.* nacido -da muerto -ta.
still life *n.* naturaleza muerta *f.*
stillness /'stɪlnɪs/ *n.* silencio *m.*
stilted /'stɪltɪd/ *a.* afectado, artificial.
stimulant /'stɪmyələnt/ *a.* & *n.* estimulante *m.*
stimulate /'stɪmyə,leit/ *v.* estimular.
stimulus /'stɪmyələs/ *n.* estímulo *m.*
sting /stɪŋ/ *n.* **1.** picadura *f.* *—v.* **2.** picar.
stingy /'stɪndʒi/ *a.* tacaño.
stipulate /'stɪpyə,leit/ *v.* estipular.
stir /stɜr/ *n.* **1.** conmoción *f.* *—v.* **2.** mover. **s. up,** conmover; suscitar.
stitch /stɪtʃ/ *n.* **1.** puntada *f.* *—v.* **2.** coser.
stock /stɒk/ *n.* surtido *f.;* raza *f.;* (finance) acciones. *f.pl.* **in s.,** en existencia. **to take s. in,** tener fe en.
stock exchange bolsa *f.*
stockholder /'stɒk,houldər/ *n.* accionista *m.* & *f.*
stocking /'stɒkɪŋ/ *n.* media *f.*
stockyard /'stɒk,yɑrd/ *n.* corral de ganado *m.*
stodgy /'stɒdʒi/ *a.* pesado.
stoical /'stouɪkəl/ *a.* estoico.
stole /stoul/ *n.* estola *f.*
stolid /'stɒlɪd/ *a.* impasible.
stomach /'stʌmək/ *n.* estómago *m.*
stomachache /'stʌmək,eik/ *n.* dolor de estómago *m.*
stone /stoun/ *n.* piedra *f.*
stool /stul/ *n.* banquillo *m.*
stoop /stup/ *v.* encorvarse; *Fig.* rebajarse. espaldas encorvadas *f.pl.*
stop /stɒp/ *n.* **1.** parada *f.* **to put a s. to,** poner fin a. *—v.* **2.** parar; suspender; detener; impedir. **s. doing** (etc.), dejar de hacer (etc.).
stopgap /'stɒp,gæp/ *n.* recurso provisional *m.*
stopover /'stɒp,ouvər/ *n.* parada *f.*
stopwatch /'stɒp,wɒtʃ/ *n.* cronómetro *m.*
storage /'stɔrɪdʒ/ *n.* almacenaje *m.*
store /stɔr/ *n.* **1.** tienda; provisión *f.* **department s.,** almacén *m.* *—v.* **2.** guardar; almacenar.
store window escaparate *m.*
stork /stɔrk/ *n.* cigüeña *f.*
storm /stɔrm/ *n.* tempestad, tormenta *f.*
stormy /'stɔrmi/ *a.* tempestuoso.
story /'stɔri/ *n.* cuento; relato *m.;* historia *f.* **short s.,** cuento.
stout /staut/ *a.* corpulento.
stove /stouv/ *n.* hornilla; estufa *f.*
straight /streit/ *a.* **1.** recto; derecho. *—adv.* **2.** directamente.
straighten /'streitn̩/ *v.* enderezar. **s. out,** poner en orden.
straightforward /,streit'fɔrwərd/ *a.* recto, sincero.
strain /strein/ *n.* **1.** tensión *f.* *—v.* **2.** colar.
strainer /'streinər/ *n.* colador *m.*
strait /streit/ *n.* estrecho *m.*
strand /strænd/ *n.* **1.** hilo *m.* *—v.* **2. be stranded,** encallarse.
strange /streindʒ/ *a.* extraño; raro.
stranger /'streindʒər/ *n.* extranjero -ra; forastero -ra; desconocido -da.
strangle /'stræŋgəl/ *v.* estrangular.
strap /stræp/ *n.* correa *f.*
stratagem /'strætədʒəm/ *n.* estratagema *f.*
strategic /strə'tidʒɪk/ *a.* estratégico.
strategy /'strætɪdʒi/ *n.* estrategia *f.*
stratosphere /'strætə,sfɪər/ *n.* estratosfera *f.*
straw /strɔ/ *n.* paja *f.*
strawberry /'strɔ,bɛri/ *n.* fresa *f.*
stray /strei/ *a.* **1.** vagabundo. *—v.* **2.** extraviarse.
streak /strik/ *n.* **1.** racha; raya *f.;* lado *m.* *—v.* **2.** rayar.
stream /strim/ *n.* corriente *f.;* arroyo *m.*
street /strit/ *n.* calle *f.*
streetcar /'strit,kɑr/ *n.* tranvía *m.*
street lamp /'strit,læmp/ *n.* farol *m.*
strength /strɛŋkθ, strɛnθ/ *n.* fuerza *m.*
strengthen /'strɛŋkθən, 'strɛn-/ *v.* reforzar.
strenuous /'strɛnyuəs/ *a.* estrenuo.
streptococcus /,strɛptə'kɒkəs/ *n.* estreptococo *m.*
stress /strɛs/ *n.* **1.** tensión *f.;* énfasis *m.* *—v.* **2.** recalcar; acentuar.
stretch /strɛtʃ/ *n.* **1.** trecho *m.* **at one s.,** de un tirón. *—v.* **2.** tender; extender; estirarse.
stretcher /'strɛtʃər/ *n.* camilla *f.*
strew /stru/ *v.* esparcir.
stricken /'strɪkən/ *a.* agobiado.
strict /strɪkt/ *a.* estricto; severo.
stride /straid/ *n.* **1.** tranco *m.;* (fig., pl.) progresos. *—v.* **2.** andar a trancos.
strife /straif/ *n.* contienda *f.*
strike /straik/ *n.* **1.** huelga *f.* *—v.* **2.** pegar; chocar con; (clock) dar.
striker /'straikər/ *n.* huelguista *m.* & *f.*
string /strɪŋ/ *n.* cuerda *f.;* cordel *m.*
string bean *n.* habichuela *f.*
stringent /'strɪndʒənt/ *a.* estricto.
strip /strɪp/ *n.* **1.** tira *f.* *—v.* **2.** despojar; desnudarse.
stripe /straip/ *n.* raya *f.;* *Mil.* galón *m.*
strive /straiv/ *v.* esforzarse.
stroke /strouk/ *n.* golpe *m.;* (swimming) brazada *f.;* *Med.* ataque *m.* **s. of luck,** suerte *f.*
stroll /stroul/ *n.* **1.** paseo *m.* *—v.* **2.** pasearse.
stroller /'stroulər/ *n.* vagabundo *m.;* cochecito (de niño).
strong /strɔŋ/ *a.* fuerte.
stronghold /'strɔŋ,hould/ *n.* fortificación *f.*
structure /'strʌktʃər/ *n.* estructura *f.*
struggle /'strʌgəl/ *n.* **1.** lucha *f.* *—v.* **2.** luchar.
strut /strʌt/ *n.* **1.** pavonada *f.* *—v.* **2.** pavonear.
stub /stʌb/ *n.* **1.** cabo; (ticket) talón

m. —*v.* **2. s. on one's toes,** tropezar con.
stubborn /ˈstʌbərn/ *a.* testarudo.
stucco /ˈstʌkou/ *n.* **1.** estuco *m.* —*v.* **2.** estucar.
student /ˈstudnt/ *n.* alumno -na, estudiante -ta.
studio /ˈstudiˌou/ *n.* estudio *m.*
studious /ˈstudiəs/ *a.* aplicado; estudioso.
study /ˈstʌdi/ *n.* **1.** estudio *m.* —*v.* **2.** estudiar.
stuff /stʌf/ *n.* **1.** cosas *f.pl.* —*v.* **2.** llenar; rellenar.
stuffing /ˈstʌfɪŋ/ *n.* relleno *m.*
stumble /ˈstʌmbəl/ *v.* tropezar.
stump /stʌmp/ *n.* cabo; tocón; muñón *m.*
stun /stʌn/ *v.* aturdir.
stunt /stʌnt/ *n.* **1.** maniobra sensacional *f.* —*v.* **2.** impedir crecimiento.
stupendous /stuˈpɛndəs/ *a.* estupendo.
stupid /ˈstupɪd/ *a.* estúpido.
stupidity /stuˈpɪdɪti/ *n.* estupidez *f.*
stupor /ˈstupər/ *n.* estupor *m.*
sturdy /ˈstɜrdi/ *a.* robusto.
stutter /ˈstʌtər/ *v.* **1.** tartamudear. —*n.* **2.** tartamudeo *m.*
sty /stai/ *n.* pocilga *f.; Med.* orzuelo.
style /stail/ *n.* estilo *m.;* moda *f.*
stylish /ˈstailɪʃ/ *a.* elegante; a la moda.
suave /swɑv/ *a.* afable, suave.
subconscious /sʌbˈkɒnʃəs/ *a.* subconsciente.
subdue /səbˈdu/ *v.* dominar.
subject /*n.* ˈsʌbdʒɪkt; *v.* səbˈdʒɛkt/ *n.* **1.** tema *m.;* (of study) materia *f.; Pol.* súbdito -ta; *Gram.* sujeto *m.* —*v.* **2.** someter.
subjugate /ˈsʌbdʒəˌgeit/ *v.* sojuzgar, subyugar.
subjunctive /səbˈdʒʌŋktɪv/ *a.* & *n.* subjuntivo *m.*
sublimate /ˈsʌbləˌmeit/ *v.* sublimar.
sublime /səˈblaim/ *a.* sublime.
submarine /ˌsʌbməˈrin/ *a.* & *n.* submarino *m.*
submerge /səbˈmɜrdʒ/ *v.* sumergir.
submission /səbˈmɪʃən/ *n.* sumisión *f.*
submit /səbˈmɪt/ *v.* someter.
subnormal /sʌbˈnɔrməl/ *a.* subnormal.
subordinate /*a, n* səˈbɔrdnɪt; *v* -dnˌeit/ *a.* & *n.* **1.** subordinado -da. —*v.* **2.** subordinar.
subscribe /səbˈskraib/ *v.* aprobar; abonarse.
subscriber /səbˈskraibər/ *n.* abonado -da *m.* & *f.*
subscription /səbˈskrɪpʃən/ *n.* abono *m.*
subsequent /ˈsʌbsɪkwənt/ *a.* subsiguiente.
subservient /səbˈsɜrviənt/ *a.* servicial.
subside /səbˈsaid/ *v.* apaciguarse, menguar.
subsidy /ˈsʌbsɪdi/ *n.* subvención *f.*
subsoil /ˈsʌbˌsɔil/ *n.* subsuelo *m.*
substance /ˈsʌbstəns/ *n.* substancia *f.*
substantial /səbˈstænʃəl/ *a.* substancial; considerable.
substitute /ˈsʌbstɪˌtut/ *a.* **1.** substitutivo. —*n.* **2.** substituto -ta. —*v.* **3.** substituir.
substitution /ˌsʌbstɪˈtuʃən/ *n.* substitución *f.*
subterfuge /ˈsʌbtərˌfyudʒ/ *n.* subterfugio *m.*
subtitle /ˈsʌbˌtaitl̩/ *n.* subtítulo *m.*
subtle /ˈsʌtl̩/ *a.* sutil.
subtract /səbˈtrækt/ *v.* substraer.
suburb /ˈsʌbɜrb/ *n.* suburbio *m.;* (pl.) afueras *f.pl.*
subversive /səbˈvɜrsɪv/ *a.* subversivo.
subway /ˈsʌbˌwei/ *n.* metro *m.*
succeed /səkˈsid/ *v.* lograr, tener éxito; (in office) suceder a.
success /səkˈsɛs/ *n.* éxito *m.*
successful /səkˈsɛsfəl/ *a.* próspero; afortunado.
succession /səkˈsɛʃən/ *n.* sucesión *f.*
successive /səkˈsɛsɪv/ *a.* sucesivo.
successor /səkˈsɛsər/ *n.* sucesor -ra; heredero -ra.
succor /ˈsʌkər/ *n.* **1.** socorro *m.* —*v.* **2.** socorrer.
succumb /səˈkʌm/ *v.* sucumbir.
such /sʌtʃ/ *a.* tal.
suck /sʌk/ *v.* chupar.
suction /ˈsʌkʃən/ *n.* succión *f.*
sudden /ˈsʌdn̩/ *a.* repentino, súbito. **all of a s.,** de repente.
suds /sʌdz/ *n.* jabonaduras *f.pl.*
sue /su/ *v.* demandar.
suffer /ˈsʌfər/ *v.* sufrir; padecer.
suffice /səˈfais/ *v.* bastar.
sufficient /səˈfɪʃənt/ *a.* suficiente.
suffocate /ˈsʌfəˌkeit/ *v.* sofocar.
sugar /ˈʃʊgər/ *n.* azúcar *m.*
sugar bowl azucarero *m.*
suggest /səgˈdʒɛst/ *v.* sugerir.
suggestion /səgˈdʒɛstʃən/ *n.* sugerencia *f.*
suicide /ˈsuəˌsaid/ *n.* suicidio *m.;* (person) suicida *m.* & *f.* **to commit s.,** suicidarse.
suit /sut/ *n.* **1.** traje; (cards) palo; (law) pleito *m.* —*v.* **2.** convenir a.
suitable /ˈsutəbəl/ *a.* apropiado; que conviene.
suitcase /ˈsutˌkeis/ *n.* maleta *f.*
suite /swit/ *n.* serie *f.*, séquito *m.*
suitor /ˈsutər/ *n.* pretendiente *m.*
sullen /ˈsʌlən/ *a.* hosco.
sum /sʌm/ *n.* **1.** suma *f.* —*v.* **2. s. up,** resumir.
summarize /ˈsʌməˌraiz/ *v.* resumir.
summary /ˈsʌməri/ *n.* resumen *m.*
summer /ˈsʌmər/ *n.* verano *m.*
summon /ˈsʌmən/ *v.* llamar; (law) citar.
summons /ˈsʌmənz/ *n.* citación *f.*
sumptuous /ˈsʌmptʃuəs/ *a.* suntuoso.
sun /sʌn/ *n.* **1.** sol *m.* —*v.* **2.** tomar el sol.
sunbathe /ˈsʌnˌbeið/ *v.* tomar el sol.
sunburn /ˈsʌnˌbɜrn/ *n.* quemadura de sol.
sunburned /ˈsʌnˌbɜrnd/ *a.* quemado por el sol.
Sunday /ˈsʌndei/ *n.* domingo *m.*
sunken /ˈsʌŋkən/ *a.* hundido.
sunny /ˈsʌni/ *a.* asoleado. **s. day,** día de sol. **to be s.,** (weather) hacer sol.
sunshine /ˈsʌnˌʃain/ *n.* luz del sol.
suntan /ˈsʌnˌtæn/ *n.* bronceado *m.* **s. lotion,** loción bronceadora *f.*, bronceador *m.*
superb /sʊˈpɜrb/ *a.* soberbio.
superficial /ˌsupərˈfɪʃəl/ *a.* superficial.
superfluous /sʊˈpɜrfluəs/ *a.* superfluo.
superhuman /ˌsupərˈhyumən/ *a.* sobrehumano.
superintendent /ˌsupərɪnˈtɛndənt/ *n.* superintendente *m.* & *f.;* (of building) conserje *m.;* (of school) director -ra general.
superior /səˈpɪəriər/ *a.* & *n.* superior *m.*
superiority /səˌpɪəriˈɔrɪti/ *n.* superioridad *f.*
superlative /səˈpɜrlətɪv/ *a.* superlativo.
supernatural /ˌsupərˈnætʃərəl/ *a.* sobrenatural.
supersede /ˌsupərˈsid/ *v.* reemplazar.
superstar /ˈsupərˌstɑr/ *n.* superestrella *m.* & *f.*
superstition /ˌsupərˈstɪʃən/ *n.* superstición *f.*
superstitious /ˌsupərˈstɪʃəs/ *a.* supersticioso.
supervise /ˈsupərˌvaiz/ *v.* supervisar.
supper /ˈsʌpər/ *n.* cena *f.*
supplement /ˈsʌpləmənt/ *n.* **1.** suplemento *m.* —*v.* **2.** suplementar.
supply /səˈplai/ *n.* **1.** provisión *f.; Com.* surtido *m.; Econ.* existencia *f.* —*v.* **2.** suplir; proporcionar.
support /səˈpɔrt/ *n.* **1.** sustento; apoyo *m.* —*v.* **2.** mantener; apoyar.
suppose /səˈpouz/ *v.* suponer. **be supposed to,** deber.
suppository /səˈpɒzɪˌtɔri/ *n.* supositorio *m.*
suppress /səˈprɛs/ *v.* suprimir.
suppression /səˈprɛʃən/ *n.* supresión *f.*
supreme /səˈprim/ *a.* supremo.
sure /ʃʊr, ʃɜr/ *a.* seguro, cierto. **for s.,** con seguridad. **to make s.,** asegurarse.
surety /ˈʃʊrɪti, ˈʃɜr-/ *n.* garantía *f.*
surf /sɜrf/ *n.* **1.** oleaje *m.* —*v.* **2.** (Internet) navegar; (sport) surfear.
surface /ˈsɜrfɪs/ *n.* superficie *f.*
surfboard /ˈsɜrfˌbɔrd/ *n.* tabla de surf *f.*
surfer /ˈsɜrfər/ *n.* (Internet) usuario -ria, navegante *m.* & *f.;* (sport) surfero -ra.
surge /sɜrdʒ/ *v.* surgir.
surgeon /ˈsɜrdʒən/ *n.* cirujano -na.
surgery /ˈsɜrdʒəri/ *n.* cirugía *f.*
surmise /sərˈmaiz/ *v.* suponer.
surmount /sərˈmaunt/ *v.* vencer.
surname /ˈsɜrˌneim/ *n.* apellido *m.*
surpass /sərˈpæs/ *v.* superar.
surplus /ˈsɜrplʌs/ *a.* & *n.* sobrante *m.*
surprise /sərˈpraiz, sə-/ *n.* **1.** sorpresa —*v.* **2.** sorprender. **I am surprised...,** me extraña...
surrender /səˈrɛndər/ *n.* **1.** rendición *f.* —*v.* **2.** rendir.
surround /səˈraund/ *v.* rodear, circundar.
surveillance /sərˈveiləns/ *n.* vigilancia *f.*
survey /*n.* ˈsɜrvei; *v.* sərˈvei/ *n.* **1.** examen; estudio *m.* —*v.* **2.** examinar; (land) medir.
survival /sərˈvaivəl/ *n.* supervivencia *f.*
survive /sərˈvaiv/ *v.* sobrevivir.
susceptible /səˈsɛptəbəl/ *a.* susceptible.
suspect /*v.* səˈspɛkt; *n.* ˈsʌspɛkt/ *v.* **1.** sospechar. —*n.* **2.** sospechoso -sa.
suspend /səˈspɛnd/ *v.* suspender.
suspense /səˈspɛns/ *n.* incertidumbre *f.* **in s.,** en suspenso.
suspension /səˈspɛnʃən/ *n.* suspensión *f.*
suspension bridge *n.* puente colgante *m.*
suspicion /səˈspɪʃən/ *n.* sospecha *f.*
suspicious /səˈspɪʃəs/ *a.* sospechoso.
sustain /səˈstein/ *v.* sustentar; mantener.
swallow /ˈswɒlou/ *n.* **1.** trago *m.;* (bird) golondrina *f.* —*v.* **2.** tragar.
swamp /swɒmp/ *n.* **1.** pantano *m.* —*v.* **2.** *Fig.* abrumar.
swan /swɒn/ *n.* cisne *m.*
swap /swɒp/ *n.* **1.** trueque *m.* —*v.* **2.** cambalachear.
swarm /swɔrm/ *n.* enjambre *m.*
swarthy /ˈswɔrði/ *a.* moreno.
sway /swei/ *n.* **1.** predominio *m.* —*v.* **2.** bambolearse; *Fig.* influir en.
swear /swɛər/ *v.* jurar. **s. off,** renunciar a.
sweat /swɛt/ *n.* **1.** sudor *m.* —*v.* **2.** sudar.
sweater /ˈswɛtər/ *n.* suéter *m.*
sweatshirt /ˈswɛtˌʃɜrt/ *n.* sudadera *f.*
Swede /swid/ *n.* sueco -ca.
Sweden /ˈswidn̩/ *n.* Suecia *f.*
Swedish /ˈswidɪʃ/ *a.* sueco.
sweep /swip/ *v.* barrer.
sweet /swit/ *a.* **1.** dulce; amable, simpático. —*n.* **2.** (pl.) dulces *m.pl.*
sweetheart /ˈswitˌhɑrt/ *n.* novio -via.
sweetness /ˈswitnɪs/ *n.* dulzura *f.*
sweet-toothed /ˈswit ˌtuθt/ *a.* goloso.
swell /swɛl/ *a.* **1.** *Colloq.* estupendo, excelente. —*n.* **2.** (of the sea) oleada *f.* —*v.* **3.** hincharse; aumentar.
swelter /ˈswɛltər/ *v.* sofocarse de calor.
swift /swɪft/ *a.* rápido, veloz.
swim /swɪm/ *n.* **1.** nadada *f.* —*v.* **2.** nadar.
swimming /ˈswɪmɪŋ/ *n.* natación *f.*
swimming pool alberca, piscina *f.*
swindle /ˈswɪndl̩/ *n.* **1.** estafa *f.* —*v.* **2.** estafar.
swine /swain/ *n.* puercos *m.pl.*
swing /swɪŋ/ *n.* **1.** columpio *m.* **in full s.,** en plena actividad. —*v.* **2.** mecer; balancear.
swirl /swɜrl/ *n.* **1.** remolino *m.* —*v.* **2.** arremolinar.
Swiss /swɪs/ *a.* & *n.* suizo -za.
switch /swɪtʃ/ *n.* **1.** varilla *f.; Elec.* llave *f.*, conmutador *m.;* (railway) cambiavía *m.* —*v.* **2.** cambiar; trocar.
switchboard /ˈswɪtʃˌbɔrd/ *n.* cuadro conmutador *m.*, centralita *f.*
Switzerland /ˈswɪtsərlənd/ *n.* Suiza *f.*
sword /sɔrd/ *n.* espada *f.*
syllable /ˈsɪləbəl/ *n.* sílaba *f.*
symbol /ˈsɪmbəl/ *n.* símbolo *m.*
sympathetic /ˌsɪmpəˈθɛtɪk/ *a.* compasivo. **to be s.,** tener simpatía.
sympathy /ˈsɪmpəθi/ *n.* lástima; condolencia *f.*
symphony /ˈsɪmfəni/ *n.* sinfonía *f.*
symptom /ˈsɪmptəm/ *n.* síntoma *m.*
synagogue /ˈsɪnəˌgɒg/ *n.* sinagoga *f.*
synchronize /ˈsɪŋkrəˌnaiz/ *v.* sincronizar.
syndicate /ˈsɪndɪkɪt/ *n.* sindicato *m.*
syndrome /ˈsɪndroum, -drəm/ *n.* síndrome *m.*
synonym /ˈsɪnənɪm/ *n.* sinónimo *m.*
synthetic /sɪnˈθɛtɪk/ *a.* sintético.
syringe /səˈrɪndʒ/ *n.* jeringa *f.*
syrup /ˈsɪrəp, ˈsɜr-/ *n.* almíbar; *Med.* jarabe *m.*
system /ˈsɪstəm/ *n.* sistema *m.*
systematic /ˌsɪstəˈmætɪk/ *a.* sistemático.

T

tabernacle /ˈtæbərˌnækəl/ *n.* tabernáculo *m.*
table /ˈteibəl/ *n.* mesa; (list) tabla *f.*
tablecloth /ˈteibəlˌklɔθ/ *n.* mantel *m.*
table of contents /ˈkɒntɛnts/ índice de materias *m.*
tablespoon /ˈteibəlˌspun/ *n.* cuchara *f.*
tablespoonful /ˈteibəlspunˌfʊl/ *n.* cucharada *f.*
tablet /ˈtæblɪt/ *n.* tableta; *Med.* pastilla *f.*
tack /tæk/ *n.* tachuela *f.*
tact /tækt/ *n.* tacto *m.*
tag /tæg/ *n.* etiqueta *f.*, rótulo *m.*
tail /teil/ *n.* cola *f.*, rabo *m.*
tailor /ˈteilər/ *n.* sastre *m.*
take /teik/ *v.* tomar; llevar. **t. a bath,** bañarse. **t. a shower,** ducharse. **t. away,** quitar. **t. off,** quitarse. **t. out,** sacar. **t. long,** tardar mucho.
tale /teil/ *n.* cuento *m.*
talent /ˈtælənt/ *n.* talento *m.*
talk /tɔk/ *n.* **1.** plática, habla *f.;* discurso *m.* —*v.* **2.** hablar.
talkative /ˈtɔkətɪv/ *a.* locuaz.
tall /tɔl/ *a.* alto.
tame /teim/ *a.* **1.** manso, domesticado. —*v.* **2.** domesticar.
tamper /ˈtæmpər/ *v.* **t. with,** entremeterse en.
tampon /ˈtæmpɒn/ *n.* tampón *m.*
tan /tæn/ *a.* **1.** color de arena. —*v.* **2.** curtir; tostar. *n.* bronceado.
tangerine /ˌtændʒəˈrin/ *n.* clementina *f.*
tangible /ˈtændʒəbəl/ *a.* tangible.
tangle /ˈtæŋgəl/ *n.* **1.** enredo *m.* —*v.* **2.** enredar.
tank /tæŋk/ *n.* tanque *m.*
tap /tæp/ *n.* **1.** golpe ligero. —*v.* **2.** golpear ligeramente; decentar.
tape /teip/ *n.* cinta *f.*

tape recorder /rɪ'kɔrdər/ magnetófono *m.*, grabadora *f.*
tapestry /'tæpəstri/ *n.* tapiz *m.*; tapicería *f.*
tar /tɑr/ *n.* **1.** brea *f.* —*v.* **2.** embrear.
target /'tɑrgɪt/ *n.* blanco *m.*
tarnish /'tɑrnɪʃ/ *n.* **1.** deslustre *m.* —*v.* **2.** deslustrar.
tarpaulin /tɑr'pɔlɪn, 'tɑrpəlɪn/ *n.* lona *f.*
task /tæsk/ *n.* tarea *f.*
taste /teist/ *n.* **1.** gusto; sabor *m.* —*v.* **2.** gustar; probar. **t. of,** saber a.
tasty /'teisti/ *a.* sabroso.
tattoo /tæ'tu/ *v.* tatuar.
taut /tɔt/ *a.* tieso.
tavern /'tævərn/ *n.* taberna *f.*
tax /tæks/ *n.* **1.** impuesto *m.* —*v.* **2.** imponer impuestos.
tax collector *n.* recaudador -ra *m.* & *f.*
taxi /'tæksi/ *n.* taxi, taxímetro *m.* **t. driver,** taxista *m.* & *f.*
taxpayer /'tæks,peiər/ *n.* contribuyente *m.* & *f.*
tax reform reforma tributaria *f.*
tax return declaración de la renta *f.*
tea /ti/ *n.* té *m.*
teach /titʃ/ *v.* enseñar.
teacher /'titʃər/ *n.* maestro -tra, profesor -ra.
team /tim/ *n.* equipo *m.*; pareja *f.*
tear /tɪər/ *n.* **1.** rasgón *m.*; lágrima *f.* —*v.* **2.** rasgar, lacerar. **t. apart,** separar.
tease /tiz/ *v.* atormentar; embromar.
teaspoon /'ti,spun/ *n.* cucharita *f.*
technical /'tɛknɪkəl/ *a.* técnico.
technician /tɛk'nɪʃən/ *n.* técnico -ca *m.* & *f.*
technique /tɛk'nik/ *n.* técnica *f.*
technology /tɛk'nɒlədʒi/ *n.* tecnología *f.*
teddy bear /'tɛdi/ oso de felpa *m.*
tedious /'tidiəs/ *a.* tedioso.
telegram /'tɛlɪ,græm/ *n.* telegrama *m.*
telegraph /'tɛlɪ,græf/ *n.* **1.** telégrafo *m.* —*v.* **2.** telegrafiar.
telephone /'tɛlə,foun/ *n.* **1.** teléfono *m.* **t. book,** directorio telefónico. —*v.* **2.** telefonear; llamar por teléfono.
telescope /'tɛlə,skoup/ *n.* **1.** telescopio *m.* —*v.* **2.** enchufar.
television /'tɛlə,vɪʒən/ *n.* televisión *f.*
tell /tɛl/ *v.* decir; contar; distinguir.
temper /'tɛmpər/ *n.* **1.** temperamento, genio *m.* —*v.* **2.** templar.
temperament /'tɛmpərəmənt, -prəmənt/ *n.* temperamento.
temperamental /,tɛmpərə'mɛntl̩, -prə'mɛn-/ *a.* sensitivo, emocional.
temperance /'tɛmpərəns/ *n.* moderación; sobriedad *f.*
temperate /'tɛmpərɪt/ *a.* templado.
temperature /'tɛmpərətʃər/ *n.* temperatura *f.*
tempest /'tɛmpɪst/ *n.* tempestad *f.*
tempestuous /tɛm'pɛstʃuəs/ *a.* tempestuoso.
temple /'tɛmpəl/ *n.* templo *m.*
temporary /'tɛmpə,rɛri/ *a.* temporal, temporario.
tempt /tɛmpt/ *v.* tentar.
temptation /tɛmp'teiʃən/ *n.* tentación *f.*
ten /tɛn/ *a.* & *pron.* diez.
tenant /'tɛnənt/ *n.* inquilino -na.
tend /tɛnd/ *v.* tender. **t. to,** atender.
tendency /'tɛndənsi/ *n.* tendencia *f.*
tender /'tɛndər/ *a.* **1.** tierno. —*v.* **2.** ofrecer.
tenderness /'tɛndərnɪs/ *n.* ternura *f.*
tennis /'tɛnɪs/ *n.* tenis *m.*
tennis court cancha de tenis, pista de tenis *f.*
tenor /'tɛnər/ *n.* tenor *m.*
tense /tɛns/ *a.* **1.** tenso. —*n.* **2.** *Gram.* tiempo *m.*
tent /tɛnt/ *n.* tienda, carpa *f.*
tenth /tɛnθ/ *a.* décimo.
term /tɜrm/ *n.* **1.** término; plazo *m.* —*v.* **2.** llamar.
terminal /'tɜrmənl̩/ *n.* terminal *f.*
terrace /'tɛrəs/ *n.* terraza *f.*
terrible /'tɛrəbəl/ *a.* terrible, espantoso; pésimo.
territory /'tɛrɪ,tɔri/ *n.* territorio *m.*
terror /'tɛrər/ *n.* terror, espanto, pavor *m.*
test /tɛst/ *n.* **1.** prueba *f.*; examen *m.* —*v.* **2.** probar; examinar.
testament /'tɛstəmənt/ *n.* testamento *m.*
testify /'tɛstə,fai/ *v.* atestiguar, testificar.
testimony /'tɛstə,mouni/ *n.* testimonio *m.*
test tube tubo de ensayo *m.*
text /tɛkst/ *n.* texto; tema *m.*
textbook /'tɛkst,bʊk/ *n.* libro de texto.
textile /'tɛkstail/ *a.* **1.** textil. —*n.* **2.** tejido *m.*
texture /'tɛkstʃər/ *n.* textura *f.*; tejido *m.*
than /ðæn, ðɛn; *unstressed* ðən, ən/ *conj.* que; de.
thank /θæŋk/ *v.* agradecer, dar gracias; **thanks, th. you,** gracias.
thankful /'θæŋkfəl/ *a.* agradecido; grato.
that /ðæt; *unstressed* ðət/ *a.* **1.** ese, aquel. —*dem. pron.* **2.** ése, aquél; eso, aquello. —*rel. pron.* & *conj.* **3.** que.
the /*stressed* ði; *unstressed before a consonant* ðə, *unstressed before a vowel* ði/ *art.* el, la, los, las; lo.
theater /'θiətər/ *n.* teatro *m.*
theft /θɛft/ *n.* robo *m.*
their /ðɛər; *unstressed* ðər/ *a.* su.
theirs /ðɛərz/ *pron.* suyo, de ellos.
them /ðɛm; *unstressed* ðəm, əm/ *pron.* ellos, ellas; los, las; les.
theme /θim/ *n.* tema; *Mus.* motivo *m.*
themselves /ðəm'sɛlvz, ,ðɛm-/ *pron.* sí, sí mismos -as. **they th.,** ellos mismos, ellas mismas. **with th.,** consigo.
then /ðɛn/ *adv.* entonces, después; pues.
thence /ðɛns/ *adv.* de allí.
theology /θi'ɒlədʒi/ *n.* teología *f.*
theory /'θiəri/ *n.* teoría *f.*
there /ðɛər; *unstressed* ðər/ *adv.* allí, allá, ahí. **there is, there are,** hay.
therefore /'ðɛər,fɔr/ *adv.* por lo tanto, por consiguiente.
thermometer /θər'mɒmɪtər/ *n.* termómetro *m.*
thermostat /'θɜrmə,stæt/ *n.* termostato *m.*
they /ðei/ *pron.* ellos, ellas.
thick /θɪk/ *a.* espeso, grueso, denso; torpe.
thicken /'θɪkən/ *v.* espesar, condensar.
thief /θif/ *n.* ladrón -na.
thigh /θai/ *n.* muslo *m.*
thimble /'θɪmbəl/ *n.* dedal *m.*
thin /θɪn/ *a.* **1.** delgado; raro; claro; escaso. —*v.* **2.** enrarecer; adelgazar.
thing /θɪŋ/ *n.* cosa *f.*
thingamabob /'θɪŋəmə,bɒb/ *n.* *Colloq.* chisme *m.*
think /θɪŋk/ *v.* pensar; creer.
thinker /'θɪŋkər/ *n.* pensador -ra.
third /θɜrd/ *a.* tercero.
Third World Tercer Mundo *m.*
thirst /θɜrst/ *n.* sed *f.*
thirsty /'θɜrsti/ *a.* sediento. **to be th.,** tener sed.
thirteen /'θɜr'tin/ *a.* & *pron.* trece.
thirty /'θɜrti/ *a.* & *pron.* treinta.
this /ðɪs/ *a.* **1.** este. —*pron.* **2.** éste; esto.
thoracic cage /θɔ'ræsɪk/ *n.* caja torácica *f.*
thorn /θɔrn/ *n.* espina *f.*
thorough /'θɜrou/ *a.* completo; cuidadoso.
though /ðou/ *adv.* **1.** sin embargo. —*conj.* **2.** aunque. **as th.,** como si.
thought /θɔt/ *n.* pensamiento *m.*
thoughtful /'θɔtfəl/ *a.* pensativo; considerado.
thousand /'θauzənd/ *a.* & *pron.* mil.
thread /θrɛd/ *n.* hilo *m.*; (of screw) rosca *f.*
threat /θrɛt/ *n.* amenaza *f.*
threaten /'θrɛtn̩/ *v.* amenazar.
three /θri/ *a.* & *pron.* tres.
thrift /θrɪft/ *n.* economía, frugalidad *f.*
thrill /θrɪl/ *n.* **1.** emoción *f.* —*v.* **2.** emocionar.
thrive /θraiv/ *v.* prosperar.
throat /θrout/ *n.* garganta *f.*
throne /θroun/ *n.* trono *m.*
through /θru/ *prep.* **1.** por; a través de; por medio de. —*a.* **2.** continuo. **th. train,** tren directo. **to be th.,** haber terminado.
throughout /θru'aut/ *prep.* **1.** por todo, durante todo. —*adv.* **2.** en todas partes; completamente.
throw /θrou/ *n.* **1.** tiro *m.* —*v.* **2.** tirar, lanzar. **th. away,** arrojar. **th. out,** echar.
thrust /θrʌst/ *n.* **1.** lanzada *f.* —*v.* **2.** empujar.
thumb /θʌm/ *n.* dedo pulgar, pulgar *m.*
thumbtack /'θʌm,tæk/ *n.* chincheta *f.*
thunder /'θʌndər/ *n.* **1.** trueno *m.* —*v.* **2.** tronar.
Thursday /'θɜrzdei/ *n.* jueves *m.*
thus /ðʌs/ *adv.* así, de este modo.
thwart /θwɔrt/ *v.* frustrar.
ticket /'tɪkɪt/ *n.* billete, boleto *m.* **t. window,** taquilla *f.* **round trip t.,** billete de ida y vuelta.
tickle /'tɪkəl/ *n.* **1.** cosquilla *f.* —*v.* **2.** hacer cosquillas a.
ticklish /'tɪklɪʃ/ *a.* cosquilloso.
tide /taid/ *n.* marea *f.*
tidy /'taidi/ *a.* **1.** limpio, ordenado. —*v.* **2.** poner en orden.
tie /tai/ *n.* **1.** corbata *f.*; lazo; (game) empate *m.* —*v.* **2.** atar; anudar.
tier /'tɪər/ *n.* hilera *f.*
tiger /'taigər/ *n.* tigre *m.*
tight /tait/ *a.* apretado; tacaño.
tighten /'taitn̩/ *v.* estrechar, apretar.
tile /tail/ *n.* teja *f.*; azulejo *m.*
till /tɪl/ *prep.* **1.** hasta. —*conj.* **2.** hasta que. —*n.* **3.** cajón *m.* —*v.* **4.** cultivar, labrar.
tilt /tɪlt/ *n.* **1.** inclinación; justa *f.* —*v.* **2.** inclinar; justar.
timber /'tɪmbər/ *n.* madera *f.*; (beam) madero *m.*
time /taim/ *n.* tiempo *m.*; vez *f.*; (of day) hora *f.*; *v.* *cronometrar.*
timetable /'taim,teibəl/ *n.* horario, itinerario *m.*
time zone huso horario *m.*
timid /'tɪmɪd/ *a.* tímido.
timidity /tɪ'mɪdɪti/ *n.* timidez *f.*
tin /tɪn/ *n.* estaño *m.*; hojalata *f.* **t. can,** lata *f.*
tin foil papel de estaño *m.*
tint /tɪnt/ *n.* **1.** tinte *m.* —*v.* **2.** teñir.
tiny /'taini/ *a.* chiquito, pequeñito.
tip /tɪp/ *n.* **1.** punta; propina *f.* —*v.* **2.** inclinar; dar propina a.
tire /taiᵊr/ *n.* **1.** llanta, goma *f.*, neumático *m.* —*v.* **2.** cansar.
tired /taiᵊrd/ *a.* cansado.
tissue /'tɪʃu/ *n.* tejido *m.* **t. paper,** papel de seda.
title /'taitl̩/ *n.* **1.** título *m.* —*v.* **2.** titular.
to /tu; *unstressed* tʊ, tə/ *prep.* a; para.
toast /toust/ *n.* **1.** tostada *f.*; (drink) brindis *m.* —*v.* **2.** tostar; brindar.
toaster /'toustər/ *n.* tostador *m.*
tobacco /tə'bækou/ *n.* tabaco *m.* **t. shop,** tabaquería *f.*
toboggan /tə'bɒgən/ *n.* tobogán *m.*
today /tə'dei/ *adv.* hoy.
toe /tou/ *n.* dedo del pie.
together /tə'gɛðər/ *a.* **1.** juntos. —*adv.* **2.** juntamente.
toil /tɔil/ *n.* **1.** trabajo *m.* —*v.* **2.** afanarse.
toilet /'tɔilɪt/ *n.* tocado; excusado, retrete *m.* **t. paper,** papel higiénico.
token /'toukən/ *n.* señal *f.*
tolerance /'tɒlərəns/ *n.* tolerancia *f.*
tolerate /'tɒlə,reit/ *v.* tolerar.
toll-free number /'toul 'fri/ teléfono gratuito *m.*
tomato /tə'meitou/ *n.* tomate *m.*
tomb /tum/ *n.* tumba *f.*
tomorrow /tə'mɔrou/ *adv.* mañana. **day after t.,** pasado mañana.
ton /tʌn/ *n.* tonelada *f.*
tone /toun/ *n.* tono *m.*
tongue /tʌŋ/ *n.* lengua *f.*
tonic /'tɒnɪk/ *n.* tónico *m.*
tonight /tə'nait/ *adv.* esta noche.
tonsil /'tɒnsəl/ *n.* amígdala *f.*
too /tu/ *adv.* también. **t. much,** demasiado. **t. many,** demasiados.
tool /tul/ *n.* herramienta *f.*
tooth /tuθ/ *n.* diente *m.*; (back) muela *f.*
toothache /'tuθ,eik/ *n.* dolor de muela.
toothbrush /'tuθ,brʌʃ/ *n.* cepillo de dientes.
toothpaste /'tuθ,peist/ *n.* crema dentífrica, pasta dentífrica.
top /tɒp/ *n.* **1.** parte de arriba. —*v.* **2.** cubrir; sobrepasar.
topic /'tɒpɪk/ *n.* *S.A.* tópico *m.*
topical /'tɒpɪkəl/ *a.* tópico.
torch /tɔrtʃ/ *n.* antorcha *f.*
torment /*n.* 'tɔrmɛnt; *v.* tɔr'mɛnt/ *n.* **1.** tormento *m.* —*v.* **2.** atormentar.
torrent /'tɔrənt/ *n.* torrente *m.*
torture /'tɔrtʃər/ *n.* **1.** tortura *f.* —*v.* **2.** torturar.
toss /tɔs/ *v.* tirar; agitar.
total /'toutl̩/ *a.* **1.** total, entero. —*n.* **2.** total *m.*
touch /tʌtʃ/ *n.* **1.** tacto *m.* **in t.,** en comunicación. —*v.* **2.** tocar; conmover.
tough /tʌf/ *a.* tosco; tieso; fuerte.
tour /tʊr/ *n.* **1.** viaje *m.* —*v.* **2.** viajar.
tourist /'tʊrɪst/ *n.* turista *m.* & *f.* *a.* turístico.
tournament /'tʊrnəmənt/ *n.* torneo *m.*
tow /tou/ *n.* **1.** remolque *m.* —*v.* **2.** remolcar.
toward /tɔrd, tə'wɔrd/ *prep.* hacia.
towel /'tauəl/ *n.* toalla *f.*
tower /'tauər/ *n.* torre *f.*
town /taun/ *n.* pueblo *m.*
town meeting cabildo abierto *m.*
tow truck grúa *f.*
toy /tɔi/ *n.* **1.** juguete *m.* —*v.* **2.** jugar.
trace /treis/ *n.* **1.** vestigio; rastro *m.* —*v.* **2.** trazar; rastrear; investigar.
track /træk/ *n.* **1.** huella, pista *f.* **race t.,** hipódromo *m.* —*v.* **2.** rastrear.
tract /trækt/ *n.* trecho; tracto *m.*
tractor /'træktər/ *n.* tractor *m.*
trade /treid/ *n.* **1.** comercio, negocio; oficio; canje *m.* —*v.* **2.** comerciar, negociar; cambiar.
trader /'treidər/ *n.* comerciante *m.*
tradition /trə'dɪʃən/ *n.* tradición *f.*
traditional /trə'dɪʃənl̩/ *a.* tradicional.
traffic /'træfɪk/ *n.* **1.** tráfico *m.* —*v.* **2.** traficar.
traffic jam atasco, embotellamiento *m.*
traffic light semáforo *m.*
tragedy /'trædʒɪdi/ *n.* tragedia *f.*
tragic /'trædʒɪk/ *a.* trágico.
trail /treil/ *n.* **1.** sendero; rastro *m.* —*v.* **2.** rastrear; arrastrar.
train /trein/ *n.* **1.** tren *m.* —*v.* **2.** enseñar; disciplinar; (sport) entrenarse.
traitor /'treitər/ *n.* traidor -ora.
tramp /træmp/ *n.* **1.** caminata *f.*; vagabundo *m.* —*v.* **2.** patear.
tranquil /'træŋkwɪl/ *a.* tranquilo.
tranquilizer /'træŋkwə,laizər/ *n.* tranquilizante *m.*
tranquillity /træŋ'kwɪlɪti/ *n.* tranquilidad *f.*
transaction /træn'sækʃən/ *n.* transacción *f.*
transfer /*n.* 'trænsfər, *v.* træns'fɜr/ *n.* **1.** traslado *m.*; boleto de transbordo. —*v.* **2.** trasladar, transferir.
transform /træns'fɔrm/ *v.* transformar.

transfusion /træns'fyuʒən/ n. transfusión f.

transistor /træn'zɪstər/ n. transistor m.

transition /træn'zɪʃən/ n. transición f.

translate /træns'leit/ v. traducir.

translation /træns'leiʃən/ n. traducción f.

transmit /træns'mɪt/ v. transmitir.

transparent /træns'pɛərənt/ a. transparente.

transport /n. 'trænspɔrt, v. træns-'pɔrt/ n. **1.** transporte m. —v. **2.** transportar.

transportation /,trænspər'teiʃən/ n. transporte m.

transsexual /træns'sɛkʃuəl/ a. & n. transexual m. & f.

transvestite /træns'vɛstait/ n. travestí m. & f.

trap /træp/ n. **1.** trampa f. —v. **2.** atrapar.

trash /træʃ/ n. desecho m.; basura f.

trash can cubo de la basura m.

travel /'trævəl/ n. **1.** tráfico m.; (pl.) viajes m.pl. —v. **2.** viajar.

travel agency agencia de viajes f.

traveler /'trævələr/ n. viajero -ra.

traveler's check /'trævələrz/ cheque de viaje m.

tray /trei/ n. bandeja f.

tread /trɛd/ n. **1.** pisada f.; (of a tire) cubierta f. —v. **2.** pisar.

treason /'trizən/ n. traición f.

treasure /'trɛʒər/ n. tesoro m.

treasurer /'trɛʒərər/ n. tesorero -ra.

treasury /'trɛʒəri/ n. tesorería f.

treat /trit/ v. tratar; convidar.

treatment /'tritmənt/ n. trato, tratamiento m.

treaty /'triti/ n. tratado, pacto m.

tree /tri/ n. árbol m.

tremble /'trɛmbəl/ v. temblar.

tremendous /trɪ'mɛndəs/ a. tremendo.

trench /trɛntʃ/ n. foso m.; Mil. trinchera f.

trend /trɛnd/ n. **1.** tendencia f. —v. **2.** tender.

trespass /'trɛspəs, -pæs/ v. traspasar; violar.

triage /tri'ɑʒ/ n. clasificación de los heridos después del combate.

trial /'traiəl/ n. prueba f.; Leg. proceso, juicio m.

triangle /'trai,æŋgəl/ n. triángulo m.

tribulation /,trɪbyə'leiʃən/ n. tribulación f.

tributary /'trɪbyə,tɛri/ a. & n. tributario m.

tribute /'trɪbyut/ n. tributo m.

trick /trɪk/ n. **1.** engaño m.; maña f.; (cards) baza f. —v. **2.** engañar.

trifle /'traifəl/ n. **1.** pequeñez f. —v. **2.** juguetear.

trigger /'trɪgər/ n. gatillo m.

trim /trɪm/ a. **1.** ajustado; acicalado. —n. **2.** adorno m. —v. **3.** adornar; ajustar; cortar un poco.

trinket /'trɪŋkɪt/ n. bagatela, chucheria f.

trip /trɪp/ n. **1.** viaje m. —v. **2.** tropezar.

triple /'trɪpəl/ a. **1.** triple —v. **2.** triplicar.

tripod /'traipɒd/ n. trípode m.

trite /trait/ a. banal.

triumph /'traiəmf/ n. **1.** triunfo m. —v. **2.** triunfar.

triumphant /trai'ʌmfənt/ a. triunfante.

trivial /'trɪviəl/ a. trivial.

trolley /'trɒli/ n. tranvía m.

trombone /trɒm'boun/ n. trombón m.

troop /trup/ n. tropa f.

trophy /'troufi/ n. trofeo m.

tropical /'trɒpɪkəl/ a. trópico.

tropics /'trɒpɪks/ n. trópico m.

trot /trɒt/ n. **1.** trote m. —v. **2.** trotar.

trouble /'trʌbəl/ n. **1.** apuro m.; con-goja; aflicción f. —v. **2.** molestar; afligir.

troublesome /'trʌbəlsəm/ a. penoso, molesto.

trough /trɒf/ n. artesa f.

trousers /'trauzərz/ n. pantalones, calzones m.pl.

trout /traut/ n. trucha f.

truce /trus/ n. tregua f.

truck /trʌk/ n. camión m.

true /tru/ a. verdadero, cierto, verdad.

truffle /'trʌfəl/ n. trufa f.

trumpet /'trʌmpɪt/ n. trompeta, trompa f.

trunk /trʌŋk/ n. baúl m.; (of a tree) tronco m.

trust /trʌst/ n. **1.** confianza f. —v. **2.** confiar.

trustworthy /'trʌst,wɜrði/ a. digno de confianza.

truth /truθ/ n. verdad f.

truthful /'truθfəl/ a. veraz.

try /trai/ n. **1.** prueba f.; ensayo m. —v. **2.** tratar; probar; ensayar; Leg. juzgar. **t. on**, probarse.

T-shirt /'ti,ʃərt/ n. camiseta f.

tub /tʌb/ n. tina f.

tube /tub/ n. tubo m.

tuberculosis /tu,bɜrkyə'lousɪs/ n. tuberculosis f.

tuck /tʌk/ n. **1.** recogido m. —v. **2.** recoger.

Tuesday /'tuzdei/ n. martes m.

tug /tʌg/ n. **1.** tirada f.; (boat) remolcador m. —v. **2.** tirar de.

tuition /tu'ɪʃən/ n. matrícula, colegiatura f.

tumble /'tʌmbəl/ n. **1.** caída f. —v. **2.** caer, tumbar; voltear.

tumult /'tumʌlt/ n. tumulto, alboroto m.

tuna /'tʌni/ n. atún m.

tune /tun/ n. **1.** tono m.; melodía, canción f. —v. **2.** templar.

tunnel /'tʌnl/ n. túnel m.

turf /tɜrf/ n. césped m.

Turkey /'tɜrki/ n. Turquía f.

Turkish /'tɜrkɪʃ/ a. turco.

turmoil /'tɜrmɔil/ n. disturbio m.

turn /tɜrn/ n. **1.** vuelta f.; giro; turno m. —v. **2.** volver, tornear, girar; **t. into**, transformar. **t. around**, volverse. **t. on**, encender; abrir. **t. off, t. out**, apagar.

turnip /'tɜrnɪp/ n. nabo m.

turret /'tɜrɪt/ n. torrecilla f.

turtle /'tɜrtl/ n. tortuga f.

turtleneck sweater /'tɜrtl,nɛk/ jersey de cuello alto m.

tutor /'tutər/ n. **1.** tutor -ra. —v. **2.** enseñar.

tweezers /'twizərz/ n.pl. pinzas f.pl.

twelve /twɛlv/ a. & pron. doce.

twenty /'twɛnti/ a. & pron. veinte.

twice /twais/ adv. dos veces.

twig /twɪg/ n. varita; ramita f.; vástago m.

twilight /'twai,lait/ n. crepúsculo m.

twin /twɪn/ n. gemelo -la.

twine /twain/ n. **1.** guita f. —v. **2.** torcer.

twinkle /'twɪŋkəl/ v. centellear.

twist /twɪst/ v. torcer.

two /tu/ a. & pron. dos.

type /taip/ n. **1.** tipo m. —v. **2.** escribir a máquina.

typewriter /'taip,raitər/ n. máquina de escribir.

typhoid fever /'taifoid/ fiebre tifoidea f.

typical /'tɪpɪkəl/ a. típico.

typist /'taipɪst/ n. mecanógrafo -fa.

tyranny /'tɪrəni/ n. tiranía f.

tyrant /'tairənt/ n. tirano -na.

U

udder /'ʌdər/ n. ubre f.

UFO abbr. (unidentified flying object) OVNI m. (objeto volador no identificado).

ugly /'ʌgli/ a. feo.

Ukraine /yu'krein/ n. Ucrania f.

Ukrainian /yu'kreiniən/ a. & n. ucranio.

ulcer /'ʌlsər/ n. úlcera f.

ulterior /ʌl'tɪəriər/ a. ulterior.

ultimate /'ʌltəmɪt/ a. último.

ultrasonic /,ʌltrə'sɒnɪk/ a. ultrasónico.

umbrella /ʌm'brɛlə/ n. paraguas m. **sun u.**, quitasol m.

umpire /'ʌmpaiər/ n. árbitro m.

unable /ʌn'eibəl/ a. incapaz. **to be u.**, no poder.

unanimous /yu'nænəməs/ a. unánime.

uncertain /ʌn'sɜrtn/ a. incierto, inseguro.

uncle /'ʌŋkəl/ n. tío m.

unconscious /ʌn'kɒnʃəs/ a. inconsciente; desmayado.

uncover /ʌn'kʌvər/ v. descubrir.

undeniable /,ʌndɪ'naiəbəl/ a. innegable.

under /'ʌndər/ adv. **1.** debajo, abajo. —prep. **2.** bajo, debajo de.

underestimate /,ʌndər'ɛstə,meit/ v. menospreciar; subestimar.

undergo /,ʌndər'gou/ v. sufrir.

underground /'ʌndər,graund/ a. subterráneo; clandestino.

underline /'ʌndər,lain/ v. subrayar.

underneath /,ʌndər'niθ/ adv. **1.** por debajo. —prep. **2.** debajo de.

undershirt /'ʌndər,ʃərt/ n. camiseta f.

understand /,ʌndər'stænd/ v. entender, comprender.

undertake /,ʌndər'teik/ v. emprender.

underwear /'ʌndər,wɛər/ n. ropa interior.

undo /ʌn'du/ v. deshacer; desatar.

undress /ʌn'drɛs/ v. desnudar, desvestir.

uneasy /ʌn'izi/ a. inquieto.

uneven /ʌn'ivən/ a. desigual.

unexpected /,ʌnɪk'spɛktɪd/ a. inesperado.

unfair /ʌn'fɛər/ a. injusto.

unfit /ʌn'fɪt/ a. incapaz; inadecuado.

unfold /ʌn'fould/ v. desplegar; revelar.

unforgettable /,ʌnfər'gɛtəbəl/ a. inolvidable.

unfortunate /ʌn'fɔrtʃənɪt/ a. desafortunado, desgraciado.

unfurnished /ʌn'fɜrnɪʃt/ a. desamueblado.

unhappy /ʌn'hæpi/ a. infeliz.

uniform /'yunə,fɔrm/ a. & n. uniforme m.

unify /'yunə,fai/ v. unificar.

union /'yunyən/ n. unión f. **labor u.**, sindicato de obreros.

unique /yu'nik/ a. único.

unisex /'yunə,sɛks/ a. unisex.

unit /'yunɪt/ n. unidad f.

unite /yu'nait/ v. unir.

United Nations /yu'naitɪd 'neiʃənz/ Naciones Unidas f.pl.

United States /yu'naitɪd 'steits/ Estados Unidos m.pl.

unity /'yunɪti/ n. unidad f.

universal /,yunə'vɜrsəl/ a. universal.

universe /'yunə,vɜrs/ n. universo m.

university /,yunə'vɜrsɪti/ n. universidad f.

unleaded /ʌn'lɛdɪd/ a. sin plomo.

unless /ʌn'lɛs/ conj. a menos que, si no es que.

unlike /ʌn'laik/ a. disímil.

unload /ʌn'loud/ v. descargar.

unlock /ʌn'lɒk/ v. abrir.

unplug /ʌn'plʌg/ v. desenchufar.

unpopular /ʌn'pɒpyələr/ a. impopular.

unreasonable /ʌn'rizənəbəl/ a. desrazonable.

unscrew /ʌn'skru/ v. desatornillar.

untie /ʌn'tai/ v. desatar; soltar.

until /ʌn'tɪl/ prep. **1.** hasta. —conj. **2.** hasta que.

Ukraine — **unusual** /ʌn'yuʒuəl/ a. raro, inusitado.

up /ʌp/ adv. **1.** arriba. —prep. **2. u. the street,** etc. calle arriba, etc.

uphold /ʌp'hould/ v. apoyar; defender.

upholster /ʌp'houlstər, ə'poul-/ v. entapizar.

upload /'ʌp,loud/ n. **1.** ascenso de archivos m. —v. **2.** subir, cargar.

upon /ə'pɒn/ prep. sobre, encima de.

upper /'ʌpər/ a. superior.

upper-case letter /'ʌpər 'keis/ mayúscula f.

upright /'ʌp,rait/ a. derecho, recto.

upriver /'ʌp'rɪvər/ adv. río arriba.

uproar /'ʌp,rɔr/ n. alboroto, tumulto m.

upset /n. 'ʌp,sɛt; v. ʌp'sɛt/ n. **1.** trastorno m. —v. **2.** trastornar.

upsetting /ʌp'sɛtɪŋ/ a. inquietante.

upstream /'ʌp'strim/ adv. aguas arriba, contra la corriente, río arriba.

uptight /'ʌp'tait/ a. (psicológicamente) tenso, tieso.

upward /'ʌpwərd/ adv. hacia arriba.

urge /ɜrdʒ/ n. **1.** deseo m. —v. **2.** instar.

urgency /'ɜrdʒənsi/ n. urgencia f.

urgent /'ɜrdʒənt/ a. urgente. **to be u.**, urgir.

us /ʌs/ pron. nosotros -as; nos.

use /n. yus; v. yuz/ n. **1.** uso m. —v. **2.** usar, emplear. **u. up**, gastar, agotar. **be used to,** estar acostumbrado a.

useful /'yusfəl/ a. útil.

useless /'yuslɪs/ a. inútil, inservible.

user-friendly /'yuzər 'frɛndli/ a. amigable.

username /'yuzər,neim/ n. nombre de usuario m.

usher /'ʌʃər/ n. **1.** acomodador -ora. —v. **2.** introducir.

usual /'yuʒuəl/ a. usual.

utensil /yu'tɛnsəl/ n. utensilio m.

utmost /'ʌt,moust/ a. sumo, extremo.

utter /'ʌtər/ a. **1.** completo. —v. **2.** proferir; dar.

utterance /'ʌtərəns/ n. expresión f.

V

vacancy /'veikənsi/ n. vacante f.

vacant /'veikənt/ a. desocupado, libre.

vacation /vei'keiʃən/ n. vacaciones f.pl.

vaccinate /'væksə,neit/ v. vacunar.

vacuum /'vækyum/ n. vacuo, vacío m. **v. cleaner,** aspiradora f.

vagrant /'veigrənt/ a. & n. vagabundo- da.

vague /veig/ a. vago.

vain /vein/ a. vano; vanidoso. **in v.,** en vano.

valiant /'vælyənt/ a. valiente.

valid /'vælɪd/ a. válido.

valley /'væli/ n. valle m.

valor /'vælər/ n. valor m.; valentía f.

valuable /'vælyuəbəl/ a. valioso. **to be v.,** valer mucho.

value /'vælyu/ n. **1.** valor, importe m. —v. **2.** valorar; estimar.

van /væn/ n. furgoneta f.

vandal /'vændl/ n. vándalo m.

vandalism /'vændl,ɪzəm/ n. vandalismo m.

vanish /'vænɪʃ/ v. desaparecer.

vanity /'vænɪti/ n. vanidad f. **v. case,** polvera f.

vanquish /'væŋkwɪʃ/ v. vencer.

vapor /'veipər/ n. vapor m.

variation /,vɛəri'eiʃən/ n. variación f.

varicose vein /'væri,kous/ variz f.

variety /və'raiɪti/ n. variedad f.

various /'vɛəriəs/ a. varios; diversos.

varnish /'vɑrnɪʃ/ n. **1.** barniz m. —v. **2.** barnizar.

vary /'vɛəri/ v. variar; cambiar.

vase /veis, veiz, vɑz/ n. florero; jarrón m.

vasectomy /væ'sɛktəmi/ n. vasectomía f.

vassal /'væsəl/ n. vasallo m.

vast /væst/ a. vasto.

vat /væt/ n. tina f., tanque m.

VAT /væt/ n. IVA (impuesto sobre el valor añadido).

vault /vɔlt/ n. bóveda f.

vegetable /'vɛdʒtəbəl/ a. & n. vegetal m.; (pl.) legumbres, verduras f.pl.

vehement /'viəmənt/ a. vehemente.

vehicle /'viːɪkəl or, sometimes, 'vihɪ-/ n. vehículo m.

veil /veil/ n. **1.** velo m. —v. **2.** velar.

vein /vein/ n. vena f.

velocity /və'lɒsɪti/ n. velocidad f.

velvet /'vɛlvɪt/ n. terciopelo m.

Venetian /və'niʃən/ a. & n. veneciano.

vengeance /'vɛndʒəns/ n. venganza f.

Venice /'vɛnɪs/ n. Venecia f.

vent /vɛnt/ n. apertura f.

ventilate /'vɛntḷ,eit/ v. ventilar.

venture /'vɛntʃər/ n. ventura f.

verb /vɜrb/ n. verbo m.

verbose /vər'bous/ a. verboso.

verdict /'vɜrdɪkt/ n. veredicto, fallo m.

verge /vɜrdʒ/ n. borde m.

verify /'vɛrə,fai/ v. verificar.

versatile /'vɜrsətḷ/ a. versátil.

verse /vɜrs/ n. verso m.

version /'vɜrʒən/ n. versión f.

vertical /'vɜrtɪkəl/ a. vertical.

very /'vɛri/ a. **1.** mismo. —adv. **2.** muy.

vessel /'vɛsəl/ n. vasija f.; barco m.

vest /vɛst/ n. chaleco m.

veteran /'vɛtərən/ a. & n. veterano -na.

veto /'vitou/ n. veto m.

vex /vɛks/ v. molestar.

via /'vaiə, 'viə/ prep. por la vía de; por.

viaduct /'vaiə,dʌkt/ n. viaducto m.

vibrate /'vaibreit/ v. vibrar.

vibration /vai'breiʃən/ n. vibración f.

vice /vais/ n. vicio m.

vicinity /vɪ'sɪnɪti/ n. vecindad f.

vicious /'vɪʃəs/ a. vicioso.

victim /'vɪktəm/ n. víctima f.

victor /'vɪktər/ n. vencedor -ora.

victorious /vɪk'tɔriəs/ a. victorioso.

victory /'vɪktəri/ n. victoria f.

video camera /'vɪdi,ou/ videocámara f.

videoconference /'vɪdiou,kɒnfərəns/ videoconferencia f.

videodisc /'vɪdiou,dɪsk/ n. videodisco m.

video game /'vɪdi,ou/ videojuego m.

videotape /'vɪdiou,teip/ n. vídeo m., magnetoscopio m.

view /vyu/ n. **1.** vista f. —v. **2.** ver.

viewpoint /'vyu,pɔint/ n. punto de vista m.

vigil /'vɪdʒəl/ n. vigilia, vela f.

vigilant /'vɪdʒələnt/ a. vigilante.

vigor /'vɪgər/ n. vigor m.

vile /vail/ a. vil, bajo.

village /'vɪlɪdʒ/ n. aldea f.

villain /'vɪlən/ n. malvado -da.

vindicate /'vɪndɪ,keit/ v. vindicar.

vine /vain/ n. parra, vid f.

vinegar /'vɪnɪgər/ n. vinagre m.

vintage /'vɪntɪdʒ/ n. vendimia f.

violate /'vaiə,leit/ v. violar.

violation /,vaiə'leiʃən/ n. violación f.

violence /'vaiələns/ n. violencia f.

violent /'vaiələnt/ a. violento.

violin /,vaiə'lɪn/ n. violín m.

virgin /'vɜrdʒɪn/ n. virgen f.

virile /'vɪrəl/ a. viril.

virtual /'vɜrtʃuəl/ a. virtual.

virtual memory memoria virtual f.

virtual reality realidad virtual f.

virtue /'vɜrtʃu/ n. virtud f.

virtuous /'vɜrtʃuəs/ a. virtuoso.

virus /'vairəs/ n. virus m.

visa /'vizə/ n. visa f.

visible /'vɪzəbəl/ a. visible.

vision /'vɪʒən/ n. visión f.

visit /'vɪzɪt/ n. **1.** visita f. —v. **2.** visitar.

visitor /'vɪzɪtər/ n. visitante m. & f.

visual /'vɪʒuəl/ a. visual.

vital /'vaitḷ/ a. vital.

vitality /vai'tælɪti/ n. vitalidad, energía vital f.

vitamin /'vaitəmɪn/ n. vitamina f.

vivacious /vɪ'veiʃəs, vai-/ a. vivaz.

vivid /'vɪvɪd/ a. vivo; gráfico.

vocabulary /vou'kæbyə,lɛri/ n. vocabulario m.

vocal /'voukəl/ a. vocal.

vodka /'vɒdkə/ n. vodca m.

vogue /voug/ n. boga; moda f. **be in vogue** estilarse.

voice /vɔis/ n. **1.** voz f. —v. **2.** expresar.

voice mail correo de voz m.

voice recognition reconocimiento de voz m.

void /vɔid/ a. **1.** vacío. —n. **2.** vacío m. —v. **3.** invalidar.

voltage /'voultɪdʒ/ n. voltaje m.

volume /'vɒlyum/ n. volumen; tomo m.

voluntary /'vɒlən,tɛri/ a. voluntario.

volunteer /,vɒlən'tɪər/ n. **1.** voluntario -ria. —v. **2.** ofrecerse.

vomit /'vɒmɪt/ v. vomitar.

vote /vout/ n. **1.** voto m. —v. **2.** votar.

voter /'voutər/ n. votante m. & f.

vouch /vautʃ/ v. **v. for,** garantizar.

vow /vau/ n. **1.** voto m. —v. **2.** jurar.

vowel /'vauəl/ n. vocal f.

voyage /'vɔiidʒ/ n. viaje m.

vulgar /'vʌlgər/ a. vulgar; común; soez.

vulnerable /'vʌlnərəbəl/ a. vulnerable.

W

wade /weid/ v. vadear.

wag /wæg/ v. menear.

wage /weidʒ/ n. **1.** (pl.) sueldo, salario m. —v. **2. w. war,** hacer guerra.

wagon /'wægən/ n. carreta f.

wail /weil/ n. **1.** lamento, gemido m. —v. **2.** lamentar, gemir.

waist /weist/ n. cintura f.

wait /weit/ n. **1.** espera f. —v. **2.** esperar. **w. for,** esperar. **w. on,** atender.

waiter /'weitər/ n. **waitress** n. camarero -ra.

waiting room /'weitɪŋ/ sala de espera.

wake /weik/ v. **w. up,** despertar.

walk /wɔk/ n. **1.** paseo m.; vuelta; caminata f.; modo de andar. —v. **2.** andar; caminar; ir a pie.

wall /wɔl/ n. pared; muralla f.

wallcovering /'wɔl,kʌvərɪŋ/ n. tapizado de pared m.

wallet /'wɒlɪt/ n. cartera f.

wallpaper /'wɔl,peipər/ n. **1.** empapelado m. —v. **2.** empapelar.

walnut /'wɔl,nʌt/ n. nuez f.

waltz /wɔlts/ n. vals m.

wander /'wɒndər/ v. vagar.

want /wɒnt/ n. **1.** necesidad f. —v. **2.** querer.

war /wɔr/ n. guerra f.

ward /wɔrd/ n. **1.** Pol. barrio m.; (hospital) cuadra f. —v. **2. w. off,** parar.

warehouse /'wɛər,haus/ n. almacén m.

wares /wɛərz/ n. mercancías f.pl.

warlike /'wɔr,laik/ a. belicoso.

warm /wɔrm/ a. **1.** caliente; Fig. caluroso. **to be w.,** tener calor; (weather) hacer calor. —v. **2.** calentar.

warmth /wɔrmθ/ n. calor m.

warn /wɔrn/ v. advertir.

warning /'wɔrnɪŋ/ n. aviso m.

warp /wɔrp/ v. alabear.

warrant /'wɔrənt, 'wɒr-/ v. justificar.

warrior /'wɔriər/ n. guerrero -ra.

warship /'wɔr,ʃɪp/ n. navío de guerra, buque de guerra m.

wash /wɒʃ/ v. lavar.

washing machine /'wɒʃɪŋ/ máquina de lavar, lavadora f.

wasp /wɒsp/ n. avispa f.

waste /weist/ n. **1.** gasto m.; desechos m.pl. —v. **2.** gastar; perder.

watch /wɒtʃ/ n. **1.** reloj m.; Mil. guardia f. —v. **2.** observar, mirar. **w. for,** esperar. **w. out for,** tener cuidado con. **w. over,** guardar; velar por.

watchful /'wɒtʃfəl/ a. desvelado.

watchmaker /'wɒtʃ,meikər/ n. relojero -ra.

watchman /'wɒtʃmən/ n. sereno m.

water /'wɔtər/ n. **1.** agua f. **w. color,** acuarela f. —v. **2.** aguar.

waterbed /'wɔtər,bɛd/ n. cama de agua f.

waterfall /'wɔtər,fɔl/ n. catarata f.

watering can /'wɔtərɪŋ/ regadera f.

waterproof /'wɔtər,pruf/ a. impermeable.

wave /weiv/ n. **1.** onda; ola f. —v. **2.** ondear; agitar; hacer señas.

waver /'weivər/ v. vacilar.

wax /wæks/ n. **1.** cera f. —v. **2.** encerar.

way /wei/ n. camino; modo m., manera f. **in a w.,** hasta cierto punto. **a long w.,** muy lejos. **by the w.,** a propósito. **this w.,** por aquí. **that w.,** por allí. **which w.,** por dónde.

we /wi/ pron. nosotros -as.

weak /wik/ a. débil.

weaken /'wikən/ v. debilitar.

weakness /'wiknɪs/ n. debilidad f.

wealth /wɛlθ/ n. riqueza f.

wealthy /'wɛlθi/ a. adinerado.

wean /win/ v. destetar.

weapon /'wɛpən/ n. arma f.

wear /wɛər/ n. **1.** uso; desgaste m.; (clothes) ropa f. —v. **2.** usar, llevar. **w. out,** gastar; cansar.

weary /'wiəri/ a. cansado, rendido.

weather /'wɛðər/ n. tiempo m.

weave /wiv/ v. tejer.

weaver /'wivər/ n. tejedor -ra.

web /wɛb/ n. tela f.

Web /wɛb/ n. (Internet) malla f., telaraña f., web m.

wedding /'wɛdɪŋ/ n. boda f.

wedge /wɛdʒ/ n. cuña f.

Wednesday /'wɛnzdei/ n. miércoles m.

weed /wid/ n. maleza f.

week /wik/ n. semana f.

weekday /'wik,dei/ n. día de trabajo.

weekend /'wik,ɛnd/ n. fin de semana.

weekly /'wikli/ a. semanal.

weep /wip/ v. llorar.

weigh /wei/ v. pesar.

weight /weit/ n. peso m.

weightless /'weitlɪs/ v. ingrávido.

weightlessness /'weitlɪsnɪs/ n. ingravidez f.

weird /wiərd/ a. misterioso, extraño.

welcome /'wɛlkəm/ a. **1.** bienvenido. **you're w.,** de nada, no hay de qué. —n. **2.** acogida, bienvenida f. —v. **3.** acoger, recibir bien.

welfare /'wɛl,fɛər/ n. bienestar m.

well /wɛl/ a. **1.** sano, bueno. —adv. **2.** bien; pues. —n. **3.** pozo m.

well-done /'wɛl 'dʌn/ a. (food) bien cocido.

well-known /'wɛl 'noun/ a. bien conocido.

well-mannered /'wɛl 'mænərd/ a. educado.

west /wɛst/ n. oeste, occidente m.

western /'wɛstərn/ a. occidental.

westward /'wɛstwərd/ adv. hacia el oeste.

wet /wɛt/ a. **1.** mojado. **to get w.,** mojarse. —v. **2.** mojar.

whale /weil/ n. ballena f.

what /wʌt; unstressed wət/ a. **1.** qué; cuál. —interrog. pron. **2.** qué. —rel. pron. **3.** lo que.

whatever /wʌt'ɛvər/ a. **1.** cualquier. —pron. **2.** lo que; todo lo que.

wheat /wit/ n. trigo m.

wheel /wil/ n. rueda f. **steering w.,** volante m.

when /wɛn; unstressed wən/ adv. **1.** cuándo. —conj. **2.** cuando.

whenever /wɛn'ɛvər/ conj. siempre que, cuando quiera que.

where /wɛər/ adv. **1.** dónde, adónde. —conj. **2.** donde.

wherever /wɛər'ɛvər/ conj. dondequiera que, adondequiera que.

whether /'wɛðər/ conj. si.

which /wɪtʃ/ a. **1.** qué. —interrog. pron. **2.** cuál. —rel. pron. **3.** que; el cual; lo cual.

whichever /wɪtʃ'ɛvər/ a. & pron. cualquiera que.

while /wail/ conj. **1.** mientras; mientras que. —n. **2.** rato m.

whip /wɪp/ n. **1.** látigo m. —v. **2.** azotar.

whipped cream /wɪpt/ nata batida f.

whirl /wɜrl/ v. girar.

whirlpool /'wɜrl,pul/ n. vórtice m.

whirlwind /'wɜrl,wɪnd/ n. torbellino m.

whisk broom /wɪsk/ escobilla f.

whisker /'wɪskər/ n. bigote m.

whiskey /'wɪski/ n. whisky m.

whisper /'wɪspər/ n. **1.** cuchicheo m. —v. **2.** cuchichear.

whistle /'wɪsəl/ n. **1.** pito; silbido m. —v. **2.** silbar.

white /wait/ a. **1.** blanco. —n. **2.** (of egg) clara f.

who /hu/ **whom** interrog. pron. **1.** quién. —rel. pron. **2.** que; quien.

whoever /hu'ɛvər/ **whomever** pron. quienquiera que.

whole /houl/ a. **1.** entero. **the wh.,** todo el. —n. **2.** totalidad f. **on the wh.,** por lo general.

wholesale /'houl,seil/ n. **at wh.,** al por mayor.

wholesaler /'houl,seilər/ n. mayorista m. & f.

wholesome /'houlsəm/ a. sano, saludable.

wholly /'houli/ adv. enteramente.

whose /huz/ interrog. adj. **1.** de quién. —rel. adj. **2.** cuyo.

why /wai/ adv. por qué; para qué.

wicked /'wɪkɪd/ a. malo, malvado.

wickedness /'wɪkɪdnɪs/ n. maldad f.

wide /waid/ a. **1.** ancho; extenso. —adv. **2. w. open,** abierto de par en par.

widen /'waidṇ/ v. ensanchar; extender.

widespread /'waid'sprɛd/ a. extenso.

widow /'wɪdou/ n. viuda f.

widower /'wɪdouər/ n. viudo m.

width /wɪdθ/ n. anchura f.

wield /wild/ v. manejar, empuñar.

wife /waif/ n. esposa, señora, mujer f.

wig /wɪg/ n. peluca f.

wild /waild/ a. salvaje; bárbaro.

wilderness /'wɪldərnɪs/ n. desierto m.

wildlife /'waild,laif/ n. fauna silvestre f.

will /wɪl/ n. **1.** voluntad f.; testamento m. —v. **2.** querer; determinar; Leg. legar.

willful /'wɪlfəl/ a. voluntarioso; premeditado.

willing /'wɪlɪŋ/ a. **to be w.,** estar dispuesto.

willingly /'wɪlɪŋli/ adv. de buena gana.

wilt /wɪlt/ v. marchitar.

win /wɪn/ v. ganar.

wind /wɪnd/ n. **1.** viento m. —v. **2.** torcer; dar cuerda a.

windmill /'wɪnd,mɪl/ n. molino de viento m.

window /'wɪndou/ n. ventana f.; (of car) ventanilla f.; (of shop or store) escaparate m.

windshield /'wɪnd,ʃild/ n. parabrisas m.

windy /'wɪndi/ *a.* ventoso. **to be w.,** (weather) hacer viento.

wine /wain/ *n.* vino *m.*

wing /wɪŋ/ *n.* ala *f.; Theat.* bastidor *m.*

wink /wɪŋk/ *n.* **1.** guiño *m.* —*v.* **2.** guiñar.

winner /'wɪnər/ *n.* ganador -ra.

winter /'wɪntər/ *n.* invierno *m.*

wipe /waip/ *v.* limpiar; (dry) secar. **w. out,** destruir.

wire /waiər/ *n.* **1.** alambre; hilo; telegrama *m.* —*v.* **2.** telegrafiar.

wireless /'waiərlɪs/ *n.* telégrafo sin hilos.

wisdom /'wɪzdəm/ *n.* juicio *m.;* sabiduría *f.*

wise /waiz/ *a.* sensato, juicioso; sabio.

wish /wɪʃ/ *n.* **1.** deseo; voto *m.* —*v.* **2.** desear; querer.

wit /wɪt/ *n.* ingenio *m.,* sal *f.*

witch /wɪtʃ/ *n.* bruja *f.*

with /wɪθ, wɪð/ *prep.* con.

withdraw /wɪð'drɔ, wɪθ-/ *v.* retirar.

wither /'wɪðər/ *v.* marchitar.

withhold /wɪθ'hould, wɪð-/ *v.* retener, suspender.

within /wɪð'ɪn, wɪθ-/ *adv.* **1.** dentro, por dentro. —*prep.* **2.** dentro de; en.

without /wɪð'aut, wɪθ-/ *adv.* **1.** fuera, por fuera. —*prep.* **2.** sin.

witness /'wɪtnɪs/ *n.* **1.** testigo; testimonio *m.* & *f.* —*v.* **2.** presenciar; atestar.

witty /'wɪti/ *a.* ingenioso, gracioso, ocurrente.

wizard /'wɪzərd/ *n.* hechicero *m.*

woe /wou/ *n.* dolor *m.;* pena *f.*

wolf /wʊlf/ *n.* lobo -ba.

woman /'wʊmən/ *n.* mujer *f.*

womb /wum/ *n.* entrañas *f.pl.,* matriz *f.*

wonder /'wʌndər/ *n.* **1.** maravilla; admiración *f.* **for a w.,** por milagro. **no w.,** no es extraño. —*v.* **2.** preguntarse; maravillarse.

wonderful /'wʌndərfəl/ *a.* maravilloso; estupendo.

woo /wu/ *v.* cortejar.

wood /wʊd/ *n.* madera; (for fire) leña *f.*

wooden /'wʊdn/ *a.* de madera.

wool /wʊl/ *n.* lana *f.*

word /wɜrd/ *n.* **1.** palabra *f.* **the words** (of a song), la letra. —*v.* **2.** expresar.

word processing /'prɒsɛsɪŋ/ procesamiento de textos *m.*

word processor /'prɒsɛsər/ procesador de textos *m.*

work /wɜrk/ *n.* **1.** trabajo *m.;* (of art) obra *f.* —*v.* **2.** trabajar; obrar; funcionar.

worker /'wɜrkər/ *n.* trabajador -ra; obrero -ra.

workman /'wɜrkmən/ *n.* obrero *m.*

work station estación de trabajo *f.*

work week /'wɜrk,wik/ semana laboral *f.*

world /wɜrld/ *n.* mundo *m.* **w. war,** guerra mundial.

worldly /'wɜrldli/ *a.* mundano.

worldwide /'wɜrld'waid/ *a.* mundial.

worm /wɜrm/ *n.* gusano *m.*

worn /wɔrn/ *a.* usado. **w. out,** gastado; cansado, rendido.

worrisome /'wɜrisəm/ *a.* inquietante.

worry /'wɜri/ *n.* **1.** preocupación *f.* —*v.* **2.** preocupar.

worrying /'wɜriɪŋ/ *a.* inquietante.

worse /wɜrs/ *a.* peor. **to get w.,** empeorar.

worship /'wɜrʃɪp/ *n.* **1.** adoración *f.* —*v.* **2.** adorar.

worst /wɜrst/ *a.* peor.

worth /wɜrθ/ *a.* **1. to be w.,** valer. —*n.* **2.** valor *m.*

worthless /'wɜrθlɪs/ *a.* sin valor.

worthy /'wɜrði/ *a.* digno.

wound /wund/ *n.* **1.** herida *f.* —*v.* **2.** herir.

wrap /ræp/ *n.* **1.** (pl.) abrigos *m.pl.* —*n.* **2.** envolver.

wrapping /'ræpɪŋ/ *n.* cubierta *f.*

wrath /ræθ/ *n.* ira, cólera *f.*

wreath /riθ/ *n.* guirnalda; corona *f.*

wreck /rɛk/ *n.* **1.** ruina *f.;* accidente *m.* —*v.* **2.** destrozar, arruinar.

wrench /rɛntʃ/ *n.* llave *f.* **monkey w.,** llave inglesa.

wrestle /'rɛsəl/ *v.* luchar.

wretched /'rɛtʃɪd/ *a.* miserable.

wring /rɪŋ/ *v.* retorcer.

wrinkle /'rɪŋkəl/ *n.* **1.** arruga *f.* —*v.* **2.** arrugar.

wrist /rɪst/ *n.* muñeca *f.* **w. watch,** reloj de pulsera.

write /rait/ *v.* escribir. **w. down,** apuntar.

writer /'raitər/ *n.* escritor -ra.

writhe /raið/ *v.* contorcerse.

writing paper /'raitɪŋ/ papel de escribir *m.*

wrong /rɒŋ/ *a.* **1.** equivocado; incorrecto. **to be w.,** equivocarse; no tener razón. —*adv.* **2.** mal, incorrectamente. —*n.* **3.** agravio *m.* **right and w.,** el bien y el mal. —*v.* **4.** agraviar, ofender.

WWW *abbr.* (World Wide Web) malla mundial *f.*

X Y Z

x-ray /'ɛks,rei/ *n.* **1.** rayo X *m.,* radiografía, *f.* —*v.* **2.** radiografiar.

xylophone /'zailə,foun/ *n.* xilófono *m.*

yacht /yɒt/ *n.* yate *m.*

yard /yard/ *n.* patio, corral *m.;* (measure) yarda *f.*

yarn /yarn/ *n.* hilo.

yawn /yɔn/ *n.* **1.** bostezo *m.* —*v.* **2.** bostezar.

year /yɪər/ *n.* año *m.*

yearly /'yɪərli/ *a.* anual.

yearn /yɜrn/ *v.* anhelar.

yell /yɛl/ *n.* **1.** grito *m.* —*v.* **2.** gritar.

yellow /'yɛlou/ *a.* amarillo.

yes /yɛs/ *adv.* sí.

yesterday /'yɛstər,dei/ *adv.* ayer.

yet /yɛt/ *adv.* todavía, aún.

Yiddish /'yɪdɪʃ/ *n.* yídish *m.*

yield /yild/ *v.* producir; ceder.

yogurt /'yougərt/ *n.* yogur *m.*

yoke /youk/ *n.* yugo *m.*

yolk /youk/ *n.* yema *f.*

you /yu; *unstressed* yʊ, yə/ *pron.* usted, (pl.) ustedes; lo, la, los, las; le, les; (familiar) tú, (pl.) vosotros -as; ti; te, (pl.) os. **with y.,** contigo, con usted.

young /yʌŋ/ *a.* joven.

youngster /'yʌŋstər/ *n.* muchacho -cha *m.* & *f.*

your /yur, yɔr; *unstressed* yər/ *a.* su; (familiar) tu; (pl.) vuestro.

yours /yurz, yɔrz/ *pron.* suyo; (familiar) tuyo; (pl.) vuestro.

yourself -selves /yur'sɛlf, yɔr- yər-/ *pron.* sí; se; (familiar) ti; te. **with y.,** consigo; contigo. **you y.,** usted mismo, ustedes mismos; tú mismo, vosotros mismos.

youth /yuθ/ *n.* juventud *f.;* (person) joven *m.* & *f.*

youth club club juvenil *m.*

youthful /'yuθfəl/ *a.* juvenil.

yuppie /'yʌpi/ *n.* yuppie *m.* & *f.*

zap /zæp/ *v.* desintegrar, aniquilar.

zeal /zil/ *n.* celo, fervor *m.*

zealous /'zɛləs/ *a.* celoso, fervoroso.

zero /'zɪərou/ *n.* cero *m.*

zest /zɛst/ *n.* gusto *m.*

zip code /zɪp/ número de distrito postal.

zipper /'zɪpər/ *m.* cremallera *f.*

zone /zoun/ *n.* zona *f.*

zoo /zu/ *n.* jardín zoológico.

SPANISH IRREGULAR VERBS

Infinitive	Present	Future	Preterit	Past Part.
andar	ando	andaré	anduve	andado
caber	quepo	cabré	cupe	cabido
caer	caigo	caeré	caí	caído
conducir	conduzco	conduciré	conduje	conducido
dar	doy	daré	di	dado
decir	digo	diré	dije	dicho
estar	estoy	estaré	estuve	estado
haber	he	habré	hube	habido
hacer	hago	haré	hice	hecho
ir	voy	iré	fui	ido
jugar	juego	jugaré	jugué	jugado
morir	muero	moriré	morí	muerto
oir	oigo	oiré	oí	oído
poder	puedo	podré	pude	podido
poner	pongo	pondré	puse	puesto
querer	quiero	querré	quise	querido
saber	sé	sabré	supe	sabido
salir	salgo	saldré	salí	salido
ser	soy	seré	fui	sido
tener	tengo	tendré	tuve	tenido
traer	traigo	traeré	traje	traído
valer	valgo	valdré	valí	valido
venir	vengo	vendré	vine	venido
ver	veo	veré	vi	visto

LAS FORMAS DEL VERBO INGLÉS

1. Se forma la 3ª persona singular del tiempo presente exactamente al igual que el plural de los sustantivos, añadiendo **-es** o **-s** a la forma sencilla según las mismas reglas, así:

(1)	teach	pass	wish	fix	buzz		
	teaches	passes	wishes	fixes	buzzes		
(2)	place	change	judge	please	freeze		
	places	changes	judges	pleases	freezes		
(3a)	find	sell	clean	hear	love	buy	know
	finds	sells	cleans	hears	loves	buys	knows
(3b)	think	like	laugh	stop	hope	meet	want
	thinks	likes	laughs	stops	hopes	meets	wants
(4)	cry	try	dry	carry	deny		
	cries	tries	dries	carries	denies		

Cinco verbos muy comunes tienen 3ª persona singular irregular:

| (5) | go | do | say | have | be |
| | goes | does | says | has | is |

2. Se forman el tiempo pasado y el participio de modo igual, añadiendo a la forma sencilla la terminación **-ed** o **-d** según las reglas que siguen:

(1) Si la forma sencilla termina en **-d** o **-t,** se le pone **-ed** como sílaba aparte:

| end | fold | need | load | want | feast | wait | light |
| ended | folded | needed | loaded | wanted | feasted | waited | lighted |

(2) Si la forma sencilla termina en cualquier otra consonante, se añade también **-ed** pero sin hacer sílaba aparte:

LAS FORMAS DEL VERBO INGLÉS

(2a) | bang | sail | seem | harm | earn | weigh
--- | --- | --- | --- | --- | ---
| banged | sailed | seemed | harmed | earned | weighed

(2b) | lunch | work | look | laugh | help | pass
--- | --- | --- | --- | --- | ---
| lunched | worked | looked | laughed | helped | passed

(3) Si la forma sencilla termina en **-e,** se le pone sólo **-d:**

(3a) | hate | taste | waste | guide | fade | trade
--- | --- | --- | --- | --- | ---
| hated | tasted | wasted | guided | faded | traded

(3b) | free | judge | rule | name | dine | scare
--- | --- | --- | --- | --- | ---
| freed | judged | ruled | named | dined | scared

(3c) | place | force | knife | like | hope | base
--- | --- | --- | --- | --- | ---
| placed | forced | knifed | liked | hoped | based

(4) Una **-y** final que sigue a cualquier consonante se cambia en **-ie** al añadir la **-d** del pasado/participio:

cry	try	dry	carry	deny
cried	tried	dried	carried	denied

3. Varios verbos muy comunes forman el tiempo pasado y el participio de manera irregular. Pertenecen a tres grupos.

(1) Los que tienen una sola forma irregular para tiempo pasado y participio, como los siguientes:

bend	bleed	bring	build	buy	catch	creep	deal
bent	bled	brought	built	bought	caught	crept	dealt
dig	feed	feel	fight	find	flee	get	hang
dug	fed	felt	fought	found	fled	got	hung
have	hear	hold	keep	lead	leave	lend	lose
had	heard	held	kept	led	left	lent	lost
make	mean	meet	say	seek	sell	send	shine
made	meant	met	said	sought	sold	sent	shone
shoot	sit	sleep	spend	stand	strike	sweep	teach
shot	sat	slept	spent	stood	struck	swept	taught

(2) Los que tienen una forma irregular para el tiempo pasado y otra forma irregular para el participio, como los siguientes:

be	beat	become	begin	bite
was	beat	became	began	bit
been	beaten	become	begun	bitten
blow	break	choose	come	do
blew	broke	chose	came	did
blown	broken	chosen	come	done
draw	drink	drive	eat	fall
drew	drank	drove	ate	fell
drawn	drunk	driven	eaten	fallen
fly	forget	freeze	give	go
flew	forgot	froze	gave	went
flown	forgotten	frozen	given	gone
grow	hide	know	ride	ring
grew	hid	knew	rode	rang
grown	hidden	known	ridden	rung
rise	run	see	shake	shrink
rose	ran	saw	shook	shrank
risen	run	seen	shaken	shrunk
sing	sink	speak	steal	swear
sang	sank	spoke	stole	swore
sung	sunk	spoken	stolen	sworn

LAS FORMAS DEL VERBO INGLÉS

swim	tear	throw	wear	write
swam	tore	threw	wore	wrote
swum	torn	thrown	worn	written

(3) Los que no varían del todo, la forma sencilla funcionando también como pasado/participio; entre éstos son de mayor frecuencia:

bet	burst	cast	cost	cut
hit	hurt	let	put	quit
read	set	shed	shut	slit
spit	split	spread	thrust	wet

EL PLURAL DEL SUSTANTIVO INGLÉS

A la forma singular se añade la terminición **-es** o **-s** de acuerdo con las reglas siguientes.

(1) Si el singular termina en **-ch, -s, -sh, -x** o **-z,** se le pone **-es** como sílaba aparte:

match	glass	dish	box	buzz
matches	glasses	dishes	boxes	buzzes

(2) Si el singular termina en **-ce, -ge, -se,** or **-ze,** se le pone una **-s** que con la vocal precedente forma sílaba aparte:

face	page	house	size
faces	pages	houses	sizes

(3) Una **-y** final que sigue a cualquier consonante se cambia en **-ie** a ponérsele la **-s** del plural:

sky	city	lady	ferry	penny
skies	cities	ladies	ferries	pennies

(4) Los siguientes sustantivos comunes tienen plural irregular:

man	woman	child	foot	mouse	goose
men	women	children	feet	mice	geese

wife	knife	life	half	leaf	deer
wives	knives	lives	halves	leaves	deer

WEIGHTS AND MEASURES/PESOS Y MEDIDAS

1 centímetro	=	.3937 inches
1 metro	=	39.37 inches
1 kilómetro	=	.621 mile
1 centigramo	=	.1543 grain
1 gramo	=	15.432 grains
1 kilogramo	=	2.2046 pounds
1 tonelada	=	2.204 pounds
1 centilitro	=	.338 ounces
1 litro	=	1.0567 quart (liquid); .908 quart (dry)

1 kilolitro	=	264.18 gallons
1 inch	=	2.54 centímetros
1 foot	=	.305 metros
1 mile	=	1.61 kilómetros
1 grain	=	.065 gramos
1 pound	=	.455 kilogramos
1 ton	=	.907 toneladas
1 ounce	=	2.96 centilitros
1 quart	=	1.13 litros
1 gallon	=	4.52 litros

Numbers/Números

Cardinal/Cardinales

one	1	uno, una	twenty-two	22	(*or* veintiuno) veinte y dos	
two	2	dos			(*or* veintidós)	
three	3	tres	thirty	30	treinta	
four	4	cuatro	thirty-one	31	treinta y uno	
five	5	cinco	thirty-two	32	treinta y dos	
six	6	seis	forty	40	cuarenta	
seven	7	siete	fifty	50	cincuenta	
eight	8	ocho	sixty	60	sesenta	
nine	9	nueve	seventy	70	setenta	
ten	10	diez	eighty	80	ochenta	
eleven	11	once	ninety	90	noventa	
twelve	12	doce	one hundred	100	cien	
thirteen	13	trece	one hundred one	101	ciento uno	
fourteen	14	catorce	one hundred two	102	ciento dos	
fifteen	15	quince	two hundred	200	doscientos, -as	
sixteen	16	dieciséis	three hundred	300	trescientos, -as	
seventeen	17	diecisiete	four hundred	400	cuatrocientos, -as	
eighteen	18	dieciocho	five hundred	500	quinientos, -as	
nineteen	19	diecinueve	six hundred	600	seiscientos, -as	
twenty	20	veinte	seven hundred	700	setecientos, -as	
twenty-one	21	veinte y uno	eight hundred	800	ochocientos, -as	

nine hundred	900	novecientos, -as
one thousand	1,000	mil
two thousand	2,000	dos mil
one hundred thousand	100,000	cien mil
one million	1,000,000	un millón
two million	2,000,000	dos millones

Ordinal/Ordinales

first	1st / 1°	primero
second	2nd / 2°	segundo
third	3rd / 3°	tercero
fourth	4th / 4°	cuarto
fifth	5th / 5°	quinto
sixth	6th / 6°	sexto
seventh	7th / 7°	séptimo
eighth	8th / 8°	octavo
ninth	9th / 9°	noveno
tenth	10th / 10°	décimo

Days of the Week/Días de la Semana

Sunday	domingo	Thursday	jueves
Monday	lunes	Friday	viernes
Tuesday	martes	Saturday	sábado
Wednesday	miércoles		

Months/Meses

January	enero	July	julio
February	febrero	August	agosto
March	marzo	September	septiembre
April	abril	October	octubre
May	mayo	November	noviembre
June	junio	December	diciembre

Signs/Señales

By appointment	Cita previa
Caution	Precaución
Closed	Cerrado
Closed for repairs	Cerrado por refaccíon
Danger	Peligro
Do not disturb	No molesten
Down (on elevator)	Para bajar
Driveway	Vado permante/Paso de carruajes
Dumping prohibited	Se prohibe arrojar la basura
Entrance	Entrada
Exit	Salida
For immediate occupancy	De ocupación inmediata
For sale	Se vende
Go (traffic)	Siga
Inquire within	Se dan informaciones
Keep to the left	Tome su izquierda
Keep to the right	Tome su derecha
Ladies'/Women's room	El cuarto de damas
Men	Señores, Hombres, Caballeros
Men's room	El servicio
Narrow road	Camino estrecho
No admittance	Entrada prohibida
No entry	Dirección prohibida
No thoroughfare	Prohibido el paso/Calle cerrada
No parking	Se prohibe estacionar
No smoking	Prohibido fumar
No tipping	No se admiten propinas
Not working	No funciona
One way	Dirección única
Open	Abierto
People working	Trabajadores
Post no bills	Se prohibe fijar carteles
Road closed	Paso cerrado
Road repairs	Camino en reparación
Same-day service	En el día
Slow	Despacio
Slow down	Moderar su velocidad
Stop	Alto
This way to...	Dirección a...
Town ahead	Poblado próximo
Up (on elevator)	Para subir
Wet paint	Recién pintado
Women	Señoras, Mujeres, Damas

Useful Phrases/Locuciones Útiles

Good day, Good morning.   Buenos días.
Good afternoon.   Buenas tardes.
Good night, Good evening.   Buenas noches.
Hello.   ¡Hola!
Welcome!   ¡Bienvenido!
See you later.   Hasta luego.
Goodbye.   ¡Adiós!
How are you?   ¿Cómo está usted?
I'm fine, thank you.   Estoy bien, gracias.
I'm pleased to meet you.   Mucho gusto en conocerle.
May I introduce . . . Quisiera presentar . . .
Thank you very much.   Muchas gracias.
You're welcome.   De nada *or* No hay de qué.
Please.   Por favor.
Excuse me.   Con permiso.
Good luck.   ¡Buena suerte!
To your health.   ¡Salud!

Please help me.   Ayúdeme, por favor.
I don't know.   No sé.
I don't understand.   No entiendo.
Do you understand?   ¿Entiende usted?
I don't speak Spanish.   No hablo español.
Do you speak English?   ¿Habla usted inglés?
How do you say . . . in Spanish?   ¿Cómo se dice . . . en español?
What do you call this?   ¿Cómo se llama esto?
Speak slowly, please.   Hable despacio, por favor.
Please repeat.   Repita, por favor.
I don't like it.   No me gusta.
I am lost.   Ando perdido; Me he extraviado.

What is your name?   ¿Cómo se llama usted?
My name is . . .   Me llamo . . .
I am an American.   Soy norteamericano.
Where are you from?   ¿De dónde es usted?
I'm from . . .   Soy de . . .

How is the weather?   ¿Qué tiempo hace?
It's cold (hot) today.   Hace frío (calor) hoy.
What time is it?   ¿Qué hora es?

How much is it?   ¿Cuánto es?
It is too much.   Es demasiado.
What do you wish?   ¿Qué desea usted?
I want to buy . . .   Quiero comprar . . .
May I see something better?   ¿Podría ver algo mejor?
May I see something cheaper?   ¿Podría ver algo menos caro?
It is not exactly what I want.   No es exactamente lo que quiero.

I'm hungry.   Tengo hambre.
I'm thirsty.   Tengo sed.
Where is there a restaurant?   ¿Dónde hay un restaurante?
I have a reservation.   Tengo una reservación.

I would like . . .   Quisiera . . .; Me gustaría . . .
Please give me . . .   Por favor, déme usted . . .
Please bring me . . .   Por favor, tráigame usted . . .
May I see the menu?   ¿Podría ver el menú?
The bill, please.   La cuenta, por favor.
Is service included in the bill?   ¿El servicio está incluido en la cuenta?
Where is there a hotel?   ¿Dónde hay un hotel?
Where is the post office?   ¿Dónde está el correo?
Is there any mail for me?   ¿Hay correo para mí?
Where can I mail this letter?   ¿Dónde puedo echar esta carta al correo?

Take me to . . .   Lléveme a . . .
I believe I am ill.   Creo que estoy enfermo.
Please call a doctor.   Por favor, llame al médico.
Please call the police.   Por favor, llame a la policía.
I want to send a telegram.   Quiero poner un telegrama.
As soon as possible.   Cuanto antes.

Round trip.   Ida y vuelta.
Please help me with my luggage.   Por favor, ayúdeme con mi equipaje.
Where can I get a taxi?   ¿Dónde puedo coger un taxi?
What is the fare to . . .   ¿Cuánto es el pasaje hasta . . . ?
Please take me to this address.   Por favor, lléveme a esta dirección.
Where can I change my money?   ¿Dónde puedo cambiar mi dinero?
Where is the nearest bank?   ¿Dónde está el banco más cercano?
Can you accept my check?   ¿Puede aceptar usted mi cheque?
Do you accept traveler's checks?   ¿Aceptan cheques de viaje?
What is the postage?   ¿Cuánto es el franqueo?
Where is the nearest drugstore?   ¿Dónde está la farmacia más cercana?
Where is the men's (women's) room?   ¿Dónde está el servicio de caballeros (de señoras)?
Please let me off at. . .   Por favor, déjeme bajar en . . .

Right away.   ¡Pronto!
Help.   ¡Socorro!
Who is it?   ¿Quién es?
Just a minute!   ¡Un momento no más!
Come in.   ¡Pase usted!
Pardon me.   Dispense usted.
Stop.   ¡Pare!
Look out.   ¡Cuidado!
Hurry.   ¡De prisa! *or* ¡Dése prisa!
Go on.   ¡Siga!
To (on, at) the right.   A la derecha.
To (on, at) the left.   A la izquierda.
Straight ahead.   Adelante.

FOOD TERMS/ALIMENTOS

apple	manzana	lemonade	limonada
artichoke	alcachofa	lettuce	lechuga
asparagus	espárrago	liver	hígado
bacon	tocino	lobster	langosta
baked	al horno	meat	carne
banana	banana	melon	melón
bean	habichuela	milk	leche
beer	cerveza	mushroom	seta
beet	remolacha	noodle	fideo
biscuit	bizcocho	nut	nuez
boiled	hervido	omelet	tortilla de huevos
bread	pan	onion	cebolla
broccoli	brócoli	orange	naranja
broiled	a la parrilla	peach	melocotón
butter	manteca	pear	pera
cake	torta	pepper	pimienta
carrot	zanahoria	pie	pastel
cauliflower	coliflor	pork	carne de puerco
celery	apio	potato	patata
cheese	queso	rice	arroz
chicken	pollo	roast beef	rosbif
chocolate	chocolate	roasted	asado
coffee	café	salad	ensalada
cognac	coñac	salmon	salmón
cookie	galleta dulce	salt	sal
crab	cangrejo	sandwich	sandwich
cream	crema	sauce	salsa
cucumber	pepino	scrambled eggs	huevos revueltos
dessert	postre	shrimp	camarón
drink	bebida	soda	soda
duck	pato	sole	lenguado
egg	huevo	soup	sopa
fillet	filete	spinach	espinaca
fish	pescado	steak	biftec
fowl	ave	strawberry	fresa
fried	frito	stuffed	relleno
fruit	fruta	sugar	azúcar
goose	ganso	tea	té
grape	uva	tomato	tomate
grapefruit	toronja	trout	trucha
ham	jamón	tuna	atún
hamburger	hamburguesa	turkey	pavo
ice cream	helado	veal	ternera
jelly	jalea	vegetable	legumbre
juice	jugo	water	agua
lamb	cordero	wine	vino